THEOLOGIANS IN THEIR OWN WORDS

THEOLOGIANS IN THEIR OWN WORDS

Derek R. Nelson, Joshua M. Moritz, and Ted Peters, editors

Fortress Press

Minneapolis

THEOLOGIANS IN THEIR OWN WORDS

Copyright © 2013 Fortress Press. All rights reserved. Except for brief quota-
tions in critical articles or reviews, no part of this book may be reproduced
in any manner without prior written permission from the publisher. Visit
http://www.augsburgfortress.org/copyrights/ or write to Permissions, Augsburg Fortress, Box 1209, Minneapolis, MN 55440.

Cover design: Michelle L. N. Cook

Library of Congress Cataloging-in-Publication Data is available

ISBN: 978-0-8006-9880-5

The paper used in this publication meets the minimum requirements of
American National Standard for Information Sciences — Permanence of Paper
for Printed Library Materials, ANSI Z329.48-1984.

Manufactured in the U.S.A.

Contents

Acknowledgments

The editors would like to thank several people who helped along the way during this book's long development. Co-editor Nelson wishes to thank Marsha Wissinger, former secretary to the faculty of Thiel College, for her cheerful clerical help at various points. Her typing of many of the previously published essays assisted greatly in bringing this book to press, and her willingness to learn all the German, Greek, and Latin terms in the texts went above and beyond the call of duty! A professor could not ask for better student workers than Kylie Czulewicz and Shea Maier at Thiel, who came through in the clutch assisting in a variety of ways. Curtis Thompson, faculty colleague extraordinaire, carefully read pieces of text and made helpful suggestions. Many thanks to you all.

Finally, hearty thanks are due to all the contributors to this volume. Most academics do not object to talking about themselves or their work. But to go the second mile of submitting that self-interpretation to public scrutiny, in the process furthering theological reflection, is noble and generous. Six of the contributors have died since their submissions were first published. We are glad that their lives and work can be honored by, at least, being remembered in print.

Contributors

Marilyn McCord Adams is Distinguished Research Professor of philosophy at the University of North Carolina, Chapel Hill. She was formerly Regius Professor of Divinity at Oxford University, and Pitkin Professor of Historical Theology at Yale Divinity School. Often associated with medieval philosophy and theology, having published *William Ockham* in two volumes, she has also written widely in the philosophy of religion, particularly on the question of evil.

Harvey Cox is Hollis Research Professor of Divinity at Harvard University, where he has taught for nearly a half-century. A prolific author, Cox is perhaps best known for his groundbreaking book *The Secular City*, first published in 1965. His most recent book is *The Future of Faith*.

Gerhard Forde (1927–2005) was at the time of his death Professor of Systematic Theology at Luther Seminary. He was the author of many books on the Protestant Reformation, its theology, and its implications for contemporary life. Active in ecumenical circles, he served for many years on the Lutheran-Roman Catholic dialogue.

George Forell (1919–2011) was Carver Professor of Religious Studies *Emeritus* at the University of Iowa. Forell was the author of many important books, including the widely popular work on Luther's social ethics, *Faith Active in Love*.

Roger Haight is presently scholar-in-residence at Union Theological Seminary in New York City. He has previously taught theology at Weston School of Theology and at Jesuit schools of theology in Chicago, Manila, and Toronto.

Philip Hefner is Professor of Systematic Theology emeritus at the Lutheran School of Theology at Chicago. He was the director of the Zygon Center for Religion and Science in Chicago, and is the author of the influential text *The Human Factor: Evolution, Culture, Religion*.

Robert Jenson retired as senior scholar at the Center for Theological Inquiry, Princeton, New Jersey and is professor of religion emeritus at Saint Olaf College, Northfield, Minnesota. His two-volume *Systematic Theology* has been regarded as one of the most important recent works in the field.

Ernst Käsemann (1906–1998) was professor of New Testament at the German universities of Mainz, Göttingen, and Tübingen. Active in the Confessing Church, which opposed Hitler, Käsemann was imprisoned by the Gestapo and wrote many historical and theological books emphasizing the central role freedom and liberation play in the New Testament.

Martin Marty is Fairfax M. Cone Distinguished Service Professor of History of Modern Christianity emeritus at the University of Chicago. The author of dozens of books and hundreds of articles, Marty has given his name to a center for the study of religion at Chicago, and to a prestigious award for the "public understanding of religion" from the American Academy of Religion.

Alister McGrath is Professor of Theology, Ministry and Education at King's College, London, where he also heads the Centre for Theology, Religion and Culture. In addition to this teaching post, McGrath is Senior Research Fellow at Harris Manchester College, Oxford University. McGrath is a prolific author whose books range from the history of theology to science and religion to apologetics.

Nancey Murphy is Professor of Christian Theology at Fuller Theological Seminary, Pasadena, California. Having earned doctorates both in the philosophy of science and in systematic theology, Murphy has written many books at the intersections of those fields of research.

Wolfhart Pannenberg is Professor of Systematic Theology emeritus at the University of Munich. His three-volume *Systematic Theology* is regarded as one of the most significant contributions to the field in the last half-century.

Ted Peters is Professor of Systematic Theology at Pacific Lutheran Theological Seminary and the Graduate Theological Union, Berkeley, California. Peters edited *Dialog: A Journal of Theology* for many years and is the author of several books, notably *God—The World's Future: Systematic Theology for a Postmodern Age*.

Clark Pinnock (1937–2010) was at the time of his death professor of systematic theology at McMaster Divinity College, Hamilton, Ontario.

John Polkinghorne is an Anglican priest and mathematical physicist. Ordained in 1982, he served various churches in England before becoming president of Queens' College in Cambridge University.

Rosemary Radford Ruether served as Georgia Harkness Professor of Theology at Garrett-Evangelical Theological Seminary, Evanston, Illinois and Carpenter Professor of Feminist Theology at the Graduate Theological Union, Berkeley, California. Author of many books, Ruether is perhaps best known for her seminal classic *Sexism and God Talk*.

Letty M. Russell (1929–2007) was professor of theology at Yale Divinity School, New Haven, Connecticut. Russell published widely in the areas of ecclesiology and human liberation. In 1999 a festschrift was published in Russell's honor, titled *Liberating Eschatology*.

H. Paul Santmire is a Lutheran pastor and author of many books on theology and the natural world. His *The Travail of Nature* is regarded as a classic in the theological interpretation of the material environment.

Hans Schwarz is professor of theology emeritus at the University of Regensburg. The author of many books in systematic theology, Schwarz has lectured widely all across the world, particularly in Asia.

Huston Smith is Thomas J. Watson Professor of Religion emeritus at Syracuse University. His book *The World's Religions* has sold over two million copies and is regarded as a classic in the field. He resides in Berkeley, California.

Paul Sponheim is Professor of Systematic Theology Emeritus at Luther Seminary in Saint Paul, Minnesota, and is the author of many books including *Love's Availing Power* and *Faith and the Other*.

Kathryn Tanner is Frederick Marquand Professor of Systematic Theology at Yale Divinity School. She was previously Dorothy Grant Maclear Professor of Theology at the University of Chicago. Her many influential books include *God and Creation in Christian Theology* and *Christ the Key*.

Ronald Thiemann (1946–2012) was Bussey Professor of Theology at Harvard Divinity School, Cambridge, Massachusetts. A former Lutheran pastor, Thiemann's books include *Revelation and Theology*, *Constructing a Public Theology*, and *Religion in Public Life*.

Introduction

Derek R. Nelson

Who are you, dear reader? How would you tell a stranger the story of your life and your life's work? And how would you put together the pieces that are invariably strewn about our fragmented lives? Families, jobs, communities—including worshiping communities—historical events that cannot be ignored. . . . All these and many other pieces, all of which are already complicated in their own right, would have to be weighed and, if the narrative were to have any coherence, fit together. This book is a collection of relatively brief attempts by major theological thinkers of the last several decades to do just that. That is to say, this book compiles intellectual autobiographies, which in every case are also theological autobiographies. All of the writers who have been asked to contribute are major thinkers in theology, biblical studies, and religion from the second half of the twentieth century up to the present day.

Some of these contributions appeared earlier in some form in the "Theological Autobiography" forum of *Dialog: A Journal of Theology*, and others have appeared elsewhere in print. Others still are newly commissioned for this book. The earliest of the autobiographies was first published over a decade ago. Some of the submissions have been updated to take into consideration later developments. Some of the submissions have changed because their writers have changed their mind about who they are and what they have achieved. And some have been left as they first appeared, perhaps as a kind of monument to the *in medias res* character of all theological thinking.

For most major theological figures of the twentieth century there are ample biographical resources. Someone interested in Barth, Bonhoeffer, or von Balthasar has many places to which they might go in order to find out the basics of these theologians' lives and thought. But this is not the case for many other theological luminaries of recent years. Thus readers may find in these pages the only source in print of basic life contours and intellectual trajectories. Whether one finds the interpretation offered of each theological self "convincing" matters little when seeking to find out the basic story.

Recent years have witnessed increasing attention being given to the categories of narrative and story.[1] Voices as varied as those from postliberal theologies,[2] interreligious dialogue,[3] and evangelical mega-churches[4] have highlighted how important narrative can be for understanding and articulating the gospel and the God to which it points. The editors of this book believe that narrative is important not just for interpreting theology, but also for interpreting theologians. After all, as E. H. Carr once argued in *What Is History?*, before studying history, one should study the historian. When a theologian is forced to piece together differing contexts, to note how particular theological content relates to a given context, and to give a narrative arc to theological development over time, the reader can eavesdrop as autobiography takes on the form of theo-graphy.

Objections to Autobiography

Some have loudly objected to the practice of reflecting theologically by means of reflection on oneself and one's life. James Wm. McClendon, for example, in his influential book *Biography as Theology*, implicitly equates autobiography with self-deception.[5] He admits that there may be a place for theological autobiography as a starting point for others to then correct its excesses and tendentious biases. Yet when he writes that "we must hear from others' experience as well as our own, and must examine self-told stories by external as well as internal light," one gets the impression that the self-told story would not have been necessary at all.[6]

It is true that some people lack the capacity to stand back far enough from their own thoughts, actions, and past to gain the perspective needed for an accurate portrayal of things "as they really are." Stanley Hauerwas and David Burrell invoke the example of Christopher Columbus never quite having understood where he had been on his travels, and what he had really done.[7]

Another form of criticism comes from Martha Nussbaum, who singles out biography and autobiography precisely as examples of literature that *do not* lead to a deepening of empathy, and thus are less satisfactory for developing an ethic of care. All they do is show us things as they happened. Poetic language, or works of fiction, on the contrary, show us how things *might be*. Thus a great novel is more likely to enhance a reader's imagination, and lead to a deepening of his or her ability to consider alternative futures, and thus to act ethically. Autobiography could conceivably supply a similar imaginative impetus, she reasons, but it would do so only to the extent to which the autobiography resembled fiction.[8]

Others object to autobiography as a theological genre not because a person cannot be expected to be fair when telling one's own story, but because the story remains about oneself, and does not say anything truthful about God. Consider, for example, the German Lutheran Johannes von Hofmann, whom Karl Barth called "the greatest conservative theologian" of the nineteenth century.[9] Von Hofmann sought to take as seriously as possible the site of revelation for the understanding of revelation itself. He used the term *Tatbestand*, which means something like "present factual situation," to name the state of affairs in which a self encounters God. Since each self has a unique history, intellect, and imagination, the theologian will have to pay attention to the situation of each person to whom God reveals Godself. For this reason, von Hofmann's thinking was dismissed by some of his peers as "Ich-theologie"[10] (a theology only of the *self*), the scorn in which appears to us to be, at best, a bit fishy.

Despite these objections, we see value in the task of narrating one's life and work for many reasons. No one writes or thinks without starting *somewhere*. No theology or philosophy can absent itself from the claims of particularity; all are necessarily perspectival and therefore culturally conditioned. The best that we can hope for, then, is for a theology that speaks from somewhere to as wide an elsewhere as possible, and from one time to as many times as imaginable. The craft of autobiography, it seems to us, will assist us in this kind of contextual theology.

POSSIBILITIES FOR AUTOBIOGRAPHY

Autobiography promises to further theological development on several fronts. One of the deepest problems for theology done in light of modern philosophy (and to some extent, even ancient philosophy) is the difficulty of navigating the chasm between subject and object. Posed decisively by Descartes, the subject-object problem has cast a long shadow over modern philosophy. It set the terms for epistemology, constricting how one could think about "knower" and "thing known." It also set the terms for ethics: Which actions are "objectively" moral and which are purely subjective caprice? Yet in autobiography, the subject becomes the object. In the task of reflecting on one's life one contextualizes, relativizes, and makes comparisons and decisions. The thinking, acting, living subject becomes, temporarily, fossilized. She is transferred to paper, so to speak, and becomes a thing that can be contemplated and considered like the other objects in the world. Roger Haight's contribution to this volume is especially perceptive in exploring the possibilities for overcoming the subject/object divide that autobiography presents.

But autobiography is not only useful in illuminating the self. Theological autobiographies are not just statements about a theologian, but are also genuine vehicles for theological reflection. In discerning patterns of continuity and change in one's intellectual development, new ground is broken. In reflecting on oneself, God is illumined, too. Patterns are detected and important influences named, which is another way of saying that divine providence is articulated. An etymological root links weaving (from *texo*, as in "textile") and text.[11] An autobiography narrates not just a text *about* a self, but in activating memory and subjecting it to scrutiny and critique, it narrates a self. Humans are narrative beings, as Paul Ricoeur has elegantly and forcefully shown.[12] And one of the characters in the story must be, however indirectly named, God. God is setting and protagonist, and sometimes perceived antagonist. God's actions within the world necessarily imply a kind of narrative, since our experience of them is folded into the story of God's redeeming love for the world.

Experience itself comes as a narrative. Stephen Crites published an influential essay in 1971 called "The Narrative Character of Experience."[13] Crites argues that whenever we do or undergo something, that acting or undergoing has a certain "style" that is not reducible to moments of time. A photograph of any experience inevitably distorts it because who we are and what we are doing only become clear over the course of time. Consciousness, he writes, "grasps its objects in an inherently temporal way" and that temporality is inherently narrative.[14] In order to make sense of experience and of the self that experiences, all we can do is pay attention to how their stories are told. Though not dependent on Crites's analyses, Alasdair MacIntyre has been especially successful in showing how the unity of one's life can only be seen in an examination of the stories and traditions in which one finds oneself located.[15]

The 2011 epic film *Tree of Life* offers a profound—if oblique—example of the importance of narrative context for making sense of experience. In that film a middle-aged man named Jack is shown brooding over the difficulties his past conveys to his present. Disaffected and free-floating, Jack cannot shake the memories of his deceased brother and their shared rocky childhood, as well as numerous other tragic losses and moral missteps. Glimpses into and vignettes from that childhood pepper the film's opening scenes. But then director Terrence Malick moves in a totally different direction. Juxtaposed against this very personal, very particular sliver of life on Earth, Malick shows breathtakingly cosmic sequences of the development of the universe, from the Big Bang to unicellular life to the dinosaurs and beyond. Critics and interpreters rightly will differ about how best to make sense of Malick's interspersions of the macrocosmic and the microscopic. But one inevitable consequence of the move is that Jack becomes able to cope with the difficulty he had been undergoing. Rather than floating about unmoored, he now sees his own life in cosmically wider perspective, and is able to move forward—in the end to a kind of blessedness and peace.

Rooted as they are in our experience of God in the church and world, those peculiar creations we call "doctrines" inevitably take form in just such a narrative setting. Soteriology, for example, has a fundamentally narrative structure. A narrative, reduced to its bare essentials, requires that there be two states of affairs, and that there be a move from the one to the other. Consider, then, the narrative of soteriology. Any articulation of a soteriology presupposes that there be a state of deprivation or corruption (sin) and a state of fullness or completion (salvation).[16] The story of Jesus, told with its significance, bridges the gap from the one to the other, supplying the needed narrative impetus. One could make a similar case for the internal logic of the doctrine of the Trinity. The procession of the Son from the Father is eternal, and thus does not originate in time, but the very terms "Father" and "Son" do not make sense abstracted from a narrative framework.[17] We could not imagine what the Trinity could possibly be like without stories of Jesus, the one on whom he called as Father, and the Advocate for us we daily experience.

THEOLOGICAL AUTOBIOGRAPHY, YESTERDAY AND TODAY

Christian autobiographical reflection has a long history. Augustine's *Confessions* must be regarded as its origin and, frankly, its high point. In this text Augustine manages not only to reflect on his life but also to take great strides forward theologically. The work functions on numerous levels. It is, chronologically, an account of his conversion from neo-Platonism to Christianity. Logically, it is a prayer to God that illumines both the one praying and the one to whom he prays. Theologically, it is a meditation on all manner of important topics, including the Trinity, time and eternity, creation, sin and redemption, and the nature of the church.

The medieval period saw numerous attempts at sustained theological interpretation of one's own life. These life stories stand in marked contrast to the dominant theological style of the day, which preferred dialectic and syllogism to narrative. Margery Kempe (c. 1373–1438) dictated what may be the first autobiography ever written in English, completed around 1438. She describes her life as a pilgrimage, and the tale is generously seasoned with accounts of her pilgrimages to various holy sites in Europe. Her difficult pregnancy, and the spiritual torments she felt in its aftermath, offer Kempe the occasion to wonder aloud about the mode of God's presence in one's life, the meaning of suffering, and the role of the church in mediating God's grace. She may have used as a model the writings of Julian of Norwich (c. 1342–1416), whom Margery met and with whom she spoke. Norwich never wrote a full autobiography, but her theological and spiritual writings frequently presuppose, and often mention, specific personal experiences Julian sought to understand and interpret. Luther and Calvin were rarely autobiographical, but not long after their writings revolutionized theology in Europe, it became commonplace to read serious autobiography. People as different as Menno Simons (1496–1561) and Jean-Jacques Rousseau (1712–1778) reflected in depth about their lives and God's presence, or absence, in it.[18]

The contributors to this volume thus stand in august company. Some of these autobiographies have the Augustinian pattern of conversion. Wolfhart Pannenberg, for example, describes his relatively secular, agnostic youth, which was interrupted by a profound experience of the presence of God. After that, everything was different. Ernst Käsemann, too, found that he had to divide his life into "before and after." Other contributions, such as Gerhard Forde's and Rosemary Radford Ruether's, have the character of an intensification of long-held beliefs. Still others, like Marilyn McCord Adams's and Nancey Murphy's contributions, appear as genuine pilgrimages to destinations that seem to have been utterly unforeseeable, much as Julian of Norwich and Margery Kempe saw their lives. Harvey Cox, like Rousseau in his *Confessions*, takes with utter seriousness the absence of God in a devastated culture.

None of the autobiographies in this volume speak only about its writer. Each in some way illumines God. And each in its own way invites us—and helps us—to detect in the narrative whole of our own lives the presence and nature of the Holy.

NOTES

[1] An important protest against this emphasis can be found in Keith Yandell, ed., *Faith and Narrative* (New York: Oxford University Press, 2011).

[2] For instance, Hans W. Frei, *The Identity of Jesus Christ* (Philadelphia: Fortress, 1975), *The Eclipse of Biblical Narrative* (New Haven, CT: Yale University Press, 1974), and William C. Placher, *Narratives of a Vulnerable God* (Louisville: Westminster John Knox, 1993).

[3] For instance, C. S. Song, *Tell Us Our Names: Story Theology from an Asian Perspective* (Maryknoll, NY: Orbis, 1984).

[4] Rob Bell's Mars Hill Church titles the statement of faith on their website "Narrative Theology," marshill.org/believe/about/narrativetheology.

[5] James Wm. McClendon, *Biography as Theology: How Life Stories Can Remake Today's Theology* (Eugene, OR: Wipf & Stock, 2002), 165.

[6] Ibid., 167.

[7] Stanley Hauerwas and David Burrell, "Self-Deception and Autobiography," in *Journal of Religious Ethics* 2, no. 1 (1974): 99–117.

[8] Martha Nussbaum, *Poetic Justice: The Literary Imagination and Public Life* (Boston: Beacon, 1995), especially ch. 1. An illuminating critique can be found in Ole Martin Skilleås, "Knowledge and Imagination in Fiction and Autobiography," *Metaphilosophy* 37, no. 2 (2006): 259–76.

[9] Karl Barth, *Protestant Theology in the Nineteenth Century*, trans. Brian Cozens and John Bowden (Valley Forge, PA: Judson, 1973), 610.

[10] Francis Pieper, *Christian Dogmatics*, 3 vols., trans. Theodore Engelder (St. Louis: Concordia, 1950–53), 1:6.

[11] On this and related matters, see James Olney, *Memory and Narrative: The Weave of Life Writing* (Chicago: University of Chicago Press, 1999). Olney examines autobiography in Augustine, Rousseau, and Samuel Beckett. He is also justly recognized for the notion that an autobiography, no matter how brief or insufficient, is a kind of metaphor for the self. He develops this argument in *Metaphors of Self: The Meaning of Autobiography* (Princeton, NJ: Princeton University Press, 1972).

[12] Paul Ricoeur, *Oneself as Another*, trans. Kathleen Blamey (Chicago: University of Chicago Press, 1985), 140–68.

[13] *Journal of the American Academy of Religion* 39, no. 3 (1971), 291–311. This article is anthologized along with many helpful related texts in L. Gregory Jones and Stanley Hauerwas, eds., *Why Narrative? Readings in Narrative Theology* (Grand Rapids: Eerdmans, 1989).

[14] Ibid., 302.

[15]"The Virtues, the Unity of a Human Life, and the Concept of a Tradition," is chapter 15 of his book *After Virtue: A Study in Moral Theory*, 3rd ed. (Notre Dame: University of Notre Dame Press, 2007): 204–25.

[16]On this, cf. Michael Root, "The Narrative Structure of Soteriology," in *Modern Theology* 2, no. 2 (1986): 145–57.

[17]It should be clear that the doctrine of the Trinity, which is necessarily narrative, is not the same as the Trinity, which is eternal, and thus non-narrative. Francesca Aran Murphy's recent protest in *God Is Not a Story: Realism Revisited* (Oxford: Oxford University Press, 2007) seems repeatedly to miss this point.

[18]Menno Simons is regarded as the father of the various Mennonite sects. An engaging interpretation of his memoirs can be found in Derek C. Hatch, "Autobiography as Theology: Menno Simons's 'Confession of My Conversion, Enlightenment and Calling,'" in *Mennonite Quarterly Review* 81, no. 4 (2007): 515–29.

1

Truth and Reconciliation • Marilyn McCord Adams

Biblical Beginnings

My first seventeen years were spent in the Bible Belt, in rural Illinois. My family were members of the Disciples of Christ. My grandfather, great uncle, second cousin, and aunt were all ministers. The Bible was our text, and we knew that our assignment was to "read, mark, learn, and inwardly digest it." There were cradle-to-grave Bible classes, meeting every Sunday to plow their way through age-appropriate syllabi. Children learned memory verses every week. Our earliest songs included "Jesus loves me, this I know; for the Bible tells me so" and "the B-I-B-L-E, yes that's the book for me; I stand alone on the Word of God, the B-I-B-L-E!" Youth groups were drilled until they knew the books of the Bible in order. There were games and quizzes on Bible facts. Older members pondered the meanings, shared insights, and worked all week long to knead the words of Scripture into the stuff of their lives. I count love of the Bible and a thorough familiarity with its text among the greatest gifts of my childhood.

In those country churches, biblical hermeneutics were not so much literalistic as "plain sense" and harmonizing. Although liberal ministers in my family read the then-new Interpreters' Bible and favored the RSV, conservatives defended the King James Version and took creation stories to be incompatible with evolution. Readings were mostly uninfluenced by academic scholarship, but they were shaped by lifelong study and minute reflection. If they had understood the question, all would have said that the Bible was the Word of God and the primary locus of authority for Christians. The Disciples of Christ was part of the Restoration Movement, which aimed to return to the primitive church and to shed accumulated distortions. Creeds were rejected as "man-made." "Tradition" and "the church fathers" were never mentioned. I learned about Methuselah, but I never heard of Augustine, Anselm, or Aquinas. Polity was congregational. The priesthood of all believers was affirmed in the sense that each Christian had the right and the obligation to study God's Word, to pray through it, and to make up their own minds about its meaning. Likewise, not the preacher but lay elders presided at the Lord's Supper. We summed up our position in song and slogan: "No creed but Christ; no book but the Bible; no name but the Divine. In essentials, unity; in opinions, liberty; and in all things, love."

Experiencing the Goodness

In Bible Belt religion, experience was also emphasized. There were revivals, tent meetings, altar calls, and dramatic conversions. Midwestern culture can be sentimental, and there was considerable focus on feelings. As a child, I did not have a Damascus Road conversion. Rather I experienced the reality of God as given as much as green grass and blue skies. Unlike corn on the cob, which was best in August, God was omnipresent like the air. I found the bigness of Divine Goodness utterly convincing. The reality of Jesus was a given, too, although the metaphysics of Christology was left vague. Jesus was confessed as "God's Son." I did not know how to ask whether that was adoptionist or Arian. What was clear was that Jesus shared the Divine property of being omni-accessible, there when you need Him; likewise, that Jesus is the Savior Who loves us. As a child, I did not believe in God and Jesus simply because adults told me so. I had—so I thought—tasted and seen corroborating realities, the way I had felt the wind and smelled the flowers. The testimony of experience and community joined to convince me in ways I could never fully escape that nothing could be more important than one's personal relationship with Jesus Christ. This was by far the greatest gift of my childhood.

Entering the Abyss

Moving through childhood toward adolescence, however, I faced realities of a different kind. My parents' home was chaotic, conflicted, and violent. By some time in grade school, I was the target of relentless physical and psychological abuse. Though mostly unconsciously deployed, their methods were textbook. Not only was I scapegoated, blamed, and beaten for things that were not my fault. Not only was I sexually molested. Not only did my parents take every opportunity to detail my faults to adults I respected. Not only did they "damned-if-you-do, damned-if-you-don't" my academic accomplishments. Not only did they put up obstacles to my maintaining peer friendships. My parents constantly ridiculed my religious attachments. I was a hypocrite. How could anyone as bad as I was, sincerely claim to be a Christian? They targeted my principal hold on meaning and purpose. Their determined effort to cut me off from God, from my personal relationship with Jesus Christ, was the cruelest of the many things they did.

In those Cold War days, the Sunday School thought experiment was this: When the Russians roll down the street with tanks, will you renounce your faith under torture? I was thirteen years old when I caved in. The cognitive dissonance was too much for me. I stood in the basement in front of the washing machine I was loading and ritualized my divorce from God by damning the Holy Spirit. In those days when family violence was unspeakable, I couldn't say, and I wouldn't have been believed if I had explained, what was really wrong. Neither were the mostly well-meaning ministers and teachers in our village equipped to cope with my easily reinvented head-trip objections to the Bible, to miracles, yes, to the very existence of God.

The more vivid my confrontation with evil became, the more my sense of the reality of God faded. Mounting and sustained abuse angered me. Looking back, I can see how the emotional static screened God out. On the surface, I didn't believe in God. But deeper down, I felt betrayed and abandoned by God. If I was so bad, why didn't the Savior come and help me learn to be good? Deep down, I felt that God hated me. My anger swelled, and I hated God back.

So, Scripture and experience set the theological agenda for the rest of my life. I had eaten of the tree of the knowledge of Good and Evil. I had tasted and seen the bigness of the Goodness, and—until I left for university right after high school graduation—I swallowed daily cups of poison. My problem was how to house God and evil in the same world, and how to contain the experiences of God and horrors within the same self.

The Existentialists

My first encounter with philosophy came when an out-of-town minister prescribed Immanuel Kant's *Critique of Pure Reason* as the cure for my religious doubts. I duly ordered the book from the state library and read it without understanding a word. My first encounter with theology came the following summer when I squandered my life savings of $75 to attend a six-week engineering program at the University of Illinois. The dorm counselor told us about Paul Tillich, and I rushed to the bookstore to find shelves of existentialist theology for under a dollar per volume. I devoured *The Shaking of the Foundations* with its reassuring note—"Accept the fact that you are accepted!"—as well as *The Dynamics of Faith* and *The Courage to Be*. I requested his *Systematic Theology* as a graduation present. When I got to university (in the summer of 1961), I took a course on contemporary religious thought that featured Bultmann, Buber, and Niebuhr. I pored over Kierkegaard, gulping down cups of bad coffee at the YMCA.

My attraction is easy to explain. Existentialist theologians began with my questions about the meaning and purpose of life and brought issues about what is at stake between us and God into the middle of their answers. Tillich's definition of "faith" as "ultimate concern for the ultimate" resonated. So did neo-orthodox pessimism about human nature. I was surprised and delighted to find that I was not alone in these struggles. There was company, smart and articulate company, that had written at length on these subjects. I eagerly read and pondered what they had to say. In my efforts to assess Bultmann, I even wrote my senior thesis on Heidegger to discover whether it was an apt conceptual framework for expressing the Christian gospel.

In the end, a variety of factors turned me away from the existentialists. The first was the sense that Heideggerian conceptuality was not apt. My primal anxiety was not about death, but about something worse: the fear that God hated me. The second was the anti-realist spin that many were putting on, e.g., Tillich's theory of religious symbols. Discussion-group leaders regularly spoke of going with "whichever metaphors work for you." However distorted their construals, I knew that I wasn't interested in adopting mere metaphors. Religious experience had convinced me of what it could never prove: that God is too big to be a social construction. What I wanted was to get back in touch with the reality of God. However philosophically underdeveloped the Christology of my childhood religion, the theologically reductive historical-Jesus and higher-critical accounts didn't fit the Jesus I had known and loved either. I had experienced Jesus *as God* without knowing how to theorize it.

Moreover, while the philosophy department at the University of Illinois was pluralistic and weighted toward history, analytic philosophy was growing in prominence. I was drawn into Bill Wainwright's and Nelson Pike's use of analytical methods to treat the problem of evil. I also discovered medieval philosophy, which was both analytical and systematic. Despite Norman Kretzmann's efforts to turn it into philosophy of language, I spied in it an extensive literature in which theology set the syllabus for philosophy.

The Anglo-Catholics

Amidst the array of thriving campus religious foundations at the University of Illinois in the early sixties, I could find only three groups that were metaphysical realists: the Intervarsity Christian Fellowship, which was too much like my childhood religion that had left me in the lurch; the Roman Catholics, whose commitment to papal infallibility was a definite and permanent non-starter; and the Anglo-Catholics, whose quarters faced the philosophy department from directly across the street. Henry Johnson, the priest who was running their graduate discussion group, was taking philosophy classes toward his Ph.D. in philosophy of education. Father "J" invited me to join in.

For me, these Anglo-Catholics embodied a liberating version of faith seeking understanding. They were intellectually flexible enough to tolerate questioning. Because their practice centered on worshipping a mystery, Anglo-

Catholics appreciated both our need to articulate what we experienced and the ultimate inadequacy of our attempts to grasp what is infinitely more than we can ask or imagine. They saw doctrinal formulations as partial and incomplete, to be worked and reworked through life. They also recognized how questioning and disputing are one way we put on the mind of Christ, one approach to integrating Christ into the whole persons that we are.

At least as liberating was the Anglo-Catholic focus on "objective" disciplines. My childhood religion emphasized feelings and claimed biblical authority for the warning: you're a liar to say you love God when you don't love your neighbor from your heart. But I was too messed up inside to have the approved feelings toward God and neighbor. In those years before pop-psychology, I didn't have a clue about how to clean up my internal act. The Anglo-Catholics taught that actions "count" whether or not the feelings are there. Feelings are not under my direct voluntary control, but I can put my body in the pew and form my mouth around the words. I can open the Bible or the Book of Common Prayer and read it. I eagerly welcomed the notion that God would take liturgical participation or fasting from meat on Friday as a friendly gesture, whether or not one had the right feelings.

The Anglo-Catholics explained that this did not have to be hypocrisy, because human beings are multidimensional. The inside and outside, conscious and unconscious, can be out of phase. The outside trains the outside toward Christ, even if the inside has a long way to go to catch up. Neither does repetition have to be vain; athletic workouts are a must, even for champions. Daily mass is there because we need to eat every day, and because we need to rehearse what is at stake between God and us, until it centers our daily lives.

More radical still was the hint that transformation could work from the outside in, that it could begin to reform our identities in advance of their being fully integrated. Liturgical participation is subversive: taking in the Body and Blood of Christ creates an imbalance in the self. Keep doing it, and comes the revolution, in which the personality will be recentered around friendship with Christ. And this was—despite the ambivalence planted by my encounters with evil—my heart's deepest desire.

The Anglo-Catholics introduced me to the idea that religious commitment should be normed by tradition—for them the ecumenical creeds and conciliar pronouncements were regulative. Following the Oxford Movement, they delved into patristic theology, somewhat to the neglect of the philosophically more rigorous medieval thinkers. Keble, Newman, and Pusey were their heroes. Later I was appalled by the conservative political thrust of the Oxford Movement (what American could countenance denying the vote to Roman Catholics?). But at the time, so much was new to me that I was splashing in an ocean of theological stimulation.

Anglo-Catholicism also forwards what I eventually regarded as a rigid ecclesiology. From the beginning, they explained that they and the Roman

Catholics were the only western churches with a valid ministry, that only clergy who were episcopally ordained by bishops in the apostolic succession could preside over valid sacraments. They also opposed the ordination of women on traditional grounds (and because it would burn bridges with Rome). In the medium run, these ideas could not stand up in the face of my Presbyterian husband and in-laws who obviously had effective ministries. In the long run, I had to break ranks when I was ordained.

In the beginning, however, the Anglo-Catholics were a safe house. They welcomed me. They put up with my heckling head-trip questions and objections to Augustine's arguments, until one day in the library I found myself overwhelmed by the reality of God. Moving fifty miles away to college had yanked me out of a hostile home environment and immersed me in intellectual work. Without constant provocation, the emotional static began to clear. When I was not studying, I was scouting for a context where I could recover my faith. The Anglo-Catholics helped me do that. I was overjoyed at the breakthrough. The Anglo-Catholics also helped me articulate my recovery and direct its energy. I was confirmed as an Episcopalian in May 1964. In their view, I could not be ordained, but I could become a theologian.

For years, I self-identified as an Anglo-Catholic. It became second nature to norm myself by ecumenical creeds and councils. Much later, during the LGBT controversies at Yale, someone challenged, "Professor Adams, your opponents have a rule of faith. Do *you* have a rule of faith?" I replied matter-of-factly to their dissatisfaction, "Of course. The Nicene Creed!" Equally influential on my theology has been the eucharistic piety into which the Anglo-Catholics initiated me. Almost fifty years of experience have made me a strong advocate of religious formation through material cult.

Medieval Philosophical Theology

The Anglo-Catholics encouraged me to pursue theology. My philosophy professors warned that mid-twentieth-century theology was methodologically at sea. Moreover, I had no money to fund theological education, while graduate school in philosophy was in those days a free ride. Graduate school in philosophy took me away from the existential questions that troubled me most. But in retrospect, I think the detour was necessary for me. I needed the rigor and discipline that analytic philosophy built into me. The Cornell Ph.D. program was scant in content but riveted on method: "truth, profundity, clarity; but the greatest of these is clarity!" We learned how to draw distinctions and how to be concise. These intellectual skills are important, not only in philosophy, but also in theology. Analytical precision and economy of expression have also made me a more accurate listener and a better preacher.

Cornell is also where I met and married Robert Merrihew Adams (in 1966). We were the only Christian students in the philosophy Ph.D. program. We courted over discussions of the Chalcedonian definition and other issues in patristic theology, which Bob had mastered "reading" theology at Oxford. His strength of character and firm faith have provided the stability and safety I needed to wrestle with God and to venture many things.

When I first arrived at Cornell in the fall of 1964, the department was in the last gasps of Wittgensteinian dominance. Syllabi were otherwise crammed with varieties of empiricism, including repeated doses of Locke, Berkeley, and Hume. To put it mildly, the ideological climate was unpromising for making progress in understanding God and evil. My way forward was pointed by Nelson Pike's regular recourse to medieval philosophical theologians, when analyzing problems about the attributes of God. Here I found mentors and conversation partners, thinkers who turned high-powered philosophical expertise to the syllabus of theology. I could not see myself simply buying into their transmogrified neo-Platonic and Aristotelian metaphysics (although I certainly find it more congenial overall than Hegelian and neo-Kantian approaches). Nevertheless, I reckoned early on that if I could figure out how medieval systems worked and discover how their methods integrated philosophy and theology, I would be well prepared for my own constructive projects. At twenty, I radically underestimated how long such "ground-work" would take.

The result was that I became, among other things, a medievalist. I have no regrets. Studying Anselm, Bonaventure, Aquinas, Scotus, and Ockham has taught me many things. First and foremost, I learned that *philosophy is and ought to be the backbone of theology.* Theologians need explicitly to take responsibility for their philosophical commitments. They should not be allowed to get by with half-baked, underdigested philosophical allusions. Second, I took from scholastic method the highly pertinent lessons that *questioning and disputing authority is not impudent insubordination but a tool of analysis* and that *vigorous disagreement is not inherently dangerous but— among fallible human beings—serves as a winnowing fork and an instrument for discovering the truth.* Most important for me was Anselm's example, making explicit how *theology is something you do with your whole self.* Between birth and the grave, the human assignment is to strive into God with all of our powers. For Anselm, that meant subjecting the will to monastic disciplines, training the emotions through spiritual exercises, and sharpening the mind by questioning and disputing authority. Each and all of the powers need training and coordination. This dynamic, played out in the *Proslogion,* brought me to another fundamental insight: that *doing philosophy and theology is itself a kind of prayer.* Anselm's job is energetic articulation that presses questions and objections. Then he pauses and awaits the Inner Teacher's "aha" disclosure, which Anselm then tries to formulate, only to question and dispute all over again. Theology is something you do with your whole self, but it is not a solo act. We are designed to function in collaboration with the Inner Teacher. Whether conscious or unconscious, insight is always the fruit of our functional partnership with God.

Even when their Aristotle is mostly bracketed, medievals have much to offer where theological emphasis and content are concerned. Key for me was the way my favorite five scholastics—Anselm, Bonaventure, Aquinas, Scotus, and Ockham—appreciate what I call "the Metaphysical Size Gap": God as immeasurably excellent is in a different ontological category from creatures, and yet is still a "personal" agent who acts by thought and will to do one thing rather than another in the created order. To my mind, analytic philosophers of religion make an idol of morality, insisting that God's perfect goodness must be moral goodness, and maintaining that we have rights against God who has obligations to us. By contrast, my favorite five were unanimous that God is too big to be networked to us by rights and obligations. Franciscans put morality in its place with their verdict: even if we were morally perfect, Divine love for us would be utterly gratuitous. "Who are we that He should show, such great love to us below?" Even from a negative angle, my existential issues with God were never that God had violated my rights (as my parents arguably had), but that God had raised expectations and inspired trust, only seemingly to abandon and betray me.

Oddly, my favorite five scholastics did not draw the converse conclusion from the Metaphysical Size Gap: that we are too small to have moral obligations to God. The anchorite Julian of Norwich (my sixth favorite) stands alone in forwarding an anthropology that relocates us in relation to Divine agency, not as adult defendants before the great judgment seat of Christ, but as infants and children who need help and discipline. I continue to find encouragement in her conception that sin is at bottom not rebellion but incompetence, and in her estimate that the worst scourge is being the dysfunctional sinners that we are.

Equally inspiring for me was the Franciscan motif of the primacy of Christ. The religion of my childhood had been Jesus-centered. But Franciscan philosophical theologians put this into cosmic perspective. Not only is the Incarnation not plan "B," regretfully adopted to solve the sin-problem; God-with-us is God's purpose in creation. Christ is the primary reason why God created anything at all!

Gathering Up the Fragments

Normally and naturally, Manichaean experience of God and of horrors fragments the self. Both realities are seared into the soul. But the unconscious fear is that Evil will swallow up the Good. It is one thing to doubt or deny the existence of God intellectually. But terror attends the prospect of erasing all experiential memory of really present Goodness. "Splitting off" is a solution, closeting memory of the Good to protect it from encounters with the devouring Bad. Unconscious memory of really present Goodness is important, because—whatever else the conscious self might think and feel, no matter what other contents the unconscious self might manage—memory-prints of Goodness fuel hope that what you see is not all you get and energize the demand to be better, to do better, and to make things better. Normally and naturally, Manichaean experience sets up a parallel polarity between love and hate, and commonly triggers the "split-off" of one from the other. Parts of me still loved God and knew that God was all I ever wanted. Other parts vehemently hated God for being dead-beat at best and treacherous at worst. Locking up the love is important, because it guards against the horror of becoming a hater through and through.

The truth, as I came eventually to see it, is that memory-prints and desires are not all we have left. Really present Goodness did not go away. God was and is omnipresent. God's real presence, like the memory of it, just went underground. Abandonment is metaphysically impossible—nothing could be or do anything if God were not there—and so merely apparent. To extend Anselm's view, this is because the Inner Teacher partners with us in all of our personal functioning, not just in generating intellectual insights. Most of the time, we are not conscious of God's presence and influences. But whether or not we recognize it, we are working together, and *God is there*. This means that it is not merely memory prints, but really present Godhead Itself that grounds our hope.

Normally, therapists and spiritual directors see fragmentation as a temporary defense that eventually needs to be undone through a process of bringing salient pieces up to consciousness and letting them "talk to each other." Before my midlife crisis, I lacked such pop-psychological knowledge of human dynamics. So much in church and society sent the message "Just suck it up and function!" After four years at the University of Michigan, we had moved to UCLA with tenure (in 1972). When I was not teaching, I spent waking hours writing my two-volume book on Ockham's philosophical theology. I attended daily mass at the Anglo-Catholic parish a mile away from our house. But God seemed distant, even abstract like the federal government that knows all about you and provides certain services but can't be greeted face-to-face.

I remained "on hold" for about six years, when an uncertain medical diagnosis got my attention. Death might be imminent. Time to take stock. I joined a prayer group. We took our 1979–1980 sabbatical in Princeton, where my father-in-law, then dean of the seminary, really was dying. I met my first spiritual director, A. Orley Swartzentruber, rector of All Saints' parish, Old Testament scholar, and ex-Mennonite missionary. His penetrating biblical preaching convinced me that he could midwife the reconnections and help me recover my personal relationship with Jesus Christ. So the internal inventory began.

Orley was influenced by the charismatic movement that stressed the healing of memories. First, one recovered the memory, then one reimagined the scene with Jesus present in it, with others praying for healing all the while. Certainly, bringing the unspeakable into community with others, along with one's sense of abandonment and betrayal, cancels the sense of isolation. Moreover, in relation to God, the exercise is an act of candor and so a gesture of trust. The point of the reimaging is to trigger a deep-level *experience* of the fact that God did not go AWOL, that God was really present in one's hour of need. Charismatic rhetoric often commended the healing of memories as if it were a "quick fix." Sometimes, such deep-structure putting two and two together happened suddenly and dramatically. Other times, the exercises and prayers were a step in a much longer complicated process. As my friend and teacher Jim Loder, a professor of Christian education at Princeton Theological Seminary, emphasized: even when the existential "aha" comes all of a sudden, its implications have to be worked through piecemeal, setting it against fragment after fragment until it saturates and reorganizes the self. Happily, Orley himself appreciated the long-haul nature of the project. The five years of work we did together did not finish the course, but they were foundational for the rest of my life.

Theology is something you do with your whole self, but—in the rough and tumble of this world—you cannot wait to do it until your self is whole. Among other things, a theologian volunteers to be a laboratory where she labors with God to accomplish God's transforming work. The theologian's job is to initiate, reciprocate, and cooperate. The theologian's task is also to watch and articulate how God saves and to map the twists and turns and obstacles on the way to becoming whole. Put otherwise, *theology is read "off the gut."* What guards against what Anglo-Catholics called "the caprice of private interpretation" is that theology is read "off the gut" *through the lens of Scripture and tradition and within the context of community.*

HOLLYWOOD DEBUT

Midlife crisis reacquainted me with my early sense of vocation to ordained ministry. Perhaps unsurprisingly, it proved much more difficult for me to get into the Episcopal church process and to clear its hurdles than it was to get a Ph.D. Rebuffed on first attempt, I decided to go to Princeton Theological Seminary anyway. Even if I didn't win a plastic collar, I could at least learn many things I wanted to know. By teaching the winter and spring quarters and attending seminary in the summer and fall (in 1983 and 1984), I was able to get two Th.M.s, with coursework evenly divided between Bible and psychology-spirituality. Twin degrees in hand, I wasn't simply going back to fishing, so I accepted then-rector David Duncan's invitation to jump-start adult education at Trinity parish in Los Angeles..

I didn't know that David had also brought in Bill Leason, an openly gay priest whose day job was bilingual education in the Los Angeles Sheriff's Department, and that gay men were flocking to our church in the wake of the AIDS epidemic. Orley and the charismatics had been vigorous in their insistence that LGBT lifestyles were incompatible with holy living. Getting real with myself, I had to admit that sexuality is a hard subject. There was nothing to do but keep my eyes and ears open. We were in emergency mode, and I had a pastor's privilege of close-range observation. I learned a lot. I observed that LGBT relationships, and the partners that peopled them, were not perfect. *And* the same was true of the heterosexual couples I knew. I saw how anti-LGBT taboos produced a lot of confusion among people who were trying hard to find ways to give and receive love. I saw sacrificial love and faithfulness persevering to the end. I saw God-with-us at work in the midst of horrendous suffering. My conclusion was that taboos are cruel and that the Church should have nothing to do with them. Taboos are social barriers erected out of fear that society will come unraveled. But fear is not what glues the Church together. What guarantees the Church's integrity is the Holy Spirit of God!

Working with returning LGBT at Trinity Hollywood was one of the greatest privileges of my life. I, who had been estranged from God for decades, who still deep down hated the God who abandons people to horrendous harm, found myself preaching God's unconditional love and unfailing solidarity, God-with-us in the worst that we can suffer, be, or do. I advertised Divine eagerness to enter into conversation with us on whichever basis we are able to start. I could not begin, as Orley had, with sin and repentance. In childrearing, discipline should be based on love. But our congregation was awash in social hate. Someone summed up my aim and proudest accomplishment: "The more I hear you talk about God, the more I like God!"

Secretly, I wondered where I got all that. I make it a rule never to preach anything I don't believe. But my sermons were so much more optimistic than my own conscious struggles let on. My conclusion was that really present Godhead had been cultivating core familiarity, teaching me about Itself all along. This learning had remained out of sight, because I hadn't been able to manage the cognitive dissonance. The urgent need of people living and dying with HIV/AIDS pulled it out of me and compelled me to proclaim the Good News of God's love in articulate speech.

I was ordained at Trinity Hollywood in 1987. Equally important, I became an honorary gay person, a member of the LGBT tribe. They were my people, and I could not afterwards deny the miracles I had seen among them. Certainly, I am as fallible as the next Christian. *But to lie about what one has seen God doing is the greatest blasphemy and forfeits all reason for being.* My experience made me an LGBT activist. I could not fail to bear witness to Orley and Jim (whom I did not convince) and the charismatics (who anathematized me). Later, when I left Los Angeles for Yale in 1993, I vowed to take the perspective of the margins to the heart of the establishment. Sure enough, I had my chance: my ten years at Yale-Berkeley Divinity School saw, not one, but three virulent LGBT controversies. Later still, when I arrived at Oxford in January 2004, I wondered why God had called me there. Two weeks in, I was asked to preach at Inclusive Church on the eve of the presentation of *Some Issues in Human Sexuality* to the General Synod. Because I didn't have English manners, I felt free to be outspoken and used my position as Regius Professor to forward LGBT causes in whatever ways I could. Because Anglican Communion controversy was firing up over the ordination of Gene Robinson (a coupled gay man) as bishop of New Hampshire, I had a lot of work to do as a public theologian opposing the Anglican Covenant and educating the Church of England about the American church.

YALE

Stimulating as urban ministry was, once I was ordained, I was increasingly dissatisfied with the "fit" of my philosophy department job. When George Lindbeck retired from Yale Divinity School (in 1993), I applied to become professor of historical theology. The move bristled with challenge and promise. The first challenge was that I was thoroughly out of sympathy with the Frei-Lindbeck Yale School, which understood theology as "grammar" or a set of linguistic rules about what to say, about which stories to tell. My jaw dropped to hear Lindbeck insist that the *Summa Theologica* was not about the metaphysics of Godhead, but about language. Yale schoolmen sometimes spoke of Christian religion as a language game sealed off from other language games (including philosophy) in such a way as not to have to interact with them. The approach was attractive to conservatives who wanted to hold content fixed without having to answer to challenges from historical and scientific disciplines. For a metaphysical realist and philosophical theologian like me, this was a non-starter. Lindbeck students regularly came up to me at conferences to say what a shame it was that I had succeeded him, because I could not and would not carry on the traditions of the Yale School.

Moreover, I had to play "catch up" when it came to the canon of twentieth-century theology. For this purpose, the annual theology seminar (for all and only theology faculty and Ph.D. students) was a help. The recipe was to take a theological locus (God, Trinity, Incarnation, soteriology, eschatology) and to read what five or six contemporary Germans (usually, Barth, Moltmann, Pannenberg, Rahner, Tillich, von Balthasar) had to say. When I arrived, Barth was very much in ascendancy, and I feared that I would have to master the whole *Church Dogmatics* to be part of the conversation. Certainly, I found Barth's lack of terminal facility trying (would that he had been disciplined in graduate school by the mandatory concision of four-page papers)! Just as irritating was Barth's animus against philosophical method in theology, when his own writings were steeped in philosophical allusions. The reconstructive programs of most of the others were underwritten by post-Kantian philosophical systems that I found philosophically uncongenial. For example, I could not get behind Hegelian-style moves of identifying God with the Absolute that is beyond the personal or impersonal, and denying that God as Ground of Being is an agent that does one thing rather than another.

Five years in, I concluded that the twentieth-century German canon was not going to bring me any closer to formulating my own constructive positions. Instead, I returned to Anglican authors. Moving forward from the Oxford Movement, I found in Gore-to-Temple the period that crystallized what attracted me so much: three-legged-stool Anglicanism that plays Scripture, Tradition, and Reason off one another in a balancing act; and a focus on the Incarnation and sacraments. The Bible, the ecumenical creeds and conciliar pronouncements, my favorite six medievals, and Gore-to-Temple Anglicans were and remain my chosen theological conversation partners.

Despite ideological misfits, I did come out of the closet as a theologian at Yale. Years before, I had told Orley that my two interests were the problem of evil and Christology. He challenged me to say how Jesus solves the problem of evil. It took a couple of decades, but eventually I wrote two books to do just that. Atheologian J. L. Mackie famously argues that theism is logically contradictory, because the existence of evil is logically incompatible with the existence of an omnipotent, omniscient, and perfectly good God. *Horrendous Evils and the Goodness of God* is directed at Christian philosophers of religion and urges them to draw on the materials of revealed religion—e.g., the sufferings of Christ and/or sufferings within the Trinity—to show how horrendous evil is logically compatible with the existence of God. *Christ and Horrors: The Coherence of Christology* is directed at theologians and explores who the Savior would have to be and what He would have to do, if His job were not primarily to solve the sin-problem but to save us from horrendous harms. The second book is a systematic Christology. Given my history of Jesus-centered religion, when I turned to systematic theology, where else could I begin?

Someone has said, "the glory of Yale is its students." Certainly, *the privilege of working with many and variously gifted Yale students was the height of my teaching career.* To begin with, Yale was a wonderful place to do historical theology. My medieval and Reformation survey was already built-in to Yale's four-semester patristics-to-twentieth-century sequence. I followed it with single-author graduate seminars on each of my favorite five, garnering enrollments from philosophy, religious studies, history, and medieval studies.

Along the way, I persuaded the most interested to learn Latin, so that we could proceed to reading courses on medieval theories of Trinity and Christology. I taught overloads and burned midnight oil, the better to seize my opportunity. Bringing to life the figures that one loves, analyzing theories that provoke, delving in and sharing the process of discovery, these are the scholar's delight, topped only by the satisfactions of watching one's students grow.

For most of my Yale years, Nicholas Wolterstorff held the Noah Porter Chair in Philosophical Theology. We joined forces to foster a program in philosophical theology, which challenged theologians with our dictum that philosophy is the backbone of theology, and sent them down the hill to the philosophy department for courses on Aristotle, Kant, and Hegel, while insisting that philosophers of religion should be at least as theologically and biblically literate as the average minister. Connections forged by the Society of Christian Philosophers brought many able students to masters' and doctoral programs at Yale. While they took our warnings with varying degrees of seriousness, the resultant cross-fertilization has enriched both fields.

Liberating for me was the way the divinity school context made it easy to integrate intellectual work into a life of worship. After all, didn't Anselm teach us, *theology is a kind of prayer?* Bob and I bought a house within walking distance of the daily liturgies of Berkeley Divinity School, the Episcopalian seminary at Yale. YDS also held mid-morning worship five days per week. When my turn came to preside at the Friday communion service, I worked with some extraordinarily feisty students to take the liturgy apart and re-assemble it into a Good-News startle. I also got involved in the preaching class, where it was so obvious that *preaching has to be done with your whole self!* I prayed and coffee-houred with Episcopal students on a daily basis. I am moved to watch so many of them taking up senior leadership positions in our Church. For me, being—in many and various ways—part of their formation was one of the great blessings of my life.

Nevertheless, my ten years at Yale-Berkeley Divinity School were institu-tionally apocalyptic. During that time (1993–2003), YDS and BDS each went through four different deans. Not only did we have three major LGBT blow-ups, there was a crisis in the Yale-Berkeley affiliation, when Yale mistakenly but publicly accused Berkeley's dean of financial wrongdoing. Caught in the whirl of bitter conflicts, lots of us tossed and turned through sleepless nights. Praying in the wee hours, it hit me: "These levels of anxiety are way out of proportion. What can they do to a tenured professor?" Then it came to me: my experience of Yale, of intense good and virulent evil existing side by side, structurally reproduced my childhood predicament. Current anxieties were drawing the stored terrors of youth up to consciousness, and these were amplifying the intensity of my adult experience. I reasoned: "No way could my childhood self have withstood these levels in her own strength—You must have been there all along!" Whew!

Several years later, institutional storms still raging, I had four hours of surgery for a broken wrist. An out-of-town friend visited that week and shared with me the latest round of sexist abuse that she had experienced from the Church. That night I woke up, still groggy from painkillers, and blurted out: "You could have got a lot more bang for your buck, if You had put my intelligence and determination into a male body! . . . and if You hadn't left a big hole where the ego-strength was supposed to be!" I drifted off and woke up again. The voice said, "I wasn't trying to get bang for my buck. I was trying to enable you to survive!" I drowsed and woke again: "and to give you something to enjoy!" A third time: "As for the ego-strength, I was planning to fill the gap with Myself."

Stunned as I was, three messages lay on the surface. First, the experience cancelled the parental curse. Even if mother and father had partly hated me, *God* wanted me to exist, and that's why I survived. Second, God-given intellectual ability was included in the survival kit, something to enjoy while I was struggling with the aftermath of childhood. Third, really present Godhead is with us always. God was there, among other things, absorbing some of the emotional energy of the conflicts, so that I was only smashed but not utterly destroyed by them. As Jim Loder predicted, some years were required for me to digest these meanings.

"Liberal"

Politically, I am a pessimistic liberal, who is convinced that no merely human being is good enough or smart enough to be entrusted with very much power. Tolerance is a corollary. Liberals agree to differ about controversial matters of great importance (e.g., belief in God, the morality of war, abortion, or euthanasia), not because they hold no conscientious beliefs, but because it would be especially wrong in such weighty matters to try to force other people's beliefs or to make them agree. Pessimistic liberals are too pessimistic to aim for purity in merely human institutions. All of them spawn systemic evils, which it becomes our duty to identify and uproot. Decision procedures exist, not to produce agreement, but to set institutional policy while the debate continues. There is nothing original in my position. It scarcely crossed my mind that it might be inconsistent with religious orthodoxy, until I moved from philosophy departments into theology.

When I arrived at Yale in 1993, I was surprised to find both left and right treating "liberal" and "Enlightenment" as dirty words. According to liberationists, Enlightenment doctrines of equality were a ruse: by remaking the whole human race in the image of the European white male, liberals had covertly cut others out of the conversation. Liberationists were carried along by a Marxian pragmatism that reduced thought to ideology and treated ideology as a tool of power. Enlightenment searches for truth were written off as at best naïve and at worst deceptive. On the right, some conservatives about sex-and-gender issues explicitly dismissed mutual respect as an Enlightenment value. God was not and Christians should not be tolerant of error!

Months and years of listening to this rhetoric made me more determined than ever. "Liberal, and proud of it," I came to say. The university is, after all, a liberal institution dedicated to seeking the truth, a medieval and enlightenment institution in which disagreement and vigorous criticism are tools of discovery. While my political objectives usually aligned with the left, I could not get on board with the *modus operandi* of either left or right. Among other things, I was and am an analytic philosopher by training and a metaphysical realist by conviction. At first, I was shocked and puzzled at the way theologies-of-engagement literature regularly distorted the texts of historical theology. Then, I realized, if thought is ideology and reality is socially constructed all the way down, why not use past thinkers to construct the enemy you need as a foil in forwarding your ideas? So-called strategic essentialism—which adopts essentialism (about race, sex, and gender) when it is politically useful to do so and switches to anti-essentialism when that appears politically advantageous—struck me as rank dishonesty and contempt for the truth. Deep-seated convictions are one thing. I have many myself. But the intolerance of both right and left struck me as a dangerous mixture of hubris and naïveté about human fallibility. The nastiness of resulting disputes was the metaphorical equivalent of drawing and quartering—the very thing that pessimistic liberalism was invented to prevent. If its "thin" values homogenize the human race, it is around the premise that each and every human being is worthy of respect and enjoys fundamental human rights. "Liberal," I say, "and proud of it!"

When I went to Oxford in January 2004, my liberal sensibilities were shocked all over again by conservatives' refusal to "agree to differ" on sex-and-gender issues within the Church of England and wider Anglican Communion debates. For Anglo-Catholics, women are not the right sort of thing to be ordained clergy. Even when made institutionally legitimate, ordinations would not "take" at the metaphysical level (the so-called "ontological change" would not happen), with the result that rites over which women presided could not be valid sacraments. The Anglo-Catholics declared that they could not tolerate remaining within the Church of England without the "protection" of a separate line of bishops whose sacramental faculties had not been compromised—to be precise, male bishops who had never laid hands on women as if to ordain.

In the wake of Gene Robinson's consecration as bishop of New Hampshire, evangelical animus against ordaining and blessing partnered homosexuals became more intense than ever. Anglicans could not remain in worldwide communion if they did not agree on "essentials" in faith and practice. For the past century and a half, this had meant adherence to Scripture and historic creeds (with variable nods to the Thirty-Nine Articles of Religion), episcopal polity, and worship somehow rooted in the 1662 Book of Common Prayer. Suddenly, essentials included "biblical morality"—most notably, the principles that sexual activity is to be restricted to the context of heterosexual marriage, and that homosexual activity is contrary to the will of God. At first, I was taken aback to see contentious ethical claims elevated to creedal status. Instancing the Church's historic flip-flop on slavery, the American church carefully distinguishes faith in the Trinity and confession of the Incarnation from evolving human understanding of what the Good News means for human life together.

These heated disputes brought polity differences out of the closet. Liberals had remained part of an institution with whose institutional sex-and-gender policies (on women and LGBT) they conscientiously disagreed, because they hoped to work within the institution to change its policies when they came into their majority. Conservatives made it clear that they could conscientiously remain within an institution only so long as their own conscientious beliefs set institutional policies. Conservatives saw liberal willingness to "agree to differ" as unprincipled, while liberals viewed conservatives as sore losers. I myself became a vocal defender of a liberal church. What sense did it make for an established Church of England, by law committed to be open to all comers, to be anything else? Surely, unholy coercion would be the result of attempts to make legally independent national churches as culturally disparate as the American Church and the Anglican Church in Nigeria agree about sexual mores!

Moving to England brought my liberal sensibilities up short another way. I had always assumed that we Americans had borrowed our democratic institutions from England. I brought along a fierce commitment to representative government, public debate, transparent majority-rule decision making. I never got over my culture shock at finding how little these values were shared in the circles in which I moved. Oligarchy was the default instinct in Oxford colleges and in the Church of England. The Senior Common Room and the House of Bishops were more like elite clubs, where people know each other and come to understandings over sherry and cigars and wouldn't think of rocking the boat enough to scandalize valued members. One head of house matter-of-factly admitted that he made all of the decisions because he knew what his colleagues wanted. Another explained how it would be shameful to have to take votes (because the defeated side would lose face?). Despite the fact that the General Synod of the Church of England is—by law—a legislature consisting of three houses, the House of Bishops still feels entitled to rule the Church of England. "Trust your betters to make your decisions for you!" When they kept proposing top-heavy polity models that further exalted the episcopacy, I was provoked to title my Bell lecture "The Episcopacy of All

Believers." I agreed that episcopacy involves an "ontological change," but I relocated it in that lived partnership with indwelling Godhead into which every Christian is initiated. Like infants growing up into a human way of being in the world, Christians need to be formed and informed by Scripture and tradition. What adult Christians are not free to do is to delegate their discernment to others. This means that our ecclesial institutions should be transparent and participatory, encouraging all believers to stretch up to their full stature in Christ.

TRUTH AND RECONCILIATION

Cathedral worship was the glory of my time in Oxford. The thousand-year-old building was—among other things—steeped in prayer. In the Latin chapel especially, there was a palpable depth of silence. It was easy to be drawn into and enveloped by its cleansing force. Choral evensong was contemplative a different way. The daily round included three services: morning prayer, eucharist, evensong or "even-said." They called me "Canon Omnipresent." I knew I had roughly six years. There was no way I was going to miss my opportunity to be a monk! I got a key, so that I could come in early before others arrived in the morning. And so the Latin chapel became the scene where I poured out my questions and accusations and arguments, the place where I made my peace with God.

That God could call me out of such toxic conflicts at Yale into the wonder of Christ Church Cathedral raised my levels of trust considerably. Week by week, I surrendered more of the defenses I had put up against God and against myself. What a relief! In those early months, the college custodians (the security men in bowler hats) asked why I was always smiling. Practicing toward English reserve which I never achieved, I replied that the architecture cheered me up!

Nevertheless, time and candor predictably brought me back into the middle of my fundamental quarrel with God. Abandonment is one thing; betrayal, another. My head knew that it was theoretically impossible for an essentially omnipresent Creator and Sustainer to go AWOL, long before experience convinced me (at Yale) that God is always there. But even if God is always there, when we've tasted and seen horrendous evils, how can we regain that Lutheran confidence that God is always there *for us*?

The rock-bottom for me was hatred: horror participation turned me into a hater. I hated my parents. I hated other abusers in my life. I hated myself. And I hated God. Didn't hatred at the core prove my parents' point: I was too bad to be a Christian? I didn't want to be a hater, but—despite years of spiritual direction and therapy—I was clueless how to stop.

For five and a half years, my early-morning plea was that God would take the hatred away. I begged to be transformed, so that I could love God with my whole self. "Speak the word only, and my soul shall be healed!" But however much I prayed and consciously willed it, the hatred didn't go away. Petition turned to grief and anger: "You must hate me! Otherwise You would uproot the hatred and enable me to love You with all I've got." Round and round I went in a vicious circle. Finally, my last holy week in Oxford, I came to "the hour of decision." The only way out was to take a leap of faith, to choose to believe that whatever God's reason for any of our torments, it's not that God hates us. I took the leap. I quit praying for God to take the hatred away. Several months later in the midst of household chores, an imaginary conversation volunteered itself in my mind: "Do you hate God?" a nameless voice inquired. "Not anymore!" I replied without hesitation. It took me several more days to tumble to the realization: God had answered my prayer after all!

CODA

In the summer of 2009, we returned to the States for tax reasons and took up research professorships at UNC-Chapel Hill. We are grateful for our time in England, and yet happy now to be within closer reach of many friends. Looking to the future, I have other books to write: a popular book on God and evil, a book on medieval views on the soul, my long-pondered monograph on Anselm, a book on ecclesiology arguing that the human side of the Church should be more like the liberal state, and a book on sacraments. In *Christ and Horrors*, I labor the question why God makes us in a world like this. I had no sooner sent it off than the issue flipped over in my mind to accentuate the positive: it is our vocation as material persons to work with God to make the material world holy, beginning with the material that we are. There is also a further spiritual exercise. At the age of sixty-five, I finally came to the point of trusting God enough to live. Now it is time to learn how to trust God enough to die!

Theology is something you do with your whole self, but it isn't something you do by yourself. Theology is read "off the gut" through the lens of Scripture and tradition and in the context of community. Recognized or unrecognized, indwelling Godhead is teacher and partner. Theology is something you do with your whole self, but you can't afford to wait to do it until your self is whole for this reason: many of us called to be theologians become whole by doing theology!

2

The Deepest Traces • Harvey Cox

For as long as I can remember I have been fascinated with the interaction of religion and politics. It is not hard to understand why.

First, religion. The house in which I grew up in Malvern, Pennsylvania (population in 1930s: 1,500) was nestled between First Baptist Church on one side and St. Patrick's Roman Catholic Church on the other. On warm days, when the windows were open, we could sometimes hear gospel hymns and the chanting of the Mass at the same time. My parents were not particularly religious. They did not attend church, but they sent my siblings and me to the Baptist Sunday School, which today would probably be called "moderate evangelical." My grandmother, however, was a Baptist churchgoer, albeit not particularly pious. As a small kid, I sat next to her on the hard wooden pew, endured the sermons but loved to sing the hymns, many of which I still know by heart years later. I also sang bass in the choir, and was president of the youth group, which often visited similar groups in the local Methodist and Presbyterian churches. As a youngster I was on friendly terms with both Father Devers, the Catholic priest who burned leaves in the lot next door as he smoked a cigar, and with a succession of young Baptist ministers serving our church, who were fascinating to me but did not smoke.

I never went inside the Catholic Church except for the parochial school's Christmas concerts, which were held in the basement, not in the sanctuary. This was decades before the Second Vatican Council, and Protestants and Catholics simply did not go into each other's churches. Still, I sometimes paused in front of it when the doors were open, and peered in. It seemed dark, even mysterious, inside, in contrast to the Baptist church, which was always flooded with light from banks of clear glass windows. Once, as I paused in front of St. Patrick's, I noticed the words inscribed over the door: "Built upon the Foundation of the Apostles and Prophets, Jesus Christ Himself Being the Chief Corner Stone." I did not know at the time that this was a quotation from the book of Ephesians. Still it seemed impressive, given that the words carved in a similar place on the front of the Baptist church said "Founded in 1874." For me, nothing was more interesting than the differences and similarities among the local churches, and I already knew as a teenager that I wanted to study religion and maybe even become a minister.

Next, the politics. If my family was not terribly religious, they were quite political indeed. My parents and grandparents were Republicans, active in local, county, and state politics. Although I changed considerably in my political views since my childhood, I still admire their persistence, dedication, and hard work. They not only believed politics made a real difference and seemed to enjoy it, even when they lost, which was frequently, especially in national elections in which they faithfully supported Hoover (1932), Landon (1936), Willkie (1940), and Dewey (1944 and 1948). But "that man in the White House" (FDR) always seemed to win. Then the local Democrats would drive through the streets honking their horns in celebration. They always paused in front of our house, and eventually my father would step out onto the porch and wave to them. He was a good loser. In those days he had to be. But he did not lose in Malvern, and at the county level Republicans had a remarkable record of success. Chester County voted for the GOP year after year from the founding of the party until 2008, when Barack Obama carried it and brought with him a Democratic Congressman.

Also, throughout my life I have been fascinated by religious diversity. Chester County was religiously mixed. My ancestors were Quakers, among the earliest settlers in Pennsylvania, and fervent abolitionists. They had also had been involved in organizing the Republican Party there in 1854. Conservative in many respects, my parents and grandparents were intensely anti-racist. The abolitionist sentiment still thrived, and I am sure this influenced me to throw myself into the civil rights movement of the 1960s where I came to know Martin Luther King Jr. and to move my small nuclear family to Roxbury, the black area of Boston, when I finished my doctoral work at Harvard.

But my immediate family was no longer Quaker. Our branch of the family became Baptist when my grandfather was "separated from meeting" some-time around 1898 for "marrying out of meeting." The outsider he married was a Baptist woman. Neither Malvern nor Chester County was religiously monochrome. The area was originally settled by religious immigrants—first Quakers, then Amish, Brethren, and Mennonites. I went to our small public school with Black Baptists, Presbyterians, Catholics, and with Mennonite kids whom my parents admired for their good manners and simplicity. Not far from our house we could see Amish people working their fields with horses and driving their buggies along narrow roads. The names of many towns in the state, like Goshen, Ephrata, and Bethlehem, echo their religious roots.

As history unfolded, Pennsylvania diversified even more. Poles, Germans, Italians, and Irish came, some to dig coal or drill in the oil fields, others to work in the factories. Gradually some moved into Malvern. Many of them were Catholics. Chester County became a center for "little steel" while the northeastern part of the state became a section of "big steel." In the 1930s and

'40s large numbers of southern black people moved to Philadelphia during the "great migration." Some found their way along the mainline railway tracks, and a number eventually settled in our little town where we all attended the same school. There were two black churches in Malvern, one Baptist and the other A.M.E. I visited both of them with my grandmother who dropped in while she was campaigning for town assessor, a position she held for many years. We were always warmly received, and this experience prepared me for the mid-1950s when I served as Protestant chaplain at Temple University in "North Philly," which has the largest concentration of blacks in that city. I became closely familiar with several of their powerful churches when I attended them with my students.

Things change, but culture lingers. When in 1966 the federal government tried Father Dan Berrigan and his associates for burning draft files, they chose the court in Harrisburg, Pennsylvania, thinking it was a conservative area (which in many ways it was, and still is). But what the feds had overlooked was that a strong pacifist and anti-military sentiment, derived from its pietistic religious past, still clung to the atmosphere, and there was considerable support for the protesters in the area. But Berrigan and his associates did not dispute what they had done. They were convicted, given short terms, and eventually paroled.

There is some evidence recently that the traditional buttoned-down conservative religious currents in Pennsylvania are not fusing well with the new political conservatism of an important segment of the Republican Party. Many traditional religious conservatives, still shaped by Quaker and Pietistic inclinations, distinctly dislike both the "showy" religion of the TV evangelists and the rancorousness of some of the candidates. There is also a long tradition of toleration, going back as far as William Penn, whose statue stands atop the city hall of Philadelphia, his "city of brotherly love." This helps explain why Obama's race seemed not to be an impediment. I sometimes wonder how my parents and grandparents would view these changes.

Malvern was a good place to be a kid in the 1930s, but when I reached seventeen I wanted to travel, so I signed on to a merchant ship headed for Europe. That turned out to be one of the most influential decisions in my life. My job was to help care for the horses on board that were being shipped by the UN Relief and Rehabilitation Authority. I was thrilled to be away, and I first set foot in a foreign country (Germany) in July 1946, just one year after the end of World War II. I say "set foot," because it was not much more than that. My footstep was onto a landing platform of a lock in Kiel during the short time it took to raise our Liberty ship, S.S. *Robert Hart*. Two shipmates and I had clambered down a ladder set up for the captain and first mate to confer with canal authorities. We were quickly chased back up by a local policeman, but I at least felt the satisfaction that I had indeed "set foot" in a foreign land. But what I noticed most about the area around the lock was how utterly devastated it was. The arms of sunken cranes still hung at precarious angles.

Two days later I climbed ashore for a longer visit in a city that was even more devastated: it was Danzig, later renamed Gdansk when it was made part of Poland after the war. Danzig/Gdansk had been both bombed and shelled many times over. When our ship tied up in its port area, called Gdynia, to unload our cargo, the crew was allowed to walk around what was left of it. At first I just stood and stared at the charred timbers and shattered chimneys. Endless blocks of skeletal ruins stretched in every direction. The acrid smell of smoke still hung on the air, probably not from the wartime attacks but from the fires the shivering populace built in the rubble to keep warm. The moment we stepped onto the dock, crowds of young prostitutes—some of them barely teenagers—swarmed around us, pathetic in their ragged skirts, torn stockings, and ridiculous makeup. Hordes of children dogged us, begging for food.

Years later I studied theology at Yale and religion at Harvard, but those early impressions of the scars of war are etched more deeply than anything I learned in the Ivy League. They deeply influenced my choice of courses and of a calling. I developed a lasting interest in World War II. In college, I studied German and majored in modern European history. After my first year in seminary I worked for a summer with a church youth program in the Lime House area of east London. Here was another war-ravaged city, even seven years after the incendiary bombs and V-2s of the blitz had leveled whole blocks. The church I worked in had been 90 percent destroyed, had not been rebuilt, and the small congregation huddled for worship in an adjacent parish hall.

A few years later, in 1956, I became the campus minister at Oberlin College where I was ordained to the Baptist ministry. That same year I led a group of students to Germany, France, and Poland on a study tour. In Berlin I left the group in the relative safety of the western part of the city and made my way to the eastern sector. That was before the wall was built, so it was possible, but "not advisable," to make the trip. Between the western and eastern parts of the city lay a vast region of wreckage, nothing but twisted metal, chimney stacks, loose wires, and ruptured streets. At night its lack of streetlights made it Hades dark.

Still, I was fascinated by Berlin. I admired the way people on both sides continued to live despite all they had been through. So, when I got a chance to spend a year there in 1962–1963, I took it. By then the wall, which had been built in 1961, cut an ugly scar through the central wilderness. But my responsibility in Berlin required me to travel back and forth between the two sectors, through "Checkpoint Charlie." Consequently I was exposed to the acres of urban desolation three times a week. But during those trips I noticed something: Places of worship remained here and there, and some had become symbols of community and hints of possibility. In the heart of West Berlin near Bahnhof Zoo, stood the jagged tower of the old Kaiser Wilhelm Memorial Church. Blasted by allied bombers, today its splintered steeple still looms above the surrounding shops and restaurants. After the war, Berliners decided not to remove the wreckage but to allow it to stand as a permanent reminder of what war does. On both sides of the Wall, I found myself immersed in the theology of Dietrich Bonhoeffer and even got to know some people who had been his co-workers. He became, and has remained, one of the principal influences on my thinking. For a year, Berlin had been both my home and my teacher. The city has always claimed a special place in my heart; consequently it was one of the most memorable days of my life when in June 2011 I was awarded an honorary doctorate at the Humboldt University of Berlin.

When I returned to America in 1963 I started a book, which was published in 1965. In it I drew on my rich experiences in Berlin, including the secularization debate, political theology, and Bonhoeffer's famous question: How do we speak of God in a *"nicht-religiose"* idiom, in a secular age? My intended title for the book was *"God in the Secular City,"* but the publisher suggested it would sell better simply as *The Secular City*. He was probably right, but the American title, without the word "God," prompted some scholars to lump me in mistakenly with the so-called "death of God" theologians of the 1960s, although I had explicitly and forcefully differed with them in *The Secular City*. But the thesis of the book was, and still is, a response to Bonhoeffer's question: How do we speak of God in a secular age?

To the publisher's amazement—and mine—the book became a bestseller. It was translated into seventeen languages and eventually sold a million copies. I still do not understand quite why. Transporting Bonhoeffer's "nonreligious" theology from increasingly secular Europe to still famously "religious" America was a daunting, perhaps even a quixotic, enterprise. Still, after nearly half a century, the book is still undergoing translation, most recently into Chinese and Bulgarian. Returning to the opening paragraph of this essay, I am pleased to note that questions about the relationship between the religious, the secular, and the political remain pressing.

There were other influences, and there were more books, a career of teaching, mainly at Harvard and—above all—my enduring gratitude for the opportunity I was given to work closely with Martin Luther King Jr. in the 1960s. But just as Melville wrote that his whaling ship, the *Pequod*, was "my Harvard and my Yale," as I reach my middle eighties, it was my little hometown and the S.S. *Robert Hart* that left the deepest traces.

3

The One Acted Upon • Gerhard Forde

Recent studies suggest that memory is not like a computer databank just waiting to be tapped when the proper button is pressed. It is rather more an artful and sometimes deceptive composition triggered as much by current wishes, experiences, and other stimuli as by exact recollection of the past. So I expect that attempting an autobiographical statement, especially a theological one, could be a misleading exercise—perhaps a bit of a fabrication of what might have been, more an *apologia pro vita mea*, than an exact account of "what actually happened." Like all autobiographies, this one should be read *cum grano salis*. I am indeed the most reliable source for what is to be said here, but I do confess to a certain bias!

BEGINNINGS

I was raised in a country parsonage just north of Starbuck, Minnesota. My father served there for most of his pastorate and my grandfather before him. It was what the old-timers in Norwegian Lutheranism would call staunch "Old Synod" territory. For those uninitiated in such historical esoterics, the "Old Synod" was descended more directly from the Norwegian State Church, was generally the least pietistic of the Norwegian synods, and tended to be more wedded to the liturgical practices of "the old country" and most inclined toward orthodoxy in its spirit and ethos. No "gospel songs," just solid chorales, if you please! This was the theological air I breathed as I grew up. Determinative also for my theology was the fact that the Old Synod was solidly "first form" in its understanding of election and predestination. That is, election takes place solely by divine decision and prerogative without any admixture of human willing or decision. The more pietistically inclined tended to be "second form," i.e., God foreknows those who will come to faith by the workings of his grace and elects on that basis. Such attempts to "have your cake and eat it too" were to be avoided at all costs. I came by my later interest in and passion for Luther's *Bondage of the Will* honestly.

Indhered, the country church where I was baptized and nurtured in the faith, with its lovely spire presiding over the surrounding countryside, was a cultural center as well as a place of worship. It actually had its own orchestra and choir, performed the *Messiah* every year, and so on. This is important for me not only because it indicates that culture was vital to the faith I learned, but also because in my later years I have come more and more to realize that my Christology and view of the atonement probably owe as much to the hearing of Handel's *Messiah*—the actual performance—as any other single source. For weeks and months before the performances—in which eventually I also participated and sometimes soloed—the parsonage rang with practices and rehearsals. I am sure that it helped to shape that which people today would like to call my "spirituality."

CATECHISM

The catechetical instruction we received was, however, the most vital shaping factor in my theological beginnings. The material was the Catechism, the Explanation to the Catechism (not Pontoppidan's—that was second form!), Bible history, and hymns. The method was memorization and recitation. We began in Sunday and released-time school memorizing the Catechism and reading Bible stories. When we got to the end we just started over. Later we progressed to hymns, Bible history, and the Explanation to the Catechism, a series of more dogmatic questions together with biblical passages to "prove" the answers. Again, when we came to the end we just started over until the whole was sufficiently in hand to permit confirmation. It was an important foundation on which to build. To this day when systematic questions arise, something of an answer with a series of biblical passages will often come to mind "out of the blue." They come from my beginnings. Say what you want about the perils of "proof-texting"; it is certainly preferable to having no text in mind at all! In some respects at least, memory may be a bank after all!

SKEPTICISM

Yet, I suppose I was never quite satisfied with the tradition. I was something of a skeptic even in Sunday School. I had a hard time believing that ax-heads could float. I was uneasy with the pious pronouncement that "there are just some things we have to take on faith!" Looking back, I think what bothered me—and what has stayed with me all my life—was not the dogmatic tradition itself, but rather that too often an insufficient case was being made for a good thing. Maybe it was that I was grasped by the gospel content but was not convinced by the scholastic method and trappings. The exhortation just to take some things on faith tended to reduce faith to the acceptance of propositions—

sometimes questionable ones, at that. At any rate, a search for a better case has always stayed with me.

I can't complete this hasty sketch of my beginnings without some mention of an event I don't remember at all but which was probably quite important. My mother was killed in an auto/train accident when I was six months old. So I never really knew her. But I suspect somehow her absence left its mark even though I was lovingly cared for, first by an aunt and then by my stepmother. But I have always felt a certain independence, not of rebelliousness (which I thought childish), but rather perhaps a skepticism, a reluctance to rely on or trust others completely, whether they be teachers or even friends. If a solution was to be found, I had to find it for myself. If it happened to agree with "the book" or with the teacher, well and good. If not, too bad! Then the search would have to continue. But a position had to be tested. The "reason" had to be found and understood. I never looked particularly for something "new." The "pull" of the ancient catechetical tradition was too strong for that. Contemporary clichés I found usually to be as vacuous as many of the ancient ones were unsupported. In the end, I was generally more interested in discovering the compelling rationale behind the ancient traditions than in multiplying contemporary confusions. The idea that the ancient traditions could or should be made "relevant" by a little modern camouflage has always seemed to me presumptuous if not slightly ridiculous. Later I have come to believe that the idea the gospel should or could be made "relevant" to old beings is one of contemporary theology's greatest miscalculations. It is about as relevant as buttermilk in a bar or marriage in a brothel. "The love of God does not discover but creates its object." So I learned later from Luther in the last of the theological theses in the Heidelberg disputation. It rang a bell. Either the tradition has something to say out of itself or it is empty. Cosmetics won't help when darkness falls.

TRANSITIONS

The "foolish" years of my life in grade and high school were spent pretty much in normal fashion trying to find out who I was. Not, however, by self-scrutiny but by grappling with the material put before me in school. I had no intention of becoming a pastor or a theologian. But then, I recall at this stage no particular intentions at all. I went to school and enjoyed it, particularly the mental competition involved. Poetry became one of my greater joys—inspired largely by my father, who could recite reams of it from memory. I also read many of the novels I found in my father's library—classics: Dickens, Hugo, Hawthorne, and so on. Because the World War II draft was still in effect I began college (Luther College) immediately following high school graduation. I signed up for the army after the fall semester and was eventually assigned to the Army Medical Corps. That was significant for my future, at least to the extent that I made up my mind I didn't want to be a medical doctor or have anything to do directly with hospitals!

Upon returning to college I decided to pursue a career in the sciences—eventually landing in organic chemistry. I was attracted to the physical sciences, I suppose, because they appeared to me to be rigorous, solid, and logical. The study came rather easily for me and I enjoyed the intellectual challenge. So I majored in chemistry and minored in mathematics and German. However, I always had in the back of my mind that I was more interested in teaching than in research. So I took some courses toward an education minor which, however, I soon abandoned in despair. I fell asleep in class too often. There is something of an irony in the fact that classes in education were the least educational of all, I thought. On the other hand, I admired the calm, judicious, thoughtful, and careful confidence of my professors in the sciences. They were, I suppose one would say today, my "role models" at the time. At the same time, I was less moved by the more strident opinions of other professors—especially some of those being presented in the required courses in religion. Those were the days of considerable strife and defensiveness in the church over against the threat of biblical criticism, liberalism, and other pernicious twentieth-century evils. The "pre-sem" students were primed in more special sessions to fight these battles. But safe in the havens of more "exact" sciences, I suppose I tolerated what the religion professors said but remained rather aloof to the fray. But it would be false to say I was a despiser. The ancient catechetical tradition was too strong for that. Nevertheless, I was still quite convinced that I didn't want to be a pastor or a theologian.

So I went on to graduate school in organic chemistry at the University of Wisconsin. There, to make a long story short, I began more seriously to question what I wanted really to do or, to put it more theologically, what I was called to do. Matters came to a head one fine fall day when I was standing at the window in the chemistry lab looking down at students hurrying here and there. Suddenly the question came to me: "What am I doing here?" At the time, organic chemists around the country were engaged in something of a race to see who could be the first to synthesize cholesterol. Up to that time it had been available only by extraction—largely from beef liver, as I recall. So I spent hours in the lab working on some little link in the chain. When I assessed what I was up to I came to the painful realization that I didn't ultimately care whether we succeeded in synthesizing cholesterol or not. Given the subsequent checkered effect of the steroid family on the human enterprise, it was perhaps a divine premonition! In any case, my lack of genuine passion for the outcome of what I was doing led me to conclude it was only honest to quit. The intellectual challenge of the scientific enterprise was stimulating, but I was not convinced it was my calling.

New Beginnings

And so eventually I started anew at Luther Seminary. How that came about I cannot exactly recall—strange as that may seem. There was no overwhelming experience, no bolt from above. There were influences, I am sure, but it is difficult to sort them out. There was a preacher in Madison who was quite moving. I don't even recall his name. There was the Lutheran Students Association, and the realization that I was more concerned about that which touches the spirit than just the body. But I suspect that through it all at bottom there was the *cantus firmus* of the ancient catechetical tradition asserting its silent but insistent witness. My older brother was at the seminary at the time, as were some of my old college roommates and friends. While visiting them as I did now and then, I chanced to pass the old patriarch Thaddeus Franke Gullixson, president of the seminary. I said hello in passing, and he responded in kind. Then slowly he stopped and turned and said to me in that magisterial voice of his with its slight quaver, "Were you looking for me?" If there has been anything like a call from God in my life, that was probably as close as you can get. I stammered something like, "Yes, I guess I am." He invited me into his office and the issue of what I was to do was decided—especially when he discovered that I had already done my time in the armed services. He was leery of students who used the seminary as means to dodge the draft!

The seminary was a new challenge for me. I soon realized I didn't know the vocabulary. To someone who came from the sciences, it was heavily philosophical. There was talk of Plato and Aristotle, Kant, Hegel and Kierkegaard, Tillich and Barth. I found it fascinating but realized I had a lot of catching up to do just to get in on the conversation. I read histories of philosophy, books on reason and revelation, and monographs on and by important theologians then in vogue, and so on. But even though I believe I got something of a handle on that vocabulary, it has never been my native tongue, and as time wore on it became apparent to me it was not where my interests lay. The suspicion that the vocabulary easily entices one on a Swiftian voyage to Laputa, the island that floats in the air, is at least in part a legacy from my scientific background. My native tongue, I think, has always been that of the ancient catechetical tradition.

Neo-Orthodoxy

But in the seminary, it soon became apparent that that ancient tradition was under attack. The attack, however, was not from without but from within. It was not, that is, the inroads of criticism and liberalism, etc., that were the ultimate source of trouble. Such inroads could temporarily, at least, be sidestepped, accommodated, or moderated. So we read Brunner (the most used in dogmatics classes as I recall), and Sittler, and Kantonen, and Nygren, and Tillich, etc., and they assured us that all was well in the "neo-orthodox" camp. Yet there was, for me at least, a certain unease. The surrender of biblical inerrancy to various versions of "truth as encounter" and other existentialist ploys seemed to lack the bite of the older views of biblical authority. Perhaps it was that something of the offense was gone. Yet there was no way back. Older views of biblical inerrancy were not an offense, they were just intellectually offensive. I was looking, I think, for something deeper and more compelling, a gospel authority that establishes itself by its own power and attractiveness, not a legal authority that simply demands submission.

Heilsgeschichte, then in vogue, dominated our theological classrooms. But it was at best a halfway house. It freed us from the older views of authority based on inerrancy but left us with rather serious questions about history. A Bible that is an authoritative mine for data to construct a historical scheme is, in the end, only slightly better than a Bible of texts used to "prove" dogmatic propositions. The inchoate desire of my younger days for a more solid foundation was not satisfied.

Influences

My real seminary experience began one day when I was impelled to set off on my own search. That certain independence and reluctance to rely just on the word of my professors once again asserted itself. While attending a class on Galatians one day, the question that was to occupy center stage for the rest of my theological career was posed, the question of the relation between "human responsibility" and divine election. The professor, bless his pious heart, stretched out his arms and said, "Men (there were only men in those days!), there are just some things we have to learn to hold in tension!" Something within me shouted NO! There are some things we no doubt might hold in tension, but not this thing, not the question of human salvation! I came to suspect that this was the real threat against the ancient tradition. I had to ask myself, "Was this the theology for which Luther was willing to see the church torn apart?" Was this the position over which he argued so desperately with Erasmus? I couldn't believe it. This touched off my quest. And that question centering around divine election, the bondage of the human will, and being a theologian of the cross accounts for the sum and substance of my theology.

The search for an answer to the question about Luther ushered me into a strange and exciting new world. Modern Luther research was just beginning to be imported from Europe. I pored over Luther on Galatians, read and reread Luther's *Bondage of the Will*; I gobbled up the essays and monographs I could find on Luther's "reformation discovery" and his theology in general

(Wingren, Nygren, Prenter, Watson, Boehmer, Pauck, Rupp, etc.), as well as on related exegetical questions about the righteousness of God, justification, law and gospel, and so on. In those days our education took place as much, if not more, in continuing conversations with fellow students in the dorm as in classes. I was blessed with an illustrious group of classmates: Robert Jenson, Carl Braaten, Clarence Lee, Harris Kaasa, Oliver Olson—to name just a few.

The quest on which I embarked was greatly stimulated and encouraged when Lennart Pinomaa, the Finnish Luther scholar, came to us to lecture for a semester. He stayed in the dormitory with us and a number of us helped him put his lectures into an English accessible to students. Needless to say, we learned a lot about the Luther renaissance. Here, I began to sense, was the real foundation for the ancient catechetical tradition for which I had been searching. I found the answers to my questions not in nineteenth- and twentieth-century attempts to transcend or remodel the tradition but rather in a probing of its own depths. In so doing I found a gospel I believed I could preach to the twentieth century. Many seem to react to the Luther renaissance as though it were a species of historical antiquarianism. I have always found Luther to be the one theologian who has something new to say—and better, one who inspires the preaching of the new.

Harvard

In any case, inspired, encouraged, and enticed by these discoveries, I thought to solidify and deepen them in a program of graduate studies. After a delightful year of "filling in" as an instructor in religion at St. Olaf, which I enjoyed immensely and which reinforced my interest in teaching, I set off for Harvard Divinity School (1956). I went to Harvard, frankly, because I was looking for a place that would allow me to continue my quest with a minimum of professorial interference! I knew pretty much what I wanted to do and also that if I were to do it in this country I would have to do it mostly on my own. I was interested still in understanding the foundation of the Reformation tradition in Luther as well as gaining some inkling of what had subsequently happened to it. This led me to take up more seriously the question of *Heilsgeschichte*. Eventually this led to a study of J. C. K. von Hofmann, the "father" of it all on Lutheran soil. There I also discovered the very interesting and significant beginnings of a controversy over the atonement among Lutherans. Much of what Gustaf Aulén said in 1929 was already anticipated by von Hoffmann and debated by his contemporaries. The intimate connection between historical revelation, Christology, atonement, law, and gospel became more apparent. The outcome of this interest was a doctoral dissertation and eventually a published book on *The Law-Gospel Debate*.

Of course I did work in other areas and on other theologians all the while, with professors who were interesting, stimulating, and broadening, even if eventually not so determinative for my theological interests: Paul Tillich, Paul Lehmann, John Dillenberger, Richard Reinhold Niebuhr, Georges Florovsky, and Milton Virgil Anastos (yes, I studied Eastern Orthodoxy!). Also, as time allowed, I listened to various famous professors "over in the yard."

Through it all, however, I continued my own more or less independent quest. I didn't really have what would be called a "doctor father." I began with John Dillenberger, but he left within the year. I then had Paul Lehmann, who introduced me to serious study of Barth, for which I am grateful, but he also left before I went to work on my dissertation. I ended with Richard Reinhold Niebuhr, H. Richard's son, who had little interest in what I was up to. The greatest help for my quest came when I was granted an LWF scholarship to study at Tübingen, Germany for a year following completion of my course work. This was one of the most enjoyable and stimulating years of my life. Here, of course, I found students and professors who "spoke the language" and knew what I was concerned about. My favorite professor was Hans Rückert, then editor of the Weimar Ausgabe of Luther's works, who lectured brilliantly on the history of dogma but published little. There were others, of course, who were helpful as well—Hermann Diem and Ulrich Mann particularly. Ernst Käsemann came the second term I was there and I listened eagerly.

The most important fruit of my year in Germany was my introduction to what writings were then available of Hans-Joachim Iwand, whom I count as my favorite interpreter of Luther, still largely unknown and unpublished in this country. I was attracted at the outset by his early essays on law and gospel and especially by his introductions to (in the München Ausgabe, Vol. 7, 1954) and essays on Luther's *Bondage of the Will* (in *Um den rechten Glauben*, a group of essays published by Chr. Kaiser Verlag in 1959). Iwand is the only interpreter I know who was able to swallow Luther's view of the bondage of the human will whole, together with all the theological presuppositions and consequences entailed in that view. He is the only one I have found who accepts the Lutheran *decretum horribile* that the *deus absconditus* has not bound himself to his word but kept himself free over all things. Virtually all of theology ever since, even to the present day, has busied itself trying by theological manipulation to banish that God from sight. It is, you might say, the favorite armchair sport of theologians. That means there is always somewhere, even among the staunchest Lutheran theologians, a reservation compelled to assert some bit of human responsibility. And that is the beginning of the end for all serious theology. This, I came to see, is where theology loses its bite. It loses its doctrine of God—the belief that God is in charge even in terrifying hiddenness. It loses its Christology—the awareness that the awesome and hidden God shows his hand concretely only in the preached word of the cross and the sacraments. Which is to say, it loses its faith in the Spirit and its ecclesiology as well. Where the word loses its bite as living address, it flattens out into a religion and enters the market where one has to look to philosophical or apologetic arguments to establish one's case.

DISCOVERIES

What I learned from Iwand is that the compulsion to hang on to some bit of human choice and responsibility over against the God of election is precisely our problem. The compulsion, the claim to freedom vis-à-vis God, is the bondage. This realization set off a chain of reasoning that has stamped my theology ever since. Iwand helped me to see that the bondage is not *theoretical* but *actual*. In its deepest sense it is not, that is, a conclusion or a deduction from the doctrine of divine necessity but an actual reaction, an act of will. As fallen beings we are compelled and driven. Our claims to freedom vis-à-vis God are precisely our rebellion against God. This is our original sin—a sin by which we are *bound*—we are not forced to it, we will it. That being the case, no theoretical or theological reformulation will help. The sinner cannot be cured by a more subtle theology. We can't sit in our studies and save people. So the conclusion became inevitable: the only remedy for the sinner is death. Thus follows the matter of becoming theologians of the cross. The old Adam or Eve must die and the new come forth who—for the time being—lives by faith alone. Somewhat in that fashion through the years, my theology took shape. As I put it in my little book on justification, it is a matter of death and life. And such death and life cannot be simply a metaphor for transformation or a change of heart. There must be a real savior, a real death, indeed, one in which we are involved and implicated, i.e., put to death, and, consequently, a real resurrection from the dead. My preoccupation with the doctrine of the atonement flows quite logically, for me, from the matter of death and life. Reshaping the doctrine in terms of death and life is one of the most prominent instances where I have sought a more adequate foundation for the tradition. The bondage of the human will works itself out finally by killing Jesus, the one who said, "You have not chosen me, but I have chosen you." And so it is. And that is our death and new life.

The basic death/life structure became determinative for all of my subsequent theologizing. It establishes the foundation for which I was searching. The word of God is not just a mine for dogma, nor a source book for the history of salvation. It is indeed both of those things. One need not deny that. But were we left only with that we would be abandoned to our own decisions. Over and above all is the realization that the word coming to us from the scriptures is a word that kills and makes alive. It is eschatological in intent and shape. It ends the old and inaugurates the new. It does this by the very fact of its unconditionality, the fact that it leaves the old Adam and Eve with "nothing to do." That is the death. The new life that follows is the sheer gift of freedom and what it inspires within us. Complaints about my being "weak on sanctification" and so forth have, of course, always swarmed around my head like angry flies. I brush them off confidently and say that if what is supposed to be Christian about our lives and deeds does not flow spontaneously from the freedom of the gospel, it has no claim to being called sanctification. It may be philanthropy or charity or other socially laudable activity, or even just plain legalism, all of it admirable and useful in this age, but it is not sanctification. As Jesus could say of the "hypocrites" who made ostentatious display of their almsgiving, "They have their reward." Public approbation *is* their reward. True sanctification has to do with the "reward" of the Father "who sees in secret." It is born out of the end and the new beginning. Theology has the task of fostering the doing of that end and new beginning in the living present. It must drive to such a proclamation, or all is lost. This is what I tried to say in *Theology Is for Proclamation*.

The fundamental death/life structure is, of course, intimately connected and indeed structurally identical with the thoroughgoing "dialectic" of Lutheran theology in general: God hidden and revealed; *simul peccator et iustus*; old/new; law/gospel; killing letter/life-giving Spirit; left- and right-hand rule of God, etc. The dialectic is compelling not only because of its inherent ability to expound the faith I learned from the beginning but also because it reflects and illumines the basic eschatological structure of the New Testament. Virtually all of my writing, teaching, and lecturing circles around these themes.

OTHERS

Other theologians have also been important to me. It is hard now to recall them all accurately and put them in any sort of rank or chronological order. The Finnish theologian Lauri Haikola was vital for the development of my understanding of law and gospel. Gerhard Ebeling's interpretation of Luther and early preoccupation with hermeneutical questions fired a constant concern about questions of interpretation and preaching. I have always believed Karl Barth to be one of the best conversation partners for Lutheran theology because he raises the right questions. Those Lutherans who were willing to listen to Barth, even if critically, I have generally found to be the most interesting. I always enjoyed teaching Barth, especially the thunderous negations of his *Romans*. Wingren has been important, perhaps as a counterbalance to Barth. His little book *Theology in Conflict* was decisive in my early struggles with Barth over law and gospel. Conversation and discussion for almost twenty years with Roman Catholic colleagues in the Lutheran/Catholic Dialogue in the U.S. have been most rewarding and have sharpened my perceptions in the ecumenical arena. Team teaching the Lutheran Confessions with Jim Nestingen has repeatedly focused and augmented my understanding of the Lutheran witness.

TEACHING

A few words about my career subsequent to the return from Germany are perhaps in order to close out this exercise. I was asked to teach the History of Christian Thought at Luther Seminary, so I shuttled back and forth between St. Paul and Harvard for a couple of years. Interpreting the history of thought in the light of what I had learned gave me the confidence that it would "fly" for prospective pastors and teachers. Teaching the next two years at Luther College following an upheaval in the religion department gave further opportunity to put my theology to the test. At stake in the upheaval were precisely the questions I had had about the ancient catechetical tradition all along, and it was challenging to have to deal with it now as a teacher. During a year's leave I had requested to finish work on my dissertation, two decisive things happened. I married my lovely and helpful wife Marianna, a Yale Ph.D. who was teaching French language and literature at Wellesley, and I was called once again to return to teach in the Church History department at Luther Seminary. So in 1964 we returned to Luther Seminary where we have remained ever since, with the exception of sabbaticals and two interesting and delightful years as Lutheran Tutor and Chaplain to Lutheran Students (of which there were hardly any!) at Oxford University. In 1971, I shifted from teaching in the Church History department to Systematic Theology. This did not represent any major transition in my thinking or teaching. My degree at Harvard was in a division they just called "Theology," as I recall, which encompassed both the History of Christian Thought and Systematics, as evidenced by professors such as Tillich and Lehmann. It did mean, however, that I have always taught systematics from a historical base—as it ought to be taught!

RADICALIZATION

It is difficult precisely to sum up what my thirty plus years teaching at Luther Seminary have meant for my theological understanding. I suppose I have said it already in what I have set down above; I am not conscious of any radical changes of mind theologically, but rather of a constant deepening and sharpening, and I would like to think, even radicalization of the views I either held or was seeking from the beginning. This I credit to ever insistent and penetrating questioning from my students and colleagues. Looking back, I think the absolute necessity of preaching a word that does the killing and making alive in the living present has been a growing conviction and the question of how one is to do that a constant preoccupation. There is no solution to the "problem" of the hidden, almighty, electing God in theology. The solution is given only if this God comes to us here and now to do the deed. That is what the preaching and the sacraments are all about. And theology must drive us to that deed. That is the breaking in of the eschatological future.

My biggest fear in the present is that the eschatological two-age structure of theology is once again simply being lost. Lost in our disregard for the new age and a life that conquers death. Lost in our constant preoccupation with the old self and its "development" and "esteem," our *causa sui* projects, as Ernest Becker put it. Lost in an ecclesiology that threatens to substitute itself for the kingdom. Lost in a turning to the historical Jesus (as in the "Jesus Seminar," etc.) rather than to the risen Christ. Lost, that is, in a theology that flattens Christianity out into a "religion" rather than the end of religion and the beginning of the new.

But now I think I have said enough, if not too much. In looking back over what I have written, I can see that I have been lured into doing what the very idea of an autobiography tempts one to do: speak too much of the self and its quest. The recently deceased John Chancellor, sagacious news analyst and commentator, is said to have remarked once that if you want to make God laugh, tell him your plans! When St. Augustine wrote his "theological autobiography," he came to realize that he finally was not the actor but rather the one acted upon. I expect that this is our only hope in the end, and that God will not have too big a laugh at our expense.

4

They Told What Had Happened on the Road • George W. Forell

Raised in a parsonage in Michelsdorf in Germany, situated in the hills of Silesia—the son, grandson, and great-grandson of Silesian pastors—I was immersed in the Christian faith and its proclamation. My paternal uncles and aunts appeared only rarely in my life. The maternal grandparents who lived in Landeshut, not far from Michelsdorf, were next to my parents the most important influence on me. My grandfather Georg Kretschmar was the superintendent of the district. Two of my mother's siblings were important members of my extended family: an aunt, my godmother, married to a pastor in Landeshut; and an uncle who was himself a pastor in the same district.

SCHOOL IN SILESIA

In 1925, when my father was called from his rural parish to Breslau, the capital and largest city of the province, to serve as *Sozialpfarrer* for Silesia (and as executive secretary of the Silesian *Frauenhilfe*) I spent six months in Landeshut getting to know my grandparents better and attending a *Volksschule*. Here I soon discovered that while being a pastor's son in the first grade might have given me status in Michelsdorf, it made me subject to hazing and beatings in the rough-and-tumble environment of this urban school where most of the other children came from what Karl Marx would have called the proletariat. Before I was six I had learned that class—and its associated dialect—was an inescapable reality. I learned to speak two languages: the Silesian dialect on the playground, and the High German expected in school and at home.

After the family moved to Breslau, I finished grade school (i.e., the first four years) in a small private school and entered the König Wilhelm Gymnasium to prepare myself to become a pastor. The Gymnasium taught Latin from the first to the last year (*Sexta* to *Ober-Prima*, nine years) and Greek starting at the third year. This emphasis on classical languages and literature—one hour for six days a week for each of these subjects—was eventually very useful to me, though at the time it seemed a meaningless exercise.

53

THE NAZI THREAT

The routine of my education was interrupted in 1933 when my father was forced into retirement (*zwangspensioniert*) as a result of Hitler's rise to power. At the time forty-four years old, he had opposed the rising Nazi tide and was forced to pay the consequences. He decided to leave Germany immediately, convinced that the evil Nazi lunacy would quickly pass. He had to find a job. A Swedish mission society concerned with the fate of refugees from Germany employed him as pastor and missionary in Vienna. He left Germany in June of 1933. My mother, my younger brother, and I stayed in Breslau until the end of the academic year—which at that time meant until March of 1934—when we too moved to Vienna.

The change from the upper-class environment of the König Wilhelm Gymnasium, attended by the children of judges, doctors, lawyers, architects, etc.—the *Gebildeten*,[1] in Schleiermacher's phrase, to the Wasa Gymnasium in the ninth district of Vienna, was an enormous culture shock. Accustomed to being part of the majority culture, I was suddenly a member of a very small minority. In a class of boys and girls who were either Roman Catholic or Jews, the Lutherans had identity problems. (About eighteen were Roman Catholics, seventeen were Jews, and three were Protestants.) Besides that, I was the only one who spoke with a foreign accent. I was a "Piefke," a boy who spoke a different brand of German. As a matter of fact, since I moved to Vienna at the age of thirteen and for the next sixty years, I hardly ever opened my mouth on any subject without people asking, "Where are you from?" I did make friends among both the Jews and the Catholics, but I had to ask myself rather early in life what it meant to be "Evangelisch, A.B." (a Protestant committed to the Augsburg Confession).

But while the Christian faith was important in my home, and I went to church and was confirmed, the overwhelming experience in these years was Viennese culture, which I devoured with enthusiasm: from opera to theater, from Austro-Marxism to psychoanalysis. In the background was always the menace of National Socialism, which had threatened briefly in 1934. In that summer, the Austrian Chancellor Dollfuss was assassinated, and the village in Styria where we were on holiday was for a day or so ruled by Austrian Nazi storm troopers.

While my Catholic and Jewish friends were mostly apolitical, I was aware of the danger especially to me and my Jewish friends. The Austrian government of the time was not devoted to democracy. It practiced its own peculiar brand of Austro-Fascism, claiming to be inspired by the papal encyclicals on social justice. Lutherans were second-class citizens. If a Lutheran and Roman Catholic had married and the marriage failed, the Roman Catholic partner could obtain an annulment from the pope, but since there was no divorce the Lutheran partner remained married to a person who soon might be married to somebody else. The result of all this was a tendency among Protestants to favor liberation from this government through *Anschluss* to the German Reich. They would not believe that the demonic evils of Nazism far outweighed the very real annoyances of Austro-Fascism.

With the exception of one committed social democrat, my friends hardly ever talked politics. We talked about soccer, art, and music, and went to the opera a couple of times a week in the section for people who were willing to stand, either on the main floor or in the gallery. We visited museums and attended professional soccer games, hiked and skied in the Vienna woods, and actually got along with each other amazingly well. I learned a great deal about Catholic and Jewish culture and the peculiar mixture of both, which was the genius of Vienna between the first and second world wars. In 1937 I graduated from the Gymnasium and began to study theology and philosophy at the University of Vienna. By that time I had decided that in the world in which I lived there were only two options.

Nietzsche vs. Christ

One was the Nietzsche option: the radical rejection of Christianity and with it all the sentimental reductionist alternatives of the Enlightenment and liberal Protestantism. God is dead and everything is permitted. I gave it some thought. My academic and political environment made it appear attractive. Nietzsche, too, was a Lutheran pastor's son. He wrote better German than any other philosopher I had ever read. He was free from the cloying religious sentimentality that says all the right things and does nothing about it. *Thus Spake Zarathustra* was one of my favorite books.

The other option was to serve Jesus, the Christ, whom I had seen as a stumbling block and foolishness to Jews and gentiles but who was the only person to whom I could be completely committed. The example of my parents, who were so obviously engaged in such service—as counseling, feeding, and clothing refugees—made the first option impossible. God had reached out to me, and my efforts to establish autonomy were doomed from the start. I had seen Christ at work through women and men of faith. Anything but discipleship to him would be inconceivable.

From Vienna to Philadelphia

I knew, of course, that I would have to get out of the doomed city of Vienna as soon as possible. The plan was to go to the Lutheran Theological Seminary at Philadelphia, where a Presbyterian friend of my father had been able to obtain a full scholarship for me. The United Lutheran Church in America still needed pastors who could preach in German and was willing to take a chance on some of us who were trying to escape the Nazi war machine. While the distinguished Norwegian writer Ronald Fangen, whom I once had given a guided tour of Vienna, had also arranged for a scholarship at Uppsala, Sweden, I decided to go to Philadelphia because my grandfather (who had never been outside the German-speaking parts of Europe) had told me, "Wolfgang, you can never become a Swede but you may become an American."

But in March of 1938 Hitler invaded Austria. My plans for an orderly journey to America to begin my studies in the fall of 1938 had to be cancelled. I had to get out immediately. Agents of the Gestapo had been at the office of the Mission. My father had not been home; he never went home again but left for Prague. I followed a day later. From there we made our way to Sweden and I tried to obtain my visa to the U.S. My application made months earlier had been lost at the embassy in Vienna. After a short stay in England and France I eventually secured a visa in January of 1939 and began my career as a theological student in Philadelphia.

After Nazi-occupied Vienna, and after London and Paris, Philadelphia represented another culture shock. Isolationism was the political mood of the time. The professor who was most kind to me, Dr. Paul Hoh, later president of the seminary, warned me never to make any political comments especially when visiting in congregations with German services. My fellow students, who were extremely kind and supportive to the greenhorn, amused by the way he handled knife and fork, had no interest in foreign policy. Those few fellow students who were politically engaged were supporters of Roosevelt and the New Deal. Especially my friend and later roommate Morgan Edwards, the son of a Johnstown steelworker who had worked as a butcher in a supermarket before coming to the seminary, introduced me to American politics. He also took me home with him and we visited his father at work in the steel mill.

Theologically I marched to a different drummer from any of my teachers or fellow students. After reading Karl Barth in Europe and especially his small book on the Apostles' Creed, *Credo*, I had become a "Barthian." The theological conflicts at the seminary—and there were very few—were between the "orthodox" and the "liberals," symbolized by Dr. Emil Fischer, who taught systematic theology, and Dr. O. Frederick Nolde, who taught religious education. Both positions seemed irrelevant to me. The emphasis on higher criticism in the interpretation of the Bible, which seemed daring and progressive to some, appeared obvious and obsolete to one who had been influenced by Barth's commentary on Romans. I had read the Old Testament commentaries based on Wellhausen—but they seemed to say nothing to the world that was about to burst into flames. While I had little patience with the question-and-answer orthodoxy of some of my textbooks, I found even that more to the point than the talk about progress and progressive revelation by the very decent and well-meaning Dr. Nolde. The war was starting in Europe and America was going to be part of it, and progress seemed not to be the category that helped explain the situation during my seminary years.

Even before I graduated from Mt. Airy in 1941 my parents, after having been briefly interned in French concentration camps, had managed to escape to America with the help of the Second Presbyterian Church in New York, and arrived in that city in October of 1940. My brother John Gotthold, who had been shipped on the notorious *Dunera* from England to Australia, was eventually allowed to join the Australian army and later studied theology in Sydney. He came to America after end of the war and served a number of Episcopal churches in New Jersey until his untimely death in 1961.

Upon my ordination I was called to serve two congregations in New Jersey (Wenonah and Woodbury) of the old Ministerium of Pennsylvania and Adjacent States and to preach every Sunday twice in English and once in German. The people in my congregations were very good to me and tolerant of my mistakes. They seemed to like my preaching—at least they liked me. They also allowed me to take one day a week—Monday—to drive to Princeton Theological Seminary to do graduate work.

FROM BARTH TO LUTHER

The two most important teachers for me were Otto Pieper and Josef Hromadka. Both were refugees. Pieper had been Barth's successor at the University of Münster, and Hromadka, a Christian socialist, had been the Czech interpreter of Barth's theology in Prague. To him, Barth had written his famous letter indicating that the Czechs had the duty to resist the Nazis militarily because of the resurrection of Christ. He allowed me to work with him on Luther's doctrine of the church. I had begun my study of the doctrine of the church at Mt. Airy and had written my B.D. thesis—still required in those days—on Paul's understanding of the church as the people of God, the true Israel. It seemed a good idea to pursue this idea in Luther. This effort produced eventually my Th.M. thesis for Princeton called *The Reality of the Church as the Communion of Saints.* I claimed that Luther, far from being an individualist, believed that God saves us into a community in which we are "baked together" like the bread in Holy Communion. Here we share all we own and hold everything in common and do not need the services of an ecclesiastical bureaucracy to sell us shares in salvation. Luther rejected the capitalist notion that undergirded the treasure of merits at the disposal of the papacy. All Christians had free access to this treasure because of the death and resurrection of Christ. Thus it was his doctrine of the church, developed very early in his career, which enabled him to stand up against what he considered the pretensions of the papacy. I published this dissertation myself in 1943. But the importance of this study was that it had forced me to read a lot of Luther. The more I read him the more

I liked him. It was the reading of Luther that slowly weaned me from Karl Barth.

Union, Niebuhr, and Faith Active in Love

In 1943, the United States was at war with Hitler's Germany. The most eloquent theological spokesman for this involvement had been Reinhold Niebuhr. I had volunteered for the chaplaincy, but as an "enemy alien" I did not qualify. I decided to continue my theological studies with Reinhold Niebuhr at Union Theological Seminary. In 1943 this was a daring move, frowned upon by the president of my synod, Dr. Emil Fischer of the Ministerium of Pennsylvania, who had moved from the seminary to this position. But I was not discouraged and began my studies at Union in the fall of 1943. I received an assistantship in church history and had the honor of working with Robert Hastings Nichols and John T. McNeill, men of faith and great scholarly achievement.

Reinhold Niebuhr was a controversial figure. Some of my best friends would not take courses from him, considering him a traitor to the pacifist cause. I admired him as a lecturer and as a theologian who had applied his theology to the gigantic problems of the day. I thought his interpretation of Luther was wrongheaded and not based on the sources but on Ernst Troeltsch. I wrote my Th.D. dissertation under him, which dealt with Luther's social ethics and was later published as *Faith Active in Love*.[2] I received much help from John Bennett and John T. McNeill, who served on my committee. From Paul Tillich, I took every course he offered and argued with him from my Barthian perspective, to his amusement and my education. He reported to my father, with whom he was associated in anti-Nazi activities, that I questioned his Christianity, but this did not keep him from befriending me especially in later years when we taught simultaneously in Hamburg and still later when we both taught in Chicago in the early sixties.

In New York I met my wife, Elizabeth Rossing, a St. Olaf graduate who was then a graduate student at Columbia, and was very intelligent, beautiful, and kind, and shared my religious and political concerns. We met in January and were married in June 1945.

It is apparent to me now that Niebuhr exerted a great influence on me. My tendency to combine an orthodox Lutheran theology with a liberal political stance was clearly influenced by him. At the time it was a peculiar combination. When, after two years as pastor at a bilingual congregation in the Bronx, I began my teaching career at Gustavus Adolphus College in 1947, this combination struck my colleagues and students as very odd. At the time the Lutheran Church in Minnesota was pretty much the Republican party at prayer. To be an active Democrat was peculiar and to combine this with serious questions concerning the agenda of theological liberalism was unheard of. I became active in the Democratic-Farmer-Labor Party in Minnesota, had a public controversy with Senator Joseph McCarthy on the campus of the college, and served as an alternate delegate to the Democratic convention in 1952. After seven years of teaching philosophy and religion at Gustavus Adolphus College, I moved to the School of Religion at the University of Iowa in the fall of 1954.

It was the year *Faith Active in Love* was published. In this book I tried to show that Luther was a social activist from the indulgence controversy in Wittenberg to his involvement with the Counts of Mansfeld at the end of his life. The book was well received, especially by Lutherans.

My new position at Iowa meant that I no longer dealt with philosophy but with "religion" and the teaching of religion in the secular university. Iowa had pioneered in this effort and from the beginning had approached it in a multireligious manner. This was a new experience for me and involved me in the valuable study of non-Christian religions. For years I taught a large course in cooperation with authorities on Judaism, Islam, Hinduism, and Buddhism that opened my eyes to the pluralistic world. While I eventually relinquished this course in order to concentrate on the course dealing with Judaism and Christianity taught jointly with my friend Rabbi Jay Holstein, the Iowa experience gave me a much broader context than my days in the parish and at Gustavus Adolphus College.

But while most of my students heard me in these large introductory courses, I continued to teach undergraduate and graduate students in the area of my graduate work—Christian ethics and Reformation studies. I believe it was this combination that involved me in the efforts of the Lutheran Church to develop an ethical stance in the controversies of the times flowing from confessional authorities of the church of the Reformation.

LUTHERAN THEOLOGY IN AMERICAN CULTURE

It seemed apparent to me that the maintenance of a Lutheran church in North America could not be justified on the same grounds as in Scandinavia or Germany. In those countries the Lutheran Church was an aspect of national identity. Practically everybody including most atheists would agree that the cultural expressions of the church, the ancient church buildings, the classical music, the rituals marking the stages on life's way from birth to death, were an inescapable component of being a Swede or German. A similar claim cannot be made in this country. Many aspects of Lutheran culture interfere with the acceptance of the Lutheran Church as part of our civil religion. Thus efforts are being made to create a Lutheran church more acceptable to the American religious sensibility, to drop the depressing emphasis on the importance of sin and to omit hymns that talk about Jesus' wounded head and the devil as the prince of this world and other gloomy subjects.

But while a Lutheran church without a Lutheran theology may be sociologically viable in Germany or Scandinavia, it is doomed in America. Without a distinctive theology, there is no reason to maintain a separate Lutheran church; its disappearance within the mainstream of culture-protestantism of the right or the left is unavoidable and by no means deplorable. There is no need for another version of the UCC or the Episcopal Church. For that matter, a Southern Baptist church with a slightly German accent is redundant.

That raises the question as to the nature of Lutheran theological identity and its significance for the life of the Christian church in this country. For years I have claimed, in season and out of season—in Lutheran theological journals and Funk and Wagnall's supermarket encyclopedia—that there are certain distinctive aspects of Lutheran theology which if lost would weaken and impoverish the Christian message in our world. Here I shall mention them only as slogans: (1) the distinction of law and gospel; (2) the Christian as righteous and sinner at the same time; (3) the finite as bearer of the infinite (with its implications for sacrament, scripture, and vocation); and (4) the theology of the cross versus the theology of glory.

Everything I have ever written has been an attempt to elucidate one or the other aspect of this message, convinced that it might help all Christians to understand their election and the resulting obligation. This proclamation is a debt Lutherans owe to the ecumenical church. It is not a sign of superiority or a reason for isolation, but rather a vocation that should contribute to the wholeness of the people of God. It would be my claim that Quakers and Jesuits, the Salvation Army and the Coptic Church may likewise have obligations to the people of God that, while not equally apparent to me, may be very obvious to them and important to all of us.

The Protestant Faith—A Post-Denominational Book

This understanding of the Lutheran tradition within the ecumenical context has been the result of my experience as a teacher of theology not only at Iowa but in Tanzania (1960), Japan (1968), India (1978), Hong Kong (1980), and Taiwan (1993), and three years as advisor to the Department of Studies of the LWF (1981–1984). I have learned that the theological insights so dear to me and clearly identified with Luther and the church of the Reformation are, if freed from the denominational label, of value to people who have no roots in the Europe of the sixteenth century. In Taiwan, my book *The Protestant Faith*[3] has been translated into Chinese, given another title more appropriate to the Chinese setting (Biblical Systematic Theology), and published without my knowledge or permission by a non-Lutheran publisher. I understand it is in the third printing and used by Christians of various backgrounds. When, while teaching at the China Evangelical Seminary at Taipei in 1993, I asked for the reason for the book's apparent popularity in a setting so very different from the Iowa students for whom it was originally written, I was told that it summarizes evangelical theology for a post-denominational Christianity in a manner they consider appropriate to their situation. It may be of some significance that while only one of my books is still in print in the USA, three are in print in Chinese.

We are, indeed, in a post-denominational age. But this does not imply that we live in a post-theological age. It is our task to express the Christian faith in words that reach people at the turn of the millennium. It is my conviction that the theology developed in the sixteenth century, briefly characterized above, supplies basic resources that can be used for the articulation of the Christian faith in our time. This task should be undertaken in the church for its members as well as for all the people on the outside who are questioning the nature and destiny of humanity.

People inside and outside the church are surrounded by innumerable ideologies soliciting their attention and demanding their loyalty. This situation is inescapable. It was always thus: as Luther observed in the Large Catechism, we trust either God or an idol; for human beings, atheism is an impossibility. Thus no other investigation is more significant than that which examines what people believe, which makes theology the queen of the sciences.

But the church is not the only place where this inquiry can be pursued. At the end of my career at Iowa I was invited to give the annual Presidential Lecture, which gave me the opportunity to explain what I had been up to for the last thirty-five years. I called it "The Sacred and the Secular: Religion in the State University," and claimed that (1) the university is a major resource to the study of religion and (2) the study of religion is a valuable resource to the academic task of the university. This is what I had tried to demonstrate while teaching the forty thousand students that had been enrolled in my classes from 1954 to 1990.

Having been brought to America more than half a century ago to preach the gospel in German, I am now apprehensive that the gospel may not be preached at all. If the church abandons its responsibility to theology to devote itself entirely to entertainment, pop-psychology, and social work, the task of helping people with the big questions will be assumed by others. If that happens, somebody will eventually write a book with the title: *The Treason of the Church*. It was at that point in a very similar condition almost five hundred years ago that Luther entered the picture. At the end of my pilgrimage I am convinced that his relevance to our situation is enormous.

Notes

1 F. Schleiermacher, *On Religion, Speeches on Religion to Its Cultured Despisers* (New York: Harper Torchbook, 1958). The term "cultured" is a somewhat inadequate translation of the German word gebildet.

2 George Wolfgang Forell, *Faith Active in Love* (New York: The American Press, 1954).

3 George W. Forell, *The Protestant Faith* (Minneapolis: Augsburg Fortress, 1975).

5

A Story of Teaching and Learning •
Roger Haight, S.J.

I wish I knew better what goes on when one writes an intellectual autobiography. In his "Apology," Socrates says that a life without self-examination is not worth living. But objective problems have occupied considerably more of my energy. In any case, when one makes oneself the subject matter of memory and reflection, one makes oneself an object. Remembering and writing convert self-consciousness into a kind of objective story. Although the storyline is not fictive, yet, as something from the past remembered in the present, it undergoes a good deal of revisionist interpretation.

The story here concerns teaching and learning, or learning and teaching, because these reciprocal activities interact to become the engine of the life of a teaching theologian. All new teachers share the surprise of how much they learn through teaching. The "banking" teacher learns in order to teach; the maieutic teacher learns through discussion with students; the two complementary processes reinforce each other. Thus much of my intellectual activity has revolved around the courses I've taught and my writing reflects this. Thus telling the story of the genesis of several books suggests itself as an "objective" way of presenting something as intimate as an intellectual itinerary. I begin with an account of how I got into a position where I could write a book.

GETTING STARTED

During the first half of my life thus far, I was getting started. It was somewhat embarrassing being still in school at the age of thirty-seven and being asked what grade I was in. I can explain what took me so long by the four major decisions that shaped my early life.

The first one was to apply for membership in the Jesuits after high school. This decision had to be accepted by the Jesuits and, when it was, it meant that every other decision I would make would not be simply my own, but would emerge from the context of the Jesuit mission and responsibility to the group. The second was to go to the Philippines at the age of twenty-two with the expectation that this would be the permanent scene of my work. During my first six years there, it became my home.

During my first ten years as a Jesuit I studied no theology, so stratified was the course of studies. Only on coming back to the United States and beginning the study of theology did I make the third decision that I wished this to be my trade within the Jesuits. This required a post-M.Div.-level graduate degree. Thus the fourth major decision that finally got me started was to enter the doctoral program in Christian Theology at the Divinity School of the University of Chicago. It is impossible to capture the fullness of the intellectual life of Chicago in a word, but some key phrases can suggest it: outstanding faculty, diverse programs and students, insistence upon depth and breadth of basic learning before specialization, self-conscious insistence on critical method. The whole school was alive, constantly moving, continually readjusting, and always in conversation.

I wrote a thesis under David Tracy on the themes of faith and doctrine in French modernism. These figures were the first, after the Tübingen School at the beginning of the nineteenth century, to make a concerted effort to confront the premodern theology in place by accepting the turn to history and to the subject in philosophy and to integrate these strategic moves into a fundamentally reconceptualized Christian apologetic. The developments in Catholic theology after Vatican II mirrored this effort. Also, the distinctions and categories that the modernists developed and that were initially condemned were proving to be sound. Their appeal to experience provided grounds for attending to the experience of other cultures and thus encouraged a process of theological inculturation in the Philippines and other parts of the developing world outside the West. When I graduated from Chicago in 1973, I was ready to get started.

THE EXPERIENCE AND LANGUAGE OF GRACE

Gathering reflections around subjects I've taught that became subjects of books provides a larger framework for recalling this history than a list of influential authors. It is difficult to sort out the relative impact of so many different and at times antithetical conceptions. In any case, I've always taught in a professional school of training for ministry. But all of these schools have had a relatively academic bent. My first course dealt with the Roman Catholic treatise on grace. In place of the objective, neo-scholastic, a-temporal analysis of various senses of this term and aspects of its ontology, I offered a historical course that spent time situating and explaining the experience and language of grace developed by Augustine, Aquinas, Luther, Trent, and Karl Rahner. These historical studies were set within the context provided by a study of

William James's *The Varieties of Religious Experience.* This set the premises of the historicity and pluralism of religious experiences.

The subject matter of the theology of grace as it was worked out in the Roman Catholic tradition is so subtle that students could finish a course and not know exactly what they had studied. One way of explaining this intrinsic subtlety lies in the object studied, which is no less than the living, dynamic relationship between God and human beings. The interaction between the two poles of God's initiative and human response shows up consistently in attention to the value of the one or the other or their mutual interdependence: Augustine and Pelagius, Luther and Aquinas. A constructive theology of grace will try to view each of these poles positively to see how they work together in a pattern broader than either/or. Such an approach led me to something like a dynamic formula of release and empowerment. These authors' descriptions of the dynamics of grace convinced me that human freedom was at stake in the very center of a Christian vision of how God entered into relationship with human beings as mediated by Jesus Christ. Human freedom had potential to be free beyond mere choices; human freedom on its own cannot realize its own potential; God releases human freedom from the internal bonds that constrain it and opens it to things beyond self-interest.

The theology of grace is a reflective reprise of the inner logic of Christian experience itself. Little can be more fundamental to and controlling of the Christian imagination than one's conviction about the structure of the relationship between God and human freedom. But this issue is so deep and mysterious that both Pelagius and Augustine can be right, and both Aquinas and Luther. An appreciation of this requires a dialectical or paradoxical imagination. This is allowed when we appreciate their assertions and make our own with a humility that respects God's mystery and transcendence and does not seek false comfort in exclusive assertions.

At the same time I began teaching the theology of grace, I also began teaching liberation theology in the context of Filipino society and culture. As a result, this book has two layers of meaning that are completely congruent. Liberation theology mirrors the theology of grace on the social level. It begins with the scandal of dehumanization, criticizes theological conceptions that support it, raises up alternative experiences, appeals to Jesus and scripture for constructive themes that negate the human negation, and measures the adequacy of theology's truth by its ability to reflect and empower liberating praxis. The distinctive insights of Augustine, Aquinas, Luther, and Rahner into the empowerment of God's grace in human existence can be translated into social expression and effectiveness. The blending of these two theological discussions provided me with a platform for the rudiments of a Christian theology of history. Whether worked out in eschatological or teleological language, history's goal in God's design and the power of God's Spirit is symbolized in what Jesus called the kingdom of God. On the ground, this vision provides Christians with a set of ideals to measure the values to which they may with confidence dedicate their freedom.

An Alternative Vision

I wrote the first draft of *The Experience and Language of Grace* in Manila; I rounded it off in Chicago while teaching at Jesuit School of Theology in Chicago. I moved to Regis College in the Toronto School of Theology in 1981 and in the course of nine years there published two books. The first was an extended interpretation of the liberation theology of Latin America titled *An Alternative Vision*.

This particular liberation theology developed in the conjunction of Vatican II and the social and cultural situation of Central and South America. As articulated by Gustavo Gutiérrez, its center of gravity lay in God's response to the suffering of the poor and the resultant imperative for a human response. Because this theology responds to God's call to react to a desperate human situation, this theology privileges graced human praxis as the source and goal of its interpretation. The practical character of this theology received far more attention than its theoretical underpinnings. Because of its direct relevance to situations of poverty and systemic injustice, it spread rapidly to all continents. But the persistent reading of it in North America construed it as a regional, or ethnic, or class, or partisan theology bound to a group and thereby failed to grasp its universal relevance. The developed nations' ability to hide the poor or marginalize them still further on the basis of middle-class or entrepreneurial values obscured or simply dismissed the significance of this theological movement in a technologically developed society and culture. I tried to internalize the fundamental intuitions of liberation theology and express them in the cultural categories of North American theology.

Liberation theology designates a genus with several species: black liberation theology, Latin American liberation theology, feminist liberation theology, and others. Not all liberation theologians are saying the same thing. For the project of reinterpreting South American thought in a North American dialect, I found the work of Juan Luis Segundo most congenial, for several reasons. He wrote from a Uruguayan situation that is largely urban and secularized; it has a large middle class. Some of his leading ideas and intellectual strategies fit a developed society and culture. "Freedom" in the sense of active creativity in society and history occupies the center of his thinking. He directly appealed to the middle class as the dynamic sector of society. He had a strong activist theology of grace that played itself out in society. Christian spirituality involved taking up God's project of the kingdom of God in history and the conviction that the kingdom that God would bring about eschatologically would also depend on graced human freedom. Here were the grounds for a liberation theology that while recognizing classes and social conflict did not privilege any with its call for participation in a joint effort to fashion more just social structures. This view of liberation theology, which bears some analogies to themes in Isaac Hecker's "Americanism" and the social gospel movement, I thought, could gain some purchase among Catholic students and in U.S. Catholic parishes. In any case, *An Alternative Vision* attempts to recast the principal doctrines and loci of theology in a liberationist idiom that supported a socially engaged spirituality. One of the problems of this book is that it does not explicitly focus and dwell on the evils of racism and the way it functions as one of the causes of poverty in the U.S.

Dynamics of Theology

This little book had an interesting provenance and marks a couple of subtle transitions. In a tradition with deep roots in medieval theological training, the course of studies leading to ordination culminated in an oral examination that considered all the central doctrines or loci of theology. This subject matter was frequently represented as a body of knowledge expressed in propositional or thematic forms. The student was expected to be able to defend by knowing and explaining or interpreting the standard classical doctrines of the Catholic Church. Every year, I and many of my colleagues would emerge from those examinations in a mild state of depression. Too many students after three years of studying theology and four months of cramming for this two-hour exam could do no better than recite the words of the doctrine; frequently the sessions never transcended the catechetical. Three years of theology had generated or confirmed rote dependence on authority. We as a faculty in many cases had simply failed to enable students to develop a rudimentary historical, critical consciousness or a creativity enabling interpretation of the meaning of a given doctrine for a particular group of people today. I decided that I would at least address the issue.

My first step was to develop a more advanced course that really covered much of the material usually associated with an introduction to the discipline. In it, I tried to communicate in a vital and relevant way for people about to take the exam I just described some essential distinctions that are presupposed by all critical theologians. I have to name these to indicate the rudimentary level I'm referring to: the absolutely transcendent character of the Holy Mystery we call God; the difference between an act or attitude of faith and belief expressed in a propositional formula; the recognition that revelation cannot be conceived of as God communicating verbal information about God's self; the historical and human dimension of biblical texts as distinct from their revelatory character; the symbolic character of all historical and linguistic mediation of God; the historical nature and hermeneutical character of all human understanding; the inescapable hold of the present on all understanding that paradoxically coexists in the human capacity of self-transcendence; the elementary co-relation with context of all understanding; and the constructive character of all interpretation. It is true that some students simply cannot take these ideas in or can only do so at rudimentary levels, but a school of theology has to help stimulate a learned and self-critical ministry.

Dynamics of Theology develops the movement of that course. The title draws on Tillich's *Dynamics of Faith*; it is meant to suggest that faith's response to reality creatively transforms the empirical world by discovering transcendent meaning in it, below it, all around it, and beyond it as a goal. Dialogue with transcendence constitutes human existence and consistently draws it forward in the exercise of personal and corporate freedom. The reduction of Christian faith to a set of propositions preserved in a hermetically sealed glass case and committed to memory really corrupts the whole divine project. Grace releases the human will and spirit from internal bonds; theology should help release the human mind creatively to interpret the meaning of Christian classics and appropriate tradition in relation to the concrete situations in which we exist.

This work was written while I was teaching in the extraordinarily cosmopolitan city of Toronto. This energetically pluralistic and yet civil city is reflected in the Toronto School of Theology where cross-registration works. This active ecumenical environment simply rules out sectarian perspectives and language and generates a healthy and satisfying experience of how pluralism works positively toward greater understanding of particularity and universal relevance. *Dynamics of Theology* is not a Roman Catholic work in a sectarian sense. It was written by a Roman Catholic, and Protestant and Orthodox readers would not have the slightest doubt about that. But it reaches out for an audience that far transcends the Roman Church. I take it that the Catholic Church's joining the ecumenical movement at Vatican II was a deliberate action; that council promised the world that its theologians would think ecumenically. The council also mandated Catholic theologians to enter into dialogue with the world in its socioeconomic problems, its cultures, and its religions. *Dynamics* offers a method and a style of theology that is aimed in that direction.

JESUS SYMBOL OF GOD

In 1990, I joined the faculty of Weston School of Theology. In the course of my first few years there I met Robert Ellsberg, who as an editor at Orbis Books asked me whether I would be interested in writing a book on Christology. I had to think about that. As far as I could see, there were two major systematic Christologies available in the early 1990s, those of Wolfhart Pannenberg and Karl Rahner. One could write a book about an aspect of Christology or collect essays on Christology, but a systematic Christology required multidisciplinary work. One had to know something about scripture and its subdisciplines of

New Testament Christology and the history and literature of the "quest for the historical Jesus." Retrieval of the historical Jesus had to have an impact on Christology. The project also required immersion in patristic authors because the classical Christological formulas still command the imaginations of the majority of Christians. Switching to systematics, despite the two minor classics I mentioned, few fields in Christian theology were more active and more pluralistic than interpretations of Jesus Christ. Also, a new extensive body of literature had arisen that dealt with Christ and the other religions. We were fast approaching a situation in which one person could no longer write a systematic Christology that was adequate to the demands of the resources. While I hesitated, I also explored ways in which I might at least attend to these several areas of research. In the end, I contracted to write a systematic Christology before I wrote it and *Jesus Symbol of God* is the result.

I have gone back and explained the method of this work and responded to objections several times, most recently in *The Future of Christology* (Continuum, 2005). But some simple observations can illumine the project as a whole. I conceived the overall logic of the work, including its suppositions and method, in terms consistent with the conception of systematic and constructive theology laid out in *Dynamics*. It addresses an audience that transcends the church in an effort at giving a rationale for Christian faith in Jesus Christ. As an apologetic work, it had to be a Christology from below, which in this case means beginning with Jesus whose human life and ministry are available and potentially comprehensible to all. Then in a sustained argument it traces the ascent of faith's interpretation of Jesus, in and through whom the disciples found God's salvation, beginning with their experience of his resurrection. Theologians frequently use the term "sacrament" to characterize the implicit logic of encountering God in historical events, or God's accommodation to the human person. But the audience, the apologetic intent, and the logical status of theological assertion recommended the broader idiom of symbol. Because the category of symbol is so fundamental to so many disciplines, few educated people are unfamiliar with the power of symbol to expand the range of human appreciation beyond empirical perception and literal predication. Rahner, Tillich, Eliade, Ricoeur, and Pseudo-Dionysius helped me here. Symbol works to open up the human imagination to new possibilities and ultimately to transcendence. If Jesus were less than symbol of God, he would not be the Christ.

Most of the criticism of *Jesus Symbol of God* has engaged the work on a serious theological level, but a good deal of it has been polemical and defensive of a position that admits no others. I have already explained that I did not and do not write to defend Roman Catholic positions against others; I believe that polemics do not serve the transcendent object of theology. Pluralism, meaning unity within diversity, defines the "natural" or intrinsic character of religious experience. I did not advance a theological position to the exclusion of others that are coherently expounded. I do not propose a single reading of Jesus, or a single New Testament Christology, or an exclusive theory of salvation, or a Spirit Christology to the exclusion of a Word Christology. I do not see how those who characterize *Jesus Symbol of God* as a "radical" Christology could know the field. It clearly and methodically argues to a formulation of faith that affirms the divinity of Jesus of Nazareth, and such a position is ordinarily taken to be a high Christology.

HISTORICAL AND COMPARATIVE ECCLESIOLOGY

Over the past seven years I have been working in a focused way in the area of ecclesiology. I hope to bring to a conclusion the trilogy, which covers fundamental theology, Jesus Christ, and the church. The church project, titled *Christian Community in History*, has two parts: the first is historical ecclesiology, and the second is a systematic ecclesiology. I tried to write the historical ecclesiology in a single volume, but it proved to be impossible and so the history of ecclesiology was divided again into "historical" and "comparative" ecclesiologies. The whole work is aimed at a systematic understanding of the church, but it is not possible to write a systematic ecclesiology of a two-thousand-year-old institution without consideration of its journey and the intellectual history of its self-understanding. I will describe some of the theological ideas that governed or arose out of the historical work and then discuss the systematic project in the next section.

Once again, a set of premises and presuppositions consistent with *Dynamics of Theology* govern the fundamental logic of this project. Thus I call it "ecclesiology from below" by appropriating the rationale that the phrase has in Christology: it means beginning with Jesus and maintaining the conjunction between theological assertion and the historical church on the ground. Also, in keeping with Vatican II's instruction that Catholic theologians think and proceed ecumenically and in dialogue with the societies and cultures of the world, I take the whole Christian movement as the primary referent governing the meaning of "church." Since the church is or includes organizational structure, I apply a formal and open sociological model for understanding organizations to the historical existence of the church. This move does not become disruptive but in fact spontaneously correlates with the major "topics" of traditional ecclesiology that consider the church's nature and mission, organizational structure, members, activities, and relationship to its world.

In some respects, these premises do not transcend the canons of the discipline of history. But two factors generate a certain complexity and ambiguity. On the one hand, this history traces the normative theological self-understanding of the Christian community. For the longest time, until the eve of the sixteenth century, ecclesiology was not a distinct comprehensive theological topic, partly because everyone more or less knew what it was to be church. On the other hand, history, the great relativizer, sets in plain view the changing character of the church across the eras and in its various social and cultural incarnations. There is little about the church that is *ubique, semper, et ab omnibus*. And yet the same church with a continuous life in history always identified with and recognized itself in the New Testament. This tension between diversity and unity, between change and sameness, can of course be asserted on a theological level: the church constantly changes with history and culture and yet remains the body of Christ animated by God's Spirit. The shift to a historical ecclesiology tries to find the traces of sameness or unchanging identity within the actual adjustments of history. To do this I consistently isolated within the historical development certain "constants" in the form of content or beliefs and principles that the whole church in any period could appeal to as its own.

With the sixteenth century and the Reformation, ecclesiology came of age. The pluralism within western Europe called forth critical and comprehensive ecclesiologies the way the division between East and West did not, probably because of territorial and cultural separation. Ecclesiologies like those of Calvin and Hooker are truly impressive, and although Trent did not formulate a comparable ecclesiology, the broad lines of Roman Catholic ecclesiology were implicit in the church's performance and more or less solidified in the canonical tradition. With the Reformation, the history of ecclesiology gained a comparative edge, one that was often explicit and openly polemical. In keeping with the initial premises of my work, which understands the church to include the whole Christian movement, and in the spirit of twentieth-century ecumenism I tried to remove the polemics from the ecclesiologies of the sixteenth century forward. But I also highlighted the "comparative" dimension. This was facilitated by the standard organizational grid used to represent ecclesiological topics in each instance. The essence of what is going on in a comparative ecclesiology of this sort is represented succinctly in the comparison between Free Church and Roman ecclesiologies. By the three criteria of faithfulness to scripture, coherence, and an ability to sustain and empower Christian life, these two very different ecclesiologies both appear to be valid. The whole church, then, is a community of communities. Each church contains the whole church theologically, but historically it constitutes a part of the church. This dialectic of whole and part, and the continual conversation between the parts that each contribute to the whole, describes the state of the church in history.

CONSTRUCTIVE TRANSDENOMINATIONAL ECCLESIOLOGY

When I began the project of a historical-comparative ecclesiology, I intended to conclude it with a historically conscious Roman Catholic ecclesiology. But this would not be a fitting conclusion given the historical/theological method I had adopted. That approach required a "transdenominational" ecclesiology. The subtle if not ambiguous object of such a work needs some commentary.

I take the work of the Faith and Order Commission of the World Council of Churches as the model for what I mean by a transdenominational ecclesiology. More specifically I have in mind the Commission's two documents, "Baptism, Eucharist and Ministry" (1982) and "The Nature and Mission of the Church" (2005). The first was a highly successful attempt to formulate in a consensus statement a theological construal of baptism, eucharist, and church ministry. That success can be measured by the six volumes of official responses to the document by different churches from around the world. It is obvious from these responses that the churches took seriously the effort of BEM to reach the largest possible constituency that could recognize the apostolicity of its theological statements. In fact, most churches affirmed the overall validity of these statements of Faith and Order in the sense of their reaching toward a current interpretation of apostolicity as distinct from complete agreement with or acceptance of the details. The overwhelming majority of the responses had questions about or reflected some particular difference with the BEM statement while at the same time recognizing that, on the whole, it reflected an apostolic faith that the churches shared in common. It will be interesting to see whether over a certain period of time the second document of the Faith and Order Commission can achieve the same success.

BEM illustrates the logic of what I've been forced unwillingly to call "transdenominational" ecclesiology for sheer lack of another term. BEM also helps define the subtle nature of its content or object. This ecclesiology does not describe or attach to a particular church in its particularity, but seeks to describe what churches share in common. In that sense, it aims at giving the fullest possible elaboration of the apostolic character of the church, that which either comes from or is compatible with the defining origins of the church. When one church recognizes the apostolicity of another church, even though the second church differs significantly from the first, this means that the first church implicitly recognizes at least a partial communion between it and the other church. The amount of this kind of consensus that is implicitly affirmed around the BEM document is quite remarkable. It means that historical consciousness, which generates the cliché that there can only be unity that at the same time accepts diversity, is actually beginning to take hold in the churches. Transdenominational ecclesiology, therefore, does not intend to construct the ecclesiology of any particular church. Yet its object exists even though this ecclesiology is by definition an abstraction. The existence of this ecclesiology lies within the churches that conceive themselves to be apostolic. The language and analysis that constitute this ecclesiology seek to formulate discursively what apostolic churches recognize as partial but substantial descriptions of themselves. I have titled this third volume of Christian Community in History *Ecclesial Existence* to indicate its simultaneously abstract and existential character: it resists complete circumscription by any particular church institution while at the same time defining in organizational terms an actual Christian spirituality or way of life.

Finally, I do not understand this communal ecclesiology as a competitor of denominational ecclesiologies; these will always be needed to define the particularities of a church tradition. But I do want to stimulate this kind of ecclesiology as a discipline running in parallel, one that keeps the lines open to other churches by comparison, contrast, and assertion of a common faith.

Such has been my itinerary thus far, and it has generated some reaction from the leadership of the Roman Catholic Church. It is difficult to respond publicly to an official disclaimer of certain aspects of one's theology without appearing self-serving and disloyal. Indeed, theological debate with legitimate institutional religious authority contains intrinsically antithetical elements that ultimately confuse the discourse. Theology and proclamation are not the same thing. In any case, my theology is not and has never been stated over against Roman Catholic teaching but addresses a broader context, envisages a larger audience, and invites extended conversation. More and more polemics and even debate seem to me to miss the inner intentionality of religious symbols generally and the positive appeal of the gospel in particular. My hope for the future is that being drawn into the incomprehensible mystery before which we all stand will elicit less contestation, more sharing, and more spontaneous reaction against the obvious sources of dehumanization that characterize our existence.

6

Theology as Interpretation of the World • Philip Hefner

"Lord, the sea is so great, and my boat is so small."

Why a sea so great and a boat so small is not mine to fathom. The art of sailing is mine to understand and practice as well as I am able. Three questions have guided my reflection: How did I get started as a theologian? What have been my intentions? What has happened along the way? The last of these questions opens up to the future.

How It Got Started

External environment—events and people—does not determine us, but it does present the menu from which we select, and since this menu is the only one available, it shapes us. We are what we select, both literally and figuratively. As the years have gone by, I have become more aware of how important the offerings of the first three decades of my life have been for me.

I grew up in the kind of frontier setting that was Denver in the '30s and the '40s, in a family that migrated into the middle class during World War II and its aftermath and that enjoyed a Lutheran church life that was suited to all of that—frontier, working class, and upward mobility. My trajectory is my family's, in that the family prepared me for it, totally supported me on the pathway, and takes pride in it. I am the product of an era and a social-class group for whom America's Dream not only worked, but was liberating for at least a quarter-century. This statement is both literally true and thoroughly ironic. By the time I was twenty-one I was aware of the ambiguity of America and its Dream.

I count my first twenty-nine years as an apprentice period, at the end of which, within a three-month period, ordination ushered me into the church's formal ministry and a Ph.D. from the University of Chicago earned me a teaching position with that formal ministry at Hamma Divinity School, a seminary of the United Lutheran Church in America. My apprenticeship took me to only a few places—all of them important to me—Denver, eastern Nebraska for college, southern Colorado and Albuquerque, New Mexico for ministerial work, study at Tübingen in Germany and travels in western Europe for a year, and Chicago for seminary and graduate school. I have lived in the same ten-block-square area of Chicago's Hyde Park neighborhood for most of my life.

These first three decades enabled me to internalize a set of values that are woven into the fabric of my theological work. School and family set a tone for intellectual excellence and pluralism of persons and ideas.

From Denver to *Una Sancta*

East Denver High School was an elite school by any standard. Its graduates in the late '40s and early '50s received more scholarship money to Ivy League colleges than any other high school in the country, and one very British English teacher was hired to devote most of his time to coaching us on how to apply and interview for elite colleges (". . . shoes shined, fingernails clean, walk directly toward the interviewer, look him in the eye, smile and extend your hand . . ."). The peer group was sensational. The student body was naturally integrated in almost equal parts: Blacks, Jews, and WASPs. My close peers were well-to-do and bright, and ended up going to those elite colleges. The bourgeoisie were there, but also John Achibold, who went into local politics, a sort of lesser Newt Gingrich of the time; John Dornberg, a Jewish refugee from Hitler, who was a socialist-communist, and became a prominent left-wing journalist; Martin Needler, a quick-witted British boy, who went on to become a social scientist of some repute. The group included the late George ("Ed") Riddick, an African American social activist. Later, we were together in Hyde Park, where he was a graduate student and, as director of research, a member of Jesse Jackson's staff in Operation Breadbasket and Operation PUSH.

Libertarians, social reformers, and power people—taking politics and societal issues very earnestly in our conversations. I did not seriously entertain *becoming* any of these things, since I was "going to be a minister," but the upshot is that I knew about them and took such people for granted as a part of ordinary life.

Church and family also admired intellectual excellence, but of a practical, nonacademic sort. The church was my "safe house" in Denver. I was an indifferent academician after the sixth grade, but belonged to a "straight-A" church family whose members were dedicated participants in whatever the local or synodical church wanted. We displayed our church activities and leadership the way some families showed off their bowling trophies. The shape of this Lutheran church life has been fundamental for me. Powerful, carefully crafted sermons and intelligent "churchmanship" (as we called it then) were top priorities; my father told stories about the brilliance of Franklin Clark Fry at the dinner table, and, for the same qualities, he admired the pastor who confirmed me.

Being vigorously active in the church was the substance of our spirituality, along with cultivating a faith that was in touch with the times and not esoteric. My father considered his work in the post office to be a Christian vocation.

Except for a Missouri Synod uncle-in-law who visited several times each year and told my dad how wrong we were, there was not much polemic or concern for theological correctness in the first thirty years. The point of the Lutheran faith I grew up in was not so much to be "right," as to be working hard and well for the church wherever one was needed and in one's secular job. To this day, when I hear my Lutheran colleagues and friends argue aggressively about being "right" or "correct," my stomach tightens and I sometimes feel physically ill. No one who does not understand the power of this early spiritual formation can understand my later theological work. Both Langdon Gilkey[1] and Richard Busse[2] suggest that I discovered this spirituality in Albrecht Ritschl, found it expressed in contemporary form in Teilhard de Chardin, and made it the centerpiece of The Human Factor.[3] They are both right, but this enduring motif goes back much farther in my personal history than the doctoral work on Ritschl.

Skipping ahead, chronologically, the experience of church as I have just described it in my Denver years was augmented, beginning in seminary years, by a catholic experience mediated by the emerging liturgical renewal movement. The movement was at first repugnant to me, because its proponents seemed to wield the liturgy as an instrument of a "high church correctness." It was Robert Wilken who opened me more positively to the richness of this experience of church. It became a basic element of my spirituality and theology in the mid-1960s, when I worked and worshiped with Wilken and Richard Neuhaus in the movement that gathered around the journal Una Sancta. My trajectory has since veered from the followers of this movement, but the fact remains that the behaviorist-activist-intellectual dimension and the ecumenical-liturgical expression of the catholic traditions have melded in a curious way to be my experience of church. This was not mediated to me by the Lutheran Confessions, as it was for the disciples of Arthur Carl Piepkorn, nor was it for me a rescue from some oppressive pietism. Neither Confessions nor pietism are indigenous to who I am, nor have I been shaped by a polemic against them. For me, the ecumenical liturgy, like churchly hard work, intellectual honesty and rigor, and concern for persons, has been a means of grace.

MENTOR MENU

Midland College in Nebraska took up the nurture where family and local congregation left off. Here I encountered serious Christian thinking for the first time, not in required religion courses, which made no impact on me at all, but in the philosophies of William Shakespeare and T. S. Eliot. A group of five professors there took me aside (there were only 250 students at the college then) and designed for me a four-year-long honors curriculum in humanities—the payoff being a Fulbright scholarship to Germany in 1954–1955. Germany and Europe blew my mind, and convinced me that I wanted to be an academic intellectual theologian. The values of intellectual seriousness and the pluralism of ideas, peoples, cultures, and social systems were greatly intensified in the European context. After that year, being an American could never be unambiguous for me. I was not only introduced to the subsistence diet and acres of rubble still left from the destruction of the war, but also to the type of European intellectual disdain that Henry James portrays in his novels. I internalized that disdain for several years. During this year I began theological study, cutting my teeth on Paul Tillich's *Protestant Era* and the first volume of the *Systematic Theology* and becoming in some sense a disciple forever after. The boy from Denver and Nebraska took also to Richard Strauss, Jean Cocteau, Jean-Paul Sartre, and the theater of the absurd (as Tillich did, too). All of them took ambiguity to a depth that seemed right.

The Chicago Theological Lutheran Seminary at Maywood included a faculty, a peer group, and an intellectual agenda that I found almost as exciting as Tübingen. The developments that were harbingers of a new day in theology and church life included ecumenism, liturgical renewal, the American appropriation of the Luther Renaissance (Luther, not the Confessions, defined Lutheran identity for us), Lundensian theology, mature historical-critical study in the form of Bultmann and his school, and the heyday of "biblical theology" in the mode of Emil Brunner, G. Ernest Wright, Gerhard von Rad, and the Kittel Wörterbuch. Karl Barth was not on the menu of this or any other theological school I attended.

The three years of doctoral studies at the University of Chicago could be divided into three equal parts: those with Jaroslav Pelikan, my advisor, those with Bernard Meland, and those with all other faculty and departments. I count Pelikan, Meland, Joseph Sittler, and Ralph Wendell Burhoe (whom I was to meet in the later '60s) as my most influential mentors, and in my own mind, I carry on the dialogue with them to this day.

Pelikan's *Explication du Texte*

Pelikan's brilliance as a historian of Christianity and an academic intellectual leader is rightly celebrated, even though his provocativeness for theology is largely unappreciated. First of all, he practiced *explication du texte* as a method; that is to say, close reading of texts is essential and needs no justification. The interpreter brings to this reading as comprehensive an apparatus as possible, not to perform a reductionism upon the text, but in the confidence that it has something to say that is intelligible and often worth hearing.

Furthermore, perhaps in a sense presaging Umberto Eco, while eschewing his trendiness, Pelikan holds that the Christian tradition *is* its texts and the particular life that animated their existence. There is a sense in Pelikan's work that true Christianity is not determined by any single normative text or set of texts, but by the totality of all its texts and the dialectics that come into play between them. Scripture is normative, not because of attributes derived from dogma, but because it is the seedbed from which all the other texts emerged. In turn, scripture's meaning is not finished as long as subsequent texts continue to emerge from its impetus. His lectures, *Jesus through the Centuries*, exemplify the method in a quintessential manner. Who is the real Jesus? All the interpretations put together are the real Jesus. This is not a positivism of texts, nor is it without critical judgments, because within the texts, normative questions are raised and judgments made.

Finally, Pelikan's interpretation of the Christian tradition, in its focus upon "what is believed, taught and confessed," makes a clear but subtle distinction between the factors that condition a text and the constructive assertion that the text articulates in, with, and under those conditioning factors. Such articulation requires the "belief, teaching, and confession" of a substantive, constructive image of Jesus that proves viable in its context. This drives the theologian into the concreteness of the texts in which Christian faith has expressed itself, while at the same time recognizing that the identity of the faith lies in the fullness of its expressions and in the give-and-take between them, acknowledging finally that the imperative for the theologian is to believe, teach, and confess a substantive, fruitful articulation of the faith.

Devoted as he was to the classical periods of Christianity, Pelikan also teaches us that our fruitful articulations of faith are to function not only as interpretations of scripture, but also as interpretation of the cultural situations in which we live. Such a theological enterprise is truly catholic. Joseph Sittler, in a style that differs sharply, asserts essentially the same qualities for the preacher.

MELAND, SITTLER, AND BURHOE

As I received them, Bernard Meland's offerings coincide with Pelikan's and Sittler's in his insistence that the actuality of life and its forms must be given first place. The dynamics of personal and cultural life play for Meland the same role that texts do for Pelikan, and reading them closely is a prerequisite for theology.

Sittler, like Meland and Tillich, read culture like a text and attended to its message. His vivid image of Christian faith as a melody that is expressed in the context of counterpoint provided by culture grows in its appeal for me. Christian faith interprets culture, just as culture is essential for taking the measure of faith's import. Sittler had a sense of being on the flank where the church meets the culture that is marked by skepticism, where he was the intermediary through whom church and culture could communicate. All of the mentors I have cited here share, each in his own distinctive manner, that dialectical togetherness of Christ and culture. A mentor who came later into my life, Ralph Wendell Burhoe, also recognized the dialectic, from his vantage point of liberal religion; scientific concepts elaborate traditional religion, they do not destroy it, and the function of theology is to interpret the evolutionary process that science describes with authority, but whose God-dimension it leaves inadequately illumined. Burhoe also insisted that the text—in his case the evolutionary process as described by the sciences—requires rigorous close reading.

If I have an agenda for my work on the religion/science interface, it embodies these two tenets: the dialectic in which classical Christian faith and scientific understandings interpret each other, and the painstakingly close reading of the basic texts of Christian tradition and the scientific descriptions of reality.

I have dwelt on the roots embedded in the first three decades because they are my constitution, and whatever my career has been and will become is a peculiar flowering of that tradition. I have never felt that my theological thought is my possession alone; it is one expression of what that tradition can and has become.

WHAT I HAVE INTENDED AND WHAT HAS COME OF IT

In my case, intentionality is an ambiguous matter. Two of my mentors are among the most disciplined workers toward a clearly defined agenda that I have ever known or heard of—Pelikan and Burhoe. I am not in that mold. More like Joseph Sittler's, my agenda has been set by what I have been asked to do. Early inputs told me that working hard to do what the church needs in my place sets the direction of one's intentionality. My synod ordained me explicitly to teach in a Lutheran seminary, and such teaching posts have always been my base of operation. Consequently, my theological work has always been a mirror of what the church has asked me to do.

However, the inputs from the apprentice decades have formed a gestalt of intentionality such that I can claim it as my own. I describe this gestalt in terms borrowed from figures as disparate as Langdon Gilkey and Thomas Aquinas. Thomas spoke of theology as the enterprise of relating all things to God, its distinctiveness residing not in the subjects it deals with—nature, humans, sin, evil, love, and such—but rather with the perspective from which it perceives those subjects: their relation to God. I take this to be the essence of what Gilkey means when he says that theology engages in the thematizing of contemporary experience by means of the Christian faith. Earlier in this essay, I spoke of theology's work of articulating Christian faith as an interpretation of contemporary culture. I am impressed by the observation of many secular intellectuals that no theologian since Reinhold Niebuhr (with the possible exceptions of Martin Luther King Jr. and Richard John Neuhaus) has made public sense of the Christian faith for the common life and destiny of the United States.

The import of this agenda for my theological work is becoming clearer for me. Just as it is not enough to define theology's mandate as maintaining the purity of traditional formulation, so, too, it is inadequate to define it as demonstrating the viability of the Christian tradition in whatever cultural circumstances it finds itself; it is still less adequate to relinquish, for whatever reason, the tradition of Christianity in favor of some other theological hermeneutic. What the tradition and its purity really mean can be discerned only as the tradition is itself engaged in the process of interpreting and redeeming the creation. The viability of the tradition is demonstrated in any cultural situation only in the tradition's ability to interpret life cogently. To abandon the tradition is to abandon also the possibility of a genuinely Christian interpretation of life.

The task of theology, then, is to uncover the actual data of contemporary life, accept them in their facticity, and then, on the basis of the Christian tradition, to construct the frameworks of meaning that will provide cogent interpretations of life and help contemporary men and women discover the meaning of their lives and the ways of living that are most commensurate with that meaning. This aim drives all of my work, particularly in the religion-and-science field, but also in my attention to other facets of contemporary life.

WRITTEN WORK

In a recent book, *The Human Factor*, I said that the Christian gospel is a message about the meaning of the world. Consequently, theology is about the task of articulating that message. However, meaning cannot exist apart from intentional behavior, particularly in an era like our own in which human behavior is the decisive factor in the survival of the human species and the planet on which it exists. The centerpiece of this book's interpretation is the concept of the created co-creator as a way of making sense of biocultural evolution and the present planetary human crisis. This is also an ethical concept, hence the emphasis on ritual and praxis.

I see in retrospect that my little 1970 book on Teilhard, as Busse suggests, does make of that thinker a model for what I believe theology should do.[4] The subtitle of the book says it all: "The Meaning of the Twentieth Century in Christian Perspective." Teilhard provides a theological interpretation of earth's evolution as a process of complexification in which human action of building up the earth in love is the cutting edge of the process. This interpretation of evolution serves both as an analysis of the causes and proposal for the solutions that are relevant to what he considers to be the crisis of human existence that was transpiring in his own time. The same could be said of my interpretation of evolution in *The Human Factor*.[5]

In *Defining America* (1974), Bob Benne and I, on the basis of traditional American symbols, proposed an interpretation of American life that could be an alternative to the proposals of civil religion.[6] My doctoral dissertation, *Faith and the Vitalities of History* (1966), approached Ritschl from the perspective of his bringing the Christian tradition to bear upon an interpretation of the rising bourgeois society of his time in terms of the kingdom of God and Christian vocation.[7] These four works, I now see for the first time, are part of a common fabric: I discovered this kind of theologizing in Ritschl, saw it elaborated in Teilhard (who could not have been more different from Ritschl!), applied it to American culture, and then to a more comprehensive range of experience that underscores scientific experience and the future of the human species and its planet.

The aim of interpreting experience in light of the Christian faith is modulated by five elaborating concerns.

The corpus of my work to date (four books and about 130 articles) shows a rough equivalence of concern for the theological tradition and for contemporary culture. This equivalence also reveals my concern for a kind of catholic theology: an action of recapitulating as much of the church's tradition as possible within the correlative action of penetrating and recapitulating as much of contemporary culture as possible, and, as the fruit of these two actions of recapitulation, attempting to articulate the Christian faith.[8] This is the first of the elaborating concerns. In my earliest book, I described it thus, drawing imagery from the cybernetic functioning of a living organism: "In each present moment, all of the organism's past and all of its contemporary awareness is recapitulated, eventuating in one temporal and spatial expression that is supremely relevant, in one way or another, to the environmental conditions in which the organism exists."[9] The tradition tells us who, up to this moment, we believe God to be, and our contemporary culture is the repository of all worldly things—à la Thomas. My book on Ritschl argued that he was possessed of a catholic intention that explains his monumental researches in church history. I faulted Ritschl for a reductionist tendency that both frustrated his own catholic instincts and rendered him less useful to us today than he otherwise could have been.

The second modulation is expressed in the medieval axiom: "grace does destroy nature, but *fulfills* it." Bernhard Stoeckle has reminded us that the Latin formulation in which this axiom occurs includes the idea that grace both *undergirds* nature and *presupposes* it.[10] Both renderings are necessary and also fruitful. No matter how prophetically critical of culture we may be, it is God's creation, designed to be fulfilled in whatever way God intends. There is no junk creation.

Nowhere in my work is this axiom more evident than in *Defining America*. I contributed the book's last two chapters. I interpreted the decades of the 1960s in terms of what God was telling Americans through the medium of their history. Building on Benne's analysis of the American Dream, I argued that the Dream was both a disclosure of God's presence for our nation and also a betrayal of that presence. Picking up Benne's themes of the power and promise of the future, as well as dedication and sacrifice for that future and the concept of covenant, I observed that these were basic Christian themes, but that the American rendering of them was demonic. I suggested that the ways in which Americans had perverted these themes were grounds for saying that America's evil, as surely as its good, resides in its Dream. Conclusion: Christians would work for a renewal of America, honoring its basic themes, but, through critique, clarifying the demonic within them and purifying them.

This is pretty clearly a rendering of the "grace does not destroy, but fulfills nature" theme. I took a similar tack in one of the few *theological* analyses of the mission of the Lutheran Church in America in terms of economic and social class, in 1977.[11] I argued that the middle-class character of the church should be viewed as the means God has given us to carry out mission, and that the middle class—under the conditions of critique and transformation, symbolized by cross and kingdom—was uniquely placed to be the servant-agent class in renovating American society.

No Pigeonholes

A third modulation of my basic theme, besides catholicity and fulfillment concerns, is an emphasis on breadth of experience. I have always resisted being pigeon-holed as anyone's disciple or as a specialist, including a specialist in religion-and-science. Even though theologians are particular creatures—

and I endorse fully Sandra Harding's notion of located knowledge—neither theology as such nor the individual churchly theologian's vocation can be comfortable with too rigid a delimitation of interest or competence. Neither the gospel nor the reality of contemporary existence allows any such comfort.

I appreciate women theologians being called to teach feminist theology, African Americans, black theology, and Latinos, Hispanic theology. My colleague Albert Pero, however, himself African American, reminds me that just as blacks were always expected to function in cultures other than their own, white theologians should also learn such competence. At least, I would argue, theologians who work within a churchly vocation should do so. The great opportunity that African American Lutherans offered me in 1986, permitting me to be an observer at the first Conference of International Black Lutherans in Harare, was a step in educating me to Pero's requirement. Even though the liberationist side of my thought is scarcely manifest in my published writings, it figures significantly in my teaching. I know that this criterion of comprehensiveness may be laid to my being white, male, privileged, and over sixty. If that analysis be true, and there is no reason why it should not be, then I own it openly as a characteristic of my particularity.

The fourth modulation of my basic work goes even more against the grain of conventional postmodern wisdom—that the challenge to theology requires constructive and synthetic theological articulation. I acknowledge the skepticism concerning overarching conceptual syntheses, since I agree that they surely serve the interests (in the sense of Jürgen Habermas) of the one who constructs them. Further, such constructs cannot claim to be objective or detached from the embodied situation in which they are framed. I also honor the incisiveness of theology that is carried on as narrative or as critical deconstructive sorties against lifeless abstractions and oppressive systems.

However, I also believe that the times need fresh constructive proposals that can put together large masses of inputs from many different sources. Interpreting experience calls for such efforts. *The Human Factor* is an attempt to provide such constructive and synthetic proposals. I try to take into account the postmodern critique of such efforts by working within the framework of Imre Lakatos's philosophy of knowledge, namely, by formulating the proposals in discussable ("falsifiable") form, insisting that they clearly rule out some competing proposals while affirming others, and that they be judged by the criterion of fruitfulness rather than correctness, that is, that they be instrumental for gaining new insights.

The emphasis on constructive synthetic articulation corresponds to the emphasis upon that which is believed, taught, and confessed. My basic proposal concerning human beings as God's created co-creators is a substantive proposal for such belief and teaching. It emerges from a larger context of scientific, philosophical, and theological reflection, but it can be received as an image in its own right and taken in directions different from those dictated by its context of intellectual origin. In any case, my argument is that the concept of the created co-creator will be a useful and wholesome response to contemporary experience of many sorts.

Apart from this recent book, my most substantial foray into constructive thought was the 1976 essay, "The Foundations of Belonging in a Christian Worldview," in which I set forth what I perceived to be the requirements for a viable worldview today and then attempted to show that the classical dogma of the Trinity could be interpreted in such a way as to fulfill those requirements for viability.[12] It is perhaps the only piece of explicit and extended metaphysical thinking that I have published.

THEOLOGICAL BRUSH-CLEARING

Fifth, and finally, the enterprise of theology as interpretation of contemporary culture requires that a lot of brush be cleared before major work can begin. I am impressed with the relatively large number of intellectually difficult questions that must be dealt with before the theologian can get on with the main task. Brush-clearing has been important in my work, and I give some examples, to illustrate some of the issues that have given me difficulty over the years. In the 1960s, I realized that the theological task of interpreting human being must reckon with certain basic assumptions and interpretations that emanate from the biological and human sciences. Two essays, "Man as Nature's Man" (1964)[13] and "Toward a New Doctrine of Man: The Relationship of Man and Nature" (1969),[14] tried simply to sort out these scientific challenges for my own thinking.

Late in the 1970s, I recognized that my thinking on the religion/science interface would have to be much more sophisticated about the problems of "is" and "ought," since one of the major criticisms of two of my mentors, Burhoe and Teilhard, was that they were careless in dealing with these issues. My 1980 article, "Is/Ought: A Risky Relationship between Theology and Science," surveys the philosophical literature on the issue and suggests a way through it.[15] It was a surprise to me to discover that philosophers have arrived at no real consensus on "is" and "ought"; the so-called naturalistic fallacy is far from universally recognized by philosophers working in this area. Also in 1980, I published a piece that surveyed the differing scientific perspectives on the question of "survival," since that concept, too, was beginning to be unavoidable for my work.[16]

SACRIFICE?

Further, 1980 saw publication of some brush-clearing I had done in the 1970s on the concept of sacrifice in the Bible and contemporary lifestyles.[17] Actually,

I published my first reflections on sacrifice while I was a graduate student, inspired in part by Markus Barth's spellbinding lecture on the theme, "Was Christ's Death a Sacrifice?"[18] On a later sabbatical, I decided to work through a fuller range of biblical scholarship on the concept. This study convinced me that the Bible does not fit the stereotypes of propitiation and relinquishment that were so often raised against it by theologians and psychologists. Also under the influence of Erik Erikson's biography of Gandhi,[19] which interpreted self-giving under the rubric of *satyagraha*, as well as the work of sociobiologists on altruism, I let all these disparate ideas flow together in my mind while I was at ease in Cambridge, England, in 1978–1979, where I was also listening to Charles Davis's lectures on critical political theology.

The result is an impossibly conceived article, in which I dared the reader to follow me through the Bible, sociobiology, and neo-Marxist critique—all under the rubric of negation. When Sittler read it, he wrote me a note: "None of us knew the dimensions of the egg you were hatching in Cambridge." Cambridge confidants Arthur Peacocke and Charlie Moule admired the effort, but thought that any attempt to resuscitate the concept of sacrifice was sheer lunacy.

This research cleared my mind, however, on what the Bible proposes as sacrifice, and I still think it is viable. Now that the feminist critique of sacrifice has taken shape, I find that I also reject the things they reject, but I do not think their critique applies to the biblical concept. Since, as Markus Barth said in the 1960s, sacrifice is the one hermeneutic for interpreting Christ's death that all New Testament writers share,[20] and since it speaks of sacrifice as a means of God's reconciling activity, rather than human relinquishment or sadism, we cannot jettison it casually. Furthermore, self-giving and self-investment under the dialectic of life and negation are central issues of our time, and these matters receive a lively interpretation in the biblical concept. The continuing importance of this research area is now made even more clear by the discussions set in motion by René Girard and Robert Hamerton-Kelly. This concept gathers together, in concert with the image of the created co-creator, the moral dimension of my thought. Churchly hard work is here, as are Ritschl's sense of vocation and Teilhard's "building the earth," but with a Lutheran sensibility for a version of the theology of the cross.

A lumberjack cannot tackle the big trees until access through the under-brush has been achieved, and gaining that access is what much of my work amounts to. It is also what is required if an honest *explication du texte*—whether the tradition's texts or culture's texts—is to be accomplished.

Voilà! This exercise set by the editor has in itself been a journey of self-discovery for me. My style of sailing is now clearer, even to me. We face a monumental challenge of reconstructing the Christian tradition for our time—theology as interpretation of the world demands it.

Notes

[1] Langdon Gilkey, "Evolution, Culture, and Sin: Responding to Philip Hefner's Proposal," *Zygon: Journal of Religion and Science* 30, no. 2 (1995): 293–308.

[2] Richard P. Busse, "Religious Cognition in Light of Current Questions," in *Ritschl in Retrospect*, ed. Darrell Jodock (Minneapolis: Fortress Press, 1995), 173, 183.

[3] *The Human Factor* (Minneapolis: Fortress Press, 1993).

[4] *The Promise of Teilhard* (Philadelphia: J. B. Lippincott Co., 1970).

[5] *The Human Factor*, 97–212.

[6] *Defining America: A Christian Critique of the American Dream* (Philadelphia: Fortress Press, 1974).

[7] *Faith and the Vitalities of History: A Theological Study Based on the Work of Albrecht Ritschl* (New York: Harper & Row, 1966; hereafter cited as *Vitalities*). See also "Albrecht Ritschl: An Introduction," in *Albrecht Ritschl, Three Essays*, ed. Philip Hefner (Philadelphia: Fortress Press, 1972), 1–50.

[8] See my "Ninth Locus: The Church," in *Christian Dogmatics*, ed. Carl Braaten and Robert Jenson, 2 vols. (Minneapolis: Fortress Press, 1984), 2:207–10.

[9] *Vitalities*, 151.

[10] Bernhard Stoeckle, *Gratia Supponit Naturam: Geschichte und Analyse eines theologischen Axioms* (Rome: Pontifical Institute of St. Anselm, 1962), 18.

[11] "The Identity and Mission of the Church: Theological Reflections on the Concrete Existence of the Lutheran Church in America," *The Church Emerging: A U.S. Lutheran Case Study*, ed. John Reumann (Philadelphia: Fortress Press, 1977), 130–81.

[12] In *Belonging and Alienation: Religious Foundations for the Human Future*, ed. Philip Hefner and W. Widick Schroeder (Chicago: Center for the Scientific Study of Religion, 1976), 161–80.

[13] In *The Christian Century*, 16 December 1964, 1556–59.

[14] In *The Future of Empirical Theology*, ed. Bernard Meland (Chicago: University of Chicago Press, 1969), 235–66.

[15] In *The Sciences and Theology in the Twentieth Century*, ed. Arthur Peacocke (Notre Dame: University of Notre Dame Press, 1980), 377–95.

[16] "Survival as a Human Value," *Zygon: Journal of Religion and Science* 15 (1980): 203–12.

[17] "The Cultural Significance of Jesus' Death as Sacrifice," *Journal of Religion* 60 (1980): 411–39.

[18] "Laetare, 1961," *The Divinity School News* 28, no. 1 (1961): 5–12.

[19] *Gandhi's Truth: On the Origins of Militant Nonviolence* (New York: W. W. Norton, 1969).

[20] Markus Barth, *Was Christ's Death a Sacrifice?* Scottish Journal of Theology Occasional Papers, no. 9 (Edinburgh: Oliver & Boyd, 1961).

7

A Theological Autobiography, to Date • Robert W. Jenson

For a Christian, autobiography and theological autobiography ought to be the same thing, since theology should not be separated from faith and works. I am, however, neither asked nor inclined to write a proper autobiography. What follows is therefore a drastic abstraction from the real story.

The account is roughly organized by chronological periods. But themes or concerns that emerge in a period will often be followed beyond the period's chronological boundary. The account will inevitably deal in decisive events and particular influences. It therefore will be over-weighted to the earlier years. In my judgment, the last ten years or so have been disproportionally productive for whatever contribution I may finally make to the church's thinking. I wrote the *Systematic Theology*. I became Senior Scholar at Princeton's Center of Theological Inquiry, where I was propelled into a frenzy of writing, often on new subjects, by the Center's projects and by a sudden flood of other requests, and where I was at the center of a worldwide ecumenical network of its own. Now I am writing biblical commentaries. And our granddaughter and I have just published recorded theological conversations, carried on when she was eight. But these riper years offer the autobiographer fewer obvious influences and turning points.

Beginnings

Let me start in college, where it first occurred to me that my inherited religion claimed to be true—and therefore might be false. That began my theological reflection, in 1947 at Luther College in Decorah, Iowa. I was very—as they say—"active" in college, but also did some studying: classics with a ferocious pedagogue who was my first intellectual hero, and as much philosophy as was available. Orlando Qualley pounded into me Greek, Latin, and love of the literature written in those languages. The tragic drama, and the theologies of Aristotle and Plato, were to become fixed poles of my thinking. On my own,

I dabbled in Nietzsche, Marx, and modernism in poetry—it will be seen that my Christianity was under some strain.

A bit of Kierkegaard and the example of a professor who contrived to be both an unyielding orthodox Lutheran and a—usually—charming intellectual, kept me on the way to seminary. I decided that one had indeed to jump into thousands of fathoms. My boat seemed to have two sides and no bow or stern. Over one side was a sort of Nietzschean empiricism. So I jumped on the other side, to what looked like it might survive Occam's razor: the time-and-space person of Jesus and whatever transcendence it was to which he called out "my Father."

The incompleteness of these identifications is obvious, and after a bit became obvious to me. But the sheer possibility of crying "Our Father . . ." with Jesus is, in my continuing conviction and life, identical with the possibility of faith. Moreover, the insistence on clinging to concrete embodiment has remained. Thus when I came to see the Resurrection as a constituting event of that "person of Jesus," I also came to insist for very life that precisely the risen Christ must be concrete in space and time, centrally on the eucharistic table. So I was prepared for Luther's Christology before I read him. The correlated distrust of doubtfully necessary metaphysical entities also continues. It is one, though only one, reason for my doubts about the reality of a *Logos asarkos*. And it is a reason for my opposition to the merest hint of Nestorianism, whether the *extra calvinisticum* or theologoumena that posit metaphysical distance between the "immanent" and "economic" trinities. I was on Karl Rahner's side before I ever heard of him.

SEMINARY

I was spared most of the first year of seminary by a wreck returning from Christmas holidays. During months in traction, I could do little but read. Besides literature great and trashy, I read through most of Kant and great chunks of Kierkegaard. This was my last sustained engagement with the latter; too much can make you crazy. But I am sure his strangeness remains in me someplace. Kant, of course, is a continual reference for any modern western thinker.

Later that year I happened on *A Faithful Guide to Peace with God* by Carl Olaf Rosenius. He was a Swedish pietist whose thinking and style were otherwise alien to me, but he made another obvious point that had not occurred to me: since unbelief is the sin in all sin, the forgiveness of sin must primally be forgiveness for unbelief. This allowed me to continue in seminary and church. And the point has remained my chief axiom of pastoral practice— of which, despite my chiefly academic vocation, there has been a surprising amount.

Luther Seminary in St. Paul was not a stellar academic institution. When I left, I vowed never to set foot in a seminary again—a disdain avenged by twenty years teaching in one. But decisive directions were set during those years. By reading books professors cautioned against— Günkel, Mowinckle, and such—I discovered that the Bible was interesting—yet another obvious point that dawned late upon me. Those psalms were actual liturgy! Those stories had actually been told, by and to interested parties! I am now active in the revolt against historical-critical hegemony in exegesis, but I have not turned against historical-critical scholarship itself. Indeed, I sometimes build critical points into theological arguments, and even—to the alarm of the professional exegetes—vice versa. The same reading made me a partisan of the Old Testament's authoritative place in Christian theology.

Luther Seminary was divided, as it had been since its founding, by controversy between orthodox Lutheranism and general Protestant pietism— and it was truly *divided*; folk took these things seriously. The specified object of controversy was one that had torn the Norwegian Lutherans since their immigration: Is God's election to belief primal, or is it made *intuitu fidei*, that is, following upon God's foresight of who will in fact freely believe? The seemingly arcane distinction opens two very different styles of theological reflection.

I took the orthodox side, represented on the faculty by Herman Preus. He led me to read the Lutheran scholastics, and reading led me to revere them. My first truly scholarly paper—disguised as a term paper for a professor on the opposing side—was on Martin Chemnitz's *De duabus naturis in Christo*. I remain in awe of the old Lutherans' intellectual power and their daring, christologically driven ontological revisions, and have hoped to follow in their steps. Insofar as I am still a recognizably Lutheran theologian, it is the hyper-Cyrillian Christology and sacramentology of Johannes Brenz—shortly adopted by Luther himself—that is the chief bond. And I continue to regard the *intuitu fidei*—which has many current disguises—as a pitiful cop-out.

Of seminary professors, one was decisive in my life. Edmund Smits was a middle-European polymath whom postwar demographic tides had washed up on the strange beach of an American denominational seminary. He introduced me to Augustine, who has remained a pole of my thought, usually but not always in concord; to psychoanalytic theory, both Freudian and Jungian, and indeed to psychoanalysis itself; and to much else, like the need for liturgy not to be overly accessible. During my last year there, he was pastor to my new wife and myself.

Two fellow students must be mentioned. Gerhard Forde put me on to Rudolf Bultmann. When I went to Heidelberg for the doctorate, I planned to write on Bultmann. I continue to honor him and have gained much also from his followers Gerhard Ebeling and Ernst Fuchs. On the famous occasion when Martin Heidegger came out of hiding in the Black Forest to lead a day-long seminar of the theologians among his old students, Günther Bornkamm had me in tow; I listened awestruck, if also Anglo-Saxon skeptical. I still have my mimeographed copy of Heidegger's paper. So there is all that in me.

The specific point of my departure from Bultmann is worth mentioning, since it continues to move my theology. Faith, said Bultmann, is "openness to the future." Good, but what is the content of that future? The Bultmannian answer had to be "openness to the future." One day this regress struck me as absurd, which left me with the abiding question: "What *describable* future does the gospel open? That is the root of my later labeling as a "theologian of hope"; though in fact I knew nothing about the movement until the book that got me the label—*Story and Promise*—was almost finished.

Carl Braaten and I were once described as two dogs circling and sniffing: he the sophisticate from the Sorbonne and relatively urbane St. Olaf College, I the defender of orthodoxy from then socially unprepossessing Luther. We greatly distrusted one another, until one day in 1957 the two graduate student couples met on the street in Heidelberg, our wives conspired to spend the evening together, Carl and I argued loudly through it, and we started becoming the best friends and regular collaborators we have been for the decades since. Carl had been Paul Tillich's teaching assistant at Harvard, and continued the process of opening me up. He has always been the initiator of our joint projects, most notably *Dialog* magazine, the Center for Catholic and Evangelical Theology (CCET), and *Pro Ecclesia* magazine.

As will have been noticed, I found seminary unsatisfying. So I moonlighted at the University of Minnesota, studying philosophy and principally modern logic. The habits of mind acquired in the latter study have never left me, and when I shortly began teaching, it was the only subject in which I was really qualified.

BLANCHE

The major theological event of my seminary years occurred during internship. I was assigned to the Lutheran student work at the University of Minnesota. There I met the counselor at the Lutheran Student House—"counselor" was a euphemism for the role of women who were pastors in all but presiding at the eucharist. We were married the following summer. And when I tell people that my books should rightly list Blanche Rockne as co-author, that is the truth.

Some will know me as a passionate ecumenist, and much of the following will talk about that. But before Blanche, I disapproved of the whole movement. She, shaped by the inevitably ecumenical ministry at state universities, converted me.

Or again, those who read me will have seen an ever-increasing use of the notion of story/narrative. It was not the labeled "narrative theologians" who pushed me that way; Blanche's critical query in fifty-two years of theological discussion/argument has ever been, "But how does this fit the biblical narrative/story?" Early in my teaching years, I was on a panel where I was going on about "the gospel." A member of the audience asked, "But what *is* the gospel?" I was taken aback. Finally I blurted, "The story about Jesus, told as a promise." I have stuck with that, except for gradually making it be ". . . about Jesus in Israel. . . ." And I have stuck with an ecumenically important entailment: "'We are justified by faith' is *not* itself the gospel."

Or yet again, when in the 1970s I developed a deep and abiding interest in specifically American theologians, wrote an enthusiastic book about the greatest of them, Jonathan Edwards, and indeed stole his aesthetic metaphysics, it was Blanche who had pushed me to read and teach the New Englanders. She knew something of American intellectual history, and thought it odd that I knew quite a lot about what happened in Germany in the eighteenth and nineteenth centuries and almost nothing about what was concurrently happening in my own country. And so forth. Note the frequent "our" in the following; it is not an authorial plural.

HEIDELBERG AND BASEL

In those days, Midwestern church colleges had to grow their own faculties, often from their alumni. I was recruited directly from seminary for Luther College's department of religion and philosophy, in the understanding that if all went well, in a year or two the college would underwrite further study. Things did not go well: my unanticipated historical-critical reading of scripture, lack of worry about evolutionary theory the department deemed too alarming for our students, and refusal to participate in religion-department policing of other departments, were thorns in the side of the man who had brought me there and who chaired the department, the aforementioned conservative intellectual. However, I did begin doctoral study with the college's support.

Blanche and I went to Heidelberg partly for the foreign experience and partly for the faculty—though I did not fully appreciate that golden age until I was there. To suggest what I lucked into, my eventual sudden-death oral for the doctorate—the *rigorosum*—was conducted by Peter Brunner, Edmund Schlink, Gerhard von Rad, Günther Bornkamm, and Hans von Campenhausen. All but Schlink influenced me importantly; but I was especially shaped by Brunner's theological care and precision, and by what he called his "bit of speculation," that God's history with his people is just so his *own* history; and by von Rad's construal of the Bible's unity as a historical unity, constituted by leapfrogging promise, fulfillment, new promise, and so on.

After I had sat a while in his seminar, Brunner, with grave misgivings, agreed to supervise a dissertation. He would hear nothing of Bultmann; work on Karl Barth's doctrine of the election of Christ was needed and I might just possibly be up to it. So that is what I did. My more immediate task, however, was catching up what I did not know that a German faculty supposed everyone did: Kant, Schelling, Schleiermacher, Hegel, etc. Only about Kant did I have a clue.

Lectures by a just-beginning *Privatdozent*, Wolfhart Pannenberg, were a big help with the others. Indeed, it was the heyday of the *Heidelbergerkreis*, a group of young enthusiasts for the theological consequences of von Rad's view of Scripture, with Pannenberg as chief spokesman. My agreement with Pannenberg dates from then and is fundamental: if there is one God and he is triune, reality must be historical, history must be a whole with an outcome, and revelation must be God's inner-historical anticipation of that outcome.

Schleiermacher, I thought, was on a wrong tack, but I learned from him, adopting particularly his analyses of "religion." In the *rigorosum* I was congratulated on my grasp of Schelling: I have forgotten what that was. As for the Hegelianism for which some now berate me, I will admit only to great profit from and disappointment by the *Phänomenologie des Geistes*, to hope that history does indeed have its own dynamic kind of logic, and to *ad hoc* use of Hegelian language and notions, which like Kantian turns are simply part of our historical situation.

When the time came to write the dissertation, we moved to Basel, where Barth was at the height of his fame. I will not dilate on how splendid and accommodating an informal adviser Barth proved to be. Enough that he read and approved the work, part of which was later published as *Alpha and Omega*.

I was never a proper Barthian—which is—I think, why Barth liked having me around, since his seminar and colloquia did not work without a foil. Blanche and I were already too catholic in our need for the church's ancient orders of worship and too Lutheran in our attitude to sacraments to become full-fledged disciples of a Swiss Protestant, however winsome.

What remains with me from the years of reading and writing about Barth is nevertheless much and decisive. First: the role of the doctrine of Trinity in the *Kirchliche Dogmatik*—not necessarily its particular development—is a mandating example. The Trinity's first function is identification of the Christian God, which leads to its wider role as the frame within which ancient and new theological puzzles can be resolved. Second: systematic theology is willy-nilly metaphysics, to be engaged on a *level* field with such as Aristotle or Hegel. Third: a perhaps implicit construal of election is always at the heart of a theology, and must be christological—Christ both elects and is the one primally elected—if it is not to paganize the whole.

Fourth: Barth's early fight against the "German Christians" teaches a fundamental lesson. Of course, e.g., theology done by Germans will differ from theology done by East Indians. But if any such difference is antecedently theorized—as racial theory or feminist theory or postcolonial theory or whatever—and this theory is then made the context within which Christian theology is construed, the result will at very best be the theology of another religion—with which interreligious dialogue might of course be appropriate. And fifth is the systematically and spiritually transforming insight that what "distinguishes [God's] eternity from time" is that "between source, movement and goal there is no conflict but only peace. . . ," not that "in eternity there are no such differences" (*Kirchliche Dogmatik*, 2/1:690).

I may as well wrap up Heidelberg. During a later sabbatical, there I was in Hans-Georg Gadamer's *Arbeitskreis*. His hermeneutics became a usually underground part of mine, insofar as I have any.

An Uproar and Its Aftermath

Degree in hand, we returned to Luther College, at the behest of the administration. The religion department quickly became even less happy with my presence than before, and launched a campaign in the college and its churchly constituency: an unsound theologian had been brought into the cherished institution, and must be removed. This devolved into a drive to bring down the college administration, with the administration's refusal to fire me or accept my resignation as the *casus belli*. At a climactic meeting of the college board, my erstwhile sponsor presented reasons why my theology could not be tolerated in a proper Christian college, and I presented reasons why his could. When the board upheld the administration, and I was asked to stay, the religion and biology departments resigned en masse.

The experience left us with abiding aversions, two of which would influence future theological choices. We do not easily trust churchly leaders; those who should then have intervened or advised looked away. And we acquired a distaste for the *rabies theologorum*—I know that some may find this implausible, but it is the fact.

As the only one left standing amidst the ruins, I found myself assigned to rebuild the religion department, and to chair and recruit a new separate philosophy department—all of which was rather heady for a green young scholar. And it got more so: a freewheeling new president gave a small group of younger scholars responsibility to shape an entire core curriculum. During our post-explosion years at Luther—1960–1966—I was therefore more occupied with philosophy and the theory of liberal education than with theology strictly as such.

Indeed, I was now officially a philosopher, and worked at it. My study in those years was bifurcated: Heidegger and such on the one hand and Russell and such on the other. The Greeks of course were always around. The straddle across the English Channel was to continue; my later book on religious language—*The Knowledge of Things Hoped For*—dealt equally with English analytical philosophers and Europeans like the Bultmannians or Gadamer.

And checking dates, I find I did write some—offbeat—theology in those years. *A Religion against Itself* was a jeremiad on the phoniness of American religion, with some backhanded praise of Christianity as the religion with an internal principle of self-criticism. *God after God* countered the "God above God" of the period's "radical" theology with an eschatological construal intended to be yet more radical. One will note a kick from Barth, and implication in the intellectual turmoil of the times.

Finally in this part, I must mention *Dialog*. Members of my generation of Midwestern Lutherans went to theological graduate school in unprecedented numbers, and returned determined to liberate Midwestern Lutheranism from its ethnic ghetto. In 1962 an otherwise rather heterogeneous group, chiefly prodded by Carl Braaten, founded the journal as one instrument to that end.

We—and of course other very differently intentioned agitators—succeeded all too well. With unbelievable rapidity, Lutheranism in this country went from isolation to being just another "mainline" Protestant denomination. This experience of unintended consequences is always present as a caution in my thinking. But the original mission of *Dialog* was great fun while it lasted.

OXFORD

Blanche and I presumed we would probably make our career at Luther College, where her protean abilities were being used in various parts of the college, and where I might have ripened as a teacher of philosophy and theologian of culture, in the latter inspired by the model and encouragement of Joseph Sittler. And indeed, I have never lost that interest: the essays collected in *Essays in Theology of Culture* appeared from 1961 through 1994; and my 2003 Maurice Lectures at King's College London had the general title "Christ as Culture"—note the switch on Niebuhr.

Our peace was interrupted by a letter. Would I spend a few years at Oxford University as the resident Lutheran? This requires some explanation. Following World War II, refugee Lutheran populations from middle Europe had landed in England, and it was thought that their churches would need to train pastors. To that end, the Lutheran World Federation arranged to "second" a post at Oxford, occupied by a Lutheran nominee but otherwise structured with Oxford's usual combination of tutoring in a college—for this post, the Reformed and at that time theologically heavyweight Mansfield—and lecturing for the university. Instead of producing candidates for ordination, however, the Lutheran groups promptly began dying out. By the time I was recruited, the Lutheran don taught the same Reformed, Anglican, and occasionally

Catholic students as other theology dons, with the LWF continuing its support as an ecumenical contribution.

So we settled into Europe again. It was my first assignment to teach theology strictly as such, and I loved it. Other things, however, were perhaps more important for the story I am to tell. We found ourselves in the heart of Anglicanism, then still possessing its seductive combination of *rabies*-free theology and the West's most faithful liturgical order, the Book of Common Prayer. And I found myself cast as a one-man ecumenical movement.

Mansfield College held public services in its chapel every Sunday of an academic term. Most Sundays of the month, I, as an ordained member of the Senior Common Room, sat up front with others of that sort and in somber garb functioned as an elder of the Reformed Church of England. One Sunday of the month, as Lutheran chaplain to the university, I celebrated "Lutheran" eucharist in quite fulsome fashion. And out of term we worshiped in the Church of England. It would have been impossible to maintain strong affective bonds to confessional distinctives, even if we had wanted to. After three years of Oxford, two at first and one later, we were on the way to being the churchly cosmopolitans—also in Lenin's pejorative sense—that we now are.

We did not go back to Luther College as planned. Instead, we went to Gettysburg Seminary. I will come back to that; here I will break with chronology altogether, to continue with my increasing involvement in and shaping by ecumenism.

Ecumenism

Back from England in 1968, I was presumed to be informed about Anglicanism and was appointed to the first round of U.S. Episcopal/Lutheran dialogue. The group quickly decided that if each party could just accept where the other located its doctrine, the Lutherans in documents and the Episcopalians in prayers, there was little that divided us but "historic episcopacy." Thereupon Reginald Fuller and I worked out the distinction between necessary *episcopé*, oversight, and the possibly variable historical ordering of that function. For compelling reasons, we said, the Anglicans retained the historical order in the sixteenth century, and for equally compelling reasons most Lutherans let it go. Each side could affirm the former action of the other, and then consider what to do now. The distinction is now standard; ours seems to have been in 1971 the first official dialogue to propose it.

I continued to be marginally involved with Episcopal/Lutheran discussions until their success—if that is what it was. This alienated me ever more from former allies. Luther Seminary became a bastion of "No bishops!," whereas I, from the first moment I considered the matter, have seen the ancient sacramentally structured governance of the church as a gift of God—and for

American Lutherans an antidote to rule by bureaucrats. Two-testament canon, creed, and monarchical episcopate notoriously emerged as a single package in the early history of the church. Why, I asked, were the first two God's will and the third not?

Next, George Lindbeck, noting that I was in a period of ecumenical under-employment, maneuvered me into Catholic/Lutheran discussions. Eventually I was appointed permanent adviser to the third round of the international dia-logue. For ten years we worked on our assignment: the relation of justification and ecclesiology. I thought of ecumenical dialogue as the attempt together to think new thoughts that might transcend otherwise intractable divisions. The Catholic members had the same view; the Lutherans did not, except for the co-chair, Bishop James Crumley, whom I came greatly to admire. Finally, a closed Lutheran caucus demanded and got my removal from the drafting committee, as being too friendly with the opposition, and all traces of my writing were stricken in the interest of not upsetting home constituencies.

Nevertheless, those were exciting years, in the course of which I became more and more committed to the ecumenical movement, more and more disgusted with Lutheran denominationalism/territorialism, and more and more catholic in churchly sensibility. And for myself I did think some new thoughts, especially about sacraments and churchly office.

In 1988, Blanche and I spent much of the year at the Centre d'Études Oecuméniques at Strasbourg, researching a book on the achievements of the dialogues and on the ecumenical blockade that was already beginning to be felt. At the time, it was thought that a "basic difference" between Catholicism and the Reformation might account for the frustrations of ecu-menical dialogue. In *Unbaptized God: The Basic Flaw in Ecumenical Theology*, we proposed instead that the problems stemmed from a "basic agreement" in an inadequately trinitarian intuition of God.

In 1990 Carl Braaten left seminary teaching—as increasingly a poor con-text for doing theology—and Carl and Lavonne proposed to Blanche and me that we should undertake an effort of theological education for pastors. Long discussions gave the project an ever more ecumenical shape; what emerged was the Center for Catholic and Evangelical Theology. And as happens with such things, the project then moved the Braatens and Jensons on its own tracks. When you spend hours every week or so plotting conferences and study projects, always concerned that speakers and topics cover at least part of the ecumenical spectrum, it changes your ecclesial perceptions.

At more or less the same time, Carl and I came to think that *Dialog*—which we had been editing by turns—had outlived its original purpose. We proposed to the board that if they would give us full control we would reshape it into a specifically ecumenical instrument. We were turned down; whereupon, with a little help from friends, we started a new journal, *Pro Ecclesia*. It quickly became a major forum for churchly theology from all wings of the ecumene. And we editors increasingly internalized the journal's stated goals.

Meanwhile, Richard John Neuhaus had invited me into his fantastically networked colloquia, on dogmatics and social ethics. There I was in conversation with a range of Christians and Jews at a level matched only by my coming experience at the Center of Theological Inquiry. Besides discussion with noteworthy Catholic and other Christian participants, my great profit from those sessions was that I came to see that discourse with such Jews as David Novak was not so much a matter of exchanging views as of joint theological work.

This view was reinforced when the connection with George Lindbeck brought me together with his student Peter Ochs, a Jewish theologian amazingly at home in Christian theology, including my writings on Trinity. Eventually, I began to lecture and write on Christian theology of Judaism, in a way that would have been unthinkable—not just for me but for the church—even a few years earlier. It is an abiding conviction: theological discourse among Jews and Christians is *not* interreligious dialogue.

In 1998 I retired from teaching, then at St. Olaf College at Northfield. But before my last semester was even finished, I was at a meeting at Princeton's Center of Theological Inquiry, when its director, Wallace Alston—who was to become a best friend much in the way that Carl is—came by and said he maybe needed a sidekick. After we exchanged self-descriptions—he decidedly Reformed, a liberal, and a drinker of Scotch, and I a catholicizing Lutheran/Episcopalian, who hung out with neocons and sometimes had a martini—we agreed on my appointment, I gave up retirement, and we moved to Princeton.

There my job for seven years—as "Senior Scholar for Research"—was to be a sounding board for and sometimes critic of resident members' projects, often from theological directions quite different from mine, and to help create and to participate in research groups and events explicitly planned to embrace widely varying perspectives and disciplines. I was like a spider sitting at the middle of a web that stretched out to theologians around the world and the ecumene. And I learned to appreciate the Presbyterians across the street.

The undoing of any residual denominationalism was complete. That is, in the semester previous to this writing, I taught "Catholic Theology since Vatican II" at the local university. So—I am often asked—will I not finally resolve the churchly cosmopolitanism in which all this has stranded us, by obeying the pull of Catholicism that I so obviously feel? If not, why not? That is matter for a whole other article.

BACKING UP: GETTYSBURG SEMINARY AND ST. OLAF COLLEGE

As earlier noted, I did not in 1968 return from Oxford to Luther College as planned. Instead I accepted a call from Gettysburg Seminary, under strong pressure from Carl to join him in the wars. After twenty years, I left seminary teaching—much as Carl was to do a little later—to return to undergraduate teaching at St. Olaf College, where I was for ten years. Together, that is two-thirds of my time in teaching.

The problem is, most of what I have to tell of those many years has already been told. I will here only fill in what has not yet been adduced. If readers have trouble coordinating the chronologies, that is no great matter. Theological reflection takes on specific qualities when you are training students for the ministry. One is that you must attend to the church for which you are training. So I returned to concern with the Reformation and Luther's insights. I wrote in *Dialog* about the grave theological problems that would beset the impending ELCA. I got involved on the infants' side of a momentarily severe inner-Lutheran controversy about "infant communion." I even co-authored a book called *Lutheranism*, with Eric Gritsch.

Gettysburg was then an active center of the liturgical renewal, with which I was already sympathetic. Gettysburg provided practice to go with theory: for several years I was dean of the chapel. Supported by most of the students and some of the faculty, we ran the changes of ancient services and crazy experiments. At the same time, Eugene Brand, a friend from Heidelberg, appointed me to the committee that drafted the Lutheran Book of Worship's eucharistic prayers —attending a service that uses them, it is still a shock to hear my own words offered by the celebrant. When I write on sacraments or ministry—or indeed on God—the experience of those years is always present.

Soon after being certified a theologian by appointment to a seminary, I was inducted into the American Theological Society, and—nominated jointly by Paul Lehmann and Paul Ramsey—into the Duodecim Society, originally founded by Reinhold Niebuhr's students. Both were at the time still clubs of the eastern and mostly liberal theological establishment, which I found—usually—impressive.

One day, Carl came with a project: that we launch and edit a multi-authored dogmatics, written by Lutherans of our generation; this became *Christian Dogmatics*. The group divided out the assignments, and I got Trinity. This proved momentous, in two ways. To prepare, I spent a year doing nothing but reading Trinitarian and christological tracts of the Fathers and a few medievals—*The Triune Identity* and chapters in the *Christian Dogmatics* are the first fruits. I have never emerged from that plunge into patristic theology; Gregory of Nyssa, Cyril of Alexandria, and Maximus are always on my mind. And the doctrine of Trinity is ever more decisively the key in all my thinking.

Finally to the Gettysburg time, the town was well located for participation in the years of protest. While at Luther College, I had been in the Washington civil rights march of 1963, and we had been locally active. Now Blanche and I joined the marches against the Vietnamese intervention; we withheld taxes; I gave speeches in hostile places; parents would not let their children associate with our daughter; and so on. And after it all, we experienced the same downer as others did: we thought there should be a straightforward move from opposition to segregation or an unjust war to opposition to killing unborn children as desired, but "the movement" and our political party went another way. I do not know precisely what effect all that has on my theology, but it must be considerable.

St. Olaf provided rewarding students—several now promising theologians—and conversation partners, and reinsertion into curricular concerns and the like. But more to the point of the present account, it greatly facilitated my writing, with a permanently reduced teaching load and a travel budget. It was in Northfield that the Braatens and we hatched and nurtured CCET and *Pro Ecclesia*, and where I wrote the *Systematic Theology*.

And finally, one joining of life and theology cannot be omitted. Concurrently with much of this, the family God gave us has been itself a theological event. The birth and growing-up of our daughter, the baptisms of our Jewish son-in-law and our step-granddaughter, and again the growing-up of our granddaughter, and their willingness to share their lives, have molded and deepened my thinking in ways not easily specified but profound.

I end this piece by summarizing the preface of the *Systematic Theology*: to be authentic, theology must be written for the undivided church that the Spirit will surely someday grant. I intend to keep trying.

8

The Freedom to Resist Idolatry • Ernst Käsemann

For several years, theology has determined my life. In our stormy century, one adventure has followed another. Such cannot be avoided in church and theology. At times we even get embroiled in the political struggle. In any event, I have had to alter my course from time to time, but have always kept faith with my beginnings.

My father fell in Russia as early as 1915. From then on my mother, really isolated in the city of Essen, had to tough it out with her two children. On my arrival at the castle Gymnasium, on the border between the Krupp colony and the more rural suburb, I found no friends. I could only have found them in the inner city where the school was also located.

Even after the war we had to queue up in front of the stores to buy anything. Then, when there was homework, there was little time for play and the outside world. I was left to read my father's books, thus at thirteen discovering Shakespeare, and in curious succession two years later Karl May (the German author of American Wild West novels) and after a similar interval the German classics and romantics. Put briefly, my youth was lonely and rather joyless.

YOUTH MINISTRY

My life first took on clarity when in my last years at school—in a way I no longer remember—I came to know the Essen youth pastor Wilhelm Weigle and his Jugendhaus situated in the city center, of which I made use twice a week after lunch. This was a preparation for and narrow entry into the study of theology. Weigle was a charismatic person such as I have not known since. Till his last breath, before and after World War I, he took care of us and like a magnet he drew thousands of youth from the working class and, when isolated from them, from the secondary schools. His theme was to bring Jesus to the youth. I venture to say that he succeeded with thousands. He made clear to me

103

what I had unconsciously sought: The Lord, to whom I could give myself and who showed me life's way and goal.

Prior to all the existentialist theology that later captivated me, and still ignorant of the St. Christopher legend, I came to know that each one's uniqueness, or in modern parlance, each one's identity, is experienced only through the Lord or through demons, to whichever one surrenders. No one belongs to him- or herself. In various ways, a person exists only in a participation to be discovered. It is not enough to demythologize texts with Rudolf Bultmann. Before doing such, the world and human beings need to be demythologized, in, say, their self-mastery, their ideology, and in the religious superstition to which they have surrendered. This takes place in the power of the gospel. It was this power that streamed forth from Weigle.

I will never forget Weigle's funeral. The procession began from the youth center, which the last mourner was leaving as the first arrived at the grave twenty minutes later. Two rows of youths and elderly crowded both sides of the street, to thank once more the one who had helped them to a radical change in life. In a way I'll never forget, Weigle showed me that German pietism preserved the Reformation heritage, though, of course, not when it was fanatical or egocentric. I have always defended that point of view, even though my theology was often damned by pietists in many countries.

Bonn

In May 1929, I became a student. Bonn lay nearest, and there also I found the friend most respected in my student years. Coming from Bultmann and Marburg, my friend intended to take his first exams at Coblenz, but still had time to ease my entry into academic life and to see to my beginnings.

His concern was not unjustified. In the university, I had attended all the lectures that piqued my curiosity, even those outside theology. Erik Peterson's Romans lecture-course fascinated me, so I also took his seminar on Augustine's *Confessions*. In addition, I took the one-hour-a-week history of religions course on Hellenism, without realizing how quickly Gnosticism was to become a chief problem of liberal, New Testament exegesis. I sensed that Peterson was resolved to convert to Roman Catholicism when during his lecture six Catholics kept stomping their feet in applause and the six irritated Protestants scraped theirs. From the first moment on, his ecclesiology had me in its spell. I was used to a church that treated youth as if it were a religious club. Now I was confronted with the worldwide body of Christ, concerning which I later took a degree in 1931. Never again, as the leadership of my church pietistically and in its programming actually still does, would I describe the care of souls as the center of theology.

Now, too, Bultmann's anthropology became problematic for me, an anthropology viewed by both Pietism and the Enlightenment as the obvious exegetical perspective. With Bultmann, however, that anthropology was not a way to psychological mastery. Existentialist theology is what occupied him— naturally, not as a worldview. Today I incline toward the venturesome thesis that the entire Bible must be read and interpreted christologically, thus, not even from a theology of creation. When Bultmann wanted to spoil for me the use of the term "humanity" as abstract, I retorted almost insolently that speaking of the "individual" was just as abstract.

In any event, the central theme of the New Testament is the worldwide lordship of the Crucified. Even the care of souls, which I have never relativized, must make that concrete in pastoral practice.

According to Paul, the task of the particular theologian is to discern the spirits. The pious person is not to become more and more pious, is not obliged to pursue or demonstrate one "religion" among others. What is required is the discipleship of the Nazarene. The individual may be a model in the fellowship. But the priesthood of all believers is not to be replaced by devotional individualism.

Every Christian exists vis-à-vis an entire world and, even when isolated in one part of it, must resist both idealism and materialism. The Christian must always confess the Lord wherever idols rule on earth, whether under the sign of greed for power or superstition or mammon. From the Christian point of view, the first commandment is personified in Christ. It is this *solus Christus* that separates the gospel from all religions and worldviews, often even from a bourgeois or proletarian Christianity. On his way to Rome, Peterson laid bare the weakness of an idealistic Protestantism. I have always been grateful to him for that.

MARBURG

My friend was suspicious. In Marburg he witnessed Peterson's power to attract New Testament Professor Heinrich Schlier, who took Peterson's route to the end. I was in danger of going that way myself. So, after the first semester, I swallowed Bultmann's historical criticism as an antidote. I naïvely agreed to go to Marburg, since I was excited about finding in Schlier the best interpreter of my Bonn master, as well as about being able to make a reasoned decision for my future career. So I asked Bultmann to take me into his seminar on "Pauline Anthropology." He replied that the usual limit had already been reached. On the recommendation of my friend, however, I was to be viewed as an exception if I could justify my acceptance with a sketch on the anthropology in Paul's letter as gleaned from Peterson's lecture course. I learned then that when success beckons, risks are not to be avoided. The risk was worth the trouble where Bultmann was concerned, though I am still astonished by it even today. Of course, in the seminar I had to pass a second test when my Christmas vacation was ruined by the requirement that in the New Year I submit a report on Kierkegaard's influence on Barth's exposition of Romans 7. When I managed this, I became a recognized member in the circle of the Marburg school. As such, I had daily to master Heidegger's philosophy as well as Bultmann's theological criticism.

My labor was rewarded in the early 1960s when the Geneva leadership of the ecumenical movement discussed the problem of whether and if so, what latitude was to be given New Testament criticism. As a representative of the Bultmann school I was asked to give a main address at the next session of Faith and Order in Montreal on the theme: "Is the Unity of the Church Based on the Unity of the Bible?" The General Secretary, Visser 't Hooft, never forgave me for deriving the variety of confessions from the variety in the biblical message. Thankfully, my thesis was adopted later. The result was obvious: discerning the spirits is a theological necessity, for which historical criticism is indispensable, and with the course of church history more and more urgent. Now, of course, I had to face up to the question as to how I could unite my pietism with radical historical criticism.

Tübingen

In the fifth semester, I changed schools once again, and, unlike most Marburgers, did not go to Barth at Münster, though I had devoured his writings ravenously. I expected greater clarity at Tübingen, above all with Adolph Schlatter, but was disappointed. This story cannot be told here and now in any detail. Schlatter loved to provoke, but was not eager to engage in public dispute. He had functioned the same way at Berlin, when in contrast to Harnack he was to maintain the balance between conservative and liberal. He never let himself be diverted from his own point of view. I profited much from him and regard him as my third teacher in New Testament. Still, he detoured around my problem.

I made use of the free time left to me. The Tübingen faculty chose the present status of Johannine research as the subject for a prize competition. Again, I naïvely plunged into one of the most difficult exegetical themes and, often till midnight and at much too young an age, came to deal with a gigantic flood of literature embroiled in dispute. Still, a semester earlier I had heard Bultmann's first lectures on the Gospel of John. I received the prize, though with the spiteful comment that I had criticized everything but Bultmann. The comment was justified. When thirty years later I held my own lectures on John, I was well prepared and had been able to give my own view greater depth.

ETHICS

Because my studies had reached their peak, after a year in an area of theology I had neglected till then, I could apply for my first exams at Coblenz. This also turned out happily, aside from an accident: I failed totally when asked about the difference between Reformation and Orthodox ethics. I had never concerned myself with the theme, but shamefacedly made up for it in the years to come.

I'll not be silent about my conclusions, although, or perhaps just because, they might be provocative. As far as I know, the concept of ethics stems from Hellenistic tradition, and is the basis of the modern idea of performance. A theory of duties makes clear what we must do or avoid, led by reason or conscience or situation and convention. When we do not adhere to that theory, we are guilty. So we are constantly responsible in thought and deed, provided we do not challenge the distinction between good and evil.

I cannot derive such a discipline, and this its watchword, from the Bible. The Bible knows of no one responsible for salvation or independent within it. Pauline theology announces the justification of the godless and in place of "ethics" sets its doctrine of the charisms, which in turn reflects the first commandment. God is the Lord who commands, but he is such as the one who delivers from Egypt and forbids giving his place to other lords and gods. In this prohibition promise is dominant. One need no longer serve other lords and gods, and like Israel which had once served in Egypt, is freed from all idolatry. Just this is at issue when Paul speaks of the charism. It is the concretion of the *charis* that favors us.

At the outset of our worship, then, stands the God who serves, who sets us free. When he commands that we serve him, he wants us to remain in the freedom he has given us, free from ideologies and illusions. Now the recipient of *charis* becomes at the same time the bearer of *charis* and its being let loose in the world. In the individual instance and always, this service becomes a witness to and realization of the divine power of human liberation—a charismatic activity.

The first commandment is truly a gospel. It calls to us to hand on what was given to us, that is, the freedom of grace. But the first commandment is made concrete in the Nazarene, and in the discipleship of the Crucified it preserves the divine power of liberation in a world beset by demons. Reason, conscience, and understanding of the situation have to play a role. In this respect, we approximate the ethics of paganism, but we are distanced from it by the fact that our freedom is expressed first of all and in flatly revolutionary ways in our resistance to the world's insanities. This was the fundamental experience of my generation. In the radical German Confessing Church we were stigmatized, because as disciples of Jesus we had to become partisans of the gospel, risking death from tyrants for the sake of Protestant freedom.

The Church Struggle with Hitler

I will omit the period of my education in the church, in order as briefly as possible to report the church struggle in my congregation at Gelsenkirchen-Rotthausen, organized through a territorial exchange among the mines from the Rhineland toward Westphalia. I have admitted earlier that from 1930 to 1933 I too voted for Hitler. My work in the congregation and for my dissertation left me little time for involvement in politics. Every night, for an entire year-and-a-half, while synodical vicar in Barmen, I was forced to experience the civil war at my very door. I eagerly longed for order. In family and at school we constantly heard that the Versailles treaty shamefully humiliated us Germans. Finally, the war left behind six million unemployed in our country. So my friends and I agreed that only a strong government could help us. I came to mistrust Hitler after his intervention on behalf of a criminal storm trooper in Silesia. But I was naïve enough to suppose that we could get rid of him at the next election in four years.

In the meantime, the party of the German Christians was formed. In the summer of 1933, its number grew from four to forty-five members among the representatives of my congregation. Then, when the so-called Reichsbischof incorporated the evangelical youth groups into the Hitler youth, and the Röhm-Putsch eliminated disputes within the Nazi leadership through mass murder, we could no longer ignore our having been handed over to criminals who unflinchingly demonstrated force and would yield only to force.

The founding of the Confessing Church at Wuppertal led to political opposition. As early as the fall of 1933, I declared that the Reichsbishof was a traitor to the evangelical church. From then on, I was hated by the Nazis; later I was denounced at the market place as a national traitor by the *Gauleiter* in Gelsenkirchen, and recommended to the higher authorities for assignment to a concentration camp. The chairman of our congregation lent support in an appeal to headquarters at Berlin. For either side there was no turning back. This became clear in sessions of the congregational representatives. As president of the congregation, I denied that those sessions had any authority in the church and assigned them a merely secular importance.

In the fall of 1934, I secretly learned that the Confessing Church was thinking of separating itself officially from the German Christians. With two colleagues and twelve members of the Confessing Church, we now resolved immediately to go on the offensive, and on the Day of Repentance and Prayer of November 15, 1934, would dismiss the forty-five German Christians from church service. In accord with church protocol, the announcement was made public at worship on the three Sundays prior, and was carried out in a solemn service on the Day of Repentance and Prayer. Before the altar forty-five members of the Confessing Church were presented as substitutes for the discharged German Christians. We were in fact the first congregation in Germany to dare such action.

What we dared to do would of course never have succeeded if what seemed miraculous to us had not happened. On the Day of Repentance and Prayer a riot was about to occur on the plaza in front of the church, and the worship service discontinued. Many women from our Ladies' Aid, the backbone of our congregation, formed the opposition. They did not threaten the men with brooms, of course, but promised to participate aggressively. Curiosity seekers of all ages and levels bordered the battle arena. Then Graf Stosch, advocate for church affairs in the district of Westphalia-North, suddenly appeared with about fifty policemen, and ordered the place cleared in the name of the state. He himself took part in the worship, which now proceeded as planned.

I preached on Jeremiah 7:1-15, an unusually compressed attack on the house of Israel, and then introduced the new Confessing Church replacements. We could see the older people weeping there. Graf Stosch had informed us the previous day that he would be commissioned by Berlin to arrest the pastors and prevent the service. When we answered "yes" to his query whether we would still keep to our resolve, he assured us of his protection. He had informed Berlin that he would guarantee order. I do not know what motivated him. Family tradition in the Silesian nobility may have prevented him from using force against the church. Perhaps he had learned from the Röhm-Putsch and the Silesian storm troopers' crimes to distance himself from tyranny. He was removed from district leadership, and became president of the Minden administrative district. I must always remember him. For me the climax of our struggle is always bound up with him.

The struggle continued, of course. Not even our synod in Westphalia regarded us as its vanguard. They wanted first to wait and see how our experiment would turn out, or so they wrote to me. Our action really isolated us. There should be no talk today of an ethics of resistance in the church of that period. We were partisans. Even after the war our inheritance was buried at Treysa (where the Evangelical Church of Germany was constituted in 1945) for the sake of the national church of the previous century. Reconciliation, in the religious sphere as well, became the watchword worldwide. Such ideology was expelled from me when in 1937 Martin Niemöller had to enter a concentration camp and seven hundred evangelical pastors also had to go to prison. At that time I had to preach at a service of intercession on Isaiah 26:13: "O Lord, our God, other lords besides thee have ruled over us, but thy name alone we acknowledge." Angry and in pain, I determined then that God's reconciliation could not be accomplished by compromising with our enemies. In the church the obverse side of freedom is and remains resistance to idolaters. On the following day, the Gestapo came and got me. The officers were very cautious and went thirty steps ahead of me. Miners can still be violent; they can deny authorities respect that the average citizen will never refuse.

I clearly recall 1937, because on Good Friday I had to hold out for seven hours in four worship services, as well as give communion on Easter week to the children and grandchildren of members of the East Prussian Prayer League. But in 1937, no less than one-third of my congregation voted for the Social Democratic Party, a communist front. At that time I did not detect any "reconciliation," but rather a fellowship of Christians and proletarians that had not existed before in Germany. Some came to worship because the pastor had visited them; others came out of curiosity, to see if my neck would finally be on the line. Night after night, for three long years before the war, we knew nothing of the security that existed only for citizens who played along. But with the exception of one co-rector who would not let me into his house, I was secure among my communist Masurians, and I will not forget what they did.

The approximately twenty-five days before being amnestied without a hearing were actually restful. I did not have to rush daily from one house to the other, or at night give communion to the dying. No one said an evil word to me. The prison inspector got me a box of Brazilian cigars, and allowed books, excerpts, and paper to be sent to me, so that I could finish my study on Hebrews, "The Wandering People of God." Now and then a guard visited me in the evening, to ask how a pastor could get himself behind bars, and how I happened to be the first in the history of Gelsenkirchen. On Sunday morning the brass choir from the hospital opposite blew, "Wake, wake, O German land; you've been long enough a-bed," and other rousing stuff. Only the fish bones in the herring soup on Wednesdays, and the anxiety at perhaps being arrested by the Gestapo on the prison steps after my release, disturbed my peace.

Up to the war, and finally with the visit of six nice women and six hardy miners to the High Consistory at Berlin, the congregation refused to be put on the defensive. When the visitors were not admitted, they sat on the steps and held out till the president, vice-president, and consistory council had only to leave their rooms to be informed about the people of Rotthausen, gently by the women, roughly by the men. We succeeded in having our records displaced till the end of the war. How that would turn out I never doubted, not even for a moment.

THE LAST WORD: "Résistez"

I would like to break off here. If I should tell how I had to be a soldier for three years, perhaps to get out of reach of the area command and seizure by the Nazis, how I finally survived the Allied camp at [Bad] Kreuznach, in which 70,000 prisoners starved, then returned to a heavily bombed congregation, and at once learned that I had been chosen as a New Testament scholar for Münster, but due to a denunciation landed at Mainz instead, would lead too far toward a biography. My students and my writings can describe the theological problems that arose at Mainz, Göttingen, and for thirty-seven years at Tübingen. I would gladly give each of them my hand and my thanks, though I cannot. Age hinders signs of friendship maintained. As a last word and as my bequest, let me call to you in Huguenot style: "*Résistez!*" For the discipleship of the Crucified leads necessarily to resistance to idolatry on every front. This resistance is and must be the most important mark of Christian Freedom.

9

Christian Theology and the Modes of Experience • Martin E. Marty

What should the stone above the buried ashes say? *Vivit* would do better than *Hic Jacet* or *Rest in Peace*, since I hope to live and not to "lie" or "rest." Then add: "*M.E.M.: He Told Stories.*" Historians in their profession tell stories; so do pastors, when they preach and counsel, or parents when they pass on familial and tribal traditions. Before "narrative theology" or "theology as story" became fashionable, theologians, or at least many theologians, also told stories and reflected on them.

Only if reflection on story gets classified as theology do I belong in the company of theologians. I define theology as "the interpretation of the life of a people in the light of a transcendent reference," that is, God. I know I am a theologian because I am in the company of scholars who are reached through a letterhead marked "Association of ELCA Theologians Teaching in Colleges, Universities and Non-ELCA Seminaries." Like everyone who touches upon religion, I also get identified as "Theologian" in the one-word subscripts conventionally used to identify participants on television talk programs.

However, those who teach systematic, dogmatic, or constructive theology at the University of Chicago Divinity School, my prime employer, or any self-respecting seminary, would not properly think of me as a card-carrying member of their profession. We historians smuggle in our God-talk in plain brown wrappers. To change the metaphor: theology forms a *cantus firmus* under the melodies that make up our stories. Now and then we are asked to open the packages and expose what passes for our theology to public view, or to play the theme of the *cantus firmus* in isolation, so it stands out. I was asked to do just that in the form of this brief theological autobiography.

Autobiographies tend to follow the trajectories of lives from birth to the time of writing. I began instead with death and an envisioned tombstone, because storytellers write in the shadows of both. Walter Benjamin: "Death is the sanction of everything that the storyteller can tell. He has borrowed his authority from death." Before my mentors St. Paul, St. Augustine, or Martin Luther prophesied the *vivit*, they reasoned from death, or from the suffering this side of it. "Christianity is suffering," wrote the great cultural historian Jacob Burckhardt—also a mentor for my role as a member of our university faculty on "The History of Culture." Burckhardt was marking his distance from "that centaur, a contradiction in terms," he called it: "the philosophy of history." His focus, our focus, instead is on "the one point accessible to us, the one eternal center of all things—man, suffering, striving, doing, as he is and was and ever shall be."

Burckhardt need not have been so polemical. Of course, there can be "philosophy of history" just as there is "philosophy of religion," toward which "philosophical theology" leans. It relates ideas to ideas. But for the historian, the storyteller who is also a person of faith, the point is to relate ideas to people and then to loop back from them into ideas. For the Christian, this means the story of "the one point accessible to us, the one eternal center of all things." The human being is seen *coram deo*, in relation to God. How connect this with God-talk? Here we have to deal with one of the "contraries waiting in the penumbra of [our] mind[s]," as French poet Paul Valéry spoke of them. In the nature of the case, or so it seems to me after forty years of thinking about it, there is nothing in the historian's workshop or toolkit that makes it possible to pierce what I call "the circle of immanence." One cannot successfully use historical methods or storyteller arts to enter "the mind of God" or prove God's existence or point definitely or definitively at acts of God in history. One calls upon faith and the language of the faith-full community to speak of God.

I began my autobiography from the end, from death, the summing up. What is my sum? I like to quote Eugen Rosenstock-Huessy to my students: "Any real book conveys one idea and one idea only. A book may deal with many elements, but even the phone book or a catalog is about one thing." So may it not also be with biography: "Any real life has one effect and one effect only"? Such may be the case if a vocational sense is strong. Jose Ortega y Gasset: "Strictly, a man's vocation must be his vocation for a perfectly concrete, individual, and integral life, not for the social schema of the career."

What is the substance, the contribution, the focus of my theological and historical vocation? None of us can see ourselves well enough to know what our core, our one thing, will turn out to be. But I expect that the plot to go with the headstone "He Told Stories" would see that the concentration of the second half of my pre-retirement life would focus on one set of ideas voiced in two words: *pluralism* and *public*. I have to say "the second half" because I do not find it clearly in the first. Schopenhauer says somewhere that we spend the first half of life writing the script and the second half interpreting it. I may have spent my first half—to age thirty-five, when, bidden by Jerald C. Brauer and Edward H. Levi, I first walked behind the teacher's desk at a university—working on the theological subscript or the *cantus firmus* of faith. That gave me the freedom then to spend the second half interpreting it in the stories of pluralism and the public.

How do I know that *pluralism* and *public* are such dominant themes? It is hard to escape them if one writes the story of American religion, or religion in America, with its wild diversities, as I am called to do. In recent years many of the stories have involved comparative studies reflecting the pluralism of "health, faith, and ethics" across religions (at the Park Ridge Center) and the diversities of public "fundamentalisms" (for the Fundamentalism Project of the American Academy of Arts and Sciences). Both of these involve varieties and project religion from the private zone into the public.

Friends and enemies consistently spot this. Even those who intentionally distort or lie about one do the service of helping to locate the focus. Thus a reviewer in *National Review* once wrote, without a shred of documentation, good will, or love or truth, that "the alpha and omega of Marty's religion is not God, but pluralism." *Damnamus.* Meanwhile, paragraphs or footnotes in a shelf-full of books also make a point of the public theme: that I coined the concept of *The Public Church* (as in a book title); or helped resuscitate Benjamin Franklin's notion of "a publick religion" (over against Rousseau's quite different "civil religion"); or was at least "present at the creation" of the theme of "public theology." If my stories have necessarily been about pluralism and the public, no doubt they reflect or force reflection upon certain theological ideas in the mind of the theologically minded. I remember that John Courtney Murray uttered: "Religious pluralism is against the will of God." I have to ask: Is it? How does one know? What does one do about what one comes to think or know? (Murray and I agreed on the next line: "But [religious pluralism] is the human condition; it is written into the script of history.")

How does one relate these themes to the main sources, if one would be grounded biblically and Lutheran confessionally? Biblical language, one is happy to note, is too concrete and often elegant to use the term "pluralism" at all, and the word "public" appears fewer than a dozen times. Scriptural writers spend considerable energy distancing themselves from the "many gods and many lords" (1 Cor. 8:5) of the surrounding culture. And much of the language of faith, while it always sees the personal in the context of community, deals little with the intermingling of communities that form a larger public.

The sectarian has it easy. She asks, in effect, "Who gives a damn about the public order? God calls the believing community out of it, to form a huddle, to be pure." I have never quite been able to square that notion with the biblical witness to God as Lord of history, all history, if Christ is the center of coherence of "all things" (Col. 1:17; and see 1 Cor. 3:21-23). Or with Luther—an idea of "good government" as part of creation and the providence of God. (See Luther's catechismal explanations of the First Article of the Creed and the Fourth Petition of the Lord's Prayer.)

Pluralism as used here is simply a name historians, social scientists, and politicians give to a society—be it global, national, or whatever—in which "any number can play," many do, and there are at least implied rules of the game to prevent each from killing all the others. Pluralism is not the subject of evangelical preaching; it is not the stuff of faith or hope or love. It does not save souls or make sorrowing hearts happy. Autobiographically: I recall walking through the snow in Manhattan on a day when cabs were unavailable, being probed by a literary agent: "Marty, in your story, what is the religion of Americans about?" Stupidly, I answered: "Pluralism." He corrected me in roughly these terms: "You will never find an American whose faith is 'about' pluralism. Faith is about making sense of suffering, coming to terms with dying, praising God, enjoying the unmerited goods and graces of life, fabricating moral responses." And if there is no personal or communal faith, there will be no interest in public faith and expression. *Pluralism* and *public* are second-order terms we give to the first-order stories of real life. But they both signal theological questions that make their demands, and to these I have addressed myself vocationally through a career.

The issue, framed by the question of contraries and inner contradictions, is this: how does one experience and interpret radical monotheist and anti-idolatrous faith, which I cherish, with the acceptance, enjoyment, and affirmation of pluralism? Or, how connect the "coexisting antagonisms" between faith that must be one's own with positive concern for a public order where faith, other faith, and nonfaith meet?

Sometimes it looks in retrospect as if my first thirty-five years were about personal, familial, tribal, confessional, local, and rooted life—and the second, spent in *partibus infidelibus*, as it were, were about the public, civil, republican, skeptical, global, and restless living that Paul Valéry sees as the mark of the modern. Now it is time to trace the two courses—this essay being assigned, after all, as theological autobiography more than argument. Finally, I will sketch a few theological addresses to the "contraries."

CONTRARIES

First, the rooting, beginning in a very provincial world: birthplace Cuming County, Nebraska. The population, in the most recent religious census, is still incredibly 100.2 percent "churched." There was shelter for a child. The biblical, catechismal, and hymnodic story came there from loving and patient parents and siblings named Emil and Louise, Mildred and Myron. That rootage never goes, or never needs to go, or I chose never to let it wane. The mark is simplicity. I have read that Pablo Casals, the twentieth century's great cellist, began every day at the piano, playing one or two of J. S. Bach's *Two-Part Inventions*. My analogue would be literally or figuratively beginning again, on each day or occasion, with the *Small Catechism* (though whatever theology I have comes from the *Large Catechism*). With this, the sign of the cross each morning, signaling a return to Baptism, since my confessional theology connects with being buried daily with Christ and rising daily with Christ.

Second, years of *gymnasium*, an educational-institutional Old World import of some breeds of Lutherans in America. It combined high school and junior college with a pre-theological option or intention. In my case, those years meant exposure to legalistic and scholastic Lutheranism. It produced an almost wholly negative reaction and took on features that denied the evangelical story. But it provided a classical education and an access to the humanities that one could easily subvert or transform into a kind of Christian humanism. In my case, this humanism was almost Erasmian—speak of contraries and contradiction, in this Lutheran world!—and has helped me ever since to be invited and at home when "humanities" is a concern, as on the boards of the National Commission of the Humanities, the Illinois Humanities Council, the National Humanities Center, the Humanities Class of the American Academy of Arts and Sciences, and the like.

How to reinforce this theologically, using resources from back then? In those prep school years we sang an uninterpreted translation of a Christmas hymn that stays with me. Praiseful believers are to "tell abroad God's goodness proudly, who our race hath honored thus, that he deigns to dwell with us." Anti-humanism seemed, ever since, to be anti-incarnational and thus antichrist. But in matters of faith, the surrounding scholasticism-and-law was at best a *paidagogus* "until Christ came" (Gal. 3:24-25).

Still, the glimmers of evangelical and pastoral thought must have been there. While preparing this article, I did what historians should do: look for documentation. My file folder "Term Papers, College and Seminary" had only three documents in it: an irrelevant paper on Cézanne, a high-graded low-grade paper I had written in Latin, and one called "Pattern." We were evidently charged to write a valedictory to pre-theology by picturing life at the end of a ministerial career, fifty years hence. Back then I wrote, as if fifty years later: "I did not know myself then, nor do I today." Now more than fifty years have come and gone, and I still don't. Or: "Though I was a conservative youth, adult conservatism annoyed me." How did I know to foresee that half-truth? Then, "I never lost contact with my background. At least I tried not to. A son of the soil through the years, I never wanted to lose contact with true, honest values. (Did the soil provide such? . . . All my life I worked against prejudice and intolerance . . .")

I also wrote: "I would rather have been a musician than anything else in the world . . . I could have been a passable artist . . . I tried poetry." Surviving companions along the way who knew me back then do remember that once upon a time I made a moonlighted half-living as a liturgical artist and designer, building in a love for art that some would pose over against my later unheroic "activism"—in the margins of the civil rights movement, and the like—as another of the "contraries" or "contradictions" of life.

How did the ministerial calling come? I relearn from the valedictory essay that "my parents, who were happy in my choice," would have gone along with other choices and that I was impelled toward pastoral ministry by an influential and much-admired grandfather. And there were tributes to parents and friends, from whom the theology that counts comes:

> Were they here "today": my grandfather, my parents, my early friends could observe and, I hope, use the words of a poet of my youth, Robert Frost: "They would not find me changed from him they knew, only more sure of what he thought was true."

Third, there were two positive Lutheran seminary experiences, at St. Louis, where Richard R. Caemmerer and company taught us *grace*, and at Chicago, where Joseph Sittler and colleagues taught us *nature*. These produced, for my cohorts and me, a kind of *Turmerlebnis*, a decisive "tower experience" that helped us realize gospel.

And there were in our cohorts classmates who became friends. Don Meyer, my genius roommate who, connecting faith and learning, Jerusalem and Athens, taught me Occamist nominalism and the *via moderna*. He died tragically young. (For those who like startling twists in the storytellers' plots: a quarter-century after his death his widow Harriet and I married, both having acquired through the loss of a spouse the prime element in Luther's credentialing of all theologians: the experience of suffering, and suffering with.)

Also, coincidentally, there was classmate Richard Koenig, Harriet's brother—formerly editor of *Lutheran Partners*, now a retired pastor and sometime seminar leader at Harvard. He exemplified to me the courage and conviction of pastoral leaders who witnessed through and beyond the Missouri Synod's turn from evangelicalism to fundamentalism. Through the years he and I have pointed and polished our Lutheran theology with amazing coincidence. Both of us have shunned "safe" Lutheran thinking, scholastic style. Valéry again, in the spirit of Paul and Luther, and for us: "faith coexists with atheism, anarchy of feeling with doctrinal views." We have both always been uninterested in the refinements of safe orthodoxies and the middling stances that make so many Lutherans uninteresting, and drawn instead to the faith/doubt dialectic in the provocations of Paul and Luther.

Most of all, Dean Lueking, best friend and (with spouse Beverly joining later) at least weekly conversation partner for forty-five years. One could write a whole theological autobiography by reference to friends! Dean reinforced the values of pastoral life through the ten years in my pastoral ministry and the decades since. He also represents a segue into stage four: congregational existence. Under William F. Bruening in Washington and Otto A. Geiseman in

Illinois, and then with the Lutheran Church of the Holy Spirit, which I helped found, and Ascension Lutheran Church, my local parish for three decades (where Paul Landahl exemplified the pastoral role so well), my theology turned congregational (not congregationalist!). Here the Third Article of the Large Catechism says it all, as does Bonhoeffer's theme, "Christ Existing as Community." To me the congregation is not "private" but "public," not "homogeneous" but "pluralist."

Two parapastoral-congregational inserts: First, if theological autobiography includes friends, it should also refer to family, which in my case has been crucial. The life and love and death of Elsa Schumacher Marty brought every important theological theme to the fore, and the presence of our offspring and an ever-changing extended family put these to the test or allowed for delicious expression. But that is a topic for other essays, on other days. Here I cite it also for its contribution to genre. I have never tried to write with the dispassion of the philosophical theologian, preferring the mode of Rosenstock-Huessy: "I am an impure thinker. I am hurt, swayed, shaken, elated, disillusioned, shocked, comforted, and I have to transmit my mental experiences lest I die. And although I may die."

Second: I have been asked how my generation came to be conscious of a theological vocation. Answer: under the tutelage of a provident senior generation. I think of President O. P. Kretzmann and a group he gathered at Valparaiso, or the pan-Lutheran voluntary group that met as the DeKoven Forum; they spotted those with interest or talent and initiated us. Do we do as well as they? And in our own generation, though I was marginal to the effort, there was the *dialog* group, which took on the establishment and soon became it.

THE SECOND HALF

Stage five: doctoral studies at and, ten years later, the beginnings of a second-half-of-life career teaching in Divinity (Religious History), Social Sciences (History), and Humanities (History of Culture), which pushed me into ecumenical, pluralist, and secular circumstances. There all the motifs of the first half of life get put to work, tested, elaborated upon. Never, in such settings, does being a Lutheran or a Christian get counted as an element in one's favor. This is the ideal circumstance for one who must work out a theology that relates to "pluralism" and "public."

In a full-length theological autobiography, I would have to ponder how I got ready for such a role, and how it relates to my life of faith, church, and theology. Joseph Sittler tells of the answer that Lutheran Church in America President Franklin Clark Fry once gave him when Sittler asked why he was not put to work in Lutheran affairs in America. Sittler was the LCA's point man in the World Council of Churches, on Faith and Order, in ecumenical encounters, on secular campuses. Fry: "You are for export only."

Sometimes I try to remember how I acquired the (I am sure, biblical) ecumenical vision, not recalling a time when it was absent. How did it come to be within the Missouri Synod of my pastoral years, a context that offered no domestic or export opportunities or encouragements; only discouragements and attempts to impose sectarian outlooks. I had to take lessons from Denis de Rougemont, who found that people he admired, Orthodox and Catholic and Protestant, were not in communion with each other, so he had to fabricate his own ecumenical movement: "I have composed my personal dialogue."

So, in a sense, it was with me. Never licensed to be at home with the alphabetized expressions (LWF, FCC, NCC, NLC, LCUSA, WCC, VCII) of ecumenism, never put to work by them, always—thanks to the invitation of one of my employers, *The Christian Century*—at the journalists' (and, usually, the critics') margins of their worlds, I found this to be a helpful vantage for ecumenical expressions that went beyond their present aspirations. Vatican II liberated most of us from confinement within the rationalized models of organized ecumenism. When the papal people put me to work, through Cardinal Franz Koenig, on a Vatican Commission, wouldn't you know it would be on the Commission on *Non Credendi*, for the study of the culture of nonbelievers? That, dear friend, is theological marginalization! And, I add hastily, another good place to be.

Ecumenism also posed contraries and contradictions. A Jewish observer at the Vatican Council once asked how I could consistently be a Christian ecumenist, seeking to recognize oneness in Christ, and a Madisonian republican, relishing pluralism in public life, with its "multiplicity of interests and sects" as safeguards in a republic. The answer would depend on the "modes of experience" occasioned by different situations. See below.

They tell me that, for all the intended devotion to the classroom and editorial offices and my love of home, I have no doubt been the "most traveled" lecturer and consultant in the history of American religious scholarship, having been to many hundreds of campuses and similar sites. My logbook records thousands of occasions. I do not know whether mention of this is bragging or complaining: it is simply a part of a vocation. I cite a friend's letterhead: *Timor Dei: Amor Peregrinationis*. Still, I love home and family, locale and roots, the Nebraska "soil" of my minority years and the Chicago "streets" of the majority of my years (1952–). In Chicago I collect Great Plains novels and get figuratively rerooted by reading Willa Cather and Wright Morris and Mari Sandoz and the rest, but would never last a week without the tumult of a metropolis. Contraries? Contradictions?

IN THE FRAY

Here one can only sketch something of the rooted, biblical-Augustinian-Lutheran sources for dealing with life *in partibus infidelibus*, in the pluralistic turmoil that I welcome and enjoy, in the public sector where no one grants favors because one is grasped by faith or preoccupied with theology. One theme is obvious: the concept of *justitia civilis*, not "die Gerechtigkeit die vor Gott gilt" but civil righteousness under the Lordship of God in Christ. Prof. Caemmerer steered us to it in the context of perfect orthodoxy: "For serving the purpose of God in the human city, for example in the St. Louis of the 1880s, it may well be that the agnostic Jewish newspaperman Joseph Pulitzer of the *Post-Dispatch* did more than any group of Christian clergy." We were taught to keep an eye on King Cyrus, Isaiah 45–46. Yahweh names him messiah, though he knew not even the Lord's name. Roland Bainton never found for us, but assumed it was there somewhere in the Weimar Edition, the very Luther-an saying that Luther may never have said: "Better to be ruled by a smart Turk than a dumb Christian." There is a rooting for "public theology," for a world where—in my *The Public Church* terminology, "saving faith" comes alongside "ordering" or "constituting-of-civil-order" faith. No theocratic impulses are needed, or allowed. Are these two righteousnesses "contraries waiting in the penumbra of the believers' minds?"

"Pluralism" represents more theological problems than "public." On Valéryan grounds, I believe that pluralism also exists within the mind, the family, the believing community. "Do we not constantly find several religions . . . represented in one family . . . and in one individual a whole armory of latent discord?" I often thought about that back in seminary days when some classmates who were future enforcers of orthodoxy scored only about 70 percent (or so) in examinations on the confessions, or, later, in pastors' conferences where one would hear thirty heresies per day concerning the Lord's Supper or predestination or the Last Judgment.

If that example is the case close to home in defined Lutheranism, what do we make of life in America, with its 222 each-split-in-two denominations in the Yearbook, its thousands of religious bodies in the Encyclopedia? Or what to make of Christianity in a world where there must be coexistence with and interplay among Christians and Jews, Muslims, Buddhists, Hindus, secularists, and more? My colleagues in History of Religion fields at the university press this on me. I see nothing in Christian witness that suggests that truth will come through the amalgamation of religions, or at their meeting points, or halfway between them, or beyond them. I emphatically see the virtues and values in evangelization, conversion, invitation, and mission—but also in conversation, encounter, and dialogue. There is no way to assure integrity in conversation if the partner must be warily watching for the moment when dialogue might convert into proselytization.

So Christian life involves "faith coexisting with atheism," "anarchy of feeling with doctrinal views," "contraries waiting in the penumbra of the mind and coming by turns onto the stage." In my case, between nonactivist art and nonartistic activism, in service of faith; between the local and the cosmopolitan, the confessional and the ecumenical, faith and doubt, evangelizing and conversing, dealing with the solemn and the humorous, using phenomenological methods in teaching and the language of personal commitment in preaching, pursuing "saving faith" through the Gospel and "ordering faith" through the Law of God. Gustaf Aulén taught me to recognize the obvious: that just as in *loco justificationis* the Gospel is the *dynamis tou theou*, the power of God, unto salvation, so, *extra locum justificationis*, when the doctrine or place of justification is not at issue, the Law is also the power of God—but unto the care of the neighbor. Does one, in the face of these contraries, turn indifferent to questions of truth? Is postmodern relativism or cynicism the route to be chosen, or imposed? Is the believer to be undecided, indecisive, wishy-washy, fickle-ly scrambling for relevance, being merely tolerant? Or, conversely, should one relish polemics, arrogantly proclaim the virtues of incivility, and hand out anathemas and *damnamus-es* with Reformation-era zest?

My sixth stage, the development of theology coherent with the story of pluralism and the public in recent years, would show me engrossed both in an anthropological and a theological set of assumptions. The anthropology is grounded in Alfred Schutz, William James, and Michael Oakeshott, and the theology again in Luther. Schutz speaks of "provinces of meaning" and "universes of discourse"; James, of "attentivenesses" to a variety of spheres or worlds; Oakeshott, to "modes of experience." A mode is a particular, consistent way in which one sees or conceives the world; it is the product of a focused and settled direction of one's attention. History, Science, Practice, Art, and Religion are such "provinces" or "modes." They are, of course, provisional and functional; one must not be guilty of what scholastics called *ignoratio elenchi* or "category-mistakes." My illustration: one does not look in the back of a French grammar for solutions to problems in mathematics. Or: the preacher, having a core and living an integral life, says "Dearly Beloved" to spouse, congregation, child, or another member of a cast member in a play—and means, must mean, very different things. Back to religion: One does not set out to convert while engaging in open-ended conversation.

Meanwhile for a second theological takeoff point, I could begin with Luther's modal theology, for he speaks of the believer being *simul justus et peccator*, at the same time justified and a sinner. Contraries? Contradictions? It all depends upon the vantage, in this case the perspective of the eye of God seen apart from and then through the activity of Christ and faith in him. But for present purposes, a third Luther concept, that of *deus absconditus*, is also helpful. This is much written about, and has troubled and inspired me from seminary days on. With boring frequency I have regaled audiences and readers with Luther's nineteenth and twentieth theses in the Heidelberg disputation. Here the theologian-as-storyteller finds a charter, over against the scholastic, the prover-of-the-existence of God, the Mystic, the contemplator:

The man who looks upon the invisible things of God as they are perceived in created things does not deserve to be called a theologian. The man who perceives the visible rearward parts of God (*visibilia et posteriora Dei*) as seen in suffering and the cross does, however, deserve to be a theologian. See Exod. 33:23.

In a recent discussion of the *deus absconditus*, Alister E. McGrath poses two themes that haunt anyone who reads Luther through the years. (McGrath makes little of and is threatened by the second.) First: "*Deus absconditus* is the God who is hidden *in* his revelation." That is the conventional one. But, second: "*Deus absconditus* is the God who is hidden *behind* his revelation." Luther had not developed this version by 1518 and Heidelberg times; it is clear in his later controversy with Erasmus in 1525 and ever after. McGrath: "We must recognize that there are certain aspects of God's being which will always remain hidden from us." There is a permanently concealed (*occulta*) will of God. Luther: "God wills many things which he does not disclose in his Word" (*Multa quoque vult, quae verbo suo non ostendit nobis*).

McGrath finds this side or mode to be only "mysterious and sinister," and catches Luther saying things in the form of "argument [that] inevitably makes theology an irrelevancy." He contends that this is so since statements that can be made on the basis of divine revelation may be refuted by appealing to a hidden and inscrutable God. Agreed; this is sinister and terrifying in certain "modes," "universes of discourse," and "provinces of meaning." But in other modes of experience and expression, when we ponder the ways of a loving and provident God, there can be a more positive reading. The God of Christian faith offers "the way, the truth, and the life" in Christ. This offer is to be taken with utter, ultimate seriousness. And *simul*, at the same time, in the world of "pluralism" and "public," what is one to make of the Cyruses and Pulitzers, the "good" Jew, Muslim, Buddhist, Hindu? Can one not work out modes of relation that do not create indifferences or relativizing in the minds and act of the believers while still witnessing to the freedom of God to have intentions not revealed, only hinted at, in scriptural disclosure? See Rom. 11:33-34 for a sample.

In other contexts I could elaborate self-criticism. This "modes of experience and expression approach" could degenerate into cowardice, muffled witness, blurring of distinctions, the loss of critical or prophetic stances, mere relativism. But in a time when republics are jeopardized, ecumenism is threatened by sectarian violence, and the tribalism of the religiously self-assured turns lethal, unlovely, and unloving, alternatives need exploration.

In the seventh stage of life, perhaps I shall be ready to pursue the fuller implications of this view of the theology of the cross, the *posteriora dei*, in the events that provide the historian's story, and the *deus absconditus*. Meanwhile, the *deus revelatus* in Christ provides that *cantus firmus* through all the doings of life, this side of death, and into the time of the proclamation and realization it elicits, the witness unto and beyond death: *Vivit!*

10

Reading Reality • Alister McGrath

In a letter written shortly after the publication of his autobiography *Surprised by Joy*, C. S. Lewis reflected on the importance of being able to discern patterns within one's life. Writing his autobiography had enabled him to discern a pattern to things that had hitherto eluded him. "The gradual *reading* of one's life, seeing the pattern emerge, is a great illumination at our age."[1] For Lewis, then aged fifty-seven, the narration of his own story was about the identification of a pattern of meaning within his life, which enabled events to be seen in their proper context, and assume their true and deeper meaning. Writing about his own life enabled him to understand himself better—not necessarily in terms of the processes within that life, but in terms of its outcomes.

Lewis makes an important point. Few plan their writing careers; they often result from the happenstance of circumstances and invitations, as much as from any deliberate planning on the author's part. It is only by looking back at the past that we realize how our life's work has been shaped decisively by the decisions of others as much as our own, by what some might call accident rather than design.

A theological autobiography allows authors to try to put into words the vision underlying their work, how this developed over time, and how it was implemented in writing projects. It offers authors the opportunity to try to discern patterns and structures within their lives, and gain a sense of how things fit together. And—as writers such as Augustine and Lewis discovered—it allowed one to track the mysterious workings of divine providence, perhaps invisible at the time, but seen more clearly from the perspective of later life. No theological autobiography can fail to create conceptual space for God, in that the narration of a life entails an implicit correlation of the "story of a soul" (Thérèse of Lisieux) with the somewhat greater narrative of God's presence and action in history.

SCIENCE AND SCIENTISM

I had no ambition to become a theologian as a teenager; I doubt if I knew what the word meant. My love in high school was for the natural sciences, and I saw my future lying in the deeper study of the world around me. I was entranced by the beauty of nature, and longed to peer further and deeper into its mysteries, convinced that something of ultimate significance lay beyond the horizon of our knowledge. I managed to build myself a small telescope to enable me to observe the moons of Jupiter. A great-uncle who had headed up the pathology department at the Royal Victoria Hospital, Belfast, gave me an old German microscope, which allowed me to explore another new world. It still sits on my office desk, a reminder of the power of nature to enthrall, intrigue, and provoke questions.

I remain unclear precisely why I became such an aggressive atheist at that time. Maybe, looking back on things, it was just part of the process of growing up. At the time, however, I saw my atheism as an act of intellectual defiance and courage, resting on the solid findings of the natural sciences. Science eliminated the conceptual space once occupied by God. Like many in the late 1960s, I was fascinated by Marxism, and saw this as an additional confirmation of the intellectual respectability of atheism. Religion was just a soporific for the intellectually challenged. If the word "Bright" had been invented back then—at least in the way to connote the independent thinker and cultural advancer who has disavowed religion as silly and harmful—I would have owned and used it proudly.

I saw myself as the accidental by-product of blind cosmic forces, the inhabitant of a universe in which one could speak only of direction but not purpose. It was not a particularly appealing idea, but I took comfort in thinking that its bleakness and austerity were certain indications of its truth. The severity and dreariness of this position were confirmations of its truth. It was axiomatic that science demanded atheism, and I was willing to be led wherever science took me. I must confess to a certain degree of smugness at this point, and a feeling of intellectual superiority over those who found solace and satisfaction in their outmoded belief in God.

In December 1970, I learned that I had won a scholarship to study chemistry at Oxford University with effect from October 1971. So what was I to do in the meantime? Most of my friends who had taken the Oxford scholarship examination had left high school in order to travel or earn some money. I decided to stay on, and use the time to learn German and Russian, both of which would be useful for my scientific studies. Having specialized in the physical sciences, I was also aware of the need to deepen my knowledge of biology. I therefore settled down to begin an extended period of reading and reflection.

After a month or so of intensive reading in the school science library, having exhausted the works on biology, I came across a section that I had never noticed before. It was labeled "The History and Philosophy of Science," and was heavy with dust. I had little time for this sort of stuff then, tending to regard it as uninformed criticism of the certainties and simplicities of the natural sciences by those who felt threatened by them. Yet by the time I had finished reading the library's somewhat meager holdings in this field, I realized that I needed to do some very serious rethinking.

Far from being half-witted obscurantism that placed unnecessary obstacles in the relentless place of scientific advance, the history and philosophy of science asked all the right questions about the reliability and limits of scientific knowledge. And they were questions that I had not faced thus far. Issues such as the underdetermination of theory by data, radical theory change in the history of science, the difficulties in devising a "crucial experiment," and the enormously complex issues associated with determining what was the "best explanation" of a given set of observations crowded in on me, muddying what I had taken to be the clear, still, and above all *simple* waters of scientific truth.

Things turned out to be rather more complicated than I had realized. My eyes had been opened, and I knew there was no going back to the simplistic take on the sciences I had once known and enjoyed. I had enjoyed the beauty and innocence of a childlike attitude to the sciences, and secretly wished to remain in that secure place. Indeed, I think that part of me deeply wished that I had never picked up that book, never asked those awkward questions, and never questioned the simplicities of my scientific youth. But there was no going back. I had stepped through a door, and could not escape the new world I now inhabited.

Was this the mysterious working of divine providence? Was I, like Augustine, moved to pick up and read these books? By the time I arrived in Oxford in October 1971, I had realized that I had a lot of rethinking to do. Up to that point, I had assumed that, when science could not answer a question, there was no answer to be had. I now began to realize that there might be limits to the scientific method, and that vast expanses of intellectual, aesthetic, and moral territory might lie beyond its scope. I had the sense of standing uncertainly on the threshold of a vast new world, tantalizingly beyond my reach, yet signaling its presence through my deepest intuitions.

I began to read more widely. Had I read Lewis at this stage—and I did not begin to read him until the winter of 1975–1976—I would have appreciated the wisdom of his remark in *Surprised by Joy*: "A young man who wishes to remain a sound Atheist cannot be too careful of his reading. There are traps everywhere."[2] A few months later, the matter was settled. I experienced an intellectual conversion to Christianity.

My initial instinct was to change course—to study Christian theology at Oxford, and abandon my study of the sciences. Yet wiser counsels prevailed. In the end, I completed my first degree in chemistry, and went on to undertake research in molecular biophysics in the Oxford laboratories of Professor Sir George Radda. Toward the end of this process, I won a scholarship that allowed me to undertake both scientific research and a first degree in theology.

My immersion in a scientific culture has been of formative importance to my thinking. Having set to one side the naïve positivism that believes science to "prove" its beliefs, I began to realize the immense implications of the dominant philosophy of the natural sciences—inference to the best explanation. A theory was to be judged by its ability to accommodate observations. Intellectual capaciousness was a distinguishing mark of theoretical truth. It was not difficult to realize the theological and apologetic implications of this. As G. K. Chesterton once put it, in a nice turn of phrase: "The phenomenon does not prove religion, but religion explains the phenomenon."[3]

EXPERIMENTS IN THEOLOGY

In the summer of 1978, I moved to Cambridge, to take up a research position in theology at St. John's College, and to prepare for ministry in the Church of England. I had already made my decision to study the theology of Martin Luther in some detail, and had been able to secure Professor E. G. Rupp—recently retired from the Dixie Chair of Ecclesiastical History at Cambridge—as my supervisor.

In the summer of 1980, I moved from Cambridge to serve as "curate"—a sort of assistant minister—at a parish church in Wollaton, a suburb of the English city of Nottingham. I hope I will not sound presumptuous in suggesting that Wollaton played a role for me not dissimilar to that played by Safenwil for Karl Barth, or Obstalten for Emil Brunner. The parish context forced me to relate theology to life; to act as an interpreter of the rich Christian tradition to the thoughts, hopes, and fears of ordinary people, trying to live out the Christian life in a perplexing world. It was a period in which I was forced to make connections, to think things through, and learn the art of theological communication.

Then, in the late spring of 1983, I saw a notice in the church press that would change my life. Wycliffe Hall, Oxford, was looking for a tutor in Christian doctrine and ethics. I sent off a letter of application, not really knowing quite what to expect. I was summoned to Oxford for interview, and was offered the job. In September of that year, my family and I moved to Oxford. I remained at Wycliffe Hall for twenty-five years, eventually serving as its Principal. It was a period of immense intellectual fulfillment and personal satisfaction. I count it one of the greatest privileges of my life to have been able to work in such a generous, caring, and supportive Christian environment.

I now had access to libraries, and the time I needed to do some serious research and writing. My research focused on three interconnecting and converging themes: the emergence of Martin Luther's reforming theology; the intellectual origins of the European Reformation; and the development of the Christian doctrine of justification. Working on these themes allowed me to sink deep shafts into the bedrock of intellectual and cultural history. Three books resulted from this research. All three are still in print.

1. A study of the shaping of Luther's theology in the late 1510s, focusing especially on continuities between Luther and certain schools of late medieval theology[4]
2. An analysis of the development of the Christian doctrine of justification from the earliest times to the 1980s, aimed at displacing Albrecht Ritschl's *Die christliche Lehre von der Rechtfertigung und Versöhnung* (1870) as the standard account of this history[5]
3. A study of the theological methodology of the Reformation, set against its intellectual context of the late Middle Ages and Renaissance[6]

Inevitably, these works established me as a historical theologian with a specialist knowledge of the Reformation, despite the fact that I saw them primarily as an aid to the mastering of the Christian theological tradition, in preparation for some serious theological reflection. My models here were the German theologians Jürgen Moltmann and Wolfhart Pannenberg, both of whom began their academic careers by cutting their teeth through some serious historical theology,[7] before going on to develop their own constructive theologies. My first foray into serious reflection on issues of constructive theology came in 1990, when I was invited to deliver the Bampton Lectures at Oxford. I was far too young for this privilege, which is normally given to scholars at the peak of their careers. However, the lectures allowed me to raise some significant concerns about "postliberal" approaches to theology, especially that developed by the Yale theologian George Lindbeck, which seemed to me to be anthropologically interesting, theologically problematic, and sociologically naïve.[8]

TEACHING AND TEXTBOOKS

Although I continued to develop my historical research, I found that my teaching of theology raised a number of pedagogical issues, above all how theology was to be taught in an age in which the inherited cultural knowledge of the Christian tradition was rapidly dwindling. My Oxford lectures on Christian doctrine set out to reclaim the Christian theological tradition, seeing this as a repository of wisdom and experience, nourished by and saturated in biblical themes, which could be reappropriated and applied in the life of the church. My Oxford publishers heard about these lectures, and asked me if I would be open to publishing them as an introductory theological textbook. After an extended period of testing material against student audiences in Oxford, North America, Asia, and Australia, I finally hit on an approach that seemed to work.

Christian Theology: An Introduction was published in 1993,[9] and immediately became Blackwell's best-selling work. The work clearly met a pedagogical need. Blackwell suggested following this with a collection of readings in theology, aimed at much the same audience. Having developed a method of engaging with texts while holding a visiting professorship of historical theology at Drew University, New Jersey, in late 1990, I was able to apply this in *The Christian Theology Reader* (1995).[10] Once more, this proved highly successful. As international interest in these works soared, Blackwell and I developed a strategy of keeping them up to date, and ensuring that user feedback was incorporated into new editions. Other textbooks followed, aiming to lay the foundations for the serious study of theology in a changing cultural situation.

As an evangelical, I was also concerned with the question of how evangelicalism could be intellectually enriched without losing its distinct identity and values. Wycliffe Hall was at that time one of the leading evangelical institutions in Great Britain, offering me an outstanding platform from which to explore such issues. My own view, which I shared with the noted evangelical writer J. I. Packer, was that evangelicalism was at its best when it saw itself as standing within the "Great Tradition" of reflection on the Bible, drawing from the strengths of past engagement, while able to discard its weaknesses.[11]

SCIENCE, NATURE, AND NATURAL THEOLOGY

After focusing on pedagogical issues, I returned to the exploration of the conceptual interaction of Christian theology and the natural sciences. I had avoided any serious engagement with this question up to this point, noting how many theologians (not without good reason) regarded the field of "science and religion" as tending toward amateurism. By 1995, I felt that I had acquired a sufficiently thorough knowledge of the Christian theological tradition to begin exploring how the working methods of the natural sciences might play a positive and constructive role in Christian theology.

Having been invited to give a lecture at the University of Utrecht on how theology might be enriched by an engagement, I expanded this somewhat exploratory lecture into a book, tentatively exploring some ways in which the working methods of the natural sciences might act as an *ancilla theologiae*.[12]

How could theology be enriched, without being reduced to some form of naturalism?

As I worked on these themes, it became clear to me that one theologian—Thomas F. Torrance (1913–2007)—had made a significant contribution to the field, which was both scientifically informed and theologically rigorous. I therefore set out to write a theological biography of Torrance, exploring how his distinctive approach developed, and assessing its significance.[13] This gave me a good sense of the theological possibilities that an engagement with the natural sciences might offer—such as providing theology with the means by which it could break free from the intellectual ghettoes of both foundationalism and anti-foundationalism. My growing interest in the form of "critical realism" developed by the social theorist Roy Bhaskar reflected the fact that this was clearly capable of bearing a significant theological load, partly as a result of Bhaskar's engagement with the notion of "social reality." This dimension of the matter, sadly lacking from other formulations of "critical realism," seemed to me to offer immense theological potential.

Over the period 2001–2003, I published three dense and substantial works on "scientific theology," exploring how a rigorous, informed understanding of both the natural sciences and Christian theology opened the way to a deepened and more intellectually capacious theological vision.[14] These volumes, representing the first theological application of Bhaskar's "critical realism," opened up some interesting new ways of understanding the theological task, while at the same time consolidating many traditional theological themes—such as the legitimacy of metaphysics in any account of reality.

The leading themes of these volumes may be summarized briefly as follows. If we are to give a responsible account of reality, we must accept the conditions under which we can investigate it—including the limitations placed upon humanity as observers of reality, the specific nature of the reality under study, and the limitations that this specificity imposes on the manner in which it is to be observed and represented. The manner in which we can interrogate the world is not of our own choosing, but is determined by the object of our investigations. We cannot lay down in advance how the world is to be investigated, but determine how its various aspects and levels are best to be explored and represented by a sustained engagement with the world. Whatever aspect of reality we are investigating, we must acknowledge the epistemological finality of reality itself, and operate under the limiting conditions that this imposes. Theological reflection is thus an *a posteriori* discipline, determined by the distinctive nature of the object of its investigation.[15] *Ontology determines epistemology.*

These three books made substantial demands of their readers. My correspondence suggests that some found the application of Bhaskar's "critical realism" to be the most significant aspect of the trilogy.[16] Others were delighted with my rigorous defense of the place of metaphysics in any engagement with reality. But most were excited at the new and positive place for natural theology made possible by a "scientific theology." Could I explore this theme in much greater detail?

Happily, I then received three invitations to give endowed series of lectures, allowing me to do this in some depth. I was invited to deliver the 2008 Riddell Memorial Lectures at the University of Newcastle. I counted this a great privilege, as C. S. Lewis had given these same lectures back in 1942, published as *The Abolition of Man*. I took as my theme the need for a renewal of the classic tradition of Christian natural theology, while insisting that this should take account both of the criticisms directed against such an enterprise by Karl Barth, and the resurgence of Trinitarianism, which offered a more robust and capacious theological framework within which to locate it. These lectures were published in a considerably expanded form as *The Open Secret*,[17] which represents a decisive move away from the older style of natural theology associated with William Paley (1743–1805).

Natural theology is here understood as the way of "seeing" and appreciating nature that arises from within the Christian faith. On this approach, "natural theology" is the Christian way of seeing nature. It does not prove God's existence, but points to the fundamental resonance between what we observe and the basic ideas of the Christian faith. This, of course, is a major theme within the philosophy of science, especially in abductive approaches such as "inference to the best explanation." I also move away from Paley's idea of natural theology as a purely sense-making activity. The traditional Platonic triad of "truth, beauty, and goodness" offers a framework for identifying the aspects of nature that are to be explored and appreciated. This approach to natural theology does not limit our encounter with the natural world to making sense of what we observe in nature, but moves on to ask how we can appreciate its beauty, and how we ought to behave within it.

So how could this approach be applied to the physical and biological realms? In my 2009 Gifford Lectures at the University of Aberdeen, I set out to explore how the physical phenomenon of "fine-tuning" can be accommodated and adapted for the purposes of such a natural theology.[18] In my 2009 Hulsean Lectures at the University of Cambridge, I set out to explore how natural theology engages the biological sciences, offering a detailed historical contextualization of William Paley's approach to natural theology, and demonstrating how my own approach engages more effectively with contemporary evolutionary theory.[19]

Taken together, these three volumes offer one of the most sustained and comprehensive approaches to natural theology, redirecting it in a more theologically sophisticated and apologetically fruitful manner. It is an area in which I remain active, and I expect to publish more in the future.[20]

Apologetics and London

I spent twenty-five years teaching and researching at the University of Oxford, and regard it as one of the most rewarding periods in my life. Oxford honored me with a personal chair, so that I became its "Professor of Historical Theology" in 1999. But I needed to move on, and find fresh pastures, partly because my work was moving in directions that did not sit easily with more traditional academic approaches to theology. One factor was my concern for theological education. Should I not be based somewhere in which issues of pedagogy were taken seriously? Where my teaching and textbooks could be enhanced through the judicious use of a rigorous and reliable philosophy of education?

Another was my growing interest in the public defense and articulation of the Christian faith, especially in the light of criticisms from leading atheists, such as Richard Dawkins. In 2004, I published a scholarly examination of his views on science and religion, which generated considerable interest.[21] When the "New Atheism" emerged in 2006, I became one of its leading critics, debating three of its leading representatives—Dawkins, Christopher Hitchens, and Daniel Dennett, and publishing a best-selling response to Dawkins's *God Delusion*.[22] My own early experiences as an atheist proved invaluable in enabling me to debate a position I once held myself, but now regard as inadequate.

In 2008, I moved to King's College London, in the heart of the British capital, as its first Professor of Theology, Ministry, and Education. My role was defined in terms of undertaking theological research, resourcing the churches, engaging in public debate and discussion on issues of faith, and developing an effective theological pedagogy. It was a wonderful opportunity, and has allowed me to champion the positive role of theology within the churches as part of a "discipleship of the mind," and as a means of enriching its ministry.[23] Most recently, I have developed my concerns for theological engagement with cultural and intellectual issues by researching a major new biography of C. S. Lewis,[24] and preparing a series of detailed studies of aspects of his thought.[25]

Providence, in Retrospect

In this autobiographical sketch, I have touched only on some highlights, and have left untouched some themes in my writings that others may feel to be important. In bringing this piece to its conclusion, a few deeper thoughts seem appropriate.

As I look back on my life, I do not really see a linear progression toward any defined goal. My life has been much more like an extended zigzag; I have traversed vast terrains, lingering in some, while always being restless, and reluctant to remain permanently in any. I seem to be a theological sojourner, rather than a settled citizen. In part, this reflects my constant questing for new ideas and insights. Back in the late 1980s, some were kind enough to suggest that I was in the process of emerging as one of the great experts on Luther. It was a generous thought, not least because I still maintain an active research interest in Luther. But I fear that I would have found any such specialization immensely dull. I had no desire to become trapped in what the historian G. M. Young so brilliantly caricatured as "the Waste Land of Experts, each knowing so much about so little that he can neither be contradicted nor is worth contradicting."[26]

My work in multiple fields has extended and enriched my vision of things, and enabled me to make connections that others might miss. Our theological vision is enhanced and enlarged by an engagement with the "Great Tradition." Others have found what I have missed, and enable me to enrich my vision through their wisdom. Perhaps there are times when I have felt that they have seen things that are not really there. Yet even here, the process of exploration, examination, and reflection that results leads to a deeper understanding. My career as a theologian has often taken the form of looking through other people's eyes, and opening other people's windows, enabling me to perceive things more clearly and to see farther.

C. S. Lewis explored this theme of the literary "enlargement of reality" at several points in his writings. His experience has been mine. Literary experience, as Lewis discovered, enables us to overcome the limitations of our particularity and individuality, without abolishing their benefits.[27]

Literary experience heals the wound, without undermining the privilege, of individuality. . . . In reading great literature I become a thousand men and yet remain myself. Like the night sky in the Greek poem, I see with a myriad eyes, but it is still I who see.

Notes

[1] Letter to Dom Bede Griffith, 8 February 1956; *Letters*, 3 vols. (London: HarperCollins, 2000–2006), 3:703.

[2] C. S. Lewis, *Surprised by Joy* (London: HarperCollins, 2002), 221–22.

[3] G. K. Chesterton, "The Return of the Angels," *Daily News*, March 14, 1903.

[4] *Luther's Theology of the Cross: Martin Luther's Theological Breakthrough* (Oxford: Blackwell, 1985). Paperback edition published January 1990. Second revised edition, 2011.

[5] *Iustitia Dei: A History of the Christian Doctrine of Justification*, 2 vols. (Cambridge: Cambridge University Press, 1986); paperback edition 1989, 1991. Second edition (in one volume) 1998. Third edition, completely revised, 2005.

[6] *The Intellectual Origins of the European Reformation* (Oxford: Blackwell, 1987). Paperback edition, 1992. Second edition, completely revised, 2003.

[7] Jürgen Moltmann, "Prädestination und Heilsgeschichte bei Moyse Amyraut," *Zeitschrift für Kirchengeschichte* 65, no. 3 (1953): 270–303; Wolfhart Pannenberg, *Die Prädestinationslehre des*

Duns Skotus im Zusammenhang der scholastischen Lehrentwicklung (Göttingen: Vandenhoeck & Ruprecht, 1954).

[8] *The Genesis of Doctrine* (Oxford: Blackwell, 1990). On this final point, see "Dogma und Gemeinde: Zur soziologische Funktion des christlichen Dogmas," *Kerygma und Dogma* (1990): 24–43.

[9] *Christian Theology: An Introduction* (Oxford: Blackwell, 1993). Second edition, 1997; third edition, 2001; fourth edition, 2006; fifth edition, 2011.

[10] *The Christian Theology Reader* (Oxford: Blackwell, 1995). Second edition, 2000; third edition, 2006; fourth edition, 2011.

[11] "The Great Tradition: J. I. Packer and Engaging with the Past to Enrich the Present," in *J. I. Packer and the Evangelical Future*, ed. Timothy George (Grand Rapids: Baker Academic, 2009), 19–27; "Faith and Tradition," in *The Oxford Handbook of Evangelical Theology*, ed. Gerald McDermott (New York: Oxford University Press, 2010), 81–95.

[12] *The Foundations of Dialogue in Science and Religion* (Oxford: Blackwell, 1998).

[13] *Thomas F. Torrance: An Intellectual Biography* (Edinburgh: T. & T. Clark, 1999).

[14] *A Scientific Theology: 1—Nature* (London: T. & T. Clark, 2001); *A Scientific Theology: 2—Reality* (London: T. & T. Clark, 2002); *A Scientific Theology: 3—Theory* (London: T. & T. Clark, 2003).

[15] "Theologie als Mathesis Universalis? Heinrich Scholz, Karl Barth, und der wissenschaftliche Status der christlichen Theologie," *Theologische Zeitschrift* 63 (2007): 44–57.

[16] For its further development, see "Transcendence and God: Reflections on Critical Realism, the 'New Atheism,' and Christian Theology," in *Theism, Atheism and Meta-Reality: Realist Perspectives on Spirituality*, ed. Mervyn Hartwig and Jamie Morgan (London: Routledge, 2011), 157–69.

[17] *The Open Secret: A New Vision for Natural Theology* (Oxford: Blackwell, 2008).

[18] *A Fine-Tuned Universe? The Quest for God in Science and Theology* (Louisville: Westminster John Knox, 2009).

[19] *Darwinism and the Divine: Evolutionary Thought and Natural Theology* (Oxford: Wiley-Blackwell, 2011).

[20] "'Schläft ein Lied in allen Dingen'? Gedanken über die Zukunft der natürlichen Theologie," *Theologische Zeitschrift* 65 (2009): 246–60.

[21] *Dawkins' God: Genes, Memes and the Meaning of Life* (Oxford: Blackwell, 2004).

[22] *The Dawkins Delusion? Atheist Fundamentalism and the Denial of the Divine* (London: SPCK, 2007).

[23] See, for example, "Erzählung, Gemeinschaft und Dogma: Reflexionen über das Zeugnis der Kirche in der Postmoderne," *Theologische Beiträge* 41 (2010): 25–38; *Mere Theology: Christian Faith and the Discipleship of the Mind* (London: SPCK, 2010). North American edition published as *The Passionate Intellect: Christian Faith and the Discipleship of the Mind* (Downers Grove, IL: InterVarsity, 2010; *Surprised by Meaning: Science, Faith, and How We Make Sense of Things* (Louisville: Westminster John Knox, 2011); "The Cultivation of Theological Vision: Theological Attentiveness and the Practice of Ministry," in *Perspectives on Ecclesiology and Ethnography*, ed. Pete Ward (Grand Rapids: Eerdmans, 2011), 107–23.

[24] *C. S. Lewis: A Life* (Carol Spring, IL: Tyndale House, 2013).

[25] *The Intellectual World of C. S. Lewis* (Oxford: Wiley-Blackwell, 2013).

[26] G. M. Young, *Victorian England: Portrait of an Age* (London: Oxford University Press, 1953), 160.

[27] C. S. Lewis, *An Experiment in Criticism* (Cambridge: Cambridge University Press, 1961), 140–41.

11

Wind and Spirit • Nancey Murphy

I was born in Alliance, Nebraska on June 12, 1951 and lived my first eighteen years on the family cattle ranch (PU-LEEZE don't call it a farm) in the Sand Hills. My parents were successful in playing "Vatican roulette"—they had (only) as many children as they wanted, when they wanted. Their only disappointment was in wanting to have the two boys first so they could be ranch hands; instead they got my sister Cathy and me first. So we became the ranch hands: we rode fences, wrastled [sic] calves, worked the hay field, and broke a few horses. We commented to one another that we could do everything as well as the boys could, and wrecked less machinery in the process. While this anecdote may be apocryphal, it nonetheless has a high degree of "truthlikeness": Mother: "Do you girls want to go with your dad to round up the wild horses, or stay here and help fold diapers?" Little wonder that we both ended up in men's worlds (Cathy is a petroleum geologist).

Growing up on the ranch has had a pervasive effect on my thinking. Scholars can be divided on the basis of their most natural construal of the word "world" as referring to the social world or to the natural world. Having lived where one can find scenes with no evidence of prior human presence, the social construction of reality seems highly improbable. I lived in a world of sand and grass, livestock and wildlife, and wind, wind, wind. Yet I lived in another world as well—one that could hardly have been more different—the world of pre-Vatican II Catholicism. My siblings and I (as had our father) attended St. Agnes Academy from kindergarten through high school. Religion classes were often my favorite, but the devotional practices taught and modeled by the Franciscan sisters were most formative. According to tradition going back to Augustine, prayer was a matter of turning inward, finding God within one's soul.

My favorite reading material was lives of the saints, and I came to believe that the highest form of human life was a life of prayer. Despite a history of teachings that played down the role of the senses, the Catholicism of my youth was a sensuous affair: choirs and bells, the scent of incense and candles. Time and space had their own special structures. The interior of the church was holy space, and the space around the altar holier still (in those days a woman could

137

go into the sanctuary only if she was pushing a vacuum cleaner). Time was structured by the church year: Advent, Christmas, Lent, Easter, and ordinary time, each season with its own liturgical color.

So I lived in two worlds: my personal version of Teresa of Avila's "interior castle" and our family's parcel of the Wild West. I didn't know whether I wanted to be a nun or a horse rancher.

ONE WORLD

My parents Richard and Shirley Murphy had both missed out on higher education. Mother was not able to attend college at all, despite her considerable linguistic talents, and my father attended for only three terms before having to return to work the ranch. It was clear that their children would not be deprived of that opportunity—we have seven degrees among us. I chose Creighton, a Jesuit university, for my undergraduate education. There my world was whole. The focus of my worship had shifted from the interiority of private prayer to the communal liturgy. A fine Gothic-revival church dominates Creighton's campus, and Saturday night dates ended there with midnight mass. Degree requirements included courses in theology. Most influential for my later studies was a course in my freshman year titled "Literature and Theology"; Virginia Shaddy showed us how modern philosophical changes could be traced first in theology and later in literature. The implicit message that came from worshipping with faculty was that faith and reason went happily together.

My determination to study psychology and pursue a career in therapy began and ended at the Nebraska Psychiatric Institute in Omaha. I attended a mental health awareness event there while still in high school and returned there in my junior year of college for an internship. The internship persuaded me to change my plans. It was the era of behavior modification, and I was not impressed by the effectiveness of "token economies" in treating psychosis.

Fortunately, at the time of my disillusionment with behaviorism I was urged to take a course in the philosophy of the behavioral sciences. I enrolled reluctantly, having already taken three required philosophy courses without being able to see much point in them. I had the opportunity many years later to meet again the professor, Robert Richards, then at the University of Chicago. I explained my wearing turtleneck shirts to his class: my pale Irish skin flushes easily, and I did not want him to mistake the obvious signs of excitement for a more common type of undergraduate passion. Richards's course convinced me to study philosophy of science. The impact philosophy could have was well illustrated by the way positivist philosophy of science had produced behaviorism in psychology.

Early in my college education, I was introduced to the concept of the hierarchy of the sciences, a helpful model for understanding the relations among the natural sciences. In social psychology I was taught that social behavior could be reduced (if only we knew enough) to individual psychology. The reduction of human behavior to biology was at once a fascinating project (I was particularly interested in biological causes of mental illness) but also troubling: what becomes of free will? These issues simmered for the next thirty years.

TWO WORLDS

At Creighton I read Paul Feyerabend's article, "Against Method," and decided immediately that I wanted to study with him.[1] I was accepted into the doctoral program at the University of California, Berkeley, and in the fall of 1973 drove my Toyota, with much trepidation, across the Continental and cultural divides between Nebraska and Berkeley.

I have never been quite sure how to account for my immediate and strong attraction to Feyerabend's work. I suspect it had to do with an unarticulated sense that Feyerabend's openness to a variety of methods of enquiry would translate into a rationale for openness to a variety of worldviews—something I would need at Berkeley as never before.

In Cal's philosophy department, I encountered philosophical atheism for the first time; I felt like the last Christian on earth. Members of the faculty were divided only over the question of whether religion was still worth arguing *against*. At the same time I joined a charismatic prayer group in the local Catholic parish. So I spent most of my week among those who took religious believers to be (at best) naïve, and several nights a week participating in a form of Christian worship that even in the eyes of many fellow Christians required a high degree of gullibility. What I found striking about the life of the charismatic, as opposed to more typical forms of Christian life, was the availability of a wide array of rather dramatic experiences that seemed to confirm the teachings. So here were two worlds, not merely different but apparently irreconcilable.

Studying with Feyerabend was a great privilege. When I arrived at Berkeley he was suffering from a serious and undiagnosed illness, adding to the pain and other health problems resulting from a war injury. He was taking very few students and was very elusive—never keeping office hours and seldom answering his phone. I made a presentation in his seminar using Imre Lakatos's account of scientific methodology to show that Sigmund Freud's was a progressive research program and therefore had to be counted scientific—despite its being one of Popper's prime examples of nonscience. Feyerabend then offered to supervise my dissertation.

I wrote a dissertation, "Progress and Proliferation in Psychiatry," arguing for Feyerabend's proliferation thesis using data on progress in treating mental illness. I claimed that the proliferation of competing theories produced a better understanding of mental illness than would have been the case if weaker theories had, in Popperian fashion, been eliminated.

By then I had married Grigor Fedán and we had a son, André. When asked about my rather prolific writing ability, I explain that anyone who can write a dissertation with a toddler underfoot can write under *any* circumstances.

Feyerabend had a remarkable personality: in the midst of the most serious arguments he was playful and full of joy. He was one of the kindest people I have known, and I was surprised by the disparaging picture he gave of his moral character in his autobiography.[2] I deeply regret that I did not take more advantage of the opportunity to spend time with him. In part, I simply could not imagine him being interested in the company of a plain vanilla creature such as myself and did not want to impose.

As I was nearing completion of my doctoral degree, I realized two things. First, not having a grasp of physics, I would never be a first-rate philosopher of science. Philosophy of science those days was largely philosophy of physics. I did not relish a career in which I would always have to be making secondhand use of science. Second, I realized that the question of the status of religious knowledge was more challenging and more existentially engaging for me than that of scientific knowledge.

The philosopher of science must answer the question, "In what does the rationality of science consist?" Few besides Feyerabend would question whether science is rational. The philosopher of religion, on the other hand, must in these days provide an apologia for the very possibility of religious knowledge. I decided to pursue this topic, and reasoned that if the philosopher of science needs firsthand knowledge of science, the philosopher of religion must need firsthand knowledge of religion. I took advantage of the presence in Berkeley of the Graduate Theological Union and enrolled for a second doctorate, in theology.

SEVEN YEARS ON HOLY HILL

The GTU is a consortium of nine seminaries, most located on a hill just north of the University of California. In my studies there, I was at a disadvantage in that I had no prior degree in theology. However, my philosophical education stood me in good stead. I recognized immediately that it is not possible to understand the development of Christian theology without knowledge of the philosophical currents of the times (Virginia Shaddy had been right). For example, Friedrich Schleiermacher, "father" of liberal theology, understood doctrines as nondiscursive *expressions* of religious feeling. Why hadn't the

Romantics' turn to experience resulted instead in a conception of religious experience as *evidence* for theological doctrines? The answer is largely that Immanuel Kant had ruled it illegitimate to argue from experience to the existence of God as *cause* of that experience. At Berkeley, Kant was of no more than historical interest, having been "refuted" by the invention of non-Euclidean geometries. Yet the theological landscape can only be understood in terms of differences in degree of indebtedness to Kant.

At Berkeley, Feyerabend had promoted the writings of Lakatos more than his own. However, it was only after embarking on theological study that I became a Lakatosian. In my charismatic days I had come to think of Christian doctrines as theories whose function is to explain the data of religion—not only the odd events at the prayer meetings such as healings and praying in tongues, but also historical facts such as those of the life of Jesus. Being a philosopher of science, I was aware that the task of justification required showing that the Christian hypothesis—to the effect that these phenomena are due to the influence of the Holy Spirit—was better supported than any competing hypotheses. The main competitor, as I saw it, was a psychological hypothesis regarding the suggestibility of the participants.

The value of Lakatos's work is that he begins with the recognition that any hypothesis can be saved from refutation by the addition of ad hoc modifications, so he provided a criterion involving prediction of "novel facts" to rule out such moves.[3] Theology, clearly, needed a way to rule out ad hoc theorizing just as much as science.

My dissertation, "Theology in the Age of Probable Reasoning," was a treatment of theological method in light of Lakatos's scientific methodology. I showed that "theological research programs" have the same structural characteristics as scientific research programs: a core theory held immune from falsification, auxiliary hypotheses, and data (here from history, scripture, and experience). In place of theories of instrumentation there are theories of interpretation that serve to justify one's use of texts. And, most important, for dealing with religious experience there are theories of discernment—accounts of how Christian communities are (or should be) able to make relatively reliable distinctions between authentic experiences of God's action and mere psychological phenomena. Given the tendency of believers' experiences to fit with prior expectations, I saw this as particularly important in that it could provide for data with some measure of logical independence from the theories they are taken to confirm. The dissertation subsequently turned into my first book, *Theology in the Age of Scientific Reasoning*.[4]

During these years my thinking was much influenced by two scholars. The first was James Wm. McClendon Jr., a Baptist professor of theology who had done postdoctoral work in philosophy at Berkeley and Oxford. McClendon was assigned as my advisor. His first advice was that I take his seminar on radical-reformation history and theology. (The radicals or

"Anabaptists"—rebaptizers—were sixteenth-century Christians who rejected church-state affiliation.) I was attracted to the theology I encountered in McClendon's seminar. The radicals' teaching seemed to fit the New Testament better than other versions of Christian thought and practice. Reading about the widespread torture and killing of Anabaptists had a profound impact on my life. It was clear to me that if Jesus had to choose between the ones being killed and the ones doing the killing, both Catholic and Protestant, he would be on the side of those who were dying. I felt a claim on my life at that time—to join a church in which nonviolence was not an optional extra.

I had become a "just-war pacifist" at Creighton during the Vietnam era. (I thought that being a pacifist, for a woman, during the draft, was a bit like being a vegetarian between meals. It didn't cost me anything.) The Catholic Church provided criteria for a just war, including proportionality, and I judged that no war, especially in our age, could meet those requirements. So I saw pacifism as consistent with Catholic teaching but not obligatory for Catholics. It was only when I moved to Pasadena, years later, that I was able to join a church explicitly Anabaptist in its self-understanding (Pasadena Church of the Brethren). I have since been ordained to the church's teaching ministry. One of my happiest acts after ordination was to preside at an ecumenical eucharistic liturgy in the chapel at the Pope's summer palace at Castel Gandolfo (the Pope, John Paul II, was not in attendance, however). It was also one of my most comic moments. When it came time to break the bread, the loaf of local bread was so tough I couldn't tear it; I had to turn to a *real priest* for help!

In the meantime my marriage to Fedán had failed. I had set out not to marry "the boy next door," and the cultural conflicts with this man of Russian parentage, raised in Colombia, turned out to be too great. I subsequently committed the grave academic sin of marrying my advisor. My marriage to McClendon ended with his death in October 2000.

The second important influence beginning during my years at the GTU was Robert J. Russell, a physicist and theologian who founded the Center for Theology and the Natural Sciences the year after I arrived there. Russell invited me to contribute my expertise in both theological and scientific methodology to various projects sponsored by the Center. Growing public and scholarly interest in the relations between theology and science meant increasingly frequent invitations to attend conferences and to lecture in that area.

Philosophy for Understanding Theology

When I completed my degree at the GTU, I set about applying for any job in philosophy, theology, or religious studies that was within commuting distance of Berkeley (enabling shared time with my son, André). I taught one year part time at the Dominican seminary in Berkeley—I introduced myself there as the un-Thomist, it being one of the few institutions whose training for ministry still follows the medieval pattern of studies. One course I taught there was Rhetoric and Theology, intended to train critical thinking skills. The reasoning texts used examples suited to college students but not to men entering the religious life: "You and your date are having an argument about which movie to attend. . . ." This led me to write a text on critical thinking specifically for theology students in which I used Stephen Toulmin's schema for analyzing arguments.[5]

Next year, I was a sabbatical replacement in the religion department at Whittier College. I quickly realized that I would never be comfortable teaching in a religious studies context, where theological issues were to be treated "objectively," because I could see that this stance toward religion was itself based on a particular set of convictions—those of the Enlightenment. That year I was invited to a conference at Princeton Theological Seminary on teaching philosophy in the seminary. I finally knew what I wanted to do when I grew up: teach theology students that which is most useful to them from the various fields of philosophy. However, my experience in the job market had already been discouraging, and this clarification of my career goals turned discouragement into despair. I knew of only one such position in the country, at Princeton, and Diogenes Allen already had the job. In my despair I turned to prayer, insisting that God not only tell me whether I would get a job for the following year, but also what kind of job it would be. Before God could answer, the phone rang—a friend calling to tell me about an opening in philosophy at Fuller Seminary in Pasadena.

Fuller is one of the largest theological institutions in the world, and self-styled "evangelical," meaning neither fundamentalist nor liberal in its theological orientation. I still had not known much of Protestant culture, and was completely new to the world of evangelicalism. Although upon careful study I was able to sign Fuller's statement of faith, I do not consider myself an evangelical, that being a description more relevant to the mainline Protestant traditions than to my adopted radical-reformation tradition. I much enjoy my Fuller colleagues and students, and my work is coming to be appreciated by evangelical scholars. Yet the culture shock persists as I move back and forth between liberal and conservative circles.

An explanation of the striking differences between these two theological worlds has been for me an intriguing problem. In my book *Beyond Liberalism and Fundamentalism* I proposed an explanation in terms of philosophy. I argued that modern philosophical assumptions had narrowed theologians' options, in many cases, to two. For example, the foundationalism of modern epistemology sent theologians in search of indubitable starting points for theological construction. There turned out to be only two options: scripture or experience. The quest for an indubitable foundation explains why conservatives would want an inerrant Bible, and also why liberals would seek a universal and self-authenticating sort of religious awareness.[6]

Shortly before I began teaching at Fuller, McClendon and I were invited to a conference on the church in a postmodern world. In 1987 the term "postmodern" was not widely used in our circles, but it was applied at this conference to the works of Diogenes Allen, George Lindbeck, and others. If these thinkers were postmodern, in what way did they differ from moderns? McClendon and I devised a characterization of modern thought by employing three intersecting axes: an epistemological axis whose end points were optimistic foundationalism on the one hand, and a skepticism on the other, based on the assumption of a need for foundations, coupled with the recognition that nothing will serve the purpose. The second is a linguistic axis whose end points were a representational/referential theory of language and an expressivist theory. The third is a "metaphysical" axis, which, when applied to humans, was bounded by individualism and collectivism. Modern thinkers, we suggested, could be located by means of "Cartesian coordinates" in this three-dimensional intellectual "space."

We defined as postmodern those thinkers who had succeeded in getting out of this modern space altogether by rejecting foundationalist, representationalist, and atomist/individualist assumptions, as with W. V. O. Quine's epistemological holism, J. L. Austin's speech-act theory, and Alasdair MacIntyre's communitarian understanding of ethics.[7]

From that point on, I took to calling myself a postmodern philosopher. It has been a nuisance having to share the term with the likes of Lyotard and Derrida (couldn't they be called *après moderne*?). Be that as it may, the distinctions we drew in that article have turned out to be immensely helpful in diagnosing cases where philosophers or theologians systematically misunderstand or talk past one another. For example, I think that "scientific realism" is a confused attempt to hold uncritically to a representational theory of language despite recognition that foundationalism doesn't work in science.

My favorite books are all narrative accounts that help to place modern philosophy in historical perspective: Richard Rorty's *Philosophy and the Mirror of Nature*; Jeffrey Stout's *The Flight from Authority*; Stephen Toulmin's *Cosmopolis: The Hidden Agenda of Modernity*; and two of Alasdair MacIntyre's books, *Whose Justice? Which Rationality?* and *Three Rival Versions of Moral Enquiry: Encyclopaedia, Genealogy, and Tradition*.

It is important to read MacIntyre's *Whose Justice* after reading the Kuhn-Lakatos-Feyerabend debates in philosophy of science. MacIntyre's account of the justification of a tradition of moral enquiry over against its rivals incorporates Lakatos's insight that rivals (paradigms, research programs, traditions) can be rationally evaluated on the basis of how they change over time in response to crises. Feyerabend's major criticism of Lakatos's methodology was that one can never know that a degenerating program will not suddenly be turned around by brilliant theorizing and become progressive in the future.

MacIntyre offers resources for answering Feyerabend. He shows that there are instances in the history of thought where one tradition is superior to its rival not only in that the rival has succumbed to an epistemological crisis, but also in that the superior tradition provides conceptual resources that explain why its rival failed and had to fail just at the point it did. This creates an asymmetry between the two traditions: It is not just that one tradition is making more progress than its rival; it also provides a more comprehensive and adequate account of how things are.

To my knowledge, MacIntyre is the only philosopher who adequately grasps the complexity of the current epistemological predicament and also provides hope for avoiding relativism. Thus I have evolved from being a Lakatosian to being a MacIntyrean. Were I to write another book on theological methodology it would be based on MacIntyre's work.

Since my shift to a self-consciously postmodern stance in philosophy, I have been uncomfortable calling myself a philosopher of religion. The distinction between philosophy of religion and philosophical theology was based on the notion that the philosopher approached these questions objectively, while the theologian was expected to start from a position of commitment to the theological tradition. Yet there is no place to stand to judge traditions from outside. Without the resources provided by a tradition of enquiry, one hasn't the resources to make a philosophical contribution. Thus, I must take a stand somewhere. Yet MacIntyre has shown that such a partisan stance need not rule out rational public debate.

I may someday give up trying to stake out a philosophical territory called "Anglo-American postmodernity." If so, I shall nonetheless identify myself as a post-analytic philosopher.

RECONCILING DISPARATE WORLDS

It is one of the great ironies of my life that I abandoned philosophy of science in order to avoid having to rely on secondhand knowledge of science, only to have been lured into the theology-science dialogue where I find myself constantly having to rely on my secondhand knowledge of science. I have expanded my focus from methodological issues to considering the relations between the content of science and that of theology. The most exciting project has been a series of conferences, sponsored by CTNS and the Vatican Observatory, examining the consequences of various scientific advances for a Christian understanding of God's action in the natural world. The first conference in 1990 considered two scientific issues: "quantum cosmology" (Stephen Hawking's idea that time would have had no directionality in the early universe and hence the universe could have had no "beginning"); and the "fine-tuning" of the laws of nature (recognition of the *a priori* improbability of having a universe in which all constants and laws fit within the narrow boundaries required for life to occur).[8]

At that conference I met George F. R. Ellis, a mathematician and cosmologist from the University of Cape Town. Ellis is a Quaker and was at that time deeply involved in the anti-apartheid struggle. It happened that we both had an extra day to spend in Castel Gandolfo (site of the Vatican Observatory). While walking around lovely Lake Albano, we asked ourselves whether the abstruse physics we had been struggling with for the past week had anything to do with real life. "Real life" for Ellis was the dangerous situation in South Africa; for me it was the buildup to the first Gulf War. Neither of us had an answer. In addition, both of us were dissatisfied with the mainline theology that seemed always to be assumed without question in theology-and-science dialogues.

Several months later Ellis sent me an outline for a book he wanted us to write together. This was a chance to investigate whether the science-theology dialogue and Anabaptist theology had anything to say to one another. The result was our co-authored volume titled *On the Moral Nature of the Universe*.[9] Here is how we summarized our position in the preface:

The (apparent) fine-tuning of the cosmological constants to produce a life-bearing universe (the anthropic issue) seems to call for explanation. A theistic explanation allows for a more coherent account of reality—as we know it from the perspective of both natural and human sciences, and from other spheres of experience such as the moral sphere—than does a non-theistic account. However, not all accounts of the divine nature are consistent with the patterns of divine action we seem to perceive in the natural world. God appears to work in concert with nature, never overriding or violating the very processes that God has created. This account of the character of divine action as refusal to do violence to creation, whatever the cost to God, has direct implications for human morality; it implies a "kenotic" or self-renunciatory ethic, according to which one must renounce self-interest for the sake of the other, no matter what the cost to oneself. Such an ethic, however, is very much at variance with ethical presuppositions embedded in current social science. Hence, new research programs are called for in these fields, exploring the possibilities for human sociality in the light of a vision modeled on God's own self-sacrificing love.

Much of the book is a synthesis and development of the work of others. We employ the philosophy of science and epistemology of Carl Hempel, Imre Lakatos, and Alasdair MacIntyre to understand the forms of reasoning that we need in order to justify our claims. Arthur Peacocke had developed a model for relating theology and the sciences that employs the idea of a "hierarchy of sciences"; he suggests that theology be understood as the science at the top of the hierarchy. What is new in our synthesis is, first, the proposal that the hierarchy be split at the higher levels into natural- and human-science branches, and, second, that the human-science branch should have at its top the "science" of ethics. It is then possible to see theology as the discipline that completes both branches—answering "boundary questions," which arise in both cosmology and ethics, yet go beyond the scope of those disciplines alone. A single account of the divine purposes in creation, then, drawn largely from the work of John Howard Yoder, provides a bridge between the natural sciences and the human sciences.

Our editor at Fortress Press quipped that we might have titled the book "All about Everything." It is my most ambitious attempt so far to bring together the very disparate worlds of science, Anabaptist theology, and current Anglo-American philosophy.

More recently, I have written on Anabaptist epistemology—an unlikely-sounding topic. As mentioned above, I believe MacIntyre provides the best resources for addressing epistemological issues in general; his work is also supremely applicable to the question that has been central to most of my academic pursuits: the rationality of Christian belief. MacIntyre's argument for the tradition-dependence of all reasoning means that Christians need not apologize for the particularity of their historical starting point. All traditions, not just the Christian tradition, depend on authoritative texts or voices. In addition, MacIntyre provides detailed historical examples and arguments to show that a plurality of traditions need not imply relativism: arguments, in the public domain, for a particular tradition's rational superiority to its rivals is in fact (sometimes) possible.

MacIntyre is consciously working within the Thomist tradition and sees his own epistemological insights as (in my terms) "theology-laden." So the question arises whether there is anything about MacIntyre's understanding of rationality of which a good Anabaptist should be suspicious. I received an invitation to contribute to a book on epistemology from the perspectives of various Christian subtraditions, which gave me a chance to show how an Anabaptist understanding of reason can be developed from MacIntyre's work. MacIntyre sees his primary rival to be the "genealogical tradition"—postmodern thinkers indebted to Nietzsche—and confesses that he has not shown that tradition to be untenable. I argue that we ought to accept the Nietzschean and Foucaultian warnings that power distorts knowledge, but then turn to the radical-reformation tradition, which in its nonviolence and other social practices provides a school for learning to live in the world without the use of worldly power.[10]

Learning to Do Philosophy of Mind in the Body

The conference on quantum cosmology and the laws of nature, mentioned above, was the first in a series of five such conferences, sponsored by the Vatican Observatory and CTNS, and usually held in the luscious setting of the Pope's summer palace. These events have been an important part of my life, providing opportunities for friendships, and constant challenges to learn more science as we have worked through the cosmology of the first conference, then the mathematics of chaos theory, evolutionary biology, the neurosciences, and quantum theory. I played a major role in editing papers from the neuroscience conference and wrote an introduction for the volume that reflected on how neuroscience and theology intersect in our attempts to understand the nature of the human person. *Neuroscience and the Person* appeared in 1999.

I had been prepared to work on neuroscience because of an earlier project undertaken with my Fuller colleagues Warren Brown and Newton Malony. Some years earlier, neuropsychologist Malcolm Jeeves gave a series of lectures at Fuller's Graduate School of Psychology. He suggested rather cautiously in the course of his lectures that developments in the neurosciences were making body-soul dualism less credible. In my response to one of his lectures I was much less cautious, and argued for a purely physicalist account of human nature. Brown was accurate in predicting that the growing prominence of the neurosciences would make this a controversial issue for Christians, especially evangelicals. So the three of us organized conferences on the nature of the person, with a number of relevant disciplines represented: evolutionary biology, genetics, neuropsychology, cognitive psychology, philosophy, biblical studies, theology, and ethics.[11]

These two books reflect my current interest: weaving together philosophy of mind, neuroscience, and the often-overlooked anti-dualist voices from the Christian tradition. I had been introduced to philosophy of mind as an undergraduate and took my only incomplete in that course due to the fact that I could not find an adequate solution to the problem of free will in only one semester. I returned to the mind-body problem while studying for qualifying exams at Berkeley but dropped the subject as soon as possible due to the sheer frustration of trying to get clear on these issues.

It is now thirty-five years since I first became intrigued by problems of reductionism and free will, and I've turned to these issues now with enthusiasm, having acquired conceptual resources in the intervening years that make them appear more tractable. The late Arthur Peacocke, whose works I first read in Bob Russell's theology-and-science classes, introduced me to resources for understanding the hierarchy of complex systems in a nonreductive manner—in particular the concept of downward causation.[12]

I then co-authored a book on brain science and free will with Warren Brown.[13] We argue that a greater appreciation for the biology of mental processes, combined with an understanding of downward causation in complex systems and a rejection of the leftover Cartesian concept of the mental as "inner" sheds light on the problems of reductionism and free will, which were truly intractable when I first encountered them.

An equally intriguing set of problems has to do with the spiritual life. Augustine's image in his *Confessions* of entering into the roomy chambers of his memory was not only the source of the now much-criticized image of the Cartesian theater, but also, as I mentioned earlier, of a life-shaping image of humans' relation to God. If we give up this picture of ourselves with chambers in our souls wherein to commune with God, then how is God to be experienced? In my personal devotional life as well as in courses on the philosophy of spirituality, I am coming to appreciate how bodily are our experiences of the divine. What could be more physical than kneeling, shedding tears of joy, a frisson in response to a numinous presence?

Tell Them I've Had a Wonderful Life

Life has been interesting and rewarding so far. André, the little stranger who appeared in my home thirty-one years ago and who took to the academic world like a cat to water, is now one of my favorite theological debating partners. I've had more delightful students and colleagues than I can count. I've been privileged to travel as far as Australia to the west, Russia and Iran to the east; from South Africa to Iceland.

I don't know how the rest of my life will go. I figure I'm 56/87 of the way through. I read somewhere that women in Nebraska have the highest rate of longevity in the country, eighty-seven years. (I wonder if you actually have to live there to reap the benefits. We used to say that if you only had two weeks to live, you should spend them in Nebraska because it would seem like a lifetime.) But I know what I want on my tombstone—Wittgenstein's last words: "Tell them I've had a wonderful life."

Notes

[1] Paul K. Feyerabend, "Against Method," *Minnesota Studies in the Philosophy of Science*, 4 (Minneapolis: University of Minnesota Press, 1970).

[2] Paul K. Feyerabend, *Killing Time: The Autobiography of Paul Feyerabend* (Chicago: University of Chicago Press, 1995). Having seen Feyerabend debating his "enemies," I now project his manner onto Jesus in his debates with the Pharisees. I haven't adopted much of Feyerabend's philosophy, but I have found that it is indeed possible to debate the most serious issues in friendship and with a lighthearted manner

[3] Imre Lakatos, "Falsification and the Methodology of Scientific Research Programmes," in *The Methodology of Scientific Research Programmes: Philosophical Papers, I*, ed. John Worrall and Gregory Currie (Cambridge: Cambridge University Press, 1978), 8–101.

[4]Nancey Murphy, *Theology in the Age of Scientific Reasoning* (Ithaca and London: Cornell University Press, 1990).

[5]Nancey Murphy, *Reasoning and Rhetoric in Religion* (Valley Forge, PA: Trinity Press International, 1994); reprint Wipf & Stock, Eugene, OR.

[6]Nancey Murphy, *Beyond Liberalism and Fundamentalism: How Modern and Postmodern Philosophy Shape the Theological Agenda* (Valley Forge, PA: Trinity Press International, 1996).

[7]See Nancey Murphy and James Wm. McClendon, Jr., "Distinguishing Modern and Postmodern Theologies," *Modern Theology* 5, no. 3 (April 1989): 191–214. These ideas have been much expanded in my *Anglo-American Postmodernity: Philosophical Perspectives on Science, Religion, and Ethics* (Boulder, CO: Westview, 1997).

[8]Proceedings of the conference are published in Robert J. Russell et al., *Quantum Cosmology and the Laws of Nature: Scientific Perspectives on Divine Action* (Berkeley and Vatican City State: Center for Theology and the Natural Sciences and Vatican Observatory Press, 1993).

[9]Nancey Murphy and George F. R. Ellis, *On the Moral Nature of the Universe: Theology, Cosmology, and Ethics* (Minneapolis: Fortress Press, 1996).

[10]This piece has not been published, as so often happens with collections. In the meantime I have decided that it should eventually be turned into a book.

[11]The fruit of our labors is *Whatever Happened to the Soul?: Scientific and Theological Portraits of Human Nature*, ed. Warren S. Brown, Nancey Murphy, and H. Newton Malony (Minneapolis: Fortress Press, 1998).

[12]See Arthur Peacocke, *Theology for a Scientific Age: Being and Becoming—Natural, Divine, and Human*, 2nd enlarged ed. (Minneapolis: Fortress Press, 1993).

[13]Nancey Murphy and Warren S. Brown, *Did My Neurons Make Me Do It? Philosophical and Neurobiological Perspectives on Moral Responsibility and Free Will* (Oxford: Oxford University Press, 2007).

An Intellectual Pilgrimage •
Wolfhart Pannenberg

Wolfhart Pannenberg

I confess that it was not without hesitation that I accepted an invitation to prepare an autobiographical account of my theological thought. I feel rather skeptical about autobiographical books or reports. They are rarely without some self-conceit. It is better to speak on the substantial issues a human life has been devoted to. But it is undeniable that there is also a personal aspect of it and maybe a legitimate interest in that aspect. Thus I decided to overcome my hesitations and offer an account of my intellectual pilgrimage. It will be related, however, to the substantial issues that occupied me, and therefore I shall present to you no less than seven short sections. The first section has to deal with the beginnings of my intellectual pilgrimage as a theologian.

BEGINNINGS

I was not raised in a Christian family. Although I had been baptized as a child, I did not receive a religious education, because in my early years my parents had left the church. My adolescence was that of a young atheist during World War II and shortly thereafter. In those early years I was enthusiastic about classical music and would have liked to become a pianist or a conductor like Herbert von Karajan.

I owe my first introduction to Christianity to a philosophical critic of Christianity, Friedrich Nietzsche, who was the son of a Protestant pastor, but became a severe critic of the pietistic spirituality of his parents' home. It was in the spring of 1944, after my family lost their home in a suburb of Berlin because of a bomb carpet laid by people who were later to become our American friends. In that situation, I looked in a public library for a book on music, and I found the title "The Birth of Tragedy from the Spirit of Music" by Friedrich Nietzsche. I was fifteen years old, and it was my first philosophical book, but I was so deeply impressed, that I managed to read everything by Nietzsche during that year.

Early in the next year, 1945, shortly before my family had to leave our new home in the East of Germany to flee from the invading Russian army, the memorable event occurred that I talked about years ago in the *Christian Century* series "How My Mind Has Changed": on January 6, 1945, on my way home from music lessons, a long walk from one town to another, I had a visionary experience of a great light not only surrounding me, but absorbing me for an indefinite time. I did not hear any words, but it was a metaphysical awakening that prompted me to search for its meaning regarding my life during the following years, while I experienced the end of the war as a German soldier, then during a summer as prisoner of war with the British.

After that I found my family again in the Eastern occupation zone and went to school once more in 1946 and 1947. There, I had the good luck of having an excellent teacher, who taught us German classical literature. He also was a professed Christian. He did not fit, however, into the type of guilt-ridden, neurotic mentality Nietzsche had described. My teacher Dr. Lange was quite lively, and in his occasional public speeches he spoke on subjects such as "Goethe and His Women," since he was a great admirer of Goethe. To the heart of a seventeen-year-old boy this came as a pleasant surprise, and I resolved that I had to find out for myself whether Christianity really had such an ascetic attitude toward life as Nietzsche claimed. That contributed to my decision that after school I should not only study philosophy, but also Christian theology. Then, after I began my studies at Berlin in 1947, I got so fascinated by theology that I became a theologian.

THEOLOGY AND PHILOSOPHY

The attraction of philosophy did not diminish after my decision to go on as a theologian. Already at the Gymnasium I had privately studied the works of Immanuel Kant. Of course, I did not understand everything in his *Critique of Pure Reason*, but enough to be fascinated. During my three terms at Berlin, I read other philosophical literature. That included Marxist writings, especially the early humanist writings of Marx, which had been published recently. It was necessary at that time at Berlin to seek information about Marxism in order to be able to form an educated judgment for oneself, especially since I often visited an aunt who had been a devoted Marxist since her youth.

But mainly I was occupied with reading the works of Nicolai Hartmann, who had been professor of philosophy at Berlin until the end of the war and afterwards changed to Göttingen in West Germany, where I had the chance to attend his lectures and seminars for two terms, in 1948 and 1949. Hartmann was probably the most knowledgeable German philosopher at that time, more so than Karl Jaspers and even Martin Heidegger. Hartmann gave the impression of carrying around with himself the entire history of philosophy. In dealing with any issue, he would start with discussing the proposed solutions from the entire history of philosophy before him. I was so impressed by this procedure, that I later adopted it somehow for dealing with theological issues in the light of their history. In one of his seminars, I was introduced to the fragments of the ancient Stoic philosophers. As a student of Hartmann, I knew I had to read carefully Plato and Aristotle, but also the pre-Socratic philosophers.

The philosophical requirement of dealing with those ancient texts made me immune against the rather arbitrary way of Martin Heidegger's interpretation and use of those philosophers, especially in his book *Holzwege*, which I had later to concern myself with in a seminar I attended at Heidelberg. I came to the conclusion, that a philosophy that leads to such distortion of the classical texts of the past cannot be true. But I could not become a disciple of Nicolai Hartmann either, for he was an atheist and I had come to think that the philosophy I was looking for should take the tradition of philosophical theism seriously and deal with the concept of God, the ultimate source of everything.

In that respect, I was not satisfied even with the philosophy of Karl Jaspers, with whom I studied in the following years at Basel, although his interpretation of human existence as related to "transcendence," which according to Jaspers is symbolized in the concept of the one God, impressed me deeply. It was only years later, when I had become a lecturer myself at Heidelberg and offered a lecture course on the modern history of Protestant theology, that I came to concern myself more closely with the work of Hegel, which I learned to regard as representing the top level of sophistication in modern philosophy and also as unsurpassed in its philosophical theology.

Nevertheless, I never became a Hegelian, although I was often labeled thus. I always had deep reservations with regard to fundamental assumptions in Hegel's thought, and these reservations became stronger in the course of the years. Still, I consider Hegel to have come closer to the Christian idea of God than any other modern philosopher, although I cannot accept his claim to definitive knowledge concerning God and history. Concerning history, I was much more deeply influenced by reading Wilhelm Dilthey.

In my later years, at Chicago in 1963, I also became involved with the Whiteheadian process philosophy. At Chicago, in those years, I could not have survived intellectually without making myself familiar with Whitehead. Some of my American friends are process theologians, such as John Cobb. But from the perspective of my European philosophical training, I always had difficulties with some Whiteheadian positions and came to prefer William James as an American philosopher. With regard to Whitehead's relationship to Christian theology, my main problem was that the God of Whitehead cannot be taken as creator of the world in the biblical sense. But in principle, a philosophical concept of God is not foreign to Christian theology. From the time of Christian patristics, the creator God of the Bible was related to philosophical monotheism, especially in the Platonic tradition, and without this close relationship with the philosophical quest for the one God the missionary success of Christianity in the ancient world cannot be properly understood. It is still indispensable presently, if intellectual confidence in the Christian faith in God is to be sustained.

Karl Barth

At this point I turn to my relationship and indebtedness to the theology of Karl Barth, the great Swiss theologian and the dominating figure in theology at the time of my student days. It was Karl Barth who reminded Christian theologians of the twentieth century of the priority of God in Christian theology, if theology was worth its name. Barth was not the first to issue this call and to fight the anthropocentrism of most theologians of the nineteenth century since Schleiermacher. But he was the most effective. It was Erich Schaeder of Greifswald who had first coined the term "theocentric theology" and in 1909 made it a program against all anthropocentric tendencies in theology. Only in the work of Karl Barth, however, this program was executed in detail and gained a deep and lasting impact. This impact was also enhanced by the fact that Barth became the leading theologian of the German confessional church in the struggle of the 1930s in Nazi Germany. In his *Church Dogmatics*, which began to appear in 1932 and was continued over the years in many volumes, Barth worked out his theocentric approach in detail, a theocentrism of God's revelation through his word in Jesus Christ, developed in terms of a trinitarian doctrine.

I was introduced into Barth's theology by my first teacher at Berlin in the late forties, Heinrich Vogel, who had been a student with Barth. When I changed to Göttingen in 1948, the impact of Barth was also very strong. I was deeply impressed by reading through the first three volumes of the *Church Dogmatics*—Barth's trinitarian doctrine of God was just the kind of approach I had missed in my philosophical studies. Thus I wanted to continue my studies at Basel, where Barth was teaching, and a scholarship from the World Council of Churches enabled me to do so in 1949. Since I was warmly recommended to Barth personally by my German teachers, I was very kindly received in his seminar and also in his home, and listened to the continuation of his *Church Dogmatics* in what was later to become his volumes on creation and then on anthropology.

I soon became critical, however, of Barth's own habit of employing analogical reasoning. In a small group at his home dealing with Barth's short publication on the Christian community and the civil society, I dared to criticize the master because he concluded from the biblical affirmation that Christ is the light, that there should be no secret diplomacy in the secular realm. I was not convinced and happened to think that the world might be better off, if not everything was immediately taken to the public media. I learned, however, that Barth did not like criticism from his students. In the course of my stay at Basel I became increasingly aware that Barth's talk about God and revelation lacked the philosophical subtlety and precision I thought desirable, and I also came to be critical of his very personal way of using biblical texts, which often seemed to be somewhat arbitrary. But that criticism gained weight only after my change from Basel to Heidelberg in 1951, where I got more seriously involved with biblical exegesis.

THE IMPORTANCE OF BIBLICAL EXEGESIS

When I first came to Heidelberg in the summer of 1950, I was in my fourth year as a student. It was unusual for a student of theology to be that far along without much concern with biblical exegesis. I had read lots of books on theology, dogmatics, but very little on biblical exegesis. This was due to the fact that I had started from an interest in philosophy and theology. There had been a number of unsuccessful attempts with exegetical courses, but it first happened at Heidelberg, in Gerhard von Rad's lectures on the Old Testament, that my mind and heart caught fire. Von Rad had a way of presenting the human reality of the ancient Israelite men and women in their relation with their God that proved fascinating with many students. He always had a big audience. I was especially impressed by von Rad's thesis that the God of Ancient Israel was a God of history showing himself to be the "God who acts," as Ernest Wright in America expressed it at the same time. The historical experience of the people of Israel was constituted by the historical actions of their God as well as through promise and fulfillment relating to those actions.

At the same time at Heidelberg, I attended the philosophical lectures of Karl Löwith on meaning in history. Löwith traced back the modern philosophy of history to the Augustinian theology of history and to its biblical roots. Although he intended his argument to deconstruct the philosophy of history, I took it as positive evidence for the connection of the modern sense of history with the biblical theology of history. In the first place I tried to find out in the New Testament, whether it shared the ancient Israelitic concern for a theology of history, and in the lectures of Günter Bornkamm on Paul I thought to find some evidence of it, which later was confirmed by the study of apocalypticism and its impact on early Christianity. In the apocalyptic literature, I found that its dependence on wisdom literature did not exclude a concern for history, motivated by the eschatological outlook that was not only to be understood as concerned for an end of history, but also for the completion of its yearning for salvation.

Discussions on these matters were lively in a circle of Heidelberg students who looked for better connections between exegesis and dogmatics and later produced the programmatic volume *Revelation as History*, which was published years after the members of that discussion circle had taken their degrees (in 1961). It was of crucial importance, of course, how Jesus' teaching and his history fitted in this context, and here discussion on the historical issue of Jesus' resurrection became important, a discussion that another one of my Heidelberg teachers, Hans von Campenhausen, professor of patristics and the New Testament, had initiated in 1952 with an investigation of the gospel tradition on Jesus' resurrection and on the discovery of his empty tomb. Campenhausen, who was considered a liberal theologian, argued that the widespread dismissal of the reports on the discovery of Jesus' empty tomb was in fact seriously prejudiced. I was very impressed by his argument. It deeply changed my attitude to the biblical Easter tradition, and I learned to appreciate Campenhausen's advice to students: you have to be critical with regard to the tradition, but no less critical regarding the critics of the tradition.

Before I turn to the further development of my own conception, I have to deal with the subject of my doctoral thesis (1953) and of my second dissertation (*Habilitationsschrift*) that was required for my first teaching position (1955).

MEDIEVAL THEOLOGY AND PHILOSOPHY

My dissertation was on the doctrine of predestination in John Duns Scotus, considered in the context of the medieval development of that doctrine. At that time, I was the only young Protestant theologian in Germany to work on medieval scholastics, and it was funny enough how I came to do so. It began in the second year of my studies, at Göttingen in 1948. I had decided to attend a seminar offered by Professor Iwand on Luther's book *The Bondage of the Will*. I wanted to write a paper for this seminar as I usually did in seminars I attended, but the list of recommended subjects for papers did not appeal to me. Professor Iwand asked me which subject would interest me, and coming from Berlin and with my Marxist readings in mind I answered, I should be interested to know whether Luther favored an idealist or materialist theory of knowledge. My professor looked a little puzzled, but then he recommended that in order to find out about that question, it might be good to concern oneself with Luther's voluntarism, and the root of that would be in John Duns Scotus. I accepted, and spent much of that winter and the following summer with reading in Scotus's commentaries on the sentences of Peter Lombard.

Finally, I delivered a paper of about one hundred pages on divine and human freedom in John Duns Scotus.

It was never returned to me, because somehow it disappeared in Professor Iwand's paper materials. Fortunately, I had kept a copy and sent it to my mentor Professor Heinrich Vogel at Berlin, and from him I received an enthusiastic response telling me that this text was almost sufficient for a doctor's dissertation. Later, at Heidelberg, Professor Edmund Schlink asked me about this, and as he was less enthusiastic with what was already at hand, I decided to seek advice from a Franciscan scholar, who advised me to rework the whole thing on the basis of manuscript evidence. So I did, and when it turned out that I would not be accepted at East Berlin for my doctor's examination after having studied for so long in the West, Professor Schlink offered me to take my degree at Heidelberg with him. So it happened in 1953.

After my dissertation was published in 1954, I was kept busy with writing reviews on books and text editions dealing with medieval theology, since there was no one else in that field. I also wrote articles for dictionaries, and one of those, on the concept of analogy and its history, made professor Schlink ask me to write my second dissertation on that subject. Now, it is easier to cover the entire history of such a concept in an article for a dictionary than to do so in one single volume. But I managed to describe and discuss that history from the pre-Socratic philosophers all the way to Thomas Aquinas and Duns Scotus, and I presented the resulting manuscript to the Heidelberg faculty in 1955. After that, I was allowed to teach in the field of systematic theology, first of all dealing with the history of theology in its modern development since Schleiermacher, but also in the Middle Ages. I was so fascinated by the history of medieval thought that I could have spent my whole life with that subject. But I was not fully satisfied with my manuscript on the history and concept of analogy. I worked on its completion for a number of years, and that provided a magnificent occasion of learning for myself. But I could not get it ready for publication, and soon there emerged more urgent matters for my attention.

FROM REVELATION AS HISTORY TO FOUNDATIONS OF CHRISTOLOGY

In the fall of 1958, I was called to the church seminary at Wuppertal, where I had to teach systematic theology. At the same time, Jürgen Moltmann came to Wuppertal. In 1961, I changed to the university of Mainz where I taught for the first time the complete course of dogmatics.

Meanwhile, in 1961 the volume *Revelation as History* was published; it had issued from the circle of former Heidelberg students that I mentioned before. We had not intended to cause a theological revolution, but only wanted to provide a more solid biblical foundation for a key concept of theology, the concept of revelation. Barth and others had devoted surprisingly little attention to it. As it turned out, our proposal was taken as a revolutionary uproar against what the parties of the hitherto all-important controversy, the followers of Barth and of Bultmann, had in common, the idea of revelation in the word of God. Our thesis was, indeed, that according to the biblical writings, it is not the word of God that is considered to reveal God as he is, but the actions of God in history, though the divine word of promise and proclamation certainly contributes to that revelatory history.

There was a passionate fight against our new heresy from both sides, Barthians and Bultmannians. That fight continued for years, until finally the attempts at silencing this new voice failed. Anyway, this was the situation during my years at Mainz from 1961 to 1967, and I had to defend myself against the vigorous attacks, as did other members of our group. In this situation I decided to choose for my next book the subject of Christology, on the basis of a lecture course I had first offered in Wuppertal. It was necessary to show that the new approach of Revelation as History was not simply a series of programmatic theses, but aimed at something more substantial. The Christology book tried to bridge the gulf between the quest for the historical Jesus and the Christology of the patristic period. In the Jesus research of historical-critical exegesis, the so-called second quest for the historical Jesus was just on its way. It was no longer concerned with a biographical reconstruction of Jesus' ministry, but with the question of whether there is substantial continuity between the apostolic proclamation of Christ and the teaching of the earthly Jesus, in spite of all the obvious differences. Some such continuity seemed to be necessary, if the church is entitled in its proclamation to call upon Jesus. Such continuity could be claimed by arguing that the apostolic proclamation of Christ makes explicit what was implicitly present already in the behavior and teaching of Jesus. Rudolf Bultmann himself had expressed such a view in 1929, when he said in a famous dictum that Jesus' call to decision in relation to his own person, when he proclaimed the kingdom of God, implies a Christology (church and doctrine in the New Testament). The proclamation of the church made this implication explicit. In this sense, in my book *Jesus—God and Man* in 1964, I tried to account for the development of Christology from the apostolic time through the patristic period in terms of implication and explication. I was not satisfied, however, to reduce that task—as Bultmann had—to Jesus' call to decision. The history of early Christianity seemed to show that a certain event, the event of Jesus' resurrection, was the precondition for that step from implication to explication. The argument of Hans von Campenhausen for the historicity of the Christian Easter tradition encouraged me to include the Easter event in the basis of a "Christology from below," as the slogan went, in terms of an explication of what was implicit in the teaching and history of Jesus.

After the publication of my Christology book, the climate of the discussion on Revelation as History improved a bit. It also reached the U.S., and I was invited to lecture on Christology at the University of Chicago in 1963. There I had some contact with Paul Tillich, who worked in the room next to my own. I also had the chance of reading papers at a number of other places. The first American doctoral student to work on my theology, Duane Priebe, was asked to write a dissertation on my Christology, which at that time was not even available in print. That way I learned that Americans are always interested in the future.

In 1964 I was invited to become a full professor at Harvard Divinity School, but I went to Harvard only as a visiting professor for one term in 1966. Subsequently I taught at Claremont, where I was reached by a call to Munich, which I accepted.

In America, I first published my ideas on the impact of eschatology on the idea of God himself: *Theology and the Kingdom of God* (1969). The God of the coming kingdom, the power of the future that will bring about the completion of everything: that has remained the guiding idea of my theology, although in later years it was explicated in the form of a trinitarian theology, especially in my Systematic Theology that was published in three volumes at the end of my normal academic duties between 1989 and the early nineties. An Australian theologian, Christiaan Mostert, pointed out brilliantly in a recent book, *God and the Future* (2002), that the trinitarian theology of my later years was not a diversion from my earlier pronouncements on God as the power of the future, but represents the full development of that idea in classical theological language.

ANTHROPOLOGY AND SYSTEMATIC THEOLOGY

Although my next publication was a book on theology and the theory of science, *Theology and the Philosophy of Science* (1973), because of the urgent actuality of discussions on the place of theology in a secular university, my main concern had become the place of anthropology in a systematic treatment of theology. I considered Barth's opposition to anthropocentrism in theology to be correct; but, still, talk about God has to be related to concern about human beings and about human nature. This need not take the form of a correlation in the sense of Paul Tillich. Yet, in dealing with the God of the Bible, theology has to claim all reality—and first of all the human reality—to be the creation of that God.

To that end, it was not sufficient to develop some idea of the human person on the basis of biblical presuppositions, but it seemed necessary to claim the human reality as it is studied and presented by the secular disciplines and to try to show that it is necessarily related to religion and to God. I was concerned for this task already in one of my lecture courses at Wuppertal around 1960. A small book of radio lectures on modern anthropology and its theological interpretation, *What Is Man?* (1962), resulted from this early work. It was widely used, even in religious instruction at schools. But I aimed at something more substantial, and in 1983 published my book *Anthropology in Theological Perspective*. I hoped that this book would occasion a new interdisciplinary discussion on the place of religion in human nature. But in the secularist climate of our culture, such a discussion did not develop. Thus the book only served the theological need of relating theological pronouncements on human nature and the human person to the secular discussion of those issues.

Credible talk about God has to be related to the reality that is claimed to be his creation. This concern motivated me to seek also a dialogue with natural science. My Heidelberg teacher Edmund Schlink introduced me into such dialogue in the fifties, when at Göttingen a group of physicists, theologians, and philosophers formed to explore the possibilities of such dialogue. It was continued in a small group at Heidelberg in the sixties, and from the discussions of that group there emerged a volume on the notions of contingency and natural law in science and in theology. Later on, I came to be involved in discussions on science and religion in the U.S. and in Britain, and I used to urge the inclusion of philosophical concerns in such a dialogue. It would help to appropriate the worldview informed by modern science to the task of theology, in this case especially to the task of a contemporary doctrine on the creation of the world and of the human being.

Credible talk about God cannot only deal with the concept of God, although it is certainly important to discuss the various problems related to the concept of God and to the atheist criticism of such a concept. But talk about God has to deal with God the creator of the world. Otherwise it would come to nothing. To deal with the creator or the world, however, requires us to consider everything to be a creature of that God, and that requires clarifying whether each single reality can be understood and has to be understood as a creature of that God. Thus a doctrine of God touches upon everything else. Therefore, it is necessary to explore every field of knowledge in order to speak of God reasonably.

It took me a long time to come to terms with the requirements of dealing reasonably with a doctrine of God. It can only be done in the form of a systematic theology, a coherent account of how the world and especially human nature and history are related to God as creative source and ultimate destination of all things. A Christian systematic theology has to deal with this task in the form of a history of the world and of the human race, a history that accomplishes the intrinsic aim of the act of creation and overcomes the failures and shortcomings of the creatures in order to fully realize the kingdom of the creator in the world of his creatures. The task of such a comprehensive and systematic theology occupied me for many years. I felt I should not wait too long with my attempt at its accomplishment, provisional as it may remain.

After all, there is only a limited span of our human life and limited strength to bring about what we feel we should at least try.

As my time is running out, I should conclude my intellectual autobiography here, though I would have liked to address some other aspects of my concerns in theology. Especially, I have been concerned for the unity of the Christian church ever since my ordination as a Lutheran pastor in 1966, and since I was introduced into ecumenical work by my teacher Edmund Schlink. I regard my ecumenical activities in the WCC and in the dialogue with the Roman Catholic Church as an important practical aspect of my commitment as a theologian to the truth of the Christian faith.

13

Still Becoming • Ted Peters

Ted Peters

"Why is it," I have asked myself repeatedly, "that I listen so intently to autobiographies?" In the decades that I have been listening to the spiritual and intellectual autobiographies of one Pacific Coast Theological Society member after another, I have found myself glued to the autobiographer's words. Why? I wonder. I know I listened closely to what Huston Smith had to say, because for nearly four decades he has been one of my intellectual heroes. But much more is happening, I think. There is some sort of sharing going on here, some sort of intertwining of consciousness. We are not alone. Author and reader both have lives; and I hope in the minutes you the reader take to read what I have written here that our lives will overlap. My two editorial colleagues— Derek Nelson and Joshua Moritz—are on the front end of promising careers in theology. Their autobiographies will be ready in the future, whereas mine is much further along. My story will have three chapters corresponding roughly to Paul Ricoeur's history of the western world: the first naïveté, the rise of critical consciousness, and then the second or postcritical naïveté.

First Naïveté

I was born in 1941, eight months before Pearl Harbor. My father told everyone he had nicknamed me "weatherstrip," because I had helped keep him out of the draft. At home they called me by my middle name, Frank, a habit I would eventually change. I was proud of my father. He was the American designer of the roto-tiller, now a very popular small farm and garden tool. Later he garnered twenty-two patents while working for General Motors. As a mechanical engineer with skills needed for the war effort, he spent those years in Norfolk, Virginia, working on ships for the U.S. Navy.

EXCOMMUNICATED BEFORE COMMUNING

I was baptized in St. John's Lutheran Church in Wayne, Michigan. St John's belonged to the Wisconsin Synod. At the age of eighteen months, the Wisconsin Synod excommunicated me. Even though I had never taken communion, I found myself excommunicated. Actually, my whole family was thrown out. My grandfather on my father's side, Oscar, had been a Wisconsin Synod pastor. Two years before his death he became ill and bedridden, and an interim pastor took over at St. John's. The interim pastor discovered rumors that during the Depression Ol' Oscar had befriended a number of jobless poor people, many of whom were not Lutheran, and he had welcomed them to the Lord's Table. This was an unforgivable sin, evidently, because when Oscar died the Synodical Conference—that is, the federation of Wisconsin and Missouri Synods—circulated a notice that no clergy were to officiate at his funeral. A pastor from the American Lutheran Church, Norman Mentor, later an ALC district president, stepped in to officiate. Both the Peters and the Tesch families united together to start a new ALC congregation only a few blocks from St. John's. My Grandpa Tesch was a carpenter, and I can still remember going with him after work over to the site to build the church, literally with hammer and nails to build what would become Prince of Peace Lutheran Church. I would bring him boards and such things while he erected the structure. All in all, my life as a child was miserable. My father was abusive. My mother and brother suffered much more than I, though spankings were a daily occurrence for me. "Let's get the strap" announced the onset of a period of time I dreaded. My only escape was into the world of the mind, into my imagination. I was not a disobedient child. Far from it. Just what the problem was I do not know. It had something to do with the old-fashioned Prussian way of ruling a family with abject terror. Living at the level of first naïveté, I presumed that this type of family life was normal. It was my lot, or destiny. I knew no other. Critical consciousness only came later. Critical consciousness regarding my family only started to dawn on an occasion in adult life after my parents had visited my wife and me and returned home. My mother phoned to observe, "Ya know, you and your wife treat your children as if they were real people." "Yes," I answered, "We treat them as real people." My church life at the level of the first naïveté was not a happy one either. The oldest memory I have of St. Paul's Lutheran Church in Dearborn, Michigan, was a spanking I received from Mrs. Niehammer, my Sunday School teacher. I was doing whatever little boys do, and I got a spanking for it. The embarrassment in front of the other children hurt more than the swats. I was only four or five at the time, and this set the tone for what would follow. St. Paul's has a magnificent sanctuary, decorated in dark brown Gothic carved wood. Beautiful to a grownup, but depressing to a child. At the beginning of each worship service the choir, which included my Aunt Edna, would march down the aisle singing. Once in the chancel choir pews, they would continue singing, "Keep Silence! Keep Silence! Keep Silence!" I took this very personally to mean, "Frankie, shut up. The grownups are in charge here." I would cease to exist for the next interminable hour. Later in life I came to realize that the words, "Keep Silence!" were scriptural and had something to do with holiness. But by the time I realized this, I was already grownup. Physically, as a little boy I was not cut out for attending church. I was energetic and restless. I could not sit still. My mother was constantly tugging and slapping me to incarcerate my constant movement. So I fought back. I broke wind. Each Sunday the story would repeat itself. The choir would tell me to keep silent. My mother would slap me into docility. Then I would break wind and fill three rows with discomforting stench. On the way to the car my father would say, "He farted again today in church. When we get home we'll have to get the strap." Now, I cannot remember for certain whether my breaking wind was an uncontrollable physiological process or something I did on purpose. If it was uncontrollable and physical, then this is conclusive evidence that I was living at the level of the first naïveté. If, on the other hand, I had done it purposely, then this could be an early sign of emerging critical consciousness.

Critical Consciousness

In 1959 about the time I was turning eighteen, I began to sense that God was calling me to a life with a purpose. I experienced what Paul Tillich called "ontological shock," yet this shock was accompanied with a sense of meaning because my personal being was taken up into divine purpose. Among other things, God was giving me something I had not gained from other sources, namely, a sense of self-respect. Exactly what this vocation would mean was not clear, but I proceeded with a higher degree of self-confidence than one would have expected from me. I looked about my community, Dearborn, Michigan, and saw only what Big Daddy saw in *Cat on a Hot Tin Roof*, mendacity. Mendacity and superficiality and meaningless activity was everywhere. All I could see was middle-class families groveling for professional status, a split-level suburban home with a two-car garage, and heading toward their graves leaving a bunch of meaningless toys behind. This kind of life was not for me. God would see to it that I would not get stuck. Much to my elation, during my freshman year at Michigan State University I found philosophers who gave voice to what I was feeling, the existentialists. Most were atheists such as Nietzsche, Camus, and Sartre. But some were Christians, most notably Paul Tillich. I read Tillich's work voraciously. Tillich himself came to MSU to lecture to a packed house. I went to hear my hero. Tillich could penetrate the mendacity of superficial life, yet in depths of life he could find grace. That was good enough for me. I have never completely left the Tillichian camp.

Seminary Secrets

Immediately after leaving Michigan State, I went to the Evangelical Lutheran Theological Seminary of Columbus, Ohio, a dreadful name. It has since been changed to Trinity Theological Seminary, an improvement. At seminary, I asked that people call me Ted instead of Frank, putting a bit of symbolic distance between me and my past. I still had the sense of call, and it seemed clear that this call would eventually take me to a poverty-stricken community in the foreign mission field. The last thing I wanted to prepare for was a middle-class parish ministry in middle America. A couple of months prior to graduation from seminary, the president called me into his office. His name was Edward C. Fendt, but we called him "Uncle Dudley" behind his back. I can still remember the presidential chair in his office. It was huge, black in color, with a tall back on it, and it swiveled. He swiveled around, put his elbows on his desk, and announced that the faculty would be very happy to see me graduate and leave the seminary. "You frighten them," he said. "Why" I asked. Then Uncle Dudley gave two reasons. First, he reminded me of an incident that occurred the first week of my first year. He told me the story as it was told among the faculty. Let me tell it from my point of view. I was up late one night doing exegesis on the book of Romans. I became intrigued at the last half of Romans 4:17 that describes God as "calling into being the things that are not" (Καλοῦντος τὰ μὴ ὄντα ὡς ὄντα). Now, as I mentioned, Paul Tillich had already become my theological alter ego. So I sat there for a while pondering Romans 4:17 in light of Tillich's notion of God as the ground of being and the existential threat of nonbeing. Then I pulled out a shirt cardboard and a felt pen and made myself a sign, a sort of motto to hang in my room. I carefully wrote out Romans 4:17 and added a little caption, "Paul the Saint or Paul the Tillich?" Proud of myself, I went to bed. The next morning found me sitting in the front row of baby systematics taught by Professor Harold Zietlow, whom we called "Zippy" behind his back. Zippy was zipping around the front of the class when he started to call to mind a New Testament passage. Just what was it? Somewhere in Romans? Yes. It had to do with being and nonbeing. He thought it might be Romans 4:17. He asked if any student had brought a Bible he might look at. Someone in the second row handed him a Bible. He looked at it quickly and handed it back. "That's English," he said. "I want a Greek New Testament." At this point I volunteered the verse: "Καλοῦντος τὰ μὴ ὄντα ὡς ὄντα," I said. "What was that?" he asked. "That is Romans 4:17 in Greek, Καλοῦντος τὰ μὴ ὄντα ὡς ὄντα," I repeated. "Oh, Mr. Peters has a Greek New Testament with him," he announced to the class. "May I have it?" "Sorry I didn't bring it," I said. "But, but, how did you know what was in Romans 4:17?" "I have it memorized." Zippy stopped dead in his tracks. A hush fell over the room. The Zippy went back to his lecture, ignoring me. Uncle Dudley reported that Zippy thought I had the entire New Testament memorized in Greek. I have never felt the need to tell him otherwise. Uncle Dudley reminded me of a second difficulty with me as a student. I had been an agitator. Things had turned out well for me at the seminary, but I must admit that I had been a thorn in the faculty's side during my first two years. By the time I had graduated from college in 1963, I had adopted the liberal platform for social change that centered in support for the civil rights movement. Less than two months after I arrived as a first semester student, I celebrated Reformation Day on October 31 by posting my own "Thirty-Five Theses." I couldn't think of ninety-five things to object to. I attacked the Lutheran Church for being too conservative and the seminary for quietism, for looking like a Republican Party at prayer. Poor seminary. I tried to rally students and faculty around what was then known as "Social Action." A number of students rose to the challenge. We met and drafted a constructive program that would take us into the wider Columbus community to work in areas of poverty, racial discrimination, delinquency, and mental retardation. I volunteered to head the program. I was proud of it. We sent it to the faculty for approval. But the faculty was not impressed. They sandbagged us. They kept postponing decisions, asking for clarifications like insurance companies who don't want to pay off. Something was wrong, but nobody was saying what. An entire year went by. It looked like it would die of a pocket veto. But I kept the pressure up. Finally, one of the professors told me they didn't like the phrase, "Social Action." It was too inflammatory. For the 1960s, it *was* inflammatory. That's why I liked it. But as long as it had this name, the answer would be "no." So, I compromised. It went through under the name "Community Service." By spring quarter of my second year we were operational. On the first round I had nearly fifty students volunteer. I sent them in teams of four to six to the state prison, the lockup at Franklin County courthouse to work with arrested teenagers, to a couple of inner-city parishes who were struggling with racial integration, to institutions for the mentally retarded and the physically impaired. We would meet and compare notes and go back out again. I had to leave campus for my third year to serve internship; so I passed the Community Service program on to new leadership. When I returned my fourth year, the program was up to eighty students participating. The new director was a new student. I slipped in as a volunteer, not telling the new director of my previous involvement. New students arriving on campus assumed that the Community Service project had existed since the time of the Garden of Eden and that it was simply expected that they would join in.

The Anti-War Movement

While on internship in 1965–1966 in Portland, Oregon, I became radicalized on the issue of the war in Vietnam. During my sermon one Sunday I thought I would explain to the congregation that the American government was an imperialist power, that President Johnson and Secretary of State Rusk were lying to us, and that hundreds of thousands of innocent civilians were suffering at the hands of the U.S. military. Between the services my supervisor, Pastor Fischer, called me into the sacristy. He was livid. "How dare you bring politics into the sermon! How dare you stand there and complain that our government is lying to us! I can't let you go out there for the second service and do that again." "But I can prove that they are lying," I said. And the whole world seemed to stop while we argued in our loudest whispers. I knew that Pastor Fischer was a reasonable and conscientious man, so he was well worth arguing with. I said, "I've been studying this for weeks. I've looked into the history. I've got statistics that contradict official government statements. This is a serious matter." "Well, if you think you can back it up, then go to it." The congregation became aroused. They asked me to arrange an open forum, to bring in experts, to help them to get to the bottom of this. I planned an extravaganza and filled the church basement. To my initial surprise, many of the families that showed up from the community had young men who were being drafted. When I returned to Columbus the next fall, I felt the need to radicalize the seminary. Poor seminary. I started with my two closest friends at the time, Phil Williams and Dean Hunneshagen. Poor Phil and Dean. I pounded away at them. I gave them literature. I persuaded them to join Clergy and Laity Concerned about Vietnam, then headed by William Sloane Coffin. We went to Washington to lobby our senators and march around the White House in the snow. Because teach-ins were the propaganda tool of the anti-war movement, I asked faculty for permission to hold a public debate on the seminary campus. Permission was granted. I got Phil and Dean to make up our team of three. Another friend, Ken Lenz, reluctantly opposed us. "Where do you stand on the war in Vietnam?" I asked Ken. He answered that he didn't have much of a position, but our government certainly must know what it's doing. That was good enough for me. "I challenge you to debate!" Poor Ken. Ken rose to the occasion. He gathered a team of three, researched the matter, and came loaded to argue. He and I were the principals with the others speaking on specific sub-issues. The seminary was packed. It was an impressive event, and the beginning of what has become one of my most treasured friendships, with Ken Lentz. Ken still complains that I cheated. The debate was being fought fairly, until I introduced the napalming of villages by U.S. bombers, and described the 400,000 village children running from their homes with their skin aflame. I had pictures of burned and maimed and dying children. Ken, himself a very sensitive person, could not counter with any justification or refutation. Had I cheated? I learned that statistical fact from the magazine *Ramparts*, and to this day I am embarrassed to say that I cannot verify its accuracy. The image of 400,000 suffering children had gripped me emotionally. It gripped the audience that night. In more recent years I have sworn not to resort to emotional appeals, trying to restrict myself to a more dispassionate analysis of confirmable data. But I was more passionate in the '60s. I believed the napalming policy to be the case, and I was deeply driven by the horrifying thought that my own nation, my own people, my own me, could be guilty of such massive destruction and desecration of human life. One of the mottoes of the anti-war movement was, "We have seen the enemy, and the enemy is us." In the years that followed, I learned something about myself I do not particularly like. When I am certain that I am right and others are wrong, I am tempted to vilify my opponents. It's called "scapegoating." How sweet to be able to consign all the evils of the world to another group or even to an individual! Especially to an administration! I could shout with throngs of marchers in the street, "Hey, Hey, LBJ! How many did ya kill today?" Some of my more dispassionate friends would chide me, "LBJ is only the president. He may be stupid, but he's not evil." As the years have gone by, I think they may have been right. LBJ was just stupid. But stupidity in high places in our complex world causes evil.

Mission, Scholarship, or Both!

My senior year in seminary found me debating whether I should go to the foreign mission field or to graduate school. I was hoping for an assignment to Tanzania. Thirty graduates that year wanted foreign posts. The church had money for four. So off I went to graduate school. My wife and I along with Ken Lentz went to Germany and the University of Heidelberg. All three of us enrolled, studied, drank in the *Gasthäuser*, and danced in the Castle ballroom. These were joyous days. I signed up for a seminar with Hans-Werner Gensichen on *Missionswissenschaft und die Weltreligionen* and listened to lectures by Gerhard von Rad, Hans-Georg Gadamer, and Edmund Schlink. In the coffee shops the students were talking about one theologian, Wolfhart Pannenberg. Ken and I bought Pannenberg's *Offenbarung als Geschichte* and went to the coffee shop. I went financially bust that year. Ken stayed on to finish his degree, but I returned home and to the University of Chicago. The Divinity School at Chicago was an intellectual orchard, delicious fruit hanging everywhere. I became particularly enthralled with Frank Reynolds, who was teaching History of Religions. Under Frank I read a pile of works by Mircea Eliade. Then I heard Eliade lecture. He was dull. So I kept on reading and listening to Frank. A *kairos* moment occurred for me during a seminar on creation taught by Joe Sittler. He was expounding the theologies of Irenaeus and Teilhard de Chardin. His eyes were up as if gazing at the majesty of the infinite cosmos. He paused just long enough for the muses to whisper phrases of heavenly eloquences into his ears, and then he said—I do not recall the exact words, which on the occasion itself precipitated aesthetic pleasure— ethics begins with a vision of the future of the world as God intends it, and then we today try to actualize it ahead of time. I heard a distinct "yes" murmured within my soul. This principle, which I now call the proleptic principle, structures the ethics chapter in my systematic theology.

Tracy and the Two Germans

At Chicago I met fellow student Marc Kolden who, like me, had become interested in Pannenberg. Marc and I picked up the coffee shop conversations I had begun in Germany, and this has led to a collegial friendship down to the present time. One day Marc announced he had gotten approval on his thesis topic, Pannenberg's theology of history. "That's what *I* wanted to write on," I thought. By this time David Tracy had become my mentor. I rushed into David's office and told him that for months I had been working toward a dissertation topic, but now Marc Kolden had taken it. Now what should I do? I was at a loss. Would David just assign me a topic? He did. He said he himself had been wondering about something. He said I should write on the influence of Hans-Georg Gadamer's hermeneutical theory on Pannenberg's theology of history. This was right next door to the topic I had lost, so why not? I agreed. We constituted the committee with David as chair and Paul Ricoeur, Schubert Ogden, and Langdon Gilkey as readers. I wrote the first half of the dissertation over the next two years. The content of the second half was clear in my mind. So it seemed prudent to me that I should consult with Gadamer and Pannenberg to be certain I was accurate. I wrote to them that I wanted to come to Germany to interview them. They agreed to my coming. I met Gadamer in his Heidelberg office and explained that in my dissertation I would show a close connection between his philosophy and Pannenberg's theology. "Oh," he said, "when it comes to theology I think of myself as closer to Bultmann." With more confidence than the situation warranted, I told him that if he were to attend more carefully to his own notion of *Wirkungsgeschichte*, it would take him away from Bultmann's existentialism toward a more historicized understanding of human knowing, like Pannenberg's. Gadamer accepted my youthful vigor and American insolence with graciousness. Yes, he remembered "young Wolfhart" as a student of his at Heidelberg. How fascinating that I would think to make a connection between the grandfather philosopher's influence and this theological upstart. How could he be of help to me? I felt like I had just struck oil. What I did not know at the moment was that I was about to be led through the doorway into a house of graduate student horrors. In the literature I had studied, I noted a controversy between Gadamer and Pannenberg over the concept of *Aussage*, that is, the role of a statement or assertion in interpretation. I will spare you the reader the details of the philosophical point at issue. Just let me say there had been a disagreement between the two Germans on this. I asked Gadamer to clarify his position. He said I would be happy to hear that in recent months he and Pannenberg vigorously debated the nature of *Aussage*. And, what's more, he and Pannenberg had come to an *Übereinstimmung* (a meeting of the minds), and no longer did they disagree. "Wow!" I said to myself, thinking like a journalist with a scoop. I took copious notes, getting all the details. My dissertation would look like the morning edition of the *Chicago Tribune* with this news. Having slain the dragon in Heidelberg, I boarded the train and headed for Munich to visit Pannenberg. This was my first meeting with him. We met at his home and he hosted me at a picnic table in his backyard. Following the routine I had established with Gadamer, I explained that my dissertation dealt with the influences of Gadamer's hermeneutical philosophy on his theology of history. "There are no such influences," he told me. My mouth dropped. "I just came from Heidelberg, and Professor Gadamer told me how he remembers you as his student." "I was never Gadamer's student. It would be wrong to make me look like an extension of Gadamer's hermeneutics." Suddenly I felt like a pile of disassembled debris lying on his patio. I tried to pull myself together. I had one ace in the hole. So, I played it. "Now to the argument you have been having with Gadamer over the issue of *Aussage*." I repeated what Gadamer told me, and I asked if he could elaborate on the *Übereinstimmung* he and the philosopher had reached. Pannenberg listened carefully. "Yes," he said, he remembered the conference and the public debate. But, he added, "*Es gibt gar keine Übereinstimmung*"(there is no agreement). Now I felt like Dresden after the allied bombing. This was the lowest point of my student career. I walked into David Tracy's office like a dog with tail between the legs. When I told David my depressing account, he laughed. "What's so funny?" I quizzed. "The problem is not with you, Ted," he said. "It's those damned Germans. They have to believe that they have a private patent on each good idea they have. They just cannot admit that they are actually part of the hermeneutical circle." We agreed that the dissertation could not go forward as originally conceived. David suggested that we change it from an account of historical influence to one of comparison. This would save my research and I could proceed. "The moral of this story," said David, "is not to write on someone who is still alive." In the years since, Pannenberg and I have developed a warm collegial relationship. I recently edited some of his writings for publication in America. Only once have I reminded him of this story. He did not laugh.

Loving Parish Ministry

One more thing about my Chicago days. I became a parish pastor and served a congregation on the south side in what we then called a "rapidly changing neighborhood." My parish was located near Lake Michigan and near U.S. Steel. My people were blue-collar steel workers, store clerks, and unemployed. It was a white congregation in an increasingly black neighborhood. Just what I wanted. I went to it with enthusiasm. My wife and I started neighborhood outreach programs, and in time our church became racially integrated. I had successfully avoided becoming a pastor in a middle-class suburb, but I came to love and respect parish ministry all the same. Eventually I left the parish for higher education, teaching first at a small Lutheran institution in South Carolina, Newberry College, and moving later to Loyola University in New Orleans. I taught Greek, various courses in philosophy and world religions, along with a little Bible and theology. I loved it.

Futurology, Eschatology, and Ecology

I joined the World Future Society in the early 1970s. It appeared to me that the real prophets in our society were not to be found in the church, but rather among the scientific and technological futurists. We are destroying life on our planet, they claimed. To back up this claim they used computer simulations of population growth, industrial and agricultural growth, depletion of nonrenewable natural resources, and production of pollution to show that the human race is headed for ecological catastrophe. Unless decisions were made to avert catastrophe, we could only expect massive starvation in the future. Furthermore, said the futurists, one of the main deleterious factors was economic injustice. The rich would simply have to share with the poor, or else all of us would suffer. The futurist vision was universal and unitary. It presupposed a destiny for both humanity and the natural world in which we were all united. Only a holistic vision could guide us. Futurology was secular theology and secular ethics. Two of my early books make the point that ethics is where eschatology and futurology meet. The first one, *Futures-Human and Divine*, made it into a second printing. Then it died. The next book, *Fear, Faith, and the Future*, died at the first printing. These were calls to action. But, I fear, very few in the churches wanted to hear that call. Our theological leadership in the 1970s turned its attention to liberation theology and feminist theology, both of which were particularistic and expressly repudiated the global vision of futurism. Theology had to be context-specific, said the liberationists, responsible only to the oppressed classes, races, or genders, not to the whole human race or to nature. Universals and meta-narratives were no good. This unfortunately fit well with the advent of the Reagan administration, which virtually snuffed out future consciousness in the wider society. One valuable but slim legacy from the '70s is the World Council of Churches' mandate that we work for a "just and sustainable" society. Only with the nuclear spill at Chernobyl in 1986 did the world wake up once again to the fact that our planet is ailing, perhaps mortally ill. With the earlier separatist phase of feminism and liberation waning, some have tried to broaden the agenda by combining justice concerns with ecology, a combination already achieved by the secular futurists of the previous generation. What bothers me is that some religious leaders in our time seem to be reacting to climate change and the ecological crisis in a religious manner, a quasi-mystical manner. A new romanticism is growing among church people that deserves all the derisive criticism the Marxists used to level against religion as the opiate of the people. Eco-spirituality is consigning religious involvement to the liturgical playpen while avoiding the difficulties of the larger world such as the need to employ science and technology to gain an understanding of the destructive forces at work in nature and society, the need to see how poverty and economic injustice are directly tied to degradation of the biosphere, and the need to see how human sinfulness in the form of ethnic rivalry and political myopia are strangling us all.

SECOND NAÏVETÉ

In 1978, I came to Pacific Lutheran Theological Seminary and the Graduate Theological Union in Berkeley. Looking forward to this move, I was hoping this would be a sort of nerd heaven for me because it combined everything this nerd wanted: work with seminarians and the life of the church; work with graduate students at the doctoral level; ecumenical contact with Roman Catholics and other Christians; interreligious dialogue with Jewish and Asian scholars; and the academic atmosphere of the University of California with the possibility of interdisciplinary scholarship. Over these many years I have not been disappointed. It has in fact been nerd heaven. What I really value about Berkeley is daily contact with some of the world's leading scholars. This is a treasure I had long coveted. The GTU has been for me a treasure box rich with accessible colleagues. My first conversation partners were Durwood Foster, Shunji Nishi, Surjit Singh, and Victor Gold. I've added countless others over the intervening years. Nerd heaven!

CENTER FOR THEOLOGY AND THE NATURAL SCIENCES

Somewhere around 1982, I was lobbied by Bob Russell to get involved with the Center for Theology and the Natural Sciences, programs that put physicists and biologists from UCB into dialogue with GTU theologians. I tried to decline. I had been interested in science and technology as cultural phenomena, and I was somewhat at home in the philosophy of science; but I had no experience talking with real Bunsen burner scientists about real science. "I've had no formal training in science. I don't know anything about science," I said. "That doesn't matter," Bob said. "The scientists don't know anything about theology either." It all sounded fair to me, and so I began wading deeper and deeper into the theology/natural science dialogue. I do not think I would have chosen to dive into this dialogue had equal opportunities been available to tread water with someone in the arts or in social science. But the pool of opportunity for interdisciplinary work at CTNS looked the most inviting, so I eventually dove in, perhaps even over my head. For most of the '80s, all of us at CTNS worked on physical cosmology and the doctrine of creation. As the '90s began, I became the principal investigator in a most ambitious CTNS research project funded by the National Institutes of Health titled "Theological and Ethical Implications of the Human Genome Initiative." Twice a year I brought together a team of more than a dozen first-rate geneticists, theologians, and ethicists to lock horns and knock heads in some of the most ruthless yet exhilarating intellectual discussion. In subsequent decades I've worked with first-rate scientists on the theological implications of genomics, stem cells, evolution, and astrobiology. Nerd heaven! Perhaps the most fruitful of my collegial relationships has been with Bob Russell. As the 1980s progressed, our two scholarly agendas began to overlap, and in some instances we deliberately chose to work on shared topics. We had much to teach each other, and much to learn from each other. More importantly, we sought to learn new things together. I write for what he edits. He writes for what I edit. A routine has developed. My telephone rings. "Bob here. Got a minute?" "Yup." The Bob tells me he is writing something or reading something. He reads a few sentences. "What do you think?" I hem and haw and cough and try to say something relevant. No matter how confused I sound, Bob always says, "That's a real good insight, Ted. You've helped me a lot. Bye." An hour or two goes by and either I call him or he calls me and we do it again. Nerd heaven.

Proleptic Eschatology

My most significant scholarly work in Berkeley has been the publication of my *magnum opus*, a complete systematic theology with the title, *GOD— The World's Future*. The many years of research and writing were difficult, although I kept a cheerful attitude for all but one of those years. I would get up each morning anywhere between 2:00 to 5:00 to put in a half-day's work before going to class. The book's central ontological concept that unites all the others is prolepsis. My colleague Carol Jacobson came up with the best analogy to explain prolepsis. She likens it to a movie preview. Seeing the movie itself is something we might do in the future. The preview tells us of the coming attraction. Yet the preview is in fact the movie itself, even if only in fragmentary and anticipatory form. In like manner, the death and resurrection of Jesus constitute the preview of the coming attraction, namely, the new creation. What the Christian faith looks forward to is the eschatological transformation of all things into the world God intends it to be;

and the Easter Christ proleptically embodied this transformation in advance, ahead of time. Thereby, he constitutes for us a promise of a still outstanding future that God intends to fulfill.

Conclusion

My life is not done yet. The year 2012 marked my professional retirement and a new marriage to Karen, a delightful and energetic partner. Who I am will be determined in large part by who I turn out to be—that is, by my future. My ultimate future, I believe, is bound up eschatologically with the resurrection of Jesus Christ and with the renewal of God's creation. In the meantime, I'll be satisfied with nerd heaven.

14

Confessions of a Postconservative Evangelical Theologian • Clark H. Pinnock

This as good a time as ever to share something of what I have learned in a life of doing evangelical theology. Toward the end of one's days, by way of retrospection, one can gain a better sense (though still limited) of how one was led. Although I am a little embarrassed to be writing alongside distinguished theologians, the laces of whose sandals I am not worthy to untie, nevertheless, I welcome the opportunity to tell my story.

I think that I may have been selected to contribute to this book because of a certain involvement in the conservative evangelical movement, not because my work reveals particular excellence compared to the other authors. I am here because I have a story to tell, one that might be of interest to any who ponder developments in the evangelical coalition, indeed how one gets free from a narrow conservatism without throwing the baby out with the bathwater. Mine is the story of a man's pilgrimage in theology, which (if you will forgive the jargon) began in the "conservative-evangelical" camp with a scholastic tendency and is finishing up (it appears) in the "postconservative" camp with the pietists and pentecostals.

In part, the story is about me but partly also (and more importantly) about a changing of the guard in evangelical theology. It is as if I discovered in the despised traditions of pietism the help I needed to overcome the debilitating impulses of fundamentalism. For my "take" on contemporary theology, see *Tracking the Maze: Finding Our Way Through Modern Theology from an Evangelical Perspective* (1990) and (with Delwin Brown) *Theological Crossfire: An Evangelical/Liberal Dialogue* (1990).

Like many of my generation, I was disappointed by developments in the Protestant mainline in regard to biblical beliefs, missional activities, and vital

Personal Background

piety. And, like many others, I found what I was looking for elsewhere in the parachurch agencies and ministries that sprang up in the years after World War II. My first teachers (I suppose) were Billy Graham, Donald G. Barnhouse, InterVarsity Christian Fellowship with John Stott, *Christianity Today* with Carl Henry, and the help given by the Reformed publishers of Grand Rapids. In this milieu (and melee!) of evangelicalism, I found faith and became part of this "interdenominational denomination" called evangelicalism. It was by the way a masterstroke to have grabbed the term "evangelical" for the movement, replacing the ugly term "fundamentalist."

In this circle, several different theological voices were heard, such as (in particular) the Reformed, Wesleyan-Arminian, pietist, dispensational, and pentecostal. (The National Association of Evangelicals was built upon this amazing diversity in 1943.) But these traditions, which were significant in their own right, were not much emphasized in this context in order to pursue more cooperative ventures. Not that they hid their light under a bushel, mind you, only that they were content to build upon what they took to be a basic consensus of faith. Certainly one could poke fun at this far-from-stale credo, but it has worked quite well. If one looks (for example) at the Lausanne Covenant, the National Association of Evangelicals' basis of faith, the Amsterdam Declaration, and other similar texts, it is plain that evangelicalism is a form of classical Christian faith, though it is not the only such example. In the early years, I had no systematic theology as such, but I did have C. S. Lewis and I did have the sages from Old Princeton and from the British Puritans, and I was made aware of some at least of the trends in theology. The Protestant faith has always been a "many splintered thing" and there has always been lots of coming and going theologically and ecclesiastically. The evangelical movement has only continued this trend.

Shifts in Theological Method

I wish to address, first, developments that I have experienced in theological method, and afterwards we can look at certain revisions of doctrine that I believe might be helpful. Conservative-evangelicals and postconservative evangelicals are theologians of a particular kind. The conservative-evangelicals are strongly traditional in beliefs and rather suspicious of doctrinal revision. They tend to think that biblical concepts are of the essence of faith and that getting the doctrines exactly right is very important. They know where to draw the boundaries and are able to identify quite confidently those who are "in" and those who are "out." They are lacking somewhat in self-criticism and are not very much aware of how they themselves have been influenced by their cultural surroundings, and they view postmodernity with great suspicion, being quite fearful of losing faith's rational grounding.

This brand of theology corresponds to the rational-propositional orientation of Carl F. H. Henry and others with him who constructed the "new evangelical" coalition and paradigm in the 1940s. It is the sort of position that I have been trying to come out of in recent years. Although we think of them as traditional in doctrine, there are exceptions, most notably the very widespread belief among conservatives of the "rapture" of the church, that is, the secret coming of Christ before the great tribulation. This novel idea had little currency before the mid-nineteenth century and yet is held by millions of "evangelicals." The doctrine promotes escapism from involvement in Christ's suffering in the latter days and enjoys little or no support exegetically from the New Testament. How "conservative" is this? It sounds like a piece of constructive liberal theology!

What about the other group, the postconservative evangelicals? These theologians are conservative too and affirm the church's main traditions, though not uncritically. (Let's not mention the widespread denial of infant baptism, which both camps agree to shelve.) They are not so nervous about fresh interpretation and promising theological moves—they welcome them. They are not afraid of thinking "outside the box." For them, the essence of Christianity lies in its power to transform human life as much as (or maybe more than) rational truths and arguments as such.

They embrace the kind of "chastened rationality" that postmodernity presents and do not fear it. In fact, they view postmodernity more as opportunity than as threat. As for revelation, they see it more in terms of history than propositional second-order language and they are comfortable with acknowledging the fact that they work in particular historical settings. The diversity that we see in contemporary theology does not worry them either but rather stimulates. This kind of postconservative thinking appeared early in the history of the movement, for instance, in the work of Bernard Ramm and at the flagship Fuller Theological Seminary. For many of us, the postconservative way of working in theology has been a breath of fresh air. It feels like we are getting free of the fundamentalist impulse that in the 1950s plagued Edward Carnell, who tried to free evangelicals of it decades ago. I myself have always struggled with it and it has (I would say) prevented me from doing my best work. The foregoing analysis of a shift in methodology was not something that I cooked up years ago but more of a gradual perception that crept upon me unawares over time. Ironically enough, "prolegomena" are often the last things to be comprehended, not the first.

THEOLOGICAL REVISIONS

Let us turn now to certain theological revisions that have accompanied the shifts in methodology. To postconservatives, theology is an ongoing and unfinished task, because we know only "in part," as Paul says, and because the situation into which we proclaim the gospel is always changing along with the historical and cultural contexts that shape our understanding and influence how we interpret truth. Owing to such factors, postconservative theologians are more open to proposing doctrinal corrections in the light of God's Word than conservative-evangelical theologians are. We wish to carry on the constructive work of theology because theology is incomplete. Remember that the Bible does not contain a single theology as such but is a multifaceted witness. Theology is something that we do to the Bible in different ways and in different contexts. The Bible is not a compendium of theology. We are called to be in conversation with this text. It is our dialogue partner.

The most fundamental shift in my work, and the most important, concerns the unbounded love of God. I had to reject restrictiveness in the Reformed model with regard to God's gift to the human race. In a nutshell, I had to embrace "the universal salvific will of God," following Wesley and not Calvin. Remember that the evangelical coalition was born amidst diversity, a major part of which was the tension between Reformed and Wesleyan-Arminian ways of thinking and in which the former has had a particularly strong influence, even dominance. Some go so far as to equate their convictions (for example, the TULIP) with evangelical theology as such. (This refers to Total depravity, Unconditional election, Limited atonement, Irresistible grace, and the Perseverance of the saints.) Right up to the present, this difference is the largest source of tension in the movement. Most of the leaders in the early days were Reformed, and their beliefs were privileged where others were marginalized and our history was written selectively and prejudicially. Pentecostals and Wesleyan-Arminians (for example) have had to resist the so-called "Presbyterian paradigm" in the telling of their story. Historian Donald Dayton has done a lot to set things straight.

Against the Reformed position, I have had to speak of the universal salvific will of God, and to avoid demeaning God's loving nature and limiting the scope of God's tender mercies because according to the scriptures God wants all to be saved and come to a knowledge of the truth. Sometimes critics portray my work, and the changes in it, as something essentially random. I think they are not. The six examples that I am about to allude to here under "revisions" are part of a single paradigm shift away from the basic "heresy" of the Reformed model, which says that God is not loving by nature though he may choose to be loving by an act of his willpower. God could just as well not love should he decide that he should show wrath, just so we know he can do that too. They seem to think that love is something God decides and not something God is. I interpret my changes as a focused effort to elicit the multifaceted implications of the truth of God's unbounded love for all mankind. God's love is not simply one attribute among others but stands at the heart of the very nature of the triune God—period. This conviction has been expressed in several of my books: *Grace Unlimited, Grace of God, Will of Man, Wideness in God's Mercy, Abounding Love,* and *The Flame of Love: A Theology of the Holy Spirit.*

It was a deliberate decision on the part of the National Association of Evangelicals to unite such believers as these two camps in a common cause in opposition to liberal theology. It can be (however) more than a little awkward at times because the differences are important and deeply held. Both consider them fundamental, so that the tension has the potential of fracturing the coalition. The debate is likely to go on as long as the coalition lasts. It broke out recently in a strong way in the debates surrounding my book *A Wideness in God's Mercy* and my book *The Openness of God.* One wonders what will happen when the Billy Graham "glue" is not there and when the postconservative theologians really get rolling. I hope that evangelicalism will remain loosely united because it is still a vital force that, in the end, we should not forsake.

Secondly, if love is the name and nature of God, how are we to understand the deity? God is a loving person who deals with us in personal and loving ways. This is the heart of the Christian faith. This is why we need a theology of what we call "the openness of God." We need a theology that can move us away from static categories like the immutability, impassibility, and nontemporality of God in the direction of a model of mutuality and relationship. If God is a personal God who loves us, then relationality is essential to who God is— a dynamic and interactive God who takes risks and faces down vulnerability. There are different kinds of relationships that God could have instituted with us. It could have been a legal one where minding your p's and q's is central. Or it could have been a deterministic one where God would have made puppets who are preprogrammed to do only what's right. But God appears to have opted for a model of mutual fellowship, deciding to make beings capable of experiencing love and returning it. In this arrangement, God genuinely interacts and enters into dynamic give-and-take relationships, leaving space for us to work in partnership with God. My primary concern then has been to highlight God's personal and relational nature as love. Loving relationships require time and change, degrees of vulnerability, and a capacity for suffering and openness to the future which is ever unfolding. Crucial here is God's willingness to lay aside prerogatives of sheer power and undertake voluntary self-limitation out of love for us. God's flexibility does not diminish God's glory but enhances it. For a presentation of "open theism," see my *Most Moved Mover* (2001).

Another issue arises in this connection, which has got people talking. It has to do with the foreknowledge of God. Why does this come up in openness theology? Part of the reason is just the novelty of the idea we have put out there that not everything of the future can be known even by God. Deeper down it has to do with the dynamic temporality of the creation project. Ask yourself a question—is the future settled in every detail or are there things still left for human agents to do? Is it worth getting up in the morning or should we just stay in bed? Can we not agree that God knows all that there is to know, given the sort of world he decided to make? So that, if God predetermined everything, then God could now know everything about the future, exhaustively and definitely. In other words, if predestined, then foreknown—of course. But what if God did not make a determined world but a dynamic temporal order instead? In that case, God would have to deal with the truth of the universe as it came down the pipe and therefore contingently. There would be an element of surprise. Just for there to be mutual relationships between God and humans, there would have to be a dynamic unfolding in time, a degree of vulnerability, and the capacity for suffering and an openness to a future that is not completely settled. Thus open theists hold that God's foreknowledge is perfect and not limited at all. God knows absolutely everything that can be known, which includes everything that will happen owing to present circumstances and everything that could happen and everything that "might happen." I do not call this "limited foreknowledge"; I call it God's infinite intelligence.

The thing is, God has established real temporal order with an open future. Creatures can even make a difference as to how things will work out. Everything is not fixed and determined. The future is not an entity out there somewhere that can be completely known right now even by God. It isn't there. The future is to an extent still the realm of possibilities as well as certainties.

Third, the shift toward Wesleyan-Arminian thinking also had an effect (salutary, I think) on the doctrine of Scripture. There was a big fight in the 1970s over whether the Bible is inerrant even in matters of history and cosmology. It was a skirmish brought on by Harold Lindsell's polemical *Battle for the Bible*. I escaped his broadside, having written a pretty feisty book of my own in the tradition of B. B. Warfield titled *Biblical Revelation* (1971). It too appealed to the supposed "biblical doctrine of inspiration and inerrancy" in the hope that certainty in theology might be achieved in a modern foundationalist way. On reflection, I had misgivings and wrote *The Scripture Principle* (1984). It dawned on me that this approach distorted the actual claims of scripture and placed them in an alien framework, that is, in a rational propositional one, which fails to notice the practical and pietist orientation of much of scripture. Though I saw it at the time merely as revisiting the data, I now see it more in relation to the shift toward Wesleyan-Arminianism. With the pietists, they too did not commit to any inerrancy tradition but focused on the transformational power of God's Word, which was a logic that would work itself out in pentecostalism. Thinking of the shift in relation to pietism also allows one to imagine a lesser divine control and a greater human contribution and with less docetism. Most importantly, I also saw a neglect of the Holy Spirit in the rational/propositionalist way of thinking about the Bible that I had fallen for in the early years.

It is good to remember that the Evangelical Theological Society invoked the term "inerrancy" but the National Association of Evangelicals did not. This fact should warn against using the word as a weapon against others and it should alert us to its limitations. The term is very difficult to define and gives the impression of imposing a standard of accuracy on the ancient text. But along with others, I retained the term even when I departed from a strict version of it. I noticed that they seldom insisted on technical precision of biblical accuracy when it came to historical and cosmological fact. The Chicago Statement on biblical inerrancy did a lot to lower the temperature by issuing a number of qualifiers and by guarding against evaluating the Bible by standards of truth that are alien to it.

Fourth, as to epistemology, I moved from a harder rational approach in my earlier work (*Set Forth Your Case*, 1967) to a softer rationality in my later work in apologetics (*Reason Enough*, 1980). Along with others, I had been finding postfoundationalism a good way to present the sort of truth claims that Christianity brings to the table. It was not a question of minimizing objective truth but of making a break with the Enlightenment paradigm. I became dissatisfied with the reliance on modern modes of thought that should not be taken on board uncritically and becoming unwanted prisoners of the secular outlook.

I prefer soft rationality in my apologetics and mount a cumulative case strategy. God does not want to overwhelm creation, as God would surely do if he dwelt "too close" and if the immediate consciousness of God's presence were too compelling. What freedom would we have then? In order to be a person, exercising a measure of genuine freedom, creation must be brought into existence, not in the immediate divine presence, but at an epistemic distance in which God is not overwhelmingly evident. I lean toward postfoundationalism in religious epistemology partly because of the postmodern ethos and partly because it seems a better way to commend our approach to knowledge.

Fifth, there is an issue to face related to the universal salvific will of God that is very problematic. How can God who is merciful send men and women to hell because they failed, through no fault of their own, to be evangelized? Conservative-evangelicals embrace restrictivism more often than not. They hold to the hard-line position that only persons who hear the gospel can be saved through faith. This has been (I suppose) the majority opinion over the centuries, though not a view held by the Greek fathers and not nowadays after Vatican II. It is said that to deny it would be to undercut the motivation for world missions. But some form of inclusivism is now held on both the Catholic and the Protestant sides on the basis of belief in the universal salvific love of God. Surely access to the possibility of the salvation of the unevangelized will not be denied to any who seek God. God is after all the rewarder of those who diligently seek him. God's love guarantees that the Spirit will pursue everyone in every age to give them access to salvation. God does not leave himself without witness. The Spirit opens windows of opportunity. This is but one more example where C. S. Lewis has helped evangelicals even though he himself is not evangelical on a number of points. Lewis affirms the finality of Jesus Christ but also holds the view that God is drawing people from all nations and religions to himself. Much in the world religions is false but what is true is perfected in Christ. And he held that eternal salvation will be given to any and all who have responded to God in this life. Such a position fits very well with a belief in the goodness of God.

I consider the move to universal access to salvation (not universal salvation itself) to be an important move in the history of doctrine. The truth of the universal salvific will of God is being recognized now and given priority on the hierarchy of Christian truths. Previously we argued over the means of grace; now we rejoice in the grace itself (*A Wideness in God's Mercy: The Finality of Jesus Christ in a World of Religions*, 1992).

Sixth, there is one more issue related to the goodness of God. It is not the fact of hell but the nature of it. In Great Britain during the last century a group of Anglican evangelicals, including John Stott, John Wenham, and P. E. Hughes, came to believe that the traditional view of the nature of hell as everlasting conscious punishing was unscriptural (and, I would add, immoral and unjust). They proposed to understand it as the second death and as life's termination after the judgment. They denied that immortality was a natural possession and saw everlasting life as the conditional gift of God. They came up with a hell as a fire that consumes rather than a fire that torments forever. This position was considered to be properly evangelical by the Evangelical Alliance in the U.K. There was a protest on this side of the Atlantic (however) from fundamentalists and conservatives who considered such a view beyond the pale and outside the boundaries of orthodoxy. On the subject, C. S. Lewis defended the traditional view of the nature of hell as ongoing but had a different spin that is also moderate. Lewis spoke of the damned as "formerly human" and as "very nearly nothing." That his view differed only slightly from annihilation was not a huge contradiction.

I have been criticized often and severely for promoting changes in doctrine such as these. On the one hand, I am puzzled because the changes are modest and supported by other more respected evangelical thinkers. Why the harsh criticism, I wonder? First, it may be because I have discovered too many such revisions. One or two might be tolerable but not six or seven! Second, it may be partly due to my continuing to be a card-carrying evangelical and symbolizing the postconservative moderation trend the conservatives do not want to own. For my own part, I hope that over the years I will have been a catalyst for the reforming of evangelical theology.

CONSERVATIVE AND CONTEMPORARY

The title of my lecture when I was installed in the chair of theology at McMaster Divinity College was "Evangelical Theology: Conservative and Contemporary." It expressed something that I have always valued—the principle that theology has a dual function: one to conserve and other to reform. On the one hand, I want continuity with the scriptures and with tradition as far as possible. I am certainly not anti-conservative, though I want to be free to challenge such antiquated ideas as there may be. The "status quo" theologically is not good enough. God's word has more to say and more light to shed. Theologians need to be both conservationists and reformers, bringing out of God's treasury that which is old and what is new (Matt. 13:52).

Keeping the balance is not so easy, given the fact that evangelicals are oriented more to conservationism than to new interpretations. So I think that we need to do a little more with reform. Evangelicalism can boast a good number of able traditionalists—what we need are a few more able reformists. We need sound theology and the new light that breaks forth from God's word ever anew, correcting traditions and reforming the church's life. The mistake that liberals are prone to make in theology is to become so enamored of innovation that they lose sight of the historic faith, while the mistake that conservatives often make is to equate the truth with a certain stage of the tradition and not see the need of ongoing reform. We need a better balance of old and new. We must not play fast and loose with the Bible or water down the fundamentals of the faith. What I hope for is that we would become better at telling the old story in new and compelling ways.

Modern evangelicalism is an essentially contested entity and a lot like a patchwork quilt theologically. It has many components as part of it. I have realized from this telling of my story that I have been caught up in the clash between scholasticism and pietism within evangelicalism. Conservative evangelicals lean in the direction of scholasticism, viewing theology as a rational discipline, somewhat apart from the life of piety. Pietists on the other hand see the message as more centrally a life-changing narrative than a matter of assenting to doctrines. Both traditions begin with God's action toward humanity. Scholastics emphasize that the saving action is recorded in scripture and expressed in doctrine, while pietists emphasize that the God who acted as recorded in scripture continues to do so. While scholasticism tends to protect the "objective" truth of scripture from contamination by "subjective" experience, pietists insist that experience is of itself very important. I am learning not to place doctrine over experience or experience over doctrine but to reject the objective/subjective dualism and seek to integrate the two—scripture and doctrine, heart and life.

15

From Physicist to Priest • John Polkinghorne

I grew up in the country and in a Christian home. My parents were regular worshippers at our local Anglican parish church and, since I was a well-behaved child, I accompanied them willingly from an early age. No particular provisions were made for children, but we had a vicar who was a skillful preacher, able to make biblical passages come alive, and I used to enjoy listening to him. I absorbed Christianity through my pores. Religion was obviously important to my mother and father, but they were people who did not naturally talk much about it and I received little in the way of formal religious instruction at home. When I was about eight an aunt of mine let me have a little book of private prayers that I had found lying around in her home, and I used these regularly and somewhat secretly.

I am, therefore, a cradle Christian. I cannot remember a time when I was not in some way a member of the worshipping and believing community of the church. The figure of Jesus has always been central for me, and no view of reality would begin to be adequate that did not fully take the phenomenon of Christ into account. I have not been given the gift of an untroubled faith—I sometimes think that Christianity might be too good to be true—but when that mood is on me I say to myself "Well, then, deny it" and I know that I could never do that. Christ's side is one on which I have to take my stand.

When I was fourteen, we moved from Somerset to Ely and I went to school in nearby Cambridge. The Perse School, which I attended, was small and very academic and for the first time I encountered clever boys who did not believe in God. We used to argue, but my faith survived that and a subsequent spell of national service in the Army before coming up to Cambridge in October 1949 to study mathematics at Trinity College.

EVANGELICAL AND CATHOLIC, ANGLICAN STYLE

In my first week as an undergraduate I was taken to a Freshers' Sermon preached on behalf of the Christian Union. The preacher used the story of

Zacchaeus's meeting with Jesus as he passed through Jericho on the way to his death at Jerusalem, as the basis of a challenge to respond to Christ right now, to take this unique opportunity. I was strongly moved and went forward at the end among a crowd of those who wished to make a decision for Christ. For some years afterwards I would have spoken of this as my "conversion," but I now understand it as a moment of deeper Christian commitment along a pilgrimage path that I was already treading.

There followed a number of years of close involvement with the Christian Union. I have mixed feelings about that time. The conservative evangelical Christianity that I embraced so wholeheartedly gave me certain gifts I continue to value and seek to retain: the importance of a personal commitment to Christ and a love of scripture. Yet it also promoted a narrow view, both of the varieties of Christian experience and of the relevance of general culture. There was a kind of defensiveness, even fearfulness, in the face of sources of truth not guaranteed as "sound." Nowhere was this more apparent than in its treatment of the Bible. I have found it immensely enhancing for my own use of scripture to be able to recognize its human and cultural character, while still discerning its inspired and normative status. The Church of England is such a broad, comprehensive church that its members are always being invited to identify themselves as adherents of one particular party or another. Today I find it difficult to choose a label for myself, but "catholic" would certainly be part of it. I value greatly the sacramental life and the accumulated insights of the Christian tradition. I feel most spiritually at home on the occasional visits I am able to make to a small community of Anglican nuns (the Society of the Sacred Cross) living a Benedictine life in the Welsh countryside.

Mathematical Physics at Cambridge

My undergraduate studies at Cambridge were in mathematics. I had chosen the subject because I was good at it and liked getting things right, and also because my mathematical imagination had been kindled at school by an outstanding master who taught me. At the university, I got interested in how one could use mathematics to understand the deep structure of the physical world, so that when I embarked on a Ph.D. in 1952 it was in the area of theoretical elementary particle physics. This was the beginning of a long career as a physicist that lasted till 1979. It was an exceptionally interesting period in the development of my subject since it spanned the long struggle, by means of experimental discovery and theoretical insight, that eventually uncovered the quark level in the structure of matter. My own work was very much on the mathematical side of this great collaborative enterprise and I attained a modest degree of professional success, becoming Professor of Mathematical

Physics at Cambridge University in 1968 and being elected a Fellow of the Royal Society in 1974.

Nevertheless, I had long thought that I would not remain in particle physics all my life. The subject was always changing in response to new ideas and new discoveries. When one was young, this state of intellectual flux was exciting; it became somewhat more tiring as one grew older. In mathematical thinking, most of us lose in middle age the flexibility of mind that is a characteristic of youth. We can still do the old tricks but it becomes harder to learn or to invent new ones. I had seen many senior colleagues get somewhat miserable as the subject moved away from them. I resolved I would leave physics before physics left me. I felt I owed this, not only to myself, but also to the young workers in the large research group I was privileged to lead. As my fiftieth birthday approached, and as a particular era in particle physics came to a close with the establishment of what is called the Standard Model, I realized the time had come for me to go. I was not leaving physics because I had in any way become disillusioned with it, but I had done my little bit for the subject and now it was time to do something else.

FROM PROFESSOR TO SEMINARIAN

I like being with people. I value the eucharistic life. I had some experience of being a lay reader (an unordained local preacher). These considerations encouraged in my mind the idea of a possible vocation to the Anglican priesthood. Fortunately, my wife Ruth concurred—it was necessarily a joint decision. The next step was to have my vocation tested and considered by a selection committee, a collection of wise and experienced people appointed by the church for that purpose. They too concurred, and I was subsequently grateful, not only for that decision but also for the care with which I felt it had been taken.

So October 1979, just before my forty-ninth birthday, saw me a beginning student at Westcott House, a small Anglican seminary in Cambridge in the liberal catholic tradition. I was the oldest person in the House, older than the Principal even! It was very odd becoming a student again—I found out how much more difficult it is to listen to a lecture for an hour than to give one—but I had a lot to learn during my two-year course. Perhaps the most important lesson of all I learned was to value the Daily Office, the round of morning and evening prayer and praise, psalmody and scripture, which it is the obligation of an Anglican priest to recite faithfully. It provides the spiritual framework for my life today.

Just before I went to Westcott, a theologically knowledgeable friend of mine suggested to me that I should read Jürgen Moltmann's *The Crucified God*. I had done a little desultory theological reading on and off over the years, but this was perhaps the first substantial theological work that I had read with serious attention. I was deeply affected by it, and Moltmann has been one of the major theological influences on me ever since. I can understand the criticisms that some make of the occasionally rather uncontrolled exuberance of his writing, but for me he is a person of exciting theological ideas that span the two horizons of the biblical witness and the demands of the century of the Holocaust.

A Scientist with Serious Theological Interests

I cared for physics, and I continue to do so, but I have come to realize that theology grips me much more profoundly than science ever did. Yet the personal paradox is that I shall never be able to become a professional theologian. I do not have the time or opportunity to recapitulate that long apprenticeship and involvement with a worldwide academic community that is the indispensable requirement of becoming a fully fledged practitioner. I do not think this means that I have nothing to contribute to theological thinking, but I am aware of my limitations. I cannot claim to be more than a scientist with serious theological interests. I have to say that I wish I knew a few more theologians who have serious scientific interests. The interdisciplinary field of encounter between the scientific and theological worldviews, which has been my predominant intellectual interest in recent years, calls from all its participants for a certain acceptance of risk and a certain charity toward the efforts of others with different backgrounds.

On ordination, an Anglican clergyman spends three years in apprenticeship to the parochial ministry. It is called serving one's title and I did mine in perfectly ordinary parishes in Cambridge and Bristol. Once licensed to go solo, I became Vicar in charge of a large village parish outside Canterbury. All in all, I did five years in this kind of work. In addition to preaching and taking services, it involved a good deal of wandering around, knocking on doors, and drinking cups of tea with people who were in some sort of trouble, such as illness or bereavement. The Church of England is a national church with a responsibility to the whole community. Only a minority of those I visited were in any way active participants in worship.

Return to Cambridge

I enjoyed this life very much, but of course there were intellectual aspects of me that were not greatly exercised in the course of it. I had thought originally that I had left the academic world for good, but I gradually came to recognize that thinking and writing about science and religion were part of my vocation, the particular way in which I might serve the Christian community. When an unsought opportunity came in 1986 to return to Cambridge as the Dean of Trinity Hall (a job equivalent to being the parish priest of that academic "village"), I decided, after some thought, to accept it. Three years later, I received an equally unexpected invitation to become the President of Queens' College, Cambridge (the Head of the College, but not its Chief Executive, rather a kind of eighteenth-century constitutional monarch in its society). This essentially secular job was possible for me because Queens', like all the ancient colleges at Cambridge, has a religious basis as part of its foundation. I continue to exercise a degree of priestly ministry as I share with our Dean in celebrating the eucharist and preaching in the College Chapel.

Writing about the Way the World Is

My main intellectual activity is writing. I love the task of composition, the search for as clear a way as possible to convey what I want to say. The late Bishop John Robinson of *Honest to God* fame (who ordained me a priest) once said to me that he could not think without a pen in his hand. I knew at once what he meant. As one reads and thinks, ideas buzz around in one's mind. It is the act of writing that causes this flux of thought to condense into some coherent thread of argument. I write all my manuscripts in scribbled longhand because, when the structure really begins to form, I cannot type fast enough to keep up with myself.

My first book in the science and religion area arose out of my experiences on leaving physics. I could not quit right away, for I had obligations to my graduate students that had to be fulfilled through an orderly withdrawal. In the eighteen months it took me to wind up my scientific affairs, I had quite a few conversations with colleagues over a cup of coffee in some laboratory canteen as they asked me what on earth I was up to. Mostly, they were probing my reasons for Christian belief. In half an hour or so I could no more do justice to that theme than I could have conveyed to an arts friend, on a similar timescale, my reasons for belief in quarks. I decided I would put down on paper what I would have said if I had had a few hours at my disposal. The result was a small book with a grandiose title: *The Way the World Is.* There isn't a great deal of explicit science in the book (the first publisher I approached rejected it on those grounds), but it exemplifies in a simple way a conviction that runs through much of my writing: that religious insight, like scientific insight, depends upon the search for motivated belief. The title was intended to convey that idea of rationally grounded understanding, rather than constituting a ridiculous claim to total metaphysical adequacy!

I did not have time for writing when I was a curate learning the trade, but as I wandered round the streets of my working-class parish in Bristol, I used to think about the similarities and differences of science and religion and what they had to say to each other about the one world of human experience. When I came to Kent as a vicar, part of the arrangement was that I should have a chance to write, and this enabled my thoughts to crystallize into *One World*, a survey of the scene that has proved a fairly steady seller.

I have never been able to see more than a book ahead, and I did not then envisage writing a trilogy of little volumes on the topic of science and religion. However, the other two offerings followed in fairly quick succession. *Science and Creation* is mainly concerned with two themes. One is the revival, as I see it, of natural theology in the modest mode of proffered insight based on the very structure of the laws of nature themselves, which seem, in their deep rational beauty and intelligibility and in their "finely tuned" anthropic fruitfulness, to point beyond science to a more profound Reality. This is an insight that is particularly appealing to someone whose scientific experience has been in fundamental physics. Biologists see a messier and more ambiguous picture of the process of the world, and the second theme I tried to address was that of an evolutionary world "making itself" in an unfolding act of continual creation, necessarily precarious and costly in its character. Here I was helped by the thoughts of my seniors, Ian Barbour and Arthur Peacocke, and by W. H. Vanstone's wonderfully insightful *Love's Endeavour, Love's Expense*, another book that I had read early in my theological studies and that has remained an abiding influence.

EPISTEMOLOGY MODELS ONTOLOGY

In chapter five of *Science and Creation*, I began the tentative exploration of a theme that has recurred in much of my subsequent writing: that we should seek to understand the relationship of mind and matter as being that of complementary poles of a single "world stuff" in flexible and open organization. The task of a proper understanding of this metaphysical issue is far beyond my modest capacity (or that of anyone today, I believe), but I have come to think that the insights of so-called chaos theory may offer a clue to a useful direction in which to wave our hands in cautious speculation.

I propose that the undoubted unpredictabilities of these exquisitely sensitive physical systems should be treated, not as unfortunate signs of epistemic ignorance, but as sources of ontological opportunity. Coining the phrase "Epistemology Models Ontology" as a slogan of scientific realism, I suggest that the ontology of deterministic equations aligns poorly with the epistemology of intrinsic unpredictabilities and that it should be replaced (as almost everyone does in the case of quantum uncertainties) by a more subtle and supple ontological account. This leads eventually to the notion of an enhanced range of causal principles in which the "bottom-up," bits-and-pieces, energetic causality of physics is supplemented by the operation of "top-down" causality of a nonenergetic, pattern-forming kind that might be called "active information." I suggest that this is how we act in the world and that it is consistent to suppose that God interacts with creation in this mode also.

My first sustained attempt to discuss divine action was in the third book of the trilogy, *Science and Providence*. Here I also took up a theme to which I have returned in later writing, the consideration of how God relates to time. Although contemporary science affords no satisfactory account of the basic human experience of the present moment, my view is "so much the worse for science!" I reject a block universe account and assert the true temporality of the world. Since God knows things as they really are, I believe that this implies that God knows creation in its temporality. In my view, there must be a temporal pole to the divine nature in addition to an eternal pole (an idea that I accept from the process theologians while rejecting a number of their other proposals), and that even God does not yet know the unformed future.

My writing has been characterized by a succession of short books. I think and read about a topic and then reach a stage at which I have to try to set down what I think about it. This seems to result in a series of volumes of just over a hundred pages. I try to write with all the intellectual seriousness and scrupulosity I can muster, but I do not write in an overtly academic style. This is a deliberate choice; I decided early on that my target audience should be twofold: the educated unbeliever whom I am wishing to persuade of the rationally motivated credibility of Christianity, and the educated believer whom I am wishing to persuade to take science seriously and to enhance Christian understanding by so doing. I do not think these aims are inconsistent with also seeking to offer some intellectual input into the interaction between science and theology.

After the trilogy, I found I wanted to return to some themes I had touched on earlier and discuss them in greater detail. This resulted in *Reason and Reality*, whose chapters seek to consolidate the consideration of how scientific and theological thinking relate to each other, the role of natural theology, and a number of issues including more discussion of how to interpret chaos theory.

GIFFORD LECTURES

The invitation to give the Gifford Lectures in Edinburgh in 1993 encouraged me to write what is my longest book to date. Rather exasperatingly, it has different titles on the different sides of the Atlantic: *Science and Christian Belief/The Faith of a Physicist*, but at least it has the same subtitle: "Theological Reflections of a Bottom-Up Thinker." The idea was to weave a discussion of Christian belief around phrases selected from the Nicene Creed, using arguments based on a bottom-up movement from experience to interpretation. Scientists know that the world is strange and exciting, beyond our prior powers of anticipation, and they are open to unexpected insights provided they are based on evidence to show that this is indeed the case. The lectures are an exercise in that search for motivated belief that is so central to my own thinking. In a sense, they are a much more developed account of the program I attempted with *The Way the World Is*. The final chapter discusses a theological problem that is much in my mind, of how we are truly to understand the interrelationships of the world's great faith traditions so obviously concerned with a common spiritual realm but so obviously making clashing cognitive claims about its nature. This unresolved diversity contrasts perplexingly with the universality of scientific understanding that has spread so readily across the globe.

After the Giffords I needed a holiday, but I love to write, so I dashed off a chatty book about science and religion, which I called *Quark, Chaos and Christianity*. It is rather a favorite of mine.

Scientists as Theologians

My valued colleagues Ian Barbour and Arthur Peacocke have also given Gifford Lectures, and comparison of the three sets reveals both many common themes but also some interesting divergences of method and conclusion, mostly relating to the question of how great a degree of conceptual autonomy has to be claimed by theology and to what extent it can harmonize its thinking with scientific patterns of understanding. In attempting the delicate task of a comparison between the three of us, I have concluded that there is a spectrum, which I characterize in *Scientists as Theologians* as running from consonance to assimilation, in which Barbour is near the integrationist end, I am near the conceptual autonomy end, and Peacocke is somewhere in between us.

I think that the science-and-theology debate is currently in an interesting phase in which the action has to some extent moved away from the obvious border areas of natural theology and the doctrine of creation into a closer engagement with central Christian questions such as Christology and eschatology. The bottom-up thinking that characterizes scientific thought has something to offer here, not as a uniquely effective method of doing theology but as a possible source of insight, comparable with the particular insights offered, in their very different ways, by black or feminist theology.

I do a fair amount of public speaking about science and religion. I quite often end a talk by saying that I am both a physicist and a priest and that I believe that I can hold these two aspects of me together, not only without compartmentalization or dishonesty, but also with a significant degree of mutual enhancement. It is to that task that I seek to devote my current endeavors.

16

My Life Journey • Rosemary Radford Ruether

In this essay I want to trace something of my life journey in terms of the interconnection between my social commitments and my intellectual production. I sometimes describe my intellectual journey as spiraling, rather than changing from one perspective and topic of concern to another. In my corpus of some forty-four books and hundreds of articles between the early 1960s and today, I seem to have addressed a vast array of issues: the church, especially Roman Catholicism, feminist theology in North America and internationally, women's history in Christianity, the history of the family, the Israeli-Palestinian conflict, anti-Semitism, racism, Latin American liberation theology, Buddhist-Christian dialogue, and ecology. For me, all these issues are deeply interconnected. Most of them have been present in my thinking since the early '70s. Early books of essays, such as *New Woman, New Earth*, and *Liberation Theology: Human Hope Confronts Christian History and American Power*, both published in the early '70s, already began to address many of these issues.

My Family

I grew up in a family that was simultaneously Roman Catholic and ecumenical, and I have expanded but maintained that combination. My mother was a Roman Catholic of English and Austrian extraction, who was born in Mexico in 1895 and grew up in Southern California. Her religion was important to her, but she had little patience with superstitious literalism or clerical authoritarianism. She passed on to me a sense that the Catholic tradition should be taken seriously, but thought about freely and critically. Nuns and priests who try to make you feel guilty about asking questions should be disregarded. The ghetto mentality of many Catholics of the 1940s and '50s was mostly absent from my experience.

My father was an Episcopalian whose religion was more of a social identity than a personal experience. I remember him dressing up to go to Trinity

Church in Georgetown where his family had belonged for generations, and I sometimes went with him. My favorite uncle was a Jew whose religion was more of a culture than a personal practice. A skilled musician and painter, he was a surrogate father during the years when my father was away in the Second World War. He imbued my two sisters and myself with a lifelong love of music and the arts.

This diversity of family religious cultures included a great aunt married to a Russian diplomat who lived many years in St. Petersburg. She was a writer and playwright who wrote stories based on Russian folklore. She was partial to the Russian Orthodox Church and to spiritualism. When her husband and son both died suddenly, she cultivated spiritualist communication with them and wrote a book called *There Are No Dead*, based on her experiences. After my father's death in 1949, our family moved to La Jolla, California, close to my mother's family home in San Diego. One of my mother's women friends was a pacifist and attended Quaker meeting, and I sometimes went to meeting with her, as well as attending mass with my mother. I also went to anti-war rallies and demonstrations for the United Farm Workers with her. From these experiences I imbibed the assumptions that one can connect with several religious traditions at the same time, without choosing between them, and should relate religion to peace and social justice.

CLASSICS, CHRISTIANITY, AND CULTURE

During my teen years, I cultivated the fine arts and aspired to be a painter. I went to Scripps College in Claremont, California in 1954 with the intention of majoring in fine art. But I was drawn instead into the study of the classics and history of Christian thought. My mentors in the classics were partial to the history-of-religions approach to the study of ancient society, and I read authors, such as Jane Harrison, who explored the matriarchal origins of Greek culture. From these studies the question of Christian origins emerged as central for me. I asked myself, "How did Christianity, as a small Jewish apocalyptic sect in the first century, manage by the fourth century to win over the ancient world in a new synthesis of Jewish and Greco-Roman thought?"

My mentor in Latin classics, Robert Palmer, did not particularly appreciate Christianity. He thought it was a shame that it won. I remember him saying sadly, when speaking of the neo-Platonic philosophy that rivaled Christianity under the reign of the emperor Julian who tried to restore paganism against the victory of Christianity, "It had everything. Why did it lose?" My question came from the other side: "Why did it win? How did Christianity manage to gather up both the most significant themes of ancient Greek philosophy and popular credibility to emerge as the winning religion of late antiquity?" But this question also assumed an appreciation of the other religious options that were erased or absorbed by Christianity: the ancient Near Eastern and Greco-Roman religions, and new movements like Mithraism and Gnosticism. They too have truths that one could still glimpse, even if dimly. No serious human religious quest is to be despised as simply wrong or false.

My questions about the relation of Christianity and classical culture continued to guide my graduate studies from 1958 to 1968, in which I earned master's and doctoral degrees at the Claremont Graduate School in Roman History and in Classics and Patristics. I also married Herman Ruether, a fellow student at Claremont in Political Science and Asian Studies, and we began a family. Between 1958 and 1963 we would have three children, even as I finished my graduate education. This experience brought me face to face with the contradictions between my aspiration to be both a mother and a scholar and the Catholic teachings forbidding birth control. Problems of Catholic teachings on sexuality and gender became urgent.

The Sixties, the Vatican, and the Klan

The early 1960s also saw the beginning of the Vatican Council and the reform vision that began to sweep the Catholic Church. I wrote several articles critiquing the view of sex and reproduction underlying the Catholic anti-contraceptive teaching. One of these became an essay in a book, edited by Gregory Baum, *Contraception and Holiness*, distributed to the bishops and theologians at the Second Vatican Council. I had become involved in church politics. Maintaining a vision of an open church where many views can be discussed has remained an ongoing commitment, even as reactionary forces seemed to take over during the pontificate of John Paul II.

Vatican II coincided with the civil rights and peace movements in the United States of the mid-1960s. The patterns of racism and classism in the U.S. began to be challenged, as well as the imperialist policies that brought it into the Vietnam War. A heady vision of a new and better world was dawning both in the church and in society. I was then in graduate school at Claremont. My friends there in the ecumenical chaplaincies committed themselves to work against racism. In the summer of 1965 our group traveled to Mississippi to work with the Delta Ministry.

That summer in Mississippi was a crucial turning point in my social consciousness. For the first time, I glimpsed America from the underside, from the perspective of poor black people

in America, and the face of white people I saw was frightening and dangerous. Our delegation was housed at Beulah, a former black college, the headquarters of the Delta Ministry. A variety of projects were underway there—plans for housing and farming cooperatives, voter registration, and a preschool program called Mississippi Headstart.

I committed myself to work with the Headstart program and traveled through the state, visiting these projects with a black colleague from Brooklyn. We had to be on the lookout for local whites vehemently hostile to our presence. One night, hooded Ku Klux Klansmen rode through the campus shooting at random at the windows of the buildings. Thereafter we stationed a nightly guard to watch for such incursions. The plan was to ring a bell warning people to get under their beds if such an event occurred again. These experiences gave me a graphic sense of living in an American war zone, one in which we had to assume that the local police were the enemy. At the end of that summer the Watts riot broke out in Los Angeles. When our group returned to the LA area, some of us got involved in Watts.

Social Justice, Anti-Anti-Semitism, and Ecofeminism

These experiences in Mississippi and in inner-city Los Angeles made social justice a key theme of my developing consciousness. This was deepened when our family moved to Washington, D.C. in the summer of 1966 where I took a job at the Howard University School of Religion, a historic black university. Black theology, as well as Latin American liberation theology, were just beginning, and I integrated this work into my own thought to interpret my experiences. Ecological crisis was also an issue that was beginning to dawn in social consciousness. I read the Club of Rome report in 1968 and began to realize that the current industrial system of "developed" nations was unsustainable. There was no way that one could bring the rest of the world into the consumer lifestyle enjoyed by affluent Americans without destroying the biosystems of the planet. Social justice demanded, not an endless expansion of the American economic system, but a conversion to a new paradigm. My first collection of feminist articles, *New Woman, New Earth*, made the ecological issue its culminating essay. This book has been called an "ecofeminist classic," although the term had not yet been coined at the time.

In the mid-1960s, race and class analysis were embraced in circles of critical thought, but gender was ignored. Neither my black nor my white colleagues in seminary or in social action thought women's oppression was worthy of discussion. Women were expected to commit themselves to the liberation of others, not to ask questions about their own exploitation. That began to change in the late '60s. Young women in the civil rights movements began a discussion of "women's place in the movement." When Stokely Carmichael jokingly responded that "the only position for women in the movement is prone," women were infuriated. This casual remark illustrated how the combined exploitation of their work and their sexuality was taken for granted by male colleagues whom they had trusted.

My first essay on sexism and theology, written in 1968, was titled "Male Chauvinist Theology and the Anger of Women." I found that this title shocked my audiences. Black men were expected to respond with anger to racism, but anger was taboo for women. In 1972–1973 I was invited to teach feminist theology at Harvard Divinity School. This year gave me an opportunity to explore the issues of sexism in Christian theological history, laying the basis for my later work in this field.

But sexism was not the only social issue I researched that year. Anti-Semitism had long been an area of concern. My relation to my Uncle David made me aware of Christian anti-Semitism even as a child. At the end of World War II the horrors of the Nazi death camps were brought to my nine-year-old consciousness by newsreels at Saturday-afternoon movies. In reading the Church Fathers I became aware of how the stereotypes of woman as "dangerous bodies" coincided with that of Jews as "bad matter." I began to examine how Christianity split from Judaism in the first century and forged a polemic against the Jews that led to a heritage of pogroms, until it was taken over by Hitler in the twentieth century in the final pogrom, the Holocaust. I taught this subject in a course that year at Harvard and wrote it up in a book published in 1974, *Faith and Fratricide: The Theological Roots of Anti-Semitism.*

By 1975, I sensed that my time at Howard School of Religion was coming to an end. Young black women were beginning to come to the seminary and wanted to discuss the issue of black women in the black church and community. But my black colleagues were resistant to this issue. One young woman wrote her master's thesis on sexism in the black church and was openly ridiculed by the faculty. When I tried to defend her, I was attacked as "racist." It was apparent that this was a no-win situation for a white feminist in a black seminary. It was time for me to move on and make room for black women professors who could address the issue in their own context. In 1976, I received an offer to be the Georgia Harkness Professor at Garrett Theological Seminary in Evanston, Illinois. This school wanted me to address both sexism and racism and was ready to appreciate my combined work in these areas.

The Seventies, Garrett, and Feminist Theology

At Garrett, I began a very fruitful collaboration with my colleague, Rosemary Skinner Keller. We began to teach together in women's history in North America. Over the next thirty years, we edited together the three volumes of *Women and Religion in North America*, and a synthesis of these volumes, *In Our Own Voices: Four Centuries of Women's Religious Writings.* In March of 2006, there appeared the three-volume encyclopedia, *Women and Religion in North America*, which covers the issues of women over four centuries and in every religious tradition, a culmination of our work together on women's religious history in North America.

In the 1970s, I also began to shape a feminist reinterpretation of Christian systematic theology. I saw this reinterpretation as a threefold process of critique and reconstruction. First, I show how Christian theology in all its theological symbols has been shaped by misogyny and negation of women. I then explore alternative traditions for a more inclusive theology and then develop a reconstruction of the basic Christian symbols of God, creation, anthropology, good and evil, Christology, church, and salvation to overcome androcentrism. This work would appear in what I still regard as my foundational work in feminist theology, *Sexism and God-talk: Toward a Feminist Theology* (1983).

My interests in feminist theology have always been practical as well as theoretical. I am interested in feminist liturgy, ministry, and church. A Fulbright scholarship in Sweden in 1984 gave me an opportunity to work on these themes with my Swedish feminist colleagues, who were also keenly interested in feminist liturgy. Many of these women were ordained priests in the Lutheran Church of Sweden and so had some opportunity to develop this work in the context of parishes and university chaplaincies. My question to women during this research was, "In what crises or transitions in your life have you felt the need of liturgical expression, but have found the church silent and unable to respond?" I got many fruitful suggestions, such as the need for lesbian marriage rites, for divorce ceremonies, for ceremonies on leaving home or moving to a new house, for healing from battering and from house break-in. This work turned into the book *Womanchurch: Theory and Practice of Feminist Liturgical Communities* (1986), still my basic work on feminist ecclesiology.

My work on Christian anti-Semitism was bringing me many invitations to speak at synagogues and Jewish-Christian dialogues. But gradually it became apparent to me that there was a hidden agenda behind many of these invitations. Christians critical of the church's terrible legacy of anti-Semitism were expected to commit themselves unreservedly to the Israeli side of the Middle East conflict. I was asked in discussion periods, "Why doesn't the pope recognize the state of Israel?" I was puzzled by these queries. One evening a synagogue mother came up to me after a lecture and whispered in my ear in a state of agitation, "They are just using you." I realized that there was a big gap in my understanding of the politics of the American Jewish community toward Israel, the Palestinians, and Arab world. I needed to learn a lot more about this.

THE EIGHTIES, JEWISH WOMEN, MUSLIM WOMEN, AND THE PALESTINIANS

In 1980, I had a chance to travel to Israel in a trip organized by Jewish women from Montreal. The trip was billed as an opportunity for dialogue and peacemaking between Christian, Jewish, and Muslim women. The hope was that women might be able to talk to each other across these divisions in ways that men had not. But it soon became evident to me that the trip was totally skewed on the side of the Israeli-Jewish view of the situation. The only Muslim woman, a Canadian from Egypt, dropped out of the trip in great distress when this bias became evident. The trip did not include visits to Palestinian areas or dialogue with Palestinians, even though we were made to believe that we were hearing "both sides."

I and several other women in the trip, including a Hispanic woman from the U.S. Southwest and Charlene Hunter-Galt, a famous African American woman, then on the McNeil-Lehrer Report, decided to use our one free day on the trip to depart from the main itinerary and meet with Palestinians. We contacted Raymonda Tawil, a Palestinian journalist (later Yassir Arafat's mother-in-law). She set up a day trip to speak to Palestinian leaders, such as the mayor of Ramallah, whose legs had been blown off by an Israeli bomb, a visit to the Palestinian women's center, In-ash el-Usra, run by the indomitable Um Khalil (who later ran for President of the Palestinian Authority against Yassir Arafat), and a visit to a refugee camp.

Our hosts were visibly upset when we returned. This intensified our impression that we had uncovered the "other" world that they did not want to address. This experience made me deeply aware that there was a very different story from the one we had been given on the other side of an invisible line just a short taxi ride away from West Jerusalem. This was the underside of the state of Israel; namely, the dispossessed Palestinians. I returned to the U.S. resolved to study the history of Zionism, the state of Israel, and the Palestinian struggle.

In the spring of 1986 my husband and I had an opportunity to spend some months at Tantur, a Christian ecumenical center on the Bethlehem road next to the checkpoint between Jerusalem and Bethlehem. I took the opportunity to teach a class on Zionism, Israel, and the Palestinians, while my husband taught a course on Islam. Our stay at Tantur made us even more aware of both the blatant and the subtle ways in which guilt for anti-Semitism was being exploited to silence Christians on the dispossession of the Palestinians, ignoring their existence. We came home from the sabbatical with an outline for a book that would put this whole story together—Christian, Jewish, and Islamic views of the holy land, the history of Zionism and the Palestinian liberation struggle, and the use and abuse of holocaust theology. This was published in 1989 as the *Wrath of Jonah: The Crisis of Religious Nationalism in the Israeli-Palestinian Conflict.*

The publication of this book made evident what we had suspected; namely, that Jewish-Christian dialogue was predicated on making Christians into docile "yea-sayers" to the policies of the state of Israel, while repressing any discussion of the treatment of the Palestinians. I was no longer welcome in Jewish-Christian dialogues, and invitations to speak in synagogues about *Faith and Fratricide* disappeared, even though I had in no way changed my mind about the evils of anti-Semitism. But at the same time, more rewarding networks of colleagues—Jewish, Muslim, and Christian—opened up, working together on a more just relationship between Israelis and Palestinians, in organizations such as the Palestinian Human Rights Campaign.

THE NINETIES AND TODAY

This organization gave me more opportunities to visit Israel-Palestine and to edit collections from its conferences, such as *Beyond Occupation: American Jewish, Christian and Palestinian Voices for Peace* (1990) and *Faith and the Intifada: Palestinian Christian Voices* (1992), with Palestinian Christian leader Naim Ateek and Jewish liberation theologian Marc Ellis. Marc Ellis was director of the Peace and Justice Center of the Maryknoll School of Theology when I first met him in the '80s. When the Maryknoll school closed, he found himself in a difficult struggle to find a new job. He had become a pariah in the eyes of the American Jewish community because of his call for Jewish repentance for injustice to the Palestinians. Finally he found at job at Baylor University in Waco, Texas, where he was made both university professor and head of a center for American Jewish studies. The irony that a Southern Baptist school in Texas felt free to hire such a controversial Jewish thinker, while Christian schools on the East Coast would not touch him, was not lost on us.

Today my work on Palestinian-Israeli peace and justice goes on primarily through Sabeel, a Palestinian liberation theology center in Jerusalem founded by Naim Ateek, a Palestinian Anglican priest-theologian, with supporting groups in the U.S., Canada, England, Sweden, and elsewhere. But the situation of the Palestinians, far from improving from 1990 to today, has greatly worsened. The so-called Oslo Peace Process was exploited by Israeli leaders to appropriate more Palestinian land in the West Bank and carve the Palestinian areas into Bantustans separated by Israeli settlements and linking roads that the Palestinians were forbidden to use. This has culminated in the building of the "wall," either a thirty-foot concrete barrier or an electrified fence that digs deeply into Palestinian land, appropriating the aquifers along the green line and separating Palestinian communities from each other and from Israel. Palestinians are being literally ghettoized, separated from opportunities for travel, employment, education, water, and agricultural land, while Israelis are forbidden from traveling to the Palestinian territories, thus seeking to prevent relations between the two peoples. The plight of the Palestinians continues to be a festering sore internationally, especially for relations between the West and the Islamic world.

However intense and absorbing the Palestinian plight, I continue to be deeply committed to other areas of concern, especially the international feminist movement and its theological expression. I have long believed that feminist theology must be multicultural and multicontextual. This includes Black, Hispanic, and Asian Christian feminisms, as well as Jewish, Muslim, Buddhist, and Wiccan feminisms in the United States. In my class on Feminist Theologies in North America, I teach this range of feminist theologies across ethnic communities and religions. In a second course, which I also teach regularly, I focus on Christian feminist theologies in Latin America, Asia, and Africa. This course studies the theological reflection of the women of the Ecumenical Association of Third World Theologians.

When the Ecumenical Association first began to meet in the '70s, feminism was ignored. But by the '80s, the women of the Ecumenical Association challenged this silencing and demanded their own network through which they could contextualize their own theological reflection. As these women put it clearly to the men of the Association, "It is not for first world women to tell us how to do this and it is not for third world men to tell us feminism is not our issue." Women from Asia, Africa, and Latin America began to gather in the '80s to discuss their own theological reflection in their own contexts. I was privileged to be able to go to some of the international meetings of the third world women theologians and to engage in dialogue with women theologians in South Africa and Zimbabwe, China, Korea and Japan, the Philippines and India, and in many Central and Latin American countries. In the last chapter of my 1998 book, *Women and Redemption*, I summarize the thought of some Latin American, Asian, and African women theologians. I continue to be enriched by this dialogue.

The interconnection of feminism and ecology in what has come to be called ecofeminism also has become central to my thinking and social concerns. The major book that tries to capture this interconnection is my 1992 volume, *Gaia and God: An Ecofeminist Theology of Earth Healing*. I also tried to bring third world women's voices on ecology, feminism, and religion to first world audiences in the 1996 volume, *Women Healing Earth: Third World Women on Feminism, Religion and Ecology*. Increasingly this connection of ecology and religion is being explored on an interfaith basis. In the mid-1990s, Mary Evelyn Tucker and John Grim organized a series of conferences on ten world religions and their ecological resources. Each conference became a volume published by Harvard University Press. I became the editor of the volume on *Christianity and Ecology* (2000), while my 2005 volume, *Integrating Ecofeminism, Globalization and World Religions*, seeks to summarize the findings of all ten conferences and connect this work with ecofeminism and the struggle against corporate globalization.

My reflection on the connections between feminism, ecology, and religion has also been enriched by twenty years of participation in Buddhist-Christian dialogue. This dialogue was begun by John Cobb and Masao Abe and for many years held a series of dialogues on Buddhist and Christian teachings on such things as ultimate reality, the physical world, the path to salvation, and the role of redemptive figures and redemptive community, comparing and contrasting the Buddhist and Christian approaches to these topics. A second round of the dialogue moved from "dogmatics" to social justice issues, comparing the Buddhist and Christian approaches to poverty and wealth, war and peace, ecological crisis and sexuality. This dialogue has been enormously enriching and has given me a comparative context through which to view Christian tradition.

Throughout this twenty-year dialogue, Rita Gross, a Buddhist feminist, and I became the main carriers of the feminist aspect of this discussion. In 1999, we did a joint dialogue on Buddhist and Christian feminism at the Grail center in Ohio. We traced the biographical roots of each of our spiritual journeys, what we found liberating and what we found oppressive in each of our own traditions and what we found helpful in the other tradition, and finally, what was useful in each tradition for ecological concerns. This dialogue found its way into the 2001 book, *Religious Feminism and the Future of the Planet: A Buddhist-Christian Conversation.*

In 2001, I retired after twenty-seven years of teaching at Garrett Theological Seminary in Evanston, Illinois. My husband and I moved to a retirement community of Christian workers in Claremont, California. But I am not at all ready to retire! For five years I taught as the Carpenter Professor of Feminist theology at the GTU in Berkeley, California, seeking to renew the teaching of feminist theology in that community of theological seminaries, Catholic and Protestant. I am now teaching feminist theology on a part-time basis at the Claremont Graduate University and Theological School.

In Claremont, I am continuing to teach my major courses on first and third world feminist theologies and on ecofeminism, but I am also struggling to define what might be called a North American liberation theology—a theology of liberation from our obsession with militarism, world imperialist domination, and belief in American exceptionalism. Toward that end, I wrote the book *America, Amerikkka: Elect Nation and Imperial Violence* (2007). My questions in this book are historical, ideological, and theological. How did the idea of America as an elect nation chosen for a unique destiny get started? How was this idea renewed in the context of new stages of expansionism through the more than two hundred years of our national history? What alternative traditions of American thought can we draw upon to critique this distorting obsession? How can we overcome theologically the fallacious ideological assumptions about God's election of our nation, American innocence and goodness, the othering of evil, and an illusory dream of our imperial destiny? How can we shape alternative, healthier ways of thinking about ourselves and other people for a sustainable future for humanity on this planet? These are the questions that shape my current writing, in what perhaps will be the culminating volume of my writing and of my journey of faith and social commitment.

CONCLUSION

As is evident from this story, my intellectual journey has always been about social commitment to right relationships. My concerns have been about help- ing us, Christians and U.S. Americans, to understand how we got into these horrible distortions of racism, sexism, militarism, imperialism, exploitation of the wealth of the planet and impoverishment of others and of the earth. And how we can imagine ways to get out of these distortions? I am not simply trying to create a better theoretical self-understanding, but one that is intimately related to an alternative practice or way of being with one another and with the earth. While criticizing ideas that have promoted distortion, I also want to recuperate those traditions that represent the best of our identity, that can help us transcend false ideologies and systems of domination and to glimpse a better world of partnership with one another and with the earth. These more healthy partnerships with one another and with the earth also are the way to understand what it means to be in life-giving relation with the God in whom we are graced to live and move and have our being.

17

Moving to the Margin • Letty M. Russell

My intellectual, social, personal, and political biography is full of margins and centers, and I am constantly on the move to find the margin and to claim it as the site of my theology of resistance. As bell hooks makes clear in such writings as *Feminist Theory: From Margin to Center*, margins are socially constructed sites that dominant groups consider the location of those of "no account."[1] These margins are not always easy to locate because they (and the social, political, economic, and ecclesial power they represent) keep moving. Margins are places of connection for those who are willing to move from center to margin. They are sites of struggle for those who choose the margin and move to the center in order to gain the ability to talk back.[2] The margins are also the sign that God's New Creation is breaking in, when the distinctions of margin and center begin to blur as all share in God's hospitality.

My discipline of liberation and feminist theologies involves knowing where the margin and center are located in order to respond appropriately. Theologians such as myself make choices about moving from margin to center, or from center toward margin, according to where we find ourselves in relation to the center of power and resources, and of cultural and linguistic dominance in any particular social structure. Our connection to the margin is always related to where we are standing in regard to social privilege, and from that particular position we have at least three choices. The first is living where we are, refusing to challenge the social construction of our identity in terms of class, gender, sexuality, or race. The second is choosing the margin, working for empowerment of people who have been marginalized by the dominant cultural, political, economic, religious, or educational systems. The third is choosing to identify with those in power in the center and to emulate the dominant group.[3]

In this autobiography, I want to look at the various social locations of my life and work, asking in what way they pushed me to keep moving to the margin as part of my commitment to share in Christ's welcome of all persons into God's household or reign. First, I will describe the way that *growing up in the center* helped to shape my theology and provide me with the roots of my Christian faith and commitment. Then I will revisit the experience of *living in the margins* that shaped the themes of my theological reflection, teaching, and writing. In closing, I will look at the ways in which my work has become more and more identified with *struggling in the center* as I have found myself located in a center of elitism at Yale University.

Growing in the Center

I must confess that my critical perspective on theology was developed at a very early age. I grew up in a Presbyterian church in Westfield, a largely white, middle-strata town in northern New Jersey where my parents expected me to attend church school and/or church each Sunday. While still in kindergarten I ran away from church school and made my way home across a number of forbidden streets. On my arrival home, I greeted my startled mother with the comment, "There just is nothing there to interest a girl like me!" Interesting or not, I continued to attend that church all the way through high school, although I drew the line at attending the youth group, because I found the Jack Benny radio program was more fun.

The support of my church and my family in my upbringing was clearly important to the development of my faith in Jesus Christ and trust in God's love. But it was only much later when I began to study religion in college that I began to notice a long heritage of church involvement on both sides of my family. Although my father seldom attended church, he grew up with a grandmother in Boston, Mary Luny Russell Charpiot, who founded the Massachusetts Home for Intemperate Women in Boston in 1881. The home housed one hundred women and was the first of its kind in the United States. My mother often stayed home on Sunday with my father, but her parents were pillars of the local church, and she herself became an active lay leader after my father died.

My feminist tendencies are connected to the fact that I was born a *misfit*. As a child, I wanted to play active games and I was what they used to call a "tomboy." I refused to learn to read until I was in the fourth grade because the books about "Dick and Jane" held no interest. One day I discovered a great book on the Vikings and read it cover to cover. The next day I told the teacher I could read and wanted to be put up in the highest reading group! In the seventh grade, I was also taller than all the boys and girls, and girls who are so tall just don't fit feminine stereotypes very well.

In college, I joined the Student Christian Movement and responded to God's call to serve in the church. But when I told my business-oriented father that I wanted to be a church worker, he said, "You will always be a *misfit*." In his view, most of the secular world would consider people who worked in the church to be odd. I became more of a misfit than he or I expected. In 1955, I was one of the first two women to enter Harvard Divinity School, and in 1958, I was one of the first women to be ordained in the Presbyterian Church. In 1974, I was one of two women teaching full time at Yale Divinity School.

What was it that gave me a *sense of entitlement* even though I often did not fit the stereotypes of white, middle-class America? Probably a very important element was the fact that I grew up as the "boy" in a family with three girls, and never felt any pressure from my parents to forsake my interest in woodworking, sports, etc. I only discovered the pain of this type of behavior when I got to adolescence. In Junior High School I discovered that being five foot eight inches tall made me tower over all the other seventh-graders. When the students asked me to play "Pistol Packing Mama" in the school musical I knew what it meant to be different! Nevertheless, I continued to think of myself as one who had a great deal of entitlement.

As the speaker at graduation, I took the opportunity to talk about *noblesse oblige.* What led to this strong sense of responsibility for others? Most certainly this was the core of what I learned in my family and I my religious education. My role model was my grandmother, Letty Mandeville Towl. She labored all her life in tireless service to her family, community, and church. Her love for others enfolded me so that, although I had a strong sense of autonomy and independence, I knew that the love and care I experienced from her was what life should be about. This was particularly important because my own father was a very rigid person whose anger toward any infringement of his authority could easily have shaped me in a different way.

The theology I grew up with was orthodox Presbyterian theology, yet this never was a theology that I took seriously enough to reject. I knew very early that there were different opinions about things because my father was a Unitarian and spent Sundays at the tennis club and not in church. Clearly, the part of my faith that was nurtured the most was that of the importance of service to others, and of responsibility for one's own actions before God.

It seemed only right, therefore, that I would arrive at Wellesley College to find its motto, *non ministrari, sed minstrare* (not to be served, but to serve) emblazoned on its crest and across the chapel chancel. I had always had the sense of entitlement that assumed I would go to college, following in my mother's footsteps to Wellesley. When I graduated from the ninth grade, my present was the registration fee for Wellesley so that I could make my application! My mother's independence in seeking out a Wellesley education and her continuing loyalty to the college was also a powerful role model. I did not miss the fact that some of the most important events in my mother's life were her opportunities to attend reunions and visit with her friends in the class of 1918.

At Wellesley, I also had a strong and continuing role model in President Mildred McAfee Horton. Having served as a commander-in-chief of the

WAVES in World War II, she was already a role model for the heroic behavior that I admired growing up during the war and wanting so much to be old enough to serve in the WAVES! Again, she was a strong, caring, faithful woman who lived out Wellesley's motto day by day. But my most important role models were my peers who joined me in the co-op dorm as scholarship students. I had chosen a school where as a white woman I would not be a misfit, but I still found that my father's low economic status and my interest in religion made me somewhat "different."

This *difference* was the foundation of my life of Christian service. I found myself living with the daughters of ministers, missionaries, and teachers who could not afford Wellesley's tuition. The businessman's daughter, who thought she had escaped compulsory church attendance on high school graduation, found herself singing in the chapel choir, daily and Sunday! The one who had thought church was boring was soon involved in a Biblical History major, with extracurricular activities centered in the ecumenical religious life on campus, and in the Student Christian Movement of New England.

If my father thought religion was marginal to what counts in society, there were many people at Wellesley who did not share this opinion, including women who were teaching theology, church history, ethics, Bible, and philosophy with no thought of gender inequality. My church history professor was Louise Pettibone Smith, a social activist and exacting scholar who was the first woman to publish in *The Journal of Biblical Literature* of the Society of Biblical Literature in 1913. She was also the only woman to appear in its pages in its first forty years![4] One of my Bible professors was Lucetta Mowry, later to be the first woman on the NRSV New Testament translation committee. Neo-orthodoxy reigned in the theology department, but this sounded like the scholarly footnotes for my Presbyterian heritage. The most important theological shift in college was that of ecumenical theology. As an officer in the Student Christian Movement of New England, I planned and attended conferences and became deeply involved in the importance of connecting the work of the church to a worldwide movement for peace and for social justice.

LIVING ON THE MARGINS

When I graduated from Wellesley, I reached for the center but soon found myself living in the margins. My ecumenical connections had led me to marry a co-leader in the SCM who was attending Harvard. Following the prescribed tapes for a middle-strata white woman in 1951, I graduated, got married, and moved to Higginum, Connecticut, to teach school, and serve as a pastor's wife while my husband began his studies at Yale Divinity School. The tapes seemed not to fit me very well! I knew something was wrong when my Methodist husband was not sure he wanted to be married to me if I believed in "predestination." By the end of our first year my husband had left Yale, and abandoned me to care for his church and continue teaching my third-grade class.

In the pain of all this, I at least recognized that if I could not fulfill my Christian vocation by being a pastor's wife, I could do it by entering ministry on my own. And so I ended up in the most challenging place I could find: an ecumenical parish in East Harlem where some of my friends in the Student Christian Movement were already at work. At least there I could learn more about who I was by living in a different culture, and by finding ways to carry out Jesus' words, "not to be served, but to serve" (Matt. 20:28). There I found a home in the margin of an interracial, low-income ghetto. By raising my salary from my home church, I was able to fund my position as a Christian education director and become a home missionary of the United Presbyterian Church.

Coming to East Harlem was like coming home. Not just because my college roommate came to work with me in the East Harlem Protestant Parish as her field placement from Union Theological Seminary, or just because I was coming out of a soul-searching crisis and life change. It was home because I discovered among a marginalized community that *in God's sight no one is a misfit*, and that it is our call to join God in practicing hospitality for all persons. The community of the Church of the Ascension where I was working and of the Group Ministry of EHPP became my extended family because they welcomed my gifts as a teacher and minister.

Nevertheless, I soon found that I needed a seminary education. First and foremost because it was clear that this was my calling to work in the church and I needed an advanced degree to do the work. I also needed more extensive theological tools in order to be able to connect our daily struggles for life with the teachings of scripture and tradition. My critical perspective was also beginning to make me increasingly aware of power issues, and it did not take long for me to notice that, even in a group ministry where everyone is "equal," one needed to be a pastor in order to carry out reforms that connected education and action with the worship life of the church. In a clerical church structure, ordination is the "union card" to conducting the worship and determining the direction of the center.

I chose to attend Harvard Divinity School because I needed space from my East Harlem involvement and I had already been supervising Union Theological Seminary students for three years. I was also excited about Harvard Divinity's reorganization under President Nathan Pusey. The renewed program was headed up by Dean Douglas Horton, the husband of my mentor, Mildred McAfee Horton, and included Paul Tillich and George Buttrick as professors. Ignoring the fact that Harvard Divinity School did not admit women, I wrote and applied and said they should change their rules. They did change, and I entered as one of two women in the M. Div. Program, along with one other woman, Judith Hoelher. The two of us moved into the maid's quarters in the home of the Dean and his wife!

At Harvard, there was no mistaking the fact that I was marginal. Most of the time I was the only woman in class, and the only one addressed by my first name. My professors and friends were all men. I didn't think it made a lot of difference, as my purpose in studying was to gain the biblical tools I needed from my professors such as Amos Wilder, Frank Cross, and Krister Stendahl, and the critical tools for understanding ways of interpreting gospel and culture from Paul Lehmann and Paul Tillich. My most important question was how to interpret ethics and the teachings of the church in different social settings. Tillich's early work on the *Protestant Era* had inspired us in East Harlem to look for new ways of being a church engaged with social issues, and Lehmann's contextual ethics held the possibility of making ethical sense in an oppressed community such as East Harlem. Just how marginal I was only became apparent in retrospect when I learned that having two women graduating at the top of the class created a problem. It seems that some of my professors were reluctant to grant top honors to us because it would reflect badly on the qualifications of the men.

I returned to the East Harlem Protestant Parish and was ordained as a Pastor of the Presbyterian Church of the Ascension in 1958. My work as a pastor in the 1960s involved me heavily in the civil rights movement and led me to develop a strongly biblical theology of liberation. I was the author of the Daily Bible Reading lectionary for inner city parishes for eight years. At the same time, I became a member of the World Council of Churches working group on the Missionary Structure of the Congregation. This ecumenical work, particularly in the area of church renewal and in Faith and Order, and the Community of Women and Men Study, has continued to shape my theology.

In order to develop this theology, I enrolled in the Th.D. program at Union Theological Seminary, taking this opportunity to study again with Paul Lehmann and to develop my interests in theological education with Robert Lynn. The most influential role model in my doctoral work, however, was Hans Hoekendijk, Professor of World Christianity. In 1968, I resigned from the parish and devoted full time to writing my thesis with him on *Tradition as Mission: Study of a New Current in Theology and Its Implications for Theological Education* (1969). This thesis helped to integrate many different streams in my theology, including the Barthian emphasis on the mission of God in which the church participates, the ecumenical emphasis on the understanding of mission as God's action in handing over Jesus Christ into the hands of all generations and nations, and the educational emphasis on liberation pedagogy. Hans Hoekendijk's teachings on church renewal provided a broader and deeper basis for the technology I had developed in East Harlem.[5]

This was a time of many shifts in my life. After graduating from Union Theological I married Hans Hoekendijk in 1970 and began five wonderful years of shared partnership in theological education until his death in 1975. I began teaching at Manhattan College, a men's college run by the Christian Brothers. Although I was the only Protestant and the only woman teaching in the Religious Studies department, it did not seem strange to me that I was on the margin. I even told a woman interviewing me for a class at Princeton Theological Seminary that my story of ministry could be easily told as one of someone who served as a "Ms, Mother, and Misfit."

The new margin in my life was that of feminism. In East Harlem I had worked as an advocate for Black and Hispanic Liberation, and I saw this work as part of my Christian ministry. Social justice was part and parcel of what God's intention for creation was all about. Gradually, as I read the testimony of other women around the world and met with them in meetings of the World Council of Churches and in the YWCA, I began to realize that women, too, are often victims of social prejudice and discrimination. Thus I began to work for justice and human dignity for women together with men. In this regard, I was not only an advocate, standing in solidarity with oppressed groups, but also someone who had herself experienced what it means to be "less than human" as a woman in a church and society dominated by men.

STRUGGLING IN THE CENTER

By the early '70s, I had come to name myself not only a Christian, but also a feminist who is committed to doing theology from a feminist perspective and to advocating renewed structures of church life that practice partnership and extend a welcome to those who have been marginalized. I began to develop this commitment when I took on an additional part-time position as the Religious Consultant to the National Board of the YWCA, USA. With the YWCA and the United Presbyterian Women, I published a Bible study booklet titled "Women's Liberation in a Biblical Perspective" in 1971. Later, while teaching at United Theological College in Bangalore, India, I wrote another study book titled *Ferment of Freedom*.

My advocacy for women led me back toward the center of the white, educational establishment as I sought out a place to teach women who were preparing for ministry. After teaching part time, I went to Yale Divinity School to teach full time in 1974. Margaret Farley had begun teaching ethics at the school, but there were no other women professors. I worked with the women students to make a proposal for a full-time position in theology. I then applied for the position and with the help of Dean Colin Williams, I was appointed as an Assistant Professor of Theology.

I had greatly feared that if I moved back into a center of white privilege, I might be co-opted into the dominant power system. This was a fear that I did not need to have, for the white, male academic system is expert at marginalizing women in educational institutions as well as in the theological tradition that is being taught. If, in addition, this is an uppity woman who insists on teaching liberation and feminist theologies, and talking about social justice, the center becomes a site of marginality. I increased this marginality by welcoming the opportunity to teach in a nontenure track as a sign of my critique of the privilege of tenure. Yet, just as one needs ordination to begin to renew a church structure as long as there is a clerical system, one needs to tenure to advocate for change in a university as long as there is a tenure system. After ten years at Yale, I was finally tenured when the university terminated the nontenure track.

Following a remark I once heard Krister Stendahl make, I began speaking of theology as "thinking about what God is thinking about when God gets up in the morning." It is obvious that God is thinking about straightening up the mess, or *mending the creation*, setting it free in all its groaning parts. As a feminist theologian, I was particularly interested in the theological methods of action/reflection that emphasized the transformation needed as we share with God in the mending of creation. In this sense my feminist theology is always concerned with eschatology as it asks what it would take to transform the present in the light of God's intention for New Creation.

An important part of my work in feminist/liberation theologies is that I began to have women colleagues for the first time. As Elisabeth Schüssler Fiorenza, Rosemary Radford Ruether, and Phyllis Trible began to teach and write, this gave me a community of critique and support that could continue to be expanded. Team teaching at Yale with Margaret Farley in a course called "Feminist Theology and Ethics" was a wonderful chance to do our work as partners with one another and with the students. This same style of teaching also supported the teaching of "Feminist Theologies in Third World Perspective," where I had the opportunity to co-teach with Katie Geneva Cannon, Shawn Copeland, and Kwok Pui Lan. Modeling a cooperative style of teaching in the classroom is very important to the authenticity of feminist theologies, and the Divinity School provided a community of students and faculty where that was possible.

At Yale, I began to publish in the area of liberation and feminist theologies, starting with *Human Liberation in a Feminist Perspective: A Theology* in 1974. This book reflected the teaching I was developing in my classes, and also expressed the connections of feminist theologies to the tradition of biblical and ecumenical theology that I had already developed. A key area of my work was that of transformation of theological doctrines from a feminist perspective. For instance, I developed a theology of *koinonia*, community or partnership, in a number of books, and finally integrated a great deal of my interest in ecclesiology and community in the book *Church in the Round: Feminist Interpretation of the Church*.[6]

Struggling in the center can only be sustained creatively if you keep moving and using the margin to reach out to others. For me, the growing edge of my work has continued to be the margin. The first area is my collaboration with and advocacy for women of color. I have continued my conviction that feminist theologies are liberation theologies and include advocacy for persons in all locations of the web of oppression. Starting with *Inheriting Our Mother's Gardens: Feminist Theology in Third World Perspective* (1988), I have sought to share in the dialogue of women of all colors about their faith and cultural traditions. This book came out of a process of networking and sharing of ideas that has continued to develop. Some of this is reflected in publications with the World Council of Churches and with the Ecumenical Association of Third World Theologians. For instance, I joined Mary John Mananzan and others to publish the report of an international women's conference of EATWOT in Costa Rica in 1994, titled *Women Resisting Violence: Spirituality for Life* (Orbis, 1996).

Since 1995, in collaboration with an ecumenical women's committee in Geneva, Switzerland, I have joined Shannon Clarkson in developing a Doctor of Ministry program with San Francisco Theological Seminary with an international feminist emphasis. With the cooperation of Walter Davis, the director of Advanced Pastoral Studies at SFTS, we developed a program that supports women leaders in their own contexts, but provides access to degrees and to the study of feminist theologies where that is not available to them.

Another area that is still on the margin of theological reflection, and full of controversy, is that of queer theologies. Reflecting on my own experience of more than twenty years of partnership with a woman, I have begun to teach courses in this area and to combine my interest in biblical theology with this to develop the area of queer hermeneutics. As the churches struggle with issues of sexuality, there is also a lot to be said for the gifts that reflection out of gay, lesbian, bisexual, and transgendered experience can bring to our understanding of the social construction of our identities and of our theologies.

My advocacy for those on the margin and for the mending of God's creation continues to inform my actions and my theological reflection. My continuing emphasis on partnership and networking was very helpful in thinking about the development of feminist theologies as I joined Shannon Clarkson in editing the *Dictionary of Feminist Theologies* (Westminster John Knox, 1996). I remembered the many women and men who have made up the web of relationships in my life, and celebrated those whose lives have shaped and sustained mine. I only pray that I can keep on moving to find the margins as sites of resistance where many of the least of Jesus' brothers and sisters are to be found!

NOTES

[1] bell hooks, *Feminist Theory: From Center to Margin* (Boston: South End, 1984).

[2] bell hooks, *Talking Back: Thinking Feminist, Thinking Black* (Boston: South End, 1989), 16.

[3] Letty M. Russell, *Church in the Round: Feminist Interpretation of the Church* (Louisville: Westminster John Knox, 1993), 24–29, 192–93.

[4] Dorothy Bass, "Women's Studies and Biblical Studies: An Historical Perspective," *Journal for the Study of the Old Testament* 22 (February 1982): 8.

[5] Hans Hoekendijk, *The Church Inside Out* (Philadelphia: Fortress, 1966).

[6] See also *The Future of Partnership* (Philadelphia: Westminster, 1979); *Growth in Partnership* (Philadelphia: Westminster, 1981); *Household of Freedom: Authority in Feminist Theology* (Philadelphia: Westminster, 1987). For a discussion of the first thirty years of my ministry, see my article "Bread Instead of Stone," in *Theologians in Transition*, ed. James M. Wall (New York: Crossroad, 1981), 177–84.

18

Ecology, Justice, Liturgy • H. Paul Santmire

When my children hear that I am working on another book, they ask, "Same old, same old?" And they are right. My publishing persona for the past four decades has been focused, not to say fixated, on the theology of nature or on what I have usually preferred to call "ecological theology." This was in large measure, I think, because I could do no other. I was a full-time pastor all those years, preoccupied with officiating at the liturgy and preaching, and with the care of souls and the public witness—not a great deal of time for a broad scope of publishing adventures. This practical bent of my professional life may also explain, in part, why I have for many years felt such a theological affinity with towering classical practitioners like Irenaeus, Augustine, Luther, and Bonhoeffer. Writing works in systematic theology has never been my métier, although I have had a longstanding intellectual passion for that kind of enterprise—witness the six years of courses that I took with Paul Tillich, beginning as an undergraduate.

Whence then my theological focus or fixation on ecological theology? This is something of a puzzle, since, in my formative theological years in the late fifties and early sixties, biblical theology was dominated by a heady and self-conscious anthropocentrism—the "God-who-acts" theology of G. Ernest Wright (with whom I took a number of courses), who pitted what he thought of as historicized biblical faith over against what Wright also called the nature religion of the Canaanites. New Testament studies were then dominated by the existential analysis of Rudolf Bultmann, a favorite of college chaplains and religion teachers. Bultmann argued, revealingly, that the groaning of the whole creation that Paul talked about in Romans 8 referred to the groaning of the *human* creation only. Like his neo-Kantian mentors and Kant himself, Bultmann handed nature, which he tended to view in mechanistic terms, over to the natural scientists. In systematic theology in those years the anthropocentric theology of "salvation history" (*Heilsgeschichte*) was much in vogue (I started reading Oscar Cullmann and Karl Barth virtually my first day in seminary in 1957). Indeed, I was told a few years later by Gordon Kaufman, the American Kantian theologian who later became my dissertation advisor at Harvard Divinity School, that "theologians need not concern themselves with nature" (or words to that effect). That I learned other things about nature in the course of my studies, above all from Luther and Tillich, is another story. That I began to see that there was another, non-anthropocentric way to approach the scriptures, especially when I read what was to become an epochal 1963 article by Krister Stendahl (who had already become a kind of role model for me), "The Apostle Paul and the Introspective Conscience of the West," is also another story. More about these things in a moment.

Nor was there much public theological discussion in the late fifties and early sixties of what was already in those years becoming a major challenge for our species, the environmental crisis. This public ecological indifference only began to give way somewhat in the wake of Rachel Carson's *Silent Spring* in 1962. I myself had no idea in those years that signs of the crisis were already apparent. I did not read the Carson book until the late sixties. I was too busy with my dissertation and a year of study in Germany.

SACRAMENTAL LUTHERAN ROOTS

Yet already in the earliest years of my theological study, I found myself fascinated with the theology of nature. Why? I think it was because of the milieu in which I grew up—call it a subculture of sacramental Lutheranism. In my case, that Lutheranism was more particularly shaped by a mostly humanizing ethnic German earthiness. That subculture extended all the way from a profound reverence for the eucharist to a lighthearted indulgence in the mundane joys of this life (I learned to drink beer at church picnics). That subculture also included, at least in my parents' case, a kind of matter-of-fact reverence for the earth. When I was young, my family lived in an exurban setting in upstate New York, near Buffalo—prosperous, yes (my father was a dentist), but it was not yet suburbia, which was just then beginning to happen. My family lived in a somewhat isolated but elegant stone house that was surrounded by woods and fields and streams. I once looked at the deed to our home for a high school history project, and found what to me were exciting references to Indian (as we said in those days) ownership of our land around 1880, which I thought of now and again as I wandered through the nearby fields and woods in solitude, contemplating redwing blackbirds, discovering pheasant nests, and overturning stones in the stream in order to observe crayfish. My father spent much of his discretionary time caring for our land, which for him especially meant planting a variety of specimen trees. The family also had a sizeable "victory garden" as many did in that World War II era, and all of us worked that garden together. I warmly remember harvesting bushels of tomatoes and helping my mother can them.

But this early experience with the earth wasn't only local. As soon as gasoline rationing ended after World War II, my parents packed my brother and sister and me into a station wagon, and we spent several weeks exploring a number of national parks in the West, among them Yellowstone, Glacier, and the Black Hills. We tented almost every evening. I still recall those awe-inspiring experiences, both driving and also taking numerous "sightseeing" walks surrounded by vast wilderness vistas. My family made several such summer trips, also to the Pacific Northwest and the Southwest. Later, as a graduate student, when I was able to turn myself loose in many intellectual directions, I suppose it was no accident that I fell in love with the writings of the nineteenth-century American naturalist and national parks advocate (and disciple of Calvin in his heart of hearts), John Muir, whose collected works I read cover to cover.

THE LUTHERAN CHURCH AND THE HOLOCAUST

But there was a dark side to this sacramental Lutheranism and its ethnicity, too, which I only discovered after I had entered into a quite different cultural world as an undergraduate at Harvard College in 1953. There a crisis of faith was thrust upon me, from which, I think, I have never fully recovered. I discovered the Holocaust, existentially. Or, better, the Holocaust discovered me. At the end of the war, I had seen some newsreel films about the liberation of some of the camps. The photos of the piles of bodies and the emaciated survivors horrified me. But I must have repressed those experiences entirely. As I recall, I never talked about them with anyone, nor was I ever called upon at home or in school or at my church to discuss what I had seen in those films. I am not sure when the very expression, the Holocaust, gained currency in my social and religious world. Remarkably, I remained consciously oblivious to the Holocaust through the end of my high school years.

All this changed one day, as I sat in a German history class when I was a sophomore. The instructor began to review the story of the Holocaust and then narrate how many "good Germans" turned the other way when the Jews were carted off to the camps. He talked, too, about Lutheranism's long tradition of hostility to the Jews in Germany, beginning in a most ugly fashion with Luther himself. He also described the Lutheran traditions of unquestioning obedience to the state, predicated on a reading of Romans 13. Those were *my* people! That was the church that had so powerfully nourished me since I had been a child! Not a few Lutherans became "German Christians," said the instructor. Me? World War II had long been over, but I had never even thought about the meaning of the Holocaust before! Why hadn't we discussed it at my church? Why hadn't synodical bodies addressed this issue, or speakers at youth rallies or Bible camps? In that class that day, I found myself at the edge of tears. I still feel those tears.

Providentially, in due time, I was befriended by a pastor during this crisis of faith: Henry E. Horn, of University Lutheran Church, Cambridge. He was later to become my senior colleague and lifetime mentor in the ministry. He introduced me to Bonhoeffer, among others, who opened my mind and heart to encounter the theology of the Confessing Church in Germany of that era. In the midst of a certain intellectual incoherence about such matters for a couple of years, I was subsequently assigned to a wonderful history tutor who took me under his wing, notwithstanding the fact that he was an agnostic and that his reading of Lutheran history in Germany was much more critical than even mine had come to be. In due course, I wrote my undergraduate honors thesis on the German resistance to Hitler, which focused on a number of leading lights of the resistance movement, among them Bonhoeffer. In those studies, I also learned that the Nazis themselves were champions, in their own way, of the theology of nature! A heroic Nordic wilderness-ethos of "blood and soil" (*Blut und Boden*) permeated much of their propaganda.

ECOLOGY AND JUSTICE

That undergraduate experience bequeathed to me two of the themes that have been at the forefront of my theological mind and heart ever since, although in different ways: the theology of nature, and the theology of justice. In light of the National Socialist celebration of nature, never again would I be able to be, if indeed I had ever been, simply a nature romantic. Nature, I had learned (although I did not know this language at that time), was in significant measure a social construction, for better or for worse. As the scales fell from my eyes when I looked at my own beloved Lutheran tradition, I would never again be able to think of the church, or anything else for that matter, without also thinking of the claims of justice for the despised and the oppressed.

This commitment to each of these themes—ecology and social justice—left me in what I perceived to be a remarkably lonely position, especially in the early years of my theological career.[1] In that era, both within and beyond the church, numerous advocates spoke up defending nature. The American scene did not lack people who championed the cause of "the land" or "the wilderness," those venerable themes from American history. Numerous advocates, again, both within and beyond the church, also dedicated themselves to fighting for social justice, as the struggles against racism and the war in Vietnam moved more and more to the front page. But few were inclined to speak and act on behalf of *both* nature *and* social justice. Often, therefore, I found myself talking justice with the ecology people and ecology with the justice people. This has been a struggle for me ever since. There is, in fact, a deep-seated tension between the concerns of the ecology party and the social justice party, a tension, indeed, that cannot merely be talked away or resolved by some higher intellectual synthesis. But I am getting ahead of myself.

By 1963, the time had come for me to settle on a dissertation topic, in the field I had chosen—"systematic and historical theology." I might have opted to work on Tillich, whose writings I thoroughly knew by then (I was a member of what I think was Tillich's last graduate colloquium at Harvard, which focused on his *Systematic Theology*). But my theological excitement in those days—and to this very day—was not first with a Tillichian "apologetic theology" that followed a "method of correlation," however important that was and is. Instead, it was first and foremost with the theology of the Word. Tillich had made a place for what he called "kerygmatic theology" and I found myself eagerly exploring that place. This was no doubt because of my existential engagement with the story of the Confessing Church, and with the figure of Bonhoeffer in particular. For these reasons, I gravitated as a matter of course toward a dissertation on Barth, who had been so deeply involved in launching the Confessing Church. Along the way, I also thoroughly immersed myself in Luther studies, under the tutelage of Heiko Oberman. I previously had worked on Luther during a year's study at the Lutheran Theological Seminary at Philadelphia with that institution's dogmatician at the time, Martin Heinecken. He interpreted Luther both historically and existentially, and was particularly helpful to me in opening up Luther's rich theology of nature. Those Luther studies formed a kind of bridge for me to Barth, who himself constantly engaged the theology of Luther (especially in Barth's long, historical footnotes in his *Church Dogmatics*). So it was the theology of the Word of God, rather than the theology of correlation, that most claimed my mind and heart—and still does.

BARTH'S THEOLOGY OF NATURE

But I chose to come at Barth (brashly perhaps) not on his own terms, but on mine. I decided that I wanted to study his theology of nature, notwithstanding the fact that Barth had announced in volume three of his *Church Dogmatics* that there is no such thing as a legitimate theology of nature. ("Nature" was then, and is now, notoriously difficult to define; I have regularly worked with the theological-phenomenological construct that nature is the biophysical dimension of God's creation.) Barth self-consciously defined theology as "the-anthropology," as a doctrine of "God and man" (as we all said in those days). I argued that by focusing his theology in such a way, Barth baptized a nontheological doctrine of nature by default—the instrumental, utilitarian, and mechanistic view championed by bourgeois society in the West. Better, I maintained, to develop a theology of nature on biblical grounds (conversant with the findings of modern science, to be sure) than to end up in that kind of theological dead end.

Although I did not deal with Barth's sacramental theology in my dissertation, that theme was very much on my mind as well. How could Barth ever envision a theology of the real presence of Jesus Christ in Word and Sacrament, as Luther did, I wondered, if nature—the world of material existence—was something to be viewed only as a symbol, as a resource, as an instrument, or even as a machine? In this respect, my thinking had been shaped by an early and careful reading of one of Tillich's most insightful essays, "Nature and Sacrament." There Tillich showed that the modern Protestant theology of nature was an expression of the spirit of the victorious bourgeoisie. Was that spirit lurking deep within the monumental argument of the *Church Dogmatics*? I concluded that it was—notwithstanding Barth's own laudable, but finally unconvincing efforts in the *Church Dogmatics* to affirm the goodness of the whole creation.

COLLEGE CHAPLAINCY

No sooner was my dissertation completed than I found myself unavoidably thrust into the sometimes silly, sometimes poignant, often passionately committed era of the late sixties and early seventies as a college chaplain, first for three years at Harvard, based at University Lutheran Church, then for thirteen years as Chaplain and Lecturer in Religion at Wellesley College. I did a lot of theology, as I thought of it in those days, on my feet. I was a mostly low-profile church activist and essayist, like many others. I stood with students who sat in on the Mallinckrodt Building at Harvard, protesting the role of Dow Chemical in the Vietnam War. I served on the steering committee of what was to become a national movement, Vietnam Summer. I walked, from time to time, with a pastoral colleague, an African American community leader, who picketed the Boston School Committee for 114 days. I stood as a wary witness in an inner-city police station once, when the call had gone out to clergy to be visibly present in such places during Boston's "civil disturbances," in order to help guard against police brutality. I stood in silent vigils in a suburban town square many times, gave many speeches against racism, against the war, and on behalf of the environment, all with the theology of the Confessing Church in the back of my mind.

It was a good era to be interested in both ecology and social justice, theologically, notwithstanding the inherent difficulties in holding these concerns together. People in those times, for better or for worse, looked to clergy for prophetic leadership. At Wellesley, I worked with a student leader named Hillary Rodham, who had a distinguished future before her; but in those days she was only one among many similar leaders who were morally driven by issues like peace and justice. I wish I had kept copies of my commencement prayers from those years, which became a kind of *cause célèbre* at the college, for reasons that I never fully understood at the time. In retrospect, it appears to me that those prayers—despite the fact that they were indeed devotionally addressed to God, or perhaps precisely because of that address—were expressions of a kind of public theology that circumstances had been calling me to develop.

In the late sixties and the seventies, I also found it relatively easy to publish op-ed pieces and other essays on the themes of ecology and social justice, in journals like *Dialog* and in the local press. In the same vein, the biologist Paul Lutz and I co-authored a book intended for popular consumption, *Ecological Renewal*.[2] Presiding over the Sunday chapel services at Wellesley also gave me the opportunity to provide a platform for, and also to meet and converse with leading lights of the late sixties and early seventies, people like William Sloane Coffin, Andrew Young, Jesse Jackson, James Cone, Jane Fonda, and progressive Catholic priests like Anthony Mullaney and James Carroll.

In those years, I discovered, too, what was for me the new wave of theological feminism. I brought people like Mary Daly and Rosemary Ruether to the college campus, and became a public advocate of their right to a hearing, in a setting where, in those days, both faculty and students were not always interested in feminist thinking. I began to develop what was to become a deep interest in theological feminism, not chiefly by any prescience, I hasten to add, but mainly out of a sense of professional self-preservation. As a male chaplain and teacher at an all-women's college, I *knew* I had to be out in front of the curve on that one. Thereafter, I was particularly taken with the developing thought of Rosemary Ruether, and with the emergence of "ecofeminism" as a central theme in her work. Although I have not written as a theological ecofeminist (for good reasons, I think), I always have consciously tried to ask the questions raised by thinkers like Ruether, and later, Sallie McFague, in order to be as sure as possible that I was "for them," however implicitly, rather than "against them." I did the same for other liberation theologians, which I read avidly in those years, above all the works of James Cone.

Such interests—the Confessing Church, the theology of liberation—have stayed with me ever since. They came to their most visible expression for me some years later, first, in an essay, "The Liberation of Nature: Lynn White's Challenge Anew,"[3] in which I argued that the liberation of nature goes hand in hand with other forms of liberation; then in my theological narrative, *South African Testament: From Personal Encounter to Theological Challenge*,[4] a book based on a firsthand engagement with the South African church and with the apartheid system at the height of its power.

BROTHER EARTH

It was while I was at Wellesley that I produced my first book, *Brother Earth: Nature, God, and Ecology in a Time of Crisis*.[5] Over against what I then called the "exclusive the-anthropology" of Barth, whereby the main objects of theological reflection were God and humanity, I proposed that both Luther and Calvin, notwithstanding their own commitments to a certain kind of anthropocentrism, in fact thought in terms of an "inclusive the-anthropology." Their theological framework was tripolar, not dipolar. They consistently thought in terms of God, humanity, *and* nature. More particularly, I explored Calvin's rich theology of divine providence in nature and Luther's profound conceptualization of God as "in, with, and under" the world of nature. (Luther once observed that there are greater miracles in a grain of wheat than there are in the Sacrament of the altar.)

I also sought to undergird my argument, necessarily so, given my commitment to a Word of God theology, by developing my own biblical interpretation throughout *Brother Earth*. I was encouraged in these efforts by Stendahl's non-anthropocentric reading of Paul, particularly by Stendahl's accent on the world-historical, even cosmic, meanings of Paul's treatment of the controversies over Jews and Gentiles in the early church. I continued the practice of doing much of my own biblical exegesis for many years, with fear and trembling. But I had no other choice, since most biblical scholars, until relatively recently, either were not interested in the theology of nature or they uncritically assumed that the Scriptures were fundamentally anthropocentric.

Brother Earth also employed a kind of correlative method, undoubtedly a sign of Tillich's influence on my understanding of the task of theology. Following the historian Perry Miller (I audited two of his courses as an undergraduate), I diagnosed a schizophrenia in American culture between nature and civilization. I suggested that in America, the ancient dichotomy between the country and the city had become a kind of sociopolitical obsession. Thus American culture did indeed have a historic fascination with the wilderness, as contrasted to the alleged impurities of the city, a theme articulated classically by Thoreau. But it also simultaneously championed "manifest destiny" and "progress"—witness Emerson's celebration of the railroad—and as a result, typically showed little regard for wilderness values. I argued that Christian faith offers an answer to that schizophrenia, that split between nature and civilization. That answer, I maintained, is evident above all in the testimonies of biblical prophets like Second Isaiah, but also in traditional Christian thinking about the kingdom of God as the end (*telos*) of all things. Nature and civilization are kin, I maintained, insofar as both are rooted and shaped by God's immanent providence and by the coming kingdom of God.

Brother Earth had a number of liabilities, I now realize. The title itself was problematic. It rightly suggested kinship as the normative human relationship with nature; but I resisted then (for some good reasons, but mostly for bad reasons) thinking of nature metaphorically as female. I also all too easily affirmed a kingdom of God theology, blithely unaware of the then-emerging feminist critique of such symbols. And, not unrelated, I was unaware that my theology of human dominion, at points, did not sufficiently guard against the inroads of the modern Protestant/Capitalist/Marxist understanding of dominion as domination. Still, I think that that book did make at least two significant contributions to the then-growing discussion of the theology of nature.

First, I insisted on the theme that God has a history of God's own with the vast world of nature, apart from nature's meaning for humans (by 1970, I was regularly talking about "the integrity of nature"). Second, I drew on the argument of one of my first published articles, "I-Thou, I-It, and I-Ens,"[6] which was a conversation with Martin Buber, to identify a human relationship with nature and with God in nature that did not turn nature into an "It." Analogous to an I-Thou relationship, I maintained, an I-Ens relationship with a tree (Buber's example), was not objectifying, but neither was it strictly personal (humans do not converse with trees). More particularly, I envisioned the human-nature relationship in terms of wonder and respectful reciprocity. All this I set forth, as a good American neo-Reformation thinker, in conversation with Luther and Calvin—and Muir. I am grateful that, beginning with Mary Daly's first edition of *Beyond God the Father*, the conceptuality of an I-Ens relation has found a place in numerous works by ecological thinkers, and even in the works of some theologians.

Brother Earth also left me with an unfinished theological agenda. The keystone of the argument of the book was its christological center. But my description of that center was underdeveloped. Perhaps that was because I had yet to come to terms, in one way or another, with Barth's famous "christological concentration," which was much under discussion in theological circles in those days. Be that as it may, I began to think about such matters more and more in the ensuing years, particularly as I came under the influence of Joseph Sittler during the 1970s. I had, of course, read Sittler's famous 1961 address to the World Council of Churches in New Delhi, where Sittler called for a new "cosmic Christology," but in those days I was preoccupied with other things, like walking picket lines. That lack of attention to Christology changed as I developed a personal relationship with Sittler, during the time when we were the theologians selected to help write the 1973 statement and theological study guide on the environment for the Lutheran Church in America. He graciously befriended me and publicly affirmed my work. In turn, I sat at his feet and particularly benefited from reading his *Essays in Nature and Grace*.[7] The theme of developing a cosmic Christology has preoccupied me and challenged me to this very day.[8]

REVISITING THE CHRISTIAN THEOLOGICAL TRADITION

But, in the late seventies, I bracketed such constructive challenges in favor of a historical task—revisiting the classical Christian theological tradition from the perspective of ecological theology. Ironically, perhaps, I only became aware of what James Nash called "the ecological complaint against Christianity" relatively late in the day. My interests in the theology of nature had been well established by the time I first read the now ubiquitously cited 1967 article, "The Historical Roots of Our Ecologic Crisis," by the historian Lynn White Jr., to which I have already referred. In that article, White charged that historic Christianity must bear a "huge burden of guilt" for the environmental crisis. That enormously popular expression of the ecological complaint against Christianity, along with my growing awareness of the severity of the environmental crisis itself, gave me a new sense of urgency about the theological path on which I had embarked. As a matter of course, then, I referred to the White thesis in the Preface to *Brother Earth* and I offered that book, in part, as an answer to White's contention that Christianity (except for St. Francis) has always been ecologically bankrupt.

During the seventies, White's argument had become the mantra of many academic critics of Christianity and even of some theologians, among them Christian feminists and advocates of Native American spirituality. Gordon Kaufman, who had supervised my dissertation on Barth and who, as he told me a few years ago, had begun to shift his own thought about the theology of nature in response to my study of Barth, publicly launched what was for him a new theological program in 1972. Kaufman came to believe, for his own systematic reasons, that, in effect, Lynn White was right: historic Christianity was bankrupt ecologically and it therefore must be totally reconstructed. I encountered that kind of judgment on many college campuses and, surprisingly, in some church circles, particularly in outdoor ministries of the church. I myself had been working all along with a quite different reading of the classical Christian tradition, so, in my available scholarly time, I began to devote myself to developing a fresh interpretation of classical Christian thought about nature. It was a long gestation period. There was much work to be done.

THE TRAVAIL OF NATURE

The eventual result was my study, *The Travail of Nature: the Ambiguous Ecological Promise of Christian Theology,*[9] thankfully endorsed by a variety of scholars, including John Cobb, Langdon Gilkey, and, *mirabile dictu*, Lynn White himself. I originally intended that book to be a shot across the bow, as it were, a kind of public theological announcement that indeed there are hidden ecological riches in classical Christian thought, notwithstanding a whole range of sometimes profound ambiguities regarding the theology of nature. I approached the subject archeologically, as I said in the book itself, only sinking down a few trenches into the tradition, so to speak, to see what I might find as a way to encourage others to begin to excavate the whole site. I singled out the following theologians for special attention: Irenaeus and Origen; the young and the mature Augustine; Thomas, Bonaventure, and Francis; Luther and Calvin; Barth and Teilhard de Chardin. Invoking a method of metaphorical analysis, I identified two major Christian ways of thinking about nature throughout the ages, the one ecological, the other spiritualizing and anthropocentric.

Soberingly, the wave of historical studies of classical Christian thought about nature that I had hoped would emerge in the wake of *The Travail of Nature* never did appear. Except for a few exceptions, historic Christian thinking about nature remains a largely uncharted territory. I have a number of ideas about why this has been the case, but I am still pondering the matter. This is not to suggest that Christians today are not interested in the theology of nature. On the contrary, the church at all levels—ecumenical, denominational, synodical, and congregational—is intensely engaged with ecological and re-lated justice issues, drawing on whatever theological resources it can muster. And the ecumenical church today does have access to a number of highly reliable ecological guides in this respect, from little-known forerunners like Joseph Sittler to highly regarded systematicians like Jürgen Moltmann. That much of this is happening, however, without benefit of substantive access to the church's classical traditions gives me pause.

Thankfully, there has been a kind of ecological revolution in biblical studies in recent years, particularly in Old Testament theology. But even if our churches today, inspired by guides like Sittler and Moltmann, do find a way to claim that theological revolution in biblical studies as their own, it would be a practice fraught with difficulties. It surely would be foolhardy to try to leap from the current situation of a world in crisis and a church seeking to minister to that world, in order to land in the midst of biblical theology and then return, without having engaged the classical tradition that continues to so deeply shape the life and thought of the church, for better or for worse. I can understand why Elizabeth A. Johnson has forthrightly called such neglect of historic traditions by the ecumenical church today irresponsible.

NATURE REBORN AND PREACHING

Notwithstanding such difficulties, and grateful for the continuing use of *The Travail of Nature* in a variety of church circles, especially among Catholics, I have persevered theologically. I find that some of my best theological work happens when I am "on the circuit," as I continue to be, well into my retirement. Should anyone wish to see a snapshot of what I say to audiences in seminary, college, synodical, and congregational settings, I invite him or her to turn to my volume *Nature Reborn: The Ecological and Cosmic Promise of Christian Theology*.[10] This little book can serve as an introduction to ecological theology in our time. I describe what I think are the theological options today: the way of the reconstructionists (Christianity is ecologically bankrupt, let us begin anew); the apologists (Christianity has all it needs in its doctrine of stewardship of creation, let us interpret it); and the revisionists, in whose ranks I number myself (Christianity has an ambiguous ecological history, let us reclaim its ecological riches wherever we can). Pursuant to my own revisionist agenda, I take issue with those who uncritically accept the ecological complaint against Christianity (with particular reference to Matthew Fox). I call attention to neglected ecological themes in biblical theology, while at the same time I argue that some major expressions of Christian theology, however relevant they might seem in this era of global crisis, are ecologically suspect (citing the exemplary case of Teilhard de Chardin). I conclude with brief discussions of the ecological dimensions of Christian ritual, spirituality, and ethics.

Nature Reborn is thus a kind of comprehensive statement of my standard "stump speech," as I travel around the country, addressing a variety of groups. A question I often hear at the end of such addresses is this: How come we never hear things like this from the pulpit? That question could come from a college professor, or even from a professional environmentalist, who happens to be a worshipper at St. John's Around the Corner. I suspect that the professor and the environmentalist *may* have heard it in their home parish, but that they might not have been prepared to take it to heart then and there. As a pastoral practitioner for many years, I am well aware of the difficulties preaching what one believes in this respect, not to speak of practicing what one preaches.

The homiletical challenges at the front lines of the church's mission in America today are enormous, from issues of making sense out of the gospel in our era "after the death of God," to coming to terms with the nihilism that dwells in the souls of many Americans in our times. Is war the only way? Does peace really have a chance? Is there any hope for a genuinely Christian family life? Why are so many young African American men in prison? Why are so many of our children being shot on the streets of our cities? Are we going to succumb to the ravages of global warming? How can we begin to see, never mind respond to, the suffering of the invisible and impoverished masses around the globe today? How can we genuinely lead lives of "voluntary simplicity" and also public witness? What are we to make of the coming cosmic death of the whole universe? And by the way, pastor, why aren't you preaching so as to fill all the pews so that we can pay all the bills and also do all manner of other good things?

We preachers therefore need all the help we can get.[11] It's not easy to preach from the church's lectionary and, at the same time, to address both themes of ecology and social justice effectively. The sermons may be biblical, incisive, and well delivered, but the congregations' readiness to hear and then respond may not be sufficient, given everything else that is on their minds. The "anguish of preaching" that Joseph Sittler talked about in 1966 is still with us, perhaps even more so than four decades ago.

Ritualizing Nature and the Eucharist

In the last few years, therefore, I have come to this conclusion, with ever-firmer conviction: the theology of the kind that comes to expression in *Nature Reborn*, in my speeches on the stump, and in my preaching, while good and true and beautiful, is not enough. Lutherans like myself have invested enormously in the theology of the Word, following Luther himself. But something, at least in our time, has been missing. This brings me to consider what I now think is the culminating stage of my theological autobiography, represented by my most recent book, *Ritualizing Nature: Renewing Christian Liturgy in a Time of Crisis*.[12] I did have a chapter on ritual in *Nature Reborn*, but this new book represents a much longer immersion in those deep waters.

Throughout the forty years of my vocational trajectory, I have, as I have already indicated, always thought things through as a practitioner, not just as an author, nor just as a kind of peripatetic theological stump speaker. If, indeed, I were to call forth one image of my vocational trajectory, before all others, I would see myself preaching and officiating at the eucharist. The liturgy of the church, and my calling to preside over that liturgy, has always been at the heart of my vocational life.

It began with a very good grounding, as I have already noted, as a protégé of Henry Horn in Cambridge. At Wellesley College, I struggled to make available the deep claims of the liturgy in the midst of a sixties and late-seventies culture that made it easy for faculty and students to assume that inherited forms of worship were either irrelevant or counterrevolutionary. During my thirteen years as an inner-city pastor in the then fourth-poorest city in the country, Hartford, Connecticut, I did preside over the transformation of a congregation from a white German-ethnic community to a racially mixed neighborhood church, and I did become the "Godfather" of an Alinsky-style neighborhood organization. But I invested still more energy encouraging that congregation to be claimed by the historic liturgy of the church. Likewise for my ministry of seven years in a large, historic downtown church in Akron, Ohio, once pastored by Franklin Clark Fry (whose countenance was later to appear on the cover of *Time* magazine, under the rubric "Mr. Protestant"). Housed in a beautiful and spacious gothic building, blessed with one of the great pipe organs in the country, and proud of its venerable Lutheran heritage, that congregation, or at least its leaders at that time, *knew* what their worship *should* be. Call this the Gothic dream of middle American Protestantism: a beautiful dream, but, in my view, much too vulnerable to the forces of acculturation, much too predisposed to foster a church that embodied what Churchill said of the Anglican church of his day—"the Tory party at prayer." It was a struggle, therefore, to introduce that congregation to some of the major reforms that emerged from the Movement for Liturgical Renewal a half-century before, let alone themes from liberation theology. But I relished that struggle.

Some things, I suppose, never change. I began my life in the church as a sacramental Lutheran and I am now concluding it as a sacramental Lutheran, although hopefully of a higher order. My ministry, both as a practitioner and a theologian, has always been shaped—insofar as it has been given me to do so—by Luther's understanding of the real presence of Jesus Christ in Word and Sacrament, and in the people of Christ ministering to each other and to the world, for the sake of "the forgiveness of sins, life, and salvation." This is why I think that my book *Ritualizing Nature* represents the culmination of my whole vocational trajectory.

FORMING CHRISTIAN IDENTITY

What does "ritualizing nature" mean? Consider this premise: liturgy is the church's mode of identity formation. Not theology, as such. Not merely preaching, which is theology as personal address (the *viva vox evangelii*). No, the church's ritual, its liturgy, makes all the difference. Such a premise reflects a wide range of cultural studies, which show that ritual, more generally, is the human mode of identity-formation. Erik Erikson, for example, argued that without rituals, the human infant would not develop what Erikson called basic trust and therefore would not be able to grow into psychological maturity. An example: morning after morning, a parent comes into a child's room and smiles at the child. This ritual inculcates basic trust. Analogously, for Christian ritual: when Christians "do this," as the Lord commanded, when they break bread and drink wine together, they are practicing, embodying, becoming habituated to the self-giving love of Christ, who "on the night in which he was betrayed" said, "do this in remembrance of me." Christian ritual thereby forms Christian character, which in turn, shapes Christian action in the world.

In *Ritualizing Nature*, I argue that *the whole liturgy must be right*, if the church's ecological and justice praxis is to be right. Practice will not make perfect. But practice—if it is good practice—will in all likelihood make possible. Consider the shape of the eucharistic prayer as a case in point. The tradition on the side of the Reformation churches has been to minimize the use of a full eucharistic prayer, for fear of introducing themes of sacrifice that contradict the gospel of the free grace of God. The tradition on the side of the Counter-Reformation church also has been to minimize the use of a full eucharistic prayer, in favor of the "words of institution," spoken silently, as the consecrating moment of the eucharist. The theology of penance, inherited from the late Middle Ages—and with that theology, the emphasis on the forgiveness of sins—has thus shaped both the Reformation and the Counter-Reformation traditions.

This has meant that a transaction addressing the individual believer's interiority has moved to the center of the liturgical experience: it is all "for me" (*pro me*). Consider, in contrast, how the post-Vatican II reemphasis on the full eucharistic prayer, in both Protestant and Catholic circles, has broadened eucharistic horizons of meaning. Now the ecumenical church gives thanks for the fullness of God's creative and redemptive activity. In that context, we are shaped by what is done; and that "what" is nothing less than what is being done by God in, with, and under the whole creation, and in, with, and under the ritual life of the church, in particular. The Reformation/Counter-Reformation liturgy thus tends to shape Christians mainly for their solitary spiritual struggles, while the post-Vatican II liturgy tends to shape them also for their communal involvement in God's wondrous and sometimes alienating works with the whole creation, as well as in God's marvelous and miraculous works within the church as a ritual community.

CLOSING WORDS

In this way, *Ritualizing Nature* brings together for me in a most gratifying and self-conscious fashion those two themes that have preoccupied me most throughout the course of my theological trajectory, ecology and social justice, each one and both together driven by the promise of the gospel, announced and formed in the church's ritual practices. As a liturgical practitioner for more than four decades, I now realize that I have been seeking to discover and embody this kind of unified theological vision my whole vocational life, in my preaching, my teaching, my writing, my counseling, my officiating, and my public witness. But now in my seventh decade, my remaining years on this earth are few. I can only hope that all these vocational labors will not have been in vain, that there might be others in the church standing ready to learn at least from some of them.

I hope, too, that the reader will understand that I am well aware—soulfully aware—that the theological trajectory I have narrated here by no means tells the whole story. It says nothing explicitly about my personal failures or losses, my times of vocational inertia or my spiritual sloth. Nor does it disclose the dynamics of my care of souls over the years or how I tried, in many modest ways behind the scenes, to be a prophetic pastoral leader. Nor, again, does it tell how grateful I am each morning when I see the daylight, smile at my wife of forty years, contemplate photos of my children and grandchildren, and begin to think about mundane things like gardening, taking a walk, or watching the Boston Celtics on TV. Neither does it tell about the ecstatic joy and the centering peace that I experience on any given Sunday morning, as I stand with the members of the inner-city congregation to which I now belong and sing my heart out. But that is another story for another time, perhaps.

NOTES

[1] I highlighted them sharply in a 1976 article in the *Christian Century*, reprinted in *Readings in Ecology and Feminist Theology*, ed. Mackinnon and McIntyre (Kansas City: Sheed & Ward, 1995), ch. 5.

[2] Philadelphia: Fortress Press, 1972.

[3] *Christian Century*, 102, no. 18 (May 22, 1985): 530–33.

[4] Grand Rapids: Eerdmans, 1987.

[5] New York: Thomas Nelson, 1970.

[6] *Journal of Religion* 67, no. 3 (July 1968), 260–73.

[7] Philadelphia: Fortress Press, 1972.

[8] See my essay, "So That He Might Fill All Things: Comprehending the Cosmic Love of Christ," *Dialog* 42, no. 3 (Fall 2003): 257–78.

[9] Minneapolis: Fortress Press, 1985.

[10] Minneapolis: Fortress Press, 2000.

[11] This is why the volume edited by David Rhoads, *Earth & Word: Classic Sermons on Saving the Planet* (New York: Continuum, 2007), to which I contributed one of the thirty-six sermons collected there, is so important for the whole ecumenical church.

[12] Minneapolis: Fortress Press, 2008.

19

Planting Trees • Hans Schwarz

I was born in 1939 just before World War II in Schwabach, known to Lutheran theologians for the Schwabach Articles, a town in the Franconian part of Bavaria in Germany. My father was a gardener and my grandparents owned a small farm. Being connected with the soil and getting my hands dirty has been natural for me. Wherever I lived, I had my own vegetable garden. This got me in touch with nature; so theology and nature for me belong together.

My family was not particularly religious. They participated in the eucharist twice a year and in the solemn service of confession the evening before. Whether they also went to church other times, I do not remember. The attitude of my paternal grandmother was: if religion does not help, at least it does not hurt. Nevertheless, one of my earliest memories is sitting next to her while she read Bible stories to me from a book illustrated with black-and-white pictures. I vividly recall the image of people drowning and a few clinging to treetops and others fleeing to a high mountain. It must be the story of the flood told to me by my grandmother. During my childhood years in the immediate World War II and post–World War II ears, children's books were unknown, and so her book with Bible stories was the only one available to me.

My grandmother, who lived with us as a member of our extended household, was an important figure for me in other ways. Whenever I returned from the university on weekends, she always cooked for me and polished my shoes. Otherwise she refused to do any household chores and left everything up to my mother. Yet I was special in her heart and she in mine.

The same relationship prevailed with my paternal grandfather. Once my grandma had passed away, he attended church every Sunday. Since he was hard of hearing due to an injury from World War I, he always sat in the front row. Never did I hear any comment about the sermon, only that the preacher was loud enough or that his voice was so low that my grandfather could not understand him. After my grandfather, then in his upper eighties, had broken a rib crossing the doorstep to church, he finally stayed home. Nevertheless, every Sunday morning he read a printed sermon in the ancient Stark's *Andachtenbuch* and every morning and night I heard him in a strong whisper pray his evening and morning prayers. In every respect for me he was a saintly person.

There is no mention of my father, because I was only three when he was killed by Russian guerrillas behind the front line in the faraway Caucasus mountains. My only memory of him is when the letter arrived stating that he had died. Fortunately, after World War II, my mother married again and now I had a father, never thinking I should call him "stepfather." Even better, soon I also had a brother.

The Seedling

Through my studying theology, my mother moved closer to the church while my father never took much interest in it, either in a positive or in a negative way. The main religious and theological influence for me was the YMCA. In Germany, the YMCA is not mainly an athletic institution as it is in the USA. Rather, as Dwight L. Moody had originally envisioned it, the "Y" strives to bring young persons to Christ. For example, the YMCA did all the youth work in our congregation. I became part of a youth group and later on part of the Bible study group. After playing games in the youth group, we usually listened to a story read by our leader and then our gathering concluded with prayers. As a young man, I remember heated discussions in our Bible study about whether it was allowed for a Christian to dance. In the Gymnasium (high school), virtually all of us attended formal dance lessons, girls at age seventeen and boys at age eighteen. Our YMCA leaders told us that dancing alone is not a sin, but dancing with others leads one astray. It was only through the perseverance of my mother that I reluctantly joined the formal dance class. I don't think this did any harm to me religiously or otherwise. Nevertheless, I was a faithful member of the YMCA and through its influence decided that I should pick up a Christian vocation.

Since my health was not that strong, I decided against becoming a missionary. Yet nothing spoke against becoming a pastor. When one of our teachers one day asked us fourteen-year-olds whether we already knew what profession we would want to pursue, I was the only one who foolhardily volunteered: "I will become a pastor." From that time on, all my classmates knew that one day I would be a pastor. But as years went by, the decision was no longer so clear for me anymore, especially since I discovered my love for chemistry. I liked the formalized language of chemical formulas and reactions and I enjoyed creating different compounds. After I had marred our bathtub, my parents gave me a separate room for a lab.

But when graduation came around, I still didn't know what to do, study theology or chemistry. I left it up to the final grades, but they were even. So the first lecture I attended at Erlangen University in 1958 was in theoretical chemistry. Nevertheless, I started with theology since I could not see myself working for a huge chemical company. Moreover, I was not sure that I would make it into basic chemical research, the area that really fascinated me. So as not to offend my parents who were not enthused about my decision to become a pastor, I left the door open to become a teacher of religion instruction in the Gymnasium, choosing English literature as my second subject.

About halfway through my studies, when I had met all the requirements in English literature, I decided to enter theology full-time and become a university professor in systematic theology. Nowadays, I would tell any similar midstream student with the same aspirations to "wait a minute." Especially in Germany, with relatively few positions to fill, becoming a university professor is risky business. One usually does not qualify before age forty and then most will not get a position. But I paid such worries little attention.

Theological Fertilizer

I asked Professor Walter Künneth for a dissertation topic and soon confronted him with the first volume of my dissertation. In my foolishness, I had thought that my dissertation topic on the understanding of miracles, a comparison between Karl Heim and Rudolf Bultmann, required at least three volumes. Yet he instructed me that one volume would be enough and I should simply condense my thoughts. Back in these days, we had very little dialogue with our professors. We had too much respect for them. I think I talked with Künneth at the most five times during the whole doctoral process. Not only was he rarely accessible, but I also had no idea what to ask him. After all, I was taught that a scholar ought to be self-motivated and able to discover things on his or her own. Yet once I was established, the annual visits at Künneth's were very natural. Künneth was interested in everything—family, theology, and world affairs. His widow even wanted me to conduct his funeral.

How did I get so deep into theology? Again, it was accidental, or rather providential, as most things in my life. One day one of my professors, Wilhelm Maurer, who taught the history of dogma, thought I looked too pale, since I was commuting each day from my hometown Schwabach to Erlangen University. So he suggested that I should live at the Martin-Luther-Bund in Erlangen, a dormitory for Lutheran theology students. I told him that this was impossible, because I was responsible back home for the Bible study group at our YMCA. His reply was persuasive: "Your duty is to study, and if the YMCA in Schwabach is so dependent on you that it cannot do without you, it should simply die!" Well, the YMCA survived without me and I entered a new phase of life. Professor Maurer was the Ephorus or the custodian of the Martin-Luther-Bund. We were just fifteen students, half of them German and the other half from other countries, including the USA. We had mandatory Matins and breakfast afterwards. Compline in the evening was voluntary. While we all revolted against so much liturgy, the five semesters I stayed there made a lasting impression on me. Liturgy is still dear to my heart. The same can be said for saying prayers at meals. This was not the custom at our home, but I picked it up at the Martin-Luther-Bund and I am thankful for that.

Budding Humor

Once a week we studied the Lutheran Confessions between Matins and breakfast, and one evening a month was reserved for a scholarly meeting when we had a guest lecturer or picked up some topic on our own, again under the guidance of Professor Maurer or our tutor who also saw to it that life in that dormitory did not get out of hand. Nevertheless, we had our own kind of fun.

For example, on the large table in the library there was a big wreath during Advent season. One evening before our scholarly gathering, some of us rigged the advent wreath. If one of us pulled a string at the other end of the room, the advent wreath slowly rose and stayed suspended behind our tutor who sat in front of the table. Of course, the uninitiated students seeing the advent wreath floating in midair, like a halo above our tutor's head, could hardly keep a straight face. Another time, we engineered the grandfather clock in our library so that whenever somebody pulled on a string that ran right through the room, the clock started to chime. Our tutor was somewhat irritated when the clock did not stop at eight, but rather continued to chime more than twenty times. As soon as he turned to the clock, the chimes stopped. Yet when he sat down, the clock chimed again. Finally he ended that intrusion, stopping the swing of the pendulum. The clock stopped. However, as soon as he sat down, the chimes nevertheless started up. So he removed one of the weights. Again the clock stopped. He was hardly down in his seat, when the chimes jingled once more. Only after he had removed all the weights was the clock finally silenced. One may call these things childish, but our scholarly evening had some built-in entertainment.

Doctoral Blossoms

Gerhard Friedrich, the famous editor of the *Theological Dictionary of the New Testament*, had asked me whether I would like to do a dissertation under him. Yet I had already set my heart on systematics and therefore politely declined. Systematics, I thought, was the theological discipline where one could not hide one's own persuasion and therefore it seemed the most decisive for me. Moreover, Walter Künneth had introduced me to Karl Heim in one of his seminars. This was exactly what I had been looking for because Heim brought together science and theology, equally important topics to me since my youth.

Yet I never made this interface my specialty. My interest was much wider than that, and I did not want to confine myself to one lifelong topic. I did not want to become a specialist, but a systematician for whom at least 75 percent of all the acquisitions in a theological library are relevant.

While Künneth was the archetype of orthodox theology, at least the way we students understood him, two things were evident: first, I wanted to be as clear as Künneth in my theological outlook, but not as narrow as I then perceived him to be. My goal was to strive for a synthesis between the breadth of Paul Althaus, the much-respected professor emeritus of systematic theology at Erlangen, and the theological clarity of Walter Künneth. Secondly, I saw that Künneth's command of the history of theology did not go any further back than the nineteenth century. I decided that this was not far enough. Therefore I was thankful that once I had completed my doctoral work *summa cum laude* in 1963, I received a scholarship to engage in my *Habilitationsarbeit*, my second thesis. I picked out a topic on Martin Luther since as a Lutheran systematician I thought knowing Luther was a must. Yet before the process was formally completed, I received in 1967 an invitation to teach in Columbus, Ohio. Therefore I left the *Habilitation* in limbo and moved to Columbus. The scholarship allowed me to read Luther's Works in the Weimar edition virtually from the first to the last volume, excerpting hundreds and hundreds of index cards. This way I got to know Luther and a lot of secondary literature, again on a topic that was most close to me: Luther and the natural world. Just before moving to the USA, I was ordained in the Lutheran Church of Bavaria.

Branching Toward America

My interest in America had been sparked through a one-year stay (1964–1965) at the Graduate School of Theology in Oberlin, Ohio as a World Council of Churches scholar. What a change that was from Erlangen! In Erlangen, virtually everything was Lutheran. In Oberlin, there were only two Lutheran students, Hans Scherer and I. His name too betrayed a German origin. This was the first time I had discovered that Lutherans can be a minority. At least we had a church historian, Richard C. Wolf, who was a Lutheran, too. Yet when I asked him for advice on my Luther studies, he told me that I knew more about Luther than he did. That was not much help. I felt like a fish out of water there, especially since all the literature I needed for my Luther work had to be ordered by interlibrary loan. Yet the librarians were extremely gracious and helpful and I got whatever I needed. Moreover, Dean Hazelton even sent me to Chicago to spend an extended weekend with Paul Tillich. This was a year of reading, learning, and expanding my vision.

The only Lutheran congregation in Oberlin was Missouri Synod. I had heard from fellow students at Erlangen that the Missouri Synod was archconservative and you did not attend there. So I worshiped at the Episcopal church. When I was invited by the Lutheran women's circle to share something with them about Germany, I thought that as a courtesy I should at least once attend the Lutheran church service. There I discovered that it was just like what I had been used to back home in Germany. From there on, I faithfully attended the Lutheran services feeling very much at home there, both with the people and with Bob Martin, their pastor. He even asked me to fill in when he was on vacation.

At the conclusion of that year I decided that I should start my teaching career in the USA. This would widen my horizon and perhaps I could be useful for the Lutheran Church there. I wrote to the ALC headquarters in Minneapolis and received an invitation from President Stewart Herman at the Lutheran School of Theology at Chicago for an interview. He was kind, but told me that they just had hired Philip Hefner, and perhaps they would not need another systematician. Just at the time when I visited with President Herman, there was a phone call from President Ed Fendt inquiring whether "that German," meaning me, was still in Chicago. I should immediately come down to Columbus, Ohio. Somehow Dr. Fendt had heard that a young man from Germany was looking for a teaching job in a Lutheran seminary in the USA. I did not even know that there was a seminary in Columbus. So I took the Greyhound bus to Columbus and talked with Dr. Fendt, president of ELTS (Evangelical Lutheran Theological Seminary), later LTS (Lutheran Theological Seminary), and now Trinity Lutheran Seminary. He told me that they had no need for me within the next two years, but after two years, especially as their student body continued to increase, they would need another systematician. This was good news, because my student visa barred me from reentering the States within two years if I wanted to teach.

In 1967, I started to teach in Columbus, first as instructor, then as an Assistant and an Associate Professor, and finally as the first occupant of the Edward C. Fendt Chair in systematic theology. Being now in the USA, I could renew friendship with two colleagues who had done their doctorate with Künneth at the same time as I did—Bill Weiblen, President at Wartburg Seminary, and Richard Trost, who was pastoring a congregation in Iowa. Though they were many years my seniors, they had worked on topics related to my own dissertation. So we had many good conversations.

In Columbus, I learned what theology is all about. As both Karl Barth and Paul Tillich had written and as I discovered there, it is a function of the church. Theology was not an individualistic scholarly pursuit. There was a camaraderie in Columbus that I enjoyed and that was rarely found anywhere else. The members of the all-male teaching staff were all Ed Fendt's "boys," and he treated us as such. Some of the faculty meetings just consisted in him telling us what decisions he had made and without even one vote taken. He was the father figure who "spanked" us when he thought we needed it and yet also protected us. For instance, when somebody inquired of the seminary whether the story of Adam and Eve was historically true, he asked who would like to answer that letter. Of course, Ron Hals volunteered, daring as he always was, but then Ed Fendt retorted: "Leave this up to me, I will answer the letter." While his leadership may have had negative sides too, this common father figure brought us closer together. He looked out for everyone. When Fred Meuser succeeded him, Dr. Fendt went to the board and told them: "I declined to have raises, because I am single, but now you have a married man and you must pay him accordingly."

Yet the camaraderie extended beyond the seminary, as I discovered in congregational life. For instance, at Redeemer Lutheran Church to which I belonged, we had Merl Hoops and Ron Hals as members. It was natural that we took turns in teaching adult education. There I would try out some manuscripts that later appeared in book form. The response of others to what I had written or said was always important to me. I do not know whether I always heard it, but at least I tried to listen.

Daily chapel also became very important for me, especially since Ed Fendt had a very persuasive idea how to get near perfect chapel attendance: you have a required course before chapel and one after chapel and you lock the library doors during chapel. Under the leadership of Stan Schneider, some of us evaluated the student sermons. Perhaps we were a little too harsh on them, but hearing them preach and analyzing their approach also taught me something on how to preach. While the students' sermons were automatically videotaped, the professors' were not. But I always insisted that I be on video, too, because I wanted to see what idiosyncrasies I had developed. Such a replay can be rather sobering, as I often discovered!

One facet that was important for me in terms of theological development at Columbus was when President David Preus sent me to the Faith and Order Commission of the National Council of Churches as one of the two Lutheran delegates. There I encountered again representatives from a wide variety of denominations. Virtually all of them were impressive representatives of the Christian faith, be it Swedenborgians, members of the Church of God of Anderson, Indiana, Southern Baptists, or Episcopalians.

Leaves of Books

During my Columbus days, I had my first encounters with the publishing world. Since most of the great theologians such as Karl Barth and Thomas Aquinas never made it to eschatology, because they died before they came to that important topic, I decided that this was not going to happen with me. I would start with eschatology. So this was my first larger publishing venture and, fortunately enough, against the predictions of Ron Hals who said that my style was too Germanic, *On the Way to the Future* even made it into a revised edition and also as a Religious Book Club selection. By now, I am fortunate to have it published in the fourth revised version, two in English, one in German, and once more in English (*Eschatology*, Eerdmans, 2000). When a former head of the book-publishing department at Augsburg talked to me about this manuscript, I mentioned to him that this was to be the first of a series of six volumes. I had picked up this idea from Karl Heim, my theological mentor. The response was just a smile. I could read what he thought: "I have heard many things like that before and none of them came true." Yet the next thing I knew, this book editor went out of business, and Roland Seboldt came on the scene. Our first encounter was at the conclusion of the American Academy of Religion conference in 1970. We started a conversation and discovered that we were both new, he at Augsburg and I in publishing. From there on ensued a lifelong friendship.

The notion of a series of six volumes on the most important theological loci never died with me. After eschatology, I addressed the issue of God (*The Search for God*), then anthropology (*Our Cosmic Journey*, another Religious Book Club selection), ecclesiology (*The Christian Church*), and finally after many years of deliberation, the doctrine of Christ (*Christology*). The latter book was especially difficult for me since so much had been written in this field. Consequently, the manuscript rested in the drawer for nearly ten years. Finally I got it out and completed it, if for no other reason than to show the readers that I indeed was interested in Christology and would not skirt that issue.

Meanwhile, a slim volume had emerged on word and sacraments (*Divine Communication*). This was more an accidental writing, since initially I had been asked by Carl Braaten and Robert Jenson to contribute two loci to the *Christian Dogmatics*. Knowing the stance of Jenson, especially on infant communion, I wondered why I had been selected for the sacraments, but did not object. It was soon evident, however, that he had his own idea of how the sacraments were to be treated and that his approach and mine were mutually exclusive. So I only contributed the portion on the Word and he did his own thing on the sacraments, and I then published separately what was originally intended for the *Christian Dogmatics*. Since then, many other book publications have appeared—more than twenty-five—some in English and German, and others just in one of the two languages.

My years in Columbus were enjoyable in many respects. First of all, I had many excellent students. The interchange with the students was the highlight of my life there. This time also allowed me to venture out into academia, especially into the American Academy of Religion. I had many good encounters there, with the group on Pannenberg under the leadership of Carl Braaten, then on Christology with Pat Keifert and Jim Moore, and finally the group in which I am still active and which I really love, Nineteenth-Century Theology, for a long time under the leadership of Claude Welch. One of the memorable events into which I was drawn and which rekindled my interest in theology and science was a historic get-together of more than forty Nobel laureates and six theologians at Gustavus Adolphus. There I struck up a lifelong friendship with John Cobb and with Ian Barbour.

Another facet that expanded my vision occurred during my first sabbatical in 1973–1974. When I was in Oberlin, I got acquainted with J. Robert Nelson, one of the *grands seigneurs* of the ecumenical movement. He was a systematician in Oberlin and initiated me into the theology of Karl Barth. My history at Erlangen meant that Karl Barth was a red flag. I still am not enticed by the redundancy of this Moby Dick. Yet the early Karl Barth was a real discovery for me. Through Bob Nelson's initiative I was invited to be the first Lutheran to teach as visiting professor at the Gregorian University in Rome. This is where the Roman Catholic Church became dear to me. There I saw a serious learnedness, a dedication to the church without any idolatry, especially by my dear colleagues at the Gregorian, such as René Latourelle and Jan Witte. When they complained how short of money they were and that they could hardly pay their bills, I suggested they should go to Paul VI, an alumnus of their university and at that time pope, so that he would make up the difference. The quick response was: "We would rather starve than become dependent!" I also never forget that some of my students volunteered to take care of our children, so we could attend the papal mass on Easter morning in front of St. Peter's Basilica, or how our kids played "ring around the rosie" with Bishop Maloney at the American College, the dormitory where the American theology students stayed.

RETURNING TO GERMAN ROOTS

Finally the years in Columbus came to a close. I did not want to spend the rest of my life in the same place, so the question was whether to move to another seminary or back to Germany. Neuendettelsau wanted me, and a friend of mine had asked me to come to Saarbrücken. Finally, out of the blue, a call came from Regensburg. I first went there, using the ninetieth birthday of my grandfather as an excuse to see whether they really had a university. It was one of those foggy days in Regensburg, in bitter-cold February. When I arrived there, I could hardly see the university buildings. I believed that there was indeed a university, not just the heap of concrete, and with some trepidation I made the move back to Germany in 1981. My fears of returning to a secular, godless university did not come true. The colleagues there may be not very close to the church, but many of them, especially in the sciences, are quite interested in religious and theological issues. I was especially fortunate to strike up a friendship with Rüdiger Schmitt, a geneticist, whose mentor Joshua Lederberg I knew very well through literature. Schmitt had also been in the

States for a few years and there was a natural affinity between us. Ever since, we have been in conversation at lectures, in meetings, or just at the dinner table.

TREETOPS AGAINST A WILD BLUE SKY

As Larry Hoffsis, then pastor of Trinity Lutheran Church in downtown Columbus, knowingly said: "So, now as a professor in Germany you have to gather your own students." Yes, a professor in a German university can be a very solitary and perhaps also lonesome figure. The other side of the coin is that within reason, which most of my colleagues possess, you can do virtually anything you please. Four areas have been important to me in that university context. The first one is interdisciplinary contacts. If theology is for people, it must be brought to the people. Therefore contacts with other disciplines, be it the sciences, humanities or medicine, are significant for me. But there are certain preconceptions about theologians. I still remember a public lecture series, "From Gregor Mendel to Genetic Engineering," to commemorate the one hundredth anniversary of Mendel's death. They wanted to conclude the series with a theologian—a nice gesture still often done in the German university system—but they did not know who I was. I was new, and sometimes theologians—so they thought—make the boldest claims out of sheer ignorance. I remember especially how uneasy one of my colleagues in biology was when I started my lecture and how relieved he was as time went on and he realized that I presented a balanced and well-researched account. From there on, the ice was broken. Yet what I glean from research they know firsthand. This is the difference between an expert in the sciences and an amateur like myself.

I have also organized several interdisciplinary symposia or lecture series to further the dialogue among colleagues and with the public. For instance, for the 1983 Luther anniversary I organized a two-semester lecture series with Roman Catholic theologians, art historians, musicologists, German studies experts, and scholars from other disciplines. Since we had enough volunteers and the art historians were especially well represented, I wanted to bump one of them. But what could I do when the one I wanted to omit asserted: "But I am Lutheran too!" Another idea was to ask how various disciplines see and understand our world, for instance history, physics, theology, philosophy, etc.

Another way to foster contacts is simply fellowship. When we entertain in our home it is never just theologians, but also colleagues from other disciplines. And, it is natural for us to start with prayers. Nobody up to now has objected. They know they are in a theologian's home.

The second area that is important for me is ecumenical contacts. Here it has been especially the Roman Catholic faculty with which I cooperate.

Almost half of the faculty members have been with me on our joint seminars in Greece taking place annually since the early 1980s, in which we discover various facets of Orthodoxy. In a small circle, we have even read together Luther's *Bondage of the Will* on account of the 1983 Luther anniversary. Many of the colleagues from the Roman Catholic faculty, such as Wolfgang Beinert, Norbert Brox, and Heinrich Petri, are close friends. Another person who figures prominently—he is still honorary professor at Regensburg—is Pope Benedict XVI.

Then there is the contact with Eastern Orthodoxy. Besides the annual one-week seminar in Greece, which has become an institution and is widely known there, I have also been asked to come to other places such as Romania and most recently Bulgaria. Again, I have good relations with Orthodox theological institutions there. As I have discovered more and more, reaching theological agreement does not primarily come through theological dialogue. Much more important is that we can trust each other, discover each other's interests, and extend friendship to each other. Orthodox bishops and abbots have been guests in our home and at our table, and that has done more to further the ties between us than many deep theological discussions. As a good colleague in the athletic department once told me: "If I have had lunch or supper with someone, the next faculty meeting will go much smoother."

My third area of interest is the cooperation with younger churches and theological institutions in Asia. I continue to have numerous doctoral students from these areas, be it India, Korea, the Philippines, or even Burma. I am also a frequent lecturer and visitor there and enjoy long-lasting friendships with numerous colleagues there. I continue to learn from them and help them with scholarships, book donations for libraries, or just through spiritual and moral support. We also have two godchildren in the Baptist Convention in the Philippines whose mother we put through seminary and who now heads the women's work in that denomination.

It has become one of my foremost tasks to help educate young leaders for various parts of the world who then assume leadership in their native theological institutions. There are deans and even a bishop among the Regensburg graduates. As two of my former assistants, David Ratke and Mark Worthing, wrote about me: "Having had students working under him from Germany, the United States, Australia, Canada, Korea, India, the Philippines, Latvia, Burma, Hong Kong, Slovakia, Rumania, the Ukraine and Cameroon who come from confessionally diverse backgrounds (Eastern Orthodox, Lutheran, Methodist, Presbyterian, Anglican, Baptist and Pentecostal churches) his doctoral seminars have often looked like a committee room of the United Nations—and sometimes the various language, cultural and confessional barriers have made dialogue as challenging!" Perhaps it is challenging for them. But for me it is fun. I have learned and mellowed without reneging on scholarly standards.

They all learn to appreciate Lutheran theology but remain firm in their own traditions. All of them, however, have returned with a broadened horizon.

I also always had a graduate research assistant from the States. This kept me in touch with "over there." Through my former assistants, Craig Nessan at Wartburg Seminary, Russell Kleckley at Newberry, and David Ratke at Lenoir-Rhyne, I did some tree planting too. Actually, I never gave up my American base. Every other year I have taught for one semester at Southern Seminary in Columbia, South Carolina. Southern grew dear to my heart because of the people there—students, colleagues, and staff. They are good examples of what a seminary community ought to be. Of course, every November I attend the Annual Meeting of the American Academy of Religion.

Then finally, there is a local church. Bob Kelley at Redeemer in Columbus was a good mentor for me. He was also good for our children. For our son Hans, Pastor Kelley was number one, then came God, and after a long distance it was finally me, his father. The church is what we as theologians work for in writing and teaching. I am also as active here in Regensburg in my local congregation as I was back at Redeemer. I am serving now the fourth six-year term on church council. With only two members continuing from the former church council, this is not a bad track record. I am also involved more in preaching in Regensburg than I was in Columbus. One reason for this is that in the States they pay you for it. But here it is simply assumed that if you are ordained and if you want to preach you do it for free, unless you are their parish pastor. For me, teaching and preaching go together. If I cannot translate what I teach into what I preach, my theology is wanting. I even started services in English here in the early 1980s, first every Sunday and now once a month. Initially it was for people waiting for political asylum in Germany. Most of them came from Africa and spoke English. Now the situation has changed. The majority applying for asylum are no longer Christians but Muslims, and most of them come to Germany for economic reasons. My assistant has taken over these services, while initially we took turns.

PLANTING TREES

So what does it mean to "plant trees"? I have planted fruit trees in our Regensburg garden. But planting trees for me also means planting young people who will continue to teach long after my own teaching career has ceased. Meanwhile I continue in that ministry of preparing others so they can prepare. But for us, it also meant planting our own family. As a father, I never had much time for our children except for the annual ski trip to Ischglin, Austria and at those occasions when they really needed me. But we are close to them and enjoy good relations with all three. Planting for me also meant being planted in a home where I have had the privilege of Hildegard, my understanding and supportive wife. After a teaching career of more than thirty-some years that is not yet at its end—God willing—Krista, our youngest, asked me recently: "Dad, are you happy with what you have achieved?" My answer was "Yes." Then she continued: "Would you do it again?" The same affirmative answer came. "I chose the right field." What is important today in theology? I do not see that the agenda has changed much. Human beings are intrinsically religious. Yet they are not intrinsically Christian. Therefore we have a task ahead to translate, to interpret, and to model. That, I think, has been the task and will remain the task. I have no recipe for how to do it; I simply plant and fertilize, and leave the harvest to someone else.

20

Bubble Blown and Lived In • Huston Smith

Socrates told his tribunal that he didn't fear his sentence because if death was the end it would be like falling into untroubled sleep, while if his soul migrated to another realm he would meet the heroes of the past and a just tribunal, which would make it no wasted journey. When I found that passage from the *Apology* inscribed on a historical marker in Athens, the words "no wasted journey" jumped out at me, for I was on my first trip around the world and they captured my mood perfectly. Not only was girdling the globe not a waste. Neither was life's journey, for I was learning so much!

I mention this because, though the prospect of writing my memories has never appealed to me (not even for grandchildren), I have toyed with the thought of what an appropriate title might be were I to do so, and in early manhood "No Wasted Journey" was the obvious choice. In my forties, though, it gave way to "That Strong Mercy," for I underwent a midlife crisis that only mercy (it felt like) pulled me through. And in these later years, "Bubble Blown and Lived In," displaces both preceding candidates. For though I am not a constructionist, it does feel (now) as if I have spent my years sweeping out a horizon of beliefs, soap-bubble thin, that I could live in.

How that bubble took shape, together with the iridescent colors that swim on its surface, I have been invited to recount. Some things that I wrote in the introduction of the book I co-authored with David Griffin, *Primordial Truth and Postmodern Theology*, apply equally to the start of my story, so my first several paragraphs will follow that earlier statement closely.

Search

I was born of missionary parents in China, and spent my formative years there. I don't suppose one ever gets over that. Because we were the only Americans in our small town, my parents were my only role models, so I grew up assuming that missionaries were what western children grew up to be. As a consequence, I came to the United States for college thinking that I would return to China as soon as I was theologically accredited, but I had not reckoned with the West's dynamism. Never mind that my landing pad was Central Methodist College, enrollment 600; located in Fayette, Missouri, population 3,000. Compared with Changshu (or even the Shanghai of that day) it was the Big Apple. Within two weeks, China had faded into a happy memory; I wasn't going to squander my life in its backwater. The vocational shift this entailed, however, was small. Instead of being a missionary, I would be a minister.

My junior year in college brought a second surprise: ideas jumped to life and began to take over. To some extent they must have gained on me gradually, but there came a night when I watched them preempt my life with the force of conversion. Returning from a meeting of a small honor society that gathered monthly for dessert and discussion in the home of its faculty sponsor, several of us lingered in the corridor of our dormitory to continue the arguments the evening had provoked—as unlikely a knot of peripatetics as ever assembled. My excitement had been mounting all evening, and around midnight it exploded, shattering mental stockades. It was as if a fourth dimension of space had opened and my mind was catapulting into it. And I had my entire life to explore those endless, awesome, portentous corridors. I wonder if I slept at all that night.

In retrospect it seems predestined, but at the time I could only see it as providential that the faculty sponsor of our discussion group was a protégé of Henry Nelson Wieman, who had founded the school of naturalistic theism almost single-handedly. Wieman was at the University of Chicago, so it was inevitable that I proceed there for my graduate study. Having earlier shifted my vocational intent from missionary to minister, I now moved next door again by opting to teach rather than preach—although in moments of misgiving I suspect that I have friends who think I never accomplished that move. When Charles Kingsley asked Charles Lamb if he would like to hear him preach, Lamb replied, "I don't think I have ever heard you do anything else." That's too close to home for comfort.

Because those vocational adjustments were obvious and small, they occasioned no soul-searching; but as I think back, I am surprised that I didn't find the collapse of my youthful supernaturalism disturbing. I entered the Divinity School of the University of Chicago a committed Wiemanite. Despite World War II—I was headed for the chaplaincy, but the war ended before I made it—Chicago was an exciting time for me. Via naturalistic theism, my vocation was clear: it would be to align the two most powerful forces in history: science and religion. I was a very young man, and fresh to the world's confusions.

I can remember as if it were yesterday the night in which that entire prospect, including its underlying naturalistic worldview, collapsed like a house of cards. It was four years later, in Berkeley—but before I relate what happened, I need to explain how I got there. Chicago proceeded as planned, with one surprise. Although in my first year I would not have believed that such a thing was possible, in the second year I discovered something better than Wieman's theology, namely his daughter. Two years later we were married. We have been married ever since.

As I was now a member of Wieman's family, he couldn't direct my dissertation, but he did suggest its topic. Stephen Pepper at the University of California had written his *World Hypotheses*, one of which was pragmatism (or contextualism, as he called it), which was close to Wieman's metaphysics; so he sent me to Pepper to explore the fit. With wife and an infant child, I spent 1944–1945 in Berkeley writing my doctoral dissertation on "The Metaphysical Foundation of Contextualistic Philosophy of Religion."

In the course of that year I chanced on a book by Gerald Hear, who is credited for moving Aldous Huxley from his *Brave New World* cynicism to the mysticism of *The Perennial Philosophy*, and reading it brought the collapse of my naturalism that I mentioned above. The mystics hadn't figured much in my formal education, but when I encountered a sympathetic presentation of their position, I responded from the soles of my feet on upward, saying, yes, yes! More than any other outlook I had encountered, it was their vision that, for me, disclosed the way things are.

Mysticism pointed toward "the mystical East," so, Ph.D. in hand and teaching now, I cut back on philosophy to devote roughly half my time (as I have ever since) to immersing myself in the world's religions; *immersing* is the right word, for I have always been devotee as much as scholar. During my eleven years at Washington University (1947–1958), this involved weekly tutorials with a swami of the Ramakrishna Order who grounded me in the Vedanta and set me to meditating. When I responded to MIT's call to strengthen its humanities program by adding philosophy to it (my years there were 1958–1973), I shifted my focus to Buddhism and undertook *vipassana* practice in Burma, Zen training in Kyoto, and fieldwork among the Tibetans in their refugee monasteries in North India. Angry at the hammerlock that analytic philosophers had on the field—in those days Harvard, Princeton, and Cornell constituted a "Bermuda triangle" in which "planes" that entered from outlying territories disappeared professionally—I welcomed a bid from Syracuse University to move from philosophy to religious studies, and invested my last decade of full-time teaching (1973–1983) primarily in its graduate program. Asia-wise, that decade brought Islam into my lived world, through Sufi shaikhs that I encountered in pre-Khomeini Iran and North Africa—their five Arabic prayers continue to frame my day. On retiring from Syracuse, we moved to Berkeley to be close to our children and their families. I continued to teach halftime: semesters here and there across the country, an occasional course at the Graduate Theological Union and the University of California. A new incursion on my religious front has been the primal religions, including work with Reuben Snake (a leader of the Native American Church) to help restore to that church the rights the Supreme Court stripped it of in its 1990 Smith decision.

This all sounds flagrantly eclectic and I can't argue that it wasn't, for the truth of the matter is that in culling from the world's religions what was of use to me, I was largely ignoring their differences. What they said about reality seemed sufficiently alike to carry me as I stepped from one to another like a hunter crossing ice floes, but I had no real idea what to do with their differences. I had been avoiding that question for some time when, in the course of a yearlong round-the-world seminar that I co-directed in 1969–1970, I ran into Professor S. H. Nasr in Iran who pointed me to a small group of thinkers who had the answer I was looking for. Referred to sometimes as Perennialists, sometimes as Traditionalists, their roots were in the *sophia perennis* and Great Chain of Being. René Guenon and Frithjof Schuon have been their chief twentieth-century spokesmen, and I also recognize the names of Ananda Coomaraswamy, Titus Burckhart, Martin Lings, and Professor Nasr himself. Meeting those men changed everything. As their position has remained in place for me since I encountered it, autobiography will enter into the rest of what I have to say only to indicate why I found its key features plausible.

Discovery

In the Foreword to his collection of essays by perennialist writers titled *The Sword of Gnosis*, Jacob Needleman puts his finger on what struck me first about these thinkers.

> [They] were not interested in the hypothesizing and the marshaling of piece-meal evidence that characterizes the work of most academicians. On close reading, I felt an extraordinary intellectual force radiating through their intricate prose. These men were out for the kill. For them, the study of spiritual traditions was a sword with which to destroy the illusions of contemporary man.

I shall come back to those illusions, but let me begin with the contrast with academicians. None of the teachers I had actively sought out—Huxley and Heard, Swami Satprakashananda, Goto Roshi, the Dalai Lama, and Shaikh Isa—had been academicians. They had served me as spiritual directors as much as informants; I know the ashrams, viharas, and monasteries of Asia better than I know its universities. When I found Schuon writing that "knowledge only saves us on condition that it engages all that we are: only when it constitutes a way which works and transforms, and which wounds our nature as the plough wounds the soil," I recognized him as standing in the line of my preceding mentors. But Schuon had two additional resources. He worked all the major traditions. And he was a theoretician, actively concerned with the way those traditions fit together.

The kingpin in constellating them, he insisted, is an absolute. Only poorly can life manage without one, for spiritual wholeness derives from a sense of certainty, and certainty is incompatible with relativism. Every absolute brings wholeness to some extent, but the wholeness increases as the absolute in question approximates the Absolute from which everything else derives and to which everything is accountable. For (as the opening lines of my *Forgotten Truth* state the point), "people have a profound need to believe that the truth they perceive is rooted in the unchanging depths of the universe: for were it not, could the truth be really important?" If human life could be completely geared to the Absolute, its power would course through it unrestrictedly and it would actually be a *jivamukta*, a soul that is completely enlightened while still in its body.

So much (momentarily) for the Absolute, the One. What of the many? As the succeeding sentence in *Forgotten Truth* puts the question: "How can we (hold our truth to be the Truth) when others see truth so differently?" As I think back on the matter, this is one of the two issues on which the perennialists have helped me most. The other is the character of the modern world, which I shall take up in my closing section.

The Relation between Religions

Having found Hindu, Buddhist, and Muslim (as well as Christian) teachers I had grown to revere, there was no way I was going to privilege one religion over the others. The question was where (within them) was there an absolute I could live by. (It needed to be an ontological absolute, not just a moral absolute like tolerance or the golden rule, for only ontological realities wield objective power.) I knew that such an Absolute couldn't be slapped together from pieces gleaned here and there, for it was obvious that the power of the historical revelations derived from their respective patterns or gestalts. To think that I could match such power by splicing *ch'l*, say, to *pratityasamutpada* and the *logos* made about as much sense as hoping to create a great work of art by pasting together pieces from my favorite paintings. Or creating a living organism from a heap of organ transplants.

The alternative seemed to be to find a single thread that runs through the various religions. This, though, ran into the problem of essentialism. Who is to say what the common essence of the world's religions is, and how could any account of it escape the signature of its proponent's language and perspective?

Caught as I was in this impasse, the perennialists called my attention to a third possibility that resolved it. Don't search for a single essence that pervades the world's religions. Recognize them as multiple expressions of the Absolute, which is indescribable. One reason it is ineffable is that its essence is single and knowing requires a knower and a known, which means that we are already in duality. The more understandable reason, though, is that descriptions proceed through forms, and the Absolute is formless.

This solution to the problem of the one and the many has satisfied me since it first came to view, but I have had to recognize that it is not widely available because most people hear formlessness as lack. To them, if formless things exist at all they are vague and abstract. Others, though, see matters differently. To distinguish the two types of people, perennialists call the first type esoterics and the second exoterics.

The lives of exoterics are completely contained in the formal world. For them, the formless is (as was just noted) abstract at best. It is incomplete. Lacking in important respects, it is not fully real. Esoterics, on the other hand, find reality overflowing its formal containers into formlessness, though this puts the cart before the horse. Because the formless is more real than the formed, the accurate assertion is that the formal world derives from the formless. The logical argument for the esoterics' position is that forms are finite and the Absolute is infinite, but for genuine esoterics the formless is more than a logical inference. It is an experienced reality. Through a distinctive mode of knowing (variously called *gnosis*, *noesis*, *intellectus*, *jnana*, and *prajna*) esoterics sense the formless to be more concrete, more real, than the world of forms. This is incomprehensible to exoterics because they conclude that an absolute that lacks formal divisions must lack the qualities those divisions fan out. But for esoterics, not only are those qualities in the Absolute; they are there in superessential, archetypal intensity and degree. Opposite of abstract, the Absolute is superconcrete.

I said that the Absolute is indefinable, but we need indications of its character and these are what the great revelations provide. In doing so, they resemble telescopes that "triangulate" the Absolute like a distant star. What in varying degrees of explicitness they all proclaim is that the Absolute is richer in every positive attribute we know—power, beauty, intelligence, whatever—than we can possibly imagine. This all the major religions assert, and we can understand the logic of their claim. For the only satisfying reason that can be given for the way things are is that it is best that they be that way, so the mind instinctively attributes to what is ultimate the best that it can conceive. The alternative is to accept meaninglessness to some degree.

The consequence of this approach for the relation between religious runs something like this. As the superconcrete Absolute includes all forms, it can deploy them at will. In anthropomorphic (which isn't to say inaccurate) idiom, it chooses to do so in the great formal constellations we call revelations, crowding as much of itself into each as is possible under the formal limitations that finitude exacts. Because the esoteric takes the Absolute to be the formless source of these revelations, he or she can endorse their plurality as alternative voices in which the Absolute speaks to be understood by different audiences.

While this format gave me exactly what I was looking for—(a) an Absolute (b) that didn't require that I rank-order the religions I work with—it carries a stubborn consequence. There is no way to satisfy both parts of this twofold *desideratum* on the formal, exoteric plane. To which hard truth perennialists add: if it is necessary to choose, it is better to adhere to the Absolute as truly and sufficiently disclosed in one's own revelation, than to displace it with the "civil liberties" principle of religious parity, which is no more than a personally arrived-at guide for conduct. Somewhere within these last two sentences I sense myself as parting company with my liberal friends in "the wider ecumenism," for they seem willing to reshape the forms of the great, originating revelations to two ends: politically, to reduce conflict by rounding off their sharp corners and rough edges; and theologically, to improve on their truths by learning from others. For my part, believing as I do that each of the enduring revelations already contains "truth sufficient unto salvation," I am not enthusiastic about tampering with them. The project smacks of precisely the sort of human fiddling with the revelations that perennialists find themselves charged with when their position is mistaken for (a) the cafeteria approach, or (b) articulated essentialism.

Continuing with that last point, the chief objection to perennialism that I hear is that its universalism rides roughshod over differences. I suspect that many such critics would shift their attack from perennialism's (presumed) New Age all-is-one-ism to its (actual) conservatism if they understood that everything that esoterics say about such things, universalism included, presupposes the formed/unformed distinction I have outlined. I was a universalist long before I encountered perennialism. Where it changed my thinking was in persuading me to balance my universalism with an equal regard for the difference that distinguishes revelations. Schuon's *Transcendent Unity of Religions* really is transcendent—radically so in being formless. In our "formal" life, forms are decisively important; so important that the forms of revelation should be respected. The cosmologies and social mores of their day (which they assume) are negotiable, but for spiritual insight we do better to plumb their pronouncements than tinker with them. For those forms are not incidental to the clarity of the message they convey, which clarity accounts for their historical power.

So much for religious pluralism. What of the modern world? Jacob Needleman warned us that for perennialists "the study of spiritual traditions [is] a sword with which to destroy the illusions of contemporary man." What are those illusions?

CRITIQUE OF THE MODERN WORLD

As long as the issue was the relation between religions, Perennialist was the appropriate name for the thinkers I identify with. When we turn to their view of modernity, it is their other appellation—Traditionalists—that makes their point.

It does so because Traditionalists consider the ethos by which people lived before the rise of modern science to be on balance more accurate than the scientistic one that has replaced it. Not (to repeat the point just mentioned) its science, which has been superseded, or its social mores, but its ontological vision. I wrote *Forgotten Truth* to celebrate that vision; and I wrote its sequel, *Beyond the Post-Modern Mind*, to expose the procrustean epistemology—again, scientistic—that has caused traditional truth to be largely forgotten. I say forgotten rather than refuted, for there has been no refutation; merely an exchange of traditional ontology for one that derives from an epistemology that (in the short run at least) caters to our material wants and wish to control, "the Old Adam." There are, of course, oceans of historical and psychological reasons for the West's having made this exchange, but no logical reasons. We simply slid into assuming that the most reliable viewfinder available to our human lot is the scientistic one that edits out spiritual truths in the way X-ray films omit the beauty of faces.

I know that this assessment will be disputed; though actually it is a good day when one encounters dispute, for typically it is simply ignored. When rejoinders are heard, they point out that the preceding paragraph doesn't even mention science; only scientism, with which (by tacit association) science is sneakily tarred.

That reply is useful, for it forces me to drop innuendo, come into the open, and say right out loud that science is scientism. I didn't have the wit (or was it courage?) to arrive at that conclusion by myself; a scientist at the University of Minnesota who teaches science to nonscience majors pointed it out to me at the close of an all-day workshop that I had devoted to distinguishing science form scientism and exempting it from the latter's pernicious effects. "Everything you said about the dangers of scientism is true," he said; "but there's one thing, Huston, that you still don't see. Science is scientism."

His assertion startled me, but on the long walk it provoked I came to see his point. If we define *science* as the procedures that scientists follow and the demonstrable results that thereby accrue, and *scientism* as the assumption that the scientific method is the most reliable method for arriving at truth and that the things that science works with are the most real things; thus defined, the two are clearly different. But here's the point. Although in principle it is easy to distinguish them, in practice it is almost impossible to do so. So scientism gets overlooked in the way the power plays that are imbedded in institutions get overlooked until the extraordinary eye of a Foucault spots them and points them out.

The cause of the blur is the one that Spinoza stated abstractly: things tend to enlarge their domains until checked by other things. This applies to institutions as much as to individuals. The vanguard of science's expansionism is scientism, and it advances automatically unless checked. Religiously, it is important that it be checked, for the two are incompatible. So where are the guardians to keep scientism from sweeping the field? The Traditionalists are the most vigilant and astute watchdogs I see. And scientism is one area where I claim expertise, for my longest tour of duty (as they say in the military)—fifteen years—was at MIT.

The chief places I have tried to keep an eye on scientism are:

1. Higher education. Rooted as the universities are in the scientific method, as a recent president of Johns Hopkins University pointed out, they are *Killing the Spirit* (Page Smith [Viking, 1990]).
2. Mainline theology. Looking up to their more prestigious counterparts at the universities, seminary professors tend to accommodate to their styles of thought. As those styles do not allow for a robust, alternative, ontological reality, our understanding of God has slipped ontologically. (When was the last time I heard the word "supernatural" from a lectern or pulpit?) This slip is having disastrous effects on mainline churches whose members are moving to evangelical churches, Asian religious, or New Age cults, and to frivolity in search of the unconventional reality that *homo religiosus* requires.
3. The science/religion dialogue, with evolution as a major checkpoint. The only definition of Darwinism that has survived its multiple permutations is that it is the theory that claims our arrival as human beings can be explained naturalistically. Scientism *must* make this claim, but the evidence for it is no stronger than that which supports its theistic alternative. Yawning lacunae in the naturalistic scenario are being papered over with stopgap, "god of the gaps" stratagems—the god here is Darwin—that are as blatant as those that theology has ever resorted to.
4. Deconstruction and postmodernism. These thinkers see through scientism, but their constructive proposals make the wrong mistake (as Yogi Berra would say) for being brilliant answers to the wrong question. The question of our time is no longer how to take things apart, but how to work responsibly at reassembling them. For as the opening speaker at the 1992, UCB, Robert Bellah–sponsored Good Society Conference put the point: "We have no maps and we don't know how to make them."

If those four one-liners seem extreme and my obsession with scientism a complete tapestry woven from a few threads of fact, I suggest that a reading of

Brian Appleyard's *Understanding the Present* (Doubleday, 1993) would alter those judgments. In it, he asks us to imagine a missionary to an isolated tribe. Conversion is slow work until a child contracts a deadly disease and is saved by some penicillin the missionary has brought along. With that single stroke, Appleyard argues, it's all over for the world the tribe had known and by extension for the traditional world generally. For the miracle its medicine men and priests couldn't accomplish, science delivers. And "science has shown itself unable to coexist with anything" (p. 9).

> Speaking for myself, if the chiefs of the tribe reason as follows:
> This white man knows things about our bodies and how to maintain them that we don't know, and we certainly thank him for sharing that knowledge with us. But it appears that knowledge of that sort tells us nothing about how we and the world got here, who we are in the fullness of our being, what happens to us after death, and whether there are beings of other kinds—immaterial beings, some of whom may be more intelligent, powerful, and virtuous than we are, the Great Spirit for example. Nor does it tell us how we should live with one another. There seems to be no reason, therefore, why we can't accept the white man's medicine with gratitude while continuing to take seriously the wonderful explanatory myths that our ancestors entrusted to us.

If, as I say, the chiefs could reason this way and hold true to that reasoning, science would not be a problem. But they can't. We moderns and postmoderns can't. And I can't not wholeheartedly, so scientized is the culture that encases me. But trying to change it is happiness enough.

21

A Living Conversation • Paul R. Sponheim

"Home Is Where We Start From" . . . Inside and Outside. I use this line from British object-relations theorist Donald W. Winnicott because much of what I think my life has been about theologically did get started at home in Thief River Falls, Minnesota. "Inside and outside" locates the differing relationships to Christian faith present in my family of origin. The dedication for my 1985 book *God: The Question and the Quest* names my sisters and brothers, and adds "to others." Certainly the range of reference in the conversation that has been my life is in some ways much wider than that represented at 519 Duluth Avenue North in that frozen northern city. And there have been other, qualitative, changes in how the relationship with a difference is best understood by a Christian. I will allude later to a transition to a posture that no longer claims a position of privilege, but still seeks dialogue with conviction. Real difference regarding faith exists; such difference challenges those who so differ. This was an important part of where I started from theologically and in many ways it is still where I live.

The Home I Started From

My parents were the first case in point for such difference. My mother was a deep and earnest Christian. She knew much physical suffering in her life, and was in practical terms "homebound" during my growing-up years. But the witness of her faith in a gracious God who wills and works for the creation's good was in my experience unwavering and clear. I recall Mother sitting in her rocker listening to the radio broadcast of the Sunday morning service from Trinity Lutheran Church, and singing vigorously the designated hymn from *The Lutheran Hymnal*.

Dad, on the other hand, was at a different place. That place was not as clear as Mother's, perhaps. He seemed interested, perhaps even somewhat pleased, when two of his kids headed for seminary. He was a dedicated listener to radio broadcasts of Handel's *Messiah* or even to special broadcasts of musical numbers from Concordia College in Moorhead. It seems a stretch to claim that his interest was only aesthetic. But he had been burned by the blaming judgment of a stupid pastor over the decision he made, as the "head of the family," to go ahead with surgery for a son suffering from a mastoid infection. The son died (my middle name was his first name and my younger brother Don's middle name his middle name). Dad's faith identity was complicated, but he surely was perceived (by me and, I think, most of the other kids) to be at a very different place than his wife. Perhaps that place had some movement within it. What am I to make of the fact that a few weeks before his death he requested and received the Lord's Supper from his youngest son, a Lutheran pastor?

We children sort of distributed ourselves across some spectrum regarding faith. The oldest son grew up to be an active churchman, a choir director who clothed an evident faith in a quiet Scandinavian reserve. The next-in-line was a child of the Enlightenment for whom science would displace religious faith, though he managed a devoted interest in William Blake's romantic flights of imagination. And so it went, with the four others of us.

I am tempted to use the now-familiar term "pluralism" to characterize our growing up in this family. But I want to stress the point that this situation was not a simple matter. The familial complexity can be illustrated by a vividly remembered argument that erupted when sister Carol as an honest atheist refused to attend the baccalaureate service that spring when she was to graduate as salutatorian of her class. It was Dad, not Mother, who insisted that she attend. His insistence was not couched in the language of faith. But why was being at that service a matter of such family pride? (She did not attend the service.)

In any case it was clear to me, growing up, that we were at different places regarding Christian faith. It is clear to me now, perhaps more so now than then, that the phrase "outside and inside" does oversimplify matters if it is understood to mean that one must be either on one side or the other. The phrase seems too simple still when I ponder my wider experience of difference regarding faith. Does a tearful cry "I want to believe, but I just can't" constitute a kind of faith without belief? Whence comes faith, anyway? The simple answers (my decision, God's determination) fail before the complex distinctions that demand recognition in a world, a family, or a person.

How was I to respond to this early experience of difference? In large measure, I identified with Mother and her clear witness. The Christian faith is good news for all people (I can still hear Mother reading Luke 2's story, which was squeezed into our family Christmas program between French horn and clarinet solos and Uncle Joe reading "Twas the Night before Christmas"). The gospel was good news, and it could be understood as such. There was a content that could be coherently, yes even cogently, explicated. The relevant Christian rubric could be evangelism, or—perhaps more closely—apologetics.

Here I offer a tribute to my confirmation pastor at Trinity, Rev. G. S. Thompson (whom I as an adult would still never call "Jerry," and Gjermund seemed unavailable). He was a fine preacher, with his words eloquently addressing the minds of his hearers. Even more to the point perhaps, Pastor Thompson was a superb teacher. I particularly well recall the winsome power or an evening series on the Augsburg Confession. Through his ministry, it became very clear to me that there was what I later learned to call a "*fides quae creditor*" and that this "faith to be believed" could be explicated and defended.

Looking back now, I think this conviction was still at work in the 1960s shaping of my first major book as *Kierkegaard on Christ and Christian Coherence*. The confessor of the faith may need to speak of paradox, but (as Kierkegaard puts it in his 500-page *Postscript* to the *Philosophical Fragments*) the faith is not nonsense. Thus in the 1980s it made sense to accept an assignment in the *Christian Dogmatics* writing team assembled by Carl Braaten and Robert Jenson. The point in that group effort was to state the faith that was "once for all entrusted to the saints" (Jude 1:3). It was thought possible to do that, even though and precisely because if it came to labeling, the editors admit that it would take at least seven labels to locate the six of us. Home is where I started from, with a strong sense for a "*fides quae*."

Those in need of my explication and defense were understood by me, I suppose, to be mainly Enlightenment types. This was true at home and for thirty years thereafter. (More recently, I have been known to complain that just when, after decades of study, I came to get [what I thought was] a clear grip on "the modern world," somebody blinked and lo the *post*modern appeared.) This sense of the conversation partners has changed, as I will later note. Among those Enlightenment types, I would name myself. In this respect, looking back I recognize myself as the son of my mother, and my dad. In *God—The World's Future*, Ted Peters writes of "three levels or stages of world-consciousness: (1) naïve world-construction, (2) critical deconstruction, and (3) postcritical reconstruction." He then adds, "I suspect that it is possible for a person of faith to live simultaneously at all three levels" (2nd edition, 22). His suspicion is right. I am not pleading for an "on the fence" position, and "inside" and "outside" can be distinguished. But the matter is complicated. I am still where I started from, in that I believe there is truth in the Christian faith for all people. But even in Thief River I asked, painfully, "Why do we get it wrong so often?" As decades passed, I came to ask, "Does not our getting it wrong so often count against the faith itself?" Both questions still trouble me.

IN THE MIDDLE OF SELF AND WORLD:
KIERKEGAARD AND WHITEHEAD

Perhaps the engagement with difference was an important part of "where I started from," but new things did enter that life. The terms "self" and "world' organize that newness, and it is useful to dramatize these changes by speaking of the young Luther League president going off to school. It was at school that I encountered the strongest voices expressing these two realities. I can be more concrete, putting names on this dynamic. The names are Søren Kierkegaard and Alfred North Whitehead. While my study and reflection on self and world have wider reference, this unlikely pair of figures does rise up in a seminal way to suggest the nexus in which my theological work took and still takes shape. And these two entered my life during something more than a decade of going to school. The schools are easy enough to locate as well, Concordia College (Moorhead, Minnesota) and the University of Chicago.

I had many fine teachers at Concordia: Sidney Rand and Gene Fevold in religion and Charles Skalert in classics, for example. But it was Reidar Thomte in philosophy who by sheer force of will drew me into the orbit of the melancholy Dane. Thomte was one of that remarkable cluster of Midwestern undergraduate teachers (Stanley Olson at Augustana, David Swenson and later Paul Holmer at the University of Minnesota, and of course Howard Hong at St. Olaf) who with Walter Lowrie and Howard Johnson at Princeton brought SK to America. Thomte was relentless in pursuit of certain students, however odd the choices may have been. A standing joke with my wife is her clear recollection of Dr. Thomte confronting her at a Fargo-Moorhead bus stop, warning her that she should not be spending so much time with Paul Sponheim, since he had plans for that student! (Fortunately for me, his warning was not ultimately efficacious.) In any case he willed me to Denmark on a Fulbright scholarship and to a close reading of SK with Niels Thulstrup.

Now, fifty years later, I still can't get rid of this guy (Kierkegaard, not Thomte—I think) and his penetrating analysis of human selfhood. In Spring term 2003, I read *The Sickness unto Death* again (for at least the twentieth time), with five independent study students, and again had my twin reactions: this guy is crazy . . . and this guy is right. Can human beings really be this "sick unto death," in so many ways? Can God's commitment to change things be truly this radical? Too dark, too bright, about right?

What about Whitehead? Well, I first read him in 1949 under, of all people, Reidar Thomte. But it was the two Bernards at Chicago, Loomer and Meland, who really got me going. In my first term at Chicago, Loomer challenged me face-to-face to be ready to respond in an eventual oral field-examination to Whitehead's challenge to true-blue Lutheran orthodoxy. But it was particularly the wise and gentle Meland with his remythologizing project that most deeply connected with me. I had a yearlong constructive theology class with Meland in which the conversation had a powerful shaping and clarifying effect.

I am linking the world side of my polarity with Whitehead and his cosmology, of course. As I read page after page in *Process and Reality* in an early term at Chicago, I came, almost reluctantly, to see how perceptive this descriptive sketch of reality was. This thoroughgoing sense of becoming, this radical sense of "internal relations" as constitutive—yes, in something like a tower experience, I came to see it was so.

In my later work with process thought, another Chicago product, John B. Cobb Jr., has been particularly helpful to me. "The world" comes through so strongly in Cobb's work, as he steadfastly refuses to let theological work be cordoned off into a tightly enclosed discipline or Christian faith itself be isolated from the claims of other faiths.

At Chicago, there were other voices strengthening that world side of things. Paul Tillich was my teacher in the Divinity School, but his investment and influence could not be neatly located there. I recall his noontime lectures scheduled for and attended by a wide range of university students and faculty. I recall him assigning me "the Pauli principle" in physics for my term paper in his course on what turned out to be Volume III of the *Systematic Theology*. Joe Sittler, with his deep sense for the cosmological importance of Christology, is also near the top of a Chicago "world" list for me. Moreover, Hyde Park, Illinois is not Moorhead or St. Anthony Park, Minnesota.

In between Concordia and Chicago, there was Luther Seminary in St. Paul. Teachers there drew me in to a deeper pondering of what it is to be a human self before God. George Aus was an eloquent and energetic exponent of "second form" Lutheranism. Aus was not unaware of the anxious questions facing any defender of a human role in faith. I sense these questions too, and deserve to be nervous about my ready response, namely, ambiguity is the epistemological correlate to the ontological reality of freedom.

Yet key seminary teachers did not give up on understanding faith in essentially relational terms, in terms I later learned to locate in the "Adamic" myth (Paul Ricoeur). Warren Quanbeck, whose every course found me enrolled, would not let the affirmation of divine sovereignty be turned into a denial of human responsibility. I came to see that the sovereign God is the continuing Creator who cannot be evicted from the universe.

One does not praise this God by cursing the creation. I link up this Lutheran affirmation of the gift and task of human selfhood with my later learning from such feminist voices as Valerie Saiving and Catherine Keller. Perhaps Lutherans have more trouble than we should in learning that being diligent in denouncing sinful pride should not lead the Christian theologian to elevate self-sacrifice as an ideal for persons (often women) who culturally are more tempted to fail to respond to the call to be/become a self. I think I finally got the point, and when I hear "trumping" moves claiming it all comes down to pride, anyway, I do dissent. I think Kierkegaard, Lutheran creation theology, Christian feminism, and my own experience all speak in that dissent.

God vs. Church

So, self and world came to be the framework in terms of which I came to do theology. But what of the church? We cannot hold back that question any longer, even though I confess that I have always been more interested in God than in the church. "So is the church"—I can imagine someone responding. That someone could have been Luther Seminary President Al Rogness, who did a remarkable job of staying with the Luther graduates doing doctoral work. Or it could have been W. Douglas Larson, my pastor at Augustana Lutheran Church in Chicago. Both men were indeed churchmen, but they seemed pretty interested in God. The God calling for much more from me than my "interest" is a continuing creator God who is everywhere present and who wills to be known. Accordingly, I have been troubled when theologians try to make Jesus-talk "cover" all God claims, as when faith in Jesus is seen as the basis for human rights. In any case, while I cannot limit our ways of knowing God to the church, I do turn to Jesus-talk as the locus for the decisive knowing of God. Where is the church to be located in relation to this self and world framework? My answer: in the middle of it, caught up in the polarity. I believe that I have been and am a theologian of the church. But I have never been able to speak of the church "by itself," as it were. Rather I have sought to speak of the church as it exists in and for self and world.

That the church exists in the world became clear to me as I came to see how the life of the church is deeply affected by the concrete context, which cannot be dismissed in praise of some ghostly "invisible" church. Geography makes a difference (as do economics, language, ethnicity, politics . . .). During seminary years, that was driven home to me when internship brought me from Lutheran Minnesota to Richland, Washington. Many of the transplanted Midwesterners had seemed to leave their church involvement on the eastern side of the Rockies. The dominant faith group in Richland was actually the Mormons. The importance of the continuity provided me by the *fides quae* became clear to me there, and that faith came into play in depth in the highly educated context featuring the Hanford atomic works site.

Later, at Chicago, Jaroslav Pelikan was my adviser and he was particularly deft at showing how the church is in the middle of time. His important 1985 book *Jesus Through the Centuries* makes emphatically clear that Jesus is not locked up in the first century or in the church. More broadly, in his teaching Pelikan demonstrated that the faith is seen differently, depending on the specific context. Two courses with him that dramatized this for me involved reading Schleiermacher's *The Christian Faith* and the *Canons and*

Decrees of the Council of Trent. Talk about difference! In my own time of teaching (more on this in the next section), I have tried to illumine this contextual element, whether in the 1960s teaching philosophy at Concordia or in the 1990s teaching something called "Reading the Audiences" at Luther Seminary.

If the church is always contextual, it follows that the study of self and world becomes a significant resource for theological inquiry. Thus I have never been able to join the large choir of voices singing a "cheap-shot" protest against the use of psychology in matters theological. Similarly, I have been an interested amateur in probing the literature of modern science for constitutive theological insight. The most direct expansion of that interest was a sabbatical study period with Arthur Peacocke in Cambridge in the 1980s. Less formally, I have tried to learn about selfhood by serving as a theological resource for Clinical Pastoral Education groups, and I have been active on the edge of a number of science and theology discussions in which the "world" is under the respective microscopes.

More on Self and World

Self and world, then—that has been my framework. Is there a problem in trying to hold these two together? I realize that one could consider thinking in these terms to be a capitulation to the modernist agenda (see Stephen Toulmin's *Cosmopolis*). But I would argue that the two need each other. To be very specific again: Whitehead and Kierkegaard need each other. Whitehead offers a rich cosmology but struggles to provide a convincing account of the continuity of personal existence. Kierkegaard probes the human self deeply, but isolates that self all too distinctly from any environing world. They need each other, and perhaps the coming together of "self" and "world" disciplines is one of the most promising developments in the emergence of the postmodern. Thanks to Thomas Kuhn, we have had nearly fifty years now to come to terms with the subjectivity of scientific work and the real-world significance of its efficacy. The postmodern recognition of the constitutive significance of relationship and of the crucial character of community bids to resist any individualizing impulse issuing from a Cartesian modernist reading of the self.

Self and world need each other, and theology can serve us as it works within this nexus. What undergirds this relational framework? The framework does not function as a metaphysical "given." Rather it is received as gift, and task, from the Creator's hand. This is where Curt Thompson is right in the Festschrift (2000) exegeting my 1970 installation address on "The Logic of an Elliptical Faith" as granting priority to God as the first of the two foci. Thus I have not ceased to speak of love as "the category proper" to be recognized in assigning any and all attributes to God. Theology has remained for me essentially God-talk, discourse about the surprising and reassuring love of God. But as the doctrine of creation has emerged for me as the basis for my theological work, I have given fuller attention to the nondivine focus, stressing the dynamics involved in the distinction and relationship of self and world. That will, I trust, be evident as I turn to suggest what has been "going on," theologically in the conversation that has been my life.

CREATING CONVERSATION: TEACHING

Teaching is one thing that has been "going on" for me—for more than four decades now. More and more I have come to see this as talking together. A Martian visiting my classroom would confirm that words are coming out of my mouth. Language, speech—yes, talking—this I do care about. The "together" part is at least not as obvious. But as I look back, after a wonderful hour in a team-taught preceptorial with Terry Fretheim or on these six decades of "doing school" since leaving Thief River, I see how much it matters that what goes on in the classroom is a happening together. I see how much I have learned in rooms where I was pegged as the instructor. There have been changes in how I see this. In 1961 when I first began to teach full-time, I saw my role to be that of outlining all the available options on the question at hand, studiously avoiding taking any particular position. The students were apparently to be treated to Spinozistic insights *"sub quadem aeternitatis specie"* or what Thomas Nagel has called the "view from nowhere."

I have come to see that teaching as conversation calls for assertion and argument. I hope to be fair in presenting the criticisms and claims of others, but I do not seek to conceal the convictions I bring to the classroom. I do not think this closes me off, for I have learned so very much from the back-and-forth that has ensued. I remember engagement with specific students—going back to Concordia (Mark, Darroll, Dorcas, Sharon, Vince) and stretching through those decades at Luther (Susan, Butch, Ann, Curt, Linda, Katherine, Jonathan . . .).

Team teaching with colleagues can intensify this learning together the more, and in this, Terry Fretheim is first among equals as I think about our working together with over a thousand students in the "God" course over the years. I have been fortunate to teach in several different structures (such as the "Integrated Quarter" with a group of students taking the same set of courses and working in contextual sites under an integrating theme), and it has dawned on me how much faculty depend on the creative and reliable service of administration and support staff. That is freshly underlined for me in my current experience of teaching a seminary credit course online. To broaden the point: "administration" is not for me a dirty word, and I did not hate my (admittedly brief) stint at Luther as Lloyd Svendsbye's first academic dean.

CREATING CONVERSATION: TALKING TOGETHER

Then there has been the talking together that has not taken place in classrooms. Who can count the number of corridor conversations that have made a difference? I can enumerate two more structured nonclassroom conversational settings. One is a couples reading group in St. Paul that has met for over thirty years. (We could still call it the YTs, but that might now be spelled out not as "Young Theologians" but as "Yesterday's Theologians." Well, let's settle for calling it "The Book Group.") We have read mostly novels—Louise Erdrich, Jon Hassler, Toni Morrison, Nadine Gordimer—and Diane Abu-Jaber's *Crescent*. We have read them *together*, for the book has always changed for me by evening's end. The other structured nonclassroom time of talking together to be cited is my time with *Dialog* and *Word and World*. There have been writing opportunities through these journals, but I want to stress the "talking together" character of the meetings of the groups charged with selecting themes and authors. There was no lack of heat and more than a little light, I believe, in the exchanges that brought printed pages to pastors' desks. Were I to say more of *Dialog*, it would be likely I would mention Carl Braaten and Robert Jenson. Their names remind me of the conversational process involved in producing the *Christian Dogmatics* and so bring me to another category.

CREATING CONVERSATION: WRITING

I have written a little. This too, I think, has been a matter of conversation. I am not Mozart, but I share with him the experience of being criticized for "too many notes." There are different "takes" available in my case, I realize. Are all those references there a hangover of the graduate student syndrome, an author anxiously trying to prove he is to be trusted because he has read two books? Perhaps. Yet I would like to believe (and somewhat more than half the time I do so believe) that this "style" is an attempt to gather a conversation to advance our consideration of a particular issue.

Early on, the conversation was perhaps a little more expository, notably in the Kierkegaard and Whitehead books. Later I have tried to introduce the conversation in the service of a constructive argument (*God: The Question and the Quest*, 1985; *Faith and the Other*, 1993; *The Pulse of Creation*, 1999). I think I see in this a parallel to the change mentioned above in teaching from objectivity to engaged intersubjectivity. It may be significant that the transition centers in the just-mentioned apologetic from 1985, where the overt conversation partner is still modern dissent, though something different seems to be entering the room. I do think of all of this writing as an effort at conversation and I want to acknowledge that on the way, conversation with teaching (read "writing") assistants served me most helpfully (many names and faces come to me: Kristen, Cordell, Jon, Steve, Corey, Erik).

Evil

In the titles and subdivisions for this piece, I have boldly used such grand phrases as "living conversation" or "creating conversation." Am I entitled to those titles? One may ask, "Did all this conversation actually create anything beyond itself?" Is any change of substance discernible over these decades? Plainly, is anything better because of what is recounted in this theological autobiography? I accept the question and wish to press it, because I believe change is needed. Moral change has been needed and is still needed. I recall that in the early *Christian Dogmatics* discussions in Carl Braaten's lakeshore apartment regarding how the loci were to be assigned, I asked for "evil." Over the subsequent years, I have explained to students that I had been doing field studies in the topic for some fifty years. I have suspected that my colleagues gave me "evil" because they doubted my competence to contribute adequately to many of the other topics. In any case, thinking about evil has been for me an absorbing theological agenda and that "standing" has been grounded existentially. Thus it was very fitting that Terry Fretheim and Curt Thompson chose "God, Evil, and Suffering" as the focus for the Festschrift.

Learning from Feminism

So has all this conversation made any difference in the face of evil? I really don't know. My most obvious efforts can be represented by some involvement in working for justice in matters of race and gender. Through the initiative of former Young Lifer Jim Nelson, I served for more than twenty years on the board of the City, Inc., an agency concerned to make things better for children on the near North and near South sides of Minneapolis. I do know that it has been inspiring to attend graduation ceremonies of the City, Inc. alternative school, when "against the grain" candidates walk up to receive their diplomas. As to gender, I have seen clearly how deeply sexism is entrenched in the structures and attitudes present in the society, definitely including the church. Does it help to serve on church task forces claiming to address sexism? Does it make any positive difference to testify unsuccessfully on behalf of a female pastor forced out of her call when she blew the whistle on the male senior pastor? Or, back at the schoolhouse, does it really help significantly to work over bibliographies of assigned texts in the terms of gender and race diversity?

I verge on the dramatic, I suppose. But there is a drama—no, an actual battle—going on out there and in here. One thing I have learned from feminism (see Sharon Welch's classic *A Feminist Ethic of Risk*) is that we need to reject an ethic of "control" in which complete success is the standard to be applied in determining what should be ventured or deemed worth accomplishing. I want to avoid "all or nothing" thinking also in reflecting on my own life and work, and I am glad for specific gains sensed. Yet I do wish I had been braver and smarter in the face of moral evil. Front and center now is the issue of how to regard gay and lesbian persons in committed relationships. In many ways it is the culture that seems to be leading the church toward the equal treatment that seems to me both wise and just. My efforts in this area (see, for example, the *Collection of Responses to the First Draft of an ELCA Social Statement* from 1994) also seem insufficient and inefficacious. At least the efficacy seems painfully slow in showing itself.

WHAT DOES IT ALL ADD UP TO?

If I am still edging around the question "What does it all add up to?" I suppose I need to face the fact that my life has been in large part about sentences: trying to understand them, trying to formulate them, getting up early and staying up late to the end that the weird phenomenon of human language is used in ways that serve the creation and thus please the Creator. I do realize that the assessment of these short years is not finally my call. But, more generally, might not a "theological autobiography" have a word of recommendation buried somewhere in the many paragraphs of report? It seems right to ask whether theological conversation can serve the Creator's will against moral evil. One can sharpen the question by asking with Kierkegaard whether the emphasis on conversation, on dialogue, does not assume with Socrates that the basic problem is ignorance. Can education be the solution if ignorance is not the problem? Will not failure result, if the basic human problem lies in the will?

I do not have an answer that can remove the question, but I would not want us to minimize the transforming power of a genuine conversation. Is this claim for conversation an expression of a rationalist streak in me, an indication that at the end of the day I am still a child of the Enlightenment? Perhaps, or perhaps, surely. But beneath and within the claim is a faith in a Creator God who still speaks to call into being things that do not exist (Rom. 4:17). This God brings strangers out of Egypt and calls on them to welcome strangers (Exod. 22:21). Genuine conversation entails not merely an exchange of ideas but a meeting of selves. Of course there are minimal conditions for genuine conversation. Here it will suffice to speak of just this: both (or all) participants in the conversation must be truly present in a speaking and listening together.

This means that I must be present to and for the other. And the other must be for me as well. Of course it is needful to recognize evil (my specialty, after all!), but the temptation to demonize the other must be avoided.

I am back to where I started from, facing the challenge of the "other." Well, perhaps not quite. I come to the conversation with conviction, certain that there is truth in Christ also for the other, all the others. I believe much of my later writing can still be located in the realm of apologetics. But I do not claim a position of privilege that seems to imply that certainty is available for me about the state of the soul of the other. Is this an untenable position? I think it is not, if I believe that the one who in Christ claims my confession is none other than the Creator God. That God cannot be evicted from any moment in the universe, including the moments and years involved in the conversation.

To Be Continued, Falling Silent

The conversation will continue, for a while. I will teach a little and do the occasional adult forum at a local congregation. I will write some. This last year there they were again: Kierkegaard and Whitehead in two of the half-dozen short pieces I produced. (There's an "inclusio" for you!) And the point about context has been there as two of the other published essays were addressed to issues of aging. There is some pretty extensive continuity covering this stretch of decades. And, yes, I am back where I started from in the sense that I am finding myself in a family. This family is once again at different places regarding faith. Once again, there is a woman of faith at the center of things. In this case, her name is Nell, whose witness in word and deed continues to call me forward to speech.

But I also see the point, in more than one way, of falling silent. In an earlier paragraph I wrote of being present in speaking and *listening*. I think of the role of silence in the Taizé worship or in the Quaker meeting. Secondly, my love affair with words surely risks making me deaf to the way in which our embodiment is much more than a prerequisite for conversation. When we fall silent as far as words are concerned, communication may well continue in a depth otherwise obscured by our verbosity and even by the misleading clarity of what we seem to be saying.

There's also a falling silent wisdom in getting out of the way of those younger folk who have something to say and need a chance to say it. What about the final silence? I look toward it, claiming the Creator's verdict that this life with its limitations is good, indeed very good. But it isn't perfect. Could there be another time, or in the language of the book of Hebrews (11:16) and James Baldwin, another country? Well, that's truly interesting. There will be, I trust, plenty to talk about. And plentiful silence, face to face.

22

Christian Claims • Kathryn Tanner

When I was in the doctoral program of Yale's Religious Studies Department in the early 1980s (working primarily with Hans Frei, George Lindbeck, and Louis Dupré), the main worries of theologians and philosophers of religion were methodological in nature: Could religious thought and language be intellectually justified? Did religious thought and language, for example, meet general standards of meaning, intelligibility, and truth? One might argue—as Frei and Lindbeck did with an ironic display of academic rigor informed by the latest philosophy, literary theory, and social science—that they need not do so to be intellectually respectable. Epistemological issues (for example, how meaning and truth were conveyed linguistically through signs and symbols) and biblical hermeneutics were the bread and butter of our studies.

Methodological preoccupations distinguished theological schools (Yale and the University of Chicago) and informed the teaching of the history of Christian thought, another mainstay of the doctoral program at Yale. Frei and Lindbeck often half-jokingly quipped that one day they would eventually do theology, rather than spend all their time talking about how to go about it. But neither, it turns out, made much headway on that front while I was at Yale as a student and then as a faculty member during the 1980s and early 1990s. Any movement by Frei in that direction was tragically cut short by his premature death in 1988, and Lindbeck's energy was increasingly taken up with response to his influential and controversial *Nature of Doctrine*, published in 1984, understood at the time not primarily as a work in comparative doctrine by a historically learned ecumenist, but as the methodological manifesto of the so-called Yale School of Theology.

CLAIMED BY A NEW GENERATION

The hopes of my teachers for their own work came to fruition with the next generation of theologians, of which I count myself a member. Typical of this new generation of theologians—whatever their methodological commitments—is a willingness to make constructive claims of a substantive

269

sort through the critical reworking of Christian ideas and symbols to address the challenges of today's world, a willingness to venture a new Christian account of the world and our place in it with special attention to the most pressing problems and issues of contemporary life. Pick up almost any work in theology at present and you are liable to find a discussion of the Trinity and its implications for politics; or a reformulation of God's relation to creation as an impetus to ecological responsibility; or a rethinking of the atonement in light of trauma theory. Frei, my old friend and mentor, at once so cautious and generous in outlook, would no doubt be astonished—grateful but perhaps a little envious too, pleasantly surprised but also taken aback by the unself-conscious boldness of this new turn in theological inquiry.

Although my teachers might have been reluctant to admit as much, this shift from methodological to substantive preoccupations has surely been in part a response to, and general incorporation of, the lessons of liberation theologies. The Enlightenment challenge to the intellectual credibility of religious ideas can no longer be taken for granted as the starting point for theological work now that theologians who face far more pressing worries than academic respectability have gained their voices, both here and around the globe. Theologians are now primarily called to provide not a theoretical argument for Christianity's plausibility, but an account of how Christianity can be part of the solution—rather than part of the problem—on matters that make a life-and-death difference to people, especially the poor and the oppressed.

Postmodern trends in the academy over the past quarter-century have also encouraged this shift away from methodological preoccupations toward substantive theological judgments and their practical ramifications. The need to find theoretical justifications for the theological enterprise in particular has become less urgent given postmodern suspicions about all claims to universality, disinterestedness, and culturally unmediated insight. Appeals to specifically Christian sources and norms of insight and the advocacy stance assumed by many theologians are less suspect than they used to be, now that the tradition-bound, culturally influenced, and politically invested character of even the "hard sciences" has become an intellectual commonplace. Judgments in the natural and human sciences cannot be exempted from the scandal of particularity so often lodged against theology; any general outlook on the world and human life, whatever its basis and no matter how ambitious its scope, is shaped by contextually specific perspectives, topics of interest, and normative orientations. The burden of proof that theology once assumed alone is lessened because every discipline finds itself in the same seemingly inescapable circumstance to some degree or other.

With the chastening of pretensions to universal and disinterested knowl-edge comes a renewed stress on the practical character of rational judgment, since all claims to knowledge now gain a topical and situation-specific focus.

Critical assessment of a claim requires consideration of who makes the claim, in what context, and for what purpose. In this academic climate, where a claim came from and the norms according to which it was generated are not as much at issue as critical assessment of the claim itself and what it has going for it. Even if sources and norms for theological proposals—such as faithfulness to scriptural witness—remain suspect in their particularity and relative immunity from criticism, thinkers believe that those proposals are saying something of wider moment about the world and our place in it, and as such are subject to challenge or support on a host of other grounds. Irrespective of their basis in sources and norms that Christians alone find credible, Christian recommendations for human life might well be plausible, aesthetically pleasing, practical, satisfying of basic human needs, and so on.

CLAIMING RELEVANCE?

The question of the legitimacy of theology shifts, in sum, from theology's ability to meet some scholarly minimum in procedure to the question of whether theology has anything important to say about the world and our place in it. How might a contemporary Christian theology promote (or not) a more adequate understanding of the world and a more just way of living? What resources, for example, does the Christian symbol system have for addressing the financial calamity and environmental degradation we must now all face up to, whether we like it or not? How would the Christian symbol system need to be creatively and critically recast in the process?

Answers to such questions require new method, and in this respect method retains its importance. Theology's closest analogue can no longer be a perennial philosophy, addressing the most general questions of human moment purportedly common to every time and place, but rather sociopolitical theory. In other words, the theologian—like a Weberian social scientist or a Gramscian political theorist—now asks about the various ways Christian beliefs and symbols can function in the particulars of people's lives so as to direct and provide support for the shape of social life and the course of social action. The theologian needs a thorough knowledge of the way these intersections of cultural meanings and sociopolitical formations have panned out across differences of time and place—a thorough knowledge of the various permutations of the Christian symbol system in all its complicated alignments with social forces, for good or ill. Such knowledge in hand, the constructive theologian is better positioned to intervene in the current situation adroitly, effectively, and responsibly, with suggestions for both rethinking Christian claims and reconfiguring their import for human life.

SHIFTS AND TURNS

My own theological trajectory has followed the general path just outlined in response to events of the times. I initially turned to theology from philosophy, which when I was an undergraduate at Yale involved (unusually for the time) the broad study of both continental and analytic philosophy and a familiarity with American pragmatism and process thought. The linguistic turn had been made, Thomas Kuhn had initiated a sociology of knowledge that chastened the objectivist ideal of science as a paradigm for all other disciplines, and deconstruction was in the air via the teaching of Geoffrey Hartman and Paul de Man and visiting lectures by Jacques Derrida; but the blurring of philosophy into anthropology and literary theory—now so common—had yet to take hold.

Theology held for me the prospect of addressing questions of meaning in a comprehensive fashion eschewed by most philosophers at the time. Theology as an academic discipline was clearly about something (not just talk about talk about talk), and its pursuit of the true and the right had significance for a community of inquiry outside itself—the church. Theology, in short, seemed to matter—to someone. Under the impact of postliberalism, which had begun to solidify around the work of Frei and Lindbeck, my work made that broader community of inquiry (which centrally involved religious people in their efforts to forge a way of life) its focus—as both subject matter and object for intervention—with a corresponding broadening of methods, away from philosophy as traditionally construed.

My first book, *God and Creation in Christian Theology* (1988), was a wide-ranging analysis of patterns of discourse about God and creation in Christian thought. It discussed the way such patterns of discourse modified habits of speech in the wider society in order to show (rather than explain) the coherence of various Christian claims about God and the world; it also discussed how those patterns of discourse were distorted and coherence lost under modern strain. Because Christian language was never adequate to the God to which it referred, the theologian was concerned not directly with that referent, but with the habits of speech and action that amounted to God's direction of Christian lives. Intellectual difficulties arising out of everyday Christian practice—for example, the inability to resolve how I am to be responsible for the character of my life while dependent, nevertheless, on God's grace—set off theological questions about the compatibility of asserting both human and divine responsibility for our actions; and those questions were resolved by altering the way we usually speak of action in common.

In *The Politics of God* (1992), I more overtly discussed the function of religious discourse in Christian lives by exploring how beliefs about God and creation shaped Christians' political stances. Discourse analysis—the method of the first book—was insufficient here; the method was now something closer to that of sociology or anthropology. This book did not simply describe

Christian practice (while commending it for its coherence, as the first book did). It argued a normative case—how beliefs about God and creation should shape Christian lives—in self-conscious opposition to the way those beliefs have commonly functioned to ill effect in the past and present.

In *Theories of Culture: A New Agenda for Theology* (1997), I raised up this new method as the primary subject for discussion, but only as a preparation for a more constructive, substantive agenda. *Jesus, Humanity and the Trinity* (2001) ventured a clear vision of the whole "Christian thing" (as David Kelsey, another of my Yale teachers, would put it); all the main topics of Christian theology, such as the Trinity, creation, covenant, Christology, and eschatology, were organized around the idea of God as gift giver, to establish a consistent Christian outlook on life and the corresponding character of human responsibilities.

Impelled by the horrendous events of 9/11 to address inequities on the global front, I developed the social principles garnered in that book from the concept of God's giving to us—principles of unconditional, mutual, and universally inclusive benefit—into an economic ethic, again with an innovative methodical twist, in a subsequent book, *Economy of Grace* (2005).

This last book brought together all the elements of the historical shift in theological sensibilities I have been discussing. The inequity of global capitalism was the specific challenge that called for a systematic rethinking of Christian themes and their implications for economic matters. Fundamental Christian beliefs, for example, have often been understood to concern a Christ who pays our debts and a God who demands repayment for goods received, parceling out just deserts to those meeting the requirements of further divine favor by their proper use of previous benefits. Rather than seeming to bring a debt economy to completion in this way, might not Christianity instead portend its end by talking about a God who in Christ extends unstinting favor to undeserving sinners, offering them all, however foreign or alienated from God's household, the full inheritance of God's own children? Rather than accepting the terms of economic life set by the wider society, Christianity, I argue, would thereby be engaging in a cultural contest with it over what the fundamental assumptions of economic life should be.

Arguing on Christian grounds for conclusions that I believe anyone might find attractive, I suggest substituting common enjoyment and use of goods for the assumed need for private property, and the ideal of a community of mutual fulfillment for a competitive winner-take-all society. I develop a method of comparative or general economy, which extends the insights of French sociologist Pierre Bourdieu, to justify including in this way both theology and economics on equal terms.

Conversations

Despite the idiosyncrasies of my personal trajectory, this sort of constructive focus on Christianity as a worldview capable of orienting social action and this investigation into the way such a focus requires conversation with social scientists are not especially unusual on the present scene. Liberation theologies, African American, mujerista and white feminist theologies, historicist- and pragmatist-influenced theologies, and those creatively developing a Tillichian form of correlation—these are often found moving in the same direction. One thing that sets my own efforts apart is the place of historical study for creatively reworking Christian ideas and symbols to meet present challenges.

Relevant to this interest in history is the fact that part of what originally drew me to theology was its oddity within the secular university and even on the contemporary scene (despite the recent rise of fundamentalism as a world-historical force). Theology had the ability to propose the unexpected, to shock and startle. It offered an escape from the taken-for-granted certainties of life by referring them to something that remained ever beyond them, resisting capture and encapsulation. The theologian respects that capacity of theology, it seems to me, not by dressing up contemporary commonplaces in religious terms, but in seeking what lies beyond a contemporary outlook and beyond the immediate context of one's work.

A theology that starts from, and uses as its toolbox for creative ends, materials gathered from the widest possible purview is, in my opinion, a theology with that imaginative expansiveness. Such a theology looks to the Christian past not for models for simple imitation but for a way to complicate one's sense of the possibilities for present Christian expression and action. It looks to the past not to restrict and cramp what might be said in the present but to break out of the narrowness of a contemporary sense of the realistic. It complements an understanding of the complex variety of premodern theologies in the West with an understanding of the complex forms of Christianity's global reach now and in the past. It moves beyond narrow denominational confines to the broadest possible ecumenical vision and sees beyond elite forms of theological expression, in written texts primarily, to the popular theologies of everyday life.

All that is what I mean by a historically funded constructive theology: the premodern, the popular, the global, and the ecumenical are put to use to shake up, reorient, and expand what one would have thought one could do with the Christian symbol system, in the effort to figure out what it is proper for Christians to think and do in today's world.

The breadth of this understanding of the historical, and the focus here on the historical complexity and variability of Christian forms of life, indicate ways that I have moved beyond my Yale training. At Yale, the talk was commonly of the biblical world and the Christian tradition. I have also refused to understand Christian ways of living in isolation from the wider culture. Christian ways of speaking and acting are not created out of whole cloth but are constituted by odd modifications to ways of speaking and acting that are current in the wider society. It is therefore impossible to understand their meaning and social point without understanding the culture of the wider society and what Christian habits of speech and action are saying about it through modifications made to it.

For example, when Christians call Jesus "Lord," it is a comment on the lords of the wider society, a comment impossible to understand without knowing what is unusual about such an attribution in the context of its use. Contrary to its usual application, "lord" in Christian employment refers to a person shamefully crucified as a criminal and enemy of the state.

Similarly, the significance of eating in church is not clear until one understands the eating practices of the wider society. Modifications to those practices in church become a kind of critical commentary on social practices—for instance, a criticism of the exclusions of ordinary table fellowship.

Theological construction—figuring out what it is that Christians should say and do in the present context—therefore requires a highly complicated and subtle reading of the whole cultural field in which Christianity figures. One is helped here again by historical analysis (in my broad sense) that incorporates such a holistic cultural perspective. Theology is always a matter of judgments regarding the practices of the wider society and about the degree and manner in which they should also figure in Christian lives. Knowledge of how Christians have made such judgments at other times and places, and one's own sense in hindsight or at a distance about whether they did so correctly (for example, in suitably Christian fashion), provide invaluable insights and practice in tackling the issues of one's own time and circumstance when the personal stakes are much higher.

BEYOND METHOD

Method, I have learned, is no safeguard for making such judgment. Karl Barth was shocked by his teachers' support for World War I into rejecting the method of Protestant liberalism. I was shocked by many of my American theological colleagues' responses to the political upsurge of the Christian right in the U.S. and to the culture wars during the late 1980s and early 1990s, which so shamefully targeted gays and lesbians at the height of the AIDS crisis, into seeing that method (as it has been traditionally conceived) is insufficient. Too many of my teachers (meaning those already established on the theological scene and from whom I expected wisdom and guidance) interpreted the upsurge of the Christian right simply as the salutary entrance of religion into the public square, promising an elevation in the seriousness with which theological exchanges would have to be taken by the wider society. What was being promulgated by the Christian right was of less interest.

Dismay and shame at the fact that Christianity could stand so publicly for this was not, as far as I could see, at a premium. Given at least superficial similarities between the postliberalism of my immediate circle of teachers and that of the religious right (for example, preoccupation with the world of the Bible, repudiation of apologetics, and opposition to liberal culture), the failure of postliberal theologians to criticize the religious right could easily be taken for an endorsement. To prevent silence from being taken for praise, the situation required, it seemed to me, only the most forceful repudiation of the Christian right's political judgments, something I tried to do in *The Politics of God*. The postliberal reluctance to be more than a witness to the wider society had to be overcome. It seemed to me, instead, that one's sense of that witness itself was to be formed in direct engagement with the political developments of the day. One should witness to a God who stood with those whom the Christian right maligned to further its own political interests— welfare mothers, sexual minorities, and the urban poor, for example.

I carried away from this time the belief that it is misguided to think that proper theological method will make clear all by itself the proper Christian stance on the contested sociocultural issues of one's day. Search for proper method with that expectation encourages blanket judgments about the wider culture as a whole—it is to be resisted, or welcomed as the ground floor for the contributions of grace, or transformed as a whole—when what is really necessary is an often more difficult and nuanced discernment about particulars.

Advocating either the Word as norm for Christian judgment with Barth or critical correlation with Tillich does not help very much when the question is the contested one of how to read the situation in a Christian light in the first place. What, for example, does feminism or the movement for gay rights represent in Christian terms? An instance of moral irresponsibility, which Christians should resist, or a movement toward full human flourishing, to which Christians should be sympathetic? Such judgments have much more to do with the substantive character of one's understanding of what Christianity is all about than they do with the method used to come up with that understanding.

To make the simplistic parallel with Barth again, Christians supported the Nazis not because they neglected the Word in favor of cultural trends but because they had a misguided understanding of Christianity. Hitler's National Socialism was wrong on Christian grounds because its material policy toward Jews (and others) was unchristian and not because it forced the neglect of the Word by making an idol of the nation-state. Clearly, if its understanding of Christianity seems to warrant it, a nation-state can, according to its own lights, be trying to respect the Word while persecuting Jews, and that fact would nevertheless merit as grave a theological condemnation as any the Barmen Declaration offers.

THE POROUS LIFE OF FAITH

Christians are always influenced, one way or another, by the cultural trends of the day—respect for the Word does not exempt them from culture's effects (as Barth himself recognized in *Church Dogmatics* I/2). It is what Christians do with these cultural influences that matters, as they grow into an understanding of their Christian commitments by way of complex processes of revision, appropriation, and resistance to them, taken one by one. One never rejects everything, since one's Christianity always remains parasitic to some extent on the wider society's forms of life. Nor (one hopes) does one accept everything, because Christian justifications even for courses of action shared with the wider society alter their sense and point.

One's judgments about different aspects of the wider society's practices need not, moreover, be uniform. For example, my grave worries about economic inequalities that are the product of global capitalism need not deny the greater economic opportunities for women that are also a feature of economic developments in the modern West. An equal resistance to both simply because they are the "world" that Christianity is to reject leads to dishonesty about the way that the world inevitably figures in even the best Christian lives and to a lazy reneging on Christian responsibilities to judge particulars with care.

Theologians need to be honest about the complexities of Christian lives and the way Christian beliefs and symbols figure there. Doing so means taking seriously what disciplines such as sociology and anthropology reveal: the often messy, ambiguous, and porous character of the effort to live Christianly. Trained historians of Christianity—particularly historians who avail themselves of the insights of those other disciplines—are not surprised by such a recommendation. Most theologians, I believe, have yet to see its force.

23

Faith Seeking Understanding • Ronald F. Thiemann

Some twenty-five years ago, I mounted the stairs to the high pulpit at Harvard's Memorial Church to deliver my inaugural convocation address as Dean of Harvard Divinity School. In addition to the faculty members, students, staff, alumni/ae, and curious onlookers seated in the pews before me, was an assemblage of persons representing the various stages on my life's way: my parents, brother, and sister; my own immediate family; members and pastors of the two Lutheran parishes I had served in Connecticut and Pennsylvania; friends from Yale University and Haverford College. Never before, and as it would turn out, never again, would I have the opportunity to gaze upon such an array of persons who had helped to shape my religious and theological commitments. As I drew a deep breath in preparation for my remarks, I could not help but wonder how a Lutheran kid from the Midwest, son of parents educated only through the eighth grade, had managed to ascend these rather dizzying heights.

Early Influences

My earliest theological influences stemmed from the situation into which I was born. My mother emigrated from Germany at the age of two, and lived into her early twenties on a tenant farm operated by her parents and her brothers and sisters. Like the rest of the family, she was forced to quit school following the eighth grade in order to assist with the farm chores. One of her brothers died of drowning when she was sixteen years old and another was left in Germany when the family immigrated to the U.S. in 1913. The latter brother never rejoined the family, grew up in Weimar and Nazi Germany, and died in the battlefields of France in 1944. These two deaths haunted my mother, and she compensated for these losses by developing a remarkably vibrant faith and a wicked sense of humor.[1]

My mother's family was part of the wave of German immigration that reached these shores in the decades prior to the First World War. Vigorously

Lutheran, they became part of the German-speaking community of the Lutheran Church-Missouri Synod that settled in the rural countryside outside of St. Louis. Despite the fact that my father was Roman Catholic, all three children were raised Lutheran.

My father was a third-generation American, his forebears having emigrated from Germany in the mid-nineteenth century. His father died when my dad was two years old, and he was raised on the family farm by his mother and grandmother. Nominally Catholic, he did not become a practicing believer until the days following the Second Vatican Council, when he became convinced that the church no longer condemned him for marrying a Lutheran and raising his children "outside the faith." Like my mother, he left school following his elementary education in order to work on the farm. Throughout most of his adult life, he was a traveling salesman, pushing Fuller brushes, life insurance, and Electrolux vacuums door-to-door. Though less prominent in my upbringing than my mother, he offered a quiet witness of faith, particularly during the years following his retirement.

Most importantly, however, my parents' marriage taught me the importance of ecumenical relations. Without knowing it, they modeled the possibility of mutual coexistence and respect for different, and sometimes conflicting, faith traditions. Particularly during the last half of their sixty-year marriage, they remained faithful to their own convictions while respecting the faith and practice of the other. Admittedly my Roman Catholic father was much better at this than my LCMS mother; yet by the end of their lives they came to share a common faith despite their divergent traditions. The endurance of their union in the face of condemnations of their "mixed marriage" by both communities was an early and indelible lesson on ecumenism and modest distrust of official church teachings.

I am one of those rare Christians in these days of denomination switching: a lifelong Lutheran. I was reared and nurtured in the Lutheran church and attended Lutheran schools exclusively for the first twenty-six years of my life. The first non-LCMS school I ever attended was Yale University, where I did my doctoral work. I had the good fortune to be educated in the LCMS at a time when the "spirit of moderation" that would ultimately lead to schism in the church was in full bloom. I learned my love of reading, music, and the life of the mind from my teachers in Lutheran elementary and high schools. Since there was virtually no tradition of reading in my family, I learned to love reading through my fascination with sports. At a very early age I discovered the sports novels of John Tunis and Claire Bee and read every volume I could find in the local school and public libraries as well as summer "bookmobiles." One day, when I was ten or eleven, the librarian of one of those traveling summer libraries put into my hand the thickest book I had ever held. "I've noticed how many books you check out every time you come here, "she said. "I think you might find this one interesting," and she placed into my hands a copy of Alexander Dumas's *The Three Musketeers*. Soon I became addicted to the literature of swashbuckling French romantics. I owe a great debt to that nameless librarian, because she introduced me to a world of literature unknown within the confines of my family, and helped me to discover the delights of narrative: plot, character, suspense, *peripeteia*, and "the sense of an ending."

Music was the other great love nurtured by my Lutheran heritage. Worship was a common experience in my life. In addition to regular Sunday services, every classroom in my elementary school conducted daily worship. Hymnody shaped my faith in those early formative years. I had an instinctive dislike for the otherworldly lyrics of pietistic hymns. I would cringe when forced to sing the words of Hymn #660, the last hymn in the blue Lutheran hymnal, "Heaven Is My Home." "I'm but a stranger here; heaven is my home. Earth is a desert drear; heaven is my home." My mother's earthy piety gave me a deep sense that Christian faith and the enjoyment of God's good creation were not inconsistent. I reveled in the soaring strains of the great hymns of praise: "Holy, Holy, Holy," "Crown Him with Many Crowns," "Immortal, Invisible, God Only Wise," and yes, "A Mighty Fortress Is Our God"—in the original sixteenth-century tempo, not the chorale version most Lutherans sing today.

Even now my spirituality is shaped more by music than by words. I can abide even the most wretched preaching as long as a service includes music that witnesses to the glory of God. Not surprisingly, my musical taste tends toward the Baroque—Schütz, Buxtehude, and, of course, Bach. Despite the pietism evident in the lyrics of his passions and cantatas, Bach's music bespeaks the grandeur and consolation of God's saving work, what the seventeenth-century scholastics termed "objective justification." In moments of great doubt and in the darkest nights of my soul, I have been sustained in my faith by the trumpets that herald the opening of Bach's "Christmas Oratorio" or Handel's "And the Trumpet Shall Sound."

My Teachers

Like most academics, I have been deeply influenced by my teachers. I experienced my first serious crisis of faith during my freshman year in college, when I realized that the rather simple piety I learned in home, church, and school could no longer sustain my belief. With typical late-adolescent romanticism, I decided to reject my parochial past and strike out on my own as a questing agnostic intellectual. This stage lasted only a few months, because during the second term of that year I entered the classroom of Walter Bouman, later to become professor of theology at Trinity Seminary. Within a matter of weeks, Walt had deconstructed the simple faith of my childhood. He savaged the otherworldly piety, the sanctimonious romanticism, and the proto-fundamentalism of my Missouri Synod background. He ridiculed the lyrics of hymns like "In the Garden," contrasting "He walks with me and He talks with me" to the *deus absconditus* of Luther's *De Servo Arbitrio*. He introduced me to the great critics of Christianity, particularly Feuerbach and Nietzsche, and showed how they devastated the anthropomorphism that characterized so much of American religion. He insisted that "Jesus loves me this I know" because the *gospel* not the Bible "tells me so."

But most importantly, Walter Bouman introduced me to the work of Martin Luther, particularly to his Christology, and through that experience both my faith and my intellect were transformed. From Luther I learned that God's grace and majesty were incarnate in the life, death, and resurrection of Jesus Christ. I came to understand that God's revelation comes always and only *sub contrario*, in the everyday, ordinary, even contemptible earthy realities of life. In Luther's Galatians commentary, I glimpsed the heart of the gospel, that "blessed exchange" whereby God in Christ becomes sin so that sinners might become righteous. Through these experiences, the natural/supernatural or sacred/profane distinction was replaced, once and for all, by the more mysterious and complex distinction between the hidden and revealed. In some sense my entire theological project has been shaped by Luther's *theologia crucis*, by the insight that God's saving grace comes to us sacramentally, in, with, and under the elements of our everyday lives. The great challenge to faith is not to believe that the divine has become human, but to believe that God has brought righteousness out of sin and life out of death.

Concordia Days

My grasp of the Lutheran theological tradition deepened considerably through my teachers at Concordia Seminary. In addition to training in systematic theology, I also learned the techniques of historical-critical exegesis. My years at Concordia (1968–1972) were remarkable, because I witnessed the full flowering of the critical but confessional theology taught by the exceptional faculty. In order to enter "the sem" at St. Louis, ministerial students had to have the equivalent of four years each of Greek, Latin, and German and two years of Hebrew. All exegesis was done in the original languages, and we learned how critical study of the Bible could be combined with a deep commitment to the Lutheran Confessions. My teacher for confessions and liturgy was the sainted Arthur Carl Piepkorn, a brilliant scholar and man of great faith, whose death, many of us are convinced, was hastened by the intemperate charge that he and his colleagues were teachers of false doctrine. Though the demise of this faculty and of the Synod would not take place for another two years, my cohorts and I witnessed the beginning of the investigations that ultimately led to the resignation of most members of the faculty and the formation of Christ Seminary in Exile (Seminex). With the destruction of the faculty, a remarkable period of American church history came to an untimely end. With the increasing polarization of American Protestantism between fundamentalist and liberal wings of the churches, centrist institutions such as Concordia could have exemplified a form of critical yet faithful inquiry, a "critical appropriation of tradition," virtually unknown in today's divisive ecclesial atmosphere. In some ways those of us who have remained "in exile" since the schism in the Lutheran Church-Missouri Synod remain committed to that model even as we labor "on the boundaries."

In addition to the fine instruction I received from my formal teachers at Concordia, my friendship with Gilbert Meilaender became an essential part of my theological development. For six years, we were classmates at Concordia Senior College and Concordia Seminary, and we engaged in theological disputes that sharpened our thinking and deepened our understanding. The bond of friendship we have shared over the years has been more than sufficient to hold us together despite our differing theological views. While we share many of the same traits of character and disposition, we disagree on a wide range of theological issues. Despite, or perhaps because of, those disagreements, he has been one of my most important teachers. Through our countless amicable debates, I learned how to respect and understand positions and persons with whom I disagree. I am a different, and a better, theologian because of my friendship with Gil.

Yale Days

When I left Concordia to enter the doctoral program at Yale, I did so with the hope that I would one day return to become professor of systematic theology. That hope died with the demise of the LCMS. Fortunately, my training at Yale equipped me marvelously for my future teaching opportunities. The single most powerful presence for me at Yale was Hans Frei, a historical and systematic theologian of enormous erudition, and a person of exceptional character.

When I arrived at Yale, I discovered that Frei had dramatically reduced his teaching load because he had become Master of Ezra Stiles College. Nonetheless, he agreed to take me on as his tutorial student for the entire first year of my doctoral program. Every Tuesday I would make the trek across the Yale campus to the Master's office at Ezra Stiles, and Hans Frei and I would study the great texts of the modern Christian tradition. Building on my deep but narrow training at Concordia, Hans (I still find it difficult to refer to him by his first name; Mr. Frei seems more appropriate) introduced me to the broad philosophical and theological literature of Europe, England, and the United States. My teaching at Haverford College in the field of modern religious thought stemmed almost entirely from these tutorial sessions. Just as importantly he taught me, by his own example, the quality of good teaching: clarity of presentation, good humor, and a commitment to students and their welfare. He worked tirelessly in behalf of his doctoral students, making sure they found teaching positions in excellent institutions. The church and academy lost a great figure when Hans Frei died, suddenly and unexpectedly, in 1988.

I was fortunate to be surrounded by an unusually gifted group of students studying theology at Yale in the mid-1970s. We met together regularly to read and discuss one another's papers, and to engage in extended, and often hilarious, conversations. After we each finished our degrees and began teaching at our respective institutions, we realized how much we missed the collegial exchange of those years. So we agreed to meet every summer, usually at the Dominican House of Studies in Washington, D.C., in order to discuss one another's book manuscripts. The Yale-Washington Theology Group has now been meeting for more than twenty years, and the group has been acknowledged in virtually all the books published by the group's membership.

During my third year at Yale I was fortunate to receive a *Deutscher Akademischer Austauschdienst* fellowship to study at the University of Tübingen. There I worked primarily with Klaus Scholder and Eberhard Jüngel and completed most of my dissertation manuscript on the christological debates between Karl Barth and Werner Elert during the tumultuous period of German politics from 1932 to 1936. In the course of my research I discovered that Elert, the theologian most revered by my teachers at Concordia Seminary, was deeply sympathetic to aspects of Nazi ideology and saw no conflict between his convictions as a Lutheran theologian and his support for the Nazi regime. My desire to understand more clearly the profound political blindness of my own Lutheran tradition led me to a serious study of the period of the late Weimer Republic and the early Third Reich. The experience also gave me a substantial dose of self-critical humility about a tradition that I still affirm and deeply love. Though I did not publish on the subject of religion and politics for nearly fifteen years, my work on the dissertation planted the seeds of my interest in the theme of theology and public life.

TEACHING AND THINKING

After teaching halftime in the Yale Religious Studies Department during the last year of my doctoral program, I was fortunate to be appointed in 1976 to the faculty of Haverford College. Haverford is one of the great teaching colleges of American higher education. The intellectual atmosphere is intense but congenial, as faculty members regularly engage in joint teaching and research projects. This interdisciplinary context provided fertile new ground for my own thinking and writing. During my first two years there I had to create eleven new courses, so it was not unusual for me to stay up until 2:00 am preparing lectures for the next day. The students were so bright that it took all my ingenuity just to stay one day ahead of them. But those first years of teaching provided the most acute educational experience of my life. Courses such as "Modern Critics of Christianity," "Narrative, Religion, and Rationality," "The German Church Struggle and the Holocaust" gave me the opportunity to explore new topics and expand my intellectual horizons. My teaching focus on Weimar and the Third Reich led to involvement with the National Conference of Christians and Jews and the American Jewish Committee, work that remains central to my vocation.

The single most important influence on my research and writing during my decade at Haverford was my colleague Richard Bernstein. Dick had just finished his book *The Restructuring of Social and Political Theory* and was beginning the research that would lead to the publication of *Beyond Objectivism and Relativism.* He invited me into his faculty research seminar, and I plunged into the literature on nonfoundational epistemology. While the technical details of the field fascinated me, I was particularly attracted to the intellectual sensibilities of nonfoundational philosophers. Those who refused to abandon the search for truth while acknowledging the absence of indubitable foundations struck me as "soul mates" of theologians who understood the significance of justification by faith.

The doctrine of justification teaches that while no earthly or temporal accomplishment can make us righteous in the sight of God, nonetheless God declares us righteous through the earthly and temporal reality of Jesus of Nazareth. The irony shared by nonfoundational philosophy and faithful theology is that only in giving up the search for certainty do we gain the confidence to affirm the truth. Dick Bernstein's eloquent description of the Cartesian Anxiety could just as easily be a theological account of the false alternatives of idolatry or despair. "The Cartesian Anxiety . . . is that grand and seductive Either/Or. *Either* there is some support for our being, a fixed foundation for our knowledge, *or* we cannot escape the forces of darkness that envelop us with madness, with intellectual and moral [we might add spiritual] chaos." These were precisely the spiritual alternatives that Luther faced while an Augustinian monk, and the doctrine of justification—by grace, through faith, for the sake of Christ—provides the theological release from this apparent dilemma.

EARLY WRITING

Revelation and Theology: The Gospel as Narrated Promise, my first book, is an attempt to rework the post-Reformation doctrine of revelation through the dual lens provided by nonfoundational philosophy and the doctrine of justification. David Kelsey once said that he liked my work because I had an affection, one that he shared, for "lost causes." When I began work on this book in the early '80s, most Protestant theologians would have agreed that the doctrine of revelation had simply outlived its usefulness and needed to be abandoned. While I agreed that most formulations of the doctrine could not hold up to careful theological and philosophical scrutiny, I was convinced that one aspect of the doctrine was essential to the Christian faith: the assertion of God's prevenience. Without this fundamental belief, the Christian affirmations of grace, faith, and salvation could not be sustained. *Revelations and Theology* set out to provide an account of God's prevenience in terms consistent with nonfoundational philosophy and the doctrine of justification.

In the course of my argument I employed the category of "narrative," and used a form of literary analysis in my interpretation of the Gospel of Matthew. Because "narrative" had become a hot topic by the time my book was published in 1985, many reviewers saw it as a type of "narrative theology," a term I despise. I understand the book to be an exercise in theological epistemology, a defense of revelation that avoids the unhappy alternatives of an anthropocentric theology that simply projects human qualities upon God or a theocentric theology that asserts the priority of God at the expense of human involvement in the drama of salvation. In the process of making this argument, I believe I develop an adequate theological reply to Feuerbach and other critics of Christianity who rely upon a theory of projection to dismiss Christian claims.

Revelation and Theology was published a few months after the appearance of George Lindbeck's influential *The Nature of Doctrine*, and many reviewers noted the formal similarities between Lindbeck's "postliberal" theology and my nonfoundational "descriptive" theology. Other critics thought they saw a connection between my work and that of Stanley Hauerwas, given our common interest in the category of "narrative," and they raised the question of whether my theological position was relevant to the world of common and public human experience. I began to pursue inquiry into the topic of public theology both as a way of answering my critics and as a means of distinguishing my work from that of Professors Lindbeck and Hauerwas.

As I argued in my next book, *Constructing a Public Theology*, I share neither Lindbeck's cultural pessimism nor Hauerwas's sectarian ecclesiology. Both thinkers offer such a bleak account of postmodern culture and liberal society as to render a public theology virtually impossible. I believe that the most important political task for the contemporary Christian community is to be a community of hope in a culture that is increasingly cynical about our common human future. Broadside attacks on liberalism or cultural despair about our de-Christianized society do not function to nurture a sense of hope about God's reconciling action in behalf of the entire cosmos. Indeed, these approaches can have the unintended but devastating consequence of discouraging Christians and other people of faith from engaging in positive political action in the public realm. But if persons formed in those communities in which the virtues of faith, hope, and love are nurtured fail to manifest those virtues in public life, then the *polis* will indeed be left to those with a shrunken and desiccated view of the possibilities of political community. My hope has been that a critical nonfoundational public theology might contribute not to the death of liberal democracy but to its moral renewal.

HARVARD DAYS AND CONTINUED WRITING

My renewed scholarly interest in the issue of the public significance of theological discourse corresponded with my move to the deanship of Harvard Divinity School in 1986. Faced with the task of the renewal of one of America's premier theological schools, I sought a way in which my scholarly project could be integrated with my primary administrative responsibilities. I did not seek the position; indeed, I feared that my own research program, which was only now emerging with genuine clarity, might be obliterated if I took such a position. But Derek Bok, then Harvard's president, was both persuasive and generous, and assured me that I could take a full semester leave from the deanship sometime during the first five years of my tenure. That leave, combined with my judicious use of my summers, made it possible for me to engage in the research that yielded *Religion in Public Life: A Dilemma for Democracy*.

This book addresses three interlocking issues: the cultural and constitutional problems raised by the doctrine of the "separation of church and state"; the philosophical and ethical problems raised by classical liberal political theory; and the religious and theological challenges raised by the phenomenon of cultural, religious, and moral pluralism. To my surprise and delight, the book was quickly discovered by constitutional scholars and has been the subject of a number of conferences at law school and law and religion societies. More recently, it has been reviewed in a number of major political science journals and has led to collaboration on projects with scholars such as John Rawls, Michael Sandel, and Robert Putnam.

Though it may not be apparent to many of the book's readers, my Lutheran commitments are once again implicit in my method. One way to think of the book is to see it as an attempt to restate Luther's *zwei Reiche Lehre* (two kingdoms doctrine) for a modern, liberal, and pluralist society. Drawing on Bonhoeffer's distinction in *Ethics* between the ultimate and penultimate, I devise an understanding of Christian truth-claiming that allows full involvement in a pluralist world while still affirming the fundamental beliefs of the Christian tradition. With the help of Nicholas Rescher's fine work on pluralism, I argue that communities of faith must come to recognize the compatibility between deep and abiding commitment to the truth claims of one's tradition and an openness and respect for the claims of other traditions. Truth-claiming and an acceptance of pluralism, I contend, are not inconsistent. In making this argument, I draw upon nonfoundational theology, classical Trinitarian conceptions of God, and a revised Lutheran understanding of God's sustaining presence in both church and world.

Looking Forward

My religious and intellectual journey has opened opportunities I would have found unimaginable just twenty years ago. And yet as I have reflected upon the course of my life, I have been struck by the number of common themes that emerge in the telling of this story. The continuing influence of parents, church, and school—particularly of my Lutheran heritage—is striking, even to me. As I look toward those unwritten chapters of my life, I hope that I can continue to be faithful to those who have helped to shape my theological autobiography, even as I seek new opportunities to grow. If faith is both a habit of the heart and of the mind, then I can think of no better motto for my life's work than the Anselmian credo, *fides quaerens intellectum*, faith seeking understanding.

Notes

[1] I reflect on these qualities as my mother faced her own death in the essay "Is There Life After Death?" in *Why Are We Here? Christian Reflections on Everyday Questions*, ed. William C. Placher and Ronald Thiemann (Harrisburg, PA: Trinity, 1996).

ions Editor	Keri Witman
d Assistant	Maureen A. Powers
ng Manager	Kevin Molloy
Production Editor	Sandra Dumas
Designer	Kevin Murphy
tion Management Services	Argosy
Photo	Old-growth in Memorial Grove, Cheguamegon National Forest, Wisconsin
	© Jeff Martin/JMAR Foto-Werks

ook was set in 10/12 Adobe Garamond by Argosy and printed and bound by Malloy Lithographing, Inc. The cover was
by Phoenix Color Corp.

ook is printed on acid-free paper. ∞

right 2003 © John Wiley & Sons, Inc. All rights reserved.

art of this publication may be reproduced, stored in a retrieval system or transmitted in any form or by any means, elec-
, mechanical, photocopying, recording, scanning or otherwise, except as permitted under Sections 107 or 108 of the 1976
d States Copyright Act, without either the prior written permission of the Publisher, or authorization through payment of
ppropriate per-copy fee to the Copyright Clearance Center, 222 Rosewood Drive, Danvers, MA 01923, (978) 750-8400, fax
750-4470. Requests to the Publisher for permission should be addressed to the Permissions Department, John Wiley &
Inc., 111 River Street, Hoboken, NJ 07030, (201) 748-6011, fax (201) 748-6008, E-Mail: PERMREQ@WILEY.COM.

der books please call (800) 225-5945.

g, Raymond A. and Giese, Ronald L., eds.
duction to Forest Ecosystem Science and Management, Third Edition
0-471-33145-7

ed in the United States of America

8 7 6 5 4 3 2 1

LIBRARY
SECC. STRAIT AREA CAMPUS
226 REEVES ST.
PORT HAWKESBURY, NS B9A 2A2 CANADA

DIAGRAM FOR THE CLASSIFICATION OF WORLD LIFE ZONES OR PLANT FORMATIONS

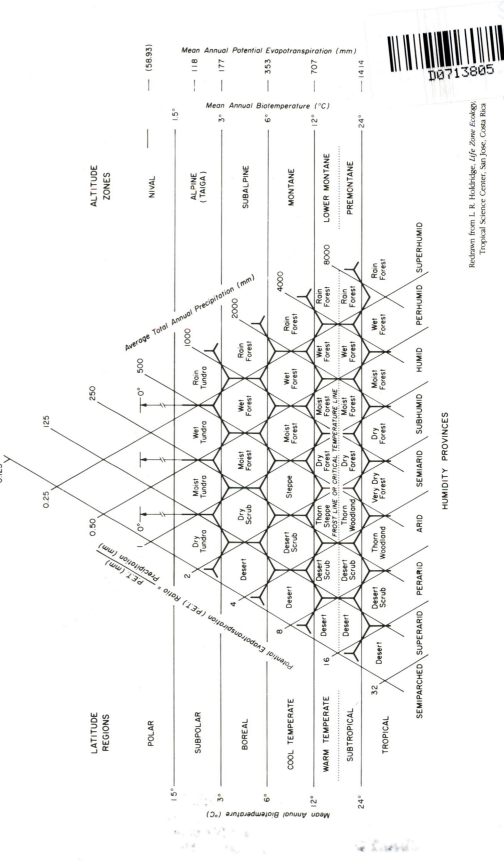

Redrawn from L. R. Holdridge, *Life Zone Ecology,*
Tropical Science Center, San Jose, Costa Rica

Kari E. Bisbee
Department of Forest Ecology and Management
University of Wisconsin–Madison
Madison, Wisconsin

Paul V. Bolstad
Department of Forest Management
University of Minnesota
St. Paul, Minnesota

Mark S. Boyce
Department of Biological Sciences
University of Alberta
Edmonton, Alberta
Canada

Diana M. Burton
Departments of Forest Science
  and Agricultural Economics
Texas A & M University
College Station, Texas

John C. Bliss
College of Forestry
Oregon State University
Corvallis, Oregon

James G. Bockheim
Departments of Soil Science and
  Forest Ecology and Management
University of Wisconsin–Madison
Madison, Wisconsin

Thomas M. Bonnicksen
Department of Forest Science
Texas A & M University
College Station, Texas

John W. Bruce
Legal Department
The World Bank
Washington, D.C.

Joseph Buongiorno
Department of Forest Ecology and Management
University of Wisconsin–Madison
Madison, Wisconsin

J. Lin Compton
Department of Forest Ecology and Management
University of Wisconsin–Madison
Madison, Wisconsin

Alan R. Ek
Department of Forest Management
University of Minnesota
St. Paul, Minnesota

Ronald L. Giese
Department of Forest Ecology and Management
University of Wisconsin–Madison
Madison, Wisconsin

Daniel W. Gilmore
North Central Research and Outreach Center
Department of Forest Resources
University of Minnesota
Grand Rapids, Minnesota

Stith T. Gower
Department of Forest Ecology and Management
University of Wisconsin–Madison
Madison, Wisconsin

Gene Grey
106 Golf Villa Dr.
Moneta, Virginia

James M. Guldin
Southern Research Station
U.S.D.A. Forest Service
Hot Springs, Arkansas

Richard W. Guldin
U.S.D.A. Forest Service
Washington, D.C.

Eric L. Kruger
Department of Forest Ecology and Management
University of Wisconsin—Madison
Madison, Wisconsin

Joe J. Landsberg
CSIRO Institute of Natural Resources
and Environment
Canberra, Australia

Wayne C. Leininger
Department of Range Science
Colorado State University
Fort Collins, Colorado

Craig G. Lorimer
Department of Forest Ecology and Management
University of Wisconsin–Madison
Madison, Wisconsin

D. Scott Mackay
Department of Forest Ecology and Management and
    Institute for Environmental Studies
University of Wisconsin–Madison
Madison, Wisconsin

David J. Mladenoff
Department of Forest Ecology and Management
University of Wisconsin–Madison
Madison, Wisconsin

A. Jeff Martin
Department of Forest Ecology and Management
University of Wisconsin–Madison
Madison, Wisconsin

George L. Martin
Department of Forest Ecology and Management
University of Wisconsin–Madison
Madison, Wisconsin

Volker C. Radeloff
Department of Forest Ecology and Management
University of Wisconsin–Madison
Madison, Wisconsin

Kenneth F. Raffa
Departments of Entomology and
    Forest Ecology and Management
University of Wisconsin–Madison
Madison, Wisconsin

Ronald Raunikar
Department of Forest Ecology and Management
University of Wisconsin–Madison
Madison, Wisconsin

Robert O. Ray
College of Agricultural and Life Sciences
University of Wisconsin–Madison
Madison, Wisconsin

Robert M. Shaffer
School of Forestry and Wildlife Resources
Virginia Polytechnic Institute and State University
Blacksburg, Virginia

Glen R. Stanosz
Departments of Plant Pathology and
    Forest Ecology and Management
University of Wisconsin–Madison
Madison, Wisconsin

John D. Stednick
Department of Range Science
Colorado State University
Fort Collins, Colorado

Thomas A. Walbridge, Jr.
School of Forestry and Wildlife Resources
Virginia Polytechnic Institute and State University
Blacksburg, Virginia

Eugene M. Wengert
Department of Forest Ecology and Management
University of Wisconsin–Madison
Madison, Wisconsin

Raymond A. Young
Department of Forest Ecology and Management
University of Wisconsin–Madison
Madison, Wisconsin

The science of forestry is a complex amalgamation of the biological, physical, managerial, social, and political sciences. Few, if any, forestry professionals are able to treat all aspects of forest science with complete authority. An edited book on forestry is thus the best method for conveying the science of forestry in one text. This third edition, formerly titled *Introduction to Forest Science*, reflects the many changes and approaches to forestry that have occurred in the field of forestry during the past 12 years, and we therefore decided, with reviewer input, to title this new edition *Introduction to Forest Ecosystem Science and Management*. The book is intended to provide beginning and intermediate students with a comprehensive introduction to the important aspects of the field of forestry. It represents a collective effort by a number of authors to present a broad view of the field. The authors give general coverage of their specialized fields within forestry and emphasize how decisions made by forest managers affect the forest ecosystem. References to other works that explore certain aspects of forest ecosystem science and management are provided for the student interested in greater depth.

It seems that there are as many approaches to the organization of a book in forestry as there are forestry professionals. In this third edition of the book, we attempt to maintain a flow from the basic cell and individual trees to the forest stand, followed by management of the forest stand, and then to acquisition of goods and services from the forest. In this new edition, we have added a new section, Forests and Society, to reflect the increasing role of human influences in forestry.

The book is arranged in four major parts. In the two chapters in the Introduction (Part 1), the development of American forest policy and the forestry profession are described. Important events that have shaped forest policy, such as the environmental movement, are treated in the first chapter and

important aspects of forestry employment opportunities are discussed in Chapter 2.

Part 2, Forest Biology and Ecology, contains information on factors affecting individual tree growth through growth of the forest stand. The first chapter in the section (Chapter 3) describes the location and composition of forests around the world as biomes. Biotic and abiotic influences on forest growth are discussed in detail in this section, and many agents affecting the complex forest ecosystem are analyzed in separate chapters on tree ecophysiology, soils, insects, and diseases. A new chapter on Landscape Ecology (Chapter 7) has been added to this third edition to emphasize the increasing importance of this subject area.

The management of the forest ecosystem for multiple uses is treated in Part 3, Forest Management—Multiple Uses. An overview of Forest Management and Stewardship is given in Chapter 9 and the significant role of private nonindustrial forests (NIPFs) is given special treatment in Chapter 10, because these forests constitute about 60 percent of all commercial forests. This is followed by two chapters emphasizing measurement and monitoring of the forest through land-based and satellite technology. Biological aspects of management are given thorough treatment in Chapter 13, Silviculture and Ecosystem Management. Separate chapters are devoted to management of forest wildlife, rangeland, watersheds, recreation, and fires in the forest. After a description of timber harvesting in Chapter 19, the last two chapters in the Management section deal with the conversion of forests to usable commodities and their valuation. In Chapter 20, the structure and properties of wood are described, and the methods for conversion to lumber, reconstituted products such as particleboard, paper, chemicals, and energy are outlined. The economics and management of the forest for wood and amenity values are analyzed in Chapter 21. An attempt is made in this chapter to assign monetary values to the amenities ascribed by humans to the forest. This chapter puts into perspective the relative value of the multiple uses we make of forests.

As already mentioned, the last section, Part 4, is devoted to Forests and Society. The increased interaction of humans with the forest, and the expectation of further intense interactions, both in urban and rural settings, has mandated specialized treatment of this subject matter. The unique situation of Urban Forests is described in Chapter 22. Social Forestry is described in detail in Chapter 23 through a discussion of community-based management of natural resources. Both regional and global emphasis are given in this important new chapter for the third edition of *Introduction to Forest Ecosystem Science and Management*.

In reality, the field of forestry cannot be separated into these four distinct sections, because of the interdependence of the many factors affecting the forest. Therefore, the reader is encouraged to refer to other sections or chapters where appropriate. Cross-references in the text designate when a specific subject is given more detailed treatment in another chapter. A glossary is also included to aid readers who are not familiar with the specialized terminology used in forestry.

As noted, a considerable number of changes have been incorporated into this third edition of *Introduction to Forest Ecosystem Science and Management* in response to changing societal needs and constructive criticism from students, colleagues, and reviewers. Fourteen of the 23 chapters, or over 60 percent of the book, have been totally rewritten by new authors and the other chapters have been extensively revised. Thus, this third edition

of *Introduction to Forest Ecosystem Science and Management* provides many new perspectives tuned to the changing values of the new millennium, especially in terms of human–forest interactions.

Also new to this third edition is the inclusion of chapter sidebars and a full-color insert. Many of the chapters contain sidebars with detailed, specialized information pertinent to the discussion in the text. The sidebars also provide additional information for the interested reader. The full-color insert has been included in this third edition to better illustrate the features of some of the more complicated figures in the book.

Students are encouraged to use the glossary for technical words that are unfamiliar. Also, the appendixes include taxonomy of forest trees as well as common and scientific names for trees and animals mentioned in the text.

As with the previous editions, the third edition of *Introduction to Forest Ecosystem Science and Management* was designed to give students a broad overview of the field of forestry but with sufficient detail that they will be able to assess their specific role as practicing forestry professionals. The book is intended to be the most advanced introductory text available. Indeed, current forestry professionals would find the text a convenient method for updating their knowledge of forest science. Certainly the book conveys the broad scope of forestry and the great challenges that lie ahead.

Raymond A. Young
Ronald L. Giese
November, 2002

Contents

8. Forest Trees: Disease and Insect Interactions   147

GLEN R. STANOSZ, KENNETH F. RAFFA, AND
RONALD L. GIESE

Part 3   Forest Management— Multiple Uses   177

9. Forest Management and Stewardship   179

JAMES M. GULDIN AND RICHARD W. GULDIN

Appendixes

Acknowledgments

The chapter authors and we have received many constructive comments on the chapters and the book from both our colleagues and outside reviewers. We are grateful to the departmental secretaries, Nancy Nehring, Marilyn McDole, and Sandy Fowler for clerical assistance along the way. Our wives, Kathryn and Maureen, deserve special thanks for their love and assistance throughout the editing process.

We are grateful to the following people for reviews or assistance with specific chapters. Chapter 5, Robert F. Powers, U.S. Forest Service; Chapter 12, Dr. Thomas Lillesand, Institute for Environmental Studies, University of Wisconsin–Madison, for thoughtful discussion; Chapter 8, UW-CALS; Chapter 17, Research Assistants Amy Sloane and Deborah Adams Ray for their critique, guidance and technical editing; Chapter 20, the late Professor John N. McGovern for contributions in the papermaking section; and Chapter 21, U.S.D.A. Forest Service, Southern Forest Experiment Station, and the School of Natural Resources, University of Wisconsin–Madison.

R.A.Y.
R.L.G.

PART 1

Introduction

T hroughout history, forests have been important to human beings. Forests provided shelter and protection, and trees provided many
products such as food, medicine, fuel, and tools.
For example, the bark of the willow tree, when
chewed, was used as a painkiller in early Greece
and was the precursor of present-day aspirin; acorns
from oak trees were an important food base to the
American Indian. Wood served as the primary fuel
in the United States until about the turn of the nineteenth century; indeed, over one-half of the wood
now harvested in the world is used for heating fuel.
Today over 10,000 products are made from wood.

Forests provide many other benefits, such as
control of erosion and flooding and reduction of
wind erosion. In addition to many utilitarian uses,
the forest provides many aesthetic features to
which quantitative values are difficult to assign.
The amenities include forest wildlife such as songbirds, fall coloration, wildflowers, and beautiful
landscapes (Figure P1.1). Urbanized society has
placed increasing emphasis on preserving the natural qualities of the forest for recreational purposes, escape, and solace. This has led to the
designation of "Wilderness Areas" intended to be
unaltered by humans.

Because of the many different viewpoints, conflicts of interest have arisen over what is considered to be the proper use of the forest in modern
American society. What a member of a preservationist group such as the Sierra Club defines as
proper management of the forest may be in conflict with how a paper industry executive views as
proper use of the forest. The forest manager,
although recognizing this conflict, must understand
both views and develop a management plan that
reflects the values involved in both points of view.

Figure P1.1 A majestic, mature stand of western
redcedar in western Washington State. Lichens
clothing the dead branches attest to a humid climate.
(Courtesy of U.S.D.A. Forest Service.)

We can now define forestry as the art, science,
and practice of managing the natural resources that
occur on and in association with forestland for
human benefit. This definition necessitates that the
forest manager consider not only the trees in the

1

forest, but also such things as protecting wildlife and preserving water systems for drinking and aquatic life. Foresters are often involved with the control of fire, insect pests, and diseases in the forest, and they can also assume the broad role of protecting the forest environment. The forester is a land manager responsible for all the goods, benefits, and services that flow from the forest (1).

The Multiple Use–Sustained Yield Act of 1960 recognized the many benefits derived from the forest: outdoor recreation, rangeland, timber, watershed protection, and wildlife and fish habitat. All need not be available at every location, but the value of each should be given equivalent recognition on a nationwide basis. Thus a clearcut for timber in a national forest should in some way be balanced by opportunities for wilderness-type experience at another location. The importance of the legislative process is further discussed in Chapter 1, Forest Policy Development in the United States.

In order to conform with legislation, managers of forests on public lands must strive to maintain a continual supply of the products, services, and amenities available from the forest. To do this, they must have a solid knowledge of science and society, a broad background in physical, biological, and social sciences, as well as administrative skills and an element of diplomacy for resolving conflicts. Clearly the task of the forest manager is a complex one requiring insight and many learned skills (2). Further discussion concerning the profession of forestry is given in Chapter 2, Forestry: The Profession and Career Opportunities.

The Forest

The forest is a biological community of plants and animals existing in a complex interaction with the nonliving environment, which includes such factors as the soil, climate, and physiography. A continuous canopy of large trees usually distinguishes forests from other types of communities. Forests are widespread, representing almost 30 percent of the earth's land surface, and typically have a predominant species composition; thus there are many forest types. The distribution of forest types or "biomes" around the world is discussed in Chapter 3, Forest Biomes of the World. The remainder of the land surface is composed of desert (31 percent), grasslands (21 percent), polar ice caps and wasteland (11 percent), and croplands (9 percent) (1).

Although trees are the predominant woody vegetation in terms of biomass,[1] trees represent only a small proportion of the total number of species present in the forest. There are thousands, perhaps millions, of different types of plants and animals in the forest. Shrubs, herbs, ferns, mosses, lichens, and fungi are present beneath the forest canopy and in the gaps of the forest cover. Large animals such as deer and bears coexist with smaller birds, insects, and tiny microorganisms. Each component makes a contribution to the flow of energy and materials through the system.

The forest is thus a dynamic ecosystem dominated by trees that is continually changing in structure and composition. Disturbances such as fire, windfall, and harvesting produce sites where new communities of trees, plants, and animals can exist and differ from the original forest. Fallen leaves and woody material that reach the forest floor decay and continue the cycling of energy and nutrients through the system. The forest community is a complex unit divided into many areas of study; these areas are treated in specific chapters in the text.

Tree Classification

Although forest ecosystems are composed of many plant and animal species, the dominant vegetation that foresters study and manipulate is the variety of tree species in the forest. Trees are generally

---

[1] Terms that may be unfamiliar to the reader are defined in the Glossary.

classified into two categories as seed plants: angiosperms with encased seeds and gymnosperms with naked seeds (Figure P1.2). The angiosperms are the dominant plant life of this geological area. They are products of a long line of evolutionary development that has culminated in the highly specialized organ of reproduction known as the flower. The seeds of angiosperms are enclosed in the matured ovary (fruit).

Two classes exist for the angiosperms, the Monocotyledones and the Dicotyledones (Table P1.1). Palms are classified as monocots, and the woody dicots are what we usually refer to as broad-leaved trees. Because the broad-leaved trees typically lose their leaves each fall, they are also often referred to as deciduous trees. However, a number of exceptions occur, such as southern magnolia or Pacific madrone, both of which retain their leaves all year. The broad-leaved or deciduous trees are also often referred to as hardwood trees, although this is a misnomer and does not refer to wood texture. Many broad-leaved trees such as basswood (linden) have soft-textured wood.

The other major class of trees is the gymnosperms, which bear their seeds in cones. The majority of the trees in this classification fall into the division Coniferophyta or conifers. A notable exception is the ginkgo tree, the only living species in the division Gingophyta. Some of the last living ginkgo trees were located by a botanical expedition in China in 1690. Subsequently, seeds from the mature tree have been planted worldwide (Figure P1.3). In recent years, extracts from the seeds and leaves have been touted for their medicinal values.

The conifers generally do not lose their needle-like leaves annually in the fall and therefore are termed evergreens. Again, there are exceptions such as larch and bald cypress, conifers that lose their needles each year like the broad-leaved trees. The conifers are also referred to as softwoods, but, like the hardwoods, the designation does not refer to the texture of the wood but to the class of tree. The terminology of hardwoods and softwoods probably originated in the early sawmills when most of the conifers used for timber were soft-textured pines, whereas most of the broad-leaved

Figure P1.2 Depiction of angiosperms (encased seed) and gymnosperms (naked seed).

Figure P1.3 The ancient ginkgo tree thrives in polluted urban environments and is planted as an ornamental worldwide. (Photograph by R. A. Young.)

Table P1.1   Scientific and Common Terms for Trees

Angiosperms (Magnoliophyta; Encased Seeds)	Gymnosperms (Naked Seeds)
Liliopsida (monocots; parallel-veined leaves)	Cycadophyta
Palms and palmettos (Palmaceae)	Cycads
Yucca (Liliaceae)	Ginkgophyta
Magnoliopsida (dicots;	Ginkgo
net-veined leaves)	Coniferophyta
Common terms for trees in this class:[a]	Common terms for trees in this class:
Hardwoods	Softwoods
Deciduous trees	Evergreens
Broad-leaved trees	Needle- (or scale-) leaved
	Conifers

[a]These terms are considered synonymous in common usage, but it is important to remember that many exceptions occur as described in the text.

trees used were hard-textured maples and oaks. It is important to recognize the synonymous terms listed in Table P1.1, since they are used interchangeably in both the literature and the common language.

Trees are referred to both by their common and scientific names. Common names are often utilized since the tree name is more recognizable in English than the Latin-based scientific names. In the text we have generally utilized the common names in reference to specific trees or stands of trees, with the scientific name sometimes in parentheses. However, it is important to recognize that common names can vary in different localities and refer to totally different trees. For example, the common name "Black Pine" is utilized for Ponderosa Pine (*Pinus ponderosa*) in the Rocky Mountain regions of the United States, while in the eastern United States, the common name "Black Pine" usually refers to Austrian Pine (*Pinus nigra*) introduced from Europe. The use of binomial scientific names, developed by the Swedish botanist Linnaeus in the mid-eighteenth century, avoids this confusion. Common and scientific names of tree species mentioned in the text are given in Appendix I.

References

1. R. D. NYLAND, C. C. LARSON, AND H. L. SHIRLEY, *Forestry and Its Career Opportunities*, Fourth Edition, McGraw-Hill, New York, 1983.
2. G. W. SHARPE, C. W. HENDEE, W. F. SHARPE, AND J. C. HENDEE, *Introduction to Forest and Renewable Resources*, McGraw-Hill, Sixth Edition, New York, 1995.

CHAPTER 1

Forest Policy Development in the United States

THOMAS M. BONNICKSEN AND
DIANA M. BURTON

All U.S. residents derive benefits from forests, either indirectly as forest product consumers or directly as participants in forest outdoor activities. Americans are making increasingly heavy and varied demands on forests. Although forest resources are renewable, there is limited land on which to produce forests. As demand rises, competition for resources also rises. Competition leads to formation of interest groups to influence elected officials and government agencies on forest resource allocation and management issues. The policy-making process resolves these differences. Understanding this process and the forest policy it generates is the principal focus of this chapter.

According to Boulding, a policy "generally refers to the principles that govern action directed toward given ends" (1). However, policies are much more. They are also hypotheses about what will happen if certain actions are taken. Whether a policy will achieve its specified ends is always in question until policy implementation results are realized. If a policy does not perform as expected, the whole policy process might be reinitiated. Thus, policy making is a continuous process that constantly attacks both new problems and those generated by past policies (2).

A society's history, philosophy, beliefs, attitudes, values, contemporary problems, and hopes are woven into its policy-making process. Thus, what is acceptable forest policy to one society in a given context may be inconceivable to another society in the same setting. Although U.S. forest policy incorporates many European forestry principles, it is a unique blend of approaches and goals tailored to American needs and circumstances. U.S. forest policy is also continually developing to accommodate change. Thus, forest policies adopted in the late 1800s differ significantly from those of a century later. Which policies are better at one time cannot be judged using standards of another time, just as forest policies appropriate to a given society cannot be judged according to another society's values.

Profile of Forest Policy Development

Throughout this chapter, the policy process is used as a framework for visualizing U.S. forest policy historical development. We look at broad periods that characterize major shifts in policies toward forests. In addition, we describe the environmental context and goals of the policy process within each period and evaluate policy results in terms of these goals. Because American forest policy is a vast topic, the scope of this text is necessarily limited. We emphasize the federal government's role and national forest management. We focus on policies stated as legislative statutes, executive orders and decrees, administrative rules and regulations, and court opinions.

Native Americans and Forests (to 1607)

The relationship between American Indians and forests varied. Forests provided building materials, food, or both. Forests were often seen as an obstacle to cultivation. For instance, the pre-Columbian northwestern coast of North America was heavily

forested and occupied by seafaring people who were highly skilled woodworkers (3, 4). Although many native peoples of the eastern deciduous forests also obtained wood from forests, the forest was principally an obstacle to the cultivation of maize, beans, and squash (5).

American Indians at times consciously favored certain tree species. In California, abundant oak trees produced acorns that were the staff of life for the Indian. The Miwok in Yosemite Valley burned grass under black oak trees in the fall to prevent growth of other trees that might shade the black oak. They also burned to clear the ground so that acorns could be easily gathered.

American Indians abided by certain rules while deriving their livelihoods from the land. These rules or guidelines were handed down from one generation to the next by word and action. Such an agreed-upon pattern of behavior, designed to accomplish a specified goal, fits the definition of a policy. Consequently, although native peoples did not have forest policies that were explicitly recognized as such, they did have rules that governed their relationships to forests. Whether modern people agree with these rules is unimportant. What is important is that American Indians had the equivalent of forest policies that enhanced their survival.

Colonial Settlers and Forests (1607–1783)

Although the world known to Europe expanded to include North America in 1492, it was not until 1607 that Europeans successfully colonized what is now the United States. The Virginia Company of London founded Jamestown, on the wooded banks of the James River, in what is now Virginia. Forests were the colonial landscape's dominant feature and a valued resource. Forests surrounding Jamestown were used to construct the town and as fuel for a thriving glass industry. However, the thick forests hid unfriendly Indians, so forests were cleared to make the area safe. Forests were also cleared for farms and roads. Thus, two attitudes toward forests developed that profoundly influenced forest policies for generations. First, forests were nuisances

Sidebar 1.1

Questions About Future Forests

America's forests have undergone pronounced changes since first seen by European explorers. Many older forests disappeared because a growing nation needed wood for fuel and construction. Clearing for agriculture and towns took the greatest toll. Even so, reforestation on federal and private lands and planting on abandoned agricultural lands have replaced much of the lost forest.

Forests now cover one-third of the United States, but they differ significantly from the original ancient forests. There are fewer old trees in today's forests than there were in ancient times, and forests are less patchy and diverse. Some change is caused by timber management, but also results from efforts to protect against lightning fires, insects, diseases, and development. The elimination of traditional burning by American Indians may have caused the most widespread changes. The lack of Indian fires and suppression of lightning fires allow debris to accumulate in today's forests. They are choked with thickets of young trees, which is slowing tree growth, increasing mortality and reducing stream flows. Thicker and more uniform forests also have less wildlife habitat. In addition, trees that grow in the shade replace trees that grow in the sun, such as Douglas fir and pine. Even more disturbing is that increasing fuels make wildfires more severe and dangerous.

Many scientists and resource managers believe that forest restoration provides the best hope for reversing American forest decline. Some predicted the forest health crisis coming several decades ago. One of the first was Aldo Leopold, who promoted forest restoration as early as 1934. Forest restoration involves using

ancient or pre-European settlement forests as models for creating sustainable forests. Restoration does not apply to forests that are dedicated to growing wood fiber. Ancient forests provided many of the things that people want from today's forests, including large trees, scenic vistas, abundant wildlife, and wildflowers. However, people also want forest products. Management that includes controlled burning and cutting can mimic processes that created and sustained the ancient forest beauty and diversity and generate forest products as well. Since ancient forests were sustainable, future forests that use them as models should also be sustainable.

Managers can produce what we want from forests by engineering new forests using modern tools and scientific principles. They do not need ancient forests as models. This is already happening in forests that are being manipulated to favor certain wildlife species, particularly endangered and threatened species, or to maximize timber production. However, are these artifical forests necessary or even desirable, and will they be sustainable? Do we really want to invent new forests, or do we want forests to look as beautiful and diverse as they did when explorers first saw them? Can we have both historic forests and engineered forests? Can the same forest serve both purposes or must they be separated? Even more intriguing, do we want forests to look the way they might look now if Europeans had not settled the continent and American Indians were still the only inhabitants? On the other hand, do we want forests to look as if no one, including Native Americans, had ever lived on the land? These are just some of the policy questions that should be

(continues)

> # Sidebar 1.1 *(continued)*
>
> pondered. The future of America's forests depends on the answers. An in-depth description of North America's ancient forests is found in *America's Ancient Forests: From the Ice Age to the Age of Discovery* (1).
>
> Source:
>
> 1. T. M. BONNICKSEN, *America's Ancient Forests: From the Ice Age to the Age of Discovery*, John Wiley & Sons, New York, 2000.

and citizens made great improvements to the land by cutting trees. Second, the seemingly unending supply of trees led to acceptance of waste and a view that American forests were inexhaustible.

Wood was the primary fuel and energy source for colonial America and remained so until 1870. Because the colonists lacked transportation, wood for fuel and building material was cut near settlements. As forests receded from settlements, it became increasingly difficult to haul wood. Although forests as a whole seemed inexhaustible, local timber supplies were limited. As a result, the first American forest policy on record was established on March 29, 1626, by Plymouth Colony. The policy forbade transport of any timber out of the colony without the governor's and council's consent. Similar policies were adopted by Rhode Island, New Hampshire, and New Jersey. In addition, William Penn directed in 1681 that in Pennsylvania ("Penn's woodland") 1 acre (0.4 hectare) of forest be left for every 5 acres (2 hectares) cleared.

Colonial policy making included political rule by a distant monarchy. Thus, forest policies reflected the perceived wants of a distant society as well as the colonists' immediate needs. The tension between these two interests seriously limited England's forest policies for the New World.

The abundance of large trees made a colonial shipbuilding industry possible. The *Blessing of the Bay*, a ship launched at Medford, Massachusetts in 1631, marked the beginning of both this industry (6) and a direct conflict with British interests in

America's forests. As early as 1609, the first shipment of masts was sent from Virginia to England (6) (Figure 1.1). Trees of sufficient size were scarce and hostile countries could easily disrupt supply lines from northern and central Europe. Great Britain was competing for European masts, so America became its principal source of supply. In order to protect its interests, Great Britain in 1691 granted a new charter to the Province of Massachusetts Bay that reserved for the crown all trees 24 inches (61 centimeters) or more in diameter growing on lands not in private ownership. This was known as the Broad Arrow policy because reserved trees were marked with a broad arrow blaze—the symbol of the British Navy. By 1721, this policy covered all colonial lands from Nova Scotia to New Jersey. The British did obtain a relatively steady supply of naval timbers under the Broad Arrow policy, which had to be enforced with large fines because colonists vigorously opposed it. In 1772, for instance, in Weare, New Hampshire, Sheriff Benjamin Whiting arrested Ebenezer Mudgett for cutting the king's white pine. The colonists reacted by seizing the sheriff in the night, beating him with rods, and forcing him to ride out of town. This event was known as the "Pine Tree Riot" (6). The Broad Arrow policy likely contributed to the American Revolution.

Building and Defending the Republic (1783–1830)

The British formally recognized United States independence in the Treaty of Paris in 1783. America

Figure 1.1   A sheer hulk stepping a mainmast. (Courtesy of Mr. Jack Coggins and Stackpole Books.)

then controlled her own forests. The social and economic problems of the new nation were exacerbated by the old belief that American forests were inexhaustible. The most significant change in the forest policy process that occurred at this time was establishing the first American government. The new government was based on the Articles of Confederation, a document designed to preserve the states as free and independent sovereignties while granting Congress limited authority. Thus, the Articles denied Congress the authority to levy taxes and to regulate commerce.

The Articles of Confederation required unanimous consent of all thirteen states. Six states were reluctant to sign because they did not have claims to large tracts of unsettled western lands. States with such lands had an advantage because land could be sold to defray Revolutionary War debts. Maryland, without western land, refused to sign the Articles of Confederation unless other states abandoned their claims. Maryland held out until March 1781, when New York surrendered its western land claims to the federal government and Virginia appeared ready to do so. Thus, ratification of the confederation also marked the beginning of the public domain. (The public domain included all lands that were at any time owned by the United States government and subject to sale or transfer of ownership under the laws of the federal government.) Congress pledged to dispose of the public domain for the "common benefit," partly to create new states and partly to make good on its promise to grant land to Revolutionary War veterans. Since Congress could not levy taxes, it used the public domain as a revenue source to discharge national debt and run the government.

Although Congress was weak under the Articles of Confederation, it managed to pass two laws that affect the landscape to this day. The first is the Land Ordinance of 1785. It provided that the Old Northwest, a territory lying between the Ohio and Mississippi rivers and the Great Lakes southern shores, should be sold to help defray national debt. The land was surveyed before sale using the now-familiar rectangular grid system of townships and sections. Only the thirteen original states and later Texas, whose admission to the union was contingent on state ownership of public lands, were not subjected to this survey system. The Northwest Ordinance of 1787 further provided that when a territory could claim 60,000 residents, it could be admitted as a state. This scheme worked so well that it was carried over to other areas of the public domain.

One problem facing the new Congress was the need for a strong navy. Congress authorized construction of six frigates in 1794, established a Department of the Navy in 1798 (6), and appropriated $200,000 to purchase timber and lands growing timber suitable for naval construction. Thus, Congress bought two islands supporting live oak off the Georgia coast. At the outbreak of the War of 1812, the United States still had only sixteen ships in its entire navy against the 800 men-of-war in the British navy. By war's end, the United States had only two or three ships left (7). Congress reacted in 1817 by authorizing the Secretary of the Navy to reserve from sale, with presidential approval, public-domain lands that supported live oak and red cedar to rebuild the navy. An 1828 act

appropriated an additional $10,000 for land purchases. These timber reserves received no more public support than had the earlier British Broad Arrow policy. Looting, or timber trespass, was common. In 1821, the General Land Office commissioner instructed his agents to stop illegal cutting on the reserves (6), but officials responsible were political appointees with little interest in confronting timber thieves. Therefore, in 1822, Congress authorized use of the army and navy to prevent timber depredations in Florida, but there was little improvement.

Important Features of the Period 1783–1830
Forest policies adopted between 1783 and 1830 produced mixed results. First, revenues derived from public land sales did not reach expected amounts. The Land Ordinance of 1785 provided that lands should be sold in blocks of at least 640 acres (259 hectares) to the highest bidder at not less than $1 per acre. Unfortunately, land could be purchased elsewhere at lower prices, and the $640 required as a minimum purchase price proved too high for most people. As a result, people in need of land "squatted" on the public domain in increasing numbers, and efforts to remove them met with little success. Naval timber reserve policies faced similar results because forests were regarded as inexhaustible. In addition, the public domain was expanding as the nation added to its land holdings through the Louisiana Purchase and like transactions, and interest in forest reserves gradually declined. However, the policy of reserving forestlands as a source of timber set an important policy precedent. Congress's right to control public lands use in the national interest was firmly established.

The Erosion of a Myth (1830–1891)

In 1830, Andrew Jackson was elected U.S. President with the support of common people. Many in the upper classes sneered at this "New Democracy," referring to "coonskin congressmen" and enfranchised "bipeds of the forest" (7). Nevertheless, politicians who could boast of birth in a log cabin had a real advantage in an election. The sturdy pioneer and forest settler were clearly in command. By the 1867 Alaska purchase, the public domain had grown by more than one billion acres (405 million hectares) and there was a need to fill these lands with settlers to protect them and make them productive. During this period more than any other, the nation's policy was to transfer land into private ownership and rely on market forces as a primary means for allocating natural resources.

Exploitation of the Forests   With seemingly inexhaustible forests, and a government dominated by western settlement and economic expansion interests, rapid resource exploitation was inevitable. Pressure on timberlands increased as wood was used to build on the treeless Great Plains, to construct railroads, to fight the Civil War and repair what it destroyed, and to rebuild four square miles (10.4 square kilometers) of Chicago burned in the Great Fire of 1871. Settlers occupying lands on the Great Plains had to import timber. Tree planting was thought to be a reasonable solution that might also increase rainfall. In 1866, General Land Office

Commissioner Joseph S. Wilson recommended that homesteaders be required to plant trees in areas lacking timber (6). Therefore, Congress enacted the Timber Culture Act in 1873. Under the law, settlers received 160 acres (65 hectares) of public land by planting 40 acres (16 hectares) with trees and maintaining them for a given period.

With the exception of railroad land grants, most policies enacted during this period focused on agricultural development. However, by 1878 it was clear that large areas of public domain were more suited to timber than agriculture and that no provision existed for timber or timberland acquisition by the public. Congress offered a remedy in 1878: the Free Timber Act and the Timber and Stone Act. The Free Timber Act stipulated that residents of nine western states could cut timber for building, mining, and other purposes without charge to aid in farms and mineral claims development (Figure 1.2). While this act was well intentioned and undoubtedly provided substantial aid to deserving settlers, it was widely abused, as enforcement was nearly impossible. The Timber and Stone Act provided that unoccupied, surveyed land principally valuable for timber or

Figure 1.2   Native Americans used wood under provisions of the Free Timber Act, Black Hills National Forest, South Dakota, in 1931. (Courtesy of U.S.D.A. Forest Service.)

stone, but not agriculture, could be purchased in 160 acre (65 hectare) tracts for $2.50 per acre in Washington, Oregon, California, and Nevada. The purchaser had to swear that the land was for personal use and not for speculation.

Throughout this period, two major forest policy problems existed. First, speculation and fraud in public land sales and transfers were rampant. Speculators and lumber executives accumulated large timberland holdings and abused public domain disposal policies. Most laws were designed to encourage small owner-operator farms, but there was little control over what the landowner did after purchase. For example, military land bounties granted to soldiers for their service and to encourage enlistment were sold to land speculators and large companies. The sales became so common that bounty warrants were quoted on the New York Stock Exchange (6). Second, some timber operators made no pretense of purchasing timberlands but simply set up lumber mills on the public domain and cut trees. In other cases, they purchased 40-acre (16 hectare) plots and proceeded to cut timber on surrounding public lots. These were known as "round forties" or "rubber forties" because of the flexibility of the boundaries.

The end of timber stealing began in 1877 with the appointment of Secretary of the Interior Carl Schurz. He immigrated from Germany where scarce forest resources were carefully husbanded. Schurz advocated a similar approach in the United States. He took exception to the popular belief of inexhaustible timber resources. In his first annual report, Schurz predicted that the timber supply would not meet national needs in 20 years (8). Schurz vigorously enforced laws against timber theft (6). He based his authority on the March 1831 Timber Trespass Law, which imposed fines and imprisonment on those who cut timber from public lands without authorization. In 1850, the U.S. Supreme Court upheld the act and extended it to include any trespass on public lands.

Conservation and Preservation of the Forests
Rapid disposal and exploitation of the public domain characterized the period from 1830 to 1891.

However, the myth that timber and other resources were inexhaustible gradually eroded, while a concern for conservation and preservation grew. As early as 1801, publications by Andre Michaux and his son, after their travels through U.S. forests, noted "an alarming destruction of the trees" and warned that increasing population would make timber scarce (6). By 1849, the commissioner of patents was also warning of timber shortages (6). In 1864, George Perkins Marsh published his famous book *Man and Nature*, pointing out undesirable consequences of forest destruction. Beginning about 1866, annual reports from the Secretary of the Interior and the commissioner of the General Land Office regularly included an expression of concern about the exhaustion of forest resources.

In 1867, this concern translated into state action when legislatures in both Michigan and Wisconsin appointed committees to investigate potential long-term consequences of deforestation. More dramatic action was taken in 1885 by New York when it created a "forest preserve" on state-owned lands in the Adirondack and Catskill mountains. In 1894, the new state constitution of New York forbade timber cutting on the preserve. In addition, in 1885, California established a State Board of Forestry and granted it police powers two years later.

Federal action aimed at forest conservation began about the same time. In 1874, an American Association for the Advancement of Science (AAAS) committee prevailed on President Ulysses S. Grant to ask Congress to create a commission of forestry (6). Congress attached an amendment to the Sundry Civil Appropriations Bill of 1876, providing $2000 to hire someone to study U.S. forest problems. This act established such a position in the Department of Agriculture and henceforth federal forest management would be primarily performed by this department. Franklin B. Hough, who had chaired the AAAS committee, was appointed to the job. He published three monumental reports containing most of what was known about forestry in the United States at that time. Later, he became chief of the Division of Forestry, which was subsequently given statutory permanence in the Department of

Agriculture on June 30, 1886. This division was the precursor of what is now the U.S.D.A. Forest Service. Also in 1886, Bernard E. Fernow, who had studied forestry in western Prussia, succeeded Hough as chief of the division.

The preservation movement had a profound effect on forest policy. In 1832, George Catlin, a painter and explorer of the American West, called for establishment of "a nation's park" in the Great Plains "containing man and beast, in all the wild and freshness of their nature's beauty!" (9). Catlin's plea for preservation was echoed by Henry David Thoreau in 1858 when he asked, in an article in the *Atlantic Monthly*, "why should not we . . . have our national preserves . . . for inspiration and our true re-creation?" (10). Other well-known preservationists such as Frederick Law Olmsted and John Muir followed Catlin and Thoreau. Together they helped to found our present system of national parks and monuments, beginning with Yellowstone National Park, which was set aside in 1872 "as a public park or pleasuring-ground for the benefit and enjoyment of the people." Yosemite Valley and the Mariposa Big Tree Grove were set aside in 1864 for public recreation, to be managed by the state of California. They became part of Yosemite National Park in 1890. Sequoia and General Grant (now Kings Canyon) became national parks that same year.

Important Features of the Period 1830–1891 The period from 1830 to 1891 saw three separate movements. One, an exploitive movement, was to dispose of the public domain and cut forests extensively. At the same time—and partly in response—two other movements encouraged scientific resource management and natural scenery preservation. One major success stands out. About one billion acres (405 million hectares), nearly the same amount of land as entered the public domain during this period, were sold to private owners (6). However, much land did not end up with small farmers but added to large corporate holdings. Another major success was the encouragement of western expansion and settlement, but the benefits were mixed with problems. A quarter-section

of land, which would have been an adequate size for a farm in the East where water was plentiful, was completely inadequate for sustaining a farmer in the arid West, and therefore many farms in the West were abandoned. Finally, prodigious amounts of timber products were produced, but subsequent generations inherited a legacy of cutover and deteriorated forestland. Nevertheless, this period ended with a rapidly growing and prosperous nation that had already taken major steps toward improving the use of its forests.

Crystallizing a Philosophy (1891–1911)

The circumstances affecting U.S. forest policy between 1891 and 1911 were different from those of any previous period. The shift from rural to urban life was accelerating. In 1790, only 2.8 percent of the population lived in cities with 10,000 or more people; by 1900, 31.8 percent did (7). An urban population often perceives natural resources differently than a rural population, whose livelihood is directly and visibly land-dependent. Thus, the conflict between the strong desire for preservation of Eastern seaboard urban residents, and the expansionist views of Western rural residents became marked.

This was the first period without a geographic frontier. In 1890, the superintendent of the census in Washington announced that a frontier line no longer existed (3). All of the United States and its territories contained settlements. The myth of inexhaustible resources had been eroding for decades. However, the loss of the frontier and the presence of large tracts of cutover land in the once heavily forested East made it obvious that something had to be done to conserve forests and other resources. People saw a "timber famine" as a real possibility. Three societal goals emerged that strongly affected forest policy: defend the rights of the people, maintain a continuous supply of timber, and prevent waste in natural resource use, particularly timber.

Creation of Forest Reserves Perhaps the most important forest policy enacted in the United States was the General Revision Act of 1891. Provisions

Sidebar 1.2

The Legacy of George Perkins Marsh

Born in Woodstock, Vermont, in 1801, Marsh grew up on America's frontier. As the fifth of eight children of the local district attorney, Marsh read intensively and ran free in the great outdoors. Graduating at the top of his Dartmouth class, Marsh taught Greek and Latin for a time at a military academy. He became a lawyer, a politician, and eventually was appointed as ambassador to Italy by President Abraham Lincoln (1). His most famous work, *Man and Nature, or Physical Geography Modified by Human Action* (1) was written during his tenure in Italy and published in 1864.

Marsh's claim that man was modifying nature was not remarkable at the time. Forests were being removed for agriculture, canals were being constructed, and a spreading population erected new towns. However, his notion that man should consider his impact on the natural environment, in part because a changed natural environment would have an impact on man, was almost radical. Marsh's thoughts anticipate by more than a century the now widely accepted idea of an integrated ecosystem:

... the trout feeds on the larvae of the May fly, which is itself very destructive to the spawn of salmon, and hence, by a sort of house-that-Jack-built, the destruction of the mosquito, that feeds the trout that preys on the May fly that destroys the eggs that hatch the salmon that pampers the epicure, may occa-

sion a scarcity of this latter fish in waters where he would otherwise be abundant. Thus all nature is linked together by invisible bonds, and every organic creature, however low, however feeble, however dependent, is necessary to the well-being of some other among the myriad forms of life with which the Creator has peopled the earth (1, p. 96).

One of the main messages in *Man and Nature* is that man ought to consider fully the impacts of his actions, not that nature should not be modified.

Marsh's ideas were taken up by many who read his works. As science progressed, the complexity of natural ecosystems became more apparent. Writers such as Rachel Carson, who published *Silent Spring* in 1962 (2), pointed out that agricultural pesticides were killing eagles through their food chain, as well as the intended crop bug targets. The Environmental Impact Statement, required by NEPA, is modern society's attempt to do what Marsh suggested: act, but act with maximum possible knowledge of consequences.

Sources:

1. G. P. MARSH, *Man and Nature*, The Belknap Press of Harvard University Press, Cambridge, Mass., 1967 (originally published 1864).

2. R. CARSON, *Silent Spring*, Houghton Mifflin, Boston, 1962.

included repeal of the Timber Culture Act of 1878 and Preemption Act of 1841, as well as imposition of restrictions on the 1862 Homestead Act to discourage speculation and fraud. What made this act so important to forestry was Section 24. It provided that "the President of the United States may, from time to time, set apart and reserve any part of the public lands wholly or in part covered with timber or undergrowth, whether of commercial value or not." The authority granted to the president by Section 24 (also known as the Forest Reserve Act) to set aside forest reserves from the public domain served as the basis for the U.S. national forest system. Less than a month later, President Benjamin Harrison established Yellowstone Park Forest Reservation. Over two years, he proclaimed an additional fourteen forest reserves, bringing the total to over 13 million acres (5.3 million hectares). A storm of protests from western interests followed, in part because the Forest Reserve Act did not include a provision for using the reserves. Consequently, the westerners' argument that forest reserves were "locked up" and could not be used was correct. Logging, mining, and other activities were illegal on the reserves. However, there was little law enforcement, so timber theft proceeded unobstructed.

A few months before passage of the Forest Reserve Act, Gifford Pinchot, who became the most famous person in American forestry history, returned from Europe where he had been studying forestry under Dr. Dietrich Brandis in France. Pinchot's motto, from the beginning of his career until the end, was "forestry is tree farming" (11). He did not believe in preserving forests but in using them "wisely."

Pinchot emerged on the national forest policy scene when he joined a National Academy of Sciences forest commission formed at the request of Secretary of the Interior Hoke Smith. The commission studied the forest reserves and their administration and made legislative recommendations that would break the Congressional deadlock over forest reserve management. The commission submitted a list of proposed forest reserves to President Grover Cleveland without a plan for their management. Pinchot argued, without success, that a plan should accompany the list so that western congressional representatives would know that the commission wanted to use the forests and not simply lock them up. President Cleveland had only ten days left in office, so he was forced to act on the commission's recommendation. On February 22, 1897, he set aside an additional 21.3 million acres (8.6 million hectares) of forest reserves.

Once again, a storm of criticism arose in Congress and legislation was introduced to nullify President Cleveland's actions. In June 1897, Congress passed the Sundry Civil Appropriations Act with an amendment (known as the Organic Administration Act). Senator Richard Pettigrew of South Dakota introduced the amendment. It provided that "no public forest reservation shall be established except to improve and protect the forest . . . for the purpose of securing favorable conditions of water flows, and to furnish a continuous supply of timber." The act excluded lands principally valuable for mining and agriculture and authorized the Secretary of the Interior to make rules for the reserves "to regulate their occupancy and use, and to preserve the forests thereon from destruction." This language dated from 1893 when Representative Thomas C. McRae introduced the first of many bills for forest reserve management. Early opposition came from western senators whose constituents were accustomed to obtaining timber from public lands without paying a fee. When a compromise was reached to handle western criticism, eastern senators continued to block passage of the bill because they feared that opening up the reserves would lead to more abuses. President Cleveland's bold action in setting aside reserves served as the catalyst to overcome the impasse. Enough votes were obtained to pass the Organic Administration Act because even some eastern senators thought the new reserves created a hardship for people in the West.

The General Land Office administered the forest reserves, an agency that Pinchot said was governed by "paper work, politics, and patronage" (11). Reform seemed impossible, so when Pinchot became head of the Division of Forestry in July 1898, he immediately set out to gain control of the reserves. His good friend Theodore Roosevelt, who became president in September 1901, after President William McKinley's assassination, aided Pinchot. Roosevelt and Pinchot were both master politicians—persuasive, dedicated, and equipped with boundless energy (Figure 1.3). The same ideas about the meaning of conservation, epitomized by such words and phrases as *efficiency, wise use, for the public good,* and *the lasting good of men*, drove them. To Roosevelt and Pinchot, conservation was the "antithesis of monopoly" and, though wealthy

Figure 1.3   Chief forester Gifford Pinchot (right) with President Theodore Roosevelt on the riverboat *Mississippi* in 1907. (Courtesy of U.S.D.A. Forest Service.)

chot wrote the letter (6). In keeping with the philosophy of the time, the letter required that the reserves be used "for the permanent good of the whole and not for the temporary benefit of individuals or companies." It also stipulated that "all the resources of the reserves are for use" and "where conflicting interests must be reconciled the question will always be decided from the standpoint of the greatest good of the greatest number in the long run" (6). These lofty, although somewhat ambiguous, goals still guide Forest Service administration.

Many landmark policies affecting U.S. forests were enacted during this period. The Forest Reserve Act's precedent was copied in the American Antiquities Act of 1906, which authorized the president "to declare by proclamation . . . objects of historic or scientific interest" on the public lands "to be national monuments." The lands had protection against commercial utilization and were open for scientific, educational, and recreation purposes. President Roosevelt used the act to set aside eighteen national monuments, including what later became Grand Canyon, Lassen Volcanic, and Olympic National Parks. Roosevelt also enlarged the forest reserves more than any other president did. When he came to office, there were 41 reserves totaling 46.5 million acres (18.8 million hectares) and by 1907, he had increased the reserves (now called national forests) to 159 and their total area to 150.7 million acres (61 million hectares) (12). Roosevelt's zealous expansion moved Congress, in March 1907, to revoke his authority to establish reserves in six western states. Roosevelt left the act unsigned until after he had reserved an additional 16 million acres (6.5 million hectares) of forestland (12).

The end of this period is marked by a controversy between Pinchot and Secretary of the Interior Richard A. Ballinger that led President William Howard Taft to fire Pinchot as chief of the Forest Service in January 1910. Actually, Pinchot had decided several months earlier to "make the boss fire him" (12). Taft's policies upset Pinchot, because, in his view, they did not carry on the traditions of President Roosevelt and the philosophy of conservation.

themselves, they both abhorred "concentrated wealth," which they viewed as "freedom to use and abuse the common man" (11). With President Roosevelt's help, Pinchot accomplished his goal to gain custody of the forest reserves. The Transfer Act of 1905 moved their administration from the Department of the Interior to the Department of Agriculture. One month later, Pinchot's agency became the Forest Service. In 1907, forest reserves were renamed national forests.

Management of forest reserves changed dramatically under the new regime. On the day the Transfer Act was signed, Secretary of Agriculture James Wilson sent a letter to Pinchot outlining the general policies to follow in managing the reserves. Pin-

Sidebar 1.3

The Father of American Forestry

You may describe a Forester from the standpoint of his specialized education and his application of technical knowledge to the protection and management of the forest, but you can not stop there. There is another concept that is equally important. Every Forester is a public servant, no matter by whom employed. It makes no difference whether a Forester is engaged in private work or in public work, whether he is working for a lumber company, an association of lumbermen, a group of small forest owners, the proprietor of a great estate, or whether he is a forest officer of State or Nation. By virtue of his profession a Forester is always and everywhere a public servant (1, p. 27).

continues

The father of American Forestry.

Sidebar 1.3 *(continued)*

Gifford Pinchot firmly believed that the forester owed his allegiance to the forest, to the land, and to the profession of forestry. Pinchot is known as the Father of American Forestry because he gave so much to the establishment of professional forestry in the United States. Long respected and practiced in France and Germany, where Pinchot went to study, the forestry profession made its debut in the United States about 100 years ago. When he took over the country's national forests in 1905, Pinchot established the Forest Service as a highly trained group of professional forest managers. On the occasion of the 1905 Transfer Act, he set forth, in the famous Pinchot letter, the decentralized management philosophy by which the Forest Service operated for most of the twentieth century.

Pinchot was a founding member of the Society of American Foresters (SAF). Founded in November 1900 in Pinchot's office, membership was limited to trained foresters. Enthusiasts such as President Roosevelt were relegated to associate member status (2). Today, the SAF remains the premier professional forestry organization.

Pinchot was instrumental in establishing the nation's first forestry school at Yale University and taught there after he left government. He wrote much, including textbooks like *The Training of a Forester* from which the previous quote is taken. This text outlines in detail all the disciplines that a forester must study in addition to silviculture, such as soil science, economics and zoology, to properly manage forest complexities. First published in 1914, the book discusses what a forester does on the job, how, and why.

Much of what modern forestry professionals learn and practice today has roots in European traditions brought to this country by Gifford Pinchot. His life of dedication to the profession, and the courage and foresight he displayed, truly make him worthy of the title Father of American Forestry.

Sources:
1. G. PINCHOT, *The Training of a Forester*, J. B. Lippincott Company, New York, 1937 (originally published 1914).

2. T. M. BONNICKSEN, *Politics and the Life Sciences*, *15*, 23–34 (1996).

Important Features of the Period 1891–1911   The period from 1891 to 1911 was one of the most colorful and active in American forest policy history. Specific goals guided forest policy throughout the period. Nevertheless, eliminating waste and bringing the management of national forests up to the standard hoped for by Pinchot and Roosevelt constituted too great a task given meager funding and little time. Creation of the Forest Service, establishment of a national forest system, and crystallization of a utilitarian conservation philosophy to guide their management represented the greatest forest policy accomplishments.

Organization, Action, and Conflict (1911–1952)

The United States faced enormous difficulties and hardships from 1911 to 1952. The world went to war twice, taking a frightening toll in human lives and property, and underwent the agonies of the Great Depression. In the United States, disastrous floods regularly ripped through settled valleys. At the same time, drought cycles and improper farming practices on the Great Plains drove farmers off the land as the soil and their livelihoods blew away during the Dust Bowl era. Intolerable working conditions and low wages also drove urban laborers to protest in the streets.

These were difficult years, but also relatively simple years, in that forest problems were clearly understood by most people and goals, though always controversial, were also clear. These goals included: 1) keeping watersheds of navigable streams and rivers covered with vegetation to reduce flooding and sedimentation, 2) keeping sufficient wood flowing out of forests to meet the nation's requirements for building its industries and successfully ending its wars, 3) protecting the nation's forests from overexploitation and losses from insects, diseases, and fire, and 4) using forest resource production from public lands to reduce unemployment during the Great Depression and to stabilize the economies of communities dependent on local forests. In addition, a small but influential segment of society inspired the public to preserve tangible parts of the United States' cultural and natural heritage.

Conservation versus Preservation   By 1910, the conservation philosophy of Catlin, Thoreau, and Muir was gaining ground as private organizations formed to represent this view. These "aesthetic conservationists," or preservationists, differed significantly from "Pinchot" or "utilitarian conservationists." Preservationists concentrated their efforts on protecting natural beauty and scenic attractions from the lumberjack's axe and miner's pick by placing them within national parks. Utilitarian conservationists' philosophy was rooted in the idea that resources must be "used." They referred to preservationists as "misinformed nature lovers" (12). This difference of opinion finally led preservationists to break away from the organized conservation movement because it was dominated by utilitarian philosophy. When conservationists and preservationists ceased to be allies, conflict over public lands disposition and management was inevitable. This conflict has grown in intensity. By the 1960s and 1970s, it dominated American forest policy.

In the early 1900s, conflict between preservationists and conservationists centered on partitioning public lands. At first, preservationists focused on creating a separate agency to manage national parks. Pinchot countered by trying to consolidate national parks with national forests. Although preservationists succeeded in gaining support from Taft and Ballinger, Pinchot argued that such an agency was "no more needed than two tails to a cat" (12). He carried enough influence in Congress to block the proposal. However, Secretary of the Interior Franklin K. Lane rescued the preservationists by placing all national parks and monuments under the jurisdiction of an assistant to the secretary. He filled the post with Steven T. Mather, a wealthy preservationist who helped usher the National Park Act of 1916 through Congress and was named first director of the National Park Service. Preservationists thus obtained an administrative home in the Department of the Interior and a champion to expand and protect the national park system.

Pinchot was no longer chief of the Forest Service, but his successors, Henry S. Graves (1910–1920) and William B. Greeley (1920–1928), were utilitarian conservationists. Furthermore, Pinchot continued to be influential with Congress, both as an individual and through the National Conservation Association. Thus, the adversaries were firmly entrenched in two separate agencies within two separate federal departments, each with its own constituency. Their first contest centered on the fact that the national forests contained most of the public land suitable for national parks, and the National Park Service was anxious to take these lands away from the Forest Service. The Forest Service was not hostile toward national parks, but as Chief Forester Graves said, "the parks should comprise only areas which are not forested or areas covered only with protective forest which would not ordinarily be cut" (8). The problem was philosophical as well as territorial. The Forest Service did not want to give up land it was already managing and therefore countered Park Service advances by vigorously resisting withdrawal of national forestland for park purposes. The Forest Service also continued its efforts to develop a recreation program that it hoped would make new national parks unnecessary.

Forest Recreation   The Forest Service recreation program represented a response to a technological innovation—the automobile—and expansion of roads pleasure-seekers used to gain access to national forests. In 1907, there were about 4,971 miles (8,000 kilometers) of roads in all national forests. The need for roads increased with automobile use, and between 1916 and 1991 over $33 million was spent on roads in and near national forests (10). These roads brought in so many recreationists that rangers, concerned about fire hazards and other conflicts with commodity uses, sought to discourage them by concealing entrances to new trails and leaving roads unposted (10). The tide of recreationists could not be turned, however, and the Forest Service reluctantly began providing for their needs.

One of the celebrated accomplishments in national forest recreation was establishment of the nation's first designated wilderness area. In 1918, a road was proposed that would cut through the Gila River watershed in New Mexico. Aldo Leopold, an assistant district forester for the Forest Service, protested against the road, claiming, "the Gila is the last typical wilderness in the southwestern mountains" (10). He then proposed designating the watershed as a "wilderness" without roads or recreational developments. No action was taken on his proposal. Then, in 1921, when an appropriation of $13.9 million for developing forest roads and highways passed Congress, he publicly expressed his proposal for wilderness protection. He defined wilderness as "a continuous stretch of country preserved in its natural state, open to lawful hunting and fishing, big enough to absorb a two weeks pack trip, and kept devoid of roads, artificial trails, cottages or the works of man" (10). This definition has remained relatively unchanged until the present. It took nearly three years for Leopold to convince the district forester of New Mexico and Arizona to approve the Gila Wilderness plan. While this was a local decision, criticism of the Forest Service by preservationists mounted and the Park Service increased its acquisition of national forests, leading Forest Service Chief Greeley to establish a national wilderness system in 1926.

The Forest Service was still a popular and aggressive agency even though it spent part of its time defending against incursions from the Park Service. The momentum of the Roosevelt–Pinchot era had slowed somewhat, but the Forest Service maintained a strong sense of mission. It advanced on four fronts: expanding national forests in the East, promoting forest research, developing the national forests, and regulating forest practices on private land.

Preservationists lobbied to add lands to the national forest system in the East. As early as 1901, the Appalachian National Park Association joined with other private organizations to petition Congress to preserve southern Appalachian forests. However, most public lands in the East had already passed into private ownership, so additional national forests would have to be purchased. Congress authorized studies but no purchases. A few years later, the Society for the Protection of New Hampshire Forests joined forces with the Appalachian group, and together they succeeded in securing passage of the Weeks Act of 1911 (11). The Weeks Act specified that the federal government could purchase lands on the headwaters of navigable streams and appropriated funds. This restrictive language reflected a congressional view that the government had the power to buy land for national forests only if the purchase would aid navigation. Naturally, advocates of eastern reserves, including Pinchot, shifted their arguments from an emphasis on forests themselves to the role of forests in preventing floods and reducing sedimentation. These arguments worked and, influenced by the great Mississippi flood of 1927, Congress accelerated acquisition of forestland when it passed the Woodruff–McNary Act of 1928 (13). By 1961, over 20 million acres (8.1 million hectares) of forestland, mostly in the East, had been purchased (8).

Forestry Research   The second major task of the Forest Service was expanding efforts in forest research. Documenting relationships between forests and streamflow accelerated forest research activity. However, reforesting cutover lands, increasing yields, and reducing waste through greater utilization of trees were also important research goals. Raphael Zon deserves much credit for the Forest Service research organization. He emphasized applied research, stating that "science . . . must serve mankind" (13). In 1908, he presented a plan to Pinchot to establish forest experiment stations on key national forests. Pinchot, recalling his response, said that "I had seen forest experiment stations abroad and I knew their value. The plan, therefore, was approved at once" (11). When Pinchot left office in 1910, he had established two forest experiment stations and authorized the construction of the Forest Products Laboratory in Madison, Wisconsin.

Congress was tightfisted with research funding over the next fifteen years. A big boost came in 1925, when enough funds were appropriated to add six new experiment stations. Yet funding was haphazard, severely limiting research activities. With Greeley's enthusiastic support, the Forest Service obtained assistance from private groups to lobby Congress for long-term research funding. Their efforts paid off in 1928 with passage of the McSweeney–McNary Act. This act raised research to the same importance as other Forest Service functions such as timber and grazing. Furthermore, the

act increased appropriations for forest research and authorized a periodic nationwide survey of timber resources in the United States.

Civilian Conservation Corps Development of national forests received increased attention when President Franklin D. Roosevelt established the Civilian Conservation Corps (CCC) by executive order on April 5, 1933, as part of his New Deal. In a March 21, 1933, document asking Congress for its support, Roosevelt detailed his goals as not only "unemployment relief" during the Great Depression but also advanced work in "forestry, the prevention of soil erosion, flood control, and similar projects." He thought of the CCC as an investment "creating future national wealth" (9). Between 1933 and 1942, when the CCC started to disband because of World War II, over two million people worked in the program with as many as a half million enrolled at one time (Figure 1.4). The Forest Service received nearly half the projects, but the Park Service and other federal agencies also received substantial aid from the program (8). Although some people criticized the CCC for hiring enrollees from lists of Democrats (8), its accomplishments

Figure 1.4 Civilian Conservation Corps camp in the territory of Alaska. (Courtesy of U.S.D.A. Forest Service.)

outweighed its problems. Young people built trails, thinned forests, fought fires, planted trees, and constructed campgrounds and other facilities. Their efforts substantially advanced the development of the national forests.

Regulation and Control of the Forests   The most controversial action by the Forest Service during the period was its attempt to regulate private forest management. The agency had played an advisory role in private timber management until passage of the Transfer Act of 1905, when much of its attention shifted to managing the newly acquired national forests. Cooperation with private owners was generally accepted as beneficial to all concerned at the time. However, Pinchot later recalled that he had been "misled" into thinking that timber owners were interested in "practicing forestry" (11).

Regulation created a split in professional forester ranks. A Pinchot-led faction favored federal control, and Forest Service chiefs Graves and Greeley led the state control fight. Pinchot argued that "forest devastation will not be stopped through persuasion" but by "compulsory nation-wide legislation" (6). Pinchot believed that the lumber industry could control state legislatures. In his view, only the federal government had the power to enforce regulations. The Forest Service argued that federal regulation was unconstitutional and the federal role should focus on cooperation rather than direct intervention in private forest management. The line was drawn and Congress became the battlefield. Bills favored each position, and both sides stood firm. Pinchot said it was "a question of National control or no control at all" (8). The bills stalled. Greeley then proposed a compromise measure that dropped regulation entirely and emphasized fire control. After all, he contended, timber cutting was "insignificant" in comparison to wildfires as a cause of deforestation (8). Pinchot agreed (8), and Congress passed the Clarke–McNary Act of 1924.

Although the Weeks Act previously authorized state and federal cooperation in fire control, Clarke–McNary expanded cooperation into other areas. It enabled the Secretary of Agriculture to assist states in growing and distributing planting stock and in providing aid to private owners in forest management. These two acts stimulated the establishment of state forestry organizations throughout the country. The Clarke–McNary Act also expanded the Weeks Act provisions for land purchases. Clarke–McNary set a precedent by authorizing purchase of land in the watersheds of navigable streams for timber production as well as streamflow protection. Purchase of timberland, particularly after it had been logged, was one approach to solving the deforestation problem on which most parties could agree. Overall, the Clarke–McNary Act is one of the most important pieces of legislation in American forest policy.

World War II increased the nation's timber appetite. Great quantities of timber were harvested from both public and private lands, and certain important tree species were in short supply. For example, loggers almost cut in Olympic National Park because of the need for Sitka spruce to build warplanes. Rapid cutting to satisfy wartime timber requirements also intensified the public-regulation controversy. Timber executives mounted a major publicity campaign to thwart further federal regulation. They were particularly concerned about attaching conditions to cooperative funds allocated under the Clarke–McNary Act.

Heightened pressure on forest resources induced by war and by proposed federal regulations motivated passage of forestry legislation at the state level. For example, the continued threat of federal control helped lumber interests decide to support state laws as the least offensive alternative. By 1939, five states had enacted legislation to curtail destructive cutting practices, but they were ineffective. The Oregon Forest Conservation Act of 1941 set a precedent for more effective state action, aimed primarily at securing and protecting tree reproduction, including several specific and quantitative guidelines. Landowners had to obtain an approved, alternative timber management plan to deviate from practices specified in the law. Likewise, the state forester could correct problems on timberlands caused by violating the law and charge the owners. Similar acts passed in Maryland (1943), Mississippi (1944), Washington (1945), California (1945), and Virginia (1948). Other states, such as Massachusetts (1943), Vermont (1945), New York (1946), and New Hampshire (1949), relied on incentives and voluntary control of cutting on private land (6).

At the federal level, Congress enacted two major forest policies in 1944. Congress amended federal income tax laws to allow timber owners to declare net revenue from timber sales as capital gains instead of as ordinary income. This law reduced taxes and helped to encourage timber owners to retain forestland in timber production. It also helped to discourage them from abandoning land to avoid paying delinquent taxes.

Congress also passed the Sustained Yield Forest Management Act of 1944. Sustained yield, in a general sense, means that an area is managed to produce roughly equal annual or regular periodic, yields of a resource such as timber. This concept can be traced back centuries in Europe where timber resources were scarce, and predictable, steady yields were essential. The U.S. frontier economy made this approach politically difficult until war-induced shortages helped to make the idea more acceptable. However, the Sustained Yield Forest Management Act focused on safeguarding forest-dependent communities from local timber shortages rather than national needs. The act authorized the Secretaries of Interior and Agriculture to establish sustained-yield units of either federal timberland or a mixture of private and public timberland. Thus, the secretaries could enter into long-term agreements with private forest owners to pool their resources with the government to supply timber to local mills. Opposition from small companies and labor unions prevented the establishment of more than one cooperative sustained-yield unit. However, the Forest Service did establish five federal sustained-yield units on national forests (8).

In 1946, President Truman signed an executive order to create the Bureau of Land Management (BLM) (22). This order combined the lands in the Department of the Interior held by the Grazing Service and those still held and managed by the General Land Office, which was established in 1812 to survey lands and manage the transfer of territory to private hands. The BLM owns great tracts of timberland in the western United States, most acquired through default of original grantees of federal lands.

The rapid and destructive cutting practices associated with the war left behind millions of acres that were not producing timber. Equally troubling was the fact that timber harvests exceeded forest growth. The Forest Service laid blame squarely on the shoulders of private timberland owners. The debate became acrimonious and technical arguments were set aside as the issue degenerated into an emotional squabble. One timber industry representative accused the Forest Service of leading the country into "totalitarian government and ultimately socialism," and even called the Assistant Chief of the Forest Service, Edward C. Crafts, a "dangerous man" because Crafts felt the public had the right to protect its interests in private land (8). Dwight D. Eisenhower settled the debate when, during his campaign, he said that he was against "federal domination of the people through federal domination of their natural resources" (8). Eisenhower became president in 1952. He appointed Governor Sherman Adams of New Hampshire, a fomer lumberman, as his presidential assistant. Adams stated earlier that natural resources could be conserved and distributed "without succumbing either to dictatorship or national socialism" (8). The Forest Service, sensing that the election might bring a philosophical change, moved to have Richard E. McArdle appointed chief, in part because he was not identified with the regulation issue (14). The decision proved sound. McArdle dropped the Forest Service regulation campaign and retained his position through the change of administrations.

Important Features of the Period 1911–1952   An evaluation of forest policies between 1911 and 1952 shows the usual mixture of success and failure. The goal of preventing forest resource overexploitation conflicted with that of furnishing wood needed to fight World Wars I and II. Maintaining forest cover in the headwaters of navigable streams was only partially accomplished. The government could not purchase all such watersheds, and purchased cutover lands were not always reforested. Technological constraints and shortages of money and workers during much of the period made it difficult to protect forests adequately from insects, diseases, and fire.

Nevertheless, the period produced at least four major accomplishments, although none of them represented a major societal goal when the period began. First, the National Park System grew in size to include the nation's most scenic areas and a new agency was established to coordinate their management. Second, the Forest Service established a wilderness system. Third, cooperative arrangements in forest management developed among state, federal, and private timberland owners. Finally, the CCC converted the adversity of the Great Depression into a significant contribution to the development of U.S. forests.

Adjusting to Complexity (1952–present)

Although the forest policy problems of previous periods were never simple, they still seem more comprehensible then the problems faced by contemporary society. Since World War II, the United States has experienced unparalleled material affluence and technological advances. A burgeoning population has heightened competition for essential natural resources. After World War II came a rapid growth in timber demand, particularly for housing construction, that resulted in a continuation of destructive logging practices. Timber needs were too great to be satisfied from private lands alone, so heavy logging reached into the national forests. At the same time, prosperity, supported by rapid exploitation of natural resources, made it possible for people to spend more of their leisure time in the nation's forests, leading to "mass recreation." The numbers of people visiting the nation's wildlands increased tremendously and the nature of those visits changed to include more cars and developed recreational sites (22). Extractive use and intensive recreational use, other than hunting, generally conflict with each other. Therefore, issues in the 1950s and 1960s were broader than issues that

divided preservationists and utilitarian conservationists in previous periods.

Global events such as the Cold War, the wars in Korea and Vietnam, and the Watergate scandal played an important role in the development of forest policy. The Government's lack of candor concerning these events caused a large segment of society to become suspicious of many public officials and, consequently, distrustful of those in authority, including professional foresters. Public demands for citizen participation in resource management decisions were largely a result of this lack of trust. Professional foresters were unprepared for this intense public scrutiny.

Most forest policy goals from 1911 through 1952 carried over into the current period. The end of Forest Service efforts to impose federal regulation on private forest management in 1952 was a major turning point for the forestry profession. Foresters accustomed to strong public support for the way they managed forests now became defensive. They also faced the challenges of reducing conflicts over resource uses, and providing a growing nation with more goods and services from a fixed land base. Achieving these goals had become more difficult in the political and economic complexity of the period and the resulting uncertainty. In 1981, tax cuts and recession created a $200 billion annual federal deficit, followed by major budget reductions in federal forestry programs (15). Then, in 1982, stumpage prices fell 60 percent because housing construction declined sharply. Consequently, the timber industry began selling timberland and cutting back on personnel and operations.

Multiple Uses of the Forests Recreational use of national forests grew steadily during the pre–World War II years, but never reached parity with timber production as an objective of forest management. Recreation achieved formal recognition as an objective in 1935 when the Division of Recreation and Lands was created in the Forest Service. However, much recreation spending was on campgrounds and other facilities to keep recreationists confined and out of the way of commodity users. Fire prevention was also an important reason for concentrating people in campgrounds (16), particularly in southern California.

Following WWII, a huge demand for forest products dominated the attention of professional foresters, but they overlooked the equally enormous growth in recreation. For example, recreation visits to national forests climbed from fewer than 30 million in 1950 to about 233 million in 1982 (17, 18). The explosive increase in recreational use revived the idea, prevalent in the 1930s, that the Park Service should administer recreation. This spurred competition between the National Park Service and the Forest Service over authority to administer recreational use of public lands.

In 1956, the National Park Service received funding for its "Mission 66," a ten-year plan to expand and upgrade recreational facilities in national parks. The Forest Service, not to be left out, responded with Operation Outdoors in 1957 to garner funds for recreation on national forests, with a focus on the more "primitive" recreation available in national forests as opposed to the more developed opportunities found in national parks. Operation Outdoors laid a critical foundation for the first Forest Service effort to emphasize nontimber uses. On the other hand, the BLM also tried for recreation dollars with its Project 2012 (to celebrate the 200th anniversary of the creation of the General Land Office), but it was less successful.

While getting funding for Operation Outdoors, Forest Service attempts to increase other recreation funding met with limited success because of a lack of statutory responsibility to provide recreational facilities on national forests (16). The Forest Service had to find a way to increase its recreational budget and at the same time protect itself from what it viewed as unacceptable demands from the timber industry, the grazing industry, and the Park Service for exclusive use of certain national forest lands. The concept adopted for defending the agency was "multiple use." In other words, the Forest Service felt that obtaining congressional endorsement to manage lands for several uses, including grazing, wildlife, recreation, watershed, and timber, would both legitimate the agency's management of all resources and enhance its funding position in Congress. The legal vehicle was the Multiple Use–Sustained Yield Act (MUSY) of 1960, through which Congress directed that national forests be managed for outdoor recreation, range, timber, watershed, and wildlife and fish purposes.

Although Edward C. Crafts said, "the bill contained a little something for everyone" (19); it was nevertheless opposed by the timber industry, the Sierra Club (a preservationist group), and the Park Service. The lumber industry thought that timber had always been given the highest priority in national forest management and that the bill would eliminate this preferential treatment by placing all resources on an equal level. Their opposition to the bill turned into mild support when the bill was amended to include the following phrase: "The purposes of this Act are declared to be supplemental to, but not in derogation of, the purposes for which the national forests were established as set forth in the Act of June 4, 1897" (10). In other words, since the Organic Administration Act of 1897 specified timber and water as the resources that forest reserves were meant to protect, they felt that these resources would be given a higher priority than other resources. However, it is generally agreed this ranking covers the establishment of national forests and does not extend to forest management (19, 20).

The Sierra Club opposed the multiple-use bill for two reasons. First, members wanted wilderness added to the resource list so that wilderness would recieve equal but separate recognition from recreation. This issue was partially resolved when the bill was amended at the request of the Wilderness Society to state that wilderness was "consistent with the purposes and provisions" of the bill (21). Second, the Sierra Club and the Park Service believed the real purpose of multiple-use was to stop the Park Service from taking national forest lands to make national parks. However, they failed to include an amendment stating that the bill would not affect creation of new national parks (19). President Eisenhower signed the Multiple Use–Sustained Yield Act of 1960 even though it did not fully satisfy the Sierra Club and the Park Service.

The Multiple Use–Sustained Yield Act has been successful in accomplishing the Forest Service's goals. The Forest Service preserved its broad constituency, its political flexibility, and its varied responsibilities. However, the boost in congressional funding for nontimber resources that was expected to follow passage of the act did not materialize. Only wildlife management received a significant average increase in funding relative to Forest Service requests (20) (Figure 1.5).

One unresolved multiple-use issue involves priorities for allocation among uses. The Multiple Use–Sustained Yield Act evades priorities entirely. It mandates that all uses mentioned are appropriate for national forest management; that all uses will be given equal consideration; that all uses will be managed according to sustained-yield principles; and that land productivity will not be impaired. Now the broader concept of "ecosystem management" integrates multiple-use management within the higher priority of sustaining an ecological system. The Forest Service adopted this concept by an administrative decision. However, this decision creates new issues because it raises the standard of sustaining an ambiguous, and possibly undefinable, ecological system above all other purposes for national forests specified in existing law.

The Wilderness System MUSY did not eliminate Forest Service problems with single-use advocates.

Figure 1.5 Bull moose in the Gallatin National Forest, Montana. (Courtesy of U.S.D.A. Forest Service.)

The wilderness issue remained. Creation of a wilderness system aided the agency in defending its boundaries, but also created a preservation-oriented constituency that wanted to protect scenic and roadless areas against Forest Service commodity use programs.

Over the years, the Forest Service added to its wilderness system and refined administrative regulations. The agency developed a classification scheme including a continuum of protection levels from primitive areas, which permitted some roads and logging, to wild and wilderness areas that prohibited these activities. In 1940, the Forest Service extended greater protection to primitive areas as well (10). However, wilderness enthusiasts watched as the Forest Service gradually reduced the size of wilderness, wild, and primitive areas. Logging roads advanced and technology increased timber utilization in remote areas, so pressures to open protected lands to harvesting increased. Because the Forest Service could change wilderness boundaries,

preservationists sought increased security from congressional action for wilderness designation. In addition, they wanted to establish wilderness on other federal lands, particularly within national parks and monuments. After eight years of debate and eighteen public hearings, Congress passed the Wilderness Act of 1964 (Figure 1.6).

The wilderness system created by the Wilderness Act set aside 9.1 million acres (3.7 million hectares) of land in fifty-four areas that the Forest Service originally identified as wilderness and wild areas. Some existing uses of the land, like grazing, could continue. Similarly, mineral prospecting could continue until 1983 (22). National Park Service lands were not included in the original wilderness areas, but Congress designated some lands for study and many wilderness areas now exist in national parks. Bureau of Land Management lands were not included under the Wilderness Act until passage of the 1976 Federal Land Policy and Management Act (22). This act legislatively authorized

Figure 1.6 Packing into the Pecos Wilderness Area of the Santa Fe National Forest, New Mexico. (Photograph by Harold Walter, courtesy of U.S.D.A. Forest Service.)

the BLM, defining a land management mission more than thirty years after executive reorganization established the Bureau (22).

One of the more interesting debates concerned the renewability of wilderness as a resource. The Forest Service stated that wilderness could not be renewed. In other words, land used for other purposes could not be restored to its original wilderness character. On the other hand, preservation groups contended that "certain areas not wilderness . . . if given proper protection and management can be restored and regain wilderness qualities" (23). This was an important issue in the eastern United States because timber production and agriculture had already affected much public land. The Forest Service felt that most of these lands no longer retained their original character, so it resisted attempts to classify wilderness areas in the East. Instead, it proposed a new eastern roadless area system that would be less restrictive and separate from the national wilderness preservation system. Preservationists refused to accept this alternative and succeeded in pressuring Congress to pass the Eastern Wilderness Act of 1975. The act added sixteen new areas to the wilderness system totaling nearly 207,000 acres (83,772 hectares). An additional 125,000 acres (50,587 hectares) in seventeen areas in national forests were set aside for the Secretary of Agriculture to evaluate for possible inclusion in the wilderness system.

Wilderness advocates could not satisfy their appetite for land. Their sights included all national forest roadless areas as well as congressionally designated wilderness study areas. The Forest Service responded in 1967 by conducting a nationwide inventory and evaluation of roadless lands within national forests for wilderness suitability. The procedure known as RARE (Roadless Area Review and Evaluation) identified 1,449 sites containing approximately 56.21 million acres (22.7 million hectares). In 1973, the chief of the Forest Service designated 235 of these sites for further study as possible wilderness areas.

Many people criticized the RARE process, so a new RARE II process began in 1977. In January 1979, Secretary of Agriculture Bob Bergland made

public the results and recommended to Congress that 15.1 million acres (6.1 million hectares) of national forests be added to the wilderness system, and that an additional 11.2 million acres (4.5 million hectares) be held for "further planning" because of a need for more reliable information on mineral deposits. There was hope that this recommendation would bring resolution to the wilderness question. However, preservationists reacted with "acute disappointment" to the recommendation, feeling that it fell short, while the timber industry argued that it was excessive (24).

Advocates were still demanding more wilderness twenty years after passage of the Wilderness Act. Therefore, the Ninety-eighth Congress added 6.9 million acres (2.8 million hectares) of wilderness to the system, bringing the total to 32.4 million acres (13.1 million hectares). The Eastern Wilderness Act and subsequent congressional actions led to a gradual change in the standards used to judge wilderness quality. Today, many groups use wilderness designation as a way to preserve areas that would not have qualified as wilderness under provisions of the Wilderness Act of 1964. In Wisconsin, for example, one wilderness area contains a red pine plantation. Likewise, current forests in many western wilderness areas are growing so thick that wildfires often burn hotter than would have occurred in the historic forests. These extremely hot fires threaten local communities and devastate the wilderness character of the land. Thus, wilderness is gradually losing its distinction as the repository of the last remnants of the historic American landscape. Clearly, wilderness issues will be around for some time.

The Clearcutting Issue Wood consumption increased in the 1970s at the same time that environmental constraints, such as air and water pollution control and restrictions on the use of pesticides and herbicides, were limiting timber production. Furthermore, net losses of timberland in all ownerships to nontimber purposes averaged about 4.9 million acres (2 million hectares) per decade. Consequently, foresters believed that wood shortages could develop at some point in the future. Although their apprehensions have not been borne out, preservationists and land managers still disagree over which methods are best for producing timber.

The focal point of the debate is clearcutting, which is a regeneration method in which all the trees on a certain area of land are cut and the site regenerated by natural seeding, seeding from aircraft, or replanting of pioneer tree species that grow in openings. Preservationists claimed that clearcutting has "an enormously devastating environmental effect which includes soil destruction, stream siltation, and a stinging blow to the aesthetic sense" (25). Where properly applied, clearcutting is less damaging than wildfire but, like a wildfire, little can be done to reduce the unpleasant appearance of a recent clearcut.

Concern over national forest management practices erupted in November 1970, when Senator Lee Metcalf of Montana released the Bolle Report, titled *A University View of the Forest Service,* and put it into the Congressional Record. Scientists from the University of Montana prepared the report at Metcalf's request. The report not only criticized Forest Service management practices, but it also uncovered a deep division within professional forester ranks. The problem began in 1968 when residents of Montana's Bitterroot Valley complained that clearcuts damaged the national forest surrounding them. Most disturbing to local residents was the Forest Service's practice of terracing steep mountain slopes to prevent erosion and improve timber reproduction. The Forest Service received a torrent of letters demanding that these practices be stopped. The Forest Service responded by appointing a task force to conduct an impartial analysis of management practices in the Bitterroot National Forest. The task force released its findings in April 1970, a full six months before the Bolle committee, and was remarkably candid. Task force members found, for example, that the attitude of many national forest staff was "that resource production goals come first and that land management considerations take second place" (26). The Bolle committee concurred with many of the findings in the task force report, but also found that "the Forest Service is primarily oriented toward

timber harvest as the dominant use of national forests" (26). In sum, the Forest Service did an outstanding job of producing timber, but it failed to adjust to changing social values.

The Forest Service modified forest management policies on the Bitterroot National Forest, but disregarded national implications of public concerns over clearcutting. A few months after the Bolle committee report was released, the Subcommittee on Public Lands of the Senate Interior and Insular Affairs Committee, chaired by Senator Frank Church of Idaho, held hearings on public lands management practices, focusing on clearcutting in the national forests, especially in Montana, West Virginia, Wyoming, and Alaska. The subcommittee concluded that clearcutting had to be regulated and found that the Forest Service "had difficulty communicating effectively with its critics, and its image has suffered" (27). Although the Forest Service had taken some actions to adjust to public concerns over clearcutting, the subcommittee felt they "have made little impact" (27). The Forest Service lost the opportunity to make forward-looking revisions in management policies and instead had to accept the Church guidelines.

The clearcutting of hardwood forests in the Monongahela National Forest in West Virginia further increased the controversy, and the issue remains unresolved to this day (Figure 1.7). Clearcutting replaced selective cutting in the Monongahela National Forest in 1964, and the reaction was almost immediate. Concerned citizens pressured the West Virginia legislature to pass resolutions in 1964, 1967, and 1970, requesting investigations of Forest Service timber management practices. A Forest Service special review committee confirmed that abuses had occurred (28). As a result, timber management policies were changed to encourage a variety of harvesting techniques. In addition, clearcuts were limited to 25 acres (10 hectares) or less, and distances between clearcuts were regulated. Since many timber sales were under contract using the old 80-acre (32-hectare) limit, Forest Service reforms could not bring immediate results (29).

These reforms failed to satisfy preservationists. They wanted all clearcutting stopped immediately.

Figure 1.7 Clearcuts (background) on the Monongahela National Forest (Gauley District), West Virginia. (Photograph by R. L. Giese.)

In May 1973, the Izaak Walton League of America and other preservation organizations filed suit alleging that clearcutting violated a provision in the 1897 Organic Administration Act stating that only "dead, matured, or large growth of trees" could be cut and sold from a national forest. In December 1973, Judge Robert Maxwell of the Northern District Federal Court of West Virginia accepted this interpretation. His ruling effectively banned clearcutting on national forests. The Fourth Circuit Court of Appeals unanimously upheld the lower court's decision in 1975, and the Forest Service halted all timber sales on national forests within the jurisdiction of the court. In 1976, the U.S. District Court of Alaska used the same reasoning to issue a permanent injunction against timber harvesting on a large area of Prince of Wales Island. These and similar lawsuits halted timber sales on national forests in six states (30).

The Monongahela decision produced a number of bills in Congress to overcome the timber production bottleneck. For example, a preservationist-sponsored bill would have instituted legislative prescriptions on timber harvesting. Acting with unusual speed, Congress passed an alternative bill titled the National Forest Management Act (NFMA). It was signed into law on October 22, 1976. The act contained many important provisions. Together with the Forest and Rangeland Renewable Resources Planning Act of 1974 (RPA) (see "Additional Legislation" later in this chapter), the NFMA requires the Forest Service to prepare comprehensive interdisciplinary forest plans for all administrative units at ten-year intervals. By 1986, twenty-five national forest plans were in final form, but most were challenged by interest groups. By the mid-1990s, all forest plans had been finalized and approved by the Forest Service Chief, though court challenges to some plans remain. The NFMA repealed the section of the Organic Administration Act of 1897 that served as the basis for lawsuits that stopped national forest clearcutting. It allows clearcutting when it is found to be the "optimal" (left undefined) silvicultural treatment. Clearcuts today are less extensive and nontimber values, such as wildlife and recreation, have a greater role in decisions about regeneration methods. While the NFMA did not completely resolve the clearcutting controversy, it did make foresters more alert and sensitive to public opinion. The act also brought forest management closer to the multiple-use ideal.

Judicial Involvement in Resource Policy Making

The Monongahela decision illustrates the growing importance of courts in forest policy development. In 1978, for example, the U.S. Supreme Court further complicated management of the national forests by handing down the Rio Mimbres decision. The Rio Mimbres flows through the Gila National Forest in New Mexico. The dispute centered on the legal right of the Forest Service to have enough water to manage the multiple uses of a national forest versus the rights of upstream water users who wanted water for irrigation and other purposes. As in the Monongahela decision, the Organic Administration Act of 1897 was used against the Forest Service. The Court interpreted the act to mean that forest reserves were set aside to maintain timber supplies and favorable waterflows. The act did not mention rights to water for other purposes. In essence, the Court ruled that the Forest Service had no legal right to Rio Mimbres water and that it would have to satisfy water needs through state water rights procedures (15). Thus, courts dramatically increased the complexities and uncertainties of national forest management.

The courts normally limit the number and scope of their reviews of administrative decisions. The judiciary gradually became more involved with administrative review as preservationists, frustrated in their dealings with administrators, turned to the courts for relief. The number of suits increased dramatically after the "Scenic Hudson" case of 1965, in which the court decided that an organization

whose principal interest is scenic beauty could sue government agencies (31). This decision opened the door to the courts and ushered in judicial involvement in resource policy-making, including the Monongahela case. Lawsuits are expensive, time-consuming, and often embarrassing to the agency involved. Thus, just the threat of a lawsuit can increase participation by citizens in formulating agency policy. Preservationists also use lawsuits as a delaying tactic.

Passage of the National Environmental Policy Act of 1969 (NEPA) and similar legislation enacted by various states greatly expanded opportunities to file lawsuits. NEPA established a detailed procedure for assessing environmental consequences of federal actions significantly affecting the quality of the human environment. These procedures require that agencies consider so many potential effects that it is difficult to fully comply with the law, which invites litigation on procedural grounds alone. Furthermore, NEPA is one of the first environmental policies using "sunshine provisions," which require that decision-making be open to public view and comment. Thus, the public is more aware of regulatory decisions and can quickly respond with legal challenges. This delays decisions and, in many cases, brings about changes in forest policy. The large volume of environmental legislation passed by Congress and the states during the late 1960s and 1970s also provided increased opportunities for lawsuits, in part because the laws included citizen suit provisions that permitted individuals to sue an agency to mandate enforcement of the law.

Additional Legislation

The Forest and Rangeland Renewable Resources Planning Act of 1974 (RPA) was perhaps the most far-reaching forest policy enacted during this period. The RPA was part of a congressional effort to gain greater control of the budgetary process. Congress was reacting to what it perceived as a decline in its authority relative to the executive branch (32). Furthermore, Congress had always shown greater support for resource programs than the executive branch, particularly the Office of Management and Budget (OMB), and RPA was one means of pressuring the president to raise budget requests for natural resources management.

RPA initiated a procedure for setting goals and formulating forest policies. The act requires the Secretary of Agriculture to make periodic assessments of national needs for forest and rangeland resources. Then the Secretary must make recommendations for long-range programs that the Forest Service must carry out to meet those needs. The act required the Secretary to tramsmit the assessment and program to Congress in 1976 and again in 1980. A new assessment was required every ten years thereafter, and the program is to be revised every five years. Subsequent assessments included comprehensive analyses of the forestry and forest products sectors in the United States and worldwide, pointing to a need for improved information to better manage forests under all ownerships. In addition, the president is required to submit a statement to Congress with each annual budget explaining why funding requests differ from the program approved by Congress.

The Forest Service took advantage of the opportunity provided by RPA. In its first budget request under RPA, the agency asked for substantial increases in funds. Congress responded favorably, and President Jimmy Carter signed the appropriations bill for the 1978 fiscal year. The Forest Service budget was raised $275 million over the funding level of the previous fiscal year (33). Subsequent budgets did not do as well. Massive federal deficits forced budget reductions that resulted in a 30 percent decline in national forest funding between 1978 and 1986 (34). While recent federal budgets have not had the sizable deficits of the past, Forest Service budgets have been largely flat or declining in both real and nominal terms as entitlement spending grows.

Although many important policies dealing with forest resources developed during this period, a series of laws adopted for other purposes profoundly affected forest management as well. These policies include enactment of NEPA (already discussed), Clean Air Act of 1970, Federal Water Pollution Control Act of 1972, Federal Environmental Pesticide Control Act of 1922, Endangered Species

Act of 1973, Toxic Substances Control Act of 1976, and Clean Water Act of 1977. Two major attributes of these policies are particularly important. First, they rely on complex and detailed federal and state regulation procedures and the exercise of federal police powers. They also mandate public involvement in the regulatory process, including public hearings and comment periods on proposed regulations. Second, they focus on broad environmental goals rather than forestry, yet they influence forest policy. For example, Section 208 of the 1972 Federal Water Quality Act amendments required the establishment of enforceable best management practices to control water pollution. These practices apply to timber harvesting and silvicultural treatments on public and private forestlands, and they further complicate the forest policy process (35).

The 1980s saw much litigation concerning forestry move through the courts and relatively little legislation move through Congress. The idea of "conflict resolution" became a natural resource management specialty because lawsuits proved too cumbersome and time-consuming for use in resolving disputes over resource use. Mediation and stakeholder meetings to collect information, assure that all viewpoints are aired, and hammer out possible solutions were hailed as the future of public natural resource management, as indeed they have become. Those most closely involved in an issue come together to work out a solution that is acceptable to everyone.

After more than a decade of litigation over the adequacy of national forest plans in meeting all of the requirements imposed by RPA, NFMA, NEPA, and various other laws, and squabbles over wilderness, the Endangered Species Act of 1973 (ESA) moved to center stage in the 1980s, 1990s, and 2000s. It may be the most important law affecting forest policy development in the United States. Although not originally controversial, the ESA became more onerous to many agencies and landowners as the U.S. Fish and Wildlife Service became more aggressive in carrying out its provisions. Thus, subsequent amendments attempted to ease the burden on affected interests, but with limited affect. For example, the 1978 amendments created the "God Squad," a presidentially appointed cabinet-level committee convened to evaluate situations where a species' critical habitat designation and recovery measures have a profound economic or other impact. Subsequent amendments allowed private landowners to be issued "incidental take permits" in return for developing a habitat conservation plan for the at-risk species where the critical habitat involves private land.

Perhaps the most well known ESA impact on forestry stems from listing the northern spotted owl as a threatened species in northern California, Oregon, and Washington. This decision curtailed harvesting of old growth forests (generally more than 200 years old) by court injunctions in 1989. Hundreds of sawmills and other processing facilities utilizing this timber shut down, causing economic depression in the myriad small towns in which these facilities were major employers. The loss of public timber also shifted the burden of meeting the nation's wood fiber needs to private forest landowners and it dramatically increased reliance on foreign imports. Since most of the remaining old growth forests in this region are on federal lands (Forest Service or BLM), government appeared on all sides of the debate: as land manager, as enforcer of the ESA, and as states and counties which stood to lose substantial revenues because so much timber harvesting had ceased. The rhetoric surrounding this issue was extreme, some local economic losses were severe, and emotions remain high. Matters reached such a level that the God Squad was convened under the ESA to determine whether some timber sales in process on BLM lands would be allowed to continue.

In the South, the red-cockaded woodpecker (RCW) was listed as endangered in 1970. The effects on Southern forestry have been much smaller than in the Pacific Northwest, in large part because remaining RCW habitat is mostly on public land, which is a small part of commercial forestland in this region.

The U.S. Supreme Court ruled on many of the issues surrounding the presence of endangered species on forested lands. In particular, the Court clarified how the ESA applies to private lands. Private property rights are a precious part of America's cultural heritage, so balancing the rights of landowners against the public interest remains a legal issue. A 1995 Supreme Court decision in *Babbitt v. Sweet Home, et al.* affirmed that the ESA applies to private lands and that a habitat conservation plan is the remedy for landowners. However, these plans are expensive to prepare and difficult to implement. Consequently, efforts are underway to find workable alternatives for small landowners. "Safe Harbor" is one proposed remedy under which small landowners can agree, as part of a statewide habitat conservation plan, to maintain some habitat on their lands for a given number of animals (36). Under "Safe Harbor," small landowners can work together by trading agreements. It is possible for one landowner to maintain all needed habitat in an area. Then other landowners compensate the owner who accepts responsibility for maintaining the habitat so that they are free to harvest timber on their lands.

A group of concerned citizens in Quincy, California, pioneered another innovative alternative to public forest management. They are known as the Quincy Library Group because they met in the town library. They succeeded in forging a compromise plan to protect their community from two interrelated problems. First, they needed a way to revitalize the local economy that had suffered from reduced timber harvests on public lands. In addition, the lack of forest management allowed trees to become denser and dead fuel began piling up underneath them. Therefore, their community also faced a growing threat from wildfires. After several years in development, their plan to resolve these issues became law in The Herger–Feinstein Quincy Library Group Forest Recovery Act of 1999, which passed in Congress as an amendment to the Omnibus Appropriations Bill. Similar programs for local participation in forest management exist in several communities, such as the Applegate Partnership in southwestern Oregon. However, the Canadian government has gone farther than any other country's in creating opportunities for local participation. They launched their Model Forests

Sidebar 1.4

Rediscovering the Local Community

Today's forest management issues frequently involve vast areas of land and national interests. Local communities that must live with decisions to resolve such issues often become victims of the policy process rather than participants. Furthermore, the grand scale of these issues makes relationships within them highly complex, which increases uncertainty about the consequences of actions designed to resolve the issues. National interest groups, who lack detailed firsthand knowledge of local conditions, further complicate such problems by ignoring uncertainties, and oversimplifying issues so that they can prescribe simple solutions. Decisions reached in this manner often generate unanticipated and undesireable social and ecological side effects. Many of these side effects are so serious that they ignite further conflict. Keeping decision making centralized at the national level cannot break the cycle of conflict, simplistic solutions, and new conflicts that such decisions inevitably generate.

Conflict can be a constructive force in an open society, but it has limits. Conflict often focuses on the outcome of a decision. The process that leads to a decision may not be as important to interest groups as winning. Further conflict then develops because the needs of losers in the process remain unfulfilled. This is another reason why conflict often fails to deliver acceptable or sustainable decisions.

Cooperation focuses on the process that leads to a decision. It represents recognition by the participants that there are no right or wrong answers, only acceptable solutions. People who work together for their individual and common interests develop a better understanding of each other and the issue being addressed. Thus, cooperation usually leads to mutual respect and it increases the likelihood of achieving a durable consensus (1).

Decades of conflicts over forest management have led to weariness with endless lawsuits and acrimonious debates. Decisions that resulted from these debates tended to ignore some groups and favor others, which led to frustration and a search for new ways to reduce conflict by promoting cooperation. What has emerged is the rediscovery of the local community. In the United States, the two best-known local groups working to resolve forest management issues are the Quincy Library Group and the Applegate Partnership. They both developed from efforts by local community leaders, loggers,

---

Program in 1992 through the Canadian Forest Service. Now the program is international, with ten forests in Canada, three in the United States, including the Applegate Partnership, and seven more in such countries as Chile, Russia, Mexico, and Japan.

Small Private Forestry Landowners who do not have a wood-processing facility are called nonindustrial private forest (NIPF) landowners (also see Chapter 10 on NIPFs). Much forest policy focuses on NIPF landowners because they own about 60 percent of the commercial timberland in the United States. For example, the Clarke–McNary Act of 1924 targets NIPFs of less than 1,000 acres (404.7 hectares). These NIPF landowners can obtain cost sharing for reforestation and technical assistance if they meet certain criteria. The Forestry Incentives Program of 1973 provided further assistance to small landowners. States administer many of these cooperative programs.

farmers, ranchers, and environmentalists who came together because conflict was damaging their communities. They are all striving to achieve the same goal: a sustainable balance between human well-being and healthy and productive forests.

The Applegate Partnership deals with issues involving all forest ownerships in the Applegate River watershed in southwestern Oregon. There is no hierarchy, nor are there officers, and the chair position rotates at each meeting. Thus, all participants have equal status and the meetings are open to everyone. Public and donated funds support the organization, and members work to ensure that all interests are respected and fairly considered in decisons.

The Quincy Library Group concentrates on national forests around the town of Quincy, California. Anyone who shows up at a meeting can join, and decisions are made by consensus, because each member has a veto. They reached a consensus on a forest management plan for the surrounding forests that was rejected by national environmental groups and the Forest Service, so the Quincy Library Group went to Congress. The result was the passage of the Herger–Feinstein Quincy Library Group Forest Recovery Act of 1999 that requires the Forest Service to carry out a national forest management plan similar to the one proposed by the group.

Canada has taken a different path to cooperation. The government, through the Canadian

Rediscovering the local community.

Forest Service, created a Model Forest Program. It encourages stakeholders, scientists, and public and private landowners to work together to develop sustainable forests that incorporate a broad range of values. The program began with ten Model Forests, but the idea is so popular that it is now part of the International Model Forest Network. To date, there are Model Forests in six countries and the list is expanding. Thus, rediscovering the local community could change the future of forest management worldwide.

Source:
1. T. M. BONNICKSEN, *Politics and the Life Sciences, 15,* 23–34 (1996).

Congress passed the Forest Stewardship Act in 1990 in response to growing concerns about the management of small private forestlands. The act includes three main provisions. First, the Forest Stewardship provision renders technical assistance, but it requires that a forest stewardship plan be prepared by a professional forester and approved by the state forestry agency. The stewardship plan must include land management objectives and strategies for multiple-use management, though the

landowner need not manage for all potential uses. The second major provision is the Stewardship Incentives Program, which provides technical assistance and cost sharing to those who have an approved ten-year stewardship plan. The third major provision is the Forest Legacy Program. This program permits landowners to retire lands of special character or lands that are environmentally sensitive in return for payments from the state. Small landowners will increasingly be required to plan with the assistance of resource professionals and demonstrate how their efforts benefit society in order to receive public monies.

Important Features of the Period 1952 to the Present An evaluation of American forest policy since 1952 shows a gradual transition to a more balanced and environmentally aware approach to resources management. The growing strength of nontimber interest groups fostered this change, but timber production remains critically important to the nation's economy and forest management. Citizen participation in local decision-making increased, and will likely continue to do so, although the traditional legislative and judicial processes continued to play an important role in forest policy development. Much work remains to achieve equity and harmony among affected interests. In spite of conflicts, and with the exception of many small communities in the West, most groups received substantially more forest resources from all ownerships, including timber products, than they obtained in any previous period.

Concluding Statement

In this chapter, we traced the history of forest policy development in the United States as seen through the policy process. This approach necessarily simplifies history, but certain general principles about forest resource policy making emerge, principles that will remain unaltered into the foreseeable future.

First, the forest policy process is inherently subjective. The preferred forest policy of one group may be seen as disastrous by another group. The search for objective measures to set goals and resolve forest policy issues has proved futile. No single criterion can ensure agreement among all contending interests as each group uses different standards to judge forest policies. Therefore, converting the forest policy process to science is not likely, nor will scientists and professionals be delegated authority to make the decisions. Active citizen participation will remain an essential part of the forest policy process.

Second, both the lack of objective criteria for assessing policies and citizen participation ensure that debate and compromise will continue to be the central means for making forest policy decisions. A professional forester or natural resource manager must be prepared not only to engage in these debates but also to compromise. The time when professional judgment was accepted without question has passed. (The following chapter discusses the forestry profession, and its responsibilities and career opportunities.)

Finally, the forest policy process is growing more complex. As demand for forest resources increases and diversity among interest groups widens, providing for society's needs in an equitable and cost-effective manner becomes more difficult. Important strides have been made in resolving forestry issues, but the unending search for creative answers remains the challenge of American forest policy.

References

1. K. E. BOULDING, *Principles of Economic Policy,* Prentice-Hall, Englewood Cliffs, N.J., 1958.

2. J. E. ANDERSON, *Public Policy-Making,* Holt, Rinehart & Winston, New York, 1979.

3. G. F. CARTER, *Man and the Land—A Cultural Geography,* Holt, Rinehart & Winston, New York, 1975.

4. H. E. DRIVER, *Indians of North America,* Univ. of Chicago Press, Chicago, 1961.

5. G. M. DAY, *Ecology, 34,* 329 (1953).

6. S. T. DANA, *Forest and Range Polity: Its Development in the United States,* First Edition, McGraw-Hill, New York, 1956.

7. T. A. BAILEY, *The American Pageant,* D. C. Heath, Boston, 1961.

8. H. K STEEN, *The U.S. Forest Service: A History,* Univ. of Washington Press, Seattle, 1976.

9. R. NASH, ed., *The American Environment,* Addison Wesley, Reading, Mass., 1968.

10. J. P. GILLIGAN, "The Development of Policy and Administration of Forest Service Primitive and Wilderness Areas in the Western United States," Vols. I and II, Ph.D. dissertation, Univ. of Michigan, 1953.

11. G. PINCHOT, *Breaking New Ground*, Harcourt Brace, New York, 1947.

12. S. P. HAYS, *Conservation and the Gospel of Efficiency*, Atheneum, New York, 1975.

13. D. C. SWAIN, *Federal Conservation Policy 1921–1933*, Univ. of California Press, Berkeley, 1963.

14. E. C. CRAFTS, "Forest Service Researcher and Congressional Liaison: An Eye to Multiple Use," *For. Hist. Soc. Publ.*, Santa Cruz, Calif., 1972.

15. J. RAMM AND K. BARTOLOMI, *J. For., 83,* 363, 367, (1985).

16. F. W. GROVER, "Multiple Use in U.S. Forest Service Land Planning," *For. Hist. Soc. Publ.*, Santa Cruz, Calif.,1972.

17. President's Advisory Panel on Timber and the Environment, Final Rept., U.S. Govt. Printing Office, 1973.

18. A. S. MILLS, "Recreational Use in National Forests." In *Statistics on Outdoor Recreation*, Part II, C. S. Van Doren, ed., Resources for the Future, Washington, D.C., 1984.

19. E. C. CRAFTS, *Am. For., 76,* 13, 52 (1970).

20. R. M. ALSTON, "FOREST—Goals and Decision-Making in the Forest Service." U.S.D.A. For. Serv., Intermountain For. Range Expt. Sta., Res. Pap. INT-128, 1972.

21. E. C. CRAFTS, *Am. For., 76,* 29 (1970).

22. S. T. DANA AND S. K. FAIRFAX, *Forest and Range Policy: Its Development in the United States*, Second Edition, McGraw-Hill, Second Edition, New York. 1980.

23. T. M. BONNICKSEN, *California Today, 2,* 1 (1974).

24. R. PARDO, *Am. For., 85,* 10 (1979).

25. N. WOOD, *Sierra Club Bull., 56,* 14 (1971).

26. A. W. BOLLE, "A University View of the Forest Servce," U.S. Govt. Printing Office, Doc. 91–115,1970.

27. U.S. Senate, "Clearcutting on Federal Timberlands," Rept., Public Lands Sub-Committee, Committee on Interior and Insular Affairs, 1972.

28. G. O. ROBINSON, *The Forest Service*, Johns Hopkins Press, Baltimore, 1975.

29. L. POPOVICH, *J. For., 74,* 169,176 (1976).

30. J. F. HALL AND R. S. WASSERSTROM, *Environ. Law, 8,* 523 (1978).

31. C. W. BRIZEE, *J. For., 73,* 424 (1975).

32. D. M. HARVEY, "Change in Congressional Policymaking and a Few Trends in Resource Policy." In *Centers of Influence and U.S. Forest Policy,* F. J. Convery and J. E. Davis, eds., School of Forestry and Environmental Studies, Duke Univ., Durham, N.C., 1977.

33. L. POPOVICH, *J. For., 75,* 656, 660 (1977).

34. N.SAMPSON, *Am. For., 92,* 10, 58 (1986).

35. J. A ZIVNUSKA, *J. For., 76,* 467 (1978).

36. R. BONNIE, *J. For., 95,* 17 (1997).

CHAPTER 2

Forestry: The Profession and Career Opportunities

RONALD L. GIESE

Forestry provides a diverse set of opportunities, which can lead to a challenging and fulfilling career. Many people are attracted to forestry by their outdoor orientation or environmental concerns, others by the mathematical and engineering applications so important in modern forestry; still others find the biological aspects of forestry to their liking. Some people find rewarding the elements of social studies in forestry such as economics, sociology, and political science. Still others are taken with applications of new technologies such as global positioning systems and satellites, or new disciplines like landscape ecology and geographic information systems in forestry. Whatever the motivation, a sense of stewardship and an appreciation of natural relationships are common denominators among those who pursue forestry as a professional career.

Events in recent decades have created momentous changes in the forestry profession. Passage of the National Environmental Policy Act and the establishment of the Environmental Protection Agency, along with various state versions of environmental and forest practices acts, require assess-

ment of the environmental consequences of forest management decisions. The Forest and Rangeland Renewable Resources Planning Act of 1974 and the National Forest Management Act (NFMA) of 1976, and the Federal Land Policy and Management Act of 1976 provided new opportunities to set national goals and formulate forest policies. Legal challenges to timber management practices on federal lands, like those arising from the Monongahela clearcutting issue, have led to changes in timber-management policies. In 1999, after 20 years of experience under the forest land management planning rules of the NFMA, the Forest Service issued new planning regulations.

The net result of these changes has been to create an institutional setting for forestry that is very different and more complex than ever before. As a society, we are now more concerned with ecosystem management and resource planning, which must deal with issues relating to diversity and biological conservation, wilderness, endangered species and the right of the people to influence the direction of resource management. Modern foresters are challenged, interested, and motivated by the complexities of their profession in a milieu of biological, quantitative and social sciences.

During a forestry career, a person usually encounters a progression of duties and expectations. Early on, foresters are very dependent on technical field skills (Figure 2.1). As they move up the career ladder into the broader aspects of land management, economics and decision-making skills become more pertinent to their professional performance. The next stage of the career often places foresters in the role of people managers who must draw broadly on a background of technology and experience in land management, as well as cope with the challenges generated by people both inside and outside their sphere of control. That such an evolution happens is evident by the fact that of over 12,000 Society of American Foresters members who reported the level of their jobs, 52 percent of these active professionals are in management, administrative, or staff specialist positions (1). The general direction of a forestry career is therefore from exercising technical forestry skills to employing business and management practices. However, the ability to communicate well and to work effectively on multidisciplinary teams is an asset at all stages of a person's career.

Paths to the Profession

Career Decisions

For students making tentative career choices, forestry is sometimes a mystery. Their perception

Figure 2.1 Students learn technical forestry skills in the field during the required summer camp experience.

of forestry may focus on operating sawmills, cutting trees, or outdoor recreation. However, as will be evident over the course of this chapter, modern forestry positions emphasize business approaches, computer science, social science, mathematics and engineering skills, as well as the life sciences. Careers in forestry can provide a variety of stimulating challenges in areas that students not primarily interested in biology usually do not consider seriously.

In planning for careers, students must use testing and classification services with caution. To a large extent the counseling services at the high school and college levels are usually out of date with respect to forestry. Vocational tests often suffer from biases and outdated bases of information. Typically, current automated testing systems picture a firefighter wearing a hard-hat or a logger with a chainsaw as characterizing forestry. These outmoded perceptions fail to do justice to the skills and education of the modern forestry professional whose background embraces computer science, ecology, operations research, business, policy, resource planning and management, engineering, and communications.

Vocational tests are widely available and generally fall into three categories: aptitude, interests, and personality. The outcomes of some of these tests are clearly wrong (based on outdated information), and others are incomplete. The Holland Classification, for example, takes interests, values and skills of individuals and combines them into six personality types (2). A combination of R (realistic), S (social), and I (investigative) types leads to forester in the Holland Code of occupations. If you undergo an analysis under this system using terms such as business management, taking risks, organizing, computing, writing, or decision-making as inputs, you will not be led, for example, to the following important aspects of forestry: planning, trade, paper processing, systems analysis, managerial activities, marketing, technical writing, or administration. Moreover, the concepts of artificial intelligence and expert systems, landscape ecology, biotechnology, and geographic information systems—each a component of forestry—have not yet found their way into the repertoire of the occupational codes or counseling services.

Some counselors and their subjects place too much credence and emphasis on test results. If taken as an end point rather than a beginning, test results are likely to lead to incorrect conclusions. This is so because the popular *Strong vocational interest* approach incorporates the Holland codes. Self-directed career searches and the *Holland Dictionary* (2) provide required educational development. However, the educational preparation specified does not include advanced mathematics or the ability to read technical literature—such a background would not even qualify a forestry program for accreditation. If you have interests or background in advanced mathematics, computer science, or statistics, an aptitude survey or vocational interest test will erroneously declare that you are overqualified for forestry. Because of the interdependency of these counseling tools, incorrect information in one of the components automatically creates flaws in the others.

If you wish to choose career possibilities with an open mind and an eye to future satisfaction, you should use testing information as only one of several sources of input. The informed person will develop a mixed strategy for choosing a career. Testing can provide some direction, but it should also stimulate questions. Interviews with counselors may help interpret the outcome of testing (Figure 2.2). Armed with vocational testing information, you can greatly enhance decisions on careers or academic majors by looking into careers, talking with advisors in college forestry departments, interviewing professionals engaged in fields that interest you, and taking a summer job to gain firsthand experience.

Never before have opportunities for exploring forestry issues been so easy and widespread. In this book, we help you to capitalize on this rich resource of information by interspersing references to websites globally. By using computers, you can expand on specialized information as interested.

Library, Nova Scotia Community College

Figure 2.2 Interactions with knowledgeable counselors can help in career choices. (Photo by W. Hoffman, UW–Madison.)

Forestry Curricula

The Society of American Foresters (SAF) defines forestry as "the science and art of attaining desired forest conditions and benefits. As professionals, foresters develop, use and communicate their knowledge for one purpose: to sustain and enhance forest resources for diverse benefits in perpetuity. To fulfill this purpose, foresters need to understand the many demands now and in the future" (3). Within this context, the SAF prescribes the curricula upon which professional forestry is built. The general requirements specified by the SAF fall into two categories, and a brief description will serve to show the diversity and strength of a forestry education.

General Education This component must provide coverage and competency in the following areas:

1. **Communications.** Oral and written competencies of communication must be demonstrated. Programs reinforce these skills throughout the entire curriculum.
2. **Science, Mathematics and Computer Literacy.** Competency is required in:
   Biological Science—understanding (a) patterns and processes of biological and ecological systems across space and time, and (b) molecular biology, cells, organisms, populations, species, communities and ecosystems.
   Physical sciences—understanding of physical and chemical properties, measurements, structure, and states of matter.
   Mathematics—understanding and using basic approaches and applications of algebra, trigonometry and statistics for analysis and problem solving.
   Computer Literacy—using computers and other electronic technologies in professional life.
3. **Social Sciences and Humanities.** Competency is required as an understanding of:
   Moral and ethical questions and using critical reasoning skills,
   Human behavior and social and economic structures, and
   Dimensions of the human experience.

Professional Education Competencies are required in the following major areas:

1. **Ecology and Biology**—understanding taxonomy, distribution and ecological characteristics of trees and their associated vegetation and wildlife; physiology of trees; genetics; ecological principles including structure and function of ecosystems; soil formation, classification and properties; silviculture including control of composition, growth and quality of forest stands, and fire ecology and use; entomology and pathology, and integrated pest management. Ability must be shown to conduct forest and stand assessments and to create silvicultural prescriptions.
2. **Measurement of Forest Resources**—identifying and measuring land areas and conducting spatial analysis; designing and implementing comprehensive forest inventory; and analyzing inventory information to project future forest conditions.
3. **Management of Forest Resources**—analyzing economic, environmental and social consequences of resource management strategies and

decisions; developing management plans with specific multiple objectives and constraints; understanding harvesting methods, wood properties, products manufacturing and utilization; and understanding administration, ownership and organization of forest enterprises.

4. **Forest Resource Policy and Administration**—understanding forest policy, processes of how local and federal laws and regulations govern forestry, professional ethics and ethical responsibility, and integrating technical, financial, human resources and legal aspects of public and private enterprises.

The mission of the Society of American Foresters is "to advance the science, education, technology, and practice of forestry; to enhance the competency of its members; to establish professional excellence; and to use the knowledge, skills, and conservation ethic of the profession to ensure the continued health and use of forest ecosystems and the present and future availability of forest resources to benefit society" (3). An important function of the SAF is the study and development of standards in forestry education and accreditation of forestry schools, and these processes further the objectives

in its mission. The SAF is recognized by the federal government as the official accrediting agency for forestry programs in the United States. A current listing of forestry schools in the United States and descriptions of their programs are available on SAF's website (4).

Forestry is atypical among professions because of the high percentage of baccalaureate-trained professionals and the small fraction of self-employed professionals, the highest percentage being employed in the public and private sectors (Table 2.1).

Although the majority of students terminate their formal education at the bachelor's level, increasing numbers are proceeding to advanced graduate degree programs, which they enter either from a forestry undergraduate curriculum, or from any number of other undergraduate majors, including mathematics, engineering, botany, and economics or other social sciences. Students who enter from another major are eligible to pursue the first professional degree at the master's level. According to the *Occupational Outlook Handbook* (5), the increasingly complex nature of forestry has led some employers to prefer graduates with advanced degrees.

Table 2.1 Employment Distribution of Society of American Foresters Membership (1)

Employer Sector	Number[a]	Percent
Government		
Federal	2,196	17
State or local	1,917	15
Other than U.S.	64	<1
Private industry	3,728	28
Self-employed		
Consulting	2,116	16
Other self-employed	705	5
College/university	1,350	10
Association/foundation	252	2
Other	341	3
Unemployed	93	<1
Not indicated	429	3
Total	13,191	100

[a]This table excludes, compared to the original information base, retirees and students (constituting over 5,000 other Society of American Foresters members) who would not normally be seeking full-time professional employment.

The relative balance among educational levels in recent forestry recruitment provides a good idea of opportunities. A 1998 report (6) noted that for entry-level forestry hirings over a two-year period, 75 percent were filled at the bachelor's level, 18 percent at the associate degree level, and slightly over 2 percent were at the master's level. A year later, another analysis was completed (7) indicating that for the previous five-year duration, 70 percent of the forestry recruitment was at the bachelor's level. Respondents to the 1998 study revealed their intentions, for the foreseeable future, to recruit people at the bachelor's level for about three-fourths of all forestry positions.

The Bureau of Labor Statistics has its *Occupational Handbook* available electronically. Information about "Foresters and Conservation Scientists" can be found at their website (5). Nature of the work, working conditions, employment, training, job outlook, and sources of information are included in the descriptive material. The handbook is updated and republished periodically so interested people can find reasonably current information in this source.

Career Opportunities

New careers in forestry continually emerge as general technology advances. Today, computer applications in forestry have become important in virtually all aspects of the field. As an example, expert systems based on principles of artificial intelligence promise exciting methods for assessing and diagnosing forestry problems in much the same way these systems are used in the medical field. Remote sensing of the environment and geographic information systems have become invaluable tools in managing forest resources. Biotechnology and genetic engineering show potential for application to forestry, especially for improving the yield and value of forest products. Scientists are modifying species to increase resistance to diseases and herbicides. There is now a greater emphasis on international forestry, and for filling these worldwide positions, skills in foreign languages and knowledge

of agroforestry practices are especially important. For an expanded discussion on the variety of specialties available in the profession, the interested reader is referred to *Opportunities in Forestry Careers* (8).

Students often fail to realize that a degree in forestry provides an excellent general education, one that can be viewed similarly to the liberal arts bachelor's degree programs offered at many institutions. Students undecided on an academic major should not miss the opportunity to explore forestry, either as a major emphasis or as a minor field to serve as a companion to a degree in statistics, mathematics, engineering, or environmental science. A forestry education provides a background for a broad variety of jobs in management, business, or computer science and students pursuing forestry degrees should not constrain their job searches just to forest management positions, especially if their interests are broader.

Though the emphasis of this book is on forestry, a group of related programs also offer coursework leading to rewarding careers. Wood science and technology and pulp and paper science majors, available at many forestry schools and colleges, typically have high placement rates for graduates.

Sources of Employment

Public Forestry in Federal Agencies

With 5,000 foresters, agencies within the federal government constitute a large employment base of professional foresters; 17 percent of the active SAF foresters in the United States fall within this group. The Forest Service (U.S.D.A.) has a total permanent work force of 29,000 people. This department is the largest federal employer of foresters. In 1999, there were about 4,000 professional foresters and 7,000 forestry technicians working in the Forest Service. This group of professionals is entrusted with managing large and widely dispersed holdings in numerous national forests comprising 191 million acres. In addition, the Forest Service works cooperatively with state and private enterprises and conducts research at its forest and range experiment stations, at the Institute of Tropical Forestry, and at the Forest Products Laboratory (Figure 2.3). An employment overview of this agency is available online and also provides links to other sites of potential interest (9).

An administrative perspective of new hires in the Forest Service is that:

> **Today's forestry professionals entering the federal workforce still need the technical skills and understanding of ecosystem functions that their predecessors possessed. However, they face a full array of new challenges in managing natural resources. The Forest Service is changing, much as the society we serve is changing. Our job is one of stewardship of public lands with lots of collaboration from the public we serve. We must all understand the concept of customer service. Our daily jobs involve satisfying many internal and external customers. How effectively we do so figures largely in our professional success. The new forester must keep in mind the long-term nature of resource management. Whereas most of our customers may look to the productivity and beauty of a forest for a decade, or for their lifetime, the forester must ensure the needs of future generations and the health of forest ecosystems far into the future (10).**

Other agencies in the U.S.D.A. that employ forestry graduates include the Natural Resources Conservation Service, Cooperative Agricultural Extension Service and the Agricultural Research Service. Elsewhere in the federal government, professional foresters are found in the U.S. Department of Interior (Bureaus of Land Management, Outdoor Recreation, and Indian Affairs, as well as the National Park Service and the Fish and Wildlife Service), Tennessee Valley Authority, and an assorted smaller number in the Departments of Defense and Commerce, the Office of Management and Budget and the Environmental Protection Agency. Hirings in federal agencies are made through the U.S. Office of Personnel Management.

Public Forestry in State Settings

Most of the states, through their departments of natural resources (or some similar title), maintain a staff of forestry professionals to carry out state policies in managing their forest resources. There are over 5,000 foresters in the state natural resource departments and they represent 15 percent of the active practicing foresters who hold membership in the

Figure 2.3 The U.S. Forest Products Laboratory in Madison, Wisconsin, is a research and development laboratory and is part of the Forest Service. (Courtesy of U.S.D.A. Forest Service.)

SAF. This represents a large pool of positions, and collectively the states now have a larger work force than the Forest Service, a condition that was the reverse until the early 1990s. In addition, the state agencies hire over 7,000 seasonal or temporary employees each year; with a wide variety of seasonal positions across the country, the states offer excellent opportunities for pre-professional experience. Together, the states also employ over 9,000 technicians; these positions are supportive in nature, normally do not require a 4-year degree, and typically the salaries in the category are lower than those for professional foresters. For the most part the forestry programs and employees are administered by the state forester, usually located in the capitol city. The National Association of State Foresters maintains a website (11) with current employment opportunities listed as well as links to each of the states' department of natural resources where local employment and program information are available.

One chief state forestry administrator summarized the setting for this sector as follows:

Foresters working in a state forestry agency are faced with the need to be proficient in a broad range of functions, from the biophysical aspects of forest resource management to complex social interactions with people and groups that have diverse interests and strongly held values relating to forests and natural resources and how they should be managed. Forestry professionals require broad-based knowledge of forest science with an integrated natural resources management perspective. They must be able to use that knowledge to develop, interpret, and implement policies and procedures to sustain and enhance functioning forest ecosystems; provide a sustainable supply of forest resources to meet human needs (material, economic, and social); protect lives and property from wildfire; and provide an economic return to citizens and corporate organizations. It is essential that graduates leave school with that basic knowledge and an initial development of those abilities (10).

Other state agencies employing foresters, though to a lesser extent, include the park services, fish and game divisions, and in some states,

departments of highways and taxation, and commissions of public lands. At about 8 million acres nationally, community forests represent an important component of public forests at the state level. Some were established over 100 years ago. Many are owned and managed by municipalities, but others may be operated by counties, schools, or other public institutions largely for multiple-use. The school forests often serve an important role in the environmental education programs of local districts.

The increasing importance of forests and trees in the urban setting has given rise to a new emphasis on urban forestry (see Chapter 22, devoted entirely to urban forestry). This emerging area requires integration of traditional forestry and arboriculture.

Forestry in Private Industry

By far the largest amount of commercial forest area in the United States is privately owned. An important part of this is held by forest products companies to provide a supply of wood for production of lumber, pulp and paper, and other wood products. Whereas federal and state resource agencies primarily manage forests, industrial firms both produce timber and utilize it to manufacture products. Thus, industry also offers a diverse set of opportunities for foresters. Industrial foresters may be involved in wood procurement as well as the management of forests. Private industry also promotes modern forestry practices through formal "tree farm" programs. The total number of professional foresters in this category is elusive; however, Wille (8) reports that about 10,000 foresters are employed by private industry. Electronic access to a large number of forest products industries can be gained through the American Forest and Paper Association (12), where an extensive roster of URLs is maintained for individual member firms nationwide and for related associations dealing with, for example, recycling, international trade, pulp, paper, plywood, veneer, and hardwoods.

From a corporate perspective, industrial forestry firms:

... seek foresters who are technically sound but also educated. New contributions from the fields of ecology and biotechnology rapidly increase the demands for an even more basic understanding of forest science and art—and social interaction with diverse stakeholders requires professionals who are broad in their thinking, who understand people, and who demonstrate clear leadership in their decisions and actions. Forestry leaders must integrate forest science, social, and business skills ... We need not just a deep scientific and technical education, not just a how-to education of forestry on the ground, but the broad professional understanding of the science, the sociology, the economics, and the politics associated with the management of complex natural resources that are important to the public ... (10).

International Forestry

One of the greatest challenges for the forestry profession is the wise use of tropical forests. Spurred by population growth and the pressure to gain foreign exchange, developing countries are experiencing depletion of vital forest resources. Nearly half of the world's population depends on wood for fuel; in fact, about 60 percent of the total production of the world's forests is consumed as fuel. An interesting paradox is that in the developed world 80 percent of the wood produced is used for industrial purposes, and in the developing countries 80 percent of the wood produced is used for energy. The Food and Agriculture Organization of the United Nations (FAO) regards the dependence of developing nations on dwindling supplies of fuelwood as a crisis. Over and above the pervasive fuelwood shortage, tropical forests are being whittled away by resettlement programs, development projects, clearing for agricultural purposes and ranching, and logging without attendant forest management. Tropical forests decline each year by an area equivalent to Austria and Switzerland (13). This rate of destruction is a major social issue of our time—so crucial that every nation has a stake in its solution. FAO is partitioned into eight departments, one of which is Forestry and Sustainable Development. The forestry program, headquartered in Rome has a website (14) with excellent global information put together with a neutral approach in a factual format.

International forestry activities are conducted along three general fronts. *Community forestry* functions in rural development, improving work opportunities and consumable goods and enhancing the environment. With the participation of local people, the community forestry approach takes into consideration the importance of forestry in land use planning and its strong relationship to watershed management, arid-zone reclamation, soil fertility, and integrating forestry and agriculture. Among the techniques available for community approaches are: *multiple-product forestry,* the use of forests for wood, edibles, and other products; *small-scale forestry,* cultivating village woodlots for the production of fuelwood; *agroforestry,* combining of forest and agricultural crops; and *silvi-pastoral systems,* controlled grazing of forest vegetation. Forest-based industries are being established, but they can benefit the country only if sustainable development of carefully managed forests is achieved. Required are intensified management and reforestation, development of appropriate harvesting, transportation and marketing systems and intelligent use of residues. The *conservation of forest ecosystems* is recognized as an important emerging area. Tropical forests help to maintain a stable global environment, provide a major genetic reservoir, and offer a source of new forest products and medicines. Wise use of these ecosystems is a high priority among international strategists.

There are numerous opportunities for contributing to the international forestry effort. The Peace Corps supports forestry projects in many parts of the developing world. Staffed primarily by volunteers, it provides excellent opportunities for professional and personal development. Nongovernmental organizations such as CARE play an important role in international forestry. The Food and Agriculture Organization collects and analyzes information on forestry, serves as a major source of technical assistance, and helps to identify investment opportunities in the forestry sector.

The U.S. Agency for International Development (USAID) pursues two strategic goals relevant to environmental protection: 1) reducing long-term threats to the global environment, particularly loss of biodiversity and climate change, and 2) promoting sustainable economic growth locally, nationally, and regionally. Forest and other natural resource management practices form a key element of many USAID assistance efforts in the agency's major spheres of action, notably sub-Saharan Africa; Asia and the Near East; Latin America and the Caribbean; and Europe. In addition to its permanent staff, USAID accomplishes forestry work by employing people for varying periods of time, for short-term consultancies as well as long-term assignment overseas. To this end the Office of International Programs within the Forest Service–U.S.D.A. maintains a large roster of individuals competent in tropical forestry. The Office of International Programs also offers technical assistance and training in forest management and forest conservation to a wide variety of international partners. In addition to its usual governmental partners, this program has recently expanded its array of cooperators to include more nongovernmental and international research organizations.

Research and Teaching

There are over 1,300 people involved as forestry faculty in educational programs at the colleges and universities in the United States. The primary functions of faculty positions are distributed approximately as follows: instruction—45 percent; research—45 percent; and extension (outreach)—10 percent. The largest number of faculty are in forest management, although well represented are the areas of: forest biology; wood science, technology, and industry; biometry; forest hydrology; forest engineering; and urban forestry. All faculty positions require advanced graduate education and, for the most part, a doctorate. Another group of over 600 foresters serves in professional staff roles in forestry departments at universities, while others teach in instructional programs at community colleges or technical schools.

An active and comprehensive organization known as the National Association of Professional Forestry Schools and Colleges serves to advance the science, practice and art of forest resource management through the encouragement and support of forest resource education, research, extension and international programs at the university level.

Some of the larger forest products firms conduct substantial research and development programs, although the number of scientists involved is unknown. The Forest Service plays a major role in research activities, and to a lesser extent, some of the major forested states also support research efforts.

Embracing forestry research on a global scale is the International Union of Forestry Research Organizations (IUFRO). Its lead office is located in Vienna, Austria; this organization is over 100 years old. IUFRO is a nonprofit, nongovernmental international network of 700 member institutions involving 15,000 participating forest scientists. The main purpose of IUFRO is to promote international cooperation in scientific studies embracing the entire field of research related to forestry. Each year over 50 conferences and symposia are sponsored around the world, and every fifth year IUFRO holds a World Congress. Like FAO, IUFRO hosts an online reference library where literature searches may be done at its website (15).

Consulting Forestry

Some professionals choose a private consulting practice. Most of the consultants operate as sole proprietors, and except for a small number of partnerships, the rest are organized as consulting firms. There are over 2,000 consulting foresters in the United States. Consultants provide advice and assistance related to forest management, marketing, and sale of forest products. Timber marking and sales, timber inventory and appraisal, timber volume estimates, timber management plans and harvesting, damage appraisal, and investment advice constitute most of the work collectively conducted by consultants. Sometimes consulting firms deal with large-scale assessments for public agencies and industry.

Over and above technical forestry understanding, from a consulting perspective, "the real key to success—for the individual forester, the consulting firm, and perhaps also for the profession—is the ability to communicate well both in writing and speaking. Opportunity in consulting is unlimited for foresters who understand the technical basics, gain field experience, see forestry in the perspective of nature and society, and can communicate ideas" (10).

Many consultants hold membership in the Association of Consulting Foresters of America. One requirement for membership is a forestry degree from an accredited university program.

Other Areas

According to the roster of members of the SAF, the remaining foresters are self-employed or involved with organizations such as the American Forest Foundation, American Forest and Paper Association, American Pulpwood Association, National Woodland Owners Association, National Hardwood Lumber Association, or various state forestry associations.

Employment

Expectations of Employers

Changes in the public's understanding of sustainability and developments in science, communications, and global markets have created a recent evolution in the practice of forestry (7). Consequently, employers now seek an expanded set of skills and competencies when hiring graduates of professional forest programs.

Table 2.2 provides an overview of technical competencies sought by employers. Based on a strategic assessment conducted by the Pinchot Institute (7) involving employers who had recently hired forestry graduates, the surveys covered all forestry sectors, with federal and state agency, industrial, and consultant participants making up 93 percent of the survey participants. The table, ranked accord-

ing to importance value, shows the twenty competencies which are most important to employers and which the majority of employers expect to be acquired at the undergraduate level. Certainly the scientific foundation of forestry forms a strong basis of the competencies, but a very high premium is placed on ethics, communications, and teamwork. This is in accord with another nationwide analysis published a year earlier by Brown and Lassoie (6) who found that the application of sound ethical principles is the attribute with the highest desirability regardless of employer category—in fact, 95 percent of the respondents said it is a requirement. This study too, showed that communication and group interaction processes are competencies required for most entry-level positions (Figure 2.4).

Also important to employers hiring professional foresters is a set of broader skills. The Pinchot Institute study (7) identified the skills most critical to hiring agencies and, at the same time, those that entry-level practicing professionals find they need for long-term success in forestry (Table 2.3). Think of these skills as the synthesis and application of certain clusters of competencies seen before in Table 2.2. For example, the ability to listen to and address public questions and concerns—the second skill listed in Table 2.3—would draw not only on specific subject matter knowledge, but would be integrated with ethics, communication, and collaborative problem-solving competencies as well.

Our society is still evolving from a somewhat autocratic mode of management to more of a shared governance model. Thus, there are gaps between how importantly a skill is perceived by employer groups and their rating of performance for the foresters they have recruited. The biggest gaps are reflected in the top two skills, teamwork and public concerns. However, positive changes have transpired in this regard during the last decade, and continued improvement will occur to narrow the gap between importance and performance.

Most forestry employers expect the undergraduate educational experience to primarily provide a sound foundation of technical competency (Table 2.2), with the development of broader integrative skills (Table 2.3) coming largely with experience,

Table 2.2 Technical Competencies Employers Expect to be Achieved at the Undergraduate Level and Their Importance (7)

Technical Competency[a]	% of employers expecting the item by end of undergraduate education	Importance to employers (1–10 scale)
Ethics	79	9.3
Written communication	86	9.2
Oral communication	78	9.1
Silvicultural systems	85	8.4
Collaborative problem solving	53	8.2
Resource management	62	8.0
Forest ecology	63	8.0
Forest inventory and biometry	86	7.8
Landscape analysis–GIS	55	7.7
Tree and plant species identification	93	7.7
Watershed management	64	7.6
Resource economics	70	7.5
Fire dynamics	67	7.3
Forest soils	80	7.2
Resource policy, law	57	7.0
Wildlife biology	78	7.0
Forest pathology	79	6.8
Conservation biology	57	6.8
Forest engineering, transportation systems	64	6.3
Wildland and protected areas management	60	5.8

[a] Terms listed only for which 50% or more of the employers expected the competency to be gained during the undergraduate experience and for which they attached an importance value greater than 5.0 on a scale of 1–10.

graduate education, and continuing education. You may notice a strong correlation between employer's expectations and curricular requirements for a degree from an accredited program discussed earlier.

Seeking Employment

Application for employment is an art and how to do it most effectively differs by industry. In the forest products industry, applicants should develop some knowledge of the company and should not set employment goals that are too narrow. Work experience, a vision of the potential employee's future, and direct contact with the company are desirable. All this requires homework. Do not

Figure 2.4 The ability to work with others is an important component of a forestry career. (Courtesy of U.S.D.A. Forest Service.)

Table 2.3   Skills Identified as Necessary for Success in Forestry, and Their Fatings of Importance and Performance by Employers [Scale of 1–10] (7)

Needed Skill	Importance	Performance
Ability to work in teams that include individuals with a variety of perspectives, both within and outside the organization.	9.0	7.3
Ability to listen to and address public questions and concerns and to explain the principles of environmentally responsible forest management practices.	8.2	6.5
Understanding of the requirements of a healthy forest ecosystem and the full variety of silvicultural and other tools available to manage that system.	8.0	7.4
An innovative approach to forest management that includes critical thinking and willingness to test new and nontraditional approaches.	8.0	7.2
An innovative approach to working with the public to address forest management problems.	7.7	6.6
Ability to evaluate and synthesize information from a variety of specialists when developing resource management plans.	7.5	7.1
Understanding of landscape-level planning of forest ecosystems and how to manage them to meet ecological, economic, and social needs.	7.3	6.9

expect most companies to interview on campus; they usually rely on résumés submitted by people seeking employment, and they purposely look for people from various geographic areas, different universities, and from diverse backgrounds.

Concluding Statement

The field of forestry offers a vast diversity of career opportunities that range from policy and social issues to highly technical, quantitative processes. Career seekers can pursue interests in conservation or timber management. The variety of organizations involved in the many aspects of forestry echoes the breadth of the field itself. Governmental agencies have active programs in forestry, and industrial firms are major players in the production of forest products. Different forestry programs span a geographic area that may be local, national or international. Regardless of agency or firm goals, the majority of forestry professionals deal with ecosystems, a theme that flows through this book.

Students with interests in forestry education should explore careers with several universities to understand curricular requirements and employment prospects. Sufficient website locations are included which, along with related sites included at each address, will provide a breadth of useful forestry information. Descriptions of, and questions regarding specific positions are best achieved by visiting with forestry-related agencies, industries, or consulting firms.

References

1. F. W. CUBBAGE, L. G. JERVIS, AND P. G. SMITH, *J. For.,* *97,* 24 (1999).

2. G. D. GOTTFREDSON AND J. L. HOLLAND, *Dictionary of Holland Occupational Codes,* Third Edition, Psychological Assessment Resources, Odessa, FL, 1996.

3. ANON., *Accreditation Handbook: Standards, Procedures, and Guidelines for Accrediting Educational Programs in Professional Forestry,* Publ. No. 86-08, Society of American Foresters, Bethesda, MD, 1994. (A new handbook was in process as this book went to press. It is based on the "Report to the Council of the Society of American Foresters" by the SAF Task Force on Forestry Education Accreditation, May, 2000. The text in this book conforms to the new standards.)

4. Society of American Foresters: Guide to Forestry & Natural Resource Education. SAFnet [22 Oct 1999]. URL: http://www.safnet.org/market/edguide/htm#A.

5. Bureau of Labor Statistics, U.S. Department of Labor, *1998–99 Occupational Outlook Handbook, Bull.* *2500.* 1998 [document online]. [21 Oct 1999]. URL: http://stats.bis.gov/oco/ocos048.htm.

6. T. L. BROWN AND J. P. LASSOIE. *J. For., 96,* 8 (1998).

7. V. A. SAMPLE, P. C. RINGGOLD, N. E. BLOCK, AND J. W. GILTMIER. *J. For. 97,* 4 (1999).

8. C. M. WILLE, *Opportunities in Forestry Careers,* VGM Career Horizons/Contemporary Publishing Co., Lincolnwood, Ill., 1998.

9. Forest Service, U.S.D.A., Employment in the Forest Service. [21 Oct 1999]. URL: http://www.fs.fed.us/people/employ/index.html.

10. "The employer's perspective on new hires." *J. For., 97,* 12 (1999).

11. National Association of State Foresters. [21 Oct 1999]. URL: http://www.stateforesters.org.

12. About AF&PA, American Forest and Paper Association. [21 Oct 1999]. URL: http://205.197.9.134/about/members.htm.

13. World Resources 1994–95: A Guide to the Global Environment. World Recources Institute, Washington, D.C., 403 pp., 1994.

14. Forestry and Sustainable Development Program, FAO, UN. [21 Oct 1999]. URL:http://www.fao.org/WAICENT/FAOINFO/FORESTRY/forestry.htm.

15. International Union of Forestry Research Organizations. [24 Oct 1999]. URL: http://iufro.boku.ac.at/iufro/.

PART 2

Forest Biology and Ecology

Trees are the largest and oldest of the known living plant species in the world today (Figure P2.1). Starting as a minute seed, they can grow to heights over 120 meters (394 ft) and accumulate as much as 1500 cubic meters (5.3×10^4 ft³) of wood in the process. In addition, trees possess a water-transporting system so powerful that it can raise water about a hundred times as efficiently as the best suction pump ever made by human beings (1). Trees are truly remarkable mechanisms of nature.

Like all other plants, trees are constructed solely of cells, the basic units of life. However, the cells in a leaf, for example, are quite different from those in the trunk and different again from those in the root. Each kind of cell is usually found in association with similar cells; groups of similar cells make up tissue and tissues combine into even more complex groups know as organs (1). Clearly the specialized organs serve different purposes in the tree. The complex functions of the tree and its component parts are treated in detail in Chapter 4, Forest Ecophysiology.

The growth and vigor of trees are a function of many factors. In addition to genetic variations, environmental factors can have a profound influence on tree growth. Minerals in the soil, water shortages, wind and climate, the availability of sunlight, and attack by insects and disease all affect the patterns of tree growth (Figure P2.2). The impact of these influences and human interaction for control of tree growth and vigor are examined in this section. The distribution of forests around the world are discussed in Chapter 3, Forest Biomes of the World. A biome is a broad classification of plant communities characterized by climate and soil. Within a biome there are numerous ecosystems. A further description of forest ecosystems and inte-

Figure P2.1 One of the oldest known living plants in the world: a 3000-year-old bristlecone pine sculptured by the wind, sand, and ice of the White Mountains in eastern California. (Courtesy of U.S.D.A. Forest Service.)

gration of the many factors that affect tree and stand growth are discussed in Chapter 6, Forest Ecosystem Ecology. The importance of ecological relationships across landscapes is then discussed Chapter 7, Landscape Ecology. Not only do landscape patterns affect organisms, but organisms can also create landscape patterns.

A forest community is a dynamic structure that responds to the laws of cause and effect, one in which all organisms intertwine to form a harmonic ecosystem (2). The classic ecological concept is that forests evolve through plant succession, the orderly replacement of one plant community or

Figure P2.2   Twisted aspens on the Grand Canyon's northern rim in Arizona are called "The Crooked Forest." The resilient trees were probably bent as saplings by deep snowdrifts, a phenomenon referred to as snow creep. (Courtesy of Life Picture Service.)

forest stand with another. Generally a temporary plant community is replaced by a relatively more stable community until a dynamic equilibrium is attained between the plants and the environment.

However, the behavior of forests frequently does not follow this classical concept. Many tree species, rather than arising during predicted periods of succession, often play a more opportunistic role. For example, red maple, which is usually considered to be a climax or final successional stage species, has light wind-borne seeds that can invade open areas and thus function as an early successional species (3). Disturbances such as those described below can also affect forest succession. The many factors affecting vegetation distribution and succession of forests are described in several chapters in this section.

Disturbances in the forest can be either natural (wind, fire, insect and disease outbreaks) or caused by human beings (forest harvesting and fire) and can result in destruction of small or large segments of the forest. The effect of disturbance is to produce sites where new communities of the trees, plants, and animals can exist. These new communities may differ from those of the native forest (Figure P2.3). The effect of disturbances are treated in several chapters in this section while the specific effects of disease and insects on forests are described in Chapter 8.

References

1. P. FARB, *The Forest*, Time-Life Books, New York, 1969.
2. H. W. HOCKER, JR., *Introduction to Forest Biology*, John Wiley & Sons, New York, 1979.
3. R. R. HICKS, JR., *Ecology and Management of Central Hardwood Forests*, John Wiley & Sons, New York, 1998.

Figure P2.3   The blast from the eruption of Mount Saint Helens in the state of Washington flattened previously lush, green forests. Ecologists are closely monitoring the return of plant and animal life. (Photograph by R. L. Giese.)

CHAPTER 3

Forest Biomes of the World

STITH T. GOWER, JOE J. LANDSBERG,
AND KARI E. BISBEE

Forests provide many ecosystem services to humans and other organisms. Forests provide timber that is used for a myriad of wood and paper products (Chapter 20). Millions of species of flora and fauna, some of which have gone, or will go, extinct before they are documented, live in forests. Forests protect the soils from erosion, minimize sedimentation in adjacent wetlands and aquatic ecosystems, mitigate flooding, and remove toxic heavy metals and organics (Chapters 5 and 16). Forests also provide recreational opportunities and have inherent aesthetic value to society (Chapter 17). Lastly, forests play an important role in global carbon budget.

The contribution of a forest biome to each of the ecosystem services and functions varies among biomes, and ecosystems within the major forest biomes. Therefore, sustainable management of forests of the world requires a fundamental understanding of the effects of environmental factors on distribution and growth of forests (Chapters 4–8), and properly matching forest management practices to the silvics of the trees (Chapters 9 and 13). Structural characteristics such as height, density, the amount of leaf area, leaf habit (e.g., evergreen versus deciduous) are important factors that differ among forest biomes, and forest ecosystems within a biome. The climate and soils of forests also influence the ecosystem services and function. Therefore, it is essential to understand how important characteristics such as species composition, climate, soils, disturbance and structural characteristics differ among major forest types. This knowledge can be used to ensure which forest should be managed for timber production, devise management plans that ensure forests are managed on a sustainable basis, identify forests that should be preserved for services other than timber production, and determine how global change may affect world forests.

The objective of this chapter is to describe briefly each of the major forest biomes. The first section describes the major factors that influence the geographic distribution of forest biomes of the world. The second section highlights the major forest biomes of the world. We describe the extent and distribution, climate, soils, important structural and functional characteristics, and management and mismanagement issues for each biome. The third section summarizes some of the major conservation concerns for forests and the susceptibility of forest biomes to global change. The treatment of each forest biome is cursory because of space limitations. The text is intended to provide the necessary background for the more detailed treatments of various aspects of forest/environment interaction in the following chapters.

Factors Affecting Vegetation Distribution

The distribution of the major forest biomes, and terrestrial biomes in general, is strongly influenced by climatic, geologic, ecological, and anthropogenic factors. Plant geographers first noted the influence of climate on the distribution of vegetation; they observed that similar climates, regardless of continent, produced vegetation with similar appearance

or physiognomy. Plants require solar radiation, water, nutrients and adequate temperatures to germinate, grow, and reproduce (see Chapters 4–7). The relative amount of these essential resources and the ecophysiology of the plants determine the species composition and structure of the forests. Climate directly and indirectly affects the distribution of biomes. Temperature and moisture availability directly affect the growth of plants. Climate also strongly influences soil development (Chapter 5), which also influences plant distribution.

The major control on climate at the global scale is solar radiation. The amount of solar radiation reaching the forest canopy is greatest near the equator and decreases toward the poles. The causes for the variation in solar radiation are two-fold: the angle at which the sun's radiation strikes the earth's surface and the length of the pathway that solar radiation must pass to reach the canopy (Figure 3.1). Solar radiation strikes the Earth's surface at a less direct angle at higher latitudes than near the equator, resulting in the radiation being distributed over a greater area—or a smaller intensity per unit land

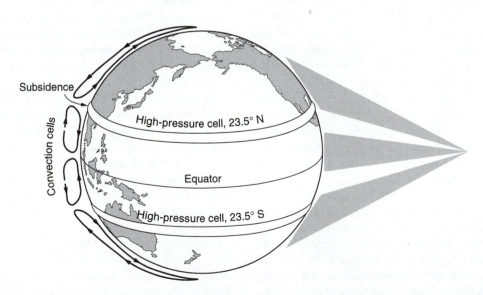

Figure 3.1 A schematic diagram contrasting the solar radiation path length at the equator and high latitude. The global precipitation patterns are determined by the convergence of air masses. Collectively, the solar radiation and precipitation patterns determine the distribution of terrestrial biomes. Adapted from Bailey (22).

surface area. Also, solar radiation travels through a greater distance of the atmosphere, increasing the reflection of solar radiation away from the earth's surface. As a result, the temperature is warmer near the equator than at higher latitudes.

Within a similar latitudinal zone, seasonal variation in temperature is much greater for a continental than for a coastal location. The pronounced differences in climate are because water has a greater thermal capacity than land. Examples of the effects of large water bodies on climate are shown in Figure 3.2. The latitude of Portland, Maine and Madison, Wisconsin are similar, but the winters are colder, the growing season is shorter and the summers are hotter in Madison than Portland. Similarly, for a similar latitude and elevation, the climate is milder and more equitable in the Southern than Northern Hemisphere. Continents are smaller in the Southern Hemisphere than Northern Hemisphere, and as a result, the mesoscale climate of the Southern Hemisphere is buffered by the greater thermal

capacity of the oceans. The large thermal buffering capacity of oceans has a pronounced effect on the distribution of forest biomes. In the Southern Hemisphere, temperate forests occur from 30° to 55° S, and within this zone broad-leaved evergreen species dominate the forest landscape. In the Northern Hemisphere, broad-leaved deciduous tree species are the dominant forest type in the lower latitudes, and boreal forests can occur as far south as 50–55° N. Axelrod (1) concluded that the temperate climates, ample rainfall evenly distributed throughout the year, and rarity of frost, favored the evolution of broad-leaved evergreen rather than deciduous forests in the temperate regions of the Southern Hemisphere.

Water availability, a function of both precipitation and drying power of the air, also influences the distribution of vegetation biomes. Near the equator, moisture-saturated trade winds rise and produce abundant precipitation (Figure 3.1). The dry subtropical high-pressure air masses centered

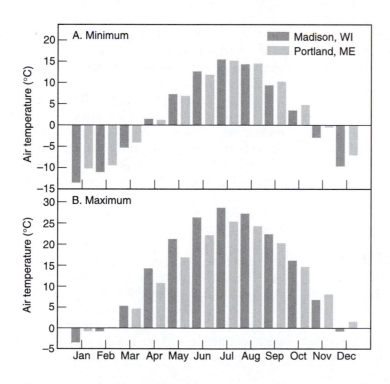

Figure 3.2 Comparison of the long-term monthly average of the maximum and minimum air temperature for Madison, Wisconsin (continental climate), and Portland, Maine (coastal climate). The two locations have approximately the same latitude. Data obtained from *http://www. worldclimate.com*.

on the Tropics of Cancer and Capricorn (23.5° N and S, respectively) produce bands that are too dry to support forests. Precipitation pattern is also influenced by continental position. Warm air passing over large bodies of water (oceans) collects water vapor. As the warm, moisture laden air mass goes over a large land mass it loses its ability to hold the water vapor, especially if the air mass must rise over a coastal mountain range. Rainfall is typically very high for these coastal regions. Forests growing on windward slopes of mountains near oceans can receive from 3.5 to 6.5 meters of rain—some of the largest annual amounts of precipitation in the world!

Soil fertility also influences distribution of vegetation. In general, evergreen plants occupy the more infertile soils while deciduous forests occur on more fertile soils. Parent material and climate influence soil fertility (Chapter 5). Hot and moist climates, such as subtropical and tropical regions increase soil weathering, causing nutrients to be removed from the soil on the time scale of millions of years. Conversely, milder climates have more fertile soils. Extremely young soils, such as those that developed since recent glacial advances, tend to be nitrogen-limited. The type of parent material that the soils develop from also influences soil fertility.

Disturbance intensity, frequency, and type of disturbance also influence biome distribution and species composition within a biome. The disturbance can be natural, such as fire, wind, or drought, or related to human activity (e.g., land clearing, harvesting, and fire suppression). Fire suppression in the midwestern United States has hastened the invasion of woody and tree species into prairies.

Forest Biomes

Vegetation Classification Systems

There are many vegetation classification systems used, although all of them use climate, physiognomy (the general appearance of the vegetation, e.g., desert, grassland, forest) and leaf habit (evergreen or deciduous) to classify vegetation. The broadest level of classification is the biome—

vegetation with a similar climate and physiognomy. Within a biome there are numerous ecosystems. For example, the temperate needle-leaved evergreen forest biome includes the coastal Douglas fir (*Pseudotsuga menziesii*) forests in the Pacific Northwest, the jack pine (*Pinus banksiana*) forests in the Lake States, and loblolly pine (*Pinus taeda*) forests in the southeastern United States. Classification systems differ in the level of detail, ranging from a simple system that has eight vegetation cover types to 30 vegetation associations. In this chapter, we provide an overview of the main forest biomes in the world. We briefly characterize the extent and distribution, the climate and dominant soils (readers are suggested to refer to Chapter 5, Forest Soils, for a detailed explanation of the different soil orders), a general description of the vegetation including some of the dominant forest genera (or families for the extremely diverse tropical forests), unique structural and functional characteristics that influence the ecology and management, and management of the major forest biomes.

For the purpose of this book, we used the vegetation classification system used by Melillo, et al. (2), because it is a reasonable compromise between complex and simple schemes. Forest biomes are based on major climatic zones (tropical, temperate, and boreal) and the physiognomy (broad-leaved evergreen, broad-leaved deciduous, and needle-leaved evergreen conifer) of the vegetation. Figure 3.3 (see color insert) shows the regions where biomes could occur, although it is unlikely that the areas concerned are completely covered by those vegetation types. The impact of humans has resulted in vegetation loss and change across very large areas of the globe.

The description of the major forest biomes is brief, but provides a general overview of the distribution, climate, soils, species composition, structure, and function, and management characteristics of the major forest biomes. The amount of information available for each forest biome varies substantially. The information provided for each forest biome is intended to provide a framework for thinking about the ecology and management of forests, as discussed in the following chapter.

Boreal Forests

Distribution and Extent Boreal forests cover about 15.7×10^8 hectares and occur only in the Northern Hemisphere (Table 3.1). The greatest single area of boreal forests is in Eurasia, where they extend from Scandinavia to eastern Siberia. The second largest boreal forest region occurs as a 500–600 km wide band from eastern Canada and the northeastern United States westward into northern British Columbia and Alaska. Boreal forests give way to arctic woodland or tundra to the north, while the vegetation to the south of the southern boundary varies. In some regions, such as eastern Canada, boreal forests transition to cold temperate evergreen needle-leaved or broad-leaved deciduous forests. In central Canada, the southern boreal forests give rise to prairies, and in Eurasia boreal forests often transition into cold steppe or shrubland.

Climate The climate of the boreal forests is one of the harshest in which trees occur. The boreal forest regions, represented by climatic data from The Pas, Manitoba, in Canada (Figure 3.4a), are characterized by long cold winters. The mean daily minimum temperature at The Pas is below 0°C for more than seven months of the year, and during the period when temperatures remain above zero, there are significant water deficits. There may be fewer than 50 frost-free days in summer (Figure 3.4a). Permafrost, a buried frozen soil layer, is common in many boreal forests. Woodward (3) suggests that the northern limit of boreal forests may be crudely defined by the number of months in which the air temperature is greater than 10°C. The length of growing season must be sufficient for evergreen conifers to construct an adequate cuticle to protect needles from winter desiccation, and mycorrhizae (root-fungus association) to facilitate nutrient and water uptake.

Soils Soil development is slow in boreal forests because of the cold temperatures; therefore soils tend to be nutrient-poor. Poorly drained soils accumulate large amounts of peat—undecomposed mosses and sphagnum. The soils are young and derived from parent material left by retreating glaciers. Permafrost, which can be less than one meter below the surface, restricts root zones and impedes soil water drainage. Few major soil taxonomic groups occur in boreal forests. Histisols, or organic soils, are common to poorly drained forests. Entisols have little or no horizon development and are typically associated with early successional riparian forests (*Populus*, *Betula*) and coarse-textured,

Table 3.1 Area (hectares $\times 10^8$) and Average Net Primary Production (NPP, tC ha^{-1} yr^{-1}) of the Forest Biomes of the World [Adapted from Landsberg and Gower (4) and Gower, et al. (6)]

Forest Biome	Area (ha $\times 10^8$)	% of total	Average NPP (tC ha^{-1} yr^{-1})
Boreal	15.7	30	4.2
Deciduous	—	—	—
Evergreen	—	—	—
Temperate	14.2	27	—
Coniferous	2.4	5	6.6
Deciduous	3.5	7	6.6
Mixed	5.1	10	—
Evergreen (Broad-leaf)	3.2	6	10.0
Tropical	22.0	43	—
Evergreen	17.4	34	8.2
Deciduous	4.6	9	8.0

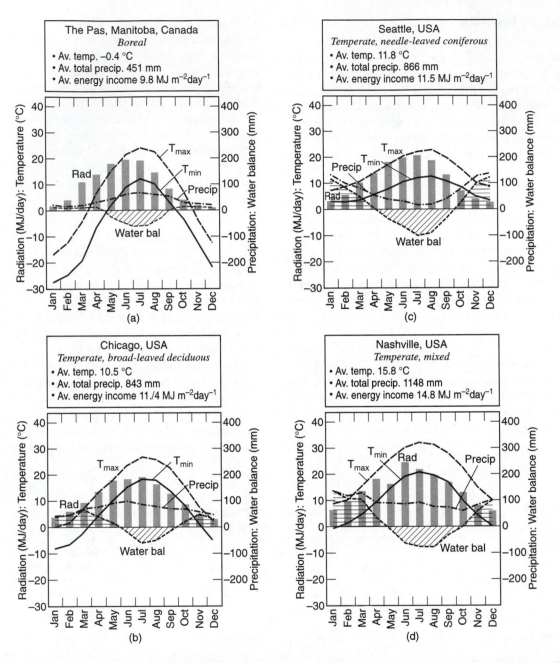

Figure 3.4 Climate diagrams illustrating the conditions in which we can expect to find: a) boreal forests; b) temperate deciduous forests; c) temperate coniferous forests; d) temperate mixed forests; e) and f) temperate evergreen forests; g) tropical evergreen forests; h) tropical deciduous forests. The diagrams show long-term monthly averages of maximum (Tmax) and minimum (Tmin) temperatures (°C), precipitation (mm) radiation (MJ m^{-2}day^{-1}) and the water balance, calculated as the difference between precipitation and evaporation using the Thornthwaite (23) equation. The diagrams were produced from data presented by Muller (24). Radiation data were not available for every station (they were missing for The Pas, Hobart, Manaus and Jamshedpur); where this

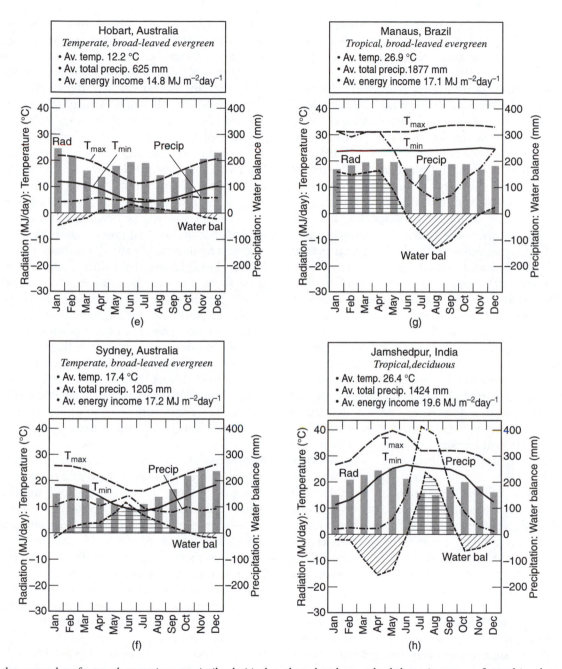

was the case, data from other stations at similar latitudes, that closely matched these in terms of sunshine hours, temperature and rainfall patterns, were used. The water balance data (precipitation–evaporation) were derived from the monthly potential evaporation figures provided by Muller (24), which were calculated from the evapotranspiration formula derived by Thornthwaite (23). This formula is based on temperature and is unlikely to provide accurate values for the water use of tropical forests. However, as Muller points out, the Thornthwaite equation is the only one that gave comparable values for every station, and it does provide a reasonable indication of evapotranspiration regimes and hence the overall water balance.

excessively drained pine forests (*P. banksiana* in Canada and *P. sylvestris* in Eurasia). Some Spodosols can be found in the wetter regions of boreal forests.

Species Composition   Tree species diversity is very poor in the boreal forests. There are only nine dominant tree species in North America, and 14 in Fennoscandinavia and the former Soviet Union (4). The low species diversity is attributed to the recent development of boreal forests following the retreat of glaciers and the harsh climate (3). In general, boreal species arrived in this region less than 2000 years ago. The distribution of species, and the species composition of stands are strongly influenced by topography and soils. Important genera include fir (*Abies*), birch (*Betula*), larches (*Larix*), spruce (*Picea*), aspen (*Populus*), and willow (*Salix*). *Picea* and *Larix* commonly occur on poorly drained lowland soils. Pines commonly occupy well-drained upland soils, while *Populus*, *Abies*, *Salix*, and certain species of *Picea* occur on the finer-textured upland soils. In North America and Europe, needle-leaved evergreen conifers tend to dominate the boreal landscape, especially at northern latitudes. However, *Larix*, a deciduous conifer, increases in importance in Eurasia and dominates the boreal treeline in Siberia (5). Ericaceous shrubs commonly dominate the understory of boreal forests. In no other forest biome do bryophytes play such an important role. Lichens (*Cladina* spp.) occur on the excessively drained sandy soils, feathermoss (*Pleurozium* spp.) forms a continuous ground layer in many spruce and pine forests of intermediate drainage and sphagnum (*Sphagnum* spp.) are the most common bryophyte on poorly drained soils.

Structure and Function   Boreal forests have low leaf area index (LAI, the amount of leaf area per unit ground surface area) and the conifer trees have very pronounced spiral canopies. The spiral canopies help shed the snow and maximize light interception when the sun is low in the horizon. Boreal forests have a low LAI because the extremely short growing season and very nutrient poor soils limit the amount of foliage area a stand

supports (Chapter 6). Aboveground net primary production (ANPP, the annual amount of organic matter or biomass trees accumulate in stem, branches, and foliage) is low, averaging 4.2 and 3.2 tC ha^{-1}yr^{-1} for evergreen and deciduous forests, respectively (6). Although live bryophytes constitute less than 1 percent of the total aboveground biomass of boreal forests, they have a profound effect on the structure and function of boreal forests. Bryophytes insulate the soil, which strongly affects the thermal regime and hence overall nutrient cycling and productivity patterns of boreal forests. Also, the productivity of bryophytes can equal or exceed that of the stem growth of trees (7).

Fire is an important natural disturbance in boreal forests. Fires, ignited by lightning, tend to cover large areas and may burn as much as 25,000 to 50,000 hectares (8). Fire frequency in the boreal forests in North America ranges from 30 to 200 years, depending on species composition and topographic position. Fire strongly influences species composition, nutrient availability and forest productivity (8). Insect damage can be important in boreal forests in some regions. Damaging summer storms are rare, and severe winter weather is unlikely to cause damage to trees.

Management   Boreal forests are one of the least managed forest biomes of the world because of the low growth rates, the extremely cold and dry climate, and inaccessibility. However, there are areas—for example, along the southern edges of the forests in Canada, Scandinavia, and in Siberia—where commercial logging occurs. A concern with harvesting boreal forests is that the rate of vegetation regrowth is very slow because of the extremely cold winters and infertile soils. Timber companies are interested in harvesting boreal forests, especially in Siberia, because of the large areas of mature forests (Table 3.1). The political instability and poor infrastructure in Siberia may be the only factor stopping large-scale harvesting of this fragile ecosystem. Plantation forests are scarce in the boreal regions. Management of natural and plantation boreal forests in the Nordic countries (Denmark, Sweden, Finland and Norway) can approach the intensity of plantation forestry, but are probably the best example of sustainable management of boreal forests. Another serious environmental threat to boreal forests is the unchecked air pollution from some of the world's largest iron ore, and nickel mines.

Temperate Broad-leaved Deciduous Forests

Distribution and Extent   Temperate broad-leaved deciduous forests cover 3.5×10^8 hectares (Table 3.1) and occur primarily between 30° to 50° N latitude (Figure 3.3). Large tracts of these forests occur in the eastern United States, Europe, western Turkey and eastern border areas of Iran, western China and Japan. The noticeable absence of deciduous forests in the Southern Hemisphere, except for the western coast of southern Chile, is because the year-round mild climate favors the evergreen over deciduous leaf habit.

Climate   In the temperate deciduous forest zone of the northern United States (represented by Chicago, Illinois, Figure 3.4b), minimum temperatures are well below freezing for at least four months of the year. The best period for growth is in the spring, when temperature and water are adequate. During the summer high, evaporation may equal or exceed precipitation, resulting in water deficits that restrict growth.

Further south, in the temperate mixed (evergreen, needle-leaved conifers and broad-leaved deciduous) region, represented by the climate at Nashville, Tennessee (Figure 3.4d), higher rainfall is not enough to prevent summer water deficits, but early-season temperatures are significantly higher than in the deciduous and coniferous areas. The deciduous trees lose their leaves during the winter, but the period when temperatures are low enough to prevent growth of evergreen conifers is relatively short.

Soils   Temperate forest soils are highly variable. Many of the mountain soils in temperate regions are Entisols, Inceptisols, or Alfisols, with the former being young and infertile and the latter being moderately weathered, but fertile. In warmer climates (e.g., southeastern United States, southern Europe) the soils have undergone greater weathering and the dominant soil order is Ultisols; these soils can be productive, especially if nitrogen and phosphorus fertilizer is applied.

Species Composition   Both tree and understory diversity are greater in temperate deciduous than temperate conifer and boreal forests; approximately 30 plant families and 65 genera occur in the overstory canopy of temperate deciduous forests (9). Species diversity of deciduous forests is highest in North America, China and Japan, where refugia for temperate forests are hypothesized to have existed during the most recent glacial periods. Species diversity is lower in Europe, perhaps because the predominantly east-west mountain ranges prevented species from retreating south to warmer climates during the most recent glacial advance. Species composition varies according to topography, soil fertility, and successional status. A few important temperate deciduous tree genera and species include maple (*Acer*), birch (*Betula*), hickory (*Carya*), beech (*Fagus*), ash (*Fraxinus*), walnut (*Juglans*), tulip tree (*Liriodendron*), *Magnolia*, aspen (*Populus*), oak (*Quercus*), basswood (*Tilia*), tree of heaven (*Ailanthus*), silktree (*Albizzia*), *Castanopsis*, and *Zelkova*. Except for stands of *Populus*, pure stands of one species are uncommon.

Structure and Function   The growing season ranges from 4 months in northern forests to 8 months in southern forests. The leaf area index of temperate broad-leaved deciduous forests tends to be higher than that of temperate evergreen forests because the evergreen conifer forests often occur on the more infertile, drought-prone soils. Net primary productivity of temperate broad-leaved deciduous forests averages 6.6 tC ha^{-1} yr^{-1}. The riparian broad-leaved temperate forests in the southeastern United States are some of the most productive forests in the world and NPP can exceed 10 tC ha^{-1} yr^{-1}. Riparian forests are also important in flood prevention, maintaining water quality, filtering harmful chemicals and sediments, and habitat for aquatic flora and fauna. A large percentage of the original temperate deciduous forests have been cleared for agriculture because these soils tend to be fertile. The drainage and conversion of riparian forests to agriculture threatens regional watersheds.

Management Present-day temperate deciduous forests do not usually occur in extensive tracts because of large-scale human activities (e.g., clearing and conversion to agriculture, pasture, and urban areas). Management may range from periodic selective tree removal to short-rotation plantations for fiber or fuel production—the most intensive form of forest management. Species commonly used in short-rotation plantations include poplars, sweetgum, willows, and sycamore. Depending upon the species, life history, and ecophysiology, both even-aged and uneven-aged management practices can be sustainable. Even-aged management is most prevalent for shade-intolerant and coppicing—regrowth of aboveground vegetation from the root stock of the trees that were harvested—species (aspen), while uneven-aged management is commonly used for shade-tolerant species. Uneven-aged management is becoming increasingly popular because managed uneven-aged forests retain many of the desirable characteristics (e.g., canopy gaps, multilayer canopies, biodiversity) of old-growth forests.

Temperate Needle-leaved Evergreen Forests

Distribution and Extent Temperate evergreen coniferous forests are largely restricted to the Northern Hemisphere and cover approximately 2.4×10^8 hectares (Table 3.1). Conifers dominate the montane forests in North America, Europe, and China and smaller areas of temperate conifers are located in montane regions of Korea, Japan, and Central America. Pines species have been planted extensively in the Southern Hemisphere. Natural temperate conifer forests tend to occur on droughty or infertile soils that cannot supply the greater water and nutrient demands of deciduous species. Evergreen conifers are the most common trees in the Pacific Northwestern United States, where dry summers and mild winters provide a more favorable environment for evergreens than conifers (10).

Climate Temperate evergreen conifers occur in a wide range of climates, such as sub-tropical, woodland, boreal forests and temperate rainforests (Figure 3.3). However, an area notable for such forests is the northwest coast of the United States, represented by Seattle, Washington (Figure 3.4c), which has cooler summers than the temperate deciduous zone, warmer winters (the average minimum temperature for any month is never below zero) and a different precipitation pattern. The largest amount of precipitation occurs in the winter months, with very little during the period of highest evaporation. As a result, significant water deficits occur and reduce tree growth during the summer. Fire can be an important cause of ecosystem disturbance, especially in exceptionally dry summers when the normal summer drought (Figure 3.4c) is extended and exacerbated by unusually hot weather and lack of precipitation.

Soils It is also difficult to generalize about temperate needle-leaved forest soils because they are extremely variable over the wide range of climatic and parent materials where these forests occur. The more common forest soil orders include: Inceptisols, Alfisols, and Ultisols. Spodosols are primarily restricted to cool to cold-temperate conifer forests that receive abundant rainfall. Many of the temperate needle-leaved conifer forests occurring on Ultisols and Spodisols respond positively to nitrogen and phosphorus fertilization treatments.

Species Composition Common genera in the temperate coniferous forests in the northern latitudes include fir (*Abies*), spruce (*Picea*), Douglas fir (*Pseudotsuga menziesii*), while hemlock (*Tsuga*) occur over a much broader range of environmental conditions. Pine, an important genera from both an economic and ecological perspective, occur in a wide variety of environments ranging from hot, arid southwestern United States to cold temperate regions of Scandinavia and Eurasia.

Structure and Function   Given the diverse environments in which temperate conifers occur, it is not surprising that the ecophysiology and structure of these forests also vary. For example, needle longevity can range from less than 2 years for loblolly pine (*P. taeda*) to greater than 40 years for bristlecone pine (*P. longaeva*). Above ground biomass of mature forests can range from a low of about 100 t ha^{-1} for *Pinus* forests in the southwestern United States to 3300 t ha^{-1} for giant redwood (*Sequoia sempervirens*) forests in northern California (11). Some of the lowest leaf area index < 1 occur in temperate conifer forests, while the highest measured leaf area index 12 was for a western hemlock (*Tsuga heterophylla*) forest in coastal Oregon (4). Aboveground net production is also quite variable, ranging from about 2 to 20 t ha^{-1} yr^{-1}, averaging 6.6 tC ha^{-1} yr^{-1} (Table 3.1).

Management   Management practices in temperate coniferous forests vary greatly; the intensity of management tends to be strongly correlated to the suitability of environmental conditions for tree growth. At one extreme these forests are allowed to regenerate naturally following disturbance such as fire or harvesting. Biomass accumulation can be substantial over several centuries, but the annual accumulation rate is very slow. The harvesting of mature, slow growing forests is controversial, because these forests provide many other valuable ecosystem services such as wilderness areas extensively used for recreation, wildlife refuges, and valuable watersheds. Because of the long growth cycle and the destruction of many of these values, harvesting these "old growth" forests more closely resembles resource mining than sustainable forest management.

Management practices of intermediate intensity are becoming more common because there is increasing pressure from society to manage mature forests on an uneven-aged basis. Managed uneven-aged stands retain structural characteristics that are similar to "old-growth" or pristine forests. At the other extreme, temperate conifers are managed at a level of intensity that rivals or exceeds agriculture. Intensive management includes mechanized site preparation and planting, use of genetically superior seedlings, application of herbicides and fertilizers during the rotation, pruning (the removal of low branches to increase wood quality), and mechanised harvesting, which can include the complete removal of all above ground biomass.

Major needle-leaved temperate conifer species used in plantations include Sitka spruce (*Picea sitchensis*) in Britain, extensive plantations of loblolly and slash pine (*P. taeda* and *P. elliotti*, respectively) in the southern United States, Douglas fir (*Pseudotsuga menziesii*) in the Pacific northwestern United States and Canada, and Monterey pine (*P. radiata*) in Australia, New Zealand, Chile and South Africa (although South Africa also uses several other softwood species).

Temperate Mixed Forests

Temperate mixed (deciduous plus evergreen) forests occur throughout the temperate evergreen and deciduous regions—particularly the southeastern United States, Europe through northern Iraq and Iran, and China—where the climates are the same as those described for temperate deciduous and coniferous forests. Mixed forests have been studied less than pure deciduous or evergreen forests. Their occurrence reflects past land use change, successional status and local variations in edaphic conditions. In the southeastern United States, conifers dominant early successional forests, mixed forests are common for mid-successional forests, and broad-leaved hardwoods dominate late successional forests. In the Lake States, needle-leaved evergreen forests dominate the xeric, infertile soils, mixed forests are most common on the soils of intermediate edaphic conditions, and broad-leaved hardwood forests occur on the mesic fine-textured soils (12). A wide range of species combinations is found in mixed forests: evergreen conifers and deciduous broad-leaved species: for example, oak and loblolly pine, Douglas fir, red alder and western hemlock, Sitka spruce and alder, larch, fir and pine, eucalyptus, and acacias.

Temperate Broad-leaved Evergreen Forests

Distribution and Extent The potential area of temperate broad-leaved evergreen forests is 5.1 × 10^8 km^2 (Table 3.1). Two categories of temperate broad-leaved evergreen forests are recognized: broad-leaved sclerophyll and broad-leaved rain forests (4). The broad-leaved sclerophyll forests occur in areas with a Mediterranean-type climate: winter rain and summer drought. The temperate broad-leaved rainforests are found in humid, frost-free climates, usually along coastal areas. The sclerophyll forests occur in scattered areas of the United States, around the Mediterranean, and over large areas of Asia from northern India through southern China. The greatest continuous areas still existing are the eucalyptus forests of Australia. Temperate broad-leaved evergreen rain forests occur in Japan, Chile, New Zealand, Australia (Tasmania), and in scattered, remnant patches in Asia.

Climate The climate at Hobart, Tasmania, Australia (Figure 3.4e) is not dissimilar to that of the west coast of South Island, New Zealand, and both areas are characterized by broad-leaved evergreen forests. The annual rainfall in Hobart is not high, but it is evenly distributed through the year and evaporation is low. Therefore, trees only experience mild water deficits during the summer. Average minimum monthly temperatures are rarely below zero, so tree growth occurs throughout the year. The climates of Sydney and Tasmania, Australia are similar (Figure 3.4e–f), although the average annual temperature for Sydney is higher (17.4°C versus 12.2°C). Higher rainfall (1200 mm or 47 inches) compensates for the higher temperatures and evaporation, so environmental conditions are good for growth throughout the year.

Soils Less is known about the temperate broad-leaved evergreen forest soils compared to other temperate forest soils. The soils of schlerophylous forests of Australia and Mediterranean areas are composed of Inceptisols and Ultisols, while the forests in Tasmania, New Zealand and South America are dominated by Alfisols and Inceptisols.

Species Composition The sclerophyll—a term that describes the thick, tough foliage of many of these tree species—forests in the Mediterranean area and the United States are dominated by oaks (*Quercus*), while the broad-leaved temperate forests of Australia are dominated by Eucalyptus. In Tasmania and Victoria, there are relatively small areas of *Nothofagus* forests; these are extensive in New Zealand and Chile. Temperate broad-leaved evergreen forests in New Zealand vary from multi-storied, mixed-species coastal forests, with tall conifers (*Podocarpus, Dacrycarpus, Agathis*), to the pure, dense-canopied montane and subalpine stands of beech (*Nothofagus*). The evergreen beech forests should not be confused with the deciduous beech forests that are native to the eastern United States. Many of the trees species have chemical compounds in the foliage that make them much more flammable than other tree species, and are therefore much more prone to catastrophic wildfires (see below).

Structure and Function The characteristic sclerophyll foliage is advantageous because it deters herbivory, helps avoid drought, and is believed to be an important adaptation to help plants cope with nutrient infertile soils. The natural structure of the sclerophyllous oak forests is a dense, often continuous canopy, less than 20 m tall. Eucalyptus canopies may vary from tall (up to 60 m in height) closed forest to shorter closed forest and woodland. The LAI of eucalyptus forests is low, especially relative to the high productivity of these forests. The forests have relatively dense shrub understory, presumably because there is adequate light and reduced evaporative demand. The NPP averages 10.0 tC ha^{-1} yr^{-1}, the highest of all the forest biomes, but this average is based on very few data. Nonetheless, temperate broad-leaved forest can be very productive when moisture and nutrient availability are high.

Management   Forests in the Mediterranean area have been used by humans for thousands of years, and in the United States cutting and clearance for agriculture and various other forms of development have been rapid. The forest industry in Australia has been based on native forests for more than 100 years. During this time, the mature forests have been either clearcut or selectively logged. Most Eucalyptus species are tolerant of fire, and the forest ecosystems are adapted to it. The native people of Australia used fire for thousands of years in a manner that appeared to be consistent with natural regimes (fires caused by lightning strikes). Since European settlement, fire has been excluded, as much as possible, from the remaining forests. The result has been fuel buildup, so that when fires do occur, they are likely to be much more intense than was normal historically (Chapter 18).

Large areas of the native Eucalyptus forests in Australia have been cleared and replaced by softwood Monterey pine (*P. radiata*) plantations. The establishment of hardwood plantations has been slow, largely because of economic and sociological reasons. Many lowland Podocarp forests have been harvested for their exotic timber. There are still large areas of beech forest. New Zealand has now virtually halted native forest logging.

The South American temperate broad-leaved evergreen forests include a range of types, from lowland to Andean slopes. The dominant species is generally *Nothofagus*. These forests have all been heavily exploited for timber. Like Australia and New Zealand, Chile now has extensive *P. radiata* plantations, which may serve to slow the destruction of native *Nothofagus* forests.

Tropical Broad-leaved Evergreen Forests

Distribution and Extent   Tropical broad-leaved evergreen forests, or rainforests, comprise the largest single forest biome in the world (see Table 3.1). The greatest single area of tropical evergreen forest is in the Amazon Basin, in the northern half of South America. Similar forests are found on the isthmus of Panama and into southern Mexico, the Congo Basin in equatorial Africa, and the southern fringe of West Africa. In Asia, tropical rainforests occur along the southeast coast of India, in Sri Lanka, the Malaysian Peninsula, the Indonesian archipelago, Borneo, Sarawak, and Papua New Guinea (collectively called Melanesia). A small remnant strip of tropical rainforest also occurs along the northeast coast of Australia. Rainfall is generally greater than 1500 mm per year and relative humidity is uniformly high. There is a broad range of subtypes within tropical forests, ranging from lowland to montane types. The large differences in climate and parent material have a pronounced impact on the structure and function of tropical forests (13), and it is difficult to make generalizations about such a large forest biome.

Climate   The tropical evergreen forests are generally considered to be wet at all times, but Figure 3.4g indicates there are periods when evaporation may exceed rainfall in the Amazon rainforests. This pattern also occurs in the African tropical rainforests, but in many of the southeast Asian areas rainfall exceeds evaporation in every month of the year. In general, diurnal variation in temperature exceeds seasonal variation in temperature.

Soils   Tropical forest soils are highly variable. An excellent summary of tropical soil distribution, extent, and key pedogenic processes that control soil fertility is provided by Sanchez (14). Oxisols and Ultisols, the two dominant soil orders in the tropics, are highly weathered and are typically infertile. Phosphorus and base cations are commonly the most deficient nutrients. They have extremely low cation exchange capacity, base saturation, and pH. Alfisols, more fertile than Oxisols and Ultisols, occur in regions with lower precipitation (e.g., tropical deciduous forest regions) than lowland wet tropical forests. Because of their higher fertility, the forests on these soils are often cleared and used for agriculture.

Species Composition   Tropical evergreen forests are the most diverse terrestrial ecosystems on earth, with the greatest number of species per unit area.

The Amazonian forests contain more than 2500 different tree species, with thousands more in the African and Asian forests. Dipterocarps are common trees in many tropical forests in the world. Eastern South America tropical rainforests contain conifers such as *Dacrydium*, *Podocarpus*, *Agathis*, and *Araucaria* (15). The African rainforests appear to be relatively poor in species compared to those of America and Asia. Characteristic species are *Lophira alata*, *Turraeanthus africana*, *Tarrieta utilis* and *Uapaca* spp. The most important commercial tree species of the evergreen forests of Africa belong to the *Meliaceae* family (16).

Structure and Function   Rainforest canopies are characterized by layered architecture. The canopy includes an upper layer of emergent trees, a main canopy layer and a subcanopy of smaller trees and shrubs. The varied canopy structure is caused by gaps of different sizes, created at different times. The aboveground biomass of tropical rainforests varies with topography, soil type, stage of development and other factors. Aboveground biomass ranges from 100 to 1500 t ha^{-1} (4). NPP averages 8.2 tC ha^{-1} yr^{-1}. The most recent summaries of NPP for different forest biomes suggest that differences in NPP between tropical and temperate forests are smaller than reported in earlier studies (17).

Millions of canopy-dwelling insects reside in wet tropical forests. These insects are part of an ecosystem in which predator–prey relationships are extremely complex. Vast numbers of these organisms consume large quantities of foliage, bark and wood.

Natural disturbances in tropical forests include cyclonic storms, wildfires and volcanic eruptions. Inland forests, in the Amazon and Congo basins, are not subject to hurricanes and appear to be at very little risk from environmental hazards, but the hazard is significant through much of the southeast Asian area, particularly in the Indonesian archipelago and Malaysia. Hurricanes are a common form of disturbance for coastal tropical rainforests.

Management   Tropical rainforests are under increasing pressure from human activities. During the 1980s (1981–90) 4.6 million hectares—or approximately 0.6 percent of all lowland tropical rainforest—were harvested or cleared. An additional 2.5 million hectares of tropical montane forests are destroyed each year. Indonesia and Brazil accounted for 45 percent of the total. Degradation and fragmentation of the remaining forests result in the loss of large tracts of unmanaged forests substantially greater than the clearing rates suggest. The causes for deforestation are numerous, and the remedies are complex. In Africa, expanding populations and constant clearance for agriculture are the primary causes of deforestation. Shifting cultivation and cattle ranching are major causes of deforestation in South America. In Asia, deforestation is caused by burgeoning human populations and poorly regulated logging. Solutions must be found for these problems—perhaps the most important will be control of human populations. Agroforestry may be a sustainable system for tropical areas. The development of viable tropical forest management systems and procedures for preserving the forests and utilizing them on a sustainable basis will require much better ecological and physiological information for the dominant tree species.

With the exception of the widely grown Eucalyptus plantations, most tropical plantations are softwoods, although hardwood plantations are beginning to gain popularity in the tropics. However, a great deal of research is necessary before the problems of managing tropical plantations to produce acceptable timber growth rates are solved.

Tropical Broad-leaved Deciduous Forests

Distribution and Extent   Tropical deciduous forests occupy 4.6×10^8 hectares (Table 3.1) and comprise 42 percent of tropical and subtropical regions (18). Tropical broad-leaved deciduous forests replace tropical broad-leaved evergreen trees as annual rainfall decreases and interseasonal differences in precipitation increase. Drought induces leaf shedding and the deciduous growth habit in trees. Deciduous tropical forests occur on the borders of evergreen forests in South America and

Africa, where the mountain forests of central Africa may be included in the deciduous category. The largest areas of tropical deciduous forests are the monsoonal forests of southern and southeastern Asia, in India, the Himalayan countries and Bangladesh, stretching through to Burma, Thailand, Laos, Cambodia, and Vietnam (16).

Climate Jamshedpur, in India (Figure 3.4h) is a monsoon climate, characterized by heavy rains for 4–6 months of the year, with high water deficits developing after the monsoon season. Temperatures are high throughout the year. A very similar climate is found in Central and South America; Managua, Nicaragua has a mean annual temperature of 27.3°C (cf. 26.4°C at Jamshedpur), and total annual precipitation of 1142 mm, most of which falls in five months.

Soils Major soils orders of tropical broad-leaved deciduous forests are Alfisols and Inceptisols. Highly weathered soils (e.g., Ultisols and Oxisols) are rare because lower precipitation prevents excessive weathering of the soil. Many of these soils are rich in base cations.

Species Composition Species diversity is typically less in tropical deciduous than in tropical evergreen forests (18). Dominant species in Africa include *Antiarus africana, Ceiba pentandra, Triplochiton scleroxolon,* and others, while important species in America are *Andira, Dalbergia*, and *Tabebuia* genera, with conifers represented by Caribbean Pine (*P. caribaea*) and *P. oocarpa* (16). Important tropical deciduous tree species in Central America include *Calcophyllum candidissimum* and *Licania arborea* in lowland forests, *Luehea seemannii* and *Guarea excelsa* in lowland riparian areas and an oak, *Quercus oleoides*, which occurs in scattered populations over a wide area (19). Deciduous tropical forests in Asia include *Tectona grandis* (teak), *Shorea robusta*, and species of *Dalbergia* and *Terminalia* (16).

Structure and Function The canopies of deciduous tropical forests tend to be shorter, less layered, and characterized by more open structure than tropical evergreen forests. Dense shrubs often occur as the second layer, presumably because of the better light environment and reduced evaporative demand at lower levels in the canopy. The productivity of tropical deciduous forests is influenced by the periods for which the trees have leaves and water relations are such that the trees can utilize radiant energy and grow relatively unchecked by water stress (see Chapter 4 on water relations and Chapter 13 on ecosytem models). Average NPP for tropical broad-leaved deciduous forests is 8.0 tC ha^{-1} yr^{-1} (Table 3.1). Fire is an important natural ecological component of tropical broad-leaved deciduous forests, and human disturbance has greatly reduced the amount and quality of these forests (4).

Management Tropical deciduous forests in all continents have been subject, over long periods, to burning and clearing for grazing and arable agriculture. Annual deforestation rates during the 1980s was 6.6 million hectares, and like the tropical broad-leaved evergreen forests, the greatest rates of deforestation are occurring in Brazil and Indonesia; human population growth in these areas will lead to continued destruction of the few remnants, with progression towards degraded forests, woodland and savannah. Soil erosion is among the many serious effects of forest destruction and degradation. Protection of these forests is an unattainable goal in many regions of the world because of rapidly growing population. The future objective should be to preserve existing pristine forests and develop sustainable management plans for disturbed ecosystems. Where damaged forests can be protected, their recovery depends heavily on the state of the soils, in terms of organic matter content, structure, and nutrient status.

Global Change and Forests

Forests are an important component of the biosphere. Forest and woodland soils contain 45 percent of the total soil carbon of terrestrial ecosystems, forest and woodland vegetation contain 84 percent of the total terrestrial vegetation carbon, and forests annually assimilate 61 percent of the total carbon dioxide removed from the atmosphere by terrestrial ecosystems (17). The role of forests in the biosphere is changing because of land use change and climate and atmospheric chemistry change. Altering the extent and spatial distribution of forests can cause feedbacks between the atmosphere and vegetation.

Habitat Protection and Land Use Change

Habitat protection is a necessary management practice to maintain or improve biodiversity—an important component of sustainable forestry. The practice is more difficult because of the need to protect large tracts of threatened ecosystems. The World Conservation Union, an independent international organization that oversees conserving biodiversity established a goal of protecting a minimum of 10 percent of each of the world's major biomes. Few of the forest biomes has the minimum 10 percent of the area protected (Figure 3.5). The temperate forest biomes have the smallest area in protected forests (2.9 to 3.2 percent). Tropical broad-leaved deciduous forests also have less than 5 percent of the total area in protected forests. Perhaps even more disturbing is there are very few temperate broad-leaved deciduous and broad-leaved evergreen forests of "low human disturbance" available for protection.

A second, and more complicated consideration, is the spatial arrangement of the protected forests. The spatial arrangement of vegetation communities is important for the survival of certain species and proper ecosystem function. For example, assuming the edge effect of harvest extends one kilometer into the intact forest, a 10×10 km clearcut would affect 143 km² of forest. However, if 100 km² is deforested as 10 strips, each 1×10 km (e.g., logging adjacent to new roads in remote forests) the affected area would be about 350 km². Skoles and Tucker (20), using repeated satellite imagery, estimated an annual deforestation rate for the entire Amazon Basin of 280,000 km² yr⁻¹, but using the

assumption outlined earlier, the area affected by clearing—the so-called rate of fragmentation—would be 380,000 km² yr⁻¹. Although the assumption made by Skoles and Tucker about the magnitude of the edge effect is controversial, they raise a valid concern, particularly for animals that require large tracts of natural forests.

An increasing percentage of timber products used in the world today, particularly pulpwood but, increasingly, sawn timber products, come from plantations rather than from natural forests. Plantations have many advantages over natural forests. Plantations can be established on prepared land, using genetically improved and uniform material at standardized spacings that allow optimum growth rates of individual trees. It is economically feasible to control weeds and use fertilizers to ameliorate problems of soil nutrition in plantations. Plantations should be used to increase the production of wood products, thereby alleviating the need to harvest the remaining native forests.

Climate Change

Changes in atmospheric chemistry also threaten the health of forest ecosystems. The concentration of greenhouse gases such as carbon dioxide (CO_2), methane (CH_4), nitrous oxides (N_2O_x) and chloroflorocarbons (CFCs) have all greatly increased and the consensus of world experts is that the increased concentration of greenhouse gases will cause the climate to change (21). One major concern is that the predicted increase in temperature is far faster than changes in climate in the geologic past and some forest ecosystems tree species may experience future climates that do not currently occur in their present-day range. There is great interest in understanding how anticipated climate change will affect the distribution and extent of future forests. Model simulations suggest that the extent of boreal forests will decrease and tropical forests will increase, although the magnitude of the change differs among the models (4).

Ozone is another atmospheric pollutant that is harmful to plant growth. Ozone is the product of complex chemical reactions in the atmosphere that

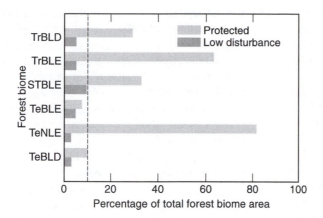

Figure 3.5 Percentage of each major forest biome area that is protected or subject to low human disturbance. The dashed line represents the goal of designating 10% of the total area of each forest biome as protected preserves. TrBLD = Tropical broad-leaved deciduous; TrBLE = Tropical broad-leaved evergreen; STBLE = Subtropical broad-leaved evergreen; TeBLE = Temperate broad-leaved evergreen; TeNLE = Temperate needle-leaved evergreen; TeBLD = Temperate broad-leaved deciduous.

involve pollutants from the combustion of fossil fuel. Reductions in the growth of agriculture crops and trees from elevated ozone concentrations are well documented (Chapter 4). A second atmospheric pollutant that is gaining worldwide attention is atmospheric nitrogen deposition. Although many forest ecosystems are nitrogen limited, chronic deposition of moderate to high amounts of nitrogen may cause forest ecosystems to function improperly, causing forest dieback and contamination of adjacent watersheds. The susceptibility of forests to nitrogen deposition is strongly dependent upon forest species, and soil type. Forest dieback attributed to stress induced from climatic change has already been suspected in many heavily industrialized areas in the temperate forests (4).

Concluding Statement

Humans have exerted a large influence on forest ecosystems of the world, and will continue to do so as the world population increases. Preserving large areas of (relatively) undisturbed forest ecosystems should be pursued wherever possible, but it is equally important to be realistic about the fact that forests must be used. The most pressing objective in forestry is to manage ecosystems on a sustainable basis. To achieve this goal, managers, politicians, and scientists must work together to develop management plans that are consistent with the ecology of each of the forest ecosystems comprising all the major forest biomes. Obtaining this goal will occur only if forest management is based on a sound understanding of forest biology (Chapters 4–8), forest fire ecology (Chapter 18), plant–animal interactions and protection (Chapters 14 and 18), and forest hydrology (Chapter 16).

References

1. D. I. Axelrod, *Evolution, 20*, 1 (1966).

2. J. M. Melillo, A. D. McGuire, D. W. Kicklighter, B. Moore, III, C. J. Vorosmarty, A. L. Schloss. *Nature 363*, 234 (1993).

3. F. I. Woodward, "Ecophysiological controls on conifer distribution." In *Ecophysiology of Coniferous Forests*, W. K. Smith and T. M. Hinckley, eds., Academic Press, San Diego, Calif., 1995.

4. J. J. Landsberg and S. T. Gower, *Applications of Physiological Ecology to Forest Management*, Academic Press, San Diego, Calif., 1997.

5. S. T. Gower and J. H. Richards, *BioScience 19*, 252 (1990).

6. S. T. GOWER, D. FELDKIRSHNER, R. J. OLSON, AND J. M. O. SCURLOCK, "Global leaf area index and net primary production data." Environmental Sciences Division Pub., Oak Ridge National Laboratory, Oak Ridge, Tenn., 2000.

7. S. T. GOWER, O. KRAKINA, R. J. OLSON, M. APPS, S. LINDER, AND C. WANG. "Net primary production and carbon allocation patterns of boreal forest ecosystems." *Ecological Applications, 11,* 1395 (2001).

8. C. T. DYRNESS, L. A. VIERECK, AND K. VAN CLEVE, "Fire in taiga communities on interior Alaska." In *Forest Ecosystems in the Alaskan Taiga*, K. Van Cleve, F. S. Chapin, III, P. W. Flanagan, L. A. Viereck, and C. T. Dyrness, eds., Springer-Verlag, New York, 1986.

9. E. ROHRIG, E. AND B. ULRICH, "Temperate deciduous forests." *In Ecosystems of the World*, D. W. Goodwall, ed., Elsevier, Amsterdam, 1991.

10. R. W. WARING AND J. F. FRANKLIN, *Science, 204,* 1380 (1979).

11. M. G. R. CANNELL, *World Forest Biomass and Primary Production Data*, Academic Press, New York, 1982.

12. J. KOTAR, J. KOVACH, AND C. LOCEY. "Field Guide to Forest Habitat Types in Northern Wisconsin." Department of Forestry, University of Wisconsin, Madison, Wis., 1982.

13. P. M. VITOUSEK AND R. L. SANFORD, JR., *Annual Review Ecology Systematics, 17,* 137 (1986).

14. P. A. SANCHEZ, *Properties and Management of Soils in the Tropics*, John Wiley & Sons, New York, 1976.

15. T. C. WHITMORE, *Tropical Rain Forests of the Far East,* Second Edition, MacMillan, New York, 1984.

16. J. BOROTA, "Tropical forests: Some African and Asian case studies of composition and structure." In *Developments in Agricultural and Managed Forest Ecology,* Elsevier, Amsterdam, 1991.

17. W. H. SCHLESINGER, Biogeochemistry: *An Analysis of Global Change*, Second Edition, Academic Press, San Diego, Calif., 1997.

18. P. G. MURPHY AND A. LUGO, *Annual Review Ecology and Systematics, 17,* 67 (1986).

19. G. S. HARTSHORN, "Gap-phase dynamics and tropical tree species richness." In *Tropical Forests: Botanical Dynamics, Speciation, and Diversity*, L. B. Holm-Nielsen, I. C. Nielsen, and H. Balslev, eds., Academic Press, London, 1989.

20. D. SKOLES AND C. TUCKER, *Science, 260,* 1905 (1993).

21. IPCC, "Intergovernmental Panel on Climate Change: Synthesis Report," World Meteorological Organization, Geneva, Switzerland, 1995.

22. R. G. BAILEY, *Ecosystem Geography*. Springer-Verlag, New York, 1996.

23. C. W. THORNTHWAITE, *Geogr. Res., 38,* 55 (1948).

24. M. J. MULLER, "Selected Climate Data for a Global Set of Standard Stations for Vegetation Science." *Junk,* The Hague, 1982.

CHAPTER 4

Forest Ecophysiology

ERIC L. KRUGER

Ecophysiology is a marriage of ecology and physiology in which the functions and activities of organisms are studied in the context of their environment. Implicit in this description is a quest to identify adaptive traits that organisms possess to cope with their often harsh and variable surroundings. Forest ecophysiology explores many of the questions and issues that emerge in related disciplines, including forest ecology, genetics, silviculture, pathology, and entomology. A good example of such an issue is forest succession, a fascinating and important ecological process involving the orderly replacement of certain plant species or communities by others through time (see Chapter 13). Ecophysiologists continue to pursue a mechanistic understanding of this phenomenon and the species adaptations that drive it. Another current focus is the generation of accurate predictions as to how forests will respond to changes in the global environment. There is cur-

rently a pressing need for these forecasts as society faces the seemingly imminent specter of marked shifts in global climate and atmospheric chemistry.

As the discipline of ecophysiology has evolved, it has expanded in scope, addressing issues at an increasingly wide range of scales. For instance, ecophysiologists have recently been studying how forest responses to changes in atmospheric chemistry will affect continental rainfall patterns, and the explanation links molecular behavior in certain leaf cells with landscape-level changes in vegetation water use. Conceptually, ecophysiology relies heavily on basic sciences such as chemistry and physics. However, it has also developed ties with ostensibly unrelated disciplines, such as economics. This has occurred because the ability of organisms to flourish in a given environment depends in part on such aspects as the efficiency in which a particular resource is used, or how effectively it is scavenged from the environment. These are critical considerations in the life of a tree, as essential resources exist in dilute concentrations in most forest ecosystems.

So where does one begin in tackling issues in forest ecophysiology? The first step is to garner a basic understanding of how trees "make a living." This step necessarily entails a coupling of tree structure and function, and there this chapter begins. From there, one can pursue any number of different paths. Here we will explore various aspects of tree response to environment, highlighting our knowledge (or lack thereof) about mechanisms underlying these behaviors. Armed with this background, we will then take a brief look at global-scale issues facing forests at present and in the future.

Coupling Tree Structure and Function

Leaves—The Tree's Solar Panels

Like all other plants, trees are made mostly from sugars as the basic building blocks. Sugars are the primary raw material from which all tree tissues (wood, bark, leaves, fine roots, flowers, etc.) are constructed. They are also the source of fuel used by enzymes and associated biochemical machinery in building and maintaining the tree. Tree leaves are sugar factories producing glucose, an organic (carbon-based) compound, by way of photosynthesis, the process of "trapping" the sun's energy. A large tree typically displays thousands of leaves that absorb sunlight and transfer its energy (by way of electrons) to carbon dioxide (CO_2), a relatively scarce gas in our atmosphere (currently ~0.037% by volume). The electron-rich carbon is then assembled to make either a disaccharide sugar, sucrose, or the closely related storage polysaccharide, starch (the general formula of both is $[C_6H_{12}O_6]_x$). A glance at the simplified chemical formula for photosynthesis, $CO_2 + H_2O \xrightarrow{light} CH_2O + O_2$, reveals that it also produces life-sustaining oxygen (O_2) when it strips electrons from water (H_2O) (see also Chapter 20, Wood Products).

This elegant process occurs in layers of leaf cells (Figure 4.1) collectively referred to as mesophyll (meaning middle of the leaf). A leaf is green because these cells contain bacterium-sized organelles called chloroplasts, which are laden with the pigment chlorophyll. The green color of chlorophyll stems from its preferential absorption of red (600–700 nm) and blue (400–500 nm) light. Thus, when looking at a leaf, we see the small amount (typically <10%) of visible light that is reflected or transmitted rather than absorbed and utilized for photosynthesis.

Chlorophyll is one of several pigments, proteins, and other components of chloroplast machinery that absorbs and converts light energy into what is essentially electric current. The energy in this current is then stored in chemical fuels that are used

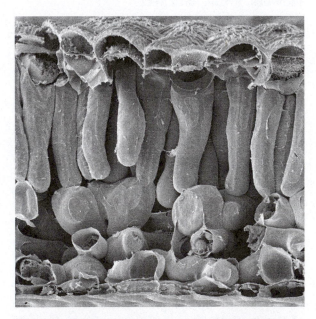

Figure 4.1 Cross-section of a Norway maple (*Acer platanoides*) leaf. The wax-coated epidermis encloses several cell types, including columnar chloroplast-laden cells called *palisade parenchyma,* amorphous spongy mesophyll (beneath the palisade cells) and vascular bundles containing xylem and phloem (not shown). All of this is packed in an envelope less than one millimeter thick.

to "fix" or assimilate carbon dioxide (CO_2) molecules into sugar. The first step in CO_2 assimilation is performed in the chloroplast by one of the most abundant and important enzymes on earth, known by the acronym "rubisco" (short for ribulose bisphosphate carboxylase–oxygenase). Rubisco, which can constitute nearly one-half of the protein in a leaf, is responsible for producing an estimated 200 billion tons of sugar around the world each year. As a frame of reference, humanity currently consumes the equivalent of roughly 10 percent of that energy, including portions of the enormous fossil fuel reservoirs that were generated by rubisco millions of years ago.

Water is a critical factor in the design of a leaf. Living cells such as the mesophyll must bathe in water, and to ensure that this is always the case, mesophyll is wrapped in the epidermis, a largely water-impermeable skin (Figure 4.1). The epidermis is impermeable because it deposits a thin wax (hydrophobic) cuticle on its exterior. However, the photosynthetic requirement for CO_2 necessitates that the mesophyll has access to the atmosphere, and therefore the epidermis has holes in it called stomates. Tens of thousands of these tiny pores typically dot a square centimeter of leaf surface. An important implication of this arrangement is that, in order to photosynthesize, the leaf must lose water, which diffuses from the moist leaf interior through the stomates to the relatively dry atmosphere. As water is generally the most limiting resource for trees and other terrestrial plants, it is essential that water loss, otherwise known as transpiration, is carefully controlled. To achieve this, stomatal pores are lined with a pair of guard cells (Figure 4.2).

Guard cells maintain a balance between photosynthesis and transpiration by opening and closing the stomatal pore in response to key environmental factors, including light, relative humidity, and even CO_2 concentration. Stomates open in response to increasing light intensity, and they close in response to dry air or high CO_2 concentrations inside the leaf. Stomates also close in response to soil drying, and this is often mediated by a chemical message from the root system. Col-

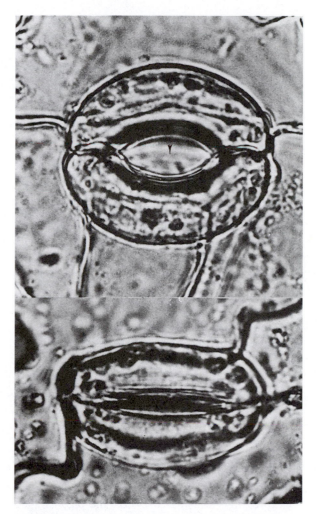

Figure 4.2 Close-up of a pair of guard cells lining a stomatal pore in the leaf epidermis. When guard cells absorb water, the stomate opens (upper photo), and when they lose water, it closes (lower photo).

lectively, these behaviors tend to minimize the amount of water lost per molecule of CO_2 assimilated.

Another essential component of leaves is the "plumbing"—the conduits through which materials are transported to and from the leaf. Water is delivered from the roots to the leaf mesophyll through a set of pipes known as the xylem. Sugar is delivered from the mesophyll to the rest of the tree through a different system called the phloem. The xylem and phloem lie adjacent to each other in vascular bundles that are imbedded in the veins pervading the leaf.

Woody Stem—The Distinctive Feature of Trees

The key feature distinguishing trees from other plants is the perennial woody stem, generally a single column that, in the case of species such as coastal redwood (*Sequoia sempervirens*), can reach massive proportions. Through the ages, arboreal forms have arisen repeatedly in unrelated plant families around the world. Why such a convergence in design? It may simply boil down to the enhanced light capture and competitive ability afforded by a tall stem.

Wood, which affords the stem sufficient strength to support a massive canopy, is essentially a matrix of lignified water conduits (Figure 4.3) that extend from the tips of the roots to the tips of the leaves. Wood (or xylem, derived from the Greek word for wood) actually owes most of its strength and density to lignin, an amorphous polymer deposited in cell walls (see Chapter 20). Much of the wood of conifers and other gymnosperms (often referred to as softwoods) is a honeycomb-like aggregate of conduits called tracheids. In dicot angiosperms (often referred to as hardwoods), the pipes, called vessels, are interspersed with thick-walled fibers that make the wood strong and dense. With few exceptions, the cross-sectional diameter of tracheids and vessels ranges from 10–500 micrometers, and only the widest of them (such as the large vessels of many oaks) are visible to the naked eye when viewing a stem cross-section.

Technically, most of the wood is dead. That is, tracheids, vessels, and fibers consist of nothing more than cell walls at functional maturity. However, in the outer band of wood, known as sapwood, there is a network of living cells, called parenchyma, which permeates the otherwise inert matrix. These cells serve as storage reservoirs for the tree's foodstuffs (mainly starch), and they help maintain the

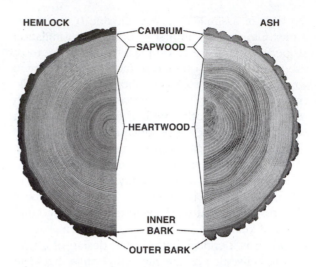

Figure 4.3   Cross-section of the stem of eastern hemlock (*Tsuga canadensis*, a gymnosperm) and white ash (*Fraxinus americana*, an angiosperm). Note in both stems the conspicuous heartwood core surrounded by sapwood and bark. Between the sapwood and inner bark (phloem) lies the meristimatic band of cells known as the vascular cambium.

integrity of the wood, by responding to injury and defending against stem-boring insects and fungi (Figure 4.4). They also participate in a coordinated abandonment of older wood as the tree stem increases in girth. This core of completely dead tissue is the heartwood, which, during the transition from sapwood, is often infused with organic chemicals (e.g., resins, gums, and oils) that deter wood-decay organisms (see Chapter 20). This imparts much of the durability and color that characterizes highly valued lumber from species such as redwood, cedar, and oak.

While water is transported through the stem sapwood from roots to transpiring foliage, a solution of carbohydrates (mostly sugar) flows from the canopy down the stem by way of the phloem, which is a thin band of cells often referred to as the inner bark (Figure 4.3). Unlike the tracheids or vessels of xylem, the plumbing in phloem tissue, consisting primarily of sieve cells (gymnosperms) or sieve tube members (angiosperms),

Sidebar 4.1

Trees are remarkable organisms.

Trees are remarkable for their size, longevity, and ability to thrive in a wide range of habitats. As for size, there are coastal redwood and giant sequoia (*Sequoiadendron giganteum*) trees in California that exceed 110 meters (360 feet) in height and 30 meters (100 feet) in basal circumference, respectively. But none of these methuselan trees has been crowned the largest organism on Earth. Instead, the current record holder is a clone of trembling aspen (*Populus tremuloides*), nick-

named "Pando," in the Wasatch Mountains of Utah. This single organism, composed of some 47,000 interconnected and genetically identical tree stems, covers about 43 hectares (106 acres) and is estimated to weigh about 6,000 tons. (The former record holder was also a forest organism—the giant shoestring fungus, *Armillaria bulbosa*, found in Michigan). Not only is this aspen stand the largest organism ever measured, it may also be the longest-lived. It is thought that the clone may have been established before the end of the Pleistocene (last glacial epoch) some 10,000 years ago. If that estimate holds true, it smashes the previous record among trees, which was held by a tena-

cious, 4,900 year-old bristlecone pine (*Pinus longaeva*) growing in the cold, high-elevation deserts in the western United States. Yet from the standpoint of an ecophysiologist, the most impressive feature of trees is the broad range of habitats in which they can survive. There are species, such as bristlecone pine, that can eke out an existence in some of the driest and coldest areas on earth. And there are others, such as bald cypress (*Taxodium distichum*), that successfully inhabit the warmest and wettest places.

Figure 4.4 In many gymnosperms, parenchyma called epitheleal cells line a network of resin ducts in the wood. When the stem is injured, these cells produce copious amounts of resin to repel the intruder and plug the wound. The presence of pitch tubes on this lodgepole pine (*Pinus contorta*) indicates that the tree has been attacked by mountain pine beetles. Sometimes the intruder is entombed in resin (like the beetle on the right). (Photo at right courtesy of Ken Raffa, copyright of Plenum Press.)

is alive at functional maturity. This contrast underscores a key difference in the mechanism of material transport between the two juxtaposed tissues. Leaf transpiration generates a tension that pulls water through the tiny capillaries of the entire xylem, which is essentially an open or porous system. On the other hand, the sugary solution in the phloem is transported by the buildup of pressure at one end of the system (e.g., the leaf). This occurs within an interconnected plasma membrane that lines all the individual sieve elements, creating something akin to a very long dialysis tube through which the pressurized fluid moves from leaves all the way to root tips.

It may seem counterintuitive that the plasma membrane, which is essential for the creation as well as maintenance of phloem hydraulic pressure, is inherently leaky. Like all cell membranes, it is semipermeable, meaning that certain substances, including water, pass easily across it while others, such as sugar, do not. The key here is that sieve elements have mechanisms to accumulate sugar from surrounding cells. In response to this sugar

loading, water flows into the sieve elements from the adjacent xylem. This phenomenon, known as osmosis, is made possible by the unique properties of the plasma membrane. Pressures exceeding ten atmospheres will commonly develop as water fills the confines of the phloem cells. Downstream, sugar is offloaded to needy tissues, and this lessens the strength with which the phloem can hold water. Consequently, water leaks out and pressure declines, creating the gradient in pressure from leaves to roots that drives phloem transport.

When one examines the cross-section of a stem (Figure 4.3), it may be a bit puzzling as to how the tree coordinates the production of new xylem and phloem tissues as the stem increases in girth. It turns out that the stem has a thin layer of meristematic cells, known as the vascular cambium, positioned between the xylem and phloem (or wood and inner bark). Each year throughout the life of the tree, the cells in this cylinder undergo innumerable divisions, producing new xylem in an inward direction, and at the same time new phloem in the outward direction.

Meanwhile, new cells are being produced in yet another meristematic cylinder that lies outside of the phloem, the cork cambium (or phellogen). The cork cambium is responsible for maintaining the protective outer bark of the tree. As the name implies, much of the tissue manufactured by this perennial cambium is cork, which is dead at maturity and has suberin, a waxy waterproof polymer, incorporated in its cell walls. This creates a barrier to water loss from the inner stem, as well as a tough guard against potential intruders. In some species, such as paper birch (*Betula papyrifera*), this skin remains fairly thin throughout the life of the tree, whereas in others, such as cork oak (*Quercus suber*), it can exceed 30 cm in thickness. (*Quercus suber* is the source of wine bottle corks.) Most of the variation in bark design that distinguishes different tree species derives from the wide array of peculiar behaviors of the cork cambium.

Until they begin to senesce, trees continuously increase in height as well as girth, and the former is accomplished by meristems at the tips of branches. These apical zones of cell division, which number in the thousands on a large tree, give rise to new stems and leaves, as well as the reproductive structures (flowers and fruits). All stem tissues originate in the apical meristem, including the vascular and cork cambia: hence, there is a continuous network of interconnected apical and lateral meristems that forms a sheath around the entire stem.

Roots—Anchorage and Access to Soil Resources

The meristematic sheath around the stem also extends below ground, surrounding the tissues of a massive root system that at times can rival the tree crown in weight and volume. Large subterranean branches, and in many species a deep-running taproot, serve to anchor the tree in the soil. From these woody "coarse roots" grows a network of ever smaller laterals, which eventually terminate in a labyrinth of fine roots. The latter, typically light brown- or cream-colored and no more than a few millimeters in diameter, are typically confined to the

upper 20 cm of the soil profile. They are the primary means with which the tree absorbs water and an array of soil elements (nitrogen, phosphorus, potassium, and at least 11 others) essential for normal growth and vigor.

While woody coarse roots resemble branches in structure, fine roots have a distinctive architecture reflecting their absorptive function (Figure 4.5). As in the case of a twig in the tree crown, the fine root terminates in an apical meristem, which lies beneath a protective root cap. Unlike a twig, the fine root's plumbing (xylem and phloem) is located in its core, which is surrounded by a band of parenchyma called the cortex. All of this is enclosed in an epidermis, from which a plethora of root hairs typically emanate. These elongated epidermal cells

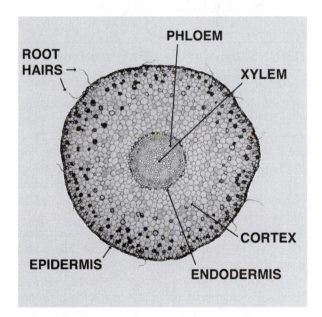

Figure 4.5 Most of the water and nutrients acquired by a tree are absorbed through fine roots with a cross-sectional structure like that shown here. Just outside of the stele (core of xylem and phloem) lies the endodermis. This acts as a barrier to unwanted materials flowing inwardly through the cortex. Primary roots such as this are short-lived; within a few months they will either die or initiate secondary growth, becoming a perennial woody root. (Photograph by Richard Dickson.)

greatly enhance the effective surface area and absorptive capacity of a root system.

One of the key functions of a fine root is to prevent the tree from accumulating potentially harmful—yet often prevalent—substances in the soil. A common example of this is aluminum, which is one of the most abundant elements in soil, and which can be toxic when in a soluble form. Between the stele (core of xylem and phloem) and the cortex lies an important cell layer, called the endodermis, which allows the fine root to discriminate between beneficial and harmful materials. The radial walls of these cells are impregnated with a plastic-like polymer (called a casparian strip) that acts as a barrier to the movement of water and anything floating in it. Consequently all materials that enter the stele must first cross the endodermal cell membranes, which are very effective filters.

Root Symbioses—Enhancing Nutrient Acquisition

One of the most intriguing aspects of root structure and function is the mutualistic partnership, or symbiosis, that fine roots of trees and virtually all other terrestrial plants form with certain fungi and in many cases bacteria as well. These ancient liaisons have been shown to enhance many facets of root function and appear to be critical for plant survival in most environments. The symbiosis between a fine root and a fungus is called a mycorrhiza (derived from the Greek words for fungus and root) (Figure 4.6). Among the several major types of mycorrhizae, two are commonly found on trees, ecto- and endomycorrhizae. These types involve different taxa of fungi and are readily distinguished from one another by general contrasts in the structure of the fungus–fine root complex. Overall, the chief benefit of this symbiosis for the host tree is an increased ability to scavenge typically scarce nutrients, such as phosphorus and nitrogen, from the soil. Much of the benefit is conferred by the network of gossamer fungal hyphae that radiate from and deliver absorbed nutrients to the mycorrhizal root, often expanding the effective size of the

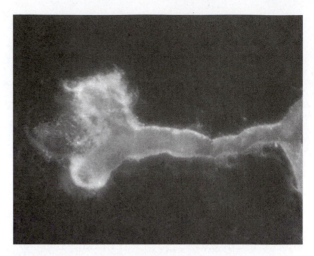

Figure 4.6   A mutualistic partnership, or symbiosis, between terrestrial plants and mycorrhizal fungi has existed for at least 400 million years. Pictured here is a fine root of red pine (*Pinus resinosa*) that has been colonized by an ectomycorrhizal basidiomycete (mushroom fungus). The telltale feature of ectomycorrhizae is the coralloid and/or bifurcated appearance of the root. The "fuzz" around this root is a matrix of fungal hyphae that permeate the soil, greatly enhancing the absorptive surface of the root. (Photograph by Glen Stanosz.)

root system by manyfold. In return, the fungus absorbs food, primarily in the form of sugars, from the host tree root.

Hundreds of tree species belong to an important group of plants that form a symbiosis with nitrogen-fixing bacteria (Figure 4.7). Nitrogen fixation is the energy-demanding process of converting atmospheric nitrogen (N_2) into a form that plants and other organisms can use—namely, ammonium (NH_4^+). (Fertilizer manufacturers currently use a tremendous amount of fossil fuel to accomplish this feat.) Typically, most of the usable nitrogen in an ecosystem is generated through this mechanism by free-living soil bacteria and blue-green algae. However, particularly in environments where soil or climatic factors limit bacterial activity, many plant species have evolved the capability of harboring certain nitrogen-fixing bacteria in

Figure 4.7 Here is yet another root symbiosis, this time involving nitrogen-fixing bacteria. These berry-like structures are root nodules of speckled alder (*Alnus rugosa*), which house actinomycete bacteria. Another group of leguminous tree species form nodules containing *Rhizobia*. Both symbioses reduce (add electrons to) large quantities of nitrogen gas (N_2) and convert it into ammonium (NH_4^+), which is a form that plants can absorb and use.

their roots (and sometimes elsewhere), in specialized structures called nitrogen-fixing nodules.

In these nodules, the host tree provides energy (small carbohydrates derived from sugar) and a favorable environment for the bacteria, and in return it assimilates the NH_4^+ that its prokaryotic guests manufacture. This partnership often allows the host tree to grow relatively well in dry, nutrient-poor and/or cold environments. Indeed, N-fixing species commonly dominate these habitats, where they exert a strong influence on the ecosystem nitrogen cycle.

Flowers, Fruits, and Seeds

Tree reproductive biology plays an important role in the ecology of forests. For example, reproductive strategies, whether sexual (seed-producing) or vegetative, often govern the distributions of different tree species in space and time. Several aspects of

sexual reproduction are critical to this role, including the timing and mode of flowering and pollination, fruit structure and chemistry, as well as seed ripening, dispersal, and germination physiology. Perhaps the most effective way to examine some of these aspects is by highlighting the reproductive characteristics of individual species.

A comparison of the flowers of northern Catalpa (*Catalpa speciosa*) and northern pin oak (*Quercus ellipsoidalis*) illustrates the key connection between flower structure and mode of pollination (Figure 4.8). The flowers of catalpa trees are "complete," in that they possess all the major flower parts, including sepals, petals, pistils, and stamens. Oak, on the other hand, has separate male (staminate) and female (pistillate) flowers, each of which is incomplete—not only because one of the sexes is lacking, but also because petals are absent. Consequently these flowers are fairly inconspicuous.

It turns out that these two species rely on different pollinators. The "showy" flowers of catalpa attract not only our attention, but that of insect pollinators as well. Insects inadvertently transfer pollen from flower to flower in their quest for sugar-rich nectar, which is secreted from tiny nectaries located in various places such as the base of the pistil. In contrast, the relatively drab flowers of oak rely exclusively on wind pollination. Thus they have no need for visual attractants such as brightly colored petals. Rather, the structure of both male and female flowers facilitates wind pollination. The female stigma is located in an exposed position, while the male anthers are born on a long catkin, which flops around in the wind, promoting pollen dispersal.

Although there are numerous exceptions, wind-pollinated species tend to flower in the spring in temperate and boreal forests, when the air is less humid (aiding pollen dispersal) and too cool for many flying insects. On the other hand, many insect-pollinated trees flower in the early summer months, when the climate is generally more favorable for insect activity. Perhaps for similar reasons, wind tends to be the dominant pollination mode in the cooler, drier climes at high latitudes and altitudes, whereas insect pollination is most common in the warm moist tropics.

Figure 4.8 With these flowers, form certainly follows function. The showy corolla (collection of petals) of northern catalpa (*Catalpa speciosa*, top) is an effective attractant for insect pollinators. The relatively drab male catkins and inconspicuous female flowers (in leaf axils) of northern pin oak (*Quercus ellipsoidalis*, bottom) rely instead on wind pollination. Results of the previous year's flowering, a developing acorn, can be seen farther back on the oak twig. Acorns of this and associated species in the red oak subgenus require two growing seasons for full development.

The seasonality of flowering and pollination is not necessarily linked to that of seed ripening and dispersal. For example, many early-flowering species common to upland temperate forests do not disperse their seeds until the fall. In contrast, most bottomland or floodplain hardwoods, such as silver maple (*Acer saccharinum*), not only flower early but also ripen and disperse their seeds in early or midsummer. These seeds germinate immediately, as it is an opportune time for seedling establishment in the newly deposited alluvium on recently flooded sites. Fall is generally not a safe time to germinate in temperate forests, and thus the seeds of most upland trees are dormant at the time of fall dispersal. These dormant seeds must be exposed to a fairly specific set of environmental cues before they germinate. The most common requirement is exposure to a period of near-freezing temperatures (typically 2–5°C), which must last for weeks to months depending on the species. This helps to ensure that seeds do not germinate before the onset of consistently warm temperatures in the spring.

Seeds of angiosperm trees are imbedded in a fruit that develops from the ovary and at times other flower parts. The chemistry and architecture of the fruit has important implications for the manner in which the seed is dispersed. The role of architecture is apparent when one observes the tiny seeds of trembling aspen floating from their capsules with the aid of a parachute-like appendage, or the winged samaras of sugar maple (*Acer saccharum*) whirling away from their parent like helicopter blades. Water is also an important mode of dispersal for many species with floating fruit, such as the coconuts of palms, which can wash up on a beach thousands of kilometers from their parents, and the acorn of overcup oak (*Quercus lyrata*), which has enough cork in its outer wall to buoy a heavy seed. Yet some other propagules are designed to avoid the vagaries of travel. A good example of this is the seed of red mangrove (*Rhizophora mangle*) (Figure 4.9).

Around the world, tree seeds and/or their fruits serve as important dietary staples for a wide array of mammals, birds, insects, amphibians, reptiles, and even fish. A fine example of this is an oak acorn,

Figure 4.9 This dagger-like structure is a red mangrove (*Rhizophora mangle*) seed. The "blade" is really a root radical that grows while the seed is still attached to the tree. This uncommon circumstance, where the seed germinates before dispersal, is called vivipary. The structure of mangrove seed is critical to its establishment in favored habitat, the muddy flats or shallows along tropical or subtropical ocean coasts. The germinant literally drops from the parent and embeds itself firmly in the mud beneath. (Photograph copyright W.H. Freeman and Company.)

which is eaten by everything from an acorn weevil to a chipmunk to a black bear. It is also an important food source in many human cultures. A number of animals hoard or cash acorns, and in the process they are often unwitting agents of acorn dispersal. For example, migrating blue jays will carry an acorn in their crops for hundreds of kilometers, dropping the seed as they attempt to consume it and the accompanying cargo.

Many animals will ingest an entire fruit, such as the drupe of a cherry tree, and subsequently excrete the intact seed after traveling long distances from the parent. In fact, some tree species have become dependent on this process as a means of promoting seed germination. Among the most famous examples of this is the large seed of the Calvaria tree, which lives on the island of Mauritius in the Indian Ocean (1). In order to germinate, the seed's tough outer coat must be softened and cracked. This used to occur when the seed was ingested and excreted by a flightless, turkey-sized bird known as the dodo. Unfortunately, dodos were extirpated from the island during the 19th century. Consequently, this tree species has not regenerated itself for many decades and is now threatened with extinction. Other species have evolved traits that deter fruit and seed predation. During development, for instance, the fleshy fruits of certain tree species, such as persimmon (*Diospyros virginiana*), contain high levels of bitter, mouth-puckering astringents, which disappear when the fruits are ripe. This trait discourages fruit consumption before the seed is mature and ready to be dispersed.

Coping with Environmental Stress

Effect of Seasonal Variation in Climate

Since they have no means of escape, trees and other sessile organisms have evolved strategies to deal with extreme seasonal variation in climate. This capability is most obvious in deciduous forests of temperate, boreal, and montane biomes around the world, where trees drop their leaves in preparation for the annual onset of potentially lethal winter temperatures. By shedding foliage, deciduous trees also avoid excessive buildup of snow or ice on their branches, which can topple the crown. On the other hand, deciduous tree species can be found in dry tropical and subtropical environments where the threat of cold temperatures is minimal. In these biomes, there are regular annual cycles of wet and dry

Sidebar 4.2

Trees don't always rely on sex.

In addition to seed production, various modes of vegetative reproduction are employed by many tree species. Perhaps the most common means of reproducing vegetatively is sprouting from the tree stump. This capability is common among angiosperms and rare among gymnosperms. A new shoot will typically emerge from underneath the bark on the stump of a tree that has been severely damaged or decapitated for any of a number of reasons. The origin of this new shoot is often, but not always, a perennial bud that remained dormant until the stem was killed. A number of angiosperms are also capable of forming new shoots from their root systems. The list of species that root sprout (often referred to as "suckering") includes trembling aspen, American beech (*Fagus grandifolia*), and several other hardwoods. Although relatively few gymnosperms can sprout from the stump or root system, many are capable of yet another trick called layering. Layering is the rooting of a living tree branch that has come into contact with the soil or some other rooting medium, such as a rotting deadfall. Eventually, that branch separates from the parent tree and becomes a whole new entity. Dense, genetically uniform stands of firs, spruces and cedars can form in this manner from just one "founder" tree. Many angiosperm trees are also able to layer, and this trait has been exploited in the vegetative propagation, or cloning, of individual trees with desirable qualities. Stem cuttings are often used to propagate poplars.

---

periods, and accordingly many species will minimize untimely water loss by dropping their foliage before or during the drought.

In many deciduous forests, an aesthetic consequence of leaf senescence and abscission each fall is the brief appearance of brilliant leaf colors. This is a byproduct of an essential recycling process that precedes leaf abandonment. The nitrogen-rich green pigment (chlorophyll) and associated photosynthetic chemicals in leaves are broken down, withdrawn and stored by the tree for use in next year's foliage. Chlorophyll degradation unmasks yellow, orange, and red pigments called carotenoids, which are actually present all summer in the green leaf. Pinks and purples, on the other hand, are anthocyanins produced by foliage largely during senescence.

In seasonally cold climates, leaf senescence is just one of many steps that trees take to prepare for winter. A number of biochemical transformations occur throughout the tree's living tissues, and collectively they allow the tree to become "cold hardy." In evergreen species, such as most of the needle-leaved conifers, cold hardiness develops in foliage as well as other tissues (Figure 4.10). The process of cold hardening may include tissue dehydration, changes in the chemical makeup of cell membranes, increases in cell sugar concentrations, and the appearance of certain dormancy proteins. These changes are quite effective, as is evident in

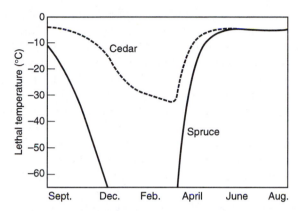

Figure 4.10 Tree species can differ markedly in cold hardiness, which is measured here as the temperature that kills 50% of the needle tissue. The relatively tolerant white spruce (*Picea glauca*) is a boreal forest species in North America. The less tolerant yellow cedar (*Chamaecyparis nootkatensis*) inhabits low-elevation sites along the northwest coast of Canada and Alaska. Note the wide seasonal oscillation in lethal temperature. Tissues are quite vulnerable to frost during the growing season, whereas during mid-winter spruce needles withstand the minimum temperature used in the study, –65°C. (Figure redrawn from Silim and Lavender, 1994, *Can. J. Bot.*, vol. 72, pages 309–316; copyright of NRC Press.)

the recent finding that needles of some evergreen conifers, such as red pine (*Pinus resinosa*), can withstand immersion in liquid nitrogen (–196°C) during the winter (2).

Trees appear to use at least two environmental cues to time the onset not only of winter dormancy but also the subsequent reawakening in the following spring. This timing of behavior is referred to as phenology. Studies have indicated that most temperate and boreal trees enter winter dormancy in response to the combination of shortened day lengths and colder temperatures. These same species break bud in the spring following the onset of warm weather. However, for temperate species in particular, there is a clever twist in this response. These trees require a period of chilling (exposure to near-freezing temperatures) before they will respond to spring warming. Just as it does in the

case of seeds, this prechilling requirement, which varies in duration from 30–120 days, prevents a tree from being fooled by spells of warm winter weather and waking up too early.

Effect of Chronic Resource Shortages

In order to persist in many ecosystems, trees and other plants must make a living in the presence of chronic shortages in resources such as light or nutrients. Tree species vary considerably in their ability to tolerate these shortfalls, and that variation leads to the differentiation of species niches (suitable positions) along environmental gradients. The litany of acclimations (short-term adjustments by individuals) and adaptations (evolutionary changes in populations) to resource limitation is too large to explore here. Instead, we will focus on the ways in which trees cope with a common stress, the minimal light availability often endured by seedlings and saplings (and mature individuals of certain species) in the forest understory. As for acclimation, most tree species exhibit light-dependent plasticity in leaf structural and biochemical properties, and this plasticity allows the tree to construct leaves that maximize photosynthetic efficiency in a given light environment (Figure 4.11). However, because both shade-tolerant and -intolerant species possess this capability, it does not afford much insight into the true nature of shade tolerance.

The amount of light reaching the regeneration layer in an undisturbed forest is typically less than 5 percent of that in an open habitat. Differences among tree species in the ability to tolerate this level of shading create the driving force for forest succession. Generally, fast-growing, shade-intolerant species, such as tulip poplar (*Liriodendron tulipifera*), are the first to colonize and dominate a site following disturbance. However, largely because of their intolerance, these early-successional species do not regenerate under themselves. Instead, they are gradually replaced by slower-growing, shade-tolerant species, such as sugar maple. While this sequence of events is predictable, the underlying physiological basis remains somewhat of an

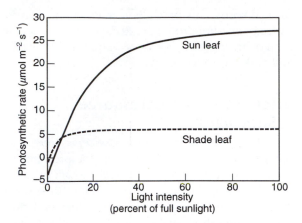

Figure 4.11 Response of leaf photosynthesis to variation in light intensity. Examples shown are leaves that have developed in sun and shade. Compared to sun leaves, shade leaves are thinner and have less photosynthetic machinery per unit leaf area. Correspondingly, they have a lower photosynthetic capacity and rate of dark respiration (when light intensity is 0). These traits allow shade leaves to be more photosynthetically efficient in low light (less than 5% of full light in this example).

enigma. Despite a considerable amount of research, there is no consensus as to why seedlings and saplings of one species are necessarily more tolerant of shade than those of another.

One prevailing hypothesis is that persistence in shade is linked with the ability to conserve valuable resources, especially carbohydrate reserves. Starch is one form of reserve that is commonly stored in trees and is available for use when photosynthesis cannot meet the demand for energy or building materials. This circumstance is likely the rule rather than the exception in dimly lit understories. Intolerant species may not maintain adequate carbohydrate reserves for two reasons. First, because they are geared for rapid growth, intolerants tend to allocate most of the photosynthate they earn to new tissue construction in lieu of reserve accumulation.

Second, and of equal importance, intolerants tend to have higher rates of dark respiration than

do tolerant species. Whereas photosynthesis utilizes light energy to make sugar, dark respiration (operating in the absence of light) generates usable chemical energy, called ATP, by breaking down a portion of that same sugar. (The chemical formula describing respiration is $CH_2O + O_2 \rightarrow ATP + CO_2 + H_2O$, which mirrors that of photosynthesis.) This catabolism (enzymatic breakdown) occurs in all living tissues and is essential because ATP powers the tree's biochemical machinery. But, high rates of respiration can deplete sugar supplies and ultimately the starch reserves from which they originate. Overall, there is an intriguing correspondence between tolerance of shade and other chronic stresses, inherently slow growth, and low rates of tissue metabolism. But the mechanistic underpinnings of this relationship remain elusive.

Effect of Variation in Resource Availability

Trees must also endure stochastic and often life-threatening variation in the availability of resources, especially water. Drought is common to most forest ecosystems around the world, and excesses of water are also problematic, particularly in lowland or flood plain forests. Trees possess a number of attributes that allow them to survive drought and flooding, and some species are much better than others at coping with water stress. Indeed these differences constitute much of the basis for the presence or absence of a given species in a particular ecosystem, and for the broad patterns of vegetation we see at the biome and continental scales.

Scientists that study drought adaptations distinguish between two general resistance strategies, drought avoidance versus drought tolerance. With few exceptions, trees and other terrestrial plants respond to the onset of soil drying by closing their stomates to conserve existing water supplies. As mentioned previously, this response originates in the root system. When the surface soil begins to dry, fine roots in that soil manufacture a small chemical messenger called abscisic acid. This hormone travels to the leaves through the transpiration stream, whereupon it triggers a set of biochemical

Sidebar 4.3

Trees can supply water to the forest.

It turns out that the role of trees in forest hydrology is not always confined to water use (evapotranspiration). Recent studies (3, 4) have revealed the importance of certain tree species as suppliers of water to the forest ecosystem. For instance, the architecture of needles, branches, and crowns of coastal redwood trees in California creates an effective collector of fog and mist, which then drips to the forest floor. Calculations of ecosystem water budgets indicate that this process is responsible for as much as 30 percent of the water input to the soil. Equally noteworthy is the phenomenon of hydraulic lift carried out by deep-rooted tree species. In this case, trees with taproots that penetrate the groundwater table are capable not only of absorbing that deep water supply, but also of

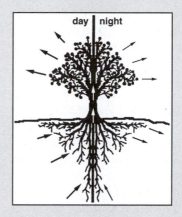

sharing it with less deeply rooted species. The mechanism of hydraulic lift works as follows: The water tension that forms during leaf transpiration allows the tree to pull groundwater through its taproot up into the tree crown (shown at right). However, especially when the surface soil of a forest is dry, some of that groundwater is pulled out of the tree's surface roots at night by the strong water tension in the soil. It is thought that during drought, this mechanism may facilitate the survival of understory herbs and shrubs located near these deeply rooted "nurse" trees.

---

events that lead to stomatal closure. The importance of this nearly ubiquitous response has been highlighted in studies of certain genotypes of black cottonwood (*Populus trichocarpa*) that do not close their stomates in response to soil water depletion. Needless to say, these trees perish during drought and thus are confined to riparian and other habitats where water is continuously in ample supply.

Perhaps the next most common characteristic is structural in nature. Many species effectively avoid internal drought (maintain adequate tissue water content) by constructing a deep-running taproot to access the ground water supply, which during drought may lie many meters below the soil surface. Species that are adapted to inherently dry

(xeric) ecosystems, such as jack pine (*Pinus banksiana*), have these deeply penetrating taproot systems. Some species from these environments are also capable of competing for scarce water through a mechanism known as "osmotic adjustment." In essence, soil drying induces these trees to accumulate unusually high amounts of sugars and other organic solutes in their living tissues. This buildup creates a large osmotic force (like that used in phloem functioning), which allows the tree to absorb (and retain) the scarce supplies of tightly held water in dry soil.

Ultimately, if drought persists there will be no way for most trees to avoid eventual dehydration. It is at this point that many species will succumb.

A few, however, possess the seemingly miraculous ability to tolerate tissue desiccation. In these cases, the cells of living tissues enter a sort of dormancy, which entails a number of membrane alterations and other biochemical changes that allow them to retain their integrity until adequate levels of moisture return. The most remarkable examples of this capability are found not in trees but in certain ferns and mosses. These plants are often referred to as "resurrection plants," because they can withstand extended dry periods, in which their tissue water contents equilibrate with that of the atmosphere, and quickly regain their original vigor following re-watering.

The ability of certain tree species to endure prolonged periods of flooding is another matter entirely. Several serious problems arise when the roots and lower stems (and at times the crown as well) are inundated for more than a few days. The most critical of these is a shortage of oxygen (O_2), the concentration of which is quite low in water as opposed to an aerated soil. A lack of O_2, known as anoxia, impairs the metabolism of plant cells and eventually kills them. But trees and other plants have a few mechanisms that delay this fate, the most important being fermentation. One might recognize this as the process used to generate ethanol (an alcohol), and that is precisely what happens in an anoxic plant cell. Fermentation is an alternative type of respiration that requires no O_2, and under anoxia it maintains a certain, albeit minimal, level of metabolism (ATP production).

This shift in metabolism is not, however, a long-term solution, and trees that survive protracted inundation undergo a number of additional changes, including the production of hypertrophied lenticels and aerenchyma in stems and root systems (Figure 4.12). These modifications can greatly enhance the diffusion of O_2 from aerial portions of the tree to the flooded roots. The development of adventitious roots is also a common flood response (Figure 4.12). These new fine roots often form on the tree stem near the water surface, presumably so that they have access to enough O_2 to allow for normal functioning. There is currently no clear understanding as to why some species, such as river birch

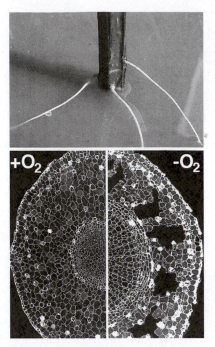

Figure 4.12 Trees that endure prolonged flooding will typically produce adventitious roots and hypertrophied lenticels (upper photo) at or near the water line on the stem. The lenticels look like little cotton balls dotting the stem. Adventitious roots, which help the tree restore its water and nutrient uptake, often have an altered structure that includes aerenchyma (lower-right photo of root cross-section), large openings in the cortex that facilitate oxygen transport to the root. (Lower images provided by Richard Dickson.)

(*Betula nigra*) can make these necessary changes while others, such as the closely related paper birch (*Betula papyrifera*), cannot. About all that appears certain is that the origin of this difference lies primarily within the root system.

Global Issues in Forest Ecophysiology

Effect of Anticipated Global Warming

At the outset of this chapter, I cited forest response to global change as one of the prominent contemporary issues addressed by forest ecophysiologists. Global change embodies two related environmental phenomena, changes in climate and atmospheric chemistry. The two are closely linked because climate is governed in part by atmospheric chemistry and vice versa. Atmospheric scientists have been utilizing global circulation models (GCMs) to derive estimates of future climates, and such calculations are influenced strongly by current and predicted future increases in atmospheric concentrations of "greenhouse gases" such as CO_2 and methane (CH_4). These and other atmospheric constituents are effective absorbers of infrared radiation, or heat, that would otherwise escape from the earth's atmosphere.

Depending primarily on future patterns of human behavior (e.g., fossil fuel consumption, land use), concentrations of CO_2 may nearly double during the 21st century (from 0.037% to ~0.07%). Consequently, the global mean for surface temperature could rise by as much as 3°C (5). GCM output also indicates that warming might be most pronounced at higher latitudes and during the winter rather than summer (in the Northern Hemisphere).

One of the charges to physiological ecologists is to generate credible predictions regarding the impact of these dynamics on the world's forests. However, the challenge of forecasting these consequences is daunting in its complexity. First of all, the effects of warming will be mediated through changes in the metabolism not only of trees, but of all life forms. Also, the nature of this change will vary depending on the manner in which climate warming is manifested. For example, a rise in the annual average for surface temperature can be brought about by a variety of changes in temperature patterns, including increases in the minimum or maximum temperatures during either the summer or winter. That these different scenarios have varying implications becomes apparent when we begin exploring the possible effects of climate warming on the spatial distribution of individual tree species and forest communities around the world. A basic assumption in ecology is that the geographic range of most plant species is governed primarily by climate and soil characteristics. In light of this,

and given that the predicted magnitude of warming is equivalent to shifting isotherms (imaginary lines connecting areas with the same average temperature) by 300–400 kilometers northward, it appears likely that warming will lead to widespread species migrations.

The U.S. Forest Service has recently published some provocative forecasts (6) of possible tree species migrations in North America (Figure 4.13). In the northern United States, they include a mass exodus of keystone northern species and an invasion by southerners. But how credible are such predictions? As with any modeling effort, they are only as good as their underlying assumptions. In this case it is fair to question the presumed link between a species' current geographic and climatic boundaries.

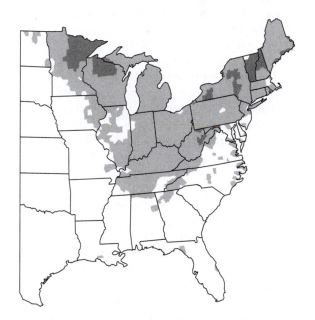

Figure 4.13 Recent predictions by scientists from the U.S. Forest Service (6) indicate that the anticipated extent of climate warming could lead to long-distance, northward migrations by certain tree species in North America. Illustrated here is the potential response of sugar maple. The light shade represents its current range, while the dark areas represent the overlap between current and predicted future ranges. (Illustration courtesy of the U.S. Forest Service.)

In fact, there are many instances where a given tree species thrives in areas where conditions are quite different from those associated with its native range. In other words, there is no certainty that a species' realized niche (the range of habitats in which it is found) matches its fundamental niche (the range of habitats that it can colonize). Moreover, there are few, if any, tree or other plant species for which scientists have identified the specific suite of environmental factors defining their fundamental niches. Further complicating this issue is the fact that these environmental factors are biotic as well as abiotic, and the former, including insects and fungi, may be very sensitive to changes in climate.

What effects will climate warming have on forest growth? Once again this is a complex issue requiring consideration of all facets of tree metabolism. Initially, it is probably most useful to focus on the balance between photosynthesis and its chief counterpart, dark respiration (Figure 4.14). Because enzymes carry out key steps in photosynthesis and dark respiration, the rate at which both processes occur is inherently sensitive to temperature. Yet, at least under current atmospheric conditions, dark respiration is relatively more responsive than photosynthesis. The net result is that increases in temperature tend to stimulate dark respiration more than photosynthesis, and thus lessen the amount of sugar produced per unit sugar consumed in fuel production. That balance equates with growth (biomass accumulation), which accordingly may decrease in response to higher growing season temperatures.

Alternatively, the most important consequence of climate warming may be an increase in the length of the growing season. Interestingly, there is a growing body of evidence, based largely on plant and animal phenologies, indicating that this is already happening (7). Such a trend would simply increase the annual duration of photosynthetic activity and growth by trees. Support for this prediction is found in a comparison of annual tree growth along latitudinal gradients in the midwestern United States. (For example, both the length of the growing season and annual rate of tree growth in Mississippi are at least twice those in Minnesota.) The upshot

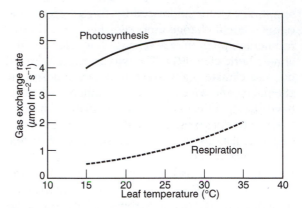

Figure 4.14 Comparison of the sensitivities of leaf photosynthesis and dark respiration to variation in leaf temperature. Rates are expressed in terms of CO_2 influx or efflux per unit leaf area per second. The example shown is a leaf from a sugar maple sapling. Under current levels of atmospheric CO_2, photosynthesis is not very responsive to changes in temperature between 20°C and 30°C. In contrast, dark respiration roughly doubles for every 10°C increase in temperature.

of all this is that there is much to be learned before the scientific community can confidently embrace any broad-scale prediction of global warming impact on forest structure or function.

Effect of Changes in Atmospheric Chemistry

The potential influences of fossil fuel combustion on forests are not restricted to alterations of global climate. Based on a wealth of evidence from laboratory and field experiments, along with some alarming trends in forest health, it appears that our emissions of CO_2 and a suite of other atmospheric pollutants may already be having direct, widespread impacts on forests and other ecosystems, especially in the Northern Hemisphere.

The burning of fossil fuels or any other organic matter results in the volatilization (conversion to gaseous forms) not only of carbon, but several other elements, including nitrogen and sulfur. These gases (mostly oxides of N, C, and S) are considered to be primary pollutants because we emit them into the atmosphere. Ironically, they do not necessarily pose a direct threat to forests, at least in the concentrations at which they presently occur. Rather, it is their subsequent conversion into secondary pollutants, namely ozone (O_3) and nitric and sulfuric acids (HNO_3, H_2SO_4), that generally causes the most concern. The latter two are constituents of acid precipitation ("acid rain"), which has been the focus of much public attention in recent decades. This stems primarily from its postulated (but not necessarily proven) role in the widespread decline in health of high-elevation conifer forests in Europe and North America that first caught the attention of the media during the 1970s.

Nitric and sulfuric acids form in the atmosphere when nitrogen dioxide (NO_2) and sulfur dioxide (SO_2) are oxidized (altered by chemical interaction with oxygen) and subsequently combined with water vapor. These acids are carried aloft in clouds and eventually deposited on the earth's surface as precipitation (rain, snow, or, especially at high elevations, fog). The acidity of this precipitation, which is expressed in terms of pH ($-\log_{10}$ of solution H^+ concentration), varies markedly among regions and elevations. For example, in pristine areas remote from major pollution sources, rain pH is about 5.6, whereas in industrialized regions of North America and Europe, rain pH often falls below 4.5. Within these regions, the extremes of exposure occur at high elevations, where clouds with a pH as low as that of vinegar (pH = 3.3) can envelop the vegetation.

Studies have revealed numerous potential threats to forests posed by chronic exposure to acid precipitation. These are typically separated into two major types, direct and indirect. Direct effects occur as a result of acid deposition on the forest canopy, and the possible consequences include destruction of leaf cuticles (waxy protective coverings), leaching of nutrients (especially potassium) from foliage, and disruption of pollination. There are potential benefits as well, including a direct fertilization of tree foliage with the essential elements N and S, when nitric and sulfuric acids are absorbed through leaf stomates.

While these impacts could be important in certain ecosystems, it is the group of indirect effects, resulting from acid deposition to the forest soil, which may prove to be most damaging in the long run. Several key properties of forest soils are sensitive to acidity and to balances of elements such as N and S. Inputs of acidity per se can accelerate leaching of valuable base cations (such as K, Mg, and Ca) from the soil profile, inhibit microbial activity (and thus nutrient cycling) and increase the solubility of toxic compounds, such as aluminum, that are naturally abundant but mostly inert in soil clay fractions. Once again, however, it is worth noting that some indirect effects, such as soil N fertilization, may be beneficial. However, even this benefit has a downside. There is increasing concern that chronically high rates of N deposition will cause detrimental nutrient imbalances in many forests, which may result in declining tree health, shifts in species composition, and disruption of ecosystem nutrient cycling. This postulated threat, coined the "nitrogen saturation hypothesis," has received much attention in the eastern United States (8).

The overall concern surrounding O_3 can be somewhat confusing, in that it involves both shortage and excess. Part of the earth's stratosphere (upper atmosphere) contains relatively high concentrations of O_3, which forms an effective barrier to much of the harmful ultraviolet light that would would otherwise strike the earth's surface (O_3 absorbs ultraviolet radiation with wavelengths between 250 and 320 nanometers). High intensities of ultraviolet radiation threaten all life forms. It appears that "ozone holes," areas of dangerously low stratospheric O_3 concentration, have been enlarging during the last few decades, perhaps because of our use and release of chlorofluorocarbons into the atmosphere.

On the other hand, concentrations of O_3 in the troposphere (~ lower ten kilometers above Earth's surface) are too high in many regions. The extra O_3, which is a potent oxidant, is produced through a complex chemical interaction among oxides of nitrogen (e.g., NO_2), oxygen and volatile organic compounds (primary pollutants resulting from incomplete fuel combustion). Notably, the process is catalyzed by ultraviolet radiation, and thus the rate of O_3 production in the troposphere is accelerated when it is sunny. Although the problem arises chiefly in urban and industrial areas, it is not confined to them; transportation, power generation, and industry pump the air full of O_3 precursors, and, while O_3 is accumulating, the polluted air mass flows into rural areas, over O_3-sensitive croplands and forests.

The threat that O_3 poses to trees and other vegetation is essentially the same as that faced by all organisms; O_3 is a strong oxidant, and as such it can damage and destroy the living tissues with which it comes in contact. (For that reason, O_3 is used to kill microbes in some municipal water supplies.) In forests, it is the canopy foliage that normally bears the brunt of this assault. Correspondingly, forest canopies are excellent "filters" of O_3 and other gaseous or particulate pollution in the atmosphere. Leaves are vulnerable to O_3 primarily because of their stomates, through which O_3 can diffuse and subsequently damage the leaf interior. One may recall that the interior, or mesophyll, houses photosynthetic machinery. Hence a loss of photosynthetic capacity is often the first functional symptom of O_3 exposure. Eventually, continued exposure will cause the death of leaf mesophyll cells, and it is at this point that O_3 damage becomes visually apparent (Figure 4.15).

Through its inhibiting effects on photosynthesis, O_3 exposure can cause large losses in growth and vigor, and thus predispose trees to other biotic and abiotic stresses such as fungal pathogens, high temperatures, and other forms of pollution. Also, it doesn't take much O_3 to cause trouble. Based on controlled laboratory and field exposures, these problems can arise when trees are chronically exposed to atmospheric concentrations of O_3 exceeding 50–60 ppb (parts per billion). In many areas of the eastern United States, concentrations commonly rise much higher than that threshold on sunny days during the growing season. Although less common, O_3 levels routinely exceed 100 ppb in some areas, and these episodes can result in acute damage to foliage.

As mentioned earlier, not all atmospheric pollution necessarily has negative consequences for

Figure 4.15 Necrotic spots on the upper surface of this trembling aspen (*Populus tremuloides*) leaf resulted from chronic exposure to moderately high ozone (O_3) concentrations (e.g., 60 ppb).

forests. For example, the gas emitted in greatest quantity, CO_2, is a primary substrate in the dark reactions of photosynthesis. Thus the recent and anticipated future increases in atmospheric CO_2 concentrations are likely to stimulate photosynthesis and growth in most terrestrial plant species. However, by what magnitude will growth be stimulated? This is a critical uncertainty in predictions of future climate (based on global circulation models), because the overall increase in atmospheric CO_2, a pivotal greenhouse gas, may be tempered substantially by the increased absorption of CO_2, and subsequent incorporation into wood, by the world's forests. This issue is viewed by the U.S. government to be sufficiently important to warrant considerable investment in research on forest responses to atmospheric CO_2 enrichment. As a result, three FACE (free-air CO_2 enrichment) facilities have been constructed in the eastern United States specifically to monitor the long-term behavior of tree stands exposed to CO_2-enriched atmospheres (Figure 4.16).

Potential Impacts of Atmospheric Pollution

To answer this question, one has only to fly over any of the infamous ore processors in North America. Consider, for instance, the large iron sinterer near Wawa, Ontario. Directly downwind from its smokestack lies a zone that is essentially denuded of vegetation. Beyond that one can see concentric bands of improving forest health and vigor as the distance from the stack increases. The total impact of that stack's emissions on its immediate surroundings extends for hundreds of square kilometers. The nearby forest quite clearly is not able to cope with the chronic exposure to a cocktail of sulfuric acid and a host of heavy metals (such as zinc and copper), which together not only kill vegetation, but also leave a legacy of soil toxicity. The impacts of this type of point-source pollution are so obvious that they require little discussion and debate.

It has proven much more difficult, however, to indict atmospheric pollution as a cause of the widespread declines of forest health and vigor that have been observed with increasing frequency during the last several decades. The most notorious of these have occurred in montane spruce forests of Germany (largely Norway spruce, *Picea abies*) and the northeastern United States (primarily red spruce, *Picea rubens*). Beginning in the 1960s, widespread episodes of crown damage, growth loss and mortality have been documented in these forests (9). No one can ignore the disturbing coincidence between these epidemics and high rates of pollutant deposition. As was mentioned previously, high elevations in polluted regions receive especially severe loadings of acid precipitation as well as O_3. Yet, to the dismay of many, decades of careful

---

Sidebar 4.4

Tree species differ in their tolerance of gaseous oxidants.

A survey of trees in urban or other polluted landscapes often reveals a great deal of variation, within as well as among species, in vulnerability to gaseous oxidants such as ozone. Norway maple (*Acer platanoides*), for example, is widely planted in urban settings partly because of its comparative pollution tolerance. Why does the foliage of one species or genotype differ from that of another in pollution tolerance? There are at least two reasons. The first is that leaves of some species do not open their stomates as widely as others (the measure of openness is stomatal conductance). Consequently, leaves with a lower stomatal conductance absorb less of the gaseous pollutant per unit time. The trade-off for this decrease in exposure is an opportunity cost, as leaves with wide-open stomates tend to have higher rates of photosynthesis. However, stomatal behavior is only part of the story. Another mechanism for dealing with gaseous pollution is the maintenance of a large pool of antioxidants and associated enzymes in leaf tissues. Species have been shown to vary considerably in foliar levels of antioxidants, such as ascorbate (vitamin C) and alpha-tocopherol (vitamin E), as well as key enzymes such as superoxide dismutase and glutathione reductase, which together quench the oxidative power of ozone and other gases before they injure vital plant components. We require a constant supply of vitamin C for the same general purpose; however, since we do not produce it, we have to eat vitamin-rich vegetables and fruit.

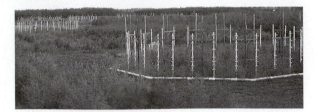

Figure 4.16 In an effort to generate accurate predictions of forest response to atmospheric CO_2 enrichment, scientists have constructed three FACE (free-air CO_2 enrichment) facilities in the eastern U.S. Each facility consists of several large rings of vertical pipes surrounding stands of trees. Based on measures of meteorology and atmospheric chemistry inside the ring, CO_2 is released from vents in a subset of the pipes. Using this approach, stands of trees can be continuously exposed to a target CO_2 concentration with otherwise minimal perturbation of their environment. The rings shown here enclose stands of trembling aspen (*Populus tremuloides*), white birch (*Betula papyrifera*) and sugar maple (*Acer saccharum*) at a facility in northern Wisconsin. (Photograph by Evan McDonald.)

experimentation and monitoring have not resulted in a consensus among scientists regarding the real culprit in these declines.

Some of the most compelling detective work in recent years has been the deciphering and synthesis of an array of data to characterize past trends in climate and atmospheric chemistry. For example, CO_2 concentrations in air bubbles trapped in cores taken from the Greenland Ice Sheet indicate that atmospheric CO_2 levels have risen more than 30 percent since the middle of the 19th century. Correspondingly, there is circumstantial evidence that at least some forests around the world may be growing faster as a result of this "CO_2 fertilization." The evidence exists primarily in the form of tree rings, the concentric layers of wood that a tree will build each year. There is a discipline, called dendrochronology, which studies historical patterns in tree ring widths to draw inferences about past climates. Wide rings usually correspond with growing seasons wherein temperatures and patterns of rainfall are most favorable. In certain cases, steady increases in ring width have occurred during the last several decades in the absence of discernible trends in monitored climatic variables (11). Many scientists implicate rising CO_2 concentration as the only remaining explanation for these growth stimulations.

Concluding Statement—Future Directions in Forest Ecophysiology

After reading this chapter, it should be apparent that some of the most interesting and important questions in forest biology remain largely unresolved. For example, ecophysiologists still do not know exactly why certain tree species are more shade-tolerant than others, and perhaps to the surprise of many, we lack sufficient information to determine how forests will respond to predicted changes in global climate. A variety of new tools are emerging to help us address these issues. Interestingly, these new frontiers promise to further expand the scale of inquiry. Exploration of biological mechanisms at very fine scales is increasingly feasible as new techniques evolve in molecular biology. This has already created new insight in plant physiology. For instance, much information has recently been generated as to how different plant hormones modify a fundamental process underlying all aspects of plant behavior, gene expression and consequent protein metabolism in plant cells. And at the other end of the scale, a number of satellites are now equipped with an array of different electro-optical sensors monitoring reflectance by vegetation in critical portions of the radiation spectrum, such as visible and infrared wavelengths. Increased availability of these remotely sensed data, along with advances in our ability to couple them with particular aspects of tree physiology, hold considerable promise in allowing scientists to monitor forest structure and function at the stand and landscape scales (see Chapter 7 and 12).

References

1. S. A. TEMPLE, *Science, 197*, 885 (1977).

2. M. L. SUTINEN, J. P. PALTA, AND P. B. REICH, *Tree Physiology, 11*, 241 (1992).

3. T. E. DAWSON, *Oecologia, 108*, 273 (1996).

4. T. E. DAWSON, *Oecologia, 117*, 476 (1998).

5. Intergovernmental Panel on Climate Change (IPPC), Climate Change 1995: The Science of Climate Change. J. T. Houghton, et al., eds, Cambridge University Press, 1995.

6. L. R. IVERSON AND A. M. PRASAD, *Ecological Monographs, 68*, 465 (1998).

7. L. HUGHES, *Trends in Ecology and Evolution, 15*, 56 (2000).

8. J. ABER, W. MCDOWELL, K. NADELHOFFER, A. MAGILL, G. BERNTSON, M. KAMAKEA, S. MCNULTY, W. CURRIE, L. RUSTAD, AND I. FERNANDEZ, *BioScience, 48*, 921 (1998).

9. A. H. JOHNSON, *Annual Review of Phytopathology, 30*, 349 (1992).

10. D. R. VANN, G. R. STRIMBECK AND A. H. JOHNSON, *Forest Ecology and Management, 51*, 69 (1992).

11. D. A. GRAYBILL AND S. B. IDSO, *Global Biogeochemical Cycles, 7*, 81 (1993).

Additional Reading

T. T. KOZLOWSKI AND S. G. PALLARDY, *Physiology of Woody Plants*, Second Edition. Academic Press, San Diego, Calif.

H. LAMBERS, F. S. CHAPIN AND T. L. PONS, *Plant Physiological Ecology*. Springer-Verlag, New York, 1998.

P. H. RAVEN, R. F. EVERT, AND S. E. EICHHORN, *Biology of Plants*, Sixth Edition. W. H. Freeman and Company, New York, 1999.

CHAPTER 5

Forest Soils

JAMES G. BOCKHEIM

Forest-soil science is a broad field involving chemistry, physics, geology, forestry, and other disciplines. Because soils have a profound influence on both the composition and productivity of a forest, it is important that persons dealing with the forest ecosystem understand the basic character of soils.

Concept of Forest Soil

There are at least four concepts of the forest soil (1). The forest soil may be viewed as a medium for plant growth. Indeed, soils are important to trees because they offer mechanical support and supply moisture and nutrients. The forest soil differs from the agricultural soil or soils under natural grassland or desert vegetation in that it contains a forest floor, tree roots, and specific organisms whose existence depends solely on the presence of forest vegetation. Soil also has been defined as a natural body with physical, chemical, and biological properties governed by the interaction of five soil-forming factors: initial material (geologic substratum), climate, organisms, and topography, all acting over a period of time. A third (hydrologic) view (see Chapter 16) holds that the forest soil is a vegetated, water-transmitting mantle. Finally, the soil may be recognized as a component of the forest ecosystem where materials are added, transformed, translocated, and lost because of natural cycling mechanisms (ecologic view). Each of these views has value in understanding the role of the soil in forest science.

Properties of Forest Soils

Forest soils may be characterized in terms of their morphological and physical properties, their organic matter and moisture contents, their populations of organisms, and their chemical properties.

Soil Morphology

A *soil profile* is a two-dimensional section or lateral view of a soil excavation. The soil profile is divided into a number of sections termed *soil hori-* *zons*, that are distinct, more or less parallel, genetic layers in the soil (Figure 5.1).

The capital letters O, A, E, B, C, and R represent the master horizons and layers of soils. The forest floor (*O horizon*) is a layer of relatively fresh and partially decomposed organic matter that overlies a series of mineral horizons. The forest floor is important as a "slow-release" source of nutrients, as an energy source for organisms, and as a covering for protecting the soil against runoff, erosion, and temperature extremes. *A horizons* are mineral horizons formed at the surface or below an O

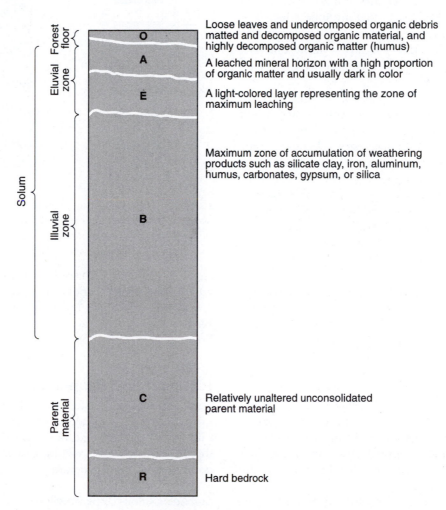

Figure 5.1   A hypothetical soil profile showing the principal soil horizons.

horizon that contain humified organic matter intimately mixed with the mineral fraction or have properties resulting from cultivation or similar kinds of disturbance. *E horizons* are mineral horizons that have lost silicate clay, iron, and aluminum, leaving a concentration of sand and silt particles of quartz or other resistant minerals. *B horizons* contain weathering products, such as silicate clay, iron, aluminum, and humus, that have either been translocated from A, E, or O horizons above or have developed *in situ*. A key property of the B horizon is that all or much of any original rock structure has been obliterated by soil-forming processes. *C horizons* are horizons or layers, excluding hard bedrock, that are little affected by soil-forming processes and lack properties of horizons described earlier. R layers represent hard bedrock that can be investigated only with heavy power equipment.

Lowercase letters are used as suffixes to designate specific kinds of master horizons and layers. For example, Figure 5.2 shows two contrasting soil profiles, along with their horizons, beneath northern hardwoods and red pine in northern Wisconsin. The soil under northern hardwoods is derived from wind-blown, silty sediments (*loess*) over an unsorted, medium-textured glacial till. The soil beneath red pine is derived from stratified, sandy glacial outwash. The profiles differ in at least two respects: (i) the profile featuring northern hardwoods contains a thick A horizon reflecting mixing of organic matter by earthworms, and the profile supporting red pine has a distinct O horizon and no A horizon; and (ii) the soil beneath northern hardwoods has a clay-enriched B horizon, designated as Bt (t = clay accumulation), and the soil under red pine has an iron-enriched B horizon, designated at Bs (s = accumulation of translocated iron and aluminum oxides and hydroxides and organic matter). In *Soil Taxonomy*, these soils beneath northern hardwoods and red pine are designated as an Alfisol and Spodosol, respectively (see section on "Soil Survey and Classification" in this chapter).

An example of a soil profile occurring beneath a northern hardwoods forest in Upper Michigan is

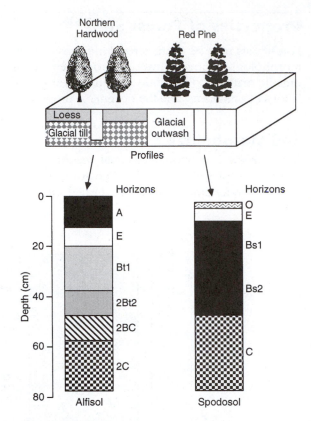

Figure 5.2   Contrasting soil profiles beneath northern hardwoods and red pine in northern Wisconsin.

shown in Figure 5.3. This soil contains a thin O horizon, followed by a dark-colored, organic-enriched A horizon, a bleached E horizon, an iron-enriched Bs horizon, and a relatively unaltered sandy C horizon.

Physical Soil Properties

Soils can be differentiated according to a range of physical properties. These properties are discussed fully in forest soils textbooks (2); therefore, only three such properties will be discussed here: soil color, texture, and structure.

Soil Color   Soils display a wide array of colors. This has been recognized by landscape artists who have

Figure 5.3 A soil profile occurring beneath a northern hardwoods forest in the Upper Peninsula of Michigan. The profile contains a thin forest floor followed by an organic-enriched A horizon, a bleached E horizon, an iron-enriched Bs horizon, and a relatively unaltered sandy C horizon.(Photograph by J. Bockheim).

sieving techniques. After such analyses are completed, particle-size data often are plotted on a soil-textural triangle, as shown in Figure 5.4. Thus, for example, a soil that contains 60 percent sand, 30 percent silt, and 10 percent clay by weight is termed a sandy loam. Texture is important because it influences other soil properties such as structure and aeration, water retention and drainage, ability of the soil to supply nutrients, root penetrability, and seedling emergence.

Sandy forest soils often support pines, hemlocks, scrub oaks, and other trees with low moisture and nutrient requirements. In contrast, silt- and clay-enriched soils usually support trees of high moisture and nutrient requirements, including Douglas fir, maple, hickory, ash, basswood, oak, elm, spruce, fir, tulip poplar, and black walnut. Soil texture is thus an important consideration in reforestation, in selection of silvicultural treatment and system (Chapter 13), and in establishment of forest nurseries.

depicted soil profiles in their paintings. Soil color is dependent upon (i) mineral composition, (ii) organic matter content, and (iii) drainage class, among other factors. For example, red colors are caused by the presence of iron oxides, and native cultures have used red soils to prepare paints. Black or dark brown colors are typical of soils enriched in organic matter. Blue and green colors may exist in soils that are poorly aerated. Soil color may be measured in the field by comparing samples of the soil to standardized soil-color charts.

Soil Texture *Soil texture* refers to the relative proportion of the various mineral particles, such as sand, silt, and clay in the soil. The U.S. Department of Agriculture developed a classification system where the particle-size fraction of sand ranges between 2 and 0.05 millimeters; silt particles range between 0.05 and 0.002 millimeters; and clay particles are less than 0.002 millimeters in diameter. Soil texture may be estimated in the field by trained people by simply feeling the soil in moist and dry states. However, soil texture is measured in the laboratory using sedimentation, centrifugation, and

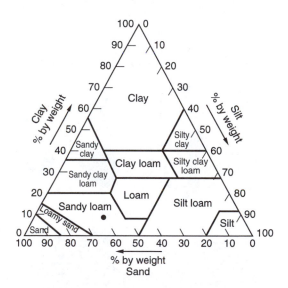

Figure 5.4 A soil textural triangle using the classification scheme of the U.S. Department of Agriculture. A soil with 60 percent sand, 30 percent silt, and 10 percent clay (designated by the point within the triangle) is classified as a sandy loam. (Courtesy of U.S. Department of Agriculture.)

Soil Structure *Soil structure* refers to the arrangement of primary soil particles into secondary units that are characterized on the basis of size, shape, and degree of distinction. Common shapes include prisms, columns, angular or subangular blocks, plates, and granules (Figure 5.5). The major causes for such differences in soil structure are chemical reactions, the presence of organic matter and organisms, and wetting and drying or freezing and thawing cycles. A well-structured soil is able to retain and transmit water and provide nutrients more effectively than a soil lacking structure.

Organic Matter

Organic matter in the forest soil serves several important functions. It improves soil structure by binding mineral grains and increases soil porosity and aeration. In addition, organic matter moderates soil temperature fluctuations, serves as a source of energy for soil microbes, and increases the moisture-holding capacity of forest soils. Upon decomposition, soil organic matter is an important source of plant nutrients.

Most organic matter is added to the forest soil in the form of *litter*, which includes freshly fallen leaves, twigs, stems, bark, cones, and flowers. Many factors influence litter production. Annual production in temperate latitudes is 1000 to 4000 kilograms per hectare. Litter is composed predominantly of cellulose and hemicelluloses (which are carbohydrates), lignins, proteins, and tannins, the characteristics of which are treated in more detail in Chapter 20. Many nutrient elements are supplied by litter, including calcium, nitrogen, potassium, and magnesium, in descending order of abundance.

Once litter reaches the forest floor, a host of macro- and microrganisms act on it. As litter is decomposed, carbon dioxide, water, and energy are released. A byproduct of litter decomposition is *humus*, which is a dark mass of complex amorphous organic matter. Organic matter may be produced below ground by the annual turnover of small roots. The organic-matter content of an undisturbed, mature forest soil represents the equilibrium between agencies supplying fresh organic debris and those leading to its decomposition. The ratio of carbon (C) to nitrogen (N) is stable in soils where this equilibrium exists. Whereas the C:N ratio of agricultural soils commonly ranges from 8:1 to 15:1, the ratio is wider in the surface mineral horizon of forest soils, usually 15:1 to 30:1.

Organic matter may be regulated in the forest soil by careful selection of a silvicultural system (i.e., shelterwood versus clearcutting) and of a utilization practice (i.e., harvesting of only the merchantable stem versus the entire aboveground portion of the tree), and by leaving the slash on the ground following pruning or thinning (see Chapter 13). Burning may be prescribed in some areas for release of nutrients from thick, undecomposed humus and slash.

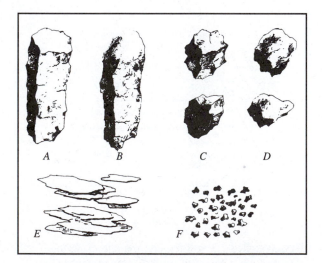

Figure 5.5 Examples of several types of structure commonly found in soils: (A) prismatic; (B) columnar; (C) angular blocky; (D) subangular blocky; (E) platy; (F) granular. (From U.S. Department of Agriculture.)

Soil Water

Moisture supplies in the forest soil are rarely at optimum levels during the growing season, as described in Chapter 4. Studies with forest trees invariably have shown growth responses to changes in soil moisture. Not only does soil water influence the distribution and growth of forest vegetation, but it also acts as a solvent for transporting nutrients to the tree root. Soil-water content influences *soil consistency* (i.e., resistance to deformation or rupture), soil aeration, soil temperature, the degree of microbial activity, the concentration of toxic substances, and the amounts of runoff and soil erosion.

The ability of the soil to retain water is influenced by adhesive and cohesive forces associated with the soil matrix and by attraction of water molecules for ions produced by soluble salts in the soil. Often soil scientists speak of "available" water—the proportion of water in a soil that can be readily absorbed by tree roots. Many factors influence the amount of "available" water in soils, including the amount and frequency of precipitation, runoff, soil storage and leaching, and the demand placed on water by the vegetation.

Water moves in forest soils under saturated and unsaturated conditions and as water vapor. Saturated flow occurs predominantly in old root channels, along living roots, in animal burrows, and in other macropores of the subsoil. Saturated flow also occurs in smaller soil pores in the surface soil during and immediately following heavy rainstorms. Unsaturated flow occurs by capillarity at the upper fringe of the water table, from the soil matrix to the tree root, and in small to medium pores in the soil matrix whenever moisture gradients exist in the available-water range.

A mode of water loss from the soil is through *transpiration*. In a humid temperate environment, trees transpire nearly as much water as will be evaporated from an open body of water. Agricultural crops transpire less than a forest because of lower leaf area indexes and a shorter growing period. However, during the peak period of growth, agricultural crops may consume more water than a forest. A measure of the efficiency of water consumption is the *transpiration ratio*, which is the grams of transpired water required to produce a gram of dry matter. While the transpiration ratio of trees commonly ranges between 150 and 350, the transpiration ratio of agricultural crops generally ranges between 400 and 800. Therefore, trees, particularly conifers, are more efficient in their use of water than are agricultural crops.

Excessive amounts of soil water may be controlled by ditching, ridging, or bedding, mechanical breakup of barriers such as a hardpan, and underplanting with species requiring high amounts of moisture. Wilde (3) described a situation where Trappist monks were able to reduce standing water and the incidence of malaria by planting eucalyptus trees. Flooding and irrigation have been used on a limited scale in areas where water deficiencies exist. Silvicultural treatments, such as thinning and herbicide application to control weed growth, may be an economical way to increase the amount of moisture available to trees in some areas.

Soil Organisms

Soil organisms play an important role in forest soils and tree growth. Soil organisms decompose organic matter and release nutrients for consumption by trees. They incorporate organic matter into the soil, thereby improving soil physical properties, soil moisture, temperature, and aeration. Soil organisms also influence soil profile development, particularly the nature of the forest floor.

Perhaps the most important organisms in the forest soil are the roots of higher plants. These roots do the following: (i) add organic matter to the soil, (ii) stimulate microorganisms via root exudates, (iii) produce organic acids that solubilize certain compounds that are relatively insoluble in pure water, (iv) hold and exchange nutrients within the soil, (v) give off toxic compounds that inhibit the establishment and growth of other plants, (vi) act as an important soil-forming agent, and (vii) protect against soil creep and erosion.

Another group of important soil organisms are *mycorrhizae* ("fungus root"), which are associations, usually symbiotic, of specific fungi with the roots of higher plants. Mycorrhizae increase the absorbing surface area of tree roots, and roots infected with mycorrhizal fungi usually live longer than uninfected roots. Mycorrhizae may also increase the ability of trees to take up nutrients, particularly nitrogen, phosphorus, potassium, calcium, and magnesium. Other types of fungi also are important in forest soils; for example, saprophytic-type fungi decompose forest litter, and parasitic fungi may cause "damping off" or may kill young seedlings by decay of the stem or roots. The influence of certain fungi on growth of forest trees is discussed further in Chapter 8.

Bacteria, microscopic unicellular organisms of different forms, are also important soil organisms. Some types of bacteria break down organic matter and others utilize nitrogen directly from the atmosphere or mutually with higher plants. A variety of other organisms occur in forest soils, such as protozoa, algae, nematodes, earthworms, insects, and small invertebrates. In terms of soil organisms, forest soils tend to contain an abundance of fungi, while agricultural soils often have a greater number of bacteria. This is mainly because fungi are favored by the more acidic forest soils, while bacteria respond more favorably to the mildly acidic or neutral agricultural soils (see section on Soil Reaction).

Chemical Soil Properties

As in the case of physical properties, soils can be differentiated according to a range of chemical properties. Since detailed discussions are provided in forest soils textbooks (2), only three chemical properties will be discussed here: soil reaction, cation-exchange capacity, and essential soil nutrients.

Soil Reaction (pH)   The acidity or alkalinity of a soil solution is measured according to the pH; a pH of less than 7 indicates an acidic solution, while a pH between 7 and 14 indicates an alkaline solution. pH is extremely important in forest soils, because it influences the microbial population of the soil, the availability of phosphorus, calcium, magnesium, and trace elements, and the rate of nitrification—that is, biological oxidation of ammonium to nitrate. Forest soils are often more acidic than grassland or agricultural soils. This is because tree litter commonly is acidic and releases hydrogen ions upon decomposition. In addition, trees

may naturally acidify the soil by taking up and storing in woody tissues calcium, magnesium, and other elements that tend to form bases in the soil. Atmospheric deposition in areas receiving pollution ("acid rain") may also acidify soils. Liming (i.e., replacing hydrogen with calcium or magnesium) commonly is used to raise the pH in agricultural ecosystems. Because of cost limitations, this practice seldomly is used in forest ecosystems, except in forest nurseries. Soil pH may decrease following fertilizer application and increase following burning of litter and slash.

Cation-Exchange Capacity   *Cation exchange* is the ability of the soil to hold and exchange positively charged forms of plant nutrients. These positively charged ions, or cations, are held on "exchange sites" on the surfaces of clay particles and humus. Dominant cations in most forest soils are hydrogen ion (H^+), aluminum (Al^{3+}), calcium (Ca^{2+}), magnesium (Mg^{2+}), potassium (K^+), ammonium (NH_4^+), and sodium (Na^+), in descending order of abundance. Cation-exchange capacity (CEC) is dependent on the amount of organic matter, the amount and types of clays, and pH. Cation-exchange capacity is low in sandy soils but higher in finer-textured soils.

Essential Soil Nutrients   In addition to carbon, hydrogen, and oxygen, which constitute the bulk of the dry matter of plants, thirteen chemical elements are considered essential for normal growth and development of trees. Nitrogen, phosphorus, potassium, calcium, magnesium, and sulfur are absorbed in relatively large amounts by trees and are referred to as *macronutrients*. Iron, manganese, boron, copper, molybdenum, zinc, and chlorine are called trace elements or *micronutrients*, because they are taken up in comparatively small but important quantities. Macro and micronutrients need to be present in the necessary forms, in sufficient quantities, and in the proper balance for normal tree growth.

The sources and available forms of the macro- and micronutrients are shown in Table 5.1. Nitrogen is present largely in the organic form in forest soils. Trees utilize nitrogen in inorganic forms, as ammonium (NH_4^+) or as nitrate (NO_3^-). Bacte-

Table 5.1 Sources and Ionic Forms of Nutrients Taken Up by Trees

Nutrient	Source	Ionic form taken up by tree
	Macronutrients	
Nitrogen	Organic matter (proteins, amino acids)	NH_4^+, NO_3^-
Phosphorus	Organic matter (phytin, nucleic acids), apatite, secondary Ca, Al, Fe phosphates	HPO_4^{2-}, $H_2PO_4^-$
Potassium	Feldspars, phyllosilicates	K^+
Calcium	Feldspars, hornblende, calcite, dolomite	Ca^{2+}
Magnesium	Mica, hornblende, dolomite, serpentinite, phyllosilicates	Mg^{2+}
Sulfur	Organic matter, pyrite, gypsum	SO_4^{2-}
	Micronutrients	
Iron	Oxides, sulfides, silicates	Fe^{2+}, Fe^{3+}
Manganese	Oxides, silicates, carbonates	Mn^{2+}
Boron	Borosilicates, borates	BO_3^{3-}
Copper	Sulfides, hydroxy carbonates	Cu^+, Cu^{2+}
Molybdenum	Sulfides, molybdates	MoO_4^{2-}
Zinc	Sulfides, oxides, silicates	Zn^{2+}
Chlorine	Chlorides	Cl^-

ria are able to convert organic nitrogen to ammonium and nitrate, a series of processes called *nitrogen mineralization*. Recent studies suggest that trees may be able to take up some organic forms of nitrogen.

Phosphorus is present in organic forms and also as secondary inorganic phosphate compounds in combination with calcium, iron, and aluminum; $H_2PO_4^-$ and HPO_4^{2-} are soluble forms taken up by trees. Phosphorus is most available under near-neutral pH conditions.

Potassium, calcium, and magnesium are contributed mainly by weathering of soil minerals. Potassium is present largely in minerals such as micas and orthoclase feldspar. Calcium and magnesium exist in dolomite, olivines, pyroxenes, and amphibole minerals. These chemical elements are available to trees as exchangeable and as water-soluble mono- and divalent cations.

Sulfur is present in organic and mineral forms and can be taken up by trees as exchangeable and as water-soluble sulfate, SO_4^{2-}. In addition, sulfur dioxide (SO_2) gas may be taken up directly by trees through their stomata (see Figure 4.2).

Micronutrients are present in mineral forms and as complexes with organic matter. Acid sandy soils, organic soils, and intensively cropped soils, such as those in forest nurseries, may be depleted in micronutrients.

Nutrient Distribution and Cycling in Forest Ecosystems

The behavior of nutrients in forest ecosystems is characterized in terms of abundance and migration. Nutrient abundance refers to the amount (mass per unit area) of an element in various compartments of the ecosystem. In forest ecosystems, these compartments generally include the atmospheric compartment, the organic compartment, the extractable or exchangeable ("available") soil compartment, and the soil and rock mineral compartment (Figure 5.6).

The distribution of nutrients within forest ecosystems is dependent on climatic zone or ecosystem type, forest type, successional stage, and site quality. Table 5.2 shows the distribution and cycling of

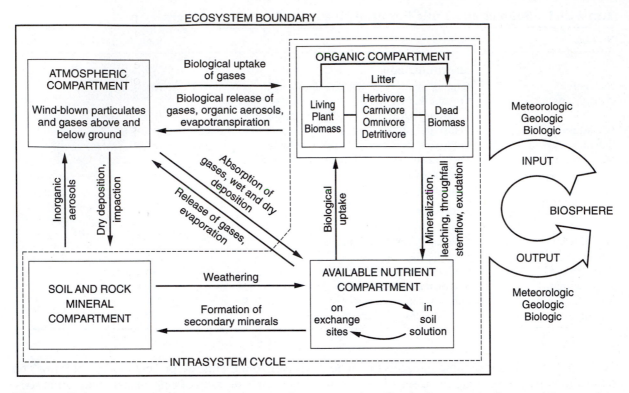

Figure 5.6 Nutrient distribution and cycling in forest ecosystems (from reference 15, Likens and Bormann).

nutrients in a 65-year-old aspen-mixed-hardwood ecosystem in northern Wisconsin. The living vegetation contains 69 percent of the dry matter in the ecosystem and from 11 percent (nitrogen) to 76 percent (potassium) of the ecosystem nutrients. The forest floor contains less than 4 percent of the dry matter and nutrients in the ecosystem.

To understand the behavior of chemical elements in terrestrial ecosystems, a knowledge of nutrient cycling is needed. Three kinds of nutrient cycles have been identified in forest ecosystems (4). The geochemical, or external cycle, refers to the balance between precipitation inputs and streamwater or leaching-loss outputs from the system. The biogeochemical cycle refers to the circulation of nutrients between the vegetation and soil compartments. The biochemical, or internal cycle, encompasses the translocation of nutrients within individual trees. To understand these cycles, meas-

urements of inputs, transfers, transformations, and outputs of chemical elements are necessary.

Atmospheric deposition is the major source (input) of nutrients in forest ecosystems, in the form of liquids (rain, fog, etc.), solids (dust), and gases. An additional input in the case of nitrogen is N fixation by free-living or symbiotic (rhizospheric) organisms. In managed forest ecosystems, chemicals may be applied as fertilizers, lime, and other additives.

There are five ways in which nutrients are lost from forest ecosystems: erosion, runoff, drainage beyond the rooting zone (leaching), gaseous losses, and product removal. Erosion and runoff contribute minimal nutrient losses in undisturbed or well-managed forest ecosystems. Gaseous losses occur primarily with regard to nitrogen in the form of ammonia volatilization and denitrification. The major source of nutrient loss in unmanaged forest ecosystems is leaching beyond the rooting zone (i.e., streamwater output.) For example, the aspen-mixed hardwood ecosystem lost between 0.047 kg/ha/yr (nitrogen) and 2.5 kg/ha/yr (calcium) because of leaching (Table 5.2). In managed forest ecosystems, product removal may constitute a major loss of nutrients. For example, if the aboveground biomass (all but roots) were to be removed in the example from northern Wisconsin (Table 5.2), 818 kg/ha of Ca and 329 kg/ha of N would be removed from the site, averaging 12 and 5.1 kg/ha/yr for Ca and N, respectively (i.e., above-

ground vegetation nutrient pool, divided by stand age), which exceeds the annual leaching losses for these elements.

Nutrient transfers involve movement from one compartment to another. For example, litterfall is the primary pathway by which most elements are returned to the forest floor (Table 5.2). Throughfall (the solution that passes through the forest canopy) and stemflow (the solution that moves along the bole of the tree) may return large proportions of the potassium and sulfur taken up by trees (Table 5.2).

Table 5.2 Distribution and Cycling of Nutrients in a 65-year-old Aspen–mixed Hardwood-Spodosol Ecosystem in Northern Wisconsin

Compartment or Flux	Organic Matter	N	P	K	Ca	Mg	S
Nutrient distribution	**mg/ha**			**kg/ha**			
Vegetation							
Roots	20	70	17	77	190	24	10
Bolewood	124	97	13	190	160	25	15
Bolebark	24	86	11	83	400	17	8.0
Branches	23	92	14	78	220	17	6.0
Leaves	3.4	54	7.0	26	38	5.0	5.0
Total	194	399	62	454	1008	88	44
Forest Floor	4.1	41	2.9	3.3	62	3.2	3.0
Mineral soil (0–30 cm)	84	3200	100	140	840	110	
Ecosystem total	283	3640	165	597	1910	201	
Nutrient cycling				**kg/ha/yr**			
Inputs							
Precipitation		5.6		2.4	5.2	0.6	4.65
Transfers							
Litterfall	4800	43	6.5	18	75	7.7	5.0
Throughfall + stemflow		3.6		20	10.7	2.0	6.35
Uptake*		59	10	60	126	13	15
Accum. in perennial tissues		26	4.1	25	6.3	5.4	9.4
Transformations							
Mineral weathering**				24	60	5.6	
Net mineralization***		69	1.8	2.4	14	2.0	
Outputs							
Leaching loss		0.047		1.1	2.5	0.8	2.6
Input-output****		5.6		1.3	2.7	-0.2	2.1

*Uptake = return in leaf litterfall + net leaching from canopy + annual accumulation in perennial tissues.

**Mineral weathering = leaching loss output – precipitation input + annual accumulation in perennial tissues of trees.

***Net mineralization = assumes release of 2.5% of mineral soil pool, 0–20 cm.

****Precipitation input – leaching loss output.

Nutrient transformations involve a change in chemical form. For example, mineral weathering releases a large amounts of calcium to the soil solution in northern Wisconsin (Table 5.2). Similarly, mineralization of soil organic matter releases large amounts of nitrogen—that can be taken up by trees.

Forest Soils and Tree Nutrition

Soil-Site Factors Related to Tree Growth

Soil-site evaluation involves the use of soil properties (as discussed earlier in this chapter) and of other site factors, such as topographic and climatic features, to predict tree growth. The ability to predict tree growth is of great value to the forester and for planning in the forest-products industry. To use the method, plots are located in stands representing the range of sites and soils found within a particular region. Measurements of tree growth and soil properties are then taken and correlated using statistical methods. The resulting equations can be used to predict site quality of stands that are heavily cut or too young for traditional site-index measurements.

Soil features important in soil-tree growth studies usually include depth, texture, and drainage (5). Site factors other than soils that are important to tree growth include slope position, orientation (aspect), and steepness. These factors influence soil moisture and temperature relations and the degree of erosion. Elevation and rainfall vary considerably in western North America and influence productivity of western conifers.

Diagnosis and Correction of Nutrient Deficiencies

Three methods are commonly used to diagnose nutrient deficiencies in forest ecosystems: 1) visual tree symptoms, 2) soil analysis, and 3) plant-tissue analysis (2, 6). Visual nutrient-deficiency symptoms include chlorosis and necrosis of foliage, unusual leaf structure, deformation or rosetting of branches,

and tree stunting. Although many of these symptoms are relatively easy to recognize, nutrient-deficiency symptoms of trees may be difficult to isolate from those caused by disease, insects, or other site limitations, such as a moisture deficiency. Thus, it is important to combine visual techniques with soil or plant analysis.

Soil testing involves determining the "available" nutrient content of the soil and relating it to productivity of a particular tree species. Two problems with this technique include: 1) selecting a chemical that will extract that portion of the nutrients available to the plant, and 2) establishing optimum levels of soil nutrients for the various tree species. Soil testing is available through most land-grant universities and from private laboratories.

The third method for identifying nutrient deficiencies is tissue analysis, which is the determination of the nutrient content of a particular plant tissue, usually the foliage, and relating it to visual deficiency symptoms and tree growth.

Nutrient deficiencies may be corrected through the use of fertilizers. Forest fertilization is generally used where the following three conditions exist: 1) forests respond to fertilization with significant increases in growth rates, 2) high demand in the region makes the price of raw wood expensive, and 3) the infrastructure for buying, transporting, and applying fertilizers exists. The practice of forest fertilization is becoming widely used especially in parts of North America. Volume gains from nitrogen average 16 percent to 26 percent in the Pacific Northwest. In a regional study employing nitrogen and phosphorus in a factorial design, volume growth of loblolly pine averaged 25 percent greater for treated than controls (7). Forest fertilization may increase not only fiber yield but also insect and disease resistance and aesthetic quality of the vegetation. However, use of fertilizers in the forest constitutes use of a nonrenewable resource for perpetuating a renewable resource. Fertilization is also expensive and may contribute to environmental pollution when not applied judiciously.

Rate of fertilizer application depends on: 1) initial soil fertility level, 2) tree species, 3) age of stand, and 4) type of fertilizer. The nutrient most commonly applied to forests is nitrogen. Nitrogen is applied at rates of 100 to 400 kilograms per hectare to stands of Douglas fir in the Pacific Northwest and at rates of 5 to 100 kilograms per hectare to pines in southeastern United States. Phosphorus is applied to pines in the southeast at rates of 30 to 100 kilograms per hectare. Fertilizer generally is applied to open land or young plantations using mechanical spreaders. In established stands and those occupying large land areas, aerial application may be used. Municipal and industrial effluents and sludges ("bio-solids") may be applied as a fertilizer substitute in some forested areas.

Soil Survey and Classification

A *soil survey* involves the systematic examination, description, classification, and mapping of soils in a particular area. Mapping of soils requires a knowledge of the interaction of five soil-forming factors: climate, initial material, relief, organisms, and time.

A soil-survey report contains soil maps at scales commonly ranging from 1:10,000 to 1:60,000 and the following information: descriptions, use and management, formation and classification of soils, laboratory data, and general information pertaining to the area. The resulting soil surveys provide the forester with valuable information for planning forest activities. For example, soil surveys can be used to locate roads and landing areas, to match harvesting systems with soil conditions for minimizing site degradation, and to match tree species with soil type during reforestation for increasing yield. These soil surveys also enable the forester to plan silvicultural treatments, such as thinning and fertilization, more efficiently. Finally, soil surveys are useful for planning recreational facilities, for evaluating potential impacts of mining, grazing, and waste disposal, and for predicting water yield and quality in forested areas.

Numerous schemes have been used to classify forest land and to predict site quality. *Multiple-factor systems* have been used extensively especially in western North America (8). These systems differentiate and classify ecologically significant segments of the landscape using landform, soil initial material, forest cover type, and soil taxonomic unit.

Single-factor systems are used to map and/or classify individual components of the ecosystem, such as vegetation or soils. The *habitat system* is an example of a single-factor system and is based on climax plant associations that can be used to predict site/successional relationships and site quality (9).

Soil Taxonomy (10) is an example of a single-factor (soil) system used to classify forest land. There are seven categories of classification in the system: 1) order (broadest category), 2) suborder, 3) great group, 4) subgroup, 5) family, 6) series, and 7) type.

Of the 12 soil orders in *Soil Taxonomy*, four are of particular importance in world forests: Ultisols, Alfisols, Spodosols, and Oxisols. *Ultisols* are forest soils with less than 35 percent of the exchange sites containing calcium, magnesium, potassium, and sodium. These soils occur in areas with moist, warm to tropical climates, with an average annual temperature of more than 8°C. Ultisols contain a yellow E horizon and a reddish, iron and clay-enriched B horizon. These soils support loblolly and shortleaf pine in the southeastern United States and oak-hickory and oak-pine in the south-central United States and tropical rainforest in central South America, equatorial Africa, southeast Asia and Oceania, and eastern Australia.

Alfisols are forest soils with greater than 35 percent of the exchange sites containing calcium, magesium, potassium, and sodium. They contain a gray E horizon and a brown, clay-enriched B horizon. These soils feature oak-hickory in the central United States, northern hardwoods in northern New York, aspen-birch in the northern Great Lakes states, and ponderosa and lodgepole pines in western North America. Alfisols are common in drought-deciduous forest and central broad-leaved forests worldwide (see Chapter 3).

Spodosols contain a grayish E horizon and dark reddish-brown B horizons that are enriched in organic matter and/or iron and aluminum oxides

(Figure 5.3). These soils develop from coarse-textured, acid initial materials under cold humid climates. Major forest cover types are spruce–fir, eastern white pine, and northern hardwoods in New England and eastern Canada, and northern hardwoods and aspen–birch in the Great Lakes region. In southwest Alaska, Spodosols support western hemlock–Sitka spruce, and in Florida poorly drained Spodosols support longleaf and slash pines. Spodosols are common in the taiga of northern Eurasia.

Oxisols are intensively weathered soils enriched in iron oxides and depleted in weatherable minerals. They occur in tropical areas, especially in equatorial South America and Africa.

Forest Soils and Environmental Quality

Forest Health, Sustainability, and Ecosystem Management

With the advent of "Ecosystem Management" (Chapters 6 and 13), a number of terms have arisen that are intended to address the long-term productivity of forest ecosystems. Because of the importance of soils in supplying nutrients to sustain productivity, it is appropriate to consider these terms in this chapter. A healthy forest ecosystem has the following characteristics (11):

- the physical environment, biotic resources, and trophic networks to support productive forests during at least some seral stages;
- resistance to catastrophic change and/or the ability to recover from catastrophic change at the landscape level;
- a functional equilibrium between supply and demand of essential resources (water, nutrients, light, growing space) for major portions of the vegetation; and
- a diversity of seral stages and stand structures that provide habitat for many native species and

all essential ecosystem processes. Basically, forest health is a condition of forest ecosystems that sustains their complexity while providing for human needs.

Forest sustainability is the continued ability of the forest ecosystem to provide a number of valued goods and services and involves 1) intergenerational responsibility; 2) maintenance of ecosystem processes and scales; and 3) use of management practices that reflect ecological conditions (12).

Timber Harvesting and Long-Term Soil Productivity

The Long-Term Soil Productivity (LTSP) program was established to address U.S. National Forest Management Act of 1976 concerns over possible losses in soil productivity on National Forest lands. Following an extensive review of the world's literature on productivity decline, authors of the cooperative LTSP concluded that soil porosity and site organic matter are the key properties most influenced by management and most related to forest health and growth within the constraints of climate and topography (Figure 5.7). The LTSP program follows standard format throughout North America with some modifications for local conditions (13). Steps consist of site selection, pretreatment measurements, treatment installation, and post-treatment measurements. About 50 experiments have been established in major commercial forest types on public and private land in North America. The treatments generally include different levels of organic matter removal and different levels of compaction. Among the important findings to date are those concerning the effects of treatment on soil physical properties affecting site productivity. For example, retaining the forest floor or logging slash keeps soils cooler in the summer and improves plant water availability by reducing evaporative losses. Another key finding is that a slight amount of compaction may actually improve the available water-holding capacity of coarse-textured, sandy soils.

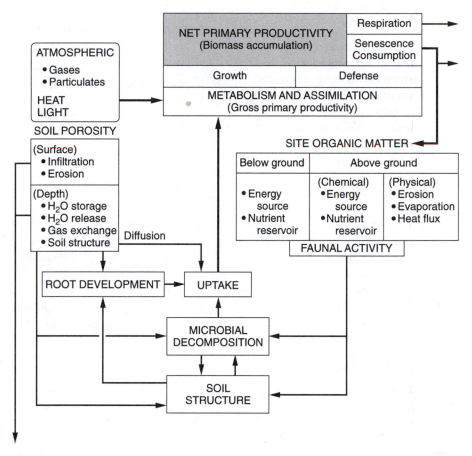

Figure 5.7 Conceptual model of how soil porosity and site organic matter regulate the processes controlling forest growth and site productivity (from reference 13, Powers et al.).

Nutrient Budgets and Forest Management

Nutrient budget and balance sheets enable the forest manager to assess the consequences of alternative management practices on long-term site quality. For example, based on data in Table 5.2, a bolewood harvest in aspen–mixed hardwoods in northern Wisconsin would remove 64 percent of the dry matter in the tree but less than 42 percent of the macronutrients (N, P, K, Ca, Mg, and S) present in the vegetation. A conventional stem harvest (bolewood + bolebark) would remove 76 percent of the dry matter but from 38 percent (P)

to 60 percent (K) of the nutrients in the tree. Therefore, if feasible, leaving the bark along with the branches, foliage and roots would conserve nutrients in this ecosystem. A more accurate estimate of the long-term sustainability of the site can be obtained by comparing the annual needs of the tree ("Accumulation of nutrients in perennial tissues," Table 5.2) with the net gain or loss of nutrients. The net gain or loss is determined by summing "Mineral weathering," "Net mineralization," and "Input-Outputs." Based on this analysis, all of the nutrients are in good supply, except possibly, phosphorus.

Concluding Statement

As the demand for forest products continues to increase, forest soils will be more intensively used. The following forest management practices may have profound effects on soil and water quality: 1) shortened rotations; 2) close utilization; 3) use of fast-growing hybrid species; and 4) mechanical and chemical site preparation.

Industrial foresters have expressed interest in *short-rotation intensive culture* (SRIC), which has also been called fiber farming or "puckerbrushing." This practice uses fast-growing hybrid cuttings that are grown at close spacings and are harvested every few years. This practice may require fertilization to supply an adequate supply of nutrients.

Site preparation refers to soil manipulation techniques designed to 1) rid areas of logging slash, 2) reduce weed competition, 3) prepare a mineral seedbed, 4) reduce compaction or improve drainage, 5) create more favorable microsites for tree planting, and 6) control diseases (14). Site preparation involves use of prescribed burning, chemical applications, mechanical techniques, and combinations of these practices. Where injudiciously applied, these practies may lead to increased erosion and runoff and an overall decline in site quality.

Improper road-building practices are often cited as a major cause of sedimentation in forest environments, particularly in steep mountainous areas. Timber removal may also contribute to sedimentation of streams, lakes, and reservoirs by exposing the surface soil, particularly during skidding and yarding operations (see Chapter 19 for methods of timber harvesting). Skidding of logs with tractors and rubber-wheeled vehicles is more likely to cause soil erosion and mass-wasting than when high-lead cable, skyline cable, balloon, or helicopter systems are employed. Wet-weather logging is especially detrimental to soils and should be avoided if at all possible.

A major concern in recent years has been the potential effects of widespread deforestation in tropical and boreal forests on carbon dioxide accumulation in the atmosphere. The accumulation of CO_2 in the atmosphere has been related to climate warming (i.e., the "greenhouse effect") and is discussed further in Chapter 4, Forest Ecophysiology.

References

1. E. L. STONE, "Soil and man's use of forest land," In *Fourth North American Forest Soils Conf. Proc.*, B. Bernier and C. H. Winget, eds., Laval Univ. Press, Quebec, 1985.

2. R. F. FISHER AND D. BINKLEY, *Ecology and Management of Forest Soils*, John Wiley & Sons, Inc., New York, 2000.

3. S. A. WILDE, *Forest Soils: Their Properties and Relation to Silviculture*, Ronald Press, New York, 1958.

4. SWITZER, G. L. AND L. E. NELSON, *Soil Sci. Soc. Amer. Proc. 36*, 143 (1972).

5. W. H. CARMEAN, *Adv. Agron., 29*, 209 (1975).

6. K. A. ARMSON, *Forest Soils: Properties and Processes*, Univ. of Toronto Press, Canada, (1977).

7. North Carolina State Forest Nutrition Cooperative, 1998: http://www2.ncsu.edu:8010/unity/lockers/project/ncsfnchpg.

8. *Proc. of the Symp. on Forest Land Classification: Experiences, Problems, Perspectives*, J. Bockheim (ed.), Dept. of Soil Science, Univ. of Wisconsin, Madison, 1984.

9. KOTAR, J., J. A. KOVACH, AND C. T. LOCEY, *Field Guide to Forest Habitat Types of Northern Wisconsin.*, Dept. of Forestry, Univ. of Wisconsin, Madison, 1988.

10. U.S. Soil Survey Staff, *Soil Taxonomy: a Basic System of Soil Classification for Making and Interpreting Soil Surveys*, U.S. Dept. Agric., Handbook 436, 1999.

11. KOLB, T. E., M. R. WAGNER, AND W. W. COVINGTON, *J. For. 92(7)*, 7 (1994).

12. TOMAN, M. A. AND P. M. S. ASHTON, *For. Sci., 42*, 366 (1996).

13. POWERS, R. F., D. H. ALBAN, R. E. MILLER, A. E. TIARKS, C. G. WELLS, P. E. AVERS, R. G. CLINE, R. O. FITZGERALD, AND N. S. LOFTUS, JR., *Sustaining site productivity in North American Forests: problems and prospects*, In Sustained Productivity of Forest Soils, Proc. 7th North Amer. For. Soils Conf., Univ. of British Columbia, Vancouver, pp. 49–79, 1995.

14. STEWART, R. C., "Site preparation," In: B. D. Cleary, R. D. Greaves, and R. K. Hermann (eds.), *Regenerat-*

ing Oregon's Forests, Oregon State Univ. and U.S. Dept. of Agric., For. Serv., Pacific Northwest For. & Range Exp. Sta., Portland, Ore.

15. LIKENS, G. E. AND F. H. BORMANN, *Biogeochemistry of a Forested Ecosystem,* Second Edition, Springer–Verlag, New York, 1995.

Website for further information on Forest Soils: http://soilslab.cfr.washington.edu/3-7.

CHAPTER 6

Forest Ecosystem Ecology

STITH T. GOWER

Ecology is the study of the interactions between organisms and the environment. The study of the relationship of a species to the environment is referred to as *autecology*. An ecosystem includes the vegetation, the soil, the organisms, as well as complex interaction of the three components. Forest ecosystem ecology is the study of the interactions between forest vegetation and organisms and the environment. The subdiscipline of ecology that focuses on all organisms and their complex interactions with each other and the environment is referred to as *synecology*.

Foresters must be well versed in both autecology and synecology to manage forests to ensure adequate regeneration, growth, and reproduction of the desirable forest tree species. In essence, forest management, or applied forest ecology, is the application of theoretical forest ecology, including topics such as species dynamics, succession, nutri-

ent cycling, and production ecology, to achieve the forest management objectives. This chapter provides an introduction to the topics of succession, nutrient cycling, and production ecology as they relate to forest management. It is essential to understand how forest ecosystems are affected by natural disturbances and harvesting, because very few forests remain unaffected by humans.

The first section of the chapter focuses on the processes that determine the species distribution in a stand. Tolerance and competition are two key processes that affect species composition. The life history patterns and associated ecological attributes affect the tolerance, and hence competitiveness, of species in a stand. The second section introduces the carbon cycle, of which plant growth, or net primary production, is one component. Plant growth is strongly influenced by the quantity and quality of organic matter in the soil, and in turn, the growth

114

rate of the vegetation influences the quantity and quality of organic matter that is returned to the soil (also see Chapter 5, Forest Soils).

Tree growth is often limited by nutrient availability, which is affected by the amount of organic matter that returns the soil. The third section provides a brief introduction to nutrient cycles. Nutrient inputs, losses, and internal cycling of nutrients are discussed and the strong linkage between the carbon, or organic matter cycle, and nutrient cycles is emphasized.

The fourth section reviews the basic concepts of succession. Forests are not static; species composition, structure and function of forests change in response to internal and external factors. One of the most important external factors is disturbance; particularly, forest harvesting. Forests provide many services to humans, such as wood, and other organisms. The last section of the chapter reviews how forest harvesting affects the long-term sustainability of forests and adjacent aquatic ecosystems.

Forest Tree Species Distribution

Tolerance and Competition

What determines the distribution of species? In Chapter 3, Forest Biomes of the World, you learned that climate, soil, and disturbance regime influence the distribution of the major forest biomes. These same factors influence the distribution of species at the local (within a stand) scale. Tree species are ranked according to their tolerance to varying environmental conditions. Tolerance to light is the ecophysiological characteristic most commonly used to classify tree species. Although the classification of species can be subjective, it has a physiological basis, and is a useful concept to guide forest managers. Table 6.1 summarizes some common forest tree species for different forest regions in the United States and their relative tolerance to light. The physiological basis for the classification is leaf photosynthesis versus light relationship. Figure 6.1 illustrates the relationship

Table 6.1 Examples of Commercially Important Tree Species for Different Forest Regions in the United States that Vary in Shade Tolerance (Adapted from Hocker [1])

Shade Tolerance Class	Forest Region			
	Eastern Deciduous	Lake States	Rocky Mountain	Pacific Northwest
Very Intolerant to Intolerant	pin cherry willow tulip poplar river birch	trembling aspen jack pine tamarack	trembling aspen lodgepole pine ponderosa pine	Douglas fir red alder western larch
Intermediate Tolerant	ash spp. oak spp. American elm sweetgum	basswood ash spp. oaks spp. red maple	blue spruce Douglas fir — —	sugar pine western white pine noble fir giant sequoia
Tolerant to Very Tolerant	sugar maple American beech hickory spp. Eastern hemlock	sugar maple yellow birch eastern hemlock	Englemann spruce subalpine fir	western hemlock Pacific silver fir western red cedar grand fir redwood

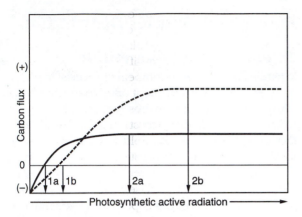

Figure 6.1 Hypothetical response curve illustrating the relationship between net leaf photosynthesis and photosynthetic active radiation, or visible light, for shade-intolerant and shade-tolerant tree species. The light compensation point, or the light intensity at which net carbon reaches zero, is lower for shade tolerant (1a) than shade intolerant (1b) species. Light saturation point, the light intensity at which net leaf photosynthesis no longer increases with increasing light, is greater for shade intolerant (2b) than shade tolerant (2a) species. (solid line—shade tolerant species; dashed line—shade intolerant species)

between net carbon balance and increasing photosynthetic active radiation (PAR)—the wavelengths of light that plants use in photosynthesis—for a shade-intolerant versus shade-tolerant tree for increasing light. The light level at which the leaf carbon balance is zero (photosynthesis equals respiration) is referred to as the *light compensation point* (LCP). The LCP is lower for shade-tolerant than shade-intolerant trees, allowing shade-tolerant plants to maintain a positive carbon budget (photosynthesis exceeds respiration) at much lower light level than shade-intolerant plants. The light level at which photosynthesis no longer increases with increasing light is referred to as the *light saturation point* (LSP). The LSP is greater for shade-intolerant than shade-tolerant tree species, demonstrating that shade-intolerant trees will outgrow shade-tolerant tree in high light environments because they can more fully utilize the higher light levels.

Despite the emphasis placed on the relationship between light availability and plant tolerance, other resources such as water and nutrients affect the ability of plants to compete and survive, and ultimately affect the distribution of plants. Plants range in tolerance to nutrient and water availability, temperature, pollution, and so forth. *Niche* is the physical environment where a species occurs. The *physiological niche* is the environment that a species can tolerate when grown in isolation and is used to infer that species can grow and reproduce successfully (Figure 6.2). Ecological niche is the environment that a species can tolerate when grown with naturally co-occurring or sympatric species. The ecological niche of species A is more restricted than its physiological niche because species B and C are better adapted than species A at edges of the physiological niche of species A. Why are species B and C better adapted than species A at edges of the physiological niche of species A? The answer to this question is not straightforward, but a partial explanation is related to the morphological or physiological adaptations of plants that enable them to more effectively compete for growth-limiting resources. This is the topic of the next section.

Life History Patterns

Numerous classification schemes have been devised to categorize plants based on the ecological niche they commonly occupy. Some classification schemes emphasize successional status, while others emphasize tolerance to light, resource limitations, and so forth. J. Grimes (2) proposed a very useful classification scheme that was based on the general life history patterns of plants. The life history refers to the ecological niche and disturbance regime that plants occupy. The Grime's life history classification scheme recognizes three categories: ruderals, competitors, and stress-tolerants. *Ruderals* are plants that occupy niches with high resource (water, nutrients, and light) availability and frequent disturbance. Many of the invasive weedy plants found along roadside cuts, railroad right-of-ways, and forest tree species that occur in recently disturbed forests are good examples of ruderals.

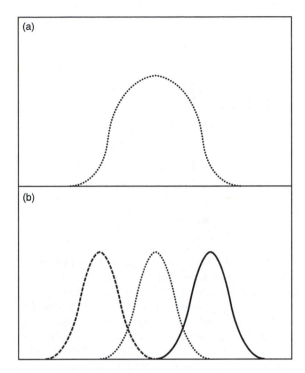

Figure 6.2 Comparison of the physiological niche (a) and ecological niche (b) for three species of varying tolerance to the availability of an essential resource required for plant growth. Note that the physiological niche is always greater than the ecological niche; the unique suite of ecophysiological and structural characteristics make species better competitors for aquiring limiting, but essential, resources for plant growth.

Table 6.2 summarizes some of the general characteristics and tree species of each of the three life history categories. Ruderal plants are characterized by rapid growth rates, prolific reproduction, and high shoot:root ratios. Competitors occupy a niche that experiences less frequent disturbance than ruderals, and competition for resources is high. Many commercially desirable forest tree species fall into this category. Stress-tolerant plants occur in the most resource-limited environments and the disturbance frequency is low. Stress-tolerant species have the slowest growth rates because resource availability is very low. Stress-tolerant species typically have a greater root:shoot ratio than ruderals or competitors to increase uptake of limiting nutrients and water. Competitors have life history characteristics that are intermediate to ruderals and stress-tolerant species.

The unique suite of morphological and physiological characteristics of each of the life history patterns makes each plant species best adapted to different environments. The different life history patterns of commercially valuable trees species require different forest management practices to promote the growth of desirable tree species and retard the growth of unwanted tree or weed species. Ruderal tree species, such as aspen, are more common to early successional forests originating from natural disturbance or timber harvesting. Stress-tolerant tree species are poor competitors in recent clearcut because of their intrinsic slow growth rates and greater allocation of biomass to roots. However, the availability of light, nutrients, and water

Table 6.2 General Life History Characteristics of Ruderal, Competitor, and Stress-tolerant Tree Species

Characteristic	Ruderal	Competitor	Stress-tolerant
Life longevity	short	intermediate	long
Leaf longevity	short	intermediate	long
% NPP allocated to reproduction	large	intermediate	small
Maximum growth potential	rapid	intermediate	slow

Adapted from Table 5-3 in Barbour, Burk, and Pitts (3)

NPP = Net Photosynthetic Productivity

changes during succession. Conversely, ruderals are poorly adapted to harsh environments, such as drought-prone, nutrient-poor soils where stress-tolerant plants occur. The boundaries between the three life history categories are not discrete, but are a continuous gradient. Nonetheless, the classification scheme is useful for categorizing tree species for both ecological and management purposes.

The Carbon Cycle and Forest Growth

The Carbon Cycle

The cycle or budget of elements such as carbon can be described by the size of the various pools, or reservoirs of the elements in the ecosystem, and the fluxes, or rates of movement of the element between the different pools. The carbon, or organic matter, cycle is composed of five major pools and the transfer of carbon among the pools. The five pools are: the atmosphere, forest biomass, animal biomass, microbial biomass, and the various forms of soil organic matter (Figure 6.3). The uptake of carbon dioxide (CO_2) from the atmosphere by the vegetation is referred to as *gross primary production* (arrow #1). The vegetation, or *photoautotrophs*, use the solar radiation (Figure 6.4) to produce their own carbohydrates that are used to build new organic matter (*autotrophs*). A portion of the atmospheric carbon dioxide taken up by the plant is released back to the atmosphere; this process is referred to as autotrophic respiration (arrow #2). *Net primary production*, the net difference between gross primary production and *autotrophic respiration*, is closely related to forest growth. Stated slightly differently, net primary production is the sum of all the new biomass (stem, branches, foliage, roots, mycorrhizae, and reproductive tissues) produced each year. A fraction of the living organic matter dies each year, and returns to the soil surface as detritus (arrow #3). There are millions of fungi and bacteria that derive their energy by decomposing dead organic matter. These organisms are referred to as *heterotrophs* because they are

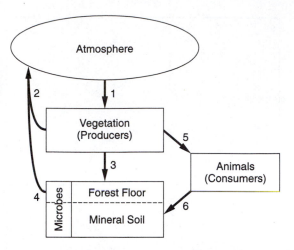

Figure 6.3 Schematic diagram of the carbon cycle. The boxes represent pools, or containers of carbon, while each arrow depicts a transfer of a fraction of carbon between pools. The corresponding names of the numbered fluxes are as follows: 1 = gross primary production (GPP); 2 = autotrophic respiration; 3 = detritus production; 4 = heterotrophic respiration; 5 = herbivory; 6 = animal mortality.

dependent upon other organisms to produce the organic matter that they consume for energy. Carbon dioxide is released back into the atmosphere as heterotrophs decompose the soil organic matter; this process is referred to as *heterotrophic respiration* (arrow #4). The net difference between the total organic matter inputs and loss of organic matter from the soil determines whether the soil organic matter is increasing or decreasing.

Understanding the carbon cycle is important for several reasons. First, an imbalance between the exchange of carbon dioxide between the atmosphere and terrestrial ecosystems increases the concentration of carbon dioxide in the atmosphere. This is important because carbon dioxide is a greenhouse gas and is suspected of being responsible for climate warming as described in Chapter 4, Forest Ecophysiology. Soil organic matter is important because of its large water and nutrient holding capacity. Maintaining the soil organic matter is an essential component of sustainable forest man-

Figure 6.4   Aerial view of a regenerating southern pine forest several years after planting (right). The location of old windrows (left) are still apparent because the nutrients in the windrows and displaced nutrients from the upper soil horizons of the surrounding area stimulated growth. Conversely, the excessive displacement of nutrients that can occur during site preparation appears to have decreased the soil fertility of the areas between the windrows.

agement. Third, the net uptake of carbon dioxide from the atmosphere by the vegetation determines the growth rate of the forest, or the ability of the forest to provide forest products for human use. A more detailed discussion of the factors that influence forest structure and growth, and soil carbon dynamics is discussed next.

Environmental Constraints on Leaf Photosynthesis

There are numerous environmental and biological factors that influence the growth rate of forests, but for simplicity, this chapter focuses on the fundamental factors that influence growth rate of forests. Where appropriate, the reader is referred to other relevant sections in the book that provide more detail. The growth rate of forests is controlled by two major groups of constraints: environmental constraints on leaf-level photosynthesis, and environmental constraints on leaf area index—an important canopy structural characteristic of terrestrial ecosystems.

Photosynthesis is the biochemical process by which carbon dioxide (CO_2) from the atmosphere, and water (H_2O), in the presence of light, are con-

verted to carbohydrates (CH_2O) as described in Chapter 4. Air and soil temperature, solar radiation, vapor pressure deficit (or how dry the air is) and foliage nutrient status are the major environmental factors that affect leaf-level rates of photosynthesis. The climate diagrams presented in Chapter 3 (Forest Biomes of the World) illustrate that the relative importance of the environmental constraints on leaf photosynthesis varies among forest biomes. Liebig's "Law of the Minimum" states that the rate of a process—photosynthesis, for example—is controlled by the most limiting resource. A useful analogy is imaging each stave of a wooden barrel as an environmental constraint (Figure 6.5). The water level in the barrel, or photosynthesis rate, can be only as high as the shortest stave, or the most limiting resource. The precise relationship between each of the above-mentioned environmental variables and leaf photosynthesis varies among species, but a general relationship exists that fits most tree species.

Extreme cold air and soil temperatures restrict photosynthesis; therefore, trees do not grow during the winter periods when temperatures drop below freezing for several days in a row. Photosynthesis increases linearly with temperature above

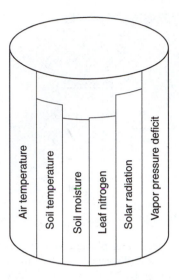

Figure 6.5 Conceptual model of Liebig's Law of the Minimum. The top of the barrel represents the theoretical maximum of a rate—in this case, leaf photosynthesis. However, the maximum rate is determined by the most limiting resource, or the greatest environmental constraint on leaf photosynthesis, which is depicted by the shortest staves in the barrel—soil moisture and leaf nitrogen, in this hypothetical example.

freezing, levels off at some optimum temperature, and declines rapidly if lethal temperatures occur (Figure 6.6a). The optimum temperature for photosynthesis for temperate and boreal tree species ranges from 15 to 20°C, and can be as high as 25°C for some tropical tree species (4). Even if air temperature is above freezing, roots cannot absorb water from frozen soil, making it impossible for trees to replace water lost by transpiration. The growing season, defined as the period of the year when environmental conditions are suitable for trees to grow, of continental boreal forests is reduced by three to four weeks in the spring because the soils remain frozen when all other environmental conditions are suitable for tree growth.

Soil moisture availability, or, more accurately, the internal water status of the plant, limits leaf photosynthesis (Figure 6.6b). The concept of internal

plant water status and pre-dawn xylem water potential as a useful index of plant water status was discussed in Chapter 4 (Forest Ecophysiology). When plants open their stomates to absorb CO_2, water vapor is lost, because the ambient air surrounding the leaf is drier than the near-saturated mesophyll inside the leaf. Extremely hot, dry days cause stomata to close because the water uptake by the roots cannot keep pace with the rapid water loss. The large vapor pressure gradient causes a rapid loss of water from high to low vapor pressure gradient until plants close their stomata. Plants, therefore, must optimize the duration and rate of stomatal conductance to maximize CO_2 uptake and minimize water loss from photosynthesis and transpiration, respectively. When soil moisture is plentiful, plants keep the stomata open for most of the day, but as the soil moisture decreases, plants will keep the stomata open during the early morning and partially or completely close the stomata during midday to avoid large water losses. During extreme droughts, plants experience severe water stress and will close stomata for days until soil moisture is replenished.

Many of the essential elements are required to construct the biochemical constituents involved in photosynthesis. As a result, photosynthesis is positively correlated to nutrient concentration, especially nitrogen over a moderately broad range of leaf nitrogen concentration (Figure 6.6d). Nitrogen is required to construct chlorophyll. Nitrogen is commonly limiting in many forests, and foliage nitrogen concentrations are typically on the linear portion of the curve.

Environmental Constraints on Canopy Structure and Forest Growth

Many of the same environmental constraints that influence photosynthesis at the leaf level also influence stand-level growth of forests by altering the biomass allocation patterns of trees. Trees use the current photosynthate to construct stems, branches, coarse and fine roots (including mycorrhizae, a symbiotic fungus—see Chapter 4), and reproduc-

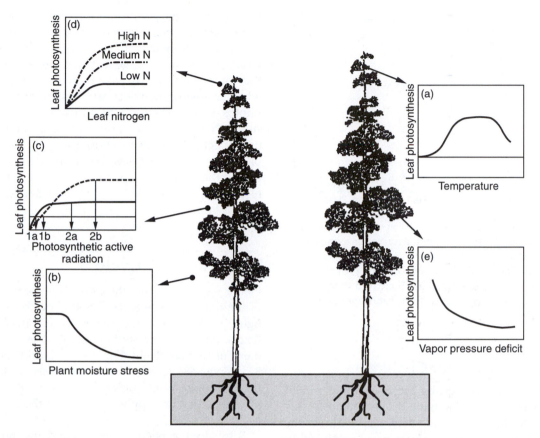

Figure 6.6 Canopy photosynthesis is limited by five major environmental constraints: (a) air and soil temperature, (b) soil moisture, (c) photosynthetic active radiation, (d) leaf nitrogen, and (e) vapor pressure deficit. Each of the environmental constraints has a different influence on leaf photosynthesis.

tive tissues, as well as storage and defense compounds. In general, trees allocate more biomass to construct tissues that will increase the availability of the most limiting resource (5). For example, trees grow fewer fine roots and mycorrhizae and more foliage when they are fertilized, because nutrients are less limiting (Figure 6.7). The increased nutrient availability often stimulates an absolute increase in foliage production. The remarkable process by which trees control the growth of different tissues is not fully understood. However, it appears that the environmental stimuli (such as drought, high vapor pressure deficit, etc.) cause plants to increase or decrease the production of different

plant growth regulators, or chemical compounds, that control the growth of different plant parts.

Water availability also influences the allocation of biomass to trees. As we have seen in Chapter 3, global patterns of precipitation, solar radiation, and temperature vary among the forests biomes of the world. Collectively, these environmental factors influence the water budget, and hence water available for plant uptake (see Chapter 16, Watershed Management).

Figure 6.8 illustrates the strong influence the hydrologic budget has on canopy structure—specifically, leaf area index (LAI)—and the positive relationship between leaf area index and forest

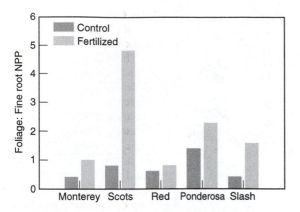

Figure 6.7 The fine root:foliage production ratio for control and fertilized conifer forests growing in contrasting environments. In all cases, fertilization caused a relative shift in priority of new growth of decreased fine root growth and increased foliage growth. Figure was adapted from Landsberg and Gower (5).

growth. The data are from forests along a precipitation gradient caused by the orographic rainfall pattern[1] as moisture from the Pacific Ocean crosses the Coastal Range and then the Cascade Mountains in Oregon. Forests that receive more precipitation have a more favorable site water balance. The average water balance of a forest is determined by the amount of precipitation minus the losses such as evapotranspiration, overland flow, and deep drainage (see Chapter 16). A large leaf area index is beneficial because there is more photosynthetic surface area to absorb carbon dioxide from the atmosphere. The amount of solar radiation absorbed and converted into carbohydrates for tree growth is directly proportional to the leaf area index.

One question that should come to mind then is: Why don't all forests support a large leaf area index to absorb all the solar radiation? The answer to this question can be found by revisiting the carbon budget of forests. Recall that a fraction of gross primary production is used to repair and maintain tissues, such as foliage. Autotrophic respiration costs occur each day regardless of whether the stomates are open and photosynthesis is occurring. In other words, supporting a large leaf area index increases the large carbon cost each day, regardless of whether environmental constraints are prohibiting photosynthesis (Figure 6.6). Consequently, plants support a leaf area index that optimizes the potential for net primary production. Excessive amounts of foliage cause excessive autotrophic respiration costs, while less than optimum amounts of foliage result in an incomplete use of light and canopy photosynthesis.

The Nutrient Cycle

Figure 6.9 summarizes the important components of the nutrient cycle for a hypothetical forest. The figure includes only the major nutrient pools and fluxes. Readers interested in a more detailed treatment of terrestrial nutrient cycles should refer to Schlesinger (8). Most of the processes shown in Figure 6.9 apply to all nutrients, but there are a few processes that are applicable only to the nitrogen cycle.

Why do we need to understand the nutrient cycles of forest? The answer to this question has both an applied and theoretical basis. From an applied or management point of view, it is important to understand how forest management affects soil fertility, because nutrients often limit forest growth. For example, can forests be harvested repeatedly without decreasing the long-term productivity of the site? If so, how frequently can they be harvested without depleting the nutrients in the soil? Also large losses of nutrients from the forest ecosystem into adjacent aquatic ecosystems can severely decrease water quality and threaten human health. Are there some forest types that are more likely to experience greater nutrient losses to groundwater following disturbance? Answers to these questions are needed if forests are to be man-

---

[1] Rainfall patterns in mountainous regions.

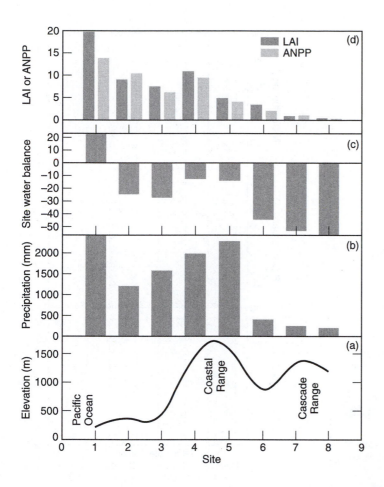

Figure 6.8 Relationship between site water balance, leaf area index (LAI), and forest growth. The data were obtained for forests in Oregon that occur along a pronounced orographic precipitation gradient along the Coastal Range and the further inland Cascade Mountains. Leaf area index is positively correlated to precipitation and available soil water, and in turn, aboveground net primary production (ANPP) is positively correlated to leaf area index. Similar relationships between the hydrologic budget and forest growth have been reported for other forest regions of the world. Data from Grier and Running (6) and Gholz (7).

aged on a sustainable basis. The effects of natural and human disturbance on nutrient cycle are discussed later in the chapter after a general introduction to the nutrient cycle is presented. From a basic point of view, there is great interest in understanding the processes that control nutrient cycling rates and nutrient accumulation in the various components of forest ecosystems.

Nutrient Distribution

Nutrients are generally not distributed equally within forest ecosystems. Figure 6.10 is a graphical illustration of the relative distribution of nitrogen (N), phosphorus (P), and calcium (Ca) in the foliage, wood, and soil (forest floor + mineral soil) for four contrasting forest ecosystems. The soil contains the

greatest fraction (80–99%) of the total nutrient content of forest ecosystems. It is important to note that although a large fraction of the nutrients are in the soil, only a very small percentage of the elements occur in a form that plants can absorb. The distributions of nutrients shown in Figure 6.10 are representative of many forest ecosystems of the world, although there are several notable exceptions. Extremely infertile forests, such as the tropical forests that occur on nutrient poor Oxisols and Spodosols, contain a higher percentage of the total nutrients in the vegetation than the soil.

Nutrient Inputs

Atmospheric deposition and weathering are two primary pathways by which nutrients enter forest

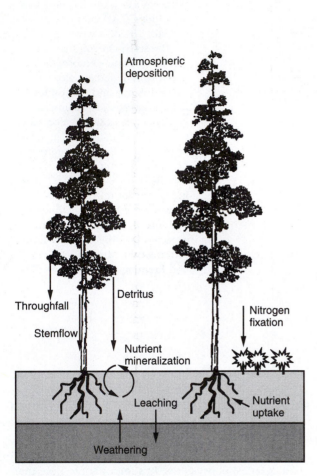

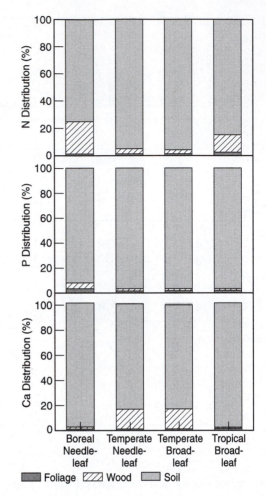

Figure 6.9 Diagram of a nutrient cycle for a hypothetical forest. The diagram illustrates the major pools and fluxes of nutrients. A complete treatment of the major terrestrial nutrient cycles is provided by Schlesinger (8).

Figure 6.10 Relative distribution of nitrogen (N), phosphorus (P), and calcium (Ca) in foliage, wood tissue, and soil (forest floor and mineral soil) for forests in four contrasting biomes. By far the greatest fraction of the total nutrient content in an ecosystem is contained in the soil, but only a small fraction of this pool is available for plant uptake. Adapted from Landsberg and Gower (5).

ecosystems, although nitrogen can enter via biological fixation (see Sidebar 6.1—Nitrogen Fixation). The amounts and types of nutrients that are present in atmospheric deposition are strongly dependent upon geographic location. Large amounts of nitrogen and sulfur deposition occur in highly industrialized areas such as the north-

eastern United States and Europe. Sodium and chlorine, originating from sea spray aerosols, are important nutrient inputs in forests that occur along the coast. The amounts and types of nutrients that become available for plant uptake from weathering are strongly dependent upon climate and parent material—or the type of rock beneath the soil (see Chapter 5, Forest Soils). Chemical weathering of limestone produces calcium, feldspars and micas release potassium when they weather, and dolomite releases calcium and magnesium when it weathers. Nitrogen is not contained in rock near the earth's surface; therefore, nitrogen is not released from weathering. As a result, nitrogen is almost always limiting in new soils derived from volcanic activity, or from unconsolidated rocks from glacial deposits.

Nutrient mineralization is the primary source of nutrients for trees in many forests. Unlike atmospheric deposition and weathering, nutrient mineralization is not a new input, but is derived from recycled nutrients contained in decaying organic matter and detritus input. Sources of decaying organic matter include dead leaves, branches, stems, and roots, as well as dead animal matter. The annual input of nutrients to the soil from detritus decreases in the order of tropical > temperate > boreal forests (5). Dead leaves and fine roots comprise the majority of the annual nutrient input in forest ecosystems. The chemical composition of the tissues and the physical environment determine the rate that the organic matter will decompose and that nutrients are released back to the soil. Leaves and fine roots have higher nutrient concentrations and lower concentrations of chemicals, and therefore decompose faster than woody tissue.

Nutrient Losses

Erosion, leaching, volatilization, and harvesting are the primary pathways for nutrient loss from forest ecosystems. The loss of nutrients via erosion is generally not a concern for intact forests because the multilayers of foliage and the forest floor reduce the physical impact of raindrops on the soil. The forest floor increases water infiltration into the soil which also helps minimize erosion. The *erosion* of the surface soil can be a large source for nutrient loss in highly disturbed forests (i.e., the canopy

Sidebar 6.1

Biological Nitrogen Fixation

A unique source of nitrogen input to terrestrial ecosystems is biological fixation of nitrogen. It is ironic that many forests are limited by nitrogen, despite the chemical composition of the atmosphere, which is 70 percent nitrogen. However, there are a small number of free-living organisms and organisms that have evolved a symbiotic relationship that can convert atmospheric nitrogen into an organic form of nitrogen that can be used by the plant or organism. There are two types of biological nitrogen fixation: symbiotic or asymbiotic fixation. *Symbiotic fixation* involves a mutualistic relationship between a plant and, often, a bacteria. Examples of symbiotic nitrogen fixation include the agriculture crop, alfalfa, and the bacteria *Rhizobium*; or black locust, a common early successional tree species in the southeastern United States, and the bacteria *Rhizobium*. Some of the highest biological nitrogen fixation rates, ranging from 100 to 300 kgN ha^{-1} yr^{-1} , have been reported for the tree species red alder (*Alnus rubra*) and the actinomycete, *Frankia*, in the Pacific Northwest. Shrubs such as *Ceanothus* in the western United States and alder in the boreal forest can also fix nitrogen. There are also many ground and tree dwelling lichens that are capable of biological nitrogen fixation. *Asymbiotic nitrogen* fixation involves only free-living microorganisms, and the rates of nitrogen fixation are much smaller than those for symbiotic nitrogen fixation. Typical rates of asymbiotic nitrogen fixation range from 5–10 kg N ha^{-1} yr^{-1}.

and/or forest floor are removed) because a large percentage of the total nutrient content of the soil is in the upper soil horizons.

Nutrient leaching below the rooting zone is a second potential pathway of nutrient loss. Nutrient leaching is detrimental because it is a permanent loss of nutrients from the soil and decreases the water quality of adjacent aquatic ecosystems. The leaching of nitrate (NO_3^-) is a common concern in agricultural ecosystems. Nitrate is derived from animal waste and excessive use of nitrogen fertilizer, and is a serious health concern. Ironically, nitrate leachate levels can exceed government standards in some natural forest ecosystems that are dominated by nitrogen-fixing trees, such as red alder. A more detailed discussion of the effects of timber harvesting on nutrient leaching is provided later in this chapter. Measurement and modeling the leaching of nutrients in forested watersheds requires a biological understanding of the cycling of nutrients and the flow of water in the soils (see Forest Hydrology, in Chapter 16).

Volatilization is the conversion of an element from the ionic form to a gas that is subsequently lost to the atmosphere. Volatilization of nutrients occurs during wildfires when the temperatures exceed the threshold for an element. Denitrification is a process similar to volatilization in that an ionic form of nitrogen is converted to a gas, but the mechanisms and environmental conditions necessary for denitrification to occur are very different. Chemoautotrophic bacteria, or soil microorganisms that derive their energy from breaking chemical bonds, are responsible for denitrification. These bacteria require anaerobic conditions and an abundant source of nitrogen. These conditions are not common in most upland forest soils, but can be important in fertile lowland soils. Denitrification is the source of large nitrogen losses in cattle and pig feedlots, because the soils are typically poorly drained and nitrogen is abundant from urine and feces. A complete treatment of the factors controlling nutrient losses in harvested forests, and the potential implications for sustainable forest management, are discussed later in the chapter.

Nutrient Transfers Within Forest Ecosystems

Nutrients intercepted by the forest canopy are either absorbed by the vegetation, drip from the canopy to the soil surface (*throughfall*), or flow down the stem (*stemflow*) (Figure 6.9). Nutrients entering the soil follow one of several pathways. Nutrients are either stored on the exchange sites of the soil, absorbed by the roots and mycorrhizae and reused by the vegetation, temporarily immobilized by soil microorganisms, which require nutrients similar to vegetation, or lost. Nutrients taken up by the vegetation are stored in the perennial tissue of the vegetation or returned to the soil surface at the end of the growing season as detritus, primarily as leaf litterfall or fine root turnover. Nutrients return to the soil as litterfall or fine root turnover (Figure 6.9). Decomposition of the organic matter releases the nutrients, completing the nutrient cycle. The amount of nutrients returned to the soil each year varies among and within the major forest biomes, but in general litterfall nutrient content decreases from tropical forests to boreal forests (5).

The mean residence time of nutrients is calculated as the total nutrient content of the compartment divided by the sum of all the inputs to an ecosystem compartment. For example, the mean residence time of nutrients in the forest floor is calculated as the nutrient content of the forest floor divided by the sum of nutrient content of litterfall (leaves and woody tissues) and fine root turnover. The nutrient residence time is a useful index of the rate that organic matter or nutrients cycle through a forest. In general, nutrient availability is inversely proportional to mean residence time. What factors influence the residence time of nutrients in forests? Warm moist climates stimulate the activity of soil microorganisms that decompose litterfall, while cold, dry climates restrict the activity of decomposers. Consequently, the organic matter and nutrient content of the forest floor is lowest in the tropical forests and highest for boreal forests (Figure 6.11). It should be of little surprise then that

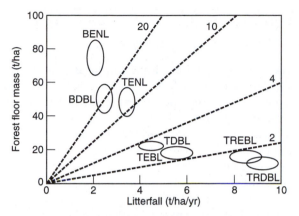

Figure 6.11 A generalized relationship for organic matter or nutrient content in the forest floor and annual litterfall organic matter or nutrient content. The mean residence times for the organic matter and nutrients in the forest floor, depicted by the dashed lines, illustrate that the time it takes for organic matter and nutrients to decompose and mineralize decreases in the order of boreal forests > temperate forests > tropical forests. The abbreviations are as follows: BENL = boreal evergreen needle-leaf; BDBL = boreal deciduous broad-leaf; TENL = temperate evergreen needle-leaf; TEBL = temperate evergreen broad-leaf; TDBL = temperate deciduous broad-leaf; TREBL = tropical evergreen broad-leaf; and TRDBL = tropical deciduous broad-leaf. The figure was adapted from organic matter data summarized by Landsberg and Gower (5).

organic matter and nutrient residence times are shortest for tropical forests, intermediate for temperate forests, and longest for boreal forests (Figure 6.11).

Forest Succession

Succession is the continuous change in the species composition, structure, and function of a forest through time following disturbance. The early stage of succession is referred to as a *successional sere*. The final stage or sere of succession, which is gen-

erally self-replacing, is referred to as the *climax sere*. There are two major types of succession: primary and secondary. Primary succession is the establishment of vegetation on bare rocks or severely disturbed soil. Secondary succession is the reestablishment of vegetation following a disturbance that killed or removed the vegetation but did not greatly affect the soil. Volcanic eruptions, retreating glaciers and colonization of bare sand dunes are examples of primary succession, while clearcutting of forests, wildfires, and hurricanes are examples of secondary succession. Hundreds to thousands of years are required for primary succession to reach climax, compared to decades to hundreds of years for secondary succession. The longer time to reach the climax sere for primary than secondary succession is because soil development must take place in primary succession. The rate of succession is dependent upon the severity of the disturbance, and the availability of seeds for recolonization. Tree species that have small, light seeds that are dispersed by wind or transported by animals recolonize a disturbed area quicker than a species with large seeds.

What morphological and ecophysiological characteristics determine the species composition and abundance in succession? In general, nitrogen fixing plants are important early succession species in primary succession because nitrogen is not derived from weathering, and little or no soil organic matter is present. Ruderals are common early successional species because of their rapid growth rates, while stress-tolerant species are common late successional species.

The structure of a forest changes during succession as well (5). Depending upon the type and severity of the disturbance, a moderate to large amount of dead organic matter from the previous forest remains on the site immediately after disturbance. The leaf area of the forest is at a minimum and slowly increases as new vegetation occupies the site. Following a stand-reinitiating disturbance, such as a blow-down or fire, the new canopy is largely composed of similar-aged, or even-aged, trees. Light, nutrient and water availability are highest during the early successional sere because the vegetation has not completely occupied the site. Canopy closure, or maximum leaf area can occur within several years after disturbance in some tropical forests, but may take 3 to 50 years in boreal forests.

The second stage of stand development is referred to as the stem exclusion stage because of the tree mortality caused by competition for light, nutrients, and water. The intense intra-species (within a species) and inter-species (between species) competition for light, nutrient and water induces mortality of plants that are shaded or have one or more life history characteristics that are not well-adapted to the changing environment. The third stage of stand development, referred to as understory re-initiation, is characterized by openings in the over-story canopy, caused by tree mortality, and the renewed growth of understory and suppressed sub-story trees in response to increased light reaching the forest floor. Consequently, the forest canopy becomes more complex, or multilayered. The final stage of stand development, climax or old-growth stage, is characterized by a species composition that in theory will continue to replace itself until a catastrophic disturbance takes place. Unique characteristics of old-growth forests include the largest accumulation of standing and fallen dead trees—referred to as coarse woody debris. Also, the annual input of litter is dominated by coarse woody debris compared to the earlier stages of stand development where leaf and fine root detritus were the dominant sources of nutrient and organic matter input to the soil.

Some vegetation ecosystems may never reach the latter stages of succession if natural disturbances (fire, flooding, hurricanes, etc.) are frequent. A pyric climax refers to an ecosystem that never reaches the potential climax vegetation defined by climate because of frequent fires. The ecotone, or boundary, between grasslands and forests is a *pyric climax,* and only with fire suppression have woodlands and forest begun to advance into these regions.

Effects of Timber Harvesting on Forest Ecosystems

The effects of timber harvesting on the long-term site productivity of forests are of great interest to land mangers and the general public. The issues surrounding timber harvesting and sustainability have many facets: deleterious effects on the physical properties of forest soils, altered microclimate, increased nutrient leaching loss, and excessive nutrient removal in the biomass. The effects of forest management on wildlife is beyond the scope of this chapter, but is discussed in Chapter 14.

Maintaining the physical properties of forest soils is essential for sustainable forest management. Increased bulk density can restrict fine root growth, thereby decreasing water and nutrient availability to trees. The use of heavy equipment for harvesting or site preparation is primarily responsible for soil compaction. Soil compaction can often be avoided or minimized by restricting heavy equipment to designated areas (logging trails and deck), the use of high flotation tires, hi-lead cable logging, or helicopter logging. Harvesting wet areas when the soil is frozen is also a management option in cold temperate boreal forests.

A second form of physical abuse of the soil is soil displacement. Soil displacement can take on several different forms, but all are deleterious to the soil. Operating heavy equipment on wet soils often results in long-term damage to the soil structure, which reduces water infiltration and water available for plant uptake. Decreased water infiltration increases overland flow and the likelihood of severe erosion. Soil displacement can also occur during site preparation if the operator of the equipment is not careful to minimize disturbance of the forest floor and upper soil horizons. The debris remaining from the harvesting is often pushed into long rows referred to as *windrows*. Significant removal of the forest floor and mineral soil to the windrows drastically decreases nutrients in the field except for where the windrows occur (Figure 6.4).

The removal of the forest canopy in some harsh climates, such as hot and dry forests, sufficiently changes the microclimate to restrict adequate regeneration. Greater extremes in temperature occur in clearcut than control forests, and even greater extremes occur in forests that are burned because the black surface decreases the albedo[2] (Figure 6.12). Small changes in the microclimate maybe insignificant for many forests, but the changes may be deleterious for hot, drought-prone forests such as those found in the Rocky Mountains and eastern slopes of the Cascades in the western United States.

Much of the discussions surrounding the potential adverse effects of timber harvesting have focused on nutrient leaching losses following harvesting and nutrient removal. Nutrient leaching is the loss of nutrients, in solution, below the rooting zone. Recall from Chapter 5 (Forest Soils) most temperate forests soils lack an anion exchange capacity, meaning that unless plants or soil microorganisms take up anions (e.g., NO_3^-, Cl^-, HCO_3^-, HSO_4^-), the anions in the soil will be leached if there is sufficient water draining below the tree roots. A cation of similar charge to the anion will also be leached because electroneutrality must be maintained. Nutrient leaching decreases the amount of nutrients available for plant uptake and decreases water quality in the groundwater or adjacent aquatic ecosystems.

Concern for the potential nutrient leaching associated with timber harvesting gained worldwide attention with the Hubbard Brook study by Likens, et al. (9). The Hubbard Brook watershed experiment involved a control (uncut) and a clearcut plus herbicide-treated watershed. The objective of the study was to better understand the natural mechanisms in a forest ecosystem that controls nutrient cycling, including nitrate leaching. To do this, the investigators removed the hypothesized primary mechanism that prevents nutrient leaching—plant uptake of nutrients. It is important to note that the objec-

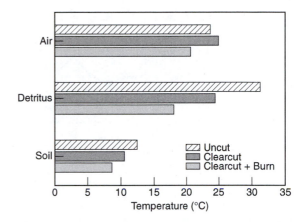

Figure 6.12 Comparison of the temperature of the air 10 cm above the forest floor surface, the forest floor, and mineral soil at a 10 cm depth for an uncut, clearcut, and clearcut and burned forest.

tive of this experiment was not to simulate a typical forest harvest. The removal of the trees (harvest) and continued suppression of vegetation re-growth (herbicide treatment) allowed decomposition and nutrient mineralization to occur, but there were few plants to take up the mineralized nutrients. Eventually the microbial demand for nutrients was exceeded and large nutrient leaching losses occurred (Figure 6.13).

How representative are the results in the Hubbard Brook study to normal forest harvesting practices? This was a question asked by both foresters and environmentalists alike after the Hubbard Brook results were published. Control and harvested paired watershed studies were conducted in the United States to quantify potential nutrient leaching losses and to better understand the mechanisms that govern nutrient leaching losses. A wide range of nutrient leaching losses were observed by Vitousek, et al. (10). Nutrient leaching losses were insignificant in some forests, but exceeded 50–100 kg N ha^{-1} yr^{-1} for other forests (Figure 6.14). In general, high nitrogen leaching losses occurred in

---

[2] The ratio of light reflected to that received.

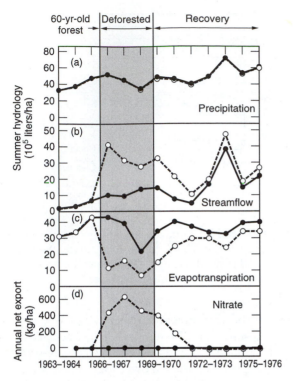

Figure 6.13 Comparison of the nutrient leaching losses from the uncut control (solid line) and harvested + herbicide (dashed line) forest. Copyright permission provided by Springer-Verlag (9).

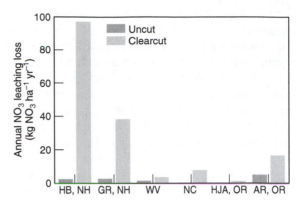

Figure 6.14 Comparison of annual nitrate leaching losses for paired control and clearcut watersheds. Abbreviations for the sites are as follows: HB, NH is Hubbard Brook, New Hampshire; GR, NH is Green River, New Hampshire; WV is West Virginia; NC is Coweeta Hydrologic Laboratory, North Carolina; HJA, OR is the H.J. Andrews Experimental Forest, Oregon; and AR, OR is Oregon. Figure was prepared from data presented in Vitousek, et al. (10).

forests that had large nitrogen mineralization rates or experienced chronic atmospheric nitrogen deposition. Conversely, forests with low nitrogen mineralization rates or small nitrogen deposition rates experienced small to non-significant nitrogen leaching losses in the clearcut forest.

ogy, and hydrology. Although, conceptual understanding of forest ecosystem ecology is required, all too often, economical, political, or social issues take precedence over ecological principles. These situations often result in mismanagement and deleterious effects to the forest. This chapter attempted to illustrate the interconnection of the water, nutrient, and carbon cycles, and how alteration of a process in one of the cycles, resulting from natural of human disturbance, affects the structure and function of the forest.

Concluding Statement

Sustainable forest ecosystem management requires a fundamental understanding of the principles of forest management and forest ecosystem ecology. I hope this chapter has provided the reader a better appreciation of the challenges of forest ecosystem ecology—a discipline in ecology that draws upon ecophysiology, soil science, micrometeorol-

References

1. H. W. HOCKER, JR., *Introduction to Forest Biology*, John Wiley & Sons, New York, 1979.

2. J. P. GRIMES, *Plant Strategies and Vegetation Processes*, John Wiley & Sons, New York, 1979.

3. M. G. BARBOUR, J. H. BURK, AND W. D. PITTS, *Terrestrial Plant Ecology*, Benjamin/Cummings Publishing Company, Menlo Park, Calif., 1987.

4. H. Lambers, F. S. Chapin, III, and T. L. Pons, *Plant Physiological Ecology,* Springer-Verlag, New York, 1998.

5. J. J. Landsberg, J. J. and S. T. Gower, *Applications of Physiological Ecology to Forest Management*, Academic Press, San Diego, Calif., 1997.

6. C. C. Grier and S. W. Running, *Ecology, 58*, 893 (1977).

7. H. L. Gholz, *Ecology, 63*, 469 (1982).

8. W. H. Schlesinger, *Biogeochemistry: An Analysis of Gobal Change*, Second Edition, Academic Press. San Diego, Calif., 1997.

9. G. E. Likens, F. H. Bormann, R. S. Pierce, J. S. Eaton, and N.M. Johnson, *Biogeochemistry,* Springer-Verlag, New York, 1979.

10. P. M. Vitousek, J. R. Gosz, C.C. Grier, J. M. Melillo, W. A. Reiners, and R. L. Todd, *Science, 204*, 469 (1979).

CHAPTER 7

Landscape Ecology

VOLKER C. RADELOFF AND DAVID J. MLADENOFF

Introduction

Ecologists recognized early the effect of the surrounding landscape on a given ecosystem. For example, a pond located within a forest will have very different ecological characteristics from a pond located among agricultural fields, even if both ponds are of the same size and depth. The forest pond is likely to be cooler because of the shade from nearby trees, and the surrounding forests provide habitat for amphibians that will lay their eggs in it. The agricultural field pond is likely to contain more nutrients from fertilizer runoff, and may be a stopover site for waterfowl during migration. These two examples illustrate how landscape patterns affect organisms (1).

However, not only do landscape patterns affect organisms, but organisms can also create certain landscape patterns. For instance, beaver create ponds in forests by building dams on creeks or small rivers. Trees that are flooded die, and beaver cut down more trees for food, thus opening the forest canopy. Once their food supply is depleted, the beaver abandon their pond, their dam breaks down and an open, nutrient-rich wet meadow remains that will gradually be recolonized by trees. Landscape ecologists study both the effects of landscape patterns and the processes that create them (2–4). The aim of this chapter is to provide an introduction to the science of landscape ecology and its application to forest management.

Definition and History

Ecology is the study of relationships between organisms and their environment. Landscape ecology is

132

the subdiscipline of ecology that focuses on spatial relationships usually over broad areas or "landscapes" (2–4).

The importance of examining ecological relationships across landscapes was recognized in the early 20th century. Carl Troll, a German geographer, coined the term *landscape ecology* in 1939 after he had studied aerial photographs of various landscapes around the globe. Aldo Leopold, an American wildlife ecologist, noted the importance of landscape patterns for game animal populations in 1933, and Alexander Watt, an English botanist, studied the relationships between patterns and processes in plant communities in 1947 (4).

Despite these early roots, landscape ecology did not gain widespread recognition in North America until the 1980s. The increasing availability of computerized spatial data (e.g., satellite images, soil maps, forest inventories) and computer programs that have the ability to analyze mapped information (e.g., Geographical Information Systems or GIS), fostered new research and applications (5). At the beginning of the 21st century, landscape ecology has become a well-established scientific discipline, and an increasingly important aspect of forest management.

Landscape Patterns and How They Are Generated

In the previous sections, we introduced the concept of landscape patterns and landscape processes. In this section, we will examine various forms of characteristic landscape patterns, and discuss how they originate. The different types of processes that cause landscape patterns are the organizing principle for this section.

Effects of Topography, Surface Geology, and Geomorphological Processes on Landscape Patterns

One of the most basic causes of landscape patterns is topography. Alpine tundra, for example, occurs in the Rocky Mountains only at the highest eleva-

tions. A map of alpine tundra therefore shows only relatively small patches of tundra that are isolated from each other (Figure 7.1).

Surface geology has a strong effect on soils as parent material and thereby on the distribution of different types of forest patches. A good example of this effect exists in northern Wisconsin, a landscape that was glaciated until about 10,000 years ago. When the glaciers retreated north, the features they left were large sandy outwash plains, moraines, and former lakebeds. Jack pine is a tree species that is well adapted to sandy soils, and the outwash plains are the only places in Wisconsin where jack pine is common, whereas the moraines, with heavier, loamy soils, are dominated by hardwoods and hemlock.

Geomorphological processes that shape landscape patterns include landslides, erosion, sand dune development, and pattern formation over permafrost. We will discuss here only one process, the fluvial dynamics that are typical of meandering

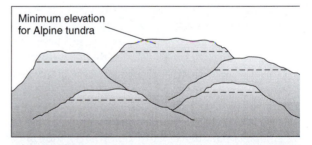

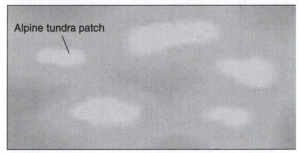

Figure 7.1 Panoramic view of a mountain range with alpine tundra at highest elevations, and a corresponding map with isolated patches of alpine tundra.

Sidebar 7.1

Key Concepts

Several concepts and terms are central to landscape ecology. The first of these are *patch* and *matrix*. A patch is a reasonably homogeneous area identifiable within a landscape. Patches are often delineated based on their vegetation. Patches are embedded in the landscape matrix (1). For example, in a forested landscape with scattered, small bogs, the bogs can be regarded as patches, whereas the forest forms the matrix.

The second important concept is the relationship of *landscape patterns* and *landscape processes* (2). The spatial arrangement of patches and matrix forms the landscape patterns of a given area. Landscape processes are dynamic processes that operate over large areas. An example of a landscape process is forest fire. In boreal forests, fires occur naturally and one fire can cover a very large area (10,000 to 100,000 hectares). After a fire, the forests regenerate and form very large patches of even-aged trees (3).

The third important issue is that of *landscape scale,* which is defined by landscape *grain* and *extent* (4). The landscape grain is the smallest spatial unit of a landscape or map representation, also termed the *resolution*. The size of the smallest patches usually determines the landscape grain. The landscape extent comprises the entire area within the boundaries of a landscape.

Scale is also very important conceptually. Different landscape processes occur at a certain scales, and need to be studied at their appropriate scale (1). For example, fires in the boreal forest operate at a very broad scale, and one has to analyze several 100,000 hectares at once to capture the dynamics of these large fire dynamics. Forest management, on the other hand, operates at a smaller scale, and a study area that captures several thousand hectares will usually be sufficient to study the effects of different forest management activities on landscape patterns (3).

Sources:

1. M. G. TURNER, *Landscape Heterogeneity and Disturbance,* Springer-Verlag, New York, 1987.

2. K. MCGARIGAL AND B. J. MARKS, *Spatial pattern analysis program for quantifying landscape structure,* Gen. Tech. Rep. PNW-GTR-351, Pacific Northwest Research Station, U.S.D.A. For. Serv., Portland, Ore., 1995.

3. J. F. FRANKLIN AND R. T. T. FORMAN, *Landscape Ecol., 1,* 5 (1987).

4. D. J. MLADENOFF AND W. L. BAKER, *Advances in Spatial Modeling of Forest Landscape Change: Approaches and Applications,* Cambridge University Press, Cambridge, U.K., 1999.

---

rivers (see Figure 7.2a in color insert). These rivers are characterized by numerous curves. These curves constantly change position because rivers erode the outside of the curves and deposit gravel and sands on the inside of the curve. When the river course forms the shape of a horseshoe, it may eventually break through, leaving an oxbow lake. Such oxbows can persist as open water bodies for quite a while, but will gradually fill in, first with aquatic

vegetation, and later with shrubs and trees. The shapes of the oxbows, however, remain, and form a very characteristic landscape pattern.

Effects of Natural Disturbance Processes on Landscape Patterns

The previous examples described how geological and geomorphological processes affect landscape pattern. One may not think of mountain ranges as a process, but underlying their development are plate tectonics and erosional forces that operate over millions of years. Glacial landscapes are shaped by 10,000–100,000 year cycles of glaciation, and rivers change their paths over centuries or decades. In contrast, the landscape processes that we focus on in this section operate at much shorter time scales. These processes are collectively referred to as "disturbances" or "disturbance regimes," because they alter the vegetation rather abruptly (6). However, the term "disturbance" is somewhat misleading because it implies that the disturbance process is not part of the natural ecosystem. On the contrary, disturbances are inherent parts of many ecosystems and are forces that often create characteristic landscape patterns and cyclic alterations in ecosystems.

A typical disturbance that was previously mentioned is fire in boreal forests (7). The boreal forest zone occurs in the Northern Hemisphere across Canada, Alaska, Siberia, and Scandinavia and reaches to the treeline, the northernmost extent where trees can grow. Fires are a natural part of the boreal forest ecoystem; they are necessary to initiate forest regeneration, and they create important habitat for many wildlife species. A single fire may last only a few days or weeks, and may cover hundreds, up to more than 100,000 hectares. The vegetation type in these landscapes depends on the time since the last fire. Recently burned patches are open, and contain only grasses and shrubs. Tree regeneration, especially by aspen and pine, soon follows, and even-aged young forests characterize a patch 20–30 years after a fire. As more time passes, the forests of the patch grow older until a new fire occurs. Fires are fairly frequent in the boreal zone, and most forests burn on average about every 100 years. The landscape pattern that is typical of boreal forests is a very large mosaic of large patches (see Figure 13.2). This landscape pattern is called a "shifting mosaic," because the landscape always exhibits a mosaic of patches of different ages, but their location shifts over time.

Quite different landscape patterns result from hurricanes, tornadoes and other winds. Wind damage to forests can also be fairly extensive, but does not typically reach a contiguous extent comparable to

boreal forest fires. Wind disturbance patches occur in very variable shapes. For example, tornadoes may cause narrow, elongated patches of windthrow, and hurricanes may cause damage across a much larger area, with very variable effects. Another unique aspect of wind disturbance is that it can blow down all or only a portion of the trees in an area. Forests that are particularly prone to wind damage include tropical forests in the Carribean, Central America, and the forests in the southeastern United States, because of the higher likelihood of hurricanes in these regions. Windthrow that can have extensive damage also occurs in north temperate regions, such as central North America, that are affected by large low pressure storms and thunderstorms. However, the frequency of wind damage even in these regions is generally much lower than the frequency of fires in the boreal zone.

The different disturbance processes of boreal and Central American forest landscapes result in a much smaller grain for the Central American forest landscape compared with the boreal landscape. An even smaller grain is typical of some temperate forests, such as the eastern United States, or tropical rain forest in Amazonia, that typically experience fire and wind damage less frequently than the regions mentioned earlier. The dominant landscape patterns of these forests are often the result of single tree gaps, caused by the death of an old tree with a large crown. Such gaps are usually not larger than 0.1 ha. An interesting case of gap disturbance is the European beech forest ecosystem. Gaps in beech forests are often 1–2 ha in size and elongated in a north-to-south direction. The reason for this is that mature beech trees often die after a few years when their trunk is exposed to sunlight. Once a single old beech tree dies, the trunks of its neighbors to the north are exposed to sunlight, and their death causes the northward expansion of the gap.

Effects of Animals on Landscape Patterns

Physical processes, such as wind, fire, and sunlight are powerful forces that shape the landscape pattern of many ecosystems, but animals also leave their mark in the landscape (1). We will again present three examples of processes that create distinctive landscape pattern, all of them being related to animal activities.

Forest insects can shape forest landscapes at large scales (8). Outbreaks of defoliating insects can occur simultaneously over many hundreds of thousands of hectares. One result of these outbreaks is that the tree species composition in the landscape is changed. For example, a spruce budworm outbreak in boreal forests will kill mainly fir and spruce thereby giving hardwoods such as aspen a competitive advantage. Spruce budworm outbreaks can also increase fire fuel loads by leaving large areas of dead trees, which may make fires more intense and/or likely.

We briefly mentioned the effect of beaver on landscape patterns in stream valleys. Beaver create dams along creeks where trees, especially young hardwood trees, are common. They maintain their dam over many years until food sources in the vicinity are depleted. Sediments accumulate on the bottom of their ponds during this period. Once a dam is abandoned, it will eventually break, thus draining the pond. What remains are nutrient-rich sediments that quickly revegetate, first by grasses and forbs, and later by tree species such as aspen. Once a new forest has formed the cycle may start again with the establishment of a new beaver dam.

Our last example for the effects of animal activity on landscape patterns is certainly not a disturbance. Jays are birds that feed on acorns among other things. One aspect of their feeding behavior is that they carry acorns, sometimes over several kilometers, and bury them in the ground. They do not recover all of these buried acorns, and some of them will germinate. This makes jays very effective seed dispersers (Figure 7.3). Trees with heavy seeds, such as acorns, are otherwise limited in that their seeds cannot travel far from the parent tree. However, activities by jays may ensure that oaks can spread relatively quickly into areas where they do not occur. This is an important advantage after a disturbance such as fire has killed the canopy across a large area. At larger spatial and temporal scales, after glaciations, seed dispersal capability determines how quickly tree species can follow the

retreating glaciers and migrate northwards. The activity of jays and other seed dispersers is one of the major processes that shape the spatial pattern of plant occurrence.

Effects of Human Activities on Landscape Patterns

All the processes described above have shaped landscape patterns for many millions of years, but during the last few thousand years, human activities have increasingly affected landscape pattern. It is important to note that humans have altered the landscape for a long time. For example, indigenous peoples in Australia and North America set fires in forests and grasslands to promote young regrowth, and thus provide better habitat for the animals they hunted. However, the impact of human activities has greatly increased with the advent of agriculture, cities, the industrial revolution, and growing world population and resource use in the 20th century.

One of the most distinct patterns of landscapes is the pattern of human settlements. These patterns are particularly striking when forested areas are being settled and often follow the patterns of transportation networks and legal boundaries. For example, in the Amazonian province of Rondonia (Brazil), roads are the most important means of transportation (see Figure 7.2b in color insert). Major roads form the backbone of what has been called "fishbone patterns." Early settlers clear land adjacent to the major roads, but soon numerous minor roads develop that run perpendicularly to the major roads. Farmers continue to clear land in the vicinity of the minor roads thus leaving only small strips of forest in the middle between them. This process of breaking up the intact forest is called *forest fragmentation*, which encompasses both the loss of the majority of the forest and a resulting pattern where forests occur only in small patches that are isolated (9). Forest fragmentation by settlement has occurred in many parts of the world over time. Most recently, it has occurred during the last 300 years in areas that were colonized by European immigrants such as the eastern United

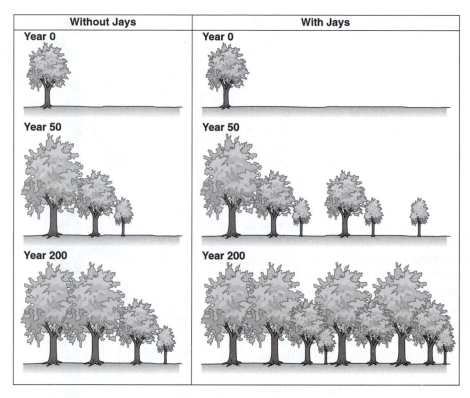

Figure 7.3   Diagram of oak encroachment with short-range seed dispersal caused by wind and squirrels (on the left) and long-range seed dispersal by jays (on the right).

States, Western Australia, and in tropical regions with rapidly growing populations.

Even where forests remain, human management will often have a strong influence on their patterns. Forest harvesting—especially clearcutting—creates very distinct landscape patterns (10–13). The actual pattern will depend on three factors, the size of the clearcuts, the rotation length (i.e., how often each forest is harvested), and how cutting units are allocated across the landscape spatially.

Both management objectives and legal restrictions determine the size of clearcuts. For instance, the state of Baden-Württemberg in Germany allows clearcuts no larger than 1 ha. Currently, the National Forests in the United States observe a 16 ha limit, whereas some clearcuts in Canada can occupy hundreds of hectares. Clearcut size will also vary

with topography, usually being larger in flat terrain, and depending on the tree species and purpose of forest management.

Rotation length determines how much of the landscape is open at any given point in time. For instance, a rotation length of 50 years translates into 20 percent of the landscape area being younger than 10 years and thus probably not containing a closed forest canopy. A rotation length of 100 years reduces the area of open patches to 10 percent of the landscape area.

The allocation of clearcuts also has a strong effect on landscape patterns. In the recent past, the most common management practice in the United States has been to disperse clearcuts as much as possible. The result is a pattern characterized by many small, open patches with narrow stands of intervening forest, creating a highly fragmented matrix (Figure 7.4). A very different approach is to allocate new clearcuts in the vicinity of previous harvests. This creates larger openings, but it also leaves large areas of continuous and undisturbed forest, and regenerates large, future patches of forest.

Subtler patterns that humans impose on landscapes are the road networks (14). Forests can be fragmented even without any forest cutting, because roads form barriers to movement of some animals. It is obvious that major highways have a strong effect even on large mammals. Highways not only cause wildlife accidents and deaths, they can also prevent migration between areas, leading to the isolation of populations and a higher potential for local extinctions (9). However, even small roads impair the movements of insects, small mammals and amphibians (15). In experiments, pedestrian beetles only once crossed a six-meter-wide, two-lane road and even single-lane roads were only rarely successfully crossed (Figure 7.5). The main reason is that the gravel makes it very easy for predators to spot their prey. This finding demonstrates that even small, rarely traveled logging roads can fragment forests.

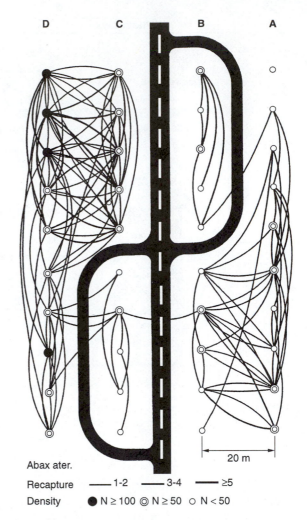

Abax ater.

Recapture ——— 1-2 ——— 3-4 ——— ≥5
Density ● N ≥ 100 ◎ N ≥ 50 ○ N < 50

Figure 7.5 Number of beetle crossings over a major and two minor roads, A–D represent trap rows; circles represent live traps. Curved lines represent the movement of a marked beetle between capture and recapture.

Figure 7.4 Clearcuts on U.S. National Forest land (on the left) adjacent to Yellowstone National Park (on the right). (Photo courtesy of J. Rotella, Montana State University.)

How Landscape Patterns Affect Forest Ecosystems

In the previous section, we outlined causes for different landscape patterns. In this section, we will examine how different landscape patterns affect forests. This includes not only direct effects on trees,

Sidebar 7.2

Temporal and Spatial Scales of Processes That Affect Landscape Patterns

It is useful to stratify landscape processes that alter forest landscape pattern according to two criteria; their return interval (i.e., how much time passes, on average, until a location is affected a second time by a process), and their spatial extent. These two aspects are somewhat correlated (i.e., processes that operate on smaller areas tend to occur more frequently). On the other hand, processes that affect very large areas, such as plate tectonics and glaciations have very long return intervals. However, there are notable exceptions to this rule, and they indicate how disturbance-prone a landscape is. For example, boreal forest fires extend over large areas, and occur relatively often. This indicates that boreal forests are particularly prone to disturbance.

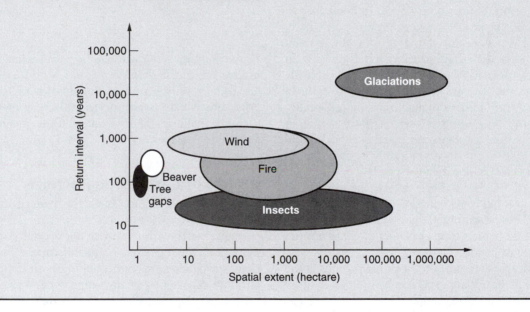

but also on other aspects of forest ecosystems. The organizing principles of this section are the different basic patterns, first, of single patches, and second, of the arrangement of multiple patches in a landscape.

Effects of Individual Patch Size and Shape

The most obvious spatial attribute of a single patch is its size. Patch size has a strong influence on many ecological processes. For example, a large forest opening, perhaps caused by a fire or a clearcut, will often experience different natural regeneration than a small one. The reason is that the ability to invade open areas differs among plant species. Tree species such as aspen have light wind-dispersed seeds. They can disperse their seeds into the center of even a very large opening. Other species, such as maple, have seeds that are heavier. Seeds such as these are not dispersed great distances and may reach only the center of small openings, but fail to colonize the center of large openings. The result is that aspen will be more dominant in larger openings than species such as maple, even if stand history, soil conditions, and climate are the same. Also, the size of an opening will affect its microclimate. For example, wind will be less pronounced in small openings, and very small openings might be partially shaded by the adjacent forest canopy.

Patch size can also determine if a patch is suitable habitat for an animal species. For example, a pair of northern spotted owls requires a patch of at least 450 ha of continuous, mature forest to successfully raise their young. The reason is that the density of their prey is relatively low. Smaller patches do not provide the necessary amount of food. The minimum value of 450 ha increases to up to 1700 ha in areas where prey is particularly sparse. However, this value is only the habitat requirement of a single pair of spotted owls. If an owl pair is isolated from other owl pairs it is unlikely that owls will persist in that location. The forest patch size required to maintain an entire population of northern spotted owls is much larger. A strong relationship between patch size and likelihood of extinction occurs not only in owls, but in many species. The size of a patch (i.e., the total amount of suitable habitat), affects the number of species it is likely to contain. This is the first law of island biogeography: larger patches (or islands) of the same habitat type are likely to contain more species than smaller ones.

Another spatial attribute of single patches is the shape of its boundary. This can be defined by how long its perimeter is compared to its area. A circular patch has the lowest perimeter compared to its area. This value increases when patches are more elongated or have complex boundaries (Figure 7.6). Patch shape is important because the forest along the edges of a patch functions differently from the forest in the interior. For example, sunlight and wind can penetrate onto the forest floor along the edges, thereby creating a different microclimate and more favorable conditions for sun-loving tree seedlings or groundlayer plants. These plant species will have an advantage in this environment over species that compete better in total shade.

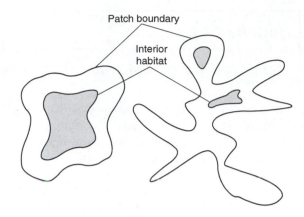

Figure 7.6   Two patches of different complexity and amount of interior habitat.

Plants or animals that survive best under intact forest are often called *interior species*, because they are usually only found in the interior of forests. Edge effects may persist up to 200–300 meter into a patch, making small woodlots often unsuitable for interior species.

Effects of Landscape Patterns

In order to understand landscape pattern fully, it is necessary to look not only at the size and shape of single patches, but also at the spatial arrangement of multiple patches on a landscape. Distances between patches or connectivity are an important attribute of patches of the same type. For example, amphibians that live in forests may be able to traverse agricultural fields up to 300 meters, and thus colonize forest patches that are less than 300 meters apart. This means that a forest patch that is devoid of amphibians is only likely to be recolonized if it is less than 300 meters away from the next forest patch. The maximum distance for recolonization varies among different species. It may be very small for ground beetles, and much larger for wide-ranging mammals or birds. The result of this pattern is that the further a forest patch is from another forest, the fewer species it is likely to contain. This is the second law of island biogeography. The combination of the first law (island size), and the second law (distance to mainland) can be used to calculate a rough estimate about the likely biodiversity (i.e., the number of species) of an island or an isolated forest patch. However, the actual number of species in a given patch is not only affected by patch size and distance to the next patch, but also by habitat heterogeneity and disturbance history, among other factors.

Most landscapes contain not only one type of patch but many. Forest landscapes are commonly a mosaic of patches of old-growth, maturing and regenerating forest, wetlands, lakes, and other vegetation types. Such landscapes exhibit a high diversity of patch or ecosystem types, exhibiting landscape heterogeneity. A diverse landscape usually provides habitat for more species than a landscape that is composed of only one vegetation type. However, biodiversity alone is not necessarily a good indicator for assessing landscapes or quantifying management effects. For example, in a region of largely young, managed forests, a large continuous block of forest may contain relatively few, but regionally rare or even endangered forest interior species. Fragmentation of this block may cause the extinction of these species in this area (9). However, the biodiversity of this area may increase at the same time, because habitat for common, open habitat species was created. Thus, it should not be a management goal to maximize biodiversity for a given forest stand, but to ensure that viable populations of all species are maintained in the landscape.

A heterogeneous landscape will also respond differently to disturbance. For example, wetlands and lakes are natural firebreaks that will limit the size of a burn. Furthermore, these areas can be important refuges during fires, where some mature trees can survive and provide seed sources for tree regeneration on the burned upland patch. A landscape that contains many wetlands will therefore regenerate differently after fires than one that contains only upland forest.

Forest management that regenerates only a limited number of tree species and age classes can reduce landscape diversity in terms of tree species.

Such management can have unexpected consequences because landscapes are complex systems, and reducing this complexity may make them less resilient to stressors. For example, insect defoliation is often more intense when tree species diversity across the landscape is low. This is because insects disperse during an outbreak into areas that are not yet infested. A landscape that is homogeneous, where host species are abundant, may result in a more rapid spread of a disturbance. In this case a high percentage of insect dispersal attempts are successful, which means that the number of insects on each tree is higher, and tree mortality may increase.

Interactions Between Landscape Patterns and Processes

In the previous sections, we discussed the origin and effects of landscape patterns. Our examples described comparatively simple one-way relationships; we discussed how a process creates a landscape pattern or how a pattern affects a process. In reality, much more complex relationships are common. This section will provide examples of feedbacks and indirect relationships that can be important but difficult to predict.

We will return in our first example of complex interactions between pattern and process to the effects of human settlements. In the European Alps, most settlements, agricultural fields and roads are located in the valley bottoms. These valley bottoms were historically the wintering grounds for red deer. Because of habitat alterations and human disturbance, red deer today remain in the forests at higher elevations during winter. Food availability is limited in these forests, and hunters often provide supplemental forage to prevent a reduction of the deer herd from starvation. High deer densities in the forest result in widespread damage to tree regeneration, both by browsing tree buds, and by peeling of the bark. This damage severely limits the regeneration of many alpine forests and threatens human settlements because forests are an important protection from avalanches. Many alpine forests have been protected from cutting for centuries to ensure that they can form a barrier against avalanches. Current landscape changes and the chain of effects described previously threaten this historic protection system and thus some of the human settlements in the European Alps themselves.

Another example of unexpected changes is related to an alteration of a landscape process. For the last half century, fires have been actively suppressed in many parts of North America, Australia, and Eurasia. This has changed many ecosystems, especially where fire was part of the natural regeneration cycle. For example, under natural conditions, ponderosa pine forests of the American West are kept open by very frequent, but low-intensity surface fires. Fire suppression altered this cycle and permitted in some areas less fire-tolerant species, such as Douglas fir, to invade ponderosa pine stands. This young Douglas fir in the understory is typically much denser than the ponderosa pine. The change in species composition and forest structure has several consequences. First, Douglas fir forests are susceptible to spruce budworm defoliation, and their outbreaks are becoming more frequent as their food source becomes more abundant in the landscape. Second, ponderosa pine seedlings are not very shade-tolerant; they can grow only under an open canopy. Dense Douglas fir prevents ponderosa pine regeneration. Third, a fire in a dense Douglas fir stand can be very intense. Ponderosa pine is adapted to light surface fires, but it cannot survive a crown fire. This means that mature ponderosa pine will disappear from the tree species mix. Once the mature trees are gone, seed sources are lacking in the landscape and the ecosystem is even less likely to revert to its original state.

Most of our examples have focused on terrestrial systems, but interactions also occur between terrestrial and aquatic systems. Our last example on complex interactions between landscape patterns and processes will address the relationship of forests and streams in the Pacific northwest. Forest management and the salmon fisheries are two major environmental issues, and these issues are widely discussed among the public and studied by scientists. What emerges is a picture of an intricate web of relationships between these two resources.

Most of the landscape in the Pacific northwest is mountainous and the forest cover is largely composed of conifers, most notably Douglas fir. The common forest harvesting practice has been to clearcut. The steep slopes are often prone to erosion once the forest cover is removed, and forest road building further increases the likelihood of landslides. This has detrimental effects on stream habitat because the silt load increases. Furthermore, water temperature rises once trees no longer shade the streams. Forest management has partly adapted to these problems, and riparian zones are often left standing during harvesting. Nevertheless, forest harvesting has been one important factor causing the decline of the salmon populations in the Pacific northwest. Other factors include commercial harvesting of salmon, and the hydroelectric power dams along the major rivers. The combined effect of all these factors is that current salmon runs represent only a fraction of their historic levels. Salmon runs comprised an important food source for many predators and scavengers, such as gulls, eagles, and bears. However, salmon not only affect the numbers of these predators along rivers, they also represent an important source for nutrient input for the forest as well as the river. Forest soils in the Pacific northwest are often limited in phosphorus, and it has been estimated that a good salmon run can result in as much as 6.7 kg/ha of phosphorus input in a forest strip of 100 meters along both sides of a stream. The effect is strongest close to the river because this is where bears leave most of the carcasses. This level of phosphorus input is comparable to the amount that is applied commercially when fertilizing evergreens. Forest harvesting thus affects not only the salmon populations, and the populations of those predators that depend on them, but also indirectly the nutrient dynamics of the forests themselves.

Methods in Landscape Ecology

The importance of landscape ecology was recognized early, but major progress has been made largely since the 1980s, when new sources of spa-

Sidebar 7.3

Critical Thresholds of Landscape Patterns

The effects of landscape pattern on process are often nonlinear, and landscape context is very important. For example, forest cutting on 10 percent of a landscape area may have very little effect if the landscape is still 90 percent forested. However, a landscape with only 10 percent forest left will change dramatically when this last 10 percent is cut.

Critical thresholds are a special case of nonlinear relationships. Systems that reach a critical threshold will change abruptly. For example, when water is heated up it does not change its properties much until reaching 100°C, at which point it starts boiling, turning to water vapor. There is growing evidence that landscapes also exhibit critical thresholds. Studies of forest fragmentation indicate that as more forest cover is cut, reducing forest cover below certain thresh-

olds can cause landscape connectivity to break down suddenly (1). The exact percentage of forest cover at which direct connectivity is lost varies somewhat among landscapes, but usually occurs with between 20–40 percent remaining forest cover. Knowledge of critical thresholds is crucial for predicting the results of management actions, but can be difficult to ascertain. Also, thresholds will vary for different species because habitat requirements differ among them, and because they have differing abilities to cross unsuitable habitat.

Source:

1. J. A. BISSONETTE, *Wildlife and Landscape Ecology— Effects of Pattern and Scale,* Springer-Verlag, New York, 1997.

---

tial data, and new techniques to analyze them, became available. Other chapters in this book provide an introduction to remote sensing, and geographical information systems (GIS). We will not duplicate the material covered there, but rather outline specifically some of the applications of these tools and methods in landscape ecology (5).

Data Collection and Analysis

Landscape ecology originated with the advent of aerial photography in the 1930s, which provided the means to accurately map large areas consistently and at comparatively low costs. Aerial photography remains an important data source for landscape ecology. Its main advantage is that it provides a spatially detailed picture. Also, for many areas historical aerial photographs have been available since the 1930s. This provides an opportunity to study

long-term changes. Air photos are commonly interpreted by outlining the boundaries of identifiable patches on them, either manually on paper prints, or digitally on scanned and computerized versions. This requires that the study purpose, land classification, and resolution be determined in advance of the mapping. Attributes, such as tree species composition, age, stocking density, or habitat values, are entered into the GIS database for each patch or polygon identified.

In the mid-1970s, satellite images of the earth's surface became available, and they have fundamentally changed the way we see and study very large landscapes. The main advantages of satellite images are that they 1) cover very large areas, 2) can be automatically classified by computer, 3) provide information for remote areas, and 4) permit the examination of changes where images from different dates are available for a given area.

Digital maps derived from aerial photography or satellite imagery can be analyzed in a Geographical Information System (GIS). A GIS is a computer system designed to retrieve, store, manipulate, analyze, and reproduce spatial data. This definition may sound dry, but the long list of attributes indicates that a GIS is a very powerful tool to work with all the information that was traditionally stored on paper maps. The vast amounts of data provided by satellites, the increasing abundance of widely available digital data, such as elevation models, forest inventories, ecosystem and habitat attributes, and climate measurements, and the need to analyze large areas, make GIS an essential tool for most landscape ecologists.

Landscape Indexes

The importance of landscape patterns for the functioning of forest ecosystems necessitates being able to describe them quantitatively. Numerous landscape indexes have been proposed to measure various spatial attributes of individual patches (Figure 7.6), and of entire landscapes. These landscape metrics help to predict the habitat suitability or other ecosystem properties of a given landscape, provide a framework for comparing different landscapes, and allow quantifying landscape change over time. Specific landscape metrics have been designed, for example, to measure patch area, the ratio of patch perimeter to patch area, and diversity of habitat types in a landscape, among many other spatial attributes. The following three examples illustrate the use of landscape metrics.

The *mean patch area index* is calculated as the average size of all patches. We discussed earlier that certain species require habitat to occur in patches of a certain minimum size in order to utilize it. Computing the mean patch area is a good way to compare landscape and to evaluate if habitat is clumped or dispersed.

The *mean perimeter–area ratio* estimates the shape of patches. Again, it is an average of a value that is first derived for every single patch. Among patches of equal area but different shape, circles exhibit the lowest perimeter–area ratio. Among

patches of the same shape, the mean perimeter–area ratio is smaller when patches are larger. There is no upper limit of the mean perimeter–area ratio.

The *Shannon Weaver Diversity Index* cannot be calculated for single patches but only for an entire landscape. It combines an estimate of the number of different ecosystems that are present in a landscape (richness) with a measurement of how much area each ecosystem type occupies (evenness). Richness is higher where more ecosystem types occur. Evenness is highest when all ecosystems occur in equal portions in the landscape.

We will not discuss these mathematical formulas of these indexes in detail, but rather point to three excellent reviews of landscape metrics and their use (16–18). Scientists have developed dozens of landscape indexes. Specialized computer software is now available to calculate landscape metrics for any type of digital data and their use is becoming more widespread. For example, scientists investigate how animals respond to landscape pattern by correlating animal censuses with landscape indexes. Forest managers use landscape indexes to examine if their management actions alter landscape pattern drastically. Also, governments use landscape indexes as indicators of ecosystem health. Landscape indexes offer a simple, objective and cost-effective way to summarize landscape characteristics for large areas. However, the relationship between the ecological question at hand, and the landscape index in use has to be kept in mind in order to attain meaningful results.

Simulation Models

Computers provide not only the means to analyze large amounts of data and to synthesize the information using landscape indexes, they also allow the use of simulation models. Landscape simulation models are unique in that they are spatially explicit; that is, they simulate processes, such as fires or animal movements, at actual locations in a landscape (19, 20). Traditional, nonspatial, forest models included processes such as fire, but they model fire only as an event that may affect any given location with a certain likelihood. What is unique about spatial landscape models is that they can incorporate neighborhood effects. For example, a fire is much more likely to spread and burn a stand that adjoins the fire than one that is far away. Only spatially explicit models can incorporate such aspects of landscape processes.

Landscape ecology and management face a challenge, because the scale of analysis required to study landscapes usually precludes the use of experiments as a tool for scientific investigation. Landscapes are in many cases simply too large to be altered for a scientific experiment. Also, there are many cases where a landscape may be unique, such as the Florida Everglades. Experimenting with such a landscape would not only be unfeasible, but also a major risk for the survival of the ecosystem under investigation. Also, a scientific experiment traditionally requires the use of controls (i.e., similar experimental units that are not altered in the experiments) and replicates (i.e., a number of similar units in which the experiment is conducted). The use of controls and replicates is obviously not feasible when a unique landscape is studied. Furthermore, landscape processes may operate over large time scales. For example, changes in fire frequency may not translate into altered landscape patterns until many decades have passed, because natural fire regimes contain high degree of variability, and broadscale ecological processes often operate slowly.

All these factors have resulted in the extensive use of simulation models in landscape ecology. Models are used for many different purposes. Some models are fairly simple and mainly used to test scientific understanding. For example, scientists built simple models simulating forest fire and regrowth to examine which fire frequency would result in the landscape pattern observed in boreal forests. Other models incorporate many processes simultaneously and are currently being tested as tools to improve complex forest management decisions (see Figure 7.7 in color insert). The results of forest management are difficult to predict over large areas. Foresters have good tools to manage single stands, but struggle to manage landscapes as a whole. This may change by using landscape simulation models, to test, for example, the effects of different forest harvesting regimes on a landscape over a century or more. Such an approach allows predicting changes in landscape pattern that result from certain management practices. It would also allow predicting, for instance, which wildlife species may increase in the landscape and which are likely to decrease. Such information allows proactive management decisions, and might help avoid ecological problems before they arise. However, these uses of simulation models are only now being explored, and time will tell if they become a widely used tool.

Concluding Statement— Management Rules

Landscape ecology is a young subdiscipline of ecology but attention to pattern and process at the landscape scale is increasing, both in forest science and forest management. Landscape ecologists recognized early the importance of the landscape context on ecosystems. Forest managers are becoming increasingly aware that ecosystem management requires looking beyond the stand level at the entire landscape and managing for all its components. The importance of landscape patterns and processes for the management of a forest will vary for different ecosystems, but a few general rules for forest managers emerge.

The first rule is to take the landscape context into account when managing an area. Questions that are important to consider before making management decisions include: Does this management area contain unique habitat types, or key resources for certain wildlife species? How important is the management area as a corridor for animal dispersal? What is the effect of management actions on neighboring ecosystems?

The second rule is to carefully choose the spatial unit of management. Traditionally, forests were managed one stand at a time. This chapter provided numerous examples of interactions between patterns and processes in forests that operate at much larger scales. Management can take these interactions into account only when it adapts the scale of management to the scale at which the most important pattern and processes of an ecosystem occur. In mountainous areas, entire watersheds are often managed as a whole, and this appears to be a successful way to define boundaries of management units based on ecological properties.

The third rule is to use natural disturbance processes as a guideline for forest management (12,21). For example, ecosystems previously shaped by extensive crown fires may be more resilient to large clearcuts than forests that exhibit only gap dynamics. The comparison of landscape pattern in managed and unmanaged forests can assist forest managers in their harvest planning.

Landscapes are inherently complex and dynamic, and much is still to be learned about the relationships between patterns and processes. Our current understanding suggests certain changes in forest management practices. However, more research is needed, and we hope that the way we manage forested landscapes will evolve with increasing knowledge about them. Landscape scale management is challenging and not all attempts will succeed. Because of the development of tools and methods that can be applied to large spatial data sets we are better equipped today than ever before to rise to the challenge. Landscape ecology as a science, and forest management as an application of the science, will have succeeded when we find ways to integrate the utilization and the conservation of forested landscapes.

References

1. J. A. BISSONETTE, *Wildlife and Landscape Ecology—Effects of Pattern and Scale,* Springer-Verlag, New York, 1997.

2. R. T. T. FORMAN AND M. GODRON, *Landscape Ecology,* John Wiley & Sons, New York, 1986.

3. D. L. URBAN, R. V. O'NEILL, H. H. SHUGART JR., *BioScience, 37,* 119 (1987).

4. S. ZONNEFELD AND R. T. T. FORMAN, *Changing Landscapes: An Ecological Perspective,* Springer-Verlag, New York, 1990.

5. M. G. TURNER AND R. H. GARDNER, *Quantitative Methods in Landscape Ecology,* Springer-Verlag, New York, 1991.

6. M. G. TURNER, *Landscape Heterogeneity and Disturbance,* Springer-Verlag, New York, 1987.

7. M. L. HEINSELMAN, "Fire and fire succession in the conifer forests of northern North America." In *Forest Succession—Concepts and Application*, D. C. West, H. H. Shugart and D. B. Botkin, eds., Springer-Verlag, New York, 1981.

8. D. G. MCCULLOUGH, R. A. WERNER, D. NEUMANN, *Ann. Rev. Entom., 43,* 107 (1998).

9. H. ANDRÉN, *Oikos, 71,* 355 (1994).

10. J. F. FRANKLIN AND R. T. T. FORMAN, *Landscape Ecol., 1,* 5 (1987).

11. E. J. GUSTAFSON AND T. R. CROW, *J. Env. Manag., 46,* 77 (1996).

12. D. J. MLADENOFF, M. A. WHITE, J. PASTOR, AND T. R. CROW, *Ecol. Appl., 3,* 294 (1993).

13. T. A. SPIES, W. J. RIPPLE, G. A. BRADSHAW, *Ecol. Appl., 4,* 555 (1994).

14. R. T. T. FORMAN AND L. E. ALEXANDER, *Ann. Rev. Ecol. Syst., 29,* 207 (1998).

15. H. J. MADER, *Biol. Cons., 29,* 81 (1984).

16. E. J. GUSTAFSON, *Ecosystems, 1,* 143 (1998).

17. K. MCGARIGAL AND B. J. MARKS, *Spatial pattern analysis program for quantifying landscape structure,* Gen. Tech. Rep. PNW-GTR-351, Pacific Northwest Research Station, U.S.D.A. For. Serv., Portland, Ore., 1995.

18. M. G. TURNER, *Ann. Rev. Ecol. Syst., 20,* 171 (1989).

19. W. L. BAKER, *Landscape Ecol., 2,* 111 (1989).

20. D. J. MLADENOFF AND W. L. BAKER, *Advances in Spatial Modeling of Forest Landscape Change: Approaches and Applications,* Cambridge University Press, Cambridge, U.K., 1999.

21. P. M. ATTIWILL, *For. Ecol. Manage., 63,* 247 (1994).

CHAPTER 8

Forest Trees: Disease and Insect Interactions

GLEN R. STANOSZ, KENNETH F. RAFFA
AND RONALD L. GIESE[1]

---

[1] Authors' note: This chapter has been revised and condensed from chapters by R. L. Giese and R. F. Patton that were included in previous editions.

147

Like all plants, forest trees are subject to injury and disease caused by adverse environmental influences, including other organisms. They may be affected at all stages in their life cycle, from seed to mature tree. Diseases and insects produce a variety of effects and can cause losses in economic, environmental, recreational, and aesthetic values produced by the forest. *Forest pathology* and *forest entomology* involve study and management of the influences of diseases and insects, respectively, on trees, forests, and forest products. Practitioners of these biological disciplines also are interested in the effects of forest management activities on the occurrence and development of diseases and insects. In the broadest sense, forest pathology and forest entomology include study of diseases and insects affecting trees in nurseries and the landscape, as well as plantations and forests. Although not discussed here, the degradation of wood products such as lumber by microorganisms and insects often is included. Thus, forest pathology and forest entomology literature is vast. Current texts and reference books emphasize the nature of damaging agents, as well as the principles and practices that are employed in their management (1–8).

Introduction

Origins and Roles of Microorganisms and Insects in Forests

Although the destructive activities of some forest microorganisms and insects are well known and often dramatic, most are beneficial to trees and forest ecosystems. The periodic epidemic or outbreak, and even the sudden, severe, and long-lasting damage resulting from introduction of exotic organisms, are exceptions rather than the rule in forests. The vast majority of microorganisms and insects have long evolved with the tree species comprising the forests they inhabit, and only a relatively small proportion of these are capable of causing severe damage.

Many activities of microorganisms and insects are of direct benefit to plants, animals, and other organisms that comprise forest communities. As pollinators, certain insects are necessary for reproduction of some forest tree species (e.g., maples and willows). A diverse group of fungi and the feeder roots of trees form mutually beneficial symbioses called *mycorrhizae* that function in uptake of both water and nutrients (9). Both microorganisms and insects are important sources of food or substrate for similar organisms and for a vast array of wildlife, including birds and mammals. In addition, many microorganisms and insects are parasites or predators of other species that can damage forest trees. They can play a major role in suppressing pest populations and reducing the damage they cause.

Microorganisms and insects, although damaging to individual trees, also have important roles in the function of forest ecosystems and in the development of forest stands. Insects deteriorate leaves, bark, and wood, which microorganisms ultimately decompose. Fungi, in particular, are essential and unique in their ability to decompose complex substrates such as wood. This process is essential in the cycling of nutrients necessary to sustain all other life. Decomposition of killed trees also reduces accumulation of fuel in forests, and therefore decreases the risk and intensity of wildfires. As microorganisms and insects kill some trees or cause damage that leads to stem breakage or "windthrow," they provide disturbance that alters forest structure. For example, mineral soil may be exposed and a gap may open in the canopy to provide light, allowing new seedlings to become established or releasing other trees from the effects of competition. Particular pathogens and insects also can exhibit host preferences or even very narrow host specificity. As they damage certain plant species and leave others unharmed, they can influence individual species distribution and the composition of the plant community. Similarly, in removing shorter-lived or intolerant "pioneer" species, pathogens and insects may be powerful forces in driving or directing the succession of forest plant communities.

Losses Caused by Forest Tree Diseases and Insects

When they interfere with the objectives of owners and managers of forest lands, both microorganisms and insects might be considered forest "pests." Activity of forest pests can inhibit production of a diversity of benefits, including aesthetic, recreational, environmental, and economic values. Although more emphasis is being placed on noneconomic values of forests, estimates of the damage caused by forest pests usually are associated with their impact on the quality or quantity of forest products such as fiber and lumber. Indeed, development of the disciplines of forest pathology and forest entomology, and continued research in these fields, is very much motivated by the potential for reducing the tremendous economic losses caused by forest pests.

A sudden and unpredictable destruction of forest trees resulting from an event of dramatic proportions can be referred to as a *catastrophe*. Examples of catastrophic events include massive ice or windstorms, wildfires, and extensive outbreaks of insects such as the mountain pine beetle or epidemics of diseases such as chestnut blight. It has been estimated that during the 20th century, almost 300 million cubic meters of timber were destroyed during catastrophes (10). Almost half of this catastrophic loss is attributed to the activity of insects.

Less spectacular but actually more important than catastrophe, is total *growth impact*, which is a continuous and pervasive feature of forests. *Growth*

impact is the result of all the various effects resulting from damaging agents, or the sum of both tree *mortality* and tree *growth loss* (10). Mortality refers simply to death from natural causes. Growth loss includes reduced rates of terminal or diameter growth, losses of accumulated growth (e.g., by decay), losses of efficiency in utilizing a site, and losses in quality.

Our knowledge of the losses caused by forest tree diseases and insects is grossly inadequate, and for lack of better figures, we continue to quote the estimates made at the time the concept of growth impact was derived in 1952, as shown in Table 8.1 (10). These estimates do, however, give some idea of the enormous annual magnitude of total growth impact. In addition, differences are apparent in the relative proportions of mortality and growth loss that are caused by diseases, insects, and other destructive agents. The growth impact resulting from diseases and insects, for example, is far greater than that resulting from fire. The majority of growth impact attributed to diseases is the result of growth loss, whereas insects cause greater losses due to mortality. More recent reports of mortality (11) and pest activity (12) confirm the enormity of losses resulting from forest tree pests, and identify the numerous and diverse diseases and insects that continue to affect the health of forest trees.

Table 8.1   Estimated Single-Year Losses Caused by Destructive Agents to Forests

Loss Factor	Total Volume Reduction*	Insects	Diseases	Fire	All Other**	
Mortality						
	Growing stock	99.4	28	22	7	43
	Sawtimber	29.9	40	18	6	36
Growth loss						
	Growing stock	217.7	10	56	19	15
	Sawtimber	73.5	11	57	21	11

*Million cubic meters.

**Includes weather, animals, suppression, logging damage.

Source: Timber resources for America's future, U.S.D.A. For. Serv. Res. Rpt. 14, 1958

Diseases and Insects Affecting Forest Trees

The health of forest trees is affected by numerous factors, including diseases and insects, that subject them to stress. At any point in time, several factors may be operating concurrently, so that the general state of health of a tree may be determined by the total effect of all stresses (13). For convenience in study and understanding, however, we separate the treatment of these factors into various disciplines, such as pathology and entomology. In each of these fields of study, damage may be classified in several ways, for example, according to the causal agent, the portion of the tree affected, the process or function disrupted, or the stage of development of the tree.

The Causes of Forest Tree Diseases

Plant *disease* can be defined as: a malfunction of a metabolic process or a disturbance of normal structure of a plant, that is caused by some abiotic *agent* or biotic *pathogen*, is influenced by the environment in which they exist, and results from continuous irritation. Abiotic agents are noninfectious and nonparasitic; biotic pathogens (e.g., a bacterium or fungus) usually are infectious and parasitic. *Injury*, as opposed to disease, also may impair vital functions or disrupt the normal structure, but it is caused by an agent such as fire, insects, or animals that affects the plant only once, briefly, or intermittently, and the irritation is discontinuous or temporary. *Damage* is sometimes used as a synonym for injury, but it usually connotes a decrease in quantity or quality of a product that decreases its economic value. A reaction (often visible) of the plant to disease is called a *symptom*, and any structure of the pathogen on or in the affected plant is called a *sign*. Symptoms and signs are used to characterize and diagnose diseases.

Abiotic or Noninfectious Agents   A number of abiotic agents cause disease in trees, including extremes of moisture and temperature, nutrient excess or deficiency, and toxic substances in the air or soil (3, 6–8). Mechanical injury may be inflicted by hail, ice, snow, and windstorms; lightning damage may kill individual trees or even trees in groups. Diseases caused by abiotic agents are often difficult to diagnose because the causal agent is no longer present or active, or because the cause and effect relationship is difficult to establish.

Temperature or moisture extremes may cause direct damage to trees or so weaken them that they are predisposed to attack by microorganisms. Sunscald canker of thin-barked trees often follows upon a sudden exposure to direct summer sun, for example, after thinning. Days and nights of high and low temperatures during late winter or early spring may cause a similar injury to bark, exposing it to sun and then freezing it again by a rapid drop in temperature at night. When warm winds in winter cause excessive transpiration, and roots in frozen ground cannot replace the water, the foliage of conifers may suffer winter injury or winter drying.

Physical and chemical characteristics of soils may have profound effects on tree growth and tree species differ greatly in their tolerance of various soil properties. Soil texture, for example, influences root development, aeration, moisture penetration, and water holding capacity. Forest tree species vary in the range of soil pH in which each may thrive, and soil must provide a balance of macro- and micronutrients within limits that also vary among species. Soil conditions in which nutrients or other chemicals are deficient or in excess may be encountered in local areas, especially in nurseries and forest plantations. As forest management becomes more intensive, forest fertilization may become almost routine, but there is also the likelihood of damage from a variety of chemicals such as fertilizers, fungicides, insecticides, and herbicides, if they are applied at excessive rates or under improper conditions.

In recent decades, air pollution has reached such high levels that forest and urban trees in industrialized regions of the world have been damaged (Figure 8.1). Many chemicals toxic to plants are introduced into the atmosphere, especially by transportation vehicles, industrial processes, and power plants. Sulfur dioxide, produced in coal combus-

Figure 8.1 Symptoms produced by aspen exposed to sulfur dioxide. (Courtesy of U.S. Department of Agriculture.)

tion and other industrial processes, and the photochemical pollutants ozone and peroxyacetyl nitrate, the main components of urban smog, are major causes of damage to conifers in particular. Eastern white pine has suffered damage from sulfur dioxide and ozone, and disease of ponderosa pine in southern California is attributed to prolonged exposure to aerial oxidants, mainly ozone. Fluorides have caused local damage to forest and orchard trees when released into the atmosphere from ore reduction, fertilizer, and ceramics installations. The potential for both wet and dry deposition of acidic substances to influence plant growth, especially that of forest trees, also is attracting considerable attention. At present, however, the effects of acidic deposition on forest trees remain unknown and the subject of continuing investigation. There are no research results indicating that acid precipitation has a direct damaging effect on forest vegetation, but the complexity of forest ecosystems makes it difficult to document such effects conclusively.

Biotic or Infectious Agents Most diseases of forest trees are caused by biotic agents, usually referred to as pathogens. These include viruses, bacteria (including phytoplasmas), fungi, parasitic higher plants, and nematodes. Of these, fungi cause the largest number of diseases as well as the greatest

total loss. Examples of diseases caused by these pathogens are described in the following sections.

Diseases Caused by Fungi

The most numerous and destructive agents causing tree diseases are fungi. The basic structural unit of fungi is the *hypha,* a microscopic threadlike filament or tube that contains the cytoplasm. Collectively, many hyphae make up *mycelium,* which comprises the vegetative body of the fungus. Mycelium is seen in the growth of the common bread mold or the white mycelial fans beneath the bark of a tree root attacked by the root rot fungi in the genus *Armillaria*. Fungi reproduce by spores produced on fruiting structures that vary in complexity from a simple hypha to complex bodies, such as the mushroom that emerges from the soil or the shelflike bracket or "conk" on the trunk of a tree with heartrot. Some fungus spores are disseminated by wind, but fungi are also distributed by rain, insects, birds and other animals, and even human beings. On a suitable substrate the spore germinates to form a simple hypha or germ tube, which then elongates and branches to form another mycelium.

Fungi are heterotrophic, requiring complex compounds that are synthesized by autotrophic organisms such as chlorophyll-containing plants. They secrete enzymes that degrade their substrates and allow absorption of nutrients from organic matter, either as *saprophytes* on dead material or as *parasites* on living plants or animals. Most fungi are saprophytes, and the deterioration of dead organic material by saprophytic fungi is often designated as rot or decay. The activities of parasitic fungi disrupt the structures or life processes of their hosts, and disease results. These diseases vary enormously in the species and parts of the tree affected, in symptoms, and in the type of damage they cause. Therefore, the effects of diseases on the production of various values of the forest and their significance to forest management are also variable; some may be inconsequential, but others may be limiting factors in growth and management of a species.

Foliage Diseases   A large number of fungi cause foliage diseases that can vary greatly in both the symptoms produced and in their ultimate effects on tree health (3, 6–8). Growth and vigor may be reduced, but the time of year of the attack and the shoot and foliage characteristics of the tree greatly influence the amount of damage caused. In wet years that favor spread of spores and repeated infection by many leaf pathogens, complete defoliation can result. Young seedlings with relatively few leaves can be severely damaged, but diseases that damage most of the leaves of even very large trees can have great and prolonged impacts on tree health.

A variety of leaf spot and anthracnose pathogens are among the most damaging fungi to broadleaved tree species. Large numbers of small leaf spots, each resulting from an individual infection, can cause leaves to drop. Defoliation of black cherry seedlings, caused by *Blumeriella jaapii*, can greatly reduce their growth or even lead to death. Anthracnose symptoms are characterized by dark discoloration and a collapse of affected leaf tissue sometimes referred to as watersoaking. As the pathogen grows through the leaf, the areas killed progressively enlarge and coalesce. The effects of sycamore anthracnose, caused by *Apiognomonia veneta*, are compounded as it also colonizes and kills buds, succulent shoots, and twigs.

Radial growth of conifers is often reduced in proportion to the degree of defoliation, and there is usually an accompanying reduction in vigor. Cosmetic damage that reduces quality also is important in ornamentals, especially in Christmas trees; a single year of attack may completely destroy marketability. The brown spot needle blight, caused by *Mycosphaerella dearnessii*, (Figure 8.2), has extensively damaged Christmas tree plantations of Scots pine, especially in the Great Lakes region. The same disease affects production of longleaf pine in the South, where it defoliates seedlings and kills young trees or greatly delays their height growth, keeping them in the "grass stage" for unacceptably long periods. In the western United States, *Elytroderma deformans*, causes a serious needle disease of ponderosa, Jeffrey, and lodgepole pines. The fungus initially infects needles, but can grow into the bark

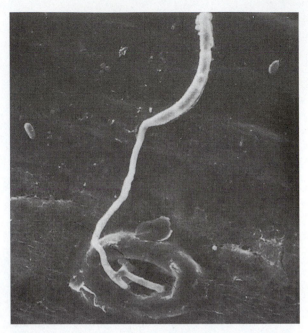

Figure 8.2   Growth of a germ tube from a spore of the brown spot fungus, *Mycosphaerella dearnessii*, on a needle of Scots pine, and development in the stomatal antechamber as seen with the scanning electron microscope.

of branches and persist for years in western forests at a low, endemic level. Under conditions that are not yet well understood, however, repeated defoliation may occur and result in mortality.

Rust Diseases   The rust fungi, so called because of the orange color of many of their spores, constitute a group of highly specialized parasites with complex life cycles. Both hardwoods and conifers are hosts of various rusts that may attack fruits or cones, leaves, and stems (Figure 8.3) (3, 6–8). Most rust fungi produce five different spore stages appearing in a definite sequence, although some species have only two. Although rust fungi often have very narrow host ranges, many require two different and widely unrelated host plants to complete their life cycle. Their different spore stages have specific functions in dissemination, survival, and reproduction. *Cronartium ribicola*, the cause of the white pine blister rust disease, produces sper-

Figure 8.3 Aecial pustules or "blisters" containing orange masses of aeciospores on a branch canker of white pine blister rust.

matia (pycniospores) and aeciospores on white pines, and three other spore forms (urediniospores, teliospores, and basidiospores) on the alternate host plants including currants and gooseberries in the genus *Ribes*.

Stem rusts of conifers are diseases of major impact in natural forests and plantations. The white pine blister rust, a native of Asia, spread to Europe and from there was introduced to North America on imported white pine planting stock in about 1900. On this continent it found a number of highly susceptible hosts in the white (five-needle) pines and it has spread to become one of the limiting factors in growth and management of these commercially important trees. The fungus produces branch and stem cankers that girdle and may kill trees of all ages and sizes, although the disease is

most important as a killer of seedlings and young trees. The fusiform rust pathogen, *Cronartium quercuum* f. sp. *fusiforme*, alternates between southern pines and oaks. Although many loblolly and slash pines are killed by development of the elongated fusiform (spindle-shaped) stem galls, longleaf pine and shortleaf pines are relatively resistant (Figure 8.4). This fungus is native to North America, but has become more damaging as management of susceptible pine species has become more widespread and intensive (24).

Figure 8.4 Spindle-shaped gall on the main stem of a loblolly pine, induced by *Cronartium quercuum* f. sp. *fusiforme*. (Courtesy of U.S.D.A. Forest Service.)

Both conifers and hardwoods are affected by a large number of foliage rust diseases. The *Melampsora* rusts of poplars are receiving increased attention as clonal plantations of hybrid poplars and cottonwoods are being established in the Pacific Northwest and the southern United States. Premature defoliation reduces growth rates, and increases susceptibility of defoliated trees to damage from other agents including cold temperatures and stem canker pathogens.

Vascular Wilt Diseases and Stain Fungi   Vascular wilts are among the most publicized tree diseases, probably because some are not relegated to the forest, but rather kill trees along city streets and in suburban yards. Vascular wilt pathogens colonize xylem vessels. Their activity reduces or inhibits normal water conduction in stems, resulting in permanent wilting of leaves and death of branches or entire trees. Dutch elm disease, oak wilt, and Verticillium wilt each can cause sudden death, killing susceptible hosts in a single growing season. The notoriety of wilt disease fungi is enhanced by their particular adaptations enabling survival and spread.

The Verticillium wilt pathogen can persist in resistant structures called *sclerotia* in the soil for many years. Sclerotia can be moved in soil with nursery stock or already be present in soil when trees are planted in the landscape. When the opportunity arises, the fungus grows from sclerotia to infect roots of maples, ashes, elms, and many other species through natural or artificial wounds. Sclerotia form in the debris of its colonized hosts, so careless landscape use of untreated chips of killed trees is a potential means of further spread of the pathogen.

The introduced fungi that cause Dutch elm disease (14) and the native oak wilt pathogen (15) are among the most destructive diseases of ornamental and shade trees. The American elm is most susceptible to the former, and species in the red oak group are most damaged by the latter. In both cities and forests, these fungi spread rapidly from tree to tree through grafted roots (Figure 8.5). They overwinter and develop fruiting bodies in their dead hosts, and failure to remove recently killed trees results in production of inoculum that is carried long distances by their insect vectors. *Ophiostoma ulmi* and *O. novo-ulmi* are carried to elms by the European elm bark beetle and the native elm bark beetle, and introduced to trees as these insects feed on or bore into stems. *Ceratocystis fagacearum* is carried to fresh wounds on oaks, such as those resulting from pruning, by beetles including some members of the family Nitidulidae. Costs for con-

Figure 8.5   Large oak wilt "pocket" in an oak forest continues to enlarge by marginal spread through root grafts.

trol of these diseases, removal of the many trees killed, and planting of replacements total millions of dollars annually.

Many other similar fungi colonize the vascular tissues of trees, imparting discolorations referred to as "stain," ranging from brown to blue to black. Although many of these pathogens are not highly aggressive, and when acting alone may have limited affects on tree health, some stain fungi are very damaging when interacting with insects in complexes or in decline diseases (described later in this chapter). In addition, discoloration of wood in standing trees or stain developing after harvest can reduce the value of pulpwood and be a cause of serious reduction in lumber grade.

Canker Diseases Cankers result when areas of the bark and vascular cambium of stems, branches, and twigs are infected and killed by a variety of fungi. There is often a discrete canker margin between the healthy and the colonized tissues, which may be discolored and deformed, sunken or swollen, and surrounded by a layer of healthy *callus* tissue. Ends of branches may be killed as they are "girdled" by cankers that coalesce or expand around their circumference, and stems weakened by cankers or subsequent decay often break. The variety of canker diseases that affect a wide range of hosts are categorized according to the duration of the association and the relative balance in the host–pathogen interaction (6).

Canker diseases may be annual or perennial. Annual canker pathogens, such as *Fusarium solani* (which affects maples and several other hardwoods), apparently are active at a particular location in the stem during a single growing season. Usually only a small area is killed, and as the tree grows it may become enclosed to form a permanent defect in the wood. A perennial canker disease usually involves a longer-term relationship between the pathogen and its host. Year after year the pathogen gradually enlarges the area it has colonized, and the host responds by development of a new layer of callus. The resulting concentric ridges or layers of callus characterize these "target cankers" such as *Eutypella* canker of maple and *Nectria* canker of various hardwoods.

The relative balance in the host–pathogen interaction also may be used to categorize canker diseases. A high level of host resistance normally dominates many interactions. Factors that induce tree stress, however, may allow relatively weak pathogens to become more aggressive and cause saprobic canker diseases. *Cytospora* canker of blue spruce, which damages older trees grown outside of their native geographic range, and some *Fusicoccum*, *Diplodia*, and *Sphaeropsis* cankers of drought-stressed trees are examples. Diffuse canker diseases are characterized by rapid growth of the pathogen through host bark with little or no callus development. Resulting from interactions that are dominated by aggressiveness of the pathogen, such diffuse cankers may girdle and kill even large trees in a single year. Damage caused by *Hypoxylon* canker of aspens, the most important disease of these species in the Great Lakes area, can decimate entire stands in just a few years (Figure 8.6).

Stem Decay When wood is used as food by fungi, cell walls are degraded to result in changes in the physical and chemical properties of wood. This process, and the resulting altered wood, are known as decay or rot. Most decay occurs in the central core or "heartwood" of nonliving wood inside trees, and may be referred to as heartrot (Figure 8.7). Decay of heartwood, which reduces harvestable volume and wood quality, has been estimated to

Figure 8.6 Stem breakage and cankering (arrows) in a stand of aspen trees severely affected by *Hypoxylon* canker.

Figure 8.7 Typical brown cubical heartrot in a log of Douglas fir. (Courtesy of Canadian Forest Service.)

partially rotted wood may be unsatisfactory for construction. Pulp yields from partially white-rotted wood may be relatively high (much of the cellulose will remain, however, whereas brown-rotted wood cannot be used for pulp). Because of changes in texture that accompany the decay process, various adjectives, including laminated, spongy, stringy, and cubical are used to describe different wood rots.

Many different species of fungi cause stem decay, but each has its own distinctive characteristics (3, 6–8). *Phellinus pini* is among the most damaging stem decay pathogens across North America. Decay columns may extend for many meters, destroying the economic value of entire stems of conifers including Douglas fir, pines, spruces, larches, hemlocks, and western red cedar. A related species, *Phellinus tremulae*, is restricted to aspens, but is the greatest cause of decay in its host species and again decay columns are often extensive. Fruiting bodies of *Oxyporus populinus* commonly are observed in old wounds, cracks, or cankers of sugar and red maples, and some other hardwoods. The decay of both heartwood and sapwood caused by this fungus often is restricted to within a meter of the conk, and therefore most of the wood in affected trees may be usable.

Although the number of trees decayed and the volume of rot generally increase as trees age, the total amount of decay in forest stands is extremely variable. The associated decay fungi, as well as the rate of decay, vary greatly among tree species. Events in the history of the stand also strongly influence decay, especially those such as fires, severe storms, and past silvicultural practices which have resulted in broken branches or trunk wounds through which many decay fungi enter trees. Determining the amount of decay in given forest stands, however, is important for the preparation of accurate inventories of present and potential growing stock upon which estimates of yield and allowable cuts are made in forests managed for wood production (see Chapters 9 and 13). Foresters can estimate the amount of decay in a stand with information from sample plot measurements and by examining trees for external indicators of decay,

be responsible for the majority of growth impact attributed to forest tree diseases. Because the effect of heartrot is largely on deadwood, it is not a major influence of tree vigor or mortality unless structural weakness leads to breakage. In contrast, decay of sapwood, which is living and has important functions in tree growth and maintenance, can strongly affect tree health. Although sapwood is relatively resistant to decay in many living trees, it can be decayed by some fungi.

Wood rots produced by fungi are commonly grouped into two main types, brown and white rots, referring to color changes characteristic of different decay processes. Brown-rot fungi decompose wood by using primarily the carbohydrates (cellulose) of the cell walls, whereas white-rot fungi utilize both the carbohydrate and lignin components of the cell wall. Chapter 20 contains further discussion of the chemical nature of wood. These differences in the mechanism of decay are important in that they can affect the utilization of decayed wood. Both types of decay weaken wood, and even such as fruiting bodies or "conks" (Figure 8.8), swollen knots, and branch stubs.

Root Diseases A large group of very different fungi causes root diseases that reduce vigor, growth, and even kill trees from every stage of development from seedling to mature tree (3, 6–8). Some attack only young, succulent roots such as the feeder roots, essentially causing tree health to deteriorate through starvation. Other fungi are root sapwood colonists, and some first kill roots by parasitic attack and then decay them. Some root pathogens also cause butt rot (decay of the basal portion of the

stem) causing a loss of growth and reduction in both volume and quality. Trees with root and butt rots also are subject to windthrow (Figure 8.9), providing gaps in the forest canopy. Development of symptoms on seedlings in clusters in nurseries and large openings in forests (sometimes called root rot "centers") may result from underground spread of root pathogens.

Many devastating root diseases are widely distributed in temperate forests throughout the world. The genus *Armillaria* (16) contains some species known as aggressive tree killers, and others that appear to be opportunistic pathogens of trees under stress. Spores disseminated from mushrooms (Figure 8.10) may be responsible for initiation of new

Figure 8.8 Fruiting bodies ("conks") of a stem decay fungus on white ash. (Courtesy of U.S.D.A. Forest Service.)

Figure 8.9 Wind-thrown trees in a *Phellinus weirii* infection center of a 50-year-old stand of Douglas fir. (Courtesy of G. W. Wallis and Canadian Forest Service.)

Figure 8.10 Clump of mushroom fruiting bodies of the root disease fungus in the genus *Armillaria* at the base of a white pine sapling killed by the fungus. Notice the white mycelial fan on the stem and the characteristic resin-infiltrated mass of soil around the root collar.

disease centers, but these fungi spread locally from colonized dead tree or stump "food bases" by black, shoestringlike strands of mycelium. Called rhizomorphs, these strands penetrate the bark of living roots to colonize new substrate as far as several meters from the original food base. *Armillaria* species and *Heterobasidion annosum* (17), another important root pathogen of conifers in much of North America and northern Europe, also can spread by root-to-root contact. Annosum root disease centers commonly begin when wind-borne spores germinate on freshly cut stump surfaces, such as those produced by thinning or other harvest of intensively managed plantations. *H. anno-*

sum continues to spread through roots of cut or killed trees, infecting residual trees and natural or planted regeneration that contact diseased roots. Similarly, *Phellinus weirii* is especially damaging to Douglas fir in the Pacific Northwest and British Columbia, persists in decaying roots of the previous stand, and infects the roots of young trees through root contact (18). Management of relatively extensive areas occupied by root pathogens for decades, or even centuries, is among the greatest challenges facing foresters today.

Other Pathogens that Cause Diseases of Trees

Viruses, Phytoplasmas, and Bacteria Viruses are extremely small and simple infectious agents visible only with the use of the electron microscope. Composed of nucleic acid and proteins, viruses utilize molecules produced by the living cells of the plants they inhabit for their own replication. Although plant viruses cause many major diseases of agricultural crops, the pathological importance of virus diseases of forest trees such as elm mosaic, birch line pattern, or locust witches'-broom is much less certain (19). As the incidence and effects of the many characterized (and many more as yet unknown) viruses of trees become better understood, perhaps they will be considered of greater significance. Moreover, because vegetative propagation perpetuates viruses, trends toward plantation forestry and vegetative reproduction of some species (e.g., poplars) might increase the threat and extent of virus diseases in commercial forest plantings.

A few tree diseases are caused by phytoplasmas that colonize the phloem of tree roots, stems, and leaves. These were previously referred to as mycoplasma-like organisms or MLOs. Phytoplasmas lack a cell wall, but possess a distinct flexible membrane and are often smaller than bacteria. Because chlorosis (yellowing) of foliage is a common symptom, these are commonly referred to as "yellows" diseases. Ash yellows is characterized by slow deterioration and eventual death of affected trees many years after initial infection (20). In contrast, elm yellows has very rapidly killed many elms in the eastern and central United States. Susceptibility of American elm to the elm yellows phytoplasma also complicates efforts to control Dutch elm disease by breeding for resistance to the introduced fungi that cause the latter.

Bacteria are known to cause relatively few diseases of forest and shade trees, but some can be serious and result in a variety of symptoms (7). Xylem-inhabiting bacteria can cause elm, oak, and sycamore leaf scorches. The bacterial canker of poplar is a serious disease in Europe, but so far is unknown in North America. No new poplar clones are released in European countries without intensive selection and testing for resistance to this disease. Presence of the bacterial canker pathogen in Europe also has led to restrictions on importation of poplars into the United States. In many species of trees a water-soaked condition of the heartwood, called "wetwood," along with discoloration and production of gas (principally methane), is associated with bacteria. The maintenance of an anaerobic situation and the presence of anaerobic bacteria, especially *Clostridium* spp. and *Methanobacterium* spp., are key factors in the production of wetwood rather than normal heartwood. Ring shake (a crack formed in the tree along an annual ring), lumber checking, and the abnormally long time required to dry lumber are problems associated with products from trees with wetwood. Bacteria also are involved in the processes causing discoloration and decay in the wood of trees.

Nematodes Plant-parasitic nematodes are microscopic roundworms of great importance as pests of agricultural and ornamental crops, yet few nematode diseases of forest trees have attracted great attention or have been well studied. Severe damage, however, has occurred in some seedling nurseries and plantations established on abandoned farmlands (21). Plant-parasitic nematodes feed by piercing cells with a needlelike stylet. Their attacks on fine feeder roots of trees can lead to browning, deformity, and death of roots or the production of root galls. Repeated and prolonged injury caused by nematodes gradually decreases the water- and nutrient-absorbing area of feeder roots. Affected seedlings may be stunted (Figure 8.11) or killed, and the growth rates and vigor of larger trees may gradually decrease.

Much more dramatic damage, including rapid death, results from pine wilt disease caused by the pine wood nematode, *Bursaphelenchus xylophilus* (22). This nematode is lethal to Japanese red pine and black pine in East Asia and has been epidemic in Japan for decades. Juvenile pine wood nematodes are vectored by wood boring beetles in the genus *Monochamus*, and enter trees through beetle feeding wounds. The nematodes feed and complete their development within tree stems. Since its identification in the United States in 1979, the pine

Figure 8.11 Healthy sand pine on left and seedling injured by lance nematodes on right. (Courtesy of U.S.D.A. Forest Service.)

wood nematode has attracted much attention and concern that it could be a serious menace to our pines. Local epidemics have appeared on two exotic pines, Austrian pine and Scots pine, and some native pines in warm regions, but the nematode does not appear to pose a threat to most conifer forests of North America. Discovery of the pine wood nematode in wood chips exported from the southern United States has had an impact on international trade. Embargoes have been enacted to prevent movement of some wood products, and heat treatment to kill nematodes has been required before shipment of lumber to countries where the nematode is not present.

Mistletoes Mistletoes are perennial evergreen seed plants that are parasitic on stems or branches of trees or shrubs. Mistletoe seeds germinate on the surfaces of their host plants. Rootlike structures emerge and penetrate through bark and into vascular tissues to obtain water and nutrients from their hosts. The leafy, or so-called true, mistletoes are well known for their ornamental and sentimental uses during the Christmas holidays. They occur chiefly on hardwoods, but some grow on a few conifer species, juniper, cypress, and incense cedar. They are most abundant in warmer regions and especially in the arid southwest. In general, the leafy mistletoes have not caused major economic damage in forest stands of the United States.

The numerous dwarf mistletoe species in the genus *Arceuthobium*, however, are recognized as the single most important disease problem in conifer forests of the western United States (23). The parasitic growth of these tiny plants (Figure 8.12) can stunt growth of the host to an extreme extent. Host tree responses to colonization include proliferation of abnormal branches in clusters called "brooms," dieback of branches, and eventual tree death. The parasite spreads in the stand by sticky, forcibly ejected seeds that may "shoot" many meters through the air to land in the crowns of other trees. In this way, large radially expanding "infection centers" develop, in which all susceptible trees may be damaged. New, distant infection centers are established when seeds are carried by birds.

Figure 8.12   Shoots of dwarf mistletoe emerging from a colonized branch of ponderosa pine. (Courtesy of U.S.D.A. Forest Service.)

Insects that Damage Forest Trees

Although often unnoticed, ignored, or unappreciated, insects can be the most numerous, diverse, and damaging animals inhabiting forests. As arthropods, insects have rigid, external *exoskeletons* and jointed appendages. The adult insect body is segmented, composed of a head, thorax (bearing three pairs of legs), and abdomen. Whether they initially hatch from eggs or are borne live, insects must periodically shed their exoskeletons to allow growth in size. Thus, as insects develop, they pass through several immature stages. These might be nymphs, that resemble the adult insect they will ultimately become, or larvae (such as caterpillars) that completely change in appearance while undergoing rather dramatic *metamorphosis* into adults. Insects "breathe" through body openings called spiracles and have decentralized, well-developed nervous systems. Their visual and chemical sensory systems often are extremely sensitive and like other animals, insects exhibit sophisticated behaviors. In either immature or adult stages, various insects may be relatively sedentary or highly mobile. Some complete their entire life cycle on a single plant; others are dispersed widely by wind or fly long distances in search of food or mates.

Insect damage to forest trees results directly from ingestion or destruction of plant parts that are fed upon, from colonization (such as tunneling or boring) of trees during feeding and reproduction, or from toxins they egest. The degree of damage that results from these activities vary widely among insect species, their various immature and mature stages, and the tree species and its stage of development from seedling to mature tree. The size of the insect population often strongly influences the degree of damage that results. Because the part of the tree that is damaged also influences whether the damage is merely cosmetic or serious, the different locations of feeding and breeding on and in trees is a convenient way to categorize groups of insects that damage forest trees.

Defoliators Defoliators eat needles and leaves. They include caterpillars, sawflies, leaf beetles, and walkingsticks (Figures 8.13 and 8.14). Some defoliators consume entire needles or leaves; others mine tunnels between the epidermal layers of the tree's foliage. Skeletonizers feed on leaf tissue between the veins. Leaf tiers attach portions of leaves to each other with silk, thereby creating a curled effect.

Insect defoliators vary greatly in their seasonal histories, biologies, and methods of feeding (1, 2, 4, 5). Some species, such as the gypsy moth are polyphagous and include many tree species in their host range. Others are oligophagous and feed only on a few hosts; examples include the European pine sawfly, which feeds on about half a dozen pine species. Defoliators that feed on a single host species such as the larch casebearer, are monophagous.

Tree response to defoliation varies greatly, depending on the individual characteristics of the tree and insect species, time of year, intensity of defoliation, and additional stresses prior to and after the defoliation event. Among conifers, complete defoliation in one growing season can cause immediate tree death (Figure 8.15). Two exceptions include the annually deciduous larch and bald

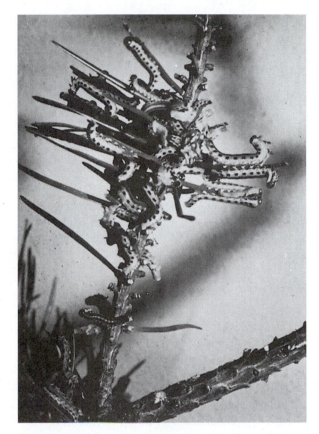

Figure 8.13 Red pine sawfly larvae are defoliators that must feed gregariously if they are to grow and develop normally.

cypress, which can tolerate nearly complete defoliation for several years with little or no mortality, and several southern pines (shortleaf and longleaf pines), which can be completely defoliated and refoliate with only rare mortality.

A single defoliation, such as that resulting from feeding of gypsy moth larvae (24), rarely causes mortality among the broad-leaved trees. Exceptions are hard maple and yellow birch, which may die if completely defoliated during mid-July to mid-August (25). As a general rule, partial defoliation (50 to 90 percent) of broad-leaved and coniferous trees reduces terminal radial growth. Tree branches rarely die until after several seasons of severe defoliation.

Figure 8.14 The walkingstick belongs to the group of pests known as defoliators.

Defoliators often cause indirect damage by weakening their hosts and rendering them susceptible to invasions by other insects, such as bark beetles and borers, that can kill trees. For example, defoliation by budworms may predispose spruces and pines to the attacks of *Ips* and *Dendroctonus* bark beetles. Cankerworms can weaken oaks so that the two-lined chestnut borer can colonize and kill these otherwise resistant trees.

Defoliator outbreaks may cover many thousands of hectares of forest. For example outbreaks of the forest tent caterpillar have encompassed most of the aspen type of north–central North America. Likewise budworm outbreaks have occurred in spruce–fir forests across the continent. Most defoliator outbreaks, however, are more locally distributed.

Bark Beetles Bark beetles are among the most devastating forest insects in the world (26). They have been responsible for the stunting and killing trees in vast areas of forests (Figure 8.16). Most species attack and kill trees that are old, or under environmental stress. However, some species infest healthy, vigorously growing trees, and often inflict serious damage. Bark beetles also have important interactions with fungi (26–28) as vectors, in pathogen–insect complexes, and as factors in the development of decline diseases, which will be discussed later.

Bark beetle adults bore through the bark and produce tunnels called "galleries" in the relatively thin area composed of the vascular cambium and adjacent phloem and xylem. After mating, females lay their eggs between the bark and the wood, either along their galleries or in special niches (Figure 8.17). After hatching, larvae feed in this area,

Figure 8.15 Jack pine mortality resulting from defoliation by the pine tussock moth.

Figure 8.16 Tree mortality on a Colorado mountainside resulting from tunneling activity of the Douglas fir beetle. (Courtesy of W. E. Waters.)

eventually extending their tunnels throughout the circumference of the trunk or branch. This girdling interrupts the translocation of nutrients and moisture, and the tree may soon wilt and die. Trees that are growing vigorously often "pitch out" or intoxify the adult bark beetles in resin. Trees possess an additional means of active defense, consisting of very high levels of toxic compounds that accumulate at the attack site. However, decadent trees and those weakened by drought or insect defoliators may not be able to repel the mining adults or larvae.

Ambrosia beetles (Figure 8.18) infest their galleries with fungi that serve as food for their larvae. Although ambrosia beetles rarely attack healthy trees, they are very significant pests of logs, stored lumber, and wood products (29). In addition to the galleries that may extend deep into the wood, economic value is reduced because of discoloration produced by the associated fungi.

Still another group of bark beetle species infests cones and seeds of pines. Many of these are in the genus *Conopthorus*. Because the activity of cone and seed beetles can cause nearly complete destruction of seed crops, they can be major seed orchard pests.

Wood Borers Wood borers, like bark beetles, bore through the outer bark of trees, but these insects

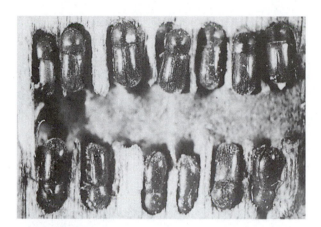

Figure 8.18 Adult stage of the ambrosia beetle, *Xyloterrinus politus*. These individuals have recently emerged from their pupal cases and will soon disperse to infest other trees.

tunnel deep into the sapwood (30). A variety of different types of insects, including beetles, moths, and wasps, comprise this group (1, 2, 4, 5). Many wood borers, such as the two-lined chestnut borer (31), attack trees that are old, dying, or suffering from environmental stress. They may also invade cut pulpwood, logs, and fire-scarred trees. A few species attack healthy, vigorous trees. This is especially true of species that have been accidentally introduced into new regions in which native trees have not evolved appropriate defenses. Devastating losses have occurred in Japan (32) and New Zealand (33) by introduced wood boring species that are much less damaging in their native range. The Asian long-horned beetle has recently been introduced into North America, and is causing serious damage to highly valued urban trees. Its potential impact on North American forests is unknown.

Two major groups of wood-destroying beetles include the long-horned or round-headed borers (Figure 8.19), and the short-horned or flat-headed borers. Females of both groups lay eggs in notches cut into the bark, and the new larvae mine for a period in the phloem. They then turn inward to feed in the wood, where they construct large and damaging tunnels. Some examples of long-horned

Figure 8.17 Galleries excavated by larvae of the smaller European elm bark beetle. Not only does this beetle inflict damage by its feeding activities, but it is also a vector of the Dutch elm disease fungus.

Figure 8.19 Larval (left) and pupal (right) stages of the poplar borer.

Figure 8.20 Spittle masses formed by immature stages (nymphs) of the pine spittle bug help the insect maintain a high-humidity environment while feeding on sap extracted from the tree.

beetles include the pine sawyer and the locust borer. Examples of short-horned beetles include the two-lined chestnut borer (which now primarily attacks oaks) and the bronze birch borer (which can be a particularly damaging pest of ornamental trees).

Sucking Insects   Sucking insects have modified mouth parts that enable them to pierce the foliage, tender twigs, or roots of trees and suck the sap or resin as food. These pests drain the vitality of healthy trees, and, if their numbers are great enough, can cause serious stunting or death of their hosts. Both coniferous and deciduous trees are attacked by sucking insects such as aphids, scales, and spittle bugs (Figure 8.20). Feeding by pine spittle bugs results in necrotic areas on stems or branches, and can cause stunting or death of many coniferous species in the eastern United States (34). Sucking insects can also introduce pathogens into trees or cause hypersensitive reactions. Some of the most damaging exotic insects pests in North America are sucking insects, such as introduced beech scale, the balsam woolly adelgid, and the hemlock woolly adelgid (35–37).

Aphids or plant lice usually attack a tree's tender new foliage or twigs, withdrawing sap and producing sugary secretions commonly referred to as "honeydew." Honeydew serves as a substrate for prolifer-ation of superficial, nonparasitic fungi known as "sooty molds." Sooty mold, therefore, can be used as an indicator of the presence of sucking insects.

Shoot and Bud Insects   Insect feeding on the growing meristem can lead to distortion and stunting of shoots and even forking of the main bole. The pine tip moths, the best known of these pests, occur throughout the world. They are especially damaging in even-aged forests, in plantations, and in ornamental beautification plantings.

The white pine weevil is the most injurious pest of white pine in northeastern North America, and one of the most damaging pests of spruce in northwestern North America (Figure 8.21). Infestation may cause permanent forking of the main bole and render the tree less marketable. Although affected trees are not killed, the recoverable volume often is of low quality.

 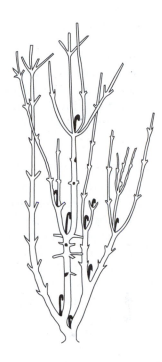

Figure 8.21   A 13-year-old spruce tree with evidence of numerous white pine weevil attacks. The weevil kills the terminal shoot, causing lateral shoots to assume dominance. The attack history is shown schematically on the right. Dead leaders appear as black crooks.

The pine shoot beetle, a bark beetle introduced from Europe, can cause significant damage to Scots pine Christmas trees. Its discovery in the United States led to imposition of quarantine restrictions that add to growers' costs and limit export opportunities.

Root Insects   Root insects cause tree stunting and death by infesting the roots and root collar regions of trees, often of planted conifers. Habits of these pests vary greatly, depending on the host species, age, and mode of attack (1, 2, 4, 5).

Female pales weevils lay their eggs in stumps of harvested trees, and the emerging adults debark newly replanted seedlings (38). Entire young plantations can be killed. The pine root collar weevil infests the trunks of living hard pines from 3 to 20 years old. Feeding by the larvae causes stunting, and severely injured trees often break off at the soil surface or die suddenly during windy periods. Sev-

eral species of caterpillars, such as the swift moth in spruce, exhibit similar behavior.

White grubs, the larvae of May and June beetles, pose serious problems to forest nurseries and new plantings. The adults feed mainly on broad-leaved trees nearby and lay eggs in areas of heavy grass and sod. Larvae feed on the roots and stunt or kill seedlings.

Tree, Pathogen, and Insect Interactions

Microorganisms and insects interact in many interesting ways and participate in unique relationships in the forest ecosystem. Some of these result in very significant damage to the health of individual trees and to forest stands that interfere with production of a variety of forest values. Insects may be *vectors*, responsible for dissemination of a variety of tree pathogens. Trees also may be affected by a fungus–insect *complex*, in which partners each play important roles in development of damage. Finally, both pathogens and insects, along with abiotic agents, can be among multiple interacting factors involved in initiation and progression of a particular syndrome recognized as a *decline disease*.

Vector–Pathogen Relationships

An insect that transfers or transmits a pathogen from one plant to another is referred to as a *vector*. Although some pathogens may grow through soil or in roots from a diseased plant to a healthy neighbor, and many are disseminated in wind or water, still other pathogens are typically carried by vectors. While other methods allow local spread, vector transmission may facilitate long-distance dissemination. Vectors also may cause physical damage (such as the wounds created during feeding) that pathogens exploit for entry into trees.

Some vector–pathogen relationships are relatively accidental, with propagules of pathogens carried externally on the bodies of the vectors. Nectar feeding and pollinating insects, such as bees, frequent rosaceous hosts including trees in *Prunus* and *Malus*. During such visits they sometimes contact oozing cankers caused by the fire blight bacterium, *Erwinia amylovora*. Bacteria contained in the ooze will stick to insect bodies, and be carried to sites of infection, including blossoms on new host trees. Similarly, fungus- and sapfeeding insects including beetles in the family Nitidulidae can vector the oak wilt fungus, *Ceratocystis fagacearum* (15). Aromatic mats of *C. fagacearum* mycelium and its fruiting bodies develop under the bark of trees colonized and killed during the previous year. Nitidulid beetles are attracted to these mats, and as they feed they also acquire spores of the fungus that are carried on their bodies. These beetles subsequently may be attracted to fresh wounds on oak trees where spores are deposited and infection occurs.

Other pathogens are internally borne by their insect vectors. Some sucking insects (including species of aphids, leafhoppers, and spittlebugs)

acquire viruses, phytoplasmas, or bacteria as they penetrate and feed from the xylem or phloem of diseased trees. Infection of healthy trees occurs when these pathogens are deposited in vascular tissues during feeding. In a very special relationship, the insect vector of a tree-invading virus may also become a "host" of that virus, supporting replication within its body. An insect vector of such a "propagative virus" can remain a source of that pathogen for long periods and may even transmit the virus through its eggs to the next generation.

Insect–Pathogen Complexes

Although the previous sections emphasize the effects that individual pathogens and insects can have on trees, these agents often act in concert. In insect–pathogen *complexes* each member contributes directly and significantly to the development of damage. Attempts to minimize the impacts of such complexes on trees are challenging, because the factors influencing each member, and their interaction, must be carefully considered. A small sample of the many insect–pathogen complexes follows.

Red Pine Pocket Mortality One commonly encountered complex that affects tree health includes bark beetles and/or root-feeding insects interacting with stain fungi. An example occurs in plantations of red pines in the northcentral United States that sometimes exhibit mortality of trees in distinct clusters or "pockets" (27). Dead and dying trees in the center of the pocket are surrounded by a zone of slowly growing trees with thin crowns of chlorotic needles. Each year the affected area expands, as trees within this zone die and as previously healthy trees immediately surrounding the pocket develop symptoms. Death ultimately results from effects of both insects and pathogens. Bark beetles, such as the pine engraver, infest and girdle the main stems of these trees. Simultaneously, trees are colonized by beetle-associated blue-stain fungi in the genus *Ophiostoma*. Although metabolites of these fungi can interfere with the tree's ability to respond to bark beetle attack, healthy red pine trees normally resist both the pine engravers and the stain fungi they vector. In these plantations, however, root weevils, other bark beetles, and their associated fungi in the genus *Leptographium* often colonize the root collars and lateral roots of these trees in advance of the stem colonizing bark beetles and fungi. Red pines can normally tolerate colonization by these root insects and black-staining fungi, but this root infestation reduces the ability of trees to mobilize defenses against the pine engraver–*Ophiostoma* complex. Expansion of the pocket is perpetuated by maintenance of populations of the insect vectors of the *Leptographium* fungi and growth of these pathogens through interconnecting root grafts into trees surrounding the pocket. The circumstances that most strongly affect root insect populations are not well understood, but appear to include factors such as very sandy soils at sites where this complex occurs.

Dutch Elm Disease The very close association of insects and fungal pathogens is illustrated by the complex of bark beetles and the Dutch elm disease pathogen (14). The aggressive, exotic fungi *Ophiostoma ulmi* and *O. novo-ulmi* quickly kill even vigorous American elms. These pathogens, however, possess neither a means of long-distance dispersal nor can they penetrate intact trees. The European elm bark beetle undergoes maturation feeding in elm twig crotches and native elm bark beetles bore into elm branches. This crown feeding does not elicit strong defensive responses, and beetles can feed in healthy as well as stressed trees. During feeding, beetles introduce spores of the pathogens, which germinate to colonize and proliferate in xylem through which the tree transports water and nutrients. Rapid wilting is induced followed by death, usually in the same year as initial infection. Dying and dead trees then provide the substrate for breeding and overwintering of the beetles. Because the fungi also overwinter in dead elms, colonizing and sporulating in beetle galleries, continued association of the beetles and the pathogens is assured. A similar relationship occurs between wood borers such as the white spotted sawyer and the pine wilt nematodes introduced into healthy pines during maturation feeding. These nematodes

can kill nonadapted hosts, and the dead trees provide the breeding material for these normally secondary beetles.

Sirex Wasps—Amylostereum Fungi Another intimate association of insects and fungi is that of *Sirex* wood wasps and their *Amylostereum* fungal symbionts, which together cause damage and death of trees in the genus *Pinus* (33). In all species of *Sirex* investigated, adult females carry a symbiotic fungus, either *Amylostereum areolatum* or *A. chailletii*, in a pair of intersegmental sacs. Spores of the fungus are inserted into the wood when eggs are deposited by female wood wasps. The fungus proliferates in tunnels produced by the feeding larvae. *Sirex* wood wasp larvae also obtain some nutrition from the fungus, and the fungus benefits from dispersal by the insect and inoculation into its host. Although wood wasps are known in many parts of the world, the *Sirex–Amylostereum* complex has caused major damage only to exotic plantations of Monterey pine in New Zealand and Australia. Attacks by *Sirex noctilio* in these plantations occurred most frequently on trees under stress.

Defoliating Insects—Opportunistic Pathogens and Insects Insects do not always act as vectors for pathogens or provide a means of entry into trees, but they also may be important in altering a tree's interaction with a pathogen or other insects. Defoliation by insects such as the gypsy moth or forest tent caterpillar often is tolerated by deciduous trees. Defoliation, however, may be followed by an increase in root disease caused by fungi in the genus *Armillaria* (16). Some *Armillaria* species are commonly found as rhizomorphs on root surfaces or in restricted lesions in roots, but colonization of vigorous trees may be limited. Defoliation causes chemical changes in root tissue, however, including alteration of the concentrations of carbohydrates and the relative abundance of certain amino acids. The increased aggressiveness of *Armillaria* fungi has been associated with these changes, and these pathogens can rapidly invade and kill previously healthy trees that have been stressed by severe or repeated defoliation. Defoliation also reduces resistance against normally "secondary" insects such as the two-lined chestnut borer, which typically does not extensively infest healthy trees. Colonization of defoliated or otherwise stressed trees can result in dieback of limbs and even whole trees. Similar relations occur among defoliators and opportunistic wood-boring insects and pathogens in conifers.

The Beech Scale–Nectria Complex   Another interaction in which insects alter the susceptibility of a tree to a fungal pathogen is the beech scale–*Nectria* complex. Feeding of the introduced scale insect, *Cryptococcus fagisuga*, on the bark of beech trees results in cellular proliferation, hypertrophy and bark cracking. This provides an infection court and reduces resistance of the bark tissues to *Nectria* fungi. The principal pathogen is *Nectria coccinea* var. *faginata*, although native species of *Nectria* also can be involved. These fungi colonize large areas of insect-altered bark on the trunks of some trees, quickly girdling and killing stems, whereas on other trees narrow strips of bark are infected, parts of the crown become chlorotic and die, and the tree survives in a weakened state for many years. Little injury is caused by each organism attacking separately.

This complex has caused massive mortality of American beech in the maritime provinces of Canada and in parts of the northeastern United States. The effects on forests last long after this complex is first observed, however. Beech root systems are not killed by this complex and sprout to produce new stems as susceptible to scale and *Nectria* as those previously present. Highly defective beech sprout thickets, therefore, can dominate stands that develop following the passage of an initial killing front. These interfere with attempts to regenerate other tree species. Beech stands in the "aftermath forest" are neither economically valuable, nor can they adequately support wildlife that depend on beechnuts produced by healthy trees.

Decline Diseases

In addition to acting alone or in particular complexes (as described earlier), it has been proposed that abiotic agents, pathogens, and insects may interact in the development of *decline diseases* (6). Decline disease does not merely refer to any gradual loss of tree health, or to any malady resulting from interaction of an agent or pathogen and an insect. Rather, a particular tree decline disease is produced by interaction of multiple, interchangeable, and ordered factors, which result in a gradual, general, and progressive deterioration in tree condition, often ending in death. Although not universally accepted, the decline disease concept can be a useful model for the study of complicated or incompletely understood phenomena affecting tree health.

Trees affected by different decline diseases often develop similar symptoms. They display reduced growth in diameter and by reduction of shoot elongation. Leaves may be chlorotic (yellow), reduced in size, and crowns may prematurely exhibit fall coloration. Symptoms of roots may include reduced carbohydrate reserves, degeneration of fine roots and mycorrhizae, and root decay fungi are often active. Twig and branch death results in crown "dieback," and epicormic shoots are common. Affected trees usually are randomly dispersed, and not aggregated (as might result from the spread of a single agent). Characteristically, symptoms and signs of pathogens and insect activity intensify over many years.

The abiotic agents, pathogens, and insects that interact to produce a decline disease are categorized as *predisposing*, *inciting*, and *contributing* factors (39). Predisposing factors diminish tree vigor from its potential optimum. Their effects may not be noticeable and they affect the tree over a long period of time (many years). Predisposing factors may include inherent attributes of the tree or characteristics of the physical environment. Inciting factors are especially damaging to trees that are already predisposed. They are relatively short-term, acting quickly and often producing very noticeable effects. Inciting factors include features of either the physical or biotic environment. Contributing factors perpetuate deterioration of trees already altered by predisposing and inciting factors. These last factors to affect trees in a decline disease typically occur over many years, and effects are very noticeable. Contributing factors often include "opportunistic" insects and pathogens, including many described earlier in this chapter. Predisposing, inciting, and contributing factors are incorporated into the decline disease spiral proposed by Manion (6), one model for the interaction of different abiotic agents, pathogens, and insects in tree decline. Though not common to all decline diseases, both insects and pathogens are thought to play important roles in development of each of the three syndromes described below.

Maple Decline   At least two different syndromes affecting sugar maples, in urban areas and in forest stands, are considered to be examples of decline diseases. In cities and especially along streets, maples may be predisposed by old age, heat associated with the urban environment, and soil factors such as compaction, poor aeration and drainage, and salt accumulation. Construction damage, especially to roots, is a common inciting factor. Contributing factors may include chronic effects of *Verticillium* wilt, opportunistic canker fungi, sugar maple borer, and *Armillaria* root disease. Decline of sugar maples in forests has been observed since the early 1900s. There this species also may be predisposed by site factors, such as shallow soils. Important inciting factors may include defoliation by moth species including the saddled prominent, forest tent caterpillar, and loopers, root damage resulting from soil freezing during winters lacking normal snow accumulation, and intense droughts. A vascular pathogen of forest maples, *Ceratocystis coerulescens*, and again, sugar maple borer, canker fungi, and *Armillaria* species are the contributing factors that are often associated with visibly deteriorating and dying trees.

Birch Dieback   The decline disease known as "birch dieback" has occurred episodically across the northeastern United States and eastern Canada. Most recently, forests of the northern Great Lakes region were affected, with mortality of millions of yellow and white birch trees during the early 1990s. Tree age appears to be the primary predisposing factor associated with birch dieback, but site factors also are suspected. Inciting factors include defoliation, caused either by insects such as the birch leaf miner or by late spring frosts. Stand opening and warmer than usual summers also are inciting factors. Resulting elevations in soil temperatures can lead to massive birch rootlet mortality. The bronze birch borer, which invades and kills branches and stems of stressed trees, and *Armillaria* root rot fungi are commonly observed contributing factors of birch dieback.

Oak Decline   Oak forests in the eastern and southern United States are periodically affected by declines. Characteristics of the site including both poorly and excessively drained soils, and tree age are predisposing factors. Inciting factors that have been important in the past include drought, frost, and defoliating insects and diseases. As the range of gypsy moth extends farther and farther, it is gaining in importance as an inciting factor. A large number of contributing factors have been associated with oak decline. These include the two-lined chestnut borer, canker pathogens that become aggressive on stressed trees, and several root and stem decay fungi.

Tree Disease and Insect Management

Despite beneficial activities that include important roles in forest ecosystems, diseases and insects can interfere with achievement of objectives established by forest landowners, resource managers, government agencies, and the public. These include production of the diversity of aesthetic, recreational, environmental, or economic benefits for which forests are valued. After careful consideration of factors that influence disease and insect occurrence and development, specialists in forest health protection employ pest management principles and select from a variety of diverse practices to prevent or suppress damage caused by diseases and insects.

Influences on Disease and Insect Occurrence and Development

Tree and Stand Attributes Attributes of both individual trees and the stands they comprise have important influences on frequency and intensity of damage resulting from diseases and insects. Tree species vary widely in their inherent resistance to particular diseases and insects. Five-needled pines (e.g., eastern white pine) are rarely damaged by the pine shoot blight and canker pathogen *Sphaeropsis sapinea*, which frequently and severely damages several species of two- and three-needled pines (e.g., Austrian pine). Oaks and poplars are highly favored feeding hosts of the gypsy moth, and thus often are severely defoliated. Other tree species, including ashes and tulip tree are not favored, and may suffer relatively little defoliation during outbreaks of this insect. Considerable variation in the damage among trees of a single species often is an indication of genetically controlled resistance, which has sometimes been exploited in attempts to manage pest impacts. Hosts also may vary widely in their ability to support both reproduction and survival of microorganisms and insects. Thus, both maintenance and growth of pest populations may be influenced strongly by tree attributes.

Size and age, and a variety of factors that influence "vigor," may affect the relative susceptibility of individual trees to pests. Young trees, such as seedlings and saplings may be severely damaged by a disease or insect that is a relatively minor pest of mature trees. Some pests exploit smaller, suppressed understory trees and very old or slowly growing trees can be particularly damaged. Thus, the ability of trees to express resistance to many pests is diminished by environmental factors that alter physiological processes of the host. An example is provided by the integrated defense system of conifers, including oleoresin exudation (40). Sticky oleoresin, or "pitch," exudes from sapwood and can flood wounds such as those produced by boring beetles. Oleoresin exudation pressure (OEP), with other preformed and induced defenses, varies by the season, time of day, weather conditions, the age of the tree, and history of other pest activity, and is closely correlated with the water balance in the tree. Trees with an impaired defense system (including low OEP) may succumb to attack by bark beetles, while those with more rapid and extensive responses are more resistant. For this reason, large and damaging infestations of conifer bark beetles are associated with older trees or stands subjected to drought or defoliation. It is important to note, however, that many pathogens and insects require no assistance from stress-inducing factors to successfully attack their hosts. Even the most vigorously growing trees are subject to damage by some pests.

Stand attributes, which can be strongly influenced by past forest management practices, also influence development of diseases and the activity of insects. As a general rule, forests with the greatest diversity of tree species are less frequently and less severely subjected to epidemics and outbreaks. Uniform age distribution functions much like species composition, in that even-aged stands may be more vulnerable to damage by some pests than those composed of a mixture of ages. More diverse stands of trees can host a greater diversity of microorganisms and insects, but usually support fewer individuals of each of these species. Thus, diversity often is associated with low levels of pest activity and stability of forest ecosystems.

Site and Weather Attributes Abiotic environmental factors associated with particular forested locations, including those of the weather or climate, directly influence disease and insect development. For example, hatch of insect eggs is influenced by temperature. These might occur earlier on warmer, south facing slopes or in areas where penetration of sunlight has increased because of opening of the stand. The generation time of insects can be reduced at higher temperatures, so that more generations of some insects might occur during an unusually warm summer. Conversely, extreme cold could adversely affect survival of overwintering eggs, larvae, or adults.

Dissemination of many pathogens, processes involved in infection, and the extent of subsequent colonization are strongly affected by conditions of both temperature and moisture. The formation and germination of basidiospores of the white pine blister rust fungus, for example, require a period of at least 18 hours of high moisture and temperatures above freezing but below 20°C. Hot, dry weather unfavorably affects development of the fungus, and chances for pine to escape infection are increased. White pines in valleys or depressions where cool, moist air collects, on sites with north-facing slopes where dew persists, and in proximity to bodies of water providing high humidity, therefore, might be considered to be at a higher risk for development of white pine blister rust.

Other site attributes, especially soil factors, have strong indirect effects on susceptibility of trees to damage by diseases or insects. Each tree species is adapted to grow within a particular range in fertility, pH, and moisture-holding capacity. At the extremes or outside of these ranges, even native tree species that are planted "off site" may be very susceptible to pests that exploit their less than optimal condition.

Pathogen and Insect Attributes Much of the research undertaken by forest pathologists and forest entomologists is directed toward gaining fundamental knowledge of pest biology. The ability of different pathogens and insects to cause damage to trees is heavily dependent on inherent characteristics of these organisms, expressed at different times during their life cycles while interacting with their hosts. Knowledge of how organisms that can be pests survive during periods unfavorable for their growth, reproduce, disseminate, recognize their hosts, and of how their activities produce damage are critical for selection of biologically rational strategies for their management (1–8, 41, 42).

Both pathogens and insects can vary greatly in their "host range," or the variety of different host species that they exploit. Some are very host specific, and a single host species might be required for life cycle completion. Others are generalists, utilizing a wide range of hosts, often in many different plant genera or even diverse plant families. Particular insects and pathogens have life cycles that include stages that alternate between host plants. For example, feeding of the Cooley spruce gall adelgid on needles can heavily damage Douglas fir. Immature females of the Cooley spruce gall adelgid, however, overwinter on spruce. In spring they mature and oviposit. Eggs hatch to produce young insects that also initially utilize spruce, feeding within galls formed on shoot tips. In midsummer, however, winged females migrate to Douglas fir, where they lay eggs to produce another generation. As mentioned previously, many rust fungi also alternate between angiosperm and gymnosperms, with presence of both hosts necessary to allow disease development.

Forest pests also vary in important aspects of population biology, including the number of generations or cycles that can be produced each year. For organisms that can only complete a single cycle each year, population growth may be relatively slower, building for many years until epidemic or outbreak levels are achieved. In contrast, the cottonwood leaf beetle (*Chrysomela scripta*) is *multivoltine*. In the southern United States, it can complete up to seven cycles from adult to egg to adult per year. Even in the northern United States, especially during prolonged warm summers when weather conditions are conducive to beetle development, rapid population growth can lead to massive and repeated defoliation of intensively, managed poplar plantations. Similarly, fungi such as the dogwood anthracnose pathogen (*Discula destructiva*) are capable of multiple cycles in a single growing season. New, sporulating lesions develop within just one to two weeks after infection. Particularly during moist weather, repeated cycles of spore dissemination, infection, lesion development, and production of additional spores are responsible for defoliation and initiation of cankers that eventually kill stems of flowering dogwood.

Forest Pest Management Principles and Practices

Knowledge of the biology of particular tree and insect or pathogen interactions may suggest one or more appropriate pest management principles.

These principles can be considered "strategies," or general approaches to minimizing the effects of damaging agents on trees and forests. Six strategies that are employed in forest pest management, including attempts to control pests of nursery seedlings and landscape trees, are:

Resistance: utilization of trees with inherent, genetically controlled characteristics that minimize pest impacts, or use of practices to increase the ability of trees to defend themselves;

Exclusion: prevention of the introduction of a pathogen or insect to an area where it is not already present;

Protection: placement of a barrier or other material (usually chemical) that interferes with interaction of the pest and the tree;

Eradication: removal or destruction of pathogen or insect life stages to reduce or eliminate pest populations;

Avoidance: utilization of locations, conditions, or practices that do not favor, or even suppress, development of disease and/or insect infestations;

Therapy: treatment to cure already diseased or infested trees (may involve employment of one or more of the other strategies listed above).

For each of these strategies, a variety of practices may be applied in managing forest pests. Different types of practices can be categorized as regulatory, physical, chemical, cultural, or biological. Selection of particular practices depends not just on availability, cost, and effectiveness, but on compatibility of the practice with forest management objectives, and environmental impacts, and societal constraints. Examples of practices that might be appropriate for each forest pest management strategy are listed in Table 8.2.

Integrated Pest Management

Integrated pest management (IPM) refers to an approach to pest control that is based on an understanding of host and pest biology, knowledge of ecological principles, and integration of methodologies from several disciplines (43). IPM plans are designed to be effective, practical, economical, and protective of human health and the environment. Both basic and applied forest research results support development and refinement of integrated pest management efforts that contribute to sustainable management of forests.

In the past, scientists in different disciplines—entomology, plant pathology, soils, forestry, and chemistry—often approached a pest problem with minimal communication with their colleagues in other fields. Sometimes methods proposed to deal with one pest were in conflict with those used to manage another, or had other undesirable effects on the forest community, including beneficial organisms. For example, thinning lodgepole pine stands to improve vigor and resistance to bark beetle attack favors spread of dwarf mistletoe and development of epidemics by this pathogen. Use of broad spectrum insecticides to kill defoliating insects also can diminish populations of parasites, parasitoids, and predators that help hold pest populations in check. It finally has been realized that it is not only feasible, but necessary to integrate pest control strategies and practices, and in so doing consider simultaneously the effects on a multitude of other factors, including other organisms, other forest management activities, and all benefits produced by the forest ecosystem.

A key element of the IPM concept is pest population monitoring. Information provided by surveys to detect and quantify insect pests and pathogen occurrence is used as a tool for decision making. Based on previous population biology and forest ecology research, numbers of insect life stages (such as egg masses) or the symptoms and signs of disease associated with unacceptable effects are determined. These are used to establish a "damage threshold" representing the population level at which attainment of desired forest values is compromised (Figure 8.22). The goal of the IPM program is to prevent pest activity from reaching this damage threshold. Therefore, a lower population level, or "action threshold" is established. Successful implementation of an appropriate pest management practice at the point when the action threshold is reached leads to the eventual decline in insect num-

Table 8.2 Examples of Practices Applied to Implement Different Pest Management Strategies

Strategy	Type of Practice	Examples
Resistance	Biological	Plant loblolly pines bred for resistance to fusiform rust
	Biological	Maintain favorable moisture regime to enhance resistance to bark beetles
Exclusion	Regulatory	Quarantine to prevent untreated wood products that could harbor insects or fungal pathogens from entering the United States
	Regulatory	Inspect nursery stock for insect egg masses before shipment
Protection	Chemical	Spray Christmas trees with fungicide to prevent infection and subsequent defoliation by needlecast fungi
	Biological	Apply the fungus *Phlebiopsis gigantea* to freshly cut conifer stumps to prevent infection by root rot pathogen *Heterobasidion annosum*
	Chemical	Treat foliage with insect feeding deterrent to reduce defoliation
	Physical	Cut root grafts to prevent spread of fungal pathogens to healthy trees through interconnected root systems
Eradication	Biological	Release insect parasites, parasitoids, and predators in infested areas
	Physical	Flood or heat treat nursery soils to reduce populations of insects, nematodes, and fungal pathogens
	Chemical	Aerially apply insecticide to kill feeding larvae of eastern tent caterpillar
	Physical	Pull gooseberry and current bushes (alternate host of white pine blister rust) in white pine production areas
Avoidance	Cultural	Increase proportion of nonfavored hosts by manipulating stands in areas subject to gypsy moth defoliation
	Cultural	Prevent logging injuries and shorten rotations to minimize losses from decay
	Cultural	Maintain diversity of stand age structure to avoid population explosions of spruce budworm
	Cultural	Utilize even-aged management in red pine to prevent dissemination of *Sirococcus* shoot blight fungus inoculum from overstory to understory trees
Therapy	Chemical	Inject systemic insecticides to kill developing wood borers
	Physical	Prune cankered branches from trees

bers or pathogen occurrence, and unacceptable damage is prevented.

Concluding Statement

Studies of diseases and insects continue to yield information that is fundamental to understanding and managing these influences on trees and forests. By definition, integrated management of forest pests brings together old knowledge, novel ideas, policy considerations, management strategies, treatment practices, monitoring, and decision making in new ways. The characteristics of trees and forest stands, site and climatic factors, and the biology of pathogens and insects discussed in this chapter are

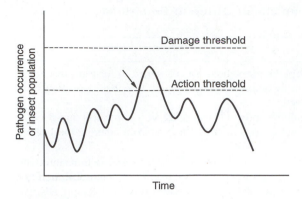

Figure 8.22 Relationship between insect population or disease occurrence, action threshold, and damage threshold. Application of an appropriate forest pest management practice at the action threshold (arrow) should prevent development of unacceptable damage.

all considered in evaluating forest pest management needs. The challenge and opportunity of forest pest managers is to employ strategies and practices so they work in concert, not in conflict, in maintaining and enhancing aesthetic, recreational, environmental, and economic benefits provided by healthy trees and forests.

References

1. R. N. COULSON AND J. A. WITTER, *Forest Entomology: Ecology and Management*, Wiley & Sons, New York, 1984.

2. A. T. DROOZE, ED., *Insects of Eastern Forests,* U.S.D.A. For. Serv. Misc. Pub. 1426, 1985.

3. R. L. EDMUNDS, J. K. AGEE, AND R. I. GARA, *Forest Health and Protection*, McGraw-Hill, Boston, 2000.

4. R. L. FURNISS AND V. M. CAROLIN, *Western Forest Insects*, U.S.D.A. For. Serv. Misc. Pub. 1339, 1977.

5. W. T. JOHNSON AND H. H. LYON, *Insects that Feed on Trees and Shrubs*, Second Edition, Comstock Pub. Associates, Ithaca, N.Y., 1988.

6. P. D. MANION, *Tree Disease Concepts*, Second Edition, Prentice Hall, Englewood Cliffs, N.J., 1991.

7. W. A. SINCLAIR, H. H. LYON, AND W. T. JOHNSON, *Diseases of Trees and Shrubs*, Comstock Pub. Associates, Ithaca, N.Y., 1987.

8. F. H. TAINTER AND F. A. BAKER, *Principles of Forest Pathology*, John Wiley, New York, 1996.

9. S. E. SMITH AND D. J.READ, *Mycorrhizal Symbiosis*, Academic Press, San Diego, Calif.,1997.

10. G.H. HEPTING AND G. M. JEMISON, "Forest protection." In *Timber Resources for America's Future*, U.S.D.A. For. Serv. Res. Rept. 14, 1958.

11. ANON., *The Outlook for Timber in the United States*, U.S.D.A. For. Serv. Res. Rept. 20, 1973.

12. ANON., *Forest Insect and Disease Conditions in the United States 1997*, U.S.D.A. For. Serv., For. Health Prot., 1998.

13. W. H. SMITH, *Tree Pathology: A Short Introduction*, Academic Press, New York, 1970.

14. M. HUBBES, *For. Chron., 75*, 265 (1999).

15. D. N. APPEL, *Ann. Rev. Phytopathol., 33*, 103 (1995).

16. C. G. SHAW III AND G. A. KILE, EDS, *Armillaria Root Disease*, U.S.D.A. Agric. Hdbk. 691, 1991.

17. S. WOODWARD, J. STENLID, R. KARJALAINEN, AND A. HÜTTERMANN, EDS., *Heterobasidion annosum: Biology, Ecology, Impact, and Control*, CAB International, Wallingford, Oxon, U.K., 1998.

18. W. G. THIES AND R. N. STURROCK, *Laminated Root Rot in Western North America*, U.S.D.A. For. Serv. Gen. Tech. Rpt. PNR-GTR-349, 1995.

19. NIENHAUS, F. AND J. D. CASTELLO, *Ann. Rev. Phytopathol., 27,* 165 (1989).

20. W. A. Sinclair, H. M. Griffiths, and R. E. Davis, *Plant Dis., 80*, 468 (1996).

21. G. W. PETERSON AND R. S. SMITH, JR., tech. coordinators, *Forest Nursery Diseases in the United States.*, U.S.D.A. For. Serv. Agric. Hdbk. 470, 1975.

22. M. J. WINGFIELD, ED., *Pathogenicity of the Pine Wood Nematode*, APS, St. Paul, Minn., 1987.

23. F. G. HAWKSWORTH AND D. WIENS, *Dwarf Mistletoes: Biology, Pathology, and Systematics*, U.S.D.A. For. Serv. Agric. Hdbk. 709, 1996.

24. C. B. DAVIDSON, K. W. GOTTSCHALK, AND J. E. JOHNSON, *For. Sci., 45*, 74 (1999).

25. R. L. GIESE, J. E. KAPLER, AND D. M. BENJAMIN, *Studies of maple blight. IV. Defoliation and the genesis of maple blight,* Univ. Wisc. Agr. Expt. Sta. Res. Bull. 250, 1964.

26. T. O. Showalter and G. M. Filip, eds., *Beetle–Pathogen Interactions in Conifer Forests*, Academic Press, San Diego, Calif., 1993.

27. K. D. Klepzig, K. F. Raffa, and E. B. Smalley, *For. Sci., 37*, 1119 (1991).

28. T. D. Paine, K. F. Raffa, and T. C. Harrington, *Annu. Rev. Entomol., 42*, 179 (1997).

29. J. A. McLean, *For. Chron., 61*, 295 (1985).

30. J. D. Solomon, *Guide to Insect Borers in North American Broadleaf Trees and Shrubs*, U.S.D.A. For. Serv. Agric. Hdbk. 706, 1995.

31. J. P. Dunn, T. W. Kimmerer, and G. L. Nordin, *Oecologia., 70*, 596 (1986).

32. F. K. Kobyashi, "The Japanese pine sawyer." In *Dynamics of Forest Insect Populations*, A. A. Berryman, ed., Plenum Press, New York, 1988.

33. J. L. Madden, *Sirex* in Australia." In *Dynamics of Forest Insect Populations*, A. A. Berryman, ed., Plenum Press, New York, 1988.

34. L. F. Wilson, *Saratoga spittlebug: Its ecology and management,* U.S.D.A. Agric. Hdbk. 657, 1987.

35. D. R. Houston, *Ann. Rev. Phytopathol., 32*, 75 (1975).

36. F. P. Hain, "The balsam woolly adelgid in North America." In *Dynamics of Forest Insect Populations*, A. A. Berryman, ed., Plenum Press, New York, 1988.

37. J. C. Jenkins, J. D. Aber, and C. D. Canham, Can, *J. For. Res., 29,* 630 (1999).

38. A. M. Lynch, *J. Ga. Entomol. Soc., 19* (issue 3, suppl. 1), 1 (1984).

39. W. A. Sinclair, *The Cornell Plantations, 20,* 62 (1985).

40. K. F. Raffa, "Induced defensive reactions in conifer-bark beetle systems." In *Phytochemical Induction by Herbivores*, D. W. Tallamy and M. J. Raupp, eds., Academic Press, New York, 1991.

41. G. N. Agrios, *Plant Pathology*, Fourth edition, Academic Press, New York, 1997.

42. A. A. Berryman, ed., *Dynamics of Forest Insect Populations*, Plenum Press, New York, 1988.

43. D. Dent, *Integrated Pest Management,* Chapman & Hall, London, 1995.

PART 3

Forest Management— Multiple Uses

The forests make up one of the earth's greatest reservoirs of renewable natural resources. Managed properly, they can provide us with essential products indefinitely and at the same time can remain a home for wildlife and a vital source of water supplies (Figure P3.1). However, the management of the forests for each of the many products, services and benefits presents a complex problem. This section presents the methods and practices by which the successful forest manager obtains these benefits from the forest without adversely affecting the environment.

In Chapter 9 an overview of forest management and stewardship is given; the approaches to management of public and private organizations, the interests of ownership, and the planning of operations are discussed. This is followed in Chapter 10 by a more in-depth treatment of small nonindustrial private forests because these forests hold a major share of the future for forest derived benefits. Almost 60 percent of commercial forestland is owned by the private nonindustrial sector.

Specific procedures for assessment of forest and timber resources are provided in Chapters 11 (Measuring and Monitoring Forest Resources) and 12 (Remote Sensing and Geographic Information Systems for Natural Resource Management). The various methods available for determining individual tree sizes and volumes and those for estimating the volume of timber in forest stands are presented. The chapter on remote sensing describes methods for evaluating stand composition, density, and the health of forests from aerial photographs and satellite data.

Chapter 13, Silviculture and Forest Ecosystem Management, describes the biological management

Figure P3.1 Our forests make up one of the earth's great reservoirs of renewable resources. Properly managed, they can provide us with essential products indefinitely and at the same time remain a home for wildlife and a vital source of water supplies. (Courtesy of U.S.D.A. Forest Service)

of the forest—how forest regeneration, species composition, and growth are regulated by biological means. Forests are used by wildlife and for rangeland, watersheds, recreation, and timber. Chapters 14 through 17 describe the important aspects of forest management for nontimber uses of the forest. Methods of integrating management decisions for protection of all the natural resources provided by the forest are described in these chapters. Extraction of timber from forests does not necessarily diminish the other benefits derived from the forest. A moderate size clearcut, for example, provides additional habitats for wildlife, and selection cutting in the forest creates areas suitable for aesthetics and recreational activities.

Although human beings cause most forest fires today, fires have always occurred in the forest due to lightning storms. The importance of fires in shaping the forest landscape is discussed in Chapter 18, Behavior and Management of Forest Fires. The use of fire as a management tool (i.e., "prescribed burns") is also described in this chapter.

A primary product of great economic importance derived from the forest is wood, and to obtain wood, the forest must be harvested. Chapter 19 shows the variety of approaches available for timber harvesting. In Chapter 20 an overview is provided of the many uses that are made of wood, from lumber and plywood to paper and chemicals. The unique characteristics and comparative abundance of wood have made it a desirable natural material for homes and other structures, furniture, tools, vehicles, and decorative objects. The structure and chief attributes that give wood these special properties are discussed in this chapter. A large percentage of harvested wood is also used for production of pulp and paper. Thousands of paper supplies are produced every year for household and industrial use. Since smaller-size logs are suitable

Figure P3.2   Log drivers wrestling Douglas fir logs on Oregon's Coos River, using long pike poles and a short peavey. These logs will roar downstream to be processed in a pulpwood mill. (Courtesy of Life Picture Service.)

for pulp production, the second growth timber in the United States is very suitable for production of these important commodities (Figure P3.2). Use of wood for paper and for energy and chemicals are also described in Chapter 20.

The final chapter in this section, Chapter 21, provides a valuable discussion of the economics and management of forests for both wood and amenity values. A thought-provoking comparison is made of the economics of forest products markets versus other forest amenities based on economic theories. The chapter demonstrates how economic reasoning can help in the wise management of forest resources.

CHAPTER 9

Forest Management and Stewardship

JAMES M. GULDIN AND
RICHARD W. GULDIN

Why manage forests? Many reasons might come to mind, but they all turn on one point—managed forests are better able to provide for the needs of society than unmanaged forests. Management of forests becomes especially important as human populations increase and forest lands decrease, and as society demands more and a wider variety of forest resources. A common thread in the history of civilization is that the practice of forestry has evolved in response to society's concerns about the scarcity of forest resources (1).

Forests do not require management to maintain their structure and function. For eons, trees have used energy from the sun to convert water, atmospheric carbon dioxide, and a handful of mineral resources into the sugars and metabolic by-products required for growth, and they have done so in a way that collectively confers productivity to the forest ecosystem. Thus, it is perhaps arrogant to discuss the value of forest resources under human administration. Forest ecosystems will be rich in natural resources even if human beings do not tamper with them. But they may not be the resources that humans want, and they may not be produced in the length of time that humans want them to be. Also, there may be unacceptable ecological and economic effects if humans use forest resources in a careless and unregulated manner.

Society has had its greatest influences on the natural patterns and processes of forests since the Industrial Revolution. One prominent influence has been the suppression of natural processes that humans find damaging or dangerous. For example, in North America, lightning has historically been, and still is, responsible for igniting wildfires annually. Before European settlement, those wildfires would have run their natural course; today, they are aggressively suppressed by firefighters. As a result, many fire-dependent forest ecosystems no longer burn as frequently as in the past. Without fire, these ecosystems can become degraded or lost. When fires do strike, the results can be catastrophic, as happened during the great Yellowstone fires of 1988 (2). (A further discussion of the behavior and management of forest fires is given in Chapter 18.)

A second prominent influence of society on forests has been the introduction of exotic species from other continents. Chestnut blight, a European fungal disease, got its start in North America when diseased chestnut logs were imported from Europe to New York in 1904. In two decades, the blight virtually wiped out the American chestnut and thereby dramatically changed the species composition of hardwood forests across the East (3). The gypsy moth, an Asian lepidopteran insect, was introduced to North America to develop a domestic silk trade. In 1898, a handful of moths escaped into a nearby forest. Today, gypsy moth causes millions of dollars of loss in oak–hickory forests in the East (3). Without advances in control technology to slow its spread, it will be found in every state east of the 100th meridian early in this century (4).

However, perhaps the single most prominent influence of society has been the deforestation of North America following European colonization. Since 1630, about a third of the forest area in the United States has been cut and converted to nonforest uses, primarily agriculture (Figure 9.1). Nearly all the rest has supported some form of timber harvesting. Two hundred years ago, forests were considered a barrier to agriculture and an inhibition to westward expansion. Today, forest resources are scarce relative to society's demand for them.

Figure 9.1 Agricultural fields taken from the forest land base in post-European settlement in North America; view looking north from Hawk Mountain Sanctuary in eastern Pennsylvania. (James M. Guldin)

A century ago timber was unquestionably the most valuable resource in the forest. Although today's society still ascribes high monetary value to timber resources, we increasingly find important nontimber values in forest resources. For example, a stand of black walnut trees growing along a stream in northern Missouri has value on many levels. It can serve as a source of beautiful cabinet lumber, as a prime squirrel habitat, and in a protective capacity by helping to maintain water quality and reduce soil erosion. It is easy to ascribe a monetary value to the lumber from a black walnut tree; it is more difficult to place a dollar value on each squirrel, each cubic foot of uneroded soil, and each unit of clarity in the stream water. Yet, society desires all these resources, and no one can dispute that maintaining squirrel habitat and water quality would be difficult if all the black walnut trees were harvested for lumber.

Moreover, the productivity and distribution of resources in any ecosystem are variable and complex. Some natural resources, such as wood fiber in a Mississippi riverfront cottonwood stand, are produced very quickly (Figure 9.2). Others are produced in very small quantities over longer periods of time. For example, the endangered red-cockaded woodpecker in east Texas constructs its nest only in the decayed heartwood of pine trees that are generally over 100 years old (5). Some natural resources require such an extended period of development that they might be considered essentially nonrenewable. The awe that many feel toward a grove of stately redwood trees in northern California is heightened by the realization that the trees are over a thousand years old.

This scarcity and complexity of forest resources, coupled with society's demand for them, is what confers value to the forests of today. Fundamental economic concepts of supply and demand, and noneconomic considerations, such as concern for preserving endangered species and maintaining environmental quality, affect the value of forest resources. Sorting out these conflicting demands, resources, and values is the domain of forest management.

Figure 9.2 A short-rotation cottonwood plantation on forest industry land adjacent to the Mississippi River in northwest Mississippi; the stand will be harvested at age 11, by which time the trees exceed 30 cm (12 inches) in diameter and 25 m (80 feet) in height. (James M. Guldin)

Forest Management

Forest management is the process of organizing a collection of forest stands so that they produce the resources that the landowner wants from that forest. The landowner might be a forest industry, a private individual or family, or the public (represented by federal, state, county, or municipal governments). The resources might be timber products, wildlife, awe-inspiring aesthetics, or any conceivable combination of these. The task of the forest management specialist is to organize the production of such resources in a sustainable manner so

that they will always be available to meet the needs of the landowner. The management techniques for accomplishing these purposes vary from the simple to the exceedingly complex.

Common goals for forest management are to produce the resources demanded by the landowner and society, to maintain a sustainable supply of resources over time, and to minimize conflicting ecological, economic, or social demands in resource use. Management typically begins with a *forest management plan* that identifies the objectives of the landowner, outlines the treatments and timetables required for each stand over the entire forest, and describes a program of resource evaluation to ensure that the ownership objectives are attained.

Forest management would be simple if all forest resources were readily renewable and if it were possible to use one resource without affecting other resources. However, nearly every practice that a forester uses to manage a particular resource also affects other resources in the forest. The more resources that are desired from a given area, the greater the likelihood that the management and use of one resource will affect another. Also, there is often a fine line between careless exploitation of a resource and a conservation-based use that ensures resource renewability.

Broadly speaking, the forest management plan is implemented using the principles of forest administration. These actions include supervising personnel, developing operational budgets, prescribing and conducting stand-level treatments, and reviewing treatments after they are completed to ensure that the outcomes desired are attained.

The degree of planning and the resources allocated for administration often depend on the size of the forest being managed and the number of resources being managed. Plans are usually more detailed if the resources of interest have high intrinsic or monetary value, because of the financial incentive to ensure that management does not adversely affect current resource quality or future resource availability. Plans also increase in complexity if a forest has multiple owners; the greater the number of owners of a particular forest, the more difficult it is to identify ownership objectives and to manage for them. Federal agencies, forest industry companies, and other large organizations have complicated management organizations that reflect their complex objectives. Conversely, small entities such as a specialized wood products plant, a cross-country ski resort, or a farm woodlot have correspondingly smaller management infrastructures. Regardless of size, forest management generally consists of two stages, each of varying complexity: planning and administration.

To develop a forest management plan, the manager assesses the landowner's objectives and evaluates the resources available to satisfy those objectives. The manager then reviews the options available for satisfying the owner's objectives. Each option must be examined from a number of aspects, including the likely desirable and undesirable effects, the financial cost compared to the budget available, and any regulatory consequences, such as permits needed and taxes imposed. The manager then selects the options that best fit the situation and summarizes them in a written plan. The plan details the methodology and treatment schedules needed to manage each stand, and demonstrates how all the stands, when combined, will provide the resources needed to meet the owner's objectives. The manager and owner then review the manager's recommendations, as well as the options not chosen and reasons why. Once accepted by the owner, the plan is finalized and becomes the basis for future action by the manager or owner.

A management plan prepared by a consulting forester for 400 acres of family-owned land in southern Arkansas may be quite simple. A management plan for the Mountain Pine Division of Weyerhaeuser Company in west-central Arkansas will be more complicated because of the value of the wood products involved, and the mills and jobs that the woodlands must support. A management plan for a national forest, such as the Amended Land and Resource Management Plan for the Ozark National Forest in northwest Arkansas, includes detailed provisions for managing all the multiple uses required by law, and reflects the diverse interests of the national forest's landowners—the citizens of the United States.

Multiple Uses

A forest has an infinite variety of uses. Trees can be used for lumber, wooden baskets, split-bark hickory chairs, maple syrup, or supports for a hammock. An outdoor enthusiast can enjoy forest fauna by hunting deer with a rifle, rainbow trout with a fly rod, or butterflies with a camera. This inherent variety of forest resources and uses reveal the challenge to modern forest management, both in choosing which resources should be used and in giving society access to them.

In the practical sense, however, the forestry profession recognizes a standard broad categorization of resources. Easy, convenient, and commonly accepted categories are those that appear in the Multiple Use–Sustained Yield Act of 1960.

The national forests are established and shall be administered for outdoor recreation, range, timber, watershed, and wildlife and fish purposes.

The Act's five categories have come to be known as *multiple uses*. The degree to which forestlands are managed for any one or more of them depends on the goals of ownership. However, because federal land is owned by the American people, the multiple uses essentially constitute a statement of the ownership objectives for the national forests. Each national forest must expressly provide an adequate supply of each of these multiple uses over a 50-year period of management.

The most dominant objective of ownership in the past has been to manage forests for timber. Timber management is often used to finance forest ownership, to support other uses more difficult to administer, or for which a financial value is more difficult to assess. In most regions of the country, trees of sawlog size bring a fairly high monetary return (Figure 9.3). Markets for smaller trees are more variable and usually depend on the species and the distance to processing facilities. These markets, if they exist, provide an opportunity to conduct treatments in young stands that improve stand condition. Finally, because trees are the dominant ecological component of a forest ecosystem, the value of nontimber resources can increase with the judicious manipulation of the timber component— or decrease by injudicious operations.

In certain situations, of course, the values of other resources far outweigh the value of timber. For example, the annual gate receipts at a 100-unit campground on nearly any national forest will exceed the value of the annual growth of the timber within the campground. Timber production is not economically feasible on sites that have low productivity or difficult access, such as ridge tops

Figure 9.3 Redwood sawlogs await manufacturing into lumber at a mill in northern California. (James M. Guldin)

or swamps. On some sites, management for timber is at odds with management that requires an undisturbed or unharvested ecosystem, such as wilderness areas, national recreational trails, or wild and scenic rivers.

Forest ecosystems provide an important watershed value by serving as living filters for precipitation. Many cities and towns throughout the United States rely on forested watersheds for abundant, clean surface waters for municipal water supplies (Figure 9.4). In many arid western states, the yield of water from high-altitude forests is increased by forest management techniques that gather more snow in the winter and prolong the snowmelt period into early summer (see also Chapter 16, Watershed Management).

Federal laws require landowners to control nonpoint sources of water pollution, such as the nutrient discharges and sedimentation associated with forest management and harvesting. The most likely source of water pollution in forestry, erosion from roads, can be minimized by proper engineering practices. Erosion of soil can also occur from stream banks or skid roads if harvesting equipment crosses permanent or ephemeral streams. An effective way to minimize streamside erosion is to retain a buffer strip of trees (called a "streamside management

Figure 9.4 The Quabbin Reservoir in central Massachusetts, source of drinking water for the Boston metropolitan area. (James M. Guldin)

zone") and to exclude forest operations from this zone.

Virtually all timber management practices affect the wildlife and fish in forest ecosystems. Wildlife species tend to be associated with certain successional stages in the forest, and practices that favor one stage of forest succession are likely to favor the wildlife that thrive in that particular stage (Figure 9.5). Forest industry landowners often manage early-successional forest ecosystems that are favorable to white-tailed deer, ruffed grouse, bobwhite

Figure 9.5 Elk grazing in a mixed conifer stand in the Canadian Rockies. (James M. Guldin)

quail, and other species that prefer the brushy habitat mosaic. As a result, the popularity of hunting on forest industry lands has increased tremendously in certain parts of the country. Some forest industry landowners have taken advantage of this; the hunting leases in the bottomland hardwood stands along the Mississippi River in Tennessee and Mississippi provide higher annual returns per acre than the timber. Even companies that lease their land to hunters for a nominal fee can expect significant nontimber income from their forest property. Game management has always been a by-product of timber management, but these recent trends demonstrate the increasing value of nontimber uses in the marketplace.

Forest management can also favor nongame species. It is common practice on industry and government forestlands to leave dead standing trees (called "snags") on a harvested site. In addition to the nesting habitat provided by these snags, the insect fauna that use them for food and shelter provide forage for nongame bird species.

The protection of populations and habitat for species found on the federal list of endangered and threatened species is common on public land, and growing in importance on private lands. For example, the endangered red-cockaded woodpecker, which under natural conditions requires old pines with heart rot for nesting, has not prospered under intensive sawtimber management regimes. Such regimes have a rotation age of 35 to 50 years, and few sawmills can produce good lumber from old pines with heart rot. A landowner who wants to manage for woodpecker populations must be willing to accept reduced timber income, or apply innovative approaches such as artificial nest box cavities in younger trees. Forest-wildlife management is treated further in Chapter 14.

A productive fish resource is generally achieved by promoting good water quality. Many of the practices that prevent turbidity, siltation, and excessive eutrophication of a stream will obviously benefit fish. An aquatic habitat can be quickly degraded by sudden changes in stream temperature. If the trees adjacent to a stream are cut, direct solar radiation on the water surface will increase stream temperature significantly, and may be detrimental to fish. For this reason, the use of streamside buffer strips of trees is beneficial for fish populations.

Range resources consist of the grasses commonly found within forest ecosystems. Grazing for domestic livestock, the primary use of rangeland resources, is prevalent in western forests (Figure 9.6). For example, ponderosa pine forests in the Southwest are sufficiently open for sunlight to reach the forest floor and promote development of grasses. The number of cattle that such forests can support is determined by research and practical experience. This number can be managed using rangeland allotments, which specify the number of

animals allowed in specific areas during a given season. Using these methods, the range manager can balance the quality and quantity of forage with the grazing intensity, both for a given area and forest-wide. Rangeland management is given further treatment in Chapter 15.

A dramatically increasing use of forestland in the United States is for outdoor recreation. Recreational use of forest resources varies, and requires different kinds of facilities and resources (Figure 9.7). Examples range from organized bus tours of national parks to solo backpacking trips in the wilderness, or from a three-week transcontinental journey to a fifteen-minute stroll in the woods. Forest recreation typically centers on the ecosystem-based resources of the forest. The challenge to the

Figure 9.6 Livestock on a national forest grazing allotment in a New Mexico ponderosa pine stand. (James M. Guldin)

Figure 9.7 Outdoor recreational activity on the Buffalo National River in the Arkansas Ozarks. (James M. Guldin)

manager is simultaneously to maintain or enhance the quality of the forest resource, and to promote conditions that satisfy the expectations of the resource user. The factors involved in managing recreation behavior are discussed in Chapter 17.

Interactions Among Competing Uses

The concept of multiple use implies that on any given acre of forestland, the opportunity exists to utilize more than one forest resource. Forest management would be simple if the owner of the forest was interested in a single resource such as timber or recreation. Multiple use is the philosophy that a forest can support the socially desirable utilization of many different resources. This is an easy philosophy to espouse, but it can be difficult to implement.

A given pair of uses can interact in one of three ways. The interaction can be *neutral*, in that one use does not particularly affect another; a wildflower enthusiast is not likely to be affected by a nearby fisherman. The interaction may be *compatible*, such as the beneficial effects of small clearcuts on wildlife species that inhabit early-successional ecosystems. Finally, the interaction may be *incompatible*: a genuine wilderness experience is impossible in an area under intensive timber management. Clawson (6) developed a qualitative model to assess the degree of compatibility of a variety of uses. The model requires specific information about the resources being used, the manner in which they will be used, and the specific forest ecosystem constraints that apply.

Conflicts may result if multiple uses of the forest are incompatible. The conflict may be between the resources themselves, as between healthy pine trees and red-cockaded woodpeckers. When incompatibility occurs, it is necessary to separate directly conflicting resources either in space, allocating resources to different areas, or in time, allocating resources to a given area in different seasons, years, or decades. The concept of *dominant use* (7), in which one use of the forest is given relative priority over others, can be implemented with

techniques such as zoning specific areas (8) and instituting seasonal controls over resources and users.

Some conflicts can occur when the techniques used to manage a particular resource are different. For example, a hiker who dislikes the visual impact of a two-year-old clearcut may not even notice a recent timber harvest in an uneven-aged stand. Under these conditions the solution may be to evaluate the range of alternative practices available for the management of the resource. The forest manager can refine or modify practices to create compatibility, such as by converting all trailside forests to an uneven-aged condition. Should this fail, it may be necessary to partition resource uses either spatially or temporally, such as by rerouting the trail or temporarily withdrawing the area from timber management.

As human populations increase, the demand for the multiple-use resources available from the forest will also increase. The challenge to forest managers is to provide a supply of forest resources that meet these projected demands and to increasingly implement the multiple-use concept on lands not restricted to a dominant or single use. Management in each of the three major ownership categories—the public forests, industry forests, and forests of the nonindustrial private landowner—must broaden its objectives. The private sector will play a key role in future resource supply, since the majority of forest land in the United States is in private hands.

Sustainability and Ecosystem Management

For most of the 20th century, forest management emphasized the timber resource. The reason is simple—pulpwood and sawlogs have been generally the highest-value products a forest can produce. Only in unusual instances do other resources rival the value of timber on a per acre basis. As a result, foresters in North America have been concerned about sustainability of timber since the rise of the profession at the turn of the century.

In the early 1900s, efforts to promote forest management were a response to concerns about widespread misuse of timber resources—abusive timber cutting practices, inadequate or no reforestation, and uncontrolled wildfire. Early attempts at forest management targeted those three issues by establishing scientific methods of timber harvest, ensuring reforestation, and controlling wildfires.

However, early forest management only ensured the sustainability of the timber resource; they did not address sustainability of other forest resources. Even if trees are properly cared for, other resources of the forests may suffer. For example, removing all the hollow trees in a stand managed for timber production would affect only a few individuals of a wildlife species that likes hollow trees; they would just look for other hollow trees in nearby stands. On the other hand, if removal of hollow trees were the standard policy for all foresters working in a large timber company or public agency, this policy would affect the numbers and distribution of the species on a much larger scale.

Research is needed on how forest management can include both the sustainability of the timber resource and the sustainability of other major resources that forests provide. However, far less is known about the needs of nontimber forest resources, because their relative value has only recently begun to be understood. This is an unfortunate byproduct of the value of timber resources relative to nontimber resources.

Many different organizations support changes in traditional approaches to forest management (9). Both public and private forestry interests have responded to this call. The National Forest System has adopted the concept of "ecosystem management," and the American Forest and Paper Association has established the "Sustainable Forestry Initiative" for managing forest industry lands. The concepts differ in some fundamental ways, but both reflect a commitment to enhance the scope of forest management beyond the usual concern with commodity production.

Ecosystem Management In 1992, the Chief of the U.S.D.A. Forest Service, F. Dale Robertson, defined ecosystem management as:

. . . using an ecological approach to achieve the **multiple-use management of national forests and grasslands by blending the needs of people and environmental values in such a way that national forests and grasslands represent diverse, healthy, productive, and sustainable ecosystems. (10)**

By this statement, the Forest Service embraced a new conceptual model for implementing the Multiple Use–Sustained Yield Act of 1960 and the National Forest Management Act of 1976.

The key to Robertson's statement is the importance given to the ecological basis for management of National Forest System lands. Traditionally, economic measures such as present net value, benefit/cost ratio, or return on investment guided forest management decisions on federal lands. Under ecosystem management, decisions are based on the ecological value they produce or sustain. Such decisions might have a secondary value economically, but the economic value is less important than whether the proposed action improves the ecological condition of the area being managed.

The most important change that underlies ecosystem management on national forest lands involves how the forester views timber production. Under ecosystem management, the focus is more on what is retained in the forest stand than on what is removed (11). The primary goal is not production of timber under optimal economic regimes, but to produce conditions in the forested landscape through stand-level actions that will maintain or restore forest health, diversity, productivity, and sustainability. Rather than harvesting simply to cut timber, harvesting is designed to achieve specified attributes in the forest that remains. These stand-level actions may produce timber as a byproduct, but the intent that underlies a practice is an ecological one.

Forest health is a key aspect of ecosystem management. If the concept of ecosystem management started anywhere, it was during the Yellowstone National Park fires of 1988. More than any recent forest event, the Yellowstone fires revealed that continued efforts to suppress fire in fire-adapted ecosystems were doomed to fail, and

Sidebar 9.1

Ecosystem Management in Action

A good example of ecosystem management in action is the restoration of shortleaf pine–bluestem in the Ouachita Mountains of western Arkansas. Consider an 80-year-old shortleaf pine stand on national forest land in west-central Arkansas. Traditional economic analyses would suggest the stand is economically mature, and should be subject to reproduction cutting. However, under ecosystem management, a district ranger might consider a different decision—to restore the pine savanna community described in early reports from the region.

Silvicultural tactics for pine savanna restoration include: 1) extending the rotation for pine sawtimber to 120+ years, 2) thinning the stand from below so as to reduce susceptibility to southern pine beetle, 3) undertaking a program of midstory hardwood control to eliminate the understory hardwoods that have sprung up in the 60-year period during which fires have been excluded from these sites, 4) reintroducing periodic prescribed fires to reestablish the native prairie flora such as the big bluestem grass and purple coneflower, and 5) installing artificial cavities in some of the pines for use by the endangered red-cockaded woodpecker. Through this decision, the ecological goal of restoring the pine–bluestem habitat, an underrepresented plant community in the area, is achieved, while still providing timber from the thinning to the local forest products economy, bobwhite quail for local hunters, and red-cockaded woodpeckers for local birdwatching enthusiasts.

The practice has the benefit of creating nesting and foraging habitat ideal for the endangered red-cockaded woodpecker. Yet, the area remains a place where an active program of timber production can still have a place, through periodic thinning and, ultimately, reproduction cutting in

A typical stand of shortleaf pine in Arkansas, prior to shortleaf pine-bluestem habitat restoration treatments.

the shortleaf pine overstory. The project has elements of forest health, diversity, productivity, and sustainability, and the implementation of creative management tactics to achieve restoration. However, even in such restoration work, the immediate needs of habitat restoration and

A different stand of shortleaf pine, which has been treated by midstory removal and restoration of a regular cycle of prescribed fire. (James M. Guldin)

recovery must include provisions to ensure a sustainable supply of those habitats over the long term. For example, the endangered woodpecker requires an adequate area in stands of suitable age and structure to provide nesting habitat, roughly defined as from 90 to 120 years old. Suitable foraging habitat for the bird can be obtained in stands from 30 to 120 years old. However, these stands do not remain static in age; over time, they will grow and mature. Young stands between 0 and 30 years in age must be established and managed as the replacement stands to fulfill future foraging needs in three to nine decades, and future nesting needs 9 to 12 decades down the road.

Thus, for long-term sustainability of the shortleaf pine–bluestem habitat, plans must be made to keep about 25 percent of the area in suitable nesting habitat, and an additional 50 percent in suitable foraging habitat. The last 25 percent in stands must be managed as very young stands between 0 and 30 years in age—a continuous supply of replacement stands for future foraging and nesting needs.

in a spectacular manner. Today, considerable effort is being made in the West and South to restore fire to fire-adapted ecosystems, either by deliberately setting understory burns (called "prescribed fires") or by allowing natural ignitions such as isolated lightning strikes to burn under controlled conditions (Figure 9.8). In both instances, foresters will limit fires to a specified area under manageable weather conditions.

Concerns about forest health in the context of ecosystem management include situations where past management practices have a negative effect on current forest conditions. For example, some managed forests in the West consist of dense, overstocked young stands of pine. Trees in such stands have low vigor, and as a result are highly susceptible to attack by insects such as the mountain pine beetle. Forest managers must choose either to develop tactics to reduce overstocking, or to allow the mountain pine beetle to do so in a way that may have unacceptable impacts within the given watershed.

Figure 9.8   Prescribed fire in a loblolly pine stand on forest industry land in southern Arkansas. (James M. Guldin)

Ecosystem management is a framework for emphasizing species diversity through habitat restoration, using methods such as thinning and prescribed fire to restore patterns and processes that have been absent in a given habitat. The target is not one specific habitat, but a spectrum of conditions that would result from varying the intensity and timing of prescribed fires and would reflect the range of naturally occurring variation in ecosystem structure and function.

Finally, sustainability is as important under an ecosystem management scenario as it is under a more traditional timber-oriented approach to forest management. Timber sustainability can be defined as a function of the species composition

and age of stands, and the cumulative area occupied by stands of different ages. These factors can also define the desired ecological habitats and conditions under ecosystem management. Thus, development of a balance of habitat conditions is as important a goal under ecosystem management as it is when timber production is a primary goal of management. Incorporating precise, quantitative descriptions of forest conditions is necessary to determine sustainability, whatever the goal of management.

Foresters working under ecosystem management are likely to face greater challenges than were faced by traditional timber-oriented forest managers. Many of these challenges are beyond the forester's control. The past 40 years have been marked by detailed Congressional legislation and by the actions of different presidential administrations, as illustrated by Robertson's ecosystem management letter in 1992 and the changes in national forest planning regulations proposed by President Clinton in 1999. These Congressional and administrative shifts in forest management policy and process reflect society's shifting attitudes toward forest management. While 40 years constitutes a long professional career for a human being and a period of 10 presidential administrations in our constitutional democracy, it is just a third of the time required to develop a regulated shortleaf pine–bluestem habitat over a large area.

As a result, it is best not to think of ecosystem management as a replacement for more traditional forms of timber-oriented forest management, but rather as the next step in the evolution of the overall theory of forest management on federal lands over time. Society, Congress, or some future administration may well come up with ways to refine or replace ecosystem management. The most realistic perspective may well be to consider ecosystem management as the latest in a long line of philosophical views that have been and will be developed to better capture society's goals for the nation's forests.

Sustainable Forestry Initiative   In the 1990s, forest industry landowners sought to play a leadership role in forest conservation on the lands that they own or manage. The result was a program called the Sustainable Forestry Initiative, which was established in 1994 by the American Forest and Paper Association (AF&PA), the nation's most influential forest industry trade association.

Under the principles of sustainable forestry, AF&PA members agree to use responsible forestry practices, maintain forest health and productivity, protect special sites, and continuously improve the practice of forest management (Figure 9.9). The guidelines that member companies follow on their own lands, and encourage landowners from whom they buy timber to follow on their lands as well, include requirements for an independent expert review of compliance, public reporting of compliance, and support of public forest policy goals for sustainable forestry

Central to the program are eight public policy goals for sustainable forestry on private and public lands. These goals include increasing growth and timber quality of forest lands, implementing appropriate ecosystem management on federal lands, reducing the risk and occurrence of wildfires, practicing integrated pest management, encouraging research on forest health and productivity, promoting continuing education in forest resources, recognizing members and others

who practice sustainable forestry, and working to help all private landowners manage forests in a sustainable manner.

It is difficult to say as yet how the Sustainable Forestry Initiative will change the practice of sustainable forestry on private lands. For example, one specific objective of the Initiative is for loggers to enroll in training courses on how to prevent erosion, stream sedimentation, and other adverse ecological effects. However, it is not clear whether this training actually leads to the desired on-the-ground improvement in harvesting practices. Similarly, member companies can agree to independent monitoring to ensure that company lands are being promptly reforested. Initiative guidelines cannot be required on outside lands that a company harvests but does not own; that decision must be made by the landowner. Like public forest managers, AF&PA members face challenges that are beyond their immediate control. Time will tell how much of an influence the Sustainable Forestry Initiative and similar efforts will have on the management practices of private landowners.

Forest Owners and Ownership

The most fundamental tenet in the practice of forestry is this: the landowner, not the forester, determines the objectives of management. The task of the forester is to implement the landowner's objectives by developing and administering a forest management plan. Foresters can and should use their professional expertise to suggest management objectives and alternatives to the landowner. At times, foresters may even be called upon to convene and facilitate discussions among landowners or with the public about land management objectives. However, the ultimate decision-making authority on forest management objectives generally rests with the landowner.

By no means does every forest landowner have or want every multiple use on his or her forest land. Owners of forest industry lands often accommodate hunting and other nontimber uses as long as they have no worse than a neutral effect on timber

Figure 9.9 A streamside management zone separates pine plantations of different age classes on forest industry land in central Arkansas. (James M. Guldin)

production. Conversely, the nonindustrial private landowner may have objectives that are not clearly defined, and that may be oriented either to a specific single use or to a specific subset of the multiple uses. Lands managed by the Forest Service are expected to provide for multiple uses at the ranger district level (generally between 50,000 and 200,000 acres) through land and resource management plans for each national forest. Thus, ownership patterns often define the uses of forests in each region of the country.

Land Ownership and Distribution

About a third of the United States is forest land—302 million hectares (747 million acres) (Table 9.1). The rest is either rangeland or other land, which includes farmland and urban and suburban areas. The 302 million hectares of forest today is about two-thirds of the land area that was forested in 1630, leaving some 123 million hectares (304 million acres) that has since been converted to agriculture and other uses. About 75 percent of the land conversion from forests to agriculture occurred in the 19th century. Between 1850 and 1910, American farmers cleared more forest than had been cleared in the previous 250 years of settlement—about 77 million hectares (190 million acres). By the 1920s, the clearing of forests for agriculture had largely ceased (12). The 1930s to 1950s saw a considerable reversion of agricultural land to forestland, especially in the South. However, those gains in

forestland were largely offset by suburban expansion and other developments.

Forestland is subdivided into three categories. *Timberland* is defined as forestland that is 1) capable of producing more than 1.4 cubic meters per hectare per year (20 cubic feet or 0.25 cords per acre per year) of industrial wood under natural-stand conditions, and 2) that is not allocated to nontimber single uses. The land may or may not be under any program of forest management, but would exceed the indicated volume growth if it were. Today, about 204 million hectares (504 million acres) are classified as timberland. The northern and southern regions contain about 69 percent of the total forestland, and about 75 percent of the timberland in the United States (Table 9.2). Within these regions timberland constitutes more than 90 percent of the total forestland base.

Reserved forestland is sufficiently productive to be timberland, but it has been allocated to specific nontimber uses such as wilderness areas, wildlife sanctuaries, and national parks. About 21 million hectares (52 million acres) of timberland (7 percent of total forestland; 9 percent of total timberland) are classified as reserved forestland, a significant resource legacy for future generations.

Other forestlands consist of slow-growing forests that are not capable of producing 1.4 cubic meters per hectare per year. Although these lands are not productive for timber, they are valuable to society for many other uses, including watershed protection, wildlife habitat, grazing, and recreation. About

Table 9.1 Land Area in the United States, 1997 (12)

Type of Land	Total Area (million hectares)	Proportion (percent)
Timberland	204	22
Reserved Forestland	21	2
Other Forestland	77	8
Total Forestland	302	33
Other Land	614	67
Total Land Area in U.S.	916	100

Table 9.2 Land Area in the United States, by Section and Type of Land, 1997 (12)

Type of Land	Total (million hectares)	North (million hectares)	South (million hectares)	Rocky Mountains (million hectares)	Pacific Coast (million hectares)
Timberland	204	64	81	29	29
Reserved Forestland	21	3	2	7	9
Other Forestland	77	1	4	22	51
All Forestland	302	69	87	58	89
Other Land	614	98	130	242	143
Total Land Area in U.S.	916	167	217	300	232

77 million hectares (26 percent of forestland) fall in this category. More than half is in Alaska and most of the rest is west of the Great Plains, ranging from arid lowland pinyon–juniper forests to high-altitude, slow-growing coniferous forests.

The National Forest System manages 19 percent of the nation's timberland, three-quarters of which is located west of the Great Plains. When national forests were created from unclaimed public lands 100 years ago, much of the lower elevation, more accessible, and productive land had already been claimed by railroads, settlers, and sawmills. Consequently, national forests tend to be on steeper terrain, at higher elevations, and have lower productivity than private timberland (12).

Although timberland on national forests is important to the economies of many communities, the timberland in private ownership plays a much larger role in meeting America's wood and fiber needs. Only 13 percent of the nation's timberland and 12 percent of the softwood growing stock is owned by forest industry, while industry timberlands provided 30 percent of the volume harvested in 1996. More than half these industry timberlands—53 percent—are located in the South, an important region in the timber economy of the nation. Most of the timberland in the United States—almost 60 percent—is owned by private individuals whose major source of income is not from their forestland. These nonindustrial private forest owners, to whom special attention is given in Chapter 10, own 71 per-

cent of the timberland in both the heavily populated North and the timber-dependent South.

Volume, Productivity, Growth, Mortality, and Removals

In 1997, America's timberland contained an estimated 25.3 billion cubic meters (905 billion cubic feet) of timber, of which 92 percent is in growing stock—live, sound trees suited for roundwood products (12). Coniferous softwoods account for 58 percent of growing stock. Softwood volume is up 12 percent since 1953, 7 percent since 1987. Western forests contain 68 percent of the nation's softwood growing stock, primarily because conifers comprise 90 percent of the growing stock in western forests. Three-quarters of these western coniferous forests are on federal lands. In contrast, more than 90 percent of the hardwood growing stock in the United States is found in the northern and southern regions. Most of this volume is on nonindustrial private land, and it varies greatly in quality.

Productivity is measured by the mean annual growth obtainable from fully stocked natural stands, a definition that varies depending on the species and site condition. Of the 302 million hectares of forestland in the United States, 73 million hectares (24 percent) are capable of producing in excess of 5.95 cubic meters per hectare (85 cubic feet per acre) annually. Half of this most productive land is in the South. Another 131 million hectares (43

Sidebar 9.2

Forest Inventory and Analysis Web Site

The power of the Internet is increasingly apparent in the federal forestry research program. No better example can be given than the National Forest Inventory and Analysis web site of the Forest Service. This web site (www. srsfia.usfs.msstate.edu) gives access to the national data base upon which Forest Inventory and Analysis state reports are prepared.

The advantage of this web page is that it enables users to customize their requests for data. For example, suppose the user is interested in building a wood-processing facility, and needs data on the availability of conifers on private lands within a given radius of the proposed location. The data entry provisions on the web page would produce the standard set of 25 tables typically found in a state report, but the tables would contain only the data specified in the parameters selected by the user. The summary tables are automatically opened in the web browser and can then be printed locally by the user.

An easier way to access inventory data— and to do so with ability to specify the area, variables, and constraints in which the user is interested—has long been a desired product from Forest Service research. This web page goes a long way toward fulfilling that promise.

percent) of forestland are capable of producing between 1.40 and 5.95 cubic meters per hectare (20 to 85 cubic feet per acre) annually. About 73 percent of this medium productivity land lies east of the Great Plains. On the 77 million hectares classified as Other Forestland, productivity is less than

1.40 cubic meters per hectare annually. Over 90 percent of these lands are west of the Great Plains and comprise over half of western forests. Reserved forestlands are not classified for productivity.

Growth has exceeded harvest in America since the 1950s, so the volume of growing stock on U.S. timberland has increased considerably the past 5 decades. Between 1953 and 1997, the net volume of hardwood growing stock increased 90 percent to 9.9 billion cubic meters (350 billion cubic feet). The hardwood volume in trees greater than 48 centimeters (19 inches) in diameter more than doubled, from 74 million cubic meters to 158 million cubic meters. For softwoods, the net volume increased 35 percent to 13.7 billion cubic meters (484 billion cubic feet), but the softwood volume in trees larger than 48 centimeters in diameter declined 6 percent. Combining both hardwoods and softwoods, net per-hectare volume rose in the 1953–1997 period in all regions—doubling in the North, increasing 76 percent in the South, rising 27 percent in the Rocky Mountains, and up 2 percent in the Pacific Coast region. Western increases were lower than the East because much of the timberland stocked with high volumes of mature or overmature timber was either harvested and regenerated with young stands, or it was shifted to the reserved forestland category (12).

Mortality is the growing stock volume that dies annually from natural causes, such as insect and disease attacks, suppression beneath the forest canopy, forest fires, windthrow, and catastrophic events. Mortality is a part of every ecosystem. In otherwise healthy stands, mortality normally ranges from 0.61 to 0.85 percent of growing stock volume. Individual dead trees are usually left standing because they are widely scattered and cannot be economically removed. Occasionally, hurricanes and other catastrophic events result in a high mortality in a localized area. In Table 9.3, mortality has already been subtracted from gross growth to obtain net growth.

Removals, which measure the growing stock volume removed from timberland, include volume removed during forest operations such as precommercial thinnings or commercial harvests, as

Table 9.3 Net Annual Growth and Removals from Growing Stock in the United States, 1996 (12)

Section and Item	All Species (million cubic meters)	Softwoods (million cubic meters)	Hardwoods (million cubic meters)
North:			
Net growth	152	33	118
Removals	79	19	60
Growth–removal ratio	1.93	1.75	1.99
South:			
Net growth	303	167	137
Removals	288	183	105
Growth–removal ratio	1.05	0.91	1.30
Rocky Mountains:			
Net growth	70	57	14
Removals	15	14	0.8
Growth–removal ratio	4.69	4.00	16.03
Pacific Coast:			
Net growth	144	126	18
Removals	72	68	3
Growth–removal ratio	2.01	1.84	5.64
United States:			
Net growth	670	383	287
Removals	454	285	167
Growth–removal ratio	1.48	1.34	1.70

well as wood removed during conversion from forest to nonforest land uses. In 1996, timber removals in the United States totaled 454 million cubic meters in comparison to total net growth of 670 million cubic meters (Table 9.3). Put another way, American forests grew 34 percent more softwood volume and 70 percent more hardwood volume than was harvested.

The South, with 64 percent of the total volume removed, has been the preeminent timber supply region in the United States for the past two decades. Its share has grown even larger with recent declines in harvesting on the public forests in the West. In several southern states, such as Louisiana, the economic value of the timber harvest exceeds the value of any other agricultural crop. But the softwood resource in the South, where removals exceeded net growth by 10 percent in 1996, will not be sustainable unless productivity increases or harvesting decreases.

Timber harvest on nonindustrial private forest lands increased by about 17 percent between 1986 and 1996, largely in response to continuing pressure to reduce harvests on national forests and other public lands (12). Nonindustrial private forest lands provided 59 percent of all timber volume harvested in 1996 compared to 30 percent from forest industry lands. The national forests accounted for only 5 percent of timber harvested in 1996, down from 13 percent in 1987. Other public lands—primarily state and county forests and Bureau of Land Management lands—accounted for the remaining 6 percent of removals.

As America's population grows in the 21st century, the nation's ability to meet its increasing wood and fiber needs depends on increasing the productivity of privately owned forestlands. Forest industry firms are investing substantial sums in increasing the productivity of their own lands and managing them on a sustainable basis. Nonindustrial private forestland owners usually need financial assistance to make equivalent investments, and professional advice on the latest scientific findings and technologies available for increasing productivity and managing as sustainably as industrial forest enterprises.

These statistics illustrate the challenge to sustainable forest management over the next several decades. Projections indicate that the forest resources desired by society, including timber, will surely increase as our country's population grows. Despite making major increases in productivity and putting increased emphasis on sustainable forest management, forest industry lands will be hard-pressed to meet projected increases in demand for softwoods two to three decades from now. Recent declines in softwood harvests on public lands have increased the pressure on nonindustrial private forestland owners to harvest available softwoods, and on forest industry to import softwoods from other countries. Further, access to nonindustrial private forestlands, also home to two-thirds of the hardwood growing stock, is becoming more difficult as the number of owners proliferates, and average tract size shrinks. Also, the pressures for access to forestlands for timber production are increasingly in conflict with forest values that arise from non-timber forestland uses.

These are the conflicts facing American forests, their owners, and their managers in the 21st century. The challenges have spawned an intense national debate over the future of both public and private forests. Two examples are the 1998 report by the National Academy of Sciences on prospects and opportunities for sustainable management of America's nonfederal forests (13) and the 1999

report by a committee of scientists who issued recommendations for stewardship of the national forests and grasslands (14). The recommendations in these two reports have helped define the forms of stewardship that should be provided for America's forests in the 21st century.

Stewardship of Public Lands

Approximately 30 percent of the nation's 302 million hectares of timberland is controlled by public owners. Four federal agencies have land management as their primary responsibility: the Forest Service of the Department of Agriculture, the Bureau of Land Management (BLM), the Fish and Wildlife Service, and the National Park Service of the Department of the Interior. Of these four agencies, the Forest Service manages 25 percent of the federally controlled forest and rangeland and the BLM 62 percent. However, the Forest Service is responsible for approximately 80 percent of the federal commercial timberland. All the BLM lands are located in the thirteen western states, mostly in the two states of Alaska and Oregon. These agencies all have other responsibilities as part of their mission. These may include educating the public about resource management options, or assisting and encouraging good management practices on private lands.

Two other federal agencies play a lesser role in land management. The Natural Resources Conservation Service (formerly the Soil Conservation Service) within the Department of Agriculture is the lead federal conservation agency for private forest land. The Department of Defense manages forestland on military reservations; although activities such as grazing, timber production, and wildlife management are permitted on some of these lands, they are primarily managed for defense purposes. It also supports the U.S. Army Corps of Engineers, which provides extremely important recreation opportunities on the nation's inland waterways.

Several other federal agencies directly administer forestlands and rangelands for various purposes, depending on the agency's particular responsibilities. Approximately 10 percent of the public forestland and rangeland is administered by federal agencies for which forestry functions are generally minor or incidental to their major responsibilities. They include the Departments of Commerce and Treasury, the State Department, the Environmental Protection Agency, the U.S. Agency for International Development, the Agriculture Research Service, the Natural Resources Conservation Service, and the Cooperative State Research Education and Extension Service.

Finally, at the state level, forest management is generally coordinated through an appropriate department or commission. At local levels, county commissions or municipal authorities manage forests within their jurisdiction, such as those affiliated with public schools.

Figure 9.10 A wilderness area overlook on the Ouachita National Forest in eastern Oklahoma. (U.S.D.A. Forest Service)

Forest Service

The USDA Forest Service is the major forest management agency within the federal government. Its origins lie in the Department of Agriculture, which established a Division of Forestry in 1876, and the Department of the Interior, which managed the nation's system of forest reserves through its Forestry Division of the General Land Office. In 1905, under the administration of Theodore Roosevelt, these agencies were combined to form the Forest Service, within the Department of Agriculture. Gifford Pinchot—a professional forester, conservationist, and associate of Roosevelt—was appointed to be the first Chief.

Today, the Forest Service manages 155 national forests, 20 national grasslands, and a variety of smaller holdings in the National Forest System, totaling over 77 million hectares (192 million acres) of land—roughly 8.4 percent of the land area of the United States, and 34 percent of the land area in the United States managed by the federal government.

The mission of the Forest Service is "Caring for the land and serving people," and reflects the long-standing commitment of the agency to conserve natural resources while providing for the needs of society (Figure 9.10). To fulfill its mission, the Forest Service takes an ecological approach to the man-agement of national forests and grasslands, to ensure a sustainable supply of timber, wildlife, water, recreation, and forage resources. This is done by developing and implementing Land and Resource Management Plans, which outline the exact goals and means by which any given national forest or grassland will be managed.

The Forest Service has a number of other important responsibilities. Its Research and Development program—the largest forestry research organization in the world—conducts research in forest resource management and conservation. State and Private Forestry is responsible for working with state forestry agencies and private landowners to enhance management of private forest lands in the nation, including support for forest health protection, rural economic development, and assistance with improved management practices on nonindustrial private forest lands. International Forestry is responsible for working cooperatively with foreign governments to promote forest resource conservation in the United States and abroad.

The Forest Service has the most advanced system of planning and administration of virtually any public or private forest management agency in the United States. This is not surprising, given the federal mandate for multiple use and the varied clientele inherent in public ownership. Guidance

Sidebar 9.3

Committee of Scientists Report

The National Forest Management Act of 1976 (NFMA) requires the Secretary of Agriculture to develop, maintain, and revise land and resource management plans for the National Forest System. Acts like this are implemented through federal regulations and internal agency directives. The regulations and directives provide guidance to planners and decision makers. The original regulation implementing NFMA was published in 1979 and revised in 1982. That regulation guided the first round of forest planning. In 1998, the Secretary of Agriculture decided to appoint a Committee of Scientists to offer recommendations on how to revise and update the federal regulation.

The Committee spent a year reviewing innovative examples of natural resource planning and management throughout the Forest Service and meeting with citizens, state and local government officials, leaders of Indian tribes, and employees of the Forest Service and other federal agencies. In their report, the Committee recommended a new vision for the Forest Service. They called for making sustainability—ecological, social, and economic—the foundation for planning and decision making. They reaffirmed that only through collaborative problem solving, where all interests are at the table and all viewpoints considered, could complex natural resource issues be resolved. They proclaimed that the best available scientific information should be used in the planning process, and they called for more involvement of the scientific community. Finally, they envisioned forest plans as "living" documents that are easy to amend and revise.

for current management of the National Forest System can be found in the Multiple Use–Sustained Yield Act of 1960, the Renewable Resources Planning Act (RPA) of 1974, and the National Forest Management Act (NFMA) of 1976. The RPA charges the Forest Service to conduct an economically based assessment that allocates forest resources among their many conflicting uses (15), and the NFMA ensures a scientific basis for management and for both scientific and public input into the planning process (16).

Planning within the Forest Service occurs at national, regional, and local levels. The Chief of the Forest Service develops long-term national goals, programs, and production levels for management of the national forests based on data generated by the RPA assessment. Regional contributions to national goals are based on regional supply of and demand for resources. Within each region, standards and guidelines are formulated on the basis of regional RPA assessments; these standards and guidelines are expressed as long-range program objectives and production levels for individual national forests within the region. At individual national forests, the planning team summarizes the management situation, establishes long-term goals and objectives, specifies in detail a plan of activities that will be conducted throughout the 10-year planning horizon for each alternative proposed, selects the desired alternative through public input and consideration of associated environmental impacts, and establishes a program to monitor plan implementation. The management plan for a national forest typically provides general directions for forestwide management and specific directions for implementing the selected alternative.

National Park Service

National Park management is probably the oldest federal forest management program. In 1872, Congress established Yellowstone National Park by withdrawing it from the public-domain lands that had been open to entry for homesteading. The early Parks were under the protection and administration of the Department of the Army. The National

Park Service (NPS) was established in 1916 within the Department of the Interior, and was given responsibility for management for the network of National Parks and Monuments.

Today, the National Park System consists of 378 areas covering more than 32 million hectares (80 million acres) in the United States and its territories. The mission of the National Park Service is to conserve the scenery and the natural and historic objects and values of the lands under its administration, and to ensure their conservation for future generations (Figure 9.11). They are not used for production of forest products, as are national forest lands. Lands in the National Park System are of such national significance as to justify special recognition and protection in accordance with various acts of Congress. The system includes not only the large National Parks such as Grand Canyon and Yellowstone, but also National Monuments, Preserves, Historic Sites, Historic Parks, Memorials, Battlefields, Cemeteries, Recreation Areas, Seashores, Lakeshores, Rivers, Parkways, and Trails.

Additions to the National Park System are generally made through acts of Congress or by executive order of the President. Under the Antiquities Act of 1906, the President has the authority to proclaim an area as a National Monument without the support of Congress, and many areas now famous within the National Park System were initially protected under this Act by Theodore Roosevelt. In the last year of his administration, President Bill Clinton used this act to set aside many additional natural areas. However, the power to establish a new National Park resides with Congress, in collaboration with the Secretary of the Interior.

Lands in the National Park System are maintained in an essentially intact condition. The challenge in this approach is that forests do not remain static. For example, the decision to suppress forest fires in western forests results in the accumulation of woody debris on the forest floor, which can lead to catastrophic wildfires. As a result, land managers are increasingly using ecological practices such as prescribed burning, fuel reduction, and habitat restoration to better manage the successional

Figure 9.11   The mission of the National Park Service includes conserving both the natural and historic objects under its care, illustrated by this view of Mount Rushmore and the surrounding forest. (James M. Guldin)

dynamics of forest stands—and thereby to maintain the health, diversity, and beauty of forest ecosystems in the National Park System.

Bureau of Land Management

The Bureau of Land Management (BLM) is responsible for managing 107 million hectares (264 million acres) of land in the United States. Major BLM holdings are in the extensive grasslands and noncommercial forestland in the West. Management practices on BLM lands include mineral exploration and extraction, grazing and timber production, recreation, wilderness, fish and wildlife habitat, and heritage resources (Figure 9.12).

The origins of the BLM lie in the Department of the Interior's General Land, which was established in the early 1800s to oversee the transfer of lands from federal holdings into private hands during the westward expansion of the nation's population. The BLM was established in 1946 by combining the General Land Office with other agencies that had responsibilities for managing the remaining federal land base in the West.

The BLM mission is to manage the lands it administers under a multiple-use framework. This mission is complicated by the increasing value that society places on recreation, conservation, and non-consumptive resources. Mining, grazing, and timber production continue to be important, but these objectives must now be integrated with the other multiple uses that do not involve extraction of resources.

U.S. Fish and Wildlife Service

The U.S. Fish and Wildlife Service, under the Department of the Interior, is responsible for managing and conserving fish and wildlife and their habitats for the benefit of present and future generations. The agency has important program responsibilities for migratory birds, endangered species, some marine mammals, and both freshwater and anadromous fish species,[1] either through direct management or through leadership in international conservation programs for migratory waterfowl and fish.

The agency manages a network of over 520 National Wildlife Refuges, encompassing over 37 million hectares (93 million acres). The majority of these are located in Alaska, but there is at least one National Wildlife Refuge in each of the 50 states. The refuges provide critical habitat for native species of plants, animals, and fish, especially for endangered and threatened species. However, the refuges are also important for recreation and conservation education, as shown by the 25 million people who visit annually.

A major program of the agency is to identify, protect, and restore the roughly 700 plant and animal species that have been identified as endangered or threatened under the provisions of the Endangered Species Act. The listing or de-listing of a species is conducted under rigorous scientific scrutiny, with

Figure 9.12 Buffalo on grasslands managed by the Bureau of Land Management in western South Dakota. (James M. Guldin)

---

[1] Anadromous fish species—those ascending upriver from the sea to spawn, such as salmon.

opportunities for public comment. When a species is listed, the agency works with landowners to develop management plans for population and habitat conservation.

Natural Resources Conservation Service

The Natural Resources Conservation Service (NRCS), formerly known as the Soil Conservation Service, is the primary federal agency responsible for conservation leadership on private lands in the United States. The NRCS has no land of its own to manage, but provides advice and program access for use in managing forests on private and nonfederal government lands. The agency traces its roots back to 1935, when the SCS was established to support conservation on private lands during the difficult years of the Depression.

The NRCS is responsible for the Forestry Incentives Program (FIP), the Conservation Reserve Program (CRP), and the Wetland Reserve Program (WRP). Each of these programs is administered and funded in slightly different ways, but they share a common goal—to assist private landowners in forest management and conservation through technical advice and financial assistance. The technical advice is usually in the form of guidance about forestry practices that qualify for federal support. If a site qualifies for assistance, management plans are prepared by foresters with NRCS or state forestry and wildlife agencies; funds are then provided to help support the financial costs of implementation, usually through some form of cost-sharing.

For example, reforestation of erosion-prone agricultural fields was a priority in the late 1990s. To determine if a particular field or pasture qualifies for assistance, a farmer might contact a county NRCS employee, county forester or state extension agent. That professional would check the site, prepare the management plan, and submit it to the NRCS for approval. If approved, federal funds will be provided to support some percentage, typically half, of the cost of the tree planting.

The NRCS works closely with state forestry and conservation agencies and private landowners to communicate the availability of program funds, to identify areas that would be of high priority for support, and to advise landowners on the conservation practices that would benefit their land. Thus, the agency best achieves its mission by providing support to landowners who want to learn more about the conservation of their land.

U.S. Army Corps of Engineers

It may seem unusual to include the U.S. Army Corps of Engineers in the list of organizations responsible for forest management on federal lands. However, most forest recreation activities involve water, and the Corps of Engineers manages over 450 manmade lakes covering nearly 5 million hectares (12 million acres). Specific legislation authorizes the Corps of Engineers to provide public outdoor recreation opportunities at these facilities (Figure 9.13).

The Corps of Engineers is the largest provider of water-based recreation in the nation. It supports over 4300 developed recreation sites, approximately 30 percent of the total found on federal lands. Annually, Corps recreation facilities support 350 million visits; about 10 percent of the population of the United States makes at least one visit per year to a Corps of Engineers recreation site.

Figure 9.13 Lake Ouachita, a U.S. Army Corps of Engineers impoundment in west-central Arkansas. (U.S.D.A. Forest Service)

Nationally, there is growing awareness that the Corps of Engineers serves a large user population and makes a significant contribution to the U.S. economy. Coupled with this is the awareness that increased support is needed to improve facilities, maintain the waterways, and manage forests adjacent to these bodies of water to enhance forest health and watershed values.

State Agencies and Other Organizations

State forestry and wildlife agencies are responsible for managing state-owned forest resources such as state parks, forests, and wildlife areas. The organization of state agencies depends largely on the amount of forestland and the importance of forestry within the individual state. States that have extensive state forest lands, such as California, Oregon, and Washington, have large forestry agencies and comprehensive procedures for management of state forest lands (Figure 9.14). In other states, activities emphasize control of wildfires, which is a major responsibility in the South. Most states also provide advice on forest management to owners of nonindustrial private forestlands.

Stewardship of Private Lands

Forest ownership in the United States is dominated by the private sector, which includes both forest industry and owners of nonindustrial private forest (NIPF) lands. Because of their importance, the NIPF sector is discussed in a separate chapter (Chapter 10).

Forest Industry

Forest industry lands are those lands owned by companies or individuals that also operate wood processing plants (17). The mission of a typical forest industry is to satisfy company goals and provide favorable economic returns to the company owners or stockholders. Their size may range from a small open sawmill with a few thousand hectares

Figure 9.14   Redwoods in Humboldt Redwoods State Park, northern California. (James M. Guldin)

of land to multinational, multiproduct conglomerates operating several dozen mills, employing thousands of people, and owning millions of hectares of productive forestland. As a result, management of lands owned by forest industry differs greatly from that of public lands.

The organization of administrative efforts also varies. Some companies employ a chief forester and staff to implement production quotas and forest management programs. Others are organized within a woodlands division, generally headed by a vice-president and subdivided into management districts (about 20,000–50,000 hectares in size), each managed by one or two foresters and a crew of technicians.

Within the company the woodlands division may exist as a separate profit center, required to show acceptable returns on all its investments from stand establishment through harvest, or the woodlands division may be part of a vertically integrated profit center, in which financial losses are acceptable if they create profit-making opportunities elsewhere or otherwise contribute to the company's goals.

A hallmark of management on forest industry lands is keen attention to productivity and growth. Practices commonly found on industry lands include the establishment of plantations using genetically improved seedlings that are bred for traits such as rapid growth and disease resistance. Seedlings are planted at precise spacing to optimize growth. The use of fertilizers to enhance early seedling growth, and herbicides to control competing vegetation (Figure 9.15), is also common. As stands mature, thinnings maintain proper spacing between trees and optimize stand volume growth (Figure 9.16). Harvests are scheduled so that the size and volume of harvested trees meet mill requirements.

A major goal of the woodlands division of the typical forest industry is to provide an even flow of wood products to the mill. Shutting down a mill for want of raw material is enormously expensive, so industry foresters develop detailed plans to

Figure 9.16 A thinned stand of loblolly pine sawtimber nearing its rotation age on forest industry land in south Arkansas. (James M. Guldin)

Figure 9.15 Applying herbicides to control competing vegetation in a loblolly pine plantation on forest industry land in central Arkansas. (James M. Guldin)

ensure a continuous flow of timber from the forest to the mill. A company's mill managers and foresters occasionally disagree about harvesting priorities in the forest, if events such as unusually wet weather or labor difficulties require logging during marginal conditions of operability, access, or when stands are not yet of optimal rotation age.

For the 21st century, managers of forest industry lands are increasingly aware of the value of resources other than timber on their lands. In response, they are pursuing opportunities to profit from managing wildlife, fish, or recreational facilities, as illustrated by the common practice of leasing forest industry lands for hunting. Nontimber resource specialists increasingly find employment with forest products companies, and their responsibilities range from encouraging hunting strategies that reduce browsing damage on seedlings to advocating for compliance with nonpoint pollution standards. In addition, the public goodwill that results from producing and accommodating nontimber resources is not lost on industrial forest managers. Even the preservation of endangered species and the protection of their habitat are increasingly viewed as a mark of good corporate stewardship.

Nonindustrial Corporate Holdings

It has become increasingly common for forest lands to be held and managed by corporations that do not own their own processing facilities but that nevertheless practice intensive management. Common examples of these are life insurance companies, real estate trusts, and other firms that look on forest management as an investment opportunity.

Similarly, a forest industry may divest its woodlands from its mills, and establish the woodlands division as a separate real estate trust. In this arrangement, the woodlands real estate trust becomes independent of the mill and responsible for making a profit. One effect of this is for the real estate trust to sell timber on the open market, where the high bidder may not necessarily be the mill that it served exclusively before the divestiture.

Generally, land or real estate trusts manage their holdings to ensure that the timber they put on the market is in demand by the manufacturing facilities in the area. Since the investment companies do not own their own processing facilities, they must produce timber with attributes—species composition, quality, volume, and operability—that are highly desirable to the forest industries that will bid on the products when they are made available for sale (Figure 9.17).

Investment firms often seek to achieve the same standards of forest management as the major forest industries. As a result, several of the largest and most prominent investment firms also subscribe to

Figure 9.17   Cull tree removal in a sawtimber-sized stand of bottomland hardwoods on real estate trust land in western Tennessee. (James M. Guldin)

the principles of the Sustainable Forestry Initiative of the AF&PA. Doing so commits the investment trust to manage its lands according to the mandatory guidelines of compliance stated in the Initiative's forest management principles.

Private Conservation Groups

A relatively new player in the field of forest management is the private conservation group. The most notable example is The Nature Conservancy, an organization dedicated to the preservation of plants, animals, and natural communities representative of the diversity of life on earth. The Nature

Sidebar 9.4

Private Conservation Groups in Action

The original forested wetland ecosystem of the lower Mississippi River Valley covered 8.5 million hectares (21 million acres) of bottomland hardwood forests. By 1991, only 2 million hectares (4.9 million acres) remained. The Big Woods of Arkansas consists of 200,000 hectares (500,000 acres) of bottomland hardwoods along the Cache, White, and lower Arkansas Rivers in eastern Arkansas, and is one of the largest remaining contiguous blocks of this vanishing forest type. Because of its rarity and the unique conservation opportunity the area represents, interest has been growing among federal and state natural resource agencies, private conservation groups, and others in developing a plan to conserve and protect the ecological diversity and promote compatible use of natural resources in the Big Woods.

The Arkansas Field Office of The Nature Conservancy (TNC) is spearheading efforts to conserve the Big Woods as a functioning ecosystem that preserves biologically significant areas. Implicit in TNC goals are mandates to connect and expand remaining forest patches and corridors, to restore natural patterns of hydrology when possible, to promote compatible human use, to conduct and encourage ecosystem research, and to reach out to local communities.

To achieve these goals, TNC has and will continue to acquire property in the area. It is working with existing landowners on afforestation and reforestation projects, and with its own scientists and others in academia to develop ecological research and monitoring in the region. Key partners include the U.S. Fish and Wildlife Service, the Arkansas Land and Development Corporation (a minority farm organization), the Natural Resource Conservation Service, Arkansas

Bald-cypress in a minor stream bottom in the Big Woods of eastern Arkansas. (James M. Guldin)

Forestry Commission, Arkansas Game and Fish Commission, Arkansas Natural Heritage Commission, Potlatch Corporation, Anderson-Tully Company, Ducks Unlimited, the Arkansas Wildlife Federation, and the Arkansas Audubon Society.

(continues)

Sidebar 9.4 *(continued)*

Ecologically, the conservation actions taken by the Conservancy represent a new direction in resource management—the conservation of significant areas through private action and development of coalitions of interested agencies, forest industry, and private citizens.

Conservancy has extended conservation protection to more than 4.4 million hectares (11 million acres) in the United States and 24 million hectares (60 million acres) elsewhere in the world.

The Nature Conservancy (TNC) achieves its results through a nonconfrontational, apolitical approach in its activities, unlike many conservation groups. If TNC identifies property as having significance for a species or habitat of interest, it will acquire it either through purchase on the open market, through donation, or through working with the landowner for a permanent conservation easement. All of these tactics have prominent tax advantages to the landowner.

After acquisition, TNC arranges for transfer of the property to the best available conservator, typically a state or federal agency. In some properties, TNC retains partial or complete ownership. The organization does not simply draw a line around its properties, though it will do so if dictated by the best science for managing a given species or habitat. However, it is common to see TNC crews engaged in active programs of forest or grassland management, especially in an ecosystem restoration context. For example, the prescribed burning crews of TNC are equal to the best of any federal or state agency, given their experience in burning prairie and woodland habitats for ecological restoration.

Stewardship Across Ownerships

If one major advance in forest stewardship can be identified in the early 21st century, it is the concept of promoting forest stewardship across ownerships. It is not that public agencies, forest industry, and private nonindustrial forest landowners cannot work alone or independently of one another; they can, and will continue to do so. However, increasingly, these three ownership sectors are finding more opportunities by working together across ownership boundaries than they would by working alone.

The collaboration starts by sharing knowledge. Forest landowners do not operate in a vacuum. They blend their personal knowledge and experience with information from many difference sources. Some of this information is scientific, such as the latest research results. Some is market-driven, such as the monthly stumpage price reports for local forest products. The local experience of forestry professionals should not be overlooked, although it tends to be more value-laden, including personal preferences, opinions, and beliefs.

Collaboration across sectors can extend to informal or formal cooperative relationships. A simple example occurs when a forest industry company buys timber from a nonindustrial private landowner on the open market. However, this simple example can extend to a formal contract for long-term management services between the company, or a private consulting forester, and the landowner. It can include partnerships between government agencies and private landowners for advice on managing special sites, or for help in preserving habitat for endangered and threatened species.

Over the past several decades, private nonindustrial forest lands have been a special concern to professional foresters. Nearly 60 percent of the timberland in the United States is in farm and other private nonindustrial ownership; these lands produce a significant share of the nation's timber, they support livestock herds, they contain unique ecological habitats, and they provide recreational opportunities for many people. Most of these forest owners hold small parcels under 400 hectares (1000 acres). Some give little thought to the management of their natural resources. Much is known about the extent of private nonindustrial forest ownership and about the resource production capabilities of their lands, but little is known about the landowners themselves.

Four types of programs provide information to forest land managers and forest landowners. *Cooperative programs* provide management and financial assistance. *Forest protection programs* deal with problems, such as wildfires or insect attacks, which commonly cross property boundaries and affect all lands irrespective of ownership. *Research programs* in various federal and state organizations exist to discover and develop new ways of applying scientific information. *Advocacy programs* exist to foster interest in specific areas and mobilize public and political support.

Cooperative Forestry Programs

Millions of hectares of forestlands are in the hands of forest industries, states, local governments, and small landowners. In recent years state agencies have become stronger and federal funds have dwindled. This situation has spawned a national effort to focus federal assistance on cooperative forestry activities that require a federal role, have multistate implications, and will provide for long-term improvements (18).

Several formal programs under the *cooperative forestry* umbrella facilitate forest management on nonfederal ownerships. Some programs provide forestry assistance to landowners, primarily nonindustrial owners of small parcels of land. Others coordinate the activities of managers of large land parcels, primarily public agencies and forest industries. The underlying premise of these programs is the need for additional financial or technical assistance to promote desirable stewardship activities.

Most cooperative programs are aimed at private lands, either by direct assistance to private landowners or by supporting programs of state forestry agencies. Cooperative programs provide technical assistance and financial assistance, often both simultaneously.

The Department of Agriculture cooperates with land grant colleges and universities to support the nationwide system of county extension agents. Some county agents provide technical advice in forestry, with the help of district or state forestry extension specialists. They focus on sharing new scientific information and technologies with landowners, consultants, and land managers. They often organize demonstration projects, teach short courses, help develop land management plans, answer questions, and may even provide a day or two of consulting to an individual private landowner who seeks their assistance.

Financial assistance includes cost-sharing incentives programs to assist nonindustrial private landowners in implementing a variety of conservation measures. It can take the form of special laws providing favorable treatment for forests, such as the capital gains provisions of the federal income tax code that use lower tax rates for income from forestry than for ordinary income. Some state property tax codes contain provisions to defer annual property taxes until the parcel generates income, usually through a timber harvest. Others require counties to assess private forest land based on its current use value rather than its value if converted to agricultural cropland, suburban housing development, or other "highest and best use" from a land value standpoint.

Finally, conservation education programs are an effective way to translate technical expertise as well. The Smokey Bear and Woodsy Owl programs are cooperative programs between the Forest Service and participating state and local agencies. Programs supported by forestry industry and state and federal agencies include Project Learning Tree (emphasizing forests), Project Wild (emphasizing wildlife), and Project Wet (emphasizing aquatic ecology). These programs use the talents of resource professionals to train primary and secondary teachers, who then use their own talents to bring environmental education to the classroom.

Forest Protection Programs

For some landowners, concerns about forest management only begin when their property is threatened. Forest protection programs are special cooperative programs set up to help public and private landowners deal with wildfires and pest outbreaks.

Wildfire policies and practices have evolved significantly in the past decade. The aggressive suppression policies of the 1950s and 1960s were encapsulated by the goal of extinguishing every wildfire fire by 10:00 a.m. the morning after the fire was detected. These policies dramatically reduced the number of hectares burned each year. However, they had some unintended outcomes that have led to a rethinking about the role of fire in ecosystems.

For those fires where suppression is appropriate, a well-coordinated initial attack framework has been established that involves federal and state forestland management agencies, Native American tribal governments and forest industry landowners. All participants have teams of employees who are trained in specific firefighting or support tasks and can be called upon to fight fires anywhere on public or private lands. The Forest Service developed a management framework, called the "Incident Command Team," through which teams and individuals from all partner agencies can quickly, cooperatively, and cost-efficiently blend their skills and resources to suppress the fire.

Pest outbreaks also call for cooperative action between federal, state, and private organizations. Like fires, pest outbreaks can occur suddenly and threaten multiple landowners. The Forest Health Monitoring Program is a joint effort by the Forest Service State and Private Forestry and participating state forestry agencies to track long-term trends in forest conditions, identify changes in health status, and evaluate causes. When pest outbreaks are identified, cooperative programs involving federal agencies, states, and municipal governments are launched to bring the pest under control. Particularly vexing are outbreaks caused by invasive species not indigenous to North America such as the gypsy moth, Dutch elm disease, and Asian longhorned beetle.

Cooperative programs are also in place to encourage land management practices that reduce the risk of infestations. For example, research has demonstrated that thinning the basal area of southern pine stands to below 17 square meters per hectare (75 square feet per acre) greatly reduces the likelihood of southern pine beetle outbreaks. Cooperative research between the Forest Service and land grant universities has led to innovative methods for controlling pest outbreaks. Chemicals that confuse insect behavior, such as artificial sex pheromones that disrupt mating, often can be used in lower doses and with fewer adverse ecological effects than pesticides. Biological controls, such as growing and releasing sterile males or natural predators of the invasive species have also been proven effective by researchers. Blending all these management tools together—silvicultural techniques, biological controls, effective chemicals, outreach activities providing technical assistance and targeted financial assistance to those in need—is called *integrated pest management (IPM)*. Because so many partners and cooperative elements are involved in integrated pest management, it is the epitome of a cooperative program for protection of forests from pest outbreaks. IPM is discussed in detail in Chapter 8 on forest diseases and insects.

Research and Development Programs

Research and development aims to discover new knowledge about ecological, economic, and social systems and to develop new ways of applying the knowledge to solve problems. In the United States, the primary research and development organizations are the Research and Development program of the Forest Service, colleges and universities, forest industry firms, and private institutes and interest groups.

The mission of the Research and Development program of the Forest Service is to "discover and develop credible new knowledge and exciting new technologies that help to sustain the health, productivity, and diversity of America's forests and rangelands and meet the needs of present and future generations." Sustainable development—meeting the needs of the present generation without compromising the ability of future generations to meet their needs—is a fundamental objective of all agency activities. They focus on sustainable development at multiple geographic scales—site, landscape, regional, national, and global.

Research is conducted through six regional Research Stations located throughout the United States, and the national Forest Products Laboratory. The core of the program is a network of 160 *research work units*, each consisting of one or more scientists holding advanced degrees as well as technicians and support staff (Figure 9.18). Unit research specialties include the spectrum of multiple uses and resources in the forest, such as silviculture, forest ecology, wood products, economics, wildlife,

Figure 9.18 Classic uneven-aged structure in a loblolly-shortleaf pine stand after 56 years of management on the Good Farm Forestry Forty demonstration area. The stand is located on the Crossett Experimental Forest, which is managed by the Monticello-Crossett Research Work Unit of the Southern Research Station, U.S.D.A. Forest Service. (U.S.D.A. Forest Service)

recreation, range science, hydrology, forest pests, and fire. Each unit has a charter that describes its mission, and that lists three or four problem areas to achieve the mission. Frequently, the problem areas are so complex that they require a number of studies focused on specific elements of a problem. The unit mission and assigned problems are reviewed every five years to assess progress and, if warranted, to adjust the mission and redirect the resources into higher priority lines of research. During these periodic reviews, research collaborators, users of the research, and members of the public at large are invited to comment on and influence the priorities of the work assigned.

Cooperation with others is a hallmark of Forest Service research activities. Every research work unit cooperates with researchers in other organizations. This cooperation is formalized in over 1000 active agreements that provide funding to partners, typically university colleagues, for collaborative research. Many of these are cooperative agreements in which university colleagues and Forest Service scientists work together to complete the studies described in the agreement.

One major Forest Service research program that depends on cooperation for its success is the Forest Inventory and Analysis (FIA) program. The FIA program has been collecting information about America's forests since the 1930s. The program uses a combination of images from remote sensing and data collected by field crews on 13,000 field plots annually to evaluate the status, condition, health, and productivity of America's forests. Without the cooperation of private landowners, state forestry agencies, and advocacy groups, the FIA program could not be successful.

Universities are the second major source of new research and development activities supporting public land managers and private landowners. Funding for university faculty involved in research comes from many sources—endowments, federal and state appropriations, cooperative agreements, and research grants from forest industry, private foundations, and government agencies. The U.S.D.A. Cooperative State Research, Education, and Extension Service provides funding to land grant institutions through formula grant funds and competitive grants. Formula grant funds are allocated according to a set of criteria, such as the acreage of forestland in a state, and support both land-grant university research (McIntire-Stennis program) and extension (Smith-Lever program) activities. Competitive grants are offered through the National Research Initiative.

The typical competitive grants process begins with the funding organization issuing a *request for proposals* (RFP) that describes in detail the particular research problem to be addressed, and the requirements for eligibility. A group of scientific peers reviews the proposals that are submitted and ranks them in order of merit. The highest ranked proposals are awarded funding. Generally, faculty who obtain grant funding will be asked to submit progress reports to the funding organization as the research is being conducted, and a final report when the research is competed.

Forest industry funds research in three categories. The first is research on the development of new products and manufacturing methods. This work is usually proprietary, often conducted by company employees, and is intended for use inside the company. A second category is for nonproprietary research available to any and all users. A few companies have their own internal research organizations that solve problems and develop improved technology for application on the firm's lands and lands of cooperating nonindustrial private forest landowners. Others conduct research activities through grants to external research partners such as Forest Service or university scientists. The third category is through alliances formed by companies to solve larger problems through industry associations or university cooperatives; member companies pool their contributions, award grants to research faculty and graduate students, and share the research results among the members. One example is Agenda 2020, a competitive grants program sponsored by the American Forest and Paper Association; another is the Southern Forest Tree Nursery Cooperative, organized by Auburn University.

Like their government and university counterparts, industry researchers and industry grant recipients usually submit nonproprietary research findings for publication in professional journals, which makes them available to the general public. Research funded by industry tends to be carefully focused on industry objectives. Thus, it sometimes tends to be of narrower scope and applicability than publicly funded research.

Advocacy groups also conduct limited forestry research. Their research usually focuses very precisely on the group's interests. It is often aimed at filling gaps in research results conducted by others, at tailoring previous results to specific sites, and at corroborating or denying previous results. The Appalachian Mountain Club, The Nature Conservancy, and the Wilderness Society are examples of advocacy groups that conduct research studies.

Advocacy Programs

Advocacy programs are run by groups of people with common interests who pool their energy and resources to create change or preserve a status quo aligned with their shared values. Advocacy programs concentrate their efforts on communications and representation activities. Working with print, broadcast, and electronic media, they gather, package, and disseminate information that describes their position management policies and options. They also contact elected and appointed officials and landowners to represent their members' interests and build support. Advocacy programs contribute to stewardship by assuring that a broad range of options are considered and that minority viewpoints get aired in the political process of making natural resource policies and management decisions. Most of the positive changes in natural resource management that occurred during the 20th century owed their success, at least in part, to support from advocacy groups and their programs.

Advocacy groups can be classified into four general categories: 1) the commodity user group, 2) the noncommodity user group, 3) the professional group, and 4) the special-issue group. It is important to recognize that a specific advocacy group may have activities in more than one category.

The commodity and noncommodity groups are both forest users. Both groups try to promote forest policies and budgets that favor their interests. A *commodity group* is composed of businesses associated with an industry that produces a marketable product such as paper, lumber, or beef. Examples are the American Forest and Paper Association and the National Cattleman's Association. A *noncommodity group* is composed of businesses or private individuals that also use the forest, but their use does not involve a marketable forest product. Rather, the primary focus of the use is enjoyment of the forest. Examples of noncommodity advocacy groups are the National Wildlife Federation, the Sierra Club, and the All-Terrain Vehicle Association. Other groups, such as the Sporting Goods Manufacturing Association, bridge this distinction.

The third category is *professional groups*. They consist of organizations whose primary purpose is to maintain and advance the technical and scientific practice and ethics of the forestry and related professions and sciences. This group includes such organizations as the Society of American Foresters, Ecological Society of America, The Wildlife Society, and the Society for Range Management.

The final category is the *special-issue group*. These are organizations that formally support or oppose a single issue. Their existence is usually limited to the duration of the issue or focused on a place having extraordinary value to the group members. However, on occasion, they take on new issues and evolve into organizations with broader interests. Examples of special-issue groups are Citizens Against Toxic Substances and Friends of the Boundary Waters Wilderness.

All these advocacy groups contribute to the stewardship of America's forests. However, the Society of American Foresters (SAF) plays an additional, very significant role as representing the forestry profession.

The SAF was founded in 1900 with the objectives of advancing the science, technology, education, and practice of professional forestry in America and of using the knowledge and skill of the profession to benefit society. The SAF publishes the *Journal of Forestry* and a newsletter, *The Forestry Forum*, each month; *Forest Science*, a quarterly research journal; and three quarterly journals with regional focus—the *Northern, Southern, and Western Journals of Applied Forestry*. In addition to serving as the voice of the forestry profession during national and regional policy discussions, SAF also maintains a code of professional ethics for foresters, accredits schools providing undergraduate or graduate forestry education, promotes continuing forestry education, strengthens international relations with foresters and forestry organizations in other countries, provides insurance for members, and develops standard references for the profession, such as a forestry dictionary and descriptions of forest cover types.

Forestry at the National Level

At first glance, the link between the practice of forestry in the woods and the nation's capital seems obscure. Other than the aesthetic appeal of the Japanese cherry blossoms during springtime on the National Mall, one does not usually think of Washington when one thinks of forestry and trees. However, in the government buildings that line the Mall—the White House, the Capitol, the Departments of Agriculture and Interior, and others—more key decisions are made about how forestry will be practiced and financially supported than anywhere else in the nation.

The balance of power is shared among three separate but equal branches of the U.S. government. Both Congress and the executive branch have active roles in forestry, and the judicial branch is often called upon for solutions to forestry issues and interests. Moreover, many people and interest groups focus their demands on forestry at the national level. The international implications of forestry cannot be ignored in Washington; many of the forests in developing nations are under public management, and the management practices of the United States are often used as the model for other countries. This diversity of interests means that the nation's policy on forestry is actually a collection of policies addressing many concerns and springing from any number of interests.

The Federal Government Role

Leadership for establishing the debate on forestry issues lies in the executive branch, and specifically in the Forest Service. Within an agency such as the Forest Service, many different staff units work together to formulate agency policy. When these staff units have different concepts about what forestry policy should be, they must work together to hammer out a policy direction for the agency's management program and the budget allocations needed to support that program. They are constrained by the limitations of the resources to be managed, the laws and regulations in effect, agency traditions, and executive orders from the president. This process goes on within a legal framework established by Congress in a single charter act or by a series of acts for different components of the agency's program.

However, the management program and budget of an agency such as the Forest Service is just a small part of the overall executive program and budget that the president seeks to enact. Forestry programs, and the budget to support them, must be balanced with other national programs such as health care, transportation systems, and defense. The central issue is the amount of federal funding to allocate to forestry programs in relation to other programs in a way that serves the American public most effectively.

The unenviable task of recommending to the president how to slice the pie falls to the Office of Management and Budget (OMB). The OMB takes all agency and department budget proposals and fits them into one or more cohesive packages. This office operates under the president's direction and with no allegiance to any one agency or department. Generally, staff members at OMB referred to as "examiners" are assigned responsibility for one agency (at

most three or four). The examiner analyzes the agency's budget proposal for use in program-balancing deliberations. The agency must provide its examiner with full information, including justifications, analyses, and assessments with each program request. If support seems inadequate, the examiner may challenge or even recommend dropping a specific program. Effective interaction with its examiner and support by the secretary and departmental staff are critical to an agency's ability to maintain its position within an administration budget.

Implementation of any part of the president's budget must await congressional action to approve the activity and its funding. Congress can of course vote to increase, decrease, or otherwise change the president's budget proposal. Congressional interest in forestry issues is evident both by members of Congress individually and by staff members of forestry-related committees or subcommittees. No single committee or subcommittee has overall jurisdiction over forestry matters. For example, committees on foreign trade consider log export issues, and committees on energy issues may consider wood fiber as an alternative energy source.

A member of Congress or a congressional staff member may have expertise in forestry matters, or may rely on an agency for such knowledge. Although most members of Congress have little background in forestry, they still may take a strong interest in particular forestry issues. The Forest Service manages land in many states and congressional districts. As a result, it is not unusual for legislators to represent the interests of their constituents in specific forestry issues during the annual congressional budget review process.

The overall role of Congress in forestry issues is somewhat similar to that of a local forest manager. Congress tries to resolve disputes over conflicting uses, but on a broader scale—that of forestry in a national context. The role of Congress is three-fold. First, Congress reviews and revises the president's program budget requests, providing direction through its annual appropriation committee reports. The budget review process provides an overview of an agency's plans and policies as specified in existing laws.

Sidebar 9.5

Joint Roles in Action on the National Level

The role of the federal government, Congress, citizens, and the courts in establishing forest policy can, in very general terms, be shown by the evolution of forestry management policy for the Forest Service.

In the 1860s and 1870s, public opinion grew to favor federal management of forests. In 1879, the American Forestry Association (AFA) and the American Association for the Advancement of Science (AAAS) petitioned Congress to reserve or set aside forested lands from public entry or disposal. In 1891, Congress passed a bill for general revision of the public land laws. When the bill emerged from House–Senate conference, a Section 24 had been added that provided authority for a president to reserve forestlands for public ownership. A month later, President Harrison set aside the Yellowstone Park Forest Reserve, south of Yellowstone Park. He proclaimed it an Executive Reserve but gave no specific direction on how or for what purpose it was to be managed.

In 1896, the president asked the National Academy of Sciences to study what had become known as the "Forest Reserves." Congress incorporated the concepts of forestry management resulting from the study into an amendment to an appropriation bill. This 1897 action, called the Organic Act, laid the groundwork for how the reserved federal forestland would be managed and used.

In 1905, the president, with congressional approval, merged the Forestry Division of the General Land Office in the Department of the Interior, which until that time had custody of the forest reserves, with the Bureau of Forestry in the Department of Agriculture. The new agency was named the Forest Service, and it was placed in the Department of Agriculture. Two years later, the former forest reserves became known as national forests. Throughout the 1900s the Forest Service managed the national forests and set specific policy based primarily on the Organic Act and the annual budget review.

In 1960, Congress stepped back into center stage by passing a new law, the Multiple Use–Sustained Yield Act, to ensure that national forests would be managed for multiple uses at levels providing a sustained yield for the future. This was a codification of policies already followed by the Forest Service.

In the early 1970s, several groups of people became concerned about how forestry was being practiced in some national forests. The citizens' groups petitioned the courts in 1975. The courts ruled that forestry practices were not in accordance with the law of 1897. More or less concurrently, Congress reentered the scene in 1974 with the Renewable Resources Planning Act (RPA). This bill requires the Secretary of Agriculture to assess natural resources periodically and to submit a five-year renewable-resources program to Congress, based on this assessment of future supplies and demands. In 1976, Congress amended the RPA legislation and enacted the National Forest Management Act (NFMA), also in response to the 1975 court action. This bill provides general guidelines for the agency by establishing the general content and process to be followed in developing national forest plans.

Thus, from the 19th century to the present day, forest policy has moved into the spotlight several times, and has been scrutinized and reshaped by public interest, the executive branch, the legislature, and the judiciary. The changes in forest policy that will occur in the future will be no less representative of these public deliberations.

Secondly, Congress affects national policy matters by enacting legislation. Laws define, redefine, or clarify the context within which agencies administer policy. Congress tends to legislate infrequently on forestry issues (although the 1970s were an exception). Legislation usually sets broad guidelines or frameworks, but defers to the agencies for the development and implementation of specific forestry policy. More specific direction is inappropriate for several reasons, including the diversity and changing demands on American forests, the size and diverse membership of Congress, and the reluctance of members to legislate on professional forestry matters. The result is that Congress usually supports and relies on the agencies that are staffed and run by professional resource managers.

A final but important role performed by Congress is monitoring and reviewing the day-to-day activities and occasional crises that occur during agency operations. These tasks are performed by two legislative branch offices, the General Accounting Office and the Congressional Budget Office, and occasionally through congressional oversight hearings. Their findings take the form of reports to or from Congress.

The executive and legislative branches sometimes employ subtle methods of reaching an agreement when establishing programs and setting program direction. The executive branch may omit from its budget recommendation programs that are enthusiastically supported by members of Congress, because the executive branch considers them lower priority. Then, in return for congressional compromise on another issue, the executive branch will include a portion of or the entire omitted program. This process may also work in reverse. Often, the key national issues of compromise often are not forestry matters, but other matters of domestic or foreign policy. Thus, professional foresters generally participate at the fringes of this process. Their role is to provide factual information on forestry opportunities and the consequences of various proposals for the forest resources and for the people who rely on these resources.

The judicial branch of the federal government is concerned with forestry issues only at the request of interested parties. Its role is to interpret and clarify actions and policies in terms of existing law and to offer redress to petitioners. The courts can either approve or prohibit specific activities and policies according to legal interpretation. They can only initiate new direction if supported by an existing legal basis, in which case an agency's operating policies may need to be changed in order to comply with the court's decision. If a law is overly broad or unclear or if controversy touches on constitutional matters, the courts may, in fact, provide considerable direction that the agency must follow. Each time a law is tested in court, new case law or precedent is established. If the law or action being tested is confirmed as being appropriate, the law or action takes on new support or strength for similar future actions.

The Public Interest

Among the most important influences on the role of the federal government are the diverse opinions of the people of the United States. Forestry at the national level cannot be understood without considering how people express their common interests and how those interests become input for forestry policy. People can make themselves heard by policymakers in many ways, from contacting management agencies and their congressional representatives, or engaging in some form of public expression.

Concern with the integration of diverse public interests into the formulation of public policy is not new to our political scene. In 1789, James Madison discussed the role and importance of what we call *public interest* or *pressure groups* in the *Federalist Papers* (19), arguing that a major function of the governmental process is to integrate opposing interests and reconcile conflicting views. Almost 50 years later, Alexis de Tocqueville, the eminent French publicist, commented on the tendency of U.S. citizens to form and join organizations, that in turn often had agendas for political action, in his book *Democracy in America*, (20).

In more recent times political scientists have suggested the "group basis of politics" as one fundamental characteristic of U.S. government. Economists have recognized "countervailing power" and interactive forces as important elements in public-policy decision making. Matters of the environment, natural resources, and forestry are presented by interest groups for consideration in developing public policy.

Several related developments in recent years have intensified both individual and group involvement in questions of forestry policy and management. One of these is a widespread and growing concern for the environment. Another is the introduction of new statutory requirements governing forestry practices, and their reinforcement by court decisions; agency responses to public views and comments are the other development.

Numerous court challenges to government agency actions have been mounted by permanent or ad hoc groups. The National Environmental Policy Act (NEPA) of 1969 provides the basis for legal challenges by requiring federal agencies to prepare environmental impact statements assessing the consequences of alternative actions. If dissatisfied with the content and rationale of such statements, citizens and groups can file suits challenging findings and other aspects of agency decisions.

Public involvement has considerably sharpened the awareness of decision makers to the consequences and alternatives of action and, in many cases, has stopped or delayed actions. Many feel that these delays have contributed to wiser decisions. Most would agree that this emphasis on impact analysis has been helped by the willingness of federal courts to give "standing to sue" to a variety of interest groups. One result has been that federal agencies have taken the requirements of the NEPA and other statutes more seriously than they might otherwise have done.

However, on any issue or set of issues, neither the involved groups nor the individual participants represent all people or all possible interest configurations. In part, the problem is one of span of attention. People cannot possibly get involved in all the issues that will affect them, nor is it clear that the decision to become involved is always rational or deliberate. Such variables as personal-ity, friendship, and presence—as well as preferences—may determine both the existence and the degree of involvement. Getting involved sometimes requires too much money, commitment, time, or understanding. Thus, it is important to recognize that less vocal citizens might be reluctant to offer their opinion before a decision is made—though they might not remain silent if a wrong decision is reached. By exercising informed judgments on what they perceive are the interests of the expressed and the silent publics, professionals and their agencies must begin to approximate the overall public interest.

In forest management, as in many resource and environmental decisions, the articulation of the public interests is often complicated by the fact that decisions made today have very long-term consequences. The responsible professional public servant must attempt to consider the future. To be sure, the crystal ball is always clouded, and there is a tendency to address the immediate crisis. Hence, analysis must substitute for prophecy and foreknowledge as much as possible. If public agencies respond only to current public outcry, the real potential public welfare may be overlooked.

The very multiplicity of interests in forestry at the national level ensures a high degree of conflict and controversy. In many situations, one set of interests will run counter to another. A major challenge to Congress and agencies is conflict resolution, that is, seeking to reconcile and choose the appropriate solution from a wide range of possible outcomes.

International Forestry

Washington, D.C., is not only a hub for national forest policy, it is also one of the world's major centers for international forestry. Headquartered in Washington are a number of U.S. government agencies, international organizations, and nongovernmental entities with international programs in forestry or natural resources.

Among the U.S. agencies, the largest international forestry program is managed by the U.S. Agency for International Development (USAID), which contributes to forestry projects in some 36 tropical countries at an annual cost of about $135 million. Assistance projects sponsored by USAID include training, disaster relief, and private-sector development efforts. The largest U.S. employer of foresters overseas, however, is the Peace Corps, which now has 550 foresters in 46 countries. The Forest Service also manages an active international program that represents the U.S. government on major world forestry issues, promotes scientific exchange and cooperative research among countries, works directly with various countries on mutually beneficial technical programs, and provides technical support to USAID (Figure 9.19). Other government agencies with international forestry or natural resource programs include the State Department, National Park Service, Fish and Wildlife Service, U.S. Geological Survey, and the Smithsonian Institution. On tropical matters, informal coordination of activities is achieved through the Interagency Task Force on Tropical Forestry.

International organizations with home offices in Washington are the World Bank, Inter-American Development Bank, and the Organization of American States (OAS). Each is active in international forestry and natural resources. The World Bank is the largest with annual forestry disbursements of about $150 million in seven countries. From 1985 to 2000, it invested approximately $1.5 billion in forestry development in 55 countries. The World Bank's policy and lending strategy on forestry emphasizes a balanced program of small-scale tree farming, institution building, and industrial projects. Activities include village forestry, environmental protection, and rural development. Some of these activities are further described in Chapter 23, Social Forestry. The Inter-American Development Bank has a growing forestry portfolio limited to the Western Hemisphere. The OAS supports forestry, agricultural research, information exchange, and training in tropical America.

Although headquartered in Rome, Italy, the Food and Agricultural Organization (FAO) of the United Nations also maintains a Liaison Office for North America in Washington. Since its creation in the early 1940s, the FAO has directed the world's leading

Figure 9.19   The main entrance to San Juan Tetla Experimental Forest, managed by the Central Region of the National Institute of Forestry and Agriculture Research (NIFAP), the federal forestry research branch of the Government of Mexico; here, as in many other experimental forests around the globe, university and government research scientists collaborate on studies of mutual interest. (James M. Guldin).

international forestry program. The FAO convenes ad hoc meetings to coordinate the activities of the world's major forestry donor agencies. Through technical meetings and publications, its Rome office facilitates the worldwide exchange of forestry information and provides assistance to developing countries. Its office in Washington coordinates policy and administrative ties to North America.

Nongovernmental organizations are playing an increasingly important role in international forestry. Many are located in Washington, such as the World Resources Institute, the International Institute for Environment and Development, and the Pan American Development Foundation. The World Resources Institute demonstrated leadership in tropical forestry by publishing a major report entitled, "Tropical Forestry: A Call for Action," which outlines problems, successful experiences, and financial resources needed to stem the rampant deforestation of tropical forests (21). The International Institute for Environment and Development emphasizes natural-resources policy and planning and often works closely with USAID on development projects.

Two major professional societies concerned with international forestry issues, the Society of American Foresters (SAF) and the International Society of American Tropical Foresters (ISTF), are also headquartered in Washington. Through its International Forestry Working Group and Committee on World Forestry, the SAF keeps its members abreast of international forestry concerns. Communication among the world's tropical foresters is facilitated by the ISTF, especially through its quarterly newsletter.

As can be seen, international forestry is a growth area for the profession. As awareness of world forestry problems grows, so will opportunities and responsibilities for the professional forester.

The Role of Forestry Research

Advocacy for research has long been a part of the national concern for forest resource management. The need for research is not a recent phenomenon. Before 1890, reports and recommendations on the nation's forests specifically called for national research initiatives. The Reverend Frederick Starr, Jr., called for "extensive, protracted, and scientific experiments in the propagation and cultivation of forest trees" in 1865. The "Report on Forestry" by Franklin B. Hough in 1882 called for research on the effect of forests on climate and for the establishment of experiment stations.

Forest management benefits from a blend of basic and applied research investigations, as well as the experience of the professional tempered through trial and error. Research projects are initiated to examine particular management questions, often at the request of resource administrators. Thus, forestry research at the national level has three functions: 1) to assist in identifying areas of major concern that require research, 2) to establish and maintain continuity between research and evolving management policy, and 3) to provide coordination and management of the nation's research programs.

National forestry policy and direction change with fluctuating social conditions and needs. Quite often, management policy options depend on new ways of monitoring uses and impacts, new methods of doing old jobs, and new means of incorporating and balancing resource needs. National forestry policy and the national research agenda are closely related; national forestry policies must be based on sound scientific information, and on occasion research findings indicate a need to change national policy.

Representatives of different research communities at the national level maintain the links between needed research and current policy. The link to policy helps determine which areas of study have high priority. High-priority research is not simply a matter of which forest problem is the greatest, but rather research that has applicability beyond a particular problem in a particular area. The other area of national responsibility for research is coordination. It is often easiest to coordinate research across agencies at the national level rather than regional or state levels, which can help avoid duplication and research voids.

Many agencies and groups have national interests in forestry research. The Fish and Wildlife Service studies the protection and management of animal resources. The National Park Service studies how to protect and manage park resources. The Environmental Protection Agency sponsors research on environmental protection and the consequences of forest activities on air and water quality. Forest Service research covers a wide spectrum of ecological, economic, engineering, and social problems related to forest and rangeland management. They emphasize opportunities for taking products from the forest; how to protect and enhance noncommodity values; and how to improve forest products.

Several special-interest groups also support research. They often do not have a national program of study but concentrate on the interests of the organization. The National Wildlife Federation has a program of grants to sponsor research by university students. The National Forest Products Association sponsors research of interest to its members. Organizations such as these study forest technology, the resource base, changing social needs, and interactions between social demands and renewable resources. Several national organizations such as Resources for the Future and the Society of American Foresters seek to focus and direct research to specific areas of concern and, when appropriate, to develop a greater understanding of the present state of the art.

University studies often depend more on an individual investigator's interests and funding sources than on overall department programs. Studies may range from social demands and needs to methods for improving product utilization. National research coordination is much more difficult to achieve among agencies, organizations, and universities than within an agency or organization. Some umbrella groups formally link federal and state research organizations, and facilitate the communication needed to set national priorities. For example, the Joint Council on Food and Agriculture Sciences fosters planning and coordination of research, extension, and higher education between U.S.D.A. agencies and the private sector. A related U.S.D.A. organization, the User's Advisory Board for National Agriculture Research and Extension, provides input into policy and program development by identifying research and extension priorities from the view of the citizen user. If formal connections do not provide a national network between scientists, informal ones often spring up among individual scientists.

People use forest environments in many ways. New knowledge is continually needed to manage the complex and changing relationships between people and forests. Research provides this knowledge.

Concluding Statement

From the resource perspective, a forest ecosystem can be viewed either as a valuable whole or as a sum of valuable parts. Multiple-use forestry is a philosophy of resource utilization that provides a theoretical basis for developing qualitative and quantitative predictions of resource interrelationships. Ecosystem management and the Sustainable Forestry Initiative provide blueprints for incorporating those multiple uses into an ecological context with sustainability as a goal.

In some instances, the valuable whole receives priority, such as in the preservation of wilderness areas and of the ecological habitats for rare or endangered species. In other instances the valuable components of a forest ecosystem, such as timber or wildlife species, receive management emphasis. However, contemporary forestry on both public and private lands must increasingly provide for the health, diversity, productivity, and sustainability of forest ecosystems.

The management of specific forest ownerships depends on many factors. First and foremost are the unique attributes of the ecosystem itself, which determine both the availability of specific resources and the degree to which management can develop the resources for economical use. The methods by which management is planned and administered affect the economic efficiency of resource utilization, which may or may not be important in bringing forest products into the market place. The objectives of the owner of the forest land—whether an individual, a corporation, or society—are another critical factor. It is the owner who decides the patterns of resource management, if any, that are implemented by the forest manager. As populations grow, demands for a diverse array of forest resources increase; but the area of timberland will probably decline through the 21st century. The centennial of forestry in North America is characterized by both redoubtable management challenges and gratifying professional rewards.

Forestry at the national level is different from that practiced at the field or technical level. It focuses on forestry issues as components of many diverse national policies. Many groups, agencies, and individuals are involved in shaping national policy; some groups are interested only in certain aspects of forestry. However, forestry is only a small part of the national agenda, and it must be viewed in a context of larger, national concerns such as employment, housing, energy, and international relations. Much effort goes into identifying how forestry can address these major national concerns.

It might be helpful in concluding this chapter to look ahead to the future of forestry from a national perspective. Because forests are renewable, they will increasingly provide some resources more economically than nonrenewable sources. The ways in which forestry issues are important to national policies will become even more complex and diverse in the coming decades as we increase our knowledge of forest ecosystems.

The complexity of forestry issues and opportunities will require agencies and other organizations to work more closely together. Such important subjects, as acid rain, global warming, and tropical deforestation require the formation of new and exciting partnerships.

Increasing public interest in and access to forestry issues will lead to questions about the roles of resource professionals and interested citizens. Forestry professionals will need to develop better ways of analyzing alternative actions and giving the public access to the decision-making process. People with little forestry background whose interests may be narrowly defined must be able to understand these processes. An increased awareness of international forestry will create new demands and will result in a broader range of issues and problems for foresters to address.

People will increasingly employ available means of influence, through all three branches of government, as they become more involved with national forestry issues. Competing interests and uses for forest resources will require new approaches to balance social needs and resource capabilities. This is the future realm of forestry at the national, regional, and local levels. The possibilities are challenging and intriguing. To serve the public in this future, foresters will need to:

- Grow more trees.
- Use more reconstituted wood products.
- Conserve more species and habitats at risk
- Improve public understanding and management of the ecosystem.
- Learn to accommodate additional segments of society in managing forests.

The future of forestry issues in national and international policies promises to be active and controversial. The coming decades will be perplexing and frustrating for professionals who continue to focus solely on the application of technical forestry principles. On the other hand, the coming decades can be a time of challenge and excitement for professionals who adopt a national perspective. For them, the future offers opportunities to make valuable contributions to forestry in the tradition of Bernhard Fernow, Franklin Hough, and Gifford Pinchot.

The following chapters in this section provide more detailed treatment of the different multiple uses made of the forests, including management approaches for different aspects of forestry endeavors.

References

1. B. F. FERNOW, *A Brief History of Forestry in Europe, the United States and Other Countries*. Third Revised Edition, University Press, Toronto and American Forestry Association, Washington D.C., 1913.
2. W. H. ROMME, *Scientific American, 261(5)*, 37 (1989).

3. G. H. HEPTING, *Diseases of forest and shade trees of the United States*. Agriculture Handbook 386, U.S. Department of Agriculture, Forest Service, 1971.

4. A. M. LIEBHOLD, K. W. GOTTSCHALK, D. A. MASON and R. R. BUSH, *J. For., 95(5)*, 20 (1997).

5. ANON., "Red-cockaded woodpecker," In *Wildlife Habitat Management Handbook*, Chap. 420, U.S.D.A. For. Serv. Handbook, Region 8. Amendment 6, Dec., 1980.

6. M. CLAWSON, *Environ. Law, 8(2)*, 287 (1978).

7. W. A. DUERR, D. E. TERGUARDEN, N. B. CHRISTIANSEN, AND S. GUTTENBERG, *Forest Resource Management: Decision-Making Principles and Cases,* W. B. Saunders, Philadelphia, 1979.

8. C. F. BROCKMAN AND L. C. MERRIAM, JR., *Recreational Use of Wild Lands*, Third Edition, McGraw-Hill, New York, 1979.

9. National Res. Council, *Forestry research: a mandate for change*. National Academy Press, Washington, D.C., 1990.

10. F. D. ROBERTSON, "Letter to U.S.D.A. Forest Service employees," 4 June 1992.

11. K. L. O'HARA, R. S. SEYMOUR, S. D. TESCH, AND J. M. GULDIN, *J. For., 92(1)*, 8 (1994).

12. W. B. SMITH, J.L. VISSSAGE, R. SHEFFIELD, AND D. R. DARR, "Forest resources of the United States, 1997." *General Technical Report*. U.S. Department of Agriculture, Forest Service, North Central Research Station, 2000.

13. ANON., *Forested Landscapes in Perspective: Prospects and Opportunities for Sustainable Management of America's Nonfederal Forests*. Board of Agriculture of the National Research Council, National Academy Press, Washington, D.C., 1998.

14. Committee of Scientists, *Sustaining the People's Lands: Recommendations for Stewardship of the National Forests and Grasslands into the Next Century*. U.S.D.A., Washington, D.C., March 15, 1999.

15. V. KRUTILLA, M. D.BOWES, AND E. A. WILMAN, "National forest system planning and management: An analytical review and suggested approach." In *Government Interventions, Social Needs, and the Management of U.S. Forests*, R.A. Sedjo, ed., Resources for the Future, Washington, D.C., 1981.

16. S. T. DANA AND S. K. FAIRFAX, *Forest and Range Policy: Its Development in the United States,* Second Edition, McGraw-Hill, New York, 1980.

17. ANON., "An Analysis of the Timber Situation in the United States, 1952–2030," U.S.D.A. For. Serv., Res. Rept. 23, 1982.

18. A. J. WEST, "Letter to Regional Foresters and Area Directors," U.S.D.A. For. Serv., June, 1986.

19. J. MADISON, A. HAMILTON, AND J. JAY, *The Federalist Papers*, I. Kramnick, ed., Penguin Books, New York, 1987.

20. A. DE TOCQUEVILLE, *Democracy in America,* Knopf Co., New York, 1993.

21. World Resources Institute, *Tropical Forests: a Call for Action. Report of an International Task Force Convened by the World Resources Institute*, The World Bank, and the United Nations Development Programme, World Resources Institute, Washington, D.C., 1985.

CHAPTER 10

Nonindustrial Private Forests

JOHN C. BLISS AND A. JEFF MARTIN

Introduction

Whose woods these are I think I know
His house is in the village, though
He will not mind our stopping here
To watch his woods fill up with snow
   —From "Stopping by Woods on a Snowy Evening" by Robert Frost (1)

Robert Frost's poem, "Stopping by Woods on a Snowy Evening," conjures up a wonderful image: a quiet winter's night, the deep silence of a forest under snow, the joy of a horse-drawn sleigh ride. The writer draws from the snowy woods comfort, solitude, and inspiration.

The values that Frost's narrator enjoyed are provided by millions of forest owners all across the United States (Figure 10.1). A private forest whose owner does not own or operate wood processing facilities (such as saw, paper, or plywood mills) is known as a *nonindustrial private forest* (NIPF). NIPF owners include individuals, families, farmers, and retirees. Hunting clubs, churches, schools, and other associations may also be NIPF owners. Even banks, insurance companies, real estate companies, pension fund companies, and other corporations are classified as NIPF owners if they own forest land but not wood-processing facilities. NIPFs range in size from one wooded acre to many tens of thousands of acres, and from sparsely vegetated tracts

221

Figure 10.1 The farm woodlot, so common when Frost penned his lines, is still common but no longer the dominant NIPF ownership type. As Frost hints in his poem, absentee landowners now control one-third of the NIPF ownerships. White-collar workers and retired individuals now own 58% of the NIPF land.

to lush, productive forests. Some NIPFs are intensively managed for production of forest products, some are held primarily for recreation and enjoyment. Many are models of forest stewardship, still others are neglected or exploited.

This chapter presents a brief overview of the nonindustrial private forest resource. We start by describing the significance of the resource and quantifying its dimensions. A section on the history of NIPF forestry sets the stage for discussion of current policies and programs. The chapter closes with a summary of emerging trends and issues affecting NIPF resources.

Significance of NIPFs

Economic Value Comprising almost 60 percent of the United State's productive forestland, NIPFs are of enormous economic, environmental, and social significance to the United States. As key suppliers of wood to the country's forest products industries, NIPFs economic significance has long been recognized. Even in the American South, where the country's industrial forests are concentrated, NIPFs supply most of the wood used by industry. In the West, the region with the least NIPF ownership, the dramatic decline of timber harvesting on National Forests has forced industry to increasingly look to NIPF sources of timber. The economic importance of NIPFs is not limited to the timber they supply to industry, however. Timber production employs people: loggers, truckers, tree planters, foresters, mill workers, gas station attendants, and grocery clerks. Moreover, the economic importance of nontimber products such as recreation, floral greens, mushrooms, and maple syrup is growing. Thus, NIPFs are vital to the economies of forest-dependent communities and regions.

Environmental Value The environmental value of NIPFs is gaining recognition as the United States becomes more urbanized, and clean air, clean water, green landscapes, and open space become scarcer. In many parts of the heavily populated East, NIPFs provide most of the available supply of such amenities. In the South, small private woodlands add diversity to landscapes dominated by large industrial and nonindustrial forest plantations. In the West, NIPFs typically occupy riparian zones alongside waterways, areas that are ecologically sensitive and that provide significant environmental values. Because of the diverse objectives of their owners, NIPFs add ecological diversity to the landscape wherever they occur.

Human Value   Less recognized than the economic and environmental value of NIPFs are the associated *human* resources. The great diversity of NIPF owners and the objectives they hold for their forests lead to the existing diversity of forest types, ages, and conditions. Many NIPF owners are vital members of rural neighborhoods and communities. Others are urban dwellers who retreat to their rural forestlands to work and recreate. They provide important links of experience and communication between urban and rural populations. As NIPF owners shape their forests through use and management, they humanize the landscape, imbuing it with human history, meaning, and values.

Dynamics Underlying NIPF Issues

Population growth, increasing urbanization, changing social values, and changes in ethnic, age, and income distribution drive two dynamics influencing NIPFs: increasing demands for forest products, values, and services, and an increasingly dynamic policy environment.

Increasing Demand   NIPF lands are under increasing pressure to produce an ever-widening array of products, services, amenities, and values. Major policy changes have led to steep declines in timber harvest levels from public lands. This in turn has resulted in increasing pressure on private forest resources to meet growing demands for forest products. In many areas, population growth is creating growing pressure for residential and commercial development of urban fringe areas, and recreational development of rural areas. Everywhere, the environmental, recreational, and spiritual values provided by forests—including nonindustrial private forests—are in high demand. These increasing demands occur at a time of unprecedented public concern over the management and condition of forest ecosystems. In other words, society is demanding more from private forests, and greater accountability from private forest owners.

Dynamic Policy Environment   The policy environment within which forest owners must make management and investment decisions is one of increasing flux. Public support continues to grow for increasingly stringent management regulations for all ownership categories. In addition to such federal laws as the Endangered Species Act and the Clean Water Act, many states have forest practices acts which regulate how forests are managed. Even counties and municipalities in some states have enacted controls over land use in their jurisdictions. Policies are dynamic, not static, which adds to the complexity of these layers of regulations. The resulting regulatory uncertainty compounds the natural and market uncertainty with which NIPF owners must contend. Indeed, regulatory insecurity may be more distressing to many NIPF owners than any possible regulations.

Moreover, new and innovative policy instruments, both governmental and nongovernmental, further complicate each forest owner's management decisions. Examples include local voluntary watershed councils, safe harbor agreements for protecting endangered species habitat, conservation easements for a wide range of conservation goals, and forest certification programs for producing and marketing forest products. Although many of these changes may prove to be positive for NIPF owners in the long run, they can be challenging, unsettling, and confusing in the short term.

The Forest Resource

Size and Distribution

About one-third of the total U.S. land area is forestland, and two-thirds of that is designated timberland, that is, forestland capable of and available for producing commercial wood crops (Figure 10.2) (2). Fifty-eight percent of all forestland and 73 percent of timberland is in private ownership. Forest products manufacturing companies own about 14 percent of the timberland. The majority of the country's private timberland (59 percent) is owned by NIPF owners, defined as private individuals, farmers, businesses, and other private groups that do not own or operate wood processing facilities (Figure 10.3).

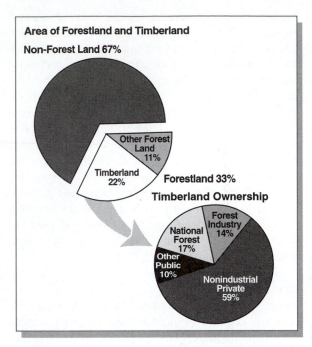

Figure 10.2   Land area and ownership of timberland in the United States, 1992 (Powell et al., 1993).

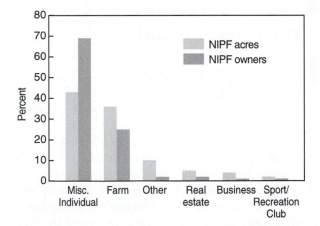

Figure 10.3   Distribution of nonindustrial private forestland ownership in the United States, 1994 (Birch, 1996).

NIPFs occur in every region of the country (Figure 10.4). About 88 percent of the NIPF timberland is in the North and South, and 12 percent is in the West. NIPFs comprise 70 percent of all timberland in the North and South, and 28 percent in the West. Total NIPF timberland declined 5.5 percent in the forty-year period between 1952 and 1992, either as a result of conversion of forest to other uses (such as urban growth) or because of changing ownership (i.e., purchase by forest industry).

Forest Productivity, Growth, and Removal

Nonindustrial private forests are an indispensable component of the nation's wood supply. NIPF lands contain 72 percent of the nation's hardwood growing stock inventory (mostly in the North and South), and 30 percent of the softwood inventory (mostly in the south and West) (2). These inventories have grown dramatically in the decades 1952 to 1992 (Table 10.1). Hardwood growing stock volume on NIPF lands increased 81 percent during the period, less than the increase on national forests, but more than that of industrial lands. Softwood growing stock volume rose 51 percent on NIPF lands in the 40 years, while other ownership groups experienced a slight decline. NIPF growing stock volume suitable for lumber manufacture increased 98 percent for hardwoods and 57 percent for softwoods. As a result of these growing inventories, NIPFs have become increasingly important as sources of wood for the nation's forest products industries.

In 1992, average net annual growth for all growing stock trees on NIPF timberland was 42 cubic feet per acre. This was less than forest industry's average of 61 cubic feet per acre but matched that on national forests and other public lands, which averaged 39 and 42 cubic feet per acre respectively.

The percentage of the national annual harvest taken from NIPF lands is about equal to the percentage of growing stock inventory that these lands contain. In 1992, for example, 67 percent of the nation's hardwood harvest came from NIPF lands— lands that contained 72 percent of the hardwood

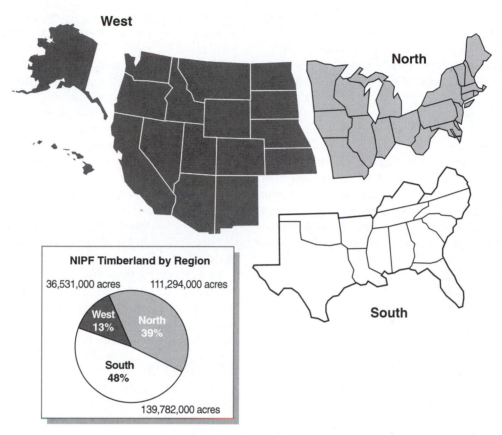

Figure 10.4   Distribution of NIPF timberland by region, 1992 (Powell et al., 1993).

Table 10.1   Net Volume of Growing Stock and Sawtimber on NIPF Timberland, 1952 and 1992

Region	Year	Growing Stock (1 million cubic feet)		Sawtimber (1 million board feet, Int. 1/4-inch Rule)	
		Softwood	Hardwood	Softwood	Hardwood
North	1992	28,514	114,967	79,133	301,272
	1952	16,048	57,054	34,163	128,880
South	1992	64,391	112,279	244,818	340,498
	1952	36,360	69,985	111,823	197,853
West	1992	50,456	15,052	236,925	41,412
	1952	42,341	6,649	211,955	18,812
U.S.	1992	143,361	242,298	560,876	683,181
	1952	94,749	133,688	357,941	345,545

Source: Powell, et al., 1993 (2)

inventory. In contrast, NIPF lands contained about 32 percent of the softwood growing stock volume, yet supplied 40 percent of the softwood harvest.

One criterion often used to indicate the productivity and condition of forestland is the ratio of net growth (that is, growth less mortality) to removals (harvests). With a growth/removal ratio greater than one, the forest adds volume to the existing inventory, even though harvests occur. Over the 1952 to 1992 period, the growth/removal ratio for NIPF lands averaged 1.5, indicating they were growing more wood volume than was being harvested. The growth/removal rate for national forests was also about 1.5, for other public lands it was about 2.0, and forest industry lands it was slightly below 1.0, indicating removals exceeded growth. From the perspective of growth/removal rates, then, NIPFs compared quite favorably with other ownerships over the 40-year period.

The Human Resource

What distinguishes NIPFs from industrial and public forests is the diversity of NIPF owners, their management objectives, capabilities, and constraints. We focus here on the 94 percent of private forest ownerships that are held by individuals and families and that collectively account for 59 percent of all privately owned forest land. Who are these people, and why do they own forest land?

Who Are the NIPF Owners?

There were 9.9 million owners of private forest land in 1994, up from 7.8 million in 1978, and their number is growing (3). Nearly 100 percent were NIPF ownerships. Why? A relatively small number of industry holders own a lot of land. Thus, although they own about 20 percent of the private forest land, they comprise less than 1 percent of the number of ownerships. About 90 percent of the NIPF ownerships are in the northern and southern regions of the United States. In 1994, the North had about 18 percent more private forest landowners

than in 1978; the South experienced a 26 percent increase, whereas the West saw a jump of nearly 67 percent.

The growing number of NIPF ownerships indicates that the NIPF resource is being divided between more and more owners. This is particularly true at the urban–rural interface, where land parcelization and urbanization are formidable trends. *Fragmentation*—large ownerships being divided into smaller ones—is also taking place in rural areas, as urbanites seek rural retreats. One estimate is that the number of NIPF tracts of 10 acres or less increased 52 percent between 1978 and 1995 (4). Fragmentation undoubtedly has contributed to the dramatic increase in numbers of NIPF owners in the West over the past two decades.

In contrast to the national trend toward fragmentation of forest ownerships, some parts of the country are experiencing land concentration, wherein large ownerships become even larger through purchase of adjacent land. This is especially evident in areas dominated by large industrial ownerships, such as parts of the deep South (5).

The demographic profile of NIPF owners is changing. The proportion of older NIPF owners is increasing: about 45 percent of NIPF owners are 45 to 64 years of age, and about 20 percent are 65 years or over. Farm ownership of NIPFs has declined from 57 percent of the NIPF timberland in 1952 to 29 percent in 1992. Today, white collar and retired woodland owners are the most prevalent occupations, together comprising over half of all private ownerships (Figure 10.5). New purchasers of NIPF land, however, tend to be younger, more highly educated, and have higher incomes than the NIPF owners of earlier decades (3).

Although 67 percent of woodland owners live on, or within one mile of, their woodlands, they tend to own their forestland for less time than did earlier generations: 40 percent of the private landowners have owned their lands for 15 years or less. Less than 10 percent of private forestland has been in the same ownership for over 45 years. This presents serious obstacles to long-term management.

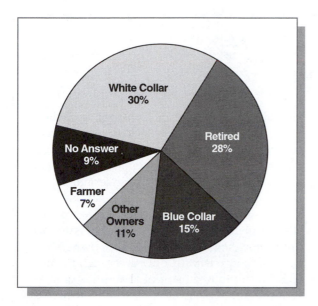

Figure 10.5 Distribution of private forestland by owner occupation, 1994 (Birch, 1996).

Several long-standing myths about NIPF owners have only recently begun to be challenged by social science research (7). Based upon generalizations that may have had more validity in the 1950s, many foresters have thought of NIPF owners as rural folks with strong family ties to the land. As such, they were assumed to be oriented toward timber production, and somewhat antagonistic toward environmentalism. They were thought to value private property rights above and beyond any other considerations, including ecological health or the public good. These truisms were thought to be especially true for owners of large tracts of forestland.

Recent research in the American South and elsewhere puts the lie to these myths. NIPF owners look increasingly like the rest of the American population and share the same values. They are more urban, better off financially, and more educated than in the past. They share the environmental values of mainstream society in the same proportions as do other U.S. citizens. And large tract owners are not nearly as different from small tract owners as formerly believed (see sidebars).

Why Do They Own Forest Land?

NIPF owners own forestland for many reasons. Some inherit forestland, or acquire it incidentally with farm or residential land. Others deliberately purchase forestland for recreation or as an investment. Most NIPF owners have a variety of reasons for owning forestland, only some of which may dominate their management decisions at particular times. In surveys, most report the following as primary reasons for owning forestland: 1) the forest is part of their residence or farm, 2) forest ownership provides aesthetic enjoyment, 3) forest ownership is a good financial investment, and 4) they enjoy forest recreation.

Relatively few NIPF owners—5 percent in a recent survey (3)—report timber production as a primary reason for owning forestland. Nonetheless, over time, most commercial timber on NIPFs is harvested—46 percent of those surveyed in 1994 had harvested timber. This is particularly true of larger NIPF ownerships, which typically receive more intensive management for timber crops.

In-depth interviews with NIPF owners (8) suggest that forest-related values and behaviors may be components of forest owners' ethnic or cultural heritage. Forest ownership and forest management provide families with opportunities to be and work together, enhancing family cohesiveness and strengthening ties between generations. For many owners, forest ownership is key to personal identity, and management gives expression to personal beliefs and values. The well-managed forest serves as a legacy of those who have been its steward. While these values are less easily quantified than income from timber sales or days spent hunting, they nevertheless help determine NIPF forest conditions.

NIPF Policies and Programs

Historical Overview

Since the 1900s, NIPF owners have received assistance with forest management planning, tree

Sidebar 10.1

A Few Own a Lot, Most Own Only a Little

The highly skewed distribution of private forest acres among owners renders discussion of average ownerships quite misleading (see Figure). Most private owners hold relatively small tracts of forestland: 59 percent have fewer than 10 acres, and 86 percent own less than 50 acres. On the other hand most of the forestland is held in very large tracts by industrial owners and NIPF owners.

Research shows that owners of large tracts are more likely than owners of small tracts to have management plans, be knowledgeable about forestry, be amenable to forest management, and to harvest timber. A 1994 study estimated that fewer than 6 percent of NIPF landowners had a written forest management plan (1). These were typically the owners of larger tracts; these 6 percent of NIPF owners owned 28 percent of the NIPF forest land. A number of studies have demonstrated that the intensity of forest management is positively correlated to the size of forest holding and the landowner's financial position. However, some recent research (2) suggests that large tract owners are not as different from small

tract owners in their opinions regarding environmental and forestry issues as has typically been assumed. For example, majorities of both groups agreed that "Private property rights should be limited if necessary to protect the environment."

The distribution of NIPF acreage among owners has significant implications for forest policy. Historically, tax-supported forestry assistance programs have favored large ownerships because contacts with only a few landowners could result in treatment of thousands of acres of forestland. However, as a result, owners of smaller tracts—many of whom may be unlikely to hire professional forestry assistance—have received less public assistance.

Sources:

1. T. W. Birch, "Private Forest-land owners of the United States, 1994." Resource Bulletin NE-134. Radnor, Penn. U.S.D.A. Forest Service NE Forest Experiment Station, 1996.

2. J. C. Bliss, S. K. Nepal, R. T. Brooks, Jr., and M. D. Larsen. *Southern J. of Applied Forestry, 21(1),* 37 (1997).

Distribution of private forestland among owners, 1994 (Birch, 1996).

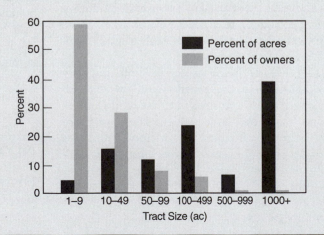

Sidebar 10.2

Environmental Values of NIPF Owners

Since the late 1960s, environmentalism has increasingly become part of the American character. Pollsters have documented a steady rise in the proportion of Americans reporting concern over dwindling supplies of clean air and water, open space, and wildlife (1). A majority of Americans support greater efforts by government to guard against environmental degradation and believe that protecting the environment should take precedence over preserving private property rights or fostering economic growth (2).

As owners of most of the country's forestland, nonindustrial private forest owners have much at stake in these policy debates. To what extent do NIPF owners share in the general public's environmental values? Research conducted over the past decade demonstrates that, in their attitudes toward forest management and environmental protection, NIPF owners are similar to the rest of the American public (3, 4). A 1992 survey in the mid-South compared the environmental attitudes of NIPF owners with those of the general public (3). The views of NIPF owners and non-owners were essentially identical on the acceptability of prescribed burning (both groups were evenly split), the use of herbicides (a majority disapproved), and the practice of clearcut harvesting (a majority dis-

approved on public land). The great majority of owners and non-owners alike favored a balance between environmental protection and private property rights that ensures environmental protection. Three-quarters agreed with the statement, "Private property rights should be limited if necessary to protect the environment." Similarly, both forest owners and non-owners sought a balance between environmental and economic values, but a balance that puts environmental protection first. In sum, the environmental values and opinions of private forest owners mirrored those of the general public.

Source:

1. R. E. DUNLAP, "Trends in public opinion toward environmental issues, 1965–90." In *American Environmentalism: The UW Environmental Movement, 1970–90*, R. E. Dunlap and A. G. Mertig, eds., Taylor & Francis, New York, 1992.

2. Times Mirror Magazines Conservation Council, *Natural resource conservation: Where environmentalism is headed in the 1990s. Times Mirror Magazine*, 1992.

3. J. C. BLISS, S. K. NEPAL, R. T. BROOKS, JR., AND MAX D. LARSEN, *J. For., 92(9),* 6 (1994).

4. M. W. BRUNSON, D. T. YARROW, S. D. ROBERTS, D. C. GUYN, JR. AND M. R. KUHNS, *J. For., 94(6),* 14 (1996).

---

planting, fire control, and other forestry activities from public agencies. Recognizing the crucial contribution NIPF lands make to U.S. timber production, the U.S. Forest Service early in its existence assigned a high priority to improving management of these lands. Government programs in this area have always been controversial. Since the inception of public forestry assistance programs in 1898,

proponents of increased government involvement in private forest management have consistently felt that regulation of harvesting on private lands is necessary to protect the public interest, and that subsidies and tax incentives are needed to ensure effective management. Critics have decried governmental interference in private-land management, arguing that the working of the free market will ensure responsible forest management in the long run. This ongoing debate has historically resulted in a mix of regulation, financial incentives, tax policies, education and technical assistance programs.

The U.S. Forest Service role in private forest land management began with Gifford Pinchot's 1898 publication of Circular 21. Pinchot believed that proper management of private forests was in the public interest. Circular 21 offered free forest management advice to farmers and other owners of large tracts of forestland.

The 1924 Clarke–McNary Act authorized a comprehensive study of state forest tax policy that was expected to reveal means of counteracting the "cut-and-get-out" pattern of forest exploitation and land abandonment, which had left behind vast areas of tax-delinquent land. The Act provided the foundation for all subsequent federal assistance to the states for private forest management and became a focal point for debate on the federal role in private forestry. Forest industry leaders lobbied vigorously against government regulation of harvesting practices on private land. A Society of American Foresters committee chaired by Pinchot argued that regulation was needed to protect the public interest. The committee's report, "Forest Devastation: A

National Danger and How to Meet It," concluded that "[n]ational legislation to prevent forest devastation should [provide] such control over private forest lands . . . as may be necessary to insure the continuous production of forest crops . . . and to place forest industries on a stable basis in harmony with public interest." Pinchot added some personal comments to those of the committee as follows:

> **Forest devastation will not be stopped through persuasion, a method which has been thoroughly tried for the past twenty years and has failed utterly. Since they will not otherwise do so, private owners of forestland must now be compelled to manage their properties in harmony with the public good. The field is cleared for action and the lines are plainly drawn. He who is not for forestry is against it. The choice lies between the convenience of the lumbermen and the public good (9).**

Despite Pinchot's concern, Congress ultimately shied away from regulation and opted for cooperation between the federal government and the states in a number of programs designed to encourage proper forest management (Figure 10.6). One historian of the Forest Service, William G. Robbins, stressed the influence of forest industries in shaping

Figure 10.6 Service foresters are the primary source of forest management information and assistance for many landowners.

Sidebar 10.3

From "The Small Woodland Problem" to "Sustainable Forestry"

The nation's nonindustrial private forests have been a major concern and research focus of professional foresters since the publication of Gifford Pinchot's Circular 21 in 1898. The profession's dominant view toward private forests has evolved in several distinct, yet overlapping phases corresponding to the concerns of the day. From the beginning, the profession has been obsessed with NIPF timber productivity. *The Small Woodland Problem* mentality arose from the view that NIPF lands were being "devastated" by exploitation and were not producing timber in volumes commensurate with their acreage. Low timber productivity was the "Problem."

From the 1950s into the 1980s this view evolved into *The Small Woodland Owner Problem,* in which the perceived under-productivity of NIPFs was attributed to the diversity of NIPF owners' objectives, their lack of forestry knowledge, and their reluctance to practice what professional foresters considered to be sound forest management. In other words, the NIPF owners themselves were the "Problem." Eventually some within the profession began to realize that "The Problem" was not the owners' problem at all, but the profession's: NIPF owners have what forest industry and the public wants—beautiful forests full of timber and wildlife (1). If foresters wanted to influence NIPF management, they first had to help achieve NIPF owners' goals.

By the early 1990s, yet another perspective on NIPFs was emerging in response to advances made in forest science. As scientists began to recognize the environmental importance of scale, ecological relationsips, and cummulative effects, foresters began considering forest ownerships within a landscape context. Under the paradigm of *ecosystem management,* timber productivity was viewed as one value among many to be managed, including water quality, endangered species recovery, and forest health. Accordingly, emphasis in NIPF research shifted from examining individual owner behavior to exploring how ownership patterns affect ecological processes and values, and how landowners might cooperate to achieve conservation goals for entire landscapes.

This paradigm is, in turn, broadening to include human and social values as well as forest and environmental values, and to concern itself with social systems as well as ecological systems. One expression of this emerging model is that of *sustainable forestry*, which explicitly considers the social, as well as the economic and environmental impacts of forest management. In this model, NIPF owners play key roles not only as resource owners but as members of rural neighborhoods, communities, and economies.

Aspects of each of these paradigms prevail within the forestry profession. The dominant perspective continuously evolves in response to changes in science, social values, and the economic and political climate.

Source:
1. W. D. TICKNOR, "Gloria reminiscences." Unpublished remarks to American Forestry Association Conference, Traverse City, Mich., October, 1985.

public policy toward private forest lands, concluding that "[i]ndustrial conditions have determined the kind and quality of federal resource programs" (10). Until the 1990s, industry's need for low-cost wood fiber was the driving force behind most NIPF assistance programs, resulting in their strong focus on timber productivity. More recently, environmental concerns (discussed later in this chapter) have dominated public policy initiatives in the NIPF arena.

The 1950s and 1960s were decades of tremendous growth in federal and state cooperative forestry assistance programs. The Cooperative Forest Management Act of 1950 provided for direct technical forestry services to all classes of private forest ownership, including small, nonfarm tracts.

During the "Environmental Era" of the late 1960s and early 1970s, several states passed legislation to protect environmental quality on private lands from poor timber harvesting practices. While many states relied upon forest taxation programs designed to encourage good stewardship of NIPF lands, other states enacted forest practices legislation to restrict and prescribe management activities. California's 1973 Forest Practice Act included the most comprehensive timber harvest regulations.

The Cooperative Forestry Assistance Act of 1978 enabled the secretary of agriculture to establish requirements for state forest resource programs. As a result of this and other legislation, the role of the federal government in private forestry assistance was largely reduced to an administrative one. In contrast to the intensive federal involvement in Depression era programs, primary responsibility for private forestry assistance was, by the 1980s, on state shoulders (10).

Contemporary Policies and Programs

Since Gifford Pinchot's 1898 publication of Circular 21, the public interest in healthy, productive private forest lands has been pursued through a combination of *financial incentives, regulations, education, technical assistance*, and *partnerships*.

Financial Incentives   *Financial Assistance:* At the beginning of the 21st century a number of government programs exist to assist owners of forest, range, or farmland protect environmental values or increase productivity of forest and related resources. Most of these programs involve a cost-share payment (the landowner typically pays 35–50 percent, the government pays the balance) to private landowners for conducting a variety of forest management practices. In addition to federal assistance programs, some states administer assistance programs aimed at enhancing management of NIPF lands (11).

Forest Taxation: Traditional property taxes are based on "highest and best use" of the land and assume production of an annual income. However, unlike agricultural lands, few NIPF ownerships produce annual income, putting forest owners at a disadvantage relative to other landowners. Several states now administer special property tax programs designed to remove such destructive effects of taxation for NIPF landowners. For those states having yield taxes, the land may be taxed annually, but the timber is not taxed until it is harvested.

Federal and state income taxes have a big impact on private forest ownership and management. Tax laws continually change, quickly rendering any summary out of date. However, rules for reporting timber sale income and deducting expenses for forestry activities are always important tax issues for NIPF landowners. Over the years, various modifications to the tax code have attempted to reduce the financial impact of forest management activities on landowners' tax obligation. Generally, timber sale income can be considered a capital gain and is thus taxed at a rate different than that of ordinary income. Forestry expenses are typically deductible from income if the landowner can demonstrate being actively involved in the management activities.

Taxes on estates, above an allowed exclusion, are high, between 37 and 55 percent of the value of the estate. Consequently, federal estate taxes are often blamed for causing landowners to break up and sell their forest lands, or to harvest their timber excessively and prematurely in order to meet their tax obligation. Proposals to lessen the negative impact of estate taxes on private forest owners include increasing the allowable exclusion and

Sidebar 10.4

Forest Products Certification

Green certification—third-party evaluation of sustainable forest management and forest products—is a rapidly growing market-based approach to improving stewardship on private and public forest lands alike. Several organizations are competing for primacy in forestry certification. One of the most established is the Forest Stewardship Council (FSC), an international organization based in Mexico. FSC developed broad principles and criteria for green certification of forest management activities, including principles regarding compliance with existing laws, the rights of indigenous peoples, workers, and local communities; environmental impacts; conservation of environmental and culturally significant resources, and management planning, monitoring, and evaluation. While most of the principles are widely accepted as central to responsible forestry, acceptance is not universal. Debate continues over whether prac-

tices such as clearcutting, plantation silviculture, and use of pesticides should be condoned.

FSC-approved foresters inspect forest owners' management plans and lands for compliance with national and regional standards. Timber products that are harvested from certified forests can then be marketed as certified, or "green." The standards of several certifying organizations comply with those of the FSC, including Smartwood, a nonprofit certifier, and Scientific Certification Systems, a for-profit certifier. It remains to be seen whether green-certified wood products will command a higher price in the marketplace and thereby become a real influence on NIPF management (1).

Source:
1. G. J. GRAY, M. J. ENZER, AND J. KUSEL, EDS., *Understanding Community-Based Forest Ecosystem Management*, Food Products Press, New York, 2001.

excluding from taxation the value of forestland placed in a qualified conservation easement.

Regulations Although NIPF owners are affected by many federal regulations, none is of more consequence than those embodied in the Clean Water Act of 1972 and the Endangered Species Act of 1973. Under the Clean Water Act, states have responsibility to monitor and manage impacts of nonpoint sources of water pollution, including forest-related sources. Many states' forest practices acts arose out of state efforts to meet the requirements of the Clean Water Act. Although normal silvicultural practices are exempt from this act, dredging or filling in wetlands (such as might be required in forest road building) requires a permit from the Army Corps of Engineers.

The Endangered Species Act of 1973 set out regulations for conserving endangered and threatened species and their habitat. In the landmark 1995 Sweet Home case, the Supreme Court upheld the government's authority to regulate endangered species habitat on private land. The Endangered Species Act has been invoked to restrain timber harvest activities in northern spotted owl habitat in the Pacific Northwest and in red-cockaded woodpecker habitat in the Southeast. Lawsuits related to this use of the act raise the issue of whether such restraints on forest management activity on private lands constitute an infringement of private property rights, and if so, whether effected landowners should be compensated.

Most states and a growing number of local units of government have passed regulations restricting the forest management practices of private forest owners. In the 1940s, a first wave of regulations covering forestry on private lands was prompted by concern over future timber availability and hence stressed regeneration standards. Subsequent regulations have mandated that forest management activities not adversely affect environmental quality, by setting minimum standards for timber-harvesting, road construction and location, and the use of herbicides and pesticides. Recent regulations have addressed long-term resource sustainability, biodiversity, improving water quality and resource conservation.

By 1997, about one-third of the nation's private timberland was covered by state forest practices acts, and a total of 38 states had at least one program regulating forest practices on private land (12). State forest practices acts typically include standards for road and skid trail construction, stream crossings, timber harvesting, size of clearcuts, slash disposal, reforestation, minimum stocking levels, riparian zones, sensitive wildlife habitat, and wetlands protection (Figure 10.7). Several states are experimenting with contingent or conditional regulations wherein best management practices are voluntary, contingent upon their widespread application. Where established forest practice standards are not followed, the state may levy penalties (12).

Recognizing the limitations of regulations to achieve conservation goals, nongovernmental organizations, state agencies, and others are working together to develop innovative conservation incentives for private land owners. In some cases, agencies and conservation organizations purchase land from private owners in order to protect the special environmental value it contains. In other cases, conservation easements are negotiated with landowners to allow some public uses or to disallow certain practices, such as the harvest of tree species or forest types that are locally threatened. Safe harbor agreements are designed to enhance protection of endangered species habitat without preventing landowners from using their land.

Education and Technical Assistance   Much of the research on NIPF owners points to education as the most effective means of influencing NIPF management decisions. A major source of information and education for NIPF owners is the Cooperative

Figure 10.7 Forest Practice regulations covering private forestlands are mandatory in some states. Other states have opted for voluntary best management practices. Most states are seeking a workable balance between regulatory and voluntary forest conservation measures.

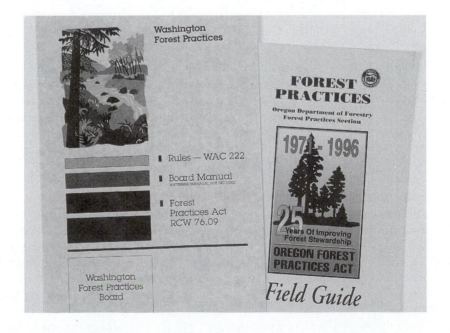

Extension Service. The CES provides educational programs and materials to NIPF landowners, professional resource managers, forest products industry personnel, loggers, policymakers, and the general public (Figure 10.8). Usually the educational service is provided through workshops, conferences, field days, TV and radio programs, "how-to" publications, the Internet, videotapes, marketing bulletins, newspaper stories, and computer programs.

As resources shrink, a number of states are adapting a volunteer training model, called the Master Woodland Manager Program, to extend their educational outreach capabilities (13). This program provides participants intensive forestry training, and, in return, each Master Woodland Manager volunteers service to other forest owners. The program aims to stimulate management activity among landowners, provide leadership in woodland management, promote woodland management to non-owners, and assist forestry extension agents in their outreach activities.

Partnerships Some of the oldest partnerships are among NIPF owners themselves, and between owners and forest industry. As of 1998, state forest owner associations existed in 31 states. Ten of these states also had local associations. Total membership in all known state and local forest owner associations was estimated to be 48,000 (14). Although the members of these associations represent a very small portion of the 9.9 million private forest owners in the nation, their influence at local, state, and national levels is growing. Through sponsorship of conferences, tours, workshops, and field days, they educate members and bring them into contact with each other and with agency personnel, researchers, and other natural resource professionals. Some associations sponsor environmental education activities for youth and the general public. Most publish newsletters, magazines, and contribute articles and editorials to local papers. Some provide timber price reporting, marketing, and insurance services to their members. Many are politically active at the state and national levels, participate in policy development, and support lobbyists.

Figure 10.8 Many woodland owners are eager to learn more about managing their lands. Field days, workshops, and conferences covering a wide range of topics are readily available, and publications abound for those seeking up-to-date "how-to" information.

Any NIPF landowner with a minimum of 10 acres of woodland and a commitment to forest management can become a member of the American Forest Foundation's Tree Farm program. As of 1998, the program boasted some 70,000 members (11). Properties meeting program criteria are certified as Tree Farms, and are re-inspected at regular intervals. Every year the program chooses state, regional, and national Outstanding Tree Farmer of the Year recipients (Figure 10.9).

Many forest products companies provide forest owners free assistance with management planning,

Figure 10.9 The Tree Farm Program provides recognition and technical assistance to NIPF owners who wish to manage their woodlands.

tree planting, vegetation management, timber harvesting, and marketing. In return for this assistance, many companies develop written agreements with landowners that guarantee the company first option on the timber crops as they become available for market. In 1994–95, nearly 11,000 landowners participated in landowner assistance programs, many in the Southeast (15).

In the past, when the public interest in private forest lands was primarily defined as one of promoting timber production, programs focused on improving the productivity of individual forest stands. As the public interest has become more broadly understood to include improvement of environmental quality, reclamation of degraded habitats, and restoration of endangered species populations, the focus on individual ownerships has become inadequate. Major conservation goals with strong public support include restoring more natural insect, disease, and fire regimes; maintaining healthy populations of aquatic and terrestrial species; and restoring endangered habitats such as the longleaf pine forests of the Southeast. Each goal requires concerted effort over large landscapes. The understanding that resource conservation requires

landscape-scale attention drives current forest management planning and policy.

Achieving conservation goals is challenging in landscapes of mixed ownership where owner objectives, capabilities, and constraints vary widely. Developing partnerships between public and private landowners and land users is one of the distinctive aspects of conservation at the beginning of the 21st century. Finding an effective mix of regulatory and nonregulatory instruments to encourage cross-boundary, cooperative solutions to environmental problems will likely be among the most daunting forest conservation policies of the first decade of the new millenium.

Emerging Trends and Issues

The beginning of the 21st century is both an exciting and frightening time for NIPF owners and for the profession of forestry. The extent and rate of change in every aspect of forestry—forest science, social values and demands, forest policies—have never been greater. This rapid change makes it difficult to predict with certainty what conditions will

Sidebar 10.5

Oregon's Salmon Plan: An Experiment in Public–Private Collaboration

To residents of the Pacific northwest, the salmon symbolizes the region's ideal of living in touch with nature. The dramatic decline in salmon populations is seen as a threat not only to the species, but also to the region's very identity. The 1995 proposal by the National Marine Fisheries Service to list coho salmon as threatened under the Endangered Species Act triggered a major, innovative experiment to avoid listing and restore salmon habitat. In 1997, the Oregon state legislature approved expenditure of $30 million—$13.6 million from a tax on forest products volunteered by forest landowners and industry—to implement what has become known as The Oregon Plan. In essence, the Plan aims to supplement existing regulations (such as the state's forest practices act) with voluntary measures designed not only to prevent "takings" of salmon, but also to restore salmon habitat and increase salmon populations. The Plan made funding available to some 60 existing or newly created watershed councils—voluntary associations of landowners, community residents, environmental organizations, and public agencies—to collaborate in restoration efforts (1). In the first year of the Plan some 1200 restoration activity reports were filed on projects including steam bank stabilization, fencing, riparian habitat restoration, culvert replacement, and "putting to bed" unused logging roads (2).

Monitoring efforts have been a major component of watershed council work. Volunteers have inventoried and mapped culverts, dams, stream crossings, forest roads, and other obstructions affecting fish passage. They have conducted salmon spawning and stream temperature surveys. Instructions for conducting and reporting these surveys are available on the World Wide Web, thereby encouraging wide participation in monitoring. An Independent Multidisciplinary Science Team monitors achievements of watershed councils through an annual audit.

This experiment in bottom-up, voluntary collaboration between state government and local stakeholders is not without controversy and risk. In 1998, a federal magistrate ruled that the National Marine Fisheries Service had violated the Endangered Species Act by not listing the coho, thereby forcing its listing. By prior agreement, that action nullified the dedicated forest products tax, thus putting Plan funding in jeopardy. It remains to be seen what effects the ruling will have on the thousands of volunteer participants in local watershed councils. Conservation groups around the country are watching to see if watershed councils will survive this blow and achieve the potential of this experiment in collaboration (3).

Sources:
1. J. CHRISTENSEN, *American Forests*, *103(4),* 17 (1998).

2. Oregon Forest Resources Institute, "Saving the Salmon: Oregonians Working Together to Manage Environmental Change." Special report, Oregon Forest Resources Institute, Portland, Ore. (No date given).

3. G. J. GRAY, M. J. ENZER, AND J. KUSEL, EDS., *Understanding Community-Based Forest Ecosystem Management*, Food Products Press, New York, 2001.

be like for NIPF owners even five years from now. Nonetheless, the following are trends and issues emerging at the birth of the new century that will likely affect ownership and management of NIPFs over the coming decade.

Rights and Responsibilities of NIPF Owners

Finding the appropriate balance between individual and public rights to private land continues to be the defining NIPF issue. Public interest in private forest lands has grown with our new understanding of the importance of these lands for environmental health. NIPF owners find themselves called upon to produce more—more timber, more wildlife, more beauty, more recreational opportunities—while at the same time being subjected to greater scrutiny. Owners in all states are subject to federal laws such as the Endangered Species Act and the Clean Water Act. However, the level of state regulation varies from states with no state regulation whatsoever over forest practices acts, to states in which most forest practices are regulated in great detail. Further complicating the regulatory scene is the profusion of municipal and county ordinances affecting management of forests and related resources. Faced with confusing, sometimes conflicting, and continuously changing rules and regulations, NIPF owners are anxious about their future ability to manage their forests.

Nonregulatory Mechanisms for Environmental Protection

This regulatory maze, together with the growing need to address environmental problems at a landscape scale, is driving a nationwide search for non-regulatory mechanisms for achieving environmental objectives. It is a time of frustration with existing policies, anxiety over the future, and optimistic experimentation with new approaches to forestry. These include promotion of voluntary Best Management Practices, cross-boundary cooperative management arrangements, conservation easements and leases, strategic alliances between environ-mental, industry, and landowner organizations, and innovative market mechanisms such as green certification.

Changing Forest Ownership Patterns

Forestland at the fringe of many metropolitan areas is being fragmented and converted to nonforest uses at an alarming rate, with an accompanying loss of green space and wildlife habitat. Urban residents decry the resulting erosion of environmental quality, and rural NIPF owners fear they will lose the right to manage their forests as residential neighborhoods proliferate. Clashes between old and new residents and their contrasting forest values are becoming more frequent. A new class of mini-forest owners is being created, with new needs for tree and forest information and management services.

At the same time, smaller NIPF ownerships in some rural areas are being consolidated into large tracts by corporate and industrial entities. Often, this change in ownership results in dramatic changes in forest composition, as the multiple objectives of NIPF owners are replaced by a stronger emphasis on commercial timber production. Loss of ownership diversity also drains a landscape of the human values NIPF owners provide. Changing ownership patterns will present multiple challenges to sustaining economic, social, and ecological health.

Changing Markets

The economic climate within which NIPF owners operate has changed significantly in the past decade, presenting new marketing and forest management challenges. Once, locally owned mills dominated local markets, determining what forest products were marketable and at what price. Such market determinations are now increasingly made in the global marketplace. Forest products produced in the United States compete with imports from Canada, South America, Pacific Rim countries, and elsewhere. U.S. environmental policy influences forestry investment decisions around the world. For example, dramatic reductions in timber harvesting on U.S. National Forests has led both to increasing harvest pressures on NIPF lands and increased imports of wood from Canada and elsewhere. In retail markets, wood and nonwood building materials compete for consumer recognition as being environmentally friendly. Green certification advocates propose to label forest products derived from sustainably managed forests, and achieve higher prices for them. All these factors combine to create dynamic and unpredictable wood markets. NIPF owners will increasingly require marketing savvy to effectively compete in complex global wood markets.

Emerging Forestry Paradigms

The profession of forestry, like all professions, evolves in response to societal changes. During the last two decades of the 20th century, the profession of forestry experienced a period of intense introspection, reevaluation, and testing of new paradigms. First derided as a mere buzzword, *ecosystem management* has become the dominant management paradigm for forestry on private as well as public lands. Ecosystem management focuses on very large geographic areas (watersheds to eco-regions) and very long time frames (up to several centuries), and emphasizes connections, processes, and desired future forest conditions. Many of the alternative policy mechanisms discussed above are attempts to find solutions to problems occurring at the ecosystem scale. Finding effective, equitable, and politically tenable means to achieving ecosystem objectives in mixed-ownership landscapes—especially landscapes dominated by NIPFs—is likely to be among the greatest challenge of natural resource managers and policy makers in the next decade.

Closely associated with ecosystem management, *sustainable forestry* encompasses many of the concepts and principles that are currently emerging within the forestry profession. Sustainable forestry goes beyond the traditional sustained yield model of production forestry to emphasize sustaining all forest values, functions, and outputs. It adds to

ecosystem management by explicitly recognizing social and economic, as well as environmental, goals for forestry. People involved in developing sustainable forestry include silviculturalists testing timber harvesting schemes that mimic natural processes, community groups searching for meaningful participation in regional forest resource planning, and forestry companies evaluating markets for green-certified forest products.

Concluding Statement

Nonindustrial private forests are of immense social, economic, and environmental value. They dominate the landscape of vast regions of the United States, are a vital component of the national economy, and play a growing role in international markets. The great diversity of NIPF owners results in a wide variety of objectives, constraints, and capabilities, which in turn create diverse forest types, ages, and conditions. This social and environmental diversity is in itself an important contribution made by NIPFs to the landscape and economy of America.

NIPF owners operate in a rapidly changing environment. Advances in forest science, growing demands for the products and values produced by NIPFs, and a dynamic policy environment all contribute to an atmosphere of instability, unpredictability, and risk. Over the coming years, NIPF owners will face changing markets, regulatory instability, and increasing demands that they cooperate with their neighbors to achieve environmental protection goals.

Each of these issues presents daunting challenges to the profession of forestry as well as to NIPF owners. Some will throw up their hands in frustration and declare the end of the forestry profession. Others will see in these challenges limitless opportunities to solve problems, serve people, improve the condition of the planet, and grow professionally. Enterprising and determined persons of creativity, patience, and energy will find the coming decade to be a wonderful time to work in the field of nonindustrial private forestry.

References

1. ROBERT FROST, "Stopping by a woods on a snowy evening." In *Favorite Poems Old and New*, Helen Ferris, ed., Doubleday & Co., Inc., Garden City, N.Y., 1957.

2. D. S. POWELL, J. L. FAULKNER, D. R. DARR, Z. ZHU, AND D. W. MACCLEERY. "Forest Resources of the United States, 1992." General Technical Report RM-234, U.S.D.A. Forest Service, Rocky Mountain Forest and Range Experiment Station, Fort Collins, Colo., 1993.

3. T. W. BIRCH, "Private Forest-land owners of the United States, 1994." Resource Bulletin NE-134. Radnor, Penn. U.S.D.A. Forest Service NE Forest Experiment Station, 1996.

4. R. J. MOULTON AND T. W. BIRCH, *Forest Farmer, 54(5),* 44 (1995).

5. J. C. BLISS, M. L. SISOCK, AND T. W. BIRCH, *Society and Natural Resources, 11(4),* 401 (1998).

6. J. C. BLISS, S. K. NEPAL, R. T. BROOKS, JR., AND M. D. LARSEN. *Southern J. of Applied Forestry, 21(1),* 37 (1997).

7. S. B. JONES, A. E. LULOFF, AND J. C. FINLEY, *J. For., 93(9),* 41 (1993).

8. J. C. BLISS AND A. JEFF MARTIN, *For. Sci., 35*(2), 601 (1989).

9. S. T. DANA AND S. K. FAIRFAX, *Forest and Range Policy: Its Development in the United States*, Second Edition, McGraw-Hill, New York, 1980.

10. W. G. ROBBINS, *American Forestry: A History of National, State, and Private Cooperation*, Univ. of Nebraska Press, Lincoln, 1985.

11. National Research Council, "Forest Landscapes in Perspective: Prospects and Opportunities for Sustainable Management of America's Nonfederal Forests." National Academy of Sciences, 1998.

12. P. V. ELLEFSON, A. S. CHENG, AND R. J. MOULTON. *Environmental Management, 21(3),* 42 (1997).

13. R. A. FLETCHER AND A. S. REED, "Extending forest management with volunteers: the Master Woodland Manager Project." In *Proceedings, Symposium on Nonindustrial Private Forests: Learning from the Past, Prospects for the Future*, Feb 18–20, 1996, Washington, D. C., Melvin J. Baughman, Minnesota Extension Service, Univ. Minnesota, St. Paul, 1998.

14. M. P. WASHBURN, "Forest Owner Associations in the United States, Linking Forest Owners to Public Policy." Unpub. Ph.D. Dissertation, School of Forest Resources, Pennsylvania State University, December, 1998.

15. J. HEISSENBUTTEL, "Forest Landscapes in Perspective: Prospects and Opportunities for Sustainable Management of America's Nonfederal Forests." Committee correspondence, American Forest and Paper Association. In National Research Council, National Academy of Sciences. Washington, D.C. 1998.

CHAPTER 11

Measuring and Monitoring Forest Resources

ALAN R. EK, GEORGE L. MARTIN,
AND DANIEL W. GILMORE

There are as many reasons to measure forests as there are uses of forests, and each use has its own specific needs for information. A forest landowner may want to sell some timber, and the determination of a fair price will require information about the species, size, quality, and number of trees to be sold. Forest managers seek to monitor forest conditions and practices and develop long-range plans concerning protection, planting, thinning, harvesting, and other treatments in their forests. These plans in turn require detailed information about the type, size, density, and growth rates of the existing stands, together with information about the location, accessibility, quality, and usage of the forest sites. Increasingly, surveys of on-the-ground silvi-cultural and harvesting practices are also conducted to understand the character, extent, and effectiveness of such activities, and particularly to assess compliance with practices deemed best for various situations. These and more detailed surveys also provide the data for forest scientists to develop an understanding of how forests grow and interact with their environment and benefit society.

These diverse information needs have led to recognition of a specialized branch of forestry, *forest measurements* (also *forest biometrics*), which focuses on techniques for the efficient measurement of forests, including their growth and response to management practices. The word *efficient* means that the measurement techniques strive to provide accurate information in a short time period at low cost.

This chapter presents an overview of some of the measurement techniques used in forestry. Both English and metric units of measurement are in use today, so both systems are described in this chapter. To help the reader become familiar with both systems, measurements in some tables and examples are in English units, and measurements in others are in metric units. The emphasis is on timber resources, but the measurement of some nontimber resources is also briefly described. Textbooks (1–3) are available for readers who want to learn more about forest measurements.

Measurement of Primary Forest Products

To appreciate how forests are measured, we first need to understand how we measure the primary products derived from forests. These primary products include *sawlogs, bolts,* and *chips.* Sawlogs are logs of sufficient size and quality to produce lumber or veneer. They must be 8 feet or more in length with a minimum small-end diameter of 6 to 8 inches. Bolts are short logs, less than 8 feet in length, and used primarily for manufacture into pulp and paper. Chips are small pieces of wood obtained by cutting up logs and sawmill wastes. They are used as a raw material for manufacturing a variety of forest products and as a source of fuel.

Scaling

The process of measuring the physical quantity of forest products is called *scaling.* During the nineteenth century the practice became established in the United States to scale sawlogs in terms of their board foot contents. Actually, the *board foot* is a unit of sawn lumber equivalent to a plank 1 foot long, 1 foot wide, and 1 inch thick. Estimates of the board foot contents of a log must take into account the portions of a log lost to saw kerf, the saw cuts between the boards, and to slabs, the rounded edges of the log. By 1910, more than forty

log rules had been devised to estimate the volume of logs in board feet, based on measurements of the diameter inside bark on the small end of the log (Figure 11.1), and the length of the log. Most of these log rules were very inaccurate and are no longer in use; however, a few managed to achieve widespread acceptance and continue to be used today: notably, the Doyle, Scribner, and International log rules.

The *Doyle log rule* was first published in 1825 by Edward Doyle of Rochester, New York. This rule is based on the simple formula:

$$V = (D - 4)^2 L/16$$

where V is the volume of the log in board feet, D is the small-end scaling diameter in inches, and L is the length of the log in feet (after allowing 3 to 4 inches for trim). The Doyle log rule grossly underestimates the volumes of logs less than 20 inches in diameter, but it continues to be used because of its simplicity and because it encourages the delivery of large-diameter logs to mills.

The *Scribner log rule* was published in 1846 by John Marston Scribner, an ordained clergyman and teacher of mathematics in a girls' school. Scribner estimated log volumes from diagrams of boards drawn on circles of various sizes corresponding to the small ends of logs. Boards were drawn with a 1/4-inch allowance for saw kerf and with the

Figure 11.1 First step in scaling: determining the diameter inside the bark on the small end of the log.

assumptions that boards would be 1 inch thick and not less than 8 inches wide. He further assumed that the logs were cylinders, so no adjustments were made for log taper. Scribner published his log rule in the form of a table, but the following formula has since been developed to describe his rule:

$$V = (0.79D^2 - 2D - 4)L/16$$

A variation of the Scribner rule is the *Scribner decimal C rule,* obtained by rounding the former rule to the nearest 10 board feet and then dropping the rightmost zero. For example, a 16-foot log with an 18-inch scale diameter would have 216 board feet according to the Scribner rule and would scale as 22 by the Scribner decimal C rule.

The most accurate log rule in use today is the *International log rule* developed by Judson Clark in 1906. Clark was a professional forester who had been bothered by the inconsistent and radically different estimates that he obtained from the Doyle, Scribner, and other log rules. He concluded that these rules grossly underestimated the volume of long logs because they did not take into account the increased board foot yield caused by log taper. In its basic form, this rule assumes a 1/8-inch saw kerf and estimates the volume of a 4-foot section. The volume of the entire log is estimated by adding the volumes of each 4-foot section and assuming a 1/2-inch increase in diameter for each section. In this way, the International rule allows for an increase in log volume owing to taper. The basic formula for the volume of a 4-foot section is

$$V = 0.22D^2 - 0.71D$$

For a quarter-inch saw kerf, this formula is multiplied by 0.905.

Table 11.1 shows that there are substantial differences between the estimates obtained with the log rules just described, especially for smaller log sizes. A wise buyer or seller will study the differences before completing any agreements.

Sawlogs can be scaled more consistently by simply estimating the volume of solid wood in the log. *Smalian's formula* is often used for this purpose,

$$V = (A_1 + A_2)L/2$$

where V is the volume of solid wood (in cubic feet or cubic meters), A_1 and A_2 are the cross-sectional areas inside bark on the two ends of the log (in square feet or square meters), and L is the length of the log (in feet or meters). Despite numerous attempts to promote cubic-volume scaling in the United States, board foot scaling still prevails.

The sawlog volume obtained with a log rule or cubic-volume formula is called the *gross scale.* A *net scale* must then be calculated by deducting for *scale defects* that will reduce the usable volume of wood in the log. Scale defects include rot, wormholes, ring shake (separation of wood along annual rings), and splits. In addition, if the log is not sufficiently straight, a scale deduction is made according to the amount of sweep or crook in the log.

Pulpwood and firewood are usually scaled by measuring the dimensions of a stack rather than measuring individual bolts. A *standard cord* of wood is a stack 4 by 4 by 8 feet and contains 128 cubic feet of wood, air, and bark. The number of standard cords in any size stack can be calculated by dividing the product of the stack's width, height, and length (in feet) by 128. Variations of the standard cord include the *short cord* or *face cord,* a stack 4 feet high and 8 feet wide with individual pieces cut to a length less than 4 feet. The dimensions of various types of cords are illustrated in Figure 11.2.

The amount of solid wood in a standard cord may range from 64 to 96 cubic feet, depending on several factors. Solid-wood content is reduced by thick bark, small-diameter bolts, crooked bolts, and loose piling, so these variables must be assessed when estimating the actual amount of wood in a given stack.

In recent years, much of the pulp and paper industry has adopted weight scaling for stacked pulpwood and wood chips. With this method, a truck carrying a full load of wood is weighed before and after it is unloaded. The difference is the weight of the wood, which can then be converted to volume or dry weight by taking into account the specific gravity and moisture content of the wood. Weight scaling is favored because it is fast and objective, and it encourages delivery of freshly cut wood to the mill.

Table 11.1   Board-Foot Volume of 16-Foot Logs for International Rule and Other Rules in Percentage of the International Rule[a]

Scaling Diameter (in.)	International[b] (bd ft)	Scribner (percent)	Scribner Decimal C (percent)	Doyle (percent)
6	20	90	100	20
8	40	80	75	40
10	65	83	92	55
12	95	83	84	67
14	135	84	81	74
16	180	88	89	80
18	230	93	91	85
20	290	97	97	88
22	355	94	93	91
24	425	95	94	94
26	500	100	100	97
28	585	99	99	98
30	675	97	98	100
32	770	96	96	102
34	875	91	91	103
36	980	94	94	104
38	1095	98	98	106
40	1220	99	98	106

D. L. Williams and W. C. Hopkins, "Converting factors for southern pine products," U.S.D.A. For. Serv., Tech. Bull. 626, South. For. Expt. Sta., New Orleans, 1969.

[a] Terms used in this table are defined in the text.

[b] Quarter-inch kerf (width of cut made by saw).

Figure 11.2   Examples of stacked-wood units, from left to right: standard cord, face cord (pieces 16 inches long), split face cord, and a split face cord piled in a small truck.

Grading

The value of forest products, particularly sawlogs, can be greatly reduced by *grade defects* that lower their strength, take away from their appearance, or otherwise limit their utility. Defects that lower the grade of sawlogs include knots, spiral grain, and stain.

Rules for grading hardwood logs emphasize the number, size, and location of defects, such as knots, that affect the amount of clear lumber that can be sawn from the log. Four classes of log use have been defined for the grading of hardwood logs (4).

1. *Veneer Class.* Logs of very high value as well as some relatively low-value logs that can be utilized for veneer. Logs that qualify as factory lumber grade 1 can often be utilized as veneer logs.

2. *Factory Class.* Boards that later can be remanufactured to remove most defects and obtain the best yields of clear face and sound cuttings. Factory lumber is typically separated into grades 1, 2, and 3.

3. *Construction Class.* Logs suitable for sawing into ties, timbers, and other items to be used in one piece for structural purposes.

4. *Local-Use Class.* In general, logs suitable for products not usually covered by standard specifications. High strength, great durability, and fine appearance are not required for the following types of products: crating, pallet parts, industrial blocking, and so on.

Rules for grading softwood logs emphasize strength and durability. The majority of softwood logs fall into the *veneer class* or the *sawmill class,* which includes logs suited to the production of yard and structural lumber. The number, location, and size of grade defects determine the grade of logs in these two classes.

Land Surveying and Mapping

Land-surveying and land-mapping techniques are used in forestry to locate the boundaries of forest properties and stands of timber, to measure the land areas enclosed within these boundaries, and to locate roads, streams, and other features of importance within the forest. Surveying techniques are also used for locating sample plots as described later in this chapter.

Forest land surveys in the United States are usually conducted with the English system of units. Distance is measured in *feet, chains* (1 chain = 66 feet), and *miles* (1 mile = 80 chains); land area is measured in *acres* (1 acre = 10 square chains) and *square miles* (1 square mile = 640 acres). In the metric system, distance is measured in *meters* (1 meter = 3.28084 feet) and *kilometers* (1 kilometer = 1000 meters), and land area is measured in *hectares* (1 hectare = 10,000 square meters) and *square kilometers* (1 square kilometer = 100 hectares). Acres and hectares are both used to describe land areas in the United States, so it is useful to remember that 1 hectare is equal to 2.471 acres or about 2.5 acres. Additional converting factors for units of distance and area can be found in Appendix III.

Distance

There are several methods for measuring distance in forest surveys, and the choice depends on the accuracy required. *Pacing* is often used for locating sample plots and in reconnaissance work where great accuracy is not required. Foresters must first calibrate their individual pace by walking a known distance—say, 10 chains—and counting the number of paces. In forestry, a pace is considered two steps, using a natural walking gait, and should be calibrated for each type of terrain encountered. Having determined the average number of paces per chain, the forester can then measure and keep track of distances by counting paces while walking through the forest. An experienced pacer can achieve an accuracy of 1 part in 80; that is, for every 80 chains traversed the error should be no more than 1 chain.

When greater accuracy is required, steel tapes are used in a technique known as *chaining*. The steel tapes may be 2 chains, 100 feet, or 30 meters in length, depending on the units desired. Chaining requires a minimum of two people to hold each end of the tape. The head chainer usually uses a magnetic compass to determine the direction of the course line while the rear chainer keeps a record of the number of tape lengths traversed. Careful chaining can achieve an accuracy of 1 part in 1000.

There are also a variety of *electronic and optical instruments* for measuring distances. Examples of such tools include laser-based rangefinders. However, these instruments require a line of sight largely free of obstacles such as trees and shrubs. For this reason, they are not well suited for timber surveys in densely wooded areas, but they are used for road and boundary surveys. Additionally, satellite linked global positioning system (GPS) units are increasingly used for establishing locations, travel routes, and boundaries.

Direction

Many of the instruments available are more accurate for measuring direction, but the *magnetic compass* is favored by foresters because of its speed, economy, and simplicity. With a magnetic compass, directions are measured in degrees (0 to 360) clockwise from magnetic north, the direction pointed by the compass needle. These direction angles are called *magnetic azimuths* and must be converted to true *azimuths* by correcting for *magnetic declination*; that is, the angle between true north and magnetic north. Many compasses allow this correction to be made automatically by the instrument. GPS units are also

supplanting compass usage where the forest cover allows links to satellites (Figure 11.3).

Land Surveys

Much of the land subdivision in the world is based on the *metes and bounds* system. Under this system, property lines and corners are based on physical features such as streams, ridges, fences, and roads. Locating such legal boundaries is often difficult, especially when descriptions are vague, corners that were once marked have been lost, and lines such as streams have moved over the years. However, most of the United States west of the Mississippi River and north of the Ohio River, plus Alabama, Mississippi, and portions of Florida, have been subdivided according to a *rectangular survey system*. This system was conceived by Thomas Jefferson at the close of the Revolutionary War, and enacted as the Land Ordinance of 1785 "to survey and sell these public lands in the Northwest Territory"

The rectangular survey system uses carefully established *baselines and principal meridians* as references for land location. The baselines run east-west, and the principal meridians run north-south. The intersection of a baseline and principal meridian is called an *initial point* and serves as the origin of a survey system. More than thirty of these systems were established as land was acquired and

Figure 11.3   Examples of GPS (with PDA) usage (left), and laser rangefinder usage (right), in the field.

development progressed westward in the United States.

Figure 11.4 shows how land is subdivided under the rectangular survey system. At intervals of 24 miles north and south of the baseline, *standard parallels* are established in east-west directions. At 24-mile intervals along the baseline and each of the standard parallels, *guide meridians* are run north to the next standard parallel. Because of the earth's curvature, guide meridians converge to the north and the resulting *24-mile tracts* are actually less than 24 miles wide at their northern boundaries.

The 24-mile tracts are then subdivided into sixteen *townships*, each approximately 6 miles square.

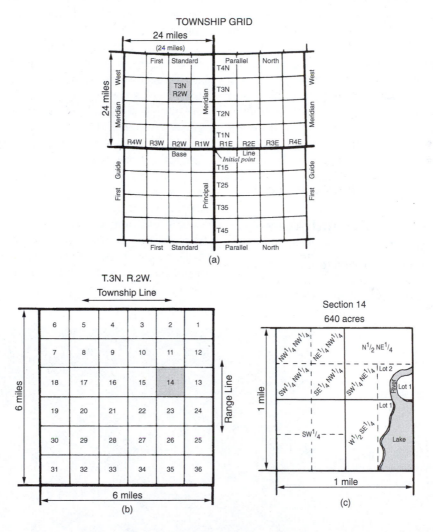

Figure 11.4 Diagram of the U.S. rectangular survey system. (a) Township grid showing initial point, baseline, principal meridian, standard parallels, and guide meridians, along with examples of township and range designations. (b) Subdivision of township into sections and the system of numbering sections from 1 to 36. (c) Subdivision of a section into quarter-sections and forties. (Adapted from the Bureau of Land Management, U.S. Department of Interior.)

Townships are numbered consecutively north and south of the baseline. Township locations east and west of the principal meridian are called *ranges* and are also numbered consecutively. For example, in Figure 11.4a the township labeled T3N, R2W denotes a township that is three townships north of the baseline and two ranges west of the principal meridian.

Townships are subdivided into thirty-six *sections,* each approximately 1 mile square and 640 acres in area. Figure 11.4b illustrates how the sections are numbered within a township. Each section is subdivided into *quarter-sections* of approximately 160 acres, which are further subdivided into 40-acre parcels known as forties. Figure 11.4c illustrates how the subdivisions of a section are identified.

A legal description for a parcel of land begins with the smallest subdivision and progresses to the township designation. For example, the forty in the northwest corner of section 14 (Figure 11.4c) would be described as NW 1/4 NW 1/4 S14, T3N, R2W.

Forest Type Mapping and Area Measurement

Forest type maps are very useful to forest managers because they show the locations and boundaries of individual forest stands, that is, areas with similar species, size, and density of trees. These maps also show nonforested areas such as lakes, rivers, and fields. Vertical aerial photographs are extremely useful for preparing forest type maps because they can be viewed with a stereoscope (Figure 11.5) to provide a three-dimensional picture of the forest.

Trained interpreters are able to identify forest stands on the photographs and outline their boundaries (Figure 11.6). Chapter 12 describes the use of aerial photographs and other forms of remote sensing in forestry.

After the forest type maps have been prepared, it is usually necessary to measure the land area within each of the stand boundaries. Forest stands normally have irregular boundaries, so their areas are often determined with a *dot grid,* a sheet of clear plastic covered with uniformly spaced dots. The grid is laid over the map and all the dots falling within the stand boundary are counted. Multiplying this dot count by an appropriate converting factor gives the land area of the stand. For example, the converting factor for a dot grid with sixty-four dots per square inch and a photograph scale of 1:20,000 is 0.996 acres per dot.[1] Suppose the number of dots falling within a given stand boundary is forty-seven; then the estimated area of the stand is

$$47 \times 0.996 = 46.8 \text{ acres}$$

Figure 11.5 Parallax bar oriented over overlapping vertical aerial photographs under a mirror stereoscope. The stereoscope facilitates three-dimensional study of the photographed scene. The parallax bar is used to determine approximate tree heights and terrain elevations. (Courtesy of Wild Herrbrungg, Inc.)

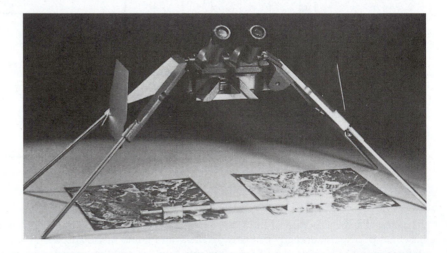

---

[1] At a photoscale of 1:20,000, one inch on the photograph represents 10,000/12 = 1,667 feet on the ground. Thus one square inch = (1667 × 1667)/43,560 = 63.8 acres. Each of the sixty-four dots then represents 63.8/64 = 0.996 acres.

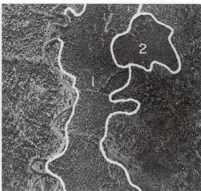

Figure 11.6 Stereogram illustrating cover-type mapping of balsam fir (1) and black spruce (2) stands in Ontario, Canada. (From V. G. Zsilinszky, "Photographic interpretation of tree species in Ontario," Ontario Department of Lands and Forests, 1966.)

Measurement of Forest Resources with a Focus on Timber

There are many variations in the types of timber focused surveys. They range from the precise measurement of individual trees on a woodlot while marking them for a timber sale, to the assessment of the timber supply in the United States, including its rate of growth and consumption. There are several major types of surveys for timber. *Strategic surveys* are used primarily for identifying overall forest conditions and to establish broad protection, management, and use policy. These are also used to determine appropriate levels of investment, both public and private, in forest management. The major example is the state-by-state nationwide Forest Inventory and Monitoring survey led by the U.S.D.A. Forest Service. This survey also measures many nontimber aspects of the forest. *Management-oriented surveys* or *inventories* are used for developing management plans for specific federal, state, private, and other forests. These ownership specific inventories are designed to provide details on the quantity, quality, and location of timber and associate site and use considerations. Typically, these surveys involve the construction of localized maps of individual stands and other important features via aerial photography and geographic information systems usage. Such information is essential to forest managers in their planning

and conduct of forest wide and local site management. *Timber appraisals* are used to determine the monetary value of a specific timber or land sale. The objectives of these surveys differ considerably as do the measurement procedures they employ. Additionally, a variety of surveys are used to monitor regeneration development, timber harvesting practices, and so forth, to inform managers about the type, extent, and sometimes the effectiveness of practices and needs as appropriate. These surveys, perhaps best labeled *practices monitoring,* are often part of ongoing management information efforts. The following discussions provide an overview of some of the more common tools and techniques used in assessing the timber aspects of such surveys.

Standing Trees

Most timber surveys require the measurement of individual trees. Standing-tree measurements may be required to estimate the volume or mass (weight) of various products obtainable from the trees, or they may be used to assess the relative sizes of trees to aid in the development of management prescriptions for the forest.

Diameter at Breast Height One of the most useful tree measurements is the diameter at breast height (dbh). This is the diameter, outside bark, of the tree stem at a height of 4.5 feet (or 1.3 meters when the metric system is used), above ground on the uphill side of the tree. The *tree caliper* (Figure 11.7) is one of the most accurate instruments for obtaining this measurement. Another instrument, the *tree diameter tape,* is a steel tape with special calibrations that convert the circumference of the tree to its corresponding diameter, assuming the cross-section of the tree is a perfect circle. Since trees are not usually circular, the diameter tape tends to overestimate tree diameters and, hence, is somewhat less accurate than the caliper. Even less accurate, but very quick and easy to use, is the *Biltmore stick* (Figure 11.8). Invented in 1898 by Carl Schenck for use on the Biltmore Forest in North Carolina, this stick is held horizontally against the tree at arm's length (25 inches), with the left edge in line with the left side of the tree. The diameter is then sighted on the stick in line with the right

Figure 11.8   Field crew in the process of observing and recording species and tree diameters on a plot. Diameters are being measured with a Biltmore stick held at a fixed distance from the eye. Observations with this instrument are based on the geometric principle of similar triangles.

side of the tree. The Biltmore stick is calibrated according to the principle of similar triangles.

Basal Area   The dbh measurement is frequently converted to basal area, that is, the area (in square feet or square meters) of the cross-section of a tree at breast height. The formula for the area of a circle (pi times radius squared), together with appropriate unit-converting factors, is used to calculate tree basal area. If dbh is measured in inches, tree basal area, *b*, in square feet is given by

$$b = 0.005454 \ dbh^2$$

If dbh is measured in centimeters, tree basal area in square meters is given by

$$b = 0.00007854 \ dbh^2$$

The basal area of a forest stand is expressed as the sum of the tree basal areas divided by the area of the stand, and is expressed in square feet per acre or square meters per hectare. Stand basal area is used by forest managers as a measure of the degree of crowding of trees in a stand (see "Stocking and Density," later in this chapter).

Figure 11.7   Forester using a caliper to measure a tree diameter at breast height (dbh).

Height There are a number of different instruments for measuring tree height, and the required level of accuracy dictates the instrument of choice. *Height poles* provide very accurate measurements for trees that are not too high. A variety of sectioned, folding, and telescoping poles are available, and they are best suited to trees with branches that allow the poles to pass readily between them but also give the poles lateral support. Height poles become too cumbersome for trees taller than 60 feet, and their use is primarily restricted to research plots for which great accuracy is required.

Tree heights can be measured indirectly with instruments called *hypsometers*. Many types of hypsometers have been devised over the years, but they all work on either trigonometric or geometric principles. Figure 11.9 illustrates the trigonometric principle, which requires knowledge of the horizontal distance between the observer and the tree, and an instrument to measure the angles between this horizontal distance and the top and base of the tree. Most hypsometers employing the trigonometric principle are calibrated in terms of the tangents of the angles, so the observer can read tree heights directly on the instrument's scale. Hypsometers employing the geometric principle must also be used at a fixed horizontal distance from the tree and, in addition, must be held a fixed distance from the observer's eye (Figure 11.10). Laser rangefinders are new tools for height measurement that allow for high accuracy and flexibility as to where the observer may stand in observing the base and top of the tree.

When trees are measured to assess the volume or weight of merchantable products in the tree, the *merchantable height* or *length* is often measured instead of the total height (Figure 11.11). Merchantable length is a measure of the usable portion of the tree above stump height (usually 1 foot) to a point on the stem where the diameter becomes too small or too irregular to be utilized.

Volume and Mass There are at present no instruments that allow the direct measurement of the volume or mass (weight) of a standing tree. Instead, volume and mass must be estimated from other

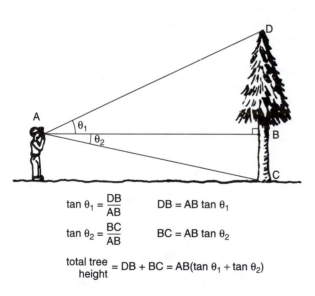

$$\tan \theta_1 = \frac{DB}{AB} \qquad DB = AB \tan \theta_1$$

$$\tan \theta_2 = \frac{BC}{AB} \qquad BC = AB \tan \theta_2$$

$$\frac{\text{total tree}}{\text{height}} = DB + BC = AB(\tan \theta_1 + \tan \theta_2)$$

Figure 11.9 Three measurements are required to determine the total height of a tree, using *trigonometric* principles: the angle θ_1 from horizontal to the top of the tree, the angle θ_2 from horizontal to the base of the tree, and the horizontal distance *AB* from the observer to the tree.

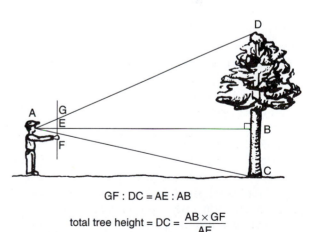

$$GF : DC = AE : AB$$

$$\text{total tree height} = DC = \frac{AB \times GF}{AE}$$

Figure 11.10 Measurement of total tree height using *geometric* principles: ratios of distances are constructed using the principle of similar triangles.

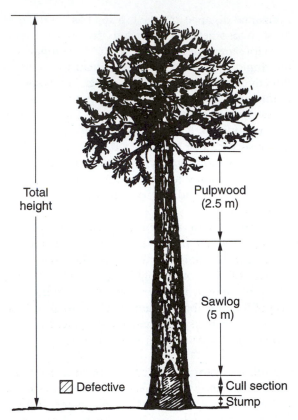

Total
height

Pulpwood
(2.5 m)

Sawlog
(5 m)

☑ Defective

Cull section
Stump

Figure 11.11   Diagram of a tree stem showing the total height of the tree and the length of merchantable sections.

tree dimensions. Tree height and dbh are most frequently used for this purpose, and many *tree volume tables* giving the average volume or mass for trees of different diameters and heights have been developed (Table 11.2).

More accurate estimates of tree volume can be obtained by measuring upper-stem diameters with instruments called *optical dendrometers* (Figure 11.12). With diameter measurements taken at various heights on the tree, volumes may be calculated for individual stem sections (see earlier section on "Scaling") and then summed.

Age and Radial Increment   Tree age is defined as the time elapsed since the germination of a seed or initiation of a sprout. Many tree species in the northern temperate region produce annual rings of wood corresponding to light-colored earlywood and darker latewood. This property makes it possible to measure tree age by using an *increment borer* to extract a core of wood and then counting the number of annual rings (Figure 11.13). The age of live trees can be determined through increment cores taken at ground level; however, stem deformaties near the ground and/or decay make it difficult to obtain a core including the tree center and all the annual rings. Consequently, cores are taken at breast height and an estimate of the time to reach that height is added to the core measure to obtain total age. The number of years for a tree to reach breast height is dependent upon the species, early competition, and site quality and can vary from 2 to 17 years (5). Annual rings are easily discernible in most conifers, but difficult to see in hardwoods such as aspen and basswood.

With young conifers having determinate height growth, age can also be estimated by counting the number of growth whorls along the stem. For older, larger trees that have lost their lower branches and evidence of whorls, this method is no longer feasible. Plantation records or records of natural disturbances which have led to new stands are also used to estimate ages. When discernible annual rings, growth whorls, or other records are missing, determination of tree and thus stand age is very difficult.

Increment borers are also used to determine the rate of tree growth by measuring the length of the last several rings in the core. This observation is called a *radial increment* and can be multiplied by 2 to estimate the diameter growth during the period.

Forest Sampling

It is seldom necessary or desirable to measure every tree on a forest property. Sufficiently accurate estimates can be obtained from measurements of a subset or sample of the trees in the forest. The process of selecting a representative sample of trees and obtaining the required estimates is called *forest sampling*.

Table 11.2 Portion of a Tree Volume Table for Approximating Merchantable Volume of Commercial Species in the Great Lakes States[a]

Diameter at Breast Height (cm)	Total height (m)					
	10	15	20	25	30	35
	Volume[b] (m³)					
10	0.021	0.024	—	—	—	—
20	0.126	0.186	0.247	0.311	—	—
30	0.292	0.429	0.570	0.718	0.853	—
40	0.524	0.767	1.017	1.281	1.523	—
50	—	1.200	1.592	2.005	2.384	2.783
60	—	1.728	2.294	2.887	3.436	4.010

Source: Adapted from S. R. Gevorkiantz and L. P. Olsen, "Composite volume tables for timber and their application in the Lake States," U.S.D.A. For. Serv., Tech. Bull. 1104, 1955.

[a] As an example of usage, a tree with a measured diameter of 30 centimeters at breast height and a total height of 25 meters would have an estimated usable volume of 0.718 cubic meter).

[b] Volume inside bark from 0.3-meter stump height to limit of merchantability—that is, to a point on the stem where the diameter inside the bark is just equal to 8 centimeters.

Sampling Units Sample trees are usually selected in groups at different locations throughout the forest. Each group of trees is called a sampling unit and may be selected in a variety of ways. One approach is to tally (count and measure) all the trees on a plot of fixed area at each location. *Sample plots* may be square, rectangular, or circular and are usually between 0.01 and 0.20 acre in area. Circular plots are often preferred because of their ease of

Figure 11.12 Observation of the upper-stem diameter with a Wheeler optical caliper.

Figure 11.13 Tree age determination with an increment borer.

installation. All trees (or all trees of merchantable size) with a midpoint at breast height lying within the plot boundary are tallied (Figure 11.14).

Table 11.3 presents an example of a forest sample obtained from 0.10-acre plots at fifteen different locations within a forest stand. Each sample tree was measured to determine its dbh to the nearest inch and its merchantable volume in cubic feet. Columns 1, 2, and 3 in Table 11.3 summarize the number of trees tallied and the total volume tallied for each dbh class. These data can be used to calculate estimates of the average number of trees, basal area, and volume per acre. The average number of trees per acre (column 5) for each dbh class is given by

$$\text{average number of trees per acre} = \frac{\text{number of trees tallied}}{nA}$$

where n is the number of sample plots (fifteen in this example) and A is the area of each sample plot (0.10 acre in this example). The average basal area per acre (column 6) for each dbh class is given by

$$\text{average basal area} = \frac{(\text{number of trees tallied})b}{nA}$$

where b is the basal area per tree, given in column 4 of Table 11.3 (see earlier section, "Basal Area," for formulas). The average volume per acre (column 7) for each dbh class is given by

$$\text{average volume} = \frac{\text{total volume tallied}}{nA}$$

Another useful type of forest-sampling was devised in 1948 by Walter Bitterlich, an Austrian Forester. This method is known as the *Bitterlich* method, *horizontal point sampling,* or *variable plot sampling.* Observers tally all trees with a dbh larger than the angle projected by a gauge viewed from each sample point (see Figure 11.15).

A variety of *angle gauges* are available for use with Bitterlich's method. Figure 11.16 illustrates the use of a stick-type angle gauge; the observer's eye corresponds to the sample point, and the stick is rotated through a complete circle while the observer views each tree at breast height to determine whether it is "in" or "out."

Instead of tallying every tree on a fixed-area plot, Bitterlich's method is equivalent to tallying each tree on a circular plot with an area proportional to the basal area of the tree. Hence, large-diameter trees are tallied on large plots and small-diameter trees are tallied on small plots. One advantage of this approach lies in the fact that large-diameter trees contribute more to stand basal area and volume than do small-diameter trees; therefore, by including more of the large trees in the sample and fewer of the small trees, more precise estimates of stand basal area and volume can usually be obtained with less effort. The geometry of Bitterlich's method gives it another advantage. If the basal area of a tree is divided by the area of its corresponding sample plot, the result is a constant, BAF, called the *basal-area factor,* and depends only on the angle projected by the gauge. Hence, each tree tallied represents the same basal area per acre regardless of the tree's area per acre and regardless of the

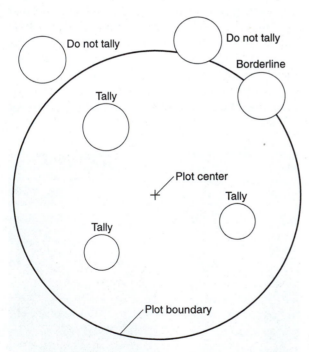

Figure 11.14 In fixed-area plot sampling, field crews tally all trees with a midpoint at breast height lying within the plot boundary.

Table 11.3　Example of a Tree Tally and Averages for a Sample of Fifteen 0.1-Acre Plots[a]

1 Diameter at Breast Height (in.)	2 Number of Trees Tallied	3 Total Volume Tallied (ft^3)	4 Basal Area per Tree (ft^2)	5 Average Number of Trees per Acre	6 Average Basal Area (ft^2/acre)	7 Average Volume (ft^3/acre)
6	89	223	0.1963	59.3	11.6	149
7	54	216	0.2672	36.0	9.6	144
8	34	204	0.3491	22.7	7.9	136
9	21	195	0.4418	14.0	6.2	130
10	15	195	0.5454	10.0	5.5	130
11	12	204	0.6599	8.0	5.3	136
12	8	160	0.7854	5.3	4.2	107
13	6	162	0.9217	4.0	3.7	108
14	3	96	1.0690	2.0	2.1	64
Total	242			161.3	56.1	1104

[a] A procedure for calculating the averages in columns 5, 6, and 7 is explained in the text.

tree's size. Thus, stand basal area can be estimated by simply multiplying the average number of trees tallied per point by the basal-area factor. This result is illustrated in the following example.

Table 11.4 gives an example of a forest sample obtained from Bitterlich points with a basal-area factor of 10 square feet per acre, at fifteen different locations within a forest stand. Each sample tree was measured as in the previous example. Columns 1, 2, and 3 in Table 11.4 summarize the

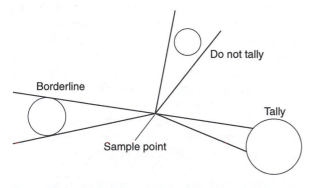

Figure 11.15　In Bitterlich horizontal point sampling, field crews tally all trees with a dbh larger than the angle projected by a gauge.

number of trees tallied and the total volume tallied for each dbh class. Again, these data can be used to calculate stand averages, but the formulas are different from those used for fixed-area plots. The average number of trees per acre (column 5) for each dbh class is given by

$$\text{average number of trees per acre} = \frac{\text{BAF (number of trees tallies)}}{nb}$$

where BAF is the basal-area factor of the angle gauge (10 square feet per acre in this example), n is the number of sample points (fifteen in this example), and b is the basal area per tree, given in column 4 of the table (see earlier section, "Basal Area," for formulas). The average basal area per acre (column 6) for each dbh class is given by

$$\text{average basal area} = \frac{\text{BAF (number of trees tallied)}}{n}$$

Notice that this formula can be used even if trees are not tallied by dbh class. For example, if only the total number of trees tallied is known (eighty-five in this example), we can use the formula just given to calculate the total basal area per acre:

$$\text{total basal area} = \frac{\text{BAF (total number of trees tallied)}}{n}$$

Figure 11.16
Use of stick-type angle gauge to tally trees on a Bitterlich horizontal sample point. Borderline trees are checked with distance tapes and careful measurement of the diameter to determine whether they are "in" or "out."

In   Out   Borderline

$$= \frac{10 \times 85}{15}$$

$$= 56.7 \ \text{ft}^2/\text{acre}$$

This result is in close agreement with the total basal area at the bottom of column 6 in Table 11.4. However, the Bitterlich method required the tally and measurement of only one-third as many trees as were tallied on the 0.1 acre plot. Thus, it can be seen that Bitterlich's method provides a very quick and easy way to obtain basal-area estimates. All one has to do is count the number of "in" trees.

The average volume per acre (column 7) for each dbh class is given by

$$\text{average volume} = \frac{\text{BAF (total volume tallied)}}{nb}$$

One of the important decisions in a forest-sampling design is the size of plot to use, or the basal-area factor of the angle gauge when using Bitterlich's method. Larger plots will include more trees, will be less variable, and will yield more precise estimates. However, if there are too many trees on the plot, the time and cost of tallying them may be excessive and there is a good chance that some

trees may be overlooked. A rule of thumb that seems to work well is to use a plot size that gives an average of 15 to 20 trees per plot. For example, a sawtimber stand may have 75 to 100 trees per acre, so a good plot size to use in this stand is 1/5 acre. A poletimber stand with 150 to 200 trees per acre would be sampled with a 1/10 acre plot.

Bitterlich's method works best if an average of 5 to 10 trees are "in" at each sample point. The important thing to remember here is that the larger the basal-area factor of the angle gauge, the fewer the number of trees tallied at each point. If the average basal area of the stand is divided by 10, the result is a good basal-area factor to use. For example, if a large sawtimber stand has a basal area of 200 square feet per acre, a good basal-area factor to use is 20. A poletimber or small sawtimber stand with 100 square feet per acre of basal area would be sampled with a 10-factor angle gauge.

Sampling Methods Once appropriate sampling units have been selected, it is necessary to decide how many units to measure and how they will be located in the forest. The total number of sample

Table 11.4 Example of a Tree Tally and Averages for a Sample of Fifteen Bitterlich Points with a Basal-Area Factor (BAF) of 10 Square Feet per Acre

1 Diameter at Breast Height (in.)	2 Number of Trees Tallied	3 Total Volume Tallied (ft³)	4 Basal Area per Tree (ft²)	5 Average Number of Trees per Acre	6 Average Basal Area (ft²/acre)	7 Average Volume (ft³/acre)
6	17	43	0.1963	57.7	11.3	146
7	14	56	0.2672	34.9	9.3	140
8	12	72	0.3491	22.9	8.0	137
9	10	93	0.4418	15.1	6.7	140
10	9	117	0.5454	11.0	6.0	143
11	8	136	0.6599	8.1	5.3	137
12	6	120	0.7854	5.1	4.0	102
13	6	162	0.9217	4.3	4.0	117
14	3	96	1.0690	1.9	2.0	60
Total	85			161.0	56.6	1122

[a] A procedure for calculating the averages in columns 5, 6, and 7 is explained in the text.

units is called the *sample size,* and the manner in which they are located is called the *sampling method.*

Random sampling is a method in which sample units are located completely at random within each stand (Figure 11.17a). Random sampling ensures that estimates obtained from the sample are *unbiased;* that is, on the average they will tend toward the true stand values. *Systematic sampling* (Figure 11.17b) is often preferred because it is easier to implement, the time it takes to walk between plots is usually less, and sketching field maps and adjusting type lines on aerial photographs is more easily done while *cruising.*[2] In systematic sampling, also *called line-plot cruising,* sample units are located at specific intervals along straight cruise lines running across the forest property. If appropriate precautions are observed, systematic sampling will not introduce undue bias. In particular, it is important to ensure that cruise lines do not force plots along a line to be in some atypical forest condition. One way, to prevent this type of bias is to run cruise lines up and down slopes, since timber conditions tend to vary, with changes in elevation.

The number of sample units located in a given stand is usually determined by the maximum allowable error that can be tolerated in the final estimates. The more sample units measured, the smaller the errors will be, on the average, in estimates obtained from the sample. Sampling errors are usually expressed as a percentage of the timber volumes or values being estimated. For example, if the objective of sampling is to determine a fair price for a large, valuable stand of sawtimber, the maximum allowable error may be set at 3 to 5 percent. If, however, estimates are desired for the purpose of making long-range management plans, less accuracy is required and allowable errors may be set at 10 to 20 percent.

Foresters can use statistical formulas to determine the minimum number of plots required to achieve a specified sampling error. The actual formula depends on the sampling method. For example, the following formula gives the number, n, of sample

[2] To *cruise* a holding of forestland is to examine and estimate its yield of forest products.

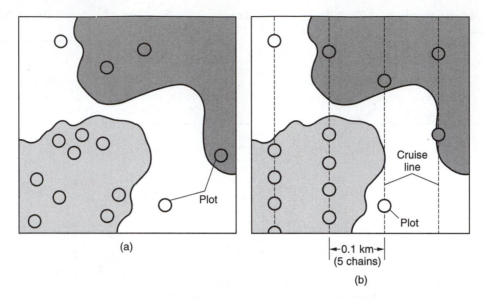

Figure 11.17 Portion of a forest tract illustrating (a) random and (b) systematic allocation of sample plots for three cover types. Sampling intensity (number of plots per unit area) varies by cover type.

units required when using random sampling in a single stand of timber,

$$n = \left(\frac{tCV}{E}\right)^2$$

where E is the allowable percentage of error, CV is the coefficient of variation in the stand, and t is a value obtained from a table of Student's t distribution.[3] The CV is a measure of how variable the size and density of timber are from place to place in the stand. A very uniform stand, like a plantation (Figure 11.18a), will have a relatively low CV. With clustering (Figure 11.18b), which can occur to varying degrees in naturally regenerated stands, CV values are higher.

The CV plays a major role in determining the required number of sample units in a given stand. Suppose the CV in a relatively uniform stand is 20 percent, the maximum allowable error for the timber cruise is set at 5 percent, and the value of t is approximately 2. In this stand, our formula gives a required sample size of

$$n = \left(\frac{2 \times 20}{5}\right)^2 = 8^2 = 64 \text{ units}$$

If the trees in the stand were clustered and the CV were, say, 40 percent, the required sample size would be

$$n = \left(\frac{2 \times 40}{5}\right)^2 = 16^2 = 256 \text{ units}$$

Because the required sample size varies with the square of the CV, a doubling of the CV (as happened in this example) means that four times as many sample units are required to achieve the same sampling error. Careful selection of efficient types and sizes of sampling units helps reduce the CVs in forest sampling designs, and can considerably reduce the required sample size and cost of a forest inventory.

---

[3] Procedures for calculating CV and determining t are explained in forest measurement textbooks (1–3).

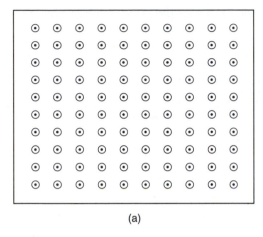
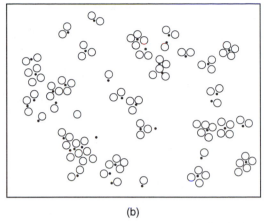

(a)   (b)

Figure 11.18 The circles in these diagrams illustrate the locations of tree stems in (a) uniform and (b) clustered forest stands.

Forest sampling is generally performed by survey crews of two people each. The crew chief is responsible for locating sample units and recording data. The second crew member is responsible for tree measurements such as dbh, height, age, and quality or condition. Data are often recorded on tally sheets and then entered into an office computer for statistical processing. However, small hand-held computers are increasingly replacing field tally sheets. Such battery operated devices are often quite rugged and may also be integrated (connected to) GPS units and other electronic measuring devices (Figure 11.19). These devices can also be programmed to help reduce the chance of data entry errors and speed subsequent data handling and compilation of results.

Statistics Estimates obtained from forest sampling are called statistics, and they will vary in detail according to the type of timber survey. In general, the most detailed statistics are required for timber appraisals and for scientific research. This level of detail may include stand and stock tables (Table 11.5) for each timber stand in the forest, together with maps showing the boundaries, area, and topography of each stand. Stand and stock tables show a breakdown of the trees and volume of tim-

ber in a stand by dbh class and species. They may also tabulate the volume of sawtimber by tree or log grades. These important factors affect the value

Figure 11.19 Sample tree measurements are entered directly into this small, battery-operated computer, which is taken into the forest. The computer is capable of performing all the statistical calculations necessary to prepare a stand and stock table (Table 11.5).

Table 11.5   Stand and Stock Table for a Red Oak Stand in the American Legion State Forest, Oneida County, Wisconsin[a]

Diameter at Breast Height (in.)	Red Oak		White Birch		Sugar Maple		Red Maple		Total	
	Trees	Cords	Trees	Cords	Trees	Cords	Trees	Cords	Trees	Cords
6			76.5	2.2	76.5	2.1			153.0	4.3
8	14.3	1.2	14.3	1.5					28.6	2.7
10	82.5	12.0	18.3	2.2					100.8	14.2
12							6.4	1.3	6.4	1.3
14	4.7	1.3							4.7	1.3
Total	101.5	14.5	109.1	5.9	76.5	2.1	6.4	1.3	293.5	23.8

[a] Values are averages per acre.

of timber, together with accessibility and distance to mills.

Inventories designed for management planning and operations usually do not require as much precision and statistical detail as appraisals. Management oriented inventories are more concerned with estimates of the species composition, average size and age of the trees, and the density and site quality of timber stands. In addition, of particular importance to management planning are the rate of growth of timber and the rate of loss through natural mortality, insects, disease, fire, weather, and harvesting.

Forest Growth and Yield

The volume of timber in a forest at a specific point in time is called *forest yield,* and the change in volume that occurs over an interval of time is called *forest growth.* The forests of North America and particularly those of Europe have been surveyed a number of times. Repeated surveys provide data for assessing the growth of a forest, changes in species composition, and the effectiveness of past management. Such surveys are the basis for regulating forests to provide a sustained, even flow of timber over long periods.

In order to reduce the effects of sampling errors on growth estimates, repeated surveys often rely on permanent sample plots that are carefully monumented so they can be found and remeasured at subsequent points in time, usually at intervals of five to ten years. Permanent sample plots also allow the growth of a forest to be assessed in terms of its basic components.

Components of Forest Growth   When a permanent sample plot is remeasured, several distinct components of growth can be observed. There may be new trees on the plot that were not present, or were too small to be tallied, at the previous measurement. The present volume of these new trees is called *ingrowth.* Trees that are alive and tallied at both measurements are called *survivor trees,* and the difference in the volume of these trees at the two measurements is called *survivor growth.* The volume of trees that were alive at the first measurement but died during the growth period is called *mortality* and is usually classified according to the cause of death. Finally, any trees that were harvested during the period can be identified by their stumps. The volume of harvested trees is called *cut.*

The net change in the volume of a forest is equal to ingrowth, plus survivor growth, minus mortality, minus cut. Important factors that affect the rate of forest growth include site quality, stocking, and density.

Site Quality Forest stands are commonly classified according to *site quality,* which indicates the productive capacity of a specific area of forest land for a particular species. Although many species may grow on the same site, they may not grow equally well. The site productivity measure most commonly used is *site index,* the average height of dominant and codominant trees at a specified index age, usually 50 years. The selection of an index age is based on the potential rotation age or timing of harvest for a given species. For example, an index age of 100 years is often used for the longer-lived West Coast species while an index age of 25 years is commonly used for fast-growing southern plantations.

When height and age have been measured, they are used as coordinates for determining site index from a set of curves (Figure 11.20). Site index curves and tables have been developed for most commercial species. Suppose a white pine stand has an average total height of 20 meters at an age of 70 years. Figure 11.20 shows that this point lies on site index curve 15. This means that the expected dominant tree height for this site is 15 meters at the index age of 50 years.

Site index has been found to be correlated with soil factors and topography related to tree growth. For example, when there is no forest stand, the site index can sometimes be predicted from such factors as the depth of surface soil, stone, silt and clay content, and slope steepness. However, the concept of site index is not well suited to uneven-aged stands and areas taken over by mixed species.

Stocking and Density The terms forest stocking and density are often used interchangeably, but Avery and Burkhart (2) do not consider them to be synonymous. *Stand density* is a quantitative term indicating the degree of stem crowding within a stand, and *stocking* refers to the adequacy of a given stand density to meet some management objective, for example, maximizing the production of sawtimber. Stands may be referred to as understocked, fully stocked, or overstocked.

Stand basal area is often used as a measure of stand density and stocking charts (Figure 11.21) have been prepared for different species that show

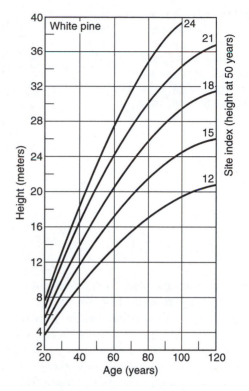

Figure 11.20 White pine site index curves. (From P. R. Laidly, "Metric site index curves for aspen, birch and conifers in the Lake States," U.S.D.A. For. Serv., Gen. Tech. Rept. NC-54, North Cent. For. Expt. Sta., St. Paul, Minn., 1979.)

acceptable ranges of basal area for stands of different average diameters. To use a stocking chart, the forester must first determine the average basal area and number of trees per acre in the stand, by using one of the forest-sampling procedures previously described. These values are used as coordinates to locate a point in the stocking chart. If this point falls between the curves labeled A and B, the stand is fully stocked. If the point falls below the B curve or above the A curve, the stand is understocked or overstocked, respectively. For example, a red pine stand with 500 trees per acre and a basal area of 200 square feet per acre would be overstocked (Figure 11.21), whereas another red

Figure 11.21 Stocking chart for managed red pine stands. (From J. W. Benzie, "Manager's handbook for red pine in the North Central States," U.S.D.A. For. Serv., Gen. Tech. Rept. NC-33, North Cent. For. Expt. Sta., St. Paul, Minn., 1977.)

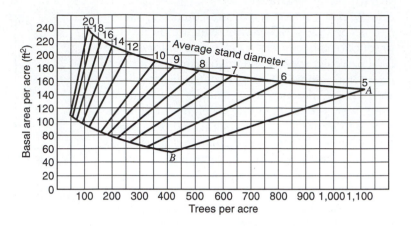

pine stand with the same basal area but only 150 trees per acre would be fully stocked.

It has been shown that height growth is not greatly affected by stand density. It has also been determined in recent years that there is not as strong a relationship as originally supposed between basal area and site quality. The main reason for the differences in volume on good sites as against poor sites is height. For many practical purposes, therefore, we can assume that basal area varies little with site quality except at the extremes.

Growth and Yield Projection Repeated surveys together with site index assessments provide a basis for projecting future stand conditions and associated yields. Growth projection models may also be used to predict stand yield for specific management practices. Table 11.6 illustrates a yield table constructed for pine stands under a particular set of management alternatives—in this instance, stand density alternatives. Notice that the model on which this table is based provides estimates of both growth and future product yields. It is important to stress that the growth and yield information for this particular forest type represents estimates based on a sample of observations from various study plots.

A variety of models have been developed to characterize growth and dynamics at the individual-tree, stand, and landscape level. *Empirical* mod-

els describe tree growth in relation to age, site index, and other easily observed variables or stand treatments such as site preparation and fertilization. These models can be used to predict yields and to determine optimal thinning and rotation ages (typically with the aid of simulation or mathematical programming techniques). Thus these models are widely used in management. In recent decades, researchers have focused on building models that attempt to quantifying growth processes. Such *process* models consider weather, site quality, the physiology of tree growth, and sometimes regeneration and disturbance in detail. These models are used by scientists to understand tree and stand response to potential climate change and increasing atmospheric CO_2, as described in Chapter 4.

Measurement of Nontimber Resources

Measurements are also made on many other resources for multiple-use management of forests. It is not possible in an introductory text to cover all the details for measurement of these resources. Brief descriptions of the rationale and the types of measurements obtained for water, wildlife habitat, recreation, and other resources are given in other chapters in this book addressing those specific

Table 11.6 Variable-Density Growth and Yield Table for Managed Stands of Natural Slash Pine[a]

Initial Basal Area (m²)	Age (years) From	Age (years) To	Site Index (m)[b] 20	25 Projected Yield (m³/ha)	30	Projected Basal Area (m²/ha)
		20	73	106	136	16
16	20	30	134	194	248	22
		40	181	262	336	25
		50	217	315	403	28
		30	102	147	189	16
	30	40	147	213	273	20
		50	184	267	341	23
	40	40	120	174	222	16
		50	156	226	289	19
		20	89	129	166	20
20	20	30	153	222	284	25
		40	200	290	371	28
		50	235	341	436	30
		30	124	180	230	20
	30	40	171	248	318	24
		50	207	301	385	26
	40	40	146	212	272	20
		50	183	265	340	23
		20	105	152	195	24
24	20	30	171	247	316	28
		40	217	315	403	31
		50	251	364	466	33
		30	146	212	271	24
	30	40	193	280	359	27
		50	229	332	425	29
	40	40	172	250	320	24
		50	209	302	387	27

Source: Adapted from equations given by F. A. Bennett, "Variable density yield tables for managed stands of natural slash pine," U.S.D.A. For. Serv., Res. Note SE-141, 1970.

[a] Cubic-meter yields and basal area as projected from various initial ages and basal areas.

[b] Base age of 50 years.

resources. Importantly, the statistical aspects of these sampling, measurement, and modeling processes are fundamentally like those used in this chapter.

With *water*, we are primarily interested in measuring quantity, quality, and timing of the water resource for particular locations. Forest character-istics affect water yield in terms of these variables. Timber harvest operations are one example of a use that could increase water yield and affect stream sediment load and temperature. There is also increasing interest in nonpoint pollution[4] and how it might be controlled by forest management practices. In

---

[4] *Nonpoint pollution* derives from a dispersed source such as agricultural activity, as compared with *point pollution*, for which a single pollution source can be identified (e.g., a factory drainspout).

this area we may be concerned with sampling and characterizing the forest resource in much the same way as we do the timber resource inventory, but with an emphasis on forest age and size class structure and associated cover, and sampling and measuring streamflow characteristics from a particular watershed. The statistical aspects of this sampling and measurement process are fundamentally like those used for the timber resource. A discussion of watersheds in forest ecosystems was given in Chapter 6 and a further discussion of watershed management is given in Chapter 16.

For measuring *wildlife* resources, management surveys usually employ census techniques to determine animal population levels directly or to develop indexes that are suggestive of relative population levels. Examples of such indexes are pellet counts or flush counts for deer and birds, respectively. There is also increasing interest in relating the forest habitat conditions, often described in large part by the timber inventory, to the population numbers and the health of the wildlife populations inhabiting or potentially inhabiting the area. The forest functions both as a food source and cover, although different features of the forest may vary in importance for either function. For wildlife, data on forest stand species and size class structure are particularly important locally. Over landscapes, forest cover type and age class distributions are fundamental habitat data. A further discussion of the interactions of the forest with wildlife is given in Chapter 14.

Management of *recreation* areas requires surveys that are primarily concerned with the numbers of users and the physical impact they have on particular sites. Thus, we may be sampling a population of users or a population of sites used by people engaged in outdoor recreation. In sampling the resource users, we frequently use questionnaires intended to get at their attitudes and likely responses to various kinds of recreation resource management. Such surveys may consider the forest as a visual resource to be experienced by the visitor. With such concepts it is possible to characterize and subsequently manage the forest environment to provide scenic forest types and opportunities that contribute to user satisfaction. A further discussion of forest recreation management is given in Chapter 17.

Urban forests are receiving much more attention, and many cities now have a forester assigned specifically to this resource. Inventories of the forest in small communities frequently take the form of a complete census of all trees. Typical information collected for each tree includes species, diameter, location (perhaps by block or lot), position (such as parkland, boulevard, or interior lot), ownership, and condition—in terms of vigor and presence of insects, diseases, and hazards. The immediate site or growing conditions are particularly important to urban tree health. For larger cities, a 5 to 10 percent systematic sample of trees or city blocks may be used. This is sometimes combined with classifications of blocks into two or three tree density classes based on aerial photos (e.g., parkland, residential, and industrial areas). Because of the diversity of species in urban areas, the field crews need considerable background in plant identification.

Given this information, the urban forest manager is in a good position to estimate future needs for tree removal and replacement and to develop annual plans for these activities. Urban forestry is further treated in Chapter 22.

Concluding Statement—Future of Measurement and Monitoring

Interest in measuring and monitoring forest resources and their use is increasing. Landowners are seeking the basic information for investments in stewardship. Governments are seeking knowledge of resources available for economic development and ways to assure resource protection. Industry seeks information about timber supply. Special interest groups ask about practices. Questions come from interests as diverse as utilization, productivity, wildlife habitat, fire protection (fuel load measurement), and outdoor recreation. Inventories and monitoring are now conducted more frequently, and long-term predictions of future forest conditions are expected. At the same time we see rapid development in technologies that provide new ways to measure the forest and to make those results readily available, such as new laser measurement tools, precise geographic positioning, satellite based remote sensing tools, and the Internet. Researchers are also gathering detailed plant and environmental data to allow for the construction and use of more sophisticated models for predicting forest conditions and use decades and even centuries ahead. The measurement of forests increasingly demands technology, quantitative skills, and integration capabilities and is likely to become even more challenging. Professionals who specialize in this area are in high demand.

References

1. B. HUSCH, C. I. MILLER, AND T. W. BEERS, *Forest Mensuration*, Third Edition, John Wiley & Sons, New York, 1982.

2. T. E. AVERY AND H. E. BURKHART, *Forest Measurements*, Third Edition, McGraw-Hill, New York, 1983.

3. B. E. SHIVER AND B. E. BORDERS, *Sampling Techniques for Forest Resource Inventory*, John Wiley & Sons, New York, 1996.

4. E. D. RAST, D. L. SONDERMAN, AND G. L. GAMMON, "A Guide to Hardwood Log Grading," U.S.D.A. For. Serv., Gen. Tech. Rept. NE-1, Upper Darby, Penn., 1973.

5. W. H. CARMEAN, J. T. HAHN, AND R. D. JACOBS. "Site Index Curves for Forest Tree Species in the Eastern United States." U.S.D.A. Forest Service Gen. Tech. Rep. NC-128, 1989.

CHAPTER 12

Remote Sensing and Geographical Information Systems for Natural Resource Management

PAUL V. BOLSTAD

Three spatial data technologies—Geographical Information Systems (GIS), Global Positioning Systems (GPS), and remote sensing—are changing how humans perceive, measure, and manage natural resources. Global positioning systems and remote sensing are aimed at answering two fundamental questions regarding natural resources: "where?" and "how much?" GIS provides a framework for organizing and analyzing this information in efficient and effective ways. These technologies are key in solving our most vexing natural resource problems, and their effectiveness has frequently been demonstrated in the preservation and recovery of endangered plants and animals, in improved planning and management of public lands, and by increased effi-

ciency and profitability of wood production on private forest lands. Spatial data technologies are found in private and public resource management agencies of all types and sizes (1–8).

Geographical information systems consist of software, hardware, and protocols for collecting, managing, analyzing, and displaying spatial data. GIS are computerized systems wherein maps and tabular data are stored in digital formats (3, 7). GIS provides the tools to enter, edit, combine, and output these digital maps in order to solve problems. GPS is a space-based system that allows users to locate positions to within a few centimeters, almost anywhere in the field with modest training and cost. Remote sensing tools provide natural resources managers with aerial photographs and satellite-based images, rapidly providing important data over large areas. GPS and remotely sensed data are useful in their own right, but their value is multiplied many times when they are combined with other data in a GIS.

The widespread adoption of GIS, GPS, and remote sensing is the result of two phenomena. First, a societal pull is driving their use, because many resource management questions require spatial analysis. For example, best forest management practices often require buffer zones around wetlands and water bodies, National Forest plans must entertain alternatives regarding where and how much land should be dedicated to competing uses, and sawmills must be located near a timber supply. Second, there is a technological push. Forest resource managers and scientists have recognized the potential for gains in efficiency and the breadth and depth of analysis through the adoption of new technologies, and many companies and government agencies have been actively developing and funding the use of GIS, GPS, and remote sensing technologies. Managers now have the tools to collect and combine disparate and previously incompatible data in novel ways to solve resource management problems.

Basic Concepts in GIS

A GIS is based on a computer-stored representation of real-world entities or phenomena (3, 6, 7). Typically, the GIS user is interested in studying or managing an area or event, for example, a wildlife refuge, forest landholdings, or the spread of invasive exotic species. These entities are represented in a GIS with cartographic objects, most often in the form of points, lines, polygons, or an array of cells. The objects are defined using a necessarily limited set of variables that are entered and maintained in a GIS. A researcher monitoring colonial nesting birds might define a bounding polygon that contains most of the colony, and count the number of breeding pairs and species. This polygon, species identifier, and count are the variables that

represent the real object (colony), and are an abstraction of the real world. Typically, a single type of object or phenomenon is represented in a data layer, with multiple layers used to represent various different types of data. Multiple data layers are often developed for an area, each layer corresponding to a different data theme (Figure 12.1). For example, forest managers may define layers representing vegetation type, soils, elevation, slope, and road location. These layers are then used singly or in combination to perform spatial analyses that aid in managing the forest.

Each data layer typically contains two distinct types of data (Figure 12.2). Geographic coordinate data are used to identify the location, size, and shapes of objects. Objects in a data layer are typically represented as points, lines, or areas. Points are objects which are considered to have no dimension (e.g., wells or feeding stations) while lines are used to represent objects conceived as one dimensional, for example, roads or streams, and areas are used to represent two-dimensional objects, such as forest stands or counties. Attribute data that correspond to the geographic coordinate

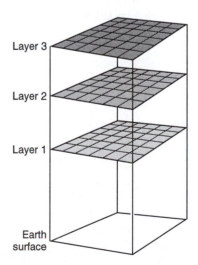

Figure 12.1 Data layers in a GIS. Different themes—for example, roads, vegetation, or political boundaries—are stored in separate, spatially-referenced data layers.

Figure 12.2 Data in a GIS are often organized into linked geographic and tabular components.

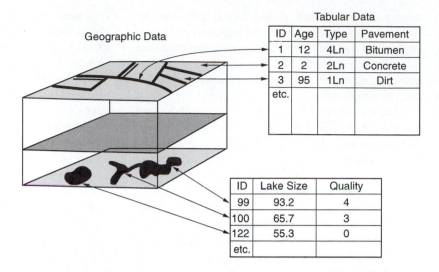

Geographic Data

Tabular Data

ID	Age	Type	Pavement
1	12	4Ln	Bitumen
2	2	2Ln	Concrete
3	95	1Ln	Dirt
etc.			

ID	Lake Size	Quality
99	93.2	4
100	65.7	3
122	55.3	0
etc.		

data are maintained—for example, the well depth and age, road name and surface type, or forest vegetation type or age. Attribute data are usually stored as tables in a relational database.

There are two common methods of structuring geographic data (Figure 12.3). When a raster data structure is used, a grid, similar to a checkerboard, is defined. Each grid cell has fixed, uniform dimensions, which correspond to the resolution of the data layer. Codes are assigned to each grid cell corresponding to the objects represented. Point objects are typically represented by a single grid cell, line features represented by a sequence of touching grid cells, and area features by a group of adjacent grid cells.

An alternative, "vector" data structure, may be used for geographic data. Features are represented by strings of coordinates. A point is represented as a single X–Y coordinate pair, a line object represented by a set of X–Y coordinate pairs, and an area represented by a closed line or set of lines. Identifiers are assigned to each point, line, or area, and linked to data in the attribute tables.

Earth coordinates are used to tie spatial data to earth locations. Latitude and longitude may be used to uniquely define locations on the surface of the

Figure 12.3 Raster and vector representations of point, line, and area features.

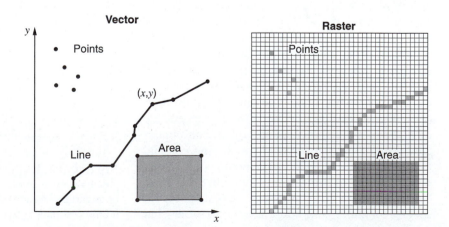

earth. However, the latitude/longitude values are unsuitable for many uses, particularly for producing planar maps. Therefore, map projections are used to convert from curved geographic coordinates to right-angle Cartesian coordinate systems. These map projections are typically defined by mathematical formulas that "project" points on the curved earth surface to points on a flat or "developable" surface. For example, a *Mercator* is a common projection type wherein points from the surface of the earth are projected onto a cylinder encompassing the earth (Figure 12.4). This surface is then "developed," in that the mathematical equivalent of cutting and unrolling the cylinder produces a flat map. Cones and planes are also common projection surfaces. Each projection introduces distortion by stretching or compressing the curved geographic coordinates on the flat map; however, this distortion can be controlled by choosing the proper map projection, and by limiting the size of the area

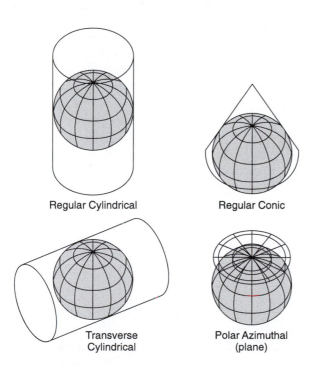

Figure 12.4 Map projection surfaces.

mapped. For example the *State-Plane coordinate system* is a standard set of projections defined for each state or portions of states. As it is used for many county-level and property line recording projects, the State-Plane coordinate system is used in GISs maintained by many county governments and other civil authorities. The State-Plane system of map projections is defined such that distance measurements using the projected coordinates do not differ from measurements on the curved earth's surface by more than one part in 10,000, or about 2 feet in a mile.

Data Entry—Digitizing

Digitizing is the process of converting data from paper maps or images into a digital data layer. Published maps contain substantial information; however, this information must be converted to digital formats to be used in a GIS. There are several methods to perform this conversion.

Manual digitizing is among the most common techniques because the equipment is relatively inexpensive and easy to learn and use. Manual digitizing requires a coordinate digitizer, typically a flat table with an attached stylus or puck. A map is fixed to the table, and the operator guides a pointer over the feature to be digitized, indicating when to collect coordinates. The coordinate information is stored in the computer, and digitizing and editing tools included in most GIS programs are used to convert these digitized data into a digital data layer. While the equipment can be quite accurate, measuring position to within 0.001 inches, it may also be quite slow and laborious, particularly when recording data from detailed maps.

"Heads-up" digitizing is a variant of manual digitizing. Satellite data or scanned aerial photographs or maps are digital images that may be displayed on a computer screen. Point, line, and area features are identified and their locations recorded by guiding a cursor on the screen. This method has become quite common in recent years, as more image data are provided in digital formats.

Automated scanning is another common digitizing method. While the equipment is typically more expensive than manual digitizers of similar accuracy, it is also much faster, and requires less human input. Maps are placed on a bed or drum of a scanning device, and transmitted or reflected light is used to record the locations of map features. All features on the maps are recorded, including legends, names, and any other annotation or symbols. These unwanted features must be removed, a process which is often aided by specialized software.

Once data are digitized, they must be edited, error-checked, and have attributes added. All digitizing methods may result in errors, caused by operator or equipment imprecision, errors in the source materials, or blunders. Location, consistency, and correctness must be checked, and attribute data entered into the tabular database and referenced to the specific geographic objects.

Global Positioning System

Global positioning system (GPS) technology is another method by which data may be entered into a GIS. GPS provides rapid, accurate positional measurements and has many uses beyond GIS data entry, including mapping, vehicle guidance, pathfinding, automatic aircraft take-off and landing, and precise scientific measurements. This inexpensive technology requires minimal training, and will be used in most future efforts when field data are collected for a GIS.

GPS is a satellite-based system operated by the United States Department of Defense. It was designed for military navigation and positioning, but civilian uses quickly emerged. The system is based on twenty-one satellites orbiting the globe, each satellite transmitting encoded signals. A field receiver measures signals from at least three satellites to determine positions on the surface of the earth. Since there are typically from six to ten satellites above the horizon at any give time, GPS can be used anywhere except under extreme terrain conditions—for example, in deep canyons.

The satellites transmit two types of signals that are commonly used by civilian receivers. One signal, called the *C/A code*, allows positions to be located to within one to a few meters. C/A code receivers are often used for field digitizing, collecting the feature locations to be entered into a GIS data layer. C/A code receivers typically operate well under closed forest canopy, take the required measurements in minutes, and are small, lightweight, and relatively inexpensive. The satellites also transmit a second, *carrier phase signal* that allows more precise position determination, down to sub-centimeter accuracies. However, because carrier-phase receivers often perform poorly under forest canopies, require longer time periods for the most accurate measurements, and are more expensive, heavier and larger, carrier-phase receivers are used primarily where higher accuracies are required, such as in property or geodetic surveys.

GPS is based on combined range measurements (Figure 12.5). A range is a distance from the receiver to the satellite. The code transmitted by the satellite contains timing and satellite position information. The receiver decodes this information to establish the satellite location and the distance to the satellite. Measurement from one satellite places the receiver somewhere on a sphere, a fixed distance away from the satellite. Measurements from two satellites constrain the location to a circle where the two spheres intersect, and measurements from

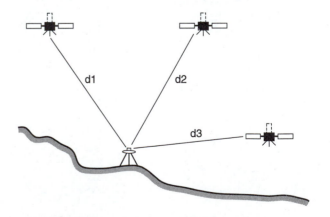

Figure 12.5 Satellite range measurements, d1 through d3, are the basis of GPS position determination.

three satellites constrain the location to two points, one of which can be discarded after a few measurements. Measurements from a fourth satellite are usually used to reduce systematic error, and additional satellites may be used to improve the position measurement. Multiple position fixes are often taken for several minutes, and averaged.

Several sources of error affect GPS measurements and lead to positional uncertainties (Figure 12.6), and the high accuracies mentioned earlier are obtained only after these errors have been removed. System delays, clock errors in range measurements, uncertainty in the satellite location, and ionospheric and atmospheric delays also add uncertainty. These errors are reduced via differential positioning, where two receivers collect data simultaneously. One receiver, a base station, occupies an accurately surveyed point. The difference between the GPS estimate and the known location at the base station can be calculated, and this dif-

ference applied to correct data collected by the roving field receiver to correct the errors. The errors are similar when the roving and base station receivers are using the same satellites, and are within a few hundred kilometers so that atmospheric and ionospheric errors are similar. A radio can be used to transmit the differential corrections from the base station receiver to the roving receiver, and accurate positions may be obtained in the field. If a radio link is infeasible, then the data may be downloaded to a computer and post-processed.

Spatial Analysis

Much of the utility of geographic information systems comes from the rich array of spatial-analytical tools they provide. These tools are applied to spatial data layers to provide information and to help solve resource management problems. The

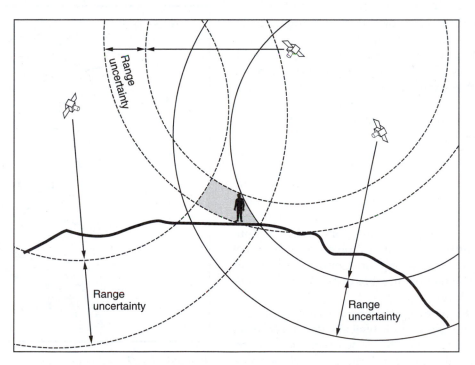

Figure 12.6 GPS signal triangulation and uncertainty caused by range error.

tools may be viewed as functions that are applied to one or more data layers. Tools typically produce summary numbers, tables, or new data layers.

Database Operations

Attribute data in a GIS are usually stored in a database; database functions are often applied to the tabular data associated with a data layer. Each row in a database may contain several variables, and these variables are used to describe each object represented in the data layer. For example, forest stands may be represented by polygons in a forest vegetation data layer. Each polygon is associated with a row in the database that contains information describing the forest stand; for example, tree species, age, average diameter, average tree height, health status, or stand area. Database operations may be applied; for example, selecting all stands over 40 years old.

Sorting, searching, and selecting are among the most common database functions. Database records are selected based on attributes and their values. Compound searches (or queries) are common, for example, selecting all aspen stands that are also greater then 80 acres in size and over 40 years old. Arithmetic or statistical functions are also commonly applied; for example, stand volume may be calculated by multiplying the average diameter, height, and area information contained in the database.

Geographic Operations

Geographic operations provide much of the unique utility found in GIS. These operations use the geometric information in a data layer or layers, and generate additional layers, tables, or summary numbers. These geographic operations may be unary, involving only one input data layer, or they may be binary or higher order, involving multiple data layers.

There are many unary geographic operators. For example, a slope layer is typically derived from an elevation data layer. The slope operation typically uses raster data input, and calculates a slope value for each output grid cell. Slope at each cell is deter-

mined from a measure of the change in elevation divided by a change in horizontal position in the neighborhood of each grid cell.

Buffering is one of the most common geographic operations. A buffer layer identifies boundaries at set distances from features in a layer (Figure 12.7). Buffers distances may be defined for point, line, or area features in a data layer. For example, timber harvesting Best Management Practices (BMPs) often exclude activities around streams or wetlands. A buffer operation in a GIS may be used to map these exclusion zones.

Cartographic overlay is another common operation. In an overlay, the geometric and tabular data are combined, and new points, lines, or regions defined that contain geometry and attributes from both source data layers (Figure 12.8). Raster overlay involves comparisons, recoding, and sometimes calculations based on grid cell values. Vector overlay of line or area features involves the intersection

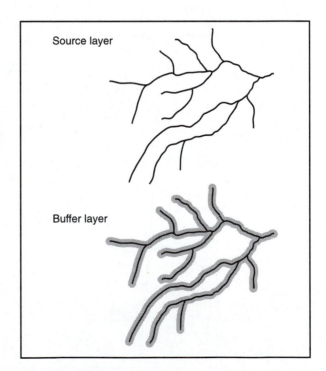

Figure 12.7   A buffer layer derived from a line data layer.

Global Vegetation

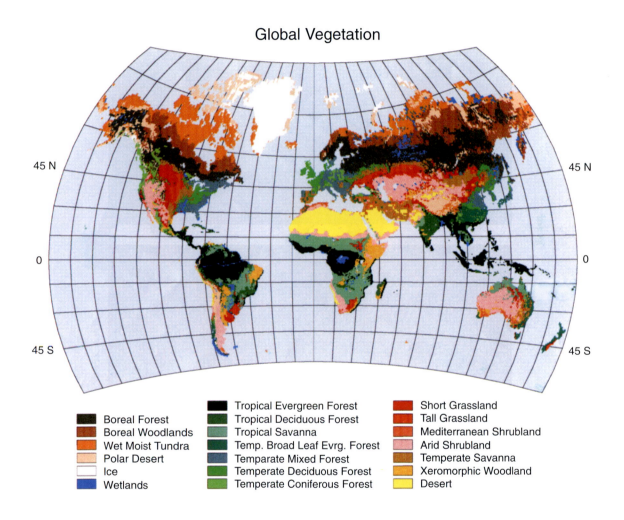

Boreal Forest	**Tropical Evergreen Forest**	**Short Grassland**
Boreal Woodlands	**Tropical Deciduous Forest**	**Tall Grassland**
Wet Moist Tundra	**Tropical Savanna**	**Mediterranean Shrubland**
Polar Desert	**Temp. Broad Leaf Evrg. Forest**	**Arid Shrubland**
Ice	**Temparate Mixed Forest**	**Temperate Savanna**
Wetlands	**Temperate Deciduous Forest**	**Xeromorphic Woodland**
	Temperate Coniferous Forest	**Desert**

Figure 3.3 Global vegetation map showing the distribution of the forest types discussed in this book. From Landsberg and Gower (4), with acknowledgements to D. Kicklighter and J. Melillo, who provided the original version of the map.

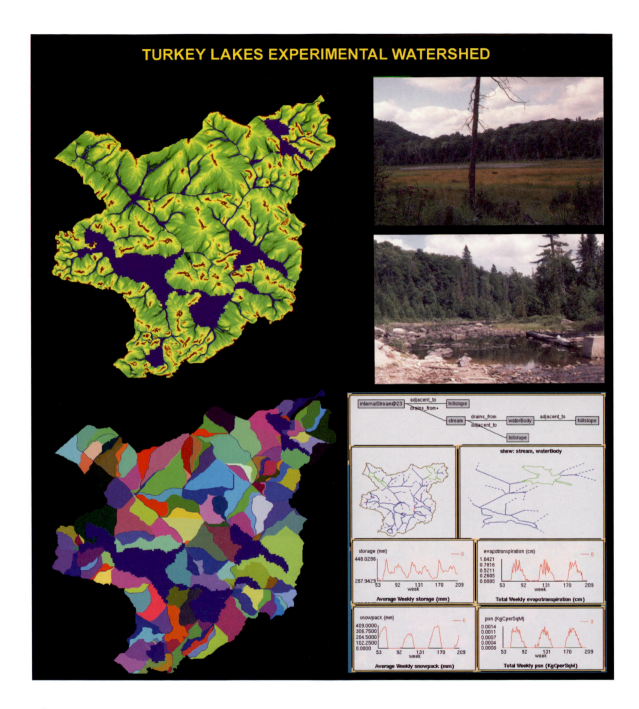

Figure 16.14 Automated tools are becoming standard methods for preparing inputs to hydrologic models. This plate illustrates some of the products (flow path analysis, segmentation of watersheds into hill-slope partitions), as well as modeling tools for making predictions.

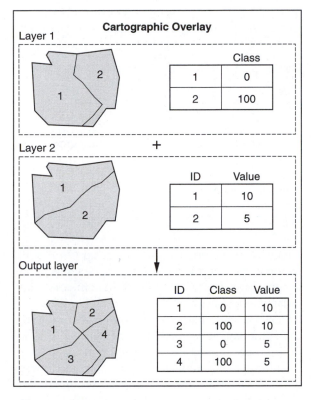

Figure 12.8 Vector data overlay.

lines and the creation of new polygons. Overlays allow the combination of features from different themes and often provide information key to the solution of many natural resource measurement or management problems. For example, land suitability is often defined by criteria based on soils (will support buildings), topography (flat), and current zoning (residential, commercial, etc.). Layers representing these three themes may be overlain in a GIS, and areas that satisfy all three criteria identified.

Geographic operations are often combined in a sequence to construct a cartographic model (Figure 12.9). A cartographic model is designed to answer a specific question, and often results in a data layer providing the answer. Operations are performed in sequence, incorporating single and multiple data layers. Intermediate data layers are generated, and combined or used with additional operations, eventually determining the needed information.

There are many additional, specialized GIS operators designed to address specific geographic problems. *Network analyses, three-dimensional GIS,* and *geostatistics* may used to optimize analyses for specific problems, and are not discussed here because of lack of space. These and many other spatial

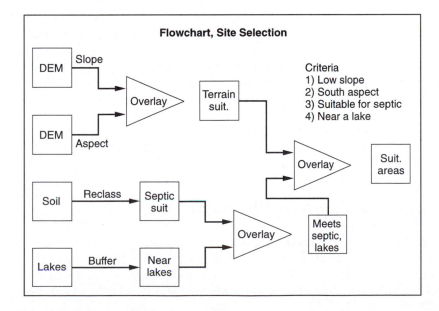

Figure 12.9 Flowchart representation of a cartographic model. Triangles and lines are operations, and squares indicate data layers (DEM = digital elevation model).

analyses are more thoroughly discussed in the references listed at the end of this chapter.

Remote Sensing

Remote sensing is the measurement of characteristics from a distance (5, 6). Practically defined for forest science applications, remote sensing is the use of airborne cameras, scanners, and satellite imaging devices to gather information about forest resources. Aerial photographs have been used in forest resource management since the 1930s, are well developed, and widely applied. The use of satellite and airborne scanner imagery in forestry is more recent, having begun in 1972. Imaging systems overcome some of the limitations in aerial photographs; however, they also introduce some limitations of their own, and so are unlikely to replace film, at least for the next few decades. Whatever the medium, remotely sensed imagery are unique and valuable data sources that are employed worldwide.

Radiant Energy and Spectral Reflectance Patterns

All remote sensing is based on the detection of electromagnetic energy. Electromagnetic energy is defined by wavelengths, and may be conveniently categorized into spectral regions (Table 12.1). A single wavelength is the distance between successive peaks in the electromagnetic energy wave. Different wavelengths have different energy intensities and are sensed as different colors. Humans sense light in the visible region (from 400 to 700 nanometers), with blue colors resulting from energy at the shorter wavelengths (400 to 500 nanometers), green in the middle (500 to 600 nanometers), and red at the longest wavelengths (700 to 900 nanometers). Intermediate colors are observed by combinations of these three wavelengths at varying intensity. Remote sensing systems may coincide with this range (true color and standard black-and-white photographs), or they may sense energy beyond the range of human vision. Infrared photographs sense

Table 12.1 Wavelength Regions of the Electromagnetic Spectrum that Are Used in or Affect Remote Sensing

Region	Wavelength (μm)
Ultraviolet	< 0.4
Visible—Blue	0.4–0.5
Visible—Green	0.5–0.6
Visible—Red	0.6–0.7
Near-Infrared	0.7–1.4
Mid-Infrared	1.4–2.9
Thermal Infrared	2.9–100
Radar–Microwave	1,000–1,000,000

energy in wavelengths just above red (700 to 900 nanometers), thermal imaging systems sense longer wavelengths (3,000 to 14,000 nanometers), and radar the longest wavelengths (1 millimeter to 1 meter). Different information may be obtained from each different wavelength, so several spectral bands of remotely sensed imagery are often used.

Differences in reflected electromagnetic energy forms the basis for remote sensing. Sunlight falling on the forest is either reflected or absorbed. Leaves absorb much of the red and blue radiation, and reflect relatively more green light, and so appear green to the human eye and on true color film. Clean, deep water absorbs most of the light in the visible wavelength regions, and so appears dark, or perhaps slightly blue. Concrete reflects strongly throughout the visible region, and so appears light gray or white. Each of these materials have different spectral reflectance patterns across the electromagnetic spectrum (Figure 12.10), and these different patterns lead to different colors, allowing a photointerpreter to distinguish between different surface features.

Aerial Photography

Cameras and Films A number of different camera types are currently available. Small format cameras, with nominal film dimensions of 35 mm or 70 mm, are routinely used by private and public

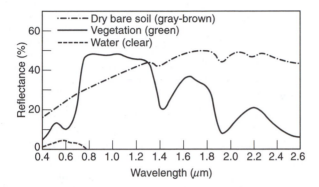

Figure 12.10 Typical spectral-reflectance curves for vegetation, soil, and water. From Lillesand and Kiefer (6), adapted from Swain and Davis (9).

types, thus infrared films are desirable when the photographs are to be used primarily for vegetation mapping. True color photographs are sensitive to the same wavelengths as the human eye, with blue, green, and red dye layers used in the film to reproduce the full range of visible colors. Color infrared films are sensitive to approximately 500 to 1100 nanometers. These films also have three dye layers; however, the blue layer is sensitive to green light, the green dye layer is sensitive to red light, and the red dye layer is sensitive to infrared light. Because vegetation reflects infrared light much more strongly than visible light, color infrared photographs are typically red in areas of dense vegetation.

organizations over much of North America. Film and cameras systems are relatively inexpensive, easy to operate, and familiar to many users. However, these film types generally cover relatively small areas with each frame, and the camera systems typically are not designed specifically for precise mapping, so geometric distortions are often unacceptably high for mapping applications. Nine-inch mapping cameras, with film sizes approximately 230 mm on a side, cover 10 to 40 times the area of the smaller formats. Furthermore, these cameras are designed specifically for mapping projects, with camera and lens components optimized to reduce geometric distortion. These cameras also come with sophisticated control and mounting systems that enable them to take photographs in rapid succession, and films are available which capture extremely fine detail. However, these cameras are quite expensive relative to smaller formats, and are most often chosen when accurate mapping over large areas is required.

Four types of photographic films are commonly used. Black-and-white panchromatic film is sensitive to the visible portion of the electromagnetic spectrum, approximately the same as human vision, from 400 to 700 nanometers. Black-and-white infrared film is sensitive to green through infrared radiation, approximately 500 to 1100 nanometers. There are large differences in the infrared reflectance characteristics among many vegetation

Photo Coverage, Scale, and Geometry

The scale of an aerial photograph is the relationship between a distance on the photograph and a corresponding distance on the ground. For example, the distance between two road intersections might be one inch on the photograph and 2000 feet on the ground. The scale is then one inch to 2000 feet. Scale is also commonly expressed as a unitless number. In our example above, the roads are 24,000 inches apart on the ground (2000 ft × 12 in/ft), so the scale might also be expressed as 1:24,000. Scale depends on the lens focal length and flying height. Mapping cameras with a 230 mm film size typically use a lens with a focal length near 150 mm, so scale is most commonly adjusted via aircraft flying height. Scale is inversely proportional to flying height, because scale is determined by the ratio of the focal length to flying height above terrain:

Photo scale = focal length/height above terrain

Photographs taken with a six-inch (150 mm) lens from a flying height of 7,920 feet will have a scale of:

Photo scale = 6 in × 1 ft/12 in/7920 = 1/15,840

This photo scale is commonly used in resource mapping, with four inches equal to one mile.

Scale is rarely constant within a photograph, because although planes may fly at a nearly constant height, the elevation of the earth surface varies below the aircraft. Variation in terrain height within an image leads to variation in scale, and differences can be substantial. Scale often varies by 5 percent or more for photos taken in mountainous areas of North America, because height above terrain may vary by that much within the image.

Photograph scale may also be affected by camera tilt. If the film plane is not parallel with the earth surface when the photograph is taken, there will be some perspective distortion in the photograph (Figure 12.11). This distortion also causes differences in photo scale, and the distortion varies by tilt direction and amount. Mapping contracts typically specify vertical photographs, meaning tilt must be less than three degrees from vertical. Because of variation in scale caused by terrain and tilt, the reported scale for a photograph should be considered an average.

Photographic coverage is related to scale and film format. The edge dimensions of the ground area covered by a photograph are approximately equal to the scale times the edge dimensions of the film. Thus, a 9-inch photograph at a scale of 1:20,000 has an edge dimension of approximately:

$$\text{Dimension} = 9 \text{ in} \times 1 \text{ ft/12 in} \times 20,000 \text{ in/in}$$

$$= 15,000 \text{ ft}$$

Increasing the flying height, and hence decreasing scale, increases the area covered in each photo. However, objects also appear smaller, and at some point it becomes difficult to identify features on the photographs. Choosing the proper photographic scale involves tradeoffs between resolution and area coverage.

The degree of overlap among adjacent photographs is another factor which may affect the number of photographs required to cover a given study area. Photographs are typically taken in parallel flight lines (Figure 12.12). Sidelap is the overlap between adjacent flight lines, and is typically 5 to 15 percent. The endlap specifies how much successive photographs overlap. Endlap is typically 15 to 65 percent of the photo dimension. Higher endlap is specified when stereoviews are required. In a stereoview, the right eye views a photograph, and the left eye views the next photograph on the flightline. If the photographs are properly oriented, a three-dimensional reconstruction of the imaged surface can be perceived. This view is based on *image parallax*, the relative horizontal shift in points based on their differences in elevation. These parallax

Figure 12.11 Geometric distortion caused by photo tilt.

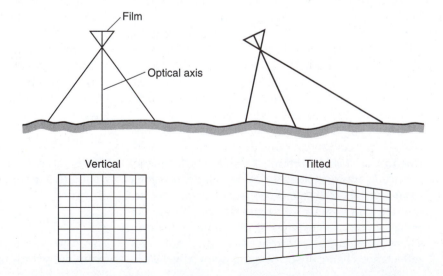

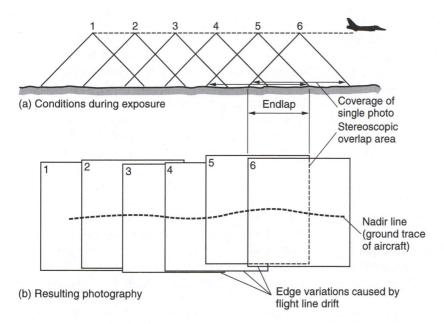

(a) Conditions during exposure

Endlap

Coverage of
single photo

Stereoscopic
overlap area

1 2 3 4 5 6

Nadir line
(ground trace
of aircraft)

(b) Resulting photography

Edge variations caused by
flight line drift

Figure 12.12
Photographic coverage along a
flight strip. From Lillesand and
Kiefer (6).

shifts result in mountains appearing higher and val-leys lower in a stereoview. Slope, terrain shape, and relative heights may be perceived in a stereoview.

The preceding discussion underscores that photographs are not maps. Most photographs, even those from the most precise mapping cameras, con-tain geometric distortion in the relative positions of features, often caused primarily by tilt and ter-rain distortion. These geometric distortions must be removed prior to the use of photographs in pre-cise mapping, before making distance or area meas-urements from photographs, or before entering them in a GIS. The level of geometric error depends on many factors, including the camera system, film format, photo scale, tilt, and terrain variation. In some instances, experience indicates uncorrected photographs will provide measurements within acceptable accuracy limits. The Natural Resource Conservation Service (formerly the U.S. Soil Con-servation Service) historically measured field areas on uncorrected 35 mm aerial photographs because they were flown at large scales, and experience indi-cated acceptable accuracies could be achieved. Many forestry organizations have mapped timber stands on uncorrected vertical 9-inch photographs.

These methods were chosen because practical experience indicated the data derived were of acceptable quality, given cost/accuracy trade-offs. However, geometric accuracy assessments and cost/accuracy comparisons should be conducted on a routine basis, particularly when data derived from the photographs will be entered into a GIS.

Photogrammetry and Photo Measurements

The science of *photogrammetry* is dedicated to pre-cise mapping and measurements from photographs (1, 2, 8). Photogrammetric engineers have devel-oped robust, well-known, reliable methods of removing photographic distortion. Until the early 1980s, most photogrammetric work was conducted on analog instruments such as a *stereoplotter* (a device based on lenses, projection, and moveable stages) to extract information from photographs and transfer the information to maps. Stereopairs of pho-tographs are viewed together, and by recreating the relative orientation of the photographs at the time of exposure, and viewing the photographs through stereographic optical systems, a three-dimensional view of the mapping area may be created. Information may then be projected to a planar base for mapping.

Since the 1980s, there has been a rapid growth in digital photogrammetry, in which the photographs are passed through a scanner and converted to a digital image. Various methods have been devised to view digital stereopairs, and photogrammetric techniques adapted to remove tilt, terrain, and other distortions from the digital images. The resulting digital photograph, called a *digital orthophotograph* (DOQ), has positive attributes of both maps and photographs. A DOQ is similar to a map because it has a uniform scale and can serve as a base for area or distance measurements, yet the DOQ also contains the detailed information visible in photographs. DOQs are easily integrated with other spatial data in a GIS, and photo interpretation may be done on-screen. DOQs are so useful that a national program has been established with the goal of making them available for the entire United States.

There are other photographic measurements in addition to area and distance. *Photomensuration* is a set of techniques to estimate tree size and wood volume. Tree heights may be measured on the photograph because trees not directly below the camera (at the nadir point) appear to lean outward away from the nadir. Measuring this form of parallax, from the base to the top of the tree, allows an estimate of tree height. Crown diameters may also be measured, and relationships between crown diameters and stem diameters may be used to estimate diameter and, hence, stem volume. Tree density may also be measured, allowing estimates of total stand volume. Relationships between photographic measurements and measured tree and stand volumes have been summarized in photo stand volume tables, where stand area, species, crown closure, tree height, and crown diameter are used to estimate stand wood volume.

Photointerpretation

Photointerpretation involves converting the variation in color and tone evident on aerial photographs into information about the location and characteristics of important resources. Forest photointerpretation is most often performed to produce a *vegetation type map*. The boundaries of homogeneous vegetation units are defined based on cues in the photograph. Color, brightness, texture or pattern, size, shape, topographic position, and proximity to other features are all used to define the boundaries between different vegetation types. Different cues may be most important for different vegetation types, and there is an art to photointerpretation gained through experience. Characteristics may change with the season, as when leaf colors for deciduous tree species change from summer to fall.

Photo characteristics for a vegetation type may vary within a single photograph. For example, colors are often brighter in the direction of the sun and darker in the direction away from the sun. In a similar fashion, colors are often lighter on slopes facing the sun than on slopes facing away. Colors may darken or change tone near the edge of the photo as a function of the camera/film/filter system. All of this variation must be integrated if the photointerpreter is to produce an accurate map.

Vegetation Types

Forest managers and scientists are often interested in mapping forest types by species, and sometimes age classes (Table 12.2) (1, 2). Classifications are sometimes hierarchical, from less detailed to more detailed classes, and in some cases it is difficult or impossible to accurately separate certain species or species groups. For example, sugar maple (*Acer saccharum*) and black maple (*Acer nigrum*) are indistinguishable from aerial photographs, and so are often grouped (on photointerpreted maps).

Figure 12.13 is a black-and-white stereopair that illustrates some of the principles of species identification using aerial photographs. A pure stand of black spruce (outlined areas) is shown, surrounded by aspen. Black spruce is a needle-leaved evergreen tree species with a slender, conical crown. Pure stands normally exhibit a regular pattern, with uniform or gently changing tree heights. Closed-canopy black spruce stands typically show a smooth, car-

Table 12.2 A portion of a forest classification system for Lakes States forests. Categories become more specific from left to right. Categories are also hierarchical, in that finer categories collapse into common coarser categories.

		Aspen < 10 years old
	Upland Deciduous Forest	Aspen ≥ 10 years old
		Red Oak
Deciduous Forest		Sugar Maple
	Lowland Deciduous Forest	Ash–Elm
		Alder
		Red Pine
	Upland Coniferous	White Pine
Coniferous Forest		Jack Pine
	Lowland Coniferous	Black Spruce

pet-like texture. Aspen is a deciduous broad-leaved species with rounded, widely-spaced crowns, and often a rougher texture. This difference in texture between aspen and black spruce is illustrated clearly in Figure 12.13.

Color infrared photographs usually allow for the finest discrimination among vegetation types, because of strong differences in the infrared reflectance properties among species. Scales between 1:10,000 and 1:20,000 are usually chosen for stand mapping, as these scales strike a balance between covering large areas with each photo, yet still allowing adequate discrimination among vegetation types. Summer photographs are often acquired. However, fall photographs are superior when distinguishing among deciduous forest types in eastern North America, and winter photographs

are better for discriminating among certain types (e.g., among needle-leaved and broad-leaved tree species). For the utmost in accuracy and discriminating ability, photos of the same area but from multiple seasons are recommended.

Regeneration, Health, and Damage Assessment

Aerial photographs are also extensively used for regeneration surveys, for forest health monitoring, and to assess disease, insect, and storm or fire damage. Photographs for regeneration surveys are typically very large scale, from 1:1,500 or larger, and often use small-format cameras because geometric accuracy is not of utmost importance. The costs of using these systems is considerably lower

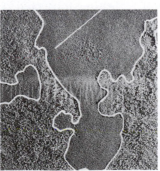

Figure 12.13 Black spruce (outlined area) surrounded by aspen in Ontario, Canada. Scale 1:15,840. Stereogram. From Zsilinszky (10), courtesy of Victor G. Zsilinszky, Ontario Centre for Remote Sensing.

than alternative mapping cameras, and large area coverage in a single photo is typically not required. Living trees on a line or in a fixed area are counted, and a proportion surviving is measured. These data help determine if regeneration was successful, or if additional treatments or plantings are needed.

Aerial photographs are also used extensively for insect pest and disease damage assessment. Most pests visibly alter the forest canopy, either by reducing vigor and changing leaf color, or by direct defoliation. These changes may be observed directly on aerial photographs. Many defoliaters are routinely monitored using aerial photographs. For example, the Gypsy moth (*Lymantria dispar*) is a serious pest in eastern deciduous forests of North America. A number of control strategies have been applied to slow the spread and reduce the severity of defoliation by this introduced pest, and aerial photographs are used in detection, the tactical planning of treatments, and assessment of effectiveness. Aerial photographs are also used for managing other species, including mountain pine beetle (*Dendroctonus ponderosae*), spruce budworm (*Choristaneura fumiferana*), the Douglas fir tussock moth (*Orgyia psueudotsugata*), and the balsam wooly adelgid (*Adelges piceae*). Management and control of insects are discussed in detail in Chapter 8.

Aerial photographs are also quite useful in assessing wind, ice, or fire damage. Wind damage can severely affect large areas, and access is often difficult because of treefall across roads. Aerial photographs, particularly three-dimensional views on stereopairs, allow accurate identification of windfall gaps and canopy openings. Aerial photographs have also proven useful in assessing the extent and severity of fire damage (also see Chapter 18, Behavior and Management of Forest Fires).

There are many other uses of aerial photographs in forest resource management, including harvest planning, property line surveys, timber and land appraisal, road design and layout, erosion evaluation, estimating wildlife populations, and recreation planning. Aerial photography is a mature technology, and will remain a valuable tool for resource managers and scientists into the foreseeable future.

Filmless Imaging

The last two decades have seen the rapid development of imaging systems that do not depend on film. One of the most amazing achievements of modern remote sensing is the engineering of imaging scanners that collect millions of observations in a few seconds, reconstructed to form geometrically accurate images. These sensors can detect wavelengths well beyond the capabilities of the human eye or film, and in wavelength ranges, or bands, specifically chosen to provide the most information. Data are digitally quantized on collection, so the images are easily transferred to computers for subsequent digital image processing. Ever-finer spatial resolutions and narrow spectral resolutions have led some to predict that these systems will eventually replace aerial photography.

Principles of Imaging Scanners

Imaging devices typically use electronic detectors to measure reflected or emitted electromagnetic radiation. Detectors are typically made from semiconductor materials when designed for the visible through thermal portions of the spectrum, while microwave and longer radiation are detected with metal antenna. Visible and thermal detectors typically change resistance or generate a voltage with the amount of electromagnetic energy striking them. The relative intensity of this energy may then be used to calculate incident energy and identify the features observed. Detectors may be designed to sense energy in a number of arbitrarily narrow wavelength bands by changing the mix of semiconducting materials, so that sensors may be designed to observed specific reflectance properties; for example, differences among vegetation types in the mid-infrared region.

Most nonradar imaging systems are passive, in that they sense reflected or emitted energy that originates from an external source. Much like film-based systems, many passive systems detect reflected sunlight or emitted long-wave radiation. Active systems, such as imaging radar, differ in that they emit energy, and then detect the reflection of that energy.

Three different designs are most commonly found in passive imaging scanners. Many older designs are based on a small number of detectors for each wave band, and a moving mirror that focuses energy on the detectors. The mirror typically scans lines perpendicular to the flight path, and forward motion of the satellite or aircraft advances the scanner over the next line. Linear arrays operate in much the same manner as moving mirror systems, except the detectors are forged in long rows, and each cell in the image (picture elements, or "pixels") is sampled at once. These systems sometimes employ prisms or mirrors to split the signal among various banks of detectors for different wavelengths. The final design type extends this progression from zero dimensions (single pixel) through one dimension (row) into two dimensions. Square arrays of detectors may be fabricated, usually on a single chip, called a *charge-coupled device* (CCD). The CCD samples an entire image at once, although several CCDs may be in one scanner, either precisely aligned to increase the sampling area, or each sampling the same area but sensitive to different wavebands to yield a multispectral image.

Radar systems (RAdio Detection And Ranging) transmit and receive radio waves from an antenna. A beam is directed at a surface, and the microwave reflectance properties and orientation of the surface govern the strength of the return. As with passive scanners, the returns can be organized in their relative positions to produce an image. Radar system characteristics are quite different from contemporary passive systems. Unlike passive systems for shorter wavelengths, radar data can be collected at night because these systems provide the energy they sense. Radar wavelengths penetrate clouds, a major advantage in many parts of the world. Because surface response to radar wavebands is often unrelated to reflectance properties at shorter

wavelengths, radar systems often provide complementary information.

Remote Sensing Systems

Landsat

The launch of the satellite Landsat-1 in July of 1972 inaugurated the civilian era of satellite-based, earth–surface remote sensing. The primary sensor of Landsat satellites 1 through 3 was the *multispectral scanner* (MSS), with an 80-meter pixel resolution and a 185-kilometer square image area. The satellites had a repeat cycle of 18 days. The scanner recorded four bands, one each in the blue, green, red, and infrared portions of the electromagnetic spectrum, so both visible and color infrared images could be produced. Landsat satellites 4 and 5 retained the MSS and added a second imaging scanner, the thematic mapper (TM). The TM incorporated many improvements based on experiences gained in analyses of MSS imagery. Among these, band widths were modified somewhat, two mid-infrared bands were included, the pixel size was reduced to 30 m, a thermal infrared band was added and a 16-day return interval was implemented.

While the MSS program was successful and pointed the way to future improvements, TM firmly established the utility of land satellite remote sensing for a diverse array of users. Public and private sector applications have been developed in agricultural and forest management, disaster assessment, oil and mineral exploration, population estimation, wildlife management, urban and regional planning, and many other fields. MSS data had two advantages relative to color infrared photos. The first was a uniformly calibrated digital image, providing data inherently amenable to digital image processing. Some analysis and interpretation could be aided or performed by computers, in part automating image interpretation. Second, the data were inexpensive relative to photographs when large areas were analyzed. Disadvantages were a coarse spatial resolution (80 m versus sub-meter for most photo scales used), and infrequent repeat times. TM provided the same digital format, and included visible, near-infrared, thermal, and new mid-infrared bands that significantly improved the utility of the data for discrimination among vegetation types. The pixel size in TM was improved to 30 m, an improvement over MSS but still much coarser than the effective resolution of most aerial photographs. TM data have been successfully applied in many disciplines, including forest type mapping, inventories, and damage assessment.

SPOT

France has led a consortium of European countries in the development and launch of four earth resource satellites known by the acronym SPOT (Systeme Pour l'Observation de la Terre). The SPOT-1 through SPOT-3 satellites carried similar instrument packages. The main imaging system, known as the HRV, employed a linear array, CCD design, a first for civilian satellite remote sensing systems. The HRV operates in two modes, a single band panchromatic mode, with 10 m resolution and 510 to 730 nanometer spectral range, and a three-band, 20 m resolution, multispectral mode, with green, red, and near infrared bands (Figure 12.14). The HRV is pointable off track, in effect reducing return times to every few days, rather than more than every two weeks as with TM and MSS. Pointable optics also allow the collection of satellite stereopairs, and thus raster elevation data may be collected. The imaged area for a single HRV scene is approximately 60 km on a side, so although the image is significantly higher resolution than typical aerial photographs, it is approximately one-tenth the area of TM and MSS imagery.

Figure 12.14 Example SPOT HRV image, Popocatepetl Volcano, Mexico. (Copyright SPOT Image, 2000, used with permission.)

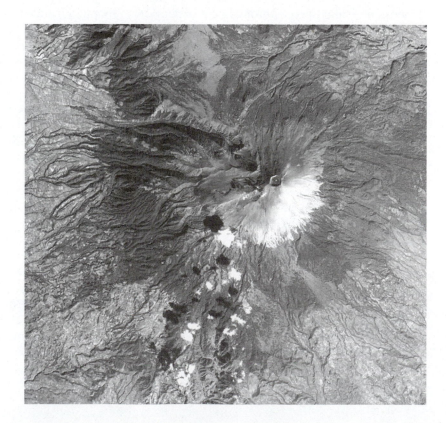

Comparison of the TM and HRV illustrates a common tradeoff in scanner system design: smaller pixel sizes typically come with a smaller imaged area. Satellite images to date have pushed the limits of data collection, storage, and transmission from space to ground stations. Smaller pixel sizes are desirable in many instances because they improve the spatial detail and type resolution available on digital images. However, each time pixel sizes decrease by a factor of two, data volumes increase by a factor of four. Thus, systems increase resolution at the expense of smaller images. Advances in data compression and transmission are allowing increasing resolution while maintaining large images; however, the tradeoff still exists.

SPOT-4 carries an improved HRV, as well as a new sensor named VEGETATION. The new HRV carries the three bands carried on previous SPOT satellites, and adds a mid-infrared band. The utility of the mid-infrared band for vegetation mapping was amply demonstrated with the Landsat TM, and is included in the HRV at a 20 m resolution. The VEGETATION sensing system operates independently of the HRV, and is designed for global vegetation productivity, health, and monitoring. The sensor has a pixel size of 1 km and a swath width of 2,250 km, and images the entire globe once a day. Four bands are recorded, a blue (430 to 470 nm), red (610 to 680 nm), near-infrared (780 to 890 nm), and mid-infrared (1580 to 1750 nm).

Radarsat

Radarsat is a side-looking satellite imaging radar system developed and operated by the Canadian Space Agency. The imaging system collects data using a 5.6 cm radar wavelength, with an effective resolution of from 10 to 100 m, depending on look angle. The orbit is repeated once every 24 days, but areas up to 500 km to the side of the orbital track may be imaged. The repeat interval is approximately 6 days at the equator, and less towards the poles. Radarsat data have been used to monitor clearcut extent, particularly in tropical regions where radar penetration of cloud cover is essential to timely measurements. Radarsat data have also been applied to problems in agriculture, hydrology, cartography, and land use.

Other Remote Sensing Systems

Several remote sensing systems are in orbit or will soon be launched that provide useful data for natural resource management. The *Advanced Very High Resolution Radiometer* (AVHRR) is a 1.1 km resolution scanner providing global coverage on a daily basis. Versions of this scanner have been carried aboard National Oceanic and Atmospheric Administration polar orbiting satellites since 1979, and the scanners sense red, near-infrared, and thermal wavelengths. Red and near-IR bands have been used to measure global phenologies and vegetation density and health, chiefly through spectral vegetation indexes such as the *normalized difference vegetation index* (NDVI). The NDVI is the ratio of the near-IR minus red divided by the near-IR plus red bands. Because water and soils absorb infrared, and vegetation reflects infrared, high NDVIs indicate high vegetation density.

A number of radar systems have been or will be launched. The ERS-1 and JERS-1 were radar systems launched by the European and Japanese space agencies, respectively, and the *Almaz-1* was launched by the former Soviet Union. These systems, taken together, sense across a range of radar wavelengths, resolutions, and sensing modes. Experience to date indicates these systems have many useful applications, among them in forest monitoring, *topographic surveys*, *landcover classification*, and *change detection*.

Scanners associated with the NASA *Earth Observing System* (EOS) will provide a wealth of research and data, much of which will prove useful in forest resource measurement and management. Landsat-7 will carry the *Enhanced Thematic Mapper* (ETM), sensing in similar wavelengths as TM, but adding a 15 m resolution panchromatic band, and increasing the resolution of the thermal band to 60 m. The *MODIS* sensor will sample 36 spectral bands at resolutions that vary from 250 m to 1 km and provide global coverage every two days. *ASTER* will sample 14 bands from visible through thermal infrared at resolutions from 15 to 90 m. As ASTER is a pointable sensor, revisit times will be approximately 6 days.

Concluding Statement

Our abilities to collect, organize, and analyze spatial data have improved tremendously over the past two decades, and will continue to develop in the foreseeable future. Remote sensing has provided new tools for rapid data collection over wide areas. GIS technologies allow us to organize and analyze these data with substantially improved speed and flexibility. Spatial data technologies serve our expanding spatial information needs. Our planet contains finite resources and an expanding human population, and spatial data and analyses will be part of intelligent identification, management, and preservation of these resources.

References

1. T. E. Avery and H. E. Burkhart, *Forest Measurements*, Fourth Edition, McGraw-Hill, New York, 1994.

2. W. Befort, *Photogrammetric Engineering and Remote Sensing, 52*, 101 (1986).

3. P. A. Burrough and R. A. McDonnell, *Principles of Geographical Information Systems*, Oxford University Press, Oxford, 1998.

4. N. Goba, S. Pala, and J. Narraway, "An Instruction Manual on the Assessment of Regeneration Success by Aerial Survey," Ministry of Natural Resources, Ontario, 1982.

5. R. C. Heller and J. J. Ulliman, "Forest resource assessments." In *Manual of Remote Sensing*, R. N. Colwell, ed., American Society of Photogrammetry, 1983.

6. T, M. Lillesand and R. W. Kiefer, *Remote Sensing and Image Interpretation*, Third Edition. Wiley & Sons, New York, 1994.

7. D. J. Maguire, M. F. Goodchild, and D. W. Rhind, *Geographical Information Systems*, Vol. 1, Longman, Green, N.Y., 1991.

8. P. R. Wolf, *Elements of Photogrammetry*, Second Edition, McGraw-Hill, New York, 1983.

9. P. H. Swain and S. M. Davis, eds., *Remote Sensing: The Quantitative Approach*, McGraw-Hill, New York, 1978.

10. V. G. Zsilinszky, *Photographic Interpretation of Tree Species in Ontario*, Ontario Dept. of Lands and Forests, 1966.

CHAPTER 13

Silviculture and Ecosystem Management

CRAIG G. LORIMER

Silviculture can be defined as the use of sustainable management practices to establish or guide the development of forest stands in order to fulfill natural resource objectives. These objectives can vary widely to include timber production, management for wildlife and biological diversity, management of aesthetics, modification of forest streamflow volume, and ecological restoration of degraded stands and landscapes. The history of silvicultural practice, like that of forestry in general, has involved a gradual broadening of objectives. A number of major "paradigm shifts" have occurred in the past six centuries in the western world, which have repeatedly redefined the scope and purpose of silvicultural treatments.

Evolution of Silvicultural Practice

European Origins

Most of the basic silvicultural practices originated in western Europe in the 14th to 19th centuries in response to fears of periodic timber famines. By the early Middle Ages, much of the European landscape had already been cleared for agriculture. England, for example, was probably not more than 10 percent forested in 1000 A.D. Population increases brought heavy pressure on the remaining fragments of woodland. These forests were heavily grazed by livestock, plundered by exploitive cutting of the best remaining timber trees, and repeatedly coppiced for small-diameter fuelwood. By the 13th century, there was sufficient alarm over the degraded condition of the woodlands and the limited supply of wood that laws were passed regulating the practice of grazing and the types of trees that could be cut (1, 2).

These early legal measures were largely protective, designed to slow the rate of exploitation and prevent continuing impoverishment of the forest. The first major paradigm shift in human use of the forest occurred as early as 1359, when managers of the city forest of Erfurt, Germany realized that if the haphazard felling of trees were replaced by a more orderly sequence of planned harvests, a perpetual supply of timber could be assured. Wise management, moreover, would actually improve the condition and productivity of the existing forest rather than simply prevent further degradation. Statutes began to specify that harvesting should be concentrated in certain sections of the forest, and subsequent regrowth protected from grazing until the saplings or sprouts were tall enough to be out of the reach of cattle (2). If an owner or government official desired to cut sprout hardwoods at an average age of 50 years, the tract could be divided into 50 sections and a different section harvested each year. These ideas were the first representation of what modern foresters would call *even-aged management for sustained yield*.

Experimentation on methods of active forest management also began to develop, particularly in Germany. In 1368, the city of Nuremberg dabbled with artificial seeding of pine, spruce, and fir. Forest officials also learned that conifer species could be regenerated naturally over large areas by leaving scattered seed trees. The "seed-tree method" of harvesting was introduced in 1454, including prescriptions for the minimum number of seed trees required for adequate stocking of seedlings. An important lesson learned from these early trials was that biological traits of tree species (silvics) imposed certain constraints on how forests could be managed. German foresters discovered, for example, that some species of trees could not be regenerated by selective or partial cutting because the seedlings could not tolerate shade. Books were written to summarize the accumulating knowledge on practical forest management and culture, such as one by John Evelyn called *Sylva, or a Discourse on Forest Trees*, published in England in 1664.

Forestry began to be guided by scientific observations and economic principles in the early 19th century. German texts covered such topics as planting and natural regeneration of new forests, thinning and improvement of existing stands, control of wildfires and disease, and estimates of forest growth and yield. The doctrine of sustained yield was modified to recognize a "financial maturity" of timber that would determine the optimal age at which trees should be harvested. As expressed in an early English document of 1810, "if profit is considered, every tree of every kind ought to be cut down and sold when the annual increase in value of the tree by its growth is less than the annual interest of the money it would sell for" (1).

Silvicultural Practice in North America: From Tree Farming to Ecosystem Management

The German model of forestry as it was practiced in the mid to late 19th century, with its typically European view of the cultivated (as opposed to wild) forest, and the view of forestry as a kind of "tree farming," is the model that was imported from

Germany by the first forestry leaders in America, such as Bernhard Fernow and Gifford Pinchot (see Chapter 1). This fact was to have great significance for the development of forestry in America and how it was practiced during most of the 20th century. Ironically, a more ecological view of forest management subsequently appeared in Germany, with "a recognition of the fact that the forest is not merely an aggregation of individual trees, but is an integrated, organic entity . . . from the smallest soil microbe to the age-old tree veteran" (2). However, this view appeared too late to have much influence on the founding fathers of American forestry. "Full utilization of the productive power of the Forests," wrote Pinchot, "does not take place until the land has been cut over in accordance with the rules of scientific forestry. The transformation from a wild to a cultivated forest must be brought about by the ax" (3).

Forest management in America never did develop fully in line with the Germanic model of the cultivated forest. There was a strong tradition in America of the wild and untamed "forest primeval," as well as the recreational and spiritual values of "getting back to nature." These values, along with increasing accessibility of remote wildland areas made possible by the automobile, fostered a great increase in the demands on use of forestlands for recreation, hunting, and fishing, leading to the doctrine of multiple use as the dominant policy in the management of public forests in the 20th century. Furthermore, foresters in the early 20th century were generally quite conservative in their management, with a tendency to prefer selective cutting methods over clearcutting, and favoring natural regeneration over planting whenever feasible.

Ironically, the clearcutting controversies in the 1960s and 70s boiled over in two sections of the country—the Pacific Northwest and the southern Appalachian Mountains—where selective logging had originally been tried but given up as silvicultural failures. Foresters then found that clearcutting was a more reliable way to regenerate the major species. However, several problems and controversies arose. Clearcutting often gave good regeneration and was economically efficient, but managers underestimated the potential extent of public disapproval. Rather than being blended into the terrain, clearcuts were often laid out as square or rectangular patches, and were sometimes excessive in size. Keeping with the Germanic tradition, natural mixed forests were often replaced by plantations of a single valuable species, such as Douglas fir in the Pacific Northwest. Finally, although the Forest Service was conducting research on management of nongame and endangered species, and this knowledge was gradually being incorporated into management plans, these changes did not satisfy those who sought more comprehensive protection for overall biological diversity.

These concerns have prompted the latest major paradigm shift in silvicultural practice on public lands. This new philosophy is generally known as *ecosystem management*. The purpose of forest ecosystem management is to manage forests in such a way that safeguards the ecological sustainability, biological diversity, and productivity of the landscape (4). The U.S. Forest Service made a commitment to using an ecosystem management approach in 1992.

Compared to the older management philosophy of sustained timber yield, ecosystem management recognizes that true long-term sustainability can be assured only if the integrity of natural ecological processes—ranging from nutrient cycling to predator-prey relations—are maintained. It is a holistic approach that evaluates sustainability of all ecosystem components over larger spatial scales and over longer time frames than traditional timber management. Unlike the traditional multiple-use philosophy, where wildlife management focused primarily on game species or on individual endangered species, ecosystem management seeks to maintain viable populations of all native and desirable non-native species, including such groups as herbaceous plants, lichens, fungi, amphibians, and arthropods. Silvicultural practices, when modified by ecosystem management principles, typically result in forests and landscapes that are more structurally complex than those maintained under traditional systems. More attention is given to retention of older trees, standing and fallen woody debris, soil organic matter, and other features. These are recognized as being important for maintaining ecosystem health and species diversity, but represent a departure from more economically driven approaches to forest management (5, 6).

Ecosystem management is considered to be a "work in progress," and therefore is under continual revision as new evidence and past experience suggest desirable changes. Managers and scientists will never have full knowledge of the forest ecosystem and management effects, but must proceed cautiously with the best evidence available. Shutting down forest management entirely on federal lands, as favored by some groups, would simply shift the burden of timber production to many less developed countries where few environmental regulations exist and where ecosystems are much less resilient.

Natural Disturbance Patterns: A Blueprint for Ecosystem Management

Even as early as 1905, Gifford Pinchot wrote that silvicultural treatments "are based on the nature of the forest itself, and are chiefly imitations of what men have seen happen in the forest without their help" (7). Ecosystem management has strengthened this principle. Harvest practices are most likely to maintain ecosystem health and species diversity if these practices mimic the patterns of natural disturbance to which organisms are locally adapted.

Natural disturbance regimes can be defined as the size, frequency, intensity, and pattern of natural disturbances in a region. Natural disturbance regimes are highly variable among geographic regions because of differences in precipitation patterns, vegetation, soils, landforms, and storm frequency. Large variations may exist even within a region that has high environmental heterogeneity. However, three common patterns can serve to illustrate the impact of disturbance regimes on forest development.

Frequent High-intensity Disturbance

To many people, forests have an aura of timelessness and permanence. However, this appearance of stability, caused by the relatively long lifespans of trees compared to humans, is deceptive. "Forests appear stable because people who admire them die," quipped one ecologist. Disturbances such as fires, hurricanes, tornadoes, insect epidemics, and even ice storms and thunderstorms routinely demolish forest canopies over thousands of hectares (Figure 13.1). U.S. land surveyors traversing vast expanses of virgin forest in the 19th century encountered thousands of extensive windfalls in which the trees were "broken and blown in every direction" (8). Catastrophic disturbances are common in nearly all temperate forest regions, but in some regions they are clearly the dominant force shaping the character of the forest landscape. Prior to the onset of fire suppression in the 20th century, large crown fires (see Chapter 18) were so common in the vast boreal forest of Canada and Alaska that the time interval between stand-killing fires was only about 50 years on average, known as the *natural fire rotation* (9). In Douglas fir forests of the Pacific Northwest, natural fire rotations ranged from about 150–400 years depending on local environmental conditions (10). Forests developing after catastrophic disturbance are said to be even-aged, because all of the trees germinated over a relatively short span of time and are approximately the same age.

Forests in regions that experience frequent crown fires tend to have three characteristics important to silvicultural practice. First, they are usually dominated by early successional species such as pines, birch, aspen, or Douglas fir. These species are adapted to disturbance and in most situations are dependent on it. Seedlings of these species normally develop well only on open sites where the previous stand has been killed by fire, partly because the small seeds require contact with exposed mineral soil, and partly because the seedlings cannot tolerate dense shade. Second, the presettlement landscape in such regions was often a coarse

Figure 13.1 An example of widespread forest destruction by natural disturbance. This photo shows pine forest in South Carolina blown down by Hurricane Hugo in 1989. This hurricane cut a wide swath across the center of the state, causing heavy damage on 500,000 hectares (1.2 million acres) of forestland. (Photo by R. M. Sheffield, U.S.D.A. Forest Service).

mosaic of large even-aged patches of different ages, with each patch dating to some past fire event (Figure 13.2). This pattern is the natural prototype for even-aged forests managed for sustained yield. Because the interval between fires was usually shorter than the maximum lifespan of the trees, succession often did not have a chance to proceed to the theoretical climax stage of shade-tolerant species. A third feature of these regions is that many animal species are also adapted to periodic severe disturbances and depend on them for suitable habitat.

Diffuse Small-scale Disturbance

In areas with fine-textured soils and a moist climate year-round, fires may be relatively uncommon. Catastrophic disturbance typically does occur in these regions as well, but intervals between such events are often long enough that trees can live out their natural lifespans. Tree mortality in these forests therefore does not usually occur synchronously in response to some cataclysmic event, but rather sporadically as scattered old trees or small patches of trees succumb to old age, wind, drought, or disease. New regeneration develops

at different times and places wherever old trees die and create canopy gaps. This pattern of disturbance leads to the development of uneven-aged stands, in which several or many age classes of trees are intermixed within a small area of forest. This disturbance pattern is the natural prototype for uneven-aged management or the selection silvicultural system.

Because of the long intervals between catastrophic disturbance and the small sizes of canopy gaps, this type of disturbance regime favors the development of late-successional, shade-tolerant species. Examples include the beech–maple forests of eastern North America, Japan, and central Europe, and the spruce–fir forests of many high mountain ranges. These species germinate readily on the shaded forest floor, and grow slowly for long periods beneath the forest canopy until a canopy gap occurs.

Frequent Low-intensity Fire

The presettlement forest in some regions was dominated by early- or midsuccessional species, such as pines or oaks, that experienced frequent light surface fires (Chapter 18). With their thick bark,

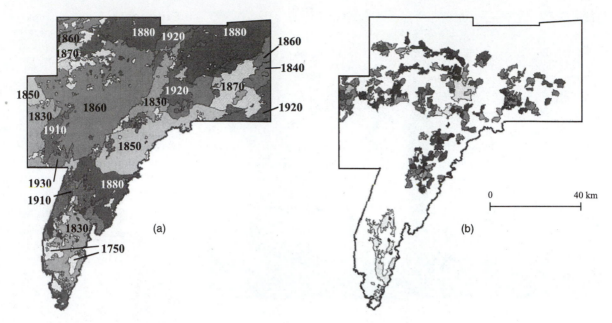

Figure 13.2 The occurrence of periodic severe fires in fire-prone ecosystems leads to a coarse mosaic of large even-aged stands on the landscape. Map (a) shows the mosaic of stands created by wildfire since 1750 in boreal forest of Ontario. Map (b) shows a much finer-grained mosaic produced by clearcuts since the 1930s. (Courtesy of Dan Welsh, Natural Resources Canada.)

these species were usually able to survive these fires, but much of the undergrowth was top-killed or eliminated, leading to relatively open stands of mature trees that were sometimes even-aged and sometimes uneven-aged.

This fire regime created a partial canopy of mature trees that provided a dependable source of seed, a favorable seedbed for early- and midsuccessional species, and partial shade to protect the young seedlings from dessication. Invasion of stands by the more shade-tolerant, fire-sensitive species was hindered, however, by the periodic fires. Good examples of forests with this type of disturbance regime were the longleaf pine savannas of the southeastern U.S., the ponderosa pine savannas of the southwest, and oak woodlands of eastern North America. This pattern of disturbance is the natural prototype for the shelterwood silvicultural system as well as the group selection system.

Growth and Development of Forest Stands

Differences in the mode of origin of even-aged and uneven-aged stands also lead to differences in their structure, manner of development, and value as wildlife habitat. An understanding of natural stand development is helpful in understanding and designing silvicultural treatments.

Even-aged Stands

Even-aged stands, in which all trees are approximately the same age, are generated in response to natural or human-caused disturbance that suddenly removed the previous stand. Even-aged stands are commonly classified by their stage of development, as reflected by the age or average size of the trees. These depend on species and location, but for many temperate forests we can recognize the following stages: seedling stands (1–5 years old), sapling stands (5–15 years), pole stands (15–60 years), mature stands (60–150 years), and old growth (> 150 years).

Young even-aged stands are often very dense, with thousands of trees on a hectare (2.47 acres) of land, but at stand maturity there will be space only for a few hundred trees on the same area. As individual trees become larger and older, competition becomes more severe. Crowns of the slower-growing trees become increasingly crowded and may finally be overtopped completely by adjacent, faster-growing trees shooting up around them. The stands therefore tend to show a certain amount of vertical stratification, and individual trees in even-aged stands are often classified by their relative position in the canopy. These *crown classes* (Figure 13.3) are defined as follows:

> *Dominant:* Trees that project somewhat above the general level of the canopy, having crowns that receive direct sunlight from above and partly from the side.
> *Codominant:* Canopy trees of average size that receive direct sunlight from above but relatively little from the sides.
> *Intermediate:* Trees with crowns extending into the canopy layer, but crowded on all sides so that only the top of the crown receives direct sunlight.
> *Suppressed:* Trees with crowns completely overtopped by surrounding trees so that they receive no direct sunlight except from occasional "sunflecks" that penetrate small gaps in the foliage above.

Once a tree in an even-aged stand has become suppressed, its chance of regaining a dominant position in the stand is slight, and the probability of imminent death is greatly increased. High mortality rates of trees in the lower crown classes result in a steep decline in the number of trees per hectare until the stand matures. In 40 years, the number of trees might be reduced by 50 to 60 percent or more. This natural decrease in numbers of trees in even-aged stands because of competition is known

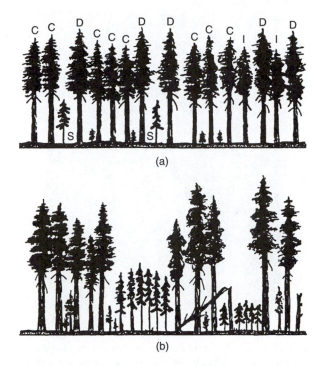

Figure 13.3 Diagrammatic profiles of an even-aged and uneven-aged forest stand. (a) Mature even-aged stand showing the various crown classes. (D = dominant, C = codominant, I = intermediate, S = suppressed.) (b) Mature uneven-aged stand. Note the irregular profile and the small openings in various stages of regrowth.

as the *self-thinning process* (Figure 13.4). Older stands tend to be more open and spacious as a result of the natural self-thinning process.

Trees vary in growth rates throughout their lifespan, often reaching a peak growth rate in early maturity and then showing a gradual decline. Because trees in even-aged stands all go through these different growth phases simultaneously, the rate of wood production for the stand as a whole is also constantly changing. The stand age at which mean annual growth rate reaches a maximum is often adopted as the optimal rotation age for most efficient volume production. The most economically efficient rotation age, however, often occurs

Figure 13.4 Two even-aged hardwood stands showing the reduction in stand density and increase in average tree size over time as a result of the natural competitive process. (a) A dense, young pole stand of oak, birch, and maple. (Courtesy of Harvard Forest.) (b) A spacious 250-year-old hardwood stand.

before this point. Some stands may be managed on extended rotations, far beyond the point of biological maturity, in order to maintain old-growth habitat.

Uneven-aged Stands

Uneven-aged stands are usually defined as stands in which at least three age classes are intermixed (Figure 13.3). Uneven-aged stands are often difficult to distinguish visually from mature even-aged stands without actual age determinations. However, the most reliable visible characteristic of uneven-aged stands is a patchy and irregular canopy of uneven height, with many canopy gaps in various stages of regrowth. That is, some of the canopy gaps will be dominated by seedlings, others by tall saplings, and others by clusters of pole trees (Figure 13.3b). This variation in canopy height and tree

size is beneficial to some species of animals, especially songbirds.

If an uneven-aged stand contains many age classes, and each age class occupies an equal proportion of the stand, it is said to be a *balanced all-aged stand*. An interesting feature of balanced stands is that the volume of wood production is approximately constant from decade to decade, unlike even-aged stands where the volume production is constantly changing. In principle, this means that if scattered individual trees are harvested in a way to maintain the balance of age classes, uneven-aged management can provide a constant and perpetual supply of timber from a single stand. While this feature is not of great importance on large landholdings, where only the yield of the entire property is normally of interest, it can be an attractive feature of uneven-aged stands for small landowners.

Pure Versus Mixed Stands

The relative merits of pure versus mixed stands have long been a subject of controversy. Increasing worldwide demand for paper has spurred the establishment of many conifer stands in which a single species has been planted in rows (Figure 13.5). These are frequently unpopular with the general public because the stands look artificial, and perhaps because they suggest that a forest ecosystem is considered by the owners or managers to be nothing more than a crop of trees to be planted in rows and harvested like corn. More importantly,

Figure 13.5 Tree plantations are often established in rows to reduce costs and simplify management. Although plantations usually have lower biological diversity than natural stands, their greater productivity can help reduce management pressures on natural forests elsewhere.

plantation monocultures often have rather low biological diversity. These can be legitimate concerns if plantation monocultures occupy a large proportion of a regional landscape.

The establishment of plantation monocultures on public land has greatly decreased in some countries such as the United States, Canada, and Britain in recent years in response to these concerns. However, there are also some countervailing arguments that would suggest that the environmentally optimal solution is not necessarily to discontinue intensive plantation management altogether. Intensively managed plantations can usually produce much more wood fiber in shorter periods of time than natural forests. Some conservationists have recognized that the higher wood yield on these plantations can have the effect of reducing management pressure on natural forests elsewhere. In effect, a certain proportion of the land is dedicated to highly efficient fiber production in the same way that we designate certain lands for agricultural use.

The species diversity issue is also more complicated than it may appear. Natural forest stands strongly dominated by a single tree species are very common in temperate regions of the world. Examples are the nearly pure stands of Douglas fir, lodgepole pine, jack pine, aspen, or black spruce that often spring up after natural fires. And despite their generally lower plant and animal diversity, forest plantations still have greater biodiversity and lower environmental impacts than the other intensive human land uses such as urban/suburban development and agriculture. A study of bird use of conifer plantations in Wisconsin, for example, revealed that they were utilized by 50 species of breeding birds, not markedly lower than the 60 species found in the surrounding natural hardwood forests (11).

Treatments to Improve Existing Stands

Silvicultural treatments applied between the time of establishment and time of harvest are called *intermediate treatments*. The purpose of intermediate treatments is to improve species composition, growth rates, and tree quality.

Intermediate treatments might or might not generate immediate revenue. Thinning a pole stand can often be done at a profit, since the trees cut may be marketable as pulpwood. However, in some intermediate treatments, no products are removed from the stand (as in pruning or fertilization), or else the trees being cut are too small or too poor in quality to have monetary value. Such treatments are considered noncommercial, and are done with the expectation that this investment in the stand will pay off later in the form of increased value of the final harvest.

Controlling the species composition of trees can have some implications for biodiversity, but this varies with forest type and intensity of practice. Sometimes, discrimination against "weedy" species such as red maple, blackgum, or scrub oaks can actually result in a forest type that more closely resembles fire-maintained forests in presettlement times. However, aggressive attempts to favor a single valuable species are less common now than in previous decades. Recent policy on public lands has recognized the need to maintain natural species mixtures, even if some low-value species are represented.

Release Treatments

Treatments to improve species composition in mixed stands are best done when the trees to be favored are still fairly young (not beyond the pole stage) and still capable of responding to release from competition. *Release treatments* are performed to free desirable seedlings or saplings from trees of competing species that have already suppressed the crop trees or are likely to do so in the near future. Release treatments are often needed to ensure successful establishment of conifer stands, since hardwood species often grow much faster than conifers at young ages. Without intervention, many conifer plantations would be crowded out by aggressive hardwoods, or development would be delayed for decades by shrub dominance.

Release treatments often require the use of herbicides, because most hardwood and shrub species resprout vigorously when the stem is cut, often regaining their former height in just a few years because of their well-developed root systems. If the competitor stems are not too numerous, herbicides can be injected in individual stems or applied to cut stumps. Otherwise, herbicides can be applied as a spray treatment from the ground, or sometimes from the air.

Improvement Cuts

Improvement cuts are treatments in pole or mature stands that remove defective, diseased, poorly formed trees, and other trees of low value. Improvement cuts differ from release treatments in that they are done in older stands, and the crop trees are often in the main canopy and not in danger of becoming suppressed. Removal of poor quality trees frees up growing space for the more desirable trees and sometimes stimulates the development of new saplings in gaps. Improvement cuts are especially important in stands that have had a long history of exploitative logging in which only the best trees were removed. Improvement cuts are therefore a valuable silvicultural tool in restoring the ecological integrity of degraded stands.

On public lands, foresters must take care not to eliminate all poor quality trees because these trees may contain cavities used by birds and mammals, and may be more suitable substrate for lichens and fungi than straight, vigorous crop trees. Both ecologically and economically, it makes sense to remove only the undesirable trees that are clearly interfering with promising crop trees that will be carried to the end of a rotation.

Thinnings

Thinnings are treatments that reduce stand density in order to accelerate the growth of the remaining trees. Trees to be cut are typically of the same species and age class as those that remain.

Thinning does not usually increase the total amount of wood produced by a forest, and may even cause a modest decrease. However, since the available light, water, and nutrients are being used by fewer trees, the remaining trees become larger than they otherwise would have been. This is the principal benefit of thinning, for large trees are more valuable than an equal volume of small trees. At the same time, less vigorous trees that would probably die anyway from competition can be salvaged for usable material. The eventual result of thinning is a more open, spacious stand of larger trees. Thus, thinning basically hastens the natural outcome of competition in even-aged stands and is a good example of how silvicultural techniques often have natural counterparts.

Several different methods of thinning are possible, but it is useful to recognize three basic approaches. In *low thinning* or "thinning from below," the trees to be cut are mostly from the lower and middle crown classes. A light low thinning would remove only suppressed and intermediate trees, while a heavier low thinning would remove some codominants as well (Figure 13.6). A heavier low thinning is usually more desirable because dominant crop trees often do not show any measurable growth response to the removal of suppressed trees. Generally, a growth increase can occur only if gaps are made in the canopy so that adjacent trees can expand their crowns and increase their total exposed leaf surface area. Low thinning is the method that most closely mimics the natural self-thinning process, but some suppressed and defective trees should be purposely retained for use by birds and other organisms.

In *high thinning* or "thinning from above," the primary objective is to create sufficient numbers of small gaps in the canopy to stimulate the growth of the better crop trees. In most cases, this will involve removing intermediate and codominant trees of smaller size or poorer quality to favor the growth of the better dominant and codominant trees. Note that a high thinning may resemble a heavy low thinning in certain respects, but the difference is that suppressed trees are not ordinarily removed in a high thinning. For this reason, a high-thinned stand may not have as much of a spacious, park-like appearance as a stand that has had a heavy low thinning.

Figure 13.6 (a) Before and (b) two years after moderately heavy low thinning and pruning in a twenty-five year old pine plantation. About 35% of the stand basal area was removed. Nearly all the dominant trees remain, but most of the suppressed and intermediate trees were cut, along with 40% of the codominants. In addition to accelerating the growth of the remaining trees, thinning has an immediate effect of creating a more open and spacious forest.

In the third basic approach, *mechanical thinning*, all trees are removed in rows or strips without regard to crown class. The greatest response therefore comes from trees whose crowns are adjacent to the cleared strip. This method is relatively quick and inexpensive and can be easily done in plantations by mechanical tree fellers, but individual tree growth is not likely to be as good as in other methods. In plantations, mechanical thinning is often accomplished simply by removing every second or third row of trees (Figure 13.5).

Although a single thinning will usually increase growth rates and upgrade the overall stand quality, such improvements are likely to be short-lived, since continued growth and competition will again render the stand crowded, usually within a decade or two. For this reason, managed stands are usually thinned at periodic intervals, such as once every 10–15 years.

In addition to increasing timber value, thinning also usually improves biological diversity by creating canopy gaps and down woody debris, and encouraging the development of understory vegetation. Thinning improves aesthetics as well, by reducing the extremely high stem density, improving visibility, and creating a more park-like appearance with larger and more widely-spaced trees. Private landowners who value their forests primarily for recreation or wildlife are often understandably reluctant to have any cutting done on their property, but careful thinning can actually hasten the development of a forest of large stately trees, such as shown in Figure 13.4b. In fact, thinning has great potential value as a tool of restoration ecology for hastening the development of old-growth structural features in younger stands, especially in regions of the world where old growth is rare. One study indicated that thinning in 80-year-old maple stands could reduce the additional time needed for trees to reach the size of old-growth canopy trees from 90 to 45 years (12).

Fertilization

Another method that can be used to stimulate growth rates of trees is fertilization of the soil. Fertilization is apt to be most successful in areas where the soils are known to contain specific nutrient deficiencies. In North America, for example, nitrogen deficiencies are common in the Douglas fir region and in boreal spruce-fir forests, whereas phosphorus is in short supply in many southeastern soils. Standard fertilizer applications may result in 15 to 100 percent increases in growth rate, which often make it an economically attractive operation. However, a decision to fertilize should be weighed carefully. Fertilizers are energy-expensive to produce and usually result in only a temporary increase in site productivity. Some forest types, moreover, show little or no response to fertilization.

Pruning

In a dense forest, lower branches of trees growing in deep shade eventually die and fall off. In some species, however, dead branch stubs may persist for decades. New wood grows around the base of the stub, producing blackened "dead knots" that reduce the strength of the lumber and may fall out when the lumber is dried. To avoid dead knots and produce clear lumber, artificial pruning of dead branches is sometimes done with pruning saws or other equipment. Clear lumber is produced once the new growth covers the cut stub.

Pruning is an expensive operation and is usually economically justified only for select crop trees of high value species. When pruning is done, it is usually limited to the best trees in a stand and limited to a height of about 17 feet.

Salvage Cuts

Salvage operations remove trees that have been killed or weakened by insects, disease, fire, drought, ice storms, wind, and other natural disturbance agents. When losses are minor, salvage cuts may be conducted as part of a thinning or improvement cut. When mortality is heavy, however, the salvage cut may have to be a final harvest operation in which most of the original stand is removed and a new stand regenerated by even-aged methods (see Figure 13.9 in section on clearcutting).

Regeneration of Forest Stands

A principal goal in silviculture is to ensure that when a stand is harvested, most mature trees removed are replaced by vigorous seedlings or saplings of desirable species. If a person is lucky, this might occur without any special effort. However, successful regeneration usually requires careful "up-front" planning. Foresters commonly have several criteria that need to be met for successful stand regeneration:

1. The condition of the ground or seedbed must be suitable for seedling germination and growth. Seedlings of many species—especially those that

are fire-adapted—have difficulty in penetrating the thick mat of leaves and partly decomposed organic matter present in most forests. Reduction of this layer by fire or mechanical means is often needed for adequate seedling establishment.

2. Openings created by tree harvest must be large enough to provide sufficient light and moisture for long-term seedling survival. Minimum acceptable opening size varies among tree species and is smallest for shade-tolerant species and largest for the very intolerant species.

3. Seedlings must initially be established in sufficient numbers to provide for a well-stocked forest, but not too dense to inhibit individual tree growth. A moderate density is usually ideal as it promotes self-pruning and good tree form. Tree seedlings should also be well-distributed to avoid large unstocked areas, although sometimes delayed occupancy by trees is desirable for biodiversity reasons.

4. Competition with other trees and shrubs already on the site is frequently severe, and often needs to be controlled to ensure the success of desired species.

5. Quality of the seed source must be considered to ensure desirable genotypes. With natural regeneration, this usually involves retention of high-quality mature seed trees. With artificial regeneration, foresters need to know the location of the original seed source and its compatibility with the environment of the site to be reforested.

If these principles are not understood or are ignored, the harvest operation may have much the same effect as exploitive logging.

The Role of Site Preparation

Site preparation is treatment of the residual vegetation and ground surface to improve the chances of successful seedling establishment. Site preparation is often done prior to natural seeding treatments as well as before planting. The three main objectives of site preparation are 1) to reduce competition from residual vegetation, 2) to reduce the fire hazard and physical obstacles to planting by chopping or burning some of the treetops and woody debris, and 3) to prepare the seedbed by reducing the depth of the litter and duff, or creating special microsites for planted seedlings.

Site preparation can be accomplished by prescribed burning, mechanical treatments, herbicide application, or a combination of these. Equipment such as the rolling brush cutter (Figure 13.7) breaks up residual wood debris, making the site easier to plant, and tears up roots of shrubs and hardwood saplings which might otherwise overtop the planted seedlings. Other equipment such as the Bräcke scarifier scalps small patches of ground to provide a suitable microsite for planting. Prescribed burning is commonly used to accomplish all three objectives of site preparation, especially on steeper slopes where use of mechanical equipment would be impractical and too likely to cause soil erosion. A very simple form of site preparation can be accomplished by having the logger drag logs across the harvested site with the skidder equipment. This causes some partial scarification and competition control.

Natural Regeneration

Natural regeneration can be a desirable way to reestablish a forest stand for several reasons. The subsequent stand will usually have a more natural appearance and spacing than a plantation, it usually maintains a greater mixture of tree species, and natural stands usually have greater biological diversity. Natural regeneration is also usually much cheaper than artificial regeneration.

The main disadvantages of natural regeneration are that it can be unreliable if all the influential factors such as seed production, weather, and seedbed conditions are not favorable, and there is less control over species composition, stand density, and genetic makeup.

There are several pathways or modes of natural regeneration in a harvested area, and so foresters relying on natural regeneration need to be aware which pathway is likely to provide the main source of young trees in each case. One pathway is germination from seed carried by wind or animals into

Sidebar 13.1

"Partial Cutting" and Forest Degradation

Small private landowners usually prefer to do "partial cutting" in their woodlots in order to retain scenic values and wildlife habitat. As commonly practiced, however, partial cutting is a major cause of forest degradation in privately owned forests around the world, leading to the formation of vast areas of "junk woodlots."

Why does this seemingly conservative practice cause so much harm? The reasons are twofold. First, unregulated partial cutting usually involves the repeated and systematic mining of only the best quality trees and most valuable species, leaving behind only low-quality trees. Many once-impressive forests of oak have been converted into junk woodlots of noncommercial species by this process. Second, the owners and loggers usually do not realize that proper seed source, light environment, and seedbed conditions must be provided to ensure regeneration of valuable species. Even if some seed trees of valuable species remain, recruitment of new trees into the canopy is practically impossible because of the dense thickets of low-value species that have been left to dominate the site.

Woodlot degradation can be avoided or reversed by having a forester develop a management plan, a service that is provided free of charge in many states and provinces. The forester will prescribe an improvement cut and competition control treatment, and can reintroduce good-quality genetic stock of the original dominant species through planting. He or she will mark with paint trees that should be removed, specifying in a contract with the timber buyer or logger that only the marked trees can be cut.

A former stand of oak on private land that has been degraded by repeated "partial cutting" of only the best quality trees and species. Although the stand retains some visual appeal, it now has little value because of dominance by defective trees and noncommercial species.

Figure 13.7 Mechanical site preparation reduces competition from advance regeneration and shrubs, and provides a more favorable seedbed for establishment of preferred species. The rolling brush cutter shown here can achieve these results without scraping away or displacing topsoil and nutrients.

the harvested area. This is generally the most unpredictable source because success is heavily dependent on the vagaries of seed production, seed dispersal, damaging insects and fungi, weather patterns, and other factors. Nonetheless, in many situations, foresters have to rely entirely on seed dissemination after the harvest because other options are not present. Success is increased by timing the harvest to coincide with a good seed year and paying careful attention to seedbed conditions and competition control.

Another source of natural regeneration is seedlings or saplings already in the forest understory that survive the harvest operation and continue to grow. These seedlings and saplings are collectively called *advance regeneration*. This is often the principal source of regeneration in the selection silvicultural system. Advance regeneration is not always abundant in forest stands, especially on drier sites, and is often composed primarily of shade-tolerant species. However, when present and of desirable species, it is one of the more reliable sources of natural regeneration.

Some tree species will resprout from dormant buds on the stumps or roots after cutting. Sprouting is rare among conifer species, but is a common and dependable source of natural regeneration

among certain hardwoods. Sprouting often causes multiple stems to develop from a single parent tree, which is not always desirable, but sprouts of certain species such as aspen and oak are commercially acceptable (Figure 13.8).

Finally, a few species of trees may regenerate from seed stored in the forest floor. This is not a common trait among commercially valuable species, but a few such as ash and yellow poplar may regenerate partly by this pathway.

Artificial Regeneration

Artificial regeneration can be accomplished either by directly applying seeds to a harvested site or by planting nursery-grown seedlings. Planting gives the forester greater control over stand establishment and growth than artificial dispersal of seeds, but both methods have the following advantages over natural regeneration:

1. Stand establishment may be more reliable because it does not depend on the occurrence of a good seed year or the distance to which seeds are dispersed by wind. If large clearcuts are made, artificial regeneration is often necessary to ensure adequate regeneration on the central portion.

Figure 13.8 Dense vegetative regeneration of aspen from root sprouts one year after clearcutting.

2. Artificial regeneration increases the chances of prompt reforestation. This issue is most important to forest industries, because long delays in reforestation can reduce financial viability of their operations.

3. There is greater control over species composition. Among forest industries that must maximize fiber production on a limited area of land, planting of the single most productive and valuable species adapted to the site is often considered the most economically efficient alternative.

4. There is greater control over tree spacing and subsequent growth. Plantations are often established in rows at a predetermined spacing to optimize stand growth, reduce variability in growth rates, and allow easier access for mechanized equipment (Figure 13.5).

5. Seeds or seedlings can be derived from genetically superior trees.

Direct Seeding Artificial dispersal of tree seed is known as *direct seeding*. It may be accomplished on the ground by hand or machine, or from the air by helicopter or fixed-wing aircraft. Direct seeding is usually cheaper than planting, but it offers less control over spacing and usually has a lower success rate. As a minimal precaution, seeds may be treated with chemical repellents to reduce pilferage by rodents and birds. Germination and survival of seedlings tend to be considerably better on

sites with some exposed mineral soil than on sites with a thick covering of litter or logging debris.

Despite its limitations, direct seeding from the air can be very useful when extensive areas must be reforested quickly, as would be the case following a large forest fire. Direct seeding is also useful on steep, irregular terrain where planting by machine would be impossible and hand planting would be difficult.

Planting High survival rates of planted seedlings and the convenience of managing row plantations has led to a great increase in plantation establishment in recent years, particularly among paper companies. Most seedlings intended for outplanting in harvested areas are grown in either large outdoor nurseries or greenhouses. Seedlings may be lifted from the beds and packaged in a bare-root condition or they may be grown in individual containers with a specially prepared potting medium. These containerized seedlings are more expensive to grow than bare-root stock, but the root systems are less likely to be damaged during the lifting and transporting process, and better survival of planted seedlings results in some cases.

Planting is often done in the spring season when soil moisture is high and root growth is most active, but it is possible at other times depending on geographic location. If the site to be planted is extensive, fairly level, and not excessively rocky, planting can be done most quickly and cheaply with mechanized equipment. Otherwise the traditional method of hand-planting crews may be used.

Despite the higher success rate of plantations compared to direct seeding, failures and losses sometimes do occur. Mice and other rodents may cause the loss of many seedlings, especially in grassy areas, and browsing by deer and other large herbivores can be a problem. Planted seedlings may face stiff competition from shrubs and stump sprouts of other trees, which may necessitate application of herbicides. Furthermore, harsh microclimates on some sites may lead to planting failures, particularly on steep slopes facing south.

Planting often represents a sizable proportion of the total cash investment in a forest stand. The cost of the seedlings reflects the expense of nursery establishment and maintenance. The planting operation itself is a fairly labor-intensive operation, and to this must be added the costs of site preparation and other measures taken to enhance planting success. For these reasons, planting is likely to be done primarily where the increased cost can be justified economically by increased returns, where natural regeneration has a low probability of success, and in cases where the funds for plantation investment are available.

Silvicultural Systems

Silvicultural systems are long-range harvest and management schemes designed to optimize the growth, regeneration, and administrative management of forest stands, usually with the goal of obtaining a perpetual and steady supply of timber. The use of silvicultural systems involves making a comprehensive prescription of stand treatments throughout the life of the stand, including the method of harvest, an evaluation of whether or not site preparation is necessary, the use of seeding, planting, or natural regeneration, and a schedule of intermediate stand treatments (Table 13.1). Silvicultural systems are generally classified by the method used to harvest and regenerate the stand. These methods vary in cutting intensity but they may readily be grouped

under the categories of even-aged, two-aged, and uneven-aged methods.

Even-aged Methods

In even-aged management the trees are harvested over a relatively short period of time, creating open, sunny conditions, and leading to the development of even-aged stands. Many species can be managed by even-aged methods, and for certain species intolerant of shade the even-aged methods may be almost mandatory, since adequate regeneration would not occur under lightly cut stands. The even-aged methods are *clearcutting, seed tree,* and *shelterwood.* They differ primarily in the span of time over which the original canopy is removed.

Clearcutting Method   In *clearcutting,* all trees on the harvest unit are felled over a short period of time. Clearcutting is appropriate in forest types in which the dominant species are intolerant of shade and dependent upon severe disturbances such as crown fire for their perpetuation. Regeneration by the clearcutting method is accomplished by natural seeding, direct seeding, or planting. If reliance is placed on natural seeding, the feasible clearcut width is limited by the effective dispersal distance of the seeds. For most conifer species, the effective dispersal distance is only about five or six times the height of the mature border trees, or a distance of about 150–230 meters (500–750 feet). For this reason, clearcuts that rely on natural seeding are usually restricted to fairly small patches or long strips. Sometimes a forester can rely on advance regeneration or stump sprouts to provide most of the regeneration after clearcutting, in which case larger harvest units are feasible. However, advance regeneration is uncommon among the early successional species normally managed by clearcutting, and many commercial species either do not sprout at all or have a low frequency of sprouting among mature trees. Because of these limitations with natural regeneration, clearcutting is often followed by planting (Figure 13.9).

While clearcutting mimics severe natural disturbance in some ways, some scientists have noted

Table 13.1 Silvicultural Information for Some Major Forest Types of North America

Forest Type	Tolerance[a] (Major Species)	Successional Status	Growth Rate	Current Commercial Value	Methods of Regeneration[b]	Ease of Regeneration[c]
Western						
Douglas-fir	Inter	Variable (site-dependent)[d]	Rapid	High	C, SH (SP, P)	M
Hemlock–Sitka spruce	Tol	Climax	Mod–rapid	High	SH, C, GS, S	E
Coast redwood	Tol	Climax	Rapid	High	GS, C, SH, S (SP)	E
Ponderosa pine	Intol	Variable[d]	Mod	Mod–high	SH, GS, S, ST, C (SP, P)	M-D
Western larch	Intol	Successional	Rapid	Mod	ST, C, SH (SP)	E-M
Engelmann spruce–fir	Tol	Climax	Slow–mod	Mod	GS, S, SH, C (SP)	M
Lodgepole pine	Intol	Successional	Mod	Low	C, SH	E
Eastern						
Spruce-fir	Tol	Climax	Slow–mod	Mod	GS, S, SH, C	E-M
White pine	Inter	Successional	Rapid	Mod	SH, GS (SP)	M-D
Jack pine	Intol	Successional	Rapid	Mod	C, ST, SH (SP)	M
Red pine	Intol	Successional	Rapid	Mod	C, SH (SP, P)	D (Nat), M (Art)
Northern hardwoods	Tol	Climax	Slow	Mod	S, GS, SH	E
Aspen–birch	Intol	Successional	Rapid	Low–mod	C (SP)	E
Oak–hickory	Inter–Intol	Variable[d]	Rapid	Mod–high	SH, GS, C (SP, P)	M-D
Southern pines	Intol	Successional	Rapid	High	C, ST, GS (SP, P)	M

[a] Abbreviations: Tol = tolerant; Inter = intermediate, Intol = intolerant

[b] Abbreviations: C = clearcutting; SH = shelterwood; ST = seed tree; GS = group selection; S = individual-tree selection; (SP, P) site preparation and planting may be necessary

[c] Abbreviations: E = easy; M = moderate; D = difficult; Nat = natural; Art = artificial

[d] Forest types with a "variable" successional status are generally successional on moist or average sites and climax on dry sites.

that forest fires, windstorms, insect epidemics, and similar disturbances are often quite patchy in their occurrence, with scattered surviving trees and clumps of trees. Also, the logs and standing dead trees remain on the site. All these features help mitigate the impact of disturbance on animal and plant species that prefer late successional forests by providing refugia for these species and a source for recolonization of the disturbed site when conditions permit. Persistence of dead wood on the site is also beneficial for maintaining site fertility. For these reasons, ecosystem management guidelines for clearcuts on public lands frequently involve retaining scattered "green trees," patches of uncut trees, snags, and fallen logs to help maintain biodiversity and productivity (Figure 13.10).

Seed-tree Method Other even-aged methods are designed to overcome some of the problems inherent in clearcutting with natural regeneration. In the *seed-tree* method, scattered mature trees are left on the site to serve as a seed source for the new stand and to provide a more uniform dispersal of seed. Although this may seem like a good solution to the

Figure 13.9 Clearcutting is sometimes done to salvage trees killed in an insect or disease epidemic. Much of the mature pine in this stand had been killed by an outbreak of the jack pine budworm. This photo was taken several years after the replanting of red and jack pine.

problem of seed dispersal, and some state laws used to mandate retention of a certain number of seed trees after harvesting, experience has shown that the seed-tree method may be unsuccessful in many situations. Sometimes the site becomes rapidly invaded by shrubs, and so few of the seeds dispersed by the seed trees actually germinate and survive. In some cases, as with oaks, newly germinating seedlings grow too slowly to compete with advance regeneration and sprouts of other species. The seed-tree method also does not work well with shallow-rooted species, since many of the seed trees will be blown down by wind. The seed-tree method is best suited to situations in which intensive site preparation is feasible and the species are reasonably wind-firm. Western larch and the southern pines are examples of species well suited to the seed-tree method.

Shelterwood Method   Seed trees are also retained in the *shelterwood method*, but in this case sufficient numbers are left standing to provide some shade and protection for the new seedlings (Figure 13.11). In the most common variant of the shelterwood method, the first major cut leaves a temporary partial overstory in which percentage of

ground surface shaded by tree crowns may vary from 30 to 80 percent, depending on species and local conditions (Figure 13.11b). Once the seedlings are firmly established, after several years, the residual trees are usually removed so that they do not retard the growth of the new saplings (Figure 13.11c).

The shelterwood method is ideal for any species or site where seedlings are not expected to germinate well under open conditions. Even some of the more intolerant species may benefit from the protection of a shelterwood overstory during the first few years when seedlings are vulnerable to desiccation; this is especially true on harsh sites. For example, the shelterwood method has been applied successfully on sites in California and Oregon where clearcutting had failed (13, 14). The shelterwood method also has the least visual impact of any even-aged method, since by the time the last of the residual overstory trees are removed, the new stand is already sapling-sized. It therefore bypasses the typically devastated look of recent clearcuts. In many situations, it probably reduces erosion hazard and nutrient loss as well.

Although the shelterwood method bears a superficial resemblance to heavy partial cutting in

Figure 13.10 On many public forests, scattered mature trees, snags, and logs are retained on clearcut sites to help maintain biological diversity and provide a more complex forest structure, as in this stand in the Pacific Northwest. (Courtesy of U.S.D.A. Forest Service.)

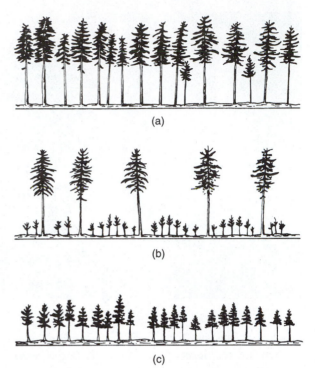

Figure 13.11 An illustration of the shelterwood method to regenerate an even-aged forest. (a) The mature stand prior to treatment. (b) The first major harvest leaves a temporary shelterwood overstory to provide seed trees, partial shade, and a scarified seedbed. (c) After saplings of the desired species are well established, the shelterwood overstory is removed to release a new even-aged sapling stand.

unmanaged forest (see figure in Sidebar 13.1), there are important differences. In the establishment phase of a shelterwood cut (Figure 13.11b), the trees to be retained are among the larger and better quality trees in the stand in order to serve as a good seed source. The overtopped, intermediate, and smaller codominants are usually removed completely. A heavy partial cutting, on the other hand, will generally accomplish just the opposite by removing many of the larger and better trees and releasing the smaller trees (which may not be of desirable species or quality). A second major difference is that after the removal cut in a shelterwood, the resulting stand is young and even-aged and composed entirely of saplings (Figure 13.11c). Such a stand will in fact differ little from a sapling stand that might have developed after a successful clearcut.

Coppice Method This method differs from all other reproduction methods in that dependence is placed on vegetative regeneration by stump sprouts or root sprouts instead of development of stands from seed. However, since coppice stands are usually harvested by clearcutting, it may be conveniently discussed with other even-aged methods. The coppice method is restricted to species that typically sprout vigorously and have sprouts capable of attaining commercial size. Good examples of such species are aspen (Figure 13.8) and oak. Coppice stands are usually managed on short rotations, and the products may be fuelwood or pulpwood. Use of the coppice method declined in developed countries in the second half of the 20th century as oil and gas became cheap and abundant fuels, but increasing demands for energy have revived some interest in coppice systems. Genetically improved species such as hybrid poplars have considerable potential as fast-growing plantations managed on short rotations.

Two-aged Management

Two-aged management is a practice developed recently as a more aesthetically acceptable alternative to clearcutting in stands of shade-intolerant species. The initial harvest in a two-aged system leaves scattered mature trees, perhaps about 15 percent of the original stand, similar to the density of trees on a seed-tree cut (Figure 13.12). Unlike a seed-tree cut, however, the mature trees are not removed once the regeneration is established, but are carried to the end of the next rotation. During this time, a two-aged stand is produced. When the younger age class is mature, the older cohort and much of the younger cohort are harvested, setting in motion another two-aged forest.

Two-aged management is designed to provide sufficient light for successful regeneration of intolerant species, while retaining some tree cover to preserve scenic values. Retention of the mature trees also probably has some value for biodiversity by creating a more complex forest structure.

Uneven-aged Methods

Uneven-aged management is accomplished by the *selection method,* in which scattered trees or small groups of trees are harvested at 10–20 year intervals. This diffuse pattern of timber removal ensures that many age classes of trees will be intermixed within a matrix of mature forest (Figure 13.13). This system can be used to perpetuate uneven-aged forests that occurred in regions with diffuse natural disturbance (such as northern hardwoods) or in areas that had frequent light surface fires that maintained uneven-aged stands of intolerant species (such as ponderosa pine).

The selection method has some unique advantages. It is the only silvicultural system in which sustained yield can be obtained from a single stand of trees. Provided that cutting is not too intense, trees can be harvested in perpetuity, while the forest canopy remains largely intact with little evidence of manipulation. There is often no need for expensive site preparation or planting. As in natural uneven-aged stands, mature trees removed in the harvest are replaced by saplings already in the understory. Erosion and disturbance to the site are minimal. Fire hazard is relatively low because of the lack of extensive piles of logging debris.

There is, however, a serious limitation with the selection system. With the exception of certain fire-resistant species that can be maintained with frequent prescribed burns, the selection system typically leads to nearly complete dominance of the forest by shade-tolerant species. The opening created by the removal of a single mature tree usually does not allow enough light for adequate survival and growth of intolerant or intermediate species. The list of such species is considerable and includes some of the most economically important species such as Douglas fir, most of the pines, larches, oaks, ashes, birches, and aspens (Table 13.1). Light cutting in stands of these species will not only fail to regenerate the species in most cases, but will actually tend to hasten the conversion to whatever shade-tolerant species happen to be in the understory. For example, use of the selection system in Douglas fir causes a conversion to hemlock and cedar, and its use in oak forests often causes conversion to maples. The shade-tolerant species often have less valuable wood than the species they displace, and are also slower-growing.

Figure 13.12 With two-aged management, scattered mature trees are retained until the end of the next rotation, helping to maintain scenic values in stands of species that otherwise require full sunlight. This photo shows two-aged management of southern Appalachian hardwoods. (U.S.D.A. Forest Service photo by R. L. Rosier.)

Other disadvantages to the selection system have been cited, but these have usually been minor or inconsistent problems. Logging costs are sometimes 20 to 30 percent higher in the selection system compared to even-aged management because logs must be skidded longer distances (15). However, for both western conifer and eastern hardwoods in North America, logging costs are often not significantly higher with the selection system when costs are expressed per unit volume harvested. This is because a greater proportion of the harvest in the selection system is contributed by large trees, which can be handled more efficiently than numerous small trees. Some authors have suggested that the selection system requires a more extensive road network than even-aged management, but it is not likely that the actual density of roads on each watershed would differ (16). Also, while selective logging can result in injury to the residual standing trees, most scientists have concluded that the problem is minor.

Some of the disadvantages of the selection system can be lessened by modification of the method of harvest. By cutting small groups of trees instead of scattered individuals, the amount of direct sunlight can be increased to the point where some

Figure 13.13 The individual-tree selection method of harvest removes scattered trees at 10–20 year intervals. Disturbance is often hardly noticeable, and old-growth features can be maintained. This example shows a hemlock–hardwood forest on the Menominee Indian Reservation in Wisconsin.

regeneration of shade-intolerant species can occur. When combined with periodic prescribed burning to control shade-tolerant competitors, this *group selection method* can be used to maintain intolerant species such as the southern pines and ponderosa pine in uneven-aged stands with comparatively small openings. Group selection is also being used in Appalachian oak forests as a more publicly acceptable alternative to clearcutting (Figure 13.14). However, the minimum opening size needed for adequate regeneration of oaks and some other species is currently uncertain. In some locations, foresters are creating group selection openings that are large enough to cause possible concerns about forest fragmentation. Especially after several consecutive entries, a patchwork of numerous large openings may become undesirable both visually as well as for certain animal species such as salamanders. Since use of group selection is likely to increase as foresters search for alternatives to clearcutting, a number of research projects have been initiated to resolve some of these issues and provide better management guidelines.

Uneven-aged management is an important and viable silvicultural system for a number of forest types—in particular, forests dominated by shade-tolerant species such as maples, hemlocks, cedars, spruces, and true firs, and a few intolerant species that can withstand periodic prescribed burning. However, in many situations it is not biologically feasible or ecologically desirable. The popular sentiment against clearcutting is so strong, however, that some legislative bills have been introduced that would virtually mandate the selection system nearly everywhere on federal lands. One environmental group drafted a platform that would seek to "end clearcutting and all its variants (i.e., all forms of even-aged management) . . . in any national forest ever." If implemented, such a provision would create extensive new landscapes of shade-tolerant species in uneven-aged stands that were virtually unknown in those regions in presettlement times and which have no natural precedent.

Silvicultural Practices and Ecosystem Integrity

Two guiding principles of ecosystem management are that current management practices should not impair or degrade the long-term productivity of the site, and they should not jeopardize the diversity

Figure 13.14 Aerial view of group selection harvests (left side of photo) in Appalachian hardwood forests. (U.S.D.A. Forest Service photo by J. N. Kochenderfer.)

and viability of native plant and animal populations. It is impossible to judge sustainability from casual visual impressions of forest management practices. However, informed assessments can be made from careful scientific measurements for each ecosystem type.

Frequently, the question of whether a management practice is sustainable depends not only on local forest type, soil conditions, and topography, but also on the intensity of the management practice. Even clearcutting, for example, can span a wide range of management intensity depending on intensity of biomass removal from the site, intensity of site preparation, and rotation length. The following sections focus mostly on clearcutting practices because they are the most intensive and controversial form of silviculture, and have been the focus of a large body of research.

Maintaining Long-term Site Productivity

Soil erosion occurs when soil is disturbed and exposed to the direct impact of rain. Although there are some exceptions, timber harvesting by itself often causes relatively little soil disturbance because the remaining litter layer and ground veg-

etation are effective in protecting the soil. Thus, scientists are usually more concerned about road-building and site preparation, since both activities can result in significant soil exposure. Many soil scientists agree that with proper road design and use of "low-tillage" site preparation equipment (or light prescribed burning), increases in soil loss over natural erosion rates will often be small, short-term, and within the recovery rate of the ecosystem (17, 18).

Conventional harvest also removes some nutrients in the tree boles, but on reasonably fertile sites, the amount removed is normally only a small fraction (usually <10%) of the total nutrient capital on the site. These amounts are often replaced within the span of one normal sawtimber rotation by nutrients added from precipitation, weathering of soil minerals, and nitrogen fixation.

For these reasons, conventional bole-only clearcut harvests with low intensity site preparation appear to be sustainable in many temperate forests. In the famous long-term clearcutting experiments at Hubbard Brook in New Hampshire, for example, the team of six scientists concluded: "our study indicates that if care is taken during logging, and if sawtimber rotation lengths are followed, there should not be major adverse effects on site nutrient capital, stand regeneration, or productivity. By the 10th year after harvest, hydrologic and nutrient budgets had returned nearly to preharvest levels" (17). Even in the highly erodible and relatively infertile Piedmont soils of the southeastern United States, a soil scientist concluded after careful monitoring that "none of the effects of clearcutting, double roller-chopping, and machine planting appear serious enough to call for special regulation . . . Fears that clearcut silviculture is depauperating soils and eutrophying streams appear unfounded in the Piedmont" (19). It is likely that the newer alternatives to clearcutting, such as green-tree retention and two-aged management (Figure 13.12), will further reduce impacts, although more research is needed.

There is, however, much greater concern about environmental effects of certain intensive practices, such as whole-tree harvesting on short rotations (Figure 13.15) and intensive mechanical site preparation such as disking and root-raking. A number of studies do suggest that these practices might lead to unacceptably high rates of soil and nutrient loss on some sites (20). It is possible that industrial firms using these practices will have to do routine fertilization and use less intensive site preparation methods in order to avoid future declines in yield. Likewise, all foresters need to be cautious about conventional even-aged harvests on soils of inherently low fertility or on high-elevation sites where much of the nutrient capital may be sequestered in the tree biomass. In such cases, some form of partial harvest and careful retention of organic matter may be required, and rotations may have to be lengthened depending on the expected rate of nutrient replacement. Foresters must also be cautious

Figure 13.15 Mechanized whole-tree harvesting reduces costs and logging injuries, while at least temporarily increasing yields. However, it also accelerates the rate of nutrient withdrawal and may not be a sustainable practice on short rotations. (Courtesy of U.S.D.A. Forest Service.)

in planning harvests in certain portions of geologically young landscapes where road-building can trigger landslides on steep, unstable slopes (20).

Maintaining Biological Diversity

Timber harvesting does not have a uniformly positive or negative effect on either the abundance of individual species or on overall biodiversity. Many species of animals and plants have preferences for certain stand ages or successional stages, reflecting their unique adaptations to the regional natural disturbance regime. A recent clearcut dominated by low shrubby vegetation, for example, is ideal habitat for the chestnut-sided warbler and the indigo bunting. After a few years, their populations will decline precipitously as their favored open habitat disappears beneath a canopy of tall saplings. At this point, the young sapling stand becomes suitable habitat for the magnolia warbler and the American redstart. In time, these species will in turn be replaced by those that prefer mature forest, such as the black-throated green warbler and the Blackburnian warbler. Thus, the harvest of mature forest typically replaces one biotic community with another. Maintenance of biological diversity requires that all stages of forest development, including old-growth forest, be represented on the landscape.

It is well known that even-aged management favors populations of game animals as well as "habitat generalists." However, contrary to popular belief, many nongame species of concern to conservationists are also favored by even-aged management. For example, 74 of the 126 species of "neotropical migrant songbirds" in the northeastern United States require early successional stages and young forest habitat, and are rare or absent in mature and old-growth forest (21). Early evidence from scientific studies suggests that green-tree and snag retention in clearcuts, as well as two-aged management practices, will further enhance species abundance and diversity over what would occur under simpler clearcutting regimes (22, 23).

Some measures taken to reduce the effects of clearcutting have had unintended negative effects on biodiversity at the landscape scale. In recent decades, foresters have kept clearcuts small and scattered them on the landscape to minimize aesthetic and environmental impacts. After several decades of this approach, however, the landscape becomes highly fragmented, and the remaining patches of mature forest lose much of their "interior forest" environment because of exposure to clearcut edges (Figure 13.16, top row). This may place some species requiring interior forest environment at risk. One lichen species in the Pacific Northwest, for example, may disappear from mature forest patches if more than 50 percent of the landscape has been clearcut in dispersed patches (5). Natural disturbance processes were less disruptive because extensive fires created a mosaic of larger stands with more interior and relatively less edge.

Clearly this creates a public policy dilemma. The public, if it is willing to tolerate clearcuts at all, will usually insist that they be small and scattered, and existing federal regulations mandate small clearcuts on U.S. national forests. Yet in much of the Pacific Northwest and boreal regions of Canada, small dispersed clearcuts clearly do not mimic the natural disturbance processes to which most species are adapted (Figure 13.2). An approach that has been suggested to overcome this dilemma is to keep clearcuts small, but aggregate them in slowly expanding clusters, rather than dispersing them (Figure 13.16, bottom row). This will help preserve the forest interior characteristic of large blocks of forest, and more closely imitate the natural disturbance regime.

Special consideration must be given to plant and animal species having very specific habitat requirements that might not be satisfied under normal forest management practices in a region. Much publicity has surrounded the controversy over the northern spotted owl and the marbled murrelet, two bird species in the Pacific Northwest that appear to require old-growth forests for nesting. There are also other less conspicuous species, such as certain lichens, fungi, and mollusks, that also may be common only in old growth ecosystems, and which may be important for healthy ecosystem functioning. For such reasons, in 1993 President Clinton's scientific advisory panel recommended setting aside

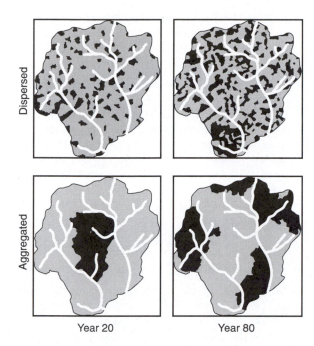

Figure 13.16 Two alternative ways of dispersing small clearcuts are shown above on maps of a watershed. If clearcuts (shown as black patches) are small and dispersed, they eventually cause forest fragmentation and loss of interior forest habitat as in the top row of maps. Aggregation of small clearcuts into larger clusters over time (bottom row of maps) helps preserve large blocks of closed-canopy forest, shown as the gray patches. White areas show streamside protection zones. From David Wallin; courtesy of Ecological Society of America (24).

a number of large "late successional reserves" on national forest land to ensure the viability of these species. It is not yet known whether silvicultural practices designed to hasten or maintain old-growth features in younger stands will be successful in maintaining the viability of such species outside of formal reserves.

Concluding Statement: Public Forests of the Future

How then, should silviculture be applied on large public landholdings such as national forests, and

what would the ideal landscape look like? There won't be one answer for all public forests, especially under ecosystem management, since practices will be attuned to the local biota and natural disturbance regime. Thus, a national forest in western Oregon will be managed much differently from a national forest in Vermont, with the selection system being used much more widely in the northern hardwoods of Vermont than in the Douglas fir forests of Oregon.

Nonetheless, it is possible to make some generalizations about how silvicultural practices under the ecosystem management paradigm will change the fabric of the landscape in the 21st century compared with what was produced under the multiple-use paradigm in the 20th century. There will be greater mixtures of tree species, representative of natural species diversity in the region. Traditional "block" clearcuts will probably be replaced largely by two-aged stands, multicohort stands, shelterwood harvests, and modified clearcuts with retention of scattered green trees and small patches of forest. Stand edges will be irregular and blended with the topography. Aggregated patches may be preferred over dispersed harvests to more closely mimic the natural disturbance regime and maintain forest interior species. Rotation ages will be longer, with many areas managed on 150–250-year rotations. Prescribed burning will be used more frequently to maintain historical patterns of species dominance and to maintain ecosystem health. There will be more use of the selection system than at present, and it will be used wherever it meets societal goals and is ecologically appropriate. Nearly all stands will have greater structural complexity, with large living trees, dead snags, and fallen logs for biodiversity. Old-growth stands will be more common in most regions than at present, both as large tracts and as small patches in a matrix of younger forest.

Although this scenario will result in landscapes with a high degree of naturalness, it will not please everyone. It does not maximize wood production in the short run, as some industries might prefer. It does not maintain maximum populations of game animals, as some hunters might prefer, and it does not restore the natural disturbance regime exactly or maintain as much old-growth forest, as some environmental groups might prefer. However, it does fulfill the goals of ecosystem management to manage vital natural resources on a sustainable basis for future generations, and to maintain the diversity and viability of native plant and animal populations.

References

1. N. D. G. JAMES, *A History of English Forestry*, Basil Blackwell, Oxford, 1990.

2. F. HESKE, *German Forestry*, Yale University Press, New Haven, 1938.

3. W. S. ALVERSON, W. KUHLMANN, AND D. M. WALLER, *Wild Forests: Conservation Biology and Public Policy*, Island Press, Washingon, D.C.,1994.

4. C. A. WOOD, *Renew. Res. J.*, *12*, 612 (1994).

5. F. J. SWANSON AND J. F. FRANKLIN, *Ecol. Applications*, *2*, 262 (1992).

6. J. W. THOMAS, *Ecol. Applications*, *6*, 703 (1996).

7. G. PINCHOT, *A Primer of Forestry*, U.S.D.A. Bureau of Forestry Bull. 24 (1905).

8. C. G. LORIMER AND L. E. FRELICH, *J. For.*, *92 (1)*, 33, (1994).

9. C. E. VAN WAGNER, *Can. J. For. Res.*, *8*, 220 (1978).

10. J. K. AGEE, "The historical role of fire in Pacific Northwest forests", In *Natural and Prescribed Fire in Pacific Northwest Forests*, Oregon State Univ. Press, Corvallis, 1990.

11. J. BIELEFELDT AND R. N. ROSENFIELD, *The Passenger Pigeon*, *56*, 123 (1994).

12. M. T. SINGER AND C. G. LORIMER, *Can. J. For. Res.*, *27*, 1222 (1997).

13. R. L. WILLIAMSON, "Results of Shelterwood Harvesting of Douglas-fir in the Cascades of Western Oregon," U.S.D.A. Forest Service Res. Pap. PNW-161, 1973.

14. P. M. McDONALD, "Shelterwood Cutting in a Young-Growth, Mixed-Conifer Stand in North Central California," U.S.D.A. Forest Service Res. Pap. PSW-117, 1976.

15. KLUENDER, R. A. AND B. J. STOKES, *So. J. Appl. For.*, *18*, 168 (1994).

16. H. C. SMITH AND P. S. DEBALD, "Economics of even-aged and uneven-aged silviculture and management in eastern hardwoods," in *Uneven-Aged Silviculture & Management in the United States*, U.S.D.A. Forest Service, Timber Management Research, Washington, D.C., 1978.

17. J. W. HORNBECK, C. W. MARTIN, R. S. PIERCE, ET AL., "The Northern Hardwood Forest Ecosystem: Ten Years After Recovery from Clearcutting," U.S.D.A. Forest Service Res. Pap. NE-RP-596, 1987.

18. R. WORRELL AND A. HAMPSON, *Forestry*, *70*, 61 (1997).

19. J. D. HEWLETT, "Forest Water Quality: An Experiment in Harvesting and Regenerating Piedmont Forest," Georgia Forest Research Paper, 1979.

20. D. A. PERRY, R. MEURISSE, B. THOMAS, ET AL., *Maintaining the Long-Term Productivity of Pacific Northwest Forest Ecosystems*, Timber Press, Portland, Ore., 1989.

21. C. R. SMITH, D. M. PENCE, AND R. J. O'CONNOR, "Status of neotropical migratory birds in the Northeast: A preliminary assessment," In *Status and Management of Neotropical Migratory Birds*, U.S.D.A. Forest Service Gen Tech. Rep. RM-229, 1993.

22. P. B. WOOD AND J. V. NICHOLS, "Effects of Two-age Timber Management and Clearcutting on Songbird Diversity and Reproductive Success," Div. of Forestry, West Virginia University, Morgantown, 1995.

23. C. L. CHAMBERS, W. C. McCOMB, AND J. C. TAPPEINER, *Ecol. Applications*, *9*, 171 (1999).

24. D. O. WALLIN, F. J. SWANSON, AND B. MARKS. *Ecol. Applications*, *4*, 569 (1994).

CHAPTER 14

Forest-Wildlife Management

MARK S. BOYCE

More than 60 percent of the world's biodiversity is associated with forests (1). From subarctic boreal forests to tropical rain forests, trees provide food and cover for many species of wildlife. Wildlife includes aquatic species such as fish, and forests may be important because they have a stabilizing effect on streamflow that provides habitats for aquatic species. Wildlife is an integral component of forest ecosystems. For example, wildlife may serve as crucial agents for seed dispersal or by selectively foraging on certain plants, can alter patterns of forest succession. Humans alter wildlife populations to assist in forest management, or, alternatively, humans manage forests because of their importance to desired wildlife species.

Wildlife Values

Wildlife most often is viewed as an amenity in forest management. This means that wildlife is viewed to be a bonus value to a forest that is not the primary reason for its management. With increasing interest in biodiversity, this view toward wildlife is changing and in some systems (e.g., the Pacific Northwest), wildlife are primary drivers in shaping priorities for forest management.

Wildlife is a source of recreational hunting and fishing in forests throughout most of the world. With careful stewardship, wildlife resources can be managed sustainably, meaning that harvesting of wildlife populations can be continued indefinitely. Each

313

Figure 14.1 Hunting constitutes a renewable use of the wildlife resource.

year many more individuals are born than can possibly survive. Human harvest or predation can remove these animals with no long-term consequences to population size (Figure 14.1).

In addition to harvest values, people around the world also value wildlife for aesthetic values. Bird-watching and wildlife safaris are becoming important sources of tourism revenue in many areas. Furthermore, most people who are actively engaged in resource extraction—for example, timber harvest, hunting, or fishing—enjoy opportunities to see bears, deer, bald eagles, songbirds and other wildlife. Also, the appreciation for wildlife is what attracts people to pursue recreational activities in forested ecosystems.

A national survey of participants in wildlife-associated recreation showed that about 14.1 million Americans hunted big and small game in 1991 (2). Expenditures for equipment, lodging, food, and transportation in pursuit of forest-associated game exceeded $12.3 billion in 1991. In the same year, approximately $3.8 billion was spent on wildlife in Canada (3). An estimated 35.6 million Americans spent $24 billion during 511 million days of fresh-water fishing. An updated 2001 survey of wildlife recreation has been undertaken and the results are reported on the following website: http://fa.r9.fws.gov/surveys/surveys.html#surv_2001.

Nonconsumptive use of wildlife has become increasingly important. The 1991 national survey showed that more than 76.1 million Americans participated in wildlife-associated recreation (2). An estimated $18.1 billion was spent in 1991 by persons engaged in "nonconsumptive wildlife-associated recreational activities." Perhaps most important, however, is the recognition that maintaining the diversity of wildlife is fundamental to ensuring the sustainability of forest ecosystems. Wildlife contributes to the very fabric of forest ecosystems and helps to ensure the availability of ecosystem services on which humans depend.

Ecological Interactions

Just as trees compete with one another for space, food, water, and sunlight, wildlife living in the forest interact with one another. These interactions occur at two levels, *intraspecifically* and *interspecifically*, and may be described as competitive, consumptive, or commensal interactions.

Many species of wildlife require certain amounts of space or territory to meet their needs. Some species defend their territories aggressively; for example, territory defense is an important function of most birdsong in the spring. Many mammals, as well as some reptiles and amphibians, maintain scent posts or other signs to mark territorial boundaries.

Consumptive interaction includes predation and herbivory and can be either interspecific or intraspecific. Some predators may occasionally kill and eat their own kind. Cannibalism among siblings appears to be frequent in the nests of hawks and owls when the parents are unable to find enough prey to feed the nestlings.

The effect of predation on wildlife populations has been controversial. For many years it was felt that predators were "bad." Then various studies began to suggest that predation was less important than some other factors in limiting wildlife abundance (4). These studies reinforced the concept of carrying capacity put forward in 1933 by Aldo Leopold, the founder of modern wildlife management (5).

This particular notion of *carrying capacity* is the number of individuals of a species that can survive in a given unit of habitat secure from predation. Carrying capacity is a measure of the adequacy of food and other resources in relation to secure cover. Once a prey species has been reduced to carrying capacity, it is no longer profitable for predators to continue hunting these animals (4). However, rather than being a fixed entity, carrying capacity varies from site-to-site; on the same site it might vary from year-to-year depending on the food available, the quality of the cover, and even snow conditions and depth.

Predators enforce carrying capacity, and in the absence of predators, some wildlife may become abundant in habitats that otherwise would be marginal. In the Cloquet Research Forest in northern Minnesota, ruffed grouse (*Bonasa umbellus*) reached a greater abundance in an aspen-pine forest when goshawks (*Accipiter gentilis*) were not nesting in that forest, but then declined sharply when these raptors returned. At the same time, grouse living in sapling aspen stands distant from coniferous cover remained relatively secure from raptor predation (6).

When large herbivorous mammals, like white-tailed deer (*Odocoileus virginianus*) or elk (*Cervus elaphus*), are living in the absence of their normal predators, available forage needed to maintain the population of animals determines the carrying capacity. When abundant, such herbivores may change the vegetation through their grazing and browsing. For some species in the absence of effective predation, territorial behavior may supplant forage availability as a factor limiting population size. Under these conditions the food and cover resources may have the capacity to support a considerably higher population of a species than intraspecific aggression will permit.

Predation is often opportunistic; that is, it most often occurs when the predator has an advantage. For some species, predation is markedly heavier along the edges between forests and openings, and especially along trails and roadways. Young and old-aged animals are usually more vulnerable than adults to predators (and hunters). Minnesota studies have shown that the percentage loss among young ruffed grouse over a seven-month period from the middle of September to the middle of April is as great as the loss among adult grouse over a twelve-month period, and numerically is about 3.4-fold greater on a monthly basis (7).

Wildlife as Components of Forest Ecosystems

Forest Habitats

Early Successional Species Vegetation succession involves a slow transition from one community to another eventually leading to a relatively long-term state termed a *climax*. Associated with each vegetative state of succession is an entire assemblage of plants and animals (Figure 14.2). Early successional species of wildlife thrive in the early stages of succession following a disturbance to the forest. For example, after fire or clearcutting, we often see increased use by moose (*Alces alces*) or white-tailed deer to feed on the herbaceous forage that is stimulated by the removal of trees. Some species, like the Kirtland's warbler (*Dendroica kirtlandii*), are restricted to early successional forests.

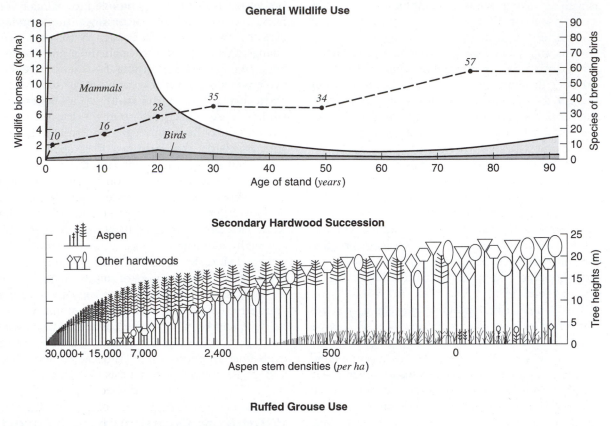

Figure 14.2 Secondary succession in a Great Lakes northern hardwoods forest, showing the sequence of dominant vegetation and the response of ruffed grouse as the forest composition changes. Also graphed is the change in animal biomass and bird species diversity associated with this succession.

Several forest types are known to undergo natural disturbance by fire that resets succession. Elsewhere, windthrow may be an occasional event resulting in gaps in the forest where early successional species would be found. Early successional habitats are often short lived, rapidly reverting to forests. The amount of early successional types on the landscape depends on the frequency and extent of disturbance. Some natural systems with high frequency of disturbance include: (a) the chaparral brushlands of California where mule deer (*Odocoileus hemionus*) are attracted after burning, (b) Rocky Mountain lodgepole pine (*Pinus contorta*) forests used by elk (*Cervus canadensis*) for foraging after fire or clearfelling (8), (c) the oak savanna of midwestern North America where the endangered Karner blue butterfly (*Lycaeides melissa samuelis*) depends on lupine (*Lupinus perennis*) that is maintained by fire, mowing, or grazing, and (d) eroded stream banks created by periodic flooding required for nesting by wood turtles (*Clemmys insculpta*).

Wildlife of Mixed-age Forests Patterns of succession on the landscape are often complex. Fires, windthrow, insect outbreaks, and other disturbances are usually patchy, creating a vegetation mosaic of early, mid-aged, and old growth forests.

Some forms of wildlife require an interspersion of trees of different ages or of different species. Primary consumers or herbivores are the most dependent on interspersion of forest resources because they use forest vegetation in several ways. Conditions favorable for the production of food resources usually differ from those providing secure cover. Additionally, forest-dwelling herbivores tend to be nonmigratory, and therefore require year-round food and cover from the habitats they occupy. Some herbivores in the Great Lakes region forests such as snowshoe hares (*Lepus americanus*), ruffed grouse, and white-tailed deer require this diversity within comparatively small areas. But mule deer (*O. hemionus*) and elk in western mountainous regions find their requirements by being migratory, often moving many kilometers from summer to winter ranges (8).

Moose require an interspersion of forest types, with the addition of streams, ponds, or lakes to provide aquatic vegetation for their summer diet. In Minnesota the proper mixture for moose on an area of 9,300 ha (21,000 acres) has been estimated to be 40 to 50 percent open land less than 20 years old, 5 to 15 percent in spruce fir, and 35 to 55 percent aspen-birch stands over 20 years old, and pond, lakes, and streams (9).

Wildlife of Old-Growth Forests At the opposite extreme from early successional wildlife are species tied to late-successional or old-growth habitats. The most celebrated example is the northern

spotted owl (*Strix occidentalis caurina*) that has been responsible for restructuring the management of forest resources in the Pacific Northwest. There are many species tied to mature forests and the unique habitats found in such forests. An ungulate example is the woodland caribou (*Rangifer tarandus*) of boreal forest regions of Canada and northern Idaho. During winter woodland caribou forage on arboreal lichens—pale-green beard-like lichens that hang from tree branches. Clearcutting of the forests has devastating consequences for the caribou because of their reliance on lichens in old trees. Selective logging might provide a creative solution, however, because some old trees are left standing, providing at least part of the lichen forage available before logging.

Edge Habitats Edges are attractive to some species because the forest provides cover and mast (e.g., acorns), whereas clearings may have more forage. Thus, by occupying the edge, individuals may gain benefits from both habitats. Aldo Leopold (5) claimed that the amount of game was proportional to the amount of edge, but this pattern appears to apply primarily to selected species such as white-tailed deer (Figure 14.3) and ruffed grouse. Although many species of wildlife prefer edge habitats, these can be dangerous places because predators often concentrate there. Several species of songbirds, for example, preferentially nest in edge habitats that become mortality "sinks" because crows (*Corvus brachyrhynchos*), jays, raccoons (*Procyon lotor*; Figure 14.4), skunks (*Mephitis mephitis*), and foxes (*Vulpes fulva*) hunt the edges of forest openings (10).

Riparian Zones Vegetation immediately surrounding bodies of water, streams, rivers, lakes and ponds, is known as the riparian zone. Waterfowl nest in riparian vegetation. Some species including semi-aquatic mammals such as beavers (*Castor canadensis*), muskrats (*Ondatra zibethicus*), otters (*Lontra canadensis*), and mink (*Mustela vison*) are found only in the riparian zone. These areas tend to be highly productive because water and nutrients are seldom limiting, and they host a high

Sidebar 14.1

Case Study: Northern Spotted Owl

Species adapted to old-growth forests are threatened by accelerated forest management. Old-growth forests typically contain trees of large size, vertical differentiation of vegetation structure, and large standing dead trees and decaying logs. Old-growth Douglas fir and redwood forests of the Pacific Northwest have these characteristics and provide habitats for the northern spotted owl. Spotted owls forage on rodents under the forest canopy, and require an open stand structure in which to hunt their prey. Young forests have trees that are too dense to permit the owls to fly.

One of the most common prey species for spotted owls, especially in California and Oregon, is the dusky-footed woodrat (*Neotoma fuscipes*). This rodent attained highest density in young regenerating stands that are too dense for hunting owls. Some of the best habitats for spotted owls are old-growth stands adjacent to younger forests that yield woodrats that disperse into the old-growth (1). Because of heavy timber harvests in recent years, young-aged forests are not in short supply. Thus, most fundamental for spotted owl habitats is the maintenance of old-growth forests.

Old-growth forests have declined by approximately 90 percent across the Pacific Northwest in the past century, and if this rate of decline were to continue the spotted owl would have been at risk of extinction within a few years. In 1990, the spotted owl was listed in the United States as a threatened species under the Endangered Species Act. Subsequently large tracts of old-growth forests on public lands have been protected, ensuring the future for the owl and associated old-growth species.

Source:

1. M. S. Boyce, *Wildl. Soc. Bull., 26*, 391 (1998).

diversity of wildlife often containing complements of both the terrestrial and aquatic fauna. Although riparian habitats occupy only 1 percent of landscapes in North America, they contain over 80 percent of our threatened and endangered species (11).

Disturbance is a fundamental component of riparian ecosystems. Periodic flooding of rivers and streams can be important in retarding succession and altering the distribution of sediments. Periodic flushing flows, to clean out gravel beds, are required to maintain spawning habitats for trout and salmon. Beavers take advantage of stream-course changes following floods where new pools are formed near aspen (*Populus tremuloides*), willow (*Salix* spp.), or cottonwood (*Populus* spp.) stands.

Dams and channelization have altered riparian forests and the disturbance processes associated with the systems. Because water levels are controlled on the Platte River in Nebraska, sand and gravel bars are becoming extensively wooded, thereby eliminating nesting habitats for least terns (*Sterna antillarum*) and piping plovers (*Charádrius melódus*). In other areas along the Platte River, cottonwood (*P. deltoides*) stands are growing decadent with no recruitment of young trees because of the absence of flooding that creates sites for germination. Solutions to the disruption of flooding cycles

Figure 14.3 White-tailed deer. Because of wildlife management efforts, this species has become the most abundant large mammal in North America.

are being found by manipulating flood-control gates to create seasonal high-water-level conditions.

Wildlife Effects on Forests

Seed Dispersal Wildlife plays a role in the distribution of seeds of many trees. Few of the birds that feed on the fruits of cherries (*Prunus* spp.), mountain ash, junipers (*Juniperus* spp.), and others, actually crush or damage the seeds. The seeds pass through the bird's digestive systems intact and ready to germinate if they are dropped in a suitable place. Indeed, passing through the gut can serve to scarify certain types of seeds enhancing their germination. The common growths of fruit-producing shrubs and trees along fences and under telephone wires or power lines attests to this function. If fruits were eaten by birds during migration seeds might be deposited many kilometers from where they were consumed.

Birds commonly carry seeds for some time in a storage pouch, or crop, before the food passes into their gizzard to be ground and digested. Predators feeding on a bird usually consume the fleshy part of the crop and leave the contents scattered where

Figure 14.4 Raccoons frequent forest edges where they will opportunistically prey on bird nests.

they eat the bird. Seeds from the crop may germinate thereby achieving dispersal.

Turtles, tortoises, lizards, and fish also transport seeds from one site to another, and if one of these animals happens to be preyed on by a bird, seeds may be moved a considerable distance. Even seeds taken by granivorous mammals may become scattered some distance from the point of origin when they are the victims of predation.

The complexity of forest-wildlife ecology is illustrated by studies of mycophagous or fungus-eating small mammals. Rodents act as vectors in the transmission of fungal spores from one site to another and may promote the establishment of conifers by distributing ectomycorrhizae important to nutrient absorption by tree roots (12) (also see Chapters 4 and 8).

Insect Predation   Birds and small mammals can consume large quantities of insects, and sometimes are known to reduce pest species. For example, netting experimentally placed to prevent birds access to trees has been shown to increase the abundance of jack-pine budworm (*Choristoneura pinus*) and western spruce budworm (*C. occidentalis*) (13). Yet, during periods of population outbreaks, these insects become so abundant that birds are unable to check populations of these pests. Insecticides may have relatively minor consequences to birds during insect outbreaks because the insects are so abundant that the birds still have plenty to eat. However, at other times broadcast spraying of insecticides can have serious consequences for birds that depend on insects for food.

Herbivory   Wildlife can be agents of disturbance maintaining systems in an early successional stage. Browsing by moose, elk (Figure 14.5), and deer can prevent woody plant establishment in grasslands (Figure 14.6) and can reduce recruitment of selected species, such as aspen, that are preferred by ungulates. Beavers can have major influences on riparian vegetation by selectively clearfelling preferred trees such as aspen and cottonwood.

Such herbivory can be the source of frustration for foresters trying to establish young trees.

Figure 14.5   The range of elk or wapiti has expanded extensively during the past 30 years and the populations of the species are now established in Wisconsin, Michigan, Pennsylvania, Kentucky, and Virginia in the United States, and Manitoba, Saskatchewan, and Ontario in Canada, as well as all Rocky Mountain states and provinces.

Figure 14.6   An exclosure on the northern range of Yellowstone National Park where native ungulate herbivory has been prevented for approximately 40 years. Few dense stands of willow can be found in portions of the park due to feeding of elk, bison, deer, and moose.

Rodents and rabbits also do a great deal of damage to forest regeneration by feeding on the tender bark of young trees. During periods when mice populations are large, stands of seedlings or sprouts may be almost completely destroyed by rodent girdling. Likewise, porcupines (*Erithizon dorsatum*) can be responsible for widespread destruction of merchantable aspen, red spruce (*Picea rubens*), balsam fir (*Abies balsamea*), and red and white pine (*Pinus resinosa* and *P. strobus*) by eating the bark of these trees.

Effects of Forest Management on Wildlife

Fire Suppression

The role of fire in forest management is controversial. Fire can cause substantial damage to the commercial value of a forest, but in many areas, fire is a natural disturbance process. For example, wildfire was responsible for maintaining the jack pine on which the Kirtland's warbler depends. Likewise, oak savannas of the midwestern United States and pine barrens of New Jersey and northwestern Wisconsin were fire-maintained systems that gradually disappeared by succession to forests as a result of protection from burning. Again, species such as the endangered Karner blue butterfly (*Lycaeides melissa samuelis*) and its food plant the lupine are dependent on disturbances such as fire. Ruffed grouse, woodcock (*Scolopax minor*), deer, moose, and elk thrive on the food and cover available in areas undergoing post-fire succession.

In contrast, for species dependent on old-growth features of the forest such as spotted owls (Sidebar 14.1), marbled murrelets (*Brachyramphus marmoratus*), ovenbirds (*Seiurus aurocapillus*), or the extinct ivory-billed woodpecker (*Campephilus principalis*), fire can be destructive.

Prescribed Burning

A number of ecosystems are maintained by disturbances such as fire, and these along with associated wildlife are becoming rare because fire is so

---

Sidebar 14.2

Case Study: Elk in Yellowstone National Park

Large herbivores can have substantial influence on vegetation. Elk (*Cervus elaphus*) in Yellowstone National Park were culled by park rangers during the middle part of the 20th century to reduce their effect on vegetation. Since 1968, however, the elk have been strictly protected inside the park resulting in substantial increases in the elk population, especially on the park's Northern Range. Clearly aspen (*Populus tremuloides*), willow (*Salix* spp.), and various shrubs are heavily browsed. Controlling herbivory by constructing fenced exclosures results in substantial changes in vegetation structure and composition (see Figure 14.6). Some people find this to be objectionable, noting that sound range management practices would not allow such heavy levels of livestock use. Others argue that we need protected places like national parks as ecological baselines where we can document the consequences of human activities outside the parks (1).

In 1995, wolves were reintroduced into Yellowstone National Park, and appear to have caused a decline in the number of elk. Current research is attempting to document response by vegetation to reduced herbivory.

Source:
1. M. S. Boyce, *Wildl. Soc. Bull., 26,* 391 (1998).

aggressively suppressed. The oak savannas and tall-grass prairies of the midwest, heathlands of the eastern coast of North America, aspen parkland of western Canada, and pine barrens of northwestern Wisconsin and New Jersey are a few examples. To ensure perpetuation of these fire-maintained ecosystems, prescribed fire is a useful management tool. The behavior and management of forest fires are further discussed in Chapter 18.

Timber Harvest

Timber harvest can be a surrogate for fire that can benefit early successional species. Florida sand pine scrub responds similarly to fire and mechnical disturbance, and timber harvest may be an acceptable substitute for natural disturbance (14). Likewise, savanna birds in the pine barrens of northwestern Wisconsin readily use openings created by timber harvest (15). Yet vegetation structure and species composition differ in several ways between openings created by fire versus those created by timber harvest (16). Therefore, although timber harvest may simulate natural disturbances, there may be differences depending on the form of disturbance that may require alternative forms of treatment, such as prescribed fire.

Forest Fragmentation

Associated with increased intensity of management of forests, generally we have seen increased fragmentation of the landscape (see Chapter 7, Landscape Ecology). Harvest patterns, road construction, and residential housing have increasingly partitioned forests into smaller and smaller units. In many areas, this has the consequence of lowering species diversity, by eliminating those species that have the largest area requirements and species that require conditions characteristic of forest interior (17). Examples of species that decline with increasing forest fragmentation include the northern spotted owl (see Sidebar 14.1) in the Pacific Northwest and ovenbirds common to woodlands

of eastern North America. Much of the decline for these species can actually be attributed to habitat loss (18), which is usually associated with fragmentation.

Effects of landscape change can be complex and fragmentation actually can benefit some species. Throughout eastern North America, forest cover has increased during the past century. Associated with this afforestation has been a decline in many bird species associated with shrublands and grasslands (19). Also, a number of game species including white-tailed deer, elk, ruffed grouse, and bobwhite (*Colinus virginianus*) are more abundant in areas with frequent forest disturbance and edge (5). For these species, forests provide cover for hiding and thermal refuge whereas open areas with greater herbaceous vegetation provide more forage. Areas with a high degree of edge afford easy access to both cover types that provide both cover and forage.

Pesticides and Herbicides

Both pesticides and herbicides may be toxic to wildlife, and many species have suffered with agricultural intensification and the expanded use of these chemicals. Raptors including peregrine falcons (*Falco peregrinus*) and bald eagles (*Haliaeetus leucocephalus*) suffered serious population declines in the middle of the 20th century from eggshell thinning caused by DDT, a pesticide developed during World War II. In the United States and Canada, many raptors have made remarkable comebacks subsequent to the ban of DDT. Unfortunately, the pesticide is still being used in many developing countries where environmental regulations are not as strict.

In addition to the direct toxicity of pesticides and herbicides, these chemicals can have serious indirect consequences for wildlife. Pesticides are designed to kill insect pests, and herbicides are designed to kill certain plants. Insects are often key foods for young birds, and most birds cannot live without them. Likewise, amphibians and reptiles are often insectivorous and elimination of their primary source of food may have devastating consequences. Plants provide cover and food for many animals, so herbicides eliminate habitats.

Wildlife Considerations in Ecosystem Management

Managing for Biodiversity

Threatened and Endangered Species The ultimate cause for at least 80 percent of known avian extinctions has been habitat loss (20). Generally the most crucial management action to prevent future extinctions is ensuring that sufficient habitats are maintained. Some species have huge area requirements; for example, grizzly bears (*Ursus arctos*) and wolves (*Canis lupus*). Species with large area requirements are often called "umbrella" species, because if we maintain large enough areas to protect these species we will also ensure the persistence of smaller species that occur in the same area but have much smaller area requirements.

Protection of habitat may not be sufficient, especially for species that require habitats maintained by disturbance. The Kirtland's warbler, for example, requires early successional jack pine stands for nesting. The Karner blue butterfly requires lupine that is maintained by fire, grazing, or mowing in oak savanna habitats of the Midwest. The red-cockaded woodpecker (*Picoides borealis*) thrives in long-leaf pine (*Pinus palustris*) stands of the southeastern United States where frequent fire prevents invasion of oaks.

Value of Downed Woody Debris One of the most important features of a forest that increases species diversity is the presence of coarse woody debris. This takes the form of downed logs on the forest floor, dead branches, snags, and standing dead trees. Deadwood then is decayed by invertebrates, fungi, and microorganisms that in turn provide food for small mammals and birds. Such woody debris is a characteristic feature of old-growth forests and is why such forests often possess high diversity. Management of forests in ways that retain woody debris is an effective way to enhance biodiversity.

Ecosystem Structure and Function

Streamside Protection Maintaining buffer zones of protected forest adjacent to streams is a common management practice to protect streams from sediment and nutrient runoff. This can be crucially important for maintaining fish habitats and failure to protect streams in the Pacific Northwest has been identified as one of the factors leading to the decline in salmon fisheries. Road crossings associated with logging are especially troublesome because of the potential for large amounts of sediment to be washed into the stream during heavy rains. Generally, the wider the streamside buffer, the more effective the protection of wildlife habitats, for example, Swainson's warblers (*Helmitheros swainsonii*) were never detected in buffers less than 300 m (984 ft) width and had higher densities in buffers >1,000 m (3,280 ft) (21). Large trees falling into the stream can be valuable components of fish habitat, so one guideline is to maintain buffers at least as wide as the height of the tallest trees (22).

Habitat Manipulation Habitats are often manipulated to enhance the value of an area for selected wildlife. Clearcutting aspen is used to stimulate shoot growth to enhance habitat for ruffed grouse, woodcock, and deer. Burning is used to enhance habitats for Karner blue butterflies, moose, elk, deer, and red-cockaded woodpeckers. Planting of food and cover crops is used to attract wildlife, sometimes to distract animals from agricultural crops or forest plantations (8).

Selective cutting of trees can hasten the development of old-growth characteristics required by northern spotted owls. Similarly, selective logging has been used in the Rocky Mountains to improve lichen

Sidebar 14.3

Case Study: Kirtland's Warbler

The Kirtland's warbler (*Dendroica kirtlandii*) is an endangered species that breeds primarily in the jack pine (*Pinus banksiana*) plains of north central Lower Peninsula Michigan and winters mostly in the Bahama Island archipelago. The natural pine barren ecosystem was historically maintained by frequent wildfires, but because of modern fire suppression techniques and alternative land uses, the amount of this habitat has decreased causing the decline of the Kirtland's warbler population. In addition, the warbler population was decreasing because of cowbird (*Molothrus ater*) parasitism. In 1972, land managers began to trap cowbirds, and in 1976, they began to plant jack pine in clearcuts to replicate wildfire habitat. Habitat management and cowbird removals have been successful at increasing the population. By 1999, the population had increased to 903 pairs with 94 percent of the birds occurring in jack pine plantations.

Large areas of low diversity are required to sustain this endangered species. The current goal for forest management is to maintain 10,340 ha of habitat for the Kirtland's warbler. Stand sizes must be greater than about 50 ha, with most

Male Kirtland's warbler.

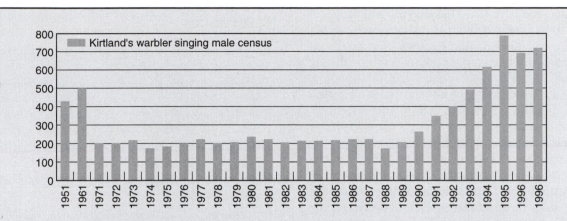

Counts of male Kirtland's warbler on their breeding range in Michigan.

birds nesting in stands greater than 100 ha. The nesting habitat for the Kirtland's warbler is almost strictly dense young jack pine stands 8–20 yrs old where the trees are 2–6 m tall. Natural habitats were typically post-fire succession, but because of modern concerns about risks associated with wildfires, current stands are typically plantations following clearcutting. Rotations of jack pine in Kirtland's warbler habitat are about 50 years with harvested trees used primarily for paper pulp.

Habitat needs for this endangered species illustrate how biodiversity conservation must be viewed on a large geographic scale. Large areas with low diversity at a local scale are required within the forest matrix to ensure the maintenance of regional diversity.

on remaining trees with the intent of enhancing habitats for mountain caribou. Foresters practicing woodlot management may selectively remove maples with little wildlife value while favoring oaks and conifers that offer greater benefits for wildlife. Another approach is manipulation of water levels, for example, in green-tree reservoirs in the southern United States, to enhance winter habitats for waterfowl (11).

Population Control

Left undisturbed, natural populations of forest wildlife will eventually reach the carrying capacity of their habitats, and over time, populations will fluctuate around this carrying capacity. However, we often find that, when abundant, wildlife may come in conflict with human interests in forest management. Hunting and trapping are probably the most common methods of population control for game species and furbearers, but sometimes these traditional methods are not practical, efficient, or socially acceptable. Under these circumstances, alternative methods of population control must be explored.

Beavers have become abundant in some areas of North America where they cut trees, dam streams flooding roads, or flood lowland forests killing valuable timber trees. Beavers can be trapped and dams destroyed with dynamite. Creative alternatives exist; for example, driving corrugated PVC pipe through a beaver dam to lower water levels.

White-tailed deer have become remarkably abundant in many regions of North America. In one sense, this points to the success of wildlife management during the latter half of the 20th century. However, deer can damage crops, browse nursery trees, and alter forest succession by selective browsing. In populated areas, automobile collisions with deer are a major concern. Although deer hunting can be used for population management, in many areas, hunter harvest has not been sufficient to achieve the desired population levels. This is especially a problem in urban areas where hunting may not be permitted. For example, the city of Milwaukee, Wisconsin has implemented deer control using professional snipers, with silenced rifles, shooting deer at bait stations. Other urban areas have trapped deer and transported them to areas outside the city. Experimental programs are being implemented in some areas using immunocontraceptives. There are no easy solutions to these control issues, because each method requires persistent treatments year after year.

Concluding Statement

Wildlife adds enormous value to the forests of the world; generally, people enjoy wildlife. Managing forests to enhance wildlife habitats often can be accomplished with little additional cost. In some instances, wildlife resources may be worth more than the traditional timber values of the forest. In other instances, wildlife can be viewed as pests by forest managers because they damage trees or interfere with regeneration. In all forests, however, wildlife contributes to ecosystem structure and function and is a key component of biodiversity, and the world is a better place to live because of it.

References

1. W. J. SNAPE, III, *Biodiversity and the Law*, Island Press, Washington D.C., 1996.

2. ANON. "1990 National Survey of Fishing, Hunting and Wildlife-associated Recreation," U.S.D.I. Fish and Wildlife Serv., Washington, D.C., 1991.

3. F. L. FILION, A. JACQUEMOT, E. DUWORS, ET AL. "The Importance of Wildlife to Canadians," Canadian Wildlife Service, Ottawa, 1994.

4. P. L. ERRINGTON, *Predation and Life,* Iowa State Univ. Press, Ames, 1971.

5. A. LEOPOLD, *Game Management,* Scribners, New York, 1933.

6. G. W. GULLION AND A. A. ALM, *J. For., 81,* 528, 536 (1983).

7. G. W. GULLION AND W. H. MARSHALL, *Living Bird, 7,* 117 (1968).

8. M. S. BOYCE, *The Jackson Elk Herd,* Cambridge Univ. Press, 1989.

9. J. M. PEEK, D. L. URICH, AND R. J. MACKIE, *Wildl. Monogr. 48* (1976).

10. N. D. NIEMUTH AND M. S. BOYCE, *J. Wildl. Manage. 61,* 1234 (1997).

11. M. S. BOYCE, AND A. HANEY, *Ecosystem Management: Applications for Sustainable Forest and Wildlife Resources.* Yale Univ. Press, New Haven, 1997.

12. J. TERWILLIGER AND J. PASTOR, *Oikos, 85,* 83 (1999).

13. T. R. TORGERSON AND R. W. CAMPBELL, *Envir. Entomol., 11,* 429 (1982).

14. C. H. GREENBERG, D. G. NEARY, L. D. HARRIS, AND S. P. LINDA, *Am. Midl. Nat., 133,* 149 (1995).

15. D. W. SAMPLE AND M. J. MOSSMAN, "Managing Habitat for Grassland Birds: A Guide for Wisconsin." *Wisc. Dep. Nat. Resour. PUBL-SS-925-97.* Madison, 1997.

16. N. D. NIEMUTH AND M. S. BOYCE, *Trans. Wisc. Acad. Sci. Arts Lett., 86,* 167 (1998).

17. S. K. ROBINSON, F. R. THOMPSON, T. M. DONOVAN, D. WHITEHEAD, AND J. FAABORG, *Science, 267,* 1987 (1995).

18. L. FAHRIG, *J. Wildl. Manage., 61,* 603 (1997).

19. R. A. ASKINS, *Curr. Ornith., 11,* 1 (1993).

20. D. WILCOVE, D. ROTHSTEIN, J. DUBOW, A. PHILLIPS, AND E. LOSOS, *BioScience, 48,* 607 (1998).

21. J. C. KILGO, R. A. SARGENT, K. V. MILLER, AND B. R. CHAPMAN, "Effect of riparian zone width on Swainson's warbler abundance." In *Proc. S. Forested Wetlands Ecology and Manage. Conf.,* K. M. Flynn, ed., Clemson Univ., Clemson, S.C., 1996.

22. M. L. HUNTER, JR., *Maintaining Biodiversity in Forest Ecosystems.* Cambridge Univ. Press, 1999.

23. J. S. MEYER, L. L. IRWIN, AND M. S. BOYCE, *Wildl. Monogr., 139,* 1–51 (1998).

CHAPTER 15

Rangeland Management

WAYNE C. LEININGER AND
JOHN D. STEDNICK

Rangelands are areas of the world that—by reasons of physical limitations: low and erratic precipitation, rough topography, poor drainage, and cold temperatures—are unsuitable for cultivation (1). They are an important source of forage for free-ranging native and domestic animals, as well as a source of wood products, water, and wildlife (2, 3). Approximately 47 percent of the earth's land surface is classified as rangeland, and of the estimated 385 million hectares of rangeland in the United States, a little over one-third is forested range (4, 5). The distribution of rangelands in the United States is given in Table 15.1.

Rangeland Grazing Management

Typically, a ranch operation in the western United States is made up of deeded land (base property) where hay is produced and cattle are "wintered," and in addition, leased land, where the livestock graze in the summer. Summer grazing on federal land is regulated by a permit system. The grazing permit entitles the user to a grazing area, a decreed number of stock, and entrance and exit dates during the summer, demarking the period when the animals can be present on the range.

Many livestock operations in the western United States depend heavily on forage produced in the forest for part of the grazing year (Figure 15.1). In Colorado, for example, approximately 45 and 50 percent of the summer forage utilized by cattle and sheep, respectively, comes from national forests (6). The number of livestock grazing in the National Forests increased steadily until about 1915. By 1918, the rising number of livestock, the long season of use, and the huge increase during the war caused most of the forest range to decline in productivity. This deterioration in the range prompted both a reduction in the number of livestock grazing in the forest and a change in the manner in which livestock were grazed. Specialized grazing systems that provided recurring systematic periods of grazing and deferment from grazing were adopted.

Deferred-rotation and *rest-rotation* grazing are two common grazing systems used in forested rangelands. Under deferred rotation, grazing on a portion of the range is delayed until after the most important range plants have set seed. Then, by rotation of the deferment over a period of years, other pastures are successively given the benefit of deferment until all pastures have been deferred (2). When this has been accomplished, the grazing cycle is repeated. In rest-rotation grazing, a portion of

Table 15.1 Distribution of Rangeland in the United States

Region	Percentage
Rocky Mountains and Great Plains	50
Pacific Region (including Alaska and Hawaii)	37
South Central	12
Other	1

Source: U.S.D.A. Forest Service data.

the range is rested for a full year. Deferring other pastures from grazing is also a part of rest-rotation grazing systems. The deferment and rest periods are designed to allow plants to increase in vigor, produce seeds, and establish new seedlings. The design and advantages of grazing systems have been extensively reviewed (1, 3, 7).

A third grazing system, *short-duration grazing,* is gaining popularity in many regions of the United States. This system employs a large number of pastures (frequently twelve or more) and short periods of grazing in each pasture (generally two days to two weeks). Intensive livestock management is required with this system, because of its high stocking density; that is, the large number of animals per area of land (7).

Major types of forests in which livestock graze in the United States include ponderosa pine, pinon-juniper, aspen, transitory, mountain meadows, and riparian zones.

Forested Rangelands

The ponderosa pine range is the most extensive forested range in the western United States. It occupies the low elevations of the mountains and foothills in many areas, but mixes with other tree species at moderate elevations (8). This type is associated with an understory of bunchgrasses and shrubs. Its value as rangeland is the highest of any of the forested range types. About 560 to 675 kilograms per hectare (dry-weight basis) of understory herbage is produced in open stands of mature pine with 500 saplings per hectare (9). As the density of pines increases, there is generally a curvilinear decrease in understory production (Figure 15.2). This range commonly serves as summer range for cattle, and spring and fall range for sheep that move to higher elevation rangeland during summer. Both rest-rotation and deferred-rotation grazing systems, under proper stocking, have been reported to benefit these forested ranges (10).

The pinon-juniper range is a woodland composed of small trees, generally less than 4.5 meters in height, growing in either open or dense stands. This range is located between the ponderosa pine forest and desert shrub or grassland. The pinon-juniper range generally occurs on rocky, poorly developed soils, and in many locations it alternates with big sagebrush, which occupies deeper soils. Understory productivity ranges from near zero on poorly developed soils to 900 kilograms per hectare on favorable sites (9, 11). Cattle and sheep

Figure 15.1 Sheep grazing in Midway Valley, Dixie National Forest, Utah. (Courtesy of U.S.D.A. Forest Service.)

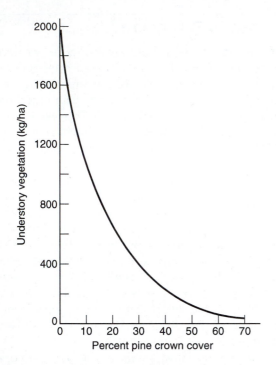

Figure 15.2 Production of understory herbage as related to the density of a ponderosa pine canopy. (After Pase [11].)

frequently graze this range in spring before moving to higher-elevation summer ranges, and again in fall as they return to their wintering areas. The pinon-juniper type is also very important as the seasonal habitat for migratory deer.

Fire suppression and overgrazing by livestock have allowed woodland to expand both upslope and downslope over the past 100+ years (12). Prescribed burns and mechanical removal of pinon and juniper trees by chaining—large tractors pulling anchor chains or cables over the land—are frequently used to reduce the invasion of this type. Desirable grasses are also commonly seeded into recently treated areas to increase forage for livestock and wildlife.

The aspen range has long been recognized for its importance to livestock and wildlife, because it creates diversity in otherwise homogeneous conifer stands. The aspen range is valued for the diversity and productivity of its understory vegetation. This type is the most productive of the forested ranges and often produces more than 2000 kilograms per hectare of understory vegetation. This amount is similar to that of many grasslands. Frequently the aspen range produces more than ten times the amount of understory that associated conifer stands do (13).

Aspen is one of the most common trees in the interior West and grows along moist stream bottoms, as well as on dry ridges and southerly exposures (Figure 15.3), on sloping embankments, and on shallow to deep soils of varied origin. The aspen range extends from Alaska to northern Mexico.

Grazing by cattle and sheep has been the primary consumptive use of the aspen range in the West (14). Livestock grazing usually occurs during summer and early autumn. Overgrazing by livestock during the first half of the twentieth century caused deleterious, long-term changes in much of this ecosystem. Excessive grazing generally changes the composition of understory species and frequently reduces productivity.

Proper management of both the aspen trees and the understory forage resource requires careful planning. Timber management should produce a variety of several aspen seral stages to maximize quantity and quality of the forage and to produce the diversity that is apparently necessary for uses of this type. Grazing guidelines have been summarized for this range (14).

Figure 15.3 Summer grazing on an open mountain meadow range with aspen stands in the background. (Photograph by J. D. Stednick.)

Transitory ranges are forested areas that are suitable for grazing for only a temporary number of years following complete or partial forest removal. After that, the overstory closes in and intercepts the light needed to produce understory forage. Major areas of transitory range in the United States are found in the South and Northwest. These regions have ample precipitation and long growing seasons. Forage yields in these regions commonly exceed 2000 kilograms per hectare in cutover forests or under sparse tree canopies (15).

Tree overstory is the most influential factor determining forage yields in transitory ranges. For example, in the southern pine-hardwood range, forage yield in most clearcuts exceeds preharvesting yields by six to twenty times (16). This substantial increase in forage can in turn be allocated to livestock and wildlife populations.

In the past, foresters had little desire to integrate livestock with timber production. Their concern was that livestock would damage seedling regeneration through trampling and browsing and therefore reduce timber production. It has been well documented that when livestock numbers, distribution, or season of grazing have not been controlled, damage to timber reproduction has frequently been unacceptable (17).

In contrast, when livestock numbers and period of grazing have been appropriate, damage to conifer regeneration has been negligible (18). Although cattle may browse or debark trees, the majority of damage to regeneration done by cattle is from trampling and rubbing. Sheep, on the other hand, primarily damage seedlings by browsing their foliage. Browsing of regeneration by livestock is normally confined to current annual growth and generally the early succulent growth (18). Recommendations for the management of livestock grazing in young timber plantations generally call for the exclusion of livestock either until seedlings are well established (two to three years) or until the terminal leader of the seedlings are out of reach of grazing livestock.

Controlled livestock grazing can potentially benefit timber regeneration in several ways. These include reducing competition, decreasing the fire hazard, preventing the suppression of seedling, and decreasing the habitat of rodents, which damage seedlings. Another important advantage of integrated timber and livestock management, called *agroforestry,* is that profits can be higher than with single-resource management. Changing markets encourage flexibility in the overall operation, because diversification provides a means of surviving poor markets.

Nonforested Rangelands

The mountain meadows range ecosystem consists of wet to intermittently wet sites in the forest zone of the western United States. Typically, this range occurs on nearly flat to gently sloping topography where surface or subsurface water accumulates in the rooting zone for at least a portion of the year (9). Grasses and grasslike plants are generally the dominant vegetation in this type of range (Figure 15.4).

Mountain meadows are extremely productive and often yield ten to twenty times more forage than surrounding uplands (19). These meadows produce very high-quality forage which remains green and nutritious late into the summer. Mountain meadows support more livestock per hectare than any other

Figure 15.4 Cattle grazing on a meadow in Saint Joe National Forest, Idaho. (Photograph by W. W. Dresskell, U.S.D.A. Forest Service.)

type of range in the United States. Because of these advantages, mountain meadows are a very important link in year-round livestock production.

In addition to their great value for the production of livestock, mountain meadows are important for the maintenance of wildlife populations, and many act as a filter to catch sediments from water flowing from surrounding slopes. Mountain meadows also provide scenic vistas and are often preferred by recreationists.

Favorable grazing conditions, coupled with proximity to water and the steepness of slopes in adjacent range types, often encourage high concentrations of livestock and wildlife in the meadows. This uneven distribution of grazing animals can result in overgrazing and deterioration of mountain meadows.

Because mountain meadows already have a great potential for productivity, improving them is frequently cost-effective. Effective range management practices designed to improve livestock distribution include the development of water, placing salt licks in upland ranges, and herding (drifting) stock away from meadows. Where meadows are sufficiently large to be fenced separately from upland ranges, it may be economical to separate the two to protect the meadows from constant use and to ensure utilization of the upland forage (19). Grazing systems that have been developed for upland ranges have generally been ineffective in improving the condition of overgrazed mountain meadows, largely because they have failed to reduce livestock concentrations in the meadow (20).

Riparian zones—areas near streams, lakes, and wet areas whose plant communities are predominantly influenced by their association with water (21)—have been estimated to occupy between 0.5 and 2 percent of western rangelands. Although these zones constitute a relatively minor proportion of any watershed area, their importance in providing places for livestock to graze, fish and wildlife habitats, and recreational opportunities is disproportionately high.

Healthy riparian ecosystems have become a vanishing resource in the West, particularly in arid and semiarid regions. Estimates are that America has lost between 70 and 90 percent of its indigenous riparian resources and badly damaged much of the rest (22). In 1977, the U.S.D.I. Bureau of Land Management concluded that 83 percent of the riparian systems under its control were in unsatisfactory condition and in need of improved management, largely because of destruction caused by excessive livestock and grazing, road construction, and other damaging human activities. Many riparian zones have been ignored in the planning process because their limited extent made them "sacrifice areas."

Cattle often concentrate in riparian zones and utilize the vegetation much more intensively than that in adjacent areas. This heavy livestock grazing has frequently decreased plant vigor and production, changed the composition of plant species, and altered the streambank channel (20). Numerous studies have reported the deleterious effects of heavy livestock grazing on the regeneration of woody vegetation and the subsequent damage to the fisheries resource (23). Riparian ecosystems are the most critical zones for multiple-use planning and offer the greatest challenge to proper management (20). Techniques of riparian zone management include:

1. Improving livestock distribution, which increases animal use of upland range and decreases stock concentration in riparian zones.

2. Maintaining a minimum amount of residual vegetation (stubble height) to help preserve plant vigor, reduce browsing of willows and other woody plants, trap sediments, and limit streambank impact (24).

3. Implementing a specialized grazing system to provide a deferment and rest from grazing.

4. Changing the kind or class of animals grazing riparian zones. Sheep are generally less damaging than cattle to riparian zones because they are more easily controlled and can be herded away from riparian zones.

5. Managing riparian zones as "special-use" pastures. This increases the flexibility of the operation in regulating the level of grazing in riparian zones and allows grazing during the least damaging period (Figure 15.5).

6. Excluding the zones from livestock grazing. Riparian zones are generally very resilient and often improve in condition within five to seven years after livestock have been removed.

7. Constructing in-stream structures. These are expensive but have generally been successful in improving the condition of riparian zones when coupled with a change in grazing management (20).

Rangeland Water Quality

The most important deleterious effect of improper range management on water quality is soil erosion and the subsequent suspended sediment. Vegetative cover and soil properties determine the infiltration rates of precipitation water and the amount of streamflow that occurs on grazed lands. Vegetative cover is the dominant factor in controlling runoff and water erosion from agricultural lands and rangelands (25). Livestock grazing may alter the natural infiltration-runoff relationships by reducing the vegetative cover, by reducing and scattering the litter, and by compacting the soil through trampling. The magnitude of these changes is determined by the physiography, climate, vegetation, stocking rate, and animal species.

Raindrops striking bare soil may dislodge soil particles and increase soil erosion. Dislodged soil particles may block soil pores, further reducing infiltration rates, while other dislodged particles may remain suspended and leave the site in overland flow. However, water yield from overland flow may be increased by the decreased infiltration rates and capacities and the soil compaction (also see Chapter 16 on Watershed Management).

Soil compaction is the packing together of soil particles, thus increasing the soil bulk density (measured in grams per cubic centimeter). As use of an area increases, the probability of soil compaction also increases. Animal bedding grounds, stock trails, watering locations, and salt licks are areas of greatest compaction. Soil texture, moisture, and the amount of organic matter influence the degree of compaction (see Chapter 5). Soil compaction may also reduce plant growth or range productivity through changes in soil aeration and soil moisture. This reduction in vegetative cover may in turn increase the occurrence of overland flow and contribute to the desertification of marginal rangelands.

Land uses that increase water yield by reducing infiltration may also increase soil erosion and the subsequent amount of suspended sediment. Vegetative cover is important in minimizing overland flow. Land uses that increase infiltration rates help

Figure 15.5 Fenceline contrast between a riparian pasture that has been lightly grazed for twenty-five years (left of fence) and an adjacent heavily grazed area. Notice the willow regeneration in the lightly grazed pasture. (Photograph by W. C. Leininger.)

to establish desired plant species and to increase the plant biomass.

Range management practices designed to increase the growth of desired plants and increase water infiltration include vegetation conversion by chaining, contour furrowing, or root plowing. Land treatment by plowing and seeding generally lowers water infiltration rates at first and increases erosion. However, after two years, less soil is usually lost, because vegetative cover is greater than before treatment. Treatment by spraying and seeding has given similar results of lower magnitude. Treatment by burning and seeding may create hydrophobic soils, reduce water infiltration, and increase soil loss (26). The impact of erosion on site productivity has not been quantified for any rangeland plant-soil complex in the western United States.

Moderate continuous grazing or specialized grazing systems that improve the production of vegetation or herbage should reduce sediment yield. If a watershed has been overgrazed, though, institution of a grazing system will not necessarily reduce sediment.

Riparian grazing systems may alter the morphology of stream channels and cause associated changes in channel hydraulics, water quality, and the accumulation of sediment. Livestock grazed along Meadow Creek in northern Oregon did not accelerate the degradation of the streambank. In this study, most streambank erosion occurred during winter periods and was independent of livestock activity during the grazing season (27). In another study in northwestern Oregon, streambank erosion and disturbance were significantly greater in areas grazed by cattle in late summer than in adjacent ungrazed enclosures (28).

Animal activity along stream channels or other open waters may change the chemical and bacterial quality of water. Specifically, animal feces may contaminate waters with bacteria or act as sources of nitrate and phosphate. Studies of two adjacent pastures along Trout Creek in central Colorado indicated only minor chemical effects of cattle grazing on water quality. The bacterial contamination of the

water by fecal matter, however, increased significantly. After the cattle were removed, bacterial counts quickly dropped to levels similar to those in the ungrazed pasture (29).

Changes in the chemical quality of water through grazing activities are generally not significant or long-lasting, unless animals and their waste products are concentrated in one area. Specifically, nitrate-nitrogen concentrations may increase and change water quality, since the nitrate-nitrogen is a mobile anion (see Chapters 5 and 16). High nitrate-nitrogen concentrations in groundwaters below feedlots are well known.

Hydrologic Evaluation of Grazing Systems

Most watershed studies have evaluated the impact of livestock grazing on hydrologic variables after grazing treatments have been in effect for several years. Treatment plots, areas, or watersheds are then compared to a nongrazed counterpart and differences are attributed to grazing. The grazing is varied in both duration and intensity. Few studies have assessed seasonal or long-term hydraulic impacts of grazing systems, and additional studies, both intensive and extensive, are needed (30).

In general, the removal of plant cover by grazing may increase the impact of raindrops, decrease the amount of organic matter in the soil, increase surface crusting (puddling), decrease infiltration rates, and increase erosion. Increased overland flow, reduced soil moisture, and increased erosion translate into greater concentrations of suspended sediment. A further discussion of the hydrologic cycle is given in Chapter 16. Other water quality impacts such as increased bacterial and nutrient concentrations do not appear to be a problem with grazing systems, except perhaps in riparian zones.

The impact of livestock grazing on watersheds has recently become a resource management issue of national proportions. Research project data have often been evaluated emotionally or according to the political advantages offered rather than by scientific and objective thinking.

The advantages between light and moderate grazing intensities for watershed protection are often not significantly different (2). Recent interest in federal grazing practices, particularly grazing allotments, may bring a reevaluation of the environmental and economic implications of grazing systems on watershed resources (Figure 15.6).

Concluding Statement

Rangelands occupy nearly half of the world's land surface, and are an important source of forage for wildlife and domestic animals, as well as water, wood products, and recreational opportunities. During the late 1800s and early 1900s, many rangelands were overgrazed by domestic livestock. A reduction in livestock numbers and the implementation of grazing systems allowed many of these areas to recover. Understory forage that is produced in

Figure 15.6 Counting cattle on Bull Mountain Allotment, Deerlodge National Forest, Montana. (Photograph by G. R. Walstad, U.S.D.A. Forest Service.)

forested communities is critical to many ranching operations in the western United States. These areas are managed with a permit system of grazing and provide summer pasture for cattle and sheep.

Livestock grazing rangelands has the potential to alter the natural infiltration-runoff relationships by reducing the vegetative cover, including litter cover on the soil surface, and compacting the soil through trampling. Animal bedding grounds, stock trails, watering locations, and salt licks are the areas of greatest compaction and have the highest risk to soil erosion. Other water quality impacts such as increased bacterial and nutrient concentrations, do not appear to be a problem with grazing on rangelands, except perhaps in riparian zones. The differences between light and moderate grazing intensities for watershed protection are often not significantly different.

References

1. J. L. HOLECHECK, R. D. PEIPER, AND C. H. HERBEL, *Range Management—Principles and Practices,* Third Edition, Prentice-Hall, Upper Saddle River, N.J., 1998.

2. L. A. STODDART, A. D. SMITH, AND T. W. BOX, *Range Management,* Third Edition, McGraw-Hill, New York, 1975.

3. H. F. HEADY AND R. D. CHILD, *Rangeland Ecology and Management,* Westview Press, Boulder, Colo., 1994.

4. R. E. WILLIAMS, B. W. ALFRED, R. M. DENIM, AND H. E. PAULSEN, Jr., *J. Range Manag., 21,* 355 (1968).

5. W. L. DUTTON, *J. For., 51,* 248 (1953).

6. R. G. TAYLOR, E. T. BARTLETT, AND K. D. LAIR, *J. Range Manag.,* 358, 634 (1982).

7. R. K. HEITSCHMIDT AND J. W. STUTH, EDS., *Grazing Management—an Ecological Perspective,* Timber Press, Portland, Ore., 1991.

8. P. O. CURRIE, "Grazing in ponderosa pine forests." In *Ponderosa Pine—The Species and Its Management,* Washington State Univ., Pullman, 1988.

9. G. A. GARRISON, A. J. BJUGSTAD, D. A. DUNCAN, M. E. LEWIS, AND D. R. SMITH, "Vegetation and Environmental

Features of Forest and Range Ecosystems," U.S.D.A. For. Serv., Agr. Handbook 475, 1977.

10. W. P. CLARY, "Range Management and Its Ecological Basis in the Ponderosa Pine Type" in *Arizona: The Status of Our Knowledge,* U.S.D.A. For. Serv., Res. Pap. RM-158, 1975.

11. C. P. PASE, *J. Range Manag., 11,* 238 (1958).

12. G. E. GRUELL, "Historical and modern roles of fire in pinyon-juniper." In *Proceedings: Ecology and Management of Pinyon-Juniper Communities Within the Interior West,* U.S.D.A. For. Serv., Proc. RMRS-P-9, 1999.

13. W. R. HOUSTON, "A Condition Guide for Aspen Ranges of Utah, Nevada, Southern Idaho, and Western Wyoming," U.S.D.A. For. Serv., Intermountain For. Range Expt. Sta. Pap. 32, 1954.

14. N. V. DeBYLE AND R. P. WINOKUR, EDS., "Aspen: Ecology and Management in the Western United States," U.S.D.A. For. Serv., Gen. Tech. Rep. RM-119, 1985.

15. W. C. LEININGER AND S. H. SHARROW, *J. Range Manag.,* 40, 551 (1987).

16. P. N. SPREITZER, *Rangelands, 7,* 33 (1985).

17. K. E. SEVERSON, *J. Range Manag., 35,* 786 (1982).

18. W. C. LEININGER AND S. H. SHARROW, West. *J. Appl. For.,* 73 (1989).

19. J. M. SKOVLIN, "Impacts of grazing on wetlands and riparian habitat: A review of our knowledge." In *Developing Strategies for Rangeland Management,* Nat. Res. Council/Nat. Academy of Sciences, Westview Press, Boulder, Colo., 1984.

20. W. S. PLATTS, "Livestock grazing and riparian stream ecosystems." In *Proc. Forum—Grazing and Riparian/Stream Ecosystem,* Trout Unlimited, Inc., Denver, Colo., 1979.

21. L. R. ROATH AND W. C. KRUEGER, *J. Range Manag., 35,* 100 (1982).

22. ANON., *The Ninth Annual Report of the Council on Environmental Quality,* U.S. Council on Environmental Quality, U.S. Govt. Printing Office, Washington, D.C., 1978.

23. A. J. BELSKY, A. MATZKE, AND S. USELMAN, *J. Soil and Water Cons., 54,* 419 (1999).

24. W. P. CLARY AND W. C. LEININGER, *J. Range. Manag., 53,* 562 (2000).

25. W. H. WISCHMEIER AND D. D. SMITH, "Predicting Rainfall Erosion Losses From Cropland East of the Rocky Mountains," U.S.D.A. Agr. Res. Serv., Agr. Handbook 282, Washington, D.C., 1965.

26. J. F. VALLENTINE, *Range Development and Improvements,* Third Edition, Academic Press, Inc., San Diego, Calif., 1989.

27. J. C. BUCKHOUSE, J. M. SKOVLIN, AND R. W. KNIGHT, *J. Range Manag., 34,* 339 (1981).

28. J. B. KAUFFMAN AND W. C. KRUEGER, *J. Range Manag., 37,* 430 (1984).

29. S. R. JOHNSON, H. L. GARY, AND S. L. PONCE, "Range Cattle Impacts on Stream Water Quality in the Colorado Front Range," U.S.D.A. For. Serv., Res. Note RM 359, 1978.

30. W. H. BLACKBURN, "Impacts of grazing intensity and specialized grazing systems on watershed characteristics and responses." In *Developing Strategies for Rangeland Management,* Nat. Res. Council/Nat. Academy of Sciences, Westview Press, Boulder, Colo., 1984.

CHAPTER 16

Watershed Management: A Regional to Global Perspective

D. SCOTT MACKAY

The Watershed

John Wesley Powell, scientist, geographer, and leader of the first expedition through the Grand Canyon, stated in 1869 (http://www.epa.gov/adopt):

> . . . that area of land, a bounded hydrologic system, within which all living things are inextricably linked by their common water course and where, as humans settled, simple logic demanded that they become part of the community

Water plays a central role in most of earth's systems and is essential for all life. Water is the medium for biochemical reactions that sustain living organisms. Water helps redistribute energy via the oceans and atmosphere. Water also contributes to the erosion and transport of minerals, organic material, and other substances. Water in the earth system has remained, on the whole, a constant for billions of years. It is moved within and between the atmosphere, lithosphere, and biosphere in a recirculatory system known as the hydrologic cycle. It may be thought of as a limited resource, which, as a result of human influence on global change, must be properly managed. Management of water resources has the primary task of preserving a supply of water of sufficient quality to meet the demands of society. Water must also be managed, in the sense that too much water may mean flooding, excessive erosion of land, and potentially loss of life. The proper management of water resources requires an understanding of how water is circulated. It also requires an understanding of how water resources interact with natural and anthropogenic processes. A framework for managing

337

water resources could consider any size system, from the entire earth down to an individual organism seeking water to survive. However, there is a need for an integrating framework that can consider systems of all sizes and organize them. The *watershed* is such a framework and it represents the basic unit for watershed management.

A *watershed* is generally defined as an area of land that drains water, sediment, and dissolved materials to a common outlet at some point along a stream channel (1). Watersheds are nature's way of dividing up the landscape. Rivers, lakes, estuaries, wetlands, streams, and even the oceans can serve as catch basins for the land adjacent to them. Ground water aquifers serve the same purpose for the land above them. The actions of people who live within a watershed affect the health of the waters that drain through it. The watershed can be defined in terms of some arbitrary spatial extent, such as 50 to 5,000 hectares (Table 16.1). More generally, the watershed is a unit area of land with well-defined boundaries that promotes the understanding of how water enters an area of interest, is stored, moved and modified within that area, and then may be exported from the area of interest.

The natural evolution of a watershed begins either with the uplifting of land as a result of collisions between moving plates of the earth's crust, or with volcanic activity. Precipitation falling on uplifted land tends to move, either on the surface or below, to the oceans with the force of gravity. Water traveling on the surface will tend to flow along preferential pathways depending upon irregularities in the surface. These preferential pathways channelize the flow of water in rills. Eventually, further erosion expands the rills to produce stream channels as the water erodes the surface. As these channels are incised, their steep slopes become sites for further erosion. Eventually, streams channels are formed. Sites nearest the channels tend to erode the most and sites furthest away from the channels erode the least. Thus, regions intermediate between channels remain at relatively high elevation and form divides. Figure 16.1 shows the basic form of the erosional watershed. A region bounded by divides and a stream channel can be viewed as a hillslope on which there are measurable flow pathways. Surface water can infiltrate the soil or run along the surface. Some of the infiltrated water may be evaporated, and the rest enters a

Table 16.1 Spatial scales of watersheds can be defined with respect to other management unit sizes.

Physical Area	Spatial Scale (order of magnitude, in hectares)	Management
Microsite	10^{-1} to 10^{0}	—
Stand	10^{0} to 10^{1}	Cutting unit[a]
Watershed	10^{1} to 10^{3}	Watershed
Landscape	10^{2} to 10^{4}	District[b]
Multi-landscape	10^{4} to 10^{5}	Timbershed[c]
Subregion	10^{5} to 10^{6}	Forest[d]
Region	10^{6} to 10^{7}	Pacific Northwest[e]

Source: Brooks and Grant (2).

[a] Timber harvest for stand replacement is generally smaller on public lands and larger on private lands.

[b] A National Forest Ranger District, for example, representing a minimum area for which community issues, such as effects of towns and groups of towns, can be usefully examined.

[c] This classification is based on timber production and processing; a timbershed contains at least one major timber-processing center, and the majority of the timber processed originates in that timbershed.

[d] National Forests in Oregon and Washington range from 100,000 to 500,000 hectares.

[e] All timberland in western Oregon is about 5 million hectares.

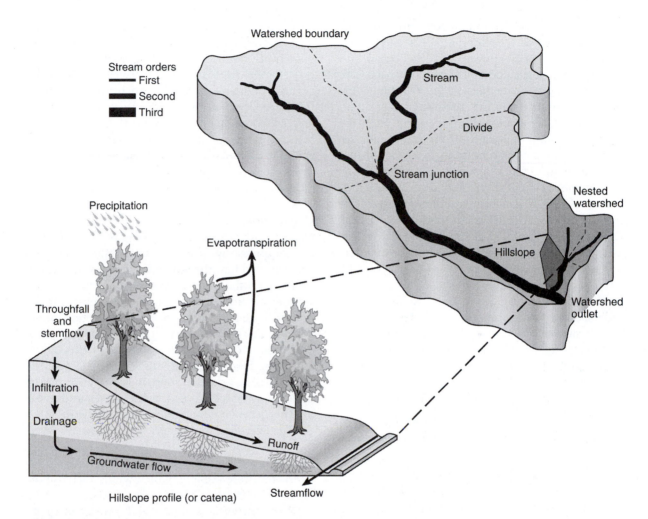

Figure 16.1 Shown are the basic components of the watershed. Stream orders are important in understanding the size of area that influences a given stream reach. Watersheds are naturally nested features, which means that smaller watersheds reside within larger watersheds. At some nesting level, it is possible to distinguish hillslopes for which hydrologic flow paths can often be directly observed. The hillslope profile indicates the major flow paths of water when precipitation falls on a vegetated slope.

groundwater flow. The surface and subsurface characteristics of a hillslope determine the partitioning of flow as surface runoff, as groundwater flow, and as evaporation. Watershed outputs of water, sediment, nutrients, and other pollutants represent the sum of these constituents generated on all hillslopes within the watershed.

It is desirable to limit the amount of surface runoff, since runoff promotes soil erosion. The

process of water movement on the surface results in sediment, organic material, and nutrients being carried with the water off the landscape and through the channels. The watershed thus provides a framework within which other resources, such as forests, agricultural crops, and urban landscapes can be managed. The view of the watershed as a unit for management with no implied spatial extent is useful, since the land surfaces of the whole earth can be divided up into watersheds with very large areas. Each of these large watersheds can in turn be divided into smaller watersheds, and so on. Furthermore, at a detailed level it is possible to measure water, sediment, or nutrient budgets on individual hillslopes and then combine them to predict watershed budgets. For instance, one might view the entire Mississippi River basin or the entire Amazon River basin as defining multistate and multination areas for management, respectively. Alternatively, the watershed drained by a tributary of a large river could be a management area. For example, we might be interested in the watershed drained by the Wisconsin River, which is a tributary of the Mississippi River. At a smaller scale, the Lake Mendota Watershed around Madison, Wisconsin, might be considered a management unit.

Once a watershed boundary is delineated, an understanding of the processes that determine the fate of water entering the watershed is needed. Since the full extent of human activity and of natural systems is global, we will begin at this spatial extent and work our way down to smaller watersheds. In this chapter we shall consider the following:

- processes responsible for the hydrologic cycle;
- interrelationships between water and terrestrial vegetation;
- issues and approaches in the management of water resources within a watershed framework;
- recent approaches to watershed management, including the transfer of responsibility from government to nongovernment organizations; and
- use of technology such as geographical information systems and remote sensing for water resource studies and management.

The Global Hydrologic Cycle

Hydrology (*Hydros*, meaning "water," and *ology*, meaning "study of") is the science that seeks to understand the processes of storage, transformation, and movement of water. These processes are collectively referred to as the hydrologic cycle, a global scale recirculatory system that links water in the atmosphere, biosphere, and lithosphere. Most of the components of the hydrologic cycle, except for permanent ice, are depicted in Figure 16.2. The various storage compartments for water include the oceans, permanent ice, ground water, soil water, fresh water bodies and rivers, the atmosphere, and the biosphere (plants and animals). The transformations between the storage compartments for water in the earth system include precipitation, evaporation, transpiration, infiltration, runoff, and groundwater flow. *Precipitation* is formed from the condensation of water in the atmosphere as it cools. *Evaporation* is the transformation of liquid or solid water to a gaseous form. It requires the input of energy, primarily from the sun. Once evaporated and released into the atmosphere, the water vapor moves with the atmospheric air circulation. Water evaporated from one location can then be transported in the atmosphere to another location where it may fall as precipitation. By altering surface properties that affect evaporation, we are in effect altering precipitation patterns. For instance, large-scale removal of vegetation, such as is occurring in the Amazon, may reduce evaporation rates and eventually reduce precipitation amounts in other areas. Climate warming associated with increased levels of atmospheric carbon dioxide may increase evaporation rates. This would in turn increase atmospheric moisture content, which would increase the intensity or frequency of storm events.

Transpiration is a specialized form of evaporation involving the release of water from photosynthesizing vegetation. Vegetation draws water from the soil through its roots, stores it within the plant and releases it to the atmosphere as part of its need to remove carbon dioxide from the atmosphere for photosynthesis. On a global scale, the biosphere stores at any given time less than 1 percent of the amount of water that falls as precipitation, and yet over 60 percent of global annual average precipitation is cycled through the biosphere. Thus, transpiration and evaporation from vegetation form important links between surface water and the atmosphere. Together they form an important contribution to atmospheric moisture levels and ultimately precipitation. It is not difficult to see that by

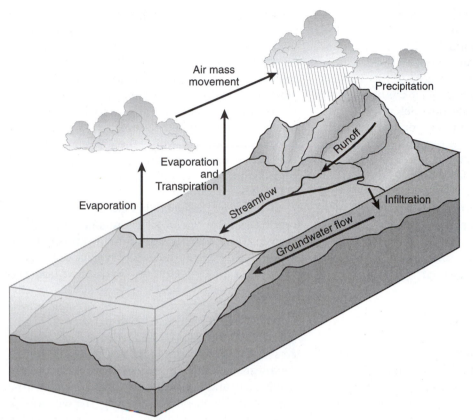

Figure 16.2 The major components of the global hydrologic cycle

altering the distribution of forests one can potentially greatly change the global distribution of evaporation and transpiration, which can in turn result in regional differences in precipitation patterns.

Infiltration and storage of water in soils helps us to link surface water with ground water, to understand spatial patterns of vegetation, to understand and predict flooding, and to trace the movement of pollutants that are carried in surface water. Water infiltrates into a soil at a rate that depends on surface characteristics, soil texture, and the amount and rate of water input (see Chapter 5, Forest Soils). Surface water that does not infiltrate must either pond at the surface or run along the surface.

At a global scale water can be considered conserved, which means that it is neither created nor destroyed.[1] This means that any part of the hydrologic cycle has a water budget that can be described in terms of water inputs, outputs, and change in storage as follows:

inputs – outputs = change in storage

For instance, the water balance equation for a volume of soil is given by:

$$\Delta S = I - (P + E + T)$$

where ΔS is the change in water stored in the soil over a defined time period, I is the amount of water

---

[1] Water can be released from volcanic activity. However, it is believed that the primary source of water on the earth's surface was derived from comets and meteorites that bombarded the earth during the first billion years after its formation.

that infiltrates into soil, P is the amount of water that percolates through the soil, E is evaporation of water from the soil surface, and T is transpiration by plants drawing water out of the soil during this time period. An equation of this form is known as a *water conservation equation*. Conservation equations can be used to describe the rate of change of water stored in any part of the earth system. We might use a conservation equation to determine groundwater storage for drinking water, reservoir storage used for hydroelectric power generation, water levels in the Great Lakes of North America, or water available for vegetation growth in different areas of our planet.

Global Distribution of Terrestrial Water and Life

Precipitation

The hydrologic cycle can be approached from any one of the storage compartments and flows represented in Figure 16.2. We will start with precipitation, because it is the primary source of water for terrestrial ecosystems. Precipitation occurs because atmospheric pressure affects air temperature, which in turn determines how much water vapor the air can hold. Like all gases, air can be compressed. The weight of a column of atmosphere above a given parcel of air exerts pressure on the parcel, which tends to compress it. When air is compressed, the molecules within it are confined to a smaller volume, which means they are more likely to collide. These collisions produce heat that warms the air parcel. The cooling (or warming) of air from a change in pressure is known as *adiabatic* cooling (or warming). When air rises in the atmosphere, it experiences a reduction in atmospheric pressure and is cooled adiabatically. Similarly, when air sinks, the atmospheric pressure on it increases and it warms adiabatically. Suppose a parcel of air is warmed by solar energy absorbed at the land surface. By warming the air, the increased energy will cause its molecules to move more quickly. Their interactions in turn exert greater

pressure, which expands the air. When a parcel of air expands, it becomes less dense. If it is less dense than the surrounding atmosphere, it is buoyant and rises. The warmed air generally continues to rise until it is cooled adiabatically to the same temperature as the surrounding atmosphere. As the parcel of air is cooled, its ability to hold water is reduced. If the parcel of air is cooled sufficiently, it may reach a point where the amount of water it holds exceeds the amount it can hold. The result is condensation, which is a source of water for clouds and precipitation.

In order to understand regional differences in precipitation, we need to know something about global climate and the ways in which precipitation is produced. Figure 16.3 shows average annual distribution of precipitation and vegetation (see Figure 16.3 in color insert). We will discuss the relationships between these later. Precipitation is generally very high in the equatorial zone. This area is known as the inter-tropical convergence zone. It gets its name from the fact that it occurs where southward-moving air masses from the northern hemisphere and northward-moving air masses from the southern hemisphere converge. The winds associated with these air masses are commonly known as the Trade Winds. As the Trade Winds move over the tropical oceans, they collect water vapor that was evaporated from the oceans. Where these winds converge, they are forced to rise upward into the atmosphere where they cool and release precipitation. Other areas of large rainfall amounts include western sides of large mountains where warm, moist air is forced to rise over the mountains. As it rises up the mountain, the air is cooled, which promotes precipitation. For example, the Pacific Northwest receives a large amount of precipitation annually (2500 mm or more). In general, midlatitude areas receive much of their precipitation from extratropical cyclones. These are eastward-moving low-pressure cells that form where arctic and subtropical air masses meet. Extratropical cyclones act as heat engines by drawing warm, generally moisture-laden air northward. At fronts separating warm and cold air masses, this moist air is forced to cool and precipitation results. More localized precipitation occurs in thunderstorms, which are the result of intense warming of moist air at the ground surface. The warm, buoyant surface air rises high in the atmosphere where it cools adiabatically and forms thunder clouds. In all cases, precipitation occurs where moisture-laden air is forced to rise and lose its ability to hold the moisture.

Deserts and semi-arid areas occur in areas where relatively dry air descends and warms adiabatically. This occurs in subtropical regions, including north-central Africa and central Australia. Arid and semi-arid areas also occur on eastern sides of large mountain ranges where air is descending after losing its water to precipitation on the western side of the mountain. Semi-arid areas are found in inter-mountain areas of western North America, which receive Pacific air masses that have released much of their moisture on the western (or windward) sides of the mountains. Midcontinental areas tend to be drier than coastal because of their great distance from oceanic sources of moisture. The eastern part of the United States and southeastern Canada experience greater quantities of precipitation from moisture evaporated from the Gulf of Mexico.

Evaporation and Transpiration

Air masses moving over water bodies and other sources of water pick up some of this water through evaporation. Evaporation is the process by which solid or liquid water on the surface is converted into vapor form and released into the atmosphere. The conversion to water vapor uses energy, most of which is received from solar radiation. Energy from the sun that enters the earth system and is intercepted at the surface is used either to heat the surface or to evaporate water. For most surfaces, some of the energy goes into surface heating and some goes into evaporating water. Wet surfaces tend to use most of the energy for evaporation, while very dry surfaces heat up (Figure 16.4). For example, when a water body absorbs solar energy, it is mostly used to evaporate water rather than warming the water. At the other extreme, deserts usually have little moisture available for evaporation and so absorbed energy here is used to heat the

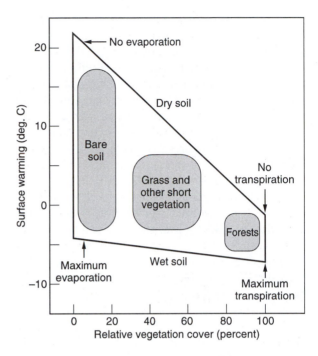

Figure 16.4 This figure shows how surfaces of different vegetation types and moisture availability partition solar radiation. In general, wet surfaces use the energy to evaporate water and dry surfaces heat up. Dense vegetation has an abundance of leaf surface area for both shedding evaporated water and heat. Bare soil has a minimal surface area exposed to the atmosphere, so its heating depends much more on energy partitioning.

land surface. Energy used for warming is referred to as *sensible heat energy* and energy used in evaporating water is *latent heat energy*. The ratio of latent to sensible heat energies is known as a *Bowen ratio*. Bowen ratios for the tropical oceans are about 10:1, and they are about 1:10 for deserts. Well-watered forests and other terrestrial vegetation have Bowen ratios that average about 1:1, which means they use about half their absorbed energy to convert water from liquid to vapor.

The rate at which water converted into vapor form is transferred from an evaporating surface to the atmosphere depends on two factors. The first is how dry the air interacting with the surface is. The second is turbulent winds that promote the uplift of water vapor into the atmosphere. As stated above, warm air can hold more moisture than cool air. Warm, dry air promotes a faster rate of evaporation than cool, moist air. We will refer to this as the evaporative demand of the atmosphere. Air masses that have moved across dry land areas tend to have low moisture contents and high evaporative demands. Alternatively, air masses that have moved through wet regions, such as over oceans, have relatively low evaporative demand. Winds traveling over rough surfaces, such as forests, tall buildings, and even grass, are forced to slow near the surface. This results in turbulence in the lower atmosphere, which promotes greater mixing of air near the surface. This mixing helps to remove evaporating water and promote further evaporation. The rougher the surface, the more efficient it is at generating turbulence. For example, tall vegetation (e.g., a tree) creates a more efficient evaporative surface than shorter vegetation (e.g., grass), because they have more leaf surface in direct contact with the atmosphere. This increased exposed surface area also allows forests to more quickly shed sensible heat, so they remain cooler than grass or bare soil.

Interception (I) is the amount of precipitation that is trapped on leaves, branches, and surface organic matter and residues. Once intercepted, this water may evaporate and thus never infiltrate into the soil. Forests have relatively large intercepting surface areas (the leaves), and as described above, these surface areas promote high rates of evaporation. The effect of interception is most evident when walking in a forest at the beginning of a rain event. There is usually a short time in which you can remain dry under the forest canopy. Once the canopy's capacity to store water has been exceeded, further rainfall will either drip down to the ground from the leaves, a process known as throughfall, or it will travel along branches and stems until it reaches the ground, a process known as stemflow.

The importance of interception in the water balance of forests depends on the ability of the canopy to intercept water, the atmosphere to dry the canopy, and the frequency and magnitude of rainfall. Small, infrequent rainfall may never reach the soil surface in dense forests. However, most of the precipitation from large or frequent events will go to throughfall or stemflow. Given enough time between precipitation events and high enough evaporation rates, interception can be a very important part of the hydrologic cycle. Numerous studies have shown that the reduction in interception when forests are harvested results in higher rates of soil recharge, greater runoff, and high potential for soil erosion. Interception can be as important or more important than water plant transpiration. Table 16.2 illustrates some typical amounts of interception for different vegetation types. Clearly, the conversion of land cover from one form of vegetation to another can have an impact on interception. For example, Law (3) found that a Sitka spruce plantation produced 280 mm less soil recharge than adjacent grasslands. Swank and Miner (4) found a 33–94 mm reduction in groundwater recharge in watersheds where deciduous cover was replaced with white pine. Hibbert (5) showed a five-to-six-fold increase in annual runoff resulting from the removal of brush and replacement with grass. Some of these differences are attributable to transpiration rates, which we will discuss next.

A special form of evaporation known as *transpiration* is the release of moisture from stomatal openings on the leaf surfaces of terrestrial vegetation. Stomatal openings permit atmospheric carbon dioxide to mix with the water and be drawn into the leaf for photosynthesis (see also Chapter 4, Forest Ecophysiology). The water is drawn from the soil through the roots, and through the xylem up to the leaves. When stomatal cells are open to the atmosphere, photosynthesis can occur. However, the stomatal openings may be thought of as small evaporating surfaces subject to the atmospheric demand for water. Water released from the stomatal cells to the atmosphere is called transpiration. When the atmospheric demand is very high or the availability of moisture in the soil is too low, the stomatal openings are closed in an effort to regulate xylem water potential. Stomatal closure reduces or shuts off transpiration and photosynthesis. The physiologic controls on transpiration dis-

Table 16.2 Estimates of the Percent of Precipitation that Is Intercepted by Different Vegetation Types

Vegetation Type	Percent Precipitation Intercepted
Forests	
Deciduous	13
Coniferous	28
Crops	
Alfalfa	36
Corn	16
Oats	7
Grasses	10–20

Source: Dunne and Leopold (1).

tinguish it from other forms of evaporation, and yet evaporation and transpiration are often combined in a single term known as *evapotranspiration* (ET). However, it is important to remember that the two forms of evaporation are different. Stomatal closure reduces both transpiration and photosynthesis. It is through stomatal control that primary production is linked to atmospheric demand and soil moisture availability, both of which depend upon precipitation. By understanding this relationship, we can interpret the global distribution of terrestrial vegetation in terms of patterns of precipitation (see Figure 16.3 in color insert). The observant reader will note that boundaries and transitions between vegetation densities and precipitation quantities correspond. The global distribution of vegetation can thus be partially related to the various controls on the distribution of precipitation.

More directly, the density of vegetation supported should depend on a balance between precipitation and ET. This can be accounted for as soil water storage. The amount of water available in the soil depends on precipitation as a source of water, ET, and hydraulic characteristics of the soils. It is often useful to consider soil moisture content as more or less constant over a long period of time. It allows us to approximate water availability for plant use using the relationship between precipitation and potential ET. Potential ET is considered to be the rate of evaporation from vegetated sur-

faces when soil moisture is high enough to keep the leaf stomata open. In general, areas with high amounts of precipitation in relation to potential ET rates can support denser vegetation canopies. High water use in areas of low precipitation will not allow this vegetation to grow and thrive (Figure 16.5). Deserts have low precipitation inputs and high evaporative demand from high solar radiation inputs, high temperatures, and dry air masses. Only vegetation that is adapted to semi-arid and arid conditions will survive in these areas. There is a tradeoff between moisture availability (precipitation) and moisture demand (energy input or temperature). Areas with lower energy inputs have lower potential ET rates. These areas can support relatively denser vegetation with lower precipitation than higher energy locations. In general, low latitude areas are warmer and so they require greater amounts of precipitation to support a given vegetation density than high latitude sites. Similarly, low altitude sites are warmer than high altitude sites, so they require higher precipitation rates to sustain the same amount of vegetation. These vegetation-water relations are adequate for explaining

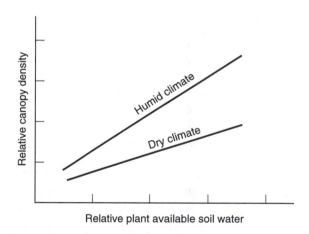

Figure 16.5 A hydrologic equilibrium can exist in which a humid climate with a large storage of soil water can support a dense vegetation cover. A dry climate will tend to require a greater amount of soil water storage in order to support the same vegetation cover supported in a humid climate.

regional to global scale patterns of vegetation, but are incomplete for watershed scales. Within watersheds, the vegetation-water relations are complicated by the need to understand patterns of soil water holding capacities and ground water flow that can produce patterns of drying and wetting based on topographic control. These are considered next.

Soil Water

Soils are made up of minerals, organic matter, water, and air. Natural field soils are porous. The pore spaces are filled with air, water, or a combination of air and water. Most soils have porosity between 45 and 55 percent of the soil volume. Soil pore spaces are pathways for the movement of water. When these pathways are completely filled with water, the soil is saturated; otherwise, it is unsaturated. The rate of flow of water through a saturated soil is called *saturated hydraulic conductivity,* and depends on the texture of the soil. Soil texture refers to the size of the individual particles that make up the soil. For mineral soils, these particles include some combination of sand, silt, and clay, which are respectively considered of coarse, intermediate, and fine texture as described in Chapter 5, Forest Soils. In general, soils with a high sand content have high hydraulic conductivities at saturation, while clayey soils tend to have low saturated hydraulic conductivities.

When a saturated soil begins to drain, it becomes unsaturated. As it does so, its rate of hydraulic conductivity decreases because of a reduction in the number of connected draining pathways. Hydraulic conductivity rates fall rapidly as the soil becomes less saturated, and at low moisture contents they are negligibly small. Soils never drain completely free of water, as there are forces that hold the water against gravity. These forces, known as *capillary forces,* exert a tension on the water within the soil pores. In order to understand the role of tension on water movement in soils, it is important to understand a few conventions in the way in which soil water tension is reported. The point where atmosphere and a saturated soil layer or free-

standing body of water meet is said to be at atmospheric pressure. Here the gravitational force exerted on a water molecule is the weight of the atmosphere that lies directly above the water molecule. Below the water surface, the pressure exerted on a water molecule is higher, since it also has the weight of the overlying water column. Capillary forces act on water molecules in all directions, not just downward. Capillary forces are caused by electrical bonds that form between the sidewall of the soil pore space and water molecules. The tension exerted by these electrical forces tends to get larger as the pore spaces become smaller, and so clay soils have greater capillarity than sandy soils. The greatest tension occurs where the moisture content on the soil pore spaces is lowest. Upward tension exerted on water that would otherwise drain freely because of gravity allows the soil to retain water against the force of gravity. Because the net downward forces exerted on water molecules held under capillary tension are less than that of free-draining water molecules, unsaturated soils have less than atmospheric pressure. By convention we usually state that atmospheric pressure is our datum, which means that the pressure is given as zero. This means that water in unsaturated soils is held under negative pressure and water in saturated soils has a positive pressure. This process of holding water at negative pressure is known as soil water retention and the relationship between moisture content and this negative pressure is known as a moisture retention characteristic. When the upward tension on the water equals the downward force of gravity on the water, drainage from the soil ceases and the soil is said to have reached *field capacity*. The field capacity of a soil is very important because it defines an upper limit normally associated with plant available water.

Plant available water is the difference between field capacity and wilting point. In order to understand what the wilting point is, it is important to recognize that plant roots are able to draw water from soils at higher negative pressures than field capacity and that water moves from a location of high pressure to a location of low pressure. Field capacity for most soils occurs at a pressure of about

−340 millibars (mb). Capillary forces within most plant roots can produce pressures much lower than soil field capacity, and can go to −15,000 mb or lower depending on the species. At pressures much lower than this, plants are unable to maintain cell turgor. Thus, at wilting point, many plant species close their stomata and may eventually be damaged.

An important property of soils is their ability to absorb incoming water from above, such as precipitation or snow melt water. Water infiltrates soils at a rate that depends on a number of properties of the soils. These include saturated hydraulic conductivity, the moisture content of the soil prior to the input of water, and the intensity of the water input. Soils with higher hydraulic conductivities have higher infiltration rates. Soils that are dry prior to a rainfall event have to be recharged, so they tend to have longer periods of high infiltration rates. As stated earlier, hydraulic conductivity depends on soil texture, such as whether the soil is predominantly sand or clay. It also depends on how compacted the soil is. A loose soil has a higher porosity than a compacted soil, and in general, near-surface soils under vegetation have high porosity that is produced by roots and organisms such as worms. Soils at greater depth tend to be more compacted by the weight of the overlying layers. At greater depth, there is also lower root and animal content. When soils are dry, incoming water generally infiltrates at a rate above the saturated hydraulic conductivity. This is caused by the combined drainage rate resulting from gravity and capillary forces that draw the water into the soil. Eventually, the rate of infiltration slows down to the rate of the saturated hydraulic conductivity as the surface soil layers become saturated. Knowing something about the infiltration capacity of a soil is key to understanding how the soil will respond to precipitation events. If rate of precipitation onto a soil surface exceeds the rate at which water can infiltrate then water will pond on the surface and eventually run off. However, if the soil has a very high infiltration capacity, as occurs in most forests, then very few precipitation events will be intense enough to produce runoff. If the rate of water infiltration into a soil is high,

but an impermeable layer, such as bedrock or highly compacted soil, or a water table, underlies the soil, then the soil may saturate from below. Once a soil is saturated, it can hold no more water and further water input runs off.

Ground Water

Ground water is water that completely fills the pore spaces of permeable materials, or ground water aquifers, below the ground surface. It includes water stored below the water table in soils and in deeper aquifers in porous bedrock. Ground water is an important part of the hydrologic cycle. It represents about 30 percent of the world's fresh water resources, and 99 percent, if permanent ice is excluded. It is an important source of water for domestic consumption, for irrigation, and for industrial uses. It is also a critical link in the terrestrial portion of the hydrologic cycle, because it links water that infiltrates into soils to streams and other surface water bodies. Ground water tends to move from upland source areas to lowland discharge areas. Through this lateral flow of water, groundwater can help to sustain riparian forests and gallery forests in valleys even in semi-arid regions.

Ground water is important both in terms of quality and quantity. Streams, lakes, and other surface water bodies can be thought of as areas in the landscape where the ground water reaches the surface. As such, water bodies can be important diagnostics of watershed health. For instance, lake acidity is a good indicator of the acid-neutralizing ability of the watershed in response to acid rain. Also, human consumption of ground water from well pumping frequently lowers regional water tables. Excessive ground water pumping may result in the land subsiding, as is occurring in some coastal areas of Texas.

Runoff

In the last thirty years, hydrologists have come to understand the mechanisms of runoff generation. Prior to the 1960s, it was believed that runoff was produced over all areas of watersheds. This runoff was believed to occur when precipitation rates exceeded the infiltration capacity of the soils. Studies have shown that most natural soils have infiltration capacities that exceed all but the highest rates of precipitation. Usually runoff is limited to only parts of the watershed, and for most precipitation events these areas remain unchanged for a given watershed. For instance, urban watersheds have fixed, impermeable surfaces. Forested watersheds with harvested areas may have low infiltration capacities and high runoff rates if the soils have become compacted during a logging operation. The low infiltration capacity sites are the most likely to produce runoff.

Most runoff in undisturbed, well-drained watersheds occurs where soils have become saturated from ground water that returns to the surface, such as near streams and in concave areas on slopes. Areas where ground water returns to the surface are usually called *seepage faces*. They occur where soils are recharging at much higher rates than in surrounding areas. This is called ground water mounding. Seepage faces also occur where thin soils are underlain with an impermeable layer, such as bedrock. Water infiltrating into the soil hits this impermeable barrier and travels down slope. In valley bottoms the water may slow down or converge, which means a water table grows upwards to the soil surface. The resultant breakout flow then runs along the surface until it reaches a stream or until it re-infiltrates in an area where the soil is not saturated. Also, precipitation that falls on a saturated soil directly runs off. Breakout flow and direct precipitation runoff are collectively known as saturation excess runoff.

Streamflow

Streams and streamflow are often the focus of watershed management. Rivers have always played a central role in human settlements. One of the earliest known human settlements, Mesopotamia (from the Greek *mesos* "middle" and *potamos* "river;" literally "land between the rivers"), developed on fertile alluvial plains watered by the Euphrates, the Tigris, and their tributaries. In addition to their importance for agriculture, rivers were historically a key for trade and commerce, transportation, as a source of food and water, and in the last century as a source of hydroelectric power. The North American fur trade relied heavily on rivers. Rivers became the focal point for the exploration and settling of both the United States and Canada. One only has to consider the commerce, culture, and growth of cities along the Mississippi and St. Lawrence rivers as illustration of the role of large streams.

Streams store very little water when viewed in terms of the world's total water budget, but they are the link between terrestrial and aquatic ecosystems. Water is moved in streams a great distance from ground water aquifers, lakes, and glaciers to the oceans. Streamflow is the cheapest and easiest to monitor of all hydrologic fluxes. Stream gauges regularly monitor most major rivers in the continental United States, Canada, and most other countries. The United States Geological Survey (or USGS) maintains a network of stream gauges, which are monitored regularly by people or by automated recording instruments. Data from these monitoring stations are routinely used by federal, state, and local regulatory agencies with a vested interest in water resources. For example, the state of California has invested considerable resources in a network of monitoring stations and experimental watersheds to improve the understanding and management of its scarce water resources.

Of concern with streamflow are low flows, which occur between precipitation events, and peak flows, which occur during or shortly after precipitation events. Low flow, called base flow, is an important source of water for human consumption and for sustaining stream ecosystems. Peak flows are regularly studied because they have the greatest potential of causing damage to ecosystems and human structures. For instance, peak flows occur during rainfall events that promote a rapid melting of snow packs in the Cascade Range in the Pacific Northwest of the United States. These events are associated with debris flows that severely damage near stream and in-stream ecosystems and wash out roads. Large streamflows may also result in stream

Sidebar 16.1

Case Study: The 1993 Mississippi Floods

The Mississippi River experienced one of its worst flooding events during late spring and summer of 1993, resulting from a combination of eight months of high rainfall followed by high amounts of snowmelt in the Rocky Mountains. From late June to late July the flood wave overtopped the river banks in Minneapolis, Minnesota, exceeded a 9.5 m levee built to contain the 500-year flood level, and reached 5.2 m above flood stage in St. Louis, Missouri. For the first time since flow records were first collected on Mississippi flooding, flood crests of the Mississippi, Missouri, and Illinois Rivers met simultaneously. Many midwestern rivers remained at flood stage until September (see Figure 16.6 in color insert). The floods resulted in 50 deaths, property damage in excess of $7 billion, evacuation of 37,000 people from their homes, flooding of 30 million ha of farmland and $3 billion in crop damage.

Weather radar and a network of rainfall and river stage gauges linked by satellite to the Army Corps of Engineers offices provided data for real-time flood-routing models. Early warning of the flood was used by the Army Corps of Engineers to open the gates of the 29 regulation dams on the Mississippi in order to release as much water as possible during the spring. However, longer warning times and improved predictive models were needed, according to the National Oceanic and Air Administration (NOAA). In addition, there has been increased questioning of policies of building levees, draining wetlands, clearing the channels and building towns on floodplains. Over the last 200 years, half of the United States wetlands have been drained, and yet these areas, along with backwaters and the floodplain, provide important storage areas for delaying runoff. The national Wetlands Reserve Program was formed to pay farmers to restore 2.5 million ha of wetlands by 1995, but as of 1994 they had rehabilitated only 125,000 ha. The U.S. National Wildlife Foundation has been campaigning to stop subsidized insurance for land owners in flood-prone areas (1).

Source:
1. J. A. JONES, *Global Hydrology: Processes, Resources and Environmental Management*, Addison Wesley Longman Limited, Edinburgh Gate, U.K., 1997.

water levels exceeding the heights of stream banks and overflowing into the surrounding flood plain. Hydrologists use probabilistic terms to describe how big a streamflow event is. The most common term used is the recurrence interval. A recurrence interval of 10 years, which may also be called a "ten-year flood," refers to a streamflow event with a magnitude that on average occurs once in ten years. Longer recurrence intervals mean larger flood events. A 100-year flood is very damaging, but will on average occur only one time in 100 years. However, hydrologists are keenly aware that a 100-year flood could happen in two consecutive years. Recent examples of large floods are the 1993 flooding of the Mississippi River valley (see Sidebar 16.1, and see Figure 16.6 in color insert), and the 1998 flooding of the Red River in North Dakota and southern Manitoba, Canada. 100-year floods result in great losses of life and property because human development occurs most frequently in floodplains, which are generally more fertile land with fewer irrigation costs.

The measured flow, Q, at a stream gauge represents water that has been concentrated from an entire watershed area over a period of time. The time taken by water as it travels from a recharge area in the watershed to the stream gauge results in a delay between the time of peak precipitation and time of peak streamflow. Measurements of streamflow over a period of time can be portrayed in a graphical form known as a *hydrograph*. The hydrograph can portray a single storm event or a sequence of events over a long period of time. The shape of the hydrograph for an event reveals much about the physical characteristics of the watershed that collects and moves water. For example, a large watershed tends to have a larger hydrograph than a small watershed. An elongated watershed tends to have longer flow path lengths, giving it a less pronounced hydrograph peak and a longer duration than a watershed with a more compact shape. A steeper sloped watershed has a higher peak and shorter storm flow duration than a shallow sloped watershed because steep slopes promote a faster acceleration of the watershed because of gravity. In addition, land cover plays an important role in delaying and reducing peak runoff amounts. Figure 16.7 illustrates the effects of urbanizing watersheds on storm runoff responses. In this case, natural vegetated surfaces are replaced with impervious surfaces, such as rooftops, roads, sidewalks, parking lots, and driveways. One consequence is that a greater proportion of annual flow in a stream comes from storm water runoff rather than base flow. In addition, as impervious cover replaces natural surfaces, there is a reduction in soil infiltration capacities, which results in reduced recharge of ground water. This can produce reduced base flow levels during long dry periods between rainfall events. Low flow amounts are considered important for aquatic ecosystems, fisheries, and municipal water supply. Storm runoff moves more rapidly over relatively smooth urban surfaces than over natural vegetation. As a result, rising limbs of storm hydrographs are steeper, have higher peaks, and recession limbs decline more steeply in urbanizing areas. The result is an overall increase in the amount of streamflow, a higher peak streamflow, and a more rapid streamflow response to a rainfall or snow melt event.

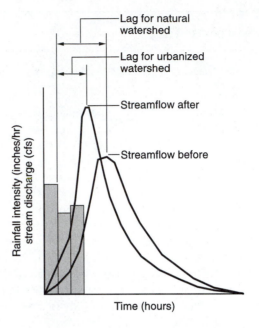

Figure 16.7   This figure shows streamflow hydrographs (curves) and input precipitation (bars), comparing a natural surface cover to an urbanized cover. The effect of urbanizing watersheds is to reduce the lag to peak flow and increase the peak flow, as a result of increased amounts of impervious surface within the watershed.

Integrated View of the Watershed and Its Management

Land Use

It should be evident that human activity has altered land cover, and this should have an impact on water resources. On a global scale, the expansion of deserts is an extreme illustration of how human land use may be causing the spread of non-arable land (see Sidebar 16.2—Land Use and the Global Expansion of Deserts). On a local to regional scale, the primary concern of watershed management is the sound use and protection of water resource quantity and quality. However, the management of water resources cannot be entirely separated from the management of other resources. All forms of land use activities influence and are influenced by water resources. For instance, forest harvesting has an immediate effect on water resources because removing the vegetation reduces interception and transpiration. However, if the forests are encouraged to grow back, then the increased water yield is short lived (3–7 years) and may result in a medium-term reduction in water yield as young forests grow to a closed canopy (Figure 16.8) (6).

Conversion of forests to agriculture or to other types of vegetation cover can have profound impacts on water balance. More precipitation falls directly on the soil surface. This in turn may increase soil water content and potential for runoff. The mechanisms of runoff generation are an important consideration in terms of watershed management. Runoff that occurs from infiltration excess tends to travel long distances, with high velocity, as sheet flow down slopes. This type of runoff promotes the erosion of soil. In contrast, runoff that occurs as saturation excess tends to either begin flowing in regions close to streams where they travel at low velocities and with little capacity for eroding soil, or they are produced in isolated depressions, travel a short distance and re-infiltrate into drier surrounding soils. Soil compaction resulting from certain forest harvest practices may result in reduced infiltration capacity with greater likelihood that the infiltration excess will result in overland flow.

Water can also serve as a means of transferring the effects to another resource. For instance, removal of vegetation in riparian areas can result in warming of streams, which can be detrimental to aquatic resources such as fish. Agricultural practices result in increased surface runoff, which erodes soil. Land cover and land use are important concerns for determining the potential for soil erosion. Energy from the impact of precipitation on bare soil surface will loosen or excavate soil from the surface, making it available for transport by runoff. By having organic materials and residues on the surface, there is less opportunity for rainfall impact to promote soil erosion. In addition, plants reduce the velocity of precipitation by intercepting and releasing it through stemflow or throughfall. After vegetation is removed, burning, plowing, or surface grading removes surface organic material. The soils are then exposed to potential erosion from precipitation impact and subsequent runoff. Erosion may occur in agricultural fields, in formerly forested areas that have been logged and where soils have been compacted under logging equipment, and in overgrazed pastureland.

Overgrazing is a classic example of how land use can dramatically alter the balance between soil protection and soil erosion. Many so-called "badlands" occur in areas where overgrazing triggers rapid soil loss. The photos in Figure 16.9 are taken from an area of badlands on the back slopes of the Niagara Escarpment in southern Ontario, Canada, where a slope composed of weathered shale has

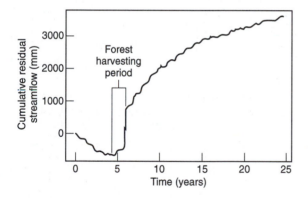

Figure 16.8 This graph shows a cumulative total of the differences between streamflow in a clearcut watershed and a fully vegetated watershed. Prior to the forest harvesting (indicated), the watershed to be clearcut has a lower streamflow. Shortly after the harvest, there is a rapid increase in streamflow in the clearcut watershed. This increase gradually declines with time. After 20 years or so, the vegetation has sufficiently recovered to show little difference between the two watersheds. (Data courtesy of the Forest Science Bank, a partnership between the Department of Forest Science, Oregon State University, and the U.S. Forest Service Northwest Research Station, Corvallis, Oregon. Significant funding for these data was provided by the National Science Foundation.)

Sidebar 16.2

Land Use and the Global Expansion of Deserts

Deserts presently cover about 37 percent of the global land cover, 7 percent of which is because of land use. The current total area amounts to about 45 million square kilometers, and this is increasing at a rate of about 60 thousand square kilometers per year (1). A key trigger appears to be the reduction of soil fertility through destruction of topsoil. One theory to explain how this happens is that devegetation along the margins of subtropical deserts results in a reduction of convective heating needed for the formation of clouds. Several feedback mechanisms can help to explain why this might happen. The destruction of vegetation, for instance through harvesting, results in rain striking soil surfaces with greater force. This seals the soil surface and may produce splashpans, which lowers the rate of infiltration, and leads to greater runoff and soil erosion. Increased runoff and erosion mean reduced storage of water in the soil and reduced soil fertility. The chances for vegetation to regenerate are thus reduced. The soils are also more likely to crack as they dry. Soil surface cracks act as channels for water and promote accelerated soil erosion rates. In addition, the dry,

cracked soil is much more prone to have its topsoil blown away. The bare soil surface reflects much more solar energy than the former vegetated surface, which means the surface absorbs less energy and heating is reduced. In addition, some of the topsoil blown off the surface is carried into the atmosphere where it increases the amount of radiation reflected back to space. This reduces the amount of energy that the atmosphere can absorb, resulting in cooler air aloft. This cooling forces the air to sink, which means it warms adiabatically and forms an inversion. The inversion suppresses strong convective uplift and cloud formation is reduced (2). This theory has been used to explain the expansion of the Sahel Desert in Africa, although the actual influence of land use is unsubstantiated.

Sources:

1. J. A. JONES, *Global Hydrology: Processes, Resources and Environmental Management*, Addison Wesley Longman Limited, Edinburgh Gate, U.K., 1997.

2. R. A. BRYSON AND T. J. MURRAY, *Climate of Hunger*, University of Wisconsin Press, Madison, 1977.

been gullied by the removal of natural vegetation by overgrazing. Once the erosion was initiated, the soils were too nutrient-poor and compacted for vegetation to re-establish. Features such as this underscore the importance of feedback between hydrological processes and land use.

Cumulative Watershed Analysis

Important considerations in watershed management are the cumulative effects of land use activities. Cumulative watershed effects stem from the con-

nectivity of different areas of the watershed because of pathways of movement of water, sediment, organic material, energy, and pollutants. Degradation of the land can potentially follow a vicious circle (Figure 16.10) (7), in which overuse of land and removal of forests leads to reduced soil infiltration rates, which promotes greater soil erosion, degradation of site quality and increased susceptibility of streams to flooding.

Specifically within the context of forest harvesting, numerous examples of cumulative effects can be identified. We will assume an order of oper-

Figure 16.9 Formation of badlands as a result of the removal of vegetation, most likely from overgrazing. The upper photo shows the transition between the vegetation pasture and the badland formation. The lower photo provides a view of the channel formation that prevents establishment of ground-protecting vegetation.

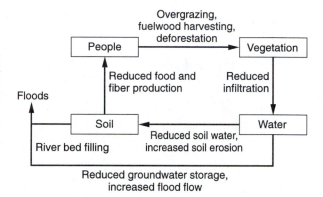

Figure 16.10 A vicious cycle exists because land use activities result in a degradation of soils, increased erosion, and flooding. To compensate for lost arable land, new land is sought and exploited, completing the cycle. (Source: Doherty and MacDonald, 1992.)

ations that includes 1) construction of logging roads, 2) actual harvesting, 3) skid trail development following harvesting, and 4) site preparation for subsequent planting. Road construction bares and compacts soil, which reduces infiltration capacities and increases runoff. Road networks in mountainous forest watersheds may increase peak streamflow by replacing subsurface flow paths with surface flow. This occurs because forest road incisions capture subsurface flow and also promote greater infiltration excess runoff. Subsurface flow is captured by the road and channeled through culverts. A study conducted in two western Wash-

ington catchments indicated that the effect of roads and culverts was to increase the effective channel network density by 64 percent and 52 percent, respectively. Model estimates indicated that this translated into about an 11 percent increase in mean annual floods (8).

Harvesting reduces transpiration, which increases runoff. Skid trails channelize water, which promotes greater runoff. Site preparation reduces ground cover, which increases the transport of sediment. These localized effects in turn accumulate downstream. During large storms, the increased peak streamflows and sediment loads in managed areas can accelerate channel erosion and sedimentation. In mountainous watersheds, an important manifestation of localized increases in soil moisture are earth flows or landslides, which send debris flows through stream reaches. A debris flow can take out much of the existing riparian vegetation and alter the shape of the stream channel. Subsequently, new riparian vegetation establishes itself on the debris. The photo in Figure 16.11 shows a stream channel covered in debris from a flow that resulted from a large buildup of snow followed by rain on the snow during the winter of 1996/1997 (see Sidebar 16.3). The resulting alteration to the channel sides

Figure 16.11 Stream channels like this are common in the Pacific Northwest. The stream bed is dominated by the remnants of a debris flow that swept through the stream channel in early 1996. It was the result of rapid melting of snow during a rainfall event, combined with storage of weathered material on an unstable slope. The effects of forest cover removal are to make slopes much more susceptible to debris flows such as this.

and bottom can severely harm stream ecosystems and domestic water supply. For example, spawning fish require cold water, high levels of dissolved oxygen, and well-aerated gravels that are free of silt and clay. Fish also require deep pools, undercut banks to protect juveniles, and overhanging riparian vegetation to provide shade for the stream ecosystem and for a source of decaying vegetation to sustain lower levels of the aquatic food chain. Lack of consideration of these factors can cause damage to economically important fish stocks, such as salmon. This has traditionally only been the concern of fisheries personnel; other land uses including forestry were considered to be competing with fisheries.

The eroded soil causes sedimentation of streams and other water bodies. In addition, pollutants attached to the sediments are also moved from the runoff-generating surface to water bodies. Pollutants include dissolved nutrients and chemicals. Pollution is normally classified as increased concentrations of these constituents over natural levels. It

occurs either from point sources or nonpoint sources. Point sources include municipal sewers and industrial waste output. Nonpoint source pollution represents by far the most significant source of pollution. By definition, nonpoint source (NPS) pollution occurs over a widespread area and is concentrated in rivers, lakes, and estuaries. In the United States, the primary source of NPS pollution is agriculture. Nutrients applied on agricultural fields are carried through streams and concentrated in lakes and other water bodies. These nutrients promote accelerated aquatic vegetation growth, such as algae blooms (see Figure 16.12 in color insert). When this vegetation dies, it remains in the water, where it decays. The decomposition of this organic material consumes oxygen, that is then depleted from the water. This loss of oxygen in surface water is called *eutrophication*. It is observable most immediately as a reduction in water clarity and decline in fish and other aquatic organisms.

A legal basis for a shift towards a more ecologically sound management of water resources began with the United States Congress passing the National Environmental Policy Act, the National Forest Management Act, and the Clean Water Act (9). These laws respectively required federal agencies to prepare environmental impact statements for projects having the potential to significantly affect the environment, directed the Forest Service to guarantee protection for all water bodies, and established Best Management Practices (BMPs) for controlling nonpoint source pollution. Section 319 of the Clean Water Act of 1987 required states to identify and submit BMPs for EPA approval to help control nonpoint source pollution. As of 1993, 41 of 50 states had EPA-approved voluntary or regulatory silviculture-based BMP programs. The state BMPs are all similar; the majority deal with roads. Montana, for example, has a total of 55 specifically addressed forest practices. Of those 55 practices, 35 deal with road planning and location, road design, road maintenance, road drainage, road construction, and stream crossings. (See Sidebar 16.4.)

Unified watershed assessments are directed at integrating state, interstate, tribal, and federal assessment programs. Priority watersheds from different agencies can be overlaid on maps for comparison. An advantage of this approach is that watersheds can be evaluated at different scales, ranging from small watersheds around single water bodies up to a regional extent. Having nested watersheds, in which smaller monitored watersheds lie within larger monitored watersheds, helps to target activities identified in watershed restoration action strategies. To make these new approaches feasible, there has been a shift of responsibility of monitoring water resources from government agencies to nongovernment agencies. Monitoring consortiums that involve partnerships between government agencies, public and private organizations are becoming common (10).

International Watershed Management: The Case of the Great Lakes Basin

Watersheds that are shared by two or more countries present unique challenges for managing water resources. High-profile examples include the Amazon River basin and the Great Lakes river basin. The Great Lakes are the largest system of fresh surface water on earth, containing roughly 18 percent of the world supply. Only the polar ice caps contain more fresh surface water. The resources of the Great Lakes basin have been central to the history and development of the United States and Canada. For the early European explorers and settlers, the

Sidebar 16.3

Case Study: Pacific Northwest Floods of 1996

Warm winds, intense rainfall, and rapid snowmelt during the winter of 1995–96 and again in the winter of 1996–97 caused major flooding, landslides, and other damage throughout the Pacific Northwest. Watershed damage included large and damaging debris flows, which are fast-moving and carry large rocks eroded from high elevation sites, fallen trees, and other debris through valley channels (see Figure 16.11). The hardest-hit areas had the worst flooding in over 30 years. Damage to roads, trails, watersheds, and water resources was widespread on National Forest Service lands. The events offered an opportunity to study the effects of severe weather, examine the influence and effectiveness of forest management techniques, and implement repairs that follow ecosystem management principles. Based on long-term access and travel requirements, road repairs were made

by relocating roads to areas outside of floodplains. Table 16.3 summarizes the major buffer strip requirements for managing stream corridors in Pacific Northwest states. These guidelines are in place for the protection of streambanks and for maintaining the health of the aquatic ecosystems. Examination of road crossings at streams concluded with the design recommendation to keep the water moving, align culverts horizontally and longitudinally with the stream channel, and minimize changes in the stream channel cross-section at inlet basins to prevent future debris plugs. Areas with stable, well-vegetated slopes and streambanks, as well as fully functioning floodplains, buffer the effects of floods. Common restoration practices include streambank stabilization and riparian plantings to aid the natural processes in these systems.

(continues)

Sidebar 16.3 *(continued)*

Table 16.3 Major buffer strip requirements for stream corridor maintenance in the Pacific Northwest. The guidelines distinguish between fisheries and water supply as primary protection areas and other impacts for secondary protection.

	Protection Areas	Required Width of Buffer Strip	Shade or Canopy Requirement	Leave Trees Requirement
Idaho	Water supply, fisheries	Fixed minimum (75 feet)	75% current shade[a]	Yes; number per 1000 feet, dependent on stream width[b]
	Other influences	Fixed minimum (5 feet)	No requirement	No requirement
Washington	Water supply, fisheries	Variable by stream width (5–100 feet)	50% (75% required if temperature>60°F)	Yes; number per 1000 feet, dependent on stream width and bed material
	Other influences	No requirement	No requirement	25 per 1000 feet, 6 inches diameter
California	Water supply, fisheries	Variable by slope and stream class (50–200 feet)[c]	50% overstory and/or understory; dependent on slope and stream class	Yes; number to be determined by canopy density[d]
	Sediment transport[e]	No requirement	50% understory[f]	No requirement[f]
Oregon	Water supply, fisheries	Variable, three times stream width (25–100 feet)	50% existing canopy, 75% existing shade	Yes; number and basal area per 1000 feet by stream width
	Significant impact downstream	No requirement[g]	75% existing shade	No requirement

[a] In Idaho, the shade requirement is designed to maintain stream temperatures.

[b] In Idaho, the leave tree requirement is designed to provide for recruitment of large woody debris.

[c] May range up to 300 feet for some types of timber harvest.

[d] To be determined by field inspection.

[e] In streams capable of sediment transport.

[f] Residual vegetation must be sufficient to prevent degradation of downstream beneficial users.

[g] In eastern Oregon, operators are required to "leave stabilization of undergrowth ... sufficient to prevent washing of sediment into Class I streams below."

lakes and their tributaries were the avenues for penetrating the continent, extracting valued resources and carrying local products abroad. By the end of the twentieth century, the Great Lakes basin was home to more than one-tenth of the population of the United States and one-quarter of the population of Canada. The United States considers the Great Lakes a fourth seacoast, and the Great Lakes region is a dominant factor in the Canadian industrial economy.

The original logging operations in the Great Lakes basin cleared the land for agriculture. Some of the wood was used in construction. Most of it was burned. By the 1830s, commercial logging

Sidebar 16.4

Case Study: Best Management Practices in Wisconsin

Nearly half of Wisconsin is forested. Its forests are critical to much of its nearly 20,000 kilometers of rivers and streams and nearly 15,000 lakes. The Wisconsin Department of Natural Resources (DNR) Forestry Divison, began a Best Management Practices (BMP) program in 1995 to determine the effects of timber harvesting on water resources. The objectives were to identify where BMPs are being used, their effectiveness, and to determine the effects of not applying BMPs. Although forestry practices contribute only 3 percent to the state-wide nonpoint source pollution, there are nevertheless important local impacts on water quality. Three primary focus areas were riparian management zones, forest roads, and wetlands. Riparian management zones are areas within about 30 meters of lakes and perennial streams. Within these zones, the highest priority BMPs designated no construction of roads or landings, that soil exposure and compaction be minimized, that no slash be placed within the zone, and that harvesting be selective. Harvesting was specified to promote long-lived species, including sugar and red maple, white and black ash, oaks, eastern hemlock, white and red pine, and cedar. Recommendations for road BMPs included planning to minimize overall road area and to not exceed road grades of 10 percent to minimize runoff. Recommendations for wetland BMPs include avoiding equipment maintenance and fueling, avoiding construction, and keeping slash away from open water.

From 1995 to 1997, individual timber sales were evaluated by teams consisting of individuals from government agencies, professional forestry organizations, environmental organizations, and the forest products industry. Only timber sales on wetlands or within 60 meters of a lake or stream were monitored. The results of the study indicated that BMPs were applied correctly 85 percent of the time when needed, and that only 6 percent of the time did the absence of BMPs have a major impact on water resources. The results of the study called for greater emphasis on BMPs for riparian management areas and forest roads. Riparian management is recommended for areas within about 30 meters of lakes and perennial streams. A key element of successful implementation will be education, because about two-thirds of the state forests are owned by about 260,000 private land owners. This includes encouraging land owners to participate in BMP training. Another recommendation of the study was to conduct further research to determine whether steep terrain or soil type correlates with the effectiveness of BMPs in some areas. This is a study that could be conducted with the application of geographic information systems and models.

began in Upper Canada (now southern Ontario), followed by Michigan, Minnesota, and Wisconsin. Cutting was generally done in the winter months, by traveling up rivers and felling trees that were floated down to the lakes during the spring thaw. Timber was eventually carried in ships specially designed for log transport. The earliest loggers harvested mainly white pine. In virgin stands, these trees reached 60 meters (200 feet) in height, and a single tree could contain 10 cubic meters (6,000 board feet) of lumber. As the forests were cleared, loggers migrated farther west and north in search of white pine. When this resource was exhausted other species were utilized. The hardwoods such as maple, walnut, and oak were cut to make furniture and specialty products. Lower-grade pulpwood would eventually support papermaking and the region became a major source of paper. With the pulp and paper industry came a mercury pollution problem on the Great Lakes until the early 1970s, when mercury was banned.

The logging industry was exploitive during its early stages. Huge stands were lost in fires, often because of poor management of litter from logging operations. In Canada, lumbering was largely done on crown lands with a small tax charged per tree. In the United States, cutting was done on private land, but when it was cleared, the owners often stopped paying taxes and let the land revert to public ownership. In both cases, clearcutting was the usual practice. Without proper rehabilitation of the forest, soils were readily eroded and lost to local streams, rivers and lakes. In some areas of the Great Lakes basin, reforestation has not been adequate and forests may be considered a diminishing resource. Pollution that had immediate local effects eventually spread throughout the basin.

An evolution in understanding how environmental damage has resulted from human use of natural resources in the basin has arisen out of the research, monitoring and commitment to Great Lakes protection by both countries. Ecosystem management requires the involvement of all levels of government, as well as industry and nongovernment organizations. Each has its own responsibilities and often work in partnership to protect the basin ecosystem. Originally, water pollution was treated as a separate problem. Eventually the connections between land, air, and water resources were better appreciated. In 1905, the International Waterways Commission was created to advise the governments of both countries about levels and flows in the Great Lakes, especially in relation to the generation of electricity by hydropower. The Boundary Waters Treaty was signed in 1909 and provided for the creation of the International Joint

Commission (IJC). The IJC has the authority to resolve disputes over the use of water resources that cross the international boundary. Water pollution was one of the first problems referred to the IJC for study. Public and scientific concern about pollution of the lakes grew as accelerated eutrophication became more obvious through the 1950s. The IJC reported in 1970 that eutrophication was the result of excessive phosphorus. The study proposed basin-wide efforts to reduce phosphorus loadings from all sources. It was recognized that reduction of phosphorus depended on control of local sources. Uniform effluent limits were urged for all industries and municipal sewage treatment systems in the basin. Research suggested that land runoff could also be an important source of nutrients and other pollutants entering the lakes. This research resulted in the Great Lakes Water Quality Agreement in 1972. It was revised in 1978 to establish target phosphorous discharge levels, 1 part per million (ppm) (mg per liter), and for the virtual elimination of toxic chemicals. In 1987, the Agreement was revised to emphasize ecosystem objectives, including nonpoint source pollution, airborne pollution, pollution from contaminated groundwater, and ecological indicators such as human and aquatic community health.

In addition to government legislation, communities, local groups and individuals play a key role in the management of the Great Lakes. The management process starts with individuals and families taking action as consumers, recyclers, neighborhood stewards and health promoters. Nongovernment organizations are taking responsibility for public education, citizen-directed projects, and for providing direction to government. Businesses are key in managing their own operations in a sustainable, ecological fashion, being partners with community and governments, and in complying with regulations set by themselves and others. Most successful management requires partnership arrangements among the various sectors in the public. People are getting involved in local decision-making processes, via groups such as Public

Advisory Committees in Areas of Concern and local community groups throughout the Great Lakes basin that exert pressure toward change.

New Technologies for Integrated Watershed Management

Recent developments in computer-based technologies are changing the way in which integrated views of watersheds are being maintained. Geographic information systems (GIS) are computer-based methods for the capture, storage, display, analysis, and output of geographically referenced information. GIS are integrative tools for spatial analysis and modeling (see also Chapter 12). A GIS can combine information of different themes that is traditionally portrayed on paper maps. A theme could represent soils, topography, vegetation, hydrography, land use, or other data collected spatially. The GIS allows for these themes to be placed in a common geographic coordinate system so that information from multiple themes can be addressed by location. Once in this form, it can be used for visualization (see Figure 16.13 in color insert), watershed modeling, and analysis. Watershed modeling tools increasingly rely on geographic data preparation as inputs and to support decision making (see Figure 16.14 in color insert).

Remote sensing is the art and science of collecting information about the earth's surface without being in physical contact with the surface. Most of the time it refers to photographs or images acquired by cameras or imaging scanners flown on aircraft or spacecraft. Information obtained using this technology is normally characterized by its spatial resolution and spectral characteristics. Spatial resolution refers to the smallest discernable element of the picture. For photographs, this depends on photographic emulsions and processing. For digital imagery, it refers to the smallest picture element. The smallest identifiable object on the ground that can be seen in a photo or image also depends on the height of the aircraft or spacecraft and the

instantaneous field-of-view (IFOV) of the camera or scanner. A low flying height and small IFOV yield the highest spatial resolution. However, a small IFOV means the sensor receives reflected or emitted energy summed from a small area on the surface, potentially giving very little information. The tradeoff between spatial resolution and spectral information content is sometimes balanced by simultaneously capturing energy over a range of wavelengths. Spectral resolution refers to the range of wavelengths from the electromagnetic spectrum that is captured by one photo or image. Photographs can capture visible wavelengths or both visible and near-infrared. These are wavelengths of energy from the sun that are reflected off the earth's surface. Image scanners can also detect thermal infrared energy emitted by the surface. In addition, there are microwave radar sensors that have shown some promise for mapping topography, detecting near surface soil moisture, and distinguishing between vegetation canopy and ground.

The most common remote sensing technologies that have been used in water resources management are aerial photography: both visible and near-infrared, and imaging scanners: visible, near-infrared, and thermal. Near-infrared energy is useful for mapping vegetation, as healthy cells in leaves are highly reflective in this part of the spectrum. In addition, chlorophyll is a good absorber of energy from the red part of the electromagnetic spectrum. By combining these two properties, researchers have developed numerous indexes of leaf quantity that correlate well with ground-based measurements of leaf area. These indexes provide a spatially large inventory of vegetation canopy density, which can be incorporated into watershed models to make estimates of transpiration. Remote sensing is increasingly being used for monitoring water quality, particularly in lakes and estuaries. Figure 16.12 shows two images over Lake Mendota in Madison, Wisconsin (see Figure 16.12 in color insert). One shows near-infrared reflectance, which highlights the presence of algal blooms. The second shows thermal infrared emitted energy, which highlights the presence of a heat plume coming from a power generation plant. The dark lines in the water are boat wakes. These appear darker because they are cooler at the surface because of mixing of the surface and deeper waters as a boat moves across the surface.

Concluding Statement

The watershed is the basic organizing framework for water and related resources management. By virtue of the nested structure of large watersheds containing smaller watersheds, a means is provided to telescope from lesser detail to greater detail. From a global level, one can telescope down to regional level, and then to a management level, and ultimately down to the hillslope level where water flow pathways can be directly measured. This allows for quantifying the storage and movement of water using conservation equations. Knowing where the water goes then assists in understanding the fate of sediment, nutrients, and other pollutants.

The distribution of global vegetation can be explained by an examination of the balance between precipitation and potential evapotranspiration (ET). When potential ET exceeds precipitation, there is generally not enough water to support dense vegetation, including forests. Forests generally occur in regions where precipitation greatly exceeds potential ET. However, for a smaller spatial extent, the presence of ground water recharge from upland to lowland sites can help offset an average water deficit by locally providing a source of soil water.

An understanding of hydrologic flow pathways is important for understanding how land use will affect the sustainability of the soils, soil erosion, and cumulative impacts on aquatic life and human water supply. Removal of vegetation can result in a decline in soil fertility, in part because of removal of nutrients and also because of a reduction in ET and soil water storage. More precipitation goes into surface runoff, which promotes the loss of soil. Pollutants attached to the lost soil are then moved into stream channels and carried out of the area of land management. In addition, there can be a vicious cycle as land use is expanded into new areas to compensate for lost soil fertility. This leads to increased loss of fertile land, and increased runoff during storms leading to greater flooding and loss of life.

An integrated view of the watershed recognizes the role of all activities within a nested watershed on water quality downstream. It requires government agencies, nongovernment organizations, and individual landowners to take on joint responsibility for the management of water and related resources. In North America and other areas in the world, there is a shift from regulation by governments towards improved education of all resource users. Best Management Practices (BMPs) are becoming widely adopted within the United States. They address the management of stream corridors to limit development in these areas that act as buffers to runoff, and as shelter for aquatic life.

BMPs and other forms of watershed management are beginning to benefit from new technologies, such as GIS and remote sensing. These tools allow for the management of large amounts of geographically referenced data to gain a broader spatial perspective on land management. By integrating these tools with models of flood prediction and nonpoint source pollution, it is possible to make better decisions for identifying priority watersheds and determining how to implement monitoring programs within limited budgets.

References

1. Dunne, T. and L. B. Leopold, *Water in Environmental Planning*, Freeman and Company, New York, 1978.

2. D. J. Brooks and G. E. Grant, *New Perspectives in Forest Management: Background, Science Issues, and Research Agenda*, Research Paper PNW-RP-456, Pacific Northwest Research Station, Forest Service, United States Department of Agriculture, 1992.

3. F. Law, *J. British Waterworks Association*, 35, 489 (1956).

4. W. T. Swank and N. H. Miner, *Water Resources Res.*, 4, 947 (1968).

5. A. R. HIBBERT, *Water Resources Res.*, 7, 71 (1971).

6. G. KUCZERA, *J. of Hydrology, 94,* 215 (1987).

7. A. DOHERTY AND M. MCDONALD, *River Basin Management*, Hodder & Stoughton, East Kilbride, U.K., 1992.

8. L. BOWLING AND D. LETTENMAIER, *Evaluation of the Effects of Forest Roads on Streamflow in Hard and Ware Creeks, Washington*, Timber-Fish-Wildlife Publication number TFW-SH20-97-001, Washington Department of Natural Resources, Olympia, Wash., 1997.

9. J. COBOURN, *J. Soil and Water Conservation*, July-August, 267 (1989).

10. U.S. Environmental Protection Agency, *Monitoring Consortiums: A Cost-Effective Means to Enhancing Watershed Data Collection and Analysis*, EPA841-R-97-006, Office of Water (4503F), United States Environmental Protection Agency, Washington, D.C., 1997.

Additional Reading

J. FRANKLIN, "Scientific basis for new perspective in forests and streams," In *Watershed Management: Balancing Sustainability and Environmental Change*, R. Naiman, ed., 1992.

K. FULLER, H. SHEAR AND J. WITTIG, *The Great Lakes: An Environmental Atlas and Resource Book*, Third Edition, Joint Publication of the Government of Canada, Toronto, and the United States Environmental Protection Agency, Chicago, 1995.

G. E. GRANT AND F. J. SWANSON, "Morphology and processes of valley floors in mountain streams, western Cascades, Oregon," In *Natural and Anthropogenic Influences in Fluvial Geomorphology*, Geophysical Monograph 89, American Geophysical Union, Washington, D.C., 1995.

WNDR, *Wisconsin's Forestry Best Management Practices for Water Quality, A Field Manual for Loggers, Landowners and Land Managers*, Forest Resource Publication No. PUB-FR-093-95, Wisconsin Department of Natural Resources, Bureau of Forestry, Madison, 1995.

WDNR, *Wisconsin's Forestry Best Management Practices for Water Quality*, Forest Resource Publication No. PUB-FR-145-99, Wisconsin Department of Natural Resources, Bureau of Forestry, Madison, 1999.

G. J. WELLS, J. FOGG, ET AL., *Stream Corridor Restoration: Principles, Processes, and Practices*, Environmental Protection Agency Report #EPA 841-R-98-900, Washington, D.C, 1998.

Managing Recreation Behavior

ROBERT O. RAY

It would be relatively easy to manage natural resources if it weren't for all the people. People are both the problem and the solution to environmental management issues. Recreational demand manifests itself as a need for participation opportunities in natural settings that hold interesting, challenging, and complex experiences for consumers. This experience-seeking behavior creates equally interesting, challenging, and complex issues that managers of natural resources must address.

While forested public lands were initially set aside for timber production and strategic reserve in a younger and more agrarian society, major changes in the structure, values, and policies of the country have had a serious impact on the management philosophy for those lands. Over time, recreation has emerged as one of the principal reasons people visit these sylvan areas. This often presents a major conflict between those who advocate wise use of resources encouraged by individuals like Gifford Pinchot and the aesthetic value of preservation fostered by Muir, Thoreau, Jensen, and others who introduced nature as an entity with value that transcends that of resource extraction (1). In more recent history, the concept of nature as a place and agent to refresh the soul and restore and cleanse the spirit, mind, and body has captured the fancy of the American public (2, 3).

This century-long trend began at a time where we moved to a more urbanized industrial base that began to separate us from the land. It was further influenced by a growth in economic affluence that permitted us the luxury of improving infra-structure (roads, airports, hotels, resorts, restau-rants, etc.) that, in turn, enhanced access to formerly remote natural areas. Current techno-logical advances in recreational equipment allow a greater number and variety of people access and opportunities for recreation that were not previ-ously available. This affluence also permits the public to set aside large areas of land, water, forests, and historical and cultural sites for the greater benefit of society.

With these changes, it is not surprising that many controversies have risen over how to best use and manage the forest resource base. For example, are the forests more useful for recreation than for tim-ber harvest, or should the forest be managed as an integral part of global environmental enhancement (clean air, water conservation, etc.)? The evolution of legislation and litigation over resource use issues has been enormous over the last century. What is more amazing is that it appears to have a good prospect for a vigorous and healthy (if not all enjoy-able) political and judicial future.

Those who manage forest-based resources have the blessings and best wishes of many as the good and faithful stewards of natural resources in some quarters. Others vilify them as demons to be feared and exorcised either because they allow exploitation and destruction of nature or because they are overly restrictive of land use. People's per-spectives on management and managers are important and critical pieces of this chapter. How do we best determine the use of the lands we have? What should they yield and to whom? Should they yield consumable products only or should they add more aesthetic and spiritual value to living? How should we manage the land, water, air, and history of the people in ways that help them respect what managers do? If we are unable to accomplish this, will the people cease to believe in us such that we will no longer be useful?

Perceptions of Forest Use

Nature has always offered an extraordinary appeal to people for countless reasons: the romance of adventure, the promise of the unexpected, the chance to find beauty, the chance to secure one's religious faith, or perhaps to find something for din-ner. The forests in particular have offered a wide range of opportunities and challenges for people that have proven strongly seductive over the course of human history. It is fair to note, however, that our love affair with the deep woods and its denizens is relatively recent in origin. Many of our ancestors carried a serious respect, distrust, and even deep fear of the forests they encountered. Evil was known to live in the form of fierce creatures and embodied in the trees, along with the prom-ises of useful resources, cool temperatures in the summer, and fresh clean water. There were many who would not set foot in the woods without seri-ous reason, good company, and something to defend against the creatures and spirits of nature.

The fear of nature began to shift in the settle-ment of the New World as our founders began the chants of "manifest destiny" with the seemingly lim-itless natural resources for exploitation in the New World. This perspective, too, changed over time, and people gradually awakened to the limits of the resources and increasingly realized that human activities could easily and quickly threaten the most abundant and desirable attributes of natural places. Along with recognition came questions that con-tinue to arise.

This chapter begins with a short description of recreation concepts, identifies typical recreation behaviors, and discusses them in the context of recreation resources management. Sketches of social change are used to present key current issues, concerns, and management strategies and their effects. Finally, the future of recreation management is addressed in light of changes in technology, social structure, user demands, population shifts, and global changes.

Throughout the chapter, readers are faced with the most difficult question faced by managers that almost never has a single, enduring answer, "What is the right thing to do?" This is followed by an almost equally difficult question, "Who says so?" This is addressed at the end of the chapter in a discussion on the evolution of new strategies for recreation management.

Some Background on Management of Recreation

Why do people pursue recreation in the out-of-doors? This is often a question that people look at, and conclude: why bother asking? However, it has evolved into probably the most important question that an area manager will face. Why? Knowing why people show up and participate allows the manager to do everything from designing an area to addressing consumer preferences and aims to managing their behavior and deciding on the most appropriate placement of amenities like rest rooms, concessions, and trash disposal sites.

Historically, inventories of recreation behavior were of only marginal interest to land and resource management agencies. This changed around late 1950s and early 1960s. It was in this time frame that the first systematic study of outdoor recreation in America was conducted by the Outdoor Recreation Resources Review Commission (ORRRC), which made its final report to Congress in 1962. The report was instrumental in reshaping the policies and approaches made to managing public lands for outdoor recreation use (also see Chapter 1). Simultaneously, legislators recognized that increased demand with a lack of systematic planning to satisfy future use and demand for outdoor recreation could be a political and natural dis-

aster. In 1960, they passed the Multiple-Use and Sustained Yield Act, which first changed the management priorities of U.S. Forest Service Lands from timber and natural resource management to include recreation as an equally important activity. The present National Forest Service is the largest provider of outdoor recreation opportunities among all federal agencies. Information in Table 17.1 illustrates the breadth and expanse of their responsibilities.

The momentum built by these landmark pieces of legislation prompted a cascade of actions that crested in the late 1960s but have never ceased being important legislative considerations over the last four decades. While space to describe in detail the elements of all legislation is not possible here, it is important to call attention to a few significant actions.

In 1963, the Outdoor Recreation Act explicitly recognized the need and desirability to assure continued access and opportunities for recreation by asking all levels of government to participate in an assessment of available recreation resources and to estimate what it would take to meet future needs. Knowing the available resources and understanding their potential to meet public demand for access and quality by current and future populations is absolutely essential. It is critical for developing and implementing appropriate management policies and practices that respond to population dynamics and resource needs. To foster participation by varied levels of government, the Land and Water Conservation Fund Act was passed in 1965. This act was one of the most significant pieces of legislation of the time, because it provided incentive in the form of funds for states and local governments to plan, develop, and maintain outdoor recreation areas that fit into a nationwide perspective.

The '60s were quite an active period for outdoor recreation legislation. Growing from the momentum created by the ORRRC report and riding public sentiment, other significant acts were passed. The National Wilderness Preservation System, the National Wild and Scenic Rivers System, the National Trails System and the National Recreation Areas creation were all products of this period.

Table 17.1   Recreation Facts, U.S.D.A. Forest Service

Information	
Land Area	
Number of National Forests and Grasslands:	177 (155 forests, 22 grasslands), 192 million acres
States, Territories, Commonwealths having National Forests and National Grasslands:	42
Wilderness Areas:	399 (34.7 million acres)
Percent of National Wilderness Preservation System Managed by Forest Service in lower 48 states:	63%
Percent of National Wilderness Preservation System Managed by Forest Service in total U.S.:	34%
Number of National Recreation Areas (NRA) (includes Land Between the Lakes NRA):	20
Number of National Scenic Areas (NSA):	9
Number of National Monuments and Volcanic Monuments (NM):	4
Total acreage of NRA, NSA, and NM (includes Land Between the Lakes NRA):	6.7 million
Recreation Roads, Trails, and Rivers	
National Forest Scenic Byways:	136 (9,126 miles)
Wild and Scenic Rivers:	95 (4,418 miles)
Trails:	133,087 miles
Scenic and Historic Trails:	6,709 miles
Sites, Facilities, and Services	
Heritage Sites:	277,000
Campgrounds:	4,300
Developed Recreation Sites:	23,000
Alpine Ski Areas:	135
Picnic Sites:	1,496
Boating Sites:	1,222
Swimming Areas:	140
Recreation Facilities:	18,000
Recreation Residences:	14,900
Resorts:	480
Outfitter/Guide Permits:	5,700
Miscellaneous Information	
Employees in Forest Service:	32,000
Total people-at-one-time capacity:	157 million
Developed sites people-at-one-time capacity:	1.8 million
Amount of recreation-deferred maintenance:	$812 million
Recreation facilities backlog:	$664 million
Trails backlog (trails and trail bridges):	$148 million

Source: http://www.fs.fed.us/recreation/recinfo/facts_sheet.shtml

The legislation slowed in the 1970s and new interests began to emerge. Among them was an effort to more closely examine the role of private landholders as participants in the recreation system. Ways to entice the landholder into participation vary but one of the more critical aspects was liability for user well-being. This is an important idea for managers to understand, since private land holdings that could be used for recreation are often held in close proximity to public recreation lands. If proper agreements for landowner protection are reached, the lands available for recreational use could be significantly expanded. This problem has been addressed in many ways, but the primary and least expensive enticement has been legislation that allows landowners who open their lands for pubic access at no charge to be relatively free of responsibilities for user liability. For the last 30 years, this has been a major concern for public land managers. The changes in liability laws effectively increased the lands accessible to participants.

Other ways to increase the access to lands for recreation continue to emerge and should be closely examined by managers. For example, gaining use of rights of way from varied utilities and services has been used for many years with considerable success. More recently, new tools have emerged. Among them include the purchase of development rights from landowners (e.g., farm and range lands). In brief, this process allows government to enter an agreement with the landowner that the land will not be developed for an activity like housing or industry in exchange for money based on the value of the profit from development. Another emergent tool has to do with collaborations between and among Non-Government Organizations (NGOs) and public agencies. For example, an NGO like the Nature Conservancy might enter into an agreement with the Forest Service for cooperative recreational use of an adjoining land for restricted purposes (e.g., birding or hiking).

As might be expected, there are always problems in new approaches to management. One recently raised by Fairfax (4) is that partnerships are often based on the assumption that partners will always have common goals that do not change over time. This may or may not happen since each partner may need to change or respond to different goals or situations that retain or conflict with initial understandings. Does this mean they should not be pursued? Absolutely not. Managers simply need to know that these changes are possible and try to find ways to either anticipate their appearance and impact or adapt to the situation by continuous dialogue with partners.

Forest-Based Recreation Management

Forests and other natural resource-based recreation management is applicable from small public resource-based recreation areas near urban centers to large, commercial forest lands. It is also appropriate for massive public land management agencies of the U.S. Forest Service, the Bureau of Land Management, the U.S. Fish and Wildlife Service and the National Park Service. The management emphasis is on the resource base and guided by decisions on the best recreation opportunities possible given the limitation of the resource, budget, and context.

A significant difference between the management of public and private lands lies in their authority and locus of control in making decisions about the use of the land. In private holding, those who own the land are able to make their own decision on what actions will be permitted (e.g., who can hunt, camp, hike, fish, or swim) on their property, whether there is a fee for use, and what the rules of use and behavior might be. As one might guess, there is quite a range of management objectives and styles among and between land owners in accommodating public use. The critical point is that a private owner does not need public input on how to manage the recreation needs of the consumer.

Those charged with management of public lands have quite a different set of needs and expectations. A brief examination of the U.S. Forest Service's document "The Recreation Agenda" (Sidebar 17.1) provides some important clues on how public agencies are trying to accommodate the continued

Sidebar 17.1

The Recreation Agenda—U.S.D.A. Forest Service

Americans cherish the national forests and grasslands for the values they provide—clean water, clean air, natural scenic beauty, important natural resources, protection of rare species, majestic forests, wilderness, a connection with their history, and opportunities for unparalleled outdoor adventure. Recreation visitors want a great deal from the Forest Service in terms of settings, experiences, facilities and services, and they will expect even more in the future. Recreation is the fastest-growing use of the national forests and grasslands.

The national forests and grasslands offer a diversity of opportunities across the Recreation Opportunity Spectrum. The Forest Service manages 63% of the wilderness system in the lower forty-eight states, and a much larger percentage of backcountry experiences. It also cares for 4,268 miles of the wild and scenic rivers system; 399 wilderness areas in the National Wilderness Preservation System; 133,087 miles of trails; 383,000 miles of authorized roads, more than 277,000 heritage sites; over 4,300 campgrounds; and 31 national recreation, scenic areas, and monuments. As outstanding as these assets are, the Forest Service is more than a custodian of a recreation infrastructure.

As Americans increasingly rely on non-federal forestlands for a variety of goods and services, the federal and non-federal sectors must work together to plan for the future. About 60% of the nation's forests are in non-federal ownership. As on federal lands, the future use of these forests is moving from product use to an anesthetic and ecological management. State and private forestry programs, state foresters, private foresters, and communities are developing an ever-increasing set of knowledge, skills, and tools to meet society's desire for open space,

management of urban sprawl, and new applications of agroforestry.

As one of the multiple benefits from these resources, the national forests and grasslands contribute $134 billion to the gross domestic product, with the lion's share associated with outdoor recreation. Resource-based travel and tourism provide a window through which an increasingly urban society can enjoy and appreciate the natural world. The Forest Service has a unique "niche" or brand of nature-based recreation to offer. This brand of recreation includes an undeveloped setting, a built environment that reinforces this natural character, and an array of services that complement enjoyment of these special wild places.

The Forest Service has the opportunity to open that window to special places and experiences even wider to reflect changes in demographic trends and recreation visitor preferences. The Forest Service serves as a catalyst among tourism professionals in working together in travel and tourism opportunities. It seeks out tourism professionals that can represent the diversity of existing and potential customers.

Both the deteriorating infrastructure, estimated at $812 million dollars, and the recreation customers are demanding more. This agenda is aimed at meeting as much of that demand as possible with the highest quality experiences and within ecological and social limits. These limits include impacts on the resource, impacts on experiences of other visitors, and capacity limits of the recreation infrastructure.

Management of these cherished resources requires a long-term viewpoint and investment strategies. Years of declining budgets and a dwindling recreation workforce have made the

(continues)

Sidebar 17.1 *(continued)*

challenges even more formidable. The Agency has responded with innovative efforts such as the fee demonstration program, permit stream-lining, nongovernmental partnerships, and help from volunteers. The Forest Service must find even more innovative ways to accomplish the work to be done.

This agenda is a guide to four goals: protect the ecosystem to guarantee that special natural settings are available for future generations, increase service satisfaction and education of Americans about their public lands, build community connections to expand available resources, and improve relationships to get the job done.

Source:
1. Adapted from U.S.D.A. Forest Service, "The Recreation Agenda," 1999, http://www.fs.fed.us/recreation/Recstrategy/recStratV70.shtml.

---

public demand for recreation on U.S. forest lands (5).

In response to increased public awareness and demand, there are enormous numbers of recreational services that are programmed into certain agencies and businesses. It is rather easy to assume if recreation is simply a set of leader-led activities, all an agency needs to do to satisfy recreational need is to hire a program designer and leader to organize and conduct recreation activities for users. In many community-based recreation agencies this is the dominant way that recreation activities and services evolve. However, once examined, recreation activities take on a more complicated view heavily influenced by individual choice and self-direction. It is interesting to note that in an e-mail discussion among professors of recreation (through SPRENET), researchers pointed out the paradox that what people say they like to do for recreation is usually *not* organized by an agency. They prefer to pursue recreation activities outside the programmed service arena (e.g., driving for pleasure, walking, and hiking). This is reflected repeatedly in recreation activity surveys. It is also important to note which are recurrent when discussing the reasons for managing an area to maximize recreation opportunity. What is it that people are looking for in recreation?

What Is This Recreation Stuff Anyway?

The question is not new and neither are the answers. There are many ways to think about recreation and there have been a number of books written on the topic. However, even though the answers are not crystal clear or uniform in their conclusions, the question has importance for management.

Recreation Is Personal

One of the most agreed-upon elements that characterize recreation is rejuvenation, or, literally, the re-creation of oneself. It implies a significant and refreshing change or departure from the activities done in the normal course of life. An assumption is that such a change is necessary for one to live a pleasant existence, and a further assumption is that what we do in the course of life has a stagnating effect on our quality of life. In short, we need a change to refresh us for a return to the ordinary activities of the world. Pieper (6) wrote of this need in his classical essay on *Leisure: The Basis of Culture*. People head to the great outdoors expecting (and usually getting) a change from the ordinary day-to-day experiences of life. Neulinger (7) added to this concept in the 1970s by identifying recreation as a psychological phenomenon characterized by the individual's perception of freedom and intrinsic motivation in pursuing an activity. Recreation is also commonly conceived as a set of usually pleasurable activities that one does as a way to counter the drudgery of day-to-day routines. There are at least three common elements that run throughout all these ideas of recreation: 1) it is individually focused; 2) it is a departure from the normal routines of life; and 3) it is a personally worthwhile experience. How can the recreation manager work to promote personal satisfaction for participants?

Recreation Can Be Seen as an Activity Free of Obligations

This concept of recreation tries to make a distinct difference between the ordinary day-to-day activities, like work, that may be seen as drudgery for many people. Going fishing is a good change of pace for many and the restorative powers are extolled by its participants. However, what happens if you need to take with you the boss or a colleague you really would like to leave behind? Or, more commonly, if one's spouse comes along and is expected to continue household responsibilities for cooking, childcare, and so forth, would the experience fit the description of recreation as a restorative activity? How much can recreation management make the experience more pleasant by assuring a change from the activities of daily living?

Recreation Is Multifaceted

There is more to hiking than a walk in the woods. Consider hiking and look at it carefully. It is easy to see there are a number of ways to understand its appeal to different people on the same day (Figure 17.1). There are people who take hiking very seriously and spend enormous amounts of time planning, obtaining the best equipment, studying the route, and anticipating the probability of extraordinary things happening. There are others who simply pass by an interesting trail or opening and decide to take a walk on a spur of the moment with no planning or strong expectations for a predictable outcome. One person may be

Figure 17.1 Hiking in the Cascade Mountains near Mount Shuksan in northwest Washington. (Photo by R. A. Young.)

interested in the physical challenge of a difficult climb, while another might be more interested in a gentle walk to a beautiful vista. Others may seek both in the same outing. Using more of this sort of probing, you can easily see that hiking is more that just a singular activity. The same reasoning can apply to most outdoor recreation activities (e.g., fishing, boating, and camping). The real trick for recreation management is to determine the range of services to offer for a single activity that might satisfy a range of reasons for participating (e.g., how many different types of fishing experiences can a particular site offer?).

Recreation Is a Multiphasic Activity

Another common understanding of the recreation experience is that it is a multiphasic activity as noted by Clawson and Knetsch (8) and Clawson (9). This means that there are different stages and phases to any recreational activity: anticipation and planning, travel to the site, on-site activity, return travel from the site, and recollection of the trip.

Knudson (10) has reduced the original five phases of the experience to four. Phase I is the *anticipatory stage* where flights of fancy begin to take shape in the mind of the participant. The actual event may or may not take place and the romance may change as realism begins to assert its presence (e.g., the constraints to the activity become more real). However, there is often a great personal or group satisfaction that may come from imagining possibilities even when the activity never takes place. Similarly, there is the potential for disappointment if the ideal does not occur.

Phase II is the *planning stage*. It is in this phase that the plans are taken from imagination to reality through preparation for the event. Gathering information, determining feasibility, assembling supplies and equipment, questioning those who have been there before, and developing the skills necessary for the event are all included as a part of this phase.

Phase III is the *participation stage*. It is in this phase where the activity actually takes place. It includes all elements from start to finish and in-

between occurrences that are both planned and unplanned.

Phase IV is the *recollection and reflection phase* of the experience. After the activity, memories begin to take hold. Reflection and reinterpretation of the events are likely to persevere long periods of time into the future. One of the ways people enhance the experience is by obtaining souvenirs, like photographs, which carry much symbolic meaning. They tend to invoke sensations apparent only to the participant. That is why it may be hard to understand why your friends are enthralled with pictures of their trip while you may be a captive audience wondering what all the excitement is about.

This multiphasic understanding is a useful way to understand recreation experience for a single person. However, it is more complex when more than one person is involved. Each person will have a unique interpretation of the experience. This makes the recollection phase far more interesting than a singular report.

An even more interesting phenomenon is the cry "Let's do it again!" It is interesting because the chance of replicating a peak experience for a recreation participant is very small. Recapturing the exact pleasure and excitement of a previous time is almost impossible to replicate. Participants often experience the same event and obtain pleasure but it is somehow different from the previous time. The place and people may be the same but they are not in the same time element. As an ancient philosopher is often quoted, "you can never step in the same stream twice." Using these elements as a starting point for understanding recreation, it seems reasonable to examine the recreation activities people pursue in the out-of-doors.

Pursuing Recreation

The outdoors has always offered an attractive array of opportunities and experiences for people. Only relatively recently has it become important to understand what people do and why as noted in the section on legislative interests. Much of this interest evolved in response to a recognition that what people do affects the natural environment incrementally over time (and vice versa). Knowing the resources and appropriately managing them for use by people will accomplish a number of goals. Among the most important is offering people high quality opportunities for a variety of experiences while keeping the natural environment healthy for current and future generations.

Outdoor recreation is highly valued for many people. In 1994, the Roper Starch Survey reported that at least two-thirds of all American adults (18 years of age or older) participate in outdoor recreation every year and at least half participate monthly. Table 17.2 shows the "important" or "very important" reasons that the respondents gave for participating in outdoor recreation.

Clearly people participate in outdoor recreation for many personally important reasons. The survey also revealed that those who were more active in outdoor recreation rated their quality of life higher than those who participated less frequently. Such benefits make outdoor recreation an important part of American culture. In 1995, the National Survey on Recreation and the Environment reported which outdoor recreation activities were the most popular (of 13 listed in the survey) (Table 17.3). Respon-

Table 17.2 **Why People Participate in Outdoor Recreation**

Reason	% Responding Either "Important or Very Important"
To have fun	76
For relaxation	71
For health and exercise	70
For family to be together	69
To reduce stress	66
To teach good values to children	64
To experience nature	64
To be with friends	60
For excitement	53
To learn new skills	48
To be alone	39
For competition	24

Source: Roper Starch Survey (39)

Table 17.3 **Most Popular Outdoor Recreation Activities**

Activity	% of People Reporting
Walking	66.7
Viewing a beach or waterside	62.1
Family gatherings outdoors	61.8
Sightseeing	56.6

Source: National Survey on Recreation and the Environment (40)

dents were at least 16 years of age at the time of the survey.

Outdoor recreation is important to and pursued by a large number of individuals. It is apparent that the trend for participation in outdoor recreation is increasing. Cordell et al. (11) compared outdoor recreation data from 1982/83 and 1994/95 and reported increases in participation for 29 outdoor recreation activities among individuals 16 years of age or older. Some examples of the percentage increases in a few selected activities are given in Table 17.4. The increases points to a more active population as noted in the visitation records from the U.S. Forest Service over a four-year period starting in 1993. The number of visits on national Forest Service lands grew from 729,474,200 ('93), to 839,238,900 ('94), 829,757,100 ('95) and 859,282,800 ('96). However, a few outdoor recreation activities declined in participation over this time period. They included horseback riding, hunting, fishing, sailing,

Table 17.4 **Change in Participation for Selected Outdoor Recreation Activities**

Activity	% Change from 1982/83 to 1994/95
Bird Watching	155.2
Hiking	93.5
Backpacking	72.7
Boating (power)	39.9
Swimming	38.2
Downhill Skiing	58.5

Source: Cordell (11; p. 239)

ice skating, and tennis. This decline poses management issues, because even though they have declined, there are still participants. The question is how to manage the recreation resource base for a smaller number of participants.

These participation trends are likely to continue and are influenced by many of the changes in population dynamics and related trends in economy and technology. It is useful to take some time to look at how these factors relate to outdoor recreation experiences and think about the implications they hold for managers.

The patterns of recreation use are always reflective of a greater set of population factors. It is useful to look at a few population characteristics to address and understand their effects on recreation behaviors. They include education, age, gender, minorities, immigration, wealth, and technology. Although these are presented separately, they are very interrelated.

Education

The average level of education in the United States has been steadily increasing since the turn of the century. According to data from the National Center for Educational Statistics (NCES), Americans had more years of education in 1998 than 1990. In 1998 among adults over 25, 83 percent had completed high school and 24 percent had completed 4 or more years of college (12). Education affects participation in outdoor recreation in many ways. Among them is the exposure to new activities and introduction to ideas and possibilities that might enhance the quality of life. Through education,

people often get new ideas for outdoor recreation which they pursue well beyond the formal school years. It is clear that more education also leads to greater sophistication in demand and greater expectations for the quality of the recreation experience. There is also a consistently strong link between education and economic success (i.e., the more formal education one has, the greater the level of income throughout the life span). With affluence, people have greater means to pursue activities in outdoor recreation experiences that would not be possible otherwise.

Age Structure

There is always an age influence in outdoor recreation, but it is sometimes difficult to draw definitive relationships with specific activities. However, there is a clear age-related trend in participation patterns represented in selected results from the 1994–95 National Survey on Recreation and the Environment shown in Table 17.5.

At the youthful end of the age spectrum there is a clear impact on outdoor recreation for higher risk, adventure, and "extreme" sports influenced by media coverage and advanced technology. These activities make management of outdoor recreation more interesting. For instance, how does one create policies for rock or cliff climbing that are compatible with public management plans and agency responsibility?

At the other end of the age continuum, vigorous and demanding physical activities tend to decline in intensity and number with advancing age. The reasons for this trend are numerous, but among

Table 17.5   Participation in Recreation Activities by Age (% of Respondents)

Activity/Age	16–24	25–29	30–39	40–49	50–59	60+
Fitness	77.2	74.7	76.1	72.0	64.0	49.7
Running	50.4	33.2	28.3	23.3	17.4	8.1
Biking	37.9	36.2	37.4	30.7	21.9	10.6
Walking	68.1	72.4	74.6	71.9	64.0	49.7

Source: National Survey on Recreation and the Environment (40)

them are the lack of time to maintain a level of fitness appropriate to the activity demand. This is often related to increased demands of adult responsibility. This lack of time also encourages people to make more deliberate choices in their activities, which means greater selectivity and the sacrifice of those deemed of lesser value or feasibility.

Activities may be pursued with adaptation across the years as well. For example, one who enjoys wilderness camping may redefine wilderness over time and pursue the adventure in areas with greater ease of access and better amenities in later years of life. Other adaptations that may be made include the use of technological advances in equipment that make continued participation possible. For example, the advances in technology for canoe construction have reduced the weight significantly and therefore the need for heroic body strength has been reduced. This one change has opened the canoe experience to many individuals who were once prohibited by the physical demands of the activity. It is important to understand, however, that this improved technology comes at a higher price that may result in restricted access just as much as age and strength.

Before leaving the issue of age, there should be a bit of warning. While there are a number of age-related effects on the physical abilities of recreationists, it is absolutely imperative to remember that Americans are in better condition now than in previous generations. Jogging, wilderness backpacking, whitewater canoeing, and many other physically demanding activities are pursued successfully into very old age by many. The good manager will not assume that age is a deterrent to participation.

Gender

The movement toward gender equity has initiated many changes in how management functions. Gaining momentum from the 1960s, these changes have increased access and opportunities for women in many areas of life and outdoor recreation participation shows significant increases for women. Outdoor recreation managers need to be thoughtful of policies and practices that are inclusive across gender lines. The most recent outdoor recreation survey data show that women participate in almost equal numbers and types of recreation as men for many categories of activities (NSRE 1994/95). For those who want to know more about gender issues related to outdoor recreation and leisure, see Henderson et al. (13, 14), Freysinger (15, 16), and Bialeschki and Walbert (17), among others.

Minority Populations

Minority populations in the United States are most commonly represented by those of African, Hispanic/Latin, Native American, or Asian ancestry. The most recent census data indicate that approximately 25 percent of the population is represented by one of these groups (U.S Census Bureau, 1994). New data from the 2000 census reflect an even larger proportion of the population, since minority populations are growing at a faster rate than the majority population. Each of these categories represents an ever greater diversity when closely examined. For instance, Hispanic/ Latin ancestry is used to designate those who may be Cuban, Puerto Rican, European, Mexican, or any number of other cultural or ethnic groups within the broader category. The growth in minority populations also means that they are likely to pursue recreation in forested areas in greater numbers (Table 17.6).

Managers need to understand that they will need to think about the implications of ethnically and racially diverse users. For example, in some areas of the southwestern U.S., it is becoming a common practice (and a necessity) to hire bilingual staff and produce signs, brochures, and other communication tools in both Spanish and English. In the West, Asian languages (e.g., Japanese, Korean, Chinese) are important to help other cultural groups learn about the area's opportunities, rules, and regulations.

Some understanding of ethnic traditions and preferred use patterns are also helpful to managers wanting to be more accommodating to these users. Equally important might be a better understanding

Table 17.6 Outdoor Recreation Participation Patterns Among Minority Groups (% of Respondents)

Activity/Group	Hispanic	Native American	Asian
Camping	21.1	27.7	18.6
Hunting	6.4	21.1	4.6
Fishing	24.9	43.1	29.2
Hiking	27.0	30.0	24.3
Picnicking	50.8	61.2	60.0

Source: National Survey on Recreation and the Environment (40)

of cultural history to avoid potential conflicts among a diverse set of users.

Most minority populations reflect settlement patterns of the dominant culture, in that they are highly urbanized. Many do not (or cannot) take advantage of the more remote or non-urban outdoor recreation environments, although their numbers are showing a slight increase. Urbanized areas present an interesting area of outreach work for managers of recreation areas. These populations can be a powerful political force in future generations. If they understand and appreciate the value of resources for recreation, they can help preserve these lands by political action. If they do not value the resource, it could prove troublesome.

Immigration

The United States has been shaped and directed in many ways by the immigration patterns of the most recent Americans. The first major waves of immigration were mostly from Europe who came seeking land and freedom and those who were brought here under less-than-voluntary circumstances (the Africans); however, both are now integral parts of our longer-tenured demography. Subsequent waves of immigration at the turn of the century again were heavily European and looked much like those who were already here. The newest surges of immigrants are of Latin and Asian ancestry. All groups bring unique contributions to the culture and all participate in outdoor recreation activities. One of the most intriguing problems recreation managers face is how policies reflect the

dominant culture's perspective. Sometimes these policies are in direct conflict with the values, traditions, and understandings of a minority or newly arrived culture, and the educational responsibilities of an agency require much more serious attention. It quickly becomes important to develop an understanding of new visitor groups and design responsive education and information programs for staff as well as visitors.

One of the first natural resource management texts to address these issues was written by Ewert, Chavez, and Magill (18) and it is still an excellent resource for understanding many of the cross-cultural issues facing recreation area managers. Chavez (19), Floyd and Shinew (20), Floyd (21), and others continue to increase our understanding of improved management strategies that accommodate multicultural understandings of recreation participation and the natural environment. Cordell et al. (11) also present useful data on outdoor recreation participation patterns by cultural, ethnic, racial, and disability categories.

These trends lead to yet another caution for recreation resource managers. Even though we need to group information on people by some common factor, remember that this is an administrative convenience and not an accurate portrayal of culture or behavior. There is enormous variation between groups and their specific cultural beliefs that can and sometimes does lead to serious user conflicts if not well understood by the manager. Further, as multiple cultures share the same space, it is simultaneously an opportunity to promote understanding and appreciation of diversity, but which could quickly become a situation promoting conflict.

Affluence

It is important to be cautious with the proclamation that individual wealth has increased dramatically. While it is true for a large sector of the population, there are still others who remain low income and live at the margins of society. However, it is true that on a national scale, personal wealth has increased dramatically and created a unique out-migration of people from urban areas to be near nature. This growing divide between affluence and poverty has had a significant impact on recreation policy. As agencies increase fees to offset declining budgets, how will access by the poor be maintained? Data from the NSRE 1994–95 survey show the direct effect of income on participation in outdoor recreation activities like boating, sailing, canoeing, water skiing, and motor boating. Where price of participation equipment is high, affluence plays a predictably prominent role.

Urbanization

From agrarian roots, we moved into the cities at the turn of the century, and over the years, became a very urbanized society. The attachment to the land became quite distant (22). Most people experience the out-of-doors in urbanized areas where some vestiges of nature continue in the forms of parks, arboretums, and urban forests. The conceptualization of nature is then colored by these settings. Media, museums, and other exhibitions have shaped an idealized and romantic concept of nature. Paired with new affluence, this has made for interesting changes to the once rural and relatively inaccessible wilderness.

Rural and small-town communities have been dramatically changed as a result of the in-migrations from urban areas (23). For example, small towns in northern Wisconsin have changed their character to serve urban tastes (e.g., fine wine and dining have replaced the bait and burger shop; four-star hotels instead of rustic cabins; and upscale furni-

ture is in demand). These situations also change recreation demands and sometimes bring conflict over use. Hunting is often disliked by those from urban areas who see all animals as desirable for non-consumptive recreation activity (e.g., bird watching), but is seen as a way of life among those who have long tenure in rural areas. The manager of a natural recreation area is likely to be found right in the middle of the debates over the proper use of a recreation site (like a national or state forest) which is often the reason people move to an area.

It is important for managers to recognize that the boundaries of a recreation area are paper agreements. The borders are quite permeable, presenting a series of concerns by residents. The protected area is actually part of an ecological region where plants, animals, and people interact with unpredictable and often uncomfortable results. Managers are required to involve the general public in design and implementation of management policies. Cases where readers might look for these issues include the Buffalo/Cattle conflict in Yellowstone (24), or user rights and control in the Boundary Waters Canoe Wilderness Area of the Superior National Forest (25).

Access to these areas is an additional result of societal affluence. Airports and superhighways now exist that allow easier access to once rural and remote areas that were at one time considered inaccessible. Increased accessibility promotes a change in the context for management. No longer is the job of the manager one of simply managing a designated area. It is now the task of the manager to see the recreation site as a part of the larger region and to promote policies, procedures, and plans that reflect that view.

Technology

This is one of the more interesting factors that has changed outdoor recreation participation in many ways, resulting in improved communications among and between employees, better record keeping, easier data base management and access to information. Conversely, each of these assumes that all the innovations are good for management. The cost of capitalization is often high, continuous training is usually needed to use the equipment properly, and maintenance is a requisite for proper function. Office management technology can also become outdated quickly and there is a continual need to upgrade. In short, it can be very expensive, but at the same time, it is much more effective and efficient, making the investment worthwhile.

On the user side, interesting consequences appear as a result of technological advances. I have had the opportunity to be in the Boundary Waters Wilderness Canoe Area on a portage where another party was passing and one member was talking away on a cell phone. Is this a proper technology for the wilderness experience? On the other hand, a cell phone or beeper could be a life-saver in cases where wilderness overwhelms the recreation participant. Should these communication technologies be encouraged, banished, or controlled in some way? How does the manager decide? Is it the manager's decision to make?

Similarly, equipment technologies have made management strategies even more interesting. Equipment like aluminum canoes that were once heavy and difficult to manage have given way to lightweight durable products like those made from Kevlar. Superhuman strength is no longer a requirement for wilderness canoe experiences. The same can be said for a wide array of recreation equipment. Off-road bicycle advances in technology permit a new access to wilderness that was impossible a few years ago. There are new versions of in-line roller skates that are designed to go across rugged terrain in addition to smooth, hard surfaces. The list of advances goes on for some length and the management implications get more intriguing. Questions for management include how to address these changes as a part of recreation policy. Is it fair to assume that all the changes are bad or that changes should be considered a fact of life? More realistically, what criteria would one invoke to make such a distinction?

Section Summary

In this section, some of the large issues for recreation managers related to innovations and change

in society have been outlined. It is impossible to separate these issues in reality, because they are all interactive. Managers need to understand the effects of complex systemic interactions like these have on achieving good management practice. What happens when managers impose selected regimes on areas? What responses of users may be forthcoming? We turn now to a brief discussion of these issues.

User Conflict

Inevitably one of the stickiest problems facing recreation managers is the conflict that occurs between and among users of a recreation area. It often seems that one of the daily tasks of management is to resolve some complaint where one group or person has infringed on the experience of another group or individual. Sometimes these are minor nuisance complaints (e.g., playing music loudly into the night) but others are quite serious (e.g., assault or other criminal behavior).

Let me address the most serious of conflicts in a brief manner. Outdoor recreation areas are not immune to illegal activities. Some sites have reported the most serious of predatory of criminal behaviors (e.g., kidnapping, drug trafficking, theft, sexual assault, and murder). These are clearly not minor conflicts and must involve authorities with police powers. In some recreation areas, staff will have some police powers and in others there may be none. Regardless, managers have policies and plans in place to confront these possibilities through joint agreements with local authorities (or with federal agencies such as the FBI and DEA) where warranted.

More frequently, managers will need to face participants who come to a site for one reason only to be confronted by other participants who have a different use of the resource in mind. For example, snowmobile operators and cross-country ski participants may share a common space (a trail) for very different and noncompatible purposes. There are numerous reports of encounters between the two groups with each complaining about the other. Similarly, runners, mountain bikers, hikers, and horseback riders may all have a common trail with multiple purposes and expectations for the experience. Lakes are also primary areas where multiples users with multiple expectations might encounter each other at close range (e.g., fishers, swimmers, sail boarders, power boaters, canoeists, and sail boaters).

Often, users resolve their diverse expectations without intervention. As noted elsewhere in this chapter, one way to resolve the conflict is to change the experience by arriving at different times to avoid or minimize undesirable interactions. Another is to relocate to another site for the experience. Finally, sometimes users can decide mutually that some modification to experience and behavior is in the best interest of all.

However, in many cases managers will need to come forward with policies, rules, and regulations that attempt to minimize conflicts among and between users. One of the first places the managers must look is into the laws and legislation creating the recreation area. Here is the place to discover what powers the agency has for making policies and rules as well as what abilities they have to enforce them.

Second, the manager needs to examine his or her personal abilities to confront and address the parties and move toward resolution. Sometimes the skills of a negotiator or arbitrator are useful when dealing with human interaction problems. Often issues of conflict arise as an exception to daily routines. For instance, a group of people playing catch with a Frisbee in an area designated for picnicking may result in a conflict where simply speaking with the parties involved might be sufficient. In situations where conflict is recurrent, it is important to reexamine existing policies and rules for applicability and enforceability. It might be possible for the manager to create and enforce a new guideline, but this also runs the risk of alienating at least one of the user groups and may lead to some legal or personal challenge.

One of the more recent evolutions in management is to create a users' advisory committee or a "Friends" group to help guide policy development and implementation. In these groups, the conflicting users must sit and discuss their concerns and develop rules that might be useful in preventing unpleasant interactions. These groups do take time and energy on part of the manager but ultimately result in better management and experience outcomes.

An example of how this process might work effectively can be found with some Lake Homeowners Associations members, who meet to determine use patterns for the lake they surround. The net effect of their deliberations results in the zoning of the lake by area, activity, and time of day. For example, power boats are not allowed on the lake before 8 A.M. and must be off by 7 P.M. Swimming is confined to a certain area where boats are forbidden. Jet skis are banned altogether. These rules are communicated to users and respected with the force of law, but mostly by assent of the users. Where people feel they are a part of the resolution of conflict, greater adherence and respect for the experiences of others increases.

This method of conflict resolution by participation is in widespread use with federal and state land management agencies. It is a very powerful tool, but requires some special talent and ability to make it work well.

Social Succession

When a management plan is implemented on an area that has been either unmanaged or managed for different experiences in prior plans, any number of outcomes are likely. The shift in management strategies may create a social succession of users and behaviors.

The net effect of succession is often displacement of one group of users by another. If the primary objective is to maintain a particular experience, the manager may change the use pattern by widening the road, improving the trail, or putting in a footbridge. Often these minor modifications of existing developments are sufficient (particularly their cumulative effect) to shift the experience enough that it appeals to a new type of user and not the traditional user. The former users are displaced by users whose expectations more closely fit the new context. Displacement is a move away from an unacceptable situation, not a move toward a desired one. This distinction is useful in differentiating displacement, a form of reactive movement, from other forms of movement which include the following:

1. *Active Migration.* People seek a suitable destination according to their values—for example, white-water canoeists seek a variety of risk and skill testing.

2. *Passive Migration.* People select a location because it is convenient, such as visiting areas to meet friends for picnics, or because other members of the participation group desire that location.

3. *Movements for Diurnal Requirements of an Activity.* People move to different locations on a lake to fish at various times of day.

Movement is then a general term, whereas displacement is a negative reactive movement (26). However, as a manager, it is possible to envision situations when one wishes to encourage displacement of one set of users who may be destructive of the environment (physical or social) by intentionally contriving the context to be less appealing for them. To effectively manage an area that facilitates user satisfaction is a serious challenge to recreation managers. It is important to examine some of the tools and practices available to managers.

The Recreational Opportunity Spectrum (ROS)

Since the types of recreational experiences desired by participants varies widely, it is difficult to provide opportunities that meet the needs of everyone. In fulfilling the mandate for multipurpose use of the forests, the managers had to think more systematically about the interaction of users with the resource base. If participants of varied interests, abilities, needs, and purposes were to derive some individual benefit from use of a common base, a tool was needed to help organize how the resource could do this (27). The solution was the Recreation Opportunity Spectrum (ROS), which was developed

to examine and categorize landscapes on a continuum from highly developed (e.g., lots of structural development) to totally undeveloped (i.e., primitive) areas. At the extremes, and between these polar ends, landscapes were categorized by descriptors that allowed a visitor and manager to better understand the types of experiences and activities available. Conceptually, the experience offered by the totally pristine environment without development would be the antithesis of the experience offered by the urban environment. While this may be a reasonable assumption of the expected outcome, it is not without argument. Indeed, for some individuals, an urbanized recreation area might prove quite an exotic and satisfying "wilderness" experience where for others even the vast open spaces of large reserves may seem too "urbanized." The point is that the ROS is a useful tool for managers to assess, describe, design, and develop the resource base; however, predicting the experiential outcome remains a speculative venture (27, 28). A simplified description of the ROS can be found in Figure 17.2 and a description of its application to the Pacific Crest National Scenic Trail is found in Figure 17.3.

Management by Design

Realizing there is great variation in the recreational experiences of individuals, it is impossible to guarantee an expected outcome for any one person. Therefore, managers must use the best tools they have available to design and develop areas that enhance the probability of a positive experience outcome for a class of users.

Obviously, it is impossible to design a site to fulfill every user's expectations. As indicated earlier, it is very important to establish a plan for area design that is compatible with the purposes of the area. The master plan needs to accommodate appropriate uses of the land based on the best available knowledge of the ecosystem (e.g., topography, soils structure, hydrology, etc.). It then needs to address the expectations of certain classes of consumers (e.g., campers, canoeists, hikers).

Figure 17.2

The Recreation Opportunity Spectrum (ROS), using the Forest Service terminology to describe specific opportunities.

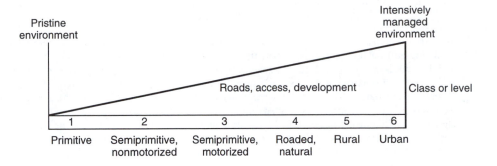

For example, the design and placement of a campground can greatly affect the recreational experience of a camper or campers. The design might accommodate the landform and consumer by its placement in an area sufficiently isolated from hazards and nuisances like busy roads, parking lots, or garbage drop areas, screened by select native trees and shrubs so a feeling of privacy exists; thus, the context is set for a pleasant experience by the visitor while the ecological integrity of the site is maintained.

Observing human behavior preferences can be helpful in other design applications. For example, most people like ease of access to recreation areas. The more challenging the access, the numbers of users declines and the characteristics of the users change. People who use the Boundary Waters Canoe Area Wilderness (BWCAW) are likely to be younger, more fit, stronger, and looking for privacy and an experience of relative isolation. Those with younger children, those who are less physically capable, or those who like or need to have service amenities close by (e.g., concessions, rest rooms) are not likely to choose the BWCAW (or any other wilderness) as their destination. In planning, it is possible to create levels of challenge as well as development to address the variations in need among participants (Figure 17.4).

One of the major purposes of a master planning process for recreation areas is determining the appropriate uses of the land and how the users

can be dispersed across the land on a continuum of use as noted in the section on the ROS. The degree of development to address certain experiences is important to consider in advance of use when possible. Anticipating the use intensity of an area clarifies the degree of site hardening required. *Hardening* refers to the degree of development for a particular site. Generally, hardening an area facilitates a greater intensity of use with less environmental damage and a greater ease of maintenance. For example, if a site is developed for high use (e.g., a public beach area with multiple activities like swimming, boating, fishing, hiking, camping, picnicking, open space for physical activities), it will likely have asphalt surfaces, grasses that tolerate heavy traffic, concessions, and so forth, with a concentration of human services for continuous maintenance and upkeep. Damaged portions can more quickly and easily be repaired and litter and waste are more easily and efficiently removed than in more remote and wild areas. More remote areas, where little or no hardening has occurred, are much more susceptible to damage and abuse that cannot be easily corrected. When wilderness areas are maintained, the cost is relatively high and the repair by nature could take many years (Figure 17.5).

Just how much development should take place? Who decides? These questions have emerged as critical points for management in a new era of forest use planning. If it is assumed that we can and

ROS Descriptions

Many believe that the Pacific Crest National Scenic Trail (PCNST) passes for the most part through wild and beautiful country. In fact, it passes through a wide variety of environments offering a range of recreational experiences. The kinds of surroundings and experiences can be viewed as a spectrum of recreational opportunities, from urban, highly developed and used by many people; to primitive, undeveloped and used by very few people. Recreation managers use this Recreation Opportunity Spectrum (ROS) to judge the appropriateness of public facilities, roads, trails, sanitation, and so forth, within particular settings, and to gauge the appropriate design for roads and timber harvest operations in areas where they are allowed. Hikers can also use the ROS to find areas that offer the hiking environment they seek.

 **Urban** The urban setting may be where you live! There are many buildings, paved roads, and a great many people. You will not experience the urban setting along the PCNST in Oregon. Hiking and biking trails through city parks and residential areas would provide an urban recreation experience.

 **Rural** The land between the cities and the forest provides a rural setting. It includes pastoral farmland, small communities, and commercial facilities, or large campgrounds and trailheads along paved highways in the forest. Expect to find many other people along these parts of the trail. These areas offer convenient day hikes and sites for off-road vehicle travel throughout the year.

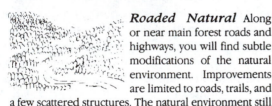 **Roaded Natural** Along or near main forest roads and highways, you will find subtle modifications of the natural environment. Improvements are limited to roads, trails, and a few scattered structures. The natural environment still dominates, but timber harvest and preparations for the next generation of trees are visible. Posted regulations as well as contacts with others are likely. In fact, there are limited opportunities to get away from others. You are farther from towns and their conveniences, so you must be self-reliant in supplying your personal needs. Substantial day hikes and opportunities for more relaxed biking and camping prevail. The PCNST trail traverses such areas as it passes near many trailheads and road crossings.

 **Roaded Modified** Along less-used forest roads you will likely find large clearcuts, skid roads, and landings dominant to the view. You will encounter more chances to get away from other recreationists, but logging operations may be dominant. No facilities are provided. You are on your own.

 **Semiprimitive** Leaving roads behind you, you become more isolated from the sights and sounds of human activity. The degree of risk and isolation increases, and recreational activities become dependent on the natural scene. No picnic tables and other improvements are provided; human comfort and satisfactions will be gained through your personal initiatives.

 **Primitive** Primitive settings are the most remote parts of the forest and are little influenced by the works of people. The natural environment dominates the setting and dictates the kinds of recreational challenges: beauty, isolation, uncertainty, risk, and discovery. Woodsmanship skills are important in providing safety and comfort.

Figure 17.3 Recreation Opportunity Spectrum: an example. Source: From the southern Oregon portion of the Pacific Crest Scenic Trail map.

Figure 17.4 The Boundary Waters Canoe Wilderness Area in the Superior National Forest provides unmatched beauty, challenge, and renewal for recreationists. (Photo by Robert O. Ray.)

should provide a spectrum of opportunities for recreational use and experience based upon the intersection of good ecosystem science, finite management resources, and human behavior, which seems to have an unlimited demand for experience, how far can and should we go in modifying the landform? This moves the discussion into a very interesting and challenging area of management.

Figure 17.5 Nature also poses interesting questions for managers. The damage from the 1999 storm in the Boundary Waters Canoe Wilderness Area introduced challenging questions related to recreational use, fire potential, and natural renewal. (Photo by Robert O. Ray.)

Limits of Acceptable Change (LAC)

The Recreation Opportunity Spectrum previously addressed is not a rigid tool for managers to impose behavior limits. It is instead a guide or index of the relationships between site constraints and visitor options. Limits of Acceptable Change (LAC) is a planning procedure that enumerates changes to the physical environment that will cause little harm to the recreational visitor's experience opportunities. An integrative procedure, LAC brings together the work of researchers on visitor expectations and the efforts of managers to understand site resource constraints. It assists managers in arriving at site management judgments by specifying the products and recreational opportunities that specific resources provide and by clarifying what would threaten their quality. However, to be successful, the process depends on a clear enunciation of management objectives.

Management by Objectives

Management by Objectives (MBO) is still an important tool in administering outdoor recreation if we are to maintain a specific identifiable recreation opportunity on the basis of resource capabilities. Simply put, management by objectives means establishing goals or outputs that are agreed on by the members of an organization. It is an effort to focus attention and resources toward a common end. An MBO exercise helps participants first to sort out a desired option from among the wide range of alternatives and then to direct their energies at providing the desired objective or product. A modification of the MBO model has the following inputs for recreation program objectives (29).

Resource Capability
Institutional Constraints
Existing Situation   } Recreation Program Objectives
User Preferences
Coordination

In this model, *resource capability* describes the overall limitations on programs, but typically agencies are more institutionally constrained by laws, regulations, or policies that effectively constrict the scope of operations for a specific agency. If the recreation pattern on a specific path has never been managed using program objectives, a certain clientele has usually developed over time. The existing situation (the norms of the existing clientele) will probably dictate the direction of the initial management planning. If other user preferences can be accommodated in the resource base, they should be included. The need and opportunity for coordination of efforts typically occurs when two or more land management authorities overlap or adjoin an area and the desire to provide continuity for the recreation experience is mutual. Interagency agreements must then be negotiated to assure that continuity is maintained.

Some Notes on Management Planning

The preceding discussion of the Recreational Opportunity Spectrum (ROS), Limits of Acceptable Change (LAC), and Management by Objectives (MBO) make the management planning process seem very straightforward and linear. It also implies that those who are the leaders in the management organization are the ones who get to set the management plans in place based upon their authority, knowledge of the ecosystem, and a belief that they know what the recreation participant prefers. There is also the implicit concept that the recreation area under consideration is a world separate from the local residents. This conceptualization of recreation area management is too narrow and needs to be revisited in light of several emerging understandings.

The multiple-use philosophy of forest management that has emerged over the last decade or more has placed a new emphasis on planning and has significantly increased the role of the public in the planning process. Forested lands in the United States have experienced a marked change in use over this time. Whereas timber production was the main reason for existence earlier in the 1900s (and continuing), there is now a much greater emphasis on managing the forests for the environmental services they render (e.g., water conservation, flood control, conservation of natural resources, and recreational use) (5, 30). Furthermore, as affluence has grown in the United States and access to these natural resources has improved, there is a growing recognition that protected areas like U.S.F.S. lands are a part of the larger communities where they are found.

As Field (31) notes,

> *The traditional philosophy of resource managers and land management agencies is that people are clients, guests, or visitors to the system. As a result, the tendency has been to consider people and their resultant behavior as a problem to solve. . . . These [parks or forests] are the places where cultural and institutional practices of the agency meet the cultural and institutional practices of the population occupying the resource on either a temporary or permanent basis.*

In recognition of these changes in philosophy and culture, there is now a larger mandate to land management agencies. As each of the sites develops a required management plan, there is a further required element for public participation in the decision making. While this is an interesting and necessary way to function successfully in a new century, it is often a confusing and challenging process that requires a set of management skills that transcends scientific knowledge of both the ecosystem and the science of recreational behavior. There is a need to understand sociopolitical processes, group dynamics, and collaborative processes with new partners. These considerations have until very recently been beyond the need of managers and planners and have resulted in the new classification of Social Forestry further discussed in Chapter 23.

It is interesting and challenging to determine first how to involve the public (e.g., whom to invite, how far to reach, what is the best format for input) and then determine what to do with their advice (e.g., does it make sense, how exclusive will the land become). Finally, how does one create a meaningful management plan with input from varied perspectives (e.g., ATV users who want no restriction on their movement, birders who want *all* vehicles banned from the area).

There are a number of models that presently exist to involve the public in planning for natural resource management. The space and focus of this chapter limits discussion of those processes but readers who are interested are encouraged to look at some recent works on collaborative planning (32–35).

All the management elements discussed (ROS, LAC, MBO) are no longer the singular product of the scientific manager. They are elements largely defined and determined by consumers. They are far more politically charged than one might first be led to believe. Creating management plans in cooperation with these new inputs is an essential, and not always easy, part of successful land management for recreation uses.

Partnerships deserve a bit more attention here. This is a relatively new phenomenon in recreation management, but there are vestiges that go back into history. Newer partnerships have evolved between governments (federal, state, and local) and organizations that were at one time distinctly separate, critical, and even hostile toward each other. Over the last decade, there has been a deliberate approach to work more collaboratively for common goals, since much of the land and water resources controlled by government, nongovernment, and private groups is in close proximity or adjacent to public lands.

Obviously, joining resources increases the ecological integrity of a region and can provide wider ranges of recreation opportunities for participants. The trick for managers is to understand how to approach these groups (or understand that how to interpret an approach from them), to arrive at common goals, monitor the processes, and help the public understand how these agreements function. It is also important to understand that these can be complex agreements with organizations that may have very different management objectives and practices. These practices may not be replicas of those endorsed by any one agency and difficult to

understand by the average user. Furthermore, leadership changes in all agencies and new leaders may bring an agenda for use that challenges the assumptions of an existing agreement. Being understanding, adaptable, and strong are important characteristics that recreation managers must maintain. Some of these "new" partners in recreation could include Lake Home Owners Associations, private timber companies, NGOs (e.g., The Nature Conservancy, Ducks Unlimited, Sierra Club), Native American Tribal Councils, or private land holders. It is an interesting task to keep these organizations working cooperatively and simultaneously holding the public concerns at the forefront in recreation management.

For many years, various agencies have addressed services by concessionaires in recreation areas. As recreation area managers begin implementing business practices to improve service, there are some lessons to be learned. For example, the state of Wisconsin moved to a centralized reservation system for campgrounds in 1999. While eventually working well, Sidebar 17.2 has warnings for new ventures that go beyond the simple rationale of decision making.

Often agencies like the Forest Service or National Park Service seek bids for specific vendors to provide a service in an area (e.g., garbage removal, food services, equipment rental). These are long-tested relationships at many levels of government where both parties contractually agree to a service or product and share in the revenue. As resources for local operating budgets decrease, this fee revenue idea has broadened. The next section addresses the evolution of fees and charges as a management tool, which are increasingly important sources of operating revenue for recreation area managers.

Fees as a Recreation Management Tool

While fees are not new to recreation on public lands, they have changed in the way they have been presented to the public and used by various

Sidebar 17.2

Public Relations and Parks Management—Change is a Challenge!

The State of Wisconsin Parks System implemented a telephone reservation system for those wishing to reserve a campsite in any of the state parks. A request for vendor applications was issued and a company outside the state was awarded the contract. In the days following implementation, complaints began to mount.

Some of the complaints were about the changes in the process. The phone reservation system replaced a mail-in reservation system that had been used for many years. A further public relations issue was created by a major change in the cost of reserving a campsite. The fee was increased from $4.00 to $9.50 per reservation and a cancellation fee of $8.50 was added. These were serious changes to the relatively inexpensive and traditional process; however, people came to understand the need for the cost increase to improve and maintain facilities for their service.

The more interesting and least anticipated reactions were to the manner in which reservations were being taken. Many of the reservation center representatives were based in California. They could not read the maps and were not familiar with the state or the parks within the system. Some also found it difficult to tell tented sites from those with motor home facilities. They mispronounced the park names and had accents that were clearly not familiar to those in the Midwest. Interestingly, one of the biggest problems that distressed local residents most was the mispronunciation of the state name. "Wes-consin" rang across the lines to the great irritation of already testy consumers.

The problem was given partial remedy when the reservation system calls were redirected to a local site that had been opened with new employees hired from a local phone-based retailer that had gone-out of business. Having people well trained in phone service and knowledgeable about the locale was critical to making an effective change in a large and outdated system.

The major lesson here is that managers must think beyond the simple logic of improved efficiency when implementing change. Public reactions are key to success in making change.

Source:
1. M. BALOUSEK, "Reserving a Campsite in "Wesconsin," Wisconsin State Journal, Sunday, July 25, 1999, p. 1C.

agencies like the U.S.F.S. In general, the practice of charging fees for the recreational use of public lands is almost a century old. Auto permit fees were issued as early as 1908 to help pay for a roadway at Mt. Rainier National Park (36). However, the debate over the use of fees for use of public spaces has been controversial over the same period of time (probably longer).

The general concerns that people have about fees can be expressed in several ways. One is that fees are a double tax on the user. Users pay into the federal general revenue fund for a wide array of goods and services. To pay a fee on top of those taxes is to pay twice. A second argument is that fees change the concept of public land to one that says the land is a commodity available to those who can most afford it. In this argument, it is possible to raise the issue that users will be treated differently based on the ability to pay. Those with more might get the campsites on the water and those who have less might find their tent pad next to the garbage drop where bears tend to gather in the night. A final argument is that a fee discourages the participation of those who are economically disadvantaged, promoting a gap between the "haves" and "have nots" of society.

Until recently, these arguments have been very effective in preventing the significant use of fees in parks and forest recreation management. Very low and no fees were the way of life for most agencies until the concept was revisited in 1996 with the implementation of the Recreation Fee Demonstration Program (PL 104-134) for the U.S. Forest Service, National Park Service, Bureau of Land Management, and the U.S. Fish and Wildlife Service. The Forest Service describes the evolution of this program in the following way (37):

More and more people recreate on national forests each year. As more and more people recreate, keeping up with the needs of those visitors and of the natural resource becomes more and more difficult. Seeing that national forests, parks, and other federal lands were suffering from the lack of funding to care for these lands, Congress passed a law to test bringing more funds to these lands in a new way.

This quotation indicates a very important change in the way that fees have been conceived, used, and desired by the agency. First there is the recognition that general revenue funds are increasingly hard to obtain from Congress for many reasons. Prior to the fee demonstration program, the site managers were given very little incentive to raise funds. Fundraising was discouraged and the assumption was that a site manager would receive an allocation from a central source. Funds might be more equally distributed, but for high-demand, high-use areas, the needs for management funds are likely higher than those in smaller, less-used areas. This placed an intense and often unpleasant internal competition for funds among the various site managers. Revenue created by a particular site was not permitted to stay at the generating site. Rather, the money was returned to the general fund of the Treasury and never returned. Under the Fee Demonstration program, a site is allowed to retain

a majority of the revenue to supplement funds allocated from the general fund (38).

This change obviously gives considerable incentive to local sites for generating extra income to do things they may never have been able to do otherwise. It is at this point where cautions again become appropriate. Some sites are so popular that affluent users are willing to pay relatively large fees to gain exclusive use of the area. The balancing act is to instill equitable access into a framework of pricing that is more market-oriented. This is a program in evolution among Forest Recreation managers. Most are not well trained in economic pricing and its effects on user patterns, so it is logical to assume that there is a steep learning curve to find the right way to establish, assess, collect, and use fees. Currently the fees retained on site are used in ways that make good sense for the site. Table 17.7 shows breakdown of uses of fee revenues for 1999 according to the Forest Service (37).

As of September 30, 1999, the Forest Service spent $42 million of the $56.6 million collected since the Forest Service began collecting these fees in 1996. Planning and time requirements for accounting and issuing contracts explains the unspent balance.

As managers become more comfortable with the mechanisms and as the public becomes more accustomed to paying for use, it is logical to assume that new applications with specific purposes might come into use. Presently, fees are rather uniform over an

Table 17.7 Revenue Spending by the U.S. Forest Service in Fiscal Year 1999

30.8% of fees on general operations, like garbage pickup and cleaning toilets
18.8% on cost of collection
18.3% on repairs and maintenance
10.3% on interpretation and signs
6.2% on upgrading facilities
6.0% on health and safety
3.5% on law enforcement
3.1% on resource preservation
2.6% on other costs
0.4% on habitat improvement

area. For instance, there might be one common fee for entry regardless of the length of stay, or size of vehicle, or need for services (e.g., a sanitary dump station). Similarly, there might be a single fee for campsite regardless of its location (e.g., waterfront costs the same as a fringe site near a traveled roadway). It is likely that different prices will be attached to sites as ways to reflect value and need. Those who need more services and those who want to use prime sites will pay more. Furthermore, managers might use differential pricing to get users into other locations. For example, a nice site that is difficult to approach might be priced lower than an equally nice site that has easier access. Thus, fees become a way to redistribute users. Similarly peak demand use may incur a higher fee than use in less popular times.

It is clear that one lesson has already been learned and shows the public is generally favorable to the use of fees in recreation sites. That lesson is that fees without explanation provoke the anger and political wrath of people. However, when people learn what the fees are for and see their use in a place they personally know (and know needs attention), their approval increases dramatically. The data in Table 17.8 illustrate the public sentiment over fees in selected recreation areas.

While it is clear that fees as a management tool will always have sharp edges and pointed debate, their use is likely to increase. It is incumbent on current and future managers to keep focused on fair and appropriate uses to benefit the entire population through creative and imaginative application.

Concluding Statement

Recreation in the out-of-doors is a passion showing no sign of decline into the future. More people than ever are seeking the possibilities of pleasure and personal renewal through activities in natural settings. Forest and range lands, wilderness, and parks are all areas where user demand is increasing at such a rate that serious and thoughtful management is needed to make sure that subsequent generations of citizens have an opportunity to enjoy the wildness of land that current generations might find. Resource managers then need to have some understanding of reasons why people come to nature and the experiences they seek. Managing human behavior requires careful and imaginative thinking along with innovative and adaptable management strategies.

The most critical thought to take from this chapter is that managing recreation is less about managing the natural resource base and more about managing human behavior. Increasing intensity and volume of use is a serious threat to natural settings, yet people need to have access for many reasons. Preserving the resource with intelligence and wis-

Table 17.8 General Opinions About Fees for Use of Recreational Resources in Percent (by Survey Locations)

Location	% Positive	% Negative
Boundary Waters Canoe Area	87	13
Vail Pass Winter Recreation Area	46	22
Desolation Wilderness	64–78	22–36
White Mountain National Forest	68–72	15–16
Cataract Lake Fee Area	64	14
Tonto National Forest	55–64	22–26
National Comment Cards	77	19
News Article Analysis	65	35

Source: U.S.D.A. Forest Service. Recreation, Heritage and Wilderness Resources web site, http://www.fs.fed.us/recreation/fee_demo/fee_intro.shtml.

dom is critical if people are to respect and enjoy nature. If we are unsuccessful in meeting this challenge, then people will have the opportunity to love nature to its death. This is an unacceptable outcome. This complex subject of forest-human interactions is treated further in Chapter 23 on Social Forestry.

References

1. R. NASH, *The Rights of Nature: A History of Environmental Ethics*, University of Wisconsin Press, Madison, 1989.

2. B. L. DRIVER, P. J. BROWN, AND G. L. PETERSON, EDS., *Benefits of Leisure*, Venture Publishing Co., State College, Penn., 1991.

3. B. DRIVER, D. DUSTIN, T. BALTIC, ET AL., EDS., *Nature and the Human Spirit*, Venture Publishing Co., State College, Penn., 1996.

4. S. FAIRFAX, "Fragmenting the Landscape: Accounting for Private Management of Public Treasures." Aldo Leopold Lecture at the University of Wisconsin–Madison, March 28, 2000.

5. U.S.D.A. Forest Service, "The Recreation Agenda," 1999, http://www.fs.fed.us/recreation/recstrategy/recStratV70.shtml.

6. J. PIEPER, *Leisure: The Basis of Culture*, New America Library, N.Y., 1952.

7. J. NEULINGER, *The Psychology of Leisure: Research Approaches to the Study of Leisure*, Charles C. Thomas Publishers, Springfield, Ill., 1974.

8. M. CLAWSON AND J. KNETSCH, *Economics of Outdoor Recreation*, Johns Hopkins Press, Baltimore, Md., 1966.

9. M. CLAWSON, *Land and Water for Recreation; Opportunities, Problems, and Policies*, Rand McNally, Chicago, Ill., 1963.

10. D. KNUDSON, *Outdoor Recreation*, Macmillan Publishing, N.Y., 1980.

11. K. CORDELL, K. BETZ, J. M. BOWKER, ET AL., EDS. *Outdoor Recreation in American Life: A National Assessment of Demand and Supply Trends*, Sagamore Publishing, Champaign, Ill., 1999.

12. National Center for Educational Statistics, 1999, http://nces.ed.gov/.

13. K. HENDERSON, *Both Gains and Gaps: Feminist Perspectives on Women's Leisure*, Venture Pub., State College, Penn., 1996.

14. K. HENDERSON, M. BIALESCHKI, S. SHAW, AND V. FREYSINGER, *A Leisure of One's Own*, Venture Publishing, Inc., State College, Penn., 1989.

15. V. J. FREYSINGER, *J. Leisure Research, 29 (1),* 1 (1997).

16. V. J. FREYSINGER, *J. Leisure Research, 27 (1),* 61 (1995).

17. M. D. BIALESCHKI AND K. L. WALBERT, *J. Leisure Research, 30 (1),* 79 (1998).

18. A. EWERT, D. CHAVEZ AND A. MAGILL, EDS., *Culture, Conflict, and Communication in the Wildland-Urban Interface,* Westview Press, Boulder, Colo., 1993.

19. D. CHAVEZ, *Trends, 29* (4), 23 (1992).

20. M. FLOYD AND K. J. SHINEW, *J. Leisure Research, 31 (4),* 359 (1999).

21. M. F. FLOYD, *J. Leisure Research, 30 (1),* 3 (1998).

22. Y. F. TUAN, *The Good Life*, University of Wisconsin Press, Madison, 1986.

23. D. MARCOUILLER, "Alternative Forest Uses and Resource-Dependent Communities: Is the Glass Half-empty or Half-full." Center for Community Economic Development, University of Wisconsin–Extension, Madison, 1999.

24. M. JENSEN, *National Parks, 71,* 43 (1997).

25. S. M. HOFFMAN, K. PROESCHOLDT, R. M. RAPSON, AND M. L. HEINSELMAN, *Environmental History. 2(2),* 226 (1997).

26. R. BECKER, B. NIEMAN, AND W. A. GATES, "Displacement of Users Within a River System: Social and Environmental Tradeoffs." A paper presented at the Second Conference on Scientific Research in the National Parks, San Francisco, Calif., U.S. Park Service, 1979.

27. United States Forest Service, *R.O.S. Book*, U.S. Department of Agriculture, Washington, D.C., 1986.

28. United States Forest Service, *R.O.S. Users Guide*, U.S. Department of Agriculture, Washington, D.C., 1982.

29. P. BROWN, "Information needs for river recreation planning and management," In *Proceedings of River Management and Research Symposium*, D. Lime, ed., St. Paul, Minn., U.S.D.A./U.S. Forest Service, 1977.

30. P. DOMBECK, "The Forest Service: The World's Largest Water Company." Public lecture at the University of Wisconsin–Madison. Madison, March 28, 2000.

31. D. Field, In *Natural Resource Management: The Human Dimension*, A. Ewert, ed., Westview Press, Boulder, Colo., 1996.

32. S. Learner, *Environmental Stewardship: Studies in Active Earthkeeping*, University of Waterloo, Department of Geography, Waterloo, Ontario, 1992.

33. D. Porter and D. Salvesen, eds., *Collaborative Planning for Wetlands and Wildlife: Issues and Examples*, Island Press, Washington, D.C., 1995.

34. R. Chambers, *Whose Reality Counts? Putting the First Last,* Intermediate Technology Publication, London, U.K., 1997.

35. R. Margolis and N. Solafsky, *Measures of Success: Designing, Managing, and Monitoring Conservation and Development Projects*, Island Press, Washington, D.C., 1998.

36. C. Harris and B. L. Driver, *J. For., 25* (1987).

37. U.S.D.A. Forest Service, Recreation, Heritage and Wilderness Resources web site, http://www.fs.fed.us/recreation/fee_demo/fee_intro.shtml, April 4, 2000.

38. C. Pratt, "Impact of Recreational Fees on Backcountry Use: The Case of Sleeping Bear Dunes National Lakeshore." Master's Thesis, University of Wisconsin, Conservation Biology and Sustainable Development, Madison Wis., 1999.

39. The Recreation Roundtable, Outdoor Recreation in America: A 1994 Survey for the Recreation Roundtable, Roper Starch Worldwide, Orlando, Florida (1994).

40. National Survey on Recreation and the Environment, U.S.D.A. Forest Service and the University of Georgia, 1994–95 National Survey on Recreation and the Environment, Athens, Georgia (1995).

CHAPTER 18

Behavior and Management of Forest Fires

CRAIG G. LORIMER

In many areas of the world, humans have historically been the principal cause of forest fires, both in the actual number of fires and in the total area burned. Yet lightning fires have probably occurred for as long as there have been regions of dense vegetation and occasional periods of dry weather (Figure 18.1). In some regions, bits of charcoal embedded in lake sediments testify to the periodic occurrence of fires over thousands of years, and it is likely that some of these were caused by lightning. Evidence of fires in the distant past can also sometimes be found on the forest site itself. Long-lived and relatively fire-resistant trees such as coast redwood and ponderosa pine often bear visible external wounds caused by fire (Figure 18.2). When the trunks of such trees are examined in cross-section, scars of fires that occurred centuries ago

Figure 18.1 Several minutes of lightning during a thunderstorm in the mountains of western North America. In this region, lightning causes 30–60% of all fires. (Courtesy of U.S.D.A. Forest Service.)

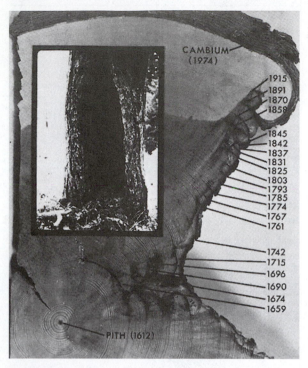

Figure 18.2 Multiple fire scars visible on a cross-section of an old ponderosa pine tree (inset) in the Bitterroot National Forest, in western Montana, reveal that twenty-one fires occurred on this site between 1659 and 1915. (Courtesy of U.S.D.A. Forest Service.)

may be evident. Even in forests that show no obvious indication of recent fire, careful examination of the lower layers of the forest floor will often reveal fragments of charcoal from fires that occurred hundreds of years ago.

Natural Fire Regimes

On a worldwide basis, it is estimated that approximately 500,000 cloud-to-ground lightning discharges occur in forested regions each day (1). Most of these discharges probably strike trees, although only about 10 percent of them actually result in fires. The frequency of lightning fires is highly variable in different parts of the world, even over relatively short distances. Lightning fires are infrequent

in tropical rain forests, and they are relatively uncommon in moist temperate areas such as western Europe and much of eastern North America. However, in some regions, such as the mountains of western North America, lightning is the single leading fire cause, accounting for 30–60% of all fires. A single storm can generate a "blitzkrieg" of lightning strikes as it passes across a mountain range (Figure 18.1), igniting more than 50 fires in a few hours. It is estimated that lightning causes about 10,000 wildland fires in the United States each year (2).

Much of the variability in lightning fire frequency can be attributed to climate and topography. Lightning fires are more common in regions with a pronounced dry season and in mountainous country that is subject to more thunderstorms. However, the nature of the vegetation seems to exert considerable influence as well. Fires are usually more common in conifer forests than in stands of broad-leaved deciduous trees, probably in part because of differences in the chemical composition, moisture content, and porosity of the fuels.

Many lightning strikes are accompanied by rain or humid weather, which can initially cause sluggish fire behavior. However, it would be incorrect to assume that lightning fires never or seldom become conflagrations. "Dry" lightning strikes in the absence of rain are common events, and even under damp conditions, a fire can smolder in leaf litter or a dead tree for days or even weeks until dry conditions return. For example, the lightning-caused Sundance Fire of 1967 in Idaho smoldered undetected for 12 days until dry, windy weather turned it into a roaring crown fire that traveled 26 km (16 miles) in only 9 hours (3). Assessment of the possibilities of lightning fires reaching a large size has become increasingly important in recent years as greater attention has been given to restoration of natural fire regimes in parks and wilderness.

The Natural Role of Fire

Given that lightning fires are common events in some regions, it is not surprising that a number of species show evidence of adaptations to periodic fire. Although the nature of this adaptation varies among species, most fire-adapted species possess characteristics that enable them to colonize rapidly and dominate severely burned areas. Some of the birches and aspens have abundant light seeds that can be transported considerable distances by wind, thus increasing the chances that seeds will reach a recently burned site. Other species, such as jack pine, lodgepole pine, and black spruce, have seeds that are held in tightly closed *serotinous cones.* Unlike the cones of most gymnosperms, serotinous cones are sealed by resin, and seeds are not released until high temperatures melt the resin and allow the cones to open. The seeds can then be dispersed even if the parent trees are killed by the fire.

Seeds of fire-adapted species germinate rapidly on charred surfaces or exposed soil, and the seedlings tend to be tolerant of the dry surface conditions and extremes of temperature common to exposed sites. As is typical of shade-intolerant species, they grow rapidly and usually outcompete other species that may arrive on the site. Many of these species are also able to produce seed at a relatively young age, which increases their chance of persisting on a landscape subject to frequent fires. In regions prone to repeated surface fires, some fire-adapted tree species also develop thick bark at maturity that makes them fairly resistant to injury from light fires.

Fire may also have subtle beneficial effects on ecosystems. In cold, dry climates, forest litter and woody debris have a tendency to build up faster than they can be decomposed. Occasional light fires can reduce this accumulation of fuel, converting nutrients that were previously locked up in organic matter into a form that is available for uptake by plants.

Influence on the Landscape

A regime of frequent low-severity fires is common in regions of the world with savanna or tree-grassland ecosystems and dry climates. In the ponderosa pine savannas of western North America, fire scars on old trees show that the average length of time between successive fires was only 6–20 years in most stands

(Figure 18.2). These frequent low-intensity fires kept the forests open and "park-like," helped maintain the grasses and pines, and discouraged invasion by shade-tolerant species. By keeping fuel accumulations low, these low-intensity fires also reduced the chances of large conflagrations.

Forests with high-severity fire regimes are usually made up of trees with flammable foliage (such as conifers or Australian eucalyptus) that occur on somewhat moister sites. Weather conditions may not be conducive to fire spread in most years, but the great buildup of fuels may make these forests susceptible to widespread conflagrations during occasional episodes of severe drought and high winds. Natural fire rotations can vary from 50 to 400 years or more (4). Landscapes in such areas are often dominated by even-aged stands of fire-adapted species (see Chapter 13), but because some fires may be variable in their intensity, two- or three-aged stands are sometimes present.

Although regions of the world with moist year-round climates often have a low fire frequency, fire can still have a significant impact on the landscape. For example, in the northern hardwood forests of North America, severe fire may occur at intervals much longer than the life span of the trees, leading to dominance of the landscape by shade-tolerant species not highly adapted to fire. However, fire may still be common on locally dry sites (such as ridgetops and sandy soils), and conflagrations can still occur on moist sites where the trees have been blown down by wind or killed by insect epidemics (5). Such episodes were historically important in maintaining a component of early successional species on the landscape.

Human Influence and Fire Policy

Human modification of the natural fire regime is not a recent development. Primitive societies commonly used fire to improve hunting and overland travel, to aid in land clearance, and to reduce insect and snake populations. The shifting pattern of slash-and-burn agriculture has been widely practiced by native peoples of the tropics. Intentional burning was also a common practice among native American tribes. For example, in 1632, a Massachusetts colonist named Thomas Morton wrote (6):

The [natives] are accustomed, to set fire of the Country in all places where they come; and to burne it, twize a yeare. . . . And this custome of firing the Country is the meanes to make it passable, and by that meanes the trees grow here, and there as in our parks, and makes the Country very beautifull, and commodius.

Early European settlers continued to use fire, especially as an aid to clearing land for agriculture. So many settlers used this method that occasionally the amount of smoke and particulates in the atmosphere was sufficient to cast semidarkness over the land. One such "dark day" in 1780, caused by fires raging in Vermont and New York, was described as follows.

The legislature of Connecticut was in session at Hartford on that day. The deepening gloom enwrapped the city, and the rooms of the state house grew dark. The journal of the house of representatives reads "None could see to read or write in the house, or even at a window, or distinguish persons at a small distance" (7).

Settlers often let these fires smolder for weeks or even months, creating a potentially explosive situation. With hundreds of these fires smoldering across the landscape, it only required a worsening drought and a strong wind to turn them into a raging inferno. This indeed happened repeatedly throughout the 19th and early 20th centuries from New England to the Pacific Northwest, with massive conflagrations ranging in size from 100,000 to a million hectares. In at least five of these conflagrations, there was also a great loss of human life, ranging from 200 to 1,500 people killed.

These repeated disasters set the stage for a policy of vigorous fire suppression. It is therefore not surprising that one of the top priorities of the American Forestry Association when it convened in 1875 was the "protection of the existing forests of the country from unnecessary waste," of which fire was the leading cause. These efforts led to passage of the Weeks Law of 1911 and the Clarke–McNary Act

of 1924, which for the first time provided federal funding to assist the states in developing a cooperative forest fire control program (see Chapters 1, 9, and 10). Although the actual amount of money provided was small at first, it did allow the construction of fire towers, hiring of fire wardens, and purchase of equipment. Fire control on publicly owned lands underwent several major changes in the 20th century. In the 1920s and 1930s, a policy of *fire exclusion* was attempted, in which all wildfires were suppressed as quickly as possible. In 1935, the "10 A.M. fire-control policy" was formulated, setting the objective of rapid and thorough suppression of all fires during potentially dangerous fire weather by ten o'clock the next morning.

Some modification of the 10 A.M. policy was required in certain areas. In parts of the western United States, labor and equipment were not always sufficient to suppress all fires, and it was recognized that such attempts had probably passed a point of diminishing returns in terms of costs and benefits. Fire suppression was therefore handled on a priority basis from about 1940 to 1960. On federal lands, fires burning in areas of highest resource values were attacked first. Remote areas of noncommercial forest with low-hazard fuels were attended to last.

Furthermore, as early as the 1920s and '30s, a few pioneering resource managers began to rediscover the beneficial effects of certain fires and realized the potential disadvantages of trying to exclude fire from ecosystems that were historically fire-dependent. The planned use of fire under specified conditions, known as *prescribed burning*, was gradually acknowledged to be useful in achieving certain objectives such as reducing hazardous fuel accumulations after logging, and preparing the forest floor as a seedbed. Initially, prescribed fires were always set by resource managers under predetermined conditions.

Beginning in the 1970s, forest fire policy on federal lands in the United States was broadened further to an overall policy of *fire management,* not simply fire control. This policy takes advantage of the beneficial effects of some unplanned forest fires while still continuing suppression of fires expected to have undesirable effects. Several features of this policy represent a bold departure from previous policies. First, it is recognized that the decision on how to handle a particular fire on federal lands should be based not only on the anticipated behavior and effects of the fire, but also on the long-range management objectives for each unit of land, and the potential costs and benefits of control. In some national forests, foresters write a management plan for each homogeneous unit of vegetation and fuels, and the degree to which fire is necessary to accomplish the objectives of the plan is clearly stated.

Second, there is a provision for allowing certain unscheduled ignitions to burn under supervision if the predictions of fire behavior indicate that the fire will help achieve the management objectives. For example, a lightning fire or other unplanned ignition may be allowed to burn under surveillance if fuel reduction is needed on that unit of land, and the current and forecasted weather conditions indicate that fire behavior and intensity would be manageable. Fires that threaten human life or property, or which have the potential to become uncontrollable, are still vigorously suppressed. However, choice of the method and equipment to be used in suppressing the fire may be determined in part by weighing the cost of these various options against the value of the resource and the potential for damage.

Finally, fire in the new policy is acknowledged to be more than simply a management tool. It is considered to be an environmental factor that may serve a necessary function not easily accomplished by other methods. Thus, although understory hardwoods in southern pine forests can be controlled by cutting down the hardwood stems and applying herbicides to the stumps, it is recognized that other beneficial effects of fire cannot feasibly be duplicated by mechanical means.

Fire Behavior

Anticipating the behavior of a fire is one of the most critical aspects of fire management. The choice of strategy in suppressing wildfires and carrying out prescribed burning depends largely on how the fire is expected to behave—its rate of spread, direction of travel, and intensity. The prerequisites for the start and spread of a forest fire are 1) flammable fuels, 2) sufficient heat energy to bring the fuels to the ignition temperature, and 3) adequate oxygen. These three factors are often referred to as the *fire triangle,* because all three factors are necessary for combustion, and further combustion can be stopped by removing any one of the three elements. Virtually all the phenomena influencing the behavior of a fire, including those related to weather and topography, can ultimately be attributed to one or more of these three factors. Thus the size, total weight, and moisture content of fuel elements partly determine the amount of heat required for ignition and the heat released by combustion. Their spatial arrangement influences the availability of oxygen. Variations in these factors are ultimately reflected in the rate at which the fire spreads and its intensity. Grass fires, for example, spread rapidly but are of relatively low intensity, whereas fires in heavy logging debris spread slowly but burn intensely.

Fuel Conditions and Fire Types

Fuels are often classified in a general manner by their spatial location in the forest. *Surface fuels* constitute a large, heterogeneous group of fuels found on or close to the surface of the ground. Included are undecomposed leaf litter, fallen twigs and branches, logs, grass, herbs, tree seedlings, and low shrubs. *Ground fuels* are found beneath the loose layer of surface litter. They include partly decomposed organic matter or duff, roots, and muck or peat in wet areas. *Aerial fuels* include all flammable material in the subcanopy layers of the forest and in the tree crowns. Fuels are classified in this manner partly because of the three distinctive types of fires associated with them: surface fires, ground fires, and crown fires.

Surface Fires   The most readily available fuels for a forest fire are the dry surface layers of litter on the forest floor, interspersed small dead branchwood, and the cured grass in some forests. This is the material consumed in most *surface fires* (Figure 18.3). Green herbs and understory vegetation are usually a deterrent to the spread of fire in the spring because of the high moisture content of the foliage, but they may contribute significantly to fire intensity and rate of spread when in a cured condition.

Although the larger fuels, such as fallen logs, may be partly or wholly consumed by the time a surface fire has died out, such material is too large and often too damp to influence the forward momentum of the fire. Thus, research indicates that the effect of fuels on the forward rate of spread of a surface fire is largely determined by the amount, arrangement, and moisture content of the fine fuels. The effect of larger surface fuels, such as fallen logs,

is to cause a more intense fire. For this reason, the most intense fires are usually those that start in logging slash or other areas of heavy fuel accumulations. In general, the higher the total weight of fuels, the more difficult the fire will be to control.

Ground Fires   In finely divided ground fuels such as peat or duff, oxygen is often limited to the point that only glowing combustion is possible. As a result, *ground fires* are often of low intensity and spread slowly. They are, however, remarkably persistent, often smoldering for days or weeks. For this reason, they present an especially serious problem, and it is often difficult to judge whether suppression activities have been successful in completely extinguishing the fire. Ironically, extinguishing ground fires that burn in bogs may require great quantities of water, much more than might be required on upland sites. One peat fire in Michigan took 36 days for containment at a size of 80 hectares, but attempts to extinguish it were not successful until a small river was diverted by bulldozers 20 days later to drown the fire completely (8).

Crown Fires   Fires that sweep through the canopy of a forest are known as *crown fires* (Figure 18.4). The susceptibility of tree crowns to ignition varies among species. Crown fires are much more common in coniferous forests than in hardwoods, because of lower foliar moisture content, flammable organic compounds, greater amounts of dead twigs, and a conical shape that allows easier access of flames to the crown. Yet even in conifer forests, the probability of a crown fire is low if the understory is sparse and the trees are mature. When they occur, crown fires often cause heavy or complete mortality of the tree canopy (Figure 18.5). Although crown fires are relatively uncommon and account for only a small percentage of all fires, they account for most of the area burned annually because of their large size.

Most crown fires start as surface fires, and the reasons why a fire may make the transition in particular cases are still not well known. The surface fire must reach a rather high intensity in order to dessicate and consume live foliage in the crown,

Figure 18.3 Surface fire. (Courtesy of U.S.D.A. Forest Service.)

Figure 18.4 Crown fire. (Courtesy of U.S.D.A. Forest Service.)

probability of ignition and fire intensity are closely related to relative humidity and fuel moisture (Table 18.1).

The rapidity of fuel response to atmospheric humidity depends on the size of the fuel elements. The "flashy" fine fuels, which normally determine the rate of fire spread, respond quickly to changes in relative humidity. As a result, fires may alternately flare up during midday when humidity is low and die down again at night when humidity is high.

Fire behavior is also affected by *atmospheric stability*, which is defined as the resistance of the atmosphere to vertical motion. An unstable atmosphere is characterized by gusty, turbulent winds, vertical air motion, and towering cumulus clouds. Crowning and erratic fires are more likely when the atmosphere is unstable, for the vertical air movement encourages the development of a strong convection column of smoke and burning debris fragments. However, if fuel moisture is at a moderate level, indicating little potential for severe fires, days with an unstable atmosphere may be preferable for prescribed burning, because smoke disperses better.

Wind has a dramatic effect on the rate of fire spread and intensity. It has long been a rule of

especially in mature forests where the lowest limbs are high above the ground. However, if conifer saplings are present in the understory, these can act as "ladder fuels," enabling a surface fire to climb into the crowns of the mature trees.

Weather Conditions

Within a given fuel type, fire behavior is regulated largely by the state of the weather. Particularly important are the effects of atmospheric moisture and wind. Fuel moisture is determined not only by the amount and duration of precipitation, but also by relative humidity during rainless periods. As humidity increases, fuels take up moisture from the air, and more of the fire's energy is used to drive off this moisture prior to combustion. As humidity decreases, fuels lose moisture to the air. Both the

Figure 18.5 Aftermath of a blowup fire, showing the numerous dead trees that can act as a fuel source for subsequent fires.

Table 18.1   Effect of Relative Humidity and Fuel Moisture on Fire Behavior

| Relative Humidity (percent) | Moisture Content (percent) | | Fire Behavior |
	Forest Litter	Small Branchwood	
>95	>25		Little or no ignition.
>60	>20	>15	Very little ignition; fire smolders and spreads slowly.
45–60	15–19	12–15	Low ignition hazard, but campfires become dangerous; glowing brands cause ignition when relative humidity <50%. Fire spreads slowly but readily; prescribed burning may be feasible.
35–45	11–14	10–12	Medium ignitibility; matches become dangerous, "easy" burning conditions. Many prescribed burns are conducted in this range.
25–35	8–10	7–10	High ignition hazard; matches always dangerous. Occasional crowning, spotting caused by gusty winds. "Moderate" burning conditions.
15–25	5–7	5–7	Quick ignition, rapid buildup, extensive crowning; any increase in wind causes increased spotting, crowning, loss of control. Fire moves up bark of trees igniting aerial fuels; long-distance spotting in pine stands. Dangerous burning conditions.
<15	<5	<5	All sources of ignition dangerous. Aggressive burning; spot fires occur often and spread rapidly, and extreme fire behavior is probable. Critical burning conditions.

Source: Adapted from Albini, 1979 (9).

thumb among fire control officials that the rate of spread is approximately proportional to the square of the wind speed; hence, a doubling of wind speed will quadruple the rate of spread.

The effect of wind on the pattern or shape of fires is illustrated in Figure 18.6. Under conditions of steady moderate or strong winds, fires tend to burn in elliptical patterns with the long axis in the direction of the wind. The strategy of fire suppression is partly based on estimates of the increase in perimeter of this elliptical zone of flames per unit time. The pattern of spread, however, can be greatly changed by abrupt wind shifts, which can turn the flank of a fire into a much expanded burning head. This greatly increases the area burned by the fire and is often a major contributing factor to the large final size of conflagration fires. Abrupt wind shifts are especially common during the passage of a cold front, which is one reason why cold fronts are often dreaded by fire control personnel (see Sidebar 18.1).

Topography

Fires burn more quickly up steep slopes, largely because heat generated by the fire front is directed more closely to the surface of the ground, thereby decreasing the moisture and increasing the temperature of the fuels ahead of the fire. Topography also has many effects on the microclimate of a particular site. Slopes facing toward the south and southwest, for example, tend to be the warmest and driest slopes because they are exposed to the direct rays of the sun during the hottest part of the day. As a result, fires are more frequent and spread more quickly on southern slopes. Topography also modifies and channels airflow patterns. Rugged, moun-

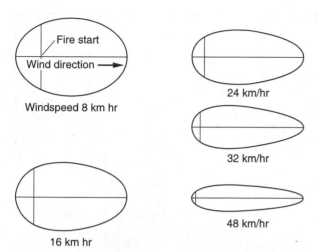

Figure 18.6 Approximate fire shapes created by winds blowing in a constant direction at different velocities. The various fire shapes are drawn to different scales. [From Albini (9).]

tainous topography often induces turbulent winds that increase fire intensity and the possibility of erratic behavior.

Erratic Behavior

Fires sometimes undergo a rather abrupt transition from a low-intensity to a high-intensity fire, which may be visibly apparent from the development of a violent convection column of rapidly rising smoke and hot gases. Such fires are often called *blowup fires* and represent an unfavorable turn of events for firefighters because they are often uncontrollable by conventional fire-fighting techniques (Figure 18.5). Blowup fires may be caused by a sudden increase in windspeed (see Sidebar 18.1) or by the start of crowning. The convection column tends to create its own "draft," which helps maintain fire intensity at a high level.

The behavior of blowup fires is frequently erratic. They may spawn tornado-like winds in excess of 300 kilometers per hour (185 mi/hr), further increasing fire intensity, as well as whirlwinds of hot air and flames that may hurl burning debris far ahead of the main fire front. Such behavior, known as *spotting,*

can start many new fires. Most blowup fires can be extinguished only by rain or snow, and human control efforts are usually restricted to attempts at blocking further lateral spread along the flanks.

Prediction of Fire Behavior

A fire researcher named H. T. Gisborne remarked at a conference in the 1940s, "I doubt that anyone will ever be able to sit down to a machine, punch a key for every factor of the situation, and have the machine tell him what to do." Be that as it may, the advent of computer simulation techniques in recent years has proved to be very useful to fire managers. Clearly it is desirable at least to have an estimate of the rate of spread and intensity of a fire, given certain weather and fuel conditions.

The quantitative study of fire behavior and prediction has been intensively pursued for several decades in research labs such as the U.S. Forest Service's Northern Forest Fire Lab in Missoula, Montana. A basic aim of this research has been to use physical laws, such as the law of conservation of energy, to describe the process of combustion and fire spread in mathematical terms (11, 12). The use of basic principles of physics to predict fire behavior has advantages over statistical approaches to studying factors influencing past fire behavior, because theoretical models are more universal in their applicability. That is, they can be used to predict fire behavior in a wide variety of forest and fuel types. Developing these equations required elaborate experimentation with fire behavior in a laboratory environment because some of the mechanisms of heat transfer and combustion were not known, and carefully controlled experiments were the only way to determine empirically the required factors.

This type of research has had handsome payoffs in practical application, one of the most useful of which has been the development of a revised *National Fire-Danger Rating System*. Various systems for rating fire danger had long been used to indicate the relative severity of fire-weather conditions, probable suppression forces needed, and other information. With the new system, more specific and accurate predictions are possible.

Sidebar 18.1

Firefighting Fatalities at Storm King Mountain

On July 2, 1994, dry lightning ignited a blaze on a ridgetop of Storm King Mountain in western Colorado. The "South Canyon Fire," as it came to be known, would not ordinarily be included even as a footnote in the annals of historic forest fires, attaining a final size of only 856 hectares (2100 acres). However, the South Canyon Fire will long be remembered for the loss of 14 elite young firefighters who were killed during the suppression attempt.

Typical of ridgetop fires, the South Canyon fire behaved sluggishly for the first several days, creeping slowly downhill through shrubby oak and pine toward the base of the canyon. There was little sense of danger. However, on the afternoon of July 6th, a dry cold front roared through the Colorado mountains, causing sustained winds of 48–72 kilometers per hour. Propelled by the strong canyon winds, fire engulfed the entire west slope of the mountain in only 10 minutes, shooting flames 30–100 meters into the air. With the fire traveling 2–3 times as fast as the firefighters could scramble uphill, 14 of the 49 firefighters were overtaken by smoke and searing heat before they could even deploy their portable fire shelters.

Although not all tragedies of this type can be foreseen or avoided, investigators raised several concerns about safety procedures during the suppression attempt. The out-of-state firefighting crew had not been briefed on the local fuels, the approaching cold front, or fire weather forecasts before being sent to the fire. The extreme fire behavior on July 6th could have

Aftermath of the South Canyon Fire of July 1994 on Storm King Mountain, Colorado. (Courtesy of U.S.D.A. Forest Service.)

been anticipated given existing fire models. Twelve of the 18 standard federal safety precautions had not been followed. The investigators concluded that the combination of fuel, weather, and topographic conditions behind the disaster were not unusual in the region, which is precisely why cases such as this should be studied carefully by firefighting crews and natural resource managers.

Included are predictions of the number of fires expected per unit area, ease of ignition, rate of spread, and fire intensity. A current limitation of the system is that it applies only to surface fires. However, it is possible to infer the likelihood of crown fire and spotting from the surface fire ratings.

As with all theoretical models of natural phenomena, these predications must be compared with the observed behavior of many fires before proper interpretation can be made.

Ratings of fire danger are computed daily by utilizing measurements of such variables as wind speed, fuel moisture, amount and duration of precipitation, lightning activity, and the condition of the herbaceous vegetation. Although some of the needed measurements can be obtained from stations maintained by the Weather Service, such stations do not ordinarily make measurements of important fire variables as fuel moisture or vegetative conditions, and the locations of ordinary weather stations (usually in valleys) are often not representative of vast tracts of forestland. A network of fire-weather stations in forested areas has been established in recent years to meet these needs. There has also been a trend toward replacing manually operated fire-weather stations with a ground network of small, remote automated weather stations (RAWS) that transmit data on weather and lightning conditions to central computing facilities via satellite signal (Figure 18.7).

Information generated by the National Fire-Danger Rating System is now readily available to the general public as well as resource managers through the Wildland Fire Assessment System website (http://www.fs.fed.us/land/wfas). National maps showing zones of fire danger are updated daily based on data provided by a network of 1,500

Figure 18.7 Fire danger in the United States is calculated daily from weather and fuel observations at weather stations. Automated weather stations, such as the one shown here, transmit data to computers via satellite signal and are gradually replacing manually operated stations. (Courtesy of U.S.D.A. Forest Service.)

weather stations (Figure 18.8). This large-scale regional view of fire danger helps managers coordinate fire prevention and suppression activities on a state or regional level, including how best to allocate fire suppression personnel and equipment.

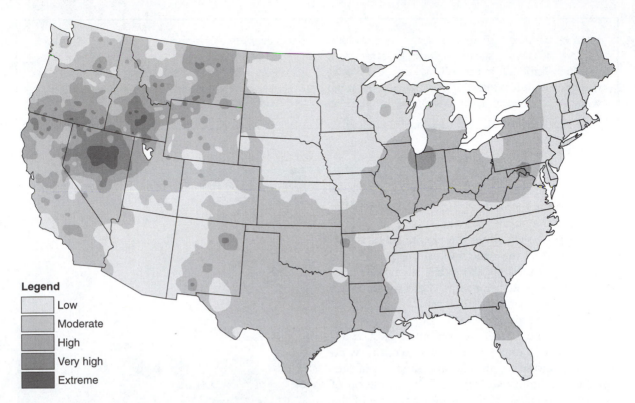

Legend

- Low
- Moderate
- High
- Very high
- Extreme

Figure 18.8 A national map showing zones of low to extreme fire danger for a specific day as predicted by the National Fire-Danger Rating System. This map is updated daily and is available on the Wildland Fire Assessment System webpage (http://www.fs.fed.us/land/wfas) The ratings are based on data from a network of 1,500 weather stations and show fire danger for the dominant fuel type at each station.

Other advances in fire modeling have enabled fire managers to obtain predictions about the shape and spread pattern of individual fires. A computer program known as BEHAVE, for example, forecasts the perimeter location of individual fires at various intervals of time (13) and forthcoming versions of the BEHAVE model will have the capability for predicting crown fire spread.

Fire Prevention

Because humans are the leading cause of forest fires in most areas, fire prevention campaigns have been vigorously promoted to reduce the number of these fires. The most visible efforts are public-education campaigns via conventional media—radio messages, signs, magazine articles, news releases, and so on. Such efforts as Smokey the Bear and Keep America Green programs have relied heavily on public education.

A recent statistical compilation of fire reports (14) indicates that in the United States, the leading cause has been arson, which has accounted for 29 percent of all fires. Other major causes have been debris burning, 25 percent; lightning, 11 percent; machine use, 7 percent; smoking, 6%; children, 5%; and campfires, 3 percent. There are some important regional variations. While arson and debris burning are important causes in all regions, lightning is usually the leading cause of fires in western states by a large margin.

This information about specific causes helps indicate where the thrust of prevention campaigns should be directed. Escaped fires from debris burning can be reduced by notifying the public of periods of high fire danger and by regulation through use of burning permits. Arson is a more difficult problem to tackle, although it is probable that education and legal action have some deterrent effect. Fires caused by sparks from mechanized equipment can be reduced by strict enforcement of regulations pertaining to the installation of spark arresters. A high frequency of fires attributable to escaped campfires in some locations may indicate the need to install outdoor fireplaces in popular but undeveloped recreation areas. Fires caused by smoking can be reduced by regular public reminders to crush cigarettes and use ashtrays, especially along highways where most cigarette fires occur.

Fire prevention can also be accomplished by hazard reduction, commonly by reducing accumulations of particularly hazardous fuels or by constructing barriers to the spread of fire. Controlled burning in areas of heavy logging slash, along railroad tracks, and even in some forests can reduce particularly serious accumulations of fuel.

Unhealthy Forests and Wildfire Risk

A particularly dramatic example of the need for hazard reduction is a fuel accumulation problem caused by decades of fire suppression in forests of ponderosa pine and larch in western North America. These once park-like forests have become invaded by dense thickets of firs and other species. Stressed by drought, blitzed by insect epidemics, and plagued by diseases such as dwarf mistletoes, millions of trees from eastern Washington state to New Mexico have been killed, creating what has been called a "forest health crisis of unprecedented proportions" (15).

The tremendous quantity of understory ladder fuels and standing dead trees have greatly increased the risk of high intensity wildfires over historic norms. Figure 18.9 shows that despite greater expenditures for fire control, the annual area burned has in fact markedly increased since the 1970s.

The suggested remedy for the forest health crisis is a combination of mechanical thinning, salvage cutting, and extensive prescribed burning. Current

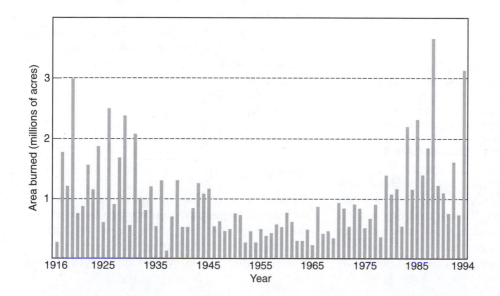

Figure 18.9
Historical trend in annual area burned by wildfires in eleven states of the western United States from 1916–1994. Despite costly expenditures for fire control, annual area burned has generally increased since the 1970s, in part because of increased fuel accumulations from fire suppression. (Courtesy of the National Interagency Fire Center.)

plans call for prescribed burning on 3 million acres annually, or five times current levels.

Politically, this is not an easy program to implement. Congress is usually more willing to appropriate money for emergency fire suppression than for preventive measures like prescribed burning. There are also environmental objections to prescribed burning ranging from endangered species protection to air pollution. However, the annual costs of widespread prescribed burning are modest compared to the billion dollars typically spent on wildfire suppression in a bad year, when suppression is often unsuccessful anyway (16), and environmental effects of prescribed burning are trivial compared to those of conflagrations. It is becoming increasingly clear that it is futile to attempt to exclude fire from fire-dependent ecosystems. Such areas will eventually burn anyway, despite vigilant fire control—but will occur with much higher economic and ecological costs.

The Urban-Wildland Interface

A social problem of even wider scope is the increasing trend toward rural housing to be built in a scattered or haphazard fashion within an extensive matrix of highly flammable wildland vegetation. This pattern of development, called the *urban-wildland interface,* couldn't be more poorly designed from a fire protection viewpoint. As one analyst remarked:

> **You could go into just about any state and find houses with wood shingle roofs, open eaves to suck fire into the attic, and firewood piled against the back wall, sitting in the midst of dense flammable vegetation, backed up against a wildland ecosystem so overloaded with fuel that it would burn with uncontrollable fury (17).**

The urban-wildland interface also creates strategic problems for firefighting agencies, and places severe strains on their budgets. When protecting a compact village in a rural area, a coherent strategy for protecting the community can be developed that relies on building a defense perimeter. Firefighting

responsibility in these cases is usually in the hands of the local fire department, which is better trained than wildland firefighters to control structural fires. Dispersed development, however, is much more difficult to protect:

> **Instead of one defense perimeter to develop . . . there may now be hundreds. Instead of relying on a community group or local fire company, now there may be virtually no organized protection other than the wildland agency itself. Access is scattered . . . and the costs of fire protection skyrocket while its effectiveness goes down.**
>
> **In the most frustrating paradox, the people who live in the [dispersed development pattern] still want fire protection, but they also want to spend less on public services, while their living patterns impose far higher costs on the community. They want to live with nature, but they don't want to pay for the real costs of that lifestyle. Not surprisingly, nobody else wants to pay it on their behalf either (17).**

Efforts toward reducing the urban-wildland interface problem initially focused on teaching landowners how to use more suitable building materials and how to reduce fire hazards in a wide zone around their homes. More recently, the federal wildland agencies have taken a more "hard-line" stance on their responsibility in protecting homes. While human life is still accepted as the highest protection priority of agencies such as the Forest Service, second priority is to "protect resources and property, based on the relative values to be protected." Decisions on the relative value of homes versus forest resources may be left up to the local incident commander.

Fire Control

Wildland fire control in the United States is administered as a cooperative venture by the Forest Service, the Bureau of Land Management, the National Park Service, and the various state governments. In some areas, private owners and industrial firms also participate in the suppression of fires. Fire control activities on large fires are usually very tightly organized, and the suppression activity itself may resemble a military campaign.

Detection

In the early 20th century, lookout towers formed the backbone of the fire detection system. Sufficient numbers of lookouts were placed on higher points of land in the area to provide reasonably thorough coverage of the landscape. Aerial detection of forest fires by systematic airplane flights, however, has gradually overshadowed fixed-point lookouts, partly because it is cheaper and allows for more complete and detailed coverage. Most agencies continue to use a skeletal system of lookouts, however. An important advantage of fire towers is that they provide continuous surveillance, so fires during dry spells are more likely to be spotted at an early stage, before they can become large and potentially uncontrollable.

Conventional aerial detection has also been supplemented with the use of *airborne infrared scanners*. These electronic devices can detect infrared radiation produced by small, smoldering fires that do not produce enough smoke to be seen by the unaided eye. Although infrared detection is not very effective through clouds, it works well at night and can detect the presence of spot fires even when obscured by a blanket of smoke. Following a major lightning storm, airplanes equipped with infrared scanners can be used even at night to plot the locations of incipient fires while they are still small. On large fires, a thermal map of the fire can be created showing the current locations of fire fronts and hot spots. Such information is useful for the fire boss in determining and updating the overall fire suppression strategy.

Suppression of Wildfires

When a fire has been spotted by a lookout or aerial observer, its location is reported by two-way radio to the dispatcher at the fire control head-

quarters. The dispatcher plots the location of the fire on a map, estimates the probable size of the attack force needed to contain the fire, and sends the needed people and equipment to the fire site.

Fire suppression can be accomplished by removing any one of the three essential "ingredients" of fire: fuel, oxygen, and heat. Fuels are removed by digging, scraping, or plowing a strip of earth known as a *fire line* in advance of the fire to halt its progress (Figure 18.10). The application of dirt, water, or fire-retardant chemicals serves to

Figure 18.10   Construction of a fire line (a) by hand tools in a western conifer forest, and (b) by a tractor and plow unit in a southern pine forest. (Courtesy of U.S.D.A. Forest Service.)

reduce both the fuel temperature and the supply of oxygen.

If the fire is not too intense, the preferred method of control is *direct attack*. The fire line is constructed near the fire edge and the flames are knocked down by water, dirt, or other means (Figure 18.10). If the fire cannot be safety approached at close range, the fire line must be constructed at a distance. In such cases, controlled burns will usually be set just inside the line and allowed to spread toward the flanks of the wildfire in order to rob the fire of fuel. This is known as *indirect attack*. As a last resort, controlled burns known as *backfires* may be set ahead of the main fire and induced to burn backwards toward the head in order to remove fuels in the path of the advancing fire front.

Although the suppression of large forest fires generally requires the use of hand tools, bulldozers, and water pumps over a period of many hours or days, significant contributions to the overall suppression effort can be made by aerial techniques. Airplanes and helicopters are used to apply water or fire-retardant chemicals to active forest fires. The usual effects of water on a fire can be augmented by adding flame-inhibiting chemicals or other additives that enhance the "wettability" of water or increase its smothering effect on the combustion of·fuels. Fine clays are often mixed with water to increase the cohesiveness of the mixture and prevent excessive dissipation during its descent from fixed-wing aircraft. These mixtures of clay and liquids are known as *slurries*. The application of slurries from the air is particularly helpful as a delaying tactic that allows time for people and equipment to arrive on the scene, especially when the fire occurs in a remote location. However, aerial retardants and slurries are not usually sufficient to extinguish a forest fire, and follow-up work by ground crews is almost always necessary.

The more intense the fire, the more problematic spotting is likely to be for the ground crews. Because spotting may cause the fire to jump the line in many places (Figure 18.11), constant surveillance for spot fires by the suppression crew is necessary. Experienced fire fighters realize that under blowup conditions, the spread of a fire is sel-

Figure 18.11 Careful surveillance is necessary to control spot fires caused by burning embers hurled across the fire line. (Reproduced from *Wildfires* with permission of the Robert J. Brady Company.)

dom restricted by the location of firebreaks. Conflagration fires can easily leap over rivers, bogs, and even lakes. Under extreme conditions, spot fires can flare up several miles ahead of the main fire front, and humans usually can do little to stop the fire's progress.

When the fire line around the perimeter of the fire has been completed and the fire is no longer spreading, it is said to be *contained*. There remains, however, the often long and tedious process of "mop-up"; all smoldering fires and firebrands near the inside edge of the fire line must be extinguished. Mop-up is necessary to ensure that the fire will not flare up again and cross the line—a quite common occurrence. Fires can even creep beneath a fire line by burning underground along root channels and then suddenly resurface on the other side of the line. Burning stumps and roots near the line may therefore have to be excavated and soaked with water. Successful mop-up will make the line safe, but the interior section of a large burned area might not be officially declared extinguished until much later, sometimes not until the arrival of winter rains or snows.

Prescribed Burning

The controlled use of fire to accomplish specific objectives is known as *prescribed burning* (Figure

18.12).There can be many reasons for controlled burning in different situations, including: 1) reduction of logging debris or "slash fuels" following clearcutting, thereby reducing the risk of intense wildfires; 2) preparation of a seedbed for tree species that require exposed mineral soil; 3) reduction of fuel accumulations in standing forests to lessen the probability of a crown fire; 4) control of understory vegetation in certain forest types, such as hardwood saplings in southern pine stands;

5) control of certain diseases such as brown spot needle blight in the southern United States and dwarf mistletoes in the western United States; 5) improvement of wildlife habitat, especially for fire-dependent species; 6) range improvement for livestock grazing in some areas; and 7) restoration of prairie habitat.

Prescribed burning requires careful planning to minimize risk and to enhance the likelihood that objectives will be accomplished. Topography and fuel conditions on the treatment area should be assessed in terms of probable effects on fire behavior and desirable location of fire breaks. Fire lines should be established in advance of any burning. Fuel weights and fuel moisture are normally assessed using standard sampling or monitoring techniques. The chances for adequate smoke dispersal must also be evaluated. This information can then be used to write the *fire prescription*, which outlines the specific objectives of the burn, the range of weather conditions under which burning would be effective and safe, the method and sequence of ignitions, and the personnel and equipment needed. A good fire prescription is very specific and includes such information as the actual amount of fuels to be reduced, the flame length and intensity needed to accomplish the objectives, and the range of acceptable windspeed, relative humidity, and fuel moisture. The National Fire-Danger Rating System can provide valuable help in deciding whether a particular day is acceptable since it gives estimates of fire spread rate and intensity under various combinations of weather and fuel conditions. Before proceeding, it is also a good idea to conduct a *test burn* on a small area within prepared lines where there is no chance of escape, in order to see whether the behavior of the fire is similar to what was expected.

Prescribed fires may be set by ground crews using a device such as a drip torch (Figure 18.13), or they may be ignited from the air by delayed-ignition devices ejected from aircraft or by a drip torch attached to a helicopter. Risk may be further reduced by burning the area in consecutive strips, sometimes with each delimited by a fire line. Regulation of fire intensity is achieved not only by

Figure 18.12 Before (a) and after (b) prescribed burning in a sequoia–mixed conifer forest in California. In addition to reducing the amount of litter, dead branches, and logs, the fire killed most of the pole-sized white fir trees shown in these photographs. (National Park Service photographs [a] by Bruce M. Kilgore and [b] by Don Taylor.)

Figure 18.13 Prescribed burning with a drip torch to reduce the fuel accumulated on the ground and to prepare the forest floor as a seedbed. (National Park Service photograph by Bruce M. Kilgore.)

selecting days with desired weather conditions but also by planning the sequence of ignitions and the direction of spread. Fires allowed to burn in the direction of the wind are known as *headfires* and have relatively fast rates of spread and high temperatures. Fires can be induced to burn against the wind by igniting the fuels on the inside edge of a fire line. Spread in the direction of the wind is therefore prevented by the fire line, and the flames move slowly against the wind. Such *backburns* are somewhat easier to control and may be preferable to head fires on days of relatively high fire hazard.

Although some of the common objectives of prescribed burning can be accomplished by other means—for example, seedbed preparation by mechanical scarification—prescribed burning is often the most economical option available and the one least demanding of petrochemical energy. The principal disadvantages of prescribed burning are the risks involved, the problem of air pollution from the smoke, and the fact that the number of days per year suitable for burning may be few in some regions.

The chances of a prescribed burn escaping control can be minimized by careful planning, but the

operation is never entirely free of risk. In May 2000, a prescribed burn on national park land in New Mexico escaped and destroyed 235 homes in the nearby town of Los Alamos, even at one point threatening the nuclear lab facilities there. Although a 30-page burning plan with detailed maps had been prepared prior to the burn, a subsequent investigative team considered the plan to be inadequate and faulted the practitioners for violating some of the standard procedures. The crew believed unpredictable weather patterns were to blame. Regardless of who or what is at fault in such situations, it is clear that even a single disastrous "escape" can be very damaging to any long-term prescribed burn program. An escaped burn in Michigan, known as the Mack Lake Fire (1980), largely shut down a program of prescribed burning for the endangered Kirtland's warbler for the following 20 years. The young jack pine habitat required by the warbler is now largely recreated through use of clearcutting and planting instead of fire.

Environmental Impacts of Forest Fires

In the 19th and early 20th centuries, observers of burned over lands frequently commented on the seemingly destructive effects of fire on the forest and site. Careful scientific measurements in recent decades, however, have resulted in a more nuanced assessment of fire impacts. The effects of fire on site productivity, for example, are so variable that generalizations are difficult to make. Some authors have noted that almost any effects of fire—positive, negative, or neutral—can be documented by the results of reputable researchers (18). Clearly the intensity of the fire, characteristics of the site, and weather conditions after the fire have much bearing on the outcome.

Most erosion following fires can be traced to either or both of the following causes: 1) exposure of bare soil through burning of the protective litter layer; 2) reduction of soil porosity (and hence increased runoff of water) through intense heating or clogging of soil pores by fine particles carried in runoff. Light or moderate fires such as most pre-scribed burns usually do not expose enough soil to cause serious erosion. Similarly, soil temperatures during prescribed burning are rarely hot enough to cause structural changes in the soil.

Crown fires or fires burning in logging slash, on the other hand, may be intense enough to alter soil structure, as well as leave bare patches of unpro-tected soil. Erosion will usually be more severe on steep slopes than on gently sloping or level sites. Following a severe wildfire in Idaho, about 30 per-cent of the sample plots on gently sloping sites showed significant erosion, compared to over 80 percent on steep slopes (19). A burned area is usu-ally revegetated by shrubs and tree seedlings within a few years, so the critical period of susceptibility to erosion does not last long.

The influence of fire on soil fertility also depends on fire intensity and location. Significant quantities of some nutrients, particularly nitrogen, can be lost to the atmosphere during the combustion of organic matter, with losses proportional to fire intensity. These losses, on the other hand, may be partly or fully compensated by an increase in available nutri-ents and processes such as nitrogen fixation. For example, thirty years of annual or periodic pre-scribed burns in South Carolina had little effect on the total amount of nutrients in the forest floor and soil layers (20).

Fires influence animal populations primarily by modifying habitat. Most fires cause little direct mor-tality to mobile animals, which usually can move away from the fire or escape beneath the ground in soil burrows. Prescribed burns may improve habitat for some animals by increasing the pro-tein and nutrient content of forage, but they may decrease habitat suitability for others that prefer the presence of dense undergrowth and woody debris. Crown fires that kill most of the canopy trees often cause a major shift in animal species composition from those that prefer mature forest to those that prefer open, shrubby habitat and early successional forests.

Smoke from forest fires has come under scrutiny in recent years as a significant contribu-tion to the overall air pollution problem. One ton of burning forest fuel releases approximately 1 ton of CO_2, 25 kilograms of carbon monoxide, 5 kilo-grams of hydrocarbons, 5 kilograms of particulates, and small amounts of nitrogen oxides. Forest fires are responsible for about 8 percent by weight of all atmospheric pollutants in the United States (21). Although open burning is restricted in many states and counties, exceptions are often granted for pre-scribed burning, partly because it does not consti-tute a major source of pollutants. It is probable that prescribed burning will be more closely regulated in the future; even now, air quality is often con-sidered in selecting days suitable for burning.

Fire in the Wilderness

In 1968, without much fanfare and on an experi-mental basis, the National Park Service began to allow certain lightning fires to burn unhindered in parts of Sequoia and Kings Canyon National Parks in California. This marked the beginning of an offi-cial policy to restore natural fire to certain wilder-ness areas. This alteration of the long-established policy of suppressing all forest fires came about partly in response to the obvious changes that were occurring in the national parks as a result of over-protecting them from fire. Like many western forests, 19th century forests in the Sierra Nevada were often park-like with little undergrowth because of frequent surface fires. By 1963, the Leopold Committee, assigned by the Department of the Interior to make recommendations on elk habitat and management in the parks, noted that much of the western slope of the Sierra Nevada was a "dog-hair thicket" of young trees and brush. The committee wondered:

> **Is it possible that the primitive open forest could be restored, at least on a local scale? And if so, how? We cannot offer an answer. But we are posing a question to which there should be an answer of immense concern to the National Park Service.**

Other pressing problems dictated a prompt response. The giant sequoias, whose preservation was entrusted to the Park Service, were not regenerating, because they lacked a suitable seedbed and because of competition with the dense understory of white fir. Moreover, understory fuels were accumulating to the point that conflagrations were likely. In 1965, prescribed burning was initiated in some sequoia groves to correct this situation.

If the goal of park and wilderness management were merely to maintain certain desirable forest environments, it is likely that the policy of fire suppression would have merely been modified to allow for an active program of prescribed burning. However, such action would seem to violate the spirit and intent of wilderness preservation. The congressional act of 1916 that created the National Park Service, to be sure, emphasized mainly protection of parklands in order to leave them "unimpaired" for future generations. However, the Wilderness Act of 1964 was much more explicit in defining wilderness to be an area that retains its "primeval character and influence," where "man himself is a visitor who does not remain," and that is managed to preserve natural conditions.

Neither prescribed burning by itself nor total fire suppression seems appropriate under this concept of wilderness—the former because it is manipulative and somewhat arbitrary and the latter because it constitutes major indirect human modification of the vegetation in naturally fire-prone environments.

The Approach

Full restoration of the natural fire regime in wilderness areas is usually not feasible, because some fires would inevitably threaten to burn beyond the park boundaries onto private land, or endanger human life inside or outside the park. The current intent of the natural-fire management policy is to allow fire to "more nearly play its natural role" whenever possible. In most wilderness areas, several management zones corresponding to different vegetation types and fuel conditions have been established. Each lightning fire is monitored, and a particular fire may be allowed to burn, or its spread may be blocked in one direction, or it may be totally suppressed. The decision is based on the

vegetation types, fuels, projected fire weather, and location of the fire in relation to human development or private property (Figure 18.14). Most fires caused by human beings continue to be suppressed. Prescribed burning is sometimes used in zones where management of natural fires is not feasible or where heavy, unnatural accumulations of fuels must be reduced artificially in preparation for natural-fire management.

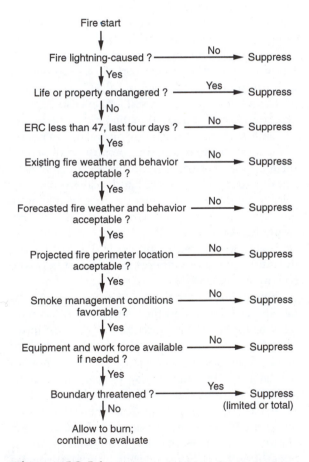

Figure 18.14 Decision flowchart for evaluating fires occurring in high-elevation areas of a wilderness tract in the Kootenai National Forest of Montana. "ERC" refers to the Energy Release Component, an index from the National Fire-Danger Rating System that indicates potential fire intensity. (Courtesy of the U.S.D.A. Forest Service.)

Thirty Years of Natural Fire Management

Wilderness fire restoration programs have been established primarily in the high-elevation zones of some major western wilderness areas, such as Yellowstone, Yosemite, Sequoia, Kings Canyon, and Grand Teton National Parks, and the Selway-Bitterroot Wilderness Area in Idaho. Everglades National Park in Florida is an example of an eastern park firmly committed to natural-fire management.

Experience with the policy in a number of different wilderness areas has shown that most lightning fires in high mountainous terrain never burn more than a small area before they die out naturally. In Sequoia and Kings Canyon National Parks, for example, 80 percent of lightning fires allowed to burn never reached more than 0.1 hectare (one-quarter acre) in size, and only 5 percent exceed 120 hectares (300 acres) (22). Yet some large and dramatic fires have also occurred since 1968. Perhaps the most difficult and controversial aspect of managing natural fires is that in certain forest types, fire cannot be harnessed to burn a small percentage of the forest at regular intervals, analogous to a forest placed under sustained even-aged management. If 1 or 2 percent of a park were to be burned in isolated patches every few years, the policy might not attract more than mild curiosity from the media and most of the general public. However, occasional large and dramatic blazes can understandably provoke opposition to the policy from some citizens and government officials, even though most conservationists have accepted natural fire management as the best way to maintain biotic diversity and wildlife habitat in wilderness areas.

The first major test of the policy occurred in 1974, when a lightning fire in a dry year burned 1,400 hectares (3,500 acres) in Grand Teton National Park (Figure 18.15). This event attracted widespread media attention, and for most people it was the first time that they had heard of the policy. The fire, although sizable, was not troublesome to manage and left a desirable mosaic of mature forest and younger vegetation. It also affected only a small percentage of the park.

Figure 18.15 A lightning fire allowed to burn in Grand Teton National Park, Wyoming, as part of a program to restore the natural occurrence and effects of fires in wilderness areas. (*Denver Post* photograph by Bill Wuensch.)

The most difficult test of the natural-fire policy occurred in the summer of 1988 in Yellowstone National Park. A natural-fire policy had already been in effect at Yellowstone for seventeen years, but fires of significant size (greater than 20 hectares) had occurred in only four of these years. Before 1988, none of the fires had ever burned more than a tiny fraction of the park's 890,000 hectares (2.2 million acres). Weather conditions in the late spring of 1988 were fairly close to normal, and a few lightning fires at that time were burning under surveillance. However, by midsummer it became apparent that drought conditions, carrying over from the previous year, were approaching a very hazardous level. In mid-July park officials shifted to a policy of vigorous suppression of all fires, regardless of origin. Because of the severe drought and high winds, however, suppression of existing and subsequent fires was virtually impossible.

By the end of the season, eight separate fires had engulfed about 45 percent of the park, although nearly half of this total area was affected by surface fires that did not kill the trees. Three of the fires, totaling 276,000 hectares (690,000 acres) were started by humans and had been fought vigorously from the time of their discovery. Park biologists pointed out that even if the natural-fire policy had not been in place, at least 25 to 30 percent of the park would have burned anyway.

There is little doubt that in naturally fire-prone environments—which include most of the western national parks—occasional large fires are inevitable, even with a policy of total suppression. However, a panel appointed to review federal policy was very critical of Yellowstone Park for not having experienced fire managers on its staff, for not having a detailed written fire management plan (such as the one summarized in Figure 18.14), and for minimal efforts at public education and public input into the plans. Other agencies in the Rocky Mountain region recognized the extraordinary drought conditions in 1988 and aggressively fought fires that season (23). Since 1988, regulations for allowing natural fires have been tightened, resulting in fewer and smaller fires.

The Yellowstone experience has also raised the question of whether even our largest parks are necessarily viable microcosms of wilderness ecosystems. Most ecologists have assumed that in order to sustain viable populations of plants and animals, a park needs to be large enough that individual disturbances cannot alter the balance of the overall park ecosystem. The 1988 fires demonstrated that Yellowstone is probably not an "equilibrium landscape," despite its vast size. Thus, while management of lightning fires and prescribed burning are likely to remain a prominent aspect of wilderness management, the details of how managers might deal with the wildly erratic fluctuations in natural fire occurrence have yet to be determined.

Concluding Statement—The Challenge of Fire Management

There is a strong consensus among ecologists and resource managers that fire should not, and ultimately cannot, be excluded from those ecosystems that were historically adapted to fire. In such ecosystems, exclusion of fire will lead to a buildup of fuels and unhealthy trees that will increase the risk of widespread conflagrations. However, several decades of experiments with natural fire manage-ment have put into sharp relief some challenges that fire managers will face in the coming years. First, it is becoming increasingly apparent that true restoration of natural fire frequency on a large scale may be impractical for many public lands because staff size, time, and funds are too limited for such a vast undertaking (24), and there are many constraints imposed by weather and private property. Second, despite careful planning, it is likely that some prescribed fires and natural lightning fires will continue to escape beyond intended bounds. This is especially likely for lightning fires in wilderness areas, since such fires often burn for months and can potentially reach an unmanageable size. Blowups and uncontrollable behavior become increasingly likely along some point of a sprawling fire perimeter if weather conditions suddenly change. Third, in less remote areas, continued development of vacation homes and tourist-related businesses dispersed within the patchwork mosaic pattern of public and private land ownership may compromise the ability of agencies to implement a large-scale program of prescribed burning.

Solving these problems may require a fundamental rethinking of land-use zoning policies in wildland areas, as well as a willingness of resource managers to set more modest goals in restoring the natural role of fire. In areas outside of parks and near human development, fire use may have to be more limited and supplemented by other methods of fuel reduction such as mechanical thinning. While such measures may not be ideal in the ecological sense, they may be the only practical solution to maintaining diversity and resilience in a landscape that is no longer governed largely by natural forces.

References

1. A. R. TAYLOR, *J. For.*, *68*, 476 (1971).

2. B. L. GRAHAM, R. L. HOLLE, AND R. E. LOPEZ, *Fire Management Notes*, *57* (2), 4, (1997).

3. H. E. ANDERSON, "Sundance Fire: An Analysis of Fire Phenomena," U.S.D.A. For. Serv. Res. Pap. INT-56, 1968.

4. J. K. AGEE, *Fire Ecology of Pacific Northwest Forests*, Island Press, Washington, D.C., 1993.

5. C. G. LORIMER AND L. E. FRELICH, *J. For.*, *92* (1), 33 (1994).

6. T. MORTON, New English Canaan, or New Canaan, Containing an Abstract of New England (1632), reprinted in *New English Canaan of Thomas Morton,* C. F. Adams. Jr., ed., Prince Society Publications, Vol. 14. Burt Franklin, New York (1967).

7. S. PERLEY, *Historic Storms of New England*, Salem Press and Printing Co., Salem, Mass., 1891.

8. R. K. MILLER, "The Keetch-Byram Drought Index and three fires in upper Michigan, 1976," In *Fifth National Conf. on Fire and Forest Meteorology*, Am. Meteorol. Soc., Boston, 1978.

9. F. A. ALBINI, "Spot Fire Distance from Burning Trees— a Predictive Model." U.S.D.A. For. Serv., Gen. Tech. Rep. INT-56, 1979.

10. F. A. Albini, "Estimating Wildfire Behavior and Effects." U.S.D.A. For. Serv., Gen. Tech. Rep. INT-30, 1976.

11. R. C. ROTHERMEL, "A Mathematical Model for Predicting Fire Spread in Wildland Fuels," U.S.D.A. For. Serv., Res. Pap. INT-115, 1972.

12. R. C. ROTHERMEL ET AL., "Modeling Moisture Content of Fine Dead Wildland Fuels: Input to the BEHAVE Fire Prediction System," U.S.D.A. For. Serv., Res. Pap INT-359, 1986.

13. P. L. ANDREWS AND R. E. BURGAN, "'BEHAVE' in the wilderness." In *Proc. Symp. and Workshop on Wilderness Fire*, U.S.D.A. For. Serv., Gen. Tech. Rep. INT-182, 1985.

14. U.S.D.A. Forest Service, *Wildfire Statistics, 1984–1990*, Washington, D.C., 1992.

15. R. W. MUTCH, *J. For.*, *92* (11) 31 (1994).

16. S. F. ARNO, "The concept: restoring ecological structure and process in ponderosa pine forests." In *The Use of Fire in Forest Restoration,* U.S.D.A. For. Serv., Gen Tech. Rep. INT-GTR-341, 1996.

17. N. SAMPSON, *Wildfire News and Notes*, *10* (2), 1 (1996).

18. C. CHANDLER, ET AL., *Fire in Forestry, Volume 1: Forest Fire Behavior and Effects*, Wiley, New York, 1983.

19. C. A. CONAUGHTON, *J. For.* ,*33*, 751 (1935).

20. T. A. WALDROP ET AL., "Long-term Studies of Prescribed Burning of Loblolly Pine Forests of the Southeastern Coastal Plain," U.S.D.A. For. Serv., Gen. Tech. Rep. SE-45, 1987.

21. J. H. DIETERICH, "Prescribed burning and air quality." In *Southern Pine Management—Today and Tomorrow*, 20th Ann. For. Symp., Louisiana State Univ., Division of Continuing Education, Baton Rouge, 1971.

22. B. M. KILGORE, *Western Wildlands*, *10* (3), 2 (1984).

23. R. H. WAKIMOTO, *J. For.*, *88* , 22 (1990).

24. D. J. PARSONS AND S. J. BOTTI, "Restoration of fire in national parks." In *The Use of Fire in Forest Restoration*, U.S.D.A. For. Serv., Gen Tech. Rep. INT-GTR-341, 1996.

CHAPTER 19

Timber Harvesting

ROBERT M. SHAFFER AND
THOMAS A. WALBRIDGE, JR.

The United States is the world's largest producer and consumer of forest products. Each American uses an average of 749 pounds of paper products and 18 cubic feet of solid wood products annually (1). As the world's economies grow, so does the global demand for paper and forest products. The U.S.D.A. Forest Service estimates that worldwide annual consumption of forest products, currently at 18 billion cubic feet, will continue to increase, reaching a total of 25 billion cubic feet by 2050 (2).

America's logging industry performs the critical process of supplying the raw wood necessary to meet the growing demand for manufactured forest products. There are approximately 35,000 independent logging firms operating in the United States today (3). These small businesses typically employ 5–15 workers and have anywhere from $500,000 to $1.5 million invested in logging equipment. Many independent logging companies contract with forest industry firms to provide timber harvesting services. Other logging firms purchase stumpage, or standing timber, directly from forest landowners, then harvest and sell the processed logs or pulpwood to consuming forest products mills. Many loggers are third and fourth generation—they often

employ other family members in their operation. Logging contractors are generally paid on a production basis, and are heavily impacted financially by factors that affect their production, like inclement weather, absentee workers, equipment breakdowns, and temporary wood inventory surplus at the mill they supply. Today's typical logging firm is characterized by high fixed costs, including substantial equipment payments, high labor turnover, high insurance costs, and a relatively low profit margin.

Today's loggers operate under intense public scrutiny. They must plan and conduct their operation so as to meet federally mandated forest water quality protection standards and minimize site impacts to ensure long-term sustainability of the forest resource. At the same time, logging contractors must operate efficiently and productively and satisfy their customers, both forest landowner and forest industry, to remain in business. Finally, they must have a high awareness and comittment for safety, since logging is one of the nation's most hazardous occupations, with an injury rate 2.5 times the average for all other industries (4). To successfully meet these challenges, many loggers regularly participate in professional education and training opportunities sponsored through state forestry associations, the Cooperative Extension Service, or forest industry firms. National and state logger associations also provide educational opportunities, as well as a voice for loggers on issues affecting their business. Additional general and technical information on the logging industry can be obtained through the websites of the Forest Resources Association [http://www.forestresources. org] and the American Loggers Council [http:// www.americanloggers.org].

Figure 19.2 This track-mounted feller-buncher generates low ground pressure and minimizes soil compaction and rutting.

Timber Harvesting Operations

The common functions of a timber harvesting operation are: 1) felling the tree; 2) delimbing and topping the tree; 3) moving (skidding, forwarding, yarding, flying) the tree from the stump to the landing or log deck (a centralized location where the trees are gathered, processed, and loaded onto a truck); 4) bucking the tree into specified merchantable lengths; 5) loading the logs onto a truck; and 6) hauling the logs to a forest products mill.

Felling can be acomplished manually with a chainsaw or mechanically with a rubber-tired (Fig-

ure 19.1) or track-mounted (Figure 19.2) feller-buncher or a multifunction machine called a harvester (Figure 19.3). Mechanical felling machines eliminate much of the safety risk involved with manual chainsaw felling, the most dangerous part of a logging operation.

Delimbing and *topping* (removing the limbs and unmerchantable top of the tree) can be accomplished manually with a chainsaw or mechanically with a

Figure 19.1 Rubber-tired feller-bunchers are productive—this highly maneuverable three-wheeled model is well-suited for thinning.

Figure 19.3 A harvester is a multifunction machine that fells, delimbs, tops, measures, and bucks the tree at the stump.

stroke (Figure 19.4) or pull-through delimber or with a multifunction harvester. Loggers can reduce the likelihood of injury by incorporating mechanical delimbing and further reducing their use of a chainsaw. Delimbing and topping may be performed at the stump or at the log landing, depending on the logging system employed.

Skidding (dragging the tree with one end suspended) the trees from the stump to the landing or log deck can be accomplished with a rubber-tired (Figure 19.5) or track-mounted skidder. Skidders are equipped with a hydraulic grapple or a winch and set of wire rope cables to support the ends of the trees above the ground. Skidders generally transport tree-length stems. A small number of loggers continue to use draft horses or mules to drag cut-to-length logs from the stump to the landing.

Forwarding (carrying the logs on the back of a machine) the trees from the stump to the landing is accomplished with a rubber-tired (Figure 19.6) or track-mounted forwarder. Forwarders generally transport log-length stems, which must be delimbed, topped, and bucked at the stump.

Cable yarding (lifting and moving suspended trees attached to an overhead cable) the trees from the stump to the landing is accomplished with a

Figure 19.5 A rubber-tired grapple skidder, combined with a feller-buncher, forms a productive and cost-efficient logging system.

stationary cable yarder (Figure 19.7) equipped with a drum winch set and tower. Yarders come in many sizes and the cable system can be set up in many different configurations. Yarders can move fully or partially suspended trees or logs either uphill or downhill along a preselected corridor.

Flying (lifting and moving fully suspended trees attached to a helicopter cable) the trees from the

Figure 19.4 A stroke delimber is a safe and effective mechanical delimbing machine for most softwood species.

Figure 19.6 A forwarder loads and transports cut-to-length logs from the stump to a roadside landing.

Figure 19.7 A skyline cable yarder system can harvest timber on steep mountain slopes with minimum soil disturbance.

stump to the landing requires a specially designed and equipped helicopter (Figure 19.8).

Bucking (cutting the tree into merchantable lengths) can be accomplished manually with a chainsaw or mechanically with a slasher saw or multipurpose harvester.

Loading the tree-length stems or cut-to-length logs onto a truck can be accomplished by a trailer-mounted (Figure 19.9) or track-mounted hydraulic knuckleboom loader or by a rubber-tired front-end loader.

Hauling the tree-length stems or cut-to-length logs to the forest products mill can be accomplished with a tractor-trailer log truck equipped with either a pole trailer or double-bunk log trailer (Figure 19.10), or a tandem-axle, straight-frame log truck.

Planning is a critical part of every timber harvesting operation (5). Good planning is necessary to meet production goals, comply with environmental and water quality protection standards, operate safely, minimize site disturbance, and meet silvicultural objectives. In several states, loggers are required to submit a timber harvesting plan to the state for review and approval before logging can begin. A typical timber harvest plan contains information on haul road location and construction techniques, location and layout of log landings, provisions for water quality and riparian zone protection measures (commonly called Best Management Practices or BMPs) (6), safe operating considerations, stream crossing locations and structures, wildlife considerations (if applicable), protection of residual timber, mitigation of site impacts, and post-harvest soil stabilization procedures.

Figure 19.8 A helicopter logging system can greatly reduce the need for logging road construction in environmentally sensitive areas.

Figure 19.9 A hydraulic knuckleboom loader is a common sight on most logging operations in the United States today.

Common Timber Harvesting Systems

A number of timber harvesting systems operate throughout the various forested regions of the United States. A particular logging system is chosen on the basis of topography, timber stand characteristics, silvicultural considerations, accessibility,

Figure 19.10 A truck with a double-bunk log trailer can haul either tree-length stems or cut-to-length logs.

local mill requirements, environmental considerations, and safety concerns. The system that is best for logging a group-selection timber sale in an oak-hickory forest on 40% slopes in the Appalachian mountains may not be the best system for harvesting a pine plantation thinning in the coastal plain region of Georgia. Professional logging engineers, logging contractors, and industrial foresters have the training and expertise to develop and match the proper logging system to each timber harvesting site to accomplish the production, safety, economic and environmental goals that will make the operation a success. The more common timber harvesting systems operating in various regions of the United States today are described in the following sections.

Manual Chainsaw/Cable Skidder System

Trees are felled, delimbed, and topped manually, skidded with a rubber-tired cable skidder to the landing where they are manually or mechanically bucked, and loaded onto a log truck with a hydraulic knuckleboom loader. This system typically produces 200–300 tons of cut-to-length logs and pulpwood per week. It requires 3–5 employees, a moderate capital investment, and can be used in a wide variety of operating conditions and harvesting applications. This versatile logging system is most common in the Northeast, Appalachian region, Lake States and Midwest, but can be found in every forested region of the country. In some areas of the mountainous West, a tracked skidder is more commonly used in this system.

Feller-Buncher/Grapple Skidder System

Trees are mechanically felled and bunched in multiple-stem piles, the bunches are skidded with grapple skidders, mechanically topped and delimbed at the landing with a stroke or pull-through delimber, and loaded tree-length onto log trailers with a knuckleboom loader. This highly productive and cost-efficient system can produce 700–1000 tons per week with 8–10 workers. It is restricted to moderate slopes and requires a capital investment exceeding $500,000. Nearly 70 percent of the wood harvested in the South is produced by this logging

system. The feller-buncher/grapple skidder system can be combined with a large wood chipping machine (Figure 19.11) to produce in-woods chips from pulpwood, which can be efficiently hauled in chip vans (modified box trailers) from the logging site to a paper mill.

Harvester/Forwarder (Cut-to-Length) System

Trees are mechanically felled, topped, delimbed and bucked at the stump with a rubber-tired or track-mounted harvester equipped with a multifunction processing head. The cut-to-length logs or pulpwood are then self-loaded onto a forwarder and transported to roadside where they are off-loaded onto double-bunk log trailers. This two-worker, two-machine logging system (not counting log truck drivers) is "soft" on the environment and can produce 400–600 tons per week on gentle topography. Capital investment for this system exceeds $600,000. The harvester/forwarder logging system originated in Scandinavia, and is beginning to find a niche in all regions of the United States.

Figure 19.11 An in-woods chipper can fully utilize the woody biomass on the site and reduce subsequent reforestation costs.

Cable Yarder (Skyline) System

Trees are manually felled, delimbed, topped, and bucked at the stump, attached by wire-rope chokers (cable fasteners) to a moveable carriage suspended from a large overhead skyline cable strung 1,000–2,000 feet or more along a corridor between the stationary yarder tower and a tail-hold stump or tree in the woods. Large mechanical drum winches in the yarder are powered to lift and reel in the carriage and attached logs along the highly tensioned skyline cable to the landing, where they are loaded onto trailers with a track-mounted hydraulic loader. Cable yarding systems are highly technical and can be configured to move logs uphill or downhill. This system is ideal for steep mountain terrain and is the predominate logging system in the Pacific Northwest. A typical operation employs 8–10 workers, has more than $1 million invested in equipment, and produces 1000+ tons of logs per week.

Helicopter Logging System

Trees are manually felled, delimbed, topped, and bucked at the stump. Logs are attached with short wire-rope chokers to a coupling device at the end of a long, high-strength cable hanging from a helicopter hovering above. The specially designed helicopter lifts a pre-measured, precisely weighted bundle of logs and flies them quickly to the landing. At the landing, the helicopter pilot carefully lowers the logs to the ground and releases them electronically from the coupling device. The logs are moved a short distance from the landing's drop zone to the truck loading area with a grapple skidder, then loaded onto trailers with a hydraulic knuckleboom loader. Helicopter logging crews can produce as much as 2,500 tons of logs per week with a crew of 10–15 workers. A helicopter equipped for logging can cost well over $1.5 million. Helicopter logging is expensive and may not be economically feasible for accessible timber harvesting sites with average timber values. However, for high timber-value sites where accessibility is difficult and road building costs are excessive, or where environmental constraints prohibit conven-

tional ground-based or cable logging systems, it offers a viable alternative. Helicopter logging systems can be found operating in challenging harvesting sites from the mountains of Alaska to the coastal plains of Florida.

Logging machines and systems are constantly evolving to meet the needs of society. Where high productivity was once the paramount criteria, minimizing environmental impact is now an equally important consideration in the development or application of new or modified timber harvesting machines or systems. For example, skidders can be equipped with super-wide, high-flotation tires to reduce ground pressure and eliminate soil rutting. Temporary bridge mats can be used in lieu of earth-filled culverts for temporary stream crossings on sites where water quality protection is critical. Cable yarding systems can be configured to provide full suspension to move logs cleanly over the tops of trees retained in a forested riparian buffer zone. Special underlayment fabric can be used with crushed rock surfacing to protect sensitive soils during haul road construction and usage.

Safety is also a major consideration in logging machine and system development. Because of its historically high injury rate, logging industry firms must pay Workers' Compensation Insurance (WCI) premium rates that are among the highest for any industry (7). Studies have shown that replacing a worker on the ground using a chainsaw with a worker in the enclosed, protected cab of a machine will dramatically reduce the incidence of accidents, injuries, and fatalities. For example, a logging contractor who replaces a worker performing manual chainsaw delimbing with a stroke delimbing machine can expect to see the firm's annual injury rate fall by nearly 50 percent (8). Accordingly, the firm's WCI premium rates will eventually decline as well, thus reducing overhead costs.

Logging Aesthetics

Modern timber harvesting has a public image problem. Overwhelming scientific evidence confirms the fact that logging, when well planned and performed properly, has little or no detrimental effect on water quality (9), site productivity, soil erosion, wildlife populations, biological diversity, endangered species, or forest resource sustainability. Forestry experts agree that timber harvesting is a critical tool to achieve silvicultural objectives such as forest regeneration, species or stocking control, or timber stand improvement. A timely and well-managed timber harvest can protect or improve forest health by surgically removing a source of insect or disease infestation, recover value through the salvage of dead and dying timber, and manage the threat of wildfire through strategic woody fuels reduction.

However, the general public often views a timber harvest as something akin to environmental devastation, simply because an unattractive landscape now exists where a mature forest of beautiful trees recently grew. To many people, it only seems logical that any operation that would create such an unattractive scene *must* be harmful to the environment, even if the area is quickly reforested. It is this line of uninformed reasoning that sometimes drives individuals to petition their local and state officials to prohibit or unduly restrict timber harvesting in their area.

In response to this issue of timber harvesting aesthetics, many logging contractors, forest industry firms, and forest landowners have voluntarily adopted techniques that can soften the initial negative visual response to a recently harvested site (10). A few of these techniques include:

- Retain a visual buffer of trees along public road corridors adjacent to the harvested area.

- Shield log landings from public view by using topography or vegetative buffers; clear landings of all woody debris, level and smooth the ground, and "green-up" the area with grass seed and mulch.

- Avoid leaving rutted haul roads or skid trails. Lop and scatter large, unmerchantable tree tops and limbs in highly visible areas.

- When clearcutting, create a natural-appearing, uneven edge, and leave small clumps of trees irregularly placed across the harvested area.

- Minimize the amount of logging debris by maximizing the utilization of each tree.

While judicious use of these and other techniques may somewhat reduce the negative aesthetics of a recent timber harvest, many people will continue to express concern any time they see an area where trees have been cut. Educating them that forests are truly a renewable and sustainable resource may be the most effective way to influence public opinion.

Logging in the 21st Century

A number of emerging technologies will likely have an impact on timber harvesting machine and system development into the 21st century (11). Among them are:

1. *Machine control systems.* Timber harvesting machines may be equipped with intelligent control systems that will enable the machine to adapt to the surrounding environment. For example, sensors will signal the machine when it is on wet or steep ground or when the wheels are beginning to lose traction. The machine will then automatically adapt to its working conditions in a way that will optimize performance and minimize environmental impact.

2. *Robotics.* Machines may accomplish systematic and repetitive functions robotically. These functions could include placing logs in a pile, acquiring a tree for delimbing, or moving ahead to the next tree. In such a system, the operator may simply point a control lever in the desired direction, and onboard computers will control the hydraulic valves and cylinders to achieve the desired function.

3. *Positioning systems.* Timber harvesting machines may be equipped with satellite-linked navigation controls based on global positioning system (GPS) technology. (See Chapter 12 for a description of GPS). The operator would deploy the machine using a map displayed on a computer screen in the cab.

4. *Machine vision.* Timber harvesting equipment in the 21st century may incorporate a form of

machine vision that will recognize and evaluate trees or logs to be handled or processed and will automatically respond accordingly. For example, an intelligent camera system will measure and select trees by diameter and form for an automated felling machine to cut.

5. *Lightweight machine components.* Lighter, stronger logging machine components constructed with aerospace materials like kevlar, aluminum, and carbon fiber will help to increase logging machine capacity and reduce environmental impacts. For example, telescoping booms made of lightweight composites could be extended on felling machines to allow operators to reach further into a timberstand to fell a tree without moving the machine, thus minimizing ground disturbance.

6. *Enhanced communications.* In the years ahead, a logging manager will be able to use a portable computer to check on the exact location of a log truck, monitor the fuel level in a skidder, or determine the up-to-the-minute production from several harvesting sites. A customer in France will be able to instantaneously send a lumber order to a sawmill in North Carolina, who will communicate the log species and size specifications needed to produce the lumber to a logging contractor at a harvest site in the forest, who will program the harvester's on-board computer to fill the order, all in the same day.

Concluding Statement

As long as there is a demand for paper and wood products, the professional logging contractors who own and operate the high-tech logging machines and systems will continue to face the challenges of efficiently and safely producing wood for a global market at a competitive cost. In addition, they must protect the environment and do their part to ensure the long-term sustainability of the forest resource.

References

1. ANON., "U.S. Forest Facts and Figures," American Forest & Paper Association, Washington, D.C., 1995.

2. ANON., "An Analysis of the Timber Situation in the United States, 1952–2030," U.S.D.A. Forest Service Research Report 23, 1982.

3. ANON., "Census Classification of Industries and Occupations," U.S. Commerce Department, Washington, D.C., 1990.

4. ANON., "Injuries in the Logging Industry," U.S. Dept. of Labor, Bureau of Labor Statistics, Washington, D.C., 1984.

5. G. STENZEL, T. A. WALBRIDGE, AND J. K. PEARCE, *Logging and Pulpwood Production*, Second Edition, John Wiley & Sons, New York, 1985.

6. ANON., "Forestry Best Management Practices for Water Quality in Virginia, Technical Guide," Third Edition, Virginia Department of Forestry, Charlottesville, 1997.

7. G. E. WILSON, "Worker's Compensation Insurance Primer for the Logging Industry," Technical Report No. 90-A-3, American Pulpwood Association, Rockville, Md., 1990.

8. R. M. SHAFFER AND J. S. MILBURN, *Forest Products Journal, 49 (7/8)*, 4 (1999).

9. N. S. YOHO, *Southern J. Applied Forestry, 4 (1)*, 27.

10. ANON., "Forestry aesthetics guide," American Pulpwood Association, Rockville, Md., 1998.

11. D. Y. GUIMIER, "Forestry operations in the next century." In *Forest Operations for Sustainable Forests and Healthy Economies*, Proceedings of the 20th Annual meeting of the Council on Forest Engineering, Rapid City, S.D., 1997.

CHAPTER 20

Wood Products

EUGENE M. WENGERT AND
RAYMOND A. YOUNG

Figure 20.1 Early European settlers to North America used the plentiful wood supply for housing, fencing, and a myriad of other essential purposes.

Importance of Wood Products

Trees produce many benefits, including watershed protection, wildlife habitat, and recreation opportunities. However, of all the benefits of trees, the greatest is probably from the wood they produce. Wood is nature's nearly perfect composite material, and it is also renewable (1).

Wood provides the fuel for cooking and heating; the material for shelters (Figure 20.1); the material for furniture, cabinets, and other "essentials" for living; and wood is the raw material for fiber-based panels, paper, and paper products (2). For millenniums, the primary use for wood has been for fuel—cooking and heating—worldwide. It is only in the so-called "developed countries" that oil and coal have replaced wood-based fuels. As a result, uses of wood in developed countries are at about the same level for both solid wood products and pulp-derived products (Table 20.1). Pulp is used to make paper and paper-related products, such as fiberboard, and chemical commodities, while sawlogs are used for lumber, which in turn is used for housing construction, cabinets, furniture, and the like (Figure 20.2).

The amount of wood used annually in the United States is tremendous—over 500 billion pounds (227 billion kilograms) annually. It is estimated that the weight of wood used in the United States is equal to the weight of applications of all metals, plastics, and Portland cement. In fact, this large amount certainly indicates that the potential for significantly reduced reliance on wood would be difficult to achieve by substitution of metal, plastics, or Portland cement.

The general term for the various uses of wood is either *wood products,* or the more general term, *forest products*, which includes nonwood items such as pine cones, nuts, Christmas trees, mushrooms,

Table 20.1 How We Use Timber in the United States

Major Uses	Volume (%)
Sawlogs for lumber	30
Pulpwood for papermaking	29
Energy and other products	27
Composite boards (MDF, OSB, etc.)	9
Veneer and plywood	5

MDF—Medium-Density Fiberboard;
OSB—Oriented Strandboard

Source: Forest Products Laboratory, U.S.D.A., Forest Service, based on 1997 data.

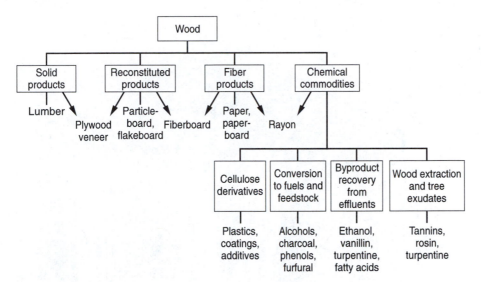

Figure 20.2
Summary of uses for wood.

and so on. Certainly in North America, as well as other developed countries, it is the monetary value received from harvesting, manufacturing and selling wood products (often called value-added processing) that allows for many timber stand improvement activities. Forest products activities result in the generation of substantial value-added income, especially in rural economies, thereby creating and generating an important source of individual and community economic viability. For example, in Wisconsin in 1998, forest products industries employed nearly 100,000 people and ranked as the #1 manufacturing industry in nearly 1/3 of the counties in the state. Forest products generated 17 percent of the value-added manufacturing income in the state.

Wood Properties

Wood is a composite product that has distinct properties, both advantages and disadvantages such as:

- renewable, complex, cellular biological material
- biodegradable—most species are easily decomposed by fungi (and bacteria) back into carbon, hydrogen, and oxygen when the moisture content is over 20 percent (oven-dry basis)

- anisotropic (different properties in different directions)
- hygroscopic (continually absorbs or desorbs moisture from the surrounding air in order to achieve moisture equilibrium)
- shrinks with loss of moisture and swells with gain in moisture
- combustible (over 400°F [200°C])
- relatively inert to most chemicals
- durable, if protected from moisture
- good insulator of sound, heat, and electricity, especially when dry
- easily cut to size required with simple tools and with little energy
- easily fastened with nails, screws and adhesives
- high strength-to-weight ratio

What Is Wood?

Wood is made of cells, which are typically long, slender (100 times longer than their diameter), hollow tubes (Figure 20.3). The role of the cells in the living tree is to conduct fluids from the roots to the leaves. In softwoods, the major cells runs vertically in the tree (called the longitudinal direction) and

Figure 20.3 Wood is made of long, hollow tubes called cells. In a softwood, more than 85% of the cells run vertically in the tree, with the remainder of the cells running horizontally from the bark toward the center of the tree. This is a resinous softwood, shown schematically.

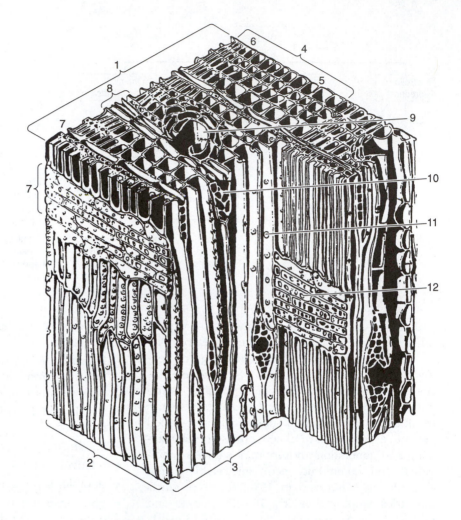

Softwood Key

1. Cross-sectional face	7. Wood ray
2. Radial face	8. Fusiform ray
3. Tangential face	9. Vertical resin duct
4. Annual ring	10. Horizontal resin duct
5. Earlywood	11. Bordered pit
6. Latewood	12. Simple pit

are called *tracheids*. Their length is 0.1 to 0.2 inches (3 to 5 mm). In hardwoods, the major cells are vessels, running longitudinally. Their length are typically 0.04 to 0.08 inches (1 to 2 mm). In addition to the longitudinal cells, 5 to 15 percent of the cells run radially (from the bark toward the center of the tree) in both softwoods and hardwoods and are

called *ray parenchyma* cells. These are short, stubby cells that are involved in the storage of starches and sugars. Parenchyma cells that run longitudinally can also be found frequently in hardwoods. Occasionally, there may be an opening between the cells. Softwoods also contain resin ducts or resin canals and hardwoods may have gum ducts. Various resins and other compounds are secreted into these ducts (3).

There are no cells that run tangent to the annual growth rings, called the tangential direction. However, each cell has numerous small openings, called pits, which connect the cells both longitudinally and radially, and provide a multitude of flow paths for water and nutrients to flow from the roots to the leaves.

The hollow spaces in the cells, called lumens in softwoods and pores in hardwoods, are filled with water, various chemicals including starches and sugars, and air bubbles. In fact, because the predominant component of wood, cellulose (discussed later in the chapter), is 1.5 times heavier than water, if the air bubbles were not present in wood, it would not float. Hemlock is one species that at times has very few air bubbles and will not float; these logs are called

sinkers and may be found on the bottom of lakes and streams where logging was a past activity.

Sometimes, various chemicals will be deposited in the lumens or pores. These chemicals, called extractives, will give wood color, odor, and certain other properties including natural decay and insect resistance. These depositions are in cells that are usually several years old or older. Such cells are no longer participating in the life processes of the tree and so are called *heartwood* (Figure 20.4). The younger cells, which start at the cambium (bark) and proceed inward, and which eventually will become heartwood cells as they age, are called *sapwood*. Sapwood is usually white-colored, may have a higher moisture content than the heartwood, has a higher porosity, and has no natural decay resistance. Some species have only a few years of sapwood cells, such as northern-grown red oak

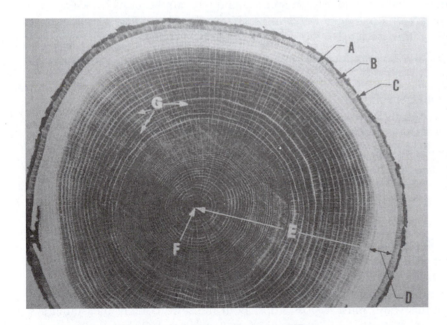

Figure 20.4 Cross-section of a white oak tree trunk: A, the cambium layer (microscopic), forms new wood and bark cells; B, the inner bark, contains living tissue and carries nutrients from the leaves to the growing parts of the tree; C, the outer bark, provides protection for the tree against physical damage, pathological damage, and drying; D, the sapwood, containing both living and dead tissue, carries sap from the roots to the leaves; E, the heartwood, containing dead tissue, is age-altered sapwood and usually contains chemicals that provide distinctive color, odor, low permeability, and decay and insect resistance; F, the pith, is the central nonwood core of the stem; G, the wood rays, running horizontally in the stem between the bark and the pith, transport liquids and chemicals, as well as store various nutrients.

Sidebar 20.1

Dendrochronology

Dendrochronology is the study of annual tree rings and is of value to scientists in a wide variety of disciplines. For example, climatic conditions can be evaluated according to the size of the rings. Narrow rings would be indicative of low rainfall or drought, while wide rings may indicate extensive rainfall (see Figure 20.4). Through the study of annual rings of very old trees, it is possible to reconstruct major climatic changes in the past. This area of emphasis is termed *dendroclimatology* and can provide information on such things as drought cycles. Of course there are other factors that influence the size of the annual rings, such as crowding by growth of other vegetation, which would reduce ring size, or harvesting and thinning operations, which would result in increased ring size. Defoliating insects could also reduce the size of the annual rings.

In 1937, Andrew Douglas founded the Laboratory of Tree Ring Research at the University of Arizona to promote the use of this approach. He utilized dendrochronology to date ancient pueblos in the Southwest by matching ring patterns from living trees, remains of fallen trees and wood samples from the ruins of the Pueblos. The dry conditions in the Southwest make this approach more viable, whereas in other, moister climates, the size of the rings are more consistent and there is greater decay of fallen and stored timber. However, dendrochronology continues to find new applications by scientists studying such things as the effects of pollution, forest fires, volcanoes, pests and earthquakes.

(perhaps 0.5 inch [1.3 cm] wide). Other species may have considerable amounts of sapwood, such as southern-grown red oak (perhaps 4 [10 cm] inches wide); yet other species, such as hard maple, are almost all sapwood, unless injured.

Moisture and Wood

In the living tree, there is about 60 percent wood and 40 percent water by weight, although there can be considerable variation from species to species, heartwood to sapwood, and tree to tree. For most uses of wood, much of this water must be removed (4).

Moisture content (MC) of wood is calculated and expressed in two different ways—the oven-dry basis and the wet-weight basis. The units are always in percent. For wood chips, particles, and pulpwood, the moisture content is:

$$MC\ (\%) = \frac{\text{Weight of water in wood}}{\text{Wet weight of wood (water + wood)}} \times 100$$

For lumber and other solid wood products, the moisture content is:

$$MC\ (\%) = \frac{\text{Weight of water in wood}}{\text{Oven-dry weight of wood}} \times 100$$

The oven-dry (O-D) weight is obtained by drying the wood in an oven at 216°F (102°C) until weight loss stops. Both moisture content measuring systems agree at 0 percent MC, but the difference between them increases as the MC increases. Considering a living Southern yellow pine tree with 50 percent oven-dry wood and 50 percent water—the MC is 50 percent MC (wet basis), but 100 percent MC (O-D basis).

Wood is a hygroscopic material, meaning that it will absorb or desorb moisture to obtain an equilibrium with the moisture in the air surrounding the wood. The relationship between the relative humidity of air (RH) and the MC varies little from species to species for most North American woods (Table 20.2). Some tropical species differ—they have lower MCs for the given RH than North American species. Wood that has been heated above 250°F (120°C), chemically treated, or irradiated with gamma rays may also have lower MC. The MC that wood achieves at a given RH is called the *equilibrium moisture* content (EMC) of the air.

The RH/EMC values (Table 20.2) are important values in that most houses and offices in North America range from 30 percent RH (winter) to 50 percent RH (summer). Most unheated buildings and most exterior climates in North America average 65 percent RH, while most coastal climates and most island climates average 80 percent RH.

If wood changes MC, then the wood will shrink (moisture loss) or swell (moisture gain) about 1/4 percent for every 1 percent MC change. MC change problems account for the vast majority of problems and poor performance with wood. However, if wood is dried to a MC close to the EMC in use, then little MC change and, therefore, little shrinkage or swelling will occur in use.

North American Wood Consumption

Wood has been an important material in the recent history of the United States. Native Americans used

Table 20.2 Key Values of RH and MC (Oven-dry Basis) for Wood

RH%	MC%	EMC%
0	0	0
30	6	6
50	9	9
65	12	12
80	16	16
100	28	28

RH—relative humidity; MC—moisture content; EMC—equilibrium moisture content

wood for heating, cooking, and shelter, as well as for implements and tools, including arrows. Early European settlers used wood for construction of commercial buildings (such as the windmill that has been reconstructed at Colonial Williamsburg), as well as for homes, implements, tools, fences, roads, piers and wharves, ships and other watercraft, and a myriad of other uses. Wood was indeed the material that built America during the last three centuries. When wood is kept dry (under 20 percent MC), it does not deteriorate, so it will last for centuries unless attacked by termites or other dry wood insects.

Today, annual wood use per capita continues to grow (Table 20.3). The uses for wood in the United States are over 60 billion board feet of lumber annually—about 75 percent of which is softwood lumber. About 1/3 of the lumber is used for new housing construction, 1/6 used for remodeling homes, 1/12 used for new nonresidential construction, 1/12 for manufacturing, and 1/12 for

Table 20.3 Per Capita Consumption of Several Wood Products in the United States over Past Years

| Product | Consumption, per capita per year | | | |
	1962	1970	1976	1986
Lumber (board feet)	210	194	205	237
Structural boards, including plywood & OSB (sq. ft—3/8")	51	69	82	107
Paper & fiberboards (pounds)	434	566	587	677

OSB—oriented strandboard

shipping (mainly pallets—over 600 million wooden pallets every year—Figure 20.5). The remaining is used for miscellaneous purposes including railroad ties, bridge timbers, and the like.

Home building is the bellwether of the U. S. economy. Although in 1991 we built only 1.0 million new homes, which is the lowest since WWII, in 1993 nearly 1.3 million homes were built in the United States. In the late 1990s, new housing construction was about 1.7 million annually, with over 1 million of these as single family units. A new home will use over 13,000 board feet of lumber (Figure 20.6) and 7,000 square feet of structural panels. This recent level of new housing growth is adequate to provide for the number of new households in the United States—in 2000 there were about 110 million households in the United States and by 2010, there will be about 121 million. In addition to strong housing, new houses today are larger and use more wood than in the previous decades—1,150 square feet in the '50s, 1,500 in the '70s, and 2,000 in the '90s. Many construction techniques today provide for more efficient use of wood (Figure 20.7). Accompanying housing growth is growth in allied products such as cabinets and furniture.

Figure 20.6   Wood frame construction is the typical construction method for homes in the United States.

Figure 20.7   Roof trusses are commonly used to speed construction and conserve natural resources. Similar truss systems are used for floors.

Figure 20.5   Wooden platforms, called pallets, are typically 40" × 48" and permit easy access by forklifts, so that large volumes of goods can be handled easily.

Conversion of Wood into Primary Wood Products

Wood products are divided into two main categories—primary products and secondary products. Primary products are those wood products made from a log. Primary products include lumber, poles, and pulp. Secondary products are those wood products made from a primary product. Secondary products include furniture, cabinets, and paper.

The procedures for converting logs into primary wood products vary depending on the product. Although the conversion efficiency also varies, it is not unusual to find that about 50 to 60 percent of the log's volume will end up in the primary wood product. Each product has certain raw material requirements as well. The following sections consider five products—lumber, plywood, particleboard, OSB (oriented strandboard), and MDF (medium-density fiberboard). Use of wood as a fuel is considered later in the chapter.

Raw Material Requirements

Each of the forest products that are produced from trees have certain quality specifications that are enumerated in the following paragraphs—straightness and diameter are usually paramount. Often, these specifications are dictated by economics, rather than by the physical properties of the wood itself. Nevertheless, it is important to consider these specifications when considering the potential uses and management for forests and forest lands. The following are generalizations.

Pulp, used primarily for papermaking, and fiber logs, used for MDF, and hardboard, can use just about any inexpensive source of wood fiber, but the fibers must be intact. Sawdust and some (recycled) papers, because of the damage to the fibers in milling, cannot always be used. Likewise, decayed wood fibers are unsuitable. The longer fibers from softwoods are often preferred for strength, but the shorter hardwood fibers can be used in many cases, especially for fine papers. Economics (specifically, transportation costs) dictate that the pulpwood sources be close to the manufacturing facility—a 50-mile radius would be ideal. Most pulpwood logs, called roundwood, will be under 8 inches (20 cm) in diameter and 4 to 8 feet (1.2 × 2.4 m) long.

Softwood lumber, used for construction, requires that logs typically be between 8 to 24 inches (20–61 cm) in diameter, although a few mills can process 6 to 8 inch (15–20 cm) logs. Logs should be as straight as possible, with no decay. Knots or knot scars, especially for large branches, are not desired. Certain species are not highly desired, for example, eastern hemlock, because of poor lumber markets, while other species are quite desirable, including Southern pine, Douglas fir, and cedars. Shake (separation of the wood within the log running parallel to the rings), bad odors, and fungal activity of any sort is usually undesirable because of the high risk of strength loss in such logs. Due to low profit margins in softwood lumber manufacturing, softwood timber should be within 50 miles of the mill (25 miles is better yet).

Hardwood logs typically are 8 inches (20 cm) and larger, up to the optimum capacity of the mill, which typically is around 24 inches (61 cm) in diameter. Log lengths are 8 to 16 feet (2.4 to 4.9 m), but the typical length in eastern mills is 12 feet (3.7 m); southern mills, 16 feet (4.9 m); and midwestern mills, 8 or 10 feet (2.4 or 3 m). Logs should be as straight as possible, but most logs are fairly crooked, with several inches of sweep being common. As most hardwood lumber is sold based on the amount of clear area in the lumber, any branches, knots or knot scars should be well spaced apart. Some species, including sweetgum, aspen, and cottonwood, have very poor lumber markets, with low lumber prices even for higher grade material; log prices are low and profits are also usually low. On the other hand, some species, such as cherry, walnut, hard maple, and red oak have very high prices and demand, with high log prices and high demand and profits. Shake, bad odors, and fungal activity of any sort are usually undesirable because of the high risk of color loss and strength loss in such logs. Hardwood timber should be within 75 miles of the mill, although 25 to 40 miles is better.

Logs used for particleboards and flake boards, including OSB, can be small diameter (as small as 4 inches [10.2 cm]), no larger than 12 inches (30.5 cm) in diameter typically, crooked or straight, knotty or clear, and short or long (typically length is 8 feet [2.4 m] long). Although almost any species can and will be used, the lighter weight species, such as aspen and yellow poplar, are preferred, as they will press together better than a denser species; nevertheless, Southern pine is also often used for OSB. Logs with decay are not acceptable. Timber should be within 25 to 50 miles of the mill in most cases to avoid excessive transportation costs.

Because of the high capital costs of pulp and fiber plants and particle board manufacturing facilities (including OSB plants), these facilities will obtain the required timber no matter what the cost, size, or distance. In short, these facilities cannot afford to run out of raw material, so they will be, at times, rather ruthless in wood procurement, even using sawlogs, or going further than 50 miles from the plant. Their critical need for raw material must be considered by a land planner that is within or near the plant's procurement area.

Lumber Manufacturing

Early sawmills used human power to move the saw through the log. However, in North America, the availability of water power led to development of water-power mills throughout the early European settlements. Lumber, especially for ship building, but also for shipping containers including barrels (called cooperage), was a critical commodity for ocean-based shipping economies during the 18th and 19th centuries. Although these historic sawmills would seem primitive without fancy computers and powerful motors, many mills produced as much or more lumber annually than an individual mill does today.

Today, there are two different mills—hardwood and softwood. A hardwood sawmill typically has 1 to 15 million board feet of annual production. Most of the lumber produced is 4/4 thick (4/4, pronounced "four quarter," is the number of quarter inches of thickness; 8/4 would be 2 inches (5.1 cm) thick). Lengths run from 4 feet to 16 feet (1.2–4.9 m); width is random. The primary quality factor is the amount of large clear areas, as hardwood lumber is seldom used "as is" but will be dried and then sawn into smaller pieces for furniture, millwork and cabinets. A softwood sawmill (Figure 20.8) typically produces in excess of 200 million board feet annually. Most of the lumber is 8/4 nom-

Figure 20.8 A sawmill can be an important source of value-added income in rural economies.

inal thickness (which would be sold as 2" [5.1 cm] by a specified width), although the actual thickness is 1.5 inches (0.6 cm). Lengths are usually 8 to 20 feet (2.4–6.1 cm); widths would typically be 4, 6, 8, or 10 inches (10.2, 15.2, 20.3, or 25.4 cm) nominal size, or 3-1/2, 5-1/2, 7-1/2, and 9-1/4 inches (8.9, 14, 19.1, and 23.5 cm) actual size. Most softwood lumber will be dried, planed, and graded, and then used "as is" without additional manufacturing, except cutting to length at times.

A modern softwood sawmill producing lumber for construction is highly automated, with high manufacturing efficiency and high production, thereby assuring good profitability and good stewardship of the natural resource. In a typical mill (Figure 20.9), logs are debarked, scanned for metal, scanned for size to determine the best sawing pattern, and sawn into lumber and cants at the headrig. Then cants are resawn into lumber. Any pieces with wane (wane is the absence of wood) are edged. Lumber is then trimmed and sorted by size. Most of these processing procedures are computer-controlled with manual override possible. Volume

Computerized Bucking	The long log (perhaps 40 feet long) is cut into shorter lengths, called sawlogs, based on log diameter, crookedness, and market demand for particular lengths.
Debarking	The bark is removed from the sawlogs so that the logs do not have any imbedded grit that would rapidly dull saws and other cutting equipment. It also ensures that any nonlumber byproducts are free of bark (required for pulp chips) and grit.
Scanning 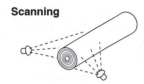	The sawlog is scanned for length, diameter, and straightness in order to determine the best (most profitable) sawing procedures. The results of this analysis include the finished lumber size, probable value and market demand, as well as the best position for the log when it enters the headsaw.
Headsawing	The headsaw is a multiple-saw machine that is usually computer-controlled. It uses the results from scanning to cut the sawlog into several flat pieces of wood of a desired thickness; these pieces are called cants. The cant usually has two flat, wide faces and two rounded edges, due to the log's round shape. The outermost piece of wood is called a slab; a slab has only one flat face, and the oppostie side is rounded.
Gang-sawing 	Large, thick cants are cut into several pieces of lumber in a multiple-saw machine called a gang-saw. Often, the cant is approximately 4 inches thick and the gang-saws are 2 inches apart; the end-products are 2" x 4" lumber, often referred to as studs.
Resawing	The slabs that are thick enough to be sawn into lumber are put through a resaw, producing a piece of lumber and a thinner slab. The resaw is also used to saw double-thickness cants into two thinner pieces.
Edging	The edger saw makes the edges of the lumber flat by removing the round edges, and also makes the two edges parallel to each other. Cants can be routed to the edger from the headsaw, gang-saw, or resaw.
Trimming	Trimming squares the ends of the lumber and removes any excess length, necessary since almost all softwood lumber is manufactured and sold in 6, 8, 10, 12, 16, 18, or 20 foot lengths. As both ends are typically trimmed, this process is also called double-end trimming.
Green-chain and Sorting	Lumber is sorted by grade, length, width, and thickness. Each size is accumulated separately. The system that conveys the lumber from the trim saw to the sorter is called the green-chain; the sorter, which typically has 30 or more bins for each size into which the lumber is dropped, is called a bin sorter or drop sorter.

Figure 20.9 The typical wood flow pattern for a softwood sawmill includes nine basic processes. It begins with a long log that has been brought in from the woods and ends with lumber that is ready to be stacked and kiln-dried, and eventually planed, graded, and packaged.

conversion efficiencies can exceed 65 percent—the 35 percent of the log not converted into lumber is used for pulp and for fuel. After the green lumber is produced, the lumber is kiln, dried, planed, and graded according to the rules of the American Lumber Standard.

Extending the Service Life of Wood Products

Wood products are subject to deterioration when they are exposed to the elements. Furniture, millwork, cabinets and other products are often coated with paints, lacquers, varnishes, and the like to retard the effects of moisture changes in the environment and the resultant shrinkage. Wood siding is often stained and coated to prevent erosion (although such deterioration is very slow) from airborne particles, water, and ultraviolet light, as well as to enhance the beauty. Poles, posts, railroad ties (also called sleepers), decks, and other wood products exposed outdoors are often treated with chemicals that are poisonous to fungi and insects. Sometimes wood is also treated with chemicals to retard or prevent ignition from fire.

In all these cases, there are tradeoffs between many factors, including the cost of the protection versus the benefit, the environmental risks or damage from applying the protection (and the risk from the ultimate disposal of the wood product), safety risks from poor performance (such as a broken electrical pole or tower, or the loss of lives in a fire), the cost of using nonwood materials, and the potential savings in wood harvested because of the longer life. The evaluation of the use of various wood treatments to prolong or enhance performance are societal issues; there is no one correct, easy answer. In fact, the answer will vary as societies change and as more knowledge is obtained.

One of the most widespread, yet controversial treatments used to prolong the service life of wood products is the use of pesticides (called wood preservatives) that are impregnated into the wood. The application and use of such chemicals is strictly controlled by the Environmental Protection Agency (EPA); quality assurance for the consumer is provided by the American Wood Preservers Association (AWPA).

Wood preservatives used today can be divided into two classes: 1) oilborne preservatives such as creosote (a coal-tar product; used for heavy timbers, ties, poles, and pilings) and petroleum solutions of pentachlorophenol; and 2) waterborne preservatives such as CCA (chromated copper arsenate; widely used for treating Southern pine, imparting a green color to the wood) and new treatments that often include copper compounds. Treatment of wood usually involves drying the wood partially to remove water so that there is room for the preservative

chemicals, and impregnating the wood with the chemicals using a combination of heat, vacuum, and pressure in a large cylinder. The wood is sometimes dried again before being put into use. The type and amount of chemical used varies depending on the expected risk of damage; for example, wood in contact with the ground (such as a post or pole) would receive more chemical than wood exposed above the ground (such as a deck). Untreated wood of many species exposed to a wet environment may last only a few years, compared to more than 50 years for treated wood.

Plywood Manufacturing

Plywood panels consist of several large thin wood veneer-type layers joined with adhesive. Some or all of the layers are sheets of veneer. Other layers, particularly in the core, may be particleboard, hardboard, lumber strips, and special materials. The fiber direction of each layer is at right angles to that of the adjoining layer. This cross-banding makes plywood more uniform and less anisotropic than lumber; its properties in the direction of panel length resemble those in the direction of panel width.

Cross-banding affects strength in a logical way in both directions of the plane, the transverse layers contribute practically no strength; plywood is roughly one-half as strong as lumber is lengthwise. But by the same principle, plywood is stronger than lumber in the direction of width and can therefore be thinner. Moreover, it does not split like solid-wood products. Plywood and lumber properties naturally are the same in the thickness direction, provided that the layers are adequately bonded together.

Cross-banding gives plywood dimensional stability. To understand this effect, consider first the fiber direction of the surface veneers. Both surface veneers and the core veneer tend to swell and shrink (move) very little, whereas the two transverse veneers or cross-bands have a very strong tendency to move. The adhesive bonds compel all five veneers to move by the same amount, somewhere between the small longitudinal shrinkage and the large transverse shrinkage of lumber. However, since wood is many times stiffer in the fiber direction than in the transverse direction, longitudinal movement dominates and the panel remains fairly stable. Similarly, in the other direction of the plane, the cross-bands dominate and restrain the movements. According to a rule of thumb, plywood shrinks and swells in directions of length and width about twice as much as lumber moves lengthwise, which is still very little. For most practical purposes, plywood can be considered to be dimensionally stable. Of course, the cross-banding does not affect movements in the direction of the panel thickness, which are large in terms of percentages but small in absolute terms and unimportant.

Many plywood panels are 6 millimeters (1/4 inch) thick; the thinnest measure about 1 millimeter, and the thickest several centimeters. In addition to house sheathing and siding, plywood is used in cabinets, billboards, furniture, bookshelves, concrete forms, skins of flush doors, paneling, boxes, in mobile homes, and for trailers.

Particleboard Manufacturing

Particleboard, also called chipboard and chipcore (Figure 20.10), is a product that was developed about 50 years ago. It uses chips, as small as 1/4

inch (6.3 mm) cubes, that are glued together. Often the chips are sawmill residue, so the raw material cost is quite low. Initially considered to be a cheap substitute for lumber when manufacturing furniture, cabinets and shelves, the product was improved and is now highly respected as an excellent building material (especially for subfloors and for counter tops) and for furniture (especially for knocked-down, ready-to-assemble cabinets and case-goods). In most cases, however, particleboards cannot withstand prolonged exposure to liquid water without developing excessive swelling and loss of integrity. Special fasteners are required to develop good joints.

The typical manufacturing flow for particleboard is sorting of the chips and breaking larger chips into smaller sizes, drying in drum dryers, spreading adhesive and waxes on the particles, spreading the particles on a conveyor in a thick layer (called a mat), compressing the mat, using heat, to activate the adhesive. After cooling, the panels are cut into the required sizes and may be sanded if required. Properties of particleboards are controlled by the amount of adhesive used and the density of the board. However, particleboard is not as strong and stiff as an equal thickness of lumber, plywood, or OSB.

Figure 20.10 Manufactured wood products include flakeboard (at top of stack), OSB (at middle of stack), and particleboard (at bottom of stack).

Oriented Strandboard (OSB) Manufacturing

OSB (Figure 20.10) is a newer product, less than 20 years old. However, because small trees and crooked stems can be effectively utilized, the raw material cost, compared to product cost, is about 38 percent ($53 out of $141 per cubic meter). Plywood requires more than double the raw material cost ($117 out of $206 per cubic meter). Lumber requires even more ($133 out of $191 per cubic meter). As a result, OSB has rapidly gained acceptance in the construction market. OSB plant capacities exceed 20 million cubic meters annually; more new plants are being constructed each year. If lumber were used to do to the same job as OSB, we would need in excess of 8 billion more board feet of lumber annually, and this lumber would have

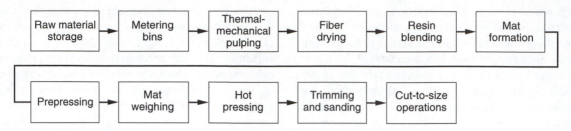

Figure 20.11 Typical material flow in an OSB facility.

to come from larger, higher-quality, more expensive trees. It is easy to understand why OSB is considered the wood product of the future in the construction business.

The typical material flow in an OSB plant (Figure 20.11) provides very high conversion efficiencies. Any "waste" is used for fuel for the manufacturing process. Logs are debarked, heated in hot water, cut into short lengths, and flaked into wafers or strands using knives. The strands are dried in large drum driers, coated with adhesive, and assembled into a thick mat. The strands in the mat are oriented to provide parallel strands in the various layers in the mat. The mat is compressed and heated, and cut to size. By controlling the panel density, the amount of adhesive, and the strand orientation, a panel can be designed and produced with properties that meet the engineering needs of the building designer and engineer.

Medium-Density Fiberboard (MDF) Manufacturing

As the name implies, MDF (Figure 20.12) is a fiber product. To obtain fibers, the log is broken down in the same manner as when wood is disintegrated for paper. However, for MDF, synthetic adhesives are added to the fibers before heating and pressing. This adhesive sets MDF apart from paper, low-density fiberboards (commonly used for ceiling tiles) and high-density boards (commonly used for pegboards and the backs of cabinets). MDF has a very smooth finished surface to which wood veneer,

paper, or plastic can be easily laminated. The surface can be directly printed on as well. Special fasteners are required to develop high joint strength.

Chemical Nature of Wood

Although the relative value of wood as a source of energy and chemicals has varied considerably through the decades, wood continues to be an important source of specialty chemicals and renewable energy, and may be even more important in the future. Here we discuss the chemical

Figure 20.12 Medium-density fiberboard (MDF) panels, which can be printed or covered with thin films and made to look like solid wood, are widely used in furniture manufacturing.

nature of wood and in the following sections provide a description of the technology for conversion of wood to pulp fibers for papermaking, to fuels for energy, and to chemicals for industry and consumers.

As described in Chapter 4, wood is like all other plant material, in that it begins with the basic photosynthetic equation in which carbon dioxide and water are combined by means of the sun's energy to produce glucose and oxygen. To understand the chemical nature of wood, we need to trace the developments in the plant starting with glucose, a basic sugar. Glucose is only one of a series of sugars that occur in nature. The sugars are generally classified according to the number of carbon (C) atoms in their structure; thus, sugars with six carbons are referred to as hexoses, and those with five carbons are referred to as pentoses. The sugars important in wood structure are the hexoses (glucose, mannose, and galactose) and the pentoses (xylose and arabinose). Because sugars are so important in our lives, a separate field of chemistry, termed carbohydrate chemistry, is devoted completely to sugar derivatives.

Sugars generally do not occur as simple compounds in wood but as higher-molecular-weight structures known generally as polymers. The concept of a polymer can be visualized by considering one sugar unit as one link, the monomer, in a long chain, the polymer. Thus, with each link an identical sugar, a chain of sugar units is formed—a polymer of sugars known commonly as polysaccharides. This linking is depicted schematically as follows:

O   O-O-O-O-O-O-O-O-O-O
Monomer   Polymer
(sugar)   (polysaccharide)

Polysaccharides are characterized by the number of sugars in the chain or the degree of polymerization (DP).

Because there are many different sugars, many different polysaccharides can be formed. A polysaccharide formed from glucose is a glucan, from xylose a xylan, from mannose a mannan, and so on. If combinations of sugars occur in one polysaccharide, a mixed polymer is formed, usually named for its predominant sugars. Thus, if glucose and mannose are present, the polysaccharide is a glucomannan; if arabinose and galactose are present, a arabinogalactan; and so on.

Polysaccharides are of paramount importance in wood and to the uses of chemically processed wood. Cellulose is the common term used for the glucan present in wood; it constitutes about 42 percent of wood's dry weight. Cellulose is the primary component of the walls of cells making up wood fibers and is the main structural material of wood and other plants. Paper, paperboard, and other wood fiber products are therefore also composed mostly of cellulose. The chemical structure of the cellulose macromolecule is shown in Figure 20.13. In the plant, the DP of cellulose is approximately 14,000.

Closely associated with cellulose in the wood structure and in paper products are other polysaccharides termed hemicelluloses. The hemicelluloses have often been labeled as the matrix material of wood. In hardwoods, the primary hemicellulose is a xylan (polymer of xylose), whereas in softwoods, the primary hemicellulose is a glucomannan, although both of these polysaccharides occur to some extent in both types of wood. The DP of the hemicelluloses is much less than that of cellulose, in the range of 100 to 200.

Table 20.4 gives a comparison of the chemical composition of extractive-free hardwoods and softwoods. (The nature of wood extractives is treated in a later section.) (5, 6) Since cellulose and the

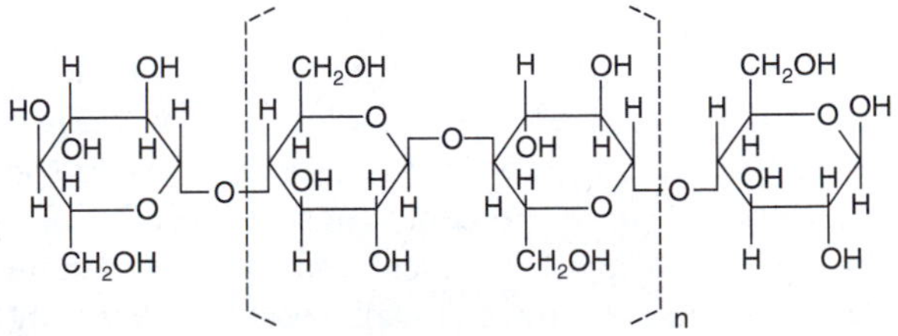

Figure 20.13 The chemical structure of cellulose; the cellulose repeat unit is shown in brackets.

Table 20.4   Chemical Composition and Fiber Length of Extractive-free Wood (by percent)

Component	Hardwood (Red Maple)	Softwood (Balsam Fir)
Cellulose	44	42
Hemicelluloses		
Xylan	25	9
Glucomannan	4	18
Lignin	25	29
Pectin, starch	2	2
Average fiber length (mm)	0.8–1.5	2.5–6.0

hemicelluloses are both polysaccharides, it is obvious that the polysaccharide component of wood is by far the dominant one, making up approximately 70 percent of both hardwoods and softwoods. Additional polysaccharides may occur as extraneous components of wood, components that are not part of the cell wall; for example, the heartwood of species of larch can contain up to 25 percent (dry weight) of arabinogalactan, a water-soluble polysaccharide that occurs only in trace quantities in other wood species.

The third major component of wood shown in Table 20.4 is lignin. Although lignin is also a polymer, it has a different chemical structure compared to that of the polysaccharides. The monomeric units in lignin are phenolic-type compounds. The spaces between fibers in wood are almost pure lignin and are termed the middle lamella (5, 6). Lignin is also considered the gluing or encrusting substance of wood and adds mechanical strength or stiffness to the tree and to wood. Higher plants are commonly referred to as lignocellulosic because of the typical joint occurrence in them of lignin and cellulose. The spaces between fibers are filled with lignin and make up the middle lamella.

A fourth class of wood components is known as extraneous material and is present in wood in amounts of 1 to 10 percent. These materials comprise a vast array of chemical compounds that are not constituents of the cell wall. Most of these compounds, because they can be extracted with water or organic solvents or volatilized with steam, are called extractives. They are considered in detail subsequently. A small portion of the extraneous mate-

rials (starch, pectin, and inorganic salts) are not extractable.

Microscopic Structure of Wood and Wood Fibers

In the tree, the cellulose polymers are laid down uniformly, the chains paralleling one another, and the long-chain molecules associate strongly through hydrogen bonds that develop between hydroxyl groups. These bonds create very strong associations between the cellulose macromolecules. These associations between the cellulose chains give a very uniform crystalline (ordered) structure known as *micelles* or microcrystallites, shown in Figure 20.14.

The micelles are also associated in the tree to give long threadlike structures termed *microfibrils* (Figure 20.14). The structure of the microfibrils is not completely uniform throughout. There are regions of non-uniformity between the micelles in the microfibrils called amorphous (disordered) regions; the cellulose microfibril therefore has a crystalline-amorphous character. Water molecules enter the amorphous regions and swell the microfibrils; ultimately, this is the mechanism by which fibers and wood swell in moist or wet environments.

The final fiber cell wall structure is essentially layers of the microfibrils or macrofibrils aligned in several different directions. The entity holding the fibers together, the middle lamella, is almost pure lignin (90 percent), as mentioned earlier. For the cellulose fibers to be separated, the middle lamella lignin must be chemically removed, a process that

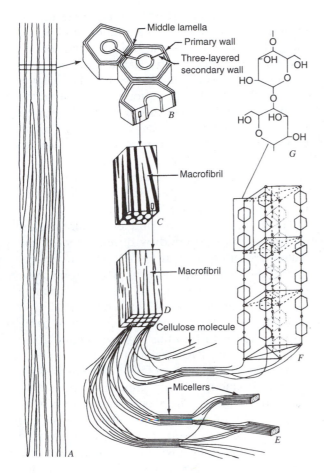

Figure 20.14 Detailed structure of cell walls. *A*, strand of fiber cells. *B*, cross-section of fiber cells showing gross layering: a layer of primary wall and three layers of secondary wall. *C*, fragment from the middle layer of a secondary wall showing macrofibrils (white) of cellulose and interfibrillar spaces (black), which are filled with noncellulosic materials. *D*, fragment of macrofibril showing microfibrils (white), which may be seen in the electron micrographs. The spaces among microfibrils (black) are filled with noncellulosic materials. *E*, structure of microfibrils: chainlike molecules of cellulose, which in some parts of microfibrils are orderly arranged. These parts are the micelles. *F*, fragment of a micelle showing parts of chainlike cellulose molecules arranged in a space lattice. *G*, two glucose residues connected by an oxygen atom—a fragment of a cellulose molecule. (From K. Esau, *Anatomy of Seed Plants*, Second Edition, 1997, courtesy of John Wiley & Sons.)

also removes most of the hemicelluloses, or mechanically degraded to free the fibers for papermaking (Figure 20.15). A paper sheet can then be formed from the separated cellulose fibers by depositing them from a water slurry onto a wire screen. The water drains away and the fibers collapse, leaving a fiber mat that derives its main strength from re-association of the fibers through many hydrogen bonds, the same type of bond that gives mechanical integrity to the fibers (Figure 20.16)

The long fibers from softwoods (Table 20.4) are usually preferred in papermaking for products that must resist tearing, such as grocery bags, whereas the shorter hardwood fibers give improved opacity, or covering power, and printability to the final paper sheet. The type of pulping process also

Figure 20.15 Scanning electron micrograph of a cluster of eastern white pine elements after pulping or maceration of a small wood cube. (Courtesy of Wilfred Côté and Syracuse University Press.)

Figure 20.16 Scanning electron micrograph of paper surface showing random arrangement of coniferous tracheid fibers in the sheet. Note the flattened or collapsed nature of the fibers in this cross-section cut with a razor blade. (Courtesy of Wilfred Côté and Syracuse University Press.)

affects the pulp properties, as described in a later section.

History of Pulp and Papermaking

The concept of making paper from the fibers from lignocellulosic materials, an integrated system of fiber separation (pulping) and reforming of the fibers into a mat (papermaking), is attributed to T'sai Lun, a court official in southeast China in 105 A.D. The first fibers were obtained from old hemp rags and ramie fishnets, but shortly thereafter, the inner bark fibers from paper mulberry trees were also utilized for papermaking. Bamboo was used as a source of fiber several centuries later. The rags were macerated into a pulp in water with a mortar and pestle; then, after dilution in a vat, the pulp was formed into a wet mat on a bamboo frame equipped with a cloth screen to drain the free water. The mat was dried in the sun. The invention was based on the need for a writing material to replace the expensive silk and inconvenient bamboo strips. The invention was a closely guarded secret for many centuries but filtered to the West at Samarkand in western China early in the eighth century. Papermaking was introduced to the United States in 1690 with the first mill near Philadelphia, Pennsylvania.

Paper was made by hand essentially as just described above, spurred by development of the Gutenberg printing press (1455), until the invention of the long, continuous wire screen machine by Louis Robert in France in 1798. The machine was subsequently developed commercially in England by the Fourdrinier brothers, whose name is associated with it to this day (see Figure 20.19 in the section on Papermaking).

Wood became a source of fiber in the mid-1840s, when a groundwood pulp grinder was manufactured in Germany. The wood was defibered by pressing against a grindstone. After 1850, several chemical methods were developed to produce chemical pulps, which will be described later. The major sources of fiber in the United States for papermaking are pulpwood (roundwood), byproduct sawmill chips, and recycled paper.

Although wood is the dominant raw material for pulp and paper in the developed world, a wide range of fibers are utilized for papermaking in other parts of the world. In many countries, pulp production is based entirely on agro-based fibers and over 25 countries depend on agro-based fibers for over 50 percent of their pulp production. The leading countries for production of pulp and paper from agro-based fibers are China and India, with China having over 73 percent of the world's agro-based pulping capacity. China mainly utilizes straw for papermaking, while India and Mexico utilize large quantities of sugar cane bagasse (fiber waste from sugar production). India also incorporates some jute fiber and large quantities of bamboo, although the supply of bamboo is not sufficient to meet demands for paper production (7). There has been considerable interest in the use of kenaf as an alternate fiber source in the United States and a number of successful press runs of kenaf-based paper (82–95%) were carried out in the pressrooms of the *Bakersfield Californian*, the *Houston Chronicle*, the *Dallas Morning News* and the *St. Petersburg Times* (7).

Practically any natural plant can be utilized as a source of papermaking fibers, but there is considerable variation in the quality of paper realized from alternate plant sources. Factors such as fiber length, content of nonfibrous components such as parenchyma tissue, contaminants such as silica, and so forth greatly influence the quality of the final sheet. Procurement of sufficient quantities of the raw material and seasonal fluctuations in supply can also pose problems. It is also necessary to use alternate pulping equipment to handle the plant materials, since the material tends to mat down in the digester, making it difficult to get uniform circulation of the cooking chemicals (7, 8).

Production of paper and paperboard in the United States constitutes about 35 percent of the world's total; papermaking in North America and Europe together made up about 75 percent of the world production. The difference in the economies of the developed and less-developed countries is shown in the accompanying tabulation by the wide range of relative per capita consumption of paper and paperboard (9):

United States	323
Japan	249
Germany	192
China	27
Russia	14
Egypt	10
India	4
Afghanistan	<1

Pulping of Wood

To prepare the wood for pulping, the standing tree in the forest is felled, delimbed, bucked to length, and conveyed to the pulp mill or sawmill (Figure 20.17). At the pulp mills the logs are usually debarked by tumbling against one another in large rotating drums, which removes the bark by impact and abrasion. The debarked logs are next taken to the groundwood mill (5 percent) or to the chipper (95 percent). After chipping, the chips are screened to remove oversize chips and fines.

Three major methods are used to pulp wood; namely, mechanical, semi-chemical, and chemical.

Figure 20.17 Unloading at a pulp mill in Kingsport, Tennessee. (Courtesy of U.S.D.A. Forest Service.)

Each process produces pulps with different properties for different applications. The major pulping
processes in use are classified in Table 20.5.

Modern mechanical pulping includes stone
groundwood pulping (SGW), in which bolts of

wood are pressed against a revolving grindstone,
and refiner mechanical pulping (RMP), in which
chips are passed between single or double rotating plates of a vertical-disk attrition mill (Figure
20.18). Recent developments in stone grinding are

Table 20.5 Wood Pulping by Process and Yield

Process	Acronym	Chemical	Mechanical	Pulp Yield(percent)
		Treatment		
Mechanical Processes				
Stone groundwood	SGW	None	Grinder	93–95
Pressure groundwood	PGW	None	Grinder	93–95
Refiner mechanical	RMP	None	Disk refiner (pressure)	93–95
Thermomechanical	TMP	Steam	Disk refiner (pressure)	80–90
Chemi-thermomechanical	CTMP	Sodium sulfite or sodium hydroxide[1]	Disk refiner (pressure)	80–90
Chemi-mechanical[2]	CMP	Sodium sulfite or sodium hydroxide	Disk refiner	80–90
Semi-Chemical Processes				
Neutral sulfite	NSSC	Sodium sulfite + sodium carbonate	Disk refiner	70–85
Green liquor	GLSC	Sodium hydroxide + sodium carbonate	Disk refiner	70–85
Nonsulfur	—	Sodium carbonate + sodium hydroxide	Disk refiner	70–85
Chemical Processes				
Kraft	—	Sodium hydroxide + sodium sulfide	None	45–55
Sulfite	—	Calcium bisulfite in sulfurous acid[3]	None	40–50
Magnefite	—	Magnesium bisulfite in sulfurous acid[4]	None	45–55
Soda	—	Sodium hydroxide	None	40–50
Soda-oxygen	—	Sodium hydroxide + oxygen	None	45–55
Soda-anthraquinone	SAq	Sodium hydroxide + anthraquinone	None	45–55
Dissolving Processes				
Prehydrolysis kraft	—	Steaming and kraft (two-step process)	None	35
Acid sulfite	—	Acid sulfite (Ca, Na)	None	35

[1] Sodium sulfite or sodium hydroxide, 2–7% of wood.

[2] Also chemical treatment after fiberizing.

[3] Also sodium, magnesium, and ammonia; pH 2.

[4] pH 5.

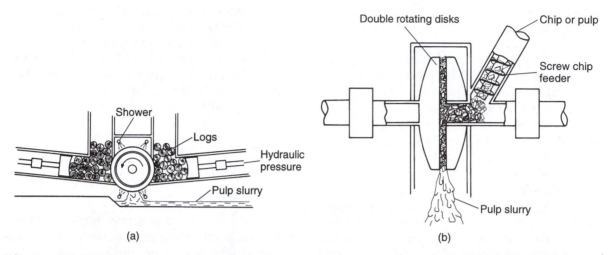

Figure 20.18 Schematic of (a) a stone grinder that pulverizes wood bolts for groundwood pulp and (b) a disk refiner that grinds wood chips for refiner and thermomechanical (TMP) pulps. Showers provide water for both methods.

applying pressure to the grinder (PGW) and controlling temperature (Table 20.5).

Basic changes in mechanical pulping technology are to pretreat chips with chemicals, steam, or both. These developments started forty years ago when chips were pretreated with caustic soda, termed chemi-mechanical pulping (CMP). Presteaming and pressure refining of chips gives a thermomechanical pulp (TMP); and when chemical pretreatment and pressure steaming are combined, the pulp is referred to as chemi-thermomechanical pulp (CTMP). There are many variations of these processes. These treatments are employed to improve pulp quality. The steam and chemicals aid fiberizing by giving a less-damaged fiber, which makes the final paper stronger.

Mechanical pulps are a major component of newsprint. The mechanical pulp imparts valuable properties to the newsprint, all of which are related to printability. These are absorbency, bulk, compressibility, opacity, and uniformity. However, because mechanical pulps are weak, up to 30 percent of a chemical pulp (described later) is blended into the pulp mixture, called a furnish, to provide greater strength. Sufficient strength is required of the newsprint to withstand the tension forces pro-

duced by the printing press. Modern mills, however, now use 100 percent TMP or CTMP to produce newsprint with sufficient strength. Mechanical pulps are also an important component of publication paper grades, which are generally coated magazine papers. Obviously, printability is important in this application as well.

Semi-chemical pulping combines a mild chemical treatment with mechanical action for final liberation of the fibers. The major semi-chemical process is neutral sulfite semi-chemical (NSSC). The semi-chemical processes were developed to improve the economic return. These processes give higher yields (75 to 80 percent) than full chemical pulping and better strength than mechanical pulps. The semi-chemical pulps are very suitable for the stiff corrugating medium in cardboard boxes. The recovery of chemicals and heat value from the semi-chemical spent liquors is well developed.

Chemical pulping is conducted on wood chips using lignin-dissolving reagents in vessels, called digesters, under elevated temperature and pressure (10). The major chemical pulping processes were developed about a century ago and are the soda (1855 in England), sulfite (1867 in the United States), and kraft or sulfate (1884 in Germany) processes.

The word "kraft" comes from the German word meaning strong. The ability to utilize all wood species, especially pines, and the excellent strength of the resulting pulp have contributed to the growth of the kraft process. Kraft pulping dominates, accounting for almost 80 percent of the total pulp production in the United States.

The mechanisms for removing lignin and separating fibers in chemical pulping are hydrolysis, which cleaves the lignin bond, and conversion of the lignin to water-soluble fractions through reactions with sulfur compounds. Recovery of spent pulping reagents is economically necessary with the kraft process and involves a series of cyclic steps. Although the kraft process has an efficient chemical recovery system, many older sulfite mills around the world have closed because of poor chemical recovery schemes for this process.

Chemical pulps, such as kraft and sulfite, and in particular, softwood kraft pulps, are generally used when considerable strength is required. Bags, stationery, and ledger and bond papers contain high percentages of chemical pulp. Sanitary tissues such as facial and toilet tissues also contain large amounts of chemical and recycled pulps. For them, a combination of softness and absorbency are sought, along with sufficient strength.

Solvent pulping is another method that has received renewed interest; organic solvents rather than the traditional aqueous sulfur pulping are used for what is called *organosolv pulping*. Since lignin is an organic polymer, it is naturally soluble in organic solvents once some of the lignin bonds have been broken by an acid, usually, or by a base included with the aqueous organic solvent. Thus, a sulfur derivative of lignin is not necessary to solubilize and solvate the lignin, and the severe environmental hazards of sulfur are eliminated from pulping and chemical recovery (11).

A variety of organic solvents have been evaluated for organosolv pulping. Two systems are alcohol pulping (50:50, ethanol/water) and "ester pulping." Ester pulping is based on three chemicals, in roughly equal proportions: acetic acid, ethyl acetate, and water. Energy costs are reduced with the ester pulping process because chemical recovery is based on a liquid-liquid phase separation after pulping. The two liquids do not mix, similar to the way water and gasoline do not mix. Since it is necessary to recover the solvent from all organosolv systems for economic reasons, the pollution hazards are considerably reduced. However solvent pulping systems have not been commercially successful to date (11).

Bleaching and Brightening of Pulp

Although pulpwood is generally light-colored and can retain its brightness in the acid and neutral sulfite processes, pulps from the dominant alkaline kraft process are dark-colored. This color is evident in unbleached kraft packaging paper and boards.

About one-half of chemical pulps are bleached to different degrees of brightness (whiteness). Substantial amounts of mechanical and chemi-mechanical pulps are also brightened to intermediate brightness levels. In bleaching, the residual colored lignin in pulp is dissolved chemically, whereas in brightening, the lignin is altered to a lighter-colored compound without removal (11).

Kraft pulps of high brightness (90 percent) are generally produced in a multistage sequence. In a series of bleaching towers, the pulp is treated with chlorine (C) or oxygen (O), caustic extraction (E), and chlorine dioxide (D), generally in a sequence of C(O)EDED. Multistage bleaching has the serious disadvantage of requiring a considerable capital investment in large, corrosion-resistant equipment with high maintenance costs. In addition, the bleaching process produces chlorinated lignin phenols, which can pose serious toxicity pollution problems. In recent years, oxygen bleaching has been substituted for chlorine in the first stage to reduce such hazards.

Regulatory agencies in Europe, and particularly in Scandinavia, have imposed even greater restrictions on emissions from pulp mill bleach plants and several new approaches have been developed. These are Elemental Chlorine Free (ECF) bleaching and Totally Chorine Free (TCF) bleaching of pulps. Generally for ECF, oxygen (O) treatment is substituted for chlorine (C) in the first stage. For TCF more radical changes are necessary with substitution of both (C) and (D) stages with ozone (O), peroxide (P), and enzyme (X) stages in a sequence such as OXZP. The use of enzymes is the newest development in bleaching technology as further described below (11).

Biotechnology—Biopulping and Biobleaching

The pulping of wood is at present based on either mechanical or chemical methods or combinations thereof, as described in this chapter. The interfiber lignin bond is broken down by the mechanical and chemical treatments to free the cellulose fibers for papermaking. In the forest, white rot fungi perform a similar task on wood left behind. The enzymes of the fungi do the work of lignin degradation. This is the basis of new biopulping approaches which have been under development for more than ten years. Wood chips or agricultural materials are treated with a white rot fungus and nutrients for about two weeks which breaks down and alters the lignin gluing substance in the lignocellulosic material. The biomass then can be much more easily disintegrated by mechanical treatment in a disk refiner (Figure 20.18b). Since some mechanical treatment is required, the method is more properly termed biomechanical pulping. Investigators at the U.S. Department of Agriculture, Forest Products Laboratory in Madison, Wisconsin evaluated hundreds of fungi for this purpose and found that treatment with the white rot fungus, *Ceriporiopsis subvermispora*, resulted in the greatest reduction in energy reqirements for mechanical disintegration and the best strength properties from the resulting paper.

Biobleaching is also possible for brightening or whitening pulp fibers in lieu of the toxic chlorine compounds utilized at present by the industry as described above. At least one enzyme based process developed in Finland has been applied commercially. The process uses xylanase to make lignin more vulnerable to oxidation by attacking the surrounding polysaccharides that protect the lignin. Another exciting application would be to use these and other enzymes for removal of lignin pollutants from waste effluents. Biotechnology should lead to safer and cleaner methods for pulping and bleaching.

Paper and Paperboard

The production of pulp of paper and paperboard for the market proceeds in three successive steps: stock preparation, papermaking, and converting to the enormous number of paper products.

Stock Preparation

The separated fibers from the pulping operation, except those in mechanical pulps, are generally not suitable for papermaking. To obtain the optimum paper properties, the fiber bonding must be improved by supplemental mechanical treatment of the fiber surface, and by imparting special properties through blending of additives and other pulps. Beating or refining, a basic step in the transition from pulp to paper, is accomplished by cutting and shortening, rubbing and abrading, and crushing and bruising the pulp fibers as they pass between the rotating and stationary bars of a beater or the disks of a refiner (Figure 20.18b). These actions promote fiber flexibility and the area of contact between the wet fibers by exposing the fibrils and microfibrils on external and internal surfaces. The close contact enables hydrogen bonds to form between the adjacent fibers on drying, as explained earlier in this chapter.

Paper is rarely made from pure fibers. The color is altered by dyes; the writing and printing capacity is improved by internal and surface sizing agents (rosin and starch, respectively); the wet strength is enhanced with resins; opacity is increased with pigments such as clay and titanium dioxide; and alum (aluminum sulfate) is added for flocculation. These additives can be introduced during the beating operation or in blending chests before the fibers go to the paper machine.

Seldom is paper made from any one kind of fiber. In addition, the pulp can enter the stock preparation system either as a pulp slurry (slush pulp) from an adjoining pulp mill integrated with the paper mill or as bales of dried pulp which need to be repulped in a beater or hydrapulper. Other functions of the stock preparation stage are control of the fiber length for sheet uniformity, removal of unwanted dirt, specks, and particles, and dispersal of the fibers.

Papermaking

The cleaned and dispersed fibers are formed or combined into a fibrous mat in the papermaking stage of the system by deposition from a dilute headbox suspension (0.5 percent solids) onto the traveling continuous wire screen of the Fourdrinier paper machine mentioned earlier (Figure 20.19). The surplus water is removed by drainage from this wire screen aided by vacuum boxes, foils, and a vacuum "couch" roll, by pressing between rolls, and by drying on steam-heated drums or in a hot-air chamber.

Other functions of the papermaking stage are to control the sheet density and surface smoothness through application of pressure and some friction in the calender (Figure 20.19). Another function is the application of a surface coating. The solids content of the paper during papermaking progresses

from 15 percent after drainage, to 40 percent after presses, to 95 percent after the drum dryers.

Finishing and Converting of Paper

The objectives in the final stage of the total papermaking system are to improve the paper surface, to reduce rolls and sheets in size, and to modify paper for special properties, by coating or embossing, for example. Paper must also be converted into finished products, such as bags and corrugated boxes, and packaged for shipping. Paper is generally coated to improve printing properties. A surface coating of a pigment, usually kaolin or china clay, calcium carbonate, or titanium dioxide; and an adhesive, starch, or casein are applied to the partially dried web by brush, blade, spray, or other method, and dried during the papermaking (on-machine) operation or in a separate operation. The paper surface is brought to a high finish by passing through calenders or supercalenders. Supercalenders are stacks of alternate steel and densified fiber rolls that create a rubbing action on the sheet, imparting an extra gloss to the sheet surface.

Recycled Paper

Wastepaper fibers can be turned back into paper, depending on the price and supply of new pulp.

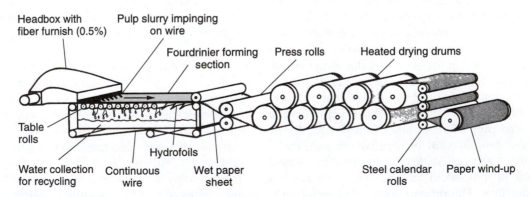

Figure 20.19   Schematic of a modern Fourdrinier paper machine.

The amount of the total recycled fiber for paper-making in the United States was 47.3 million tons in 2000, for a recovery rate of 45 percent. The United States is a major exporter of wastepaper—over 4 million metric tons per year.

The majority of the wastepaper exported from the United States goes to "fiber-poor" countries. These countries have much less virgin fiber and therefore recycle greater quantities of paper. Countries that recycle over 50 percent of their paper include the Netherlands, Japan, Mexico, South Korea, Argentina, Hungary and Switzerland. A variety of problems are associated with paper recycling, such as collection, distribution, and wild cyclic swings in the market. However, with landfill sites at a premium and paper representing about 40 percent of municipal solid waste, it makes good sense in the long run to promote paper recycling, which reduces both landfill needs and the consumption of virgin timber (9).

Pulp is produced from sorted wastepaper (paper stock) by separating the bonded fibers in the recovered paper and paperboard through mechanical action. This is done in water in a hydrapulper, which is a tub equipped with a powerful propeller rotor and auxiliary equipment to separate rags, wire, and other coarse contaminants. During the repulping operation, sodium hydroxide loosens the ink, called de-inking. The coarse contaminants are first removed by screening and cleaning equipment; then the pulp is given an extra fiberizing treatment and finally subjected to fine screening and cleaning. For use in newsprint, tissue, fine and toweling grades, the de-inked pulp requires bleaching in single and multistage processes (9).

Environmental Protection

The manufacture of pulp and paper is a chemical process industry and produces air emissions, effluents, and solid and toxic wastes that are potential hazards. The paper industry uses large volumes of water as a fiber carrier and as a chemical solvent. An increasing volume of water is recycled, but makeup water is still required to cover losses. A bleached pulp and paper mill may use 100 cubic meters (26,400 gallons) of fresh water per metric ton of product and 50,000 cubic meter (13.2 million gallons) daily for a plant producing 500 metric tons of products. In addition to this aqueous effluent that the mill must clean up, it must also contend with polluted air and solid and toxic wastes. Pulp and paper mills are considered to be minor toxic waste offenders. In this connection, the paper industry has generally been in good compliance with governmental environmental regulations, although at considerable capital expense, which amounts to about 10 percent of the cost of the mill.

In the 1970s, procedures for removal of the fibers and clay from the paper mill effluents were incorporated through settling or clarification or primary effluent treatment. About the same time secondary effluent treatment (biochemical treatment) of the pulp mill effluent was necessary to remove pulping residuals. The purpose of this treatment is to reduce the biological oxygen demand (BOD) of the effluent, which, if untreated, reduces the oxygen content of the stream to a level incapable of supporting aquatic life. The most common method uses microorganisms that react with the wood sugars and other oxygen-consuming compounds in the spent liquors; this is called the activated-sludge method. The products of primary and secondary treatments are sludges.

Solid wastes represent the ultimate in mill residues and include the accumulated refuse of the mill and the sludges from primary and secondary effluent treatment. There is difficulty in removing water from the secondary sludge; the primary and secondary sludges are often mixed to aid in water removal, which is important if the sludge is to be incinerated for disposal. The sludges from pulp and paper mills are handled mostly as landfill, and sometimes, if not toxic, they are spread for agricultural purposes.

Most mill solids are slightly toxic, predominantly from chlorination compounds in the wash waters from bleaching. This toxicity can be reduced with lime pretreatment and biological treatment. Toxicity has been the main concern of governmental regulating bodies.

Two objectionable air emissions have characterized pulp mills for years: the sulfur dioxide of the sulfite pulping mill and the malodorous reduced sulfur compounds (TRS) (mercaptans and hydrogen sulfide) of the kraft mill. Still another less noxious air emission is the particulate matter from steam boilers. Coal-burning boilers also emit sulfur dioxide, as is well known.

Cellulose Derivatives

Although most wood pulp fibers are produced for papermaking as described in the previous section, a small percentage (3 percent) are produced as dissolving pulp for the production of other cellulose based commodities. As shown in Table 20.5, the yield from dissolving pulp processes is only 35 percent. The percentage is low because all the hemicelluloses, in addition to the lignin (and some low-molecular-weight cellulose), are removed in the pulping process to give an almost pure cellulose fiber pulp. This pulp is then the raw material for the chemical and textile industries (12, 13).

Fibers and Films

Rayon and cellophane are produced from dissolving pulps and cotton linters by modifying the cellulose with carbon disulfide in caustic solution to give a cellulose derivative, namely, cellulose xanthate. The cellulose xanthate is then soluble in dilute alkaline solution, and when dissolved, the pulp fiber structure is lost. The resulting viscous solution of cellulose xanthate is termed viscose. This viscose can be "spun" into fibers by extrusion of the solution through tiny-holed spinnerets or cast into films by forming a thin sheet of the viscose. The original cellulose is regenerated by contact of the viscose with an aqueous acid bath, which splits off the carbon disulfide to give regenerated rayon fibers or cellophane films. The first textile fibers were produced from cellulose and were termed "artificial silk."

Cellulose acetate is formed from dissolving pulp or cotton linters by reacting the fibers with acetic anhydride using sulfuric acid as a catalyst. The cellulose acetate is then soluble in organic solvents such as acetone and can also be spun into fibers and cast to films. The cellulose is not regenerated but remains as cellulose acetate. The "acetate" fibers are used for textile fabrics and cigarette filters. The films are used in photographic products and as excellent osmotic membranes (13).

Chemical Commodities

Cellulose nitrate is one of the oldest cellulose derivatives and today is most widely used as an explosive (gun cotton) and as an ingredient in "smokeless powder." Alfred Nobel, who bequeathed the Nobel prizes, combined gun cotton with nitroglycerin to form a jellylike substance (blasting jelly) that was more powerful than dynamite. Nitrocellulose is also used as a lacquer coating material.

Carboxymethylcellulose (CMC) is a large commercial-volume cellulose ether. The nontoxic nature of CMC makes it very useful in the food, pharmaceutical, and cosmetic industries. It is used as a sizing agent, an emulsion stabilizer, a paint thickener, an oil-well-drilling mud, and a superabsorbent material (in the fibrous form). Methylcellulose and ethylcellulose are also cellulose ethers, but with quite different properties. Ethylcellulose provides exceptionally durable films and is used where extreme stress is encountered, such as in bowling pin coatings. Other uses include paper coatings, lacquers, and adhesives. Hydroxyethylcellulose became a commercial product in the 1960s and is chiefly used as a component of latex paints (13).

Conversions of Wood to Energy, Fuels, and Chemicals

The net photosynthetic productivity (NPP) of the earth has been estimated at 140×10^9 metric tons of dry matter per year. Forests account for about 42 percent or 59 billion metric tons of the NPP, which is equivalent to more than the annual world consumption of fossil fuels. In the United States, the equivalent of 80 quads of energy is produced each year as total plant biomass; however, much of this is inaccessible, uneconomical to collect, or already utilized for agricultural crops or forest products. It has been estimated that there are approximately 200 quads of standing timber in the nation's forests today. Thus, if an attempt were made to have wood as the sole source of energy in the United States, the country would be totally depleted of this reserve in two years. Woody biomass will therefore never be a panacea to an energy crisis, but certainly a greater contribution to the overall energy diet can be supplied by this important resource.

Probably the most significant advantage of biomass is the renewability. The U.S. Department of Energy has estimated that the equivalent of about 8 quads of energy in the form of biomass is produced annually in the nation's forests, but roughly one-half or the equivalent of 4 quads is already harvested annually for lumber and paper products. Much of the forest that is not harvested is inaccessible or under harvesting restrictions. Thus, the major contribution from woody biomass will probably be in the form of more efficient use of residues and waste.

If all types of waste are included in the scenario of biomass utilization, including urban and agricultural wastes in addition to wood wastes, these wastes and residues represent close to 1 billion metric tons or the equivalent fuel value of approximately 15 percent of the total energy needs of the United States. Wood, in the form of logging and manufacturing residues, accounts for about 25 percent of this figure. In addition, roughly 40 percent of most municipal waste is composed of wastepaper, which represents the wood cellulose ultimately derived from the forest. Thus, a significant energy contribution could be made by efficient utilization of waste material. The use of wood as a primary source of industrial chemicals decreased dramatically in the 1940s when oil became the preferred raw material. The term *silvichemicals* is sometimes used to refer to wood-derived chemicals analogous to petrochemicals.

The use of wood for energy, fuels, and chemicals can be conveniently divided into four major categories: direct combustion, saccharification-fermentation (SF), thermal decomposition, and thermochemical liquefaction (9). Each of these methods is discussed in more detail in the following sections.

Direct Combustion

The concept of using wood as a source of energy through direct combustion dates back to the very beginning of human existence. As soon as early people learned to use fire, wood became the major source of energy. It is important to note that even now approximately one-half of all the wood harvested worldwide is used for fuel by direct combustion. Thus, direct combustion is probably the most important method for deriving energy from wood.

Wood has certain advantages over fossil fuels, the most important of which is that it is a renewable resource. In addition, it has a low ash content which is easily and usefully disposed of on land as mineral constituents essential for plant growth. The sulfur content of wood is low, usually less than 0.1 percent, so that air pollution from this source is negligible, although particulates may cause a serious problem. Generally, wood fuel is used close to where it is grown; thus the need for energy in long distance transport is reduced. The use of fossil fuels unlocks the carbon that has been stored in them for ages and increases the carbon dioxide content of the atmosphere. In contrast, wood fuel releases the same amount of carbon dioxide that the forest has recently fixed.

Wood does have disadvantages as a fuel. It is a bulky material, and in contrast to other fuels, it has a low heat of combustion. The gaseous and liquid fuels, from methane to petroleum have a higher potential heat content because they do not contain oxygen.

All wood species consist of essentially the same chemical compounds; therefore, the various woods differ little in heat content per pound. The differences noted in the fuel value of different woods when compared by volume are caused by differences in density. One cord of hickory, a dense commercial wood, for example, gives two times more heat than one cord of low-density species such as aspen or spruce. The heat values and densities of important woods grown in the United States are shown in Table 20.6 (4, 14). An exception to the density rule of thumb are coniferous woods, which contain energy-rich resin. These species can contain up to 12 percent more heat potential.

Green wood at 50 percent moisture content has only about one-half the fuel value of dry wood. The amount of energy released in a fire depends on the wood moisture content more than on any other factor. Moisture affects the energy release in two ways, by consuming heat for moisture evaporation, and by causing incomplete combustion (2).

Incomplete combustion has several other bad effects in addition to wasting fuel. Gases from burning wood contain formic and acetic acids; these acids, when condensed, corrode stovepipes. The corrosion can be so severe that the pipes may need to be replaced after only one year of operation. Other condensed vapors form creosote, a brown or black stenchy liquid that may leak out of stovepipe joints and cause unsightly stains. Prolonged exposure to heat converts the creosote to a flaky layer of carbon known as soot. Carbon particles in the fire effluents tend to aggregate and adhere to the inside surfaces of stoves, stovepipes, and chimney flues, augmenting the accumulation of soot. These deposits insulate and hinder flow of gases; with unusually hot fires, these deposits can ignite as chimney fires, which can crack the chimney and ignite the house. For this reason, chimneys should be cleaned periodically depending on the amount of use and completeness of combustion. Hot, oxygen-rich fires reduce chimney deposits, but hot effluents also carry heat out of the chimney (2).

Wood-burning units have evolved over centuries of use in homes around the world (2). Many old-time stoves in Europe relied on immense heat-storing masses of fireclay, firebrick, and other masonry. Hot, oxygen-rich fires facilitated complete combustion, and the fire effluents passed through a long labyrinth of flues to deliver the heat to the solid mass. The Russian-Ukrainian type of stove, still in use today in rural areas, was constructed with a low cooking section containing the combustion chamber, and a much larger (6 to 8 feet) flue section with an immense, flat top surface, which provided warm sleeping quarters for the whole family.

The German Kachelofen or tile stove was a showpiece in the living room; many small tile stoves still heat rooms of homes, particularly farmhouses throughout Europe. All stoves store some heat, but modern types lack the storage capacity and versatility of the old brick monsters.

Many Americans have become more interested in burning wood in their homes to reduce heating costs. Household wood burning varies considerably with the region of the country; roughly 50 percent of the residents of Maine, Vermont, and Oregon burn more than one-third of a cord of wood annually, but fewer than 10 percent of the residents of most southern states burn this much wood.

Many hundreds of different types of stoves, furnaces, fireplaces, and accessories for heating with wood have appeared on the market as a result of the increased interest in wood burning. A few of these are discussed further in the following paragraphs.

Fireplaces The open built-in fireplace is the least efficient heating device. Warm air bypasses the fire, as shown in Figure 20.20a, and escapes through the chimney. This draft pulls equal amounts of cold outside air through joints at doors and other openings into the house so that, in very cold weather, the use of the fireplace may actually cool rather than heat the house. A fireplace door obstructs the bypass of the air and, with the help of a baffle between the grate and door (Figure 20.20b), can eliminate the bypass of air so that the fireplace will heat more efficiently. Whatever the design, watching and hearing a crackling fire has a gratification not to be matched, and people have enjoyed it since the dawn of humanity.

Stoves and Furnaces In stoves and furnaces, the air takes various paths through the wood fuel. In all these variations, the intent is to have the air pass through the burning wood pile to promote combustion, heat the air, and then pass to the outlet at the top or back of the stove. There is no intrinsic

Table 20.6 Densities and Heat Values at 12% Moisture Content[a] of Important Wood Grown in the United States

Tree Name	Density(g/cm³)	Heat Value[b] (million kJ/m³)	Heat Value[b] (million Btu/cord[c])
Hardwoods			
Live oak	0.99	17.60	40.32
Shagbark hickory	0.81	14.40	32.99
White oak	0.76	13.60	31.16
Honeylocust	0.72	12.80	29.32
American beech	0.72	12.80	29.32
Sugar maple	0.71	12.60	28.86
Northern red oak	0.71	12.60	28.86
Yellow birch	0.69	12.40	28.40
White ash	0.67	12.00	27.49
Black walnut	0.62	11.00	25.20
Sweetgum	0.58	10.40	23.82
Black cherry	0.56	10.00	22.91
American elm	0.56	10.00	22.91
Southern magnolia	0.56	10.00	22.91
Black tupelo	0.56	10.00	22.91
Sycamore	0.55	9.80	22.50
Sassafras	0.52	9.20	21.08
Yellow poplar	0.47	8.40	19.24
Red alder	0.46	8.20	18.79
Eastern cottonwood	0.45	8.00	18.33
Quaking aspen	0.43	7.60	17.41
American basswood	0.41	7.40	16.95
Softwoods			
Longleaf pine	0.66	12.63	28.92
Western larch	0.58	11.13	25.49
Loblolly pine	0.57	10.92	25.00
Shortleaf pine	0.57	10.92	25.00
Douglas fir	0.54	10.27	23.53
Bald cypress	0.52	9.85	22.55
Western hemlock	0.50	9.00	20.62
Ponderosa pine	0.45	8.56	19.61
White fir	0.44	7.80	17.87
Redwood	0.43	7.60	17.41
Eastern white pine	0.39	7.49	17.16
Engelmann spruce	0.39	7.49	17.16
Western red cedar	0.36	6.40	14.66

Source: Densities from reference 4, heat values from P. J. Ince, U.S.D.A. For. Serv., Gen. Tech. Rept. FPL 29, Forest Products Laboratory, Madison, Wis., 1979.

[a] Moisture content based on weight of ovendry wood.

[b] Heat values include heat in fire effluents. Calculated on the basis of British thermal units (Btu) per pound of ovendry wood, 9200 Btu for resinous-wood species.

[c] One cord equals 128 cubic feet or 3.6246 cubic meters; it is assumed that the pile is two-thirds wood and one-third air (between the pieces); hence, one cord contains 2.4164 cubic meters of solid wood.

Figure 20.20
Movement of air (a) through an open built-in fireplace and (b) through a fireplace with a door to obstruct bypass of air.

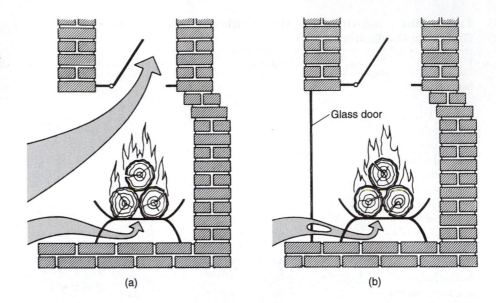

(a)   (b)

reason why one type is better than another as long as the air passes through the burning wood in an efficient manner. Hot air streams naturally upward, but the air velocity depends mainly on the chimney draft and can be regulated with vents and dampers. Modern "airtight" stoves provide the best air control and thus more efficient heating.

A completely different heating appliance, the stick wood furnace, was developed at the University of Maine (Figure 20.21). In this stove, long sticks or logs stand in a tight jacket. Air enters only at the bottom where burning of the sticks takes place. To confine the burning to just the bottom end of the stove, water cools the jacket and can then be used for hot water in the home. The sticks burn slowly at the bottom and are self-feeding because of their own weight. Theoretically, the stick wood furnace can be used to burn whole-tree stems.

Saccharification–Fermentation

The saccharification–fermentation (SF) method is based on the breakdown or hydrolysis of the polysaccharides in wood to the constituent monomeric sugars. The six-carbon or hexose sugars (glucose, galactose, and mannose) are then fermentable to

ethyl alcohol (ethanol or grain alcohol, C_2H_5OH) by yeast fermentation in the same way that ethanol is produced from grains or fruits. Obviously the concept is not a new one; the polysaccharide character of wood has been known for over 100 years.

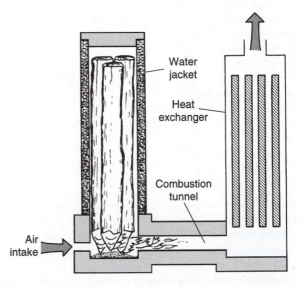

Figure 20.21   A stick wood furnace.

The limitations to the use of wood for ethanol production have been primarily the difficulty in separating and hydrolyzing the crystalline cellulose component in wood. Both acids and enzymes can be used to hydrolyze the cellulose to glucose, but only acids have been utilized commercially for wood hydrolysis to sugars, and only in foreign countries.

Interest in producing alcohols from wood was revitalized by the dramatic increase in the price of petroleum in the 1970s and the push to decrease oil imports by substituting gasohol, which is one part alcohol in nine parts gasoline, for 100 percent gasoline at gas pumps. Both ethanol and methanol can be used in gasohol blends. Because of the high oil prices, the country of Brazil took the dramatic step of shifting to much greater use of fuel alcohol. Most of their sugars are produced from sugarcane. One wood hydrolysis plant was constructed, but it was uneconomical to operate and was shut down. However, their experience demonstrates that fermentation ethanol (95 percent ethanol and 5 percent water) is a perfectly satisfactory motor fuel. At least 500,000 Brazilian automobiles operated on undried alcohol continuously, and most of the rest of their fleet operated on this fuel on weekends when only alcohol was available at the gas stations (9). A number of methods can be used for production of ethanol from wood.

Thermal Decomposition

A number of terms are used interchangeably for thermal decomposition of wood and generally refer to similar processing methods: carbonization, pyrolysis, gasification, wood distillation, destructive distillation, and dry distillation. All result in the thermal breakdown of the wood polymers to smaller molecules in the form of char, tar (a condensible liquid), and gaseous products. A liquid fuel derivable from wood by this method is methyl alcohol (methanol or wood alcohol, CH_3OH). A wide variety of other chemicals are also derivable from wood by thermal decomposition, a method with a long history of applications.

During World War II in Germany, automobiles were fueled by the gases produced from thermal decomposition of wood, and research is active today on more efficient gasification of wood. Destructive distillation has been used throughout most of recorded history to obtain turpentine from pinewood; this is discussed further in the section on wood extractives. The range of chemicals derivable from thermal decomposition of wood is summarized in Figure 20.22.

Charcoal and Other Chemicals Production of charcoal and tars by destructive distillation is the oldest of all chemical wood-processing methods. Charcoal was probably first discovered when the black material left over from a previous fire burned with intense heat and little smoke and flame. For centuries, charcoal has been used in braziers for heating purposes. Destructive distillation of hardwoods has been performed seeking charcoal as the desired product, with volatiles as byproducts; for softwoods (pines), volatiles were the principal products (naval stores, discussed later), with charcoal considered a byproduct.

Basic techniques for producing charcoal have not changed over the years, although the equipment has. Charcoal is produced when wood is burned under conditions in which the supply of oxygen is severely limited (15). Carbonization is a term that aptly describes the thermal decomposition of wood for this application. Decomposition of carbon compounds takes place as the temperature rises, leading to a solid residue that is richer in carbon than the original material. Wood has a carbon content of about 50 percent, whereas charcoal of a quality suitable for general market acceptance can be analyzed as follows: fixed carbon, 74–81 percent; volatiles, 18–23 percent; moisture, 2–4 percent; ash, 1–4 percent. Charcoal with a volatiles content over 24 percent will cause smoking and is undesirable for recreational uses.

Thermochemical Liquefaction

Although a reasonable amount of research effort has been expended on thermochemical liquefaction of wood, extensive commercialization of this process is not anticipated in the near future. The

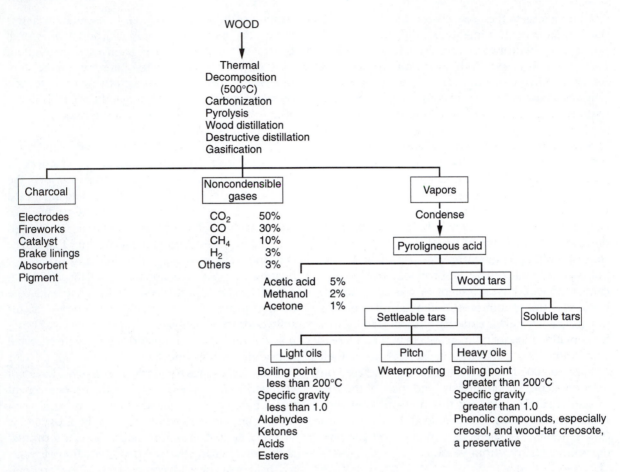

Figure 20.22   Products obtained from the thermal decomposition of wood.

basis of the method is a high-pressure and high-temperature treatment of wood chips in the presence of hydrogen gas or syngas to produce an oil instead of a gas. The low-grade oil produced could potentially be substituted for some present petroleum uses.

Wood Extractives

All species of wood and other plants contain small (mostly) to large quantities of substances that are not constituents of the cell wall, as pointed out previously. The entire class is called extraneous components. Extractives are the largest group by far of

this class. The extractives embrace a very large number of individual compounds that often influence the physical properties of wood and play an important role in its utilization. Colored and volatile constituents provide visual and olfactory aesthetic values. Certain phenolic compounds lend resistance to fungal and insect attack with resulting durability, and silica imparts resistance to the wood-destroying marine borers (16).

Extractives can also have a detrimental effect on the use of wood. Alkaloids and some other physiologically active materials may present health hazards. Certain phenols present in pine heartwood inhibit the calcium-based sulfite pulping process and cause pitch problems. The loss of water absorbency properties of wood pulps can also result from extractives. Extractives from cedarwood and the woods of a number of other species can cause severe corrosion problems in the pulping operation (16). A wide variety of extractives are utilized commercially, as will be described.

Two broad classes of extractives occur in wood 1) those soluble in organic solvents, such as wood resins including turpentine, rosin, fat, and fatty acids; and 2) those soluble in water, mostly polyphenolic material including tannins and lignans and the polysaccharide arabinogalactan.

Extractives Soluble in Organic Solvents

The largest aggregate volume and value of industrial extractives are those derived from pinewoods. These materials, which include turpentine, rosin, and fatty acids, are also often referred to as *naval stores*. This term derives from the use of pitch and tars from pine extractives as caulking and waterproofing agents for wooden ships in early American history. The term naval stores has remained in use and now mainly refers to the turpentine and rosin derived from pine trees.

There are three sources of naval stores: *gum*, *wood*, and *sulfate*. *Gum naval stores* are produced by wounding pine trees and collecting the oleoresin. The oleoresin is a sticky substance composed of an essential oil, turpentine, and a resin, rosin. Since turpentine is a low-boiling, volatile material, the two products can be separated by a distillation process (9, 17).

In this country, the gum naval stores industry is based on two Southern pine species, slash and longleaf, and is centered in the state of Georgia. Though very important in the past, this method today accounts for only a few percent of U.S. rosin and turpentine production. Typically the oleoresin is collected in containers by cutting grooves in the tree so that the wound opens the resin ducts (Figure 20.23). Various means have been used to stimulate oleoresin production such as repeated wounding and spraying with sulfuric acid or the herbicide paraquat. The so-called lightwood, high-

Figure 20.23 Scarification of pine trees for collections of oleoresin. (a) View of stand. (b) Close-up of tree wound. (Courtesy of University of Georgia, College of Agriculture.)

oleoresin-content wood, then contains up to 40 percent resin (17).

Wood naval stores are obtained by organic-solvent extraction of chipped or shredded old pine stumps. The old pine stumps have lost most of the outer sapwood through decay and are made up primarily of the oleoresin-rich heartwood where the extractives are mainly deposited. Turpentine and crude resin fractions are obtained by this method.

Sidebar 20.2

Cholesterol-Lowering Margarine

Benecol margarines and spreads are based on stanol esters, a class of sterols that are obtained from waste-pulping liquors from kraft pulping of pine species. Recent studies have shown that by regular use of these products, the so-called "bad cholesterol" can be reduced by up to 14 percent. Raisio, a Finnish company, built plants in Finland and Charleston, S.C., to make the ester from sterols extracted from tall oil pitch supplied by such firms as Arizona Chemicals. The Raisio company has also embarked on a $50 million project with a tall oil refiner in Chile to build the world's largest sterol extraction plant.

The product has been a large commercial success in Finland; however, the American market has been much more subdued. The Food and Drug Administration has allowed labeling of Benecol foods with a statement that they have been proven to lower cholesterol and may lower the risk of heart disease, which may increase sales. This is an excellent example of how continued research on plant and waste materials can lead to new important medicinal products in the market.

Sulfate naval stores are derived as byproduct streams from the kraft pulping process. As pine chips are treated in the digester to produce pulp, the volatilized gases are released and condensed to yield a sulfate turpentine.

Turpentine was used as a solvent in its early history, particularly as a paint solvent. Today this use is small, and turpentine is used for the most part as a feedstock for manufacture of many products, including synthetic pine oil, resins, insecticides, and a variety of flavor and fragrance chemicals. Flavors and fragrances derived from turpentine include lemon, lime, spearmint, peppermint, menthol, and lilac. The synthetic pine oil is further converted to terpin hydrate, a cough expectorant. Obviously, turpentine has become a valuable byproduct of the forest and pulp-and-paper industry (17).

Rosins are usually used in a form modified by further chemical reaction. Rosin found considerable use at one time in laundry soap (38 percent in 1938), but this use is negligible today. Rosin soaps are at present important as emulsifying agents in synthetic rubber and chemical manufacture and for paper sizing. The sizing is used to reduce water absorptivity of paper. Rosin is also used in surface coatings, printing oils, and adhesives. Typically pressure-sensitive tapes such as "scotch" tape contain considerable quantities of rosin (17).

Water-Soluble Extractives

The most important group of water-extractable compounds are the polyphenolics. These substances are generally extractable with water at 80–120°C from the heartwood and bark of many trees. Of the polyphenolics, only the tannins have shown commercial value. The traditional source of tannins in the United States was chestnut wood and bark, but this source was removed when the chestnut blight of the 1930s devastated the chestnut tree in North America. The South American tree, quebracho, is now the major source of tannins. Acacia bark extracts, called wattle or mimosa, are also an important source of tannins, and together with quebracho extractives, amount to a production of 250,000 tons per year (5, 18).

The primary use of tannins is for manufacture of leather from hides. The natural tanning agents continue to dominate the market, even though synthetic tanning agents are available. The extractives from each different wood species provide their own unique color and properties to the leather.

Wattle tannins have also been successfully substituted for phenol in phenol-formaldehyde adhesives in South Africa. The phenol-formaldehyde adhesives are used in the production of plywood, particleboard, and laminated beams.

Biotechnology Chemicals

As with pulping and bleaching, biotechnology could also have a considerable impact on the production of chemicals from wood and other forms of plant biomass. The effects of biotechnology will probably first be noticed in areas of enzymatic hydrolysis of polysaccharides and fermentation technology.

It should be possible to improve the efficiency of the cellulose enzyme complex for hydrolyzing cellulose to glucose. The enzyme complex contains decrystallizing and hydrolysis enzymes that work together to convert cellulose to glucose. Isolation of the specific enzymes and genetic engineering could provide a more efficient complex.

As discussed earlier in this chapter, enzymes are also the basis for yeast conversion of hexose (six carbon) sugars, such as glucose and mannose, to ethanol. These enzymes could also be genetically engineered to improve the efficiency of alcohol production, and several biotechnology firms are exploring this possibility.

Many other chemicals can be obtained from both yeast and bacteria fermentation of sugars and pulp mill effluents. Potential fermentation products from wood hydrolysates include acetone, organic acids (acetic, butyric, lactic), glycerol, butanediol, and others (18).

Concluding Statement

The unique properties and the renewable nature of wood make it a very desirable material for a great variety of uses. Even with the advent of new polymers, plastics, and high technology materials, wood products are still pervasive in our life. The ready availability and workable properties of wood make it valuable for building materials and furniture. Mechanical and chemical disintegration allows us to convert wood into a myriad of paper products so important to communication and packaging. Finally, a wide variety of chemical commodities are derivable from wood from cellulose superabsorbents to flavors, fragrances and fuel alcohols. Truly, wood is one of nature's most attractive and, useful products.

References

1. W. M. HARLOW, *Inside Wood—Masterpiece of Nature*, American Forestry Assoc., Washington, D.C., 1970.

2. H. KUBLER, *Wood as a Building and Hobby Material*, Wiley-Interscience, New York, 1980.

3. A. J. PASHIN AND C. DE ZEEUW, *Textbook of Wood Technology*, Vol. 1, *Structure, Identification, Uses and Properties of the Commercial Woods of the United States and Canada*, Fourth Edition, McGraw-Hill, New York, 1980.

4. ANON., *Wood Handbook: Wood as an Engineering Material*, U.S.D.A. For. Serv., Forest Products Laboratory, U.S. Govt. Printing Office, Washington, D.C., 1999.

5. D. FENGEL AND G. WEGENER, *Wood: Chemistry, Ultrastructure, Reactions*, Walter de Gruyter Publisher, New York, 1984.

6. E. SJÖSTRÖM, *Wood Chemistry: Fundamentals and Applications*, Academic Press, New York, 1993.

7. R. A. Young, "Processing of agro-based resources into pulp and paper," In *Paper and Composites from Agro-based Materials*, R. Rowell and R.A. Young, eds., Lewis Pub., CRC Press, Boca Raton, Fla., 1997.

8. R. A. Young, "Vegetable fibers," In *Encyclopedia of Chemical Technology*, Vol. 10, Kirk, ed., John Wiley & Sons, Pub., New York, 1994; 2003.

9. R. A. Young, "Wood and wood products," In *Riegel's Handbook of Industrial Chemistry*, J. A. Kent, ed., Van Nostrand Reinhold, New York, p. 207–272, 1992; 2003.

10. J. D. Casey, ed., *Pulp and Paper, Chemistry and Chemical Technology*, Third Edition, Wiley-Interscience, New York, 1980.

11. R. A. Young and M. Akhtar, eds., *Environmentally Friendly Technologies for the Pulp and Paper Industry*, Wiley-Interscience, New York, 1998.

12. R. A. Young and R. M. Rowell, eds., *Cellulose: Structure, Modification and Hydrolysis*, Wiley-Interscience, New York, 1986.

13. R. M. Rowell and R. A. Young, eds., *Modified Cellulosics*, Academic Press, New York, 1978.

14. P. J. Ince, "How to Estimate Recoverable Heat Energy in Wood or Bark Fuels," U.S.D.A. Agr. Handbook 605, South For. Expt. Sta., U.S. Govt. Printing Office, Washington, D.C., 1985.

15. Anon., "Charcoal Production, Marketing and Use," U.S.D.A. For. Serv. Rept. 2213, Forest Products Laboratory, Madison, Wis., 1961.

16. B. L. Browning, ed., *The Chemistry of Wood*, Robert E. Krieger Pub., Huntington, N.Y., 1975.

17. D. F. Zinkel, *J. Appl. Polymer Symp., 28*, 309 (1975).

18. G. J. Hajny, "Biological Utilization of Wood for Production of Chemicals and Foodstuffs," U.S.D.A. For. Serv. Rept. 385, Forest Products Laboratory, Madison, Wis., 1981.

CHAPTER 21

Economics and the Management of Forests for Wood and Amenity Values

JOSEPH BUONGIORNO AND
RONALD RAUNIKAR

Foresters, be they practitioners or students, often accept only reluctantly that economics has any role to play in their profession. They chose this career for their love of the woods. The counting of money seems foreign, indeed contrary, to the powerfully romantic attraction of the wild forest. Yet, the current forest endowment of nations is to a large extent the result of past economic forces. Among them, the industrial revolution of Europe and the settlement of America's New England are economic watersheds that have changed forever the nature and extent of forests. Presently, the economic development of Latin America and Africa are largely deciding how much forest, if any, will remain in the Amazon and the Congo basin.

Furthermore, economics deals with much more than money, and contrary to common opinion, it does have something to say about value. In the words of Ludwig Von Mises: "Everybody thinks of economics whether he is aware of it or not. In joining a political party and in casting his ballot, the citizen implicitly takes a stand upon essential economic theories" (1). More specifically, Nobel prize economist Paul A. Samuelson defines economics as "the study of how people and society end up choosing, with or without the use of money, to employ scarce productive resources that could have alternative uses, to produce various commodities and distribute them for consumption, now or in the future, among various persons and groups in society. It analyzes the costs and benefits of improving patterns of resource allocation" (2).

In this spirit, this chapter considers the wide array of goods and services that are provided directly or indirectly by forests. They include wood products that we use in our daily lives: lumber, plywood, particleboard, and other panels for houses and furniture; paper for newsprint, books, and stationery, fuelwood for heating, and many chemical derivatives. Services from forests include their protective role against erosion and avalanches in mountain areas, the aesthetic and other pleasures that one derives from hiking through them, and their role as biodiversity preserves and carbon sinks. The purpose of this chapter is to review briefly how economic reasoning can help in the wise management of forest resources.

Economics of Timber Production

Because wood has been throughout human history an essential element of civilization, for fuel, construction, transport, and defense (3), the art of forest management has long been organized in a set of general principles founded on the scientific method. Over time, this has led to elaborate rules to optimize forest harvests in sustainable fashion. In the process, some foresters realized early on that economic principles were more important to forestry than to perhaps any other production activity. Few other ventures require as much time between initiation of production and sale of the product. Instead, much of the rest of the economy evolves in a groping process with inefficient firms losing to more efficient firms. In relatively short order, firms know whether they have a positive cash flow given the prices consumers are willing to pay. The firms either learn to operate efficiently enough to stay in business or they quickly disappear. They learn by internally developing insights or by using the example of more successful firms. Although forestry enterprises do also partake of this economic selection process, the results are generally slower, and simply doing the same as others is not always the best. Thus, for forest managers, well-considered economic reasoning is of paramount importance.

This importance has been long recognized, and solutions of some forest economic problems predate the discovery of similar principles in general economics. The most famous example is probably Martin Faustmann's rigorous derivation of the value of forestland (4). General economists largely missed Faustmann's insight, and it was not until the 1930s that, extending beyond the work of Irving Fisher and others, the general theory of investment was formulated as soundly as Faustmann's forestry formula. Interestingly, Fisher, though possibly "the greatest sin-

gle economic writer on interest and capital," gave a poor solution to Faustmann's problem (5).

The Value of Forestland and Faustmann's Formula

In seeking the value of forestland, Faustmann recognized that it must be equal to the value of the net returns that one could expect from that land, if it were used in forestry. However, much of these returns would occur only very far into the future, so that they would be worth less now; that is, they must be discounted at a suitable interest rate. Thus, the land value had to be equal to the net present value of the full future stream of costs incurred and benefits derived from the forest. This insight seems ordinary now with the common use of benefit-cost analysis to evaluate projects and policies, but it was remarkable at the time. It defines unambiguously the general principle to follow in choosing between forest management alternatives and different land uses: maximize the land expectation value.

By simplifying the forest management problem to only the value of wood harvested from a stand of trees, Faustmann showed that the economic optimal rotation is less than the rotation that produces the maximum average annual biological yield. This conclusion seems to contradict the intuition that higher average annual production must also mean higher income. Faustmann's insight was to recognize that, besides the magnitude of the harvests over the rotation, their timing also matters.

Cutting and selling early gives income to either consume or to reinvest in forestry or alternative investments. The interest rate reflects this opportunity cost of postponing a harvest. One elegant aspect of Faustmann's method is that it recognizes the opportunity to plant a new stand of trees earlier when the rotation age is shortened. By summing the costs and revenues of an infinite series of replanted stands, Faustmann accounts for the opportunity cost of these future stands. Alternatively, he could have maximized the present discounted value of a single rotation, and included the land rental value of the bare land left at the end of the rotation. However, the calculation of the appropriate market land rental rate is fraught with difficulties. It is one of the notable advantages of Faustmann's approach that the land rental value is not needed, but that instead it results directly from his formula.

In its simplest form, the Faustmann model can be symbolized as in Figure 21.1. We begin at time 0, with a piece of bare land, we plant trees and let them grow for R years, the rotation. All the trees are harvested at rotation age. Immediately after the harvest, we establish a new plantation, identical to that of time 0. The trees then grow exactly as in the first rotation, and they are harvested at the same rotation age. This sequence is assumed to continue indefinitely.

In this simple model, let V_R be the volume of timber per unit area at age R, c the reforestation cost per unit area, p the price of timber per unit of volume net of harvesting cost, and i the interest rate per year. The volume V_R depends only on the age of the trees, and the parameters R, c, p, and i are assumed to be constant over time, for example, equal to their current value.

It can be shown that the discounted value of all future returns, net of all costs is:

$$LEV = \frac{pV_R - c}{(1 + i)^R - 1} - c \qquad (1)$$

where the first term on the right is the present value of all future harvests net of reforestation cost ($pV_R - c$) recurring every R years, indefinitely, and the second term is the cost, c, of establishing the initial plantation, at time 0. The result is the *land expectation value, LEV*; that is, value of bare land used in this kind of forestry. This result, is, in a very simplified form, Faustmann's great finding, a fundamental contribution to forestry economics, and also a precursory insight into the general theory of investments (5). Faustmann also gave an extension of formula 1 to calculate the value of a stand with trees younger than the best rotation.

Economic Comparison of Alternative Land Uses

Equation 1 has numerous applications, to compare different land uses, or to compare different forest management strategies. For that purpose, it usually includes much more detail such as density in plantations, commercial and pre-commercial thinning, and so forth. As an illustration, equation 1 can be used to find the best economic rotation, R; that is, the rotation that maximizes the land value, LEV. This economic rotation can be determined with simple calculations in a spreadsheet, along the lines illustrated in Table 21.1.

In Table 21.1, the first column is tree age, from 20 to 100 years. The second column shows the volume per unit area. It is largest for 100-year-old trees. The third and fourth column show the gross and net return, respectively, from harvesting the trees at different ages. The fifth column shows the present value of $1 paid every R year, indefinitely. The interest rate is 2.5% yr^{-1}. For example, the present value of a perpetual series of $1 paid every 20 years is $1.57. However, if the same $1 is paid every 40 years, the present value is only $0.59.

The land expectation value, in column 6 is the product of columns 4 and 5 minus c. It is negative for $R = 20$ years. Thus, if the trees were cut when they were 20 years old, the present value of the returns would be less than that of the present value of the costs, so that this would be a bad policy indeed. A rotation of 60 years is best from a purely financial viewpoint because for that age, the land expectation value is highest, at $1387 ha^{-1}. Note that this is not the age at which the trees are largest or

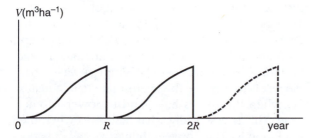

Figure 21.1 Stand growth and harvest in simple Faustmann model; V is the stand volume, per unit area, and R is the rotation age.

Table 21.1   The best economic rotation leads to the highest land expectation value, *LEV*; it is shorter than the best biological rotation.

(1)	(2)	(3)	(4)	(5)	(6) = (4) × (5) − c	(7)
R (yr)	V_R (m³ha⁻¹)	pV_R ($ha⁻¹)	$pV_R - c$ ($ha⁻¹)	$\dfrac{1}{(1+i)^R - 1}$	*LEV* ($ha⁻¹)	V_R/R (m³ha⁻¹yr⁻¹)
20	29	377	−117	1.57	−677	1.5
40	274	3,562	3,068	0.59	1,327	6.9
60*	530	6,890	6,396	0.29	1,387	8.8
80**	728	9,464	8,970	0.16	951	9.1
100	868	11,284	10,790	0.09	504	8.7

p=13 \$/m³, c=\$494/ha, i=2.5%/yr, *=economic rotation, **= biological rotation.

most valuable, nor is it the age of highest physical productivity. As shown in the last column, the highest physical productivity, in m³ ha⁻¹ yr⁻¹ occurs at age 80. Indeed, the economic rotation age is always shorter than the biological rotation age set by physical productivity alone. This is because financially, $1 next year is worth only $1/(1+i)$ now.

The land expectation value obtained by Faustmann's formula, $1,387 ha⁻¹ in this example, is the highest possible return from land used in this kind of silviculture. It is, therefore, the price a buyer would pay for this kind of land, and it is also the price at which an owner would be willing to sell. This land expectation value can then be compared with the land·expectation value for alternative land uses (obtained with the equivalent of Faustmann's formula, regardless of the land use). A necessary condition for sustainable forestry in a free market economy is that the land expectation value obtained with a crop of trees be at least as large as the highest land expectation value obtainable by other land uses, such as agriculture, cattle grazing, or urban development. It is because the land expectation value for forestry is much lower than for agriculture or ranching that large areas of the tropical forests are currently being converted to those other uses.

Faustmann extended his approach to compute the value of immature forest stands, that is, stands younger than rotation age. The method has also been generalized to the case of uneven-aged or selection forests, forests where some trees are always left standing. In such a stand, the land expectation value is equal to the net present value of future returns minus the value of the remaining trees. Again, the sequence of harvests that leads to the greatest land value (i.e., the greatest return to the fixed input) is best, from a purely economic viewpoint. Faustmann's formula can also be generalized to include benefits in addition to harvested wood. The difficulty, of course, is in determining this nontimber value of forests, a question to which we shall return, below. Another difficulty not addressed here, lies in choosing a proper interest rate (6, 7).

Dealing with Risk

Risk of natural catastrophe and other uncertainties are ignored in the simplifying assumptions of the Faustmann analysis, but dealing with biological and economic risk and uncertainty are important in practical forest economics (8). The simplest way to handle risk is to increase the interest rate, i, in equation (1) when the risk is high, and to lower it otherwise. This is essentially what banks do when they lend money. They protect themselves against possible losses by charging higher interest for loans in risky ventures. In forestry, other things being equal, a higher interest rate will lead to a shorter economic rotation. This is consistent with the intuition that would suggest to cut trees earlier if there is a definite risk of a natural catastrophe, such as tornadoes or fires.

The problem with handling risk by changing the interest rate is that it is hard to know by how much to change the rate. For that reason, other approaches use the same interest rate, regardless of risk level, but recognize risk explicitly in the production function, that is, in the second column of Table 21.1, and in the price level, p. One approach, called simulation, consists in calculating *LEV* many times, each time with a different production function or price, in a pattern similar to what might happen in reality. The economic rotation is then the one that gives the highest *LEV* on average, or the one that insures the lowest variation in *LEV*, and thus the lowest probability of a major loss. Another approach is the Markov decision process model (MDP). It describes changes in the forest stand and other variables (especially prices) with a table of probabilities: each being the probability of a future stand and market state given the current state. Hool (9) first proposed such a model for even-aged forests, but the first operational application was Lembersky and Johnson's work with Douglas fir plantations (10). Other applications of MDPs to forestry have shown that they are adaptable to uneven-aged forests. With them it is possible to investigate management strategies with economic and ecological criteria as objective functions or constraints, while taking full account of risk (11).

Economics of Forest Product Markets

Key to the evaluation of the economics of timber production with Faustmann's formula and its derivatives is a correct assessment of interest rates, prices, and costs. In particular, future prices depend on the demand and supply conditions in the wood products markets. Here again, economics gives foresters useful tools to better understand what causes prices to change, and help predict their future direction, if not their exact level.

Demand and Supply

The simplest abstraction, or model, of a market consists of two equations: one representing demand, the other supply. For economists, demand is a relation, not a quantity. Figure 21.2 shows such a relation. Assume that it represents the demand for timber in the United States. On the horizontal axis is the quantity of timber consumed, Q_d (m^3yr^{-1}); on the vertical axis is the price of timber, P ($\$m^{-3}$). A downward-sloping line, such as D_1 represents the demand for timber. It shows that other things being equal, the higher the price, the lower the consumption. Of the two demand lines in Figure 21.2, the one farther from the origin, D_2, corresponds to the higher demand, since it leads to higher consumption at a given price. For example, in the United States, much lumber goes into houses. Therefore, as the number of houses built increases, the demand for lumber increases, and the demand line in Figure 21.2 shifts to the right. Another way to represent the United States demand for timber is with an equation:

$$Q_d = a - bP + cH \qquad (2)$$

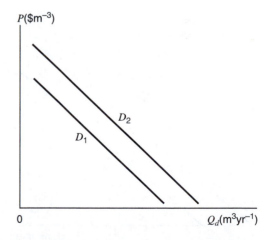

Figure 21.2 Every point on a demand line represents the quantity demanded at a given price. The lines slope downward because demand decreases as price increases. Lines that are farther from the origin correspond to higher demand.

where P stands for the price of timber, and H stands for the number of houses started in a given year, and a, b, c are parameters that can be estimated with statistical methods. The equation shows that demand for lumber is a derived demand. We do not consume lumber directly like food, but instead we use it to build houses. Thus, the demand for lumber and most of the other wood products derives from the demand for housing.

Like demand, the term "supply" for economists also means a relation rather than a quantity. For example, Figure 21.3 symbolizes the supply of timber in the United States. The private supply is an upward sloping line, S_1, indicating that as the price increases, private producers have an incentive to produce more timber. However, a good part of the timber is produced in the United States by government from federal and state forests. Government supply is set by policy and is usually independent of price. In Figure 21.3, the distance Q_g represents government supply.

We can express the total supply with the following equation:

$$Q_s = dP - ei + Q_g \qquad (3)$$

where the positive coefficient d means that private timber production increases as price increases. Instead, the negative coefficient $-e$ implies that private supply decreases as i, the interest rate decreases. Both of those facts derive from the Faustmann's formula 1, which shows that at a higher price, timber production becomes more profitable (LEV increases), while at a higher interest rate, timber production becomes less profitable (LEV decreases). The cumulative effect of all those changes in each private property leads to the aggregate national supply response symbolized by equation 3. Q_g is the government supply, independent of interest rate or price.

Market Equilibrium and Price

By overlapping Figures 21.2 and 21.3, one gets a picture of a market equilibrium, as in Figure 21.4. At the intersection of the demand and supply lines, the quantity of timber demanded in the United States is just equal to the quantity supplied, that is, $Q_d = Q_s = Q^*$, and the price paid by demanders of

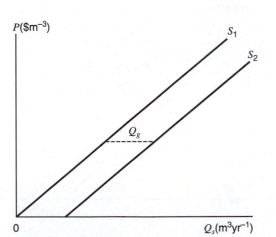

Figure 21.3 Every point on a supply line represents the quantity of timber supplied at a given price. The lines slope upward because production rises as price increases. Lines that are farther right correspond to higher supply.

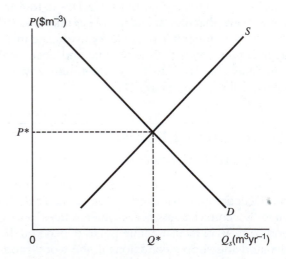

Figure 21.4 The market for timber is in equilibrium when demand is equal to supply. This is the quantity Q^* where the supply and demand lines intersect. A single equilibrium price, P^* corresponds to the equilibrium quantity.

timber is just equal to the price received by suppliers, P^*. We say that the market is in equilibrium.

The equilibrium can also be computed by solving the demand equation 2 simultaneously with the supply equation 3, under the condition that quantity demanded be equal to quantity supplied. Since, at equilibrium, $Q_s = Q_d$, we get:

$$dP - ei + Q_g = a - bP + cH$$

which gives the equilibrium price:

$$P^* = f + hi - kQ_g + mH \qquad (4)$$

And, by substituting the equilibrium price in the demand equation 2, we get the equilibrium quantity:

$$Q^* = u - vi + wQ_g + zH \qquad (5)$$

The parameters in equations 4 and 5 are defined completely by the parameters of equations 3 and 4. The price equation 4 shows that the price of timber in the United States increases with the interest rate and the number of houses started, while it decreases with the amount of timber produced from public forests. The quantity equation 5 shows that the quantity of timber consumed (and produced) decreases with the interest rate, and increases with public timber production, and it also increases with the number of housing starts.

Forecasting and Policy Analysis

Forest economists estimate the parameters in demand-and-supply equations like 2 and 3 by statistical methods with regional, national, or international data, depending on the context. Econometric models of this kind have a long history (12). After calibration, the model can be used for forecasting and policy analysis. For example, above, given the equilibrium condition of demand-supply equality, the two-equation demand-supply system 2, 3 has been solved for price as a function of the demand and supply shifters (interest rate, housing starts, government supply). This price equation 4 can then be applied to predict price, conditional on the future values of interest rate, public timber supply, and housing starts. Presumably, interest rate and housing starts are themselves predicted

by macroeconomists and demographers, and in that way the forest sector is linked to the rest of the economy. The public supply variable, Q_g, instead, is a policy variable, since the government can choose how much timber to produce from public forests. Equation 4 can be used to predict the effect of this government policy on timber prices. Such a price projection is important for benefit-cost analysis, including calculations with Faustmann's formula to decide whether to begin, continue, or stop forest production activities on private as well as public lands.

Economic forest sector modeling of this kind has progressed greatly during the past thirty years. The models are used extensively to help set national forest policy (13). Even at the international level, multi-country models of production, consumption, trade, and prices of wood products now help to study policy issues (14). These models are based typically on the equilibrium theory sketched above, whereby at every point in time there exists a unique set of prices that equilibrate markets for all products in all countries. Their implementation often involves a combination of statistical and mathematical techniques (12).

Forest sector models represent a significant advance in how forest policy is decided, and forest decisions are made. This is because the methods and assumptions are transparent, facilitating greatly the communication of ideas, their critique, and ultimate progress. Still, current forest sector models lack accuracy. At best, they give an indication of possible direction of changes, given an internally consistent set of assumptions, but the future may turn out quite differently from what the models predict. Thus, in the foreseeable future, the timber prices that foresters should use even in the simplest Faustmann's formula will always be greatly uncertain. In addition, foresters must deal with the rising importance of the complex nontimber values of forests.

Non-Timber Values and Benefit-Cost Analysis

As the ecological value of forestland is increasingly recognized and understood by foresters and by the public, the nontimber value of forests that stems from their variety of life forms and functions is of growing interest. Economic theory can help define these values in monetary terms, and econometric techniques can be used to measure them. Hartman (15) reanalyzed Faustmann's optimal harvest age problem after including nontimber values of a mature forest such as flood control, recreation, and wildlife. He showed that if the services of the mature forest are valued more than the services of a newly planted forest, then it is best to extend the harvest age beyond the Faustmann rotation computed with timber prices only. Strang (16) showed that it might be preferable never to cut an existing old growth forest, even if it is optimal to eventually harvest the same land if initially barren. This is because of the considerable nontimber values embedded in the old-growth forest.

Forest Externalities

Often, values that derive from the presence of forest cover, such as flood and erosion control, may benefit others than the forest owners, so the owners do not include such benefits in the *LEV* calculation. These values are externalities for the firm making the economic decision. Since, by definition, externalities do not profit the owners, the amount of the externality is incidental to their decisions. If the externality is good, like erosion control, then society at large might desire more than the private owners will provide spontaneously. The private owners may guard against excessive erosion during harvest to a degree because they want to preserve the land fertility, but a municipal water processing plant downstream will want more effective erosion control so they have less silt to remove.

One approach to achieving the socially best level of erosion control is direct regulation, that is, decreeing and enforcing standards to control erosion. As another example, cedar rust is a disease that is incubated in red cedar and that attacks the leaves and fruit of apple trees. A 1914 law of the state of Virginia gave apple orchards the right to remove all red cedar trees within two miles of an orchard (17). Though draconian, the law was an attempt to force cedar owners to bear the cost of the damage they inflicted on orchards.

Another approach is taxation. For example, to control erosion, a tax could be waged on the forest owner for each ton of silt in the runoff. If the tax is set at the right level, the forest owner will choose the socially optimal degree of erosion prevention. Discovering the correct tax rate is the main difficulty in this approach.

A third approach is to establish clear property rights. To pursue the water pollution example, if the water plant had the right to silt-free water then the forest owners must pay the water plant for adding silt to the water. In this way, the forest owners incur an added expense for each ton of silt they add to the water, so they consider that cost in their management decision. The cost of enforcing the property right can make this approach impractical. Monitoring erosion on all the watersheds and estimating how much purification costs increase for each incident of erosion might be more costly than ignoring the right.

In some cases, property rights are impossible to establish. The beauty of the forest and the protection of threatened species are public goods that anyone can enjoy freely without preventing others from doing the same. A public nontimber forest good, such as its beauty, may be valuable to the owners, yet it tends to be underprovided compared to the social optimum. The combined value of a public good for all citizens is greater than the value to each, so as forest owners make the best decisions for themselves, they provide less than what all citizens desire.

Benefit-Cost Analysis of Forestry Projects

While externalities are common for private forests, nothing is external for a public forest. Thus, managers of public forests must consider many constituencies in setting policy. Benefit-cost analysis (BCA) helps in this process by including all known costs and benefits with a project or policy change. In the United States, ideas about a quantitative approach to policy formation began to emerge in the 1930s. In particular, the Flood Control Act of 1936 required BCA for all flood-control projects. The introduction of quantitative methods into management was accelerated by the logistical needs of World War II. BCA was at first limited to governmental projects, but was later increasingly applied to evaluate policies and regulations. Currently, BCA has many champions who believe that it is a rigorous approach that will become adopted internationally (18). In particular, the transparency of the BCA process leaves less room for corrupting influences in countries with weak democratic institutions (19).

In the United States, BCA is required on federal lands. Both the Bureau of Land Management through the Federal Land Policy and Management Act of 1976 and the Forest Service through the National Forest Management Act of 1976 must use BCA to set policy. The Forest Service's procedures include U.S.D.A. Forest Service directives, which require that lands be managed to maximize net public benefits (20). This public BCA includes not only financial flows but also any benefit or cost accruing to all U.S. citizens. Therefore, as applied to forestry, BCA is essentially a generalization of Faustmann's reasoning, to include all the goods and services that derive from the land and the trees that it carries.

Nevertheless, an emerging school of thought questions the use of BCA in policy formation. For example, Vatn and Bromley argue that rather than trying to maximize anything, policy formation should deal with how to achieve a desirable future state (21). In this view, BCA is useful only to determine if that future state is achievable. Indeed, a most difficult part of BCA is to quantify how much we value particular outcomes. If instead we implement a process to set as a goal the future state we most value, then one of the main objects of BCA is achieved, by definition. Determining the socially desired future state is not a simple process, but it could at least be more transparent than the convoluted valuation methods of BCA.

In public forest management, the limitations of BCA, revealed by the numerous lawsuits brought by interest groups to stop management plans on National Forests, have led to attempts to replace them with multidimensional decision methods. For example, Niemi and Whitelaw divided forest "clients" into four interest groups. They cataloged all effects of a change on each group, without trying to convert them in money. They formalized a process by which balanced policy decisions could be made and they illustrated its application in southern Appalachia (22). However, such methods are still experimental, and far from being as institutionalized as BCA is. The attractiveness of BCA is that it deals with monetary value, a dimension that every decision maker would like to have, and that lawyers covet.

The crucial step in BCA is assigning a monetary value to all costs and benefits. To bring some order to this complicated issue, benefit-cost analysts classify the value of the many qualities or output of forests as use-value, option-value, bequest-value, or existence-value. *Use-value* derives from a particular use of the forest or its products. For example, timber has a use-value, and so do hunting, grazing, and nonconsumptive uses such as recreation and flood control. *Option-values* pertain to forest resources that might have value in the future. A pharmaceutical use for a biochemical compound produced by an understory species might be discovered in the future. We maintain the option of collecting this value as long as forest conditions allow the species to survive.

Bequest-value is the value of maintaining a resource to pass on to future generations. The satisfaction we gain from the idea of passing a forest intact to future generations is its bequest-value to us. Last, the value that individuals and society derive from the forest merely being there now is its existence-value. *Existence-value* may be, but is not necessarily related to, some use values. An individual who greatly values the beauty of a forest is using the forest while viewing it, yet the greater part of the value of sightseeing might be confirming the existence of the forest. Others might value the existence of rare animal species harbored by the forest even though they might never see or in any other way use them. As suggested by the subtlety of their definitions, quantifying their value is no easy task.

Measuring Social Welfare

Economists have developed many techniques to do benefit-cost analysis. The easiest use-values to estimate in monetary terms are those that are bought and sold at a "market price." Suppose the good is timber, traded in a region where there are many small private forests, and a large public forest. Under the current policy, the public forest produces nothing, so that the upward sloping line, S_1, in Figure 21.5 represents supply (all private), while the downward sloping line, D, represents demand.

Demand and supply cross at B, the quantity of private timber sold and bought is F(m³yr^{-1}), and the equilibrium price is A ($\$$m^{-3}). Suppose that the managers of the public forest consider producing timber independently of price level. This policy would result in a shift in the total regional supply line from supply S_1 to supply S_2. The new equilibrium would them be at a lower price, C, for a larger volume bought and sold, G. However, the amount sold by private forests would decrease from F to J. Consequently, there would be an increase in the welfare of timber buyers, measured by the area of the polygon $ABEC$, but a decrease in the welfare of private sellers, equal to the area $ABHC$. There would then be an increase in total welfare of consumers and producers, equal to the area BEH. This is an example of complete welfare accounting, with a full evaluation of benefits and costs, and of winners and losers. It still demands work to esti-

mate the necessary demand and supply relations, and it is not possible without a market.

Assessing the Value of Forest Amenities

It appears, then, that for public goods, even those with use-value, such as forest scenery, the assessment of value in monetary terms is difficult. If we knew the demand schedule for the good, we would calculate the value of, say, a change in supply as we did above, but there are usually no market data to estimate the demand schedule. We can count the number of sightseers and tabulate the time they spend viewing forest scenery, but short of a wall hiding the forest and a tollbooth, we can neither limit sightseers nor charge them a fee. In this example, the ability to limit access to or charge for the public good is difficult or impossible; so most consumers will "free ride," that is, benefit without paying to view the scenery. One can observe the quantity of a public good that free riders use at zero cost, but construction of the full demand equation requires the methods described later.

In another example, the absorption of air pollution by forests provides clean air that anyone can use without paying. Without a way of charging for the use of that clean air, we cannot observe how use of clean air changes with price. As private forests purify the air, owners rarely consider the

Figure 21.5 As public timber supply increases, the welfare of society increases by the amount measured by the area of the triangle BEH.

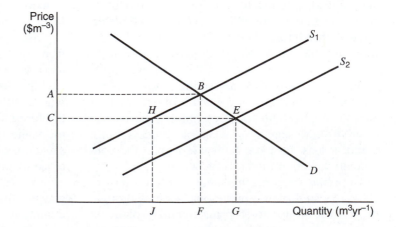

value of the clean air to others. In choosing to build houses where there was forest, the air cleaning capacity of the forest is typically not considered by the builders, so we cannot directly infer the value of air cleaning by observing the behavior of land developers.

For resources with option-value, such as the unknown medicinal value of forest flora, we might observe a value in an options market. Since the option-value exists because of a potential future market good, rights to that resource could be traded and a market value observed. For example, the pharmaceutical company Merck bought the right to bioprospect in Costa Rica for $1 million plus royalties (23). The biotech company Diversa paid the U.S. National Park Service $175,000 plus a percentage of profits to do the same in the Yellowstone hot springs (24). To the extent that those deals were competitive, they should represent the expected value of patentable biological discoveries over costs for the companies. However, these two companies are searching for short-term value in the genetic material, which we as a society have retained the option to use by maintaining the ecosystems with those life forms. The uncertainties Merck and Diversa face in finding valuable biological material are small compared to the difficulty of evaluating longer-term option values.

Effective markets for long-term option-value are hard to envision with the short profit horizon typically important to businesses. The option-value of future nonconsumptive goods is also not subject to market valuation. In the Midwest of the United States, the existence value and recreational value of traditional tall grass prairie ecosystems has been discovered in the last few decades after the destruction of all but small remnants. The option of re-creating prairies was preserved in the plants left in those areas. Since not so long ago few would have predicted that the prairie would some day have a nonconsumptive value, they would have had a hard time guessing its option-value.

The bequest-value and existence-value of forestlands are in part revealed when forestlands are bought and sold. These non-use values are part of the price paid. But separating bequest values and

existence values from the total price paid for the complex bundle of goods represented by the forest is not a simple task. Furthermore, if the price data come from private transactions, to obtain the total value of the forestland, we must add its value to the rest of society to the private value.

Economists use three kinds of methods to estimate the value of forest goods that are not traded directly and unambiguously: travel cost, hedonic pricing, and contingent valuation. In the *travel cost approach,* the cost of travel to the forest is used to infer the value of visiting the forest for an individual, and also the value of different forests for different people. Hanley and Ruffell used the travel cost method to determine the value of the physical characteristics of forests in Canada (26). Fix and Loomis found that a mountain bike trip to Moab, Utah was worth $205 (27).

In the *hedonic pricing method,* a market good is viewed as a bundle of attributes. The value of each attribute is inferred from price differences between goods with various amounts of attributes. For example, the price of houses can be used to estimate the amenity value of a neighboring forest. Along with pure housing attributes such as square footage, number of bedrooms, and so forth is access to the forest, measured for example by its distance from the house. Given a sufficient number of houses bought and sold, we calculate by statistical methods the best equation to relate house price to the attributes. We can then infer how much more an otherwise equivalent house is worth just for being near the forest. From this hedonic price analysis, we have inferred the amenity value of the forest as the amount a household is willing to pay for being close to it. With this technique, Li and Brown found that a house is worth $250 more near a conservation area and $2800 more next to a recreation area (28). Examples of application of hedonic pricing in forestry include Turner, et al. (29), and Roos (30) who inferred the value of particular characteristics of forest estates, such as their location. Scarpa and Buongiorno estimated the amenity value of a stand of trees as the difference between what the owners could have gotten had they tried to maximize profits (according to Faustmann's rule), and what they actually cut. By then comparing the amenity value of many different stands, they inferred the amenity value of trees of different species and size. They found that for most owners, the amenity value of trees was much larger than their timber value (31).

The travel cost approach and hedonic pricing use market prices; for example, the cost of gasoline or the price of a house, to infer the nonmarket value of forest amenities. These methods are based on actual choices of people who reveal their preferences by their actions. In the *contingent valuation method* (CVM), instead we ask individuals about how much they are willing to pay for a particular nonmarket good or service supplied by a forest. One advantage of contingent valuation is that it can deal with non-use values such as the existence of a healthy forest, as well as use-values such as viewing that healthy forest (32). As a result CVM is used extensively in benefit-cost analysis. For example, Crocker asked forest visitors their willingness to pay for a visit to a forest if the trees showed slight, moderate, or severe damage from air pollution (33). With these data he estimated the public willingness to pay to prevent damage to trees. Mattson and Li used the CVM to quantify the value of on-site consumptive use (berry and mushroom picking), on-site nonconsumptive use (hiking, and camping), and off-site visual experience (34). Still, there is much controversy concerning the theory and techniques of CVM, such as how to design surveys for public opinion polling, and the magnitude of biases in the assessment of willingness to pay for a nonmarket good (35).

Opportunity Cost of Non-Timber Objectives

While measuring the economic value of forest amenities is difficult, determining the opportunity cost of a decision to preserve or enhance some amenities values is much more straightforward. For example, it is hard to tell how much the spotted owl is worth, but it is much easier, and yet useful, to determine the cost of protecting the spotted owl, in terms of revenue foregone by curtailing timber production in the Pacific Northwest. To take a sim-

pler example, refer again to Table 21.1, and assume that instead of cutting trees at their economic age of 60 years we wanted to keep them growing for one century, possibly because of the aesthetic and ecological superiority of stands of old trees. Then, Table 21.1 shows that the land expectation value for a rotation of 100 years would be $504 ha^{-1} only. This would be $1,387 ha^{-1} − $504 ha^{-1} = $883 ha^{-1} less than the land expectation value of the purely economic policy.

The opportunity cost of the "big tree" policy would then be $883 ha^{-1}. If the forest were public, this is what citizens would have to be willing to give up in order to enjoy the bigger trees. In the case of a private forest, the opportunity cost gives an estimate of what would have to be paid to private owners to induce them to keep trees growing beyond the age of financial maturity. Knowledge of such opportunity costs is precious for objective policy making, and it is well within the capacity of standard economic tools.

Concluding Statement

From Faustmann's classic valuation of forestland to the complex multidimensional choices in modern forest policy, economic principles and methods have contributed much to forest management decisions. Economics help foresters grapple with the fundamental issue of opportunity cost, as it applies to time, alternative land uses, and conservation. It also gives us the framework and tools to handle risk objectively. Applied to the timber sector, economics is essential to predict the demand, supply, and prices of wood products. In the more difficult realm of amenity values, the methods of benefit-cost analysis are put to work constantly to measure the full social value of forests. As economic theory and methods continue to develop, new opportunities open for their application to the management of forests. The amenity value of forests is likely to grow in importance, and to take more time in the day-to-day concerns of forest managers. Economics is helping in the assessment of these values.

Nevertheless, there are definite limits to economics. Some forest policy issues, such as the preservation of species, far transcend the purely economic dimension, and reach into the realm of ethics and religion. One may, then, question whether economic methodology can truly give a definitive measure of value in those circumstances. Conservation goals will most likely be set on more grounds than purely economic considerations. Nevertheless, the means to achieve conservation will certainly have an important economic dimension. They involve budgets, reallocation of resources, and sacrifices in current consumption. In sum, there is a very real opportunity cost to any forestry decision. It is the role of economics, and its power to determine this cost exhaustively and accurately.

References

1. L. E. VON MISES, *Human Action: A Treatise on Economics*, Yale University Press, New Haven, Conn., 1949.

2. P. A. SAMUELSON, *Economics*, McGraw-Hill, New-York, 1976.

3. R. K. WINTERS, *The Forest and Man*, Vantage Press, New York, 1970.

4. M. FAUSTMANN, *Allgemaine forst-un jagd-zeitung*, *15*, 441 (1849).

5. P. A. SAMUELSON, *Econ. Inquiry*, *14*, 466 (1976).

6. A. C. FISHER AND J. V. KRUTILLA, *Quarterly J. of Econ.*, *89*(3), 358(1975).

7. A. LESLIE, *Unasylva*, *39*(1), 46 (1987).

8. D. A. PERRY AND J. MAGHEMBE, *For. Ecol. and Management*, *26*, 123 (1989).

9. J. N. HOOL, *For. Sci. Monograph*, *12*, 1 (1966).

10. M. R. LEMBERSKY AND K. N. JOHNSON, *For. Sci.*, *21*(2), 109 (1975).

11. C. R. LIN AND J. BUONGIORNO, *Management Sci.*, *44*(10), 1351 (1998).

12. J. BUONGIORNO, *International J. of Forecasting*, *12*, 329 (1996).

13. D. M. ADAMS, R. J. ALIG, B. A. McCARL, ET AL., *For. Sci.*, *19*, 343 (1996).

14. S. ZHU, D. TOMBERLIN, AND J. BUONGIORNO, "Global Forest Products Consumption, Production, Trade and Prices: Global Forest Products Model Projections to 2010." Working paper GFPOS/WP/01, Forest Policy and Planning Division, FAO, Rome, 1998.

15. R. HARTMAN, *Econ. Inquiry*, *14*, 52 (1976).

16. W. J. STRANG, *Econ. Inquiry*, *21*, 576 (1983).

17. W. J. SAMUELS, *The George Washington Law Review*, *57*, 1556 (1989).

18. D. W. PEARCE, *Environ. and Dev. Econ.*, *2*, 210 (1997).

19. A. RAY, *Environ. and Dev. Econ.*, 2, 215 (1997).

20. C. S. SWANSON AND J. B. LOOMIS, "Role of Nonmarket Economic Values in Benefit-Cost Analysis of Public Forest Management." General Technical Report PNW-GTR–361, U.S.D.A. Forest Service, 1996.

21. A. VATN AND D. W. BROMLEY, *J. of Environ. Econ. and Management*, *26*, 129 (1993).

22. E. NIEMI AND E. WHITELAW, "Assessing Economic Trade-offs in Forest Management," General Technical Report PNW-GTR-403, U.S.D.A. Forest Service, 1997.

23. FT Asia Intelligence Wire, "Basmati—biodiversity and Germ Plasm Issues," *THE HINDU*, May 6, 1998.

24. T. KUPPER, "Diversa's Studies in National Park are Halted," *San Diego Union-Tribune*, March 27, 1999, p. C-1.

25. J. B. BRADEN, C. D. KOLSTAD, AND D. MILTZ, "Introduction," In *Measuring the Demand for Environmental Quality*, North-Holland, New York, 1991.

26. N. HANLEY AND R. RUFFELL, "The Valuation of Forest Characteristics," Queen's Institute for Economic Research, Discussion Paper: 849, 1992.

27. P. FIX AND J. LOOMIS, *J. of Environ. Planning and Management*, *41*(2), 227 (1998).

28. M. M. LI AND H. J. BROWN, *Land Econ.*, *56*(2), 125 (1980).

29. R. TURNER, C. M. NEWTON, AND D. F. DENNIS, *For. Sci.*, *37*(4), 1150 (1991).

30. A. ROOS, *Scand. J. of For. Res.*, *10*, 204 (1995).

31. R. SCARPA, AND J. BUONGIORNO, "Assessing the Non-timber Value of Forests: A Revealed-Preference, Hedonic Model." Unpublished paper, Department of Forest Ecology and Management, University of Wisconsin, Madison, 1999.

32. P. H. PEASE AND T. P. HOLMES, *So. J. Applied For.*, *17*(2), 84 (1993).

33. T. D. CROCKER, *Land Econ.*, *61*(3), 244 (1985).

34. L. MATTSON AND C. LI, *Scand. J. of For. Res.*, *8*, 426 (1993).

35. R. T. CARSON, "Constructed markets," In *Measuring the Demand for Environmental Quality*, North-Holland, New York, 1991.

PART 4

Forests and Society

Social forestry seeks to understand the relationships among human behavior, social systems, natural resources, and the environment. Because natural resource issues are embedded in social and cultural contexts, future forest managers must consider the changing relationships between the biophysical and social environments that shape forest communities and the people who depend on them (Figure P4.1).

Specialization in this area includes studies of forest-dependent communities, sociology of natural resources, forest and environmental history, forest and resource policy, park and protected area management, sustainable forestry, human dimensions in ecosystem management, urban forestry, international forestry, and economic development of forests, including nontimber forest products and agroforestry.

Figure P4.1 Community forestry project in Algeria. (United Nations Photo.)

Underlying all areas of social forestry is the understanding of how people shape and are shaped by natural resource systems through their social institutions and cultures. Central to social forestry is the recognition that people and human behavior are natural components of ecosystems. We have already been introduced to some of the management issues in social forestry in Chapter 17, Managing Recreation Behavior.

The two chapters in this section deal with additional various aspects of social forestry. Chapter 22 on urban forestry treats the unique situation of management of trees and forests located in urban environments. Finally, Chapter 23 provides a description of community-based management of natural resources, which has applications both domestically and internationally. The many issues and challenges of this complex subject are described in detail based on global experiences.

Urban Forestry

GENE GREY

Urban forestry concerns the care of trees and related organisms within the environs of cities, towns, and other developed areas, and is a specialized application of forest science (and art) to the dynamic physical, social, and political environments in which people live and work. Totaling an estimated 69 million acres, the nation's urban forests are complex mixtures of planted and naturally occurring trees and related vegetation in close proximity to the structures and activities of human life. In simplest terms, "urban" areas are made up of trees and other vegetable and animal organisms, structures, and people (Figure 22.1). It is the challenge of urban forestry to make trees and other organisms compatible and serviceable within and to this environment (1–7).

Urban forestry merges the knowledge and skills of traditional forestry—of working with natural forest

Figure 22.1 The urban forest is a dynamic environment of manmade structures, such as buildings and streets, and organisms, such as plants and trees.

ecosystems and planted forests—with disciplines involving landscape plant materials and design, arboriculture, urban wildlife, engineering, planning, legal matters, and social and political science. The complexity of the urban forestry environment requires no less.

The language of urban forestry can sometimes be confusing. For example, the very word "urban" can give the impression that only large metropolitan areas are involved, even though the principles and practices are equally applicable to tiny hamlets. To counter this impression, the term "community forestry" is often used. Also, the title of urban forester often goes by other names, such as city forester, city arborist, or even city horticulturist. To avoid confusion, the term "urban forestry" is used throughout this chapter, as is the word city, being generic to all human habitat situations. Furthermore, the term urban forest manager is used except when referring to the specific public office of the person responsible for urban forestry within a city. In such cases, the term "city forester" is used.

Although, in any given city, many individuals are involved in urban forestry as professionals or volunteers, overall responsibility is usually vested in the office of city forester. Operating under ordinances specific to the urban forest, the city forester is responsible for coordination of activities relating to the needs of the entire forest.[1] To be effective, the city forester and other urban forest managers must have a thorough working knowledge of the urban forestry environment—of what the urban forest needs, how to plan and budget for necessary management programs, and how to implement them successfully. The following sections discuss each in more detail.

---

[1] Please note that the following approach from the perspective of the city forester does not ignore or diminish the role in and contribution to urban forestry of countless other professionals and volunteers in public agencies and private business; nor does it fail to recognize that the function of city forester is often carried out by volunteer boards or committees and that some programs are successfully conducted without formal ordinances.

The Urban Forestry Environment

The total urban forestry environment (the environment in which urban forestry must operate) includes all the physical (including biological), institutional, social, legal, and political factors that either facilitate or inhibit care of the urban forest.

Physical Environment

To understand the physical environment of the urban forest, one first needs an overall vertical perspective, as from an aircraft or aerial photograph. Below is an extremely complex mixture of land-use situations—streets, roads, highways, railways, utility corridors, business and industrial areas, parking lots, athletic fields, parks, residential areas, riparian areas, and other natural forests—most having trees and related vegetation in varying degrees. A further look at the ground reveals how trees and other vegetation serve and relate to each situation, particularly in context with buildings, utilities, and other structures. As noted above, trees make up an integral element in cities and are thus a part of the urban infrastructure, providing aesthetic and other environmental benefits (Figure 22.2). The totality of trees and other vegetation in all areas within a city is properly the urban forest.

The physical environment also involves the nature of the forest itself, its composition (by species, age, and size), condition, and distribution, over all land use situations. In a later section, Determining What the Urban Forest Needs, we will explore composition and distribution in more detail.

It is important to understand also that the urban forest is extremely dynamic, and that expansion into natural woodlands, construction within the city, and the simple fact of vegetation growth and death cause continual changes in composition, condition, and distribution.

Socioeconomic Environment

Perhaps the most important aspect of the urban forestry environment is who is responsible for man-

Figure 22.2 Design of streetside landscapes is an important component of urban forest management.

agement. As suggested by the aerial overview, there are myriad owners, both public and private—city and other government, business, institutions, industry, and homeowners—each influencing the state of the urban forest within its area of responsibility. Ownership is not absolute, however, in that rights for the greater society must be given. In the case of the urban forest, such rights are manifested by easements for public utilities, giving electrical, telephone and other utility providers authority for treatment of trees on such areas. Thus, there are four general categories of "managers" of the urban forest: 1) city government, generally with direct authority for parks and streetsides; 2) other government agencies, particularly state highway departments; 3) private owners, especially homeowners; and

4) public utilities. From the perspective of the city forester, responsible for coordination of management of the total urban forest, these categories represent the four principal audiences for his or her efforts.

Critical also within the urban forestry environment are those individuals and organizations that influence or have the potential to influence management of the urban forest: neighborhood associations, advocacy and volunteer groups, civic clubs, the media, and service individuals such as arborists and nursery people. This is, in part, related to the political environment, which will be discussed later.

A final factor in the socioeconomic environment concerns attitudes of people regarding trees and other vegetation. Attitudes, obviously, vary greatly by individuals, having been formulated by past experiences—physical, cultural, and economic. Of these, economics is perhaps the most important, as care of trees may be an unaffordable luxury to some, or may be the ultimate expression of ownership pride by others. Economics may also effect community pride, with resulting influences on budgets for public urban forestry programs.

Legal Environment

The legal environment of urban forestry has three major aspects: management responsibility and authority; tree protection and landscape matters; and safety and liability. Management responsibility and authority is normally established by city ordinances that establish and define the office of city forester, outline responsibilities, and grant authority for operations. In most cities, ordinances give city foresters responsibility for streetside and park trees and for vegetation on other city-owned areas. Commonly called management ordinances, such statutes typically have the following elements, although items 5, 6, and 7 may be included in a separate "Standards" section:

1. Definitions
2. Designation of City Forester
3. Establishment of citizen tree board
4. Responsibility for trees on city property and easements

5. Planting regulations (permits, official species, spacing, location)
6. Maintenance standards
7. Tree removal requirements and standards
8. Catastrophic authority on private property (condemnation and treatment)
9. Requirements for private contractors
10. Violations and penalties

Tree protection ordinances concern special trees and groves (because of size, species, scarcity, historical or cultural significance, or environmental contribution) and allow them to be set aside and maintained. Landscape ordinances generally relate to development and construction, and concern maintenance of tree cover and protection of individual trees. Tree cover requirements for developers are normally expressed as a percent of total land area, stems per acre, or percentage of crown cover. Critical drainage areas, wetlands, special wildlife habitat, and other ecosystems may also be delineated.

In addition to city ordinances, the legal environment of urban forestry is extended by state and federal regulations concerning rare, threatened, or endangered species; wetlands or critical habitats; point and nonpoint source pollution; pesticides; and workplace safety. Also, many subdivisions have specific regulations concerning establishment and care of trees and other vegetation. Generally, such regulations are based on concerns for maintenance of property values, public safety, and protection of the environment.

Safety is of utmost concern within the urban forest. Trees can be threats to life and property. Accidents because of fallen trees or limbs, slippery leaves and fruit, and obstructed views often leave property owners and those responsible for management liable for damages. Liability is based on the tort law principle of prudent and reasonable care; thus property owners and their agents have a responsibility to exercise due care concerning trees and related vegetation. With the trend of increasing litigation and higher damage awards by the courts, the issue of liability is extremely important in urban forestry, calling for increased emphasis on hazard prevention (discussed in a later section).

Political Environment

The political environment of a city has to do with those who influence decisions. Budget decisions are of particular importance, as there is generally intensive competition for funds, and those programs and services having key political support are usually well funded. Every city has its political structure, within city government, but also made up of influential citizens and leaders of civic, service, and business organizations. Identifying and working with such people is essential to successful urban forestry programs, since, ultimately, political support is a manifestation of the public's concern for trees.

Management Structure

The Office of City Forester

As indicated, responsibility for coordination of overall urban forest management is legally vested in the city forester. Varying by cities, the function of city forester may be in a separate department or may be included in other governmental units such as Public Works, Parks and Recreation, or Land Management. In larger cities, forestry departments may be divided into divisions according to responsibility, such as streetside trees and park trees.

Tree Boards

Many cities have tree boards, a generic title for citizen's groups with official support or administrative responsibilities for urban forestry programs. Known variously as commissions, committees, or boards, such groups have official roles which may be advisory, policy making, administrative, or operational. *Advisory boards* are charged with giving counsel on urban forestry matters—to study, investigate, and make recommendations. *Policy-making boards* have broader responsibilities, including program planning and even budgeting. *Administrative*

boards are independent commissions with full program responsibilities and independent funding, often from specific tax levies. The city forester is directly responsible to the administrative board, whose duties include long-range planning, policy development, budget approval, and program evaluation. *Operational boards* usually function in tiny communities lacking the resources to support a municipal program. Such boards assume the function of city forester, doing it all, from program planning to actually caring for trees.

In addition their various duties as indicated above, tree boards provide invaluable service as advocates for trees and by giving strong program support. Normally made up of respected, public-spirited citizens, tree boards give added importance to urban forestry, by their presence and through special activities aimed at building support for trees.

Determining What the Urban Forest Needs

Fundamental to planning and implementing a successful urban forestry program is knowledge of the urban forest—its distribution, composition, and condition—and ultimately what is needed to set it in order. Called *structural information*, this knowledge includes health, vigor, safety, diversity, stocking, functionality, and aesthetics. All this must be translated into quantifiable needs for the future—numbers of trees to be established, pruned, removed, or otherwise treated—within the context of ensuring safety, diversity, functionality, and aesthetics.

While general information about what the urban forest needs can be gained by observation, from past work records and other documents, and by simply listening to complaints, comprehensive information can be obtained only by formal surveys or inventories. The beginning point is with aerial photographs to develop cover type maps, identifying general vegetative situations such as riparian areas and other natural woodlands, park lands, homogeneous residential areas, and tree cover in business and industrial areas. Ground checks can confirm or refine type identification. If cost-effective and otherwise practical, this process may be facilitated by use of Geographic Information Systems (GIS) and computer technology to scan visual images from photographs and maps, allowing cover types and other features to be featured as layers (see also Chapter 12).

For many areas, such as natural woodlands and passive parks, such cover type information, coupled with ground observations, will be sufficient to develop prescriptions for management. For other situations, however, such as streetsides, active parks, and other areas where intensive management is needed, more detailed information must be obtained (Figure 22.3).

The amount of information to be gathered by surveys or inventories must be determined by the need and the capability to use the information. For example, if the need is for information sufficient to develop a long-range plan in the hopes of establishing a city forestry program, which has been the case in countless small cities in recent years as urban forestry has expanded, more general, non-site-specific information is needed. If, however, the need is for information to enable an established city forestry department to more intensively manage streetside and park trees, a detailed site-specific inventory—that is, where individual trees are located on the ground—is necessary. Thus, the dis-

tinction: surveys are non-site-specific and are generally for long-range planning purposes; and inventories are site-specific and are for intensive management purposes. There are, of course, degrees of need within both, but the distinction is important, because both, especially inventories, are expensive and time-consuming.

Surveys

Cover type maps from aerial photographs are essential to urban forest surveys, in that they allow areas of homogeneity to be identified. Once identified, selective sampling systems can then be developed. One such system that works extremely well for streetside trees is to drive sample streets, recording trees by species, size, and condition class. From a slowly moving vehicle, trees on both sides of the street are recorded by species, estimated diameter (DBH), and condition class. Condition classes are as follows.

- *Good*. Healthy, vigorous tree. No apparent signs of disease or mechanical injury. Little or no corrective work needed. Form representative of species.

- *Fair*. Average condition and vigor for area. May be in need of some corrective pruning or repair. May lack desirable form characteristic of species. May show minor insect injury, disease, or physiological problem.

- *Poor*. General state of decline. May show severe mechanical, insect, or disease damage, but death not imminent. May require major repair or renovation.

- *Dead or dying*. Dead, or death imminent from mechanical, disease, or other causes. Removal needed.

Vacant spaces in need of planting are also identified. Compiled data allows species and size diversity, stocking, and condition to be determined. From this information, reasonable conclusions may be made as what is needed to set the streetside urban forest in order: number of trees to be removed, pruned and planted; and species to be favored or avoided in future planting. Such information is

Figure 22.3 Urban forests of residential areas often include natural woodlands, riparian zones, church yards, cemeteries, parks, and golf courses.

absolutely essential to long-range planning, as will be discussed in a following section.

Inventories

Inventories serve the need of intensive management and thus must be more precise, identifiable to individual trees. Consequently, inventories are more costly, requiring on-site decisions as to tree location and condition. Only that information which is directly applicable to future management should be collected, since too much (or too little) information can be excessively costly. The information needed may be summarized as: what the tree is; what it needs; and where it is. Data collected concerning each tree then becomes:

What it is:	Species, diameter, crown spread
What it needs:	Pruning (by type), mechanical work (cabling or bracing), insect or disease treatment, soil treatment, removal of physical impediment, tree removal
Where it is:	Street name, lot number or other location method

Decisions as to what the tree needs can either be made on site, or indicators of need recorded: trunk, branch, crown, and leaf condition; and environmental factors such as proximity to overhead wires, root-zone restrictions, apparent soil problems, and other inhibitors of growth and vigor. Generally it is best to record such factors, since on-site judgments of need are for a single point in time and do not indicate the causes of need. Knowing where trees are is critical to management. Work crews must be able to unfailingly locate individual trees, as the wrong tree treated or removed can have unfortunate consequences. Trees (and tree spaces) may be located by lot number or by sequential numbering within city blocks.

Most inventories are computerized, including automatic data entry from the field. Multiple cross tabulations allow near-instant retrieval of information, including virtual reality displays of streetside situations and individual trees. A common short-coming of inventories is that they are not continuous and quickly become obsolete, with life spans rarely exceeding 5 to 7 years. Hence, a system for information feedback and an allowance for tree growth is necessary. Effective information feedback ensures that everything that changes a tree—prescribed treatments, construction disturbance, accidents, storm damage, other—is recorded.

In addition to streetside tree management, inventories may be for other special purposes, such as land condemnation, wildlife habitat evaluation, species or ecosystem preservation, and tree hazard evaluation. In such cases, objectives must be clearly defined and systems designed to meet specific needs. Inventories of park trees normally involve a grid system for locating individual trees (Figure 22.4). GPS can also be a valuable aid in park tree inventories.

Planning and Budgeting for Urban Forestry

Planning, no matter how detailed, has five basic elements: 1) an assessment of what you have; 2) a vision of what you want it to be; 3) how to get there; 4) what it will take to get there; and 5) an "occasional" look at how you are doing. Applied to urban forestry planning, this simply means that planning must start with an assessment of the forest situation from surveys, as discussed in the preceding section. A vision of what the urban forest should be—safe, healthy, fully stocked, diverse, functional, and aesthetically pleasing—should next be developed, with each visionary element becoming an objective of a long-range plan. Strategies can then be developed for each objective, priorities determined, estimates made of costs, and a timetable developed to carry out each strategy. Evaluation is ongoing, allowing adjustments to be made as necessary, according to the factors of change within the urban forestry environment. Thus, urban forestry planning must be ongoing.

Urban forestry planning must begin with a long-range plan. As indicated above, the long-range plan states the vision, identifies objectives, determines

Figure 22.4 Parks may be designated for either active or passive uses.

priorities, estimates costs, and provides for evaluation, thus providing the framework within which operational plans and budgets are developed. Operational plans which are normally annual, depending on a city's fiscal cycle, are expressions of what must be done within a given year to achieve the objectives of the long-range plan. In such plans, annual goals are set—number of new trees to be established, amount and kind of pruning to be accomplished, number of trees to be removed, and other activities—and budgets developed to meet the goals. Budgets so developed thus have a solid planning basis, rather than being simply annual adjustments for inflation, as is unfortunately the case with many urban forestry programs. Plans of work are then developed, listing activities and timetables by various personnel. Finally, a system of evaluation is implemented, involving monitoring and end-of-the-year program evaluation. Thus, the long-range plan provides the framework, operational plans follow, budgets are derived from operational plans, plans of work facilitate annual goals, and evaluation is both ongoing and retrospective. The planning "flow" is summarized as follows.

- *Long-range plan.* States the mission and defines objectives. Identifies strategies and sets priorities

to achieve objectives. A function of tree board and city forester.
- *Operational plans.* Usually annual. Based on long-range plan. Set incremental goals, establish procedures, and identify resources for meeting goals. A function of city forester.
- *Budgets.* Based in items in operational plans and reflect resources needed to accomplish goals.
- *Plans of work.* Internal documents, giving tasks and timetables.
- *Evaluation.* Ongoing, often with emphasis on end-of-year review.

Long-range planning, as indicated above, is normally conducted by tree boards in conjunction with the city forester, and often with other involved citizens. Such planning must utilize accurate information, from surveys and other sources, and must consider all other urban forestry environmental factors, particularly the rights and needs of people. Such planning is fundamental to urban forestry, as it is the basis for all that follows.

In addition to planning as discussed, there is a need for emergency planning. No city is immune to natural disasters, such as severe storms, fires, floods, or even earthquakes. Such planning, coordinated with other city departments, should consider the role of the city forester, tree board, and other urban forest managers concerning such disasters, giving first priority to public safety, followed, in order, by clean up, repair, and replacement of trees. Obviously, if a disaster happens, the strategies and priorities of long-range plans may have to be revised.

Program Implementation

Fundamental to urban forestry program implementation is a working knowledge of the technical aspects of *arboriculture*—how to correctly establish, prune, and do whatever else is necessary to maintain trees and related vegetation. This knowledge, coupled with the working concept of the urban forest as a complex ecosystem, allows each operation to be in context with overall objectives.

The urban forest has four basic and interrelated management needs: establishment; maintenance; protection; and removal. Each need, with its various elements, must be addressed in meeting long-range objectives as identified in the planning process.

Tree Establishment

Tree establishment is a continuing need in the urban forest: to replace mortality; to enhance existing stands of trees; and to landscape new developments. Although most often referred to as *tree planting*, tree establishment is a more accurate term, as it reflects the broader need—to ensure that trees are properly selected, located, planted, and given adequate care until they are able to thrive on their own. Thus, planting is but one of five steps (evaluation should also be included) in tree establishment.

Location and Selection

"The right tree in the right spot" is a common, and accurate, expression concerning the urban forest, and means simply that all factors of site and species adaptability must be considered. Tree establishment must be in context with long-range objectives for the urban forest, as summarized by the following four "rules."

1. Tree establishment must be in accordance with the needs (numbers and locations) as identified in urban forestry plans.
2. Tree establishment must maintain or enhance diversity of the urban forest.
3. Trees selected must be consistent with the limiting factors of planting sites (soil, space, climate, other).
4. Trees selected must meet the remaining criteria as identified by objectives in long-range plans (safe, healthy, diverse, functional, other).

Three factors are paramount in tree selection: the tree's purpose in the landscape; what the site will allow; and how much care will be needed. Although most trees will also have secondary purposes, such as shade, wind protection, screening, enframement, accent, contrast, or wildlife attraction, the primary purpose is the first factor in narrowing the choices. In most urban forest situations, the precise planting spot will largely determine the primary purpose.

Virtually all planting sites will impose constraints, primarily because of soils and space, both above and below ground. In many urban forest situations, particularly streetsides and building sites, soils are less than ideal for tree establishment because of compaction, lack of depth, pollution, low fertility, alkalinity, or acidity. In some situations, depending on costs, it is necessary to amend the soil, replace it entirely, or build special drains or other structures (Figure 22.5).

Restricted space is perhaps the largest (and costliest) single problem with urban trees. There is often a proliferation of overhead wires, underground utilities, buildings, and pavement. There may also be constraints because of sun, shade, wind exposure, and air pollution. The challenge of urban forest tree establishment is to match trees by purpose to their planting sites. Fortunately, nature, with help by scientists, has designed trees with enough characteristics to provide choices in nearly every situation.

Figure 22.5 In central business areas where paving is common, trees are often located in special planters.

Trees must be adaptable to local climates, with the primary limiting factor being cold hardiness. Plant hardiness zone maps should be consulted, with the understanding that such zones are based on average minimum temperatures and do not take into account extremes, nor do they allow for local microclimates because of terrain or other factors. Additionally, as indicated above, trees must be tolerant to site-specific factors of sun, shade, wind, air pollution, and soil.

To fit space restrictions, trees may be grouped into three general mature size classes: small (30 feet); medium (60 feet); and large (100 feet). Additionally, landscape trees have characteristic forms, or shapes, created by branch structure and growth habit: irregular, vase, oval, pyramid, fastigiate (narrow), round, and weeping (Figure 22.6). Such

shapes allow trees to be fitted to specific situations. For example, vase-shaped trees are generally best for streetsides, as their ascending branches allow for lateral clearance. Conversely, pyramid-shaped trees do not serve well as streetside trees, as excessive pruning of lower branches is necessary to allow for pedestrian and vehicle passage.

Negative characteristics must also be considered: excessive fruiting, bad odors, heavy leaf fall, surface rooting and suckering, attraction to nuisance wildlife and insects, dense foliage that shades out grass, and excessive production of pollen.

Finally, but not least, cost of planting stock, relating to size, type, and planting sites must be considered. Planting stock varies by size and type. Sizes are usually expressed by height in feet or trunk caliper in inches. Stock types are bareroot, balled and burlapped, containerized, container-grown, or machine transplanted; hence, costs vary greatly. Generally, bareroot planting stock is least expensive; however, not all species can be successfully transplanted in bareroot condition.

Planting

Planting should be considered as a process following selection and location, and involves quality assurance, contracting for plant materials and for implementation, site designation, and implementation. Quality assurance begins with the ability to recognize good planting stock. Standards for planting stock have been published by the American Association of Nurserymen and should be the criteria for contracting for plant materials. Quality can be further assured by proper handling of stock

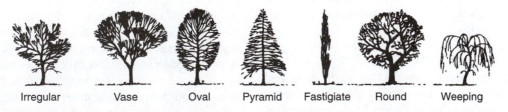

Irregular   Vase   Oval   Pyramid   Fastigiate   Round   Weeping

Figure 22.6 Typical shapes of landscape trees.

during delivery and during storage prior to planting.

Precise spots where individual trees will be planted must be designated, with assurance that the correct tree will be planted in each spot. Underground utilities must first be checked. In many cities, excavators, including tree planters, are required by law to give notification of planned excavations. Planting spots can be marked on the ground with stakes, flags, or by spray paint with species code designations identifiable to planting crews.

From a management perspective, implementation of tree planting involves logistics of plant materials, equipment, supplies, and labor. Also involved is quality control, proper handling of planting stock, hole digging, back filling, mulching, and other details. Implementation also involves internal and external public relations. Internal coordination with other agencies of city government (as is necessary in all other urban forestry activities) helps ensure safety and minimizes public inconvenience. External public relations are directed primarily toward making people, particularly nearby residents, aware that trees are being planted and to gain support in protecting "their" trees.

Aftercare

Aftercare involves treatments after planting to ensure health and vigor: corrective pruning, watering, mulching, removing staking materials (needed only in special cases), monitoring insects and diseases, and repairing wounds. An established tree is one that will thrive on its own after a given period of time, generally two to four years.

Evaluation

Tree establishment evaluation is quite important in making future decisions, allowing comparisons to be made between species, by size and type of planting stock, among nursery sources, by planting sites, and by management activities. Timely and accurate monitoring is necessary. Of particular importance is determining the causes of mortality.

Maintenance

Maintenance involves everything necessary between establishment and removal to ensure the optimum quality of the urban forest. While all are interrelated, there are three basic areas of maintenance: hazard management, plant health management, and tree quality improvement (primarily pruning).

Hazard Management

Safety must take top priority as a management activity in the urban forest. Trees, by their very nature, can be dangerous. Branches may fall or entire trees may topple during storms, leaves and fruit are discarded, roots may heave sidewalks, and trunks and branches may pose physical or sight barriers. Consequences can be disastrous in terms of human suffering and because of liability obligations of urban forest managers. Thus, tree hazard management requires a continuing commitment in urban forest management. Two elements are necessary for hazards: trees predisposed to any of the preceding, and the presence of someone or something of value (targets) (Figure 22.7). Thus, hazard management involves prevention and correction of tree "problems" and removal of targets.

Hazard prevention is integrated with all other management activities and involves the following:

- *Species selection:* avoiding species with inherent problems that may make them unsafe; and selection of high-quality planting stock to ensure strong future branching structure and tree vigor.

- *Planting location:* judicious location of planting sites to avoid making trees, by their presence, hazards.

- *Health care:* insect and disease management, correction of soil problems, water management.

- *Pruning:* to develop strong scaffold branches, to discourage decay entry to wounds, and to provide physical and visual clearance for pedestrians and vehicles.

- *Protection during construction:* root-zone protection, and prevention of trunk and branch wounding.

Figure 22.7 For a tree hazard to exist, there must be a potential for tree failure (i.e., the possibility of a limb falling off), as well as a target (i.e., a playground).

Hazard correction is also a major need, particularly in urban areas with substantial populations of older trees. Correction requires recognition and anticipation of potential hazards—recognition of current unsafe situations, and anticipation of predictable events such as fallen leaves, fruit, and other materials potentially hazardous to people and property. Effective recognition requires periodic inspections, identifying indicators and signs of potential tree failure, followed by timely treatment, generally by pruning or other arboricultural measures. In some instances, particularly in cases of large, decadent trees of historic or other value where pruning or other practices cannot ensure safety, "tar-

get" removal may be required, by fencing, signing, or otherwise prohibiting public access.

Plant Health Management

Plant health management requires an understanding of the interrelationships of the biological environment of the urban forest, with emphasis on soils, sites, physiological needs of plants, and life cycles of insect and disease pathogens. A major objective is maintenance of health and vigor, so that insect and disease impacts will be minimized, thus reducing the necessity of direct treatments, particularly chemical pesticides (see Chapter 8). Plant health management is integrated with other management and includes such activities as plant selection and location, enhancement of the growing environment, pruning, wound prevention and repair, direct and indirect insect and disease control, public education, and monitoring and recording.

Tree Quality Improvement

Quality improvement applies to individual trees and primarily involves pruning, although site enhancement by fertilization, soil amendments, and other methods is sometimes done. Few landscape trees in the urban forest go without the need for pruning during their life spans—for hazard prevention, for health and vigor, and for physical and visual clearance. Pruning is, in fact, the largest single item in most city forestry budgets, and is also a major cost item for utility providers. Ideally, pruning should be a part of programmed or cycled maintenance, according to varying needs of the total tree population, depending on growth characteristics of individual species and other factors. Emergency pruning, however, will also be needed as hazards are identified, or in the aftermath of storms or accidents.

Programmed pruning requires a pruning cycle, or the number of years required to prune all trees in a particular area—a 5-year pruning cycle meaning, for example, that one fifth of the trees will be pruned every year and each tree will be pruned every 5 years. Optimum pruning cycles are determined by marginal cost and return analysis, accord-

Sidebar 22.1

Florida Citrus Canker Program

Urban foresters can encounter many political as well as technical problems when managing trees in urban settings. An example of a very controversial approach was the plan developed by the Florida Department of Agriculture and Consumer Services for eradication of the citrus canker of citrus trees in south Florida in the late 1990s. The citrus canker is a bacterial disease that is harmless to humans but scars fruit and causes it to drop prematurely, although the fruit remains edible. This highly contagious disease threatened the state's $8.5 billion citrus industry, so the decision was made to eradicate all infected trees, as well as all healthy trees within 1,900 feet of the infected trees. The tree removal was mandated for both citrus plantations and all residential areas. Thus, many homeowners were very disturbed when healthy trees were removed from their yards, often without prior notification. Some south Florida residents brandished guns, padlocked gates and let guard dogs run free around their citrus trees. Citizens of several counties, including Miami-Dade, Broward, and Palm Beach, filed a lawsuit to stop the eradication program. To placate homeowners who lost trees, a $100 voucher was offered, regardless of how many trees were removed, which could be redeemed for replacement trees or garden supplies. However, the canker program prohibits replanting citrus trees for two years. It is esti-

mated that it cost the state $80 million to reimburse homeowners for the estimated 800,000 trees removed in residential areas at the end of the eradication program. However, the small monetary reimbursement did not quell the anger of many homeowners some of whom lost orange and grapefruit trees that were with families for generations.

---

ing to separate situations of age, species, and other factors within the total tree population.

Pruning of city-owned trees may be accomplished by city forestry department crews or by contract with private arboricultural firms, with decisions whether to prune with city crews or by contract based largely

on economics. Most cities find contracting the preferable alternative. Pruning standards have been developed by the National Arborists Association and are used in most contract situations. In some cities, usually those with smaller populations, streetside tree pruning and other maintenance is the responsibility of adjacent property owners. In such cases, the role of the city forester or tree board is largely educational, directed toward helping property owners better care for their trees.

Removal and Utilization

Trees, by nature, discard various things—leaves, fruit, dead branches, and such—and ultimately die. In natural forests, such materials decay on the forest floor and are a part of nature's continuing process. In urban forests, however, much of what is discarded, and dead trees themselves, must be removed. Some of what is removed can be used—fuelwood, for example—but such utilization is minor when all that must be removed is considered: dead trees, hazardous trees, oversize or competing trees, trees in the way of construction, stumps, and occasionally roots, hazardous branches, other branches removed during pruning, leaves, obnoxious or hazardous fruit, seeds and seed carriers, and sometimes even flower petals.

Except in cases of storms or other disasters, most removal can be anticipated and removal work can be scheduled according to season and proximity to people. As suggested, some material can be utilized: trunks and branches for fuelwood; leaves for compost; and occasionally, seeds and seed carriers for ornaments and novelties. Timber products may also be produced, but utilization is limited because of volume, inconsistency of supply, and metal and other foreign objects in logs.

Removal and utilization can also be difficult because of public sensitivity to trees being cut down and because of noise and disruption. Thus, there is the need for effective public relations explaining the necessity of such work in context with long-range objectives for the urban forest.

Other Management Considerations

The preceding discussion has concerned the primary things necessary to meet the basic establish-

ment, maintenance, protection, and removal needs of the urban forest. There are, however, other interrelated considerations, each quite important to the well-being of the forest.

Trees and Construction

Construction is a near-continuous activity in most urban forests: erection of buildings and other structures, street widening, and trenching for utilities. Such activities may cause wounds to trunks and branches, but the main concern is for root-zones of trees, by severing of roots, soil compaction, changes in grade, and alterations of water tables. Coordination with construction planners and developers by urban forest managers is necessary. Alternative locations for construction may be found in cases of historic or other extremely valuable trees, but the largest need is for on-site protection measures, particularly for tree root-zones (Figure 22.8).

In addition to protecting individual trees, the impact of long-term development on the urban forest must be considered: watershed values, wetlands, critical wildlife habitat, and threatened or endangered species. Concerning such, there are three basic considerations: 1) How may the values of natural forests be protected and enhanced during development? 2) Are such values recognized and

Figure 22.8 Construction activity can have severe negative impacts on root-zones of trees.

provided for by planners, administrators, developers, and other decision makers? and 3) If such values are not recognized, what measures are necessary to ensure them? By addressing these questions, urban forest managers can play an important role in comprehensive city planning and development.

Fire Protection

Except in areas where subdivisions have been developed in natural forests, particularly in the arid West, fire protection is of relatively lesser concern to urban forest managers. The primary focus of fire protection in urban areas is on structures, and "forests," if considered, are looked upon as "carriers" of fire. Fire protection in urban forests is usually the responsibility of city or other local fire departments. The urban forest manager's role is often cooperative with such agencies, providing input in protection planning and disaster recovery.

Urban Wildlife

While some urban forestry management practices (particularly removal of dead branches and trees) are detrimental to urban wildlife, many wildlife species abound in cities, some existing in even greater numbers than in natural habitats. For example, most large cities in the nation now have resident populations of Canada geese and abundant raccoons. People generally value urban wildlife highly, delighting in feeding and watching birds and observing other creatures (Figure 22.1). Wildlife can cause problems, however, by being dangerous to traffic, having annoying habits (noisy, destructive, messy), and occasionally carrying diseases. Urban wildlife management has three general aspects: 1) providing and enhancing habitat; for example, by establishing wildlife-friendly plants, protecting natural vegetation in new developments, providing travel lanes, and leaving dead trees and branches in nonhazard areas; 2) providing for viewing or consumptive opportunities, through such methods as construction of trails, viewing platforms, and boat ramps; and 3) controlling damage or nuisances by exclusion, lessening attractions, or reducing populations.

Urban Forest Valuation

Because of casualty losses or condemnation of properties to be developed, valuation of individual trees and urban woodlands is often necessary. Generally, woody plants in the landscape have no real value unto themselves; their only value being in their influence on real estate values. The appropriate method for assigning monetary values to woody plants depends on plant size, species, condition, function, location in the landscape, and other situational factors. Valuation can be subjective, and the urban forest manager must offer his or her best professional judgement in determining the method to use and in the appraisal process. Methods of appraisal are: direct replacement cost; compounded replacement cost; present value of future returns; cost of repair; cost of cure; forest product value; crop value; and trunk formula.

Of the above methods of appraisal, *trunk formula* is most commonly used with larger, specimen trees. This method, developed by the Council of Tree and Landscape Appraisers, begins with a base value derived from the cost per square inch of trunk diameter of the largest locally available transplantable tree of the same species of the tree being appraised. This value is applied to the total square inch trunk area of the appraisal tree and then reduced by species class, condition, and location in the landscape.

Information Management

The importance of information management cannot be overemphasized. Keeping accurate records and being able to retrieve information is absolutely essential to effective urban forest management. *Records:* reveal what has been done to trees and serve as the basis for future care; allow program evaluation; are essential to planning and budgeting; and furnish proof of care in disputes involving liability. Modern computer technology allows massive amounts of information to be efficiently handled. The key, however, is information entry, reasonably recording everything that happens to the urban forest—planting, pruning, insect and disease infestations and control, construction disruptions, fire, accidents, storm damage, tree removal, and such. Without such information, the basis for making reasonable judgements is greatly reduced.

Information management is not limited to internal records. Computers allow Internet access to virtually all topics concerning urban forestry. Many urban forest managers have their own websites, and communication with contemporaries worldwide is commonplace. Computer software is available for tree inventories, planning, budgeting, cost accounting, program analysis, tree selection, and other management applications.

Program Needs Analysis

Information management is the basis for program analysis. Program analysis begins with the simple question: Is the program as effective as it should be in meeting the needs of the urban forest? Program analysis must be done at both the macro and micro levels. Macro-analysis is an administrative function, and addresses the six elements necessary for comprehensive management of the urban forest: a central organization with responsibility and authority; knowledge of the total urban forestry environment; knowledge of what the urban forest needs; plans for meeting the needs; adequate budgets; and effective implementation (Figure 22.9). If any element is missing completely, comprehensive management cannot occur. If any element is partially missing, management cannot be as effective as possible. As missing parts are identified, the questions then become: Why is it missing? What are the barriers to putting it in place? and how may the barriers be overcome? The answers identify what should be the highest priorities for urban forestry program administrators. Micro-analysis looks within the program to identify strengths and weaknesses, and must be ongoing. The basic questions involve what is wrong and how it might be fixed, and what works well and whether more of it should be done.

Figure 22.9 The urban forest often includes areas of mature natural forests.

Indirect Management

The preceding text was concerned primarily with urban forestry activities on streetsides, parks, and other areas where trees and other vegetation are managed directly by the city forester. A major portion of the urban forest, however, from private yards to business and industrial sites, is not the direct responsibility of the city forester. While the arboricultural and landscaping practices discussed are applicable to these areas, the city forester can influence their enactment only indirectly. The objective of indirect management is for other owners to better care for their parts of the urban forest. Thus, there are two approaches: information dissemination; and working with those who service the urban forest.

Information Dissemination

The objective of information dissemination is education, in the hope that new knowledge will be applied to the urban forest. Information may be addressed to the generic needs of the urban forest, as identified in the long-range plan (safety, diversity, health, function), or may be specific, as related to storm damage, insect or disease infestations, poor arboricultural practices, or other situations. Each need can be addressed according to the following principles and practices of information dissemination:

- *Principles:* identify specific audiences; use methods appropriate to audiences; take advantage of the teachable moment; be specific as to what should be done; keep the message simple; use others to tell your story; and repeat, repeat, repeat.
- *Practices:* public meetings; tours and demonstrations; flyers, door-hangers, and posters; newsletters; inserts in newspapers and utility statements; newspaper special editions; newspaper articles; telephone hotlines; television and radio through programs or public service announcements; and direct mail.

Of the above principles, getting others to tell your story is especially important, as many credible "others" have the ready capability to extend information. Cooperative Extension Service agents, state forestry agency personnel, garden editors of newspapers, arboricultural and nursery firms, and even the clergy are examples.

Working with Those Who Service the Urban Forest

Those who service the urban forest have a direct positive or negative influence on its well-being. No one is in a better position to do good or harm to the urban forest than the person with a saw in his or her hand, or the person who supplies and plants trees. Hence, upgrading the knowledge and skills of such individuals must be of high priority for urban forest managers. An additional goal should be to have each service individual and firm (commercial and utility arborist, and nursery people) dedicated to the long-term objectives for the urban forest. Approaches involve: sharing of long-range plan information; sponsoring pruning schools and other training sessions; publishing newsletters; encouraging arborists to become members of professional associations; and aiding nurseries in furnishing diverse planting stock.

Program Support

Urban forestry programs at the city level are supported by various volunteer, technical, and financial resources. Volunteers are generally from local sources, while technical support may come from state or national organizations. Financing is largely from local sources, but other opportunities are sometimes available.

Volunteers

Volunteers provide valuable services to the urban forest and are utilized in virtually every successful city forestry program in the nation. Volunteers may be unaffiliated individuals or may be members of a group. Volunteer groups may be advocacy-, project-, or program-oriented.

- *Advocacy-oriented groups:* generally focused on specific causes or single issues; strong emphasis on fundraising and lobbying.
- *Project-oriented groups:* often part of a larger organization (civic or service club, business, youth organization); focused on individual projects, such as tree planting or environmental improvement.
- *Program-oriented groups:* focused on broader, long-range concerns (tree boards are an example).

Volunteers are a valuable resource for urban forest managers. Not only do volunteers provide labor, but they can also, particularly in the case of advocacy and program-oriented groups, be a source of involved program support. It is especially important for urban forest managers to consider the role of volunteers during annual program planning, with a "plan" for recruitment and utilization. Recruitment can be facilitated by working through various community organizations such as project-oriented groups, as above.

Technical Support

Technical support for local urban forestry programs, in the form of information and direct assistance, is available from a number of governmental and private sources. A primary source is the State Forestry Agency. Supported by the U.S.D.A. Forest Service, each state has an urban forestry coordinator with responsibility for facilitating development and better implementation of local programs. Specific activities include consultation, guidance in developing new programs, coordination of conferences and training events, administration of special projects, and direct assistance with application of new technologies. The Cooperative Extension Service is also a valuable resource. Backed by university specialists in areas pertaining to urban forestry, extension agents sponsor educational events such as workshops, field days, demonstrations, provide publications, and access research findings on special topics. Other sources of assistance are materials suppliers, arboricultural firms, nurseries, state arborists' associations, and national organizations such as the International Society of Arboriculture, the National Arborists Association, the American Association of Nurserymen, The National Arbor Day Foundation, and American Forests.

Financing

The majority of local urban forestry program funds are from public monies allocated through the planning and budgeting process. Such monies are usually from the city's general fund, but may come from specific tax levies. Occasionally there are also special (usually one-time) assessments for special projects, most generally tree establishment in a specified area. Opportunities for additional funds for general operations are rare. Funds provided through recurring budget cycles provide for continuity consistent with planned long-range objectives. Although often useful, funds from other sources, particularly those earmarked for tree planting, can result in more trees than can be established and maintained by regular program funds. There are, however, special needs that will not result in additional unfundable costs over time, such as tree inventories, systems for processing information, new technologies, and staff or tree board training. There may also be need of special funding for insect, disease, or storm emergencies. Sources of special funding are state and federal agencies, and grants by various philanthropic organizations.

Concluding Statement

It is the challenge of urban forestry to make trees and other organisms compatible and serviceable within an environment largely dominated by people and structures. In so doing, urban forestry merges the knowledge and skills of traditional forestry with disciplines such as landscape plant materials and design, arboriculture, engineering, planning, legal matters, and social and political science. The urban forest manager must have a working knowledge of the physical, social, legal, and political environment of the urban forest, of how to plan and budget for necessary management programs, and how to successfully implement them.

The urban forest has four basic and interrelated needs: vegetation establishment; maintenance; protection; and removal—each to be met in an extremely dynamic natural and human-influenced environment. From the perspective of the city forester, management is both direct and indirect; the former requiring physical attention to the four basic needs of the urban forest, and the latter directed toward various public audiences in an attempt to influence better management.

References

1. D. J. Nowak, *J. For., 92* (10), 42 (1994).

2. L. Westphal and G. Childs. *J. For., 92(10),* 31 (1994).

3. G. W. Grey, *The Urban Forest—Comprehensive Management,* John Wiley & Sons, New York, 1996.

4. G. W. Grey and F. J. Deneke, *Urban Forestry,* Second Edition, John Wiley & Sons, New York, 1986.

5. R. W. Harris, *Arboriculture—Integrated Management of Landscape Trees, Shrubs, and Vines,* Second Edition, Prentice Hall, Inc., Englewood Cliffs, N.J., 1992.

6. R. W. Miller, *Urban Forestry—Planning and Managing Urban Green Space,* Prentice Hall, Inc., Englewood Cliffs, N.J., 1988.

7. A. L. Shigo, *Modern Arboriculture—A Systems Approach to the Care of Trees,* Shigo and Trees Associates, Durham, N.H., 1991.

CHAPTER 23

Social Forestry: The Community-Based Management of Natural Resources

J. LIN COMPTON AND JOHN W. BRUCE

Social forestry is rapidly gaining the attention of those concerned about the continuing degradation of the environment around the world. The need to find solutions to the global environmental crisis becomes more critical daily. Scientists, legislators and policy makers, development program administrators, and enforcers of laws do not have all the answers to the complex problems and issues confronting that segment of the world's population that lives in close proximity to or that is in some manner or degree dependent upon forest resources. Neither do impoverished rural people who, caught up in the struggle to survive, sometimes pursue practices of forest and forest product use that work to diminish the very resource upon which their continued survival may depend. During the past two decades, many efforts have been launched in a variety of locations around the globe to deal with deforestation and resulting land degradation. Much has been tried and much has been learned about the requirements of an effective response to this environmental crisis. The purpose of this chapter is to present a selection of those experiences and the lessons learned from them and to highlight some of the issues and challenges ahead.

Social forestry revolves around a complex set of concepts and propositions concerning the *community-based management* of natural resources. Social forestry as an action strategy is seen as one means to promote rural development and maintain forest biodiversity and forest health (Figure 23.1). The major proposition is that this can be done by simultaneously producing income and empowering people while promoting sound forestry practices. In some settings, forest user groups, having rights to trees but not to the land, have taken an active role in protecting, harvesting, and regenerating

Figure 23.1 The tropical forest in the heavily populated city-state of Singapore is under many competing utilization pressures. (Photo by R. A. Young.)

forests. Specific collective activities range from establishing home gardens, carrying out alley cropping, setting up tree nurseries, and operating woodlots to meet wood needs, to practicing contour farming by integrating trees into hedgerows to prevent soil erosion and campaigning for local natural heritage development. Such activities may be integrated with efforts to improve animal production and the propagation of improved varieties of crops and species of trees. Strategies to support local social forestry efforts range from legislative activities, to overseeing quality control, to fostering effective relationships among participating institutions. In the following sections, examples drawn from world-wide experience in social forestry will be given and concepts and principles imbedded within these experiences highlighted. Finally, some of the continuing and major issues and challenges will be discussed.

Global Experience in Social Forestry

In April 1995, Prabinder Das, the Chief Forest Conservator for West Bengal State in India, visited Hayfork, a town in northern California, under Ford Foundation funding. A month later, a community organizer from Orissa State followed him. They were consulting with the Watershed Research and Training Center in this forest-dependent community in Trinity National Forest, sharing experiences of community forestry.

There is less old growth forest in Trinity now, and environmental legislation has also constricted production. Hayfork residents set up the Center to help them explore ways to diversify and to think through ways to get more of the existing revenue from forestry for local people. India has pioneered a program of joint forestry management (JFM) in which local communities manage areas of state forest for the Forestry Department, and the people in Hayfork were interested (1).

Hayfork is not alone. American forestry was wasteful of forest resources for generations, but in recent decades there has been a broad recognition of the need for sustainable production and the sustainable livelihoods that this can bring with it (2). The boom and bust progression historically associated with forestry-dependent communities has been too costly in human terms. Because of mill closures, these communities have found themselves thrust from rugged self-sufficiency into a life on remittances. The results are devastating, with the ideology and images of forestry long outliving its economic viability (3).

Even where bust is averted, scholars have noted that forestry-dependent communities that have moved out of the boom stage exhibit persistent poverty. Sociological studies of poverty in forest-dependent communities have identified root causes and suggested solutions. Current thinking suggests that stability is a vain hope, and that sustainability means something different: an acceptance of the inevitability of change by these communities and a lively and creative response by them to the challenges and the opportunities posed by change. There is a renewed interest in social capital issues in these communities. Scholars are asking exactly what that capital consists of, and how best to build it (4, 5).

Where communities can respond effectively, what are some of the strategies for social forestry that have been identified as promising? One strategy is to assure greater diversity of species and products within the timber industry, thus decreasing vulnerability to change. More processing locally and more exploitation of nontimber forest products reduce risks. The development of complementary enterprises when timber is still booming can make things easier later. Scaling up of operations may be important. Large enterprises may be better able to make the investments that will enable them to survive in a harsh competitive environment. Strong local markets and diversified production may provide insulation from major ups and downs of national markets for timber. Investment is more likely where there is local ownership of forests and forest product industries and when less money from forestry flows out of the community.

This last point brings to thinking about American forestry a radical critique developed in recent years in the Third World. Forest-dependent communities exist in the midst of a rich endowment of natural resources, and yet often they are subject to persistent poverty. There is little capital accumulation and investment in those communities, because the resource belongs to government or to large private forest landholders. This phenomenon is not limited to forest-dependent communities, but applies to natural resource–dependent communities more generally, such as communities that rely on tourism for their major income (6).

This is why Hayfork is interested in joint forestry management in India and other models of forestry in which local communities assume control over forest resources, and there is a large body of experience from the Third World to be consulted. Beginning in the early 1980s, a series of experiments in village forestry in India led to a national program that gives village forestry committees access to state forests, mostly small areas of degraded state forest in need of reforestation. An agreement between the Forestry Department and the village forestry committee sets out a co-management scheme, in which the Forestry Department assists the community in replanting the area and the community undertakes to exploit it in accordance with an appended Forest Management Plan. Communities own the trees they grow, but market them through the Forestry Department, which recovers its own costs of production from the sales before passing along the community's share. The purpose of the program is to turn around communities whose members had sometimes been engaged in degrading these resources, and create incentives in those communities for the conservation and good husbandry of the resource (7, 8).

Many programs in developing countries aim to increase community participation in forestry and provide new incentives for sustainable forestry. All have as an essential component a reduction of emphasis on enforcement and a new stress on creating incentives for local communities to support sustainable resource use by giving those communities more direct control of forest resources and improved income opportunities generated by access to those resources. In the Philippines, a community stewardship program gives long-term leaseholds of large areas of land with forests to local foundations, often ethnic territories of minority groups represented by those foundations (9). In Thailand, the government has been experimenting with "forest villages." Villagers reafforest areas of state plantations around villages within the plantation, but also have fields for family agricultural production around the village. In China, villages now hold the ownership of substantial areas of mountain land and have initiated tree planting under a variety of institutional patterns including village (local government) forestry, village shareholder associations, and long-term leases to family partnerships (10).

In Africa, an innovative management program for Niger's Guesselbodi National Forest organized local users bordering the forest into cutters cooperatives and licensed them to cut in the forest (11) (Figure 23.2). In the Mgori Forest of central Tanzania, five communities have become the active guardians of a large miombo woodland; which was in danger of disappearing because of uncontrolled wood extraction, shifting cultivation, and settlement. Through a collaborative arrangement with government, the villagers are recognized not only as the prime users, but as the controlling managers and potentially, owners of the forest, for as long as they protect the forest from damaging use or diminishment. Their main tools of management include village forest management plans, detailed rules concerning forest use, vigilant patrolling of the forest by forest "watchers," and the establishment of a monthly forum in which representatives

from the five villages meet to discuss and resolve problems of mutual concern (12).

In mountainous Yunnan, China, an innovative project is underway for the testing of two models for sustainable management of upland forest-based ecosystems: 1) a model for the adaptive co-management of the buffer and development zones surrounding nature reserves by villagers and government reserve staff, and 2) a model for multi-village watershed ecosystem management councils and interwatershed forest ecosystem management councils. Mountain dwellers depend upon the timber, nontimber forest products, and the headwaters of streams located within the forests of such upland areas to sustain their livelihoods. Additionally, as the lives of lowland dwellers have been increasingly affected by the soil erosion, river siltation, and flooding caused by deteriorating upland ecosystems, the government has become more inclined to mobilize and support the ecosystem management efforts of local mountain communities (13) (Figure 23.3).

In South America, there are a variety of new institutional models being used to provide forest-dwelling peoples with more control over the forest resource or at least to protect their access to it (14). Mexico's *ejidos* have in the past decade taken over direct management of the forests they have long owned from concessionaires. In Canada, the Kedgewick Loggers Co-op, New Brunswick, is now exploiting a former private forest whose exploitation had come to be regarded as uneconomic by the owner (15). In Quebec, the provincial forest department began leasing out large holdings of provincial forest to individuals under a forestry sharecropping program (16).

Many of these programs have yet to prove themselves economically. The JFM program in India is still awaiting an adequate economic evaluation of benefits to villagers. Mexico's *ejidos* need to restructure for greater efficiency in the face of stiff competition from cheap lumber coming into Mexico under the liberalized trade regime of NAFTA. However, the response in the local communities to these opportunities has engendered an intense interest in such programs and motivated the Ford Foundation

Figure 23.2   Felling of okoume in Gabon, W. Africa. Okoume is a major raw material for plywood in Europe. (Photo by Neuhoff, Center for Tropical Forestry, France.)

Figure 23.3 Hillside reforestation in Vietnam. (F. Mattioli, World Food Program, UN-FAO.)

to sponsor a research program to explore the potentials of community forestry in the United States.

The new interest has led to new assessments of the potential of community forestry (17) and has focused attention on previously unsung cases of community forestry at home. Wisconsin, Michigan, and Minnesota boast county forestry programs. In Wisconsin, the counties are the largest forest landowners in the state, with 2.3 million hectares in 28 counties (also see Chapter 10, Nonindustrial Private Forests). The county forest ownership originated in Depression-era tax defaults that caused the land to revert to the counties, providing the legal basis for local government forestry (18).

Also, in Wisconsin, 25 miles west of Green Bay, there is an important example of Native American community forestry. Menominee Tribal Enterprises (MTE) has a forest of 220,000 acres on its reservation of 235,000 acres. The Menominee have been engaged in commercial timbering since before the turn of the last century, and managed to avoid the

"allotments" of land to individuals that broke up so many reservations in the region in the early and mid-1900s. MTE operates its own sawmill and grows a diversity of species that both reflect traditional values and allow it to access specialized market niches (19).

Managers of federal forests in the west are seeking to respond to demands for new modes of collaboration with local communities (20), and urban forestry is receiving new attention, not only for ornamental and recreational purposes, but also for reservoir and watershed management around cities (21). These programs seem to have a potential for engendering new enthusiasm for forestry in these communities (see Chapter 22, Urban Forestry).

Social forestry programs draw upon strengths in the community itself. One of those strengths that has been recognized in many Third World community forestry programs is the indigenous knowledge of the sustainable use and management of both timber and nontimber forest products within local ecosystems that local people possess. In northern Thailand, the traditional watershed ecosystem management practices of the Karen ethnic minority have been carefully studied and highly acclaimed for the soundness of underlying scientific principles, principles that have been worked out through centuries of discovery learning within the micro-environments inhabited by the Karen (22). Tree, crop, soil, water, animal, and wildlife relationships are managed to promote sustainability of the ecosystem (Figure 23.4).

The indigenous or local experiential knowledge of such groups as the Karen, as well as all such indigenous knowledge everywhere, can be conceptualized as falling into six categories or levels: 1) indigenous technical knowledge (ITK), the cognitive structure of indigenous knowledge and its language forms; 2) indigenous knowledge about local social organization, how people organize themselves to use ITK in relation to, for example, the conservation and use of resources; 3) indigenous knowledge about decision-making processes and patterns, how knowledge regarding resource conservation and use is employed by individuals

or groups to decide courses of action; 4) indigenous knowledge about innovations and experimentation, how knowledge is developed and refined; 5) indigenous knowledge as manifested in values and beliefs systems, how people feel about their knowledge; and 6) indigenous knowledge about teaching-learning transactions and communication, how people share or exchange their knowledge. Such local, experience-based indigenous knowledge about biological or natural phenomena may often contain scientific principles or, through careful scrutiny, yield new insights into important relationships specific to a particular location or ecosystem or perhaps generalizable to other similar settings or contexts.

Sometimes indigenous knowledge may be the only knowledge which exists about such phenomena, as particular insect-plant interactive relationships. Just as important, if not more so, is the improved communication that can occur between the lay population and scientists when the language for expressing the local knowledge is known. Scientific information can then be translated into the local language forms. Such communication is

Figure 23.4 A newly planted hillside in Thailand. (UN-FAO photo.)

needed to close the current gap between scientist-derived knowledge and indigenous, experience-based knowledge, to facilitate the functioning of an additional laboratory for scientific investigation, to identify and correct weaknesses or errors in either knowledge system, and to facilitate further discovery. The sustainable management of community forests in the future may depend upon the progress made in closing this gap (22).

Indigenous knowledge of how to sustainably manage natural resources exists wherever people have been actively engaged for decades in meeting the challenge. The Menominee of Wisconsin, mentioned above, practice logging by starting at one end of the reservation and, over a period of several years, progressively moving toward the opposite boundary of the reservation, selectively cutting only mature trees before returning to the initial starting point to restart the process. The Menominee have found that this procedure enables them to take mature trees for timber, maintain the integrity and quality of the forest ecosystem, and provide a continuous source of livelihood for the community.

In the Philippines, farmers in mountain communities have joined together to develop multi-story systems of agroforestry, which allow the growth of a variety of tree crops within the same plots, taking advantage of the photosynthesis, shade requirements and tolerance, and soil nutrient needs of such trees and plants as coconut, banana, papaya, and pineapple. Many combinations of such intercropping have been tested and found effective by the local farmers through their own experiments and the intergenerational transmission of the resulting and gradually accumulating knowledge. Other farmers have developed ways to reinforce hillside terraces, where agricultural crops are produced, by planting deep-rooting trees along the edge of terraces to hold soil in place, thereby preventing or reducing soil erosion (Figure 23.5). The trees selected (e.g., calliandra) also provide a steady supply of fuelwood and leaves for fodder for animals (23).

In many areas of the world, cooperation among government organizations in the delivery of services to community-based social forestry programs is still rare or weak. In some areas, progress is being made in strengthening such interagency cooperation. In Thailand, the Royal Forestry Department and Department of Community Development, recognizing each other's respective strengths, have joined forces in a pilot experiment for supporting

Figure 23.5 Palm trees incorporated in terraced hillside planting in Indonesia. (Photo by K. L. Young.)

local participation in community forestry and natural resource conservation. The two government units, with advisory inputs from faculty at two universities, aim to establish a model to guide the provision of the technical expertise of the 400 forestry staff members and the social organization expertise of 6,000 community development workers to the country's 60,000 village communities in the promotion of the sustainable management of community forests. Using a participatory land-use planning strategy and raised topographical maps as a tactile device for fostering visual clarity, villagers are encouraged to identify, agree upon, and implement needed changes in the conservation and use of the natural resources in the surrounding area. The work thus far has resulted in significant changes and improvements in both agricultural practices and forest resource management in the pilot villages.

Improved patterns of cooperation also are needed among communities having access to the same resource base. For example, forest conservation efforts are often located within watersheds containing a number of village communities, requiring cooperation in the management of common-pool forest and water resources. Laos, with assistance from the UNDP, has begun the piloting of watershed ecosystem-based development emphasizing technical analysis of watershed resources, constraints, and potential; the decentralization of governmental authority; local participation in intervillage watershed ecosystem management councils; and mobile district management teams that include training and monitoring and evaluation specialists. The rules governing the sustainable use and management of forest resources are determined locally and enforced by the communities themselves. The major issue encountered in the project to date has been failures in the devolution of power from government bureaucracies to local communities, even though the project objectives previously agreed upon were to do exactly that. It seems that entrenched bureaucracies are difficult to change and are frequently an obstacle to the achievement of community-based management of natural resources in many settings (24).

Efforts to alleviate rural poverty through the promotion of community-based agroforestry programs have had mixed degrees of success. The Forestry Bureau of Yunnan, China, discovered that the increased apple production stemming from Bureau provision of tree saplings to mountain communities resulted in a flood of apples into the market and the lowering of prices so drastically that farmers became disinclined to further expand production. The basic problem seems to have been an insufficient range of agroforestry crops that would allow farmers to adjust to changing market demands (Figure 23.6). A subsidiary issue is the singular control of tree nurseries by the Forestry Bureau, a policy that inhibits possibilities for diversification and provision of tree stocks that are in line with farmer preferences. Field studies of villager interests in the cultivation of various types of trees and their preferences for planting trees in different locations within their farm area, showed clear choices of specific trees for different locations (near family dwelling, at edge of fields, near streams, on a hilltop) and purposes (shade, windbreaks, soil conservation, wildlife habitat). Yet the Bureau was not able to respond to these choices and preferences (25).

Community-owned and -operated tree nurseries can sometimes provide an answer to the diversity of needs and preferences for tree stocks. Commu-

Figure 23.6 Agroforestry development in Amazonia. (UN-FAO photo.)

nity forestry programs in Costa Rica have empha-sized the establishment and control of tree nurs-eries by the communities themselves. The saplings nurtured are those desired by the community. In some communities, a deliberate effort has been made to turn the responsibility for the management of the nurseries over to the most impoverished segment of the community's inhabitants. Oftentimes the managers are women who find nursery man-agement work and sales correspond conveniently with other family or household responsibilities. The income earned from the sale of the saplings also goes directly to meeting family needs.

In Andhra Pradesh State of India, one joint for-est management (JFM) project has enabled villagers to become self-sufficient with money earned from timber and bamboo (Figure 23.7). "Poverty was caused by environmental degradation. So we made poverty alleviation our primary target through envi-ronmental regeneration," says one spokesman for the project. The project was implemented in an area under the control of the Naxalite movement, which started as a revolt against the inequitable distribution of land and water. Vana Suraksha Samiti (VSS) or Forest Protection Committees were

established and govern the redistribution back to the villagers of all income earned from timber and bamboo (26).

Issues and Challenges

In addition to the lessons, principles, strategies, problems, needs, questions, issues, and challenges described thus far, there are several others that war-rant mentioning, because they will be the focus of scientific endeavors and development work during the decades ahead.

Participation and Local Initiative

Local citizen participation in social forestry programs and schemes seems to be critical to success. Yet considerable disagreement exists over the nature and amount of participation that is desirable, obtain-able, and sustainable. Creating a participative envi-ronment, one that contains an appropriate incentives structure and works to positively affect and sustain interest and active participation, appears to remain an elusive goal in most programs

Figure 23.7 Fuelwood supply and collection is a critical problem in many developing countries, shown here in India. (Photo by R. A. Young.)

and projects. How to stimulate local initiative and a sense of ownership for a social forestry program among local groups from the very inception of an activity, how to assure participation in an equitable distribution of benefits, and how to assure co-learning by both local citizens and project facilitators remain challenges for the developers of the science and practice art. Failure to set the right tone in participation can lead local people to misunderstand and react negatively to the whole enterprise, and at worst, can lead local people to feel that government is asking them "to plant government trees on their land." The design and testing of mechanisms for facilitating empowerment, autonomy, self-realization, and community-based management seem to be in an early stage of design and testing and will need to be developed or refined in the years ahead.

Community Control

Another key to effective social forestry is community control of forest resources, related money flow, and local capacity for money management. Reports on social forestry programs around the world suggest these are some of the most critical factors in determining success. Often little information exists regarding either the land and forest resources available or the nature of the conditions of the surrounding human population. Community forest resource assessments have sometimes been carried out to help secure tenure and rights to forest resources, seek compensation for lost or threatened resources, provide an information base for use in managing forests sustainably, and monitor biodiversity for conservation. Securing tenure, creating appropriate economic incentives, and strengthening institutional capacity for social forestry programs require considerable managerial ability and mutual understanding and cooperation, that is, a *modus cooperandi* writ large, between people and their governments. Yet many local groups seem to lack, for one reason or another, the requisite skills needed to effectively manage, especially within collective arrangements, valuable and scarce natural resources and related organized human

behavior. The training of citizens for administrative tasks, the local provision of technical assistance and economic advice, and for forestry-related business roles to promote independence, self-reliance, and sustainability remain important challenges that warrant much attention.

Program Planning and Development

The achievement of success in social forestry programs and in the advancement of the science and art of the field of practice calls for much reflection, theory building, skills development, planning, implementation, and evaluation. Community-based management of forests entails participatory land-use planning and management, the development of land stewardship, a continual reinvestment of benefits derived, and an ensuing strengthening of the social dimension of local communities. Many issues, questions, and propositions concern the nature of such local natural resource planning: 1) the necessity of decentralization of decision-making and responsibility in support of community-based management of forests, 2) the nature and degree of top-down and bottom-up interactions in program planning and implementation, 3) ways and means of arriving at appropriate site-specific recommendations, 4) the nature of formats and processes for comprehensive planning of social forestry programs, and 5) the problems of and prospects for co-management of social forestry and for mediating system incompatibilities. One choice seems to be that of finding common ground between state and local management in the benefit distribution of collective forest resources, on the one hand, as against having a local state-sponsored entity managing forestry activities. A question seems to be whether this is the best course for local social and ecosystems. The design and testing of more site-specific management plans based on considerations of indigenous knowledge systems and defined in terms of local needs and benefits must go forward. In this regard, China's contract responsibility system may be a model with potential for worldwide applicability.

Legal and Policy Environment

A people's approach to social forestry also requires the formation of supportive policies. Social forestry can only occur within a supportive legal and policy environment. Such policy must be blended with both culture and legislation. There needs to be clarity in terms of access to resources, contractual accountability, and regulatory responsibility. When local communities and their members are asked to make forestry a more important part of their livelihood strategies, they need to be provided with clear terms on which to do so and assurance that government is committed to those terms. In parts of Africa, social forestry has been discouraged when national governments grant tree-cutting concessions to urban elites, who so empowered show up to cut forest resources which communities have been husbanding. More studies of the range of factors and forces that hinder or enhance policy implementation are needed.

Ecological Settings and Processes

Social forestry is practiced in a wide variety of geophysical landscapes such as hillsides, mountain tops, river valleys, watersheds, arid plains, wetlands, buffer zones around protected areas, and degraded lands. Each of these provides unique features and parameters that influence if not dictate the nature of social forestry activities which take place. Sometimes the major concerns are forest disturbance, transformation, or recovery, while at other times the major concern is with the nature of practices and rates of utilization of forest resources that are sustainable within each context. Because of insufficiency in laws and regulations for governing forest use and in forestry personnel to enforce them, locally organized community-based groups for supervising forest use are essential in many locations if forest-based ecosystems are to be restored and sustained.

Watershed Management

There are many locations around the world where an ecosystem approach to natural resource management will frequently involve the conservation and protection of forests by multicommunity groups that reside within the same watershed. A better understanding of how such groups can work together to protect and sustain the watershed ecology is needed in many areas. How to approach and work effectively with such groups remains a major challenge for most government and nongovernment organizations.

Land and Tree Tenure

People's social forestry–related behavior is affected by their real or perceived security of ownership or user rights to land and land-based natural resources. A sense of security influences human motivation and ability to protect forests from exploitation by outside forces. *Tenure* itself is a broad concept. In reality, it may include a variety of tenure "niches": state-controlled lands, trees in communal areas, sacred sites, resettlement areas, or individual lands, for example. Other tenurial contexts such as private timber lands, collective tree tenure, and private tree tenure will also influence the nature of social forestry activities. Tenurial processes within changing forest use patterns need to be clearly understood. Often land or tree tenure is based on gender, and the stability of such rights, especially those of women, varies from one area or culture to another. The length of time for which tenure is awarded also affects the motivational base of land husbandry and forest stewardship and the type of practices of agriculture and forest protection and use. In some locations, it has become necessary to award long-term stewardship certificates to local communities as a basis for encouraging desired behaviors.

Land Use Patterns

Changes in landscapes frequently result from large-scale infrastructural developments such as hydroelectric dams of major streams, vast irrigation and electricity networks, new roads or other transportation systems, oil or gas pipelines and storage facilities, and the setting aside of lands as biosphere reserves or natural parks and recreation sites. How such developments affect land use patterns and the practice of social forestry by local populations or the adaptations they make to these large macrospective infrastructural changes that are beyond their control is a subject that warrants much study.

Agroforestry

As stated by the previous Director-General of the International Center for Research in Agroforestry (ICRAF) in Kenya, the world's farmers are far ahead of the scientists in regard to knowledge of and experience with crop/soil/tree/animal/water relationships because they have been doing it for thousands of years. One strategy for efficiently advancing our scientific understanding of such relationships is to study what farmers are already doing and then testing and measuring observed concepts and relationships for validity and utility under varying conditions. In much of the world, the "agroforestry" of fuelwood, food, fiber, livestock, soil fertility, water, and income generation is central to social forestry concerns (Figure 23.8). Working with groups of farmers or even whole communities, it may become possible to find acceptable ways to

resolve such issues as the conversion of forests to pasture, of preventing soil erosion in hilly regions with tree reinforced contours, or preventing wind erosion through strip planting, and which type of tree crops to use in which locations as a means of nitrogen fixation.

Forest and Woodland Management

More frequently today, local communities or social groups are formed to manage forests and woodlands, quite often because there are not sufficient government personnel to do such work, sometimes because of the realization that local people may be highly motivated to do the work well. Thinking and action regarding forest management ranges from scientific certification systems for sustainable forest management to indigenously derived systems for managing the sustainable extraction of renewable wood and nonwood resources. Issues exist concerning whether to practice selective, or partial, or clearcutting of trees, and under what conditions and why; the feasibility of compartmental management of forests; the solving of differences in ideal choice of tree species and type of forest cover versus local preference; whether local peo-

Figure 23.8 Roadside fuelwood plantation in Tanzania. (Photo by B. K. Kaale, World Food Program, UN-FAO.)

ple (especially the rural poor) can be sufficiently trained and entrusted with the tasks of managing tree nurseries and tree planting; and the validity of indigenous methods and locally created "appropriate" technologies. Social forestry provides a context for the search for answers to such questions and resolution of such issues.

Wood Industry

In many parts of the world, the ups and downs of the wood industry are tied inextricably to local community acceptance of or resistance to the extraction rates and patterns practiced by timber companies. Controversy over the nature and length of timber leases has pitted local communities concerned with the ecological basis of their own economic survival against the voracious appetites of timber companies and sometimes corrupt forestry officials. The mobilization of community protests against destructive wood industry practices is a major theme in many parts of the world. These problems are so pervasive that during the last four years of the 1990s, the World Bank has refused to fund any projects involving commercial logging. A recent evaluation of the Bank's policy pointed out, however, that this had simply left a lucrative area of lending open to private lenders who lack the Bank's compunctions.

Reforestation and Ecological Restoration

Invigorating the biophysical and socioeconomic landscape of severely denuded and impoverished regions becomes a more realistic and necessary proposition as the human population continues to expand and the number of suitable alternative placements decrease. The challenge of restoring degraded areas to ecologically desired states requires the cooperation of governments and local communities. Certainly, in many locations, current policies of removing inhabitants from areas under restoration represents a debatable issue. The root causes of ecosystem degradation, whether social, political, economic, or natural/environmental, must

be addressed and ways and means must be sought to help local forest-dependent communities find economic opportunities that will enable them to survive while protecting their forest resources. Much community forestry work is based on the failure by weak governments to enforce negative sanctions effectively, and the hope that providing an interest in the preservation of the forest to local people will give them the necessary incentive to help police the resource. An integrated set of actions may be needed: from improving logging practices, to diversifying local economies, to identifying incentives so that local people will feel that they have a "stake" in the restoration efforts, to strengthening local governance, to formulating and enforcing policy reforms. Social forestry will be of central importance to success in these actions.

Biodiversity Conservation

Much current social forestry focus is on the rationale for and means of creating effective buffer zones around biosphere reserves. Buffer zones are envisioned as means to resist land speculation, reduce negative forest edge effects, increase biodiversity, deflect forest pressures, and improve community conditions. The conceptual and programmatic links to community development are potentially strong but require the formulation of means to promote a wise use of nontimber forest products (NTFP), to alleviate fuelwood pressures, reduce environmentally destructive and, therefore, unsustainable agricultural practices, and optimize community participation in the protection of the nature reserves. Prospects for the establishment of effective buffer zone programs will also depend on the extent to which appropriate and locally accepted forms of economic and legal freedom are achieved because capacity for direct enforcement by government authorities is too limited. Cultural factors must also be considered. In Africa and Asia, "sacred forests" are proving an important source of biological diversity, preserved by indigenous systems of sanctioning including religious prohibitions. Obviously, social forestry must encompass such considerations.

Sociocultural Context

Various sociocultural factors affect the prospects for sustained health of forest resources. Some progress is now being made in understanding the differences between Western property laws and indigenous tenure systems, of how local life is often intertwined with various aspects of a forest, and the perceptions of different ethnic groups regarding forest-people reciprocity. Studies that have explored the cultural basis of human interaction with natural resources should be assessed for insight into the cultural basis of social forestry.

Indigenous Knowledge Systems (IKS)

The prospects for designing site-specific social forestry plans that will be implemented on a sustained basis by the people inhabiting a target area will largely hinge upon the extent to which local, indigenous knowledge is studied, understood, and taken into account. Such knowledge may often become the foundation from which sustainable programs can be built. They can be the curriculum from which a "conscientization" or awareness-building process can be launched. In some locations, this may be the only way, outside of external economic or legal inducements, that sustained local participation can be achieved. The process whereby local communities or groups adapt to changes taking place around them in order to survive calls for a dynamic interaction between indigenous, experience-based knowledge systems and scientist-derived knowledge systems. This proposition poses as much of a challenge to scientists today as it does to local people because the process and methods for learning from indigenous experience require a considerable investment of valuable time and energy. Hope for blending the traditional governance of local societies and cultures with the functioning of an international economy in a mutually beneficial manner may rest, at least in part, upon the extent to which IKS is brought into the equation.

Gender and Poverty

Women comprise the majority of the world's population and suffer the effects of gender-based biases and inequalities. The importance of integrating women into decision-making processes concerning the management and use of natural resources is undeniable. In social forestry, a major need today is understanding the differentiation of gender-specific tasks based on tree species, products, and local culture. In Africa, there are some cultural practices that interfere with women participating in social forestry, such as prohibitions of tree planting by women, tree planting being treated as a men's activity, or taboos that will not allow women to deal with certain tree species. On the other hand, the example of rural poor women in Costa Rica taking on the task of operating tree nurseries as a means of earning income while simultaneously providing a service essential to the restoration or reforestation of degraded areas suggests a potentially fruitful direction. It is also an example of the type of social forestry activities that need to be designed and tested. The alleviation of rural poverty in degraded resource areas constitutes a major challenge for many governments, many having already experienced significant difficulty in finding effective means of improving the quality of life of the weaker sections of their population.

Migration and Settlement

Of increasing concern to environmentalists is the shifting and resettlement of human populations, as a part of nomadic traditions, as a result of natural disasters, as a result of the overcrowding of urban areas, or just because of formal government plans to occupy or create more favorable human environments (Figure 23.9). It is likely that the pressure for this will become larger in years ahead as the world's base population expands. Much work needs to be done in designing and testing the nature and extent of services required by new settlements in forested areas and in finding ways and means of working effectively in partnership arrangements

Figure 23.9 Creation of logging roads, such as this one shown in Papua, New Guinea, opens access for migration and settlement in forest regions leading to further decline of tropical forests.

with such new communities to promote a viable form and level of human existence while sustaining the surrounding forests.

Economic Change

Several key economic questions and issues surround social forestry: 1) the design and conduct of cost-benefit analyses of programs and activities; 2) the determination of rates of return for social investments; 3) the distribution of benefits from collective endeavors; 4) the efficiency of community-based forest enterprises; 5) the economic viability of state monopolies versus farmers responding to free markets; 6) the required nature and degree of reinvestment of derived benefits at the local level to maintain sustainability; 7) the balancing of community economic development with forest sustainability; 8) the formation and functioning of forestry cooperatives as a means to protect the environment and improve the local economy; 9) the division of profits for reinvestment and for individual and group benefits; 10) estimating the costs

of forest assessments (labor, capital, maintenance, professional expertise); 11) managing for the market versus managing for biodiversity and maintaining a choice among species; 12) the clash of interests between community forest enterprises (CFE) and world trade efficiencies; and 13) the nature and amount of compensation required for "ecological" services delivered by the poorer segments of the population, for example, community tree nurseries run by women in impoverished rural villages in Costa Rica. What types of socioeconomic alternatives exist to thwart the excessive use of forest and forest products or what alternatives might be developed? What incentives are necessary for individuals to become willing to consider such alternatives?

Interorganizational Collaboration

Integrated service delivery remains an elusive goal for many government and nongovernment organization-sponsored social forestry projects. Appropriate and timely response to local needs and perceptions of the same is not easily achieved. Social forestry programs are not immune from this aspect of programming failure. Some success has been experienced when agencies or organizations move from acting as patrons of local efforts to becoming encouragers and facilitators of local initiative and responsibility. The big challenge in the community-based management of natural resources continues to be the acceptance and use of adaptive and facilitative styles for dealing with diverse forests and the human users of the same. Ways and means of achieving and maintaining interorganizational collaboration in such responsive programming need to be sought, tested, and adapted to fit varying local circumstances.

Conflict Resolution

Disputes over access to and the control and management of natural resources occur; 1) within communities; 2) between communities; 3) in contests between public versus private property rights; and 4) between individual rights and the community good. In many cases, organizational structures and dispute settlement mechanisms for "mediating" democratic processes of conflict resolution often exist for categories 1 and 4, but not for 2 or 3.

Extension

Key concepts and issues regarding the role of extension in social forestry programs are: 1) forester credibility; 2) prospects for fostering farmer-to-farmer exchanges regarding agroforestry practices; 3) establishing and working effectively with farmer associations to arrive at group decisions on policies and practices; 4) achieving accuracy in target grouping; 5) the willingness to revamp strategies in a continuing quest to increase relevance, effectiveness, and efficiency in program actions; 6) improving communications with clientele; 7) improving rural people's understanding of the limits on forest use; and 8) extension staff willingness to serve as catalysts and facilitators working among the ranks of (and not trying to serve as representatives for) the people they serve.

Measurement and Evaluation

There are serious social, ecological, and economic implications attached to the types of evaluation and measurement methods and techniques used in social forestry programs. The results of using or emphasizing one method or approach over another may influence the balance of ecological parameters with the marketplace or the balance between promoting income generation and maintaining resource base integrity. Assessment methodology has advanced rapidly in recent years as a result of the development of: 1) remote sensing capacities; 2) pairing geographic information systems (GIS) with thematic mapping using participatory rapid appraisal (PRA) or participatory land-use planning (PLP) techniques; 3) conducting continuous forest or timber inventories; 4) mapping resource boundaries; and 5) inventorying nontimber forest products (NTFP). A related issue is the use of different

monitoring and evaluation methods by different organizations and agencies working in the same service area, resulting in varying kinds and levels of data being collected and, therefore, different interpretations being given to local conditions and needs. This situation often seriously reduces the chances for effective interorganizational response to local community forestry efforts. Additionally, most measurement science assumes the involvement of local citizens, yet ways need to be designed and tested for properly introducing it to them and effectively developing their abilities and willingness to employ it themselves.

Concluding Statement

Social forestry as a science and practice art is evolving rapidly in response to increasing pressures on forest resources and forest-based ecosystems around the globe. A recognition of the necessity to mobilize human communities to assume a greater responsibility and role in conserving the earth's natural resources has gradually emerged. Yet the consolidation of the principles and lessons from decades of experience in diverse settings and situations remains an unfinished task.

An ecosystem approach to local management of natural resources will require collaboration at all levels, but community responsibility will remain the key to success. It has been and will continue to be a challenge to combine an ecosystem approach and community management because communities may not be organized for natural resource management at the ecosystem scale. It will continue to be necessary to: 1) raise levels of public awareness, understanding, and appreciation of the need for and nature of community-based natural resource management; 2) create capacities for intercommunity collaboration in ecosystems occupied by several communities; 3) develop the forestry science that must undergird such work, 4) identify the policy frameworks necessary to support community control and initiative; and 5) empower local groups with a wide variety of skills critical for getting the job done well. Much of what will be needed has been discussed in the preceeding sections. Much more will need to be discovered or developed.

References

1. C. Danks, "Developing Institutions for Community Forestry in Northern California," *Rural Development Forestry Network Paper 20a,* Winter 1996/97. London: Overseas Development Institute, 1996.

2. J. H. Drielsma, J. A. Miller, and W. R. Burch, Jr., "Sustained yield and community stability in American forestry," In *Community & Forestry: Continuities in the Sociology of Natural Resources*, R. G. Lee, D. R. Field and W. R. Burch, Jr., eds., Westview Press, Boulder, Colo., 1990.

3. E. C. Weeks, "Mill closures in the Pacific Northwest: The consequences of economic decline in rural industrial communities," In *Community & Forestry: Continuities in the Sociology of Natural Resources*, R. G. Lee, D. R. Field and W. R. Burch, Jr., eds., Westview Press, Boulder, Colo., 1990.

4. L. Fortmann, J. Kusel, C. Danks, L. Moody, and S. Seshan, "A comparative rapid rural assessment of seven forest communities," In *Well-Being in Forest-Dependent Communities*, Vol. 1, Kusel and Fortmann, Department of Forestry and Natural Resource Management, UC-Berkeley, Berkeley, Calif., 1991.

5. T. M. Beckley, *Society and Natural Resources, 8*, 261 (1995).

6. N. L. Peluso, C. R. Humphrey, and L. P. Fortmann, *Society and Natural Resources, 7,* 23 (1994).

7. J. M. Lindsay, "Law and Community in the Management of India's State Forests, Lincoln Institute for Land Policy Working Paper," Lincoln Institute of Land Policy, Cambridge, Mass., 1994.

8. M. Hobley, "Participatory Forestry: The Process of Change in India and Nepal." *ODI Rural Development Forestry Study Guide 3,* London, 1996.

9. O. F. Lynch, and K. Talbott, "Balancing Acts: Community-Based Forest Management and National Law in Asia and the Pacific," World Resources Institute, Washington, D.C., 1995.

10. J. W. Bruce, S. Rudrappa, and L. Zongmin, *Unasylva, 46 (180),* 75 (1995).

11. J. Heermans, *Rural Africana, 23/24,* 67 (1985).

12. L. Wily, "Collaborative Forest Management—Villagers and Government: The Case of Mgori Forest, Tanzania," FAO/SLU-WP, Rome, 1995. (http://www.trees.slu.se/publ/online/wilycove.htm).

13. M. R. Teuke. and S. Pigorsch, *On Wisconsin. 97*(1), 22 (1995).

14. S. H. Davis and A. Wali, *Ambio, 23*(8), 485 (1994).

15. P. N. Duinker, P. W. Matakala, F. Chege, and L. Bouthillier, *The Forestry Chronicle, 70*(6), 711 (1994).

16. J. Kazi, "The Lower St. Lawrence Model Forest: Entrusting Communities with Their Forests," Paper prepared for the Who Owns America II Conference, Land Tenure Center, University of Wisconsin–Madison, 1998.

17. J. C. Bliss, S. K. Nepal, R. T. Brooks, Jr., and M. D. Larsen. *J. For., 92,* 6 (1994).

18. R. D. Lindberg and H. J. Hovind, "Wisconsin Forests, an Assessment," Bureau of Forestry, Department of Natural Resources, Madison, Wis., 1985.

19. P. Huff, "Menominee tribal enterprises: A case study" In *Case Studies of Community-Based Forestry Enterprises in the Americas,* Land Tenure Center and Institute for Environmental Studies, University of Wisconsin–Madison, 1994.

20. R. Barker, "Forestry in the Next West," In *The Next West; Public Lands, Community and Economy in the American West*, J. A. Baden and D. Shaw, eds., Gallatin Institute, Island Press, Covelo, Wash., 1997.

21. R. W. Miller, "The urban forest," In *Urban Forestry: Planning and Managing Urban Greenspaces*, Second Edition. Prentice Hall, Upper Saddle River, N.J., 1996.

22. J. L. Compton, "Multi-agency and Local Participatory Cooperation in Biodiversity Conservation in Yunnan's Upland Ecosystems," UNDP/Global Environmental Facility (GEF) Project Proposal, Rome, 1996.

23. J. L. Compton, "Extension and Communication in a Farming Systems Development Project–Eastern Visayas (FSDP–EV), Philippines," Cornell University International Agriculture Program, Ithaca, N.Y., 1983.

24. J. L. Compton, "Eco-Development and Irrigation Project: Institutional Assessment, Vientiane, Laos," UNDP/UNCDF, Rome, 1998.

25. U. Tan-Kim-Yong, J. L. Compton and C. J. Compton, "Evaluation Report of the Yunnan Social Forestry Project, Beijing," Ford Foundation, N.Y., 1995.

26. R. Mahapatra, "A Quiet Revolution," *Down To Earth 8/21—Special Report,* 2000.

Common and Scientific Names of Tree Species Mentioned in the Text

Common Names	Scientific Names
Acacia	*Acacia* spp.
Achin	*Pistacia mexicana*
Ailanthus or tree of heaven	*Ailanthus altissima*
Alder, common or European	*Alnus glutinosa*
red	*Alnus rubra*
Aliso	*Alnus jorullensis*
American hornbeam (see Beech)	
Ash, American mountain	*Sorbus americana*
common	*Fraxinus excelsior*
flowering	*Fraxinus ornus*
green or red	*Fraxinus pennsylvanica*
mountain	*Eucalyptus regnans*
Oregon	*Fraxinus latifolia*
white	*Fraxinus americana*
Aspen (European)	*Populus tremula*
largetooth or bigtooth	*Populus grandidentata*
quaking or trembling	*Populus tremuloides*
Bald cypress (see Cypress)	
Balsa	*Ochroma pyramidale*
Bamboo	*Cephalostachyum pergracile*
Basswood, American or American linden	*Tilia americana*
small-leaved linden	*Tilia cordata*
white	*Tilia heterophylla*
Beech, American	*Fagus grandifolia*
blue, or American hornbeam	*Carpinus caroliniana* (*Carpinus betulus virginiana*)
common or European	*Fagus sylvatica*
eastern hornbeam	*Carpinus orientalis*
European hornbeam	*Carpinus betulus*
southern	*Nothofagus* spp.
Bigcone Douglas fir (see Fir)	

Common Names	Scientific Names
Birch, gray or field	*Betula populifolia*
river	*Betula nigra*
silver	*Betula verrucosa*
sweet or black	*Betula lenta*
white or paper	*Betula papyrifera*
yellow	*Betula alleghaniensis* (*Betula lutea*)
Blackgum (see Gum)	
Blue beech (see Beech)	
Box elder (see Elder)	
Buckeye, Georgia	*Aesculus georgiana*
yellow	*Aesculus octandra*
Butternut	*Juglans cinerea*
Camaron	*Alvaradoa amorphoides*
Caoba	*Swietenia humilis*
Carob tree	*Ceratonia siliqua*
Castano bellota	*Sterculia mexicana*
Catalpa, northern or hardy	*Catalpa speciosa*
southern	*Catalpa bignonioides*
Cedar, Alaska yellow	*Chamaecyparis nootkatensis*
Alantic white	*Chamaecyparis thyoides*
eastern redcedar	*Juniperus virginiana*
incense	*Libocedrus decurrens*
Japanese	*Cryptomeria japonica*
northern white, or eastern arborvitae	*Thuja occidentalis*
Port Orford	*Chamaecyparis lawsoniana*
prickly juniper	*Juniperus oxycedrus*
western juniper	*Juniperus occidentalis*
western red cedar	*Thuja plicata*
Cherry, black	*Prunus serotina*
cornelian	*Cornus mas*
pin	*Prunus pensylvanica*
Chestnut, American	*Castanea dentata*
Spanish	*Castanea sativa*
Chinatree or chinaberry	*Melia azedarach*

Common Names	Scientific Names
Chinkapin, golden	*Castanopsis chrysophylla*
Chokeberry	*Aronia* spp.
Coffeetree, Kentucky	*Gymnocladus dioicus*
Cottonwood (see Poplar)	
Crape myrtle	*Lagerstroemia indica*
Cucumbertree or	*Magnolia acuminata*
cucumber magnolia	
Cypress, bald cypress	*Taxodium distichum*
Monterey	*Cupressus macrocarpa*
Montezuma	*Taxodium mucronatum*
Dogwood, flowering	*Cornus florida*
Douglas fir (see Fir)	
Doveplum	*Coccoloba diversifolia*
Elder, box	*Acer negundo*
Elm, American or white	*Ulmus americana*
English	*Ulmus procera*
Japanese	*Ulmus japonica*
rock or cork	*Ulmus thomasii*
Siberian	*Ulmus pumila*
winged	*Ulmus alata*
Eucalyptus	*Eucalyptus* spp.
False mastic	*Sideroxylon foetidissimum*
Filbert (see Hazel)	
Fir, alpine, or subalpine	*Abies lasiocarpa*
balsam	*Abies balsamea*
bigcone Douglas fir	*Pseudotsuga macrocarpa*
California red	*Abies magnifica*
Douglas fir	*Pseudotsuga menziesii*
Fraser	*Abies fraseri*
grand or lowland white	*Abies grandis*
noble	*Abies procera (Abies nobilis)*
Pacific silver	*Abies amabilis*
silver	*Abies alba*
white	*Abies concolor*
Fish poison tree, Florida	*Piscidia piscipula*
Ginkgo tree	*Ginkgo biloba*
Gmelina	*Gmelina arborea*
Goldenrain tree	*Koelreuteria paniculata*
Gum, black or black tupelo	*Nyssa sylvatica*
red or sweetgum	*Liquidambar stryaciflua*
swamp tupelo	*Nyssa sylvatica biflora*
tupelo or water tupelo	*Nyssa aquatica*
Gumbo-limbo	*Bursera simaruba*
Hackberry	*Celtis occidentalis*
Hazel, European or filbert	*Corylus avellana*

Common Names	Scientific Names
Hemlock, eastern	*Tsuga canadensis*
mountain	*Tsuga mertensiana*
western	*Tsuga heterophylla*
Hickory, bitternut	*Carya cordiformis*
mockernut	*Carya tomentosa*
pignut	*Carya glabra*
shagbark	*Carya ovata*
Holly, American	*Ilex opaca*
Honeylocust	*Gleditsia triacanthos*
Hoja fresca	*Gilbertia arborea*
Hophornbeam, eastern	*Ostrya virginiana*
European	*Ostrya carpinifolia*
Hornbeam (see Beech)	
Horsechestnut (Buckeye)	*Aesculus hippocastanum*
Huisache	*Acacia farnesiana*
Ironwood	*Dialium guianense*
Judas tree	*Cercis siliquastrum*
Juniper (see Cedar)	
Karri	*Eucalyptus diversicolor*
Kentucky coffeetree (see Coffeetree)	
Larch, American, eastern, or Tamarack	*Larix laricina*
European	*Larix decidua (Larix europaca)*
subalpine	*Larix lyallii*
western	*Larix occidentalis*
Laurel, bay	*Laurus notilis*
California, Oregon-myrtle	*Umbellularia californica*
Leadwood	*Krugiodendron ferreum*
Lemonwood	*Psychotria capensis*
Lignum vitae	*Guaiacum sanctum*
Linden (see Basswood)	
Locust, black or yellow	*Robinia pseudoacacia*
Madrone, Pacific	*Arbutus menziesii*
Magnolia, cucumber (see Cucumbertree)	
southern	*Magnolia grandiflora*
Mahogany, West Indies	*Swietenia mahagoni*
Mangrove, black	*Avicennia nitida*
red	*Rhizophora mangle*
Maple, bigleaf	*Acer macrophyllum*
Norway	*Acer platanoides*
red (including trident)	*Acer rubrum*
silver	*Acer saccharinum*
sugar	*Acer saccharum*

Common Names	Scientific Names	Common Names	Scientific Names
sycamore	*Acer pseudoplatanus*	Paulownia	*Paulownia tomentosa*
vine	*Acer circinatum*	Pecan	*Carya illinoensis*
Melina	*Gmelina arborea*	Persimmon, common	*Diospyros virginiana*
Metasequoia	*Metasequoia glyptostroboides*	Pine, aleppo	*Pinus halepensis*
		apache	*Pinus engelmannii*
Monkeypod, monkey puzzle	*Araucaria araucana*	bishop	*Pinus muricata*
		black or Austrian	*Pinus nigra*
Mulberry, red	*Morus rubra*	bristlecone	*Pinus aristata*
white	*Morus alba*	Caribbean	*Pinus caribaea*
Nettle tree, European	*Celtis australis*	Chihuahua or piño chino	*Pinus leiophylla* var. *chihuahuana*
Oak, black	*Quercus velutina*		
blackjack	*Quercus marilandica*	Coulter	*Pinus coulteri*
bur	*Quercus macrocarpa*	Digger	*Pinus sabiniana*
California black	*Quercus kelloggii*	eastern white	*Pinus strobus*
California live	*Quercus agrifolia*	foxtail	*Pinus balfouriana*
California white	*Quercus lobata*	jack	*Pinus banksiana*
canyon live	*Quercus chrysolepis*	Jeffrey	*Pinus jeffreyi*
cherrybark	*Quercus falcata pagodaefolia*	Khasia	*Pinus kesiya*
		knobcone	*Pinus attenuata*
chestnut	*Quercus prinus*	limber	*Pinus flexilis*
cork	*Quercus suber*	loblolly	*Pinus taeda*
durmast	*Quercus petraea*	lodgepole	*Pinus contorta*
English	*Quercus robur*	longleaf	*Pinus palustris*
holm	*Quercus ilex*	maritime	*Pinus pinaster*
Hungarian	*Quercus frainetto*	Merkus	*Pinus merkusii*
live	*Quercus virginiana*	Mexican weeping	*Pinus patula*
northern red or eastern red	*Quercus rubra (Quercus borealis)*	Monterey	*Pinus radiata*
		Norfolk Island	*Araucaria heterophylla*
Oregon white	*Quercus garryana*	pinabete	*Pinus ayacahuite*
overcup	*Quercus lyrata*	piño colorado	*Pinus teocote*
pin	*Quercus palustris*	piño de Montezuma	*Pinus montezumae*
post	*Quercus stellata*	piño prieto	*Pinus oocarpa*
pubescent	*Quercus pubescens*	pinyon	*Pinus edulis*
scarlet	*Quercus coccinea*	pitch	*Pinus rigida*
silky	*Grevillea robusta*	pond	*Pinus serotina*
southern red	*Quercus falcata*	ponderosa or western yellow	*Pinus ponderosa*
swamp chestnut	*Quercus michauxii*		
turkey (United States)	*Quercus laevis (Quercus catesbaei*	(Rocky Mountain form)	*Pinus ponderosa* var. *scopulorum*
turkey (Europe)	*Quercus cerris*	red or Norway	*Pinus resinosa*
water	*Quercus nigra*	sand	*Pinus clausa*
white	*Quercus alba*	Scotch or Scots	*Pinus sylvestris*
willow	*Quercus phellos*	shortleaf	*Pinus echinata*
Olive	*Olea europaea*	slash	*Pinus elliotti*
Oriental plane	*Platanus orientalis*	southwestern white	*Pinus strobiformis*
Osage-orange	*Maclura pomifera*	spruce	*Pinus glabra*
Oyamel	*Abies religiosa*	stone	*Pinus pinea*

Common Names	Scientific Names	Common Names	Scientific Names
sugar	*Pinus lambertiana*	Norway	*Picea abies*
Virginia or scrub	*Pinus virginiana*	red	*Picea rubens*
western white	*Pinus monticola*	Sitka	*Picea sitchensis*
whitebark	*Pinus albicaulis*	white	*Picea glauca*
Poplar, California or black cottonwood	*Populus trichocarpa*	St. Johns bread (see Carob tree)	
eastern or eastern cottonwood	*Populus deltoides*	Strangler fig, Florida	*Ficus aurea*
		Strawberry tree	*Arbutus unedo*
swamp cottonwood	*Populus heterophylla*	Sugarberry	*Celtis laevigata*
yellow, or tuliptree	*Liriodendron tulipifera*	Sugi (see Cedar, Japanese)	
Prickly ash, lime	*Zanthoxylon fagara*	Sumac, winged	*Rhus copallina* var. *copallina*
Quebracho	*Schinopsis* spp.		
Redberry eugenia	*Eugenia confusa*	Sweetbay, southern	*Magnolia virginiana*
Red cedar (see Cedar)		Sycamore, American	*Platanus occidentalis*
Redwood	*Sequoia sempervirens*	Tamarack (see Larch)	
Rompezapato or saffron-plum	*Bumelia celastrina*	Tamarind, wild	*Lysiloma bahamensis*
		Tanoak	*Lithocarpus densiflorus*
Rosewood	*Dalbergia* spp.	Teak	*Tectona grandis*
Royal palm, Florida	*Roystonea elata*	Torreya, California	*Torreya californica*
Sassafras	*Sassafras albidum*	Tree of heaven, see Ailanthus	
Sequoia, giant	*Sequoiadendron giganteum*		
		Trumpet wood	*Cecropia mexicana*
Silk-cotton tree	*Ceiba pentandra*	Tupelo (see Gum)	
Silktree	*Albizzia julibrissin*	Walnut, black	*Juglans nigra*
Soapberry, wingleaf	*Sapindus saponaria*	Willow, black	*Salix nigra*
Sourwood	*Oxydendron arboreum*	Yellow-poplar or tuliptree	*Liriodendron tulipifera*
Spruce, black	*Picea mariana*	Yew, common	*Taxus baccata*
blue	*Picea pungens*	Pacific	*Taxus brevifolia*
Engelmann	*Picea engelmannii*		

Common and Scientific Names of Animal Species Mentioned in the Text

Common Names	Scientific Names
Insectivores	
Mole, eastern	*Scalopus aquaticus*
Shrew	*Sorex* spp.
Hares and Rabbits	
Hare, snowshoe	*Lepus americanus*
Cottontail, eastern	*Sylvilagus floridanus*
Rodents	
Beaver	*Castor canadensis*
Gopher, pocket	*Thomomys* spp.
Mouse, white-footed deer	*Peromyscus maniculatus*
Porcupine	*Erethizon dorsatum*
Squirrel, flying (southern)	*Galucomys volans*
Squirrel, ground	*Spermophilus* spp.
chipmunk least	*Eutamias minimus*
(western)	
Squirrel, tree	
gray, eastern	*Sciurus carolinensis*
pine or chickaree	*Tamiasciurus douglasi*
red	*Tamiasciurus hudsonicus*
Voles	*Microtus* spp.
Carnivores	
Bear, black	*Ursus americanus*
grizzly	*Ursus horribilis*
Coyote	*Canis latrans*
Fisher	*Martes pennanti*
Fox, gray	*Vulpes fulva*
red	*Urocyon cinereoargenteus*
Lynx	*Lynx canadensis*
Mink	*Mustela vison*
Mountain lion	*Felis concolor*
Otter	*Lutra canadensis*
Raccoon	*Procyon lotor*
Wolf, gray or timber	*Canis lupus*
Wolverine	*Gulo luscus*

Common Names	Scientific Names
Even-Toed Ungulates	
Caribou, woodland	*Rangifer* spp.
Deer, mule	*Odocoileus hemionus*
white-tailed	*Odocoileus virginianus*
Elk (wapiti)	*Cervus canadensis*
Moose	*Alces alces*
Birds	
Bluebird, eastern	*Sialia sialis*
Catbird	*Dumetella carolinensis*
Chickadee, black-capped	*Parus atricapillus*
Cranes	*Grus* spp.
Creeper, brown tree	*Certhia familiaris*
Crossbill	*Loxia* spp.
Dove, mourning	*Zenaida macroura*
Duck, American golden-eye	*Glaucionetta clangula*
Barrow's golden-eye	*Bucephala islandica*
black	*Anas rubripes*
buffle-head	*Bucephala albeola*
hooded merganser	*Lophodytes cucullatus*
mallard, common	*Anas platyrhynchos*
wood	*Aix sponsa*
Eagle, bald	*Haliaeetus leucocephalus*
Falcon, peregrine	*Falco peregrinus*
Finch	*Carpodacus* spp.
Flycatcher, least	*Empidonax minimus*
Grosbeak, evening	*Coccothraustes vespertinus*
Goose, Canada	*Branta canadensis*
Grouse, blue	*Dendragapus obscurus*
prairie chicken or	*Tympamuchus cupido*
pinnated	
ruffed	*Bonasa umbellus*
sharp-tailed	*Pedioecetes phasianellus*
spruce	*Dendragapus canadensis*
Hawk, broad-winged	*Buteo platypterus*
goshawk	*Accipiter gentilis*

Common Names	Scientific Names	Common Names	Scientific Names
red-shouldered	*Buteo lineatus*	mountain pine	*Dendroctonus ponderosae*
Heron	*Ardea* spp.	native elm bark	*Hylurgopinus rufipes*
Jay, pinyon	*Gymnorhinus cyanocephalus*	smaller European elm bark	*Scolytus multistriatus*
Kestrel	*Falco sparverius*	southern pine	*Dendroctonus frontalis*
Kingbird	*Tyrannus* spp.	western pine	*Dendroctonus brevicomis*
Magpie	*Pica pica*	Borer, bronze birch	*Agrilus anxius*
Martin, purple	*Progne subis*	hemlock	*Melanophila fulvoguttata*
Merganser, hooded	*Lophodytes cucullatus*	poplar	*Saperda calcarta*
Nuthatch, white-breasted	*Sitta carolinensis*	two-lined chestnut	*Agrilus bilineatus*
Oriole, Baltimore	*Icterus galbula*	Budworm, jack pine	*Choristoneura pinus*
Osprey	*Pandion haliaetus*	spruce	*Choristoneura fumiferana*
Ovenbird	*Seiurus aurocopillus*	Casebearer, larch	*Coleophora laricella*
Owl, barred	*Strix varia*	Engraver, fir	*Scolytus ventralis*
horned	*Bubo virginianus*	pine	*Ips pini*
saw-whet	*Aegolius acadicus*	Looper, hemlock	*Lambdina fiscellaria*
Quail, bobwhite	*Colinus virginianus*	linden	*Erannis tiliaria*
Raven	*Corvus corax*	Moth, gypsy	*Lymantria dispar*
Redpoll	*Carduelis* spp.	shoot, European pine	*Rhyacionia buoliana*
Siskin	*Carduelis pinus*	Douglas-fir tussock	*Orgyia pseudotsugata*
Swallow, tree	*Iridoprocne bicolor*	pine tussock	*Dasychira plagiata*
Swift, chimney	*Chaetura pelagica*	white-marked tussock	*Hemerocampa leucostigma*
Thrush	*Hylocichla* spp.		
Turkey, eastern	*Meleagris gallopavo silvestrii*	Pitch nodule maker	*Petrova albicapitana*
		Sawfly, European pine	*Neodiprion sertifer*
Vireo, red-eyed	*Vireo olivaceus*	European spruce	*Diprion hercyniae*
Warbler, black-and-white	*Mniotilta varia*	jack pine	*Neodiprion pratti banksianae*
blackburnian	*Dendroica fusca*		
Kirtland's	*Dendroica kirtlandii*	larch	*Pristiphora erichsonii*
Waxwing	*Bombycilla* spp.	red-headed pine	*Neodiprion lecontei*
Woodcock	*Philohela minor*	red pine	*Neodiprion nanulus nanulus*
Woodpecker, downy	*Dendrocopus pubescens*		
flicker	*Colaptes auratus*	Swaine jack pine	*Neodiprion swainei*
hairy	*Dendrocopus villosus*	Sawyer, southern pine	*Monochamas titillator*
ivory-billed	*Campephilus principalis*	white spotted	*Monochamus scutellatus*
pileated	*Dryocopus pileatus*	Scale, pine tortoise	*Toumeyella numismatica*
red-cockaded	*Dendrocopus borealis*	Spanworm, elm	*Ennomos subsignarius*
yellow-bellied sapsucker	*Sphyrapicus varius*	Spittlebug, pine	*Aphrophora parallela*
		Saratoga	*Aphrophora saratogensis*
Wren	*Thyrothorus* spp.	Tent caterpillar, eastern	*Malacosoma americanum*
		forest	*Malacosoma disstria*
Insects		Walkingstick	*Diapheromera femorata*
Aphid, balsam woolly	*Adelges piceae*	Wasp, wood	*Sirex* spp.
Beetle, Douglas-fir	*Dendroctonus pseudotsugae*	Weevil, pales	*Hylobius pales*
		pine root collar	*Hylobius radicis*
Japanese	*Popillia japonica*	white pine	*Pissodes strobi*

APPENDIX III

Unit Conversion Table

Linear Measure

	cm	m	km	ft	mile	chain	link
1 centimeter	1	0.01	10^{-5}	0.0328	6.214×10^{-6}	4.971×10^{-4}	0.04971
1 meter	100	1	0.001	3.2808	6.214×10^{-4}	0.04971	4.971
1 kilometer	10^5	1,000	.1	3,280.84	0.6214	49.7097	4970.97
1 foot	30.4801	0.3048	$3,048 \times 10^{-4}$	1	1.8939×10^{-4}	0.01515	1.5152
1 mile	160,934.4	1,609.344	1.6093	5,280	1	80	8,000
1 chain	2,011.68	20.1168	0.02012	66	0.0125	1	100
1 link	20.1168	0.2012	2.0117×10^{-4}	0.66	1.25×10^{-4}	0.01	1

Mass Measure

	kg	m ton	pound	short ton
1 kilogram	1	0.001	2.2046	1.1023×10^{-3}
1 metric ton	1,000	1	2204.6226	1.1023
1 pound	0.4536	4.5359×10^{-4}	1	0.0005
1 short ton	907.185	0.9072	2,000	1

Area Measure

	m^2	ha	ft^2	$chain^2$	acre	$mile^2$ (section)
1 hectare	10,000	1	107,639.1	24.7105	2.4711	0.0039
1 square meter	1	1×10^{-4}	10.7639	2.4711×10^{-3}	2.4711×10^{-4}	3.8610×10^{-7}
1 acre	4,046.86	0.4047	43,560	10	1	1.5625×10^{-3}
1 square mile	2.5910×10^6	258.999	27,878,400	6,400	640	1
1 township	—	9,323.9892	—	—	23,040	36
1 section	2,589,988	258.9997	27,878,400	6,400	640	1
1/4 section	647,497	64.7499	6,969,600	1,600	160	0.25
1/4-1/4 section	161,874	16.1875	1,742,400	400	40	0.0625

Volume Measure

	cm^3 (ml)	m^3	in^3	ft^3	L	qt
1 cubic centimeter	1	1×10^{-6}	6.1024×10^{-2}	3.5315×10^{-5}	0.001	1.0567×10^{-3}
1 cubic meter	10^6	1	6.1024×10^4	35.3147	1,000	1,056.688
1 cubic inch	16.3871	1.6387×10^{-5}	1	5.7870×10^{-4}	1.6387×10^{-2}	1.7316×10^{-2}
1 cubic foot	28,316.85	2.8317×10^{-2}	1,728	1	28.3169	29.9221
1 milliliter	1	1×10^{-6}	6.0124×10^{-2}	3.5315×10^{-5}	0.001	1.0567×10^{-3}
1 liter	1,000	0.001	61.0237	3.5315×10^{-2}	1	1.0567
1 quart	946.3529	9.4635×10^{-4}	57.75	3.3420×10^{-2}	0.9464	1

APPENDIX IV

Taxonomy of Selected Forest Trees

MAGNOLIOPHYTA (angiosperms)
Magnoliopsida (dicots)

Willow family (Salicaceae)
    Poplars, aspens *(Populus)*
    Willows *(Salix)*

Birch family (Betulaceae)
    Alders *(Alnus)*
    Birches *(Betula)* .

Beech family (Fagaceae)
    Chestnut, chinkapins *(Castanea)*
    Beeches *(Fagus)*
    Oaks *(Quercus)*

Elm family (Ulmaceae)
    Hackberries *(Celtis)*
    Elms *(Ulmus)*

Magnolia family (Magnoliaceae)
    Tuliptree *(Liriodendron)*
    Magnolia *(Magnolia)*

Laurel family (Lauraceae)
    Sassafras *(Sassafras)*

Witch-hazel family (Hamamelidaceae)
    Sweetgum *(Liquidambar)*

Sycamore family (Platanaceae)
    Sycamore *(Platanus)*

Mulberry family (Moraceae)
    Mulberry *(Morus)*

Maple family (Aceraceae)
    Maple *(Acer)*

Basswood (linden) family (Tiliaceae)
    Basswood *(Tilia)*

Legume family (Fabaceae)
    Honeylocust *(Gleditsia)*

Locusts *(Robinia)*

Olive family (Oleaceae)
    Ashes *(Fraxinus)*

Walnut family (Juglandaceae)
    Hickories, pecan *(Carya)*
    Walnuts *(Juglans)*

Buckeye family (Hippocastanaceae)
    Buckeye, horsechestnut *(Aesculus)*

Rose family (Rosaceae)
    Hawthorns *(Crataegus)*
    Mountain ashes *(Sorbus)*

Liliopsida (monocots)

Palms and palmettos family *(Arecaceae)*

Lily family (Liliaceae)
    Yucca *(Yucca)*

CONIFEROPHYTA (gymnosperms)
Pine family (Pinaceae)
    Pines *(Pinus)*
    Firs *(Abies)*
    Spruces *(Picea)*
    Hemlocks *(Tsuga)*
    Douglas-fir *(Pseudotsuga)*
    Larches *(Larix)*
    True cedars *(Cedrus)*

Bald cypress family (Taxodiaceae)
    Bald cypress *(Taxodium)*
    Redwood *(Sequoia)*

Cypress family (Cupressaceae)
    Junipers *(Juniperus)*
    Cypresses *(Cupressus)*
    Cedars *(Chamaecyparis, Thuja)*

Yew family (Taxaceae)
    Yew *(Taxus)*

Glossary

A

Abiotic factors. Nonliving elements (factors) of the environment—that is, soil, climate, physiography.

Abscission. Dropping leaves, flowers, fruits, or other plant parts following the formation of a separation zone at the base of the plant part.

Absorbance. A measure of the ability of a surface to absorb incident energy, often at specific wavelengths.

Absorbed light. Light rays that are neither reflected nor transmitted when directed toward opaque or transparent materials.

Absorption. A process of attenuation through which radiant energy is intercepted and converted into other forms of energy as it passes through the atmosphere or other media.

Absorption band. A range of wavelengths over which radiant energy is intercepted by a specific material that may be present on the earth's surface or in the atmosphere.

Adaptation. Genetically determined character or feature of an organism that serves to increase reproductive potential or chance of survival.

Adsorption. Adhesion of the molecules of a gas, liquid, or dissolved substance to a surface, particularly of water molecules to the internal surface within the porous walls of wood and bark cells.

Advance regeneration. Young trees that have become established naturally before a clearcut is made.

Adventitious. Plant part that develops outside of the usual position or time or both.

Aerial film. A specially designed roll film supplied in many lengths and widths to fit aerial cameras. See *Color*, *Color infrared film*, *Infrared*, and *Panchromatic*.

Aerial photograph, oblique. An aerial photograph taken with the camera axis directed between the horizontal and the vertical.

Aerial photograph, vertical. An aerial photograph made with the optical axis of the camera approximately perpendicular to the earth's surface and with the film as nearly horizontal as is practical.

Aerial photographs, composite. Aerial photographs made with a camera having one principal lens and two or more surrounding and oblique lenses symmetrically placed; the several resulting photographs may be rectified in printing to permit assembly as verticals with the same scale.

Agrisilviculture. System of cultivation combining agriculture and forestry whereby tree plantations are interplanted with agricultural crops (the crops can yield a fast return while trees slowly mature).

Agroforestry. A system of planting agricultural crops in a compatible fashion with tree species, often in the forms of plantations.

Air-dry. Of timber or wood dried to equilibrium with the surrounding atmosphere.

Albedo. The percentage of the total illumination of a planet or satellite that is reflected from its surface.

Albuminous cells. Certain ray and axial parenchyma cells in gymnosperm phloem; associated with sieve cells.

Alkaloid. Nitrogen-containing toxins produced by plants that serve as defense compounds.

Allelopathy. Suppression of germination, growth, or the limiting of the occurrence of plants when chemical inhibitors are released by some plants.

Allogenic succession. Ecological succession resulting from factors (such as prolonged drought) that arise external to a natural community and alter its habitat (i.e., changes the vegetation).

Amorphous. Formless.

Anadromous. Ascending upriver from the sea to spawn; relating to such fishes as salmon.

Analog. A form of data display in which values are shown in graphic form, such as curves. Also, a form of computing in which values are represented by directly measurable quantities, such as voltages or resistances. Analog computing methods contrast with digital methods in which values are treated numerically.

Angiosperm. Vascular flowering plants that produce seeds enclosed in an ovary. Include monocotyledons (grasses and palms) and dicotyledons (herbaceous and woody plants).

Angle of incidence. The angle formed by a straight line, ray of light, or the like, meeting a surface and a normal to the surface at the point of meeting.

Anisotropic. Of a material whose properties vary according to the direction of measurement. The anisotropy of wood corresponds to the main features of wood structure and the marked anisotropy of the cellulose long-chain molecules.

Annual ring. One growth layer as seen in cross-section of a woody plant stem. Formed by contrast of springwood and summerwood.

Apical dominance. Influence exerted by a terminal bud in suppressing the growth of the lateral buds.

Apical meristem. Growing point at the tip of the root or stem. Gives rise to primary tissues.

Autecology. Study of the relationship between an individual organism and its environment.

Autogenic. Involving or resulting from a reaction between or in living organisms.

Autotrophic. Referring to green plants that make their own food by photosynthesis, and of bacteria that can grow without organic carbon and nitrogen. Self-nourishing.

Auxin. A plant growth-regulating substance. Among other effects, it controls cell elongation.

Avifauna. Bird life of a given region.

Axil. Angle between the upper side of a leaf or twig and the supporting stem.

Axis. Longitudinal support on which organs or parts are arranged; the stem and root; the central line of the body. Axial, adjective.

Azimuth. The geographic orientation of a line given as an angle measured clockwise from north.

B

Backfire. Fire set along the inner edge of a fire line to consume the fuel in the path of a forest fire, to change the direction of the fire, or both.

Bark. All tissue outside the cambium.

Basal area. Area of the cross-section of a tree stem, generally at breast height (1.3 meters or 4.5 feet) and inclusive of bark.

Bast fiber. Any of several strong, ligneous fibers obtained from phloem tissue and used in the manufacture of woven goods and cordage.

Bedrock. Bottom layer, lowest stratum; unbroken solid rock, overlaid in most places by soil or rock fragments.

Bilateral aid. Aid based on a formal agreement between a single donor country and the recipient; in contrast to multilateral aid, which originates from several countries, usually through an international agency.

Biltmore stick. A graduated stick used to estimate tree diameters.

Binder. Extraneous bonding agent, organic or inorganic, used to bind particles together—for example, to produce particleboard.

Biological control. Regulation of pest species through the use of other organisms.

Biomass. Quantity of biological matter of one or more species present on a unit area.

Biome. Usually terrestrial ecological communities of very wide extent often defined by botanical habitat and characterized by soil and climate; the largest ecological unit.

Biosphere. Part of the earth's crust, water, and atmosphere where living organisms can subsist.

Biotic factors. Relation of living organisms to one another from an ecological view (as opposed to abiotic or nonliving elements).

Black liquor. Liquor resulting from the manufacture of pulp by alkaline processes and containing, in a modified form, the greater part of the extracted lignin and sugar degradation products.

Blowup fire. Sudden increase in intensity and rate of flame spread, often accompanied by a violent convection column of smoke and hot gases.

Board foot. Unit of measurement represented by a board 1 foot long, 1 foot wide, and 1 inch thick (144 cubic inches), measured before surfacing or other finishing. Abbreviations: b.f., bd ft, ft.b.m.

Bole. Tree stem of merchantable thickness.

Bolt. Any short log, as a pulpwood or veneer bolt.

Boreal. Of or pertaining to the north.

Brightness. Blue reflectance of a sheet of paper, a measure of the maximum whiteness that can be achieved with proper tinting.

Browse. Leaves, small twigs, and shoots of shrubs, seedling, and sapling trees, and vines available for forage for livestock and wildlife.

Bryophyte. Any plant of the division Bryophyta, a division containing the liverworts and mosses. These plants do not possess a vascular system.

Buck. To cut a tree into proper lengths after it has been felled.

Bud primordium. Embryonic shoot formed in the axil of a leaf.

C

Calender. Machine in which cloth, paper, or the like is smoothed, glazed, or otherwise manipulated by pressing between revolving cylinders.

Caliper. An instrument for directly measuring tree diameters.

Canopy. More-or-less continuous cover of branches and leaves formed collectively by the crowns of adjacent trees or shrubs. See *Understory*.

Capillary water. Water that fills the smaller pores less than 0.05 millimeter in diameter and that by adhesion to the soil particles can resist the force of gravity and remain suspended in the soil. This water constitutes the major source of water for tree growth, except in soils having a high water table.

Carbonization. Decomposition by heat of organic substances in a limited supply of air accompanied by the formation of carbon. See *Destructive distillation*.

Carnivore. Organism that consumes mostly flesh.

Carrying capacity. Number of organisms of a given species and quality that can survive in a given ecosystem without causing its deterioration.

Cation. Positively charged atom or group of atoms. Cation exchange capacity is the total capacity of soil colloids for holding cations.

Chain. A unit of linear measurement equal to 66 feet.

Chaining. Using a surveyor's chain or tape for linear measurements along the ground.

Charge-coupled device (CCD). A solid-state sensor that detects light; a microelectronic silicon chip.

Chipper. Machine for cutting logs or pieces of logs into chips.

Chlorophyll. The green pigment of plant cells, necessary for photosynthesis.

Chloroplasts. A plastid in algal and green plant cells in which chlorophylls are contained; site of photosynthesis.

Chlorosis. Abnormal yellowing of foliage, often a symptom of mineral deficiency, infection, root or stem girdling, or extremely reduced light.

Chlorotic. Leaf tissue that has yellowed because of chlorosis.

Chromosome. Body in the cell nucleus containing genes in a linear order.

Clearcutting. Silvicultural system in which the entire timber stand is cut. See *Seed-tree method*, *Shelterwood method*.

Climatic release. Relaxation of environmental resistance factors and the recurrence of favorable weather for several successive years. Together, these conditions allow a pest species to approach its reproductive potential.

Climax community. Community that has achieved the maximum possible development. The end point of a sere.

Clinal variation. Variation occurring in a continuous fashion along a geographic or environmental gradient.

Clone. All the plants produced by asexual means (e.g., grafting, layering, budding) from a common ancestor and having identical genetic constitutions.

Collenchyma. Supporting tissue containing elongated living cells with irregularly thickened primary cell walls; often found in regions of primary growth in stems and leaves.

Color. The property of an object that is dependent on the wavelength of the light it reflects or, in the case of a luminescent body, the wavelength of light that it emits.

Color-composite image. A color image prepared by projecting individual black-and-white multispectral images in color.

Color infrared film. A color film consisting of three layers in which the red-imaging layer responds to photographic infrared radiation ranging in wavelength from 0.7 to 0.9 micrometer. The green-imaging layer responds to red light and the blue-imaging layer responds to green light.

Combustion. Consumption by oxidation, evolving heat, and generally also flame and incandescence.

Community. Unit of vegetation that is homogeneous with respect to species composition and structure and occupies a unit area of ground.

Companion cell. Specialized parenchyma cell in angiosperm phloem; associated with sieve tube members.

Conifer. Division of gymnosperm; plant producing naked seeds in cones, mostly evergreen, with timber known commercially as softwood.

Coppice system. Silvicultural system in which crops regenerate vegetatively by stump sprouts and the rotation is comparatively short.

Cord. Volume measure of stacked wood. A standard cord is 4 × 4 × 8 feet and contains 128 cubic feet of space. Actual wood volume varies between 70 and 90 cubic feet per cord. A face cord is a short cord in which the length of the pieces is shorter than 8 feet (Figure 11.2).

Cordillera. Entire chain of mountain ranges parallel to the Pacific Coast, extending from Cape Horn to Alaska.

Cork cambium. Lateral meristem that produces cork toward the outside of the plant and phelloderm to the inside.

Cortex. Ground tissue of the shoot or root that is located between the epidermis and the vascular system; a primary-tissue region.

Cotyledon. Embryonic leaf, characteristic of seed plants; generally stores food in dicotyledons and absorbs food in monocotyledons.

Crown fire. Fire that burns the tops of trees and brush.

Cruise (timber). Survey of forestlands to locate and estimate volumes and grades of standing timber.

Cutting cycle. Period of time between major cuts in an uneven-aged stand. See *Rotation age.*

Cytoplasm. Term commonly used to refer to the protoplasm of the cell exclusive of the nucleus.

D

dbh (diameter at breast height). Tree diameter at breast height, 1.3 meters (4.5 feet) above the ground as measured from the uphill side of the tree.

Deciduous. Perennial plants that are normally leafless for some time during the year.

Decurrent. Having a leaf base elongated down the stem. See *Excurrent.*

Deferred-rotation grazing. A system of range management whereby grazing is delayed on a portion of the land until after the most important range plants have gone to seed. Then grazing is deferred on adjacent portions in rotation over a period of years so that all pastures receive the benefit of deferment.

Defoliation. Loss of a plant's leaves or needles.

Deleterious. Harmful, injurious, or destructive.

Dendrology. Branch of botany dealing with classification, nomenclature, and identification of trees and shrubs.

Dendrometer. Instrument for measuring the dimensions of trees or logs.

Denitrification. Process by which nitrogen is released from the soil (as a gas) to the atmosphere by denitrifying bacteria.

Density. Proportion of cell wall volume to total volume of wood. The number of individuals (trees, animals) per unit area at a given time.

Derived demand. Demand for a good coming from its use in the production of some other good; for example, timber is demanded not by consumers but by firms that manufacture wood products.

Desertification. Exhaustion of the soil, often because of removal of vegetative cover in semi-arid regions, leading irreversibly to an unproductive desert.

Dessicated. Dehydrated.

Destructive distillation. Decomposition of wood by heating out of contact with air, producing primarily charcoal, tarry distillates, and pyroligneous acid.

Detritus. Any organic debris.

Diameter tape. A tape measure specially calibrated to convert circumference of the tree to its corresponding diameter, assuming the cross-section of the tree to be a perfect circle.

Diapause. State of arrested physiological development of an insect.

Dicotyledons. One of two classes of angiosperms; a plant whose embryo has two seed leaves.

Differentiation. A process by which a relatively unspecialized cell undergoes a progressive change to a more specialized cell; the specialization of cells and tissues for particular functions during development.

Diffuse-porous wood. Wood (xylem) of hardwoods in which the vessels are small in diameter; vessels in springwood do not have much greater diameters than those in summerwood. See *Ring-porous wood*.

Digital computer. A computer that operates on the principle of counting as opposed to measuring. See *Analog*.

Digital elevation model. Model resulting from the matrix of elevation data obtained by systematically scanning a stereomodel.

Digital image. An image having numeric values representing gray tones; each numeric value represents a different gray tone.

Digital image processing. Computer manipulation of the digital values for picture elements of an image.

Digitize. Using numeric values to represent data.

Dioecious. A condition in which staminate and pistillate flowers (or pollen and seed cones of conifers) are borne on different individuals of the same species. See *Monoecious*.

Dominant. Pertaining to trees that project somewhat above the general level of the canopy, having crowns that receive direct sunlight from above and partly from the side. See *Suppressed*.

Dormancy. A special condition of arrested growth in which the plant and such plant parts as buds and seeds do not begin to grow without special environmental cues.

Duff. Organic matter in various stages of decomposition on the forest floor.

E

Ecology. Science that deals with the relation of plants and animals to their environment and to the site factors that operate in controlling their distribution and growth.

Econometric. Pertaining to a system of analysis of economic affairs using a specialized statistical technique for large masses of assembled data.

Ecosystem. Any complex of living organisms with their environment considered as a unit for purposes of study.

Ecotone. Transition zone between two adjoining communities.

Edaphic. Pertaining to soil conditions that influence plant growth.

Edge. Boundary between two or more elements of the environment, for example, field-woodland.

Elasticity. Relationship, expressed mathematically, between a percentage change in one variable and the resulting percentage change in another variable, when all other things are held constant. The price elasticity of demand (supply) is the percentage change in quantity demanded (supplied) when price changes by 1 percent, with all other variables such as income and population held constant.

Electromagnetic energy. Energy propagated through space or through material media in the form of an advancing interaction between electric and magnetic fields; also more simply termed *radiation*.

Electromagnetic spectrum. The ordered array of known electromagnetic radiations, extending from the shortest cosmic rays, through gamma rays, X-rays, ultraviolet radiation, visible radiation, infrared radiation, and including microwave and all other wavelengths of radio energy.

Emulsion. A suspension of photosensitive silver halide grains in gelatin that constitutes the image forming layer on photographic materials.

Endemic population. Natural low population level of most species native to an area.

Energy exchange. Flow of energy through the ecosystem beginning with the capture of radiant solar energy by photosynthesis and ending when the energy is lost back to the environment as heat through metabolism.

Entomology. Study of insects.

Entomophagous. Feeding on insects.

Environmental resistance. Physical and biological factors that inhibit the reproductive potential of a species.

Ephemeral. Short-lived; completing the life cycle within a brief period.

Epicormic growth. Growth of lateral buds after the apical bud is damaged.

Epidermis. Outermost layer(s) of cells on the primary plant body.

Ericaceous. Belonging to the heath family of plants, including the heath, arbutus, azalea, rhododendron, and American laurel.

Ethanol. Ethyl alcohol, C_2H_5OH; a colorless, volatile liquid manufactured from starchy or sugary materials by fermentation; also synthetically produced.

Eutrophication. Aquatic succession characterized by gradual nutrient enrichment and subsequent depletion of dissolved oxygen.

Evapotranspiration. Combined loss of water through evaporation and transpiration from the soil and vegetal cover on an area of land surface.

Even-aged stand. Stand in which relatively small age differences exist between individual trees, usually a maximum of 10 to 20 years.

Excurrent. Tree with the axis prolonged to form an undivided stem or trunk (as in spruces and other conifers).

Exotic. Not native; foreign; introduced from other climates or countries.

Extractive. In wood, any part that is not an integral part of the cellular structure and can be dissolved out with solvents.

F

False color. See *Color infrared*.

Fecal coliform. Colon bacilli, or forms that resemble or are related to them.

Fermentation. Change brought about by an agent such as yeast enzymes, which convert sugars to ethyl alcohol.

Fiber. Narrow cell of wood (xylem) or bast (phloem), other than vessel elements and parenchyma; includes tracheids. Or a cell material with a length-to-diameter (l/d) ratio greater than 20:1.

Fiberizing. Separation of wood and other plant material into fibers or fiber bundles by mechanical (sometimes assisted by chemical) means.

Field moisture capacity. The greatest amount of water it is possible for a soil to hold in its pore spaces after excess water has drained away.

Filter, optical. A material that, by absorption or reflection, selectively modifies the radiation transmitted through an optical system.

Fines. Pulp fractions having very short or fragmented fibers.

Fire line. Strip of plowed or cleared land made to check the spread of a fire.

Fluvial. Pertaining to or formed by a river.

Food chain, food web. Chain of organisms existing in any natural community such that each link in the chain feeds in the one below and is eaten by the one above; at the base are autotrophic (green) plants, eaten by heterotrophic organisms including plants (fungi), plant-eating animals (herbivores), plant and animal eaters (omnivores), and animal eaters (carnivores).

Forb. Any herbaceous plant that is not a grass or grass-like—such plants as geranium, buttercup, or sunflower.

Forest yield. The volume of timber in a forest at a specific point in time.

Forties. Term applied to 40-acre parcels of land, equal to one-sixteenth of a township in the standard rectangular survey system.

Fourdrinier. Name associated with the wire-forming section or the entire papermaking machine. Originally developed by the Fourdrinier brothers in England (1804).

Fruit. In angiosperms, a matured, ripened ovary containing the seeds.

Furfural. Oily liquid aldehyde, $C_5H_4O_2$, with an aromatic odor, obtained by distilling wood, corncobs, bran, sugar, and other ingredients with dilute sulfuric acid.

Fusiform initials. The vertically elongated cells in the vascular cambium that give rise to the cells of the axial system in the secondary xylem and secondary phloem.

G

Gall. Pronounced, localized, tumor-like swelling of greatly modified structure; occurs on plants from irritation by a foreign organism.

Gamete. Male pollen cell or a female egg cell, typically the result of meiosis, capable of uniting in the process of fertilization with a reproductive cell of the opposite sex.

Gasification. Conversion of a solid or liquid substance to a gas.

Gene. Unit of heredity; portion of the DNA of a chromosome.

Gene flow. Migration of genes from one population to another via the dispersal of individuals, or of propagules such as seed or pollen.

Gene pool. Sum total of genetic information distributed among the members of an interbreeding population.

Genetic drift. Change in gene frequency in small breeding populations because of chance, in contrast to a similar change under selection.

Genotype. Total amount of genetic information that an individual possesses. See *Phenotype*.

Geographic information system. An information system that can input, manipulate, and analyze geographically referenced data to support the decision-making processes of an organization.

Girdle. To destroy tissue, especially the bark and cambium, in a rough ring around a stem, branch, or root. Girdling often kills the tree.

Globose. Pertaining to a tree having the shape of a globe or globule; approximately spherical.

Grade. Established quality or use classification of trees, timber, and wood products; to classify according to grade.

Gross national product (GNP). Total value at current market prices of all final goods and services produced by a nation's economy, before deduction of depreciation and other allowances for consumption of durable capital goods.

Ground fire. Fire that not only consumes all the organic materials of the forest floor, but also burns into the underlying soil itself—for example, a peat fire. See *Surface fire*.

Ground tissue. Tissues other than the epidermis or periderm and vascular tissue; conjunctive parenchyma, fundamental tissue.

Growth impact. Pervasive, ongoing destruction of forests because of growth loss and mortality. See *Growth loss*, *Mortality*.

Growth loss. Difference between potential and actual tree growth, caused by destructive agents such as insects, diseases, or weather. See *Growth impact*, *Mortality*.

Gymnosperm. Vascular plants that produce seeds not enclosed in an ovary.

H

Habitat. Immediate environment occupied by an organism. In forestry, habitat usually refers to animal habitat.

Habitat type. Unit of land capable of supporting a single climax community type.

Hardpan. Indurated (hardened) or cemented soil horizon. The soil may have any texture and is compacted or cemented by iron oxide, organic matter, silica, calcium carbonate, or other substances.

Headbox. Final holding container of pulp slurries for regulation of flow onto the moving papermaking-machine wire.

Head fire. Fire spreading, or set to spread, with the wind.

Heartrot. Decay in the central core of a tree, usually caused by fungus.

Heartwood. Inner core of a woody stem, wholly composed of nonliving cells and usually differentiated from the outer enveloping layer (sapwood) by its darker color. See *Sapwood*.

Height poles. Sectioned, telescoping poles used to measure the height of trees.

Hemicellulose. Any of the noncellulosic polysaccharides of the intercellular layer and of the cell wall that can be extracted with aqueous alkaline solutions and are readily hydrolyzable by acids to give sugars.

Hemocoel. General insects' body cavity in which blood flows.

Herb. Any seed-producing plant that does not develop persistent woody tissue above ground. Includes both forbs and grasses. May be perennial. *Herbaceous*, adjective.

Herbivore. Organism that consumes living plants or their parts.

Heritability. Proportion of any observed variability that is caused by genetic effects, the remainder being attributed to environment.

Heterotrophic. Referring to organisms dependent on the environment for obtaining organic food because they are unable to synthesize organic material. All animals, fungi, and many bacteria are heterotrophs. The obtain almost all their organic material either directly or indirectly from the activity of autotrophs.

High grading. Type of exploitation cutting that removes only trees of a certain species, or of high value.

Hogged wood. Wood reduced to coarse chips—for example, for fuel or manufacture of wood pulp or chipboard.

Horizon, soil. Layer of soil roughly parallel to the land surface, distinguished from adjacent layers by different physical, chemical, or biological characteristics.

Hue. The attribute of a color that differentiates it from gray of the same brilliance and that allows it to be classed as blue, green, red, or intermediate shades of these colors.

Humus. Decomposed lower part of the soil organic layer, generally amorphous, colloidal, and dark-colored.

Hydrarch succession. Primary succession beginning on a substrate of water, usually a pond or lake.

Hydration. Chemical combination of water with cellulose or hemicelluloses (usually in fibers) to give a swollen structure; endowing fibers with an increased capacity for water retention through mechanical beating.

Hydrolysis. Conversion, by reaction with water, of a complex substance into two or more smaller molecules.

Hypertrophy. The excessive growth or development of an organ or tissue.

Hypha. A single tubular filament of fungus; the hyphae together constitute the mycelium.

Hypsometer. Device for measuring tree height.

I

Improvement cutting. Silvicultural treatment in which diseased or poorly formed trees or trees of undesirable species are removed.

Inbreeding depression. Loss of vigor that frequently results from mating closely related individuals.

Incident energy. Electromagnetic radiation impinging on a surface.

Increment.   Increase in girth, diameter, basal area, height, volume, quality, or value of individual trees or crops.

Increment borer.   Auger-like instrument with a hollow bit, used to extract cores from trees for the determination of growth and age.

Infection court.   Site of infection by a pathogen.

Infiltration.   The amount of water that penetrates the soil, governed by the texture of the soil, vegetation cover, and the slope of the ground.

Infrared.   Energy in the 0.7- to 15-micrometer wavelength region of the electromagnetic spectrum; for remote sensing the infrared wavelengths are often subdivided into near-infrared (0.7 to 1.3 micrometers), middle-infrared (1.3 to 3.0 micrometers), and far-infrared (7.0 to 15.0 micrometers); far-infrared is sometimes referred to as *thermal* or *emissive infrared*.

Ingrowth.   The increase in timber volume of a given stand owing to new trees that were not measured in previous surveys. See *Survivor growth*.

Inhibition.   Prohibition, or checking, of an action or process.

Initial.   Undifferentiated cell that remains within the meristem indefinitely and adds cells to the plant body by division.

Initial point.   The origin point of the standard rectangular survey system, the intersection of a baseline and a principal meridian.

Inland Empire.   Area lying between the crests of the Cascade Mountains and Bitterroot Mountains, and extending from the Okanogan Highlands to the Blue Mountains of northeastern Oregon. Timber production is very important in this region.

Integration (economics).   Expansion of a firm into production of other, often closely related, types of products (horizontal integration) or into prior or later stages of the production of a given product (vertical integration).

Intercellular space.   Space between the cells of a tissue.

Interception.   (1) The process by which rainwater is caught and held on the leaves of trees and vegetation and is returned to the air by evaporation without reaching the ground. (2) The part of precipitation caught by vegetation.

Internode.   Portion of a stem or branch that is between two successive nodes.

Intolerance, shade.   See *Shade tolerance*.

Ion.   Electrically charged atom or group of atoms.

J

Juvenile wood.   Wood formed close to the central core of the tree that contains a high percentage of thin-walled cells.

K

Kerf.   The narrow slot cut by a saw advancing through the wood.

Kiln-dry.   Dried in a kiln to a specified range of moisture content.

Knot.   Portion of a branch enclosed in the xylem by the natural growth of the tree.

Kraft pulp.   Chemical wood pulp obtained by cooking—that is, digesting wood chips in a solution of sodium hydroxide (caustic soda) and sodium sulfide.

L

Lammas shoot.   Abnormal shoot formed late in the summer from expansion of a bud that was not expected to open until the following year.

Landsat.   An unmanned, earth-orbiting satellite of the National Aeronautics and Space Administration that transmits images to earth receiving stations; designed primarily for collection of earth resources data.

Larva.   Immature, wingless, feeding stage of an insect that undergoes complete metamorphosis.

Lateral meristems.   Meristems that give rise to secondary tissue; the vascular cambium and cork cambium.

Lattice.   Crossed strips with open spaces between to give the appearance of a screen-like structure.

Leaching.   Removal of soluble substances (e.g., from soil or timber) by percolating water.

Leaf primordium.   Lateral outgrowth from the apical meristem that will become a leaf.

Lenticel.   Small breathing pore in the bark of trees and shrubs; a corky aerating organ that permits gases to diffuse between the plant and the atmosphere.

Lesion.   Circumscribed diseased area.

Lignification.   Impregnation with lignin, as in secondary walls of xylem cells. See *Lignin*.

Lignin.   Noncarbohydrate (phenolic), structural constituent of wood and some other plant tissues; encrusts the cell walls and cements the cells together.

Lignocellulosic.   Of materials containing both lignin and cellulose; a characteristic of higher forms of terrestrial plants.

Lignosulfonic acid.   Soluble derivative of lignin produced in the sulfite pulping process and present—in the form of salts (lignosulfonates)—in the waste liquor.

Limiting factor.   Environmental factor needed by an organism but in shortest supply.

Linear programming.   A mathematical programming technique that either maximizes or minimizes a single, linear objective function. The objective function may be subjected to sets of linear equalities or inequalities, called constraints.

Lithosphere.   Crust of the earth.

Littoral.   Of vegetation growing along a seashore or very large lake. See *Riparian*.

Loam.   Rich friable soil containing a relatively equal mixture of sand and silt and somewhat smaller proportion of clay.

Loess.   Particles, mostly silt-sized, transported and deposited by wind.

Log rule.   Table showing the estimated or calculated amount of lumber that can be sawed from logs of given length and diameter.

Lumen.   Cell cavity (often hollow).

M

Macerate.   To soften, or separate the parts of a substance by steeping in a liquid, with or without heat.

Mast.   Nuts and seeds of trees, serving as food for livestock and wildlife.

Mature.   Stage of tree growth when height growth slows and crown expansion and diameter increase and become marked. See *Seedling, Sapling, Pole, Senescent*.

Megasporangium.   The ovule-bearing structure in gymnosperms.

Mensuration, forest.   Science dealing with the measurement of volume, growth, and development of individual trees and stands and the determination of various products obtainable from them.

Merchantable height.   The height above the ground, or in some cases above stump height, to which the tree stem is salable.

Meristem.   Undifferentiated plant tissue from which new cells arise. See *Apical meristem, Lateral meristems*.

Mesarch succession.   Primary succession beginning on an intermediate substrate that is neither open water nor solid rock, such as a recent mud-flow or glacial moraine. See *Hydrarch, Xerarch succession*.

Mesophyll. Parenchyma tissue in a leaf between the upper and lower epidermis.

Methanol. Methyl alcohol, CH_3OH; a colorless, volatile liquid, a product of the destructive distillation of wood, derived mainly from the lignin; also manufactured synthetically.

Microclimate. Climate of small areas, especially insofar as this differs significantly from the general climate of the region.

Microsporangium. The pollen sac of a staminate cone in gymnosperms.

Microwave. A very short electromagnetic radiation wave between 1 meter and 1 millimeter in wavelength or 300 to 0.3 gigahertz in frequency.

Middle lamella. Layer of intercellular material, rich in lignin and pectic compounds, cementing together the primary walls of adjacent cells.

Mineralization. Breakdown of organic compounds in soil releasing inorganic constituents that can be taken up by plant roots.

Monocotyledones. One of the two classes of angiosperms; a plant whose embryo has one seed leaf.

Monoculture. Crop of a single species, generally even-aged. See *Even-aged stand*.

Monoecious. A condition in which both staminate and pistillate flowers (or pollen and seed cones of conifers) are borne on the same plant. See *Dioecious*.

Monophagous. Feeding on a single host species.

Morphology. Study of form and its development.

Mortality. Volume of trees killed by natural causes in a given time or a given forest, exclusive of catastrophes.

Multispectral scanner. A scanner system that simultaneously acquires images in various wavelength regions of the same scene.

Mutagen. Substance known to induce mutations.

Mutation. Sudden, heritable change in the structure of a gene or chromosome or some set thereof.

Mycelium. The mass of interwoven filaments or hypae making up the vegetative part of a fungus, as distinct from the fruiting body.

Mycoplasmas. Smallest of free-living organisms, lacking a cell wall, but possessing a distinct flexible membrane.

Mycorrhizae. Symbiotic association between nonpathogenic or weakly pathogenic fungi and living cortical cells of a plant root.

N

Naval stores. Historical term for resin products, particularly turpentine and rosin from pine trees, previously also pine tars and pitch.

Necrosis. The localized death of plant or animal tissue; for example, the response of a leaf to invasion of a pathogen. An affected area is described as being *necrotic*.

Necrotic. An area of dead plant tissue from necrosis.

Nematodes. Parasitic or free-living, elongated smooth worms of cylindrical shape; roundworms.

Niche. Status of a plant or animal in its community—that is, its biotic, trophic, and abiotic relationships. All the components of the environment with which an organism or population interacts, especially those necessary to its existence: its habitat.

Nitrification. Process whereby protein, amino acids, and other nitrogen compounds in the soil are oxidized by microorganisms, with the production of nitrates.

Nitrogen cycle. Worldwide circulation of nitrogen atoms in which certain microorganisms take up atmospheric nitrogen and convert it into other forms that may be assimilated into the bodies of other organisms. Excretion, burning, and bacterial and fungal action in dead organisms return nitrogen atoms to the atmosphere.

Nitrogen fixation. Conversion of elemental nitrogen (N_2) from the atmosphere to organic combinations or to forms readily utilizable in biological processes.

Node. Part of a stem or branch where one or more leaves or branches are attached.

Nodules. Enlargements or swellings on the roots of legumes and certain other plants inhabited by symbiotic nitrogen-fixing bacteria.

O

Oblique photograph. A photograph acquired with the camera axis intentionally directed between the horizontal and vertical orientations.

Oleoresin. Group of "soft" natural resins, consisting of a viscous mixture of essential oil (e.g., turpentine) and nonvolatile solids (e.g., rosin) secreted by the resin-forming cells of the pines and certain other trees.

Optical dendrometer. An instrument for measuring the upper stem diameters of trees to aid in accurate product scaling.

Organ. Structure composed of different tissues, such as root, stem, leaf, or flower.

Organic compounds. The compounds containing carbon that pertain to living organisms in general, and those compounds formed by living organisms.

Orthographic projection. Projection in which the lines are perpendicular to the plane of projection.

Orthophotograph. A photographic copy prepared from a perspective photograph in which the displacements of images caused by a tilt and relief have been removed.

Osmoregulation. Regulation of the osmotic pressure in the body by controlling the amount of water and salts in the body.

Osmosis. The diffusion of water, or any solvent, across a differentially permeable membrane. In the absence of other forces, movement of water during osmosis will always be from a region of greater water potential to one of lesser water potential.

Oven-dry. Of wood dried to constant weight in a ventilated oven at a temperature above the boiling point of water.

Overgrazing. Grazing above and beyond the level that a given range can sustain without change.

Oviposit. To lay eggs or deposit eggs by means of an ovipositor.

Ovipositor. The tubular organ at the extremity of the abdomen in many insects by which the egg are deposited.

P

Pacing. A simple method for measuring linear distance for surveys, when great accuracy is not required, whereby a person's individual premeasured pace is used as the measuring tool.

Panchromatic. Pertaining to films that are sensitive to a broad band of electromagnetic radiation, such as the entire visible part of the spectrum, and are used for broadband photographs.

Parallax. The apparent displacement of the position of an observed body with respect to a reference point or system, caused by a shift in point of observation.

Parallax wedge. A simplified stereometer for measuring object heights on stereoscopic pairs of photographs.

Parasite. Organism that lives in or on another living organism of a different kind and derives subsistence from it without returning any benefit. See *Predator, Saprophyte*.

Parenchyma. Tissue composed of living, thin walled, brick-shaped cells; primarily concerned with the storage and distribution of food materials. Axial parenchyma cells are vertically oriented; ray parenchyma are laterally oriented.

Pathogen. Organism directly capable of causing disease in living material. See *Saprogen*.

Pectin. Complex organic compound (polysaccharide) present in the intercellular layer and primary wall of plant cells; the basis of fruit jellies.

Ped. Visible structural soil aggregate—for example, crumb, block, or prism.

Perforation. Gap in the cell wall lacking a pit membrane; occurs in vessel members of angiosperms.

Pericycle. Root tissue located between the epidermis and phloem.

Periderm. Outer protective tissue that replaces the epidermis; includes cork, cork cambium, and phelloderm.

Perspective projection. Projection in which the lines converge at an arbitrarily chosen station point, to represent on a plane the space relationships of natural objects as they appear to the eye. The perspective projection of the camera lens causes scale variations and displaces image positions.

pH. A measure of acidity; the logarithm of the reciprocal of the hydrogen ion concentration. The value 7 pH is neutral; the values above are alkaline; and the values below are acid.

Phelloderm. Tissue formed toward the inside of the plant by the cork cambium.

Phenol. Hydroxyl derivative of benzene, C_6H_5OH.

Phenology. Study of biological events as related to climate.

Phenotype. Outward appearance or physical attributes of an individual. See *Genotype*.

Pheromone. Hormonal substance secreted by an individual and stimulating a physiological or behavioral response from an individual of the same species.

Phloem. Tissue of the inner bark; contains sieve elements through which carbohydrates are transported.

Photogrammetry. The art or science of obtaining reliable measurements by means of photography.

Photograph. A representation of targets formed by the action of light on silver halide grains of an emulsion.

Photographic scale. An expression or ratio stating that one unit of distance on a photograph represents a specific number of units of actual ground distance.

Photoperiod. Duration of daily exposure to light; length of day favoring optimum functioning of an organism.

Photosynthesis. Synthesis of carbohydrates from carbon dioxide and water by green plant cells in the presence of light, with oxygen as a byproduct.

Phototropism. Growth movement in which the direction of the light is the determining factor, as the growth of a plant toward a light source; turning or bending response to light.

Physiography. A general description of nature or natural phenomena; the science of physical geography.

Physiology. Study of the vital functions of living organisms. *Note:* Differences in physiological character may not always be accompanied by morphological differences.

Phytochrome. Chemical compound used by plants to detect daylength.

Piedmont. Plateau between the coastal plain and the Appalachian Mountains.

Pioneer community. First stage in the ecological development of a community.

Pit. Gap or recess in the secondary cell wall that facilitates the interchange of materials between cells.

Pith. Ground tissue occupying the center of the plant stem or root, within the vascular cylinder; usually consists of parenchyma.

Pixel. A picture element or cell within a spatially ordered matrix of numbers.

Planer. Machine for surfacing sawed timber.

Plasmolysis. Contraction of the cytoplasm because of removal of water from the protoplast by osmosis.

Pole. Still-young tree larger than 4 inches (10 centimeters) dbh, up to about 8 inches (20 to 23 centimeters) dbh; during this stage, height growth predominates and economic bole length is attained. See *Seedling, Sapling, Mature, Senescent.*

Polymerization. Transformation of various low molecular-weight compounds (monomers) into large molecules—that is, polymers.

Polyphagous. Feeding on many different host species.

Predator. Any animal which preys externally on others; that is, hunts, kills, and feeds on a succession of hosts. See *Parasite.*

Prescribed burning. Controlled use of fire to further certain planned objectives of silviculture, wildlife management, fire hazard reduction, and so forth.

Present net worth. Single amount measuring the net current value of a stream of future revenues and costs.

Price index. Price of a good or group of goods in any year divided by the price of the same good or group of goods in a base year. See *Relative price index.*

Price leadership. Determination of prices by one or a few firms, with other producers in the industry tacitly accepting the prices thus determined.

Primary growth. Growth originating in the apical meristem of shoots and roots. See *Secondary growth.*

Primary succession. Succession beginning on a substrate that did not previously support vegetation, such as open water, fresh glacial moraine, or bare rock. See *Secondary succession.*

Primordial. A cell or organ in its earliest stage of differentiation.

Profile, soil. Vertical section of the soil through all its horizons and extending into the parent material.

Progeny. Offspring produced from any mating.

Progeny test. Evaluation procedure in which parents are rated based on the performance of their offspring.

Protoplasm. Living substance of all cells.

Protoplast. Entire contents of the cell, not including the cell wall.

Provenance. Natural origin of seeds or trees, usually synonymous with "geographic origin," or a plant material having a specific place or origin.

Pulp. Fibers separated by mechanical or chemical means; the primary raw material from which paper is made.

Pupa. Insect in the nonfeeding, usually immobile, transformation stage between larva and the adult. *Pupae* (plural).

Pyric climax. An ecosytem that never reaches its potential climax vegetation because of frequent fires.

Pyroligneous acid. Aqueous portion, after separation of the tar, of the liquor obtained during the destructive distillation of wood; a complex mixture of water (80 to 90 percent) and organic compounds. See *Destructive distillation*.

Pyrolysis. Subjection of wood or organic compounds to very high temperatures and the resulting decomposition. See *Destructive distillation*.

Q

Quad. Unit of energy measure; 1×10^{15} British thermal units (Btu).

R

Radar. Acronym for radio detection and ranging, an active form of remote sensing that operates at wavelengths from 1 millimeter to 1 meter.

Radial increment. The diameter growth over a given period obtained by measuring the length of the last several annual rings in a core sample.

Radiation. The propagation of energy in the form of electromagnetic waves.

Rangeland. Areas unsuitable for cultivation, which are a source of forage for free-ranging native and domestic animals.

Ray. Laterally oriented, ribbon-shaped tissue extending radially in the xylem and phloem; functions in the lateral transport of water and nutrients.

Ray initial. An initial in the vascular cambium that gives rise to the ray cells of secondary xylem and secondary phloem.

Recombination. Formation of new combinations of genes as a result of segregation in crosses between genetically different parents.

Recurrence interval. Frequency of fires in a given stand.

Reflectance. The ratio of the radiant energy reflected by a body to that incident upon it.

Reflectance, spectral. Reflectance measured at a specific wavelength interval.

Refugia. Areas that have escaped alteration during glaciation.

Regeneration. Renewal of a tree crop, by natural or artificial means.

Regulated forest. Forest that produces a continuous flow of products of about the same size, quality, and quantity over time.

Relative price index. Price index for one good divided by the price index for another good or group of goods. The divisor is usually the wholesale or consumer price index.

Release cutting. Silvicultural treatment in which larger trees of competing species are removed from competition with desired crop trees.

Relief. The vertical irregularities of a surface.

Relief displacement. The geometric distortion on vertical aerial photographs. The tops of objects are located on the photograph radially outward from the base.

Remote sensing. Collection of data by a device that is not in physical contact with the object, area, or phenomenon under investigation—for example, aerial photography or satellite imagery.

Reproductive potential. Ability of a species to multiply in the absence of countervailing forces.

Resin. Pitch; the secretions of certain trees, oxidation or polymerization products of the terpenes, consisting of mixtures of aromatic acids and esters insoluble in water but soluble in organic solvents; often exuding from wounds.

Rest-rotation grazing. A system of range management whereby one portion of the land is left ungrazed (rested) for a full year; the next year another portion is rested.

Rhizome.   Horizontal underground stem, usually containing stored food.

Rhizomorph.   A densely packed strand of fungal tissue with the appearance of a root that is produced by some higher fungi such as *Armillaria*. Rhizomorphs enable fungi to spread.

Rickettsia.   Bacteria-like microorganisms of the genus *Rickettsia*, parasitic on arthropods and pathogenic for human beings and animals.

Ring-porous wood.   Wood (xylem) of hardwoods in which the earlywood vessels are much larger in diameter than vessels in the latewood; the vessels generally appear as a ring in a stem cross section. See *Diffuse-porous wood*.

Riparian.   Of vegetation growing in close proximity to a watercourse, small lake, swamp, or spring. See *Littoral*.

Root cap.   Thimble-shaped mass of cells covering and protecting the growing root tip.

Root hairs.   Tubular outgrowths of epidermal cells of the young plant.

Rosin.   Solid residue after evaporation and distillation of the turpentine from the oleoresin of various pines, consisting mostly of rosin acids.

Rotation age.   Period of years required to establish and grow timber crops to a specific condition of maturity. Applies only to even-aged management. See *Cutting cycle*.

Roundwood.   Timber or firewood prepared in the round state—from felled trees to material trimmed, barked, and crosscut.

Ruderal.   Plant that occupies a niche with high resource availability (water, nutrients, and light) and frequent disturbances. Also a plant living on wasteland in built-up areas.

S

Saccharification.   Conversion of the polysaccharides in wood or other plant material into sugars by hydrolysis with acids or enzymes.

Sahel.   Semi-arid region of Africa between the Savannas and the Sahara extending through Senegal, Mauritania, Mali, Niger, Sudan, northern Nigeria, and Ethiopia. Since the late 1960s, this region has been afflicted by devastating drought leading to the starvation of hundreds of thousands of people.

Sapling.   Young tree at least 1 meter (3 feet) high, but not larger than 10 centimeters (4 inches) dbh; crowns are well elevated and usually many lower branches have started to die. See *Seedling, Pole, Mature, Senescent*.

Saprogen.   Organism capable of producing decay in nonliving organic material. See *Pathogen*.

Saprophyte.   Plant organism which is incapable of synthesizing its nutrient requirements from purely inorganic sources and feeds on dead organic material. See *Parasite*.

Sapwood.   Predominantly living, physiologically active wood; includes the more recent annual layers of xylem that are active in translocation of water and minerals. See *Heartwood*.

Savanna.   Any large area of tropical or subtropical grassland, covered in part with trees and spiny shrubs.

Sawlog.   A log considered suitable in size and quality for sawn timber.

Scale.   Estimated solid (sound) contents of a log or group of logs.

Scanner.   An optical–mechanical imaging system in which a rotating or oscillating mirror sweeps the instantaneous field of view of the detector. The two basic types of scanners are airborne and stationary.

Scarification.   Wearing down, by abrasion or chemical treatment, of the bark or outer coat.

Scion.   Detached living portion of a plant grafted onto another plant.

Sclerenchyma.   Supporting tissue composed of cells with thick, often lignified secondary walls; may include fiber cells or sclereid cells.

Sclereid. Sclerenchyma cell with a thick, lignified secondary wall.

Sclerophyll. A term that describes the thick, tough foliage of many tree species of the Mediterranean area and parts of the United States and Australia (i.e., eucalyptus).

Secondary growth. Growth derived from lateral meristem; results in increase in girth. See *Primary growth*.

Secondary succession. Succession starting after the disturbance of a previously existing plant community. See *Primary succession*.

Sedimentation. Deposition or accumulation of mineral or organic matter.

Seedling. Youngest trees from the time of germination until they reach a height of 1 meter (3 feet). See *Sapling, Pole, Mature, Senescent*.

Seed orchard. Plantation of trees established to provide for the production of seeds of improved quality.

Seed-tree method. Silvicultural system in which the mature timber is removed in one cut, except for a small number of seed trees left to provide a source of seed for the next crop. See *Clearcutting, Shelterwood method*.

Selection. Any discrimination by natural or artificial means that results in some individuals leaving more offspring than others.

Selection cutting. Silvicultural system in which scattered trees or small groups of trees are cut, providing sustained yield from an uneven-aged stand.

Selection differential. Difference between the value of a selected individual (or mean value of a selected population) and the mean value of the original unselected population.

Senescent. Growing old; aging stands at this stage are over-mature; losses from mortality and decay may exceed additions in volume. See *Seedling, Sapling, Pole, Mature*.

Sensor. A device that receives electromagnetic radiation and converts it into a signal that can be displayed as data or an image.

Serotinous cones. Cones of some species of gymnosperms that are sealed by resin, requiring high temperatures to open the cones and release seeds.

Serpentine. Common mineral, hydrous magnesium silicate, $H_2Mg_3Si_2O_2$.

Shade tolerance. Capacity of trees to reproduce and grow in the shade of and in competition with other trees.

Shelterwood method. Silvicultural system in which the mature timber is removed, leaving sufficient numbers of trees standing to provide shade and protection for new seedlings. See *Clearcutting, Seed-tree method*.

Shifting cultivation. Itinerant forms of agriculture, common in tropical regions, whereby the farmers clear a parcel of the forest and cultivate the soil until it becomes unproductive, then move onto another area where the process is started anew.

Shoot. Aboveground portion of a vascular plant.

Short-duration grazing. A system of range management employing a large number of separate pastures grazed individually for short periods of time, generally two days to two weeks.

Shrub. Woody perennial plant, seldom exceeding 10 feet in height, usually having several persistent woody stems branching from the ground.

Side-looking radar. An all-weather, day/night remote sensor that is particularly effective in imaging large areas of terrain; it generates energy that is transmitted and received to produce a photo-like picture of the ground. Also called *side-looking airborne radar*.

Sieve element. Cell of the phloem concerned with the long-distance transport of food substances. Classified into sieve cells (gymnosperms) and sieve tube members (angiosperms).

Silvichemicals. Chemicals derived from wood and trees.

Silviculture. Manipulation of forest vegetation to accomplish a specified set of objectives; controlling forest establishment, composition, and growth.

Site index. A particular measure of site quality based on the height of the dominant trees in a stand at an arbitrarily chosen age.

Site quality. A loose term denoting the relative productivity of a site for a particular tree species.

Size, sizing. Additive introduced to modify the surface properties of manufactured board or paper.

Skidding. Loose term for hauling logs by sliding, not on wheels.

Slash. Open area strewn with debris of trees from felling or from wind or fire; the debris itself.

Slurry. Watery suspension of insoluble matter— that is, pulp slurry.

Snag. Standing dead tree from which the leaves and most of the branches have fallen.

Soil-plant-atmosphere continuum. The continuous column of water that begins in the soil, travels across the roots, up the xylem within the roots and stem, through the xylem in leaf vascular bundles, to the wet surfaces of the mesophyll cells, and continues by evaporating into the atmosphere, all of which results in a close coupling of evaporation and uptake of water by a siphonlike action.

Specific gravity. As applied to wood, the ratio of the oven dry weight of a sample to the weight of a volume of water equal to the volume of the sample at some specific moisture content.

Spectral reflectance. The reflectance of electromagnetic energy at specified wavelength intervals.

Spectral-reflectance curve. A plot of the reflectance of electromagnetic energy for a series of wavelengths.

Spectral response. The response of a material as a function of wavelength to incident electromagnetic energy, particularly in terms of the measurable energy reflected from and emitted by the material.

Spectral-response envelope. The range of frequencies in which the spectral response is greatest.

Spectrum. A continuous sequence of energy arranged according to wavelength or frequency.

Sporangium. A hollow unicellular or multicellular structure in which spores are produced.

Spot fire, spotting. Fire set outside the perimeter of the main fire by flying sparks or embers.

Stand density. The average total basal area per acre of a given stand.

Stand table. A table showing the number of trees by species and diameter (or girth) classes, generally per unit area of a stand.

Stenotopic. Organisms limited to a very specific habitat.

Stereogram. A stereopair of photographs or drawings correctly oriented and permanently mounted for stereoscopic examination.

Stereomodel. A three-dimensional mental impression produced by viewing the left and right images of an overlapping pair with the left and right eye, respectively.

Stereopair. A pair of photographs which overlap in area and are suitable for stereoscopic examination.

Stereoplotter. A device that will plot as a contour map data obtained from aerial photographs; operates by means of a stereo-scopic instrument.

Stereoscope.   A binocular optical device for viewing overlapping images or diagrams to obtain the mental impression of a three-dimensional model.

Stereoscopic image.   The mental impression of a three-dimensional object that results from stereoscopic vision.

Stereoscopy.   The science or art which deals with three-dimensional effects and the methods by which these effects are produced.

Stomata.   Openings in the surface of a leaf through which water vapor, carbon dioxide, and oxygen pass.

Stratification.   Placing dormant seeds between layers of moist material, usually a sand and peat mixture, and exposing them to low temperatures to satisfy the pre-germination chilling requirements.

Structure, soil.   Combination or arrangement of primary soil particles (e.g., sand, silt, clay) into secondary particles called peds. See *Ped*.

Stumpage.   Value of timber as it stands uncut; uncut marketable timber.

Suberin.   Fatty material in cell walls of corky bark tissue.

Subsoil.   Bed or stratum of earth or earthy material immediately under the surface soil.

Substrate.   Underlying material; the soil beneath plants or animals; the material on which an enzyme or fermenting agent acts, on which adhesive is spread, or on which a fungus grows or is attached.

Succession.   Change in community composition and structure through time.

Sulfite pulp.   Chemical wood pulp obtained by cooking—that is, digesting wood chips in a solution of bisulfites and sulfurous acid.

Suppressed.   Pertaining to trees with crowns completely overtopped by surrounding trees so that they receive almost no direct sunlight. See *Dominant*.

Surface fire.   Fire that burns only surface litter, loose debris of the forest floor, and small vegetation. See *Groundfire*.

Survivor growth. The increase in timber volume of a given stand owing to the continuing growth of previously measured trees. See *Ingrowth*.

Sustained yield.   Yield a forest can produce continuously, such as timber.

Sweep.   Curve in stem or log as distinct from an abrupt bend, generally as a reaction to environmental conditions.

Symbiosis.   Mutually beneficial relationship between two dissimilar living organisms, called *symbionts*. In some cases, the symbionts form a single body or organ, as in mycorrhizae or lichens.

Synecology.   Study of the community and its environment.

Syngas.   Synthesis gas; a synthetically produced gas containing two parts hydrogen (H_2) and one part carbon monoxide (CO).

Systemic.   Of a pathogen, capable of spreading throughout its host. Of a pesticide, absorbed by a plant so as to be lethal to agents that feed on it.

Systems analysis.   Method of analysis which deals with the movement of energy or materials to different parts or components of a complex system.

T

Tall oil.   Byproduct of the kraft pulping of resinous woods (e.g., pine), consisting mainly of resin acids and fatty acids.

Tannins.   Complex extracellular water-soluble substances, generally formed from a variety of simpler polyphenols; part of wood extractives.

Terpenes.   Class of hydrocarbons, with their derivatives, commonly occurring in many species of wood and generally having a fragrant odor; characteristically noted with pine trees.

Texture, photo image.   The frequency of change and arrangement of tones; descriptive adjectives for textures are fine, medium, or coarse, and stippled or mottled.

Texture, soil.   Relative proportion of the various mineral particles such as sand, silt, and clay, expressed as a textural class—for example, sandy loam, clay loam.

Thermal band.   A general term for middle-infrared wavelengths that are transmitted through the atmosphere window at 8 to 13 micrometers; also used for the windows around 3 to 6 micrometers.

Thermal radiation.   The electromagnetic radiation emitted by a hot blackbody, such as the filament of a lamp.

Thermal scanner.   A detector which sweeps the instantaneous field of radiant energy across the terrain in either the 3- to 5-micrometer or 8- to 14-micrometer region of the spectrum.

Thermochemical liquefaction.   Decomposition of organic compounds to smaller molecules often in the form of an oil. The reaction is usually carried out in the presence of a catalyst and hydrogen or synthesis gas at high pressure and temperature.

Thinning.   Silvicultural treatment in which stand density is reduced to accelerate diameter growth in remaining trees.

Threshold dosage.   The minimum dose necessary to produce a measurable effect in a given organism.

Throughfall.   All the precipitation eventually reaching the forest floor—that is, direct precipitation plus canopy drip.

Tissue.   Group of similar cells organized into a structural and functional unit.

Tissue system.   Tissue or group of tissues organized into a structural and functional unit in a plant or plant organ.

Tone.   Each distinguishable shade of gray from white to black on an image.

Tracheary element.   Tracheid or vessel member.

Tracheid.   Elongated, thick-walled conducting and supporting cell of xylem. Has tapering ends and pitted walls without perforations. Found in nearly all vascular plants; the main fibrous component of wood. See *Vessel member*.

Tree.   Woody perennial plant, typically large and with a single well-defined stem and a more or less definite crown.

Triploid.   Individual having one set of chromosomes more than the typical number for the species.

Trophic, -troph, tropho-.   Pertaining to nutrition, feeding.

Trophic levels.   Steps in the movement of energy through an ecosystem.

Turgor.   Normal distention or rigidity of plant cells, resulting from the pressure exerted from within against the cell walls by the cell contents.

Turpentine.   Essential oil that can be obtained by distilling the oleoresin of conifers, particularly pines, consisting of a mixture of terpenes. Most turpentine is now obtained as a byproduct of the kraft pulping of pines.

U

Understory.   Any plants growing under the canopy formed by others. See *Canopy*.

Uneven-aged stand.   Stand in which more than two distinct age classes and a range of size classes (seedling, sapling, pole, etc.) are present.

Ultraviolet radiation.   Electromagnetic radiation of shorter wavelength than visible radiation but longer than X-rays; roughly, radiation in the wavelength interval between 10 and 4000 angstroms.

Uptake. Amount of water and nutrients absorbed by vegetation.

V

Vascular cambium. Cylindrical sheath of meristematic cells, the division of which produces secondary xylem and secondary phloem.

Vascular tissue. Specialized conducting tissue in plants forming a vascular system—in woody plants making up the whole of the xylem and phloem.

Vector. Any agent capable of transporting a pathogen or saprogen to a host.

Veneer. Thin sheet of wood of uniform thickness, produced by rotary cutting or by slicing.

Vessel member. Elongated cell of the xylem characterized by perforations. Its function is to conduct water and minerals through the plant body. Found in nearly all angiosperms and a few other vascular plants. See *Tracheid.*

Visible radiation. Energy at wavelengths from 0.4 to 0.7 micrometer that is detectable by the eye.

Volatiles. Essential oil distilled from plant tissues, generally characterized by a low boiling point.

Volume table. Table showing the average cubic contents of trees or logs by diameter and merchantable length in a specified unit of volume.

W

Watershed. Total area above a given point on a river, stream, or other waterway, that contributes water to the flow at that point.

Watershed management. The analysis, protection, repair, utilization, and maintenance of drainage basins for optimum control and conservation of water with regard to other resources.

Water stress. Stress or negative pressure exerted on a water column in a plant owing to transpiration.

Water table. Upper surface of the groundwater. A perched water table is one separated by relatively impermeable material from an underlying body of groundwater; may be seasonally impermanent.

Wavelength. The distance between successive wave crests, or other equivalent points, in a harmonic wave. The symbol is λ.

Weathering. The physical and geothermal processes by which rock minerals are broken up and decomposed.

Wholesale price index (WPI). Weighed average of wholesale prices of a representative bundle of goods and services produced by the economy. The rate of increase (decrease) in the WPI is one measure of the rate of inflation (deflation) in the economy.

Wood. Secondary xylem.

Woody plants. Trees or shrubs exhibiting secondary growth.

X

Xerarch succession. Primary succession beginning on a substrate that is solid rock and therefore has minimal water-storing capacity.

Xeric. Of, pertaining to, or adapted to a dry environment.

Xylem. Tissue containing tracheary elements through which water and minerals are transported; wood is secondary xylem.

Y

Yard. To haul logs to a central spot to prepare them for transport.

DATE DUE

May 30 07				
OCT - 5 2009				